TURKEY

REAL GUIDE CREDITS

Series Editor: Mark Ellingham
Editorial: Martin Dunford, John Fisher, Jack Holland, Jules Brown,
    Jonathan Buckley, Richard Trillo, Greg Ward
US Text Editor: David Reed
Production: Susanne Hillen, Kate Berens, Andy Hilliard
Typesetting: Gail Jammy

The authors would like to **thank** the following individuals, who helped out in the planning and research stages of this guide: Ahmet Ersoy, Press Attaché, and İrfan Acar, First Secretary, at the Turkish Embassy in London; Selami Karaibrahimgil at the Turkish National Tourist Office in London; Orhan Taşan and Yusuf Tavus of the Press and Information Office in İstanbul; and Anya Schiffrin for valuable İstanbul listings.

Thanks also to Catherine Mulvenna for valiant proofreading; Matthew Yeomans for information from the US; Gail Jammy for typesetting far beyond the call of duty; and, last but not least, Martin Dunford and John Fisher for marathon patience.

Individually, the authors would like to thank . . .

Rosie: Kâmil Eryavuz; Ayşe Peker; Gordon Dobie; Ümit Küçükoğlu; Ufuk Uras; Amelia French and Metin Güneş, as well as the staff of the İstanbul tourist office; Derya and İsmet Toymuş from the Nevşehir tourist office; Kaymakam Ümit Karahan and Muammer Sak in Ürgüp; Yildirim, Ekrem, and Kadir in Göreme; Ender Yaşar and Doğan Bey in İsparta; John and Ferda in Üçağız; Bilgi Sakir in London; and Jayne Creamer, Ruth Ayliffe, and Billy for all kinds of support everywhere.

Marc: Nurten Çelikkaptan at the İzmir tourist office; Asuman Akpolat at the Marmaris tourist office; Necip Albayrak of the Trabzon tourist office; Muhammet Yoksuç at the Erzurum tourist office; Omur Uzunoğulları in İzmir; Çiçek Park in Çeşme; Mustafa Ok in Kuşadası; Mete Amca on Bozcaada; Chris Hellier, Joelle Blanc, and Leylâ Akbaba in Ankara; Adrian Higgs, Emil Galip Sandalcı, Leylâ Navarro, Haldun Aydıngün, and İzzet and Rosette Keribar in İstanbul; Enver Lucas in Antalya; Mevlut and Meşgüre Kaya in Pamukkale; Simon Palmour for tips on the Black Sea and bicycling; Suzanne Anderson and Sue Crimlisk on the road from Artvin to Kars; and those intrepid Euphrates kayakers from the universities of Aberystwyth and Edinburgh.

John: Aitor Santillan, Taner from the Çadir Hotel in Ayvalık, Ali Yalçın, owner of the İlk Pansiyon in Amasya; Mustafa Çelik in Urfa; Salim Tuğan in Hakkâri; Ahmet Önel in Midyat; Mehmet Nalbant in Diyarbakır; Genda Makoto; and the man from the Safranbolu PTT office, whose name I never found out.

Illustration credits

"Basics", David Loftus; "Contexts", Henry Iles; incidental illustrations in Parts One and Three, Edward Briant.

Published in the United States by
Prentice Hall Press
A division of Simon & Schuster Inc.
15 Columbus Circle
New York, NY 10023

Prentice Hall Press and colophons are registered trademarks of Simon & Schuster Inc.

Typeset in Linotron Univers and Century Old Style to an original design by Andrew Oliver
Printed in the United States by R.R. Donnelley & Sons.

752pp. includes index

Cataloguing-in-Publication Data is available from the Library of Congress.

THE REAL GUIDE
TURKEY

Written and researched by

**ROSIE AYLIFFE, MARC DUBIN,
AND JOHN GAWTHROP**

PRENTICE
HALL
PRESS

NEW YORK LONDON TORONTO SYDNEY TOKYO SINGAPORE

HELP US UPDATE

We've gone to a lot of effort to ensure that this first edition of *Turkey: The Real Guide* is up-to-date and accurate. However, things do change—opening hours are notoriously fickle, restaurants and hotels come and go, previously remote areas become disovered—and any suggestions, comments, or corrections would be much appreciated.

We'll credit all contributions, and send a copy of the next edition (or any other Real Guide if you prefer) for the best letters. Please write to:

Martin Dunford and John Fisher, The Real Guides, Prentice Hall Trade Division, 15 Columbus Circle, New York, NY 10023.

CONTENTS

Introduction viii

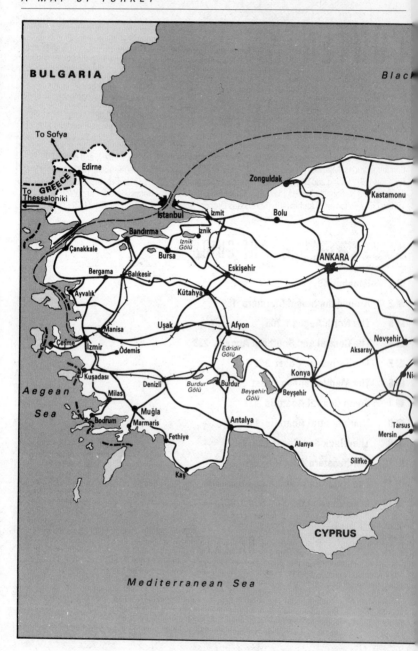

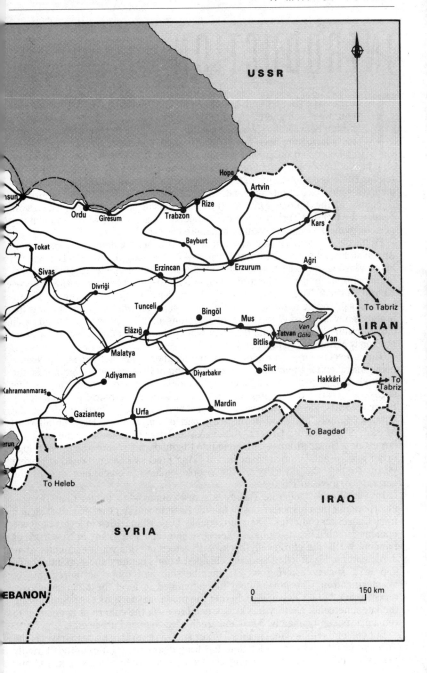

INTRODUCTION

Turkey is a country with a multiple identity, poised uneasily between east and west—although, despite the tourist-literature cliché, it is less a bridge between the two than a battleground, a buffer zone whose various parts have long been fought over from all directions. The country is now eager to be accepted on equal terms by the west: it has aspirations to membership in the European Community, and is the only NATO ally in the Middle East region. But it is by no stretch of the imagination a Western nation, and the contradictions—and fascinations—persist. Mosques coexist with Orthodox churches; remnants of the Roman Empire crumble alongside ancient Hittite sites; and, despite the fact that Turkey is a secular state, there are strong Muslim fundamentalist tensions drawing the country in a more easterly direction.

Politically, modern Turkey was a bold experiment, founded on the remaining, Anatolian kernel of the **Ottoman Empire**—once among the world's largest, and longest-lasting, imperial states. The country arose out of the defeat of World War I, almost entirely the creation of a single man of demonic energy and vision—**Kemal Atatürk**. The Turkish war of independence, fought against those victorious Allies intending to pursue imperialistic designs on Ottoman territory, was the prototype for all Third World "wars of liberation" in this century; it led to an explicitly **secular republic**, though one in which almost all inhabitants are at least nominally **Muslim** (predominantly Sunni).

Turks, except for a tiny minority in the southeast, are not Arabs, and loathe being mistaken for them; despite a heavy lacing of Persian and Arabic words, the **Turkish language** alone, unrelated to any neighboring one, is sufficient to set its speakers apart. The **population** is, however, ethnically remarkably **heterogenous**, despite official efforts to bring about uniformity. When the Ottoman Empire imploded in the early part of this century, large numbers of Muslim Slavs, Kurds, Greeks, Albanians, and Caucasians—to name only the largest non-Turkic groups—streamed into the modern territory, the safest refuge in an age of anti-Ottoman nationalism. This process has continued in recent years, so that the diversity of the people endures, constituting one of the surprises of travel in Turkey.

By Old World standards, Turkey is a vast country—it's bigger than Texas—incorporating the characteristics of Middle Eastern and Aegean, even Balkan and trans-Caucasian countries. There are equally large **disparities** in levels of development. İstanbul boasts clubs as expensive and exclusive as any in New York or London, yet in the chronically backward eastern interior you'll encounter standards and modes of living scarcely changed from a century ago—an intolerable gap in a society aspiring to EC membership and other accoutrements of **Westernization**. The government has attempted to level the differences over recent years, but it's debatable whether the modernization process begun during the late nineteenth century has struck deep roots in the culture or is doomed to remain a veneer, typified by a fax- and credit-card-equipped urban elite.

But one of the things that makes Turkey such a rewarding place to travel is the Turkish people, whose reputation for friendliness and **hospitality** is richly deserved; indeed, you risk causing offense by refusing to partake of it, and any transaction can be the springboard for further acquaintance. Close to the bigger resorts or tourist attractions, some of this is undoubtedly mercenary, but in much of the country the warmth and generosity is genuine—all the more amazing when recent Turkish history has demonstrated that outsiders usually only bring trouble in their wake.

Turkey has been continuously inhabited and fought over for close to ten millennia, as the layer-cake arrangement of many **archaeological sites** and the numerous **fortified heights**, encrusted with each era's contribution, testify. The juxtaposed ancient monuments mirror the bewildering **succession of states**— Hittite, Urartian, Phrygian, Hellenistic, Roman, Byzantine, Armeno-Georgian— that held sway here before the twelfth century. There are also, of course, an overwhelming number of graceful **Islamic monuments** dating from the eleventh century on, as well as magnificent city **bazaars**, which are alive and well despite the encroachments of more recent shopping practices. The country's modern architecture, which is partly the consequence of returned overseas workers eager to invest their earnings in real estate, is less pleasing—an ugliness also manifest in the **coastal resorts**, where the beaches are rarely as good as the tourist-board hype. Indeed, it's **inland** Turkey—Asiatic expanses of mountain, steppe, lake, even cloud forest—that may leave a more vivid memory, especially when accented by crumbling *kervansarays*, mosques, and castles.

Where to Go

Western Turkey is not only the more economically developed but also by far the more visited half of the country. **İstanbul**, straddling the straits linking the Black and Marmara seas, is touted as Turkish mystique par excellence, and understandably so: it would take months to even scratch the surface of the old imperial capital, which is still the cultural and commercial center of the country. Flanking it on opposite sides of the **Sea of Marmara** are the two prior seats of the Ottoman Empire, Bursa and Edirne, each with their complement of attractions and regal atmosphere. The sea itself is flecked with tranquil, frequently overlooked islands, ideal havens when the cities get too much—and just beyond the Dardanelles and its World War I battlefields lie two larger Aegean islands, only recently opened to outsiders.

Moving south, the classical character of the **North Aegean** comes to the fore in the olive-swathed country around Bergama and Ayvalık, perhaps the two most compelling points in the region. Just outside **İzmir**, the old Ottoman princely training ground of Manisa and the onetime Lydian city of Sardis, lost in vineyards, make another fine pair, while İzmir itself is the functional introduction to the **Central and Southern Aegean**, a magnet for travelers since the eighteenth century. The archaeological complex at Ephesus overshadows in visitors' imaginations the equally deserving ancient Ionian sites of Priene and Didyma, and the extensive ruins of Aphrodisias, Labranda, and Alinda in old Caria. Be warned that the coast itself is heavily developed, although the main resorts—of which Çeşme is perhaps the quietest and Bodrum the most characterful—make comfortable bases from which to tour the interior. Don't overlook such evocative hill towns as Şirince, Birgi, and Tire, which still exist in something of an Ottoman time warp.

Beyond the huge natural harbor of Marmaris, the Aegean becomes the Mediterranean; the level of tourism drops slightly and the shore becomes more convoluted and piney. Yacht and schooner cruises are the thing to do here, and are easily arranged in Marmaris or the more pleasant town of Fethiye, the principal center of the **Turquoise Coast**. Two of the finest and largest beaches in the country are at Dalyan and Patara, close to the eerie tombs of the Lycians, the fiercely independent locals of old. Kaş, another busy resort farther east, is a good place to rest up and an excellent base for explorations into the mountainous hinterland. Beyond the relatively untouched beaches around ancient Olympos, Antalya is Turkey's fastest-growing city, a sprawling place located at the beginning of the **Mediterranean Coast** proper. This is a lengthy shore, reaching as far as the Syrian border, with extensive beaches and archaeological sites—most notably at Perge, Side, and Aspendos—although its western parts get swamped in the high season. Once past castle-topped Alanya, however, the numbers diminish, and the stretch between Silifke and Adana offers innumerable minor points of interest, particularly the Roman city of Uzuncaburç and the romantic offshore fortress at Kızkalesi.

There are, perhaps, more spectacular attractions inland, in **South Central Anatolia**, where you're confronted with the famous rock churches, subterranean cities, and tufa-pinnacle landscapes of Cappadocia, in many ways the centerpiece of the region. The dry, bracing climate, excellent local wine, the artistic and architectural interest of the area—not to mention the chance to go horseback-riding—could occupy you for as much as a week here, taking in the largest town in the area, Kayseri, with its bazaar and tombs, on the way north. You could also pause at Eğirdir or Beyşehir—historic towns on the shores of two of the numerous lakes that dot the region—or in Konya, which, for both its Selçuk architecture and associations with the Mevlevi dervishes, makes for an appealing stopover on the way to or from the coast.

Ankara, hub of **North Central Anatolia**, is Turkey's capital, a planned city whose contrived Western feel gives some concrete indication of the priorities of the Turkish Republic; it also has an outstanding museum. Highlights of the surrounding region include the bizarre, isolated temple of Aezani, near Kutahya to the west; the Ottoman museum-town of Safranbolu; and the remarkable Hittite sites of Hatuşaş and Alacahöyük. If you're traveling north to the Black Sea, you should also look in on the Yeşilırmak Valley towns of Sivas, Tokat, and Amasya, each with their quota of early-Turkish monuments. The **Black Sea** shore itself is surprisingly devoid of architectural interest other than a chain of Byzantine-Genoese castles, but the beauty of the landscape and beaches goes some way to compensate. The oldest and most interesting towns between utilitarian Samsun and Zonguldak are Sinop, the northernmost point of Anatolia, and Amasra, also easily reached from Safranbolu. East of Samsun, the coast gets wilder and wetter until you reach fabled Trabzon, once the seat of empire and today a base for visits to the marvelous monasteries of Aya Sofya and Sumela.

The Ankara–Sivas route also poises you for the trip along the Euphrates River and into the hitherto invisible "back half" of Turkey—the East. Your first stops in **Northeastern Anatolia** might be the outstanding early-Turkish monumental ensembles at Divriği and Tercan. You'll inevitably end up in Erzurum, Turkey's highest and bleakest major city, from which you can visit the temperate and church-studded valleys of southern medieval Georgia or go trekking in the Kaçkar Mountains, Turkey's most popular hiking area, which wall off the area from the Black Sea. Dreary Kars is worth enduring for the sake of nearby Ani, the ruined medieval Armenian capital, and various other Armenian monuments in the area—although many of these require some ingenuity and resourcefulness to seek out.

South of here, the **Euphrates Basin** and the adjacent coastal region of the **Hatay** represent Turkey at its most Middle Eastern; indeed, nearby Syria has long had designs on this part of the country, which may become more manifest in the wake of the Gulf War. Antakya is the heart of the Hatay, and has good connections with the Euphrates Basin city of Gaziantep—once again a functional place, but a gateway to some centers of genuine interest. Urfa and nearby Harran are biblical in both appearance and history; Mardin, with its surrounding monasteries, is the homeland of Turkey's Syrian Orthodox minority. The colossal heads of Nemrut Dağı, though, glimpsed ad infinitum on brochures and travel posters, are the real attraction here, and still mighty impressive, if very commercialized these days. East from here, by the time you reach wall-encased Diyarbakır you're verging on the largely Kurdish **Lake Van** basin, which opens out just beyond the canyon-flank town of Bitlis, overlooking the unearthly blue alkaline lake. Urartian, Selçuk, and Armenian monuments abound along the shore, most notably at Çavuştepe, Ahlat, and Akdamar, although you'll almost certainly have to stay in the town of Van, an oasis sprawling on the eastern shore behind its ancient, rock-hewn citadel. East of Van looms the fairytale Kurdish castle of Hoşap, although excursions into the spectacular Cilo-Sat Mountains beyond may be limited by the prevailing political situation. A day's journey north of Van, just outside of Doğubeyazit, you'll find another isolated monument, the İşakpaşa castle, which stares across to Mount Ararat—the very end of Turkey.

When to Go

Turkey has a range of climates, and there's a good chance that no matter when you want to go, somewhere in the country will be at least tolerable, if not ideal—although you should also pay attention to the basic seasonal patterns of tourist traffic.

Of the coastal areas, **İstanbul** and the area around the **Sea of Marmara** have a relatively damp, Balkan climate, with muggy summers and cool, rainy (though seldom snowy) winters. Bear in mind that competition for facilities between June and August can be a drawback. Things are similarly busy during summer on the popular **Aegean and Mediterranean coasts**; climatic conditions, too, can be difficult during July and August, especially between İzmir and Antakya, where the heat is tempered only slightly by offshore breezes. Perhaps the best time to visit these coastal regions is in spring or fall, when the weather is gentler and the vacation crowds a little thinner; indeed, even during winter, the Turquoise and Mediterranean coasts—except for brief rainy periods in January and February—still fairly pleasant, and beyond Alanya winters can be positively balmy, although you still might not want to brave the water. The **Black Sea** is something of an anomaly, with temperate summers and exeptionally mild winters for so far north; rain is likely during the nine coolest months of the year, lingering as mist and humidity during summer—but it does have the advantage of being less crowded than the Aegean.

Anatolia is a natural fortress, its entire coast backed by mountains or hills that cut off the interior from any moderating maritime influences. **Central Anatolia** is mostly semi-arid steppe, with a healthy, bracing climate—warm but not unpleasant in summer, cool and dry in the relatively short winters—although Ankara is exceptionally nasty during the winter on account of the noxious soft coal burned for heating. Cappadocia in particular is a colorful, quiet treat throughout spring and fall (indeed well into December). As you travel east, into **Northeast**

Anatolia and around **Lake Van**, the altitude increases and conditions are frigid and deeply snowy between October and May, which means that high summer is by far the best (in some cases the only) time to visit, when you'll also find things more comfortable and less populated than on the teeming coast. Swinging into the lower **Euphrates Basin** and the **Hatay**, a Middle Eastern influence exerts itself: winters are no worse than in central Anatolia, but summers can be torrid— and often without the compensation of a nearby beach.

AVERAGE HIGH TEMPERATURES IN °C AND °F											
	JAN	FEB	MAR	APR	MAY	JUN	JUL	AUG	SEPT	OCT	NOV	DEC
İSTANBUL	6	6	7	12	17	21	24	24	20	16	12	8
	43	43	45	54	63	70	75	75	68	61	54	47
İZMIR	9	10	12	16	21	25	28	28	24	19	15	11
	48	50	54	61	70	77	82	82	75	66	59	52
ANTALYA	11	12	13	17	21	23	29	29	25	21	16	12
	52	54	56	63	70	77	84	84	77	70	61	54
ANKARA	1	1	5	12	17	20	24	24	19	13	8	3
	34	34	41	54	63	68	75	75	66	56	47	37
TRABZON	8	8	9	12	16	20	23	24	20	17	14	10
	47	47	48	54	61	68	73	75	68	63	57	50
VAN	-3	-3	1	7	13	16	22	22	17	11	5	-1
	26	26	34	45	56	65	72	72	63	52	41	30
DİYARBAKIR	2	4	9	14	20	26	31	31	25	18	10	5
	35	39	48	57	68	79	88	88	77	65	50	41

PART ONE

THE
BASICS

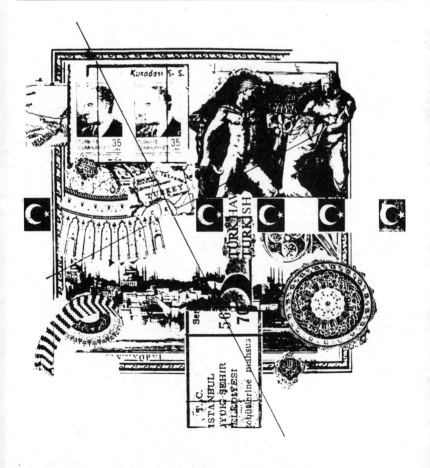

GETTING THERE

The easiest way to reach Turkey direct from the United States is by air. While the country has a number of gateway airports, most international flights from the US go via İstanbul. If you have the time, you may prefer to take a train to Turkey from one of the major European cities or travel by ferry via Italy or the Greek islands. It's also possible to take a bus across Europe, but this is very time-consuming, uncomfortable, and no cheaper than flying direct.

BY PLANE

Turkish Airlines (*THY*; ☎212/986-5050) is the only carrier that flies direct to Turkey from the United States, with **New York (JFK)–İstanbul** flights four times a week. APEX fares purchased 21 days in advance and valid from 7 to 60 days start at $780 in low season, rising to $1007 in high season. *Pan Am* (☎1-800/221-1111) and *TWA* (☎1-800/221-2000) offer a semi-direct service to İstanbul (with a change of planes in a European hub city); *Pan Am* flies daily, with APEX fares valid up to six months going for $1210 in low season but rising to $1409 during summer. There's also a "Eurosaver" program with prices slightly higher than *THY* and conditions more restrictive.

From just about anywhere else in the US, *Pan Am* or *TWA* provide a connecting service to JFK, which will add an extra $300–400. Remember, also, that these fares are "sticker prices," and many airlines sell discounted tickets through specialist travel agents, as described below.

DISCOUNT TICKETS

Travel agents are often the best bet for cheap deals to Turkey. The *Turkish Air Travel Bureau* (*Tursan Travel*, 20 East 49th St., New York, NY 10017; ☎212/888-1180) has special arrangements with both *Turkish Airlines* and *KLM*, with low-season fares starting at $750 round-trip. *KLM* flies four times a week to İstanbul from New York. *Club America Travel* (51 East 52nd St., New York, NY 10017; ☎212/972-2865) offers low rates on *Turkish Airlines* as well as on other major carriers. It's also worth checking the travel pages of the major Sunday papers for charter fares and cut-price agents, as well as the discount agents such as *STA* and *Council Travel* (see next page for addresses). These last two agents are particularly good if you're **under 26** or a full-time **student**.

FROM CANADA

The single **direct** Toronto–İstanbul flight, handled by *PIA* (☎212/370-9158), is an expensive option at CDN$2200. However, a number of European carriers provide **indirect** service with fares often comparable to those out of New York. *Swissair* (☎1-800/221-4750) flies daily from **Montreal** to **İstanbul** via Zurich, and twice weekly from Montreal and **Toronto** to **Ankara**. APEX fares vary between CDN$1227 and CDN$1415, depending on the time of year. *Lufthansa* (☎1-800/645-3880) offers a daily service via Frankfurt from Montreal and Toronto to both İstanbul and Ankara, at more expensive APEX fares. *KLM* (☎1-800/777-5553) flies daily to Amsterdam from Toronto, and five times weekly from Montreal, with onward connections to Istanbul six days a week. APEX fares weigh in at $CDN1286–1415, with tickets valid for up to six months. From **Vancouver**, *KLM* and *Lufthansa* between them provide a one-stop service to İstanbul through their European hubs five days a week.

VIA THE UK

If you're traveling to Turkey via the UK as part of a wider European tour, the simplest option is to take one of the daily scheduled flights direct to the country from London's Heathrow Airport. *British Airways* offers high-season, round-trip fares of £380 (£280 low-season) to İstanbul, a little more to Ankara. Other carriers offer indirect flights, for substantially cheaper fares: *İstanbul Airlines*, for

COUNCIL TRAVEL IN THE US

Head Office: 205 E. 42nd St., New York, NY 10017; ☎212/661-1450

CALIFORNIA

2486 Channing Way, Berkeley, CA 94704; ☎415/848-8604

UCSD Price Center, Q-076, La Jolla, CA 92093; ☎619/452-0630

1818 Palo Verde Ave., Suite E, Long Beach, CA 90815; ☎213/598-3338

1093 Broxton Ave., Suite 220, Los Angeles, CA 90024; ☎213/208-3551

4429 Cass St., San Diego, CA 92109; ☎619/270-6401

312 Sutter St., Suite 407, San Francisco, CA 94108; ☎415/421-3473

919 Irving St., Suite 102, San Francisco, CA 94122; ☎415/566-6222

14515 Ventura Blvd., Suite 250, Sherman Oaks, CA 91403; ☎818/905-5777

COLORADO

1138 13th St., Boulder, CO 80302; ☎818/905-5777

CONNECTICUT

Yale Co-op East, 77 Broadway, New Haven, CT 06520; ☎203/562-5335

DISTRICT OF COLUMBIA

1210 Potomac St., NW Washington, DC 20007; ☎202/337-6464

GEORGIA

12 Park Place South, Atlanta, GA 30303; ☎404/577-1678

ILLINOIS

1153 N. Dearborn St., Chicago, IL 60610; ☎312/951-0585

831 Foster St., Evanston, IL 60201; ☎708/475-5070

LOUISIANA

8141 Maple St., New Orleans, LA 70118; ☎504/866-1767

MASSACHUSETTS

79 South Pleasant St., 2nd Floor, Amherst, MA 01002; ☎413/256-1261

729 Boylston St., Suite 201, Boston, MA 02116; ☎617/266-1926

1384 Massachusetts Ave., Suite 206, Cambridge, MA 02138; ☎617/497-1497

Stratton Student Center MIT, W20-024, 84 Massachusetts Ave., Cambridge, MA 02139; ☎617/497-1497

MINNESOTA

1501 University Ave. SE, Room 300, Minneapolis, MN 55414; ☎612/379-2323

NEW YORK

35 W. 8th St., New York, NY 10011; ☎212/254-2525

Student Center, 356 West 34th St., New York, NY 10001; ☎212/643-1365

NORTH CAROLINA

703 Ninth St., Suite B-2, Durham, NC 27705; ☎919/286-4664

OREGON

715SW Morrison, Suite 600, Portland, OR 97205; ☎503/228-1900

RHODE ISLAND

171 Angell St., Suite 212, Providence, RI 02906; ☎401/331-5810

TEXAS

2000 Guadalupe St., Suite 6, Austin, TX 78705; ☎512/472-4931

Exec. Tower Office Center, 3300 W. Mockingbird, Suite 101, Dallas,TX 75235; ☎214/350-6166

WASHINGTON

1314 Northeast 43rd St., Suite 210, Seattle, WA 98105; ☎206/632-2448

WISCONSIN

2615 North Hackett Avenue, Milwaukee, WI; ☎414/332-4740

STA IN THE US

BOSTON

273 Newbury St., Boston, MA 02116; ☎617/266-6014

HONOLULU

1831 S. King St., Suite 202, Honolulu, HI 96826; ☎808/942-7755

LOS ANGELES

920 Westwood Blvd., Los Angeles, CA 90024; ☎213/824-1574

7204 Melrose Ave., Los Angeles, CA 90046; ☎213/934-8722

2500 Wilshire Blvd., Los Angeles, CA 90057; ☎213/380-2184

NEW YORK

17 E. 45th St., Suite 805, New York, NY 10017; ☎212/986-9470;☎ 800/777-0112

SAN DIEGO

6447 El Cajon Blvd., San Diego, CA 92115; ☎619/286-1322

SAN FRANCISCO

166 Geary St., Suite 702, San Francisco, CA 94108; ☎415/391-8407

TRAVEL CUTS IN CANADA

Head Office: 187 College St., Toronto, Ontario M5T 1P7; ☎416/979-2406

ALBERTA

1708 12th St. NW, Calgary T2M 3M7; ☎403/282-7687. 10424A 118th Ave., Edmonton T6G 0P7; ☎403/471-8054

BRITISH COLUMBIA

Room 326, T.C., Student Rotunda, Simon Fraser University, Burnaby, British Columbia V5A 1S6; ☎604/291-1204. 1516 Duranleau St., Granville Island, Vancouver V6H 3S4; ☎604/689-2887. Student Union Building, University of British Columbia, Vancouver V6T 1W5; ☎604/228-6890 Student Union Building, University of Victoria, Victoria V8W 2Y2; ☎604/721-8352

MANITOBA

University Centre, University of Manitoba, Winnipeg R3T 2N2; ☎204/269-9530

NOVA SCOTIA

Student Union Building, Dalhousie University, Halifax B3H 4J2; ☎902/424-2054. 6139 South St., Halifax B3H 4J2; ☎902/424-7027

ONTARIO

University Centre, University of Guelph, Guelph N1G 2W1; ☎519/763-1660. Fourth Level Unicentre, Carleton University, Ottawa, K1S5B6; ☎613/238-5493. 60 Laurier Ave. E, Ottawa K1N 6N4; ☎613/238-8222. Student Street, Room G27, Laurentian University, Sudbury P3E 2C6; ☎705/673-1401. 96 Gerrard St. E, Toronto M5B 1G7; ☎ (416) 977-0441. University Shops Plaza, 170 University Ave. W, Waterloo N2L 3E9; ☎519/886-0400.

QUÉBEC (known as *Voyages CUTS*)

Université McGill, 3480 rue McTavish, Montréal H3A 1X9; ☎514/398-0647. 1613 rue St. Denis, Montréal H2X 3K3; ☎514/843-8511. Université Concordia, Edifice Hall, Suite 643, S.G.W. Campus, 1455 bd de Maisonneuve Ouest, Montréal H3G 1M8; ☎514/288-1130. 19 rue Ste. Ursule, Québec G1R 4E1; ☎418/692-3971

SASKATCHEWAN

Place Riel Campus Centre, University of Saskatchewan, Saskatoon S7N 0W0; ☎306/343-1601

NOUVELLES FRONTIÈRES

In the United States

NEW YORK 19 W. 44th St., Suite 1702, New York, NY 10036; ☎212/764-6494

LOS ANGELES 6363 Wilshire Blvd., Suite 200, Los Angeles, CA 90048; ☎213/658-8955

SAN FRANCISCO 209 Post St., Suite 1121, San Francisco, CA 94108; ☎415/781-4480

In Canada

MONTREAL 1130 ouest, bd de Maisonneuve, Montréal, P.Q. H3A 1M8; ☎514/842-1450

QUÉBEC 176 Grande Allée Ouest, Québec, P.Q. G1R 2G9; ☎418/525-5255

---

instance, charge £140–180 round-trip, depending on the time of year. A more time consuming but far more interesting option is to travel overland, by a combination of train, bus, and ferry.

BY TRAIN

The principal routes to the Balkans from the UK run via France, Switzerland, and Italy, or through Belgium, Germany, and Austria. Service standards gradually diminish as you cross Yugoslavia, Greece, and Bulgaria, so if you're not keen to sample Balkan rail systems you might consider taking a train as far as Ancona or Venice and covering the last leg of the trip by sea (see p.6).

Standard rail fares are not cheap, however—a round-trip ticket currently costs £328—though **students and those under 26** qualify for the discounted BIJ fares offered by

Eurotrain (£239 round-trip via Bulgaria, £122 one-way). If you're planning to travel extensively around Europe before arrival in Turkey, some of the rail passes offered by **Eurail** might be worth considering. The "Youthpasses" available only to those under 26 currently cost $425 per month, $560 for two months. The adult passes, however, are frankly exorbitant, and are not valid in Turkey itself. If you wish to pursue the railpass option, contact *STA* or *Council Travel* (see above), or call ☎1-800/777-0112 for the latest prices.

TRAVELING THROUGH BULGARIA OR YUGOSLAVIA: VISAS

In order to travel **through Bulgaria**, US citizens do not require a visa (and may stay for up to 30 days), but Canadian citizens do. These must be obtained from a Bulgarian embassy or consulate

---

BULGARIAN EMBASSIES AND CONSULATES

USA: Consulate: 11 East 84th St, New York 1028 (☎212/737 4790); Embassy: 1621 22nd St 667 3870, Washington DC 20008 (☎202/387-7969).

CANADA: Consulate: 100 Abelaide Street West, Suite 1410, Toronto (☎416/363-7307).

BRITAIN: 188 Queen's Gate, London SW7 5HL (☎071/584 9400) (Mon–Fri 9:30am–12:30pm).

TURKEY: Consulate: Yıldız Posta Sok. 15, Esentepe, İstanbul (☎166 2605). Embassy: Atatürk Bul 124, Kavaklıdere, Ankara (☎126 7456).

YUGOSLAV EMBASSIES AND CONSULATES

USA: Embassy: 2410 California St NW, Washington DC 20008 (☎216/621-2093); Consulates: 1375 Sutter St, San Francisco, CA 94709 (☎415/776-4691); 17th Floor, 767 Third Ave, NY 10017 (☎212/838-2300).

CANADA: Embassy: 17 Blackburn Ave, Ottawa, Ontario K1N 8A2 (☎613/233-6289); Consulate: 377 Spadine Rd, Toronto, Ontario N5P 2V7 (☎416/481-7279).

---

in advance—they're not available at the border. There are two kinds of visa: transit visas which allow you to stay in Bulgaria for thirty hours and cost $40 or $60, depending on whether they're valid for single or double entry, and (rather better) **tourist visas**—valid for three months and permitting thirty days' stay. The latter cost $80 and seem to be regarded more favorably by the border guards; they also give the option of stopping off for longer if you wish—especially worthwhile if you're using a rail pass. Applying in person at a Bulgarian embassy or consulate should get you either kind of visa on the same day. Postal applications take about a week; enclose your passport, a note specifying the type of visa required, a photo, cash, or postal order as payment (no checks), and an SASE.

Traveling **through Yugoslavia**, nationals of both the United States and Canada need a visa; they're available free from a Yugoslav embassy or consulate, or for a fee at the border (time-consuming and officially discouraged).

BY BUS

You're not going to make any substantial savings traveling to Turkey **by bus**, and you can count on spending nearly four days on the road. Services from London are run by **Eurolines**, 52 Grosvenor Gardens, London SW1 (☎071/730 0202), and tickets can be reserved through most travel agents. Buses leave London's Victoria Coach Station on Sunday, Thursday, and Friday at 9pm, arriving roughly seventy hours later. Fares are £219 round-trip (youth fare £165), £123 one-way (youth fare £92). **Discount agents**, advertised in newspapers and listings magazines, will knock a few pounds off the standard fare.

BUSES FROM OTHER PARTS OF EUROPE

Thanks to the presence of large numbers of Turkish workers in northern Europe there are reliable **bus services from various European cities**—Brussels, Munich, Paris, Zürich, and Vienna—charging around $300 equivalent for a round-trip ticket. For further information contact: *Deutsche Touring GMBH*, Am Römerhof 17, 6000 Frankfurt 90 (☎069/790 3249); *Bosfor Turizm*, Seidlstr. 2, 8000 München (☎089/594 002); Gare Routière Internationale, 8 Place de Stalingrad, 75019 Paris (☎1 12 01 70 80); Argentinierstr. 67, Südbahnhof, 1040 Wien (☎222 65 65 93); Mete Cad 14, İstanbul-Taksim (☎11/143 2525); or *Varan Turizm*, Josefstr. 45, 8005 Zürich (☎1/440 477); Südbahnhof Südtirolerplatz 7 (☎1 44 04 77); or İnönü Cad 17, İstanbul (☎1/143 2187).

FERRIES FROM ITALY OR GREECE

Coming overland to Turkey, particularly by train, concluding the journey with a **boat ride** from Italy or Greece is tempting. There are two main alternatives. From mid-May to mid-October, *Minoan Lines* run a weekly (usually Fri) ferry from **Ancona to Kuşadası** on the Aegean coast, with stops at several Greek islands and Piraeus. Total journey time is two and a half days, with one stopover allowed. Fares for the whole distance range from $82 deck class to $146 for a mid-range cabin berth; a car costs $148. From Piraeus to Kuşadası the deck class fare is just $36. Prices include embarkation taxes, and although no student or railpass concessions are given, round-trip fares are ten percent cheaper.

From late March to early November, *Turkish Maritime Lines* offer a weekly (usually Sat) ferry from **Venice to İzmir**, with a stop in Piraeus except during July and August. The two-and-a-half-day crossing is relatively pricey, however, at about $150 for a pullman seat, $250 for a third-class cabin; depending on the time of year, cars can cost an additional $150, and taxes are not included. Better value in terms of sea-miles covered is *TML*'s identically priced weekly service from **Venice to Antalya**, a three-day sail offered between mid-May and the end of September.

Many travelers take the **short-hop** ferries over from the Greek islands of Lesvos, Hios, Samos, Kos, and Rhodes, to the respective Turkish ports of Ayvalık, Çeşme, Kuşadası, Bodrum, and Marmaris. Except for the Lesvos and Samos services, these still run after a fashion in winter, but you may have to wait a week or two between boats. One-way prices of $25–40 make it an expensive way to get to or from Turkey, vastly overpriced for the distances involved; full details of services are given in Chapters Three and Four.

One thing to bear in mind if you're vacationing in Greece is that a quick overnight jaunt over to the Turkish side on one of these ferries will, if you're on a charter flight, **invalidate** the return half of your ticket, since the Greek government, having subsidized cheap landing fees for charter airlines, is loath for you to spend your money elsewhere. Day excursions (i.e. not staying in Turkey overnight) are exempt from this, but otherwise there is no way around it, since the Turkish authorities will clearly stamp your passport both when you enter the country and when you leave.

PACKAGES AND SPECIAL INTEREST TOURS

Turkey is growing as a tourist attraction for American and Canadian visitors, and a small number of firms in the US now offer a range of **organized tours** with the emphasis on outdoor and adventure activities.

Inner Asia and *Wilderness Travel* are two long-established California-based companies offering nearly identical twelve-day *gulet* cruises along the Turquoise Coast, and a week's trekking in the Kaçkar as part of a 17-day trip. *Inner Asia* also offers more sedate, two-week bus tours of monumental and scenic highlights in eastern and western Turkey. Prices at both companies weigh in at about $1900 for the trekking package, $1800 for the coastal cruise, and $2700 for the bus trips. (These figures do not include airfare.) *Journeys* and *Overseas Adventure Travel* are relatively new companies whose broadly similar offerings might be worth investigating.

If you're really game for physical involvement, *Sobek Expeditions* will take you rafting down the Çoruh River for nine days as part of a two-week, early summer package in eastern Turkey; the land-only cost is just over $2100. Finally, *Kosmos* is one of the few Turkish companies worth singling out, offering a wide range of one- or two-week trekking, sailing, and converted-truck trips along the Turquoise Coast, through Cappadocia, and the Toros or Kaçkar ranges. They have long acted as outfitters for UK-based adventure companies, but will in theory sign up customers on the spot, for far cheaper than you'd pay overseas: citing prices is difficult, since these are dependent on the current Turkish lira exchange rate.

Pacha Tours caters to a more sedate audience, running a variety of one-to-three-week tours, usually on buses, in groups of up to 35 customers. The company follows a variety of regional routes ("Western Turkey", "Eastern Turkey & Black Sea Coast") and pursues cultural/religious themes ("The Sepharidic Legacy" or "In the Steps of St Paul"). Prices range from $745 for the eight-day Turquoise Coast cruise, to $3590 for the 24-day "Grand Turkey" tour, with meals, and often air fare, included. *Pacha* also prepares customized, individual, itineraries.

PACKAGE TOUR OPERATORS

Inner Asia, 2627 Lombard St., San Francisco, CA 94132 (☎415/922-0448 or 800/777-8183).

Wilderness Travel, 801 Allston Way, Berkeley, CA 94710 (☎415/548-0420).

Journeys, 3516 NE 155th St., Seattle, WA 98155 (☎1-800/345-4453).

Overseas Adventure Travel, 349 Cambridge, MA 02139 (☎617/876-0533).

Sobek, PO Box 1089, Angels Camp, CA 95222 (☎209/736-4524 or 800/777-7939).

Kosmos, Cumhuriyet Cad 243/3, Harbiye, Istanbul (☎141 5253).

Pacha Tours, 1560 Broadway, New York, NY 10036 (☎212/764-4080).

RED TAPE AND VISAS

All American and Canadian citizens need to enter Turkey is a passport—no visas are required. Americans are allowed to remain in Turkey for three months, and Canadians two months, before having to apply for an extension. During this time it is forbidden to take up employment.

If you want to stay longer you can apply for an *ikamet tezkeresi* or residence permit. In order to get one of these you'll have to give evidence of means of support—either savings, a steady income from abroad, or legal work in Turkey (not easy to find—see "Finding Work," p.43). Many people more commonly nip into Greece or Bulgaria (even Northern Cyprus) every three months for at least 24 hours and re-enter for a

new, three-month stamp, rather than go to the trouble of applying for a residence permit.

BORDER INSPECTIONS

Entering Turkey usually entails a very cursory customs inspection: current commodity import **limits** worth knowing about include 400 cigarettes, one kilo of loose tobacco, five liters of spirits (foreign booze is now readily available in Turkey, for broadly overseas prices), and 1.5 kilos of instant coffee; you might bring this as gifts for friends, since it's exorbitantly priced in Turkey. A record of cameras, video recorders, etc may be made in your passport to ensure that you take them out with you when you leave. **Vehicles** will most definitely result in a passport entry, making it impossible for you to leave Turkey without it—unless you can prove that the vehicle has been either wrecked or stolen (see "Getting Around").

Checks **on the way out** may be more thorough, and you should arrive at the airport or ferry dock in good time in case the customs officers decide to be slow and inquisitive. Only an idiot would try and take drugs through Turkish customs, although it's more likely that the guards will be on the lookout for **antiquities**. Penalties for trying to smuggle these out include long jail sentences, plus a large fine. For details of what constitutes an antiquity, see the advice in "Bazaars and Shopping."

HEALTH AND INSURANCE

No special inoculations are required before visiting Turkey, although if you don't want to take any chances, jabs against cholera, typhoid, and tetanus are suggested, particularly if you're traveling to the southeast. Some visitors also take the precaution of getting a gamma globulin injection against hepatitis A. Only if you're visiting the southeast in late spring or early summer need you consider malaria preventative tablets.

HEALTH PROBLEMS AND HAZARDS

You're unlikely to encounter many health problems in Turkey. Many people experience bouts of **mild diarrhea**, and the chances of this happening increase the longer you stay in the country. As a precaution take *Lomotil* or similar anti-diarrhea tablets with you (you'll be able to buy locally produced remedies if you forget). It's probably best to avoid drinking the tap **water**, heavily chlorinated though it is, and with bottled water widely available you shouldn't have any need to.

In the east, particularly during the hot summer months, more serious **food poisoning** is a possibility. In restaurants, avoid dishes that look as if they have been standing around for a while, and if you have a sensitive stomach make sure that meat and fish is well grilled. Also, don't, whatever you do, eat mussels in summer. If you're struck down, the best thing is to let the bug run its course and drink lots of fluids like sweetened tea (without milk), *gazoz* (lemon-flavored soda), and bottled water; plain white rice and a bit of yogurt will also help stick you together again.

Turkey has a few animal hazards. **Adders** and **scorpions** can lurk among the rocks and stones of archaeological sites. **Mosquitos** are a problem in some places, and since no good repellents are available in Turkey, you should bring your own—the roll-on varieties are best. At night they're most easily dispatched with locally sold incense coils (*spiral tütsü* in Turkish), or an *ESEM Mat*, a small electrified tray that slowly vaporises an odorless pyrethrin disc during the course of a night. Malaria is sometimes a seasonal problem (April–July) in the regions between Adana and Mardin (mainly the area covered in Chapter Eleven).

Rabies is perhaps the greatest potential danger; the giant Sivas-Kangal sheepdogs, while rarely aggressive unless their flock is closely approached, are the most obvious possible source. Be wary of any animal which bites, scratches, or licks you, particularly if it's behaving erratically. First aid involves flushing a wound with soap and water after encouraging limited bleeding; apply antiseptic and bandage if necessary, but do not suture. As soon as possible— within a maximum of 72 hours—embark on a six-injection course of human diploid cell vaccine (HDCV)—given in the arm and nowhere near as painful as the old abdominal shots—followed by one of human rabies immunoglobulin (HRIG). If you've been pre-immunised, you'd only need two doses of HDCV and no HRIG.

MEDICAL ATTENTION

For **minor complaints** head for the nearest *eczane* or pharmacy. Even the smallest town will have at least one, where you'll find remedies for ailments like diarrhea, sunburn, and flu. In larger towns, *eczane* staff may know some English or German. Pharmacies are able to dispense formulas that would ordinarily require a prescription in North America. Medication prices are kept low by a combination of government control and cheap local production, but it may be difficult to find exact equivalents to your home prescription, so bring it, and a good supply of the actual medication, along. Night-duty pharmacies are known as **nöbet(ci)**; a list of the currently open one(s) is posted in every pharmacy's window.

For more **serious ailments** you'll find well-trained doctors in the larger towns and cities. Most of these, however, are specialists, advertising themselves by means of street signs outside their premises. A *diş tabibi* or *hekimi* is a dentist; a *tıbbî doktor* will treat ailments of all kinds, while an *operatör* is a qualified surgeon.

If you're not sure what's wrong with you, it's best to go instead to a *klinik* or **hospital**, indicated by a blue street sign with a large white "H" on it. Hospitals are either public (*Devlet Hastane* or *SSK Hastanesi*), or private (*Özel Hastane*); the latter are vastly preferable in terms of cleanliness, shortness of lines, and standard of care, and since all foreigners must pay for any attention anyway, you may as well get the best available. Fees are lower than in North America but still substantial enough that you'd want insurance cover (see below). Admission desks of private hospitals can also recommend their affiliated doctors if you don't want or need to be an in-patient, and your consulate or the tourist information office may also be able to provide you with the address of an English-speaking doctor.

INSURANCE

Travel insurance can buy you peace of mind as well as save you money. Before you purchase any insurance, however, check what you have already, whether as part of a family or student policy. You may find yourself covered for medical expenses and loss, and possibly loss of or damage to valuables, while abroad.

For example, **Canadians** are usually covered for medical expenses by their provincial health plans (but may only be reimbursed after the fact).

Holders of **ISIC** cards are entitled to $2000 worth of accident coverage and 60 days ($100 per diem) of hospital in-patient benefits for the period during which the card is valid. University **students** will often find that their student health coverage extends for one term beyond the date of last enrollment.

Bank and charge **accounts** (particularly *American Express*) often have certain levels of medical or other insurance included. **Home-owners' or renters'** insurance may cover theft or loss of documents, money, and valuables while overseas, though exact conditions and maximum amounts vary from company to company.

SPECIALIST INSURANCE

Only after exhausting the possibilities above might you want to contact a **specialist travel insurance** company; your travel agent can usually recommend one—*Travelguard* and *The Travelers* are good policies.

Travel insurance offerings are quite comprehensive, anticipating everything from charter companies going bankrupt to delayed (as well as lost) baggage, by way of sundry illnesses and accidents. **Premiums** vary widely—from the very reasonable ones offered primarily through student/youth agencies (though available to anyone), to those so expensive that the cost for two or three months of coverage will probably equal the cost of the worst possible combination of disasters.

A most important thing to keep in mind—and a source of major disappointment to would be claimants—is that *none* of the currently available policies insures against **theft** of anything while overseas. North American travel policies apply only to items lost from, or damaged in, the custody of an identifiable, responsible third party, i.e. hotel porter, airline, luggage consignment, etc. Even in these cases you will still have to contact the local police to make out a complete report so that your insurer can process the claim.

BRITISH POLICIES

If you are **transiting through Britain**, policies there cost considerably less (under £20/$32 for a month) and include routine cover for theft. You can take out a British policy at almost any travel agency or major bank; check agencies detailed in the "Getting There" section for addresses. ISIS, a "student" policy but open to everyone, is reliable and fairly good value; it is operated by a company called *Endsleigh*, and is available through any student/youth travel agency.

REIMBURSEMENT

All insurance policies—American or Canadian—work by **reimbursing you** once you return home, so be sure to keep all your receipts from doctors and pharmacists. Any thefts should immediately be reported to the nearest police station and a police report obtained; no report, no refund.

If you have had to undergo serious medical treatment, with major hospital bills, contact your consulate. They can normally arrange for an insurance company, or possibly relatives, to cover the fees, pending a claim.

COSTS, MONEY, AND BANKS

While no longer as rock-bottom cheap as it was a decade ago, much of Turkey is still less expensive than most Mediterranean travel destinations. Prices at the main resorts, however, have steadily crept up to a little less than those in Greece, Yugoslavia, and Portugal. Domestic inflation runs at seventy or ninety percent annually, depending on which set of statistics you believe; outsiders are spared the full effect of this by a constant devaluation of the Turkish currency against hard currencies, amounting to about sixty percent a year. We've therefore quoted all prices in the guide in

$US, and, with minor upward adjustments from year to year, these should give a reliable idea of what you'll be paying on the spot.

COSTS

You can pretty well spend as much or as little as you want in Turkey, given the wide disparity in prices between the coastal resorts and relatively unvisited spots in the interior. In terms of a **daily budget**, a frugal existence relying exclusively on coaches, food from simple soup kitchens and the cheapest grades of accommodation won't set you back more than $15 a day per person. If you're entitled to one, a student identity card—FIYTO being more influential than ISIC—will shave a bit more off the cost of museum and entertainment tickets and some transportation. For any degree of comfort, including rooms with en suite bath and the occasional splurge on a moped or at the bazaar, allow an average daily expenditure of $25–30. Incidentally, you won't save much by buying picnic ingredients—even the poorest Turks eat out frequently, and you may as well too.

As for specifics, **accommodation** costs range from about $3–4 per person in the most basic backwoods flophouses, to five-star resort hotels with every luxury at $100–140 per person, with well-amenitied mid-range hotels weighing in somewhere between the two at $10–15 per person in large provincial towns and coastal centers. **Food** also varies widely: it's difficult to spend more than $6 apiece for a meal once off the tourist circuit, but easy to drop twice that amount or more in a resort town. **Transport** is more consistent—coach fares hover around $2 per 100km traveled, slightly more for popular routes and top-flight companies. The better long-distance trains cost about the same, with small surcharges for sleeping facilities. Domestic air ticket prices are rapidly approaching parity with those in North America, but a pullman seat or third-class cabin on the admittedly limited long-haul ferry network is still good value.

MONEY AND BANKS

The Turkish **currency** is the lira, abbreviated everywhere as TL. Coins still exist in denominations of 25, 50, 100, and 500TL, although the smallest two have strictly nuisance value except in paying for public toilets. Paper notes come as 1000, 5000, 10,000, and 20,000. Most newcomers confuse the similar-looking 1000 and 10,000 notes, so be alert; additionally, all bills below 1000TL have been withdrawn—don't accept any obsolete ones as change.

Rates for foreign currency are always better inside Turkey, so don't bother buying TL at home unless you know you'll be arriving in the dead of night at some obscure land border, in which case a token amount is advisable. Because of the TL's constant devaluation you should only change money as you need it, every few days.

Banks are open Monday to Friday, 8:30am to noon and 1:30 to 5pm; foreign exchange transactions won't be undertaken after 4:45pm. Most banks charge no **commission** (komisyon in the Frenchified Turkish); if they do, go somewhere else. Between April and October most coastal resorts between Çanakkale and Alanya have **weekend and evening hours** at specific nöbetçi (duty) banks; a list is posted in the window or door of each branch telling you who's open that week. Main bank branches themselves vary in their efficiency, with the time spent filling in triplicate forms and obtaining counter-signatures ranging from a few minutes to nearly an hour in some cases. As a rule of thumb, the more remote and less touristed a place is, the longer you'll wait—often with tea served in the meantime. In certain east Anatolian towns only one or two banks are authorized to accept foreign currency. If you have a choice, the Türk Ziraat Bankası, the Yapı Kredi Bankası, and the Türk Ticaret Bankası are the most competent; Eti Bank, Akbank, and İşbank, which charges whopping commissions of $2–5 a transaction, should be avoided. Most others fall somewhere in between.

Both during and **outside of bank hours**, you can also use the **special exchange booths** run by banks in coastal resorts, airports, and ferry docks—a good reason to take advantage of an enforced halt in such places—where service is usually quicker and commissions nonexistent. The local **post and telephone office (PTT)**, particularly in a sizable town, is also often able to change foreign currency (though not always traveler's checks)—helpful if you've just stepped off a train in Konya at 6am and are running low on cash.

Incidentally, keep all **foreign exchange slips** with you until departure. They can help prove the value of purchases made in case of queries by customs, and they entitle you to re-exchange excess TL. Normally, token amounts of up to about $100 in value can be reconverted to hard currency without comment. In any event, don't leave Turkey with unspent TL—it's not illegal up to $3000, but the stuff is utterly worthless once out of the country.

Having money transferred from overseas to a Turkish bank is inadvisable. All of the above caveats about bank bureaucracy will apply fivefold, with waits measured in days, commissions and fees in the tens of dollars. If you have a credit card it's far cheaper and quicker to get a cash advance (see below).

CASH, TRAVELER'S CHECKS, AND PLASTIC

It's wise to carry a fair wad of overseas **cash** with you in Turkey: theft and pickpocketing is not an overriding problem except in İstanbul, you can often pay for souvenirs or accommodation with it directly (prices for both are often quoted in hard currency), and it reduces bank bureaucracy considerably. Bear in mind also that the **black market** for foreign cash, referred to as "Tahtakale" after the İstanbul bazaar district

where it originated, offers up to a ten percent premium over the official rates and isn't illegal—the most reliable outlets are jewelers' or goldsmiths' shops, who will serve you quickly and without taking commission.

Traveler's checks, available from your downtown bank for a one-percent commission, go with slightly more difficulty—the bank must have a specimen for the brand you carry, or they'll refuse to serve you. This is less of a problem with *Thomas Cook* and *American Express* checks; *Visa* checks will be harder to change. For both cash or traveler's checks transactions, $US, sterling, or DM are the preferred currencies.

A major **credit card** is invaluable for domestic ferry and plane tickets, and also for waiver of a huge cash deposit when renting a car. You can also normally get **cash advances** at any bank displaying the appropriate sign. In addition, you can use a *Visa* card in the widespread Automatic Telling Machine network of the *Yapı Kredi Bankası* to get a cash advance in TL—subject, of course, to the usual surcharges.

COMMUNICATIONS: MAIL, AND PHONES

The Turkish postal and telephone service is run by the PTT (*Post Telefon ve Telegraf*), easily identifiable by their black-on-yellow logo. In the larger towns and tourist resorts, the phone division of the main PTT building is open 24 hours, with mail accepted from 8am until 7pm. Elsewhere expect both facilities to be available from 8am to 10pm Monday to Saturday, 9am to 7pm on Sunday.

THE MAIL

Letter rates are rapidly approaching uniformity with those in North America; stamps are only available from the PTT. The outgoing service is efficient, but make sure that the clerk has charged you for air mail (*uçakla*) and not the cheaper and painfully slow surface rate. *Acele* (Express) service is available for a hefty, $25 surcharge, with delivery to the US promised within four days.

Mailboxes are clearly labeled with categories of destination: *yurtdışı* for overseas, *yurtiçi* for inland, *şehiriçi* for local. **Street-corner boxes** are rare, and shouldn't be mistaken for look-alike rubbish bins. To receive mail **poste restante**, articles should be addressed to you, c/o Postrestant, Merkez Postanesi, (City), Turkey. If you carry *American Express* traveler's checks, however (they charge an inquiry fee otherwise), you may be better off having mail sent and held at the İstanbul or Ankara branches of *Türk Ekspres*, the local **American Express agent**.

The best advice on sending **packages** is not to—at least not anything over two or three kilograms. If you must, do it in a medium-sized town

INTERNATIONAL TELEPHONE CODES

To reach **a number in Turkey from overseas,** dial your country's international access code, then ☎90 for Turkey, then the city code and subscriber number.

USEFUL NUMBERS IN TURKEY

Local directory assistance ☎011

Long-distance directory assistance ☎061

Intercity operator ☎031

International operator ☎032 (only for reverse charges calls)

Express calls, intercity ☎091

INTERNATIONAL DIALING CODES

| USA ☎9 9 1 | AUSTRALIA ☎9 9 63 | BRITAIN ☎9 9 44 |
| CANADA ☎9 9 1 | NEW ZEALAND ☎9 9 64 | IRELAND ☎9 9 353 |

with an airport and enlist the help of a sympathetic supervisor who understands the rules. Boxes must be left open for inspection, though at main branches folded packing kits are sold. Always come prepared with tape, twine, indelible marker, glue, scissors, supporting invoices and certificates—and plenty of patience.

PHONES

The PTT is also the best place to make **phone calls**. Inside or just adjacent there is usually a range of alternatives: a *jeton* (token) phone, a card phone, or a *köntürlü* (metered, clerk-attended) phone, sometimes in a closed booth. Phones elsewhere are relatively rare, though you will find them in public parks and at gas stations.

Jetons theoretically come in small (*küçük*), medium (*orta*), and large (*büyük*) sizes, for local, intercity, and international use respectively, though the two larger sizes are often in short supply. Fractionally used tokens are not returned, so don't use bigger sizes for local calls; despite notices to the contrary, you can usually exchange unused ones for postage stamps. While you're in Turkey it's a good idea to always carry a few on you—they're not always for sale when you need them. You drop at least one token in the slot before dialing; when the red light comes on and a warning tone sounds, you have about ten seconds to feed in more. Never attempt to call from a *jeton*-operated phone box where the square, red "out of service" light is illuminated.

For intercity or overseas calls, **phonecards** (available in denominations of 30, 60, and 120

units) or **metered booths** are better value, the latter also tending to be quieter. Phonecards are used in the same manner as European ones, though wait for the number of units remaining to appear on the screen before dialing. Remember, too, that card-phone booths are only common in the west and in big resorts; don't buy the biggest size card and expect to be able to use it in eastern Anatolia.

Once the connection is made, the system is generally excellent—it had a major overhaul in 1984–85. Direct-dial, long-distance calls can be made at any phone booth bearing the label *Şehirlerarası* (Intercity) or *Milletlerarası* (International). For Turkish **long-distance calls**, dial 9 (wait for a change in tone), and then the city code (a list of major towns is usually provided) plus the subscriber number without a pause in between. Excluding the initial "9," all Turkish numbers—code and subscriber together—must total eight digits. As the network expands, local codes tend to shorten, with the final digit becoming part of the local prefix—though sometimes a different digit is used to lengthen local numbers. Thus be wary of old phone numbers on last year's tourist literature. We've listed phone numbers throughout the guide; otherwise the directories in PTTs are usually the most current sources.

Overseas rates are not cheap: over $3 per minute to North America or Australasia, and around $1.70 per minute to Britain. But there is a 25 percent discount on normal rates after 10pm and on Sunday. To make an international call, dial 9 twice (waiting for two changes in tone), then the country/area codes, and finally the local number.

INFORMATION AND MAPS

Before you leave it's worth a visit to the Turkish tourist office (officially the Information Office of the embassy), where you'll be able to pick up a few very basic maps and glossy brochures. Don't overload your luggage with these, though; much the same range (or often the same scarcity) of stuff is available in Turkey itself. What you should do before setting off is invest in decent regional and town plans, since those on sale in Turkey are generally inadequate.

INFORMATION IN TURKEY

Most Turkish towns of any size will have a *Turizm Danişma Bürosu* or **tourist information office** of some sort, in smaller places lodged inside the public library or *belediye* (city hall). However, outside of the larger cities and obvious tourist destinations there's often very little actual information available, and the staff may well try to dismiss you with a selection of useless and very general brochures. It's more constructive, really, to approach these offices with specific questions, such as exact bus schedules, festival ticket availability, or revised museum opening hours, although there is no guarantee that there will be anyone who can speak English. Lists of accommodation for all budgets are sometimes a useful feature at the more heavily patronized offices; the staff, however, will generally not make reservations.

We've given precise **opening hours** of tourist information offices in most cases; as a general rule they adhere to standard 8:30-to-12:30, 1:30-to-5:30, Monday-to-Friday schedules. In big-name resorts and large cities summer hours extend well into the evening and over much of the weekend.

MAPS

Stock up on **maps** *before* you leave, as Turkish ones are usually not particularly detailed and sometimes rather inaccurate.

The best available **touring maps** are the German *Reise und Verkehrsverlag* (RV) "Turkey, West" and "Turkey, East (With Cyprus)" ($11.95 each). They cover the entire country at a scale of 1:800,000 and are detailed and fairly accurate, showing major and minor roads, railroads and some basic topographical detail, with basic street plans of the major cities. The only comparable alternative is the *Kümmerly-Frey* double-sided map of east and west Turkey at $7.95, but this doesn't show the rail network. If you're just visiting the Aegean or Mediterranean, *Hallwag* produces a 1:2,000,000 map of the whole country with coastal insets at a scale of 1:750,000 for $7.95.

As well as our own **city maps**, the tourist offices in İstanbul, Ankara, and İzmir stock reasonable complimentary **street maps**, although the İstanbul one is restricted to downtown and lacks detail. The quality of local plans available at provincial tourist offices varies widely, though as a rule of thumb, the more tourists a place gets the better the maps tend to be.

There are very few maps of Turkish cities on sale, and when available they are in any case rarely good value. A notable exception is the exhaustive **A–Z atlas of İstanbul** published by *Asya* (about $12 at better bookstores), a worthwhile investment if you plan to spend a lot of time in the city. Otherwise, *Hallwag* does a good street map of central İstanbul for $6.95, and the *Falk Plan* of İstanbul ($7.95) is also acceptable, with additional coverage of more outlying districts.

It's virtually impossible to obtain large-scale topographical maps of specific areas for **trekking**; don't bother asking in Turkey, and overseas you're mostly restricted to a 1:200,000 series prepared with German assistance in 1944. Even laying hands on these in North America is tedious, since the Turks have security protocols with other NATO countries, and permission may have to be obtained from military authorities. You might try the map room of a major university library. Usable enough maps for the most popular trekking areas can be found in *Trekking in Turkey* ($9.95, Lonely Planet).

TURKISH INFORMATION OFFICES ABROAD

USA 821 United Nations Plaza, New York NY 10017 (☎212/687-2194).

UK First Floor, 170/173 Piccadilly, London W1V 9DD (☎071/734 868).

GETTING AROUND

Public transit is fairly comprehensive in Turkey, and only on major routes and public holidays do you need to book tickets in advance. Where a destination is not part of the rather skeletal train network, private bus companies more than compensate, in a system that is cheap and efficient. Although terminals can be nightmarish at times, assiduous attention is paid to your comfort and safety while you're in transit. Short stretches are best covered by *dolmuş*—either shared taxis which run in towns and cities, or minibuses linking rural villages. Moving around under your own steam is also an option, though car rental rates are among the highest in the Mediterranean, and road conditions can be challenging. The domestic ferry network is now confined to the upper Aegean and Black Sea coasts, while the internal plane network is constantly expanding as demand rises and new private companies are allowed to compete with the state carrier *THY*.

TRAINS

Turkey's **train network**, run by the *TCDD* or *Turkish State Railroads*, is far from exhaustive, and it's best used to span the distances between the three largest cities and the main provincial centers. When the Germans laid the track in the late nineteenth century they were paid by the kilometer, with the result that trains often follow ludicrously tortuous routes and take up to twice as long as buses. They do, however, have the advantage of additional comfort at comparable or lower prices.

The better services west of Ankara, denoted "**mavı tren**" or "**ekspresi**," almost match long-distance buses in speed and frequency; in the east, however, punctuality and general service standards begin to flag. Avoid any departure labeled *posta* (mail train) or *yolcu* (local)—they're excruciatingly slow; in the chapter-end travel details we've only given data for the best trains. Portable **timetables** in any language are nonexistent; the only way to get reliable information is to go to the station in person, scan the placards, and then confirm with staff. On major train routes it's a good idea to make a **reservation**. You can do this for any journey in the country in İstanbul and Ankara, where the system is computerized. **Basic—second class—prices** on the better trains are about the same per kilometer as the buses. Reckon on paying around $17 for a one-way ticket, İzmir–Ankara, with a couchette; buying a return ticket brings the fare down by thirty percent. **Inter-Rail** passes are valid all over Turkey; Eurotrain tickets however, only take you as far as İstanbul, and Eurail passes are not honored. Within Turkey, foreign **students** with an ISIC card are entitled to a ten percent discount on rail tickets.

On long-haul journeys you have a choice between a first- and second-class **seat**; some shorter runs are still equipped with dilapidated third-class carriages. **First class** features pull-man-style seats, and, in summer, air conditioning, and is expensive; **second-class** wagons have continental-style, six-person compartments with narrow corridors on one side, and cost around half as much as first class. **Third class**, where it still exists, consists of uncomfortable wooden seats but it is at least very cheap. In second- or third-class carriages, **single women** traveling alone will be looked after by the conductor, which generally means delivered into a family or mixed-sex compartment. **Non-smoking** cars are always available on first- and second-class trains; ask for an *içmeyen vagon* when booking.

There's almost always a **dining car** on trains west of Ankara—the limited menus aren't so bad or expensive as to require bringing your own food, though no one will object if you nurse a Coke. In the east you'd be well advised to check on the availability of food and drink, or bring your own.

There are two different kinds of **sleeping facilities** on a Turkish train. **Küşetli** is a couchette in a six-seat, second-class compartment, where you'll share with strangers and pay a supplement of about $7. **Yataklı** wagons have first-class, three-bed suites that cost up to three times as much as *küşetli*. You're heavily penalized price-wise for booking one of these alone, and they're really intended for families or groups.

LONG-DISTANCE BUSES

An immensely popular form of transport, the Turkish **long-distance bus** is a crucial part of the country's modern culture. There is no national bus company in Turkey; most routes are covered by several firms, with ticket booths both at the *otogars* (bus terminals) from which they operate, and also downtown. To further complicate matters, there's no such thing as a comprehensive timetable, although individual companies often provide their own. This makes for a bewildering selection from which to choose. Prices vary slightly between the best and scruffiest companies, though convenience of departures and on-board service are equally important differences. The *otogars* are full of touts waiting to take you to the company of their choice once you state your destination—though it may not have the soonest departure, or the best service and seats. As a broad example of **fares**, İstanbul to Antalya costs around $8.

When buying tickets, ask to see the **seating plan**: if you crave fresh air, request front-row seats behind the driver's window, which may be the only open ventilation on the coach. If in doubt, inspect the vehicle out in the loading bay (*peron* in Turkish), and ask at the *gişe* how long the trip will take. It's worth bearing in mind that long-haul journeys (over 10hr) generally take place at night, and that buses rarely cover more than 60km an hour, no matter what you're told. Unacquainted women and men are not allowed to sit next to each other, and you may be asked to switch your assigned seat to accommodate this convention.

Be warned that most buses play music— either *arabesk* or some Western equivalent— until the lights go out. **Non-smoking** zones don't exist on the cheaper Turkish buses—and most Turks hate open windows or vents. Partial compensation for this is the avid attention of the **muavin** or driver's assistant, who can supply drinking water on demand, and will appear several times in a journey with pungent cologne for freshening up. Every ninety minutes there will be a fifteen-minute *mola* (**rest stop**) for tea and toilet visits, and less frequent half-hour pauses for meals at roadside cafeterias.

To avoid the worst drawbacks of Turkish bus travel, particularly on the main intercity lines, you might consider going with the two **premium coach companies**, *Ulusoy* and *Varan*. Their seats are more comfortable than most and they have non-smoking areas, although they don't segregate single passengers by sex. *Pamukkale* and *Kamil Koç*, while not quite as enlightened, are two of the best "standard" outfits.

DOLMUŞES

The Turkish institution of the **dolmuş** or shared transport could profitably be imitated in the West: it's practical, economical, and ecologically sound. The idea is that a vehicle—a car or mini-bus—runs along set routes, picking passengers up and dropping them off along the way. To stop a dolmuş, give a hand signal as for a normal taxi, and if there's any room at all (the word *dolmuş* means "stuffed"), they'll stop and let you on. To get out, say either *inecek var* (literally, "there's a getting out") or *müsait bir yerde* (literally "at a convenient place").

On busy **urban routes** it's better to take the dolmuş from the start of its run, at a stand marked by a "D" sign in blue, black, and white, sometimes with the destination written out— though generally you'll have to ask to find out the eventual destination, or look at the dolmuşes themselves, which generally have their journey's end written on a windshield placard. On less popular routes the driver will often depart before the vehicle is full, in which case you're likely to be taken aboard wherever you flag it.

Inter-town and -village dolmuşes are always twelve-seater minibuses. For the remotest villages there will only be two services a day: to the nearest large town in the morning, back to the village in mid-afternoon. Generally, though, dolmuşes run between 7 or 8am and 7pm in summer, stopping earlier to match the hour of sunset in winter. In the chapter's-end travel details we've given broad frequencies within this period unless otherwise stated.

There's no strict **vehicle specialization**—minibuses can and do serve as dolmuşes in most cities, particularly in İzmir—but in İstanbul classic Chevrolets and Fords, sold off by US military and embassy personnel 35 years ago, have the monopoly on most routes. Yellow taxis, confusingly still bearing signs saying "TAKSI," operate as dolmuşes in many towns—if you're not sure, ask; in İstanbul the older dolmuş saloons have a checked stripe on their flank. In the text we've always said "dolmuş" but the context and location will make it clear if we mean a minibus or sedan.

Fares are low, hardly more than urban bus prices and about the same between towns, but it's always difficult to know how much to pay if you're only going part-way. Everybody else will know, however; just state your destination and hand over a pile of coins or notes, and you'll invariably get the right change. If you sit near the front, you'll have to relay other people's fares and repeat their destinations to the driver—no mean feat if you don't speak the language.

CITY BUSES AND TAXIS

In larger towns the main means of transit are red-and-white **city buses**, which take **pre-purchased tickets**, available from kiosks near the main termini, from newsagents, or from touts for slightly inflated prices. The only **exceptions** are the blue city buses in İstanbul, whose drivers have been known to take cash in place of tickets.

Yellow city **taxis** are everywhere, and ranks crop up at appropriate places, though at rush hour finding a free cab can be difficult. Flagging one down in the street is the best way to find a cab; radio cabs don't exist, but in suburban areas there are useful street corner telephones, from which you can call cabs if you can make yourself understood. Urban vehicles all have working, digital-display meters, and fares are among the lowest in the Mediterranean. Within city limits, it's illegal to ask for a flat fare, though attempted rip-offs of foreigners aren't unheard of. Out in the country, you'll have to bargain.

HITCHING

Hitching is a viable option where public transit is scarce or unavailable, and rides tend to be frequent and friendly. You may be expected to share a glass of tea with the driver on reaching your destination. It is polite to offer a little money, though it will almost always be refused. Rural Turks hitch as well—if you see large numbers at roadsides waving you down in your own car, it's a good bet that no bus or dolmuş is forthcoming, and you'd be peforming a useful service by giving them a ride.

On routes that are well served by buses and dolmuşes, the general consensus among Turks is that there's little point in hitching since public transit is so cheap, and they will be less inclined to view hitchhikers favorably.

Contrary to what's been written elsewhere, you do sometimes see Turkish **women**—older, conservatively dressed villagers—hitching near the Aegean coast. However, you also see prostitutes soliciting truck drivers along the main highways, and on balance it's not a good idea for foreign women to hitch alone, especially in the east of the country. With company, it need be fraught with no more peril, and possibly less, than elsewhere around the Mediterranean.

DRIVING

Given the excellent bus services, you don't need to **drive** in Turkey to get around, but it can make it possible to see more of the country more quickly, particularly in the central and eastern regions.

Roads are usually adequate, although often dangerously narrow. This is not so much of a problem in the relatively uncrowded east, but it makes driving quite hair-raising in the west. You **drive on the right**, and yield to oncoming traffic on your right. **Speed limits**, though seldom observed, are 50km/hr in towns, 90km/hr on the open road and expressways.

Typical **hazards** include the local flair for passing right, left and center, sometimes even on bends, and huge trucks ambling along at walking pace or whizzing past at kamikaze speeds. At **night**, be prepared for vehicles with no taillights, one headlight or just parking lights and even more lumbering long-distance trucks. Oncoming cars will flash their lights at you for no apparent reason, whether or not your brights are on.

Foreigners are rarely stopped by the **police** at the frequent checkpoints, but if you are you may have to produce your drivers' license and proof of ownership of the car (or car rental papers). You may also be stopped and given an on-the-spot fine for not wearing a seatbelt, for speeding, or disregarding no-turn or one-way signs.

Archaeological sites or other points of interest are marked by big **black-on-yellow** signs; however, side roads to minor sites and villages are often inadequately posted, and inaccurately shown on maps. Information from the nearest gas station is usually reliable—they'll be able to tell you, for instance, that a tempting-looking side road is now submerged under a new dam.

Petrol stations are amazingly frequent throughout the country, and open long hours, so it's pretty difficult to run out of fuel. Diesel is **mazot**; gas is **benzin**, available in normal and *süper* grades, though *süper* can be hard to find in remote areas. Check with the pump attendant if you're not sure which your car is supposed to take; car rental firms like you to fill up with *süper*. You may be in for a problem if you bring a car with a catalytic convertor, since **kurşunsuz** or lead-free gas is extremely difficult to come by outside the largest cities. Many outlets of the *Petrol Ofisi* chain have it, and they issue a useful pamphlet detailing their locations.

Car **repair** workshops and **spare-parts** dealers are located in industrial zones on the outskirts of towns called *sanayis*. Turkish mechanics can fix almost anything and charge very little for labor.

CAR RENTAL

Car rental in Turkey is expensive, with rates equalling or exceeding those in Europe. This is partly a consequence of the high accident rate—second in the Mediterranean after Portugal—but mostly because of the surprisingly high cost of Turkish-produced cars.

Minimum on-the-spot rates of the largest **international chains** are close to $90 a day in summer. Turkish **local chains** charge twenty to thirty percent less, and just occasionally you'll find a **fluke outlet** in a relatively untouristed town that's willing to let a car go for less than $30 a day out of peak season. If you insist on renting from *Hertz, Avis,* or *Budget*, you'll have to exploit every discount scheme available to bring the price down to about equal with Turkish companies. Frequent Flyer cards, *THY* boarding passes presented at airport rental desks, and discount vouchers obtained at home before departure are all effective ways of cutting costs a little. If you're willing to sacrifice some flexibility, and can commit to long (2- or 4-week) rental periods, you can also sometimes pre-book special rates from North America, either with the major chains or as part of a **fly-drive package** prepared by your local travel agent. Otherwise, you're almost always better off dealing face-to-face with Turkish companies—especially in spring or autumn.

Prices and contract conditions on a given day within the same town may appear to be uniform, but there's often considerable scope for comparison—and bargaining. **Unlimited kilometrage** is invariably a better deal than any time-plus-distance scheme. Basic **insurance** is usually included, but **CDW** (Collision Damage Waiver) is not, and taking this is virtually mandatory. If you have a good travel insurance policy, you needn't sign on for the extra **personal insurance**. Along with the **KDV** (Value Added Tax), all these extras can push up the final total considerably. The **minimum age** is generally 21 years, with a **driver's license** held for a minimum of one year. An **International Driving Permit**, obtainable from the *AAA*, is not essential but very helpful. You'll need to flash a **credit card** or leave a substantial cash deposit to cover the estimated rental total.

The bottom-of-the-line **models** which most companies offer are either the Serçe, the Turkish equivalent of a Fiat 124, or the somewhat sturdier Renault Toros 12X. Either costs around $350–400 a week, all told, during spring or autumn, and quite a bit more during high summer—less any reductions you're able to negotiate.

TTOK OFFICES

İstanbul: Halaskârgazi Cad 364 Şişli (☎1/131 46 31).

Ankara: Adakale Sok 4/1, Yeneşehir (☎4/131 76 48).

Mersin: Mücahitler Cad 55, Kat 2/10 (☎741/20492).

İskenderun Mareşal Çahmah Cad 8/12 (☎881/17462).

İzmir: Atatürk Bul 370, Alsancak (☎51/217 149).

Trabzon: Cami Sok 17/11, İskender Paşa Mahalle (no phone).

Gaziantep: Fuat Cebesoy Cad 50 (☎851/25224).

Note that most rental cars in Turkey are stick-shift; if you really need an automatic it's advisable to arrange rental a long time in advance, and be preapared to spend in the region of $800 for a one-week rental of a Ford Taurus or similar.

If you have an **accident** of any kind, even if it's just a scratch in which no other car is involved, go immediately to the nearest police station and get them to type out a *kaza raporu* or accident report—otherwise the insurance won't cover you. Insurance never covers **smashed windshields**, for which passing trucks churning up barrages of gravel are the main culprit, so give them a wide berth.

For advice on insurance and related matters, your best bet is to contact the **TTOK** (Turkish Touring and Automobile Association), the Turkish equivalent of the *AAA*. *TTOK* have branches in İstanbul, Ankara, İzmir, İskenderun, Trabzon, Kuşadası, Mersin, Gaziantep, Taşucu, and almost every land border post. They have a breakdown service, which you will have to pay for unless you are a member of an AIT-affiliated organization, or you protect yourself before you leave.

The *AAA* has no reciprocal arrangements with the *TTOK* in terms of emergency roadside service; if you break down while driving your own vehicle in Turkey, you'll have to pay for whatever assistance is rendered, by the *TTOK* or others.

BICYCLING

Touring Turkey by **bicycle** isn't as crazy as it sounds, so long as you avoid the hottest months and the busiest roads. Flying in with one in your luggage is no more complicated than to any other destination, and often it's not even charged as excess baggage.

You do, however, have to be prepared for the **lack of maintenance** facilities, and your own **novelty value**. The only pushbikes Turks are used to seeing are old clunkers used strictly for sedate pedaling around town. A homegrown mountain bike industry is emerging in İstanbul,

but you should bring **spares** of everything, and not count on the admittedly ingenious local mechanics to improvise parts. Because you'll probably opt for back roads where few foreigners pass by, you'll draw crowds at any rest stop. Accept the inevitable and consider that bike and bags are usually more rather than less secure guarded in this manner while you go have tea.

The main **dangers** to you and your rig will be potholed pavement and the elements; most backroad drivers are surprisingly courteous, perhaps because they're so stunned at the sight of you, though be prepared for some gratuitous horn-honking. It would be unpleasant, not to mention suicidal, to pedal through İstanbul, and you're not allowed on the Bosphorus bridges anyway. You can skirt many potential trouble spots, or skip boring stretches of Anatolian steppe, by judicious use of the ferry and train network, on which you can transport your machine for free. **Rentable pushbikes** are as yet few and far between in Turkey; the few outlets we know about are mentioned in the text.

Much the same caveats apply to driving around Turkey on a **motorbike**, though they'll be charged at their own special rates on the ferries, and not transported free. In larger resorts and big cities it's generally possible to find at least one **motorbike rental agency**, or car rental companies which also rent out motorbikes and mopeds (*mobilet* in Turkish). You'll need a driver's license to rent a moped or motorbike, and most companies insist that this have been held for at least a year. Before renting any kind of bike, particularly a moped, make sure it's physically capable of coping with the terrain you want to use it on.

FERRIES

All of Turkey's **ferries** are run by the *Türkiye Denizcilik İşletmesi* (literally "Turkey Maritime Services"), more commonly rendered as Turkish Maritime Lines (*TML*). There are three kinds of ferry: short shuttle city services, short-hop links to islands and across the Sea of Marmara, and longer-haul services connecting major domestic and international centers. The **city lines**, mainly serving foot passengers and connecting points within places like İstanbul and İzmir, are frequent, cheap and efficient, running to very tight schedules, so they don't hang around waiting for passengers. Timetables (*saat tarifeleri*) are available from the ticket window (*gişe*) at the various docks. The municipality of İstanbul also operates the *Deniz Otobüsleri* or "Sea Buses," a fleet of hydrofoils supplementing the steam ferries across the Bosphorus but which also call at more remote points such as Yalova and the islands of the Sea of Marmara. In general they're twice as fast—and twice as costly—as conventional boats.

In addition to these are **short-hop ferries**, some of which serve foot passengers only, while others have provision for **vehicles**. Useful examples of the former include the services from İstanbul's Kartal, Kabataş, or Sirkeci docks to Yalova, and from Sarayburnu to the islands of the Sea of Marmara. Vessels accepting both foot passengers and cars include the lines from İstanbul's Sarayburnu across the Marmara Sea to Bandırma or Mudanya, the Harem–Sirkeci shuttle in İstanbul, and the Darica–Topcular crossing of the Gulf of İzmit. Any of the trans-Marmara links save time compared to the road journey, but are relatively expensive with a vehicle: İstanbul–Bandırma, for example, costs $32 for two in a car, $16 without.

Long-haul domestic ferries are now restricted to the coastal stretches where the road network is substandard, specifically between İstanbul and Trabzon—with intermediate stops—and direct from İstanbul to İzmir. They also run internationally, from İzmir or Antalya to Venice, and Taşucu, Mersin, or Alanya to Girne in Northern Cyprus. All long-haul services are enormously popular, and **reservations** must be made well in advance through one of the authorized *TML* agencies in the appropriate ports. Exact addresses or phone numbers are given in the town accounts, though the İstanbul headquarters at Karaköy, right behind the jetty on Rihtim Caddesi, is the best equipped. **Schedule pamphlets** in English, Turkish, and German are issued yearly, though prices and timetables are subject to change.

There are five classes of **cabin** on long-haul ferries, depending on their position in the boat.

All are comfortable enough, if ruthlessly air conditioned, with attached showers and toilets. It's also possible to reserve a *pulman koltuk* or reclining chair, but if you leave reservations to the last minute you won't even get one of these. No one will mind if you sleep up on **on deck**—bring a sleeping bag and mat, or just crash out on the chaise longues provided—but you will need to have a confirmed seat reservation to be allowed on the boat in the first place. **Fares** are reasonable—about $40 in a third-class cabin İstanbul–İzmir, for example—and **students** with ISIC enjoy a fifty percent discount; there are also concessions for groups and children. **Cars** cost almost as much again as a passenger berth, but most drivers consider the difference well worth it in terms of wear and tear saved.

Once aboard, the **atmosphere** is extremely convivial; the long-haul services are essentially budget cruises. However, the mediocre **food and drink**, whether at the bar, the self-service cafeteria, or in the dining room, is marked up seventy percent over the average, and only available in exchange for prepaid, nonrefundable **chits**, which you get from the purser's office on board.

PLANES

The state of domestic **air transport** in Turkey is in constant flux. *THY*, the state airline, has recently been subjected to competition from smaller private companies, and the list of destinations served tends to change rapidly as the market fluctuates and marginal routes are shed to the newcomers. The general trend, though, is one of better services to established airports, and steadily climbing fares.

As of this writing, *THY* still flies—in decreasing order of frequency—between İstanbul and Ankara and İzmir and most other major Turkish centers except Bursa and Edirne. Most flights to the east involve a connection in Ankara, with frequently long stopovers there. Of the competitors, the next largest airline is *THT*, actually a subsidiary of *THY*, which essentially runs "air dolmuşes"—small and relatively slow turboprop planes with plenty of stops—out of either İstanbul or Ankara to Samsun, Antalya, Sivas, Erzincan, Elâzığ, Kars, Şanlıurfa, Batman, and Denizli. *Sönmez* is thus far just a Bursa–İstanbul shuttle; *İstanbul Hava Yolları* (*İstanbul Airlines*) flies between İstanbul and Adana/Antalya/ Dalaman/Trabzon/İzmir, as well as to selected overseas airports. *Greenair*, a new Soviet-Turkish venture, is similar but with a much smaller flight network to date. We've listed the addresses and/ or phone numbers of airlines or their agents throughout the guide.

Fares vary by fifteen percent at most when more than one carrier serves a particular destination. *THY* is usually the most expensive, and no longer offers any domestic student discount. Most airlines do, however, offer family and child **discounts** of ten to ninety percent—worth bearing in mind when comparing prices.

SLEEPING

Finding a bed for the night is generally no problem in Turkey, except in high season at the busier coastal resorts and larger towns. Lists of category-rated hotels, motels, and the better pansiyons are published by local tourist offices, and we've listed the best options throughout the guide, although in practice where you end up tends to be luck of the draw—and which tout, if any, you decide to follow.

Prices, while cheap by most west European standards, are no longer rock-bottom. To some extent facilities have improved correspondingly, though not surprisingly you often get less for your money in the big tourist meccas. In the guide we've quoted the least expensive single and double occupancy prices in dollars; Turkish domestic inflation being what it is, TL prices are fairly meaningless. Singles generally cost just over half what a double does, since proprietors are well used to lone (male) business travelers. Rooms with attached bath are generally about 25 percent more than unplumbed ones; triples are also usually available, costing about thirty percent more than a double. Prices posted on the

wall or door of the room should be discreetly compared to those over the reception desk—they are the maximum permissible.

The foremost criterion when **choosing a room** is noise avoidance. Pick a room away from main thoroughfares or mosque minarets (not easy). You'll never cause offense by asking to see another room, and you should never agree on a price for a room without seeing it first. **Water** should be tested to verify claims of *devamlı sıcak su* (constant hot water). Though break-ins aren't the norm in Turkey, **security** should be at least a token consideration. **Bargaining** is often in order, especially if you're visiting out of season or remote areas.

HOTELS AND MOTELS

Turkish **hotels** are graded on a scale of one to five stars by the Ministry of Tourism; there is also a lower tier of unstarred establishments rated by municipalities. At the four- and five-star level you're talking Sheraton-type amenities—and prices, at $75–150 per double. Two- or three-star outfits are less expensive and may have slightly more character; cheaper still are the wide variety of one-star establishments, which range in price from $12 to $22 a double. Their exact price depends on the location and the presence or absence of bath, and to some extent on the season; out of season you can bargain prices down considerably. Breakfast, on the occasions when it's available, is sometimes included in the rates—but almost invariably unexciting; exceptions are noted in the text.

Motels, also graded from one to five stars, tend to be more expensive than hotels of the same class, and conform more to American notions of the term; they're essentially aimed at the drive-in trade, and often have imposing beachfront or panoramic settings to compensate for a nondescript layout. However, unless you're touring by car their locations—generally way outside city centers—are too inconvenient to be of much use. Be warned also that the term "motel" is sometimes used to add a touch of class to an otherwise mediocre hotel.

The **unrated** hotels licensed by municipalities can be virtually as good as the lower end of the one-star class, sometimes with wall-to-wall carpeting, attached baths, and bedside phones. On average, though, expect spartan rooms with possibly a wash-basin and certainly a shower (never a tub), with a squat toilet down the hall. Count on $4–10 per person for such comforts, with showers often carrying a separate $1 charge. Some places are jail-like flophouses where the bedding, winter or summer, tends to be a thick quilt wrapped in a seldom-laundered slipcover anchored with safety pins.

At the **roughest**—and not particularly recommended—end of the spectrum you may pay by the bed $1–3 apiece—rather than the room, so potentially sharing quarters with strangers; there will usually be no shower in the building. Such places tend to be patronized by villagers in town on business and thus attract an exclusively male clientele; often they have a less than salubrious location as well.

PANSIYONS AND APARTMENTS

Often the most pleasant places to stay are **pansiyons** (pensions), small guesthouses which may or may not have attached plumbing and which proliferate anywhere large numbers of holiday-makers do. If there are vacancies in season, touts in the coastal resorts and other tourist targets descend on every incoming bus, dolmuş, or boat; at other places or times, look for little signs with the legend *Boş oda var* (Empty rooms free).

The typical Turkish breakfast is almost always available for about $1.25–1.75 per person, often served in the common gardens or terraces which are this kind of accommodation's strong point. Rooms tend to be sparse but clean, furnished in one-star hotel mode and always with two sheets (*çarşafs*) on the bed. Hot water is generally solar heated at seaside locations, out of wood- or coal-fired boilers elsewhere. Laundry facilities—even if only just a drying line and a plastic bucket—are almost always present, a big advantage over most low-grade hotels. In addition the proprie-

tors, often members of an extended family, are apt to be younger and friendlier than the hotel-staff norm—though this may be manifest in an unduly attentive attitude to lone female guests. Prices are often rigidly controlled by the local tourist authorities, according to what category the establishment is rated at, and you should expect to pay $10–20 a double with attached bath, $4–12 without. Hot showers are rarely charged for separately; if they are, count on an extra dollar a go as in modest hotels.

Kitchenette apartments are just beginning to become widespread in coastal resorts, and are mostly aimed at vacationing Turks, or foreigners arriving on pre-arranged packages at the larger resorts. If you come across any—either on the spot or through the local tourist office—they're certainly worth considering for an extended stay. The major negotiable outlay will be for the large gas bottle feeding the stove.

CAMPING, CHALETS, HOSTELS

Wherever pansiyons are found, there will also be **campgrounds**—often run by the same people, who in the absence of a proper site may simply allow you to crash out in the pansiyon's garden. Charges per head run from a couple dollars for such an arrangement to $7 in a well-appointed, if sterile, ground at a major resort in season, plus fees of around $3–4 per tent. You may also be charged for your vehicle—anything from $5 to $20 depending on the site and season. Campgrounds often rent out tents to those showing up without canvas, or provide **chalet** accommodation which can be anything from a stuffy garden shed with a bed inside to a fairly luxurious affair with bathroom. Value for money of chalets varies tremendously, as does their architecture; prices will be anything between $10 and $20.

Various **impromptu roadside "kampings,"** essentially nothing more than some clumps of trees with parking space for Turkish weekenders, are unlikely to appeal to most foreigners. **Camping rough** is not illegal, but hardly anybody does it except when trekking in the mountains, and, as you can expect a visit from curious police or even nosier villagers, it's not really a choice for those who like their privacy.

What with the abundance of budget pansiyons and downmarket working-men's hotels, there are relatively few **hostels** outside İstanbul; sometimes a pansiyon in a major resort will have roof space or a "group room" set aside. Most other hostels—called *yurts*—are rather pokey dormitories aimed at local students on summer vacation and are unlikely to cater to you, making the purchase of a AYH card before you leave a waste of money. The only exception might be if you've signed up on some sort of work-camp or student/youth exchange tour, in which case your accommodation at such places will have been arranged in advance anyway. See p.43, "Finding Work."

HAMAMS

One of the highlights of a stay in Turkey, especially during the cooler months, is a visit to a hamam or Turkish bath. A nearby hamam will also make a shower-less but otherwise acceptable budget hotel more palatable. Many tourists never partake because they (usually wrongly) anticipate sexual hassles or intense culture shock; in fact, after a day at the ruins or in the bazaar, a corner of the bathhouse is likely to be an oasis of tranquility in comparison.

VISITING A HAMAM

Virtually all Turkish towns of any size have at least one hamam per neighborhood; about the only exceptions to this pattern are some of the coastal resorts which were formerly populated by Greeks, who didn't build such structures. Baths are usually **signposted**, but if in doubt look for the distinctive external profile of the roof domes, visible from the street. Baths are either permanently designated for men or women, or sexually segregated on a schedule—look for the words *erkekler* (men) and *kadınlar* (women) followed by a time range.

On entering, you will usually leave your **valuables** in a rather small locking drawer, the key of which (often on a wrist/ankle-thong) you keep with you for the duration of your wash. Bring soap, shampoo, and a shaving mirror, which are either not supplied or are expensive; the basic **admission** charge varies depending on the level of luxury, but except in smart or tourist-oriented baths it should never be more than $3 per person, and is normally clearly posted by the front desk. Men are usually **supplied** with a *peştamal*, a thin, wraparound sarong; both sexes get *takunya*, awkward wooden clogs, and later a *havlu* or proper drying towel. Changing cubicles (*camekân* in Turkish), equipped with a reclining couch, are sometimes shared and rarely lock except in the better hamams—thus the safe-drawer.

The *hararet* or **main bath chamber** itself varies from the plain to the ornate, though any hamam worth its salt will be dressed in marble at least up to chest height. The temperature inside varies from tryingly hot to barely lukewarm, depending on how well run the baths are. Unless you're with a friend, it's one customer to a set of taps-and-basin; refrain from making a big soapy mess in the basin, which is meant for mixing up pure water to ideal temperature. Use the plastic or metal scoop-dishes provided to sluice yourself, being careful not to splash your neighbors; on Fridays especially they may have just completed their *abdest* (ritual ablution), and would have to start all over again if touched by an "infidel's" water.

It's also not done for men to drop their *peştamal*: **modesty** is the order of the day, and washing your lower half through or under the cloth is an important acquired technique.

Women are less scrupulous about covering up, though they too keep their panties on. More than one foreign female visitor has been brought up short by the sight of a matronly figure advancing on them, beckoning with a straight razor: religious Turkish women **shave** *all over*, though usually not at the baths. Alternatively the locals stalk about swathed to waist height in green depilatory paste like so many New Guinea mud-women. Men, incidentally, are expected to shave themselves in the *tıraşlık*, a section of the *soğukluk* cooling-down room located between the foyer and the main chamber.

Heart of the hamam is the *göbek taşı* or "**navel stone**," a raised platform positioned directly over the wood-fired furnaces which heat the premises. In a good bath this will be piping hot, and covered with prostrate figures using their scoop-dishes or special pillows as headrests. It's also the forum for vigorous (to say the least) **massages** from the *tellâk* or masseur/masseuse, whose technique owes more to medieval rack-and-wheel practice than New Age touchie-feelie methods—be warned. A *kese* (**abrasive mitt**) session from the same person beside your basin, in which untold layers of dead skin and grime are whisked away, will probably be more to most people's tastes. Agree in advance with the *tellâk* on terms, which (including a small tip) should be about equal to the basic bath charge. If you prefer, you can buy a *kese* at any pharmacy and rub yourself down. Finally, it's considered good etiquette to clean your marble slab with a few scoopfuls of water before leaving.

Upon return to your cubicle you'll be offered tea, soft drinks, or mineral water, any of which are a good idea since the baths dehydrate you. These, like a massage, are **extras**; if in doubt consult the price placard over the reception desk. Except in the heavily touristed establishments, tips above and beyond the listed fees are not required or expected.

EATING AND DRINKING

At its finest, Turkish food is some of the best in the world. There are enough climate zones in the country to grow most ingredients locally, and the quality of the raw materials has not yet been compromised by modern marketing standards. Prices, except for the fancier cuts of meat and seafood—and of course at the major resorts, where standards have sadly declined as tourism has taken hold—won't break your budget either; when in doubt, eat where the local tradesmen do. Unadventurous travelers are prone to get stuck in a kebab rut, and come away complaining about the monotony of the cuisine; in fact, though, all but the strictest vegetarians should find enough variety to satisfy them.

BREAKFAST AND STREET SNACKS

The usual Turkish **breakfast** (*kahvaltı*) served at hotels and pansiyons is almost invariably a pile of day-old bread slices accompanied by a pat of margarine, a small slice of cheese, a dab of jam and a couple of olives. Only the tea is likely to be available in quantity; seconds are likely to be charged for, as are English-style extras like *sahanda yumurtalar* (fried eggs).

You can eat better by simply using street stands or snack joints, many of which serve some of Turkey's best food alternatives. Many workers **start the morning** with a *börek*, a rich, flaky, layered pastry containing bits of ground meat or cheese; these are sold either at a tiny *büfe* (stall-café) or from street carts. Others content themselves with a simple *simit* (bread rings speckled with sesame seeds), or a bowl of *çorba* (soup) with lemon.

Later in the day, vendors hawk *lahmacun*, small, round Arab-style pizzas with a thin, meat-based topping. Kebabs, which are considered takeout food in some parts of North America, are not generally considered so in Turkey; try instead a sandwich (*sandviç*) with variable fillings (often *kokoreç*—offal—or fish); in coastal cities *midye tava* (deep-fried mussels) are often available, as are *midye dolması* (mussels stuffed with rice, pine nuts, and allspice).

Not to be confused with *lahmacun* is *pide*, Turkish pizza—flat bread with various toppings, served to a sit-down clientele in a *pideci* or *pide salonu*. The big advantage of this dish is that it's always made to order; typical styles are *peynirli* (with cheese), *yumurtalı* (with egg), *kıymalı* (with ground meat), or *sucuklu* (with sausage). It would be another ideal breakfast food, but many *pidecis* don't light their ovens until 11am or so, making it an obvious lunchtime treat.

Other snacky specialties worth seeking out are *mantı*—traditional central Asian meat-filled ravioli served drenched in yogurt and spice-reddened oil—and *gözleme*, a crêpe-like delicacy often served at the same places. In any sizable town you'll also find at least one **kuru yemiş** (dry munchies) stall, also known as a *leblebeci*, where nuts and dried fruit are sold by weight—typically 100g a shot. Aside from the usual, keep an eye out for *cezeriye*, a bar made of carrot juice, honey, and nuts; *pestil* or pressed fruit, most commonly apricot and peach, and a winter/spring snack; or *tatlı sucuk*, a fruit-nut-molasses roll not to be confused with meat *sucuk*.

RESTAURANT FOOD

Several kinds of eateries fill the need for more substantial food. A **lokanta** is a restaurant, as is a "*restoran*," but the term means little on its own. A *çorbaci* is a soup kitchen; *sulu* or *hazır yemek* means precooked dishes kept warm in a steam tray; *izgarada(n) yemek* indicates meat dishes grilled to order. A *kebabcı* or *köfteci* specializes in the preparation of kebab and *köfte* respectively, with a limited number of side dishes—usually just salad, yogurt, and desserts.

Most budget-priced restaurants are *içkisiz* or alcohol-free; any place marked *içkili* (serving booze) is likely to be more expensive. A useful exception is a **meyhane** (tavern), in its truest incarnation a smokey dive where eating is considered secondary to tippling; in the fancier ones, though, the food—mostly unusual delicacies—can be very conspicuous, very good and not always drastically marked up. No self-respecting Turkish woman, however, would be caught dead in most of them, and unfortunately very few *meyhanes* are the sort of spot where an unaccompanied foreign woman can go without comment, and some will seem marginal to western men also—deviations from this pattern are noted in the guide. That said, any foreign men or couples bold enough to visit the more decorous *meyhanes* will be treated with the utmost courtesy. In restaurants unaccompanied women may be ushered into the *aile salonu* (family parlor), usually upstairs or behind a curtain.

Prices vary widely according to the type of establishment: from a dollar or two per person at a simple boozeless soup kitchen, up to $10–12 at the flashier (and often more exploitative) resort restaurants. **Portions** tend to be tiny, so if you're a big eater you'll need to order two main courses. Many places don't have **menus**; you'll need to

ascertain the prices of the most critical main courses beforehand, and review the tab carefully when finished. Tallying up items you never ate, or presenting diners with dishes they didn't order, are fairly common gambits by waiters; so is having your plate whisked away before you're done with it. This last habit is not so much a ploy to hurry you along, but derives from the Turkish custom of never leaving a guest with an "empty" plate before them.

WHAT TO EAT

In a *sulu yemek* kitchen, soup (*çorba*) and salad (*salata*) predominate. The most frequently encountered **soups** are *mercimek* (lentil), *ezo gelin* (rice and vegetable broth—grainy enough to be an appetizing breakfast), *paça* (lamb foot), or *işkembe* (tripe). *Çoban* (shepherd's) *salatası* is the generic term for the widespread cucumber, tomato, onion, pepper, and parsley **salad**; *yeşil* (green) salad is only seasonally available.

Move up a notch in surroundings, to any *içkili restoran* or *meyhane*, and you'll find more of the **mezes** (hors d'oeuvres, appetizers) for which Turkey is justly famous—usually a bewildering array of rich purees, vinaigrettes, and fried-then-chilled dishes kept (sometimes for too long) in refrigerated display cases. Along with dessert (see below), they're really the core of Turkish cuisine, and are far too numerous to list exhaustively. The best and most common include *patlıcan salatası* (eggplant mash), *piyaz* (white beans vinaigrette), *semizotu* (purslane weed), *mücver* (zucchini croquettes), *sigara böreği* (tightly rolled cheese pastries), *beyin salatası* (whole brain), *turşu* (pickled vegetables), *imam bayıldı* (cold baked eggplant with onion and tomato), and *dolma* (any stuffed vegetable).

Bread is good if it's an hour or two old but otherwise is spongy and stale, best kept for scooping up *meze*. The flat unadorned *pide* served during Ramadan (not to be confused with the almost identical *pide* served with toppings) and at many *kebabcıs*, and very rare *kepekli* (bran; only from a *fırın* or bakery) loafs afford the only relief. In villages, *yufka*—like an ultra-thin tortilla—also makes a welcome respite, as does *bazlama* (similar to an Indian paratha).

Main courses are nutritious if often plainly presented. In *sulu yemek* restaurants, *kuru fasulye* (bean soup), *taze fasulye* (French beans), *turlu sebze* (vegetable stew), and *nohut* (chickpeas) are the principal **vegetable** standbys. Vegetarians should, however, be aware that even though no meat may be visible floating in these dishes, they're often prepared with lamb- or chicken-based broth. If all else fails, *bulgur* (cracked wheat) with yogurt is a safe bet. Other casserole dishes more obviously containing meat include *mussaka* (not as good as the Greek rendition), *karnıyarık* (a much better Turkish version), *güveç* (clay pot fricassee), *tas kebap* (a meat/vegetable combo), and *saç kavurma*, an inland Anatolian specialty, made from meat, vegetables, spices and oil, fried up in a *saç* (the Turkish wok).

Full-on **meat** dishes served up from the *ızgara* (grill) include several variations on the stereotypical kebab. *Adana kebab* is spicy, with a sprinkling of purple sumac herb betraying Arab influence; *İskender kebab*, best sampled in Bursa, is heavy on the flat bread and yogurt. *Köfte* (meatballs), *şiş* (stew meat chunks), and *çöp* (bits of lamb or offal), usually mutton or beef, are other options. When ordering, you should specify if you want *bir buçuk* (one-and-a-half—adequate) or *çift* (double portion—generous). Grilled dishes normally come with a slice or two of *pide* and a green garnish.

Potentially more exciting are tidbits like *pirzola* (lamp chop), *böbrek* (kidney), *yürek* (heart), *ciğer* (liver) and *koç yumurtası* (ram's egg) or *billur* (crystal)—tha last two euphemisms for testicle. A *karışık ızgara* (mixed grill) is always good value. Any size serving comes with garnish. Chicken (*piliç* or *tavuk*) is oddly expensive in Turkey and not as common as you'd think.

Fish and seafood is good, if usually pricey, and sold by weight more often than by item. Buy with an eye to season, and don't turn your nose up at humbler items, which in all likelihood will be fresher because they turn over faster. Budget mainstays include *sardalya* (sardines—grilled fresh, and vastly superior to the canned kind), *palamut* (autumn tuna—ditto), *lüfer* (bluefish), *kefal* (grey mullet, a south Aegean specialty), and *sargoz* (bream).

DESSERTS AND SWEETS

After the occasionally functional presentation of main dishes, Turkish chefs pander shamelessly and elegantly to the sweet tooth. Sticky-cake addicts and pudding freaks will find every imaginable concoction at the closest *pastane* (sweetshop).

The syrup-soaked **baklava**-type items are pretty self-explanatory upon a glance into the glass display cabinet— all variations on a sugar, dough, nut, and butter mix. More mysterious, less sweet and healthier are the **milk-based** products, which are popular all over the country. *Süpangile* ("süp" for short) is an incredibly dense and rich chocolate pudding; more modest are *keşkül*, a vanilla/nut crumble custard, or *sütlaç* (rice pudding)—one dessert that's consistently available in ordinary restaurants. Top honors for elaborateness go to *tavukgöğsü*, a cinnamon-topped morsel made from hyper-boiled and strained chicken breast, semolina starch, and milk. *Kazandibi* (literally, "bottom of the pot"), is *tavukgöğsü* residue with a dark crust on the bottom—not to be confused with *fırın sütlaç*, which looks the same but is actually *sutlaç* pudding with a scorched top baked in a clay dish.

Grain-based sweets are some of the best Turkey has to offer. If you coincide with the appropriate holiday (see below) you'll get to sample *aşure*, a sort of jello laced with pulses, wheat berries, raisins, and nuts.* The best-known Turkish sweet, *lokum* or "Turkish delight," is pretty much ubiquitous, available from *pastanes* and the more touristy shops. It's basically solidified sugar and pectin, flavored (most commonly) with rosewater and sometimes pistachios and sprinkled with powdered sugar. There

---

*Aşure is the Turkish variant of a food with deep religious symbolism, found in Muslim, Christian, and Jewish communities throughout Anatolia and the Balkans. The word is derived from the Arabic word for "ten," referring to *aşure günü* or the tenth of the month of Muharrem, when Hasan and Hussein, sons of the fourth caliph Ali and grandsons of Muhammad, were slain, becoming martyrs for the Shiites and their allied sects in Turkey, the Alevîs and the Bektaşis. The latter have incorporated *aşure* fully into their ritual: after fasting for the first ten days of Muharrem, Bektaşi elders invite initiates to a private ceremony where the fast is broken over a communal meal of *aşure*. It is supposed to be made from forty different ingredients, courtesy of a legend which claims that after the Ark's forty-day sail on the Flood, and the first sighting of dry land, Noah commanded that a stew be made of the remaining supplies on board—which turned out to number forty sorts of food. An alternative name for the dish is thus "Noah's pudding," but today you'll be fortunate to find half that number of ingredients, even in a devotional recipe. You can also buy bags of prepackaged *aşure* mix in Turkish markets, and many kebab joints or *pastanes* serve it much of the year.

are also nearly a dozen recognized sorts of *helva*, including the tahini-paste chew synonymous with the concoction in the West, although in Turkey the term usually means any variation on the basic theme of baked flour or starch, butter, sugar, and flavored water.

Ice cream is an excellent summer treat, provided it's genuine *Maraşlı dövme dondurma* (whipped in the Kahraman Maraş tradition—a bit like Italian *gelato*), not factory-packed garbage. Consistent warm weather prompts the stationing at public parks, sea promenades and so on of outlandishly costumed young men with swords selling the stuff. Being served is half the fun: you may be threatened or cajoled at (blunted) sword point into buying, after which the cone is given to you on the point of the sword after a twirl or three, and a bell rung loudly to celebrate the transaction.

If none of the above appeals, your last resorts include *kabak tatlısı*, candied squash usually served in autumn with walnut chunks and *kaymak* (cream), or summer **fruit** (*meyva*), which generally means *kavun* (Persian melon) or *karpuz* (watermelon).

DRINKING

Beverages are consumed in Turkey with or without food, on the hoof or sedately, in the open-air setting of a tea garden or café or the boozy environs of what are essentially all-male clubs.

TEA, COFFEE, JUICES

Tea, grown along the Black Sea, is the national drink and an essential social lubricant—it's virtually impossible to be in Turkey more than twenty minutes without being offered some. It's properly prepared in a double-boiler apparatus, with the larger water chamber underneath the smaller receptacle containing dry leaves, to which a small quantity of hot water is added. After a suitable wait the tea is decanted into tiny tulip-shaped glasses, then diluted with more water to taste: *açık* is weak, *demli* or *koyu* steeped. Sugar comes as cubes on the side; milk is never added. If you're frustrated by the usual tiny glass at breakfast, ask for a *düble çay* (a "double," served in a juice glass).

Coffee is not as commonly drunk, despite the fact that the Ottomans first introduced the drink to Europe. Instant—usually Nescafé—is relatively costly but increasingly popular; much better

is the traditional, fine-ground Turkish type, brewed up *sade* (no sugar), *orta şekerli* (medium sweet), or *çok şekerli* (cloying). For an extended session of drinking either tea or coffee, you retire to a *çay bahçesi* (tea garden), which often will also serve ice cream and soft drinks.

Herbal teas are also popular in Turkey, particularly *ıhlamur* (linden flower) and *ada çay* ("island" tea), an infusion of a type of sage common in all coastal areas. The much-promoted *elma çay* (apple tea) in fact contains strictly chemicals and not a trace of apple essence.

Certain **traditional beverages** tend to accompany particular kinds of food or appear at set seasons. *Sıcak süt* (hot milk) is the perennial complement to *börek*, though in winter it's fortified with *salep*, the ground-up tuber of *Orchis mascula*, a phenomenally expensive wild orchid gathered in coastal areas—and a good safeguard against colds. *Ayran*, watered-down yogurt, is always available at *pidecis* and *kebabcıs*, and is good cold but not so appetizing if—as it sometimes is—it's lukewarm and lumpy. In autumn and winter, you'll find stalls selling *boza*, a delicious, mildly fermented millet drink. Similarly tangy is *şıra*, a faintly alcoholic grape juice acceptable to devout Muslims and available in late summer and fall.

Fruit juice or *meyva suyu* can be excellent if it's pulp in a bottle, available in unusual flavors such as *kayısı* (apricot), *şeftali* (peach), and *vişne* (sour cherry). The new wave of thinned, preservative-spiked juices in cardboard cartons is distinctly less thrilling. The good stuff is so thick you might want to cut it with *memba suyu* (spring water), found at the tableside in most restaurants, or fizzy *maden suyu* (mineral water). *Meşrubat* is the generic term for all carbonated **soft drinks** such as *Coca Cola*, *Fanta*, and the like—available pretty much everywhere now.

BEER AND WINE

Despite inroads made by Islamic fundamentalists, **alcoholic drinks** (*İçkiler*) are available virtually without restriction in resorts, though you may have some thirsty moments in interior towns like Konya or Van.

Beer (*bira*) is sold principally in bottles but also in cans (expensive) and on tap (cheaper). There are two main brands, *Efes Pilsen* and *Tuborg*, along with a new label, *Venus*, though this is actually produced by Tuborg. The *birahane* (beer hall), an imitation-German notion, has

A FOOD AND DRINK GLOSSARY

Basics

Su	Water	*Makarna*	Pasta	*Sirke*	Vinegar
Buz	Ice	*Yoğurt*	Yogurt	*Yağ*	Oil
(Kepekli) ekmek	(Whole bran) bread	*Süt*	Milk	*Tuz*	Salt
		Yumurta	Eggs	*Şeker*	Sugar
Pilav, pirinç	Rice	*Tereyağı*	Butter	*Kara biber*	Black pepper
Bulgur	Cracked wheat	*Zeytin*	Olives	*Bal*	Honey

Useful Words

Başka bir...	Another...	*Çatal*	Fork	*Peçete*	Napkin
Bardak	Glass	*Kaşık*	Spoon	*Hesap*	Bill, tab
Tabak	Plate	*Bıçak*	Knife	*Servis ücreti*	Service charge

Cooking Terms

Ezme	Puree, mash	*Pılakı*	Vinaigrette, marinated
Haşlama	Meat stew without oil, sometimes with vegetables	*Buğlama*	Steamed
		Sıcak/soğuk	Hot/cold
		İyi pişmiş	Well cooked
Kızartma	Fried, then chilled item	*Pişmemiş*	Raw
Zeytinyağli	Vegetables cooked to limpness in their own juices, spices and olive oil (*zeytin yağı*), then allowed to steep and chill for a day	*Yoğurtlu*	In yogurt sauce
		Soslu, salcalı	In red sauce
		Yumurtalı	With egg (e.g., *pide*)
		Sucuklu	With sausage
		Kıymalı	With mince
İzgarada(n), ızgarası	Grilled	*Peynirli*	With cheese
Tava, sahanda	Deep-fried, fried	*Etli*	Containing meat
Fırında(n)	Baked	*Etli mi?*	Does it contain meat?

Soup (*Çorba*)

Mercimek	Lentil	*İşkembe*	Tripe
Tarhana	Yogurt, sour grain and spice soup	*Yayla*	Similar to *tarhana*
Ezo gelin	Rice and vegetable broth	*Düğün*	"Wedding": egg and lemon
Paça	Sheep or goat foot	*Yoğurt*	Yogurt, rice and celery greens soup
Tavuk	Chicken		

Appetizers (*Meze* or *Zeytinyağlı*)

Çoban salatası	Chopped tomato, cucumber, parsley, pepper, and onion salad	*Burulce*	Black-eyed peas
		Patlıcan esmesi	Eggplant pate
		Piyaz	White beans, onions, and parsley vinaigrette
Yeşil salata	All-green salad		
Zeytin	Olives	*Barbunya*	Red beans, marinated
Turşu	Pickled vegetables	*Sigara böreği*	Cheese-filled pastry "cigarettes"
Amerikan salatası	Mayonnaise-and-vegetable salad: Russian salad renamed in a pique of NATO patriotism	*Yaprak* or *yılancı dolması*	Stuffed vine leaves
		Cacık	Yogurt, grated cucumber, and herb dip
Tarama	Red fish-roe	*Semizotu*	Purslane vinaigrette
Haydarı	Dense garlic dip	*Müçver*	Zucchini fritatta
Beyin salatası	Lamb brains	*İmam bayıldı*	Cold baked eggplant, onion, and tomato
Pancar	Beets, marinated		

Meat (*Et*) and Poultry

Sığır	Beef	*Çöp kebab*	Literally, "bit kebab"—tiny chunks of offal or lamb
Dana	Veal		
Koyun	Mutton	*Orman kebab*	Roast lamb (expensive)
Kuzu	Lamb	*Döner kebab*	Compressed meat
Keçi	Goat	*İskender* or *Bursa kebab*	Döner drenched in yogurt and sauce
Domuz, jambon	Pork (very rare)		
Pastırma	Cured meat	*Karışık ızgara*	Mixed grill
Tavuk	Boiling chicken	*Beyti*	Lamb shoulder chop
Piliç	Roasting chicken	*Yürek*	Heart
Pirzola	Chop, cutlet	*Ciğer*	Liver
Bonfile	Small steak	*Böbrek*	Kidney
Köfte	Meatballs	*Dil*	Tongue
Adana kebab	Spicy southern kebab	*Billur, koç yumurtası*	Euphemisms for testicle
Şiş kebab	Shish kebap		

Fish (*Balık*) and Seafood

Barbunya, tekir	Red mullet	*Palamut, torik*	Two types of bonito (autumn)
Kefal	Grey mullet (Aegean)		
Sargoz	Bream (Aegean)	*Kalkan*	Turbot
Levrek	Bass	*Karagöz*	Black bream
Alabalık	Trout	*Çipura*	Gilt-head bream
Mezgit	Gobby, bogue	*Kılıç*	Swordfish
İstavrit	Horse mackerel (Black Sea)	*Orfoz*	Giant grouper
Hamsi	Anchovy (Black Sea)	*Kalamar*	Squid
Uskumru	Atlantic mackerel	*Ahtapod*	Octopus
Kolyoz	Club mackerel	*Midye*	Mussel
Lüfer	Bluefish (autumn, İstanbul)	*Yengeç*	Crab
Sardalya	Sardine	*Karides*	Prawns
Mercan	Coral fish	*İstakoz*	Salt-water crayfish

Vegetables (*Sebze*)

Domates	Tomato	*Mantar*	Mushrooms	*Bakla*	Broad beans
Salatalık	Cucumber	*Kabak*	Courgette, marrow	*Patlıcan*	Eggplant
Soğan	Onion			*Karnabahar*	Cauliflower
Sarmısak	Garlic	*Acı biber*	Hot chilis	*Havuç*	Carrot
Maydanoz	Parsley	*Sivri biber*	Skinny peppers, hot or mild	*Bamya*	Okra
Marul	Lettuce (rare)			*Bezelye*	Peas
Lahana	Cabbage (usually stuffed)	*Nohut*	Chickpeas	*Ispanak*	Spinach
		Kuru fasulye	White beans	*Patates*	Potato
Turp	Raddish	*Taze fasulye*	French beans		

Snacks

Menemen	Stir-fry omelet with tomatoes and peppers	*Pide*	Elongated Turkish "pizza"
		Lahmacun	Round Arabic "pizza"
Börek	Rich, layered cheese pastry	*Cezeriye*	Carrot-honey-nut bar
		Pestil	Pressed dried fruit
Su börek	"Water börek"—sort of a cross between pasta and a filled pastry	*Badem*	Almonds
		Fıstık	Pistachios
		Yer fıstığı	Peanuts
Kokoreç	Mixed innard roulade	*Leblebi*	Roasted chickpeas
Midye dolması	Mussels stuffed with rice, allspice, pine nuts	*Fındık*	Hazelnuts
		Kuru üzüm	Raisins

Typical Dishes

Turlu sebze	Vegetable stew	*Karnıyarık*	More consolidated eggplant-and-meat dish
Tas kebap	Meat and vegetable stew		
Güveç	Meat and veg clay-pot casserole	*Mantı*	Asian "ravioli" with yogurt
Saç kavurma	"Wok" fried medley	*Gözleme Yufka*	(crepe-like village bread) with various toppings
Mussaka	Crumbly compared to Greek, no bechamel sauce	*Otlu peynir*	Herb flavored cheese, especially around Lake Van

Cheese (*Peynir*)

Beyaz	White; like Greek feta	*Kaşar*	Kasseri, more or less aged
Çerkez	Like edam	*Tulum*	Dry, crumbly, parmesan-like cheese made in a goatskin
Dil	Like mozzarella or string cheese		

Fruit (*Meyva*)

Elma	Apple	*Mandalin*	Tangerine	*Erik, papaz*	Plum, green	*Düt*	Mulberries
Armut	Pear	*Şeftali*	Peach	*(hoca) erik*	plum	*Karpuz*	Watermelon
Üzüm	Grapes	*Muz*	Banana	*Kayısı*	Apricot	*Kavun*	Persian melon
Portakal	Orange	*Kiraz*	Cherries	*Çilek*	Strawberries	*İncir*	Figs
Limon	Lemon	*Nar*	Pomegranate	*Böğürtlen*	Blackberries	*Ayva*	Quince

Sweets (*Tatlı*)

Pasta	Any pastry or cake	*Sabuniye helvası*	Starch helva
Acı badem	Giant almond cookies		
Kurabiye	Almond-nut cookie dusted with powdered sugar	*Asûde helvası*	Starch and rosewater helva
		Tahin helvası	Sesame paste helva
Baklava	Layered honey-nut pie	*Keşkül*	Vanilla/almond custard
Kadayıf	"Shredded wheat" in syrup	*Krem karamel*	Creme caramel
Lokum	Turkish delight	*Sütlaç*	Rice pudding
Mustafakemalpaşa	Syrup-soaked dumpling	*Muhallebi*	Rice flour and rosewater pudding
Kadın göbeği	Doughnut in syrup	*Süpangile*	Ultra-rich chocolate pudding
Komposto	Stewed fruit	*Fırın sütlaç*	Baked rice pudding
Aşure	Pulse, wheat, fruit, and nut jello	*Kazandibi*	Browned residue of *tavukgöğsü*
Tavukgöğsü	Chicken fiber, milk and semolina taffy	*Zerde*	Saffron-laced jello
		Dondurma	Ice cream
İrmik helvası	Semolina and nut helva	*Kaymak*	Clotted cream

Drinks

Çay	Tea	*Meyva suyu*	Fruit juice
Ada çay	Sage tea	*Memba suyu*	Spring water (non-fizzy)
Kahve	Coffee	*Maden suyu*	Mineral water (fizzy)
Salep	Orchid root powder-based drink	*Bira*	Beer
Ayran	Drinking yogurt	*Rakı*	Aniseed-flavored spirit distilled from grape pressings and seed
Boza	Fermented millet drink		
Şıra	Grape must	*Şarap*	Wine

Common toasts

The closest equivalents to "Bottoms up" are:

The following are more formal . . .

Şeref'e, şerefiniz'e or	To honor, to our honor	*Sağlığınız'a*	To our health
		Mutluluğ'a	To happiness
Neşe'ye	To joy	*Cam cam'a değil, can can'a*	Not glass to glass, but soul to soul

cropped up in many towns but there's often a distinctly aggresive atmosphere compared even to a *meyhane*—they're best avoided. **Wine** (*şarap*), from vineyards scattered across western Anatolia between Cappadocia, Thrace and the Aegean, is often better than average; names to watch for include Kavaklıdere, Doluca, Turasan, or Kavalleros. Red is *kırmızı*, white *beyaz*, rose *roze*. In shops, count on paying $2–5 for a bottle of wine.

SPIRITS AND HARD LIQUOR

The Turkish national **aperitif** is *rakı*, not unlike Greek ouzo but rougher and stronger. It's usually drunk over ice and topped up with bottled water. The *meyhane* routine of an evening is for a group of men to order a big bottle of *rakı*, a bucket of ice, a few bottles of water, and then slowly drink themselves under the table between bites of *meze*, or nibbles of *çerez*—the generic term for pumpkin seeds, chickpeas, almonds, etc, served on tiny plates. **Stronger stuff**—domestically produced *cin* (gin), *votka* (vodka), and *kanyak* (cognac)—was long the province of the "Tekel" or government monopoly, but recently import duties on foreign-bottled items have plummeted and you needn't subject yourself to Tekel's gut-rotting properties any longer.

MOSQUES, MUSEUMS, AND SITES

There's no admission fee for entry to mosques but you may be asked by the caretaker or *imam* to make a small donation. If so, put it into the collection box rather than someone's hand. Larger mosques which are frequented by tourists are kept open all the time; others open only for *namaz*, or Muslim prayer, five times a day. Prayer times, which last around twenty minutes, vary according to the time of year, but basically occur at dawn, mid-morning, midday, sundown, and early evening; often a chalkboard will be posted outside the door with exact hours for that day. Outside of prayer times it's sometimes possible to find the *imam* and ask him to open up; just ask passers-by where his house is.

Whether or not you're required to, it's a **courtesy** for women to cover their heads before entering a mosque, and for both men and women to cover their legs (shorts are considered particularly offensive). In some mosques pieces of material for this purpose are distributed at the door. Shoes should always be removed, and unless there's an attendant outside, pick your shoes up, carry them inside, and place them on the racks located near the door for this purpose. It's better to wait until prayer is finished and then go in, rather than to enter while it's in progress, although whenever you enter you will find a few individuals at prayer. As long as you keep your distance and speak quietly you won't disturb anyone unduly.

MUSEUMS AND SITES

Museums are generally open from 8am or 8:30am until 5pm or 6pm, and closed on Monday, though in the case of some smaller museums you may have to find the *bekçi* (warden) yourself and ask him to open up. All sites and museums are closed on the mornings of public holidays. İstanbul's Byzantine palaces are generally closed on Mondays and Thursdays.

Major **archaeological sites** have variable opening hours, but are generally open daily from just after sunrise until just before sunset. Some smaller archaeological sites are only guarded during the day, and left unfenced, permitting a free wander around in the evening. Others are staffed until after dark by a solitary warden who may have enough English to give you a guided tour, for which he will probably expect a tip.

Never pay an **entrance fee** unless the warden can produce a ticket, whatever other documentation s/he may have. Admission varies from the current equivalent of $1 at minor sites, to $5 for five-star attractions like Ephesus. FIYTO **student cards** should ensure free admission to museums and sites; ISIC cards will usually—though not always—get you a fifty percent reduction.

Some of İstanbul's most fascinating smaller Byzantine monuments, like the Fethiye Camii and Aya Irene, are only accessible **by permission** from the Directorate of Aya Sofya, located in the grounds of Aya Sofya. Certain Armenian monuments along the Soviet border also require permission to visit—but this is granted only by the military authorities in Ankara.

BAZAARS AND SHOPPING

Consuming interests are high on the agenda of most visitors to Turkey. Even those who come determined not to buy will be shortly persuaded otherwise by the myriad street merchants and store owners who cannot resist the hard sell—as traditional to Turkish culture as tea and hospitality—and by the high quality of goods available.

THE BAZAARS

There are several kinds of bazaar in Turkey, with a common denominator of interest, if you're not too intimidated by the barrage of pestering touts or proprietors trying to guess your nationality and inveigle you into their premises.

First there are the **covered bazaars**, found in large towns like İstanbul, Bursa, and Kayseri. These are basically medieval Ottoman shopping malls, comprising several *bedestens* or domed buildings from which particular types of goods are sold, linked by various covered arcades, which in turn were also originally assigned to a particular trade.

Surrounding these covered bazaars are large areas of **small shops**, essentially open-air extensions of the covered areas and governed by the same rules: each shop is a separate unit with an owner and apprentice, and successful businesses are not allowed to expand and merge. Prices on the street are often slightly lower than in the *bedestens* owing to lower rents.

In addition there are weekly or twice-weekly **street markets** in most towns or in different areas of cities, arranged on the same lines as those in northern Europe, and selling roughly similar everyday household products. More exotic are the semipermanent **flea markets** (*bit pazarı* or literally "louse markets"), ranging in quality from street stalls where old clothes are sold and resold among the homeless, to lanes of shops where you can buy secondhand clothes, furniture or occasionally an antique of real aesthetic or monetary value.

Apart from the variety and visual impact of goods on sale in Turkish bazaars, and the tantalizing prospect of picking up something worthwhile, the main reason to frequent them is for the challenge of **bargaining**. As a guideline, start at a figure somewhat lower than whatever you are prepared to pay, usually around half of your shopkeeper's starting price. Once a price has been agreed on, you are ethically committed to buy, so don't commence haggling unless you are reasonably sure you want the item. There are other psychological tactics to engage in, such as inquiring about several articles in a shop before you even look at the thing you really want, or proposing to go elsewhere for some comparison shopping, but you'll only perfect your act with practice.

THE WARES

Turkish **carpets and kilims** are world famous, and can still be bought relatively cheaply in Turkey. The selection is best in İstanbul, whose shopkeepers scour the countryside, with the result that there are relatively few rugs on sale near their source. A *kilim*, or pile-less rug, is flat woven on a loom, while a *cicim* is a kilim with additional designs stitched onto it.

Special attention must be paid when shopping for any kind of floor-covering; it's easy to pay excessively for inferior quality. One useful test, to ensure that the colors of the product aren't going to run the first time you try to clean off a coffee stain, is to wet a rag and rub the carpet, then check to see if any color has come off. If it has, it doesn't bode well for the future, and the dyes certainly aren't natural. Since elderly, handmade, natural-dyed rugs are getting rarer all the time, various artificial aging techniques have been resorted to by dealers, including solar or chemical bleaching, or applied dirt. Genuine collector's items are often salvaged from deteriorated larger works, and more or less skillfully repaired.

It's worth finding out as much as you can about the origins of the carpet, the symbolic meanings of its motifs, and the techniques used in its production. This will increase the nostalgic value of the product, and during such discussions you should be able to decide if your dealer is trustworthy, and whether his final price will be fair or not. If you're very serious about carpet-buying, a visit to an ethnological museum or two—and a read of some of the recommended titles on the subject in "Books," in *Contexts*—might be a worthwhile use of time.

Jewelry should also be bought with care, since imitations abound. Fake amber can be identified with a naked flame, because it melts, but a test isn't advisable without the permission of the proprietor. Gold, silver, and semiprecious stones, of which amber and turquoise are the most common, are sold by weight, with almost total disregard for the disparate level of craftsmanship involved. One particularly intricate method is *telkâri* or wire filigree, most of which comes from eastern Turkey, particularly Diyarbakır and Trabzon. Bear in mind that the per-gram price of silver or gold can be bargained down, making a substantial difference to the eventual total. Also remember that sterling silver items should bear a hallmark—anything else could well be a nickel or pewter alloy.

Copperwork is not as common as in the days when it was an essential part of a newly-wed couple's household furnishings, and very little of it is still hammered out from scratch, or really heavy-gauge. Still, the articles are very handsome, and occasionally functional; if you want to buy at the source, keep an eye out in the bazaars of eastern Anatolia. Since copper is mildly toxic, vessels intended for use in the kitchen must be tinned inside—one layer for use as a tea kettle, three for use with food. If the layer is absent or deteriorated, have it (re)done at the nearest *kalaycı* or tinsmith. If you live in a hard-water area, or the pot is from such a place in Turkey, a layer of mineral deposits will quickly build up, serving the same protective function.

Turkey's **clothing** industry has raised its profile since Rifat Özbek appeared on the international scene with a line of orientally influenced designer clothing, and Turkish designs are beginning to match the quality of local fabrics—including Bursa silk and Angora wool; they are also generally cheaper than anything to be found in North America. Otherwise most outlets (and street vendors) concentrate on imitation Lacoste, Levi's and Benetton items of varying quality.

There are always a number of well-stocked **leather** outlets in any important tourist center, though the industry was originally based in western Anatolia where alum deposits and acorn-derived tannin could aid the tanning process. Today İzmir and İstanbul still have the largest workshops, though the retail business also booms on the Mediterranean coast, particularly in Antalya and Alanya, where specialist (biker, gay) tastes may be catered to. Jackets are the most obvious accessory, the prices of which vary from a paltry $60 to over $300, with a minimum of about $120 for anything half decent. If you're not interested in big outlays, wallets—especially Maraş brand—are excellent and durable.

The *nargile* or **hookah** is doubtless one of those Ottoman holdovers, like fezzes and dervishes, that Atatürk might have wished to consign to the dustheap of history. However it's still around, indulged in by the hour throughout northwestern Turkey by cafés-full of contentedly puffing gentlemen.

A functional *nargile* is not a plastic toy or objet d'art as sold in so many trinket shops, but should be fitted with a lamb's leather, wire-reinforced tube, all-brass or lathed hardwood plumbing, and a clear glass or crystal chamber. If you find an older, crystal item, it will be an antique, and worth upwards of $50. Expect to pay $25 for a quality 18-inch model with a blown glass bowl; cast ones with visible mold marks aren't so valuable. A wood superstructure looks better but brass ones last longer.

If you intend to use the *nargile* when you get home, remember to buy *tömbeki*, or compressed Persian tobacco, as you won't find it easily outside of Turkey. You'll also have to convince customs authorities that your *nargile* isn't narcotics paraphernalia, and you'll need a source of live coals to drop into the *sönbeki* or brazier end—matches don't work well.

MUSEUM PIECE OR COLLECTOR'S ITEM?

Some of the more popular **archaeological sites**, particularly Ephesus, Pamukkale, and Ani, are the haunt of characters peddling "*antiks*" of doubtful authenticity. These freelance salesmen are remarkably tenacious but in the majority of cases you would simply be throwing money away; in the unlikely event you were sold something genuine, you would be liable for prosecution. Under Turkish law it is an offense to buy, sell, attempt to export or even just possess museum-caliber antiquities. Exact age limits are not specified in the lawbooks, which suggests that decisions by customs officials are arbitrary and subjective.

In the case of **carpets** handled by established dealers, you run a very slight risk of investing a lot of money in a supposed "collector's item" which turns out to be collectable only by the Turkish Republic. If you're apprehensive about a proposed purchase, you should ask the dealer to prepare both a **fatura** (invoice) stating the exact purchase price—also necessary to satisfy customs—and a declaration stating that the item is not an antiquity. If you're still not satisfied, you may want to summon staff of the nearest museum; if the dealer's not being straight, such a proposal will put the fear of Allah in him, and you'll soon know the whole story.

Should you be caught **smuggling** anything out, the Turkish authorities will be unimpressed by any excuses or connections, and will very likely make an example of you—as they did an American woman in 1986, who unsuccessfully claimed ignorance of a purchase's vintage, and served six months of a much longer prison sentence before escaping with the assistance of her lawyer.

Traditional Turkish **musical instruments** are sold cheaply all over Turkey. The most easily portable are the *ney*, a Turkish flute made from a length of calamus reed or bamboo, the *davul* or drum, and the *saz*, the long-necked Turkish lute. In İstanbul the main sales points are along Atatürk Bulvarı below the Valens Aqueduct, and across from the Mevlevi *semahane* near the top station of the Tünel in Beyoğlu. In İzmir, there is a row of shops next to Basmane train station. You are less likely to get a "toy" version if you buy instruments at specialist shops like these, or from craftsmen themselves. A *kaval* (end-blown flute) is compact and inexpensive at about $7, and a *saz* is good value for around $30 and up.

A **tavla** or backgammon set makes another good souvenir of Turkish popular culture, since it is played in dives all over the country. The cheapest wooden sets cost around $4; a medium-size apparatus of inlaid, painted cedar wood (*şedir*) runs about $20, and you can pay anything up to $100 for inlaid mother-of-pearl and ivory. Most of the boards come from Damascus, as any reputable dealer will admit; if you're not confident that the inlay material is genuine and not just stencilled on, it's better to settle for the painted-wood kind, which is more difficult to fake. Dice and pieces should be included, and many boards have a chess/checkers grid on the exterior; an olive-wood chessmen set will set you back another $6.

Other possible memorabilia easily found in the shops of any covered bazaar are probably best obtained from the towns in which they originate. These include **meerschaum pipes** carved from *lületaşı* stone quarried near Eskişehir; **Karagöz puppets**, representing the popular folk characters Karagöz and Hacıvat, preferably made from camel skin in Bursa; **towels and silk goods**, again in Bursa; **onyx**, available all over Cappadocia but especially Hacıbektaş; and **Kütahya ceramics**, which may not be the finest ever produced in Turkey, but since the kilns of İznik closed down are the best available. Enameled tiles suitable for kitchens or bathrooms won't cost more than $2 apiece at either of the two Kütahya factories making them.

FESTIVALS AND NATIONAL PUBLIC HOLIDAYS

There are two kinds of celebrations in Turkey: religious festivals, observed all over the Islamic world on dates determined by the Muslim calendar, and Turkish national holidays, which commemorate significant dates in the history of Ottoman and Republican Turkey. In addition there are a number of annual cultural or harvest extravaganzas held in various cities and resorts across the country.

RELIGIOUS FESTIVALS

There are four important **religious festivals**, though since the **Islamic calendar** is lunar, their dates tend to drift backward eleven days each year relative to the Gregorian calendar. See the accompanying box for the specific dates of forthcoming religious festivals.

The month of **Ramadan** itself (*Ramazan* in Turkish) is perhaps the most important, the Muslim month of daylight abstention from food, water, tobacco, or sexual relations, occurring during late winter in the 1990s. Ramadan is not a public holiday; life carries on as normal despite the fact that half the population is fasting from sunrise to sunset. Some restaurants close for the duration, others discreetly hide their salons behind curtains, but at most establishments you will be served with surprisingly good grace. **Kadir Gecesi** takes place the 23rd and 24th days of the month of Ramadan, when Muhammad is supposed to have received the Koran from God, an event hailed with night-long prayer in mosques.

The three-day **Şeker Bayramı** (Sugar Holiday) is held at the end of Ramadan, celebrated by family get-togethers and giving of presents and sweets to children, and restrained general partying in the streets and restaurants. The four-day **Kurban Bayramı** (Festival of the Sacrifice), in which the sacrificial offering of a sheep in place of Abraham's son Ismael—a Koranic version of the biblical story—is marked by the slaughter of over 2.5 million sheep. Only the wealthiest families can afford to buy a whole animal, so part of the meat is distributed to the poor of the neighborhood. Sheep are brought from all over Anatolia to the big cities (subject of the Yılmaz Güney film *The Herd*), and sold on street corners in the weeks leading up to the festival. They are killed by the traditional Islamic method of a slit gullet in any open space available (apartment-house gardens are a favorite).

During *Şeker* and *Kurban Bayrams*, which are also public holidays, **travel** becomes almost impossible: from the first evening of the holiday (a Muslim festival is reckoned from sunset) public transit is completely booked up, and unless you also plan in advance you won't get a seat on any long-distance coach, train, plane, or ferry. Many shops and all banks, museums, and government offices close during the holiday periods (although corner grocery stores and most shops in resorts stay open). It's worth noting that when these festivals occur close to a national holiday the whole country effectively grinds to a halt for up to a week, with resorts packed for the duration.

UPCOMING DATES OF RELIGIOUS FESTIVALS	
Şeker Bayramı	*Kurban Bayramı*
16–18 April 1991	23–26 June 1991
5–7 April 1992	12–15 June 1992
24–26 March 1993	1–4 June 1993

CULTURAL FESTIVALS

Cultural festivals are most interesting in the larger cities and tourist resorts with the resources to accommodate and attract international name acts. Just about every sizable town will have some sort of yearly bash, though many are of limited interest to outsiders; we've tried to select the best below.

The most important event is the **International İstanbul Arts Festival**, which runs from the middle of June to the middle of July. This includes Turkish and European opera, music, and ballet in places all over the city, including the Rumeli Hisarı, Aya Irene church, and Topkapı Palace, where Mozart's opera *Abduction from the Seraglio* is performed. The **International İzmir** festival, which takes place at the same time, runs a close second, with the majority of performances at Ephesus and Çeşme. Another festival of interest to visitors is the **İstanbul Film Festival**, held in early April, when recent Turkish and foreign films are screened at a large number of forums, particularly the Atatürk Culture Center and the movie theaters on İstiklâl Caddesi. It provides a rare opportunity to see Turkish films with English subtitles.

Less spectacular but still **meriting a look** if you happen to be in the area are the Ephesus Festival, in the second week of May; the Bergama Festival in late May or early June; the Bursa Festival in July; the Foça Festival in late July; the Çanakkale Festival in mid-August; the Konya Art and Culture Festival in mid-May; the Bodrum Festival in early September; the Antalya Altın Portakal Film and Art Festival in early October; and the Noel Baba (St Nicholas) Festival at Demre in early December.

A number of more **unusual events** are also worth catching, not least **camel wrestling** at Selçuk, which takes place in mid-January, though bouts (between two camels) occur throughout the province during December and January. You might also try and see the **grease-wrestling** in Kırkpınar near Edirne in early summer, and the **bull-fighting**—again *between* beasts—which forms the climax of the Kafkasör Yayla Festival at Artvin in June. Camel- and grease-wrestling are national sports with an exotic appeal for foreign visitors; if you can't make live performances, they make compelling TV viewing.

One of the few public performances of a religious nature—and the emphasis is on the word "performance"—is the **Mevlana Festival** at Konya on 14–17 December, one of the few occasions when the so-called "Whirling Dervishes" appear in public. Preferable, however, are the more genuine Mevlevi turning ceremonies that take place at the same time in İstanbul—a marked contrast to the basketball-court setting at Konya. The only other public devotional observance or mass pilgrimage is the Hacı Bektaş Veli commemoration at the namesake village near Avanos, in mid-August, when Bektaşis, and their affiliates the Alevîs, converge for a weekend of ritual singing and dancing.

Folk dance festivals are always worth a detour, providing an opportunity to see some of the country's best dance groups displaying a

---

NATIONAL PUBLIC HOLIDAYS

National public holidays are generally marked by processions of schoolchildren or the military, or else by some demonstration of national strength and dignity, like a sports display. Banks and offices will normally be closed in these days; where they are not, we have said so.

1 January Yılbaşı—New Year's Day.

23 April Ulusal Egemenlik ve Çocuk Bayramı—Independence Day and Children's Day, celebrating the first meeting of the new Republican Parliament in Ankara.

19 May Gençlik ve Spor Günü—Youth and Sports Day, also Atatürk's birthday.

29 May Festival to commemorate İstanbul's capture by Mehmet the Conqueror in 1453 (İstanbul only).

1 July Denizcilik Günü—Navy Day (banks and government offices open).

26 August Armed Forces Day (banks and offices open).

30 August Zafer Bayramı: Celebration of the Turkish victory over the Greek forces at Dumlupınar in 1922.

28–29 October Cumhuriyet Bayramı: commemorates the proclamation of the Republic by Atatürk in 1923.

10 November The anniversary of Atatürk's death in 1938. Observed at 9:05am (the time of his death), when the whole country stops what they are doing and maintains a respectful silence for a minute. It's worth being on a Bosphorus ferry on this morning, when all the engines are turned off, and the boats drift and blow their foghorns mournfully.

sample of the widely disparate Turkish dances and costumes. There are folk festivals in Diyarbakır in late March, in Silifke in May, and in Samsun in July. Less organized, more spontaneous, and therefore more difficult to track down is the gypsy music and dance season in Thrace during early summer.

Agricultural festivals play an important part in Turkish rural life. The Diyarbakır Watermelon Festival in mid-September is basically a competition for the most outsized of the regions' over-grown fruit. Ürgüp's Grape Harvest Festival in mid-September culminates a season of celebrations in the Cappadocia region, including not only the above-noted Hacı Bektaş ceremonies but also a Tourism and Handicraft Festival at Avanos during August. The trodden grape is honored by drinking some of Turkey's finest white wines from the local thimble-size, earthenware vessels. Other agricultural products are ingested at the Mengen/Bolu Chefs' Contest in August; the region is purportedly home to the country's best cooks.

THE MEDIA

Newspapers and magazines weren't even allowed in Turkey until the mid-nineteenth century but since then lost time has been made up for with a vengeance. Dozens of mastheads, representing the full gamut of tastes from respectable to gutter, compete for readers' attention. The airwaves have until recently been exclusively state-controlled, but with satellite dishes a reality, private stations are not far off.

NEWSPAPERS AND MAGAZINES

Doyen of the **quality newspapers** is *Cumhuriyet* (Republic), a serious, mildly left-of-center institution in the same mold as *The Washington Post*. Stories and features are soundly analytical, but the Turkish used is university level and thus hardly material for beginners. Foreigners will mainly be interested in the daily entertainment listings on pages four to six—just about the only way to find out about live events in İstanbul, Ankara, and İzmir, aside from keeping an eye out for wall posters.

In terms of circulation, *Cumhuriyet* is outstripped by the more right-wing *Hürriyet* and is fielding a stiff challenge from *Güneş*, lately revamped to overtake *Hürriyet* in the sweepstakes for second most serious paper. It's got a Saturday supplement mag, *Ekran*, with comprehensive TV and radio listings. *Güneş* is also flagship of the huge media fleet still owned, as of this writing, by Asil Nadir, the notorious North Cypriot tycoon who made his first fortune in London's East End clothing industry before diversifying into fruit-canning, consumer electronics, and publishing.

His umbrella company, Polly Peck, crashed spectacularly in the autumn of 1990; whether he'll be forced to sell off all or part of his media empire to satisfy creditors is currently a hot topic in Turkey.

The top-selling daily *Günaydın*, also part of the Nadir chain, occupies the **middlebrow** territory. The once-proud *Tercüman* is now a declining right-wing rag, and *Milliyet* trails both in reader numbers and influence behind the quality papers. Though no rival to Nadir's, another small family-run press cartel, based in İzmir, produces the middle-of-road *Sabah*, which recently and unsuccessfully tried to expand nationwide, and *Yeni Asır*, the self-styled "Voice of the Aegean." At the **lower end of the spectrum**, cornering the girlie, crime, and sports markets, are such four-color fish-wrappers as *Tan* (yet another Asil Nadir property) and *Bügün*.

The principal **weeklies** are *Nokta*, a news-and-feature magazine again controlled by Asil Nadir, and *Panorama*, a picture-spread affair a bit like the original North American *Life*. *İkibin'e Doğru* (Towards 2000), an influential leftist weekly with regular provocative scoops, was closed down permanently by the authorities in June 1990 after numerous temporary bannings; a successor, *Yüzyıl* (Century), has appeared, and its staff have immediately run afoul of the powers that be. *Sokak* (Alley), a features and current affairs journal, folded in April 1990, after financial troubles were aggravated by a hostile official response to an article questioning the necessity of conscription.

Such incisive, topical coverage is exceptional; the main explanation for the frequent timidity of press coverage in Turkey is the simple fact that hard-hitting scoops can be hazardous to journalists' health. Publishing an article deemed to "damage the respectability and dignity of Turkey abroad," or "weaken national feeling," or "incite strife by exploiting class, race, religious, sectarian, or regional differences," as defined by the **Devlet Güvenlik Mahkemesi** (the State Security Tribunal, in session in each province), can net both reporter and editor a maximum seven-year term in the slammer, *per article*. Despite an alleged commitment to the full return of civil liberties in Turkey, such indictments by the *DGM* are still returned with depressing regularity. Most "infractions" have to do with alleged insults or impertinence to government officials, accounts of official misdeeds and financial scandals, the history or current status of Kurds or Armenians, and anything resembling advocacy of communism (banned in Turkey).

Mostly immune from any such processes are the various weekly **satirical comic revues**, whose format, often quasi-pornographic, delivers an at times political message, even for non-readers of the extremely street-slangy text. *Gırgır*, the oldest, was long the largest selling worldwide adult comic after America's *Mad* and the Soviet Union's *Krokodil*. With such a winning formula, proprietor Asil Nadir (again!) until recently let well enough alone, but in late 1989 a dispute between management and cartoonists over the copyright ownership of artwork resulted in a massive staff walkout. *Gırgır's* loss was the gain of a host of competitors such as *Limon*, *Hıbır*, and particularly *Avnı*—a cooperative venture begun by the ex-*Gırgır* personnel—who have forged ahead in terms of scurrilousness and pungency, leaving *Gırgır* a rather tame magazine by comparison.

English-language publications, sold wherever foreigners congregate, include the *Turkish Daily News*, published in Ankara and pretty turgid, and the more incisive and literate weekly *Dateline Turkey*, based in İstanbul and owned by *Hürriyet*. *Dateline* has intelligent features, good reviews of ongoing events or exhibits, and a pull-out directory section. Also worth looking out for—if it's still around—is the glossy bimonthly magazine *Turquoise*, which despite a preponderance of ads and featurettes on coastal real estate deals and expensive antique stores, often has stories on destinations and topics rarely found elsewhere. For a good **overseas** summary of Turkish affairs, consult *Turkey Briefing*, a rather critical though

nonpartisan bimonthly digest. It's available only on a subscription basis (£12 yearly individual, £5 student) from 87 Glebe St, London W4 2BB, UK.

British newspapers tend to be three days old on the rare occasions they're available; **North American** ones never are. For up-to-date news in English you're better off with the *International Herald Tribune*, or the American weeklies *Time* and *Newsweek*.

TV, RADIO, AND MOVIES

TV and radio are largely government-monopolized, and ubiquitous. As many as five **television** channels of **TRT** (Turkish Radio and Television), broadcasting from roughly 5:30am to just after midnight, are available depending on where you are. Satellite dishes have also begun to proliferate, catching CNN and other private European networks—including Magic Box, a German-Turkish pirate station run by an ex-chief of TRT.

Most **public programming** veers between foreign historical drama series dubbed in Turkish, American films (also dubbed), and talking-heads-type panel discussions-plus-news, punctuated by classical Turkish musical interludes, variety shows, soaps, and chirpy, American-style ads. It may still be true that the original soundtrack of dubbed foreign films is simulcast on radio at FM 94.7. **TRT2** often has slick international music videos on Sunday afternoon, and foreign concert clips in the evenings; the same channel also broadcasts an English-language news program every day at 10:45pm. The third channel, **GAP** (*Güney Anadolu Programı* or "South Anatolian Program") is reserved for re-runs and general pap aimed at the Kurdish-and Arabic-speaking areas of the country. Channel 5 only broadcasts between 7pm and midnight.

Radio is a bit more accessible, with up to four stations broadcasting between roughly 7am and 1am, though certain channels start earlier or end later. Because of the overwhelming number of transmitters and frequencies, precise details are fairly pointless, but by playing dial roulette on your Walkman you can often capture some amazingly good jazz, rock, blues, or classical programs. The **Third Program** broadcasts the highest proportion of Western music, and airs the news in English at 9am, noon, 2pm, 5pm, 7pm, 10pm, and 12:55am; it's most commonly found at 88.4, 94, and 99mHz.

Movie theaters are only found in the largest towns, and subsist mostly on a diet of shoot-em-ups, kung-fu flicks, and Indian musicals. Films are subject to heavy censorship, with many western releases banned outright. Most foreign products are dubbed, but you may strike lucky in İstanbul, Ankara, or İzmir and find a decent movie in English. Examine the posters outside for clues (*Asıl ses* means "original voice") and then ask the ticket seller. *Seans* (screening) times, up to six daily, occur from about midday to late evening. This means that films are often cut to fit the time slot as well as the censors' considerations, and intermissions are similarly arbitrary.

SEXUAL HARASSMENT ... AND WOMEN IN TURKEY

Mutual mistrust and misapprehension are the hallmarks of relationships between Western women and Turkish men. Each approaches the other with woeful stereotypes fueled partly by myth, partly by reality: Turkish men are supposed to be lecherous punks out for a good time with any passing piece of skirt, while foreign women are an easy lay, and rich to boot.

Turkish society is deliberately gender-segregated, and if you want to avoid men completely, even if you're traveling alone, it's not too difficult. Simply seek the company of Turkish women at every opportunity, and you will generally be protected by them. Turkish women suffer from **harassment** themselves, and their methods of dealing with it can be imitated successfully. Avoid eye contact with men, and try to look as confident and purposeful as possible. When all else fails, the best way of neutralizing harassment is to make a public scene. You won't elicit any sympathy by swearing in Turkish, but the word *Ayıp* (Shame!) spoken very loudly generally has

the desired effect—passers-by or fellow passengers will deal with the situation for you. *Defol* (get lost), or *bırak beni* (leave me alone) are stronger retorts.

WOMEN'S STATUS

Turkish women, particularly Western-style feminists, are presently organizing to fight back, picking up a thread which has always run through Turkish society. Among the pre-Islamic Turkic tribes, men were only allowed one wife (as they are in today's Republican Turkey) and the king and queen ruled as equals, so that a decree was only valid if issued in both their names. Historically Turkish women have had support from some impressive quarters: the two best known Sufi mystics, Hacı Bektaş Veli and Celâleddin Rumi (aka Mevlana), both strongly endorsed the need to educate women and treat them as equals, and Atatürk, the founder of the Turkish Republic, made numerous speeches on the subject of women's rights, lending support to efforts which culminated in full women's suffrage in 1934. Nowadays abortion is available on demand with or without the father's consent, and contraceptives are readily available over the counter.

But **feminism** still has a long way to go, both in the cities and rural areas. The veil is becoming more prevalent rather than less, girls' education is still marginalized in village schools, and women are rarely seen outdoors after dark, alone or accompanied. Women have long worked as public employees and in private white-collar jobs, but are almost totally absent from the bazaars, restaurants, and bars, even in tourist resorts, due to the fact that women must be certified prostitutes to work anywhere alcohol is served. Conversely, pornography is conspicuously exhibited daily on newsstands across the country, perhaps two racks down from the handful of women's magazines pitched at an urbanized, educated audience.

Nowhere is Turkish women's subordinate status more apparent, however, than in Turkey's numerous **brothels**. Strange as it may seem in a nominally Muslim culture, prostitution is legal and highly organized—the idea being that some women protect the virtue of others by acting as foils for male lust. Prostitution tends to be a feature of certain obvious hotels in a town's bazaar area, or more commonly is concentrated in special compounds, complete with gate and police guard, known as the *genel evler* ("general" or "public" houses). Activity is more widespread in the south and east of the country, where single men may receive offers of red-light tours from taxi drivers ("Just to look, sir . . .")—a rather sordid sort of voyeurism.

The **prostitutes** themselves are licensed, and supposedly examined regularly for VD, but are effectively the chattel of the mobsters who run most of the business nationwide. If they attempt to flee the brothels, the police are likely to work them over before returning them to their workplace. Many of the women have literally been sold by their families or ex-spouse for real or imagined transgressions of the rural moral code; a like proportion are dosed with amphetamines or other drugs much of the time, and few have a life expectancy of over 35 years. The UK-based Anti-Slavery Society has begun a preliminary investigation into the racket, but little remedial action seems possible other than helping individual women escape the *genel evler*. Perhaps the greatest obstacle to full civil rights for prostitutes is official policy; the Constitutional (Supreme) Court, for example, ruled in 1989 that the rape of a prostitute shall carry a prison term only one-third as long as that for other rapes.

CAMPAIGNS AND ORGANIZATIONS

In the face of such entrenched reactionary attitudes, feminists face an uphill struggle. **Campaigns** like the *mor iğne campanyası*, the "purple needle campaign" of 1989, in which activists gave out purple-ribboned hat-pins to women on İstanbul buses and ferries—urging them to use them in response to harassment—and the *mor çatı* or "purple attic," a newly opened refuge for battered women, are clearly only a beginning. The problem of raising male and female awareness without provoking a spectacular Islamic backlash is still to be resolved.

Mor Çatı, the organization running the women's refuge in İstanbul, is located at Cumhuriyet Cad, Fransız Hastanesi Sokak, Özbakır İşhanı 3/2, Harbiye (☎148 6045). There's a **women's study and information center** at Fener Mahalle, Abdülezel Paşa Caddesi, İstanbul (Mon, Sat & Sun 10am–7pm, Tues, Thurs & Fri 1–7pm; ☎523 7408).

POLICE AND TROUBLE

Despite popular stereotypes, you're unlikely to encounter any trouble in Turkey. Violent street crime is uncommon, theft is rare, and the authorities treat tourists with courtesy. Keep your wits about you and an eye on your belongings just as you would anywhere else, make sure your passport is with you at all times, and you shouldn't have any problems.

THE POLICE AND THE ARMY

Although the country returned to civilian rule in 1983, Turkey's huge armed forces still play a fairly high-profile role in maintaining law and order. **Civilian police** come in a variety of subdivisions, treated with a healthy respect—mixed with fear—by the locals.

The green-uniformed *Polis* are the everyday security force in the towns and cities; the most you'll probably have to do with them is a request for help in finding a street. The *Trafik Polis*, recognizable by their white caps and two-toned Renault 12s, are a branch of this service, and their main responsibility seems to be controlling intersections and doing spot checks on vehicles. In the towns you're also likely to see the *Belediye Zabitası* or navy-clad market police, who patrol the markets and bazaars to ensure that tradesmen aren't ripping off customers. If you have reason for complaint while shopping, your best recourse is to approach one of the *Zabita* force.

In most rural areas, particularly as you move farther east, law enforcement is in the hands of the *Jandarma* or **gendarmerie**, a division of the regular army charged with law enforcement duties. Gendarmes wear military uniforms with distinguishing red arm-bands; most of them are conscripts and will be courteous and helpful if approached.

Another branch of the army much in evidence (again, particularly in the east), are the **military police** or *Askeri İnzibat*. You'll recognize them by their white helmets bearing the letters '*Az İz*', white holsters and lanyards. Officially they are supposed to keep order among the large numbers of conscripts you'll see on the streets of Turkish towns.

PROBLEMS AND RESTRICTED AREAS

In addition to the caveats on drugs and antiquities, there are a number of other **situations to avoid**. Don't insult Atatürk or Turkey in any way, even in jest. Don't take photographs near the numerous, well-marked military zones. Try not to be drawn into serious disputes, since while things rarely turn violent in Turkey, when they do they can turn *very* violent—if anybody seems to be insulting or provoking you, walk away. And lastly, don't engage in any missionary or proselytization activities among the locals, or attempt to import evangelical literature. Touring the Christian sites with the Bible or a scholarly work is certainly okay, but any tract intended for distribution isn't. Many foreigners have recently been arrested and/or deported for offending Muslim sensibilities on this point.

In the southeastern provinces still under **martial law** the army patrol the streets in the towns and cities, and man checkpoints on rural roads. In the mountains around the towns of Hakkâri and Siirt, and between Kemah and Tunceli, there's an intermittent guerilla war going on. You're highly unlikely to have any direct experience of this but you will notice a certain level of tension in the nearby urban areas.

In extremely **remote areas** of the east you may attract the attention of the military or the police, who'll want to know what you're doing and where you're going. This may involve, at most, a rather tedious day or evening of polite interrogation. The only areas where you absolutely need a **permit** are within 5km (sometimes 10km) of the borders with the USSR and Iran, and we've detailed the specific instances in the guide. Areas under threat from insurgent activities fall into a sort of gray zone: while it is not, strictly speaking, illegal for outsiders to visit them, the authorities will prevent you from going if they can, and will take no responsibility for your safety should you manage to get past the roadblocks. Currently this isn't recommended; were you to meet any guerillas, you could probably count on a fairly unpleasant reception, or getting caught in crossfire.

SPORTS AND OUTDOOR ACTIVITIES

The Turks have been sports fanatics since the inception of the Republic, but success in the international arena has thus far been confined to Naim Süleymanoğlu's spectacular Olympic weight-lifting coup in 1988, when everyone in the country was treated to infinite television replays of his winning clean-and-jerk.

SOCCER

Soccer claims pride of place in the hearts of Turks, with the history of organized teams going back to the first decade of this century. Stadiums are mammoth, and matches, usually Saturday or Sunday afternoons between September and May, are well attended. The most **conspicuous teams** are the three İstanbul rivals *Beşiktaş*, *Galatasaray*, and *Fenerbahçe*, and the surprisingly good provincial sides *Trabzonspor*, *Adanaspor*, and *Konyaspor*. Oddly enough, İzmir's *Karşıyaka* and *Altay* are continually threatened with relegation to minor-league status. Foreign players have begun to appear but are limited to two per team.

Unfortunately Turkish soccer has been quick to adopt some of the more **unsavory aspects** of western European play. Charges of bribery and corruption are regular, and crowds, while generally less liquored up than abroad and not yet up to levels of hooliganism elsewhere, can get rowdy. It's not unknown for a losing team to be attacked by their own supporters after a game, while victories are celebrated deliriously, with flag-waving maniacs leaning on the horns of cruising cars embroiled in massive traffic jams.

SKIING

Turkey is normally thought of as a summertime holiday destination, but if you're around during the cooler seasons there are a number of serviceable **ski resorts**, though none are as yet up to North American standards. The oldest, most famous, and perhaps the most overrated resort is Uludağ above Bursa, with easy and intermediate runs, but tourism authorities are pinning current hopes on the Saklıkent complex in the Beydağları near Antalya—potentially ideal for an early spring sea-cum-ski holiday, though snow cover is apt to be thin. Roughly midway between İstanbul and Ankara, near Bolu, Kartalkaya is probably better than either of these two, with a mixture of beginners' and intermediate runs, but only one T-bar lift. The best snow conditions and toughest, half-hour runs are at Palandöken near Erzurum, where the Turkish Olympic team trains, and Sarıkamış, near Kars, the highest and snowiest runs in the country. Other facilities are planned throughout Turkey but up to now this has meant just a rather token, antiquated resort at Tekir Yaylası on Erciyes Dağı near Kayseri.

MOUNTAINEERING AND HIKING

Although the Turks themselves are just beginning to **trek and hike** for pleasure, there is plenty of scope for these activities; if you're interested, get hold of a copy of *Trekking in Turkey* (Lonely Planet, $9.95), co-written by one of the authors of this book. If you're daunted at the prospect of going alone, contact one of the adventure travel companies listed under "Packages" in the "Getting There" section, p.7.

At present, the **Kaçkar Dağları** running parallel to the Black Sea is the most rewarding area for extended treks, and a number of companies organize expeditions there. The **Cilo and Sat massifs** along the Iraqi border are reportedly even more spectacular but have regrettably been off-limits to outsiders for most of the past twenty years owing to the ongoing Kurdish troubles. Next up in interest are the **Taurus (Toros) ranges**, which form a long chain extending from central Turkey to above the main Turquoise Coast

resort areas; again various tour companies can point you to the best places.

Aside from this, **mountaineering** in Turkey consists mostly of climbing the volcanoes of the central plateau—not nearly as satisfying; Ağrı Dağ (Ararat) is likely to be a crashing non-event for most and Erciyes or Hasan Dağı near Cappadocia little better.

If you go alone, you'll need to be fully equipped, since alpine huts are nonexistent. **Water** can be a problem in the limestone strata of the Taurus, **detailed maps** are usually unavailable for security reasons, and **trails** (when present) are faint. But the unspoiled quality of the countryside and the friendliness of the mountaineers goes a long way in compensation. You'll find details on specific hiking routes through the Kaçkar Dağları in Chapter Ten, and a selection of walks on Bursa's Uludağ in Chapter Two.

OTHER ACTIVITIES

Opportunities for engaging in various **watersports** abound at the Turkish coastal resorts. You can count on renting windsurfing, kayaking, and snorkeling gear just about anywhere, and at the more developed sites water-skiing, sailing, and yachting will be offered—the yachts chartered either bare-boat or (more likely) as part of a guided, skippered three-to-fifteen-day **coastal cruise**. For possibilities of pre-booking a sailing trip, again see "Getting There"; for advice on arranging something on the spur of the moment, see Chapter Four, "Marmaris."

Because of the presumed number of antiquities still submerged off Turkey, **scuba diving** is strictly regulated and is principally available out of Bodrum, Fethiye, and Marmaris, where there's something appreciable to see.

Only two rivers—the Çoruh, in the Kaçkar, and the Göksu, in the Taurus mountains—are suitable for **white-water rafting**, and both are under threat from hydroelectric projects. The Çoruh gets some occasional attention from one North American outdoor travel concern; on the Göksu you're strictly on your own. For more details, see Chapter Ten.

FINDING WORK

Turkey has a surplus of qualified graduates, a high unemployment rate relative to North America, low wages, and no special privileges for foreigners—hardly a bright picture for potential job-seekers. Still, many foreigners do work in Turkey for varying periods, even on a tourist visa, though this is strictly speaking illegal.

TEACHING

Year-round employment and reasonable working conditions are best achieved by **teaching English** as a foreign language in one of the major cities. Even so, contracts should be examined carefully. In government-run institutions, including universities, high schools, and *Anadolu Liseleri* (the equivalent of British grammar schools), you will need some kind of degree, and your first pay packet can be delayed until the confirmation procedure (checking your credentials and political background), which can take up to three months, is completed. Other schools generally—but not always—want proof of teaching qualifications and experience, though smaller schools often just want native English speakers, so it's worth inquiring for work even if you're not qualified.

Teaching posts in the bigger outfits are advertised in Britain—in the *Guardian*, the *Times Educational Supplement*, and the *International Herald Tribune*—but private schools are probably best approached on the spot, since the work will be temporary anyway. Check whether the job will enable you to apply for an *ikamet tezkeresi* or residence permit, because if it doesn't you will have to leave the country every three months. The better organizations will in any case normally take care of the legalities for you.

OTHER OPTIONS

There is always plenty of work available in **tourist resorts**, at least during the summer months. Very little of it is legal, but since the authorities generally turn a blind eye this simply means you will find yourself crossing a border into some neighboring country every three months to renew your tourist visa.

Foreigners are not allowed to work as tour guides—one rule that is enforced—though tour companies may employ you to do PR work in the office, or to meet groups from the airport and take them to their hotel. Carpet and leather shops will often employ English-speakers on a commission basis, in which case you will work long hours trying to pull in your quota of likely tourists, but the pay can be rewarding. Bars, restaurants, and hotels also like English-speaking staff, particularly women. You won't be well paid but board and accommodation should be free. Yacht and *gület* crews are also often prepared to take on foreign staff to cook and clean, or host guests.

Voluntary work in Turkey is organized by *Gençtur*, Yerebatan Caddesi 15/3, Sultanahmet, Istanbul (☎1/526 5409, 512 0457). Their camps generally involve manual labor in Turkish villages or in holiday resorts. Basic accommodation is provided either in guesthouses or in the village school, and food is prepared by the villagers. *Gençtur* is affiliated with the *International Voluntary Service*, 162 Upper New Walk, Leicester LE1 7QA, UK (☎0533/549430).

DIRECTORY

ADDRESSES In Turkish addresses street names precede the number; if the address is on a minor alley, this will be incuded after the main thoroughfare it leads off. If you see a right-hand slash between two numbers, the first is the building number, the second the flat or office number. A letter following a right-hand slash is more ambiguous: it can mean either the shop or unit number, or be part of the general building number. Standard abbreviations, also used in this book, include "Cad" for *Cadde(si)* (avenue or main street), "Bul" for *Bulvarı* (Boulevard), "Meyd" for *Meydan(ı)* (Square), and "Sok" for *Sokak/Sokağı* (alley). Other useful terms are *kat* (floor), *zemin* (ground floor), *han(ı)* (office block), *mahalle* (district or neighborhood), and *çıkmaz(ı)* (blind alley). *Karşısı* means "opposite to," as in *PTT karşısı*. A five-digit zip-code system has been introduced, but is sporadically used; it is much more important to include the district when addressing mail. For example: Halil Güner, Kıbrıs Şehitler Caddesi, Poyraz Sokak, Ulus Apartmanı 36/2, Kat 1, Deliklıçınar, 34800 Direkköy, which means that Halil Güner lives on Poyraz Sokak no. 36, just off Kıbrıs Şehitler Caddesi, on the first floor, Flat 2 of the Ulus apartments, in the Deliklıçınar area of a larger postal district known as Direkköy.

BARGAINING You can bargain for souvenir purchases, minor repair services, rural taxis, car rental, hotels out of season, and meals at eateries where a menu is absent. You shouldn't have to bargain for dolmuş or bus tickets, though some of the stewards collecting fares on long-distance coaches are less than honest; if in doubt check to see what others are paying for the same distance.

BRING . . . A water container for ruin-tramping; a flashlight for dark corners of same; roll-on mosquito repellent; a mini-alarm clock for early transport; sunscreen cream exceeding Factor 15; photo film (see below); and contact lens accessories—only very antiquated solutions for hard lenses are available. A powerful Walkman is also useful for when you tire of the Turkish pop played on long bus journeys.

CAMPING GAS CARTRIDGES One factory near İzmir has begun making it, but it's mostly imported from Greece and nearly impossible to find—bring lots unless you're flying in.

CHILDREN They're adored in Turkey; childless couples will be asked when they plan to have some, and having children along guarantees red-carpet treatment almost everywhere. Three- or four-bedded hotel rooms are easy to find, and airlines, ships, and trains offer substantial discounts. Baby formulas are cheap and easily available; disposable diapers aren't.

CIGARETTES AND TOBACCO SMOKE Turkish ones can be rough, but if you're eager to try them, *Maltepe* are the most smokable—though even these are not recommended in large quantities. Better are the cigarettes made in Turkey under license from foreign brands, notably *Marlboro*, which are milder than their European equivalent. If you don't smoke, tobacco smoke can be a major nuisance. There are designated no-smoking cars on most trains, and smoking is forbidden on all domestic flights, but in buses—except for those of one or two premium companies—and enclosed waiting areas you are more or less at the mercy of a national habit.

CONTRACEPTIVES Birth control pills (*doğum kontrol hapı*) are sold over the counter at pharmacies, although you should have your own brand with you to check against the Turkish formula. Condoms used to be rare but are now sold in most pharmacies and off street carts, though you'll want to bring a supply along. Should you need them on the spot, the "proper" word is *preservatif*, the slang term *kılıf* ("hood"). Barely 100 cases of AIDS have been recorded thus far in Turkey, but nasty strains of gonorrhea are prevalent.

DEPARTMENT STORES The two chains are *Vakko* and *Yeni Karamürsel*, with outlets in İstanbul, İzmir, and Ankara.

DEPARTURE TAX None currently charged.

ELECTRIC POWER 220 volts, 50 cycles, out of double round-pin sockets. North American appliances need both a plug adaptor and a transformer (except dual-voltage shavers, which need only the former).

EMERGENCIES Police ☎055 or 666 666; fire brigade ☎000; ambulance ☎077. These calls cost one small *jeton*.

FILM This is expensive in tourist resorts and provincial towns; most Fuji products are reasonable if bought in the bazaars of İstanbul, İzmir, and Ankara, though it's best to bring enough with you. You won't find anything faster than ASA 100 outside of the three largest cities. The *Refo* chain used to offer decent E-6 processing but quality has taken a tumble of late—wait till you get home.

GAY LIFE Homosexual acts between adults over 18 are legal, but "spreading homosexual information"—i.e. advocating the lifestyle—isn't. The few gay bars in İstanbul have been raided in the past by the police, who forced customers to submit to venereal disease testing. Public attitudes are generally intolerant—or closeted—except in resorts like Bodrum, Side, or Alanya; *ibne* (catamite, passive male partner) is a deadly Turkish insult, while there is no specific word for the other role. Against such a backdrop, the *Radical Gay Group* (Sıraselviler Cad 176/5, Taksim, İstanbul) does what it can.

LAUNDRY Laundromats don't exist except for one in İstanbul (see Chapter One), but there are dry-cleaning (*kuru temizleme*) establishments in most large towns.

LUGGAGE CONSIGNMENT An *emanet* (luggage-consignment) service is available at virtually all *otogars* and train stations; there are no lockers, you pay the attendant upon delivery of article(s) in exchange for your claim ticket. Prices vary according to the amount of insurance applicable—for nice foreign backpacks or duffels, staff will charge you the most expensive rate, about $1.

NUDISM Best to assume that it's not on, though in the more decadent resorts like Side or Alanya you could get away with some discreetly topless sunning.

OPENING HOURS White-collar workers keep conventional Monday-to-Friday, 9am–6pm schedules with a full lunch hour; civil servants in theory work 8:30am–5:30pm, but in practice hours can be much more erratic, including two-hour lunches—don't expect to get important official business attended to the same day after 2:30pm. Ordinary shops are open continuously from 8:30 or 9am until 7pm or 8pm, depending on the owner. Craftsmen and bazaar stallholders keep marathon hours, often working from 9am to 8pm or 9pm, Monday to Saturday, with only the hastiest of breaks for meals, tea, or prayers. Even on Sunday the tradesmen's area may not be completely shut down—though don't count on this.

TAMPONS Tampax are available from pharmacies in the bigger towns, for slightly more than in North America; avoid *Orkid*, the disastrous domestic brand of "sanitary towels."

TIME Almost always ten hours ahead of EST; daylight savings is observed between the last weekend in March and the last one in September, so for much of October Turkey is only nine hours ahead of New York.

TOILETS Except in the fancier resort hotels and restaurants, most public ones are of the squat-hole variety, found either in public parks or (more infallibly) next to any mosque. They usually cost about 15¢, so keep small coins handy. Also keep a supply of toilet paper with you (available in Turkey)—Turks wash themselves off either with the bidet spout or the special vessel filled from the handy floor-level tap. You may well become a convert to this method, reserving the paper—which shouldn't be thrown down the hole—for drying yourself off.

VALUE ADDED TAX (VAT) The Turkish variety, known as *Katma Değer Vergisi* or *KDV*, is included in the price of virtually all goods and services. Look for the notice *Fiatlarımız KDV Dahildir* (VAT included in our prices) if you think someone's trying to do you for it twice.

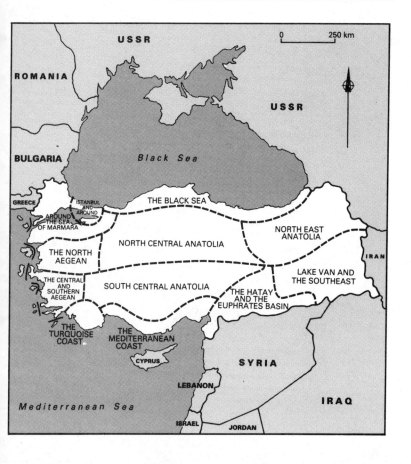

CHAPTER ONE

ISTANBUL

A rriving in İstanbul comes as a shock. You may still be in Europe, but a walk down any backstreet will be enough to convince you that you have entered a completely alien environment. Traders with handcarts, *hamals* (stevedores) carrying burdens of merchandise twice their own size and weight, limbless beggars and shoeshine boys all frequent the streets around the city center, proclaiming their business loudly until late at night. Men monopolize bars and teahouses, while women scurry about their business, heads often covered and gaze ever downcast. In summer, dusty trails take the place of sidewalks, giving way in winter to a ubiquitous slurry of mud. Where there are sidewalks, they are punctuated at intervals with unmarked pits large enough to swallow you without trace. And this is before you even begin to cross any bridges into Asia.

Yet İstanbul is the only city in the world to have played capital to **consecutive Christian and Islamic empires**. Their legacies are much in evidence, nowhere more prominently than in the cultural center of the city, where the great edifices of **Aya Sofya** and **Sultan Ahmet Camii** glower at each other across a small park. The juxtaposition of the two cultures would be fascinating enough in itself, and it's made more so by the fact that the transition between them was a process of assimilation and adoption. The **city walls** of Justinian have been preserved because they were refortified by Mehmet the Conqueror, and most of the city's **churches** were reconsecrated as mosques—not least Aya Sofya itself, which was a constant source of inspiration to Islamic architects.

Monumental architecture aside, the very confusion of sights and sounds— initially so alienating—soon becomes one of İstanbul's greatest fascinations. Even if the city did not have such a varied and vivid history, it would still take any number of return visits to begin to discover the source and meaning of the cacophony. Exploration reveals ancient **bazaars**, many of them still functioning today, including the **Kapalı Çarşı**, the largest covered bazaar in the world. The modern city, located around **Taksim Square**, offers further diversions: the sense of space created by the square's vast emptiness affords to some a feeling of relief after days spent in crowded, dirty backstreets, while night gives Taksim a new lease on life as the streets which in daylight are frequented by suited business types are taken over by club-, theater-, and opera-goers; transvestites, prostitutes, and their potential clients. The area has much to offer in the way of nightlife: the Atatürk Cultural Center on Taksim Square; most of the city's theaters and movie theaters as well as several bars and clubs—mainly seedy—in the area between Taksim and Galata; and some of the city's best restaurants. The **Bosphorus**—the straits dividing Europe and Asia—should be visited as often as possible during the course of a trip, since how much you enjoy İstanbul may well depend on how often you can escape to its shores. The **coastal villages** offer incredible views as well as some of the city's most interesting historical sites, parks, and even open

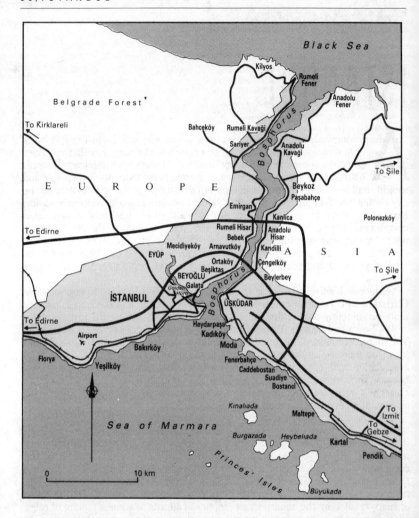

forestland, and the best fish restaurants in this part of the world. The **Princes' Islands**, a traditional refuge from political turmoil on the mainland, should be visited for their unspoiled natural beauty and for the possibility of finding a secluded beach an hour's ferry-ride away from Eminönü.

Perhaps one of the most pleasant aspects of a visit to İstanbul lies in the fact that an appreciation of its merits plays a part in the consciousness of locals of every race and creed, particularly evident in a diffident pride in the city's past. Ankara may have replaced İstanbul as the capital of Turkey, but the old imperial capital will never be replaced in the affections of the populace. Yaşar Kemal, in *The Sea-Crossed Fisherman*, summed up these feelings well:

In the distance, sunk in shadow, its leaden domes, its minarets and buildings only vaguely discernible in the bluish haze, İstanbul was still asleep, its face hidden from the world. In a little while the city would awaken, with its buses, cars, horsecarts, its ships, steam launches, fishing boats, its hamals sweating under their loads of heaped crates, its streets and avenues overflowing, its apartment buildings, mosques, bridges, all surging, interlocking in a furious turmoil and, pressing through the tangle of traffic, wondering how this city could still move, was not entirely paralyzed, people would be making superhuman efforts to reach their destination. Fishvendors in their boats by the waterfront would be setting up their gear, lighting their coals or butane cookers, heating the oil into which they would drop the flour-coated fish, and soon the odour of fried fish would spread through the early-morning air right up to Karaköy Square, to the Flower Market and to the fruit-trading wharf. Hungry workers, tramps who had nowhere to sleep but had somehow got hold of a little money, carousers with a hangover, drowsy young streetwalkers, homeless children who subsisted by picking pockets, sneak-thieving or selling black-market cigarettes would line up in front of the bobbing boats to buy a slice of bluefish, a quarter of tuna, three or four pickerel or scad, sandwiched in a half-loaf of bread, and devour it hungrily, the fat dripping down their chins. And the dull heavy roar of the awakening city would reach us from across the sea, and gradually the domes and minarets, and also the ugly apartment buildings so out of keeping with the city, would emerge from the haze, and like a strange giant creature İstanbul would spread itself out in the light of day, down to its age-old battlements along the seashore.

Some History

Considering that this city was to have such an auspicious history, its origins were surprisingly humble. While there is archaeological evidence of a **Mycenaean settlement** dating to the thirteenth century BC on the old acropolis, little is known about it, and popular tradition has it that the city was founded by **Byzas the Megarian** in the seventh century BC—hence the original name of Byzantium—and inhabited by what one ancient historian described as "a feeble colony of Greeks" until the third century AD. The site was chosen in accordance with a Delphic oracle instructing the settlers to found a city "opposite the city of the blind," and they concluded that this must refer to Chalcedon, modern-day Kadıköy, since the earlier settlers had built their city in blithe ignorance of the obvious strategic merits of the peninsula, Saray Burnu, in front of their eyes.

Over the next thousand years, Byzantium became an important center of trade and commerce, but always as a vassal of one overlord or other, and it was not until the early fourth century AD that a decision was taken that would elevate the city to the pinnacles of wealth, power, and prestige. For more than 350 years, Byzantium had been part of the Roman province of Asia. On the retirement of Diocletian in 305, Licinius and **Constantine** fought for control of the empire. Constantine finally defeated his rival on the hills above Chrysopolis (Üsküdar) and chose Byzantium as the site for the new **capital of the Roman Empire**.

It was a fine choice. Rome itself was virtually uncontrollable—hidebound by tradition and effectively ruled by the mob. The seven hills on which Constantine was to build the new capital (a deliberate echo of Rome: indeed the city was originally to be called New Rome) commanded control of the **Bosphorus** and had easy access to the natural harbor of the **Golden Horn**. The site was protected by water on two sides, and its landward side was easily defensible. It was also well placed for access to the troublesome frontiers of both Europe and the Persian Empire.

In 395 the division of the Roman Empire between the two sons of Theodosius I left Constantinople as capital of the eastern part of the empire, which rapidly began to take on its own distinctive character, disassociating itself from Rome and adopting the Greek language and **Christianity**. (Despite Constantine's earlier espousal of the religion, Christians were still in the minority during his reign.) Long and successful government was interrupted briefly by the Nika riots during the reign of Justinian (in 532), after which the city was rebuilt on an even grander scale than before. The church of Aya Sofya, particularly, was rebuilt to proportions hitherto unimagined.

Half a century later, however, the dissolution of the Byzantine Empire had begun, as waves of Persians, Avars, and Slavs attacked from the north and east. The Emperor Heraclius stemmed the tide with a brilliant military campaign, but over the following centuries decline was constant, if slow. The empire was overrun by Arabs in the seventh and eighth centuries, and by Bulgars in the ninth and tenth centuries, and it was only the Theodosian land walls that saved the city of Constantinople itself from attack and invasion. At the beginning of the thirteenth century, however, not even the city's great fortifications could keep out the **Crusaders**. They breached the sea walls in 1204 and proceeded to sack and destroy the city. By the time the Byzantines, led by Michael Palaeologus, had regained control, not only had many of the major buildings fallen into disrepair and disuse, but the empire itself had greatly diminished in size.

Parallel to this decline ran the increasing strength of the **Ottoman Empire**, whose capital moved between Bursa and Edirne in the century preceding the capture of Constantinople, and whose territory effectively surrounded the city long before it was taken. Most importantly, in 1452, Mehmet II demanded and received land on the Bosphorus, the lifeline of the fading city, on which to build the fortress of Rumeli Hisarı. This enabled him to besiege vital supply lines and starve the city into submission.

The **siege** of the city lasted seven weeks, and ended when the Ottoman forces breached the land walls at their weakest point, between Topkapı and Edirnekapı. After the capture and subsequent pillage, **Mehmet the Conqueror** (Fatih Sultan Mehmet) began to rebuild the city, beginning with a new palace to replace the Great Palace of Byzantium. Later the Mosque of the Conqueror (Fatih Camii) and many smaller complexes were established. This did not mean that other religions were not tolerated—indeed Mehmet actively encouraged Greeks and Armenians to take up residence in the city, a policy followed by his successor Beyazit II, who settled Jewish refugees from Spain in an attempt to increase the flagging population figures and inject life into the economy and expertise into the workforce.

In the century following the conquest the victory was reinforced by the great military achievements of **Selim the Grim**, and by the reign of **Süleyman the Magnificent** (1520–1566), "the Lawgiver." This greatest of all Turkish leaders was confounded in his plans for domination in the Western hemisphere only at the gates of Vienna, and the wealth gained in military conquests was used to fund the greatest of all Ottoman architecture, the work of Mimar Sinan.

It was another century after the death of Süleyman before the empire began to show signs of **decay**. Territorial losses abroad combined with corruption at home, which insinuated its way into the very heart of the empire, Topkapı Palace itself. The institution called the Cage, introduced by Ahmet III (see p.77), had proved a less than humanitarian solution to the custom of fratricide committed by newly crowned sultans, since many of its occupants were completely insane by the time their turn came to take office. Many of the sultans preferred to spend their time in the harem rather than on the battlefield, and the women of the harem became involved in intrigue and power struggles on a grand scale.

By the end of the eighteenth century these problems could no longer be ignored. As the Ottoman Empire lost more and more territory to the West, succeeding sultans became more interested in Western institutional models. This movement of **reform**, which began with Selim III's new model army, culminated in the first Ottoman constitution and a short-lived Parliament in 1876. Parliament was dissolved after a year by Abdül Hamid II, but eventually the forces of reform led to his deposition in 1909. After the War of Independence, Atatürk created a new capital in Ankara, a small provincial town in central Anatolia. İstanbul retained its importance as a center of trade and commerce, however, and although the modern offices, hotels, and apartment buildings may not have the glamorous appeal of the finer imperial architecture, they are evidence that the city still plays an important part in the life of its country.

Modern İstanbul

The **population** of İstanbul has increased from 1.8 million in 1960 to nearly ten million today, almost a fifth of the country's total, and is still on the rise: 350,000 Anatolian peasants pour into the capital every year, and an estimated ninety percent of the city's population consist of first-generation arrivals. The effects of the consequent overcrowding on the city are obvious even on a whistle-stop visit. According to a recent survey İstanbul has less **green space** per capita than any among a random sample of twenty European cities (2 square meters per head, as opposed to Stockholm, which has 80 square meters per head). **Slum clearance programs** initiated under the former right-wing mayor, Dalan, and continued, notwithstanding election promises, by leftist Sözen have marginally improved the appearance of some of the key tourist centers of the city while giving impetus to **highrise development** on an ever-growing radius. It is thus becoming increasingly difficult to escape the city's perimeters, especially since traffic congestion and an overcrowded public transit system, combined with an apparent conspiracy between the municipal authorities and taxi drivers to carry out constant repairs on all major through roads, make it very hard to move at all, even within the city boundaries.

> The İstanbul **area telephone code** is ☎1.

Arriving and Getting Around the City

İstanbul is cut in two by the **Bosphorus**, a narrow strait that runs roughly southwest between the Black Sea and the Sea of Marmara, dividing Europe from Asia. At right angles to the strait is an inlet which feeds it, the **Golden Horn**, commencing in two small streams about seven kilometers from the mouth of the Bosphorus. The majority of İstanbul's suburbs are located along the shores of the Sea of Marmara and on the hills above the Bosphorus, while the quarters along the Golden Horn are dominated by light industry.

İstanbul effectively has two city centers, separated by the Golden Horn but both situated on the European side of the Bosphorus. The **Sultanahmet** district

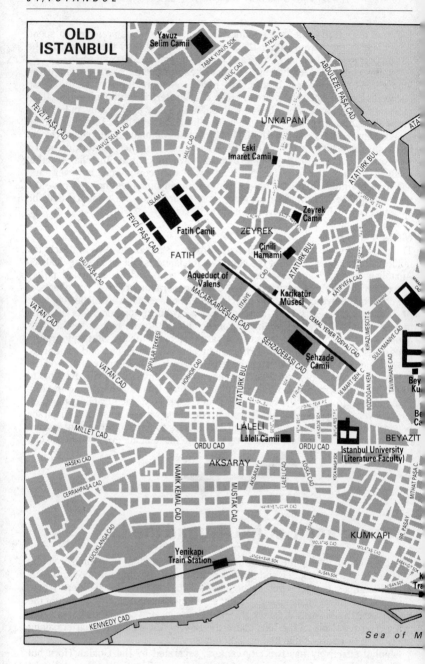

OLD ISTANBUL

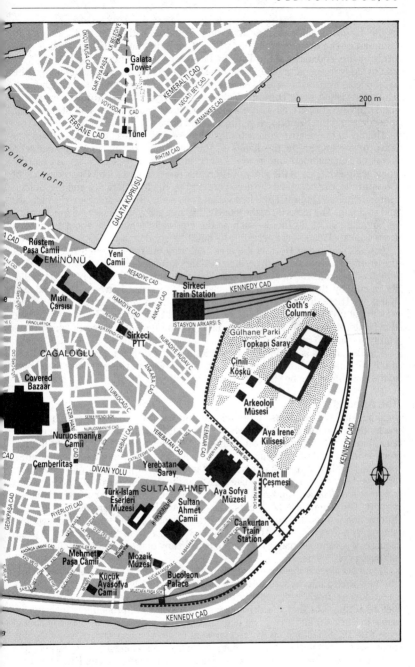

is the historical core of the city, while **Taksim** is the heart of culture and commerce. The two can easily be made out from the water, distinguished respectively by the landmarks of the Topkapı Palace and the Sheraton Hotel. As a visitor you're likely to spend much of your time in and around the Sultanahmet area, the symbolic as well as the actual center of both the Byzantine and Ottoman empires. The most-visited sites, **Topkapı Palace**, **Aya Sofya**, **Sultan Ahmet Camii**, and the **Hippodrome**, are all within a stone's throw of each other, and of the major museums and the **Kapalı Çarşı**, the covered bazaar.

Thanks to the relative concentration of these major sites, it's an easy matter to leave fellow tourists in the hands of the numerous self-appointed guides who frequent Sultanahmet, and head off alone in search of lesser-known but equally convincing evidence of the glory of İstanbul's imperial pasts. The Byzantine city of **Constantinople** occupied the area bordered by the Marmara Sea and the Golden Horn, delimited landward by Theodosius's city walls, the greater part of which are still standing. The majority of the sites in this area are within easy walking distance of Sultanahmet, and others—such as the city walls, which are about four miles from Topkapı Palace—are accesible by bus, train, or dolmuş.

Across the Golden Horn is the area centering on Taksim, often referred to as the **modern city**, although it includes the former Genoese colony of Galata which is as old as the acropolis itself. The two sides of the inlet are connected at its mouth by the **Galata Bridge**, spanning the water between Eminönü and Karaköy. There are buses and dolmuşes from Eminönü to Taksim, and a great way to get up the steep hill to Galata and Istiklal Caddesi from Karaköy is to take the **Tünel**, the ancient French-built underground funicular railroad, which takes eighty seconds to reach its destination.

The Bosphorus is spanned by two **bridges**, the original Boğaziçi Köprüsü and the Fatih Sultan Mehmet Köprüsü, opened in 1988. The villages along the shores of the Bosphorus can be visited by ferry, in small rented motorboats or by bus.

The Airports

İstanbul has two **airports**, international and domestic, situated within 5km of each other, and **buses** run between the two at half-hourly intervals (between 7am and 9pm; service is erratic at other times). Unfortunately these double as the bus service into İstanbul, so if you choose to make use of this service from the international terminal your first experience of public transit in Turkey may include an endless delay as you wait for a late arrival at the domestic airport. The bus stops are marked "Havaş," and are situated outside the main door of the domestic airport and immediately across the parking lot from arrivals at Atatürk International Airport. The service into İstanbul costs $1 and goes via Topkapı bus station and Aksaray (see "Finding a Place to Stay") to Şişhane, near Taksim Square. It's a simple matter to take a bus from any of these into İstanbul's centers of tourism or business.

If you decide that the bus journey is too grim a proposal at this stage then—until the new metro line between Atatürk airport and Ataköy train station comes into operation—you will have to resign yourself to the mercies of a **taxi** driver. Insist before setting out that the driver uses his taxi meter (pronounced exactly the same in Turkish) and ensure on departure that he switches it on. The trip should cost $10–15, depending on where you want to go. You can save money by going only as far as the nearest train station, in Ataköy, and taking a train to Sirkeci (the last stop on the line). You buy a *banliyö* ticket of fixed price (around 30¢) from the *gişe* (ticket office) on the platform and then hop any train going east. From Sirkeci you can either take a bus (see below) or another taxi up to the hotels in Sultanahmet. If you're heavily laden with luggage, take the taxi all the way.

The Train Stations

İstanbul has two mainline **train stations**, one in Europe, at Sirkeci, the other, Haydarpaşa, across the Bosphorus in Asia. Trains from Western Europe arrive at **Sirkeci station**. From here it's easy to find a taxi to the hotels in Sultanahmet or Lâleli, and there are any number of buses (for example #80, #84 and #86) going in that direction from the Eminönü bus terminal, 100m away on the waterfront.

Trains from Moscow, Baghdad and all of Asian Turkey, with the exception of İzmir, arrive at **Haydarpaşa station**. If you want to cross the Bosphorus to Sultanahmet, the easiest way is to board a ferry immediately in front of the station; this will take you to Karaköy, from where buses cross the Galata Bridge to Sultanahmet. Alternatively it's a two-kilometer walk to the hotels farther along the waterfront in Kadıköy, or you can take a #12 or #14 bus to Üsküdar, also on the Bosphorus. There's a taxi stand outside the main entrance, on the road between the station and the wharf.

Otogars

Again there are **two major otogars**, situated at Topkapı (an outlying suburb of the city taking its name from a gate in the city walls, some 6km from the Topkapı palace in Sultanahmet) in Europe and at Harem in Asia. Buses from European cities generally terminate at **Topkapı**, though some will go on to Harem after that; most Asian buses also call at both. The #84 bus goes from Topkapı via Lâleli and Sultanahmet to Eminönü. From **Harem** there are dolmuşes every few minutes to Kadıköy. These leave from the south side of the complex, beyond the ticket offices surrounding the main courtyard, and taxis are also easily found in this area.

City Transportation

For any one journey within İstanbul there's invariably a whole gamut of possible permutations of route and modes of transportation, the sole common denominator being that they're all exceptionally time-consuming. The only efficient forms of public transit are the **metro**, also known as the *hızlı tramvay* service, which presently runs only between Aksaray and outlying suburbs to the northwest, and the **seabuses**, *deniz otobüsler*, which ply between Asia and Europe. For once İstanbul's municipal authorities have put residents before tourists: while these services are extremely useful to commuters they do not as yet cover major tourist routes.

What you are left with is an antiquated, idiosyncratic system of **public transit** which can either be pleasantly diverting or intensely distressing, depending on whether you're in a hurry or not.

Buses

There are two kinds of **buses** in İstanbul, **mavı** (blue) buses which are rented out by the government to private contractors, and municipality-run or **belediye** buses. There's not much to choose between the two, although the blue ones are generally more dilapidated and they can be slower as drivers tout for business along the way, but their drivers will generally accept cash on the sly instead of tickets.

Otherwise you'll need to buy **tickets** in advance. They're sold at otogar ticket offices; newspaper, cigarette or fast-food booths; some small grocery stores and newsstands; or by ticket touts who sell at slightly inflated prices around some bus terminals. It's worth stocking up on tickets whenever you get the chance, since you can walk for miles trying to find one in more remote areas of the city. Tickets are sold in blocks of ten: full price (*tam*) at around 25¢ each, or half-price green tickets for students and teachers with passes issued by Turkish educational institutions. Recently a new system has been introduced whereby you need two tickets on certain buses. These are identified with the sign "*iki bilet gecilir,*" while buses for which only one ticket is required have a sign saying "*tam bilet gecilir.*" When in doubt, watch what everyone else does. Tickets should be deposited into the metal dispensary next to the driver upon boarding (don't be alarmed if this is on fire, tickets are disposed of in this way).

Trains

The **municipal train network**, consisting of two lines, one on each side of the Bosphorus, is hardly comprehensive. The trains however are frequent and cost the same as buses. Tickets are bought on the platform and should be retained until leaving the station as there is a fine for traveling without one.

Dolmuşes and Minibuses

One of the most economical yet elegant forms of public transit, the **dolmuş** is an endearing Turkish institution. The basic principle is one of a shared taxi with a predetermined route, and set fares for all or part of that route. The cars employed for the purpose were exported to Turkey as part of the Marshall Plan in the decade or so after World War II, and the fact that so many of them are in perfect running order—some even appear to be in mint condition—is as much a credit to Turkish workmanship as to the cars themselves. Enthusiasts will enjoy a working museum of 1950s Fords, Cadillacs, Dodges, Plymouths, and Chevrolets, while others can take a back seat and relish the ride. Less comfortable and romantic but equally practical **minibuses** run on the same principle but along different routes.

Both should have their point of departure and destination displayed somewhere on the windshield, and you can get on or off wherever you want en route. Flag down either as you would a taxi and ask to get out at a convenient place with the polite *müsait bir yerde* or simply *inecek* (pronounced "inejek") *var.*

Ferries and Motorboats

Many useful routes are covered by the various **passenger boats** which work the waterways of the city, including crossings of the Bosphorus and the Golden Horn, and regular services to the Princes' Islands in the Sea of Marmara. The boats get extremely crowded during rush hour (8–9am and 5:30–8pm) but otherwise are uniquely relaxing: however frantic the hurry you may be in you might as well resign yourself to your fate on this leg of your journey since the boats always take more or less the same time to cross. On board, you can drink tea or *sahlep* (a sweet drink made from a kind of root and sprinkled with cinnamon) or take a tour of the ship to admire wooden and brass fittings, or possibly a steam engine. Crossing from Asia to Europe by ferry is now free; crossing the other way you'll need a small **token**, a *jeton* (30¢), which you can buy at the kiosks by the entrance or from ubiquitous touts at slightly inflated prices. Smaller boats make trips up and down the

Horn, between Bostancı and the islands, and between Üsküdar and Beşiktaş: on these, cash fares are generally collected by one of the passengers.

Finding a Place to Stay

Finding **somewhere to stay** in İstanbul is rarely a problem, as supply generally exceeds demand and new hotels appear all over the place every year. But this doesn't mean that you will necessarily be able to get into the place of your choice: it's best to **phone ahead** to avoid a lot of trudging from one full pansiyon to the next, and in mid-season it's advisable to **make reservations** anything up to a week in advance, especially if you're hoping to stay somewhere pleasant that's also good value and central.

It's essential, and expected, that you should have a look at a room before you take it, even though **prices** are generally a reliable indication of the kind of accommodation on offer (if rates are quoted in Turkish lira, for example, you probably won't have a bathroom in the room, and the emphasis will be on function rather than appearance). **Hotels** (as opposed to pansiyons or youth hostels) generally quote prices in a strong currency—at present this is US dollars, which is a help if you've just arrived. Prices should by law be displayed in the foyer, but don't feel you can't **bargain**—especially in cheaper places, out of season, or if you intend to stay for a few nights.

There is a current trend for converting **old buildings** into hotels, or—in order to get planning permission despite tricky laws protecting old buildings— dismantling a building, using some of the original materials in a completely new construction, and calling it "renovated." Perhaps the saddest victim of free enterprise in İstanbul is the old **Çırağan Palace** on the Bosphorus. This former imperial palace was until recently the attractive setting of one of the few public outdoor swimming pools in İstanbul but is now being converted into a luxury hotel. Other buildings of lesser historical interest have been converted with a degree of sensitivity and respect for their original appearance, and some of these have been included in the listings.

Sultanahmet

Some of the city's nicest small hotels and pansiyons—and many of its worst hostels—are situated in **Sultanahmet**, right in the most touristed part of İstanbul. You will have to weigh up whether you want to be offered the same guidebook as you step out of the front door each morning, but for short visits the hotels surrounding the Hippodrome couldn't be much better placed—without actually being part of the imperial harem—to give an on-location sense of history. The highest concentration of cheap accommodation is to be found in and around **Yerebatan Caddesi**. Rooms can also be found in the less prominent but equally atmospheric backstreets between the Sultan Ahmet mosque and the sea, or in the streets running down to the sea parallel to the wall of Topkapı Palace.

AROUND THE HIPPODROME

Hotel Antique, Küçük Ayasofya Cad, Oğul Sok 17 (☎516 4936, 516 0997). Ideally located in a quiet street behind the Hippodrome. Terrace bar in summer, central heating in winter. Comfortable, quiet, clean and, if you're looking for a room with its own bathroom, good value. $25 a night double, no singles.

Optimist Guesthouse, Hippodrome (☎516 2398, fax 516 1928). Pleasant and basic, situated at the southeast end of the Hippodrome, beyond the Turk-Islam Eserleri Müzesi. Rooms extremely clean; some overlooking the busy little Terzihane Sokak, others with access to the roof from which there is the most amazing view of the Hippodrome and Sultanahmet. Tables outside where breakfast is served virtually on the Hippodrome. Make reservations well in advance as it's very small. Double $30 with bath, $20 without, including breakfast; singles $25/15; discounts out of season.

Optimist Pansiyon. Apply at the Guesthouse above and you'll be taken to the pansiyon. Rooms leading off a central, communal lobby are rather dark and poorly furnished but clean. Shared shower with hot water. $10 single, $12 double including breakfast.

Hippodrome Pansiyon, Üçler Sok 9 (☎516 0902). Cheap and convenient, with clean rooms and friendly staff. Single/double $10, triple $15, one bathroom for every two rooms.

Hacıbey Pansiyon, Özbekler Sokak. Small, cheap and pleasantly situated in an atmospheric backstreet near Sokullu Mehmet Paşa mosque. Shared facilities. Single $3, double $5.

Turkoman Hotel, Asmalı Çeşme Sok 2 (☎516 2956, 516 2957). Upscale converted house furnished in nineteenth-century Turkish style, situated off the Hippodrome (up Üçler Sok). Each room takes the name of the carpet on the floor, and carpets are for sale in the breakfast room downstairs. Single $40, double $50.

AROUND TOPKAPI AND DOWN TO CANKURTAN AND THE SEA WALLS

Yücelt Interyouth Hostel, Caferiya Sok 6/1 (☎513 6150, 513 6151). As the literature says, this hostel is in the Shadow of Aya Sofya, but it's in the shadow of a lot of nicer hostels too. As a member of the IYHF it should be non-profit, but all facilities are extra, including luggage storage, and you have to pay in advance. Double $7 per person, dorm $5.

Hotel Büyükayasofya, Caferiya Sok 5 (☎522 2981). A low-price, friendly hostel next door to the Yücelt. $7 without a private shower, $9 with, roofspace $2.

Topkapı Hostel, Işakpaşa Cad, Kutluğun Sok 1 (☎527 2433). Simply furnished, five rooms to each bathroom, but excellent location. Double $20, dormitory $8, roofspace $6.

Berk Guesthouse, Kutluğun Sok 27 (☎511 0737). Family run, with only half-a-dozen rooms, all with baths—great view of the old prison from the terrace. $30 double.

Hotel Park, Utangaç Sok 26 (☎522 3964). Clean and friendly. Single with shower $16, without $8, double with shower $18, without $10.

Side Pansiyon, Utangaç Sok 20 (☎512 8175). A good place with f5riendly staff, clean rooms, and a pleasant tea garden, five bedrooms to one bathroom. Double $10, triple and dorms $4 per person.

Orient International Youth Hostel, Akbıyık Caddesi no. 13 (☎516 0171, 516 0194). Campbeds and no carpets but clean. Five bedrooms per bathroom. Dormitory $3, triple $4 each, double $10.

Sultan Tourist Hostel, 2 Akbıyık Cad, Terbiyik Sok 3 (☎516 9260). Pleasant hostel with a friendly atmosphere and garden, but lone females have reported problems. Rooms with private bathrooms, $18 double; without bathrooms $8 double, $11 triple.

OFF YEREBATAN CADDESI

Elit Hotel, Yerebatan Cad, Salkım Söğüt Sok 14 (☎511 5179, 519 0466). Above a carpet shop: clean, fairly quiet rooms with private facilities. $22 double.

Hotel Anadolu, Yerebatan Cad, Salkım Söğüt Sok 3 (☎512 1035). Small rooms without private showers, but very quiet. $8 per person, free hot showers.

OFF DIVANYOLU CADDESI

Hotel Klodfarer, Klodfarer Caddesi 22 (☎528 4850). Opposite the Binbirdirek Byzantine cistern, one of a number of cheap hotels along here. Dark and old-fashioned, but cheap. Rooms with shower $13 single, $19 double.

Aksaray and Lâleli

If you can't find anywhere in Sultanahmet but want to stay relatively close to the center, İstanbul's other main concentration of hotels is situated about a mile up Ordu Caddesi, past İstanbul University, in the areas called **Aksaray** and **Lâleli**. If you're coming from Topkapı bus station or the airport late at night and want to be sure of finding somewhere immediately, this would be the place to head; the disadvantage is that the area has been carved up by divided highways, and Ordu Caddesi in particular is totally devoid of charm, madly frenetic and noisy. The farther you stray off the main thoroughfare, north (into Lâleli) or south (into Aksaray), the more chance you'll have of finding peace and quiet.

The main concentration of places is south of Ordu Caddesi, between Aksaray and Koca Ragip caddesis, and there's also an enclave of nice hotels between Atatürk Bulvarı and Büyük Reşit Paşa Caddesi up as far as Şehzade Camii in Lâleli. Expect to pay around $20–30 single, $30–50 double, although there are a few cheaper pansiyons in the area. Since there's so little to choose between the hotels and they're so numerous, it's easy to walk around and find one that suits you. The following are a few that we consider reasonably good value.

IN LÂLELI

Hotel Kul, Büyük Reşit Paşa Cad, Zeynep Kamil Sok 27 (☎526 0127, 528 2892). Basic rooms with own shower, $15 single, $22 double.

Hotel Neşet, Harikzadeler Sok 23 (☎526 7412, 522 4474). Old place, but friendly and cheap. $14 single, $22 double.

Hotel Burak, Fethi Bey Cad, Ağa Yokuşu 1 (☎511 8679, 522 7904). Fairly ordinary but well situated and cheap. Single $17, double $26.

Hotel Mine Pansiyon, Gençturk Caddesi 54 (☎511 2375). Clean rooms, shared facilities, friendly staff. They have four-bedroom apartments with kitchen, bathroom, and television lobby. These are hardly palatial but would be ideal for a group traveling on a budget. $32 per apartment. Singles $8, doubles $12.

IN AKSARAY

Hotel Cevher, Mesihpaşa Caddesi 66 (☎520 9669, 511 1782). Convenient but pretty shabby. $16 single, $26 double.

Hotel Cidde, Aksaray Caddesi 10 (☎522 4211, 522 4212, 522 4213). Large, a bit gloomy and none too friendly, but otherwise good value, with a reasonable bar. Single $16, double $25; extra bed $6.

Taksim and Around

Taksim may be the city's business center, but it's also a remarkably convenient base for sightseeing. It affords easy access to the Bosphorus and comes into its own at night, when it becomes the center of entertainment and cultural and culinary activity. At the other end of İstiklâl Caddesi, seedy, cosmopolitan **Beyoğlu** has several well-established hotels, and frequent buses to and from Beyazit and Eminönü.

Family House, Gümüşsuyu Kutlu Sok 53 (☎149 7351, 149 7396, fax 149 9667). Worthwhile if there are enough of you and you intend to cook for yourself, since apartments have fully equipped kitchens, and transportation to and from the airport and a baby-sitter service are available. Interiors are fairly gloomy and cheaply furnished but the building is situated in a pleasant, quiet backstreet. Prices vary according to time of year, number of people and even the position of the room in the building: June–Aug, 4 people, $150 a day, 6 people $180; Sept–May, 4 people $100–110, 6 people $120–130. In season you should reserve in advance.

Plaza Hotel, Sıraselviler Caddesi, Aslanyatağı Sok 19/21 (☎145 3273, 145 3274). Follow Sıraselviler Caddesi from Taksim Square and it's the second building on the left, next to the Hotel Cihangir. Definite old-world comfiness and charm about this place—bathrooms have real bathplugs! Ask for room with sea view and veranda as they all cost the same, and the view across the Bosphorus is something else. Single $22, double $43; 20 percent winter reduction.

Hotel Oriental, Cihangir Caddesi 60 (☎145 1067, 145 1068). Possible fallback if the above is full and you particularly want to stay in this area. Garden café, lobby and restaurant, some rooms with sea view and balcony. Single $34, double $46, 20 percent reduction in winter.

Hotel Dünya, Mesrutiyet Caddesi 79, Tepebaşi (☎144 0940). Run-down and peeling but clean and cheap, with views of the Princes' Islands from the seventh floor. Single with bathroom $7, double $11. Double without bathroom $6.

Otel Alibaba, Meşrutiyet Caddesi 119, Tepebaşi (☎144 0781). Plain and simple but a bit dusty and run-down. $20 double with bathroom, $16 without, no singles.

Pera Palace, Meşrutiyet Caddesi 98–100, Tepebaşı (☎151 4560). Built in the nineteenth century to accommodate passengers of the Orient Express, this contender for classiest hotel in İstanbul deserves a visit, if only for a cup of coffee in the chandeliered American Bar and a visit to the "powder room." You don't need to worry about mixing with the hoi polloi here either: the list of dignitaries, film stars and even royalty who have preceded you includes Jackie Onassis, Zsa Zsa Gabor, and General Tito. Single room $99, double $148.

Büyük Londra Oteli, Meşrutiyet Caddesi 117, Beyoğlu (☎149 1025, 145 0670). Mid-nineteenth-century, Italian-built and palatial, with a good restaurant and cocktail bar. Rooms are well furnished, some with fridges—ask for a view across the Golden Horn. $30 single, $50 double, $60 triple.

Erişen Hotel, Galipdede Caddesi, Şahkulu Sok 10, Tünel, Beyoğlu. (☎149 9169). Downbeat and rather gloomy, generally a haunt of traveling Turkish businessmen rather than tourists. Situated in the backstreets of the old Genoese neighborhood of Galata, which will appeal if you like cobbled alleyways and local color. Men's and women's bathrooms for every seven rooms. Single $4, double $10.

The Bosphorus

The suburbs and villages along the shores of the Bosphorus are—ideally—relaxing places to spend time and get to know the country while still not too far from the city center. There are several **cheap hotels** on the **Asian side** in Kadıköy and Üsküdar, the former being almost devoid of tourist sites (and tourists), lively, scruffy, and genuine; the latter retaining some of its Ottoman character and buildings, and a friendly small-town atmosphere. Between the two is Harem with its bus station, car ferry, and a few hotels. A word of **warning**, though, about Kadıköy hotels: the *Deniz*, on the front, the *Yeniefes* (Damga Sok 17, near the Eminönü ferry station) and the *Asya* (Recaizade Sok 13) are all unwelcoming to single women, the *Yeniefes* in particular having a reputation as a bordello.

Hotel Okur, Rıhtım Cad, Reşitefendi Sok 3, Kadıköy (☎336 0629, 337 8079). The best of several on this street. $12 single, $20 double with bath.

Hotel Girne, Rıhtım Cad, Reşitefendi Sok 7, Kadıköy (☎336 9077). Clean and basic at $6 single, $8 double, $3 each in three- or four-bed room.

Hotel Engin, Rıhtım Cad, Recaizade Sok, Kadıköy (☎338 6651). Two streets along the front beyond the *Okur*. Rooms a bit cramped, but fairly comfortable. Single $14, double $20.

Harem Otel, 81170 Selimiye, Harem (☎333 2025). Large modern hotel in busy but convenient location above the bus station. Swimming pool and bar. $28 single, $33 double, $50 triple.

Otel Zümrüt, Molla Eşref Sok 4, Üsküdar, opposite Migros supermarket (☎333 0802). Only one bathroom for fourteen rooms and no hot water, but all very clean. Single $5, double $8.

Yeni Saray Oteli, Selmanipak Cad, Çeşme Sok 33, Üsküdar (☎333 0777, 334 3485). Pleasant family hotel with restaurant, bar, café, and a terrace overlooking the Bosphorus. Single $26, double $38.

Konut Oteli, Selmanipak Caddesi 25, above Kanaat Lokantası, Üsküdar (☎333 2284). A bit grim but reasonably clean; eight rooms to one bathroom, no hot water. Single $5, double $9, triple $12.

Hidiv Kasrı, Çubuklu (☎331 2651, 322 3434). Way up the Bosphorus, beyond the second bridge in the quiet and charming village of Çubuklu, this is one of the nicer conversions carried out by the Touring Club under the guidance of Çelik Gülersoy. Decorated in Art Nouveau style in the early 1900s for the last Khedive of Egypt, it has been attractively restored and furnished and commands a formidable position on a hill above the Bosphorus. Cheapest rooms are $36 single, $47 double—no bath for this but you still get the romantic setting. To get there, take a cab or walk from Çubuklu village.

The Princes' Islands

The paradisical nature and proximity to İstanbul of these romantic retreats make it well nigh impossible to find accommodation on the Princes' Islands in the summer months, and the closure of most hotels in the off-season means that the same is generally true in winter. It's certainly worth some time and patience to search something out, however, since there is no nicer place to stay in the vicinity of İstanbul.

Ideal Otel Pansiyon, Kadıyoran Caddesi 14, Büyükada (☎382 6857). Walk straight from the ferry landing to the clock tower, round the phallic symbol and take the second street on the right past the fountain. Next take the street to the left of the police station and at the top the road forks; Kadıyoran Caddesi is the right fork. This attractive, ramshackle old wooden house is packed in summer with vacationing Turks, and empty (but open) in winter because there's no heating and it's so cold and damp that it's practically uninhabitable. Rooms are generally rented out for four-month periods ($1200), but you might be lucky and find the management "between lodgers," in which case a room costs around $7 a night.

Villa Rifat, Yilmaz Turk Cad, Büyükada (☎382 3081, 382 6068). Quite a walk from the town center and beaches on the shore road running around the east side of the island, but pleasant and comfortable nonetheless. $20 per person for bed, breakfast and evening meal.

Panorama Hotel, Ayyıldız Cad, Heybeliada (☎351 8543). Comfortable and old-fashioned, if rather run down; friendly staff. Rooms have own bathrooms. Situated on the seafront with an outdoor café. Around $25 per person.

Halki Palace, Refah Şehitler Caddesi 88, Heybeliada (☎351 8543). This nineteenth-century villa used to belong to the Greek Orthodox Patriarchate, and was used as a guesthouse for the families of students at the Greek Orthodox school on Heybelli. It's been converted most stylishly and is extremely comfortable and attractive, laying claim to a swimming pool and a boat for ferrying residents from Bostancı. Single $22, double $44.

Campgrounds

The city's campgrounds are all located along the Marmara coast between the airport and the city center. Coming into town on the E5 or E25—from Edirne and Tekirdağ respectively—follow signs to Yeşlköy.

Ataköy Tatil Köyü, Rauf Orbay Cad, Ataköy (☎559 6000, 559 6001). Ten minutes from the airport (taxi $3), with an attractive setting on the Marmara Sea, 16km from city center. Bar, pools, disco, and tennis courts, but a bit close to the main road for comfort so make it clear you want a seaside position if you reserve ahead. #82 bus into town via Kumkapı to Unkapanı.

Londra Camping, on the Eski Londra Asfaltı five minutes from airport (the *Havaş* buses pass it on the way in). Crowded, badly located site with swimming pool and adjoining hotel and restaurant. Buses and dolmuşes run from here to Aksaray.

Florya Tourist Camping, Yeşilköy Halkalı Caddesi Florya (☎573 7991). Pleasant and leafy, well served by public transit, and run by the municipality, so it's cheap. About 25km from the city by #73 bus from Taksim, Florya–Topkapı dolmuş, or train from either Eminönü or Ataköy—the train station is 500m away.

Long-term Residence

Apartment-hunting in İstanbul can be a time-consuming business. Most landlords want prohibitively vast sums of money upfront—generally a month's deposit and six months' rent—and banks are reluctant to lend money without collateral even to known customers.

The best way to go about finding a place is to choose an area you find particularly attractive and then look around for *kiralık daire* (apartment to let) signs in windows. This way you will avoid paying agents' fees, generally another month's rent. Otherwise house agents (*emlak*) control much of the best property in İstanbul and they will generally be able to offer you something as soon as you can come up with the money.

The other problem about rentals is that they're almost bound to be unfurnished: Turkish people don't generally move from the parental home until they marry, and they don't usually marry until they can afford to furnish a house. Still, buying furniture in the flea markets (*bit pazarları*) of İstanbul can be good fun, especially if you enjoy bargaining.

THE IMPERIAL CENTER

The area bordered by Constantine II's city walls, by the city's natural harbor of the Golden Horn, and by the Marmara Sea to the south is termed the **Old City**, or "Stamboul" in some books. This quarter has been a **seat of government** since Byzas the Megarian founded his colony here, and there is enough evidence of this illustrious past—from the palaces and places of worship of successive empires to their city walls and cisterns—to imbue the entire area with a sense of history.

But the old city is also very much alive today, with its own particular dilemmas and idiosyncracies. Between İstanbul University and the offices of the nation's press in Cağaloğlu occur frequent **demonstrations**, orchestrated by any of a number of political factions and occasionally erupting into violence, to which the members of the nation's press have become increasingly vulnerable. Tahtakale, the area between the covered bazaar and Eminönü, is the home of İstanbul's **black market** money-changers, who have usurped the official Bourse on the other side of the Golden Horn, while the ramshackle houses in the suburbs along the Theodosian city walls are rumored to be centers of **hard drug manufacture**. Fatih and surrounding districts are strongholds of Islamic fundamentalism, though they coexist peaceably enough with the nearby Christian and Jewish districts of Fener and Balat.

Poverty is rife, but accompanied by a paradoxical generosity. You will probably find that the farther you wander from the tourist center of Sultanahmet into the poorer districts toward the city walls, the more favorable will be the impression you receive of what is essentially a caring society.

Sultanahmet

Initial impressions of **Sultanahmet**—for many their first experience of Turkey—will almost certainly be negative. The very worst of the country's most persistent **hustlers** gather here to plague new arrivals, who haven't yet learned to deal summarily with such irritants. **Women**, alone or together, are particularly prone

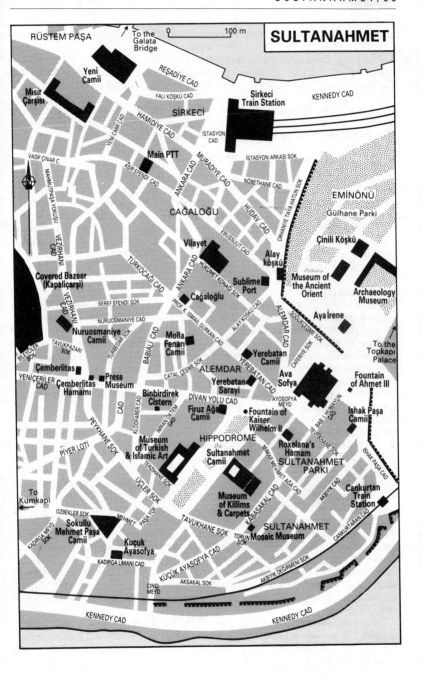

SULTANAHMET

RÜSTEM PAŞA
To the Galata Bridge
0   100 m

Yeni Camii
REŞADİYE CAD
Mısır Çarşısı
YALI KÖŞKÜ CAD
Sirkeci Train Station
KENNEDY CAD
HAMİDİYE CAD
SİRKECİ
YENİ CAMİ CAD
İSTASYON CAD
VASIF ÇINAR C.
Main PTT
MURADİYE CAD
İSTASYON ARKASI SOK
MAHMUTPAŞA YOKUŞU
AŞİR EFENDİ CAD
ANKARA CAD
NÖBETHANE CAD
EMİNÖNÜ
Gülhane Parki
CAĞALOĞLU
HÜDAV. CAD
ORHANİYE TAYA HATUN SOK
EBUSSUUT CAD
Çinili Köşkü
VEZİRHANİ CAD
Vilayet
HÜKÜMET KONAĞI SOK
Alay köşkü
Museum of the Ancient Orient
Covered Bazaar (Kapaliçarşi)
TURKOCAĞI CAD
ANKARA CAD
Sublime Port
ALEMDAR CAD
SAĞUNCEŞME SOK
Archaeology Museum
VEZİRHANİ CAD
SEREF EFENDİ SOK
Cağaloğlu
PROF. K. İSMAİL GÜRCAN CAD
ALAY KÖŞKÜ CAD
Aya İrene
NURUOSMANİYE CAD
Nuruosmaniye Camii
BABIALİ CAD
TÜRBEDAR SOK
Molla Fenari Camii
CAFERİYE SOK
BİLEYCİLER SOK
TAVUKPAZARI SOK
Yerebatan Camii
YEREBATAN CAD
To the Topkapi Palace
Çemberlitaş
ÇATAL ÇEŞME SOK
ALEMDAR
Yerebatan Sarayi
Ava Sofya
Fountain of Ahmet III
YENİÇERİLER CAD
Çemberlitaş Hamami
Press Museum
Binbirdirek Cistern
DİVAN YOLU CAD
AYASOFYA MEYD
BABI. HÜMAYUN
İshak Paşa Camii
CAD
KLODFARER CAD
İMRAN ÖKTEM
Firuz Ağa Camii
Fountain of Kaiser Wilhelm II
TEVFİKHANE SOK
PEYKHANE SOK
PİYER LOTİ
Museum of Turkish & Islamic Art
HIPPODROME
Roxelana's Hamam
SULTANAHMET PARKI
ISHAK PAŞA CAD
TERZİHANE SOK
MİMAR MEHMET AĞA CAD
Sultanahmet Camii
To Kumkapi
UÇLER SOK
Museum of Killims & Carpets
KABASAKAL CAD
AKBIYIK CAD
Çankurtan Train Station
ÖZBEKLER SOK
MEHMET PAŞA YOK.
TAVUKHANE SOK
TORUN SOK
SULTANAHMET Mosaic Museum
CANKURTARAN CAD
Sokullu Mehmet Paşa Camii
KADIRGA MEYD.
SOK
Kuçuk Ayasofya
KADIRGA LİMANI CAD
KÜÇÜK AYASOFYA CAD
AKBIYIK DEĞİRMENİ SOK
CİNCİ MEYD
AKSAKAL SOK
KENNEDY CAD
KENNEDY CAD

to unwanted attention and may be driven to purdah (or murder, depending on their disposition) during the course of a visit.

And yet a large percentage of short-stay visitors spend all their time in the Sultanahmet district, for here are the **main sightseeing attractions**: the Topkapı Palace, heart of the Ottoman dynasty; Sultan Ahmet itself, known as the Blue Mosque; and the greatest legacy of the Byzantine Empire, the church of Aya Sofya. Here also are the ancient Hippodrome; the Museum of Islamic Culture, housed in the former Palace of İbrahim Paşa; the Yerebatan underground cistern; and the Kapalı Çarşı, the largest covered bazaar in the world.

Aya Sofya

For almost a thousand years **Aya Sofya** (or Haghia Sophia; 9:30am–5pm, galleries 1–5pm; closed Tues; $5) was the largest enclosed space in the world, designed to impress the strength and wealth of the Byzantine emperors upon their own subjects and visiting foreign dignitaries alike. Located between Topkapı Saray and Sultan Ahmet Camii on the ancient acropolis, the first hill of İstanbul, it must have dominated the city skyline for a millennium, until the domes and minarets of Sinan's mosques began to challenge it in the sixteenth century.

Some History

Aya Sofya—the Church of the Divine Wisdom—was **commissioned** in the sixth century by the Emperor Justinian after its predecessor had been razed to the ground in the Nika revolts of 532. The architects, **Anthemius of Tralles** and **Isidore of Miletus**, were to create a building combining elements in a manner and on a scale completely unknown to the Byzantine world, and no imitation or rival would subsequently be attempted until the sixteenth century. It remained an important symbol of Byzantine power long after the empire itself had been destroyed, and it proved fatal to at least one Ottoman architect—**Atik Sinan**, who was executed by Mehmet the Conqueror when the dimensions of the dome of Fatih Camii failed to match those of Aya Sofya—and became the inspiration, not to say obsession, of the greatest of all Ottoman architects, **Mimar Sinan**, who devoted his lifetime to the attempt to surpass its technical achievements.

For a hundred-foot wide **dome** to hover over a seemingly empty space, rather than being supported by solid walls, was unprecedented, and the novelty and sheer dimensions of the projected structure meant that the architects proceeded with no sure way of knowing that their plans would succeed. The building was initially constructed in five years, but various crises arose during the process which suggested that the design was unsound. Twenty years and several earthquakes later the central dome collapsed. By this time both the original architects had died, so the task of rebuilding the dome went to **Isidorus the Younger**, the nephew of one of the original architects. He increased the height of the external buttresses and of the dome itself, and it is possible that he effected the removal of large windows from the north and south tympana arches, thus initiating the gradual blockage of various windows which has resulted in the half-light in which visitors now grope.

First impressions on entering are of an overwhelming gloom and general neglect. It's sad to see the dome in such a bad state of repair, but judging from a letter written by Mary Montague Wortley the process of decay had begun well before she arrived there in 1717:

. . . the whole roof [is] mosaic work, part of which decays very fast and drops down.
They presented me a handful of it.

Considering the vicissitudes undergone by the building over the centuries, and
bearing in mind its size and the cost of its upkeep—a crippling burden to the
Byzantines themselves, once decline had set in and the population of Byzantium
had decreased in the Middle Ages—it's perhaps surprising to find it still standing
at all.

The worst **desecration** of the church occurred in 1204, when it was ransacked
by Catholic soldiers during the **Fourth Crusade**. The altar was broken up and
shared among the captors, the hangings were torn, and mules were brought in to
help carry off silver and gilt carvings. A prostitute was seated on the throne of the
patriarch, and she "sung and danced in the church, to ridicule the hymns and
processions of the orientals." One of the Crusaders said that Constantinople
contained more holy relics than the rest of Christendom combined and that "the
plunder of this city exceeded all that has been witnessed since the creation of the
world."

Two and a half centuries later, in 1452, the Byzantine church became Catholic in
the hope that western powers would come to the aid of Constantinople against the
Turks, but they were too late. On May 29, 1453 those who had said they would
rather see the turban of a Turk than the hat of a cardinal in the streets of
Constantinople got their way when the city was captured. **Mehmet the
Conqueror** rode to the church of Aya Sofya and stopped the looting that was
taking place there. He had the building cleared of relics and its "idolatrous
images" covered over, and he said his first prayer there on the following Friday.
Later a wooden minaret was built at the southwest corner of the building, not to be
replaced until the late sixteenth century, when Mimar Sinan was called upon to
restore the building.

Extensive restorations were carried out on the mosaics in the mid-nineteenth
century by the Swiss **Fossati brothers**, but they were later covered over again,
and even the angels the Fossatis painted in the west pendentives of the nave, to
match the two mosaic angels in the east pendentives, were given medallions to
hide their faces.

The building continued to function as a **mosque** until 1932, when further renovations were carried out, and in 1934 it was opened as a museum. To the credit of
progressive members of the Turkish government, they have not yielded to popular pressure—which has included a petition of several thousand signatures—to
convert Aya Sofya back into a mosque.

The Museum

The **exterior** of Aya Sofya gives no hint of the delights within. Always rather
hidden by the heavy buttresses which were added after the first dome collapsed,
it is now crowded in by buildings on two sides which make it almost impossible
to get a good look at the exterior. This may be just as well, as it has been covered
in cement which is given a new coat of increasingly lurid paint every few years:
currently it is an interesting deep pink.

The main body of the building approximates a **domed basilica**, although a
more accurate description of its form would be a basic octagonal shape split in
two with a domed rectangle inserted. Thus Aya Sofya is both centralized and
domed—forms which were gaining in popularity for prestigious monuments of
the sixth century—but it retains a longitudinal axis and side aisles. At the

diagonals of the octagon are semicircular niches (*exedrae*). The galleries, which follow the line of these exedrae around the building, are supported by rows of columns and by four piers, which are also the main support of the dome.

Most interesting of the internal decorations are the **marbles** and the **mosaics**. The former include purple-colored Egyptian porphyry which was not quarried at the time, so must have been pilfered from elsewhere. In revetments, small pieces are given undulating edges to conceal the joints, and the disparate sizes of the porphyry columns in the exedrae are compensated for in their pedestals. The columns supporting the galleries and the tympanum walls are verd antique marble while those in the upper gallery of the exedrae are Thessalian marble. These ranges of columns, above and below the gallery, are not aligned one above the other, an irregularity which was thought outrageously daring by contemporaries who considered it structurally unsound as well as a dangerous departure from classical norms. Of those in the exedrae the poet Paul the Silentiary wrote: "One wonders at the power of him, who bravely set six columns over two, and has not trembled to fix their bases over empty air." Upstairs in the western gallery a large circle of green Thessalian marble marks the position of the **throne of the empress**.

Byzantine **mosaics** were designed to be seen in lamp- or candle-light. These conditions show off the workmanship to its best advantage: flickering light reflected in pieces of glass or gold which had been carefully embedded at minutely disparate angles gave an appearance of movement and life to the mosaics. Nowadays visitors must rely on natural light, frequently lacking in İstanbul, and consequently the effect can be disappointing. What remains of the abstract mosaics and the large areas of plain gold which covered the underside of the dome and other large expanses of wall and ceiling dates from the sixth century. Some of the prettiest of this abstract work can be seen under the arches of the south gallery and in the narthex (the entrance porch), from which some impression can be gained of what the original four acres of such mosaics must have looked like.

The **figurative mosaics**, all of which date from after the Iconoclastic era (726–843), are located in the narthex, the nave, the upper gallery, and the vestibule. Some of the most impressive are in the south gallery, where, beyond a pair of false marble doors on the west face of the pier, is a comparatively well-lit mosaic of a **Deisis**, depicting Christ, the Virgin, and Saint John the Baptist. Although this mosaic is partly damaged, the three faces are all well preserved and there is no problem in making out their expressions. The face of John the Baptist is especially expressive, showing great pain and suffering, while that of the Virgin has downcast eyes and an expression of modesty and humility.

On the east wall of the gallery, contiguous with the apse, is a **mosaic of Christ flanked by an emperor and empress**. The inscriptions over their heads read "Zoë, the most pious Augusta," and "Constantine in Christ, the Lord Autocrat, faithful Emperor of the Romans, Monomachus." It is believed that the two figures are those of Constantine IX Monomachus and the Empress Zoë, who ruled Byzantium in her own right with her sister Theodora before she married Constantine, her third husband. The explanation of why the head of Constantine and the inscription over his head have been changed may be that they were formerly those of one or other of his predecessors. The other mosaic in the south gallery, dating from 1118, depicts the **Virgin and Child between the Emperor John II Comnenus and the Empress Irene**, and their son Prince Alexius, added later. This is a livelier, less conventional work than that of Zoë and Constantine, with faces full of expression: the Virgin appears compassionate while Prince Alexius, who died soon after this portrait was executed, is depicted as a wan and sickly youth, his lined face presaging his premature death.

Other mosaics include a Virgin and Child in the apse and, one of the most beautiful of all the Aya Sofya mosaics, a **Virgin and Child flanked by two emperors**. The latter is located in the Vestibule of Warriors, now serving as an exit, and to see it you have to turn around and look up after passing through the magnificent Portal of the Emperor. Dated to the last quarter of the tenth century, it shows Emperor Justinian, to the right of the Virgin, offering a model of Aya Sofya, while the Emperor Constantine offers a model of the city of Constantinople. This is the only mosaic that has been properly spotlit, and the effect must be similar to that originally intended by the artists.

What is left of the structures from Aya Sofya's time as a **mosque** are a *mihrab*, a *mimber*, a sultan's loge and the enormous wooden plaques bearing sacred Islamic names of God, the Prophet Mohammed, and the first four caliphs. These and the inscription on the dome by the calligrapher İzzet Efendi all date from the time of the restoration by the Fossati brothers.

Topkapı Palace

The **Topkapı Palace** (daily 9:30am–5:30pm, closed Tues in winter; $5) was both the symbolic and the actual center of the Ottoman Empire for nearly four centuries, from the construction by Mehmet the Conqueror of its oldest buildings—of which the present-day arms museum is the most complete example—to the removal of the imperial retinue to Dolmabahçe, by Sultan Abdül Mecid I, in 1853. It is a beautiful setting in which to wander and contemplate the majesty of the Ottoman sultanate, as well as the cruelty exemplified by institutions like the harem and "the Cage."

In accordance with Islamic tradition, the palace consists of a collection of buildings arranged around a series of courtyards, similar to the Alhambra in Granada or a Moghul palace in India. The effect is extremely satisfying aesthetically, but creates an initial impression of disorder. In fact the arrangement is meticulously logical, and the various adjustments made to the structure and function of the buildings over the centuries are indicative of shifting emphases in power in the Ottoman Empire (for example a passageway was opened between the Harem and the Divan during the "Rule of the Harem," and in the eighteenth century, when the power of the sultan had declined, the offices of state were transferred away from the "Eye of the Sultan"—the window in the Divan through which a sultan could monitor proceedings—and indeed from the palace altogether, to the Sublime Port).

Originally known as *Sarayı Cedid*, "**the new palace**," Topkapı was built between 1459 and 1465 as the seat of government of the newly installed Ottoman regime. It was not at first a residence: Mehmet the Conqueror had already built what would become known as the old palace on the present site of İstanbul University, and even after he himself moved, his harem stayed on at the old site. The first courtyard was the service area of the palace, open to the general public, while most of the second court and its attendant buildings were devoted to the Divan, the Council of State, and to those who had business with it. The pavilions of judges were located at the Orta Kapı (the entrance to the palace proper, between the first and second courtyards) in accordance with the tradition that justice should be dispensed at the gate of the palace.

The third courtyard was mainly given over to the palace school, an important imperial institution devoted to the training of civil servants, and it is only in the fourth courtyard that the serious business of state gives way to the more pleasurable aspects of life. Around the attractive gardens here are a number of pavilions erected by successive emperors in celebration of their respective victories and of the glorious views and the sunsets to be enjoyed in privileged retreat from their three- to four-thousand-member retinue.

The First Courtyard and Aya Irene

Entering the first courtyard from the street through Mehmet the Conqueror's **Bab-ı Hümayün**, the great defensive imperial gate opposite the fountain of Ahmet III, all is taxi stands and buses and disembarking tour groups—it's hard to believe that this is the outer courtyard of a former imperial palace. Such a melee, however, is entirely in keeping with the origins of the first courtyard, which, as the service area of the palace, was always open to the general public. The **palace bakeries** are located behind a wall to the right of the courtyard, and the buildings of the **imperial mint and outer treasury** are located behind the wall north of Aya Irene (none of these are currently open). In front of Aya Irene stood the quarters of the straw-weavers and carriers of silver pitchers, around a central courtyard in which the palace firewood was stored, while the former church itself was variously employed as an armory and storage space for archaeological treasures.

Today, **Aya Irene**, "the Church of the Divine Peace," is closed to visitors, and it's next to impossible to obtain the necessary entrance papers. If you are prepared to enter into lengthy negotiations, you should approach the Directorate of Aya Sofya, located at the entrance of Aya Sofya, and proceed from there. Otherwise, occasional concerts of the İstanbul festival are held in the former church. The original church was one of the oldest in the city, but it was rebuilt along with Aya Sofya after being burned down in the Nika riots of 532. Around the semicircular apse is the only **synthronon** (seating space for clergy in the apse of a church) in İstanbul to have survived the Byzantine era. It has six tiers of seats with an ambulatory running behind the fourth tier.

The Second Courtyard and the Divan

To reach the second courtyard you pass through the Bab-üs Selam, the Gate of Salutations, otherwise known as the **Orta Kapı** or Middle Gate. To the right of the gate, still in the first courtyard, is a ticket office and a useful list of the rooms and exhibitions open for viewing on the day in question. You'll need to pay again for the guided tour of the Harem when you get there. Entering through Orta Kapı, with the gateway to the third courtyard straight ahead of you, the **Privy Stables of Mehmet II** (closed to the public) are on your immediate left, while beyond them are the buildings of the Divan and the Inner Treasury, and the entrance to the Harem. Opposite the Divan, on the right side of the courtyard, is the kitchen area.

The gardens between the paths radiating from the Orta Kapı are planted with ancient cypresses, plane trees, rose bushes, and lawns. Originally they would also

have been resplendent with peacocks, gazelles and most importantly with fountains. Running water, considered to have almost mystical properties by Muslims,
was supplied in great quantity to the palace from the Byzantine cistern of
Yerebatan Saray (see p.89). This **second courtyard** would have been the scene
of pageantry during state ceremonies, when the sultan would occupy his throne
beneath the Bab-üs Saadet, the Gate of Felicity. At all times, even on one of the
four days when the courtyard was filled with petitioners to the Divan, silence
reigned here, as people obeyed the rules of conduct imposed in the
presence—actual or potential—of the sultan.

The buildings of the **Divan**, to the left of the courtyard just beyond the
entrance to the harem, are historically fascinating, and it's a pity that they should
be closed to the public as they are at present. Peering through the windows, you
should be able to make out the metal grille in the Council Chamber (the first
room on the left), through which the sultan could listen to the proceedings of the
Divan, the eminent institution which took its name from the couch running
around the three walls of this room (this grille was "the Eye of the Sultan"). The
building dates essentially from the reign of Mehmet the Conqueror, though
subsequently much altered. The Council Chamber was restored to its sixteenth-
century appearance in 1945, with some of the original İznik tiles and arabesque
painting. The other two rooms of the Divan have retained the Rococo decorations
of Ahmet III.

The **Divan tower** is visible from many vantage points all over in the city. It was
rebuilt in 1825 by Mahmut II to replace a squat-looking version with a pyramidal
cap. The classical lines of the octagonal structure, with its tall windows between
engaged Corinthian columns and lead-covered conical spire, look rather out of
place here, but it's certainly an impressive landmark, and a nice foil for the domes
of the Divan.

Next to the Divan is the **Inner Treasury**, another building dating from
Mehmet the Conqueror's original palace. This is a six-domed hall preceded by a
double-domed vestibule, and supported internally by three piers. The **exhibition
of arms and armor** here includes much exquisite craftsmanship along with
barbaric-looking exhibits, such as a seventeenth-century executioner's sword
(which looks more like a meat cleaver) and some seven-foot-long double-handed
swords which wearied Europeans were relieved of during various Turkish
campaigns. It is also interesting to compare the swords of various Ottoman
sultans—that of the Conqueror appears altogether more effective than the more
finely wrought example attributed to a patron of the arts such as Süleyman the
Magnificent.

Across the courtyard are the **palace kitchens**, with their magnificent rows of
chimneys (best seen in profile from a distance, for example from Kennedy
Bulvarı which runs around the Marmara shore). Much of this complex was
destroyed by fire in 1574, and the chimneys were reconstructed by Mimar Sinan,
as were eight of the ten domes behind them (the two southernmost domes date
to the reign of Mehmet the Conqueror). The ten kitchens, which had a staff of
1500, all served different purposes. The two at the far end, where desserts and
helva were made, have been restored complete with a fascinating array of utensils. The other rooms of the kitchen complex house a collection of some of the
finest porcelain in the world, an ever-changing display continually replenished
from the vast Topkapı collection.

The Third Courtyard

Passing through the **Bab-üs Saadet**, the Gate of Felicity, the throne room is immediately in front of you. This building, mainly dating from the reign of Selim I, was where the sultan awaited the outcome of sessions of the Divan in order to give his assent or otherwise to their proposals. The gray marble building at the center of the third courtyard, the **library of Ahmet III**, is not generally open to the public. It is restrained and somber compared to his highly decorative fountain outside the gates of the palace.

On the southwest side, on either side of the Bab-üs Saadet, are the rooms of the **Palace School**, where boys aged ten or more recruited from Christian families (a process known as the Devşirme) were converted to Islam and educated to become members of the janissary corps or even future administrators of the empire. The room to the left of the entrance houses a collection of embroidery and a very small selection from the imperial costume collection. The latter includes a charming little outfit of Selim I's—red with yellow circles—begging the question of where he could have acquired his epithet "the Grim." Beyond the school to the right are the **Seferli Odasi**, used as lodging or a gym for pages, and the hamam of Selim the Sot, who fell there in a drunken stupor and died later of his injuries.

The Treasury

The **Pavilion of the Conqueror** takes up most of the southeast side of the third courtyard, to the right of the entrance. The building is on two floors, and a colonnaded terrace leads from the courtyard into the lower rooms, which would originally have been employed as service rooms. The interior plasterwork of these apartments, including shell-shaped niches, stalactite capitals, and ogee (slightly pointed) arches over the windows, is typical of the fifteenth century. The first two rooms—the righthand one of which was used as the *camekân*, or changing room, of the hamam of Selim II—are beautifully proportioned and domed. The last two rooms are at right angles, with an attractive loggia at the angle where they meet.

The **Topkapı Treasury** is housed in these four rooms of the Conqueror's Pavilion. The first room contains a number of highly wrought and extremely beautiful objects, including a delicate silver model of a palace complete with tiny crabs and birds in the trees, a present to Abdül Hamid II from Japan, and a seventeenth-century music box decorated with palm trees and an elephant. The next two rooms—memorials to the excesses and bad taste of the megalomanic—are always thronged, and there are certainly plenty of thrills to be had if you like your gemstones big and your precious metals abundant. In any case you might as well give up struggling with your sense of proportions and resign yourself to the larger-than-life dimensions of imperial wealth and ostentation.

The big crowd-puller in room two is the **Topkapı Dagger**, which starred alongside Peter Ustinov in the Sunday-matinee classic *Topkapı*. A present from Murat I to Nadir Shah, which was waylaid and brought back when news of the Shah's death reached Topkapı, the dagger is decorated with three enormous emeralds, one of which conceals a watch (suggesting rather different attitudes to time and mortality than those you'll find in modern-day crime fiction, where watches are more likely to conceal weapons than vice versa).

In room three the **Spoonmaker's Diamond**, the fifth-largest diamond in the world, is invariably surrounded by a gawking throng, who perhaps give some impression of the effect it must have had during its first public appearance, on

Mehmet IV's turban at his coronation in 1648. The golden ceremonial throne, which was presented by the governor of Egypt to Murat III on his accession in 1574, is accompanied by an unfortunate photograph of Selim III made to look dreadfully puny and insignificant by its odd dimensions. The rest of this room is a succession of increasingly grotesque and jewel-studded exhibits, and you might well be tempted to bail out early.

Room four boasts another jewel-studded throne (believed to have been presented to Mahmut I by Nadir Shah, who never received his return gift of the Topkapı Dagger), and the hand and part of the skull of John the Baptist, but otherwise it's a relative haven of restraint and good taste. Ivory and sandalwood objects predominate, refreshingly simple materials whose comparative worth is determined by craftsmanship rather than quantity, so you don't feel obliged to make interminable calculations of the current market value of every object on display.

Across the courtyard from the treasury, the **Pavilion of the Holy Mantle** houses the Holy Relics brought home by Selim the Grim after his conquest of Egypt in 1517. The relics were originally viewed only by the sultan, his family and his immediate entourage on days of special religious significance, but were opened to the public in 1962. They include a footprint, hair, and a tooth of the Prophet Mohammed as well as his mantle and standard, swords of the first four caliphs, and a letter from the Prophet to the leader of the Coptic tribe. The most precious of the relics are kept behind glass, attractively arranged and lit.

Next to this, the former Hall of the Treasury now houses a selection from Topkapı's **Collection of Paintings and Miniatures**. The miniatures date from the reign of Süleyman the Magnificent to that of Ahmet III, the Tulip Age, but above all they come from the reign of Murat III. He commissioned three works, the *Hürname* (the "Book of Accomplishments"), the *Shahanshahname* (the "Book of the King of Kings") and the *Surname* (the "Book of Festivals"), the first two of which glorified the exploits of the sultans, while the last was a depiction of the circumcision ceremony of the sultan's son (nowadays Turks make home videos on the same theme). One of the illustrations from the *Surname*, "A Parade of Mule Drivers," shows the Serpentine Column from the Hippodrome (see p.82) complete with its three heads, and the sultan seated in a pavilion next to the Palace of İbrahim Paşa. A very small selection of the works of Siyah Kalem ("the Black Pen") are also on display. These unique and beautiful works depict a selection of wrinkled old men and highly animated devils, as well as meticulously observed animal life. No longer believed to be from the hand of a single artist, they are thought to relate to a fourteenth- or fifteenth-century nomadic society, from either Turkestan or Transoxania, holding shamanistic beliefs.

The Fourth Courtyard

The **fourth courtyard** is entered through a passageway between the Hall of the Treasury and the display of clocks and watches in the Silahdar Treasury (currently closed). It consists of gardens graced with pavilions where sultans would take their pleasure. There are spectacular views of the setting sun and the sea, and sprawling gardens complete with fountains and darkened retreats. The most attractive of the pavilions, from which you get a totally new perspective of the city from Galata to Fatih, are located around a wide marble terrace beyond the tulip gardens of Ahmet III.

The **Bağdad Köşkü**, the cruciform-shaped building to the north of the terrace, is the only one currently open to the public. It was built by Murat IV to celebrate

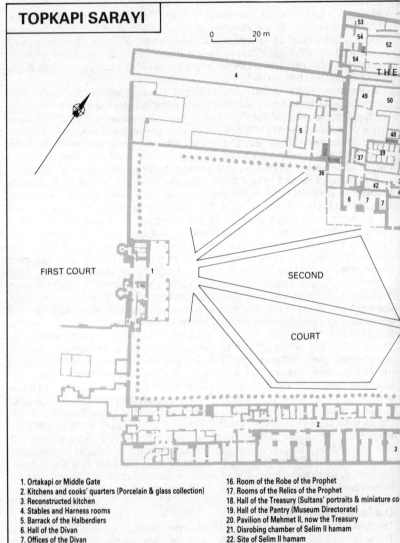

TOPKAPI SARAYI

0   20 m

FIRST COURT

SECOND

COURT

THE

1. Ortakapi or Middle Gate
2. Kitchens and cooks' quarters (Porcelain & glass collection)
3. Reconstructed kitchen
4. Stables and Harness rooms
5. Barrack of the Halberdiers
6. Hall of the Divan
7. Offices of the Divan
8. Inner Treasury (Arms & armour collection)
9. Gate of Felicity
10. Quarters of the White Eunuchs (Costume collection)
11. Throne room
12. Ahmet III library
13. Mosque of the school, now the library
14. Harem mosque
15. Court of the Room of the Robe

16. Room of the Robe of the Prophet
17. Rooms of the Relics of the Prophet
18. Hall of the Treasury (Sultans' portraits & miniature co
19. Hall of the Pantry (Museum Directorate)
20. Pavilion of Mehmet II, now the Treasury
21. Disrobing chamber of Selim II hamam
22. Site of Selim II hamam
23. Site of Selim II hamam boilers
24. Hall of the Expeditionary Force
25. Circumcision Köşkü
26. Terrace and bower
27. Pool
28. Baghdad Köşkü
29. Pool
30. Revan Köşkü

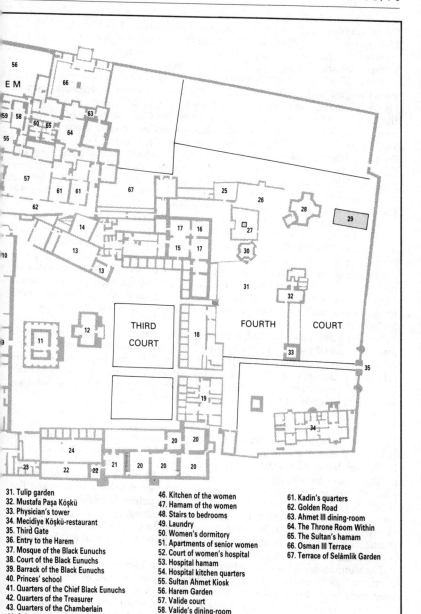

31. Tulip garden
32. Mustafa Paşa Köşkü
33. Physician's tower
34. Mecidiye Köşkü-restaurant
35. Third Gate
36. Entry to the Harem
37. Mosque of the Black Eunuchs
38. Court of the Black Eunuchs
39. Barrack of the Black Eunuchs
40. Princes' school
41. Quarters of the Chief Black Eunuchs
42. Quarters of the Treasurer
43. Quarters of the Chamberlain
44. Aviary gate
45. Courtyard of the Women of the Harem

46. Kitchen of the women
47. Hamam of the women
48. Stairs to bedrooms
49. Laundry
50. Women's dormitory
51. Apartments of senior women
52. Court of women's hospital
53. Hospital hamam
54. Hospital kitchen quarters
55. Sultan Ahmet Kiosk
56. Harem Garden
57. Valide court
58. Valide's dining-room
59. Valide's bedroom
60. The Valide's hamam

61. Kadin's quarters
62. Golden Road
63. Ahmet III dining-room
64. The Throne Room Within
65. The Sultan's hamam
66. Osman III Terrace
67. Terrace of Selâmlik Garden

the conquest of Baghdad in 1638. The exterior and cool, dark interior are tiled in blue, turquoise, and white, and the shutters and cupboard doors are inlaid with tortoiseshell and mother of pearl. Only the recent repainting of the dome—red on leather—is out of keeping with the general effect.

If you think the pavilion is redolent of unseemly excess, take a look at the attractive pool and marble fountain on the terrace, scene of debauched revels between İbrahim I and the women of his harem. Deli İbrahim, also known as **İbrahim the Mad**, emerged from 22 years in the Cage dangerously insane, his reign culminating in a fit of sexual jealousy when he ordered death by drowning—in the Bosphorus—for the 280 concubines of his harem. Only one of them lived to tell the tale. She escaped from the sack in which she was bound and was picked up by a passing French ship and taken to Paris. In one of his calmer moments İbrahim had built the **İftariye Köşkü**, the little balcony with a bronze canopy set into the white marble balustrade of the terrace, naming it after the evening meal at which the day's fast is broken during Ramadan.

The **Sünnet Odası** (Circumcision Room), in the Portico of Columns above the terrace, also dates from the reign of İbrahim the Mad. During renovation you'll have to peer through the windows to get any idea of the interior, but outside it's covered in İznik tiles of the sixteenth and early seventeenth centuries. There doesn't seem to be much of a design about these—any number of different patterns are represented—but they include some of the most beautiful panels from the very best İznik period. At the other end of the Portico of Columns is the Revan Köşkü, built to commemorate the capture of Erivan in the Caucasus by Mehmet IV.

The **Mecidiye Köşkü**—the last building to be erected at Topkapı—commands the best view of any of the Topkapı pavilions; on a clear day from its garden terrace you can identify most of the buildings on the Asian shore of the Bosphorus, and appropriately it's been opened as a restaurant and terrace **café**. It's pricey, so best not to time things so that you arrive here famished, but it's a lovely place to while away a few hours over a long drink.

The Harem

The **tour of the Harem** (10am–4pm, departing hourly from the entrance to the Harem in the second courtyard; $2.50) may be the most popular aspect of a visit to Topkapı, but it can also be the biggest disappointment. Many of the more interesting rooms—the dining room of Sultan Ahmet III with its fruity frescoes; the Cage, in which the heir to the throne would have been incarcerated; and the women's dormitories—are regularly closed to the public. In addition, the obligatory guided tour is rarely very informative or interesting. The itinerary does change from time to time, however, renovations are proceeding on the women's dormitories, and you can always spice a tour up (and slow it down) by asking pertinent questions at every available opportuntiy.

The word *harem* means "forbidden" in Arabic. In Turkish it refers to the suite of apartments in a palace or private residence where the head of the household lived with his wives, odalisques (female slaves) and children. The harem in Topkapı is located between the sultan's private apartments—the Circumcision Room, the Revan Pavilion, and the Apartment of the Holy Mantle of the Prophet—and the apartments of the Chief Black Eunuch. It consists of over four hundred rooms.

THE CAGE

The Cage was adopted by Ahmet I as an alternative to fratricide, which had become institutionalized in the Ottoman Empire since the days of Beyazit II. To avoid wars of succession, a sultan should execute his brothers upon his accession to the throne. The Cage was introduced as a way around this practice, but in the event it proved a less than satisfactory solution. After the death of their father, the younger princes would be incarcerated along with deaf mutes and a harem of concubines, while their eldest brother acceded to the throne. They remained in the suite of rooms of the harem known in Turkish as *Kafes* (the Cage) until such time as they were called upon to take power themselves. The concubines never left the Cage unless they became pregnant, and great care was taken to prevent this, either by the removal of their ovaries or by the use of pessaries, since if it did occur they were immediately drowned.

The decline of the Ottoman Empire has in part been attributed to the institution of the Cage. The sultans who spent any length of time there emerged crazed, avaricious, and debauched. Osman II, for example, enjoyed archery, but only when using live targets, including prisoners of war and his own pages. He was assassinated by the janissaries, to be replaced by Mustafa I, who had all but died of starvation in the Cage, and was even more insane than his predecessor. He was also assassinated. The worst affected of all, however, was İbrahim, better known as Deli İbrahim or İbrahim the Mad. He spent 22 years in the Cage, and when they came to take him out he was so sure he was about to be assassinated that he had to be removed forcibly. His reign was characterized by sexual excess and political misrule (his mother Köşem once complained that there was not enough wood for the harem fires, and he responded by having his grand vizier executed). Eventually, in response to a rumor of harem intrigue, İbrahim had all of his 280 concubines (excluding his favorite, Şeker Para) drowned in the Bosphorus.

The **harem women** were so shrouded in mystery that they became a source of great fascination to the world in general. The most renowned among them was probably Haseki Hürrem, or Roxelana as she was known in the West, wife of Süleyman the Magnificent. Prior to their marriage, it was unusual for a sultan to marry at all, let alone to choose a wife from among his concubines. The marriage, and the subsequent installation of the harem women in the palace, established the women of the harem, and especially the **Valide Sultan** (the mother of the reigning sultan), in a position of unprecedented power. This was the beginning of a new age of harem intrigue, in which women began to take more control over affairs of state.

Roxelana began this new order in characteristic style: she persuaded Süleyman to murder both his grand vizier, İbrahim Paşa, and his son, the heir apparent, Mustafa—the latter in order to make way for her own son, Selim the Sot. The favorite of Selim the Sot, **Nur Banu**, made a significant change in the layout of the harem when she became Valide Sultan in her turn. She moved her suite of apartments from one end of the Golden Road to the other, so that it was located next to that of her son, Murat III. She was now lodged near the entrance of the Divan, and could easily listen in on affairs of state. Nur Banu encouraged her son in debauchery (he fathered a total of 103 children, 54 of whom survived him) and persuaded him to murder his most able minister, the grand vizier Sokollu Mehmet Paşa.

The number of **odalisques** employed in the harem increased steadily with the decline of the Ottoman Empire. During the reign of Mahmut I (1730–1754) there were 688 odalisques in Topkapı, excluding those who served the sultan personally. Most of these were servants to the Valide Sultan, the first wives, and favorites. By the reign of Abdülaziz (1861–1876) this number had increased to 809. Many of the Ottoman odalisques were imported from Georgia and Caucasia for their looks, or were prisoners of war, captured in Hungary, Poland, or Venice. Upon entering the harem, they became the charges of the *haznedar usta*, who taught them how to behave toward the sultan and the other palace inhabitants. The conditions in which the majority of these women lived were dangerously unhygienic, and many of them died from vermin- and water-borne diseases, or from the cold of İstanbul winters. The women who were chosen to enter the bedchamber of the sultan, however, were promoted to the rank of imperial odalisque, given slaves to serve them and pleasant accommodation, and if they bore a child, they were promoted to the rank of favorite or wife, with their own apartments. If the sultan subsequently lost affection for one of these women, he could give her in marriage to one of his courtiers. The following account of life in the Topkapı harem, given by Hafsa Sultan, a wife of Mustafa II (1695–1703), dispels a couple of popular myths about life there:

> *The claims that the sultan throws a handkerchief at the girl he prefers are quite untrue. The sultan asks the Chief Black Eunuch to call whichever of the girls he desires, and his other women take her to the baths, perfume her body and dress her gracefully in clothes appropriate to the circumstances. The sultan sends the girl a gift, and afterwards goes to the room where she is. There is no truth either in the claim that the girl crawls to the sultan's bed.*

THE BUILDINGS

The harem centered around the suites of the sultan and the Valide Sultan. Around these, in descending order of rank, were the apartments of the wives, favorites, sultan's daughters, princes, housekeepers, maids, and odalisques. It was connected to the outside world by means of the **Carriage Gate**, probably so-called because the odalisques would have entered their carriages here when they went on outings. To the left of the Carriage Gate as you enter the harem are the barracks of the Halberdiers of the Long Tresses, who carried logs and other loads into the harem. The Halberdiers, who also served as imperial guardsmen, were only employed at certain hours, and even then they were blindfolded. The Carriage Gate and the Aviary Gate were both guarded by black eunuchs, who were responsible for running the harem, but only allowed to enter during daylight hours. At night the female housekeepers took charge, and reported any unusual occurrences to the Chief Black Eunuch.

The **Court of the Black Eunuch**, the first area to be visited on a tour, dates mainly from a rebuilding program started after the great fire of July 24, 1665. The fire, started by a malicious servant, damaged most of the harem as well as the Divan. The tiles in the Eunuchs' quarters all date from the seventeenth century, suggesting that the originals were destroyed in the fire.

The *Altın Yol*, or **Golden Road**, ran the entire length of the harem, from the quarters of the Black Eunuch to the Fourth Courtyard. It was down this road in 1808 that the last of the great Valide Sultans, Aimée Dubbucq de Rivery, fled with her son Mahmut to escape the deaf mutes, hired assassins of the janissaries. The life of the prince was saved by a Georgian odalisque named Cevri Khalfa, who flung a brazier of red-hot coals into the faces of the pursuers. The prince escaped to become Mahmut II, later to be given the title of "reformer." Strategically located at the beginning of the Golden Road were the **apartments of the Valide Sultan**, also rebuilt after 1665. They include a particularly lovely domed dining room. A passageway leads from her apartments to those of the women she controlled, the senior women of the court. These were well-designed, compact apartments, with an upper gallery in which bedding was stored, windows, and a hearth.

Beyond the Valide Sultan's apartments, to the north, are some of the most attractive rooms of the palace. These were the apartments and reception rooms of the *Selamlık*, the sultans' own rooms. The largest and grandest of these is the **Hünkar Sofası**, the Imperial Hall, where the sultan entertained visitors. Another important room in this section is a masterwork of the architect Sinan: the **bedchamber of Murat III**. This is covered in sixteenth-century İznik tiles, including an inscription of verses from the Koran, and furnished with a marble fountain and, opposite, a bronze fireplace surrounded by a panel of tiling representing plum blossom.

The northernmost rooms of the harem are supported by immense pillars and vaults, providing capacious basements used as dormitories and storerooms. Below the bedchamber is a large indoor **swimming pool**, with faucets for hot and cold water, into which Murat is supposed to have thrown gold to the women that pleased him. Next to the bedchamber is the light and airy **library of Ahmet I**, with windows overlooking both the Golden Horn and the Bosphorus, and beyond this is the **dining room of Ahmet III**, the walls of which are covered in wood panelling painted with bowls of fruit and flowers, typical of the extravagant tulip-loving sultan. To the southwest of the bedchamber are two rooms which were originally thought to be **the Cage**, but this is no longer believed to be the case—the Cage was actually situated in various rooms on the floor above.

Other rooms which you may visit on a tour of the Harem are the **dormitories** of the favorite women, located up stone stairs on a beautiful terrace overlooking the fourth courtyard, and the **boating pool** of Murat III.

It's usual for tours to depart from the harem by way of the **Aviary Gate**, or Kuşhane Kapısı. One of the most infamous of all the Valide Sultans, Mahpeyker Sultan, also known as *Köşem*, "the leader," was assassinated here. She was the de facto ruler of the Ottoman Empire during the reigns of her two sons, Murat IV and İbrahim the Mad, and since she was not banished to the old palace after the death of İbrahim (which would have been in accordance with custom), she also ruled during the reign of her grandson Mehmet IV. She was eventually murdered on the orders of a jealous rival, the new Valide Turhan Hatice, by the Chief Black Eunuch. At the age of eighty the toothless old woman was stripped naked and strangled, after allegedly putting up a ferocious struggle.

Gulhane Parkı, the Çinili Köşk, and the Archaeological Museums

Gulhane Parkı was once the gardens of Topkapı Palace. It is now a public park, serving as the location of free open air concerts. Performers include *arabesk* musicians and belly dancers, neither of which can be broadcast by the Turkish media because they're considered to be low-class and Arabic influenced. The park is also home to a rather sordid little **zoo**, among whose exhibits are caged dogs—seeing man's best friend behind bars gives a new dimension to the issue of caged animals.

The graceful **Çinili Köşk** (Tiled Pavilion) is the oldest secular building in İstanbul, and its design and decoration is influenced by Selçuk art. Built in 1472 as a kind of grandstand from which the sultan could watch sporting activities like wrestling or polo, it now houses a **museum of ceramics** which unfortunately is closed to the public at the moment. Beside it is a pleasant **tea garden**, where you can appreciate the slow emergence of faces and torsos from the marbles lying about the courtyard; these include part of a Medusa's head of the type which was revealed when Yerebatan Saray was dredged (p.89).

The **Archaeology Museum complex** (9:30am–4:30pm, closed Mon; entrance $2.50) can be entered either through Gulhane Parkı or from the first courtyard of Topkapı Sarayı. The first of the museums, the **Museum of the Ancient Orient**, contains a small but dazzling collection of Anatolian, Egyptian, and Mesopotamian artifacts. The late-Hittite basalt lions flanking the entrance look newly hewn, but they actually date from the ninth century BC, giving a taste of the incredible state of preservation of some of the exhibits inside.

These include the oldest peace treaty known to man, the **Treaty of Kadesh** (1280–1269 BC), which was signed when a battle fought on the River Orontes (today's Ası Nehri in Anatolia), between Pharaoh Ramses II and the Hittite king Muvatellish, ended in a stalemate. It includes an agreement of bilateral ceasefire and pledges of a mutual exchange of political refugees, and was originally engraved on silver tablets. None of these survive, but it was also inscribed in hieroglyphics on the mortuary temple of Ramses II in Thebes, and the copy on display in the museum was uncovered during excavations at the site of the Hittite capital of Hattuşaş (see p.510). A recent copy of it decorates the entrance to the UN building in New York.

The blue-and-yellow **animal relief** in the corridor (room 2) beyond the first room dates from the reign of Nebuchadnezzar (604–562 BC), the last hero-king of Babylonia, when it would have lined the processional way in Babylon leading from the Ishtar Gate to a sanctuary where New Year festivities were held. Other exhibits in the museum were taken from the palace-museum of Nebuchadnezzar, located at the Ishtar Gate. Another massive relief, in room 8, depicts the **Hittite king Urpalla** presenting gifts of grapes and grain to a vegetation god three times his own size, wearing a rather attractive pair of curly-toed boots. This is a plaster copy of a relief found at İvriz Kaya near Konya, dating from the eighth century BC.

Other exhibits include a **Sumerian** love poem and a tablet of Sumerian proverbs dating from the eighteenth century BC, and a figure of a duck (room 2) bearing an inscription identifying it as a standard weight belonging to a priest called Musallim Marduk. It weighs about 30 kilograms and has been dated to around 2000 BC, making it the oldest known standard measure.

Across the courtyard is the **Archaeological Museum** itself, built in the nineteenth century to house the antiquities which had previously been stored in the Çinili Köşk and the recent acquisitions of the director of ancient antiquities, Hamdi Bey. It was his excavations at Sidon in 1887 that brought to light the group of sarcophagi, including the Alexander Sarcophagus, the Sarcophagus of the Mourning Women, and the Lycian Sarcophagus, which are the chief exhibits of the museum. The monuments found at Sidon are of Phoenician origin but of quite disparate styles, evidence of the variety of influences absorbed into Phoenician culture from neighboring civilizations.

The upstairs rooms of the museum are currently closed for restoration, but most of the major exhibits are still on display downstairs. The **Alexander Sarcophagus** is located immediately to the left of the entrance lobby, in room 8. It's covered with scenes of Alexander the Great hunting and in battle, but since Alexander himself is known to have been buried in Alexandria this is no longer believed to be his own sarcophagus. Despite its Hellenistic influences, different sources variously ascribe it to a ruler of the Seleucid dynasty or to the Phoenician prince Abdolonyme, but there seems to be agreement in dating the sarcophagus to the end of the fourth century BC. The metal weapons originally held by the warriors and huntsmen were stolen prior to the excavations of Hamdi Bey, presumably when the burial chambers were looted.

The Ionic architecture of another of the Sidon sarcophagi, the **Sarcophagus of the Mourning Women**, is repeated in the exterior of the museum itself. This one shows eighteen women, members of the harem of King Straton who died in 360 BC, in various poses of distress and mourning. To drive the point home a funeral cortege is shown proceeding around the lid of the sarcophagus. As with the Alexander Sarcophagus, traces of the original paintwork can still be seen on the surface of the marble.

The **Lycian Sarcophagus** (room 9) depicts centaurs, sphinxes, and griffins, as well as scenes from Greek mythology. It is in the Lycian style, but the carvings show Peloponnesian influence in the stocky bodies and broad faces of the human figures. In the same room are the anthropoid sarcophagi from Sidon, which illustrate the fifth-century BC fashion for Egyptian models in Greek sculpture. The **Tabnit Sarcophagus**, the oldest Sidon discovery, is in fact Egyptian in origin. A hieroglyphic inscription on the chest of this alabaster mummy case states that it belonged to an Egyptian commander named Penephtah, and a later inscription suggests that Tabnit, himself the father of a pharaoh, was its second occupant.

The **Sidamara Sarcophagus** (room 3) dates from the third century AD, and is the most important remaining example of its type. This room is full of similar sarcophagi, discovered elsewhere in Anatolia; on many of them a drill has been used for much of the carving, especially of the foliage, which is roughly executed in comparison with the Sidon Sarcophagi.

The Hippodrome

The arena of the **Hippodrome**, formerly the cultural focus of the Byzantine Empire, is now the site of a long and narrow municipal park, the **At Meydanı** or Square of Horses. This rather unprepossessing strip of land, which has a road running around its perimeter, is overshadowed by the Palace of İbrahim Paşa on one side and Sultan Ahmet Camii on the other, but its historical significance predates that of most other major monuments in İstanbul.

Nowadays taxis rather than chariots perform laps of honor around the stadium, which was originally constructed by the Byzantine Emperor Septimius Severus in 200 AD, and later enlarged by Constantine the Great, for the performance of court ceremonies and games. The original orientation and dimensions of the 480-meter-long arena have been more or less preserved by the present-day park, although its amphitheater was destroyed in the construction of the Sultan Ahmet mosque, and its semicircular south end is now the site of the Marmara University rectory. Part of an arcade of columns was still in place at the south end until 1550,

CROWD TROUBLE IN CONSTANTINOPLE

The **Hippodrome factions** originated in ancient Roman trade guilds, which in Byzantine times developed further associations: "the Blues" were generally upper-class, politically conservative, and orthodox regarding religion, while "the Greens" were from the lower classes and more radical in their political and religious views.

The factions were a focus of serious rivalry in Constantinople, centered on the circus events in the Hippodrome. In 532 the rivalry was forgotten when members of the Blue faction combined forces with the Greens against the Emperor Justinian in protest at heavy taxation, and in the resulting riots—which derived their name from the battle cry "*Nika!*" or "Victory!"—much of the city, including the church of Aya Sofya, was destroyed. It was the former courtesan, the Empress Theodora, who eventually shamed Justinian into action, and as a result 30,000 Greens and a few hundred Blues were trapped and massacred by the forces of General Belisarius in the Hippodrome. Chariot racing was banned for some time after this, and it was a number of years before the Green faction recovered to the point of being able to compete in either the sporting or the political arena.

when it was pulled down to be used as building material. But, as can be seen from miniatures in the *Surname* of Murat III (see p.75), the Hippodrome continued to be a focus of state ceremony for the Ottoman sultans.

The large open space would now be little more than a pleasant respite from the surrounding hubbub if interest in its origins were not aroused by the monuments strewn in seemingly haphazard fashion throughout its length. Down at the south end of the park are three survivors of the array of obelisks, columns, and statues that originally adorned the spina, the raised central axis of the arena, around which chariots raced.

The northernmost of these, the **Egyptian Obelisk** was originally 60m tall, but only the upper third survived shipment from Egypt in the fourth century. The obelisk itself was commissioned to commemorate the campaigns of Thutmos III in Egypt during the sixteenth century BC, but the scenes on its base depict its erection in Constantinople under the direction of Theodosius I. Among the figures are dancing maidens accompanied by musicians, Theodosius and his family watching a chariot race (south side), and a group of captives kneeling to pay homage to Theodosius (west side).

The **Serpentine Column** comes from the Temple of Apollo at Delphi, where it was dedicated to the god by the 31 Greek cities who defeated the Persians at Plataea in 479 BC. It was brought to Constantinople by Constantine the Great. The three intertwining bronze serpents originally had heads, which splayed out in three directions from the column itself. The jaw of one of the serpents was lopped off by Mehmet the Conqueror on his arrival in Constantinople, as a gesture of defiance against such symbols of idolatry, and the rest of the heads were probably removed in an act of vandalism at the beginning of the eighteenth century. As a result of this dismemberment and of the discoloration of the bronze, the statue is now sadly lacking in grace or beauty. One of the heads is supposedly kept in the archaeological museum, but isn't on display due to renovation work.

The third ancient monument on the spina is a huge lump of masonry, a 32-meter-high column of little or no aesthetic or practical merit. The Emperor

Constantine Porphyrogenitus was presumably of the same opinion in the tenth century, since he restored the pillar and sheathed it in gold-plated bronze. This ornamentation was taken and melted down by the Crusaders during the Sack of Constantinople in 1204. The origins of the column, known erroneously as the **Column of Constantine**, are uncertain, but an inscription records that it was already decayed when Constantine restored it.

A work of rather more aesthetic merit at the north end of the park is the **fountain of Kaiser Wilhelm II**, funds for which were donated by said kaiser to Abdül Hamid II in 1895—evidence of the powerful effect this sultan had on his European contemporaries. As crown prince, Wilhelm had been charmed by the sultan and described his meeting with him as "one of the most interesting encounters I have ever had with foreign princes."

Sultan Ahmet Camii: the Blue Mosque

It is impossible to remain long in the Hippodrome without becoming aware of the **Sultan Ahmet Camii**, the Blue Mosque, on its southeast side. In the unlikely event that the mosque's imposing size fails to impress itself upon you, your attention will doubtless be drawn to it by some persistent youth who wishes to guide you around it. Despite its fame, however, Sultan Ahmet is not really the place to start developing a taste for oriental interiors: here it's size and visibility that counts, rather than any architectural or aesthetic merits.

Before construction began, in 1609, objections were raised to the plan of a **six-minareted mosque**—partly because it was said to be unholy to rival the six minarets of the mosque at Mecca, but also because it would be a great drain on state revenues at a time when the empire was contracting in size. The true cause of the objections, however, probably had more to do with the need to destroy several palaces belonging to imperial ministers to make way for construction.

From the **outside**, the building is undeniably impressive, particularly on the all-important approach from the Topkapı Palace. An imposing hulk of gray stone, it's visible for miles around on its hilltop vantage point and instantly recognizable because of its six minarets. Above the level of the courtyard the mosque is a mass of shallow domes and domed turrets, hardly broken by a single straight line. Its courtyard is best approached from the west portal, attractive and graceful—apart from the redundant little dome on top—and bearing a calligraphic inscription by the father of the travel writer Evliya Celebi. The courtyard is surrounded by a portico of thirty small domes, recently repainted, and has the same dimensions as the mosque itself.

All this is extremely pleasing, and it's only when you enter the mosque itself that things start to go wrong. Here four **"elephant foot" pillars** (so called because of their size and clumsiness), five meters in diameter, immediately impose their disproportionate dimensions, appearing squashed against the outer walls and obscuring parts of the building from every angle. The pillars also tend to dwarf the modest dome they support, which in turn renders their immense proportions ridiculous. The mosque has a four-leaf-clover shape, with semidomes flanked by smaller semidomes to north, south, east, and west, and is rendered more interesting by a balcony running around three sides. The corners are a pleasing arrangement of semidomes and stalactite pendentives, with arches connecting the pillars to the wall.

The name "Blue Mosque" is derived from the predominantly blue color of the decoration. The walls and arches are covered with **arabesque stencilling**, unattractive and of poor quality. The **windows** are brightly colored but badly designed—the original stained glass was best-quality Venetian but even that caused an effect of gloominess—and many of the carpets on the floor are worn.

The main attraction are the **tiles**: over twenty thousand of them, constituting such a tall order that the İznik kilns were practically exhausted. Still in evidence are the clear bright colors of the best period of late sixteenth-century İznik ware, including flower and tree panels as well as more abstract designs. They're difficult to see in the gloominess of the interior, and the best panels, in the galleries, are all but obscured by the columns of the arcades while renovation continues.

A more serious obstacle is the **fence** that bars non-Moslem visitors from entering two-thirds of the mosque interior. This renders any examination of the attractive *mihrab* and *mimber* and the sultan's loge impossible, so after a cursory inspection of what is visible from behind the fence it might be as well to curtail your visit in favor of some other more welcoming environment.

Elsewhere in the Sultan Ahmet complex are other buildings of some interest. At the northeast corner of the complex is the **royal pavilion**, approached rather unusually up a ramp, and giving access to the sultan's loge inside the mosque. Walking past this building and down beside the mosque you arrive at the **Fil Ahırı**, the elephant stables, which house a **Kilim Museum**, currently closed for restoration.

The Tomb of Sultan Ahmet

Outside the precinct wall to the northwest of the mosque is the *türbe* or **tomb of Sultan Ahmet** (9:30am–4:30pm, closed Tues). Buried here along with the sultan are his wife and three of his sons, two of whom (Osman II and Murat IV) were rulers in their turn. This successive rule of brothers was only possible because Sultan Ahmet had introduced the institution of the Cage to the Palace, thus relieving himself and his sons of the responsibility of fratricide upon accession to the throne. Unfortunately both Ahmet's own brother Mustafa and his son Osman were completely insane and unfit to rule by the time they left the Cage to take up the reins of office, and Murat IV only escaped this fate by succeeding to the throne at the age of ten, before the conditions in the Cage had affected him. The tomb, like the mosque, is tiled with seventeenth-century İznik tiles and contains various **holy relics**, including a turban from Yahya Efendi's tomb.

İbrahim Paşa Sarayı—Türk ve İslam Eserleri Müzesi

İbrahim Paşa Sarayı (the Palace of İbrahim Paşa), on the other side of the Hippodrome, was recently opened as the Türk ve İslam Eserleri Müzesi, the **Museum of Turkish and Islamic Art** (Tues–Sun, 10am–5pm; $2.50), an attractive, well-planned museum containing what is probably the best-exhibited collection of Islamic artifacts in the world. It is certainly more impressive than the Museum of Islamic Art in Paris, partly because the sixteenth-century setting of cool, darkened rooms around a central garden courtyard obviate the necessity for expensive technology to keep the sun off the exhibits, but also because the museum gives a better idea of the wealth and complexity of Islamic art and culture than does its western counterpart.

The İbrahim Paşa Sarayı is one of the few private Ottoman residences to have survived the fires which periodically destroy large areas of the city, and even this has only survived in part. Much of the building has disappeared, and what remains was rebuilt in stone—according to the original plan—in 1843.

Completed in 1524 for the newly appointed grand vizier of Süleyman the Magnificent, İbrahim Paşa, the palace is a fitting memorial to one of the most able statesmen of his time, whose abilities were matched only by his accumulation of wealth and power. His status can be judged from the proportions of the rooms of his palace, and by its prominent position next to the Hippodrome; later sultans were to use its balconies to watch festivities below. İbrahim controlled the affairs of war and state of the Ottoman Empire for thirteen years, and fell from grace partly as a result of the schemings of Süleyman's wife Roxelana. Even so, it doesn't seem unreasonable that Süleyman should distrust a servant who could say to a foreign ambassador: "If I command that something should be done, and he (the sultan) has commanded to the contrary, my wishes and not his are obeyed." The body of İbrahim Paşa was found in a room of the Topkapı Palace with strangulation marks around its neck. Süleyman the Magnificent ordered it to be buried in an unmarked grave, and his possessions, not the least of which being the palace, reverted to the crown.

The main concentration of **exhibits** in the museum deals with Selçuk, Mamluk, and Ottoman Turkish art, but there are also several important Timurid and Persian works on display.

The Selçuk Empire, centered in Konya, preceded that of the Ottomans in Anatolia and it is interesting to trace influences between the two cultures. Ceramic techniques, for example, were obviously well developed by the Selçuks, judging from the wall tiles on display in the museum, and the wood carvings from Konya also suggest a high level of craftsmanship and artistry which may have influenced later Ottoman work.

Other impressive exhibits include sixteenth-century Persian miniatures, which like many Ottoman works defy the Islamic stricture against depicting human or animal forms. Pictures in lacquer and leather-bound Persian manuscripts portray a tiger ripping an antelope, and a dancing girl dated 1570. The tiny Sancak Korans were meant for hanging on the standard of the Ottoman imperial army in a Jihad (Holy War), so that the word of God preceded the troops into battle.

The **Great Hall** of the Palace, İbrahim Paşa's magnificent audience hall, is devoted to a collection of Turkish **carpets** that is among the finest in the world. It includes tattered remains dating from the thirteenth century. On the ground floor, in rooms off the central courtyard, is an exhibition of the **folk art** of the Yörük tribes of Anatolia. This includes examples of a *Kara Çadır* (literally "black tent," a domicile woven from goat hair still to be seen in central and eastern Anatolia) and a *Topakev* (a tent constructed around a folding frame, which was used by nomads in Anatolia and Mongolia for over a thousand years). There is also an invaluable if somewhat faded exhibition concerning the dyes used in Turkish kilims and carpets, and the plants and insects from which they are derived. The use of natural dyes was almost forgotten in Anatolia after the introduction of chemical dyes in 1880, and the exhibition pays deserved homage to the work of Marmara University's government-sponsored project, piloted in the province of Çanakkale, to encourage the rediscovery of natural dyes in the carpet- and kilim-making processes.

The Hamam of Roxelana

The double-domed building between the Sultan Ahmet Camii and Aya Sofya is the **Hamam of Roxelana** (9:30am–5pm, closed Tues), built by Mimar Sinan in 1556 to replace the Byzantine baths of Zeuxippus on the same site. The 75-meter-long hamam served the worshippers at the mosque of Aya Sofya. The hamam has been restored with stained glass windows and varnished wooden doors, and original marble fountains in the changing rooms, but the effect is rather diminished since after renovation the building was converted into a salesroom for handwoven carpets.

One of the consequences of this unfortunate decision is that the hamam now has electric lighting, which destroys the characteristic effect produced by the skylights in the dome of a hamam, which is especially attractive when viewed through a veil of steam. The salespeople are collecting signatures for a petition aimed at persuading the Ministry of Tourism to employ the building in its original purpose, or at least as a museum, but in the meantime it merely provides a pleasant surrounding in which to listen to more sales patter.

Sokollu Mehmet Paşa Camii

A pleasant walk from the southwest corner of the Hippodrome leads down the steep Mehmet Paşa Yokuşu to **Sokollu Mehmet Paşa Camii** (open at prayer times only, but the *imam* may be around to unlock the door during the day). This, one of Mimar Sinan's later buildings (1571), appears to have been omitted almost entirely from tourist itineraries. **Sokollu Mehmet Paşa**, who commissioned the mosque, was the last grand vizier of Süleyman the Magnificent, and it was his military expertise that later saved the Ottoman empire from the worst effects of the dissolute rule of Selim the Sot. He was eventually assassinated as a result of the intrigues of Nur Banu, the mother of Murat III, who was jealous of his power.

The large mosque **courtyard** is surrounded on three sides by the rooms of the *medrese*, now occupied by a boys' Koran school (the boys, ten- to twelve-year-olds, inhabit the dervish lodge at the back of the mosque and can be seen seated in the porch studying the Koran during the school year). At the center of the courtyard is a handsome fountain with a pretty upcurved parapet to its dome.

The **interior** of the mosque is notable for the height of its dome and the impressive display of İznik tiles on its east wall. These are from the best period of Turkish ceramics: the white is pure, the green vivid, and the red intense. Calligraphic inscriptions are set against a jungle of enormous carnations and tulips, and the designs and colors are echoed all around the mosque and in the conical cap of the *mimber*, the tiling of which is unique in İstanbul. While the stained glass windows are copies, some of the original, extremely delicate **paintwork** can be seen in the northwest corner below the gallery and over the entrance. Embedded in the wall over the entrance and above the *mihrab* are pieces of the Kaaba from Mecca.

Around three sides of the mosque, a **gallery** is supported on marble, lozenge-capitalled columns. With permission from the *imam*, who will hover during your visit, you can have a look up here and see the mosque interior from a different angle.

Küçük Ayasofya Camii

Like its namesake Aya Sofya, the **Küçük Ayasofya Camii** (the small mosque of Aya Sofya; Küçük Ayasofya Camii Sok, Küçük Ayasofya Cad, continuing down from the Mehmet Paşa Camii; open at prayer times only) was built as a church in the sixth century. It was originally named after two Roman soldiers, **Sergius** and **Bacchus**, who were martyred for their faith and later became the patron saints of Christians in the Roman army, but was renamed, aptly, because of its resemblance to Aya Sofya. It is believed to have predated the larger church, but this is not certain; all that is known is that it was built between 527 and 536 to service the palace of Hormisdas. This means that the church was part of the vast rebuilding program carried out by Justinian to accommodate a growing population and to encourage the spread of Christianity, and also to consolidate his power after near-humiliation in the Nika riots. The church was converted into a mosque comparatively late, at the beginning of the sixteenth century during the reign of Beyazit II.

Despite imperfections in its execution, this is an attractive building, and it makes an interesting comparison with Aya Sofya because the smaller building is virtually a scale model of the larger one. The lesser dimensions mean that the various component parts are easier to comprehend as a whole.

Like most Byzantine churches of this era, its **exterior** is of unprepossessing brick, and only inside can its satisfying proportions be properly appreciated. It is basically—like Aya Sofya—an octagon with exedrae at its diagonals, inscribed in a rectangle, but both these shapes are extremely irregular. The irregularities have been variously ascribed to a pragmatic solution to an awkward space at the planning stage or to shoddy workmanship, and while the latter seems to be the more likely explanation, the irregularities certainly don't detract from the general effect. The original marble revetments and gold leaf have all vanished, but a frieze honoring Justinian, Theodora, and Saint Sergius runs around the molding under the gallery. Again it's worthwhile, for the sake of the view, to ask permission to visit the **gallery**—but put on a pair of wooden clogs before you go up because it's dirty upstairs, and the *imam* won't tolerate dirty feet on his mosque carpet.

The Sea Wall and the Byzantine Imperial Palace

At the Küçük Ayasofya Camii you're almost down at the Marmara, and close to the best-preserved section of the **sea wall**, built by Cyrus, Prefect of the East, in 439. These originally stretched from Saray Burnu all the way to the city walls of Constantine the Great, and were later extended by Theodosius to meet his land walls. Thirteen gates pierced the eight-kilometer barrier. In the ninth century Theophilus, the last Iconoclast, rebuilt the walls against the possibility of an Arab invasion.

Nowadays the best way to see the walls is by **train**, since the tracks run along their length and on out of the city; indeed, parts were destroyed when the rail lines were built. The best-preserved remains are a stretch of a couple of kilometers between Ahır Kapı, near the Cankurtan train station, and Kumkapı, but they are difficult to follow on foot—unless you brave noisy Kennedy Caddesi on the sea side—since numerous detours are necessitated by dead ends.

About halfway between the Küçük Ayasofya Camii and Cankurtan train station, the facade of the **Palace of Bucoleon** is one of the most melancholy and moving survivors of Byzantine Constantinople. This is a last remnant of the Great Palace of the Byzantine emperors, which once covered an enormous area from the Hippodrome down to the sea walls (see the Mosaic Museum, below). It was begun by Constantine and added to by later emperors, until the Comneni dynasty abandoned it. Later it was rehabilitated, however, and a description by one of the Crusaders explains why they took up residence after the Sack of Constantinople in 1204:

> *Within the palace there were fully 500 halls all connected with one another and all made with gold mosaic. And in it were fully 30 chapels, great and small, and there was one of them that was called the Holy Chapel, which was so rich and noble that there was not a hinge or a band nor any other small part that was not all of silver, and there was no column that was not of jasper or porphyry or some other precious stone.*

By the time the Latins left in 1261, however, the palace was virtually destroyed, and funds were never found to repair it. Mehmet the Conqueror was so saddened by what he found there that he is said to have recited lines from the Persian poet Saadi:

> *The spider holds the curtain in the Palace of the Caesars*
> *The owl hoots its night call in the towers of Aphrasiab.*

It's easy to miss what's left of the Bucoleon Palace, especially if you're speeding past it along Kennedy Caddesi. It is draped in beautiful red vine, set back from the road with a little park in front of it. Three enormous marble-framed windows set high in the wall give glimpses of the remains of a vaulted room behind. Below the windows, projecting marble corbels give evidence of a balcony that would have projected over a marble pier (the waters of the Marmara once reached almost as far as the walls of the palace). For the rest, you'll need a lively imagination.

Walking from Küçük Ayasofya Camii along Kennedy Caddesi in the other direction for about ten minutes you come to the little suburb of **Kumkapı**, the fish center of Istanbul. A large number of increasingly expensive but excellent fish restaurants here cater to both locals and visitors, and there's also a fabulous **fish market**, which should be visited between 5 and 6am in the morning. At that time you'll witness the daily catch from the Marmara Sea—a vast array of marine life from squid and tuna to thousand upon thousand of *hamsi*—performing its death throes under the disrespectful boots of fishermen, vendors, hoteliers, and restaurateurs. The atmosphere of the place is frantic, but if you find a safe place from which to observe you'll be practically ignored in favor of the business of the day.

Mosaic Museum

The only other remains of the Great Palace are the mosaics displayed in the **Mozaik Müzesi** (9:30am–5pm; $1), inland from here on Torun Sokak. Walk along Kennedy Caddesi to Ahır Kapı (Stable Gate), just before Cankurtan train station, and double back along Ahırkapı Sokak to the Akbıyık Camii, located on a square which is also graced by an ornately carved, eighteenth-century Baroque fountain. From here, walk up Akbıyık Caddesi, take a left onto Mimar Mehmet Ağa Caddesi, then the first left onto Torun Sokak. The museum can also be reached by running the gauntlet of salespeople in the Arasta Çarşısı (formerly Kabasakal Caddesi), a newly renovated street selling tourist gifts, whose shops originally paid for the upkeep of the nearby Sultan Ahmet Camii. The street was built on part of the site of the Great Palace, and until recently parts of the mosaics, now removed to the museum, could be seen in the shops themselves.

The museum is basically a quonset hut-type structure placed over the mosaics, many of which are still in place, so that some idea of their original scale and purpose can be imagined. The building has been constructed so that some of the mosaics are first viewed from a catwalk above but can also be examined more closely by descending to their level. The remains in the museum were part of a mosaic peristyle, an open courtyard surrounded by a portico. To the south of the portico and down to the Bucoleon on the Marmara were the private apartments of the emperor, while the public sections of the palace were located to the north. The mosaics, which probably date from Justinian's rebuilding program of the sixth century, feature various animals, both in their natural habitats and in domestic scenes. They include a vivid portrayal of an elephant locking a lion in a deadly embrace with its trunk, and two children being led on the back of a camel.

From Sultanahmet to Beyazit

Beyazit, which centers around the buildings of İstanbul University and is also home to the covered bazaar, is relatively little explored by tourists, but it's a quarter that deserves some time. The university and its surrounding mosques—Nuruosmaniye, Beyazit Camii, and Süleymaniye—are all interesting, and of course there's the bazaar itself, as well as the most famous of İstanbul's second-hand book markets.

The Yerebatan Saray

Before leaving Sultanahmet, it's worth making a detour along Yerebatan Caddesi to the Basilica Cistern or **Yerebatan Saray** (Sunken Palace; Tues–Sun 9am–5pm; $2.50), one of several underground cisterns that riddle the foundations of the city. This is the only one that has been extensively excavated and renovated, and although it's always thronged it's worth devoting time to a prolonged exploration of the furthest recesses. Probably built by Emperor Constantine in the fourth century, and enlarged by Justinian in the sixth century, the cistern was supplied by aqueducts with water from the Belgrade Forest, and it in turn supplied the Great Palace and later Topkapı Saray.

The cistern seems to have fallen into disuse in the century after the Ottoman conquest and its existence was only brought to public attention in 1545 by the Frenchman **Petrus Gyllius**. He had been led to it by local residents, whose houses were built over the cistern and who had easy access to it. They had sunk wells into it and even kept boats on the water from which they could fish its depths (Gyllius's interest was allegedly aroused when he found fresh fish being sold in the streets nearby).

Restorations were undertaken in 1987: 50,000 tons of mud and water were removed; the walls were covered to make them impermeable; and eight of the columns were sheathed in concrete to fortify the structure. The construction of concrete pathways to replace the old boats may seem a desecration, but they do facilitate a leisurely examination of interesting bits of masonry, as does the careful spotlighting. Piped music and the café at the exit add an additional element of mystery to the place: their purpose is wholly obscure.

The largest covered cistern in the city, measuring 140 by 70 meters, Yerebatan holds 80,000 cubic meters of water. The small herringbone **domes** are supported by 336 columns, many of which have Corinthian capitals, and the whole fragile-looking structure supports the buildings and a busy main road overhead. There is evidence that building material for the cistern was pillaged from elsewhere. The two **Medusa heads** at the southwest corner, brought to light when the cistern was drained, are thought to have been used simply as construction material, since they would have been totally submerged and invisible. The marble **columns** may also have been recycled: some are square shaped, others in two parts, and one has a tree-trunk effect patterned on its surface, resembling the remains of columns found beyond the university on Ordu Caddesi.

Divanyolu

The main approach to Beyazit is along **Divanyolu**, a major thoroughfare which, if you're staying at one of the hotels in Lâleli or Aksaray, you may well be following in the other direction on your way to the better-known sights around Sultanahmet. It gained its name because it was the principal approach to the Divan, and hordes of people would pour down it three times a week to make their petitions to the court. It's still hideously overcrowded, its narrow sidewalks barely passable at any hour of the day or night, its shops run down, the restaurants shabby, and the major attractions, hemmed in by buildings, are easy to miss as you struggle along the street below. Nevertheless there's plenty to see as you push your way through.

The **Binbirdirek Cistern**, or Cistern of a Thousand and One Columns, is on the Binbirdirek Meydanı at the end of Işık Sokak, to the left off Divanyolu as you walk away from Aya Sofya, underneath a small building currently serving as the regional *muhtarlık* (municipal directorate). If you ask there, the *muhtar* should produce the keys and take you down a flight of stone steps to view the cistern, dimly lit by holes in the wasteland behind the *muhtarlık*. The second largest cistern in the city, measuring 64 by 56 meters, Binbirdirek contains 224 columns, twelve of which were walled in not long after the cistern was completed. Originally the hall would have been over twelve meters high—the columns actually consist of two separate units placed one on top of the other—but it's filled with soil almost to the top of the lower columns. The cistern is thought to have been built originally under the palace of Philoxenus, one of the Roman senators who accompanied Emperor Constantine to the city, and was restored and enlarged under Justinian. It dried up completely sometime around the fifteenth century, and was later used as a spinning mill until the beginning of the twentieth century.

Continuing on Divanyolu itself you'll come to a burnt column of masonry known as Çemberlitaş or the Hooped Stone. This is the **Column of Constantine**, erected by Constantine the Great in 330 AD to commemorate the city's dedication as capital of the Roman Empire. For the next sixteen centuries the city was known as Constantinople, and the Christian religion Constantine introduced was to be associated with the city for almost as long. The column itself was originally sheathed in porphyry (the most prestigious of the colored marbles, found only in Egypt) and surmounted by a statue of the emperor. The iron hoops from which it derives its Turkish name were bound around the joints in the porphyry after an earthquake in 416 damaged the column and threatened its imminent collapse.

Across Vezirhanı Caddesi from the column is the **Çemberlitaş Hamamı** (☎522 7974; daily 9am–7pm; $3 without massage), founded in the sixteenth century by Nur Banu, one of the most powerful of the Valide Sultans. Thanks to its central location the masseurs are well used to foreigners, and this might not be a bad place to be initiated into the rites of the Turkish bath.

If you head up Vezirhanı Caddesi you'll come to the **Nuruosmaniye Camii** behind the covered bazaar; coming from the other direction, the courtyard provides a refreshing open space after the bazaar's dark convolutions. Nuruosmaniye, begun by Mahmut I in 1748 and finished seven years later by Osman III, was the first and most impressive of the city's Baroque mosques, setting the fashion in Baroque and Rococo architecture for the following century. The designer is unknown—it has been attributed to both Turkish and foreign architects—but since it was such a radical departure from anything that had gone before it seems likely that foreign influence was at work.

The Covered Bazaar

İstanbul's Kapalı Çarşı (Mon–Sat 9am–7pm) is said to be the largest **covered bazaar** in the world, though whether it beats the Galleria in Los Angeles is debatable. The comparison isn't as ludicrous as it sounds: the bazaar works along much the same lines as a western supermarket or mall—simple to use once you know how to find what you're looking for, and with the same opportunities to shop under cover and in comfort, with plenty of refreshments.

The whole thing is laid out street by street, so that a particular type of shop is found in a certain area. There are several good **carpet** shops around the fountain at the intersection of Keseciler and Takkeciler Caddesis, and cheaper, somewhat scruffier places on Halıcılar Çarşısı Caddesi (Carpet Sellers' Market Street). Carpets can also be bought at **auction** on Wednesdays at 1pm in the Sandal Bedesteni, but you'll need a good grasp of your numbers in Turkish and some idea of what you want. You'll notice that the dealers inspect anything interesting with some care before bargaining, and many avoid the place altogether since you can't really see what you're buying, but it's fun to watch. Other auctions are of furniture and ornaments (Tuesday) and jewelry (Thursday; also at 1pm in the Sandal Bedesten). The best old **silver** is sold in and around the old bazaar or **Iç Bedesten**, more or less at the center, and traditionally reserved for the most precious wares because it can be locked at night. **Ceramics** can be found along Yağlıkçılar Sokak and off it in Çukur Han; leather and kilim **bags** are sold on Keseciler Caddesi; and glittery, mainly poor quality **gold** is sold around Kuyumcular Caddesi (the Street of the Jewelers) and Kalpakçılar Başı Caddesi. For details of specific shops, see under "Shops and Markets," p.151.

When you need a break, the nicest **café** in the bazaar is the *Şark Kahvesi*, on Yağlıkçılar Sokak almost opposite Zenneciler Sokak. Here you can play backgammon and drink strong tea while devising your plan of attack or gloating over hard-won booty.

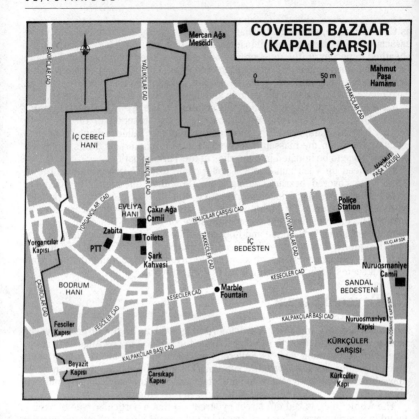

In Ottoman times the bazaar was a vital part of the town and consisted of both a covered and an open area centered on a *bedesten*, where foreign trade took place. In İstanbul the commercial center was based around two bedestens, both inside the Covered Bazaar. The **İç Bedesten** probably dates from the time of the conquest, while the **Sandal Bedesten** was added during the reign of Süleyman to cope with the quantity of trade in fine fabrics that the capital attracted in the sixteenth century. In effect the bazaar extends much farther than the limits of the covered area, sprawling into the streets that lead down to the Golden Horn, and the whole area was controlled by the strict laws laid down by the trade guilds, which reduced competition between traders. Each shop could support just one owner and his apprentice, and successful merchants were not allowed to expand their businesses. Similar unwritten laws control market forces among traders in the covered bazaar even today.

Whether or not you actually enjoy the **experience of the bazaar** is very much a matter of temperament and mood: you'll either find the hassle from traders intolerable, or you'll be flattered at being paid more attention in one afternoon than you've received in your entire life. The only way to avoid it would be to go out of season, dress a la Turk, and move so fast they can't see you: in normal circumstances you might as well resign yourself to the bantering hard sell. If you have time to spend in idle chat you may discover some of the more interesting characters who work in these parts, and everyone is at least friendly and cheerful, in summer anyway. In winter the bazaar goes into hibernation: profit and loss are assessed, the ranks close, and the season's sport is soccer—played in the alleys between shops—rather than tourist-baiting.

Beyazit Meydanı

If you continued straight up the main road, you'd arrive at Beyazit Meydanı, the main square of Beyazit and the principal approach to İstanbul University. Here also, approached through a small *bit pazarı* or flea market, is the famous **Sahaflar Çarşısı**, the secondhand booksellers' market, a little enclave of wonderful shops run by some of the quarter's best-known and worst-tempered characters. The Ottoman book market dates back to the eighteenth century, but long before that it was the site of a Byzantine book and paper market. After the Conquest it lost its original identity to the spoonmakers, but gradually other tradesmen were replaced by booksellers as printing and publishing were legalized in the Ottoman Empire in the second half of the eighteenth century. On the west side of the square this tradition is reflected in a small **Museum of Calligraphy** (Tues–Sat 9am–4pm; $1.25), which contains some interesting examples of this highly developed Ottoman art form. It occupies an attractive old building, formerly a theological college.

To the east of the square, **Beyazit Camii**, completed in 1506, is the oldest surviving imperial mosque in the city. It has a beautiful, somber courtyard full of richly colored marble, including twenty columns of verd antique, red granite, and porphyry. Inside, the building is a perfect square of exactly the same proportions as the courtyard (although the aisles make it feel elongated), and its plan is basically a simplified version of Aya Sofya, with the same balancing semidomes to the east and west but without the lateral galleries. The sixteenth-century fittings, including the carvings of the balustrade, *mihrab*, and *mimber*, are all highly crafted and beautiful. If you walk straight past the mosque from Beyazit Square and on through the Sahaflar Çarşısı, you'll arrive at another entrance to the covered bazaar.

The University

Located on the site of the Old Palace of Mehmet the Conqueror, **İstanbul University** commands an impressive position on the crown of one of the city's seven hills. The fire tower located in the grounds, the Beyazit Tower, is a landmark all over the city, and the main building and some of its subsidiaries have a certain style and grandeur, especially when approached through the main gateway (the time to do this is 9am during the academic year, when the national anthem, the *İstiklâl Marşı*, is played, and everyone in the vicinity freezes for the duration).

There's a possibility that as a foreigner you won't be permitted to enter the grounds, since the gates are periodically manned by police who check identity cards. İstanbul University is a center of political activity of both the left and Muslim fundamentalists, and this occasionally erupts in demonstrations, lock-ins, and even violence on the campus. Since this is used as a reason for the police presence on the campus, it is rumored that trouble is often encouraged by the presence of *agents provocateurs*. Whoever is demonstrating, one of the main causes of

campus unrest is *YÖK*, the Higher Education Council. This controversial body controls all higher education in Turkey, determining the national syllabus (which still includes compulsory classes on the life of Atatürk and the history of the republic) and laying down the protocol which forbids headscarves and beards on campus and bans all but one, officially controlled, society per university.

The **Old Palace** of Mehmet the Conqueror was the official imperial residence from its inception, after the Conquest of İstanbul in 1453, until it burned to the ground in 1541, when the residential quarters and harem were relocated next to the Divan in Topkapı Palace. The Old Palace was then rebuilt to serve as a residence for concubines who had been retired after the accession of a new sultan. However, most of the buildings now serving as draughty lecture halls were constructed by the French architect Bourgeois in 1866, and housed the Ministry of War until this moved to Ankara along with the other departments of state. At that time the university, which until then had been scattered around the city in various *medreses* of the imperial mosques, was relocated here.

Apart from the monumental gateway through which the campus is entered, the most impressive building on the site is a small *köşk*, to the right of the entrance, now used as the staff dining room. This is part of the original Bourgeois complex and has retained its Baroque interior decoration.

The Süleymaniye

Heading downhill through the university grounds, you will emerge in front of a collection of buildings considered to be the finest of all the Ottoman mosque complexes. Built by the great architect Sinan in honor of his most illustrious patron, Süleyman the Magnificent, they are arguably his greatest achievement.

When the imperial entourage moved to Topkapı Saray, the grounds of the Old Palace were given over to the new building, in what must have been a most attractive location overlooking the Golden Horn and its waterside parks and gardens. **Süleymaniye Camii** and its satellites, completed in just seven years between 1550 and 1557, are built along traditional Islamic lines—the mosque is centralized beneath a dome and is also at the very center of the entire complex—but the whole achieves a perfection of form and a monumentality of appearance, dominating the skyline from Galata and the Horn, which set it apart from other Ottoman architecture.

Approaching from the university side, the first street encountered before entering the mosque area is **Tıryakı Meydan**, the Street of the Addicts. The name derives from the fact that the coffee houses on this street, whose rents augmented the upkeep of the foundation, also used to serve hashish, to be smoked on the premises or taken away. They have been replaced by a line of student cafés which, while seedy, are evidently nowhere near as interesting as the earlier establishments.

Behind the shopfronts in this street is the famous **Süleymaniye Library**, housed in the Evvel and Sani *medreses*. These buildings, mirror images of each other, are situated around shady garden courtyards. The library was established by Süleyman in an effort to bring together collections of books scattered throughout the city; works were brought from eleven palaces, and date from the reigns of six different sultans. The library is open to the public and all the works are on microfilm, to protect the originals. There is also a book restoration department, where the original bindings are closely imitated.

Other buildings of interest in the vicinity include the **Türbe of Mimar Sinan**, on the corner of Sıfahan and Mimar Sinan caddessis. This is located in a triangular garden, which was the location of the architect's house during construction work. At the corner of the triangle is an octagonal eaved fountain. Perhaps there is no better way to be remembered than by providing the gift of water to passing strangers, but in Sinan's case it nearly caused his downfall: the fountain, as well as Sinan's house and garden, were liberally supplied with water, but when the mosques farther down the pipeline began to run short, Sinan was charged with fraudulently diverting the water supply for his household needs. The garden beyond the fountain now contains Sinan's tomb, its magnificent carved turban standing as a measure of the architect's high rank. The eulogy written on the south wall of the garden picks out the bridge at Büyükçekmece as Sinan's greatest achievement.

MIMAR SINAN (1489–1588): MASTER BUILDER

Many of the finest works of Ottoman civil and religious architecture throughout Turkey can be traced to one man, a genius who had the good luck to come of age in a rich, expanding empire willing to put its considerable resources at his disposal. **Mimar Sinan** served as court architect to three sultans—Süleyman the Magnificent, Selim II, and Murat III—but principally to the former, who owed much of his reputation for "magnificence" to this gifted technician.

Little is known of his early life except that he was born in a small village near Kayseri, the son of Greek or Armenian Christian parents; even his birthdate is open to question, since it is established that he was conscripted into the janissaries in 1513, which would have made him a good ten years older than the typical recruit. In any case, prolonged military service in all the major Ottoman campaigns of the early sixteenth century compelled Sinan to travel the length and breadth of southeastern Europe and the Middle East, giving him the opportunity to become familiar with the best Islamic—and Christian—monumental architecture in that area. Sinan was immediately able to apply what he learned in his job as military engineer, building bridges, siegeworks, harbors, and even ships that earned him the admiration of his superiors. These included Sultan Süleyman, who in recognition of his abilities appointed him Court Architect in April 1536.

During Sinan's first twelve years in the job, he did little out of the ordinary, undertaking only relatively minor public works such as aqueducts, bridges, hamams, *kervansarays* and *imarets* throughout Anatolia and the Balkans. In 1548 he completed his first major religious commission, İstanbul's Şehzade Camii, and shortly thereafter embarked on a rapid succession of ambitious projects in and around the capital, including the waterworks leading from the Belgrade Forest and the Süleymaniye Camii. After presumably exhausting the potential of the great city, Sinan again turned his matured attention to the provinces, gracing Edirne with the Selimiye Camii in 1569–75, and a decade later fulfilling a longstanding wish as a devout Muslim in overseeing the restoration of the Harem-i-Şerif mosque in Mecca.

Unusually for his time, Sinan could make an objective assessment of his talents: he regarded most of his pre-1550 works as apprentice pieces, and posterity has generally agreed with the self-evaluations in his memoirs, the *Tezkeret-ül-Bünyan*. Despite temptations to luxury he lived and died equally modestly, being buried in a simple tomb he made for himself in his garden on the grounds of the Süleymaniye Camii—a tomb which was perhaps the last of more than 500 of Sinan's constructions, large and small, throughout the empire.

Otherwise, the buildings of the Süleymaniye complex served the usual functions: on Sıfahan Sokak are a soup kitchen (*imaret*), which used to be the museum of Turkish antiquities and is usually open to wander around, and a *kervansaray*; a *mektep* or primary school stands on the corner of Tıryakı Çarşısı and Süleymaniye Caddesi; and there are Koran schools and a language school that taught the proper pronunciation of Arabic for reading of the Koran. The **hamam** on the corner of Mimar Sinan Caddesi and Dökmeciler Hamamı Sokak is a beautiful building in a terrible state of repair, and there's also a wrestling ground, located to the south of the cemetery.

The **mosque** and **cemetery**, enclosed by a wall with grilled openings, are located in the midst of these buildings, part of a harmoniously integrated ensemble, but at the same time independent enough to dominate the whole, and to be visible from all sides.

The mosque is preceded by a rectangular courtyard whose portico is supported by columns of porphyry, Marmara marble and pink Egyptian granite (which are said to have come from the royal box of the Hippodrome), and by four tapering minarets. In the center of the courtyard stands a small rectangular fountain that serves to emphasise the size of the open area. On the exterior of the mosque itself, semidomes supporting the huge central dome to the east and west alternate with arches, in front of which are a set of three domes. The east and west flanks of the mosque are distinguished by two-storey loggias, accessible from within the mosque, which support an eave protecting those performing their ablutions at the faucets below.

The doorway into the mosque is high and narrow, with wooden doors inlaid with ebony, mother of pearl, and ivory. Inside, a sense of light and spaciousness is paramount, the majestic effect only slightly tempered by the tackiness of more Fossati interior decor. The proportions are perfectly balanced: a dome 53m high (twice its diameter), surmounting a perfect square of 26.5m. The effect of space is helped by the fact that there are no side aisles; and the airiness is enhanced by 200 windows, including 32 in the central dome and 23 in each tympanum, whose double panes ensure softly filtered light.

The dome collapsed during the earthquake of 1766, and in the nineteenth century further damage was done by the Fossati brothers, whose attempt at Ottoman Baroque redecoration jars with the simplicity of other aspects of the building. The original crystal lamps have also been replaced by glassware supported on a rather cumbersome iron frame, which is a bit distracting. The original stained glass of İbrahim the Mad remains, however, above a simply graceful marble *mimber*, along with a few İznik tiles, a first cautious use of tiling by Sinan before he was swept away by enthusiasm in the Rüstem Paşa Camii down the hill.

In the **cemetery** (Wed–Sun 9:30am–5pm) are located the tombs of Süleyman the Magnificent and of Haseki Hürrem, or Roxelana, his powerful wife. Süleyman's tomb is particularly impressive: passing through doors inlaid with ebony and ivory, silver and jade, and a peristyle supported by four verd antique columns, you're confronted by the huge turban of Süleyman the Magnificent. Above, the inner dome has been restored in red, black, and gold inlaid with glittering ceramic stars. Here and in the neighboring tomb of Roxelana, you'll see the original very beautiful tiles, and some of the stained glass, which have survived.

Eminönü and the Golden Horn

Descending from Beyazit down the hill to Eminönü is not an experience for the faint-hearted. The streets are steep, narrow, and badly paved, and invariably thronged with *hamals* (stevedores) bent double under burdens of merchandise twice their size. Even the smallest of these roads is open to traffic, and the resulting confusion can be awesome to behold.

Immediately below the covered bazaar is the region known as **Tahtakale**, the unofficial moneychangers' market. This is also the place to buy a secondhand camera (or buy back one you thought you'd lost) from stallholders who set up shop here on Saturdays. The whole area around the bazaar and down to Sirkeci, generally known as **Eminönü**, is in effect an extension of the covered bazaar, with streets specializing in ironware, wooden implements, cheap rugs, dentists' chairs, or small nameless pieces of cheap metal. Farther east, below Divanyolu, is the area known as **Cağaloğlu**, best known as the location of the nation's press, whose offices are mainly located along Babıali Caddesi and Turkocağı Caddesi. In recent years increasing violence—including a murder in 1990 over a bad restaurant review—have established journalism as one of Turkey's high-risk industries, providing ample copy for the most sensationalist among them. Turkish *Playboy* also has its offices in Cağaloğlu, soft porn being one of the country's major growth industries.

For visitors, though, Cağaloğlu's major attraction is its **hamam** (Yerebatan Caddesi 34, women's entrance on Cağaloğlu Hamam Sok; 7am–10pm for men, 8am–9pm for women), the most popular baths this side of town, famous for their beautiful *hararets* (steam rooms), open cruciform chambers with windowed domes supported on a circle of columns. The baths were built in 1741 by Mahmut I to pay for the upkeep of his library in Aya Sofya, and the arches, basins and taps of the hot room, as well as the entries to the private cubicles, are all magnificently Baroque. Western weight-watchers should take note of the masseurs in the baths to appreciate what pride of bearing can do for a little fat.

Sirkeci, the area immediately below the main railroad station, is a major ferry port, with boats for the Princes' Islands, the Bosphorus and the Golden Horn all leaving from landings around here. Seen from the Galata Tower across the Horn, the buildings above the water form a foreground to the skyline of Beyazit and Sultanahmet, with Yeni Cami directly below Nuruosmaniye, the Egyptian Bazaar below Beyazit Camii, and Rüstem Paşa Camii below the Beyazit fire tower. The old Galata bridge is currently located in front of Yeni Cami, while the new one is nearing completion alongside it.

Yeni Cami and the Spice Bazaar

The **Yeni Cami** is a large, gray, and frankly ugly building, whose steps form a popular stamping ground for hawkers, pickpockets, and pigeons. It was the last of İstanbul's imperial mosques to be built in the classical era, however, and its history gives an interesting perspective on harem power struggles. It was built for the Valide Sultan Safiye (The Light One, a beautiful Venetian woman who some said was a Venetian spy), mother of Mehmet III and one of the most powerful of the Valide Sultans, who ruled not only the harem but in effect the whole empire through the weaknesses of her son. Apart from this complex no other imperial *külliye* was built during the reign of her son, and the site she chose was regarded as wholly inappropriate. It occupied a slum neighborhood inhabited by a sect of Jews called the Karaites, who were relocated down the Horn in Hasköy, and a synagogue and church had to be demolished to make room for it. The site was also dangerously close to the water's edge, and the building program was constantly plagued by seepage from the Horn. The foundations that eventually withstood this seepage are a series of stone "bridges" reinforced with iron.

An even greater plague to the building program, however, was court politics. The original architect was executed for heresy, and the work was interrupted again by the death of Mehmet III and the banishment of his mother to the old palace. Construction had reached as far as the lower casements when it was halted, and the Karaites returned to camp out in the rubble; sixty years passed before the Valide Sultan Turhan Hatice, mother of Sultan Mehmet IV, completed the building. Today the mosque, which is more or less a copy of the Şehzade Camii, is characterized above all by its gloominess, partly due to the heavy eaves that overhang the washing area, but also a result of the heavy layer of soot from the nearby ferry port that covers its walls and windows. The interior is dominated by arabesque stencilling and poor-quality tiles.

Mısır Çarşısı

The nearby **Mısır Çarşısı** or Egyptian Bazaar, also known as the **Spice Bazaar** because the main bulk of produce sold here has always been spices, was part of the same complex and is far more atmospheric. Still a good place to buy anything from saffron to spice mixtures sold as aphrodisiacs, the bazaar is nowadays also good for towels, bed linen, *lokum* (Turkish delight), and basketware, while the large courtyard outside is lined with aviaries crowded with parrots and lovebirds as well as house plants and garden supplies. Completed a few years before Yeni Cami, the L-shaped bazaar was endowed with customs duties from Cairo (which explains its Turkish name). It has 88 vaulted rooms and chambers above the entryways at the ends of the halls; one of these, over the main entrance opposite the ferry ports, now houses the famous Greek *Pandeli Restaurant*, moved here after anti-Greek riots in 1955.

Rüstem Paşa Camii

One of the most attractive of İstanbul's smaller mosques, the **Rüstem Paşa Camii**, lies just a short walk west of the Spice Bazaar. Built for Süleyman the Magnificent's grand vizier Rüstem Paşa (who was responsible along with Roxelana, for the murder of the heir apparent Mustafa), the mosque is dated to the year he died, 1561, and was probably built in his memory by his widow Mihrimah, Roxelana's daughter.

Despite its setting in the midst of the bustling bazaar area of İstanbul, surrounded still by darkened backstreets of workshops and store rooms, Rüstem Paşa is no workaday piece of architecture. Designed by Sinan on a particularly awkward site, above a tangle of streets that seem to offer no room for such a building, you are hardly aware of its presence as you wander about in the streets below. At street level an arcade of shops occupies the vaults, and climbing up to the mosque itself is like ascending to some higher realm. There are steps up to the terrace from the Golden Horn side of the mosque and from Kutucular Sokak behind it. Through an attractive entrance portal on the Golden Horn approach, you encounter a wide courtyard and a tiled double portico along the west wall. It's almost like entering a theater, the tiles of the portico being the backdrop, and the mosque interior—the dimensions of which are not immediately realized—being "backstage."

The **tiles**, inside and out, are among the most profuse in any mosque in Turkey, and mainly of the very best quality from the finest period of İznik tile production, when the technique for producing tomato-red—slightly raised above the other colors—had been perfected. Designs, covering the walls, piers, and pillars, and decorating the *mihrab* and *mimber*, include famous panels of tulips and carnations, as well as geometric patterns, in such profusion that it pays to concentrate on them panel by panel to appreciate the subtlety of individual designs.

Inside there are galleries supported by pillars and marble columns, and about as many windows as the structure of the mosque will allow. This airiness was common in sixteenth-century mosques, a paradoxical contrast with a simultaneous Dark Age in learning, when sciences and logic were suppressed in favor of religious orthodoxy. Here it ensures that there is plenty of light to appreciate the surface irregularities of the tiles. Even the pendentives are tiled, with circular medallions containing inscriptions and surrounded by designs of flowers; only the ugly nineteenth-century painting, thoroughly incongruous and jarring, detracts from the overall effect.

Ancient Hans

The area behind Rüstem Paşa is a warren of antiquated streets, containing a few of the buildings that were there when the mosque was built. These alleys and their peculiar little specialist shops are interesting in themselves, but detailed exploration uncovers one of the best of all the city's Byzantine buildings, fascinating for its simple ordinariness. This is the remains of a commercial warehouse known as the **Balkapan Hanı**, the Han of the Honey Store. Situated on Balkapan Sokak off Hasırcılar Caddesi, this is one of several ancient *hans* in the neighborhood (others include Kızılhan and Hurmalı Han) about which practically nothing is known apart from their Byzantine origins. Aside from the original courtyard, which is now surrounded by later Ottoman structures, the remains of the Balkapan Hanı are all underground. The space is still being used to store imported goods—Japanese watch parts rather than Egyptian honey these days—but it's possible to look around with the help of one of the workmen who can be found in the courtyard. Steps down to the vaults are found in the middle of this courtyard, and below is a gloomy, cavernous space whose herringbone-brick vaulting is supported by rows of columns. The vaults are reminiscent of a Byzantine cistern, but the fact that they are still used for their original purpose, and that they are practically unknown to tourists, makes them all the more exciting to visit.

Galata Bridge and the Golden Horn

Back on the waterfront, the most prominent and popular landmark is one that's about to be shipped off to a destination still unknown at the time of writing. The **Galata Bridge** floats on pontoons, so that early every morning the central section can be towed out to allow ships a passageway between the Horn and the Bosphorus. Its two tiers have long been a focal point of the city's low-life, providing a marketplace for hawkers and a perch for fishermen. Few locals will eat in the disreputable restaurants along the lower level, but they are popular among those with an eye for a romantic setting. The bridge, which was built in 1912, is currently being replaced by another two-tier, six-lane monster, which will also have shops and restaurants on a lower tier. The new bridge will open upwards in the center to provide a passageway for ships.

One way of visiting the Horn is to ride one of the small ferries that ply up and down from the Galata Bridge to Eyüp, beyond the city walls. The boat service isn't as effective as the one serving the Bosphorus, being infrequent and none too strictly timetabled, but it's an enjoyable ride of ten minutes to Fener, 35 minutes to Eyüp. Times are posted on blackboards outside the boat stations.

The derivation of the name **Golden Horn**, *Chrysokeras* in Greek, is obscure (*Halic*, the Turkish name, simply means "estuary"), but one suggestion is that it was coined during the Turkish siege of the city, when all the gold and precious objects that the Byzantine citizens could collect were thrown into the inlet. Whatever the story, the name has become singularly inappropriate in recent years, since this stretch of water has become a dump for the worst of the city's filth and pollution. A clean-up program was initiated by İstanbul's former right-wing mayor Dalan, but the best time to make a trip up the Golden Horn is still winter, before the stench gets too high. Yaşar Kemal's description of the Horn from *The Sea-Crossed Fisherman* still rings true for those who have experienced the reek of this once-beautiful stretch of water:

> *The Golden Horn, that deep well surrounded by huge ugly buildings and sooty factories, spewing rust from their chimneys and roofs and walls, staining the water with sulphur-yellow rust, a filthy sewer filled with empty cans and rubbish and horse carcasses, dead dogs and gulls and wild boars and thousands of cats, stinking . . . A viscid, turbid mass, opaque, teeming with maggots . . .*

Despite its unwholesome condition, the Golden Horn is still one of the finest natural harbors in the world, and its fortunes have been closely linked with those of the city it serves. On two separate occasions, the capture of the Horn proved to be the turning point of crucial military campaigns. The first occasion, in 1203–1204, was when the Crusaders took the Horn and proceeded to besiege the city for ten months, until they breached the walls separating the inlet from the city. The second was a spectacular *tour de force* on the part of Mehmet the Conqueror, who was prevented from entering the Horn by a chain fastened across it, and so carried his ships overland at night and launched them into the inlet from its northern shore. Mehmet then proceeded to construct a pontoon across the top of the Horn across which he transported his army and cannons in preparation for the siege of the land walls, which were finally breached in 1453.

For the Ottoman Empire the Horn was a vital harbor, supplying the Genoan, Venetian, and Jewish trading colonies that had become established on its northern shore. Nowadays the shipyards at Hasköy turn out Turkish copies of Scandinavian naval vessels and cruisers in a convincing attempt to establish Turkey as a seafaring nation.

Both banks of the Horn have long been settled by İstanbul's minority communities, and the suburbs of **Balat** and **Fener** were once respectively Jewish and Greek ghettos. Nowadays these areas retain much of their individual character through the buildings, institutions, and community life of their respective faiths. Fener is still the location of the recently refurbished Greek Patriarchate, as well as of a number of churches and the gigantic red-brick Greek Lycée, high on a hill overlooking the water. If you are thinking of taking to the water, however, the most interesting trip would be to the Muslim district of **Eyüp** (p.117), a center of pilgrimage for the Islamic world.

Lâleli and Aksaray

Heading west from Beyazit up Ordu Caddesi you arrive at an appalling tangle of road intersections, the main focus of **Aksaray** (to the southwest) and of **Lâleli** (to the northeast). Both districts are run-down and short of any sense of community, partly because of the dispiriting effect of the roar of traffic on the main street but also because, in Lâleli especially, many of the inhabitants have not really settled or been accepted in Turkey, being Iranian refugees and Arab students. Turks often express antagonism or at least emphasise their cultural differences from other Islamic ethnic groups, and in Lâleli this manifests itself in a feeling of ill will which is certainly more pronounced than anything you are likely to feel in an area of İstanbul with a predominantly Greek or Jewish community.

Both quarters, though, have interesting mosques and converted churches, and it's certainly worth wandering away from the main road to explore some of them, especially if you're staying around here.

Lâleli Camii

The **Lâleli complex**, right on Ordu Caddesi, is in the Ottoman Baroque tradition of Nuruosmaniye and the Ayazma Camii in Üsküdar, but the mosque itself owes more to traditional Ottoman architecture. It was founded by Mustafa III, whose octagonal *türbe* is located at the southeast gate; Selim III, who was assassinated by his janissaries, is also buried there.

The main Baroque elements are the use of ramps, including one which the sultan would have ridden up to his loge; the grand staircases; and the detail, for example in the window grilles of the *türbe* and in the carved eaves of the *sebil*. Inside, a profusion of pillars dominates, especially to the west where the columns beneath the main dome seem to crowd those supporting the galleries into the walls. The paintwork is coarse and dull, enlivened only a little by a flood of light from the huge windows in the dome; in fact one of the few reasons for entering is to have a look at the sign at the entrance, asking you not to wear mini skirts or shorts and thanking you very much for your "coordination."

Back outside, the foundations of the mosque have been exploited to make space for a covered **market** or *arasta*. This is supported on eight pillars and its central hall is lit by high windows, adding an extra tier to the west facade of the mosque. The market is very much in use today, selling the cheapest of cheap clothes and acting as an inducement for the local populace to worship at the mosque.

Around Aksaray—some Minor Mosques

Aksaray spreads to the south and west beyond the Lâleli Camii, with a number of interesting but scattered sites. The **Murat Paşa Camii**, at the intersection of Millet Caddesi (the continuation of Ordu) and Vatan Caddesi, is one of two mosques in İstanbul in the old Bursa style, with rooms, leading off a central hall, that at one time were used as hostels for traveling dervishes. The mosque is beautifully carpeted and its two domes prettily painted, the westernmost one resting on an arrangement of triangles.

The **Külliye of Bayram Paşa**, five minutes' walk off Haseki Caddesi on the left, is worth a look for the small octagonal building in the courtyard which served partly as a *mescit* and also as a dervish ceremonial hall, where dervishes would perform the rituals of their particular sect. Farther along, walking away from Millet Caddesi, Haseki Caddesi becomes Hekimoğlu Ali Paşa Caddesi. Off to the left here, Davutpaşa Medresesi Sokak, leads to the remains of the **Davut Paşa Medrese**, which can only be investigated by asking a shopkeeper for access: surrounding shops use its courtyard as storage space, and the whole thing is in a glorious state of disrepair, grazed by the occasional wandering goat. A series of small brick domes are supported by reused Byzantine columns and capitals, creating rooms that once served as student cells.

Back on Hekimoğlu Ali Paşa Caddesi, three blocks farther along, the **Hekimoğlu Ali Paşa Camii** (1734–5) shows evidence of Baroque experimentation in elements like the Rococo-style carvings around the *sebil* in the courtyard, and its two-room *türbe*. The most interesting feature, however, is the domed chamber above the entrance portal, which was designed and still serves as a library. It is reached by a ladder, and the librarian seems happy for visitors to inspect the beautiful painted wooden cages that still contain books and manuscripts.

Another small but fascinating mosque in the vicinity is the **Ramazan Efendi Camii**, two side streets farther along, on a side street called Kuru Sebil Sokak. This may have been badly restored, with a flat wooden ceiling in place of its original wooden dome, but it's still one of the most famous of the Sinan mosques thanks to its extraordinary panels of faience tiles. These include some with geometric intertwining designs as well as other more traditional, but still exceptionally beautiful ones depicting vases of tulips and carnations. It is thought to be the last mosque built by Mimar Sinan, dating to his ninety-fifth year (1586).

The Aqueduct of Valens and Kalenderhane Camii

An alternative route from Beyazit into Lâleli takes you up toward the Şehzade Camii following the line of the magnificent **Aqueduct of Valens**. Currently undergoing renovation, the aqueduct was built as part of the late fourth-century waterworks rebuilding program carried out by the Emperor Valens, part of a distribution network that included the reservoirs in the Belgrade Forest and various cisterns located around the city center. It was in use right up to the end of the nineteenth century, having been kept in good repair by successive rulers, who maintained a constant supply of water to the city in the face of both drought and siege (which is more than can be said for the present administration). More than six of its original ten kilometers are still standing in the valley between the two hills of Fatih and Beyazit, and its height above Atatürk Boulevard is 18.5 meters.

The ninth-century Byzantine Church of Kyriotissa, near where the aqueduct now ends (Kalenderhane Camii Sok, 16 Mart Şehitler Cad; open for *namaz* only), was renamed **Kalenderhane Camii** after the Kalender dervishes who converted it into a *tekke* after the conquest. It has the cruciform groundplan typical of Byzantine churches of its time, but few original features remain inside: where mosaics once covered the walls and ceiling only bare brick is now visible (though this has been scrupulously restored and some of the original colored marble revetments and sculptural decoration have survived); the apse has been closed off (the *imam* doesn't know why, or where the key to the door is); and a truly vile carpet laid on the floor. Worst of all, the famous fourteenth-century frescoes of the life of St Francis of Assisi were removed after restoration in the 1970s, and are no longer on public display.

From upstairs in the *Café Plaza* next to the church you can get a good look at the exterior, with its layers of brick and stone, its windowed dome, and its newly leaded roof. During the school year the café is popular with bored-looking students playing *Okey* or some such mind-numbing pastime.

Şehzade Camii

Şehzade Camii, the Mosque of the Sultan's Son, was commissioned in 1543 on the death of Şehzade Mehmet, the 21-year-old heir to the throne and eldest son of Süleyman the Magnificent. The mosque complex was the first major commission of Mimar Sinan, and only the fourth imperial mosque in the city. Again, the exterior of the mosque is its strength. The entire complex stands on a terrace in a fairly open space so it can be viewed from some distance. The courtyard is the same size as the mosque itself, and is bordered by a portico whose arches have attractive pink and white marble edges. The two minarets are also worth a look: they are decorated in relief with stalactite *şerefes* (balconies) and terracotta inlay. Along the north and south flanks of the mosque are colonnaded galleries which disguise the buttresses and present attractive facades.

The interior is often criticized for being boringly symmetrical, the work of an engineer rather than a master architect. The central dome sits on a square room, and is supported by four semidomes and four huge piers. The idea, as with all Sinan's subsequent mosques, was to create an open, centralized interior, with as little obstruction of the *mihrab* as possible. On this occasion, though, it was achieved at the expense of the graceful aspects associated with Sinan's later works, and the decorations are charmless, the painting dull, and the carpets pretty shabby.

Sadly, the **tombs** which are perhaps the most impressive aspect of the complex are closed to the public. They are said to contain one of the finest collections of İznik tiles in the country. The *türbe* of Şehzade Mehmet himself was designed, according to an inscription over the door, to mirror paradise. It is tiled, mainly in apple green, in the *cuerda seca* technique, so that all the colors are outlined with a thin black line. The *türbe* also contains original sixteenth-century stained glass, almost as rare as the tiles themselves.

Outside the main door of the mosque courtyard, to the west of the complex, there's a pleasant **park** with a good view of the mosque, the Valens Aqueduct, and Fatih Camii. Immediately northeast is the **Burmalı Mescit Camii**, an attractive little mosque dating from the middle of the sixteenth century. Its twisted minaret (Burmalı means "with twists") is unique in İstanbul and it has four pilfered Byzantine Corinthian capitals in the porch (since restoration, these are in fact copies). The graveyard has a fine display of carved tombstones that have also been restored to good effect, revealing the minor differences between the various carved turbans and fezes on the stones which were meant to indicate the rank of the men buried here.

Zeyrek

Across Atatürk Bulvarı, the aqueduct continues into **Zeyrek**, an attractively seedy area notable for its steep, cobbled streets, and ramshackle wooden houses interspersed with small mosques. There are also wonderful views of the Süleymaniye mosque complex. Crossing Atatürk Bulvarı can be something of an ordeal, as local drivers seem to regard it as a Grand Prix test track. Once across, follow İtfaiye Caddesi, turn onto Zeyrek Caddesi and then right onto Yeni Akıl Sokak, and continue straight up İbadethane Arkası Sokak to reach **Zeyrek Camii**, the former Church of the Pantocrator.

This twelfth-century church was converted into a mosque at the time of the Conquest and is officially open only at prayer times, though you may be able to persuade the *imam* to open the door for you (his house is up the stone steps behind the wooden door, next to the mosque). The building originally consisted of two churches and a connecting chapel, built between 1118 and 1136 by John II Comnenus and the Empress Irene. The chapel was built as a mausoleum for the Comneni dynasty, and continued to be used as such by the Paleologus dynasty. Although the tombs have been removed, there is still evidence of the graves beneath the pavement. The Empress Irene also founded a monastery nearby which was to become one of the most renowned religious institutions in the empire, and later the official residence of the Byzantine court, after the Great Palace had been reduced to a ruin. No trace remains of the monastery nor of its hospice, asylum, or hospital.

The mosque, which occupies the south church, is also in an advanced state of dilapidation, and it's difficult to believe that it was once an imperial mausoleum. Among the surviving features are the revetments of the south apse and the original marble door frames. The floor, naturally, is covered in carpets, but the *imam* may pull one of these back to give a glimpse of the colored marble underneath: an interlacing geometric pattern with figures of animals in its borders.

Another attractive Byzantine church can be found within walking distance, albeit on a rather convoluted route. To get there, return to İbadethane Sokak, and follow this to Çirçir Caddesi. Take a right onto Hacı Hasan Sokak, at the end of which is the Eğri Minare Camii, the Mosque of the Crooked Minaret. Turn right and then left onto Küçük Mektep Sokak, and you'll see the church, now known as the **Eski İmaret Camii**, ahead of you. To get in you'll need to arrive at *namaz* time or hope to find the *imam* at home (his house is connected to the mosque down a flight of stone steps). Founded at the end of the twelfth century by Empress Anna Delessena, the mother of Alexius I Comnenus, it is a four-column structure similar to the south church of the Pantocrator, evidence of a return to traditional Byzantine forms, perhaps in reaction to the encroaching political threat from east and west.

It has one of the most interesting exteriors of all the Byzantine churches in İstanbul. As ever it's hemmed in by surrounding buildings, but in this case the wooden houses as you approach down Küçük Mektep Sokak provide an attractive frame. The roof and twelve-sided dome retain their original curved tiles, while the eaves are decorated with a zigzag of bricks. Other designs in the brickwork include swastikas and Greek keys. Inside, some of the original fittings remain, notably the red marble door frames and a floral decoration around the cornice supporting the dome. The two side apses also retain their original windows and marble cornice.

Back toward the aqueduct, the **Çinili Hamam** or Tiled Baths on İtfaiye Caddesi make a refreshing antidote to sightseeing. This double hamam was built for the great sixteenth-century pirate-admiral Barbarossa and has been beautifully restored to working order, with a particularly friendly atmosphere. Notice the huge dome and the marble floors and fountain of the *camekân*, the enormous octagonal marble massage table in the main room of the *hararet* (the steam room), and the toilets, which are continually flushed by water draining from the *hararet*. There are still a few of the original tiles on the walls in the men's section, but none are evident through the continuous clouds of steam in the women's baths. The blissful bath experience can be nicely rounded off in the *Gül Lokantası*, behind the basketball court on the other side of İtfaiye Caddesi. This little basement kebab joint has a discreet but friendly atmosphere peculiar to establishments in areas slightly off the tourist agenda, and as such is a rarity in İstanbul.

The **Karikatür Müzesi**, or Museum of Caricatures (Tues–Sun 10am–5:30pm; $1), is back on Atatürk Bulvarı between Cemal Yener Tosyalı Caddesi and the aqueduct, housed in the rooms of a *medrese* arranged around a pretty garden courtyard with a marble fountain. Cartoons are an important popular art form in Turkey: most papers employ a number of cartoonists, and the weekly *Gırgır* was the third-best-selling comic book in the world before many of its employees left to set up the rival *Avni*. The exhibition changes every week, and silk screen and other workshops, including some for children, are organized by the museum.

Fatih

Initial impressions of the area called **Fatih** (The Conqueror) may be favorable: it is quieter than the center of town, and can at first seem to have a more relaxed atmosphere. In fact this is one of the few areas in İstanbul, and even in Turkey generally, where Islamic orthodoxy is coupled with an air of intolerance toward visitors of different religious and cultural persuasions. If you spend any time here, you'll notice that people dress differently—there are more covered women in the streets, many of them in full *chador*, little girls wear headscarves, while old men sport long white beards and knitted caps—and even the language spoken on the streets is different, full of guttural-sounding Arabic borrowings long ago discarded elsewhere in Turkey. People are more likely to take exception to naked limbs, or (perhaps understandably) to having their picture taken without due warning. All of which is not to say you shouldn't visit: only a very small minority of people are likely to show hostility toward foreigners even in Fatih, and it's certainly worth braving such a minor cold front to see the Selimiye, Fenarı İsa, and Fethiye mosques.

To get to Fatih, simply follow the line of the Valens Aqueduct from the north side of Atatürk Bulvarı and keep going in the same direction when you run out of aqueduct, or from Sultanahmet take any bus going to Edirnekapı and get off at the Fatih mosque complex. On the southwest side of the aqueduct, nearest to the main road, a pleasant tea garden is situated in a park alongside the **Fatih monument**. This bronze statue commemorates the events of 1453, when İstanbul fell to Mehmet II, the Conqueror (Fatih Sultan Mehmet as he is known in Turkish). The Conqueror and his horse are suspended from a concrete pillar between two groups of figures, one of learned men in turbans, including Mehmet's *hoca* (teacher), and the other of his standard bearer and two janissaries. The inscription notes that the monument was erected not in memory of the conquest but of the Conqueror, universally remembered for effecting the transition between two eras, and that even the figure of Ulubatlı Hasan, the standard bearer, has not been give a weapon for this reason.

Fatih Camii

The **Mosque of the Conqueror**, on İslambol Caddesi, was begun ten years after the conquest of İstanbul, in 1463, and completed in 1470. In 1766 it was almost completely destroyed in an earthquake: only the courtyard, the entrance portal of the mosque, the south wall of the graveyard, and the bases of the minarets survived; the rest was rebuilt.

The **outer precinct** of the mosque—which is always open—is large enough to accommodate the tents of a caravan. It is enclosed by a wall and, to north and south, by the *medrese* buildings, which accommodated the first Ottoman university. The inner courtyard of the mosque is one of the most beautiful in the city. Verd antique and porphyry columns support a domed portico with polychrome edges, and the eighteenth-century fountain with its wide canopy is surrounded by four enormous poplar trees. Over the windows outside the courtyard in the west wall the first verse of the Koran is inscribed in white marble on verd antique, while at either end of the mosque portico there are inscriptions in the early İznik *cuerda seca* technique. The inscription over the mosque portal gives the date and dedication of the mosque and the name of the architect, Atık Sinan, who was supposedly executed the year after the completion of the mosque on the orders of Mehmet because the dome wasn't as large as that of Aya Sofya.

The **interior**, painted in drab colors without a tile in sight, is most remarkable for being so well frequented that it is rarely empty even outside prayer times. It appears to be a social meeting place as well as a center of serious Koranic study for both women and men. As in all mosques, the men occupy the main body of the building while the women's section is confined to the anterior regions, where there's an unusual old bronze water pump with silver cups here.

The **tombs** of Mehmet II and one of his wives, Gülbahar, (Wed–Sun 9:30am–4:30pm) are situated to the east of the mosque. The originals were destroyed in the earthquake, and while that of Gülbahar is probably a facsimile of the original, the *türbe* of the Conqueror is sumptuous Baroque. **Çorba Kapısı**, the Soup Gate, to the southeast of the mosque, is original, inlaid in porphyry and verd antique. The gate leads to the nearby *tabhane*, the hospice for traveling dervishes, which has recently been restored and is now used as a Koran school.

Other Mosques in Fatih

Yavuz Selim Camii, on Yavuz Selim Caddesi, is a twenty-minute walk from Fatih Camii. Alternatively, you could take a ferry up the Golden Horn from Eminönü to Aykapı İskelesi and walk up to the mosque, again about twenty minutes. Built on a terrace on the crest of one of İstanbul's seven hills (the fifth, counting from Topkapı's), the mosque holds a commanding position over the surrounding suburbs, and viewed on the approach down Yavuz Selim Caddesi it presents one of the most impressive facades to be seen in the city. This is mainly because of its position next to the **Cistern of Aspar**, one of three open cisterns built during the fifth and sixth centuries in Constantinople; more recently the space contained market gardens and a village, but these were cleared away as part of Mayor Dalan's slum-clearance program, and although a brand-new covered market was promised in its place, the cistern is still a wasteland, across which you get a clear view of the mosque.

The mosque of Yavuz Selim, **Selim the Grim**, was probably begun in the reign of Selim and completed by Süleyman, but its dates are not certain. Close up, the exterior is rather bleak, a fitting memorial to a man with such a reputation for cruelty. Here is no pretty cascade of domes and turrets, just a large dome squatting above a square room with a walled courtyard in front of it. Once **inside** the walls of the courtyard, however, this simple, restrained building emerges as one of the most attractive of all the imperial mosques. The central fountain is surrounded by tall cypress trees and the floor of the portico is paved with an attractive floral design, while its columns are a variety of marbles and granites.

The **domed rooms** to the north and south of the mosque—which served as hostels for traveling dervishes—are characteristic of early Ottoman architecture, seen particularly in the Yeşil Camii at Bursa. In the mosque itself, long pendentives alternate with tall arches supporting the great shallow dome, which is hardly painted at all but is inset with stained-glass windows. The lack of decoration, combined with an expanse of green carpet and gray marble, is very attractive. Under the sultan's loge (supported on columns in a variety of rare marbles) is paintwork in designs reminiscent of the delicacy of Turkish carpets or ceramics—a great relief after an excess of arabesque stencilling; in places, bunches of flowers are tied with painted bows which cannot predate the eighteenth century, but the rest of this paintwork may be original.

The **tomb of Selim the Grim** (Wed–Sun 9:30am–4:30pm), beside the mosque, has lost its original interior decorations, but retains two beautiful tiled panels on either side of the door. Other **tombs** in this complex include that of four of Süleyman the Magnificent's children, probably a work of Sinan.

A comfortable fifteen-minute walk from Yavuz Selim Camii—follow Daruşşafaka Caddesi northwest until it becomes Manyasizade Caddesi—is Fethiye Camii, the former **Church of Theotokos Pammakaristos**. This twelfth-century church was one of the few that remained in the hands of the Byzantines after the Conquest, and was home of the Greek Orthodox Patriarchate from 1456 to 1568. Mehmet II would come here to discuss matters of theology with the Patriarch Gennadius, leading to the supposition in the West that he intended to convert to Christianity. The church and chapel were reconsecrated as a mosque in 1591 and called Fethiye (Victory) Camii to commemorate the end of the Persian wars. At the time of writing it's not worth making this trip unless you've received permission to visit in advance from the Directorate of Aya Sofya, located in the grounds of Aya Sofya museum—you won't be admitted to see the mosaics without some kind of official sanction, preferably a written document.

The **mosaics**—which are really what you come here to see—are all located in the memorial chapel erected in memory of General Michael Doukas Glabas Tarchaniotes, who died in 1310, by his widow Maria. This small chapel, crammed with mosaics, is located to the south of the mosque, closed off by partitions, and can only be opened by its curator. Among the highlights are, in the dome, Christ Pantocrator surrounded by twelve Prophets; a Deisis with Christ in the apse; the Virgin on the left wall; John the Baptist on the right; and four archangels in the vault above. There is also a mosaic of the baptism of Christ on the vault of the south aisle. The inscription on the south wall, in gold letters against a blue ground, is a poem by Manuel Philes commemorating the love of Maria for her husband:

> *Therefore I will construct for thee this tomb as a pearl-oyster shell,*
> *Or shell of the purple dye, rose of another clime,*
> *Even though being plucked thou art pressed by the stones*
> *So as to cause me shedding of tears . . .*

Ask to climb the stairs to the little balcony to the west of the chapel, as there is a better view of some of the mosaics from this angle.

Fener

Walking from Fethiye Camii toward the Horn, you're entering the district of **Fener**. The **Greek Orthodox Patriarchate** here, the spiritual headquarters of the church, is located on Sadrazam Ali Paşa Caddesi. Its most interesting feature is the gate, where the patriarch Gregory V was hanged in 1821 for treason against the Ottoman Empire. Since then it has been welded shut and painted black. Inside, the Patriarchal Church of St George on the lefthand side is a wooden-roofed basilica of the simplest early Byzantine style (domes and masonry roofs were forbidden to Christians in Ottoman İstanbul). It contains the patriarchal throne, whose origins are claimed to be fifth century but which in reality probably dates from the end of the Byzantine period.

The City Walls

İstanbul's old **land walls** are among the most fascinating Byzantine remains to be found in Turkey. Remnants in varying states of preservation can be found along the whole of their six-and-a-half-kilometer length, and in places modern reconstruction work provides a working model of the original walls.

A walk along the walls takes at least a day—longer if some of the major sites scattered along the way are to be explored at the same time. They currently provide shelter for many of İstanbul's homeless and destitute, and there are also gypsy encampments in the localities of Topkapı and Edirnekapı. If you show respect for peoples' privacy and don't barge through anyone's yard you'll probably be left to your own devices, but it can be alarming to be followed along the walls, especially since in places they are quite remote and secluded. If you're likely to feel threatened, don't go alone.

The land walls were named after Theodosius II, even though he was only twelve years old when construction began in 413. The inner walls—stretching from the Marmara to Tekfur Saray some two kilometers farther out than the previous walls of Constantine—were planned by Anthemius, Prefect of the East, to accommodate the city's expanded population. They were all but destroyed by an earthquake in 447 and had to be rebuilt in haste, since Attila's forces were on the verge of attack. An ancient edict was brought into effect whereby all citizens, regardless of rank, were required to help in the rebuilding, and the Hippodrome factions of Blues and Greens provided 16,000 laborers and finished the project in just two months. The completed construction consisted of the original wall, five meters thick and twelve meters high, plus an outer wall of two meters by eight and a half, and a twenty-meter-wide moat. This was sufficient to repel Atilla's Huns: they numbered several thousand but didn't have the skill or patience for siege warfare.

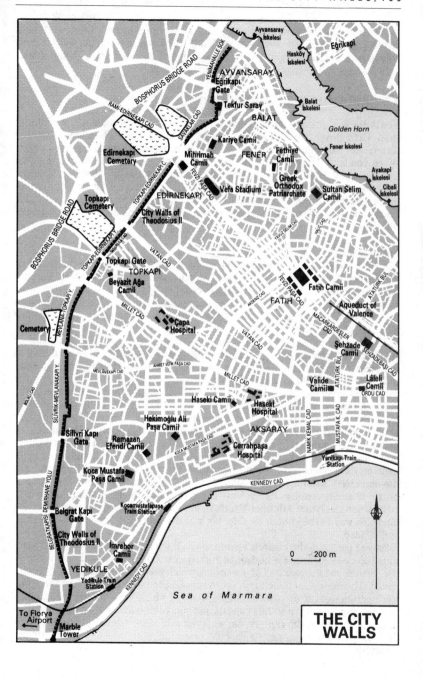

THE CITY
WALLS

Buses to the walls from Eminönü and Sultanahmet include #80 to Yedikule, #84 to Topkapı, and #86 to Edirnekapı, but the best way to reach the walls is probably to take a local *banliyö* train to Yedikule, on the Marmara shore. Bring a flashlight if you want to explore the fortifications thoroughly.

Yedikule and the Golden Gate

Yedikule is a quaintly attractive quarter, full of churches since it is a center of Rum Orthodoxy: the dwindling congregations of such churches, scattered throughout İstanbul, are the last remaining descendants of the Byzantine Greeks. When you leave the train station, on Yedikule İstasyon Caddesi, head away from the sea along Halit Efendi Sokak and you reach İmrahor İlyas Bey Caddesi, Yedikule's main street. Here you'll find a concentration of quaint, Greek-influenced houses and some attractive churches, as well as a few reasonable restaurants and cafés where you can stop before setting off on your exploration of the walls.

İmrahor Camii

The only ancient building of any note in the vicinity of Yedikule is the **İmrahor Camii**, the former Church of St John of Studius, at İmam Aşır Sokak, off İmrahor İlyas Bey Caddesi. Even this is almost completely ruined. To get there, walk straight up Halit Efendi Sokak from the train station and you'll see the remains on your right. Whatever anyone may suggest to the contrary, there is no entrance fee to see them.

The church, built in 463, was connected to a monastery of the *akoimetai* or "unsleeping," who prayed in relay round the clock. The monks lived according to the strict rules of Saint Basil: even melancholy was considered a sin and the monks were required to keep before them the specter of death by repeating the words "We shall die!" over and over. They still found time, however, to transcribe books for mass circulation, and even Russian monks came to the monastery to learn the trade and prepare books for distribution in Russia. The monastery gained particular renown under the auspices of the **Abbot Theodore**, an outspoken defender of images and critic of the Byzantine court, who established it as the center of a renaissance of Byzantine scholarship. Although he died in exile on the Princes' Islands, the reputation of the institution survived him, and the monastery was home to the University of Constantinople during the first half of the fifteenth century. Its greatest claim to historical fame, though, came in 1042, when the tyrant **Michael V** took refuge here from a popular revolution. He made his way to the church by ship, but was discovered, dragged from the altar, and blinded.

As you approach the **church entrance** you'll see four large columns with acanthus capitals supporting a horizontal carved entablature. This is the entrance to the narthex and the east wall of the atrium, which was square, and probably colonnaded. The interior of the church was a simple, almost square basilica; the aisles were partitioned off by rows of columns, six of which have survived, and again they are capped with acanthus capitals and support a horizontal entablature. The interlace floor is twelfth century, but what remains of the original fittings suggests that the church was sumptuously decorated in comparison with its simple structure.

The Yedikule Fortifications

The most impressive sections of wall here have been designated the **Yedikule Museum** (Tues–Sun 9am–5pm; $1), situated to the southwest of İmrahor Camii on Yedikule Meydanı Sokak, Yedikule Caddesi. Follow Kuyulu Bakkal Sokak (or, from the station, Yedikule İstasyon Cad) straight to the entrance.

The **Golden Gate**, flanked by two marble towers, was constructed on this site by Theodosius I in 390, before even the walls themselves. This monumental entrance stood alone, a triumphal arch in the path of important visitors of state and conquering emperors (generals were never permitted to pass through the gate even after successful campaigns). Nowadays the shape of the three arches is still visible on both sides of the wall, but it takes a degree of imagination to invest the structure with the glamor and dignity it must once have possessed. Michael Palaeologus was the last emperor to ride through the gate in triumph, when the city was recaptured from the occupying Crusaders. Afterwards the empire went into such decline that the gold-plated doors were removed and the entrance bricked up.

The other five towers of the Yedikule (Seven Tower) fortifications were added by Mehmet the Conqueror, and with their twelve-meter-high curtain walls they form the enclave which can be seen today. Despite appearances this was never used as a castle, but two of the towers served as prisons and others as treasuries and offices for the collection of revenue of the *Vakıf*, or Pious Foundation.

For those of a morbid disposition, the two **prison towers** are those immediately to the left of the entrance, the Tower with Inscriptions, and the tower on the south side of the Golden Gate. The inscriptions around the outside of the first of these were carved into the walls by prisoners, many of whom were foreign ambassadors on some hapless errand. The prison in the second doubled as an execution chamber: the wooden gallows and Well of Blood, into which heads would roll, are still to be seen, and the occasional instrument of torture can be found lying about outside in the courtyard. The most famous victim of the execution chamber was Osman II, deposed and murdered in 1622 by his janissaries, thus providing Ottoman history with its first case of regicide.

Yedikule is worth spending some time over, climbing around the battlements with the lizards. **Views** include the Marble Tower, where the sea and land walls meet beyond the rail line on the Marmara coast, and a good stretch of the walls to the south. There are also marvelous vantage points for train enthusiasts and for those with an active interest in the Turkish tanning industry. Notice also the **graveyards** outside the walls: the Turks buried their dead beyond the boundaries of the city, and until recently the city of İstanbul was still physically delimited by the line of the ancient city walls.

Toward Topkapı

Leaving Yedikule to walk along the walls you'll pass the first public gate, the **Yedikule Kapısı**. This is still in use: self-appointed and official traffic cops vie to direct traffic through the narrow entry, while a Byzantine eagle cut in the blackened marble above remains serenely oblivious to the commotion.

Most of the outer wall and its 96 towers are still standing, and their **construction** can be examined in detail if you don't mind clambering through the dirt and brick dust. The stone used is limestone, while the bricks, about a foot square and two inches thick, were sometimes stamped with the name of the manufacturer or donor and bear the name of the emperor in whose reign they were made. Cement mixed with brick dust was used liberally to bind the masonry. The towers had two levels, separated by the small brick domes used in Byzantine architecture to strengthen roof structures so as to support the weight overhead.

You can walk between the first gate and the second, **Belgrade Kapısı**, on a path leading along the top of the inner wall and then down to the terrace between the two walls. Belgrade Kapısı was a military gate, distinguished from the public variety by the absence of any bridge across the moat beyond the outer walls. It was named after the captives who were settled in this area by Süleyman the Magnificent after his capture of Belgrade in 1521. The walls here have been substantially renovated—they're floodlit at night—and a cannonball from the cannon of Mehmet the Conqueror has been stuck into the wall with the claim that it became embedded there during the siege of Constantinople in 1453.

Silivri and Mevlevihane Gates

From Belgrade Kapısı it's possible to continue walking along the inner wall for some distance, but at the end you'll encounter a nasty descent to ground level or a less difficult path to the terrace between the walls. Alternatively, coming from the center of town, there is a minibus-dolmuş service from Beyazit to **Silivri Kapısı** (the final destination being Zeytinburnu, which should be written somewhere on the vehicle). A diversion from Silivri Kapısı, requiring about an hour to complete, takes you through the Muslim and Christian graveyards to the east of the walls. Cross the main Belgratkapı–Demirhane Yolu Caddesi to the road leading off nearly opposite the gate, Seyit Nizam Caddesi, and take a right fork at the sacrificial sheep shop to Silivrikapı–Balıklı Caddesi. On your left along this street is the **shrine of Zoodochou Pigis**, the "Life-Giving Spring," called Balıklı Kilise or the "Church of the Fish" in Turkish. Buried in the graveyard here are several patriarchs of the Greek Orthodox Church, including the last patriarch, whose body was returned from the U.S. in 1972. The gravestones bear interesting masonic symbols, and marks of vandalism perpetrated during the anti-Greek riots of 1955.

The Christian shrine was built by Leo I and dedicated to the Virgin Mary, although it is thought that it could rest on the site of a pre-Christian sanctuary of Artemis. Successive emperors visited the shrine once a year, on Assumption Day, and it was rebuilt several times during the Byzantine period, although the present building dates from 1833. A flight of steps leads down to the chapel of the sacred spring, where you can peer into the sacred depths for fish.

Back at the walls, the walk to Mevlevihane Kapısı is best done along the backstreets on the other side to the main road, partly because the walls themselves are in too bad a state of repair to be worth exploring, but also because these are interesting suburbs, where wooden houses are interspersed with foundries and other fascinating workplaces.

There is more restoration work at the **Mevlevihane Kapısı**, and also some interesting inscriptions on the outer wall. The Theodosian walls reached completion at this gate, since the Greens, building from the Marmara, met the Blues, who were working southward from the direction of the Golden Horn. A Latin inscription to the left of the gate celebrates this fact: "By the command of Theodosius, Constantine erected these strong fortifications in less than two months. Scarcely could Pallas herself have built so strong a citadel in so short a time."

Topkapı Gate and Around

The Topkapı Gate is barely 1km farther on, but again it's difficult to walk along the walls themselves because of the gypsy encampments on this stretch. It's probably better to stick to the backstreets. Just south of Topkapı the walls have been destroyed to make way for the enormous thoroughfare of Millet Caddesi, and you will somehow have to cross this to reach Topkapı itself. On the other side follow the steep, stony path from Millet Caddesi to Paşa Odaları Caddesi until you reach the area called Kaleiçi and the **Topkapı Gate**. The "Gate of the Cannonball" is named after the most powerful cannon of Mehmet the Conqueror (see below), some of whose enormous stone cannonballs have been placed around the inside of the gate. To get here by public transportation, you can take a dolmuş from Karaköy, or any of a number of buses from Sultanahmet or Eminönü marked "Topkapı".

On the other side of the walls is the site of a national and international bus depot, the noise and general confusion of which is quite disorientating. This is also home to the **Topkapı Bit Pazarı** (literally "louse market"), where poverty reveals its worst in the painful sale and resale of grubby, disintegrated pieces of clothing.

At Kaleiçi you can get a decent lunch at any of the *lokantas* and *pide* or kebab joints on Topkapı Caddesi. At the bottom of the street, on the left, is the **Ahmetpaşa Camii**, a Sinan mosque dating from 1554. In the porch there are original tiles made in the *cuerda seca* technique, and despite some heavy-handed renovation it's worth having a look inside at the original arabesque paintwork under the galleries.

Another attractive mosque in this region is on the other side of the Trakya Otogarı on Topkapı–Davutpaşa Caddesi (not to be confused with nearby Davutpaşa Cad). The wooden **Takkeci İbrahim Çavuş Camii** (open for *namaz* only) is delightful and retains much that is original, including its wooden dome and some fine tile panels from the best İznik period (a few botched copies only serve to highlight the beauty of the real thing). The underside of the galleries and the stalactite pendentives also retain their original paintwork. The mosque was founded in 1592 by the eponymous *takkeci*, a maker of the distinctive felt hats (*takke*) worn by dervishes. The income of an artisan could not have been equal to the cost of building a mosque, however modest, and around this fact no doubt has grown the myth of its origins.

It is said that the hatmaker was told in a dream to go to Baghdad, where he would find a great treasure buried under a vine tree in the garden of an inn. He duly set off on his donkey and, arriving at the place of his dream, he began to dig under said vine. The innkeeper came out and inquired his business, admonished him and advised him to return to the place from which he had started his journey. On arriving back in Topkapı he found two bags of gold on the present site of the mosque. Burying one in the ground, he used the other to finance the building of his mosque, the idea being that if this mosque were destroyed then another could be built in its place with the buried gold. The *imam* who tells this story to visitors points out a panel of faience tiles depicting plump red grapes hanging on vines, jokingly suggesting that these are corroborative evidence of his story. And in such a poor parish, who can blame him for clinging to the fond hope that sufficient funds are buried beneath the wooden mosque to finance its rebuilding should the need arise?

Toward Edirnekapı

Between Topkapı and Edirnekapı there is a pronounced valley, formerly the route of the Lycus River, now occupied by Vatan Caddesi. At this point the walls are at their least defensible, since the higher ground outside gives the advantage to attackers. The famed **Orban cannon** of Mehmet the Conqueror was trained on this part of the walls during the siege of 1453—hence their ruinous state—and it was here that Constantine XI rode into the midst of the Turkish army after he realized that all hope of holding out was gone.

Beyond Vatan Caddesi, just inside the walls, lies **Sulukule**, where late at night travelers are persuaded to part with vast sums of money by gypsy dance troupes who live in the ramshackle houses in this area. The idea is that the brothers play *kemençe* and change your money into smaller denominations, which you duly offer to their sisters, who will dance for you, while you eat mother's home cooking. Turks who used to frequent the place will no longer go near it; but if you don't mind being ripped off to the tune of forty or fifty dollars in an evening it's an enjoyable place to lose it. It's advisable to go with someone who knows the area, though, or at least a Turkish-speaker, since it's potentially a little dangerous for lone foreigners.

Edirnekapı itself is a small-time suburb with a large bus station and no decent restaurants. The gate of Edirnekapı takes its name from the route to modern Edirne, which passed through here even in Byzantine times. Also left over from the Byzantine era is the smallest of the ancient city's open cisterns, located about 50m from the bus station on the left of Fevzipaşa Caddesi, below the level of the road. It's now the site of the Vefa sports stadium, but the original dimensions of the cistern can still be seen. Buses straight to Edirnekapı from town include the #28 from Eminönü.

The **Mihrimah Camii** is to the left of the bus station as you face the walls. Mihrimah, the favorite daughter of Süleyman the Magnificent, had a passion for architecture as great as that of her husband Rüstem Paşa, and the couple commissioned many of Sinan's early works, both in İstanbul and elsewhere. The Mihrimah Camii, situated on the highest of İstanbul's seven hills, dates from somewhere around the middle of the sixteenth century. Raised on a platform, the area beneath which is occupied by shops, it can be seen from all over the city and especially as you approach from Edirne.

The mosque and its outbuildings have suffered in two earthquakes, the second of which brought the minaret tumbling down onto the mosque itself, and during renovation the interior was filled with twentieth-century arabesque stencilling. Other aspects of the interior compensate, however, especially the light flooding in through the vast number of windows—fifteen in the tympana of each arch—and the graceful white marble *mimber*. Notice the skillful fake marbling of the arches under the eastern gallery. The mosque's nearby **hamam** has also been poorly restored but at least is still functioning.

Kariye Camii

To get to **Kariye Camii** (Wed–Mon 9:30am–4:30pm; $2) from Edirnekapı, take Yeşilcedirek Sokak off Fevzipaşa Caddesi. Bear left at Neşter Sokak and follow this around to Kariye Meydanı, where you'll see the mosque, grouped together with a Touring Club hotel and lilac-colored café. According to its own literature "this purple building with its white wooden carving, rather resembling a bird's nest or the old-fashioned Turkish cherry pudding with cream on top, bears the unmistakable Çelik Gülersoy stamp." Çelik Gülersoy is the president of the Touring Club, which undertakes much of the restoration work in İstanbul.

Whatever its surroundings, the former church of Saint Saviour in Chora does contain a series of superbly preserved frescoes and mosaics that are among the most evocative of all the city's Byzantine treasures. The church was probably built in the early twelfth century on the site of a building which predated the walls—hence the name "In Chora," meaning "in the country." The nave and central apse are all that remain of that church. Between 1316 and 1321 the states-man and scholar Theodore Metochites rebuilt the central dome and added the narthexes and mortuary chapel.

The **mosaics and frescoes** date from the same period as the renovations carried out by Metochites, and depict the life of Christ in picture-book sequence. The first series to be followed is a set of dedicatory and devotional panels located in the two narthexes. On entering the church, the most prominent of the mosaics is that of Christ Pantocrator, bearing the inscription "Jesus Christ, the Land of the Living." Opposite this, above the entrance, is a depiction of the Virgin and angels, with the inscription "Mother of God, the Dwelling Place of the Uncontainable." The third in the series is located in the inner narthex and shows Metochites offer-ing a model of the building to a seated Christ. The hat he is wearing is called a *skia-don*, or "sunshade." Saints Peter and Paul are depicted on either side of the door leading to the nave, and to the right of the door is a depiction of Christ with his Mother and two benefactors, Isaac (who built the original church) and a female figure, described in the inscription as "Lady of the Mongols, Melane the Nun."

In the two domes of the inner narthex are medallions of Christ Pantocrator and the Virgin and Child; and in the fluting of the domes, a series of notable figures—starting with Adam—from the **geneaology of Christ**. The **Cycle of the Blessed Virgin** is located in the first three bays of the inner narthex. The mosaics are based on the apocryphal gospel of Saint James, which gives an account of the birth and life of the Virgin, and was very popular in the Middle Ages. Episodes depicted here include the first seven steps of the Virgin (taken when she was six months old); the Virgin caressed by her parents, with two beautiful peacocks in the background; the Virgin presented as an attendant at the temple (where she remained from the age of three to twelve); the Virgin receiving a skein of purple wool, as proof of her royal blood; Joseph taking the Virgin to his house, in which is also depicted one of Joseph's sons by his first wife; and Joseph returning from a six-month business trip to find his wife pregnant.

The next cycle, located in the lunettes of the outer narthex, is that of the **infancy of Christ**. The mosaics can be followed clockwise, starting with Joseph dreaming, the Virgin and two companions, and the journey to Bethlehem. Apart from well-known scenes like the Journey of the Magi and the Nativity, there are depictions in the seventh bay (farthest right from the main entrance) of the Flight into Egypt, which includes the apocryphal Fall of Idols (white and ghostly look-ing figures) from the walls of an Egyptian town, as the Holy Family passes by. In the sixth bay is a scene depicting the Slaughter of the Innocents, complete with babies impaled on spikes. The inscription accompanying the picture of Herod says: "Then Herod, when he saw that he was mocked of the Wise Men, was exceeding wroth and sent forth and slew all the children that were in Bethlehem, and in all the coasts thereof, from two years and under."

The Cycle of Christ's Ministry fills the vaults of the outer narthex, and parts of the south bay of the inner narthex. It includes wonderful scenes of the Temptation of Christ, with dramatic dialogue (Matthew 4:3–10), which could almost be in speech bubbles, beginning:

> Devil: If thou be the son of God, command that these stones be made bread.
> Christ: It is written, Man shall not live by bread alone, but by every word that proceedeth out of the mouth of God.

Other scenes in this cycle deal with the miracles.

In the nave, the main frescoes echo the mosaics, depicting the death of the Virgin, over the door, and to the right of this a depiction of Christ with the inscription "Jesus Christ, the Land of the Living." To the left, the inscription accompanying the picture of the Virgin reads "Mother of God, the Dwelling Place of the Uncontainable." The best known of all the decorations in the church, however, are the frescoes in the **burial chapel**. These comprise depictions of the Resurrection, the Last Judgement, Heaven and Hell, and the Mother of God. Below the cornice are portraits of the saints and martyrs.

Most spectacular is the depiction of the **Resurrection**, also known as the Harrowing of Hell. The picture is a dramatic representation of Christ in action, trampling the gates of Hell underfoot and forcibly dragging Adam and Eve from their tombs. A black Satan lies among the broken fetters at Christ's feet, bound at the ankles, wrists, and neck, but still writhing around in a vital and lively manner. To the left of the painting animated onlookers include John the Baptist, David, and Solomon, while to the right Abel is standing in his mother's tomb, and behind him is another group of the righteous.

Other frescoes, in the vault of the east bay, depict the **Second Coming**. In the east half of the domical vault Christ sits in judgment, saying to the souls of the saved on his right, "Come ye blessed of my Father, inherit the kingdom prepared for you from the foundation of the world." To the condemned souls on the left he says: "Depart from me, ye cursed, into everlasting fire, prepared for the devil and his angels." Below, a river of fire broadens into a lake in which are the souls of the damned. Their torments are depicted in the lunette of the south wall, and comprise the Gnashing of Teeth, The Outer Darkness, the Worm that Sleepeth Not, and the Unquenchable Fire.

The **tomb** in the north wall of the paracclesion has lost its inscription, but it is almost certainly that of Theodore Metochites, the donor of the church.

Tekfur Saray

The remains of a late thirteenth-century Byzantine palace, **Tekfur Saray**, originally known as the Palace of the Pophyrogenitus, are located between Edirnekapı and Eğri Kapı alongside the walls. A sign above the entrance proclaims the entrance fee as 200Tl, but the occupants of the cottage inside the palace walls may try to charge you more. In actual fact, entrance is free. What you'll see are the bare walls of a simple rectangular structure—originally it was three-storied—decorated with brick and marble geometric designs, especially on the north facade of the courtyard.

From Tekfur Saray toward the Horn, the Theodosian walls were replaced in the twelfth century by a single, thicker wall without a moat, with strong, high towers placed close together. This section is currently being restored in gaudy white cinderblocks and red brick. Arriving at the Horn, whose newly laid-out gardens—part of Mayor Dalan's clean-up program—have yet to mature into convincing parkland, a right turn onto Demirhısar Caddesi will take you back toward the suburbs of Balat and Fener.

Eyüp

Beyond the walls, although more obviously reached up the Golden Horn, there's one final place worth seeing. **Eyüp** is the last ferry stop before the Horn peters out into two small streams (there are bus and minibus services from the city center), or it's an attractive walk from the walls. The only problem is crossing the Bosphorus Bridge arterial road; once you've done this, head north along Aşhane Sokak (where there's an attractive little mosque, the Aşçıbaşı Camii) and continue in the same direction, parallel to the Horn, until you come out at **Eyüp Camii**. This beautiful mosque complex is famous above all as the site of the tomb of Eyüp Ensari, the Prophet Mohammed's standard-bearer. One of the small group of companions of the Prophet, Eyüp Ensari was killed in the first Arab siege of Constantinople (674–678); a condition of the peace treaty following the siege was that his tomb be preserved. Later, the complex hosted the investiture ceremonies of the Ottoman sultans, described here by Pierre Loti (see below):

> *In the holy mosque of Eyoub, amid scenes of great pomp, Abdül Hamid girded the scimitar of Osman. After this ceremony, he marched at the head of a long and brilliant procession all through Stamboul, on his way to the Palace of the old Seraglio, pausing at every mosque and funerary kiosque in his path to pay the customary acts of worship and prayer . . .*
> *On the heights of Eyoub were massed a swaying multitude of Turkish ladies, their heads veiled with the white folds of the yashmak, while their graceful forms, in vivid silken draperies that swept the ground, could hardly be distinguished from the painted and chiselled tombstones beneath the cypresses.*

The mosque and tomb are about a ten-minute walk from the ferry dock on Camii Kebir Caddesi. They face each other across the courtyard that was the scene of the girding of the sultans, the exact site marked by a raised platform surrounded by railings, from which two plane trees grow. The original mosque, built by Mehmet the Conqueror in honor of Eyüp Ensari, was destroyed in the eighteenth century, probably by the same earthquake that wiped out Fatih Camii. The present Baroque replacement, filled with light, gold, pale stone and white marble, was completed in 1800. The **türbe of Eyüp Ensari** is far more compelling, however (footwear should be removed and women should cover their heads before entering). Its facade and vestibule are covered in tile panels from many different periods, and although the overall effect is a bit overwhelming, the panels constitute a beautiful and varied display of the artform—you could spend weeks visiting individual buildings to see as many different designs and styles.

Eyüp is still a popular burial place, and the hills above the mosque are covered with beautiful Ottoman tombstones. To the north of the mosque, off Silahtarağa Caddesi, Karyağdı Sokak leads up into the Eyüp Cemetery. Following the signs up this lane through the graveyard—most beautiful at sunset—you'll reach the **Piyer Loti Café**, where waiters in Ottoman costume serve up Turkish coffee. The cafe was made famous by the autobiographical novel of Pierre Loti (pen name of Julien Marie Viaud), a young French naval officer and writer of romantic novels and travel books who fell in love with the green eyes of a Circassian harem girl called Aziyade, in nineteenth-century İstanbul. Perhaps his most fitting memorial is this romantic little café overlooking the Golden Horn.

ACROSS THE HORN: TAKSİM AND AROUND

Life across the Horn revolves around the massive open plaza of **Taksim**, the modern business center of İstanbul. Such a large open space—wholly atypical of traditional Islamic city planning—is a glorious relief after you've been grubbing around in the backstreets of the old quarters, but as an imitation of a Western-style plaza it's not a great success because it lacks the essential monumental architecture to balance the size of the open space. *Taksim* in Turkish means "distribution," and in late Ottoman times the reservoir at the top of İstiklâl Caddesi was the main water distribution center for the whole city.

You're most likely to arrive on this side of the Horn via the Galata Bridge to Karaköy and the old Levantine areas of **Galata** and **Pera**, formerly inhabited by İstanbul's various ethnic minorities. The first of these were the Genoese, who built one of the city's most famous landmarks here, the Galata Tower. Not far from the northern end of the bridge is the entrance to the **Tünel**, İstanbul's subway system, which runs less than a kilometer up to the start of İstiklâl Caddesi. Built in 1875 by French engineers, this is one of the oldest subways in the world. From the top you can follow İstiklâl Caddesi all the way through to Taksim.

The wayward carousing that takes place in the drinking establishments, broth-els, strip joints, and more recently in the transvestite bars of the European quar-ters of İstanbul have afforded it notoriety since the sixteenth century. Taksim is still central to İstanbul's nightlife, whether this be classical opera and ballet, movie theaters, gay bars, or sex shops. At night, the suited business types give way to transvestite prostitutes who cruise the square and the city's gay bars, located on Siraselviler Caddesi off Taksim Square. Daytime pleasures across the Horn include a number of interesting monuments and museums, the brand-new İstiklâl tramway, and the opportunity to explore—away from the tourist trail—the steep, mysterious backstreets of İstiklâl, with their hidden bars, junk shops, and hamams.

Any number of **buses** cross the Horn via the Galata and Atatürk bridges. Take ones marked *Beyoğlu* or *Taksim* from Aksaray, or buses to *Karaköy* or *Taksim* from Eminönü. It's also pleasant to walk up to Beyoğlu, taking the steep Yüksek Kaldırım Caddesi past the Galata Tower and on up to Galipdede Sokak, well known for its book and musical-instrument stores.

Galata and Beyoğlu

The settlement at **Galata** is as old as the city itself. In the fifth century the area already had city walls, which Justinian restored, and toward the end of the century Tiberius is said to have built a fortress on this side of the Horn to facili-tate the closure of the water to enemy shipping.

The **Genoese** occupation of Galata began when they gave active support to Michael Palaeologus in his attempt to drive out the Crusaders. In return he signed a treaty in March 1261, granting them preferential treatment throughout his dominions, present and future, and signing Galata over to them as a semi-independent colony. From that date until the Turkish Conquest of Constantinople, the Genoese busied themselves with fortifying their stronghold and expanding its territory. The Byzantines no doubt lived to regret the privileges granted to the colony when the Genoese repaid them with neutrality during the final siege of Constantinople by Mehmet the Conqueror. The new sultan, however, showed his gratitude by allowing the Genoese to retain their commercial and religious establishments, although arms were to be handed over and walls torn down.

During the early centuries of Ottoman rule, Galata became established as the city's **European quarter**. Jews invited them from Spain by Beyazit II settled here, as well as Moorish, Greek, and Armenian refugees. In time, foreign powers established their embassies in the area, and it was also a popular haunt of visiting merchants, seamen, and dignitaries. Lady Mary Montague Wortley wrote in a letter in 1718 that very few Europeans were prepared to brave the journey across the Horn to "Constantinople," or old Stamboul:

> *Christian men are loath to hazard the adventures they sometimes meet amongst the Levents or seamen . . . and the women must cover their faces to go there, which they have a perfect aversion to do. 'Tis true they wear veils in Pera, but they are only such as serve to show their beauty to more advantage, and which would not be permitted in Constantinople. Those reasons deter almost every creature from seeing it, and the French Ambassadress will return to France (I believe) without ever having been there.*

The word **Pera** is Greek for "beyond" or "across," and it was originally used interchangeably with Galata to refer to the area across the Horn. Later it came to refer to the district above Galata, present-day **Beyoğlu**, to which the European quarter, in particular the diplomatic corps, gradually spread as Galata became too crowded. The *Pera Palas Hotel* was built in the late nineteenth century to accommodate a new influx of travelers from Europe, encouraged by the completion of the Orient Express in 1889. Around the same time Pera became a favored haunt—and subject matter—of a school of artists heavily influenced by European "salon" painting of the nineteenth century. The best-known member of the Pera school was Osman Hamdi Bey (1842–1909), the first Ottoman Muslim painter to have his work displayed abroad.

The **nightlife** of the quarter was notoriously riotous even in the seventeenth century, when Evliya Çelebi could write:

> *Whoever says Galata says taverns, because they are as numerous there as at Leghorn or Malta. The word Gumrah (seducing from the road) is most particularly to be applied to the taverns of Galata, because there are all kinds of playing and dancing boys, mimics and fools flock together and delight themselves day and night.*

By the nineteenth and early twentieth centuries, the area had become fashionable for its operettas, music halls, taverns, movie theaters, and restaurants; and it was only after the exodus of the Greek population from İstanbul in the 1920s that Galata and Pera began to lose much of the cosmopolitan flavor on which they had thrived. Other minorities followed, partly as a result of the wealth tax imposed on

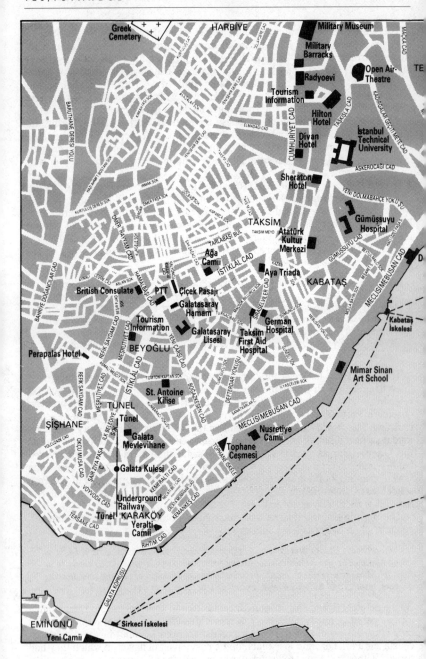

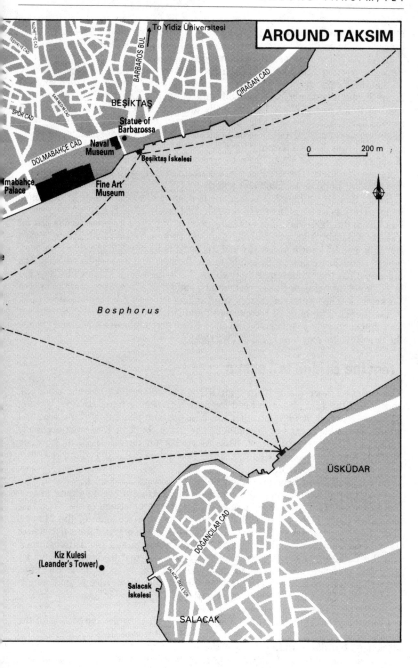

AROUND TAKSIM

To Yidiz Üniversitesi

BARBAROS BUL

ÇIRAĞAN CAD

BEŞİKTAŞ

SPOR CAD

SALHANE CAD

NÜZHETİYE CAD

TEŞVİKİYE CAD

Statue of
Barbarossa

DOLMABAHÇE CAD

Naval
Museum

Beşiktaş İskelesi

Imabahçe
Palace

Fine Art
Museum

0   200 m

Bosphorus

ÜSKÜDAR

DOĞANCILAR CAD

SALACAK SAHİL ESK

Kiz Kulesi
(Leander's Tower)

Salacak
İskelesi

SALACAK

ethnic communities between 1942 and 1944, and until recently it looked as if the area would be entirely destroyed by office building and lack of planning.

In recent years, however, there have been moves to restore the appearance of Beyoğlu, starting with its most famous food emporium, the *Çiçek Pasajı*. It may be that the facelift given to this seedy, thronging restaurant arcade killed some of its spirit, and it certainly frightened off some of the musicians and characters who used to frequent the place, but gradually the Pasaj is regaining its relaxed and riotous flavor, and it doesn't lose much for being vaguely clean. Next in line for a historical revamp is Beyoğlu's main boulevard, **İstiklâl Caddesi**, once known as the Grand Rue de Pera. Ground-floor businesses have been forced upstairs, and shopfronts are to be given over to museums and art galleries or to quality commercial outlets. The street is now a pedestrian mall, with İstanbul's only tram-line running along its 1.2 kilometer length.

So far, though, nothing has been done to destroy the sleazier side of Beyoğlu's image. The city's official **brothels** (known collectively as İki Buçuk, or "two-and-a-half," from the days when that was their price in lira) are located in Galata just off Yüksek Kaldırım Sokak; Sıraselviler Caddesi, running from Taksim back toward Beyoğlu, is best known for its gay and transvestite bars; while the side streets off İstiklâl Caddesi are lined with "adult" movie theaters and nightclubs which are as big a rip-off as their counterparts anywhere else in the world. Meanwhile, Beyoğlu is still good for bars, *meyhanes*, restaurants, and art movie houses, and the best of Turkey's clothing outlets are reappearing among İstiklâl's rejuvenated shopfronts. While there's little hope of recapturing the district's cosmopolitan past, when it was almost entirely populated by the city's European minorities, given the chance the new Beyoğlu may flourish in its own right.

From the Bridge to Taksim

The **Galata Tower** (daily 10am–6pm; $1) is the area's most obvious landmark and one of the first places to head for on a sightseeing tour, since its viewing galleries, reached by elevator, offer the best possible panorama of the city, and are an invaluable means of orientation. The tower, built in 1348, was originally known as the Tower of Christ. The inscription on its side records how, on Tuesday May 29, 1453, the Genoese surrendered the keys of the colony of Galata to Mehmet the Conqueror.

As you walk from here up Galipdede Sokak toward Taksim, an unassuming doorway on the right leads to the courtyard of the **Galata Mevlevihane** (Tues–Sun 9:30am–4:30pm), a former monastery and ceremonial hall of the "Whirling Dervishes" (see p.443). The building now serves as a museum of the Mevlevi sect, which was banned by Atatürk along with other Sufi organizations because of its political affiliations. Exhibitions include instruments and dervish costumes, and the building itself has been beautifully restored to late-eighteenth-century splendor, complete with the fake marbling that was so popular at the time. Dervish ceremonies take place sporadically at the Mevlevihane, and almost certainly on December 17, the annual Mevlana holiday—information on this should be available at the museum.

Continuing to the bottom of İstiklâl Caddesi, you pass the top station of the Tünel. Although the shops, seedy nightclubs, and movie theaters are the real attraction, **İstiklâl Caddesi** is also the location of an impressive number of churches. One of the best known of these is the **Church of St Antoine**, located in a courtyard just after Postacılar Sokak at number 325. A Roman Catholic church run by Franciscan monks, it was demolished to make way for a tramway at the beginning of the century but rebuilt in 1913, a nice example of red-brick neo-Gothic architecture. Also located at the Tünel end of İstiklâl Caddesi, in the grounds of the Dutch consulate, is the **Union Church of İstanbul**, a seventeenth- or early eighteenth-century building whose basement once served as a prison. At the Taksim end, next to the *Haci Baba Restaurant* at Meşelik Sok 11/1, **Aya Triada** is a large Greek Orthodox church founded in the late nineteeth century (open at 4pm for daily mass).

Taksim Square

The size of **Taksim Square** is undeniably impressive, which is just as well since there's little else to be said in its favor. Poor planning and confused traffic rob it of any real atmosphere; a busy bus station on the north side does little to enhance the ambience, nor do the large, impersonal hotels—including the luxury *Etap Marmara*—and other examples of misguided modern architecture that surround it. One exception to the otherwise gray and uninviting prospect is the **Atatürk Cultural Center**, to the east of the square. Its attractive foyer provides an ideal viewing gallery from which to observe the action below, whether this be daytime traffic jams or street life at night. Another plus is that the streets leading off the square, including Inönü Caddesi and Tarlabaşı Bulvarı are the best place in town to find classic 1950s **dolmuşes**.

The immediate environs of the square are disappointing if you're looking for decent **food**. There's a *McDonald's* at the beginning of Cumhuriyet Caddesi, whose novelty is beginning to wear off even for the Turks, and a café, *Sütiş*, on the square itself, which has good snacks but the rudest service in all of Istanbul.

The Military Museum

The **Military Museum** (Wed–Sun 9am–5pm), about 1.5km north of Taksim Square along Cumhuriyet Caddesi, is worth visiting mainly for the band that plays outside every afternoon that it's open, from 3–4pm. To get there, turn right after İstanbul Radyoevi and follow the road around to the left behind the military barracks; continue along this road, Gümüş Sokak, past the *Lutfi Kırdar Spor Salonu*, and the museum is on the right.

The **Mehter Band** originated in 1289 when the Selçuk Sultan Alâeddin Keykubad II sent a selection of musical instruments to Osman Gazi, founder of the Ottoman Empire. The band became an institution, symbolizing the power and independence of the Ottoman Empire; its members were janissaries, and they accompanied the sultan into battle. During public performances, members of the band sang songs about their hero-ancestors and Ottoman battle victories. They had considerable influence in Europe, helping create new musical styles such as Spanish *a la turca*, and inspiring numerous composers (examples include Mozart's *Marcia Turca* and Beethoven's *Ruinen von Athens Opus 113*). The kettledrum (*kös* in Turkish) was also introduced into the West as a result of interest in the Mehter bands. The band was abolished by Mahmut II along with the janissary corps in 1826, and only re-established in 1914, when new instruments were added. The pieces played nowadays include some that date from the seventeenth and eighteenth centuries, and others written by Giuseppi Donizetti for Mahmut II's new army.

Inside the museum you'll find an assortment of Ottoman armor and weaponry, along with various campaign memorabilia including the tent used by warring sultans, and a collection of miniature janissary costumes.

THE BOSPHORUS

One of the world's most eulogized stretches of water, the **Bosphorus** is a source of pride for İstanbul's residents—even those who have to commute across it daily on perilously overcrowded ferries—and admiration for visitors. The 30-kilometer strait divides Europe and Asia and connects the Marmara and Black seas. Its width varies from 660m to 4.5km, and its depth from 50 to several hundred meters. The main current flows from the Black Sea to the Marmara, while a strong undercurrent flows in the opposite direction. The importance of the Bosphorus can be measured by the extent and variety of traffic it supports, but its recreational assets are equally evident, whether you're boating or enjoying one of the many bars and restaurants overlooking the water.

For residents, the straits are a daily fact of life, one of İstanbul's most important transport arteries; as a visitor, too, you can use the Bosphorus to get around, but the ferry journeys often turn out to be a pleasure in themselves, if not one of the city's highlights. Along the way *yalis*, or waterside residences, mostly in a state of precarious disrepair, overhang the banks. There are also numerous mythical and historical associations: indeed the very name is derived from the Greek myth of Io, lover of Zeus, whom the god transformed into a cow to conceal her from his jealous wife Hera. She plunged into the straits to escape a gadfly—hence Bosphorus, or "Ford of the Cow." The Bosphorus was also visited by Jason in his quest for the Golden Fleece.

The regular ferryboats that weave their way up and down from shore to shore share the waterways with oil tankers, ocean liners, and cargo ships of every nationality. But despite the resulting pollution, the Bosphorus is full of **fish**: from porpoise and swordfish to red mullet and *hamsi* (a small fish belonging to the anchovy family). These are caught by professionals and amateurs throughout the year, and the shores are lined with restaurants from the Galata Bridge to the Black Sea.

There are various ways of touring the Bosphorus and its shoreside villages by **public transportation**, but the best way is probably to use a combination of ferries, buses, and dolmuşes so that you can see exactly what you want to in your own time. If you prefer to have your itinerary planned in advance, however, there are special **sightseeing boats** throughout the year (two daily in winter; three on weekdays and five on Sundays in summer) which leave from the first ferry landing in Eminönü. They're expensive (about $6), and only take an hour and forty minutes to get to their final destination in Anadolu Kavağı, but you can always get off and wait for the next one at a landing stage on the way. To ensure a good seat in summer, arrive at least half an hour before departure—it's not worth making the trip if you have to sit in the bowels of the boat with screaming children and no views.

To explore more economically and with greater independence you'll need a **ferry** timetable (*vapur tarifesi*, normally available from ferry *gişe*) and a handful of ferry tokens (*jetons*; also from any *gişe*) and bus tickets. The normal ferries are reasonably frequent, and if you get stranded up the Bosphorus after they stop running (the last one from Anadolu Kavağı in summer is at 5, 3pm) you can always resort to a bus or dolmuş, both of which run and European shores from village to village. There are jetties village on either side of the strait, but you only need jetons on side—it's free to come the other way.

The European Shore

The **European Shore** of the Bosphorus borders the modern city for some distance, and almost as far as the Bosphorus Bridge it's really the backyard of Taksim and commercial İstanbul. A backdrop of shipping companies and merchant banks, not to mention the central sorting office of the PTT, make **Karaköy** something less than a tourist mecca, while **Beşiktaş** is dominated by major roads and a bus terminal. Farther up towards the Black Sea the scenery mellows, but a result of their relative proximity to the center of town is that the most charming villages on this side—traditionally **Bebek** and **Trabya**, but now **Ortaköy** and **Arnavutkoy** too—are becoming popular haunts for the rich and careless who are responsible for the growing commercialization of what were once attractive waterside retreats.

Beşiktaş

Most visitors to **BEŞİKTAŞ** are here to see the Dolmabahçe Palace, successor of Topkapı as the residence of the Ottoman sultans. It's worth spending time in the neighborhood, however, since it's also the location of the naval museum, as well as of a couple of decent art galleries and the Yıldız Parkı and Palace.

Dolmabahçe Palace
Dolmabahçe Palace (Dolmabahçe Caddesi; Oct–Feb 9am–3pm, March–Sept 9am–4pm, closed Mon & Thur; guided tours only, $4) is the largest and most sumptuous of all the palaces on the Bosphorus built in the nineteenth century by various members of the Balian family. To the contemporary eye it's not so much magnificent as grotesque, a grossly excessive display of ornament and ostentatious wealth, suggesting that good taste suffered along with the fortunes of the Ottoman Empire. Classical Turkish architectural forms were being replaced by those of eighteenth- and nineteenth-century Europe, and while elsewhere these were successfully adopted into an oriental idiom, in Dolmabahçe there's a feeling that the wholesale adoption of western architectural forms constitutes a last-ditch effort to muster some respect for a crumbling and defeated empire.

The palace is situated on the site of the harbor from which Mehmet the Conqueror launched his attack on Constantinople, later to be used as a conveniently public location for **naval ceremonies** of the Ottoman fleet. The harbor gradually silted up and was completely filled in at the beginning of the seventeenth century (Dolmabahçe means "filled garden"). It later became a **waterfront grove** set aside for imperial use, with a number of small palaces and pavilions, which were destroyed to make way for Sultan Abdül Mecid's new enterprise: a palace to replace Topkapı as the imperial residence of the Ottoman sultans. This was built by the Armenian architect Karabet Balian and his son Nikoğos between 1843 and 1856.

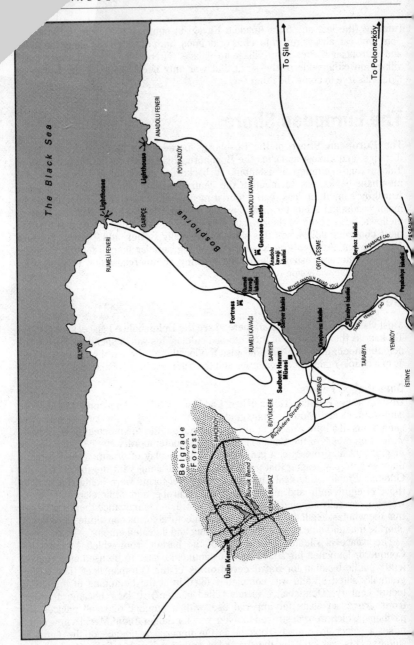

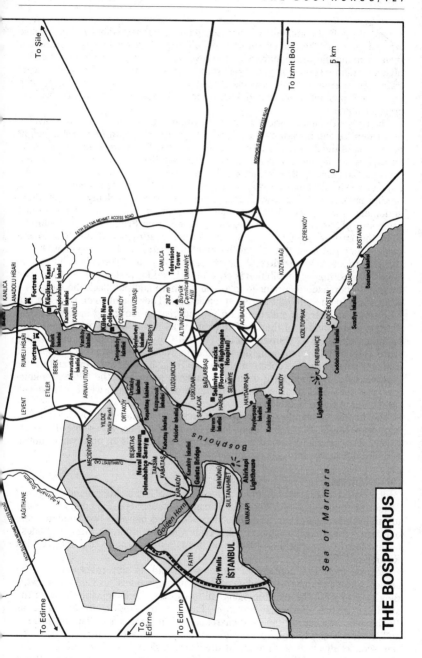

THE BOSPHORUS

To Şile

To İzmit Bolu

5 km

BOSPHORUS BRIDGE ACCESS ROAD

FATİH SULTAN MEHMET ACCESS ROAD

KANLICA
ANADOLU HISARI
Fortress
Küçüksu Kasrı
Anadoluhisari İskelesi
Kandilli İskelesi
KANDİLLİ
Kuleli Naval College
CENGELKÖY
HAVUZBAŞI
Çengelköy İskelesi
Vaniköy İskelesi
BEYLERBEYİ
Beylerbey İskelesi
ÇERENKÖY
CAMLICA
Television Tower
UMRANIYE
282 m
Büyük Çamlıca Hill
ALTUNIZADE
ACIBADEM
KOZYATAĞI
KIZILTOPRAK
ÇADDEBOSTAN
SUADIYE
BOSTANCI
Lighthouse
Caddebostan İskelesi
Suadiye İskelesi
Bostancı İskelesi
FENERBAHÇE
KADIKÖY
HAYDARPAŞA
Haydarpaşa İskelesi
Kadıköy İskelesi
SELIMIYE
HAREM
Harem İskelesi
Selimiye Barracks (Florence Nightingale Hospital)
BAĞLARBAŞI
ÜSKÜDAR
SALACAK
Üsküdar İskelesi
Kuzguncuk İskelesi
KUZGUNCUK
Ortaköy İskelesi
ORTAKÖY
Beşiktaş İskelesi
BEŞİKTAŞ
YILDIZ
Yıldız Parkı
MECİDİYEKÖY
CUMHURİYET CAD.
TAKSİM
KABATAŞ
Kabataş İskelesi
Naval Museum
Dolmabahçe Sarayı
KARAKÖY
Karaköy İskelesi
Galata Bridge
EMİNÖNÜ
Ahırkapı Lighthouse
SULTANAHMET
KUMKAPI
FATİH
City Walls
İSTANBUL
Golden Horn
Kâğıthane Stream
KAĞITHANE
LEVENT
ETİLER
RUMELİ HISARI
Fortress
BEBEK
Bebek İskelesi
Arnavutköy İskelesi
ARNAVUTKÖY
Yeniköy İskelesi
Çengelköy İskelesi

Bosphorus

Sea of Marmara

To Edirne

To Edirne

To Edirne

One of the first comments of your tour guide, whatever language he is speaking, will no doubt be that everything you will see colored yellow is **gold**. Rather than spending the whole tour trying to prove him wrong, you could more profitably use the time screening your eyes from the worst of the excesses and concentrating on more wholesome aspects of the tour, like the inlaid parquet floors, the translucent pink alabaster imperial baths, or the famous double staircase with its crystal balusters.

The palace retains an oriental feel in the organization of its rooms: it is divided into **selâmlık** and **harem** by the 36-meter-high **throne room** (double the height of the rest of the rooms). The ceremonies conducted here were accompanied by an orchestra playing European marches and watched by women of the harem through the *kafes*, grilles behind which women were kept hidden even in these days of westernization and reform. Other onlookers included members of the foreign press, from their own balcony, who certainly had plenty to keep them scribbling within these decadent walls. The four-ton chandelier in the throne room, one of the largest ever made, was a present from Britain's Queen Victoria.

In the east wing of the palace, the former apartments of the heir to the throne—entered from the side of the building nearest to Beşiktaş—now house the **Resim ve Heykel Müzesi**, or **Museum of Fine Arts** (Wed–Sun noon–4pm). The permanent exhibition is currently closed for restoration, but you may be able to persuade a curator to take you up there and pull back the curtains a crack to let in enough light to view the paintings. They mainly date from the late nineteenth and early twentieth centuries, and give an intriguing insight into the lifestyle and attitudes of the late Ottoman Turks. Some of the most interesting paintings are those by **Osman Hamdi** (1842–1910) and the impressionist painter **Ruhi** (1880–1931). Comparing these paintings with the miniatures on display at Topkapı Palace, the European influence on Turkish art is apparent, and rather disappointing. It would have been interesting to know how the Ottoman miniature and the works of artists in the tradition of Siyah Kalem would have developed without western influence.

The nineteenth-century **Dolmabahçe aviary** and Hareket Köşkü (Oct–Feb 9am–4pm, March–Sept 9am–6pm, closed Mon & Thur) are accessible via the art gallery. Peacocks and swans can be observed, and there's an observation house and bird infirmary in the same complex.

Deniz Müzesi

Back toward the ferry landing in Beşiktaş, the Deniz Müzesi or **Maritime Museum** (bus #25, #25A; Wed–Sun 9:30am–noon & 1–5pm) is one of the really fun museums in İstanbul. The collection is divided between two buildings, the one facing the water housing seagoing craft while the other, on Cezayir Caddesi, is devoted to the maritime history of the Ottoman Empire and the Turkish Republic.

Despite the dusty confines of the museum and its silly rules (stick to the carpets and don't turn the handles of the "working models" or God knows what they'll do to you), the **exhibits** can't fail to capture the imagination of even the strictest pacifist. Barbaros Hayrettin Paşa, better known in the west as **Barbarossa**, was one of the most charismatic of all figures from Turkish history, and **Turgut Reis**, his pirate colleague, is almost as fascinating. The two men were consecutively first admirals of the Turkish fleet, and there are extensive displays in the museum concerning their histories. Elsewhere most of the labels are in Turkish, but many of the exhibits, such as the enormous wooden figure-heads depicting tigers and swans, and the display of items from Atatürk's yacht, the **Savarona**, need little explanation.

Next door, the exhibition continues with a display of **caiques** belonging to the sultans—some with models of the oarsmen in fez and şalvar—and a piece of the chain used by the Byzantines to close off the entrance of the Golden Horn in 1453.

Other Sights: Yıldız Parkı

In the main square in front of the Beşiktaş ferry station, a **statue of Barbarossa** stands on a base inscribed with the poem, "From Whence This Sound of Cannons on the Horizons of the Sea?," by Yahya Kemal. Opposite the statue is his tomb, an early work of Mimar Sinan.

A short walk from this main square takes you past the **Çirağan Palace** (once a burned-out shell of a summer palace, now being converted into a hotel) to the entrance of **Yıldız Parkı** (winter 9am–5:30pm, summer 9am–6pm), a vast wooded area dotted with *koşks*, lakes, and gardens, which was the center of the Ottoman Empire for thirty years during the reign of Abdül Hamid. The buildings in and around the park constitute **Yıldız Palace**, a collection of structures in the old Ottoman style, and a total contrast to Dolmabahçe. The park and pavilions were restored by the Touring Club of Turkey in 1979, but not landscaped to such an extent as to detract from the natural beauty of their superb hillside location. Since then Yıldız Parkı has become one of the most popular places in İstanbul for city-dwellers thirsting for fresh air and open spaces—on holidays the park is always crowded.

Most of the **pavilions** date from the reign of Abdül Aziz, but it was Abdül Hamid—a reforming sultan whose downfall was brought about by his intense paranoia—who transformed Yıldız into a small city and power base. Among its many buildings were the Mabeyn, the great palace used for official business; the Şale Köşkü, where receptions were held; and the Küçük Mabeyn where the sultan lived; also in the park were a factory for Yıldız porcelain and a theater.

The most important surviving building is the **Şale Köşkü** (Oct–Feb 9:30am–4pm; March–Sept 9:30am–5pm, closed Mon and Thur; $1.50), designed to resemble a Swiss chalet. It was built for the first visit of Kaiser Wilhelm II in 1889, and presumably its dimensions were meant to impress: the Hereke carpet in the Ceremonial Hall is so big (approximately 400 square meters) that part of a wall had to be knocked down to install it.

To reach the other palace buildings you need to return to the main square in Beşiktaş and take any bus or minibus up Barbaros Bulvarı (it's not far to walk, but it's a steep hill). Follow the signs to Yıldız Üniversitesi and Şehir Müzesi off to the right. The main buildings of the palace are not open to the public, but subsidiary structures house a small art gallery occasionally used for exhibtions of popular modern artists; the **Belediye Şehir Müzesi**, or State Museum (8am–4:30pm; closed Mon, Tues and Thur); and the **Sahne Sanatları Müzesi**, or Museum of Theater. The former includes a miscellaneous collection of knick-knacks, ornaments, and paintings from the eighteenth and nineteenth centuries, many of them peculiar to the Ottoman way of life, such as an instrument for making *tesbih* (Islamic worry beads) and a janissary's chin support. The theater museum has a fascinating collection of items illustrating the history of Turkish theater from its Armenian roots to its heightened respectability under the patronage of Atatürk.

Ortaköy and Arnavutköy

The two villages on either side of the first suspension bridge across the Bosphorus, built in 1974, are former Bosphorus backwaters which are becoming increasingly popular haunts of "Bağdat children," İstanbul's yuppy youths. To get to Ortaköy take a #23B, #B2, #40A, or #40 bus from Taksim, or a #25 from Eminönü, or take a bus or ferry to Beşiktaş and walk (about fifteen minutes). The latter is the best bet on holidays and weekends, since the traffic is terrible on this road. The village now has a **Sunday market** largely frequented by the *entel* set, intellectuals with a penchant for large crowds and small talk; the stalls aren't very exciting but you can find some nice ceramics. Ortaköy is also a popular **evening haunt** of the same crowd, and consequently restaurant decors and prices have gone way up the scale; anything on the waterfront will certainly be overpriced.

The small **Sinan hamam** in the center of town, by contrast, is much better value than many of the larger baths, at under $3 per person ($4 with a massage). The waterfront is a favorite spot for fishing, and it's also the location of an attractive little Baroque mosque and some of the liveliest teahouses on the Bosphorus.

Farther up the European Shore

It's an easy enough matter to get up the Bosphorus as far as the delightful fish restaurants in SARIYER and RUMELI KAVAĞI, but you may have trouble getting back again. The last boat back is the special Bosphorus tour boat which leaves Rumeli Kavağı at 5:20pm in summer, 3:10pm in winter. If you're intending to make an evening of it, the last bus from Rumeli Kavağı to Eminönü, the #25A, leaves at 10pm from the bus stop near the jetty. The last dolmuş to Sariyer leaves at 11pm, and there are later buses from there.

On the way up there are various sites worth looking into, notably the **fortress of Rumeli Hisarı** (Tues–Sun 9:30am–5pm; $2.50). Larger and more commanding than its counterpart across the straits, this early Ottoman fortress is an impressive sight, especially bearing in mind that it was constructed in just four months, in 1452, before the Ottoman conquest of the city.

Belgrade Forest

The land west of Sariyer is occupied by the **Belgrade Forest**, originally a hunting preserve of the Ottomans. The only sizable piece of woodland in the vicinity of the city, Belgrade Forest has always been popular among Turks, as well as expatriates seeking a pastoral—not to say elite and Christian—retreat from the rigors of the city. The forest and Belgrade village, of which only a few remnants remain, were inhabited since Byzantine times by the caretakers of the reservoirs that supplied the city with water.

The name came about after the capture of Belgrade in 1521, when a community of Serbian well-diggers, prisoners-of-war of Süleyman the Magnificent, were settled here to take over the care and upkeep of the water supply system. In the seventeenth century its attractions were discovered by the foreign community of İstanbul, who came to the village to seek refuge from a particularly nasty pestilence which was wiping out half the city, and for the next century or so many wealthy Christians had second homes here. In the 1890s the village was evacuated by Abdül Hamid II, who in his paranoia believed that the inhabitants were polluting the city's water supply.

To get to the forest take a **dolmuş** from Çayırbaşı, between Sariyer and Büyükdere on the Bosphorus, to BAHÇEKÖY, which is at the edge of the forest.

A sophisticated system of dams, reservoirs, water towers, and aqueducts is still in evidence around the forest. The water towers, or *su terazı*, were an ingenious device for transporting water over long distances and storing it en route: water descends into underground conduits where pressure builds up and forces the water up into the tower. When the tank is full the water is sent underground with enough force to travel up into the next tower, and so the process continues. By this means, and by aqueducts, water was brought from the forest to the city.

The most impressive of the aqueducts in the forest is the Uzun or **Long Aqueduct**, beyond Kemer Burgaz on the way to Kısırmandıra. Its tiers of tall, pointed arches across the Kağithane Suyu (one of the streams that feeds the Golden Horn) were built by Sinan for Süleyman the Magnificent in 1563. Easier to get to from Bahçeköy is the **Büyük Bend** reservoir. Follow the blue sign marked "Bentler" out of the village to Neşet Suyu, half an hour's walk from the town, where there's a small tea garden and a first-aid station. From here it's another beautiful half-hour (2km) walk to the reservoir. Gymnastic equipment, including parallel bars and a wooden horse, can be glimpsed through the trees on the road between the Neşet picnic area and Büyük Bend, having been provided for the benefit of the amateur athletes who make for the forest in droves to partake in jogging and working out away from the fumes of the city. The reservoir, which was originally built in Byzantine times, is one of the oldest parts of the water system.

Sadberk Hanım Museum

Back on the Bosphorus, one more essential place to visit is the **Sadberk Hanım Müzesi**, located 300m south of the Sariyer jetty at Piyasa Caddesi 27–29, Büyükdere (10:30am–4pm, closed Wed; $1.20). Bus #25 to Sariyer from Eminönü and Beşiktaş passes by it. This excellent collection of miscellaneous archaeological and ethnographical objects is located in a wooden house that formerly belonged to an Armenian civil servant who became a politician and died in the Great Beyoğlu Fire of 1922. The nucleus of the display is the collection of Sadberk Hanım, wife of the millionaire business enterpreneur Vehbi Koç. The artifacts in the museum are well-lit and beautifully displayed (the interior decor of the building is mainly black marble), with excellent commentary explaining the significance of the objects on display—a rare virtue in a Turkish museum. The oldest exhibits include sixth-millennium mother goddesses and Hittite cuneiform tablets from the second millennium BC. In the ethnography section there are maternity and circumcision beds, needlework, clothing and jewelry, and a thorough examination of İznik and Kütahya pottery.

The Asian Shore

The vast suburbs and small villages on the Asian side of the Bosphorus all have one thing in common: they are virtually unknown to tourists. The best base for exploring this area is probably **Üsküdar**, one of the most beautiful of all the

Bosphorus suburbs, with some impressive imperial and domestic architecture and a uniquely tranquil atmosphere. There are a few good hotels here (see p.62) and buses leave regularly to all the other villages up and down the Bosphorus from the main bus station in front of the İskele Camii.

Kadıköy to Üsküdar

KADIKÖY, which sprawls dirtily between the Bosphorus and the Marmara, may at first seem to have only views of the European shore to recommend it, but despite an unpromising appearance it's a lively and busy place, with good shops, restaurants, and movie theaters. After dark the ferry landing area comes alive—it's a good place to buy a bottle of cheap alcohol after closing time, which may explain the number of drunken brawls in the area—and there are scores of street vendors along the windswept shorefront esplanade who'll sell you a disposable watch or pair of socks for next to nothing. The main road south from Kadıköy to Kartal is **Bağdat Caddesi**, part of the old silk route from China. Nowadays the street is better known as a place to pose and shop for clothes to pose in (labels should be external, prominent, and preferably foreign). As all good Bağdat people know, the best way to see Bağdat Caddesi is from daddy's BMW, but failing that you can take a seabus to Bostancı—from Bakırköy, Yenikapı, Karaköy, or Kabataş—and then a dolmuş from behind the *Dolphin Hotel* back to Kadıköy (Bağdat Caddesi is one-way, so you can't tour it from Kadıköy). Dolmuşes can be hailed anywhere along the street, which is just as well since the stores, although generally massive, are pretty far apart and you may not feel like walking between them. Best areas for shopping are Şaşkın Bakkal and Suadiye (see "Shops and Markets" for more information), and there are good restaurants the whole way along.

In Kadıköy itself the best place for clothes is Bahariye Caddesi, but there's more fun to be had sorting through the great mounds of junk, including a few old carpets and kilims, that can be found for sale in the **Bit Pazarı** on Özellik Sokak. **Moda**, the district to the south of Kadıköy jetty, reached by taking the shore road (Mühürdar Cad) away from Haydarpaşa and turning left up any of its side streets. is a pleasant area for aimless wandering, and particularly popular among "courting couples." On Moda Caddesi there's an art gallery, the *Benadam*; the *Café Bonjour;* and at no.266 a very well-known ice-cream parlour, *Ali Usta*, that attracts vast lines on summer evenings. Round the corner on Feritele Sokak, the *Café Kırıntı* serves *durum*, a delicious meat sandwich affair, and at the end of the street is a nice little tea garden overlooking the sea.

The Selimiye Barracks
The **Selimiye Barracks**, home of the former **hospital of Florence Nightingale** (daily 9:30am–5pm; free), are on the road between Kadıköy and Üsküdar in Haydarpaşa. To get there take a dolmuş between Kadıköy and Üsküdar and ask for the Selimiye Kışlası, or walk about fifteen minutes from Kadıköy up Haydarpaşa Rıhtım Caddesi, which becomes Rıhtım and then Tıbbiye Caddesi. After passing the military hospital and the imposing turreted building that now houses Marmara University's law and medicine departments, turn left onto Çeşme-i Kebir Sokak and continue straight toward the sea until you reach the entrance of the massive Selimiye Barracks to your left. Despite appearances to

the contrary, parts of this building are open to the public, although you'll be required to take a **guided tour**, probably given by a conscript thanking his lucky stars that military service has turned up such an easy option.

The barracks were originally built by Selim III in 1799 for his western-style *Nizam-i Jedid*, or **New Order**, which was established to undermine the power of the janissaries. The building was positioned some distance from the city so that the new corps wouldn't cause too much trouble among the janissaries, but in this it failed and Selim was forced to dissolve the corps. The barracks were burned down in 1808, the same year that Selim was deposed and assassinated, but were rebuilt in stone in 1828, two years after Mahmut II finally destroyed and massacred the janissaries. Additional wings were added by Abdül Mecit in 1842; as it stands today the building has more than 1100 exterior windows.

The northwest wing was used as a hospital by the British during the **Crimean War** (1854–56), and **Florence Nightingale** lived and worked in the northern tower. This section has been organized as a Nightingale museum by the Turkish Nurses' Association, who have preserved the original furnishings and some of her personal belongings. During her stay here she reduced the death toll among patients from twenty to two percent, and established universally accepted **principles of modern nursing**. Some of the pamphlets written by Nightingale, such as *Notes on Nursing for the Labouring Class* and *The Sanitary State of the Army in India, 1863*, are on display here, as is a copy of the lady's lamp (rather more oriental in design than that pictured in history books).

Haydarpaşa

On the opposite side of Çeşme-i Kebir Caddesi, on Selimiye Camii Sokak, is the **Selimiye Camii**, constructed, along with the nearby hamam, for the use of soldiers of the New Order. With its imposing entrance portal and window-filled tympanum arches, it does more than justice to the quiet and attractive suburb in which it is situated, elevated above the surrounding streets in a garden of sycamore trees.

Also in Haydarpaşa, not far from the hospital, is the **British War Cemetery**, with casualties of the Crimean and two world wars. To find it, return to Tibbiye Caddesi and walk in the direction of Kadıköy, past the Marmara University law and medicine building; take a left turn on the road between the university and the military hospital (Burhan Felek Caddesi) and continue past the entrance to the hospital down the leafy lane which leads to the cemetery. It's a beautifully kept, peaceful spot, though not as romantic as many of the Ottoman graveyards around the city.

The largest Muslim graveyard in İstanbul, the **Karaca Ahmet Mezarlığı**, is a ten-minute walk away on Tibbiye Caddesi in the direction of Üsküdar. A beautiful, sprawling place shadowed by ancient cypresses, it's ideal for wandering around in and studying Ottoman gravestones. Women's graves are marked by carved flowers, each bloom of which signifies a child, while men's are surmounted by headgear signifying the lifetime office of the deceased. The **Karaca Ahmet Türbesi**, on Tunus Bağı Caddesi at the north end of the cemetery (easily reached by making a right off Tibbiye Caddesi through the graveyard), commemorates a sainted warrior who fought beside Orhan Gazi. It is still used as an almshouse and a kind of youth club by the Bektaşi dervishes, where boys and girls learn poems and the ritual *sema* of these Sufi mystics, whose activities were first restricted during the reign of Mahmut II because of their connections with the janissaries.

Üsküdar

Although there's plenty of evidence of religious conservatism in ÜSKÜDAR (formerly Scutari), particularly in the dress of its inhabitants, the town has a relaxed ambience, and a feeling of old-fashioned hospitality and of a prosperity more akin to Black Sea villages than to İstanbul's suburbs. The atmosphere may have been affected by dervish attitudes of religious tolerance and open mindedness, since it has long been a center of Islamic mystical sects, but whatever the reason it's certainly a more comfortable and friendly place than other similarly conservative centers (eg Fatih). Although there are some fine imperial mosques in and around the suburb, modern Üsküdar is primarily renowned as a shopping center for Bosphorus villagers. In the main square, trucks park in a big circle to sell produce in bulk, while the small streets roundabout peddle fresh fish and vegetables, as well as all kinds of kitchen hardware. Secondhand furniture and ornaments are sold at the Üsküdar Flea Market in Büyük Hamam Sokak, and there are some reasonable jewelry and even clothes shops.

Despite the relaxed atmosphere in these parts, as yet nothing resembling a nightclub has emerged, but along the waterfront at **Salacak** there are some good restaurants, sidewalk cafés and bars, and fantastic views of Topkapı Palace and of İstanbul generally. To get to Üsküdar take a **ferry** from Eminönü or Beşiktaş, a #500B bus from either Edirnekapı or Mecidiyeköy, or from Kadıköy a #12 or #14 bus or a dolmuş. Üsküdar's main square and waterfront is an enormous bus stand. **Buses** up the Bosphorus, as far as Anadolu Hisarı, leave from in front of the İskele Camii on Paşa Liman Caddesi. It's also possible to get dolmuşes from here to Çengelköy and Beykoz.

The **İskele** or **Mihrimah Camii** is located opposite the ferry landing on the İskele Meydanı, sitting on a high platform with an immense covered porch in front of it. This porch is a favorite viewing platform where old men in knitted hats shelter in all weather and complain about the changing times while they peruse the square below. Inside it's all fairly gloomy and cluttered, and the lateral domes are dwarfed by the large central dome. Designed by Sinan and built in 1547–8, this is the only Ottoman mosque with three semidomes (as opposed to two or four), a result of the requirements of a difficult site against the hillside behind.

Directly across the main square from the İskele Camii is the **Yeni Valide Camii**, and it's worth being in the vicinity of these two mosques for the call to prayer: the two *muezzin* call and answer each other in a poignant refrain across the bus park below, where, by popular consensus, they are studiously ignored. The Yeni Valide Camii, built by Ahmet III in honor of his mother between 1708 and 1710, is most easily identified by the Valide Sultan's green, birdcage-like tomb, whose meshed roof was in fact designed to keep birds out while allowing rain in to water the garden tomb below (now rather untidily overgrown). There is an attractive *şardıvan* (ablutions fountain) in the courtyard: the grilles of its cistern are highly wrought and their pattern is echoed in the carvings in the stone above.

Minibuses to Ümraniye from the main square run past the foot of **Büyük Çamlıca**, the highest hill on the Asian side. If you get off at Kısıklı Camii you can walk up Kısıklı-Büyük Çamlıca Caddesi, turning right just before the *Büyük Çamlıca Et Lokantası* to reach the park, a walk of fifteen minutes or so. The effort is rewarded by refreshingly cooler temperatures and spectacular views, not only of İstanbul but also of the Uludağ mountain range to the south, near Bursa. Büyük

Çamlıca used to be covered with shantytown *gecekondu* dwellings, but these were demolished in a slum clearance program to make way for a park and another of the Turkish Touring Club's overpriced cafés (daily 9am–midnight). The atmosphere in the café is very phony, and the waiters look profoundly uncomfortable in their traditional Ottoman costumes, but on winter evenings the blazing fire can be mighty welcome if you've crunched through snow drifts to get up here. Otherwise, the *Et Lokantası* on the way up is a cheaper option for a decent meal.

On to Beylerbey

The next village along the Bosphorus, just before you reach the first bridge, is **KUZGUNCUK**. There's a good fish restaurant on the shore here, with a fine view of Ortaköy Camii on the other side, and another cemetery—this time Jewish—a half-hour walk from the village up İcadiye Sokak. From a distance this **Jewish cemetery** looks like a hill littered with pieces of white paper: this is because the white marble gravestones, some of which are coffin-shaped, lie flat on the ground instead of standing upright. The Jewish presence in İstanbul goes back to 1492, when Beyazit II gave refuge to Jews escaping the Spanish Inquisition. As the Spanish economy suffered from the exodus, so the Ottomans benefited from the commercial activities and know-how of the Jewish community, which still plays an important part in the Turkish economy.

The main attraction of **BEYLERBEY**, the next village along, is the **Beylerbey Palace** (9:30am–4pm, closed Mon & Thur; $1.50, guided tours only). This nine-teenth-century summer residence and guesthouse of the Ottoman sultans was again built by members of the Balian family (in this case Sarkis and Agop). Its grounds are entered through a 130-meter-long tunnel, part of the imperial road between Üsküdar and Beykoz which was constructed at the time of Mahmut II. At the Üsküdar end of the tunnel are two original fire hose pumps—ironic, since the wooden palace built on the site by Mahmut II was destroyed by fire.

The present palace, built for the Sultan Abdül Aziz and completed in 1865, was much admired by contemporary visitors from Europe. The Empress Eugénie, after her stay in 1869, had its windows copied in the Tuileries Palace in Paris, and the palace is still popular among western visitors who are repelled by the extrava-gances of Dolmabahçe. The interior decoration was planned and designed by Sultan Abdül Aziz himself, while some of the furniture, including the matching dining chairs in the harem and the *selamlık*, were carved by Sultan Abdül Hamid II during his six years of imprisonment in the palace (he died here in 1918). Downstairs, the reception room was lit by three Bohemian crystal chandeliers, and a marble pool and fountain cooled the air of the building. The central stair-case, with its fanciful twisting shape, is perhaps the individual highlight, but all kinds of details, from the neo-Islamic patterns on the ceilings down to the beauti-ful Egyptian *hasır*, the reed matting on the floor, are worth spending time to investigate.

Çengelköy to Anadolu Hisarı

ÇENGELKÖY's fish restaurants are overpriced, its locals not particularly friendly and its main attraction, the *kuleli*, closed to the public, so there's not much point stopping here unless you want a good look at the **Baroque fountain** in the square. The *kuleli* is the long yellow building on the shore beyond the village. It was originally built, along with the Selimiye Barracks, as a military training school and barracks by Selim III, and like that building it served as a hospital under the direction of Florence Nightingale in the Crimean War. Since the end of World War I the building has been an officers' training school, offering the best education to be had in Turkey in exchange for the adult working life of its students.

Küçüksu Kasrı, the Palace of Küçüksu (9:30am–4pm, closed Mon & Thur; 50¢), is a ten-minute bus ride from Çengelköy. After passing a boatyard on the left you'll cross a bridge over the Küçüksu Deresi; get off at the next stop and walk back to the sign saying *"Küçük Saray Aile Bahcesi."* At the end of the drive is the Küçüksu Kasrı.

This is another Balian palace, built this time by Nikoğos Balian, son of the architect of Dolmabahçe. Its exterior is ornate with Rococo carving which is probably best seen from the Bosphorus, the intended angle of approach. From the water you also get the best impression of the staircase, which doubles back on itself to create the illusion of being free of any means of support. Inside is another attractive staircase, and the whole of the interior is decorated with lace and carpets from Hereke and lit by Bohemian crystal chandeliers. The floors are mahogany, inlaid with rose, almond-wood, and ebony. Upstairs is an ebony table on which Sultan Abdül Aziz was wont to arm-wrestle with visitors of state.

The **Göksu Deresi** and the **Küçüksu** farther down the Bosphorus are the streams formerly known to Europeans as the "Sweet Waters of Asia." Their banks were graced by picnicking parties of Ottoman nobility, and the vision they presented was much admired by European visitors. The Ottoman castle of **Anadolu Hisarı**, a short walk through the village on the other side from Küçüksu Kasrı, is open at all times to wander around and clamber over, but its main interest is historical. Close as they were to Constantinople, this and the fortification across the Bosphorus were built while the city was still in Byzantine hands, this one in around 1390 by Beyazit I and the other sixty years later by Mehmet the Conqueror. The Anatolian fortress is by no means as impressive as its counterpart across the water, but nevertheless it's a measure of the extent of decline of the Byzantine Empire that the Turks could build such fortifications on the shores of a stretch of water that was so important strategically and economically.

On the coastal path toward Anadolu Hisarı there is a **tea garden** serving *midye tava* (fried mussels), with a good view of Rumeli Hisarı across the Bosphorus. Just before the Göksu Deresi, behind the *spor klübü*, is the *Hisar Köftecisi*, a tiny **café** where you can eat a basic meal of steak or *köfte* and salad for next to nothing. The unsightly pieces of reinforced concrete littering the field next to the restaurant are the supports on which the second Bosphorus bridge was made. There are **boats for rent** at Anadolu Hisarı: smaller ones on which you can take a trip up the Göksu Deresi or larger ones ($13) to tour the Bosphorus at your leisure.

On to Anadolu Kavağı

KANLICA, the next stop up, is famed for its yogurt, which can be eaten at any of the little waterfront restaurants. Not far beyond is the glass factory of **Pasabahçe**, which once produced fine, delicate glassware, still to be found in secondhand shops around Turkey. Standards have slipped, however, and nowadays the factory shop doesn't yield much excitement, although it might be fun to get a group of people together for a tour of the factory (☎322 0018; tours, for a minimum of ten people, leave at 2:30 and 4:30pm, Mon–Fri).

The road to **ANADOLU KAVAĞI** is in theory closed to foreigners, and if you attempt to take it you may find yourself ejected from your bus and detained at a military checkpoint to await its return. You may, of course, be lucky and pass unnoticed, but it's probably a safer bet to arrive in Anadolu Kavağı by ferry, either on the Bosphorus tour from Rumeli Kavağı or on a rented boat from Anadolu Kavağı Hisarı.

The village has a distinct if dilapidated charm—balconied houses with boat moorings in place of garages overlook the Bosphorus, and the main street is lined with restaurants and food stands—but the real reason to make the trek (1hr 40min by ferry from Eminönü) is to visit the **Byzantine fortification** from which the village takes its name, on the hill above the town. This used to be part of a military base and has only recently been opened to the public: there are still a number of apartment buildings housing military families on the steep road up to the fortress, and various signs forbidding entry. These appear to be universally ignored, but proceed with caution anyway in case the situation has changed again.

To get there, take Mirşah Hamam Sokak from the dock and walk uphill for half an hour. The fortress sprawls across a hilltop overgrown with currant bushes, gorse, heather, and grasses, affording excellent views of the Bosphorus and of migratory birds in spring. The best approach to the castle itself is to walk to the top of Anadolu Kavağı Fener Yolu, with the defenses on your left, to the upper-most entrance. The fortress is sometimes known as the Genoese Castle, since it was controlled by them after the mid-fourteenth century, but approaching from above you'll see various Greek inscriptions, and even the imperial motto of the Palaeologus dynasty (a cross with the letter "b" in each corner, which stands for "King of Kings, who Kings it over Kings"), as clear evidence that it was in fact Byzantine in origin.

FARTHER OUT: ESCAPES FROM THE CITY

İstanbul is surrounded by sea, and if the city's crowds and noise finally become too much it's not hard to escape for a day or more to one of the nearby beaches. While those in the immediate vicinity suffer from pollution and overcrowding, both the Sea of Marmara and the Black Sea offer attractive alternatives.

The **Princes' Islands**, in the Sea of Marmara between 15 and 30km southeast of the city, have always been a favorite retreat from the mainland. Nowadays four of the nine islands are easily accessible by ferry from İstanbul, and summer holidays bring a steady stream of visitors threatening to destroy the peace and tranquility of these sleepy havens. Many Turkish families take full advantage of the proximity of the islands and move out here for the duration of İstanbul's sticky summer. In the other direction, the **Black Sea** offers the daytrippers' delights of Şile, Kilyos, and lovely Ağva. It's also surprisingly easy to find open countryside if you know in which direction to head: the Belgrade Forest is an obvious example; Polonezköy, all but unknown to foreign tourism, a less obvious one.

The Princes' Islands

The Princes' Islands have been inhabited since classical times, but their first claim to fame derived from the copper mines of Chalkitis (Heybeliada), which have long since been exhausted but are still visible near Çam Limanı. In the Byzantine era numerous convents and monasteries were built on the islands, and these became favored—because of their proximity to the capital and ease of surveillance—as luxurious prisons for banished emperors, empresses, and princes (often after they had been blinded).

After the Conquest, the islands were largely neglected by the Ottoman Turks, and they became another of the city's refuges for Greek and Armenian communities. Armenian Protestants acquired **Heybeliada** from the Turkish government in 1821. In 1846 a ferry service was established from the mainland to the islands; they became popular with Pera's expatriate community, and in 1857 the British Ambassador Sir Henry Bulwer bought Yassıada and built a castle there. But it was only in the early years of the Republic that the islands entered popular Turkish culture as İstanbul's most visited summer resort. Mosques began to appear in the villages, hotels and bougainvillea-draped villas followed, and many beautiful wooden *konaks* were built, which contributed to the turn-of-the-century Ottoman gentility of the larger islands. A Turkish Naval College was established on Heybeliada, and the islands received the rubber stamp of Republican respectability when Atatürk's private yacht was moored here as a training ship.

Not all of the islands have romantic connotations, however. **Sivriada**, which is not inhabited or visitable, gained public notoriety in 1911 when all the stray dogs in İstanbul were rounded up, shipped out there, and left to starve; and **Yassıada** is best known as a prison island, used for the detention of high-risk political prisoners. It was here that Adnan Menderes and two of his former ministers were executed on the night of Sept 16, 1961. Menderes, who has recently been publicly rehabilitated and his remains reburied in a mausoleum on the mainland, was hanged after a military coup that sought to prevent a religious revival and political repression on a level that threatened the stability of the Turkish Republic.

Recently, **development** has become a serious worry. Apart from unsightly building projects—legislation restricting the height of new buildings has been flouted, and many exceed the 7.5-meter, two-storey limit—other direct results of the new development on the islands include deforestation and pollution caused by earth being dumped into the sea. Little is being done by the authorities to prevent any of this: a couple of years ago a preservation order lasted for about six weeks before the islands were once again opened up to development, and two years later Büyükada and Heybeliada were declared centers of tourism, offering substantial incentives to would-be developers.

All this means that the islands are changing rapidly, but at least they are still traffic-free. Plans to introduce a bus service were eventually dropped by the municipality under pressure from *Ada Dostları* (Friends of the Islands), and this pressure group is doing what it can to preserve what's left of the islands heritage. Despite the changes, the essence of a day trip to the islands is still escape from the noise, stress, and pollution of the city.

Getting There

The Princes' Islands are all too easy to get to. The farthest is less than two hours by boat from Sirkeci, and there is even a sea bus (*Deniz Otobüs*) service three times a day on weekends and holidays from Kabataş (near Beşiktaş on the Bosphorus) and Bostancı (on the Asian shore) to Büyükada, which takes about twenty minutes.

Island-hopping between the four larger islands—**Büyükada, Heybeliada, Burgazada,** and **Kınalıada**—is a simple matter as long as you check the ferry times at the dock and don't simply rely on a timetable: the service is notoriously changeable. In season there are around twenty boats a day from Büyükada to Heybeliada alone. The other islands are equally well served by the steady old boats, some of which are steam-powered, beautifully trimmed in varnished wood, and furnished with armchairs and tables like something out of an Agatha Christie novel.

Büyükada

BÜYÜKADA (the Great Island, the original *Prinkipo*, or Prince's Island in Greek) is the largest of the islands and has always been the most popular and populated of them. It is also the best-known place of exile. Long-term visitors to the convent of Saint George included the granddaughter of the Empress Irene, and the royal princess Zoë, in 1012. Another well-known exile to take advantage of the island as a luxurious retreat was Leon Trotsky, who lived here from 1929 to 1933.

The island consists of two hills, both surmounted by monasteries, with a valley between them. The south of the island is wilder and unpopulated, and is most easily visited by **phaeton** (horse and carriage). These expensive tours (the small tour is $7, large tour $10, leaving from the main square off Isa Çelebi Sok) are evidence of the island's considerable tourist development, as are donkey rides, good hotels, and admission charges at beaches. There are **bike rental** shops (Çınar Caddesi 10B and 51A, around $2 an hour); good cheap **meals** (for example from the *Konak Et ve Balık Lokantası*, Balıkçıl Caddesi 87; ☎382 5479); and **donkeys** to ride up the hills, starting from a little park up Kadıyoran Caddesi from the center of town (about $2 a ride).

The southernmost of the two hills, **Yüce Tepe**, is the location of the **monastery of Saint George**, probably built on the site of a building dating from the twelfth century. Lady Hornby described riding up to the monastery in the nineteenth century: "Perched on the very highest peak of mountain above, it looks no bigger than a doll's house, left there by some spiteful fairy, to be shaken by winter tempests and scorched by the summer glare." Close up, it consists of a series of chapels, currently undergoing renovation work, on three levels, with the oldest, containing a sacred spring, being on the lowest level. In Byzantine times the monastery was used as an insane asylum, and iron rings set into the floor of the chapels were used for restraining the inmates. The monastery on the northernmost hill, **İsa Tepe**, is a nineteenth-century building. Three families still inhabit the premises, and there are services in the chapel on Sundays.

The convent of Saint Irene, once located on Yılmaz Türk Caddesi near the *Villa Rifat Pansiyon*, has now been ppulled down and replaced by tennis courts. This seems horribly appropriate in the light of the changes sweeping across the islands.

Heybeliada

HEYBELİADA, or the "Island of the Saddle-Bag," is popular for its natural beauty and for the beaches to which İstanbul residents flock in their hundreds at weekends. It is also the location of a yacht club—situated near Değirmen Burnu on the northwest side of the island—whose $4000 annual membership fee gives you an idea of how fashionable the islands are becoming. Heybeli has retained much of its village identity, however, and there is a strong community spirit among its permanent residents. The unique character of the island is enhanced by a plague of cats, who stalk the streets and feed off the rats and mice living in the old wooden buildings of the village.

Heybeli is not completely devoid of motorized **transportation**, but what there is is either *Belediye-* or naval-owned, so there's no chance of hitching any rides. Once again, you're at the mercy of semi-wild animals and their taciturn owners in your travels: prices for **phaetons** from Ayyıldız Caddesi (which runs parallel to the shore) to various destinations around the island are posted on a board in the street, and tours of the island are also available (short tours for $4, longer ones $8). The **restaurants** cater to locals year-round, and consequently are generally good, simple, and cheap. Most are on Ayyıldız Caddesi: at no. 75, for example, there's a cheap *pide salon* where you can eat Turkish pizza for next to nothing. The *Güleryüz* restaurant on the same street is slightly classier, and there's an extremely good cake shop, *Mehtap Pastanesi*, down toward the dock.

If you do take a tour of the island, one of its most prominent landmarks is the nineteenth-century **Greek Orthodox School of Theology**, the Aya Triada Manastiri, which is the site of an important collection of Byzantine manuscripts. The school, majestically situated on the peak of the island's northernmost hill, is only accessible with permission from the Greek Orthodox Patriarchate in Fener. Other buildings you'll be shown include the Heybeliada Sanatorium, a private home for TB sufferers located off Çam Limanı Yolu on the south side of the island; and the Naval School (*Deniz Harp Okulu*) on the east side of the island along the coast road from the main ferry dock. The school was originally located on the Golden Horn, but was moved here by Sultan Mahmut II after a fire in 1821.

Walking is a better way to enjoy Heybeli, though, and its pine forests and hills make for scenic rambles. The best way to find an isolated **beach** is to head up Refah Şehitler Caddesi out of the village until you arrive at Alp Görüngen Yolu, which encircles the western half of the island. The northern shore, before you reach Alman Köy, is a particularly good bet for a quiet swim if you climb down from the road to one of the tiny pebble beaches below. You can also reach Yeni İskele, the new dock, from Refah Şehitler Caddesi, and from here it costs around $4 to take a small boat across to KAŞIKADI (Spoon Island, so called because of its shape), which may still be worth doing if the developments now in progress aren't too overwhelming.

Burgazada and Kınalıada

The other two islands served by public ferry are Burgazada and Kınalıada, both small and relatively unspoiled, although development is proceeding apace. They are still popular with escapees from the strict Islamic codes more evident in mainland İstanbul, and vacation homes already outnumber those of permanent residents on both islands. In winter the villages around their docks are practically ghost towns, with little to see or do.

BURGAZADA has a small, pleasant guesthouse, the *Villa Maria* at 2 Sarnıç Sokak (at the top of the steep Yeni Kuyu Sokak; closed in winter) with an Art Nouveau conservatory full of plants. There's also a fascinating small **museum** (Tues–Sun 10am–noon & 2–5pm, Saturday 10am–noon; free) at 15 Burgaz Çayırı Sokak, on the other side of the square from the Church of St John the Baptist (the dome of which is the town's most prominent landmark). The museum is dedicated to the novelist Sait Faik (the "Turkish Mark Twain"), who once lived here, and the house has been so carefully preserved—as if the writer were still there—that as a visitor you get an unsettling sense that you're trespassing. This becomes stronger when you go up to the bedroom and find a pair of pyjamas neatly folded on the bed and a towel on the rack beside it. You also get an immediate sense of the man, whose exceptional character is evidenced by the simple bohemian style of furnishings in his island home (the floor is covered in reed matting generally associated with impoverishment, and on the living-room wall is a portrait of a naked man).

KINALIADA, Henna Island, takes its name from the red coloring of its eastern cliffs; in Greek it was known as Proti (First), since it's the nearest of the islands to the mainland. Like Heybeliada, Kınalıada's history is notable for exiles, including Romanus IV Diogenes, deposed after his disastrous defeat at the battle of Manzikert by the Selçuk Turks. Nowadays its population is seventy percent Armenian.

The island is rather bare and barren, with no hotels. There are a few reasonable **restaurants**, though: the *Mimosa*, to the left of the ferry landing, is probably the best, but only open in the summer season; the *Çinaraltı Lokantası*, Çinar Tepe 12, is nothing special but is open year-round. There's a pebble beach, frequented by ominous-looking black crows, to the left of the dock, and a luxurious beach club with outdoor pool, sauna, and massage to the right of the dock.

West to the Black Sea

The Black Sea and a few of its resorts are easily accessible from İstanbul, and if you're staying in the city for any length of time and want a short break, these seaside villages make ideal day trips or weekend breaks. Kilyos, on the European side of the Bosphorus, is accessible by dolmuş from Sariyer along a direct road of about 12km. Şile is a two-hour drive from Üsküdar, with buses from the western-most bus depot every hour on the hour from 9am—it's another half hour to Ağva. Tickets are sold from several small booths on Balaban Caddesi and Balaban Sokak, and cost $1.50 to Şile, $2 to Ağva. If you're driving, the easiest route to take out of İstanbul is along the coast road via Beykoz (a quicker route is via Kısıklı, near Büyük Çamlıca, but it's not as well marked).

Şile

As the closest real resort to the metropolis, **ŞILE** suffers from over-familiarity: as far as locals are concerned it's all right for a lark at the weekend, but if you get the chance to go farther afield, then take it. Consequently the place is sad and abandoned—and peaceful like no other Turkish beach resort—during holiday periods, but jam-packed on weekends. Without the crowds it's undeniably attractive, perched on a clifftop overlooking a large bay and tiny island, with white sandy beaches stretching off to the west. To add to the holiday feel, there's a pretty black-and-white striped lighthouse and the romantic remains of a fourteenth-century Genoese castle on a nearby island.

Şile's main historical claim to fame is that it was visited by Xenophon and his Ten Thousand, the army that was left leaderless when its officers were all murdererd by the Persians. They stayed in Şile, then known as Kalpe, and in his memoirs Xenophon wrote about how well the site suited the establishment of a city.

Hotels are plentiful, but be aware that prices go up on weekends. One of the best places to stay, 2km from town on the İstanbul road, is the attractive and comfortable *Kumbaba Hotel* ($35 per person) and campground. Try also the *Rüya Motel* (☎1992/1070), with cabin-type rooms overlooking the beach (which isn't suitable for swimming because the water's too shallow) for $11 single, $15 double; or the *Yasemin Pansiyon* and Restaurant at Vali Muhittin Caddesi 1 (☎1992/1358), where pleasantly furnished, modern rooms go for $20 a head. Food is also readily available at several **restaurants** along the main street of the village, some with outdoor terraces overlooking the sea below. Along the beach you can rent deck chairs and umbrellas in season.

Ağva

A little farther along the coast from Şile, **AĞVA** is a lovely, quiet, and sleepy little haven, even more worthy of the journey from İstanbul. To get there, take one of the Şile buses from Üsküdar, which continue another hour to Ağva and cost $1 more. Be warned that the last buses from Ağva back to İstanbul leave at 7pm in summer, in winter at 5pm on weekends, 3pm on weekdays.

There are a few small **hotels** in the village, some with fish restaurants attached. The best of them is the *Göksü Apart Motel* (☎1992/8265, 8174), a building with spotless, fully equipped apartments that are popular with groups of students during the university holidays. There's also plenty of camping space, including a makeshift **campground** under pine trees next to the beach.

The beauty of this tiny village lies in its location between two rivers, the Yeşilçay and the Göksü, both of which are fished to provide for the livelihood of the local community. It's an easy matter to take a boat around the cove to Karabatak beach (also accessible from the Kilimli road out of Ağva), where it's possible to camp in absolute seclusion, and there's a good chance of spotting a school of dolphins in these waters.

Polonezköy

The small Polish village of **POLONEZKÖY** can be visited on your way to the coast if you're driving, but it's not easy to reach by public transportation. Quaintly pretty, it makes a refreshing trip out of town, but its most interesting aspect is its unusual history. Polonezköy (Village of the Poles) was established in 1848 by **Prince Czartorisky**, the leader of the Polish nationals who was granted exile in the Ottoman Empire from Russian oppression in the Balkans. His main aim, along with other Eastern European exiles like the poet Adam Mickiewicz and Hungarian nationalist leader Kossuth, was to establish a union of the Balkan races, including Romanians, Circassians, and Turks, to counteract Panslavic expansion. He continued this work during his years of exile, while establishing the community which still survives on the plot of land sold to him by a local monastery, the site of Polonezköy. The present inhabitants of the village are the sixth generation of Poles in İstanbul. Since the establishment of the Turkish Republic they have not been allowed to educate their children in Polish and now just under half of the fifty-member permanent community of the village speak Polish.

The village became known to tourism in the 1970s, when it was popular among İstanbulites in pursuit of illicit pork, which is hard to come by in İstanbul itself. A change has taken place in recent years, however, and the new generation of visitors to the village is more interested in sex than sausages. Consequently the latter are practically unobtainable, while a number of insalubrious madams offer rooms for rent at hourly rates.

The main problem in visiting the village is that getting there is so difficult—there is no longer public transit from İstanbul. Possible options are to take a taxi from town, or ride the #15K bus from Üsküdar to Cavuşbaşı and hitch the final thirteen kilometers. To get there by car, take the first turn off the Mehmet the Conqueror bridge on the Asian side and follow the signs from Ruzgarlıbahçe to Polonezköy. Alternatively, ask for the Polonezköy road from Paşabahçe on the Bosphorus.

The best place to eat the local fried chicken—which has now replaced pork on local menus, although pigs are still kept for private consumption—is at the **restaurant** owned by Daniel Ohotsky, Polonezköy 21 (☎1839/3130 99). A meal should come to around $8 a head, and a pleasant **room** with attached bath here is $32, including dinner.

Kilyos

Another of İstanbul's tiny satellite vacation villages, this time on the European shores of the Black Sea, **KİLYOS** is nothing exceptional, but it's an attractive place with an impressive stretch of beach. This fine expanse of sand, complete with umbrellas, deck chairs, and other resort parapheralla in season, is kept spotlessly clean. The most imposing monument, the medieval Genoese castle perched on a cliff above the town, is closed to the public because of the Turkish army unit installed there. To get here, take a minibus, marked Kilyos, from the Bosphorus suburb of Sariyer, and it's a thirty-kilometer ride from there.

There are a couple of restaurants down near the shore, and plenty of **hotel** options, although accommodation tends to be pricey. The plush, modern *Kilyos Kale Hotel* in Kıyıköyü, on a cliff overlooking the sea, has pansiyon rooms beneath its expensive hotel rooms for $12 per person. Another cheaper option is the *Kilyos Yuva Hotel* (☎1882/1043), near the minibus stop some distance from the beach, where clean, basic rooms are $10 per person.

THE FACTS

İstanbul may not be the political capital of Turkey, but in terms of culture, gastronomy, and consumption it certainly leads the nation. Despite twenty percent unemployment and average wages of around $40 a month, it's not at all difficult to part with large amounts of cash when you go out to eat, drink, or shop. For food and nightlife, the liveliest areas of the city are across the Horn in Taksim and Galata, although there are restaurants everywhere; shopping is most satisfying in the bazaars of the old city, but for practical stuff or designer clothes you'll find the going easier along İstiklâl Caddesi or over the Bosphorus on Bağdat Caddesi.

Restaurants

Eating out is an everyday activity for most Turks, and the best restaurants in Turkey—some would say in the world—are located in İstanbul. Good places are listed below, but if you're just after a snack you can find it almost anywhere. **Street-food** options in İstanbul vary from the excellent fish sandwiches served from boats by fishermen in Kadıköy, Karaköy, and Eminönü, to disgusting piles of sheeps' innards (*kokoreç*) which are sold from booths in less salubrious areas. There's no real way of knowing what standards of hygiene to expect from these places, but then there isn't in a restaurant either, however much you pay.

Taksim and Galata

Most of İstanbul's best restaurants and bars are located around Taksim and Galata, catering to theater- and cinema-goers and people who want to spend all night over a meal and a bottle of *rakı*. For the latter, the **Çiçek Pasajı** (the Flower Passage, İstiklâl Cad, opposite Galatasaray Lisesi) seems to be back in business, regaining some of its seedy old-world glamor after a facelift that looked as if it might have improved the place beyond recognition. Many of the old characters have returned to ply their trade around the tables of this arcade of tiny restaurants, from jugglers and shoe-shine boys to the old Armenian woman who plays Scottish ballads on her accordion. It's not the best or cheapest food in town by any means, but if you like your meals eventful and your fellow customers loud, this is the place to head. Don't be surprised, however, if a street fight is staged for your benefit.

For those of a nervous disposition, a less traumatic culinary experience can be had at any of a number of *lokantas*, restaurants, and cafés scattered around the same area, some of which are listed below.

Under $10 a Head

Hacı Abdullah, Sakızağacı Cad 19, Beyoğlu (☎144 8561). Opposite the Ağa Camii, the only mosque on İstiklâl Caddesi. A really excellent little place, unusually decorated with huge jars of pickles. Well-known among locals as a cheap, reliable alternative to the flashier places on İstiklâl. The only catch is they don't serve alcohol.

Hasır I, Kalyoncu Kulluğu Cad 94/1, Tarlabaşı, Beyoğlu (☎150 0557). Very popular Turkish *meyhane*, about ten minutes' walk from the PTT on İstiklâl Caddesi. Excellent food, lots of vegetarian options. Order a minimal selection from the menu, as the best food is periodically brought around on large trays.

Burç Pastanesi, İstiklâl Cad 463–465, Beyoğlu (☎144 0574, 144 2890). Good breakfasts and snacks.

Han Restaurant, Kartçinar Sok 16, Karaköy (☎152 5452). Located in a 600-year-old Genoese building, used as a soap factory before it was converted into a restaurant. A good, cheap lunchtime option in the Galata Tower region; nowhere near such a wide selection by the evening. Open 11am–2pm & 7:30–10:30pm.

Ferman Restaurant-Bar, Cumhuriyet Cad 87/1, Elmadağ (☎146 6685). None too special food, but a well-stocked bar.

Hasir II, Nevisade Sok 21/A, behind the *Çiçek Pasajı* (☎144 3942). Not as good as its namesake—listed above—but a quiet, reasonably priced alternative to the *Pasajı*.

Ayazpaşa Russian Restaurant, İnönü Cad 77/1, Taksim, entrance on Miralay Şefik Bey Sok (☎143 4892). Basement restaurant with friendly atmosphere and good service, serving a selection of Russian favorites like borscht and *palaçinka*, although the interpretation of some is unmistakably Turkish. The eventual outcome is OK though, and it's cheaper than *Rejans*.

C Fischer Restaurant, İnönü Cad 51/A (☎145 2576, 145 3375). Not unlike Ayazpaşa (above)—similar menu at the same prices, but with the addition of some German fare.

Cafe Süt, Sıraselviler Cad. 24, Taksim (☎143 6353). Clean, functional place serving cheap snacks like *menemen* and *köfte*. Open 7am to 1pm.

Restaurant Tuncel, Meşrutiyet Cad 129/1, Tepebaşı, Beyoğlu. (☎145 5566, 151 4443). Reasonably priced and open from midday to midnight.

Kral ve Ben, Turnacibasi Sok 10 (☎144 9688, 143 3641). Reasonably priced pizzas and burgers. All-you-can-eat pizza on Fridays after 5pm.

Over $10 a Head

Çatı Restaurant and Bar, İstiklâl Cad, Piremeci Sok 20, Baro Han, Floor 7, Tünel, Beyoğlu (☎145 1656, 151 1642). Well established among İstanbul's intelligentsia but unknown to tourists, this attractive restaurant deserves its reputation. The food is a little pricey but good, the bar has a discreet atmosphere and a wonderful night-time view of the lights of the Golden Horn. Open Mon–Sat 12am–3pm & 6:30pm–midnight.

Garibaldi Bar-Rôtisserie, İstiklâl Cad, Perukar Çikmazı 1, Beyoğlu (☎149 6895, 151 9591). Excellent cheap salad bar and some good Turkish standards as well as a dubious selection of "international" dishes. Jazz and Turkish folk music as background accompaniment.

Rejans, Olivo Geçidi 15, İstiklâl Cad, Tünel, Beyoğlu (☎144 1610). Frequented by diplomats from the nearby consulates and generally by people who know where to eat, this famous establishment was founded by White Russians in the 1930s and thrives on a well-earned reputation. Considering the quality of food and service it's not expensive. Closed Sun.

Hacı Baba Restaurant, İstiklâl Cad 49 (☎144 1886, 145 4377). Somewhat overpriced, but the food is good and there's an attractive, peaceful balcony in back overlooking the churchyard of Aya Triada in Beyoğlu.

Galata Tower Restaurant, in the tower. Expensive, and no real atmosphere. It's better to go up in the daytime for the views and eat elsewhere.

Ottoman

Revan Restaurant, Sheraton Hotel, Taksim (☎131 2121). A fixed menu of ten courses for around $30 without drinks, and the ingredients are the best from all over Turkey.

Far Eastern

Tegik, Recep Paşa Cad 20, Talimhane, Taksim (☎154 7172). Newly opened, Korean-owned restaurant serving a selection of Korean, Chinese, and Japanese food at reasonable prices.

Yu Me Ya, Cumhuriyet Cad 39/1, Taksim (☎156 1108). Japanese food at the kind of prices you'd expect for a restaurant catering to a mainly business clientele.

Italian

Little Italy, İstiklâl Cad 251–253 on the second floor of *Örs Turistik İş Merkezi*, next to the new British Council premises (☎143 1718). Newly opened and very stylish, this promises to be popular. Reasonable prices make it a possibility for lunch or a snack, although you may feel uncomfortable if you don't dress up a little.

Vagabondo's, İstiklâl Caddesi 315–318 (☎149 0481). Good, cheap food, including 23 varieties of pizza and fantastic ice cream, but overloud pop music and overpriced drinks.

International

Four Seasons, corner of İstiklâl and Şahkula Bostanı Sok (☎145 8941). Popular with expats for its classy old-world charm and dessert trolley. Not cheap, but you get what you pay for. Closed Sun.

Taksim Sanat Evi, Sıraselviler Cad 69/1, Taksim (☎144 2526, 152 0273). Large, well decorated, with a splendid Bosphorus view; popular with media people. Excellent menu includes Chinese, Turkish, and Albanian food for around $25 a head. Open noon–3:30pm & 10pm–2am.

Desserts

Saray, on İstiklâl just above Çiçek Pasajı. Emphasis on milk-based desserts; classic and cheap.

Saray, Tezvikiye Cad, just east of the police station. No relation to the above but just as good, serving simple egg and noodle snacks until 2am. A ten-to-fifteen-minute walk from the War Museum or Dolmabahçe.

Around Sultanahmet

As good a reason as any to evacuate the Sultanahmet and Beyazit regions at dusk is the appalling dearth of decent restaurants to be found in these parts. This is hard to understand, considering the demand created by the number of hotels around, but you might as well face facts and get out when you've seen all you want to of the sights. Cheap eateries for lunch are abundant at least, and some of these, listed below, are excellent value. Otherwise, for evening meals, head down to Kumkapı, on the Marmara Sea, where you'll find some of the city's best fish restaurants.

Subaşı Restaurant, Kılıçlar Sok 48/2 (☎522 4762). A spit-and-sawdust place (with real sawdust) located under the Nuruosmaniye Camii near the Covered Bazaar. Excellent lunchtime food—far better than anything else in the same price range and area. Go early (noon–1pm), as it gets packed at lunchtimes and the food may run out.

Havuzlu Lokantası, Gani Çelebi Sok 3, Kapalı Çarşı (☎527 3346). This is probably the best eating establishment in the Covered Bazaar, reasonably easy to locate since it's next to the PTT. The lofty, unadorned hall gives a good impression of the architecture of the bazaar. After an explosion in 1954 cooking gas was banned in the bazaar, and the food is cooked on cast-iron coal-fired stoves to good effect.

Altın Sofrası, Süleymaniye Cad 33 (☎522 5518). A good bet for lunch on a visit to Süleymaniye—certainly much better than any of the touristy restaurants that face the mosque.

Sarnıç, Soğukçeşme Sok, Sultanahmet (☎512 4291). A Touring Club venture located in a thousand-year-old Byzantine cistern. Atmospheric if you can overcome any reservations you may have regarding the misuse of such an historically important building, but overpriced.

Honey Balık Restaurant Kürkçü Kuyu Sokak 27, Kumkapı (☎512 7011). One of the many good restaurants in the Kumkapı area. Try also the **Merkez**, Çaparı Sokak (no phone), which serves excellent fish stews and the region's specialty dessert of honey, cream, and nuts.

Lâleli and Aksaray

There are a few worthwhile options not far from Beyazit in Lâleli and Aksaray. As with the hotels in this area, it's best just to wander and find one that suits your tastes, but here are a few possibilities:

Ramada Hotel Dynasty Asian Restaurant, Ordu Cad 226, Lâleli (☎513 9300 ext 5092). Well-cooked Chinese food: *dim sum* lunch served from noon to 3pm for around $10, but dinner will set you back $20–30. The Ramada's Turkish restaurant, the **Lale** (ext 5054), is similarly priced and a good bet for superlative Turkish food which hasn't been standing in trays since mid-morning. The hotel, which comprises several buildings on opposite sides of the street brought together under one roof, and renovated beyond recognition, is worth a look anyway.

Konyalı Kebabcı, İnkilap Caddesi 8-10, Aksaray (☎586 6083). Simple, basic, and cheap.

Aksu Oçakbaşi, Aksaray Cad, Azımkar Sok 5, Lâleli. Well-prepared, interesting food, not too expensive, friendly service.

Eminönü and Sirkeci

Pandeli, Misir Carsı (☎522 5534). Unusually for a commercial establishment, this restaurant is deliberately located out of the way: as a result of anti-Greek riots in the 1950s it was moved here on the advice of then-prime minister Adnan Menderes. To get in, go through the main entrance of the Mısır Carsısı and turn back to look toward the doorway. On your right is a staircase leading up to the restaurant. The restaurant is run by a Greek and a Turk, and the food is some of the best to be found anywhere in İstanbul. Open 11:30am to 3:30pm

Borsa Lokantasi, Yalıköşkuşkü Işhanı 60/62, Eminönü (☎522 4173). Excellent restaurant: pricey, but you won't find better Turkish meat dishes anywhere in the country.

Konyali, Ankara Caddesi 233, Sirkeci (☎513 9610). Excellent pastry shop frequented by the quarter's business people, who eat their breakfast standing at the marble-topped counters. Open 7am–6pm weekdays, 7am–5:30pm Saturday, closed Sunday. Tucked away around back in Mimar Kemalettin Caddesi is one of the city's best **self-service restaurants**, part of the same establishment, serving excellent meat stews and pastries.

The Bosphorus

The straits dividing Europe and Asia certainly provide the most romantic settings in which to eat fish, drink *rakı*, and muse over how your budget will be affected by the evening's final outcome. The best value and the best fish are to be found way up near the Black Sea, in Rumeli Kavağı and Sariyer on the European side, but if you don't have your own transportation it can be difficult to get back into town afterwards. Otherwise you can try your luck in Ortaköy (which has gotten expensive as a result of its recent rise in popularity), Arnavutköy, or possibly one or two of the villages across the straits. Don't expect the fish to be cheap, though, especially if there's a good view as well. There's less chance of meeting other tourists if you take the trouble to work out ferry times and cross the straits to the Asian side.

European Shore

İskele Balik Lokantası, İskele Meydanı 4/1, Rumeli Kavağı (☎142 2273). Rather large and impersonal, but the food's good.

Bosfor Restaurant, Çayirbaşı Cad 312–314, Büyükdere (☎142 0364). No Bosphorus view to speak of—it's on the wrong side of the main road—hence reasonable prices, and good service.

Süper Yediğün, Rumeli Kavağı Iskele Cad 27, Sariyer (no phone). Reasonably priced fish restaurant (around $10 a head), with an open terrace on the roof.

Borsa Lokanta, Fener Kalamış Cad 87, Kalamış Fenerbahçe (☎348 7700). Recently taken over by the Borsa chain (see Eminönü), this restaurant lives up to the reputation: food and service are marvelous, and unusually, it all takes place in an enormous greenhouse affair. If you sit too near the windows you may feel a bit exposed.

Tahta Kaşık, Muallim Naci Cad 90, Ortaköy (☎161 9443). Good for lunchtime snacks, with meat dishes and desserts as well as tripe soup; views, too.

Mor Fil Izgara Salonu, Osmanzade Sok 27, Ortaköy (☎136 0169). Another lunchtime place, this time a more basic snack bar.

Çinar, İskele Meydanı, Ortaköy (☎159 7358). Most of Ortaköy's classier restaurants are now along here.

Yaselam Arabian Restaurant, Cevdet Paşa Cad 294, Bebek (☎157 7795, 157 7796). Excellent Arabic food in chintzy, extravagant decor. Restaurant overlooks the harbor and has a pleasant garden in back. Open noon to midnight.

Hasir, Beykoz Korusu, Beykoz (☎322 2901, 322 2902). Good food and a bar in plush modern surroundings with a Bosphorus view. Around $10 a head without drinks.

Ahtapot, Köyiçi Kilise Meydanı 50, Beşiktaş (☎161 9148). Small, friendly fish restaurant located near the fresh produce market in lively Beşiktaş. Serves all the standards but cheaper than establishments right on the Bosphorus.

Dergah Pastanesi, Yıldız Yolu 20, Beşiktaş. Very good strawberry cakes and pastries.

Asian Shore

Uludağ Kebabcısı, İskele Cad 8, Caddebostan, off Bağdat Cad (☎358 3386, 358 7580). There's only one item on the menu here, and the atmosphere is like a school dining room, but the İskender Kebab is the best to be had outside Bursa.

2ler Et Lokantası, Bağdat Cad 289, Caddebostan (☎355 2253). Meat restaurant with a good reputation, though sometimes the service isn't all it could be.

Idris Pizza and Kebab Salonu, Bağdat Cad 374, Şaşkinbakkal (☎358 3230). Good value little restaurant serving lunchtime snacks, such as delicious *durum*, a kind of pastry meat sandwich. The kebabs are also excellent.

Divan Pasthanesi, Bağdat Cad 319, Erenkoy (☎358 5451). Very classy joint selling the best pastries and cakes on the street. You can sit outside and watch the Bağdat people as you indulge yourself. Also does attractively boxed sweets and *lokum* (Turkish delight).

Huzur Restaurant/Arabin Yeri, Salacak, Üsküdar (☎333 3157). Run by Arabic-speaking Turks from the Hatay, specialties include *içli köfte*, a kind of bulgur-covered meatball from that region. The restaurant has an old-world, rather shabby charm, and a wonderful view of the Bosphorus, but unfortunately the service is often plain shabby.

Kanaat Lokantasi, Selmanipak Cad no. 25, Üsküdar (next to Migros). Recently renovated with copies of İznik tile panels from the Selimiye in Edirne and a copper chimney piece. Meals, though not as good as they used to be, are still reasonably cheap at about $3 a head. Despite the waiters—grumpy and taciturn at best—this is probably the area's best *lokanta*.

Café Çamlıca, Büyük Çamlica hill, Ümraniye. Set in beautiful gardens with views of the whole of İstanbul and, on a good day, even of Uludağ near Bursa. A little expensive but the snacks are good, and in winter, when the hill is often snow-clad, a real fire makes the place.

Nightlife: Clubs, Bars, and Discos

Traditional İstanbul **nightlife** revolves around restaurants and *gazinos* (clubs where *meze* are served, accompanied by singers and oriental dancers), but new bars and Western-style clubs are gaining in popularity among the younger middle class and *entel* (pseudo-intellectual) set. They are generally uncomfortable imitations of Western models with little real atmosphere, but a few of them have the charm of a good location, or attract an interesting clientele that provides a distraction from bad decor or obsequious service. Most are located around Taksim and its nearby suburbs; and along the Bosphorus, mainly on the European side.

Bars

On the Bosphorus

Bebek Hotel Bar, Cevdet Paşa Caddesi 113, Bebek (☎163 3000). Popular with expats and older examples of the local beautiful people. Nondescript inside, so only worth it in the summer when you can sit by the water: be prepared to wait for an outside table, especially on weekends. Open 1pm to 2am daily.

Bukalemun, Dereboyu Cad 22, Ortaköy (☎159 1972). A newer *entel* bar run by one of Turkey's foremost artists, whose aim was to open a bar that would not be out of place in Manhattan. The walls are covered with Bedri Baykam's paintings and graffiti, and a broken wall leads through to the dark and gloomy bar. Turkish groups often perform, but lack of outdoor seating is a disadvantage in the summer. Open 8pm–2am daily.

Kalem Bar, Cevdetpasa Cad 306/1, Bebek (☎165 0448). This unstylish bar is popular with students from nearby Bosphorus University and rich kids from the neighborhood. The tiny balcony is packed in summer and there's a jazz pianist most nights. Open noon to lam daily.

Memo's, Muallim Naci Cad, Salahanesi Sok 10/2, Ortaköy (☎161 8304). When *Memo's* opened it was *the* place for İstanbul's yuppies. Its aggressively modern (and western) approach, which includes suited bouncers and imported Italian chairs, took İstanbul by surprise and then turned out to be just what everyone wanted. The "international" restaurant downstairs is totally overpriced, considering the quality of the food. Open 6pm–1:30am.

Yelkovan, Muallim Naci Cad 71/3, top floor, Ortaköy (☎160 5199). A bit like going to a bad student party or a relaxed informal bar, depending on your view. Furnished with throw cushions and low tables, *Yelkovan* is a hangout for the hippyish types that have made Ortaköy their own in recent years. The outside terrace has a great view of the mosque and there is live music most nights: sometimes it's Turkey's only "reggae" band, other times it's a Joan Baez lookalike strumming on a guitar. Open 6pm–2am daily.

Ziya Bar, Muallim Naci Cad, just past Ortaköy (☎161 6005). One of the older, more established bars. In the winter it caters more to the middle-management business crowd, whose bosses might be found at *Memo's*. The summer is much livelier, thanks to the big garden and outdoor bar. Open daily noon–1am.

Naima, Arnavutköyderesi Sok 1, Arnavutköy (☎163 0578). *Naima* is owned by jazz percussionist Selim Selçuk who wants to have a "genuine" jazz bar in Turkey. Foreign and Turkish musicians play, and Sunday nights there's a jam session open to the public. An intimate, dark, wood-paneled kind of place, *Naima* gets unbearably loud and crowded on weekends. Snacks are American style, burgers, sandwiches, etc. Open 10:30pm–12:30am, lam at weekends. Jazz brunch on Sundays.

Kedi Bar, opposite *Naima*, Arnavutköy. Although *Kedi* only opened a couple of years ago it feels ancient, mainly because it's the hangout of much of İstanbul's sizable 1968-worshiping population. The music, mostly cover versions of old Bob Dylan tunes, adds to the atmosphere. Despite this, *Kedi* is very popular with the aspiring *entel* set. Open till lam.

Kalem Bar, Cevdet Paşa Cad 306/1, Bebek (☎165 0448). Intimate, expensive, and *entel* with its English-captioned arty photos.

Baca, Boyaciköy, Emirgan Yolu 58 (☎177 0808). One of the newer yuppie bars and a good place for a quiet drink. Located on a hill overlooking the Bosphorus, the view is outstanding, especially in summer when the roof bar is open. The clientele consists mainly of older businessmen and their wives, so the atmosphere is very pedestrian. Open 8pm–4am daily.

Bilsak, Soğancı Sok 7, Cihangir; or after May 15, Köybaşı Cad 87, Yeniköy (☎162 4713). Winter *Bilsak* is an aspiring cultural center with a restaurant, small informal bar and occasional music. The summer venue is more formal, and famous for the jazz festival (usually at the end of summer) which attracts international musicians. Open noon to midnight; closed Sundays in the winter.

Uno, Bağdat Cad 406, Suadiye (☎350 2399). Chrome-and-glass aquarium bar with occasional singers. Not worth making a detour for, but if you're over on this side of the Bosphorus it has quite a relaxed atmosphere.

Around Taksim

Cartoon Bar, Maçka Bronz Sok 4–2, Nişantaş (☎147 5496). Newly opened, this bar is brightly lit and decorated with posters of Tin Tin and Donald Duck as well as video monitors that double as tables. This bar epitomizes the new wave of İstanbul's after-work scene, and is packed from 6–9pm. The weekend crowd is older. Open 6:30–11pm, till lpm on Fri, closed Mon.

Kortan Café, Hakkak Yumni Sok 15, Emirgan (☎177 0445). The out-of-the-way location (take a taxi—tell the driver it's the left past the gas station) is the only drawback; otherwise, this is an out-of-the-way café with a stunning view and very low prices. Virtually devoid of foreigners, *Kortan* is known by local teenagers whose parents came here when they were young. Open 11am–midnight daily.

Taksim Sanat Evi, Sıraselviler Cad 69/1, Taksim (☎144 2526). Looks like an airport lounge but has a good view of Cihangir, popular with film people as well as older housewives and their businessmen husbands. A cover band plays jazz classics on the weekend. Food is available; the beans (cooked with a local beef sausage) are exceptionally good. Open daily noon–2am, 4am on weekends.

Cep Sanat Evi, Tünel Mueyyet Sok 11, second floor, Beyoğlu. Another low-key bar, *Cep* is in a building filled with artists' studios so it sometimes attracts an interesting crowd but it's dead in the early part of the week. Filled with a hodgepodge of building fixtures and antiques.

Zihni, Bronz Sokak l/B, Maçka (☎146 9043). The first of the new bars, *Zihni* was opened by a local sculptor who is often seen mixing drinks. The walls are covered with Ottoman calligraphy and most of the furniture is antique, resulting in a fairly tranquil atmosphere. After work *Zihni* is crowded with local bankers meeting their wives; during the day it's a good place for lunch (if you happen to be shopping in the area). The menu has salads and brunch-type dishes as well as more substantial meat and seafood. Open noon–10pm.

Dancing

Near Taksim

29, located in winter at Nispetiye Cad 29, Etiler (☎163 5411); in summer in Çubuklu, reached by frequent launch from Istinye, beyond the big ships in this little bay. Winter *29*, which is also known for its excellent downstairs restaurant, was designed with the help of the owner's cousin Rıfat Özbek. It looks like a sophisticated bordello, with red walls and leopard-skin seats. Summer *29* is a large outdoor club right on the water—with tables shaded by canvas umbrellas and lit by flaming torches. Music is basically disco; the crowd is all ages and very energetic. Certainly the best in İstanbul.

Régine Diskotek, Cumhuriyet Cad 16/2, Elmadağ, Taksim (☎147 5730, 148 6220). Attracts an older crowd of business types. Open daily 10pm–4am, minimum charge $8 with a drink.

Hydromel, Cumhuriyet Cad, Elmadağ (☎140 5893) Small, intimate, and reasonably priced, attracting a young crowd; has an unfortunate tendency to play albums in the early hours of the night. Open 9:30pm–4am, entry $8.

Cinema Bar, Maçka Bronz Sokak 4-2, Nişantaş. (☎147 5496). Newly opened, sultry disco with a movies theme, featuring old theater seats in back. Music is live salsa, clientele the same as at the next-door *Cartoon Bar*. One drawback is that the balcony is a casualty to urban planning and now overlooks a road instead of the Bosphorus. Open 10:30pm–3am, closed Sun.

On the Bosphorus

Caz Bar, Korukent Recreation Center, Levent, Ortaköy (☎166 4493). *Caz Bar* has been around for a while—it's not especially trendy, but can be a good place to dance. Decor is dark and mirrored, some kind of jazz combo plays frequently. Open 9pm–4am daily.

Nostalji, Tayyareci Suphi Sok 44, Arnavutköy (☎165 2911). A tiny bar located above an art gallery and decorated with kilims and work by local painters. *Nostalji* has a beautiful view and on weekdays is very quiet. Music is jazzy records and on weekends there is a guitarist who plays country and pop hits (no admission charge but the first drink costs a fortune; subsequent drinks are the usual $6 or so). Open 6pm–1am, till 2am Sat, closed Sun.

Şamdan Etiler, Nispetiye Cad 30, Etiler (☎163 4898, 165 7048). One of the top discos in town, catering to the local high-society types. Downstairs is a very good restaurant ($45 a head), upstairs a glittery bar filled with tables surrounding a small dance floor. By 1am everyone is bopping and the place is packed. Open 8:30–4am weekdays, till 5am weekends. Closed in summer. First drink $16, weekends $12. Reservations essential.

Gay İstanbul

Despite the widespread enthusiasm for transvestite and transsexual singers and entertainers in Turkey, homosexuality is still a taboo subject and it is possible to be arrested for cruising. The following are all located around Taksim, the main center of the Turkish gay scene.

1001, Sıraselviler Cad. Transvestite bar and disco serving food.

Valentino, Taksim Square. Male gay bar open 10pm–7am.

Vat 69, 7 Imam Adnan Sok, İstiklâl Cad. Western-style disco open 11pm–4am. Most gay activity takes place on weekends, otherwise it's fairly straight.

Ceyland, Abdülhak Hamit Cad, Belediye Dükkanları 14 (☎156 2121). Gay bar frequented by all ages.

Cabaret

Yeşil, Abdulhak Hamit Cad 61, Taksim (☎155 2020). Frequented by the film and acting crowd, *Yeşil* is owned by one of the leading local actors who is into preserving old cabaret culture. Shows change, but past ones included a selection of cabaret scripts from the 1920s and a drama about daily life in the Ottoman empire performed partly by men in drag. $35 admission includes five local drinks or three foreign ones. Show starts at midnight. Closed for part of the summer, reservations necessary.

Noyan & Noyan, Sehit Muhtar Cad 56, Taksim (☎153 4544, 153 4527). A dark, cosy bar with about twenty tables, owned by a husband-and-wife team who perform much of the show themselves. The revue includes wonderful old scratched jazz records from the 1930s, live jazz music, and the Noyans telling jokes and singing classic songs in Turkish and Ladino (medieval Spanish which is still spoken by Turkish Jews) as well as calypso hits and old American spirituals. Audience participation is welcomed and the atmosphere is very friendly. They also perform in English if they see foreigners in the audience. Not to be missed if you want a taste of cultured contemporary İstanbul. First drink $24; show starts at midnight; reservations suggested. Closes for part of the summer.

Kervansaray, Cumhuriyet Cad 30, Harbiye (☎147 1630). A huge pillared and chandeliered hall where you aren't going to feel comfortable without dressing up a bit. Expensive at $56 per person with a meal ($30 without food), but the club has an excellent reputation for its floor show, which includes oriental and folk dancers. Open 7:30pm–midnight.

Maksim, off Taksim Square (☎144 3134, 144 5869). A sophisticated club located in a turn-of-the-century concert hall. The show is long and fairly comprehensive, consisting of oriental and folk dancing, as well as Turkish classical music. Fixed menu, with drinks, is $52.

Shops and Markets

At times İstanbul seems like one enormous bazaar, and as long as you know where to look you can purchase anything. Knowing where to look is always the tricky part, of course: the best and cheapest shopping is as elusive in İstanbul as in any major city. Given that there's a fairly comprehensive public-transit system, however, nothing is inaccessible once you start finding your way around.

Clothes

Turkish **fashion** designs are beginning to compete on the European catwalk, thanks to Rıfat Özbek, the darling of the fashion world. Other names to watch out for in Turkey are Neslihan Yargıcı, Zeynep Tunuslu, and Arif Ilhan, all of whom are working with the best Turkish fabrics, including leather so fine that it is now processed for the Italian market and sold at inflated prices under Italian labels; Bursa silk; and the universally famous Angora wool. While Turkish designers often imitate European styles, they do occasionally flirt with eastern motifs and designs to interesting effect.

Leather is big business in Turkey, which isn't surprising in a country where so much meat is consumed: something has to be done with all those hides after *kurban bayram* (the annual ritual slaughter). Turks wear a lot of leather and, increasingly, designs are matching the quality of the raw material. Prices are also attractive to foreigners—if you go home without buying a leather item then count yourself in the minority. The classiest outlets are listed below; cheaper shops are located in and around the covered bazaar, particularly in Vezirhan Sokak. Bursa **towelling**, among the best in the world, is available from *Özdilek* in Galeria.

Clothing outlets in İstanbul are mainly located in Nişantaşi, Osmanbey and Şişli beyond Taksim in the modern city (buses leave from Taksim square and Cumhuriyet Caddesi); Bağdat Caddesi on the Asian side of the Bosphorus; and Galeria, a modern shopping complex in Bakırköy. İstiklâl Caddesi in Beyoğlu is also gaining prestige as a result of its new facelift.

Galeria is a five-minute walk along the main Bakırköy highway (Rauf Orbay Cad) from the seabus landing. It's designed to incorporate western features, such as an ice-skating rink surrounded by fast food cafés, but the shops are grouped by genre in typical Turkish bazaar fashion. The best of Turkish names as well as some European chains like *Printemps*, have outlets here, and contrary to expectations their prices don't seem to be inflated although the rents for premises are phenomenal.

Designer Clothes

Neslihan Yargıcı, Kuyulu Bostan Sok 6, Nişantaşı.
Yargıcı, branches in Nişantaşı on Valikonağı Cad 30; in Galeria; and on Bağdat Cad 313/1.
Park Bravo, Halazkargazı Cad 214/D and Bağdat Cad 399.
Beymen, Halazkargazı Cad 230, Şişli.
IGS, Galeria and Halazkargazı Cad 198, Şişli.
NN Club, Galeria, Bağdat Cad 306, and Matbaacı Osmanbey Sok 71, Osmanbey.
Vakko, İstiklâl Cad123–5.

Shoes

Hotiç, two outlets on Bağdat Cad and one on Teşvikiye Cad135/1.
Bally, Bağdat Cad 308, Erenköy.

Casual Clothes

Mudo, Rumeli Cad 44, Osmanbey, and Bağdat Cad 395/1A.
BM Club, Galeria, Rumeli Cad 81, Osmanbey, and Bağdat Cad 310/1.
Vakkorama, Osmanlı Sok 13, Taksim, and Bağdat Cad 407.
Tiffany and Tomato, Rumeli Cad 67, Osmanbey, and Bağdat Cad 396/2, Suadiye.

Leather

Derishow, Bağdat Cad 381, Suadiye, and Akkavak Sok 18A, Nişantaşı.
Derimod, Sahilyolu Cad, Beşkardeşler Durak 28, and Teodem, Rumeli Cad Şafak Sok 27/29, Osmanbey.

Angel Leder, Vezirhan Cad 67.

De-Sa, Ortakazlar Cad 8–10 in the Covered Bazaar; carries a good selection of leather and kilim bags.

Groceries

The best places for grocery shopping are the **Halk Pazarları**, located in residential areas all over the city. These are permanent markets with small cubicle-like shops including grocers, butchers, and delicatessens, usually open from Saturday to Monday, and specializing in fresh, cheap produce. If you're looking for specialist foods and Western commodities that you can't find elsewhere, the best place is the Balıkpazarı, the **fish market** off İstiklâl Caddesi behind the Çiçek Pazarı. You can buy otherwise unobtainable pork and bacon at a shop called *Şutte*, Duduodalar Sok 21. Exotic and hard-to-find **spices** (such as curry spices) are available at Duduodalar Sok 26 and 32, and you can find Western-style sauces and other specialist **imports** at *Saraylar*, Balıkpazarı 17. Another outlet for spices is *Faruk Ersöz*, Halıcılar Cad, 40–42 in the Covered Bazaar.

Books

Only a few stores in İstanbul carry English-language books, and foreign publications are hideously expensive. It's often rewarding to spend time and energy raking the secondhand bookmarkets and shops, however. The best-known of the *Sahaflar Çarşısı* (old book markets) is the one at Beyazit, where antique and new history and art books, English novels, language textbooks, and even old prints can all be bought (at a price).

Haşet Kitabevi, İstiklâl Cad 469, Beyoğlu (☎144 9470). Good selection of guides and art books in English.

ABC Kitabevi, İstiklâl Cad 461. Reasonably up-to-date foreign newspapers and magazines.

Redhouse, Risapaşa Yokuşu 48, Tahtakale (☎522 8100). Highly respected publishing house. You may have to knock in order to obtain entrance, or phone ahead, since the shopfront is closed.

Narmanlı Han, İstiklâl Cad 390, practically opposite *Haşet*. This small *Sahaflar Çarşısı* has one particularly good shop called *Karma*, one of the best places to root for bargain antiques and books on the history of the city.

Beyoğlu Sahaflar Çarşısı. Another good book market, in the *Çiçek Pasajı*, where there are several shops, some of which specialize in English-language texts.

Zamba Koğlu, Altıpatlar Sok 63, off Turnacıbaşı Sok. Good antiquarian bookshop where you can also find old magazines and sheet music.

Gallery Alpha, Hacıoğlu Sok 1/A, Beyoğlu. Old prints, maps, and documents as well as antiquarian books.

Carpets and kilims

There are carpet shops all over the city, particularly in and around the Covered Bazaar (Takkeciler Cad has a good concentration), but also in the flea markets of Kadıköy and Üsküdar and in secondhand shops around Altıpatlar Sokak off İstiklâl Caddesi. Buying a carpet involves a psychological game called bargaining. The rules of the game are learned by playing it with the right people, and it's probably a good idea to bear this in mind before you even look at the carpets.

Markets

Flea markets or *bit pazarları* (literally "louse markets") make for excellent shopping: whether you're settling in the city and need furniture or simply looking for souvenirs, it's well worth having a root around these areas, which are basically streets full of junkshops. Remember that while antiquities may be bought and sold, it's illegal to export them (punishable by five to ten years imprisonment).

The **Cihangir** *bit pazarı* is located in the streets below the Galatasaray Hamam off İstiklâl Caddesi, particularly Çukurcuma Sokak. It includes some very classy antique shops, some of which are listed below. **Üsküdar**'s *bit pazarı* is on Büyük Hamam Sokak, off Hakimiyet-i Milliye Caddesi, and **Kadıköy**'s *bit pazarı*, selling mainly furniture, is off Soğutluçeşme Cad, on Özellik Sokak.

The **arts and crafts market** in Ortaköy may be pretentious and trendy, but it's an enjoyably relaxing place to spend a Sunday afternoon if you don't mind crowds. Among the best stands are those selling obscure music cassettes and dissident literature. It's held every Sunday on the waterfront square (take the road leading off the main street to the Bosphorus, from behind the gas station).

Open-air **street markets** are also an important aspect of the city's commercial life. The biggest is probably the *Salı Pazarı*, the **Tuesday Market**, which confusingly takes place every Tuesday and Friday at Altıyol in Kadıköy, but every residential district has its own little string of stalls on a particular day of the week. They are very much what you'd expect, selling cheap fresh produce, spices, kitchen utensils, and clothing.

Listed below is an assortment of **market stalls**, and odd shops selling **crafts** and **antiques**.

In the Covered Bazaar

İç Bedesten. Known as the Old Bazaar, this is where the most precious objects have always been kept because the doors can be locked at night. It's the place to go for antiques of every kind, from Ottoman hamam slippers to pistols. There are also a number of shops here selling silver jewelry.

Sarnıçlı Han, Çadırcılar Cad 5. A wholesale and handicrafts bazaar; lots of copperware.

Gül, Outside Çarşıkapi at Nuruosmaniye Cad 18. An attractive little souvenir shop selling mainly copperware and some ceramics.

Emin Çömez, Yağlikçılar Cad 101–103. Excellent hat stall in the Covered Bazaar, well stocked with Russian and Turkish wool, leather, and fur in winter. This street is also good for handprinted cloth and other Anatolian textiles.

Sofa, Nuruosmaniye Cad 42, Cağaloğlu. Old prints, maps, calligraphy, and ceramics.

In Cihangir and Beyoğlu

Leyla Seyhanlı, Altipatlar/Çukurcuma Cad 30, Cihangir. Antique lace shop.

Aslı Gunsıray, Çukur Camii Sok 72/A. Antique furniture and prints.

Gallery Alpha, Hacioğlu Sok 1/A, Firuzağa, Beyoğlu. Prints, maps, postcards, and ephemera relating to Turkey and İstanbul.

In Ortaköy

Medisa, Cami Sok 6. Glassware painted with *ebru* marbling techniques and modern ceramics.

Ayşe Gallery, İskele Sok. Designer jewelry, some inspired by Ottoman motifs, some hi-tech.

Artisan, İskele Sok, next door to the above. Specializes in Kütahya pottery.

Directory

Airlines Most major airlines have main offices on Cumhuriyet Caddesi, Harbiye. *American Airlines* (☎130 2211) are at no. 269; *British Airways* (☎134 1300) at no. 10; *Olympic Airlines* (☎132 9426) at 171/A; *THY Turkish Airlines* (☎145 2454) at 109–201 and on Mustafa Kemal Paşa Caddesi, Aksaray (☎586 5514, 586 7793); *Pan Am* (☎131 2339) in the *Hilton Hotel*, Cumhuriyet Caddesi, Elmadağ; *Austrian Airlines* (☎132 2200) in the *Sheraton Hotel*, Cumhuriyet Caddesi, Elmadağ; *Sabena* (☎150 4390) and *Iberia* (☎155 19 68) are both on Topcu Caddesi, Taksim; *KLM* (☎130 0311) Abdi Ipekçi Cad, Ünsal Apt 6–8, Nişantaşı; and for **domestic flights**, *THT* (☎574 7240) Atatürk Airport, Yeşilköy; *Greenair* (☎141 0293) Cumhuriyet Cad Adlı Işhanı 279; *İstanbul Airlines* (☎570 3400) Incili Caddesi, 50 Bakırköy; *Sönmez Holding Hava Yollan* (☎573 9323, 573 7240) Atatürk Airport, or through *Moris Sey Acentesi*, Tünel Pasaji 11, Beyoğlu (☎149 8510) or *Anadolu Turizm*, Cumhuriyet Caddesi 261 (☎146 8045).

Airport Domestic and international flights from Atatürk Airport, Yeşilköy: for international flights (*Dış Hatları*) call ☎573 4093; domestic flights (*İç Hatları*) ☎574 2443 or 573 2920. Half-hourly buses to the airport leave from the *THY* office in Şişhane (☎145 4208), near the top of the *tünel* from 7am–9pm.

Art galleries Good ones include: *Edpa*, Husrev Gereda Cad 126, Teşvikiye; *Almelek*, Nispetiye Aytar Cad, Nil Apt 24/6, Levent (☎169 8014); *Benadam*, Moda Cad 220/226, Moda, Kadıköy; *Derishow*, Ihlamur Caddesi, Beşiktaş (☎159 7255); and *Galeri Vinci*, Teşvikiye Ihlamur Yolu, Günol Apt No. 1 (☎133 0619).

Banks Opening hours Mon–Fri 9am–12:30pm and 1:30–5pm. The *Garanti Bankası* in Sultanahmet stays open through lunchtime, and *İşbank* at the airport is open 24 hours a day. The change window in Sirkeci station is open on weekends from 9am–5pm, and takes travelers' checks. Don't pay commission unless you're really strapped for cash: you can always change money in the covered bazaar or in Tahtakale, İstanbul's unofficial exchange (located in the streets below the bazaar), at a better rate than you'll get in the banks.

Books See "Shops and Markets."

Buses For information on city services see "City Transportation," and for getting out of the city see "travel details." The main bus terminals are located at Topkapı (☎577 5617) and Harem (☎333 3763); two of the better bus companies, *Pamukkale* and *Ulusoy*, can be reached at ☎582 2934 and ☎582 6845 respectively.

Car rental Local companies offering good deals are: *Airtour*, Cumhuriyet Caddesi, Dr. Celal Öker Sok 1/1, Harbiye (☎132 8486, 132 8488); *T Tour*, Kuşdilli Caddesi 99, Kadıköy (☎337 9373, 346 0315), and at İstanbul Airport international arrivals (☎573 3779, 573 2920); *Step Rent a Car*, Cumhuriyet Caddesi 287, Harbiye (☎140 3577, 148 2040); *Master Rent a Car*, Ordu Caddesi, Ceylan Sokak 2/1, Aksaray (☎527 4821, 512 8988); *Çelebi Car Rental*, Cumhuriyet Caddesi 141/1, Elmadağ (☎130 0900). International companies—with the advantage of countrywide outlets—include *Hertz*, Divanyolu Cad, Şeftali Sok 16, Sultanahmet (☎526 1465); *Europcar*, Cumhuriyet Cad 47/2, Taksim (☎154 7788); and *Avis* at Atatürk Airport (☎573 1452).

Car repairs İstanbul mechanics are highly skilled and used to keeping old cars roadworthy; and they charge very little for the service. Mechanics and auto-parts shops are located at *Oto sanayi* in outlying areas of the city. Nearest to Sultanahmet is the *sanayi* at Topkapı, on the other side of the walls off Davutpaşa Caddesi around Latif Ağa and Gürün Sok. There's a large repair shop, *Esin*, at Molla Şeref Mah, Halicilar Köşkü Sok 18, Vatan Cad (☎523 5399). Most spare parts can be found at Tarlabaşı Caddesi in Taksim.

Consulates *United States*, Meşrutiyet Cad 104–108, Tepebaşı, Beyoğlu (☎151 3602); *Canada*, Büyükdere Cad 107/3, Begun Han, Gayre Hepe (☎172 5174); *Britain*, Meşrutiyet Caddesi 34, Tepebaşı, Beyoğlu (☎149 8874, 144 7540); *Ireland*, Cumhuriyet Cad 26/A, Elmadağ (☎146 6025); *Soviet Union*, İstiklâl Cad 443, Tünel, Beyoğlu, (☎144 2610, 144 1693); *Germany*, Inönü Cad, Selim Hatun Camii Sok 46, Ayazpaşa, Taksim; *France*, İstiklâl Cad 8, Taksim (☎143 1852); *Greece*, Ağa Hamam Sok, Beyoğlu (☎145 0596); *Netherlands*, İstiklâl Cad 393, Galatasaray, Beyoğlu (☎149 5310); *Norway*, Rihtim Cad Frank Han 277, Karaköy (☎149 9753).

Crime Turkey as a whole is relatively crime-free, but pickpocketing is on the rise in İstanbul. More worrying, there is an increase in the use of sleep-inducing drugs on victims who are subsequently divested of all their valuables. The police are generally sympathetic to foreigners. Reports of theft or loss should be made to the Tourist Police, Alemdar Cad 6, Sultanahmet, (☎528 5369), while any commercial misdealings should be reported to the *Zabita* (see "Police," below).

Dentists *Unident Dış Merkezi* at the Pastör Fransiz Hospital, Taşkışla Cad 3, Taksim (☎133 0707) has adults' and childrens' clinics. There's a 24-hour emergency service run by *İrfan Cezmi Şirin* at Millet Caddesi 169/2, Şehremini, on the way to Topkapı (☎585 8085). Across the Bosphorus try *Kadir Demirkazık*, Hasan Amir Sokak 5/2, Bağdat Caddesi, Kızıltoprak (☎348 2990, 338 9979).

Festivals The International Film Festival (late March to mid-April) takes place at movie theaters all over town; information and reservations from the *Atatürk Kültür Merkezi* in Taksim (a program is published in *Cumhuriyet* in early March). This is the only chance you'll get to see the best of the previous year's Turkish films with English subtitles. The festival has lost credibility in past years by censoring foreign films. The İstanbul Book Fair is held in the *İstanbul Sergi Sarayı* on Meşrutiyet Caddesi, near the *Pera Palas Hotel*, in late October, and the İstanbul Festival of Arts and Culture runs from mid-June to mid-July. Its venues include the *Atatürk Kültür Merkezi* on Taksim Square, the *Açik Hava Tiyatrosu* (Open Air Theater) on Taşkışla Caddesi, Harbiye, the Aya Irene church, Sultanahmet, and Topkapı Palace, and the program includes international classical, jazz, and rock music as well as opera, ballet, and traditional dancing. Tickets available from early June from the *Atatürk Kültür Merkezi*, Taksim.

Hamams The most central, and most frequented by tourists, are *Çemberlitaş Hamam*, on Divanyolu; *Cağaoğlu Hamam*, on Hilali Ahmed Caddesi 34, Cağaloğlu; and *Galatasaray Hamam*, Turnacıbaşı Sok (for men), Çapanoğlu Sok (for women), Beyoğlu. Other good ones are the *Çinili Hamam* off Itfaiye Caddesi in Zeyrek, the *Ortaköy Hamamı*, the *Beylerbeyi Hamamı*, and the *Turistik Aga Hamam* on Turnacıbaşı Sokak, Beyoğlu, which is cheaper and friendlier than *Galatasaray Hamamı*.

Hospitals Most Turkish hospitals, especially the state-run ones (*devlet hastaneleri*, preceded by the initials SSK), are dangerouly overcrowded, understaffed, and under-resourced. Foreign-funded establishments are better off. They include the American *Admiral Bristol Hospital*, Güzelbahçe Sok 20, Nişantaşı (☎131 4050); French *Pasteur Hospital*, Taşkışla Caddesi 3, Harbiye (☎148 4756); *German Hospital*, Sıraselviler Caddesi 119, Taksim (☎151 7100, 143 8100); *International Hospital*, İstanbul Cad 82, Yeşilköy (☎574 7802, 574 7803); and the *Italian Hospital*, Defterdar Yokuşu 37, Cihangir. Otherwise, the teaching hospitals are a safer bet than state hospitals. The *Cerrahpaşa Faculty of Medicine* is at Cerrahpaşa Caddesi 97, Cerrahpaşa (☎585 2100); the *Çapa Medical Faculty Hospital* is at Millet Caddesi, Çapa (☎525 9230); and the *Marmara University Hospital* is at Fahrettin Kerim Gökay Cad, Okul Sok, Altunizade (☎340 0100). The *Taksim First Aid Hospital* is at 112 Sıraselviler Cad (☎152 4300).

Laundry You might find a laundry service in your hotel or pansiyon, otherwise there's a laundry, the *Hobby*, at Caferiya Sokak 6/1, Sultanahmet (☎513 6150, 513 6151; 9am–8pm). Prices, though, are high (about $1 a kilo) and dry cleaners (*kuru temizlemecisi*) may work out cheaper. There's a good one, *Morve-Site*, at the far end of the Hippodrome from Sultan Ahmet, at Üçler Sok 4/A.

Luggage storage Offices (*Emanet* in Turkish) can be found in both Sirkeci and Haydarpaşa train stations. Charge per item.

Libraries The *American Culture Center* has a library in the American Consulate (Meşrutiyet Cad 104–108, Tepebaşı, Beyoğlu). The *British Council* library is in the *ÖRS Turistik İş Merkezi*, İstiklâl Cad 251/253, third floor (☎152 7474 152 7478). The *Turkish Touring Club* maintains a library on the history of İstanbul, on Soğukçeşme Sok, Sultanahmet (☎512 5730), open Mon 10am–noon, Wed & Fri 2–4pm.

Opticians Turkish opticians are invariably cheaper than their American counterparts, and their frames are mostly imported from Western Europe. There are a number of outlets in Sirkeci, particularly on Hamidiye Caddesi.

Phone cards A few payphones in İstanbul now take plastic stored-value cards, which don't get eaten as fast as tokens. You can find card phones at Sirkeci and Kadıköy PTTs, and in seabus stations.

Police The Tourist Police headquarters is at Alemdar Caddesi 6 (☎528 5369), and there are *Zabita* offices all over town, including a handy one in the city center, at the far end of the Hippodrome from Sultan Ahmet. For work and resident permits, contact the *Yabanci Sübe* of the *Emniyet Müdürlüğü*, next to the *Vilayet* on Hükümet Konağı Sok, Cağaloğlu.

Post offices The main post office is on Yeni Posthane Cad in Sirkeci, open 9am–5:30pm (8am–8pm for stamps). Large branch offices, for example those at İstiklâl Caddesi in Galatasaray, Kadıköy İskele Meydanı, and Hakimiyeti Milliye Cad in Üsküdar, are open for air mail and parcels from 8:30am–12:30pm and 1:30–5pm; for normal mailings from 8:30am–8pm; and for telegraph and phone *jetons* from 8:30am to midnight. Small branch offices are open 8am–6pm, Mon–Fri.

Post restante Address to Büyük PTT, Yeni Posthane Cad, Sirkeci.

Soccer Soccer is Turkey's national sport, and top teams, most of which are İstanbul-based, receive fanatical support across the country. Major games are played at İnönü Stadium, on Kadırgalar Cad between Taksim and Beşiktaş, and Fenerbahçe Stadium on Bağdat Caddesi, in Kızıltoprak.

Swimming pools Public pool at the *Burhan Felek Spor Sitesi*, Nuh Kuyusu Cad, Bağlarbaşı (on the minibus route between Kadıköy and Üsküdar); indoor pools in the *Ramada Hotel*, Ordu Cad 226 (☎513 9300), and the *Büyük Sürmeli Hotel*, Saatçı Bayırı Sok, Gayrettepe (☎172 1160); outdoor pools at the *Hilton*, Cumhuriyet Cad 152, Harbiye (☎131 4646), the *Sheraton Hotel*, Mete Cad, Taksim (☎131 2121), and the *Harem Hotel*, above the bus station in Selimiye, Üsküdar (☎333 2025); pools connected to gymnasiums include the *Riviera Pool*, Dr Eşat Işik Cad 39/A (☎346 9938), and the *Moda Kondisyon 2000*, on the ground floor of the Moda Deniz Külübü, Moda, Kadıköy (☎346 2126).

Taxis Ubiquitous; insist they use the meter or get out and find another, and don't let them charge you ten times what's displayed on it.

Trains There are two city lines, one running from Haydarpaşa out to Göztepe, Bostanci, and along the Gulf of İzmit to Gebze, and the other from Sirkeci out to Yedikule, also along the shores of the Marmara. They are frequent, cheap, and crowded at rush hour. Buy a $0.50 ticket (flat fare) and keep it for the duration of your journey. Enquiries: Sirkeci (☎527 1816).

Tourist offices The Regional Directorate of Tourism (☎143 3472) is located at Meşrutiyet Cad 57 (Mon–Fri 9am–5pm). They are extremely helpful and well informed, and it's worth making some effort to visit them. Otherwise there's an office in Sultanahmet on Divanyolu Cad (☎522 4903) near the Hippodrome (daily 9am–5pm), which might be able to spare you a map in the tourist season (they're completely useless in the off-season), and another in the *Hilton Hotel* arcade on Cumhuriyet Caddesi (Mon–Sat, 9am–5pm).

Travel agents For plane and bus tickets try *Marco Polo*, Divanyolu Cad 54/11, Sultanahmet (☎519 2804), or *Imperial*, Divanyolu Cad 30, Sultanahmet (☎513 9430).

Turkish language classes The *Turkish-American Universities Association (TAUA)*, Osmanbey (☎147 2188) runs a five-week summer course (3 hours each weekday) for $250, and courses throughout the year on a trimester basis; *English Fast* in Mecidiyeköy (☎175 4398), Kadıköy (☎338 9100) and Bakırköy (☎542 5627) offers an intensive, five-day-a-week course for $124 a month, or three days a week for $60 a month; *Bosphorus University* (☎163 1500 ext 623/613) offers an intensive eight-week summer course for $1,250, and a regular two-semester Turkish course ($336 a semester); and the *Tömer* school in Gümüşsuyu (☎152 5154) runs an intensive three-week summer school, fifteen eight-hour teaching days for $90. It also runs courses through the year.

Turkish Maritime Lines Rihtim Cad, Karaköy (144 0207).

Turkish Touring and Automobile Association Halaskargazı Cad, Şişli (☎131 4631).

Women's movement An active women's group meets at Türkbeyi Sok 33/1 in the "Pink Apartment" in Pangaltı (☎148 8683), currently on Wednesdays (7pm) and Saturdays (noon–5pm). They are running a campaign against male violence and have recently established a women's refuge, the *Mor Çatı*, for its victims.

travel details

Buses

Mediterranean and Aegean Coasts
(Served by *Varan, Pamukkale, Kamil Koç*)
Alanya (hourly; 14hr); Şide (*Pamukkale*, 1 daily; 13hr); Antalya (several in the evenings from 6pm; 12hr); Fethiye (hourly; 15hr); Marmaris (4 daily; 13hr); Datça (*Pamukkale*, 1 daily; 17hr); Bodrum (4 daily, evenings only; 12hr); Kuşadası (3 daily; 10hr); İzmir (hourly; 9hr 30min); Ayvalik (hourly; 9hr).

Black Sea Coast
(Served by *Ulusoy, Trabzon, As Turizm, Findikkale*) Karabük (*Ulusoy*, 4 daily; 6hr); Zonguldak (3 daily; 6hr); Samsun (6 daily; 12hr); Ordu (3 daily; 14hr); Trabzon (7 daily; 19hr); Rise (4 daily; 20hr); Hopa (*Ulusoy*, 1 daily; 22hr); Artvin (*As Turism* 1 daily; 23hr).

Western Turkey
(*Kamil Koç, Pamukkale, Varan, Uludağ, Hakiki Koç*) Ankara (hourly; 7hr); Balikesir (3 daily; 8hr); Bursa (hourly; 4hr 30min); Bandirma (hourly; 6hr); Denizli (hourly; 10hr); Kütahya (*Uşak Özlem*, 4 daily; 5hr 30min); Uşak (*Uşak Özlem*, 4 daily; 8hr 30min); Çanakkale (hourly; 5hr 30min).

Cappadocia
(served by *Nevtur, Göeme Seyahat, Ulus, Mersin Co.*)
Avanos (5 daily; 12hr 30min); Göreme (5 daily; 12hr 30min); Kayseri (4 daily; 13hr); Nevşehir (5 daily; 12hr); Urgüp (5 daily; 12hr 30min).

Eastern Turkey
(*Esadaş Turizm, Mersin, Lüx Akdeniz Expres, Özkaymak*)
Tokat (3 daily; 16hr); Konya (7 daily; 11hr); Adana (2 daily; 19hr); Urfa (1 daily; 21hr); Antep (1 daily 20hr); Erzurum (3 daily; 18hr); Diyarbakir (3 daily; 19hr); Mardin (1 daily; 22hr); Antakya (*Esadaş Turizm*, 2 daily; 18hr); Iskenderun (*Esadaş Turizm*, 2 daily; 18 hr); Doğu Beyazit (*Esadaş Turizm*, 1 daily; 24hr).

Trains

From Haydarpaşa Station
Ankara (6 daily; 9hr/ 7hr 30min express); Gaziantep (Tues, Thurs and Sun; 5hr 25min); Denizli (1 daily; 14hr 25min); Tatvan (Mon, Thurs, Sat; 43hrs); Konya (2; 13hr 35min); Kars (Tues, Fri; 45hr); Afyon (3; 13hr 30min); İzmir (2; 11hr); Arifiye (3; 3hr) Eskişehir (3; 6hr 20min); Adapazarı (11; 2hr 45min); Gebze (2/3 hourly; 30min).

From Sirkeci Station
London (1 daily; 65hr); Paris (1 daily; 52hr); Moscow (1 daily; 39hr); Rome (1; 51hr); Milan (1; 46hr); Venice (1; 41hr); Munich (1; 39hr); Vienna (1; 37hr); Belgrade (1; 23hr); Zagreb (1; 26hr); Thessalonica (1; 12hr); Athens (1; 32/46hr); Sophia (1 daily; 14hr); Edirne (1; 5hr 10min); Halkalı (4; 45min); Üzünköprü (2, 6hr 5min).

Boats

From Saray Burnu
Bandirma (2 daily; 4hr 15min); Mudanya (5 weekly; 3hr); İzmir (3 weekly; 19hr); Sinop (1 weekly; 68hr); Samsun (1 weekly; 62hr); Ordu (1 weekly 39hr); Giresun (1 weekly; 31hr); Trabzon (weekly, 41hr); Marmara (1 daily June –Sept, 2 weekly Oct–May; 5hr).

From Kabataş
Yalova (3 daily; 2hr).

Domestic Flights

From Yeşilköy Airport
Bursa (6 daily; 30min); Ankara (10 or more daily; 55min); Antalya (2 or more daily; 65min); Dalaman (1 daily; 75min); Kayseri (2 weekly; 75min); Trabzon (1 or 2 daily 1hr 30min); İzmir (6 or more daily; 55min); Konya (3 weekly; 1hr 10min); Van (5 weekly; 3hr); Gaziantep (6 weekly; 3hr); Diyarbakir (1 or 2 daily; 4hr); Adana (4 weekly); Dalaman (2 weekly; 1hr); Batman (3 weekly; 4hr); Denizli (2 weekly; 1hr); Elaziğ (3 weekly; 3hr); Kars (2 weekly; 3hr 30min); Samsun (4 weekly; 1hr); Sivas (2 weekly; 2hr 30min); Şanlıurfa (3 weekly; 3hr 30min).

CHAPTER TWO

AROUND THE SEA OF MARMARA

D espite their proximity to İstanbul, the shores and hinterland of the Sea of Marmara are the part of Turkey most neglected by foreign travelers. This is not altogether surprising—here the country is at its most Balkan and, at first glance, least exotic—but there are good reasons to come: above all the exquisite early Ottoman centers of **Edirne** and **Bursa**. If your appetite is whetted for more of the same, **Lüleburgaz** and **İznik** make good postscripts to the former imperial capitals.

For many citizens of Commonwealth nations, a pilgrimage to the extensive and moving World War I battlefields and cemeteries on the **Gallipoli Peninsula** may involve personal as well as national history. The north-Marmara port of **Gelibolu** makes a good base for excursions to the memorial sites, although Çanakkale (see Chapter Three) is the more commonly used jump-off point.

With more time at your disposal you might consider sampling some of the **coastal resorts**, notably **Şarköy** on the north shore or **Erdek** on the south, or the three inhabited and easily accessible **islands** in the sea. But don't expect too much: they're all much too close to İstanbul, Edirne, and Bursa to have been spared extensive development, and in many cases you'll be the only foreigner in town—they're almost exclusively locals' havens. For evocative—but again, hardly pristine—inland scenery, visit **Uluabat Gölü** or **Uludağ**, both easily reached from Bursa.

Before 1923, much of the Marmara region's population was Greek Orthodox; following the establishment of the Republic and the exchange of populations, massive immigration—both internal and from abroad—combined to fill the vacuum. The result is an ethnic stew that includes people of **Çerkez** (Circassian), Artvinli, and Greek Muslim descent, but consists predominantly of **Pomak, Bosnian**, and **Macedonian Muslims**, and especially **Bulgarian Turks**. All of them had in fact been trickling in since well before the turn of the century, as Austro-Hungarian and Christian nationalist victories in the Balkans made their previous homes inhospitable to Turks or Slavic Muslims.

This trend received a huge reinforcement following the disturbances in Bulgaria in 1989, when hundreds of thousands of ethnic Turks fled to Turkey. Cars with Bulgarian plates are now a common sight on every road around the Marmara. Many of their owners have officially immigrated; some—taking advantage of the open borders and Bulgaria's new liberalized regime—are just visiting relatives or shopping; but a good number are ambivalent, maintaining a wait-and-see attitude toward the shifting winds in Bulgaria and the increasingly strained reception they're experiencing in Turkey. At the time of writing, more than a third of them have in fact officially returned to Bulgaria.

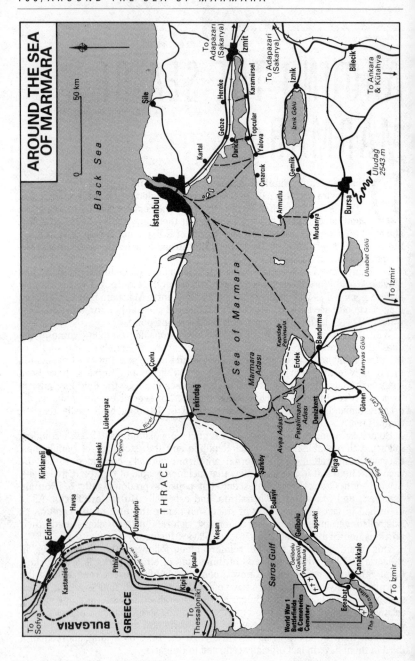

THRACE (TRAKYA)

Thrace, the historic term for the territory bounded by the Danube and Nestos rivers and the Aegean, Marmara, and Black seas, is today divided roughly equally between Greece, Bulgaria, and Turkey. In ancient times it was home to warlike, stock-breeding tribes credited by various historians with bizarre religions and habits, and with being a continual headache for rulers bent on subduing them.

Contemporary life is decidedly less colorful, and the three-percent proportion of Turkey lying in continental Europe is best regarded as the anteroom to the country. The terrain is mostly nondescript, monotonously rolling hills flecked with thickets of stubby oaks; it's a major agricultural area too, with the grain and tobacco fields green or dun-colored according to season. Until the late 1960s nearly all of it was a military security zone, off-limits to foreigners; most is open to travel now, but all towns remain heavily garrisoned, and no major tourist attractions were revealed by the new ease of access.

The modern highway from İstanbul to Edirne almost exactly follows the route of the Roman and Byzantine **Via Egnatia**, which later became the medieval route to the Ottoman holdings in Europe: keep an eye out for various fine **old bridges**, which, like the road itself, may be Ottoman reworkings of Roman or Byzantine originals. The best of these is the quadruple **Büyükçekmece** span, crossing the neck of an estuary a few kilometers west of İstanbul and built by the great architect Sinan in 1563. Not surprisingly, many towns along the road began life as Roman staging posts, a role they continued under the Ottomans, who endowed each with a civic monument or two. Yet few places have anything else to detain you; except for those detailed below, they can be glimpsed well enough from the window of a passing vehicle.

Edirne and Around

More than just the quintessential border town, **EDİRNE** makes an impressive and easily digestible introduction to Turkey. It's a lively and attractive city of nearly half a million, occupying a rise overlooking the meeting of the Tunca, Arda and Meriç rivers, a short distance from the Greek and Bulgarian borders. The life of the place is derived from day-tripping foreign shoppers, heavy trucks and their drivers, a growing number of discerning tourists, students (the University of Thrace is here) and, more sadly of late, Bulgarian Turkish refugees in transit. Downtown, teeming bazaars, horse-drawn carts, cobbled streets, and elegant domestic architecture almost distract you from the clutch of elegant, early-Ottoman monuments that lift Edirne out of the ranks of the ordinary. The best of these, crowning the town hill and sufficient reason in itself for a detour here, is the architect Sinan's culminating achievement, the **Selimiye Camii**.

There has always been a settlement of some kind at this strategic point, and its military importance has fated it to be captured—and sometimes sacked for good measure—repeatedly over the centuries. Thracian Uscudama was refurbished as Hellenistic Oresteia, but the city really entered history as **Hadrianopolis**, designated the main center of Roman Thrace by the emperor Hadrian. Under the Byzantines it retained its significance as a forward base en route to the Balkans—or, more ominously from the Byzantine point of view, as a stepping-stone for invaders marching on İstanbul. Unsuccessful besiegers of Constantinople habitually vented their frustration on Hadrianopolis as they retreated, and a handful of emperors met their end here in pitched battles with Thracian "barbarians" of one sort or another.

By the mid-fourteenth century, the **Ottomans**, who were more disciplined and enduring than the usual marauders, had enmeshed the Byzantines in a web of mutual defence treaties and links by marriage, and gained their first permanent foothold on the coast of Thrace. In 1361 Hadrianopolis surrendered to the besieging Murat I, and the provisional Ottoman capital was effectively transferred here from Bursa. A century later Mehmet the Conqueror trained his troops and tested his artillery here in preparation for the march on Constantinople; indeed, the Ottoman court was not completely moved to the Bosphorus until 1458, and because of its excellent opportunities for hunting and falconry, Edirne, as the Turks renamed it, remained a favorite haunt of sultans for three more centuries.

Decline set in during the 1700s, prompted partly by a fire and an earthquake six years apart. During each of the Russo-Turkish wars of 1829 and 1878–79, the city was occupied and pillaged by Czarist troops; far worse were the Bulgarians, who presided over a four-month spree of atrocities in 1913. The Greeks, as one of the victorious World War I Allies, annexed Edirne along with the rest of Turkish Thrace from 1920 to 1922, and Turkish sovereignty over the city was only confirmed by the 1923 Treaty of Lausanne. Though most physical marks of this turbulence have long since been repaired, the litany of invasions makes it easier to understand the persistent atmosphere of tension between Greeks and Bulgarians. Never an easily defendable strongpoint, Edirne is once again an appetizer, in all senses, for İstanbul.

Arrival, Information, and Services

From elsewhere in Turkey, you'll most likely arrive at Edirne's **otogar**, a little more than 2km southeast of the city center; red city buses or dolmuşes will whisk you to points opposite the town hall. The **train station**, a likely entry point from other European cities, is another kilometer out in the same direction. If you're coming directly from the Greek or Bulgarian highway border posts, see the next section for details.

There are two **tourist information offices**, both on Talat Paşa Caddesi: the main one, about 500m west toward the Gazi Mihal bridge at no. 76/A (☎11518), which stocks plenty of glossy handouts on all of Turkey as well as Edirne, and the equally important annex (daily 8:30am–9pm summer, 8:30am–5pm winter) up near Hürriyet Meydanı, Edirne's "Ground Zero" by the traffic signals. There's also a booth at the Bulgarian (Kapıkule) border.

If you need to **change money** you'll find several banks along Talat Paşa Caddesi; from mid-April to mid-Oct, one of them stays open on weekends—to find out which, check the list posted on the door of all banks. The **PTT**, open 24 hours, is on Saraçlar Caddesi. The **Bulgarian consulate** (Mon–Fri 9am–12:30pm; ☎11069) is out on Talat Paşa Asfaltı, about halfway to the otogar; the **Greek** one is on Cumhuriyet Caddesi in Kale İçi district (same hours, ☎11074). There's a **hospital** behind the Bulgarian consulate.

The **Sokullu Paşa Hamamı** on Hükümet Caddesi, across from the Üç Şerefeli Cami (open 6am–10pm for men and women in separate wings; $2) is neither as friendly, hot, nor well maintained as it might be, especially when you consider its pedigree: it was built by Mimar Sinan, for more on whom see later.

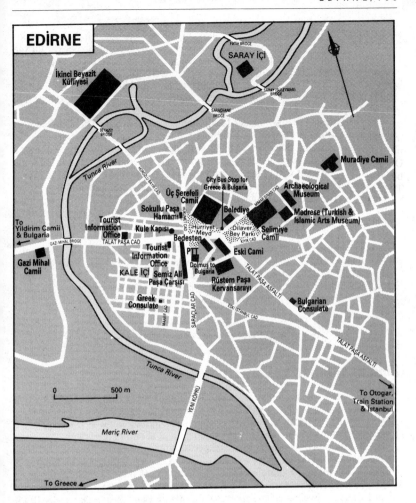

Border Crossings

At the time of writing, the **Turkish-Greek** border posts are only open from 8am to 1pm daily; the Turkish station of Pazarkule, separated from the Greek one at Kastaniés by a kilometer-wide no-man's-land, is 7km west of Edirne and 2km beyond the last Turkish village of Karaağaç.

Red **city buses** (15¢) run from Edirne to Karaağaç every twenty minutes from in front of the Belediye building; **dolmuşes** (25¢) depart with similar frequency from 200m away, behind the town hall. Depending on the prevailing mood between the two countries, however, you may be prevented from walking the final stretch—inquire about the current situation at the tourist information office before setting off, and if you can't walk take a **taxi** ($4) all the way from Edirne to

Pazarkule. Once at Pazarkule, you'll have to take a Greek taxi to the Kastaniés post; this applies to travelers coming from Greece, too—budget $5 per car for the 1000-meter gap! On the Greek side three daily trains, and about as many buses, make the three-hour run down to Alexandhroúpoli, the first major Greek city, between 8am and 1pm, with a couple more later in the day. If all this seems too much trouble, compare it with the more southerly rail and road crossings into Greece on p.170.

The **Bulgarian-Turkish** border is slightly less problematic. The vast complex at Kapıkule, 18km northwest of Edirne, straddles the busy E5/100 expressway and is open around the clock. Unless the new Bulgarian government has a change of heart on such matters, most nationals will still need a **visa** of some kind: $12 for a transit visa obtained from the Edirne consulate, $16 for one issued at the border, and $19 for a tourist visa with a more generous time limit.

Getting to Bulgaria is no problem: red **city buses** shuttle to the border six times daily between 6:45am and 6:40pm, and *Yıldırım Ko-op* **dolmuşes** ply the route half-hourly from 6:30am to 9pm, both for a fare of 40¢. A taxi will set you back well over $10.

If your interest lies farther afield in the Balkans, consider the conveniently timed daily international express **train**, with sleeping-berths, which passes Edirne at 11pm (2am in summer) and theoretically arrives in Sofya nine hours later, with connections to all other European capitals. The overnighter from Sofya arrives in Edirne at 5am during the summer, 8am in the off-season.

> The Edirne area telephone code is ☎181.

Finding a Place to Stay

If Edirne ever experiences a major tourism boom, the accommodation situation could become impossible—with the few genuinely budget hotels either substandard or booked solid by truck drivers, things are tight enough as it is, and you'll probably have to opt for a mid-range establishment at mid-range prices.

The tourist office usually points backpackers toward nearby **Maarif Caddesi**, where the *Otel Anil*'s deceptive exterior at no. 8 conceals a rough, grim flophouse charging $4 single, $7 double, while the *Konak* next door is little better at $5 single, $8 double. The *Aksaray*, Alipaşa Ortakapı Cad 8 (☎26035) on the corner of Maarif Caddesi, is cleaner and more salubrious, but not great value at $8–10 for cell-like singles, $12–14 for doubles.

Some better budget options are a bit farther south and east, along and around **Saraçlar Caddesi**. *Otel Açıkgöz*, Tüfekçiler Çarşısı, Sümerbank Arkası 74 (☎11944), is probably the best deal at $6–8 single, $13–15 double, some with baths; the *Otel Kent* (☎11070), just in front of it on Saraçlar Caddesi proper, is cheaper but noisier. The *Otel Saray*, east of Saraçlar at Eski İstanbul Cad 28 (☎21457), is comparable but quiet at $6–7 single, $11–12 double.

Among the more comfortable places, the calm *Park Hotel*, Maarif Cad 7 (☎14610), is the least expensive option at $16 single, $26 double. Dead central, and thus noisier, is the similarly priced *Kervan Oteli*, Kadirhane Sok 134 (☎11167, 11382). On the far side of the Eski Cami from the *Kervan* stands the **Rüstem Paşa Kervansarayı**, renovated in recent years as a deluxe hotel: you pay $38 single, $69 double for the atmosphere (and noise from the rather dubious bar downstairs).

Campgrounds are liberally sprinkled around Edirne, lining the roads in every direction—but they're geared mainly for RVs. *Fifi Mocamp*, 8km along the E5/100 toward İstanbul; *BP Kervansaray*, near the otogar; *Turing*, along the Kapıkule road; and *Söğütlük*, en route to Karaağac, just past the Yeni Köprü, are your choices. The price for one person and a tent aren't much cheaper than what you'd pay for a decent single room in town.

The City

You can tour the main sights of Edirne on foot, but as the Ottoman monuments are widely scattered you'll need a full day to do it. If the weather's fine this is a pleasure, especially since you'll walk along the willow-shaded banks of the Tunca River for some distance. It's difficult (if not impossible) to get between the outlying sites by public transportation, which is arranged radially, and renting a taxi will probably be more trouble than it's worth.

The logical starting point is the **Eski Cami**, the oldest mosque in town, right across from the Belediye. This boxy structure, topped by nine vaults arranged three by three, is reckoned to be a more elaborate version of Bursa's Ulu Cami. Emir Süleyman, son of the luckless Beyazit I, began it in 1403, but it was his younger brother Mehmet I—the only one of three left alive after a bloody succession struggle—who dedicated it eleven years later. Currently the interior is something of a mess as restoration proceeds; a gaudy late-Ottoman paint job threatens to overshadow the giant calligraphy for which the mosque is famous.

Just across the way Mehmet constructed the **Bedesten**, Edirne's first covered market, a portion of whose revenue went to the upkeep of the nearby mosque. The barn-like structure, with its fourteen vaulted chambers again indebted to a Bursa prototype, has recently been restored, but nothing will make the junky plastic goods on display yield to the precious wares of times past.

The other main covered bazaar in Edirne is the nearby **Semiz Ali Paşa Çarşısı**, whose north entrance lies about 250m west on the corner of Talat Paşa and Saraçlar caddesis. This was begun by Sinan in 1568 at the behest of Semiz Ali, one of the most able and congenial of the Ottoman grand viziers. Like the Bedesten it's of no more than middling interest, the merchandise within being only marginally more appealing than its neighbor's—some jewelry, leather, and shoes are all that's pitched at foreigners. Just opposite the north entrance looms the **Kule Kapısı** (Tower Gate), sole remnant of the town's Roman/Byzantine fortifications; the Ottomans, in a burst of confidence after expanding the limits of empire far beyond Edirne, demolished the rest. Today the gate is occupied by the fire department. West of the Semiz Ali market sprawls the **Kale İçci** district, a rectangular grid of streets dating from Byzantine times and lined with much-interrupted rows of medieval houses. A stroll through here will also uncover some surviving stumps of Byzantine wall.

For the moment, though, head slightly north from Semiz Ali and Hürriyet Meydanı to the **Üç Şerefeli Cami**, which replaced the Eski Cami as Edirne's Friday mosque in 1447. Ten years in the making, its conceptual daring represented the pinnacle of Ottoman religious architecture until overshadowed by the Selimiye Camii a short time later. The name, meaning "three-balconied," derives from the presence of three galleries for the muezzin on the tallest of the four whimsically idiosyncratic **minarets**; the second-highest has two balconies, the others one, and each base is different. Each of the multiple balconies is reached by a separate stairway within the minaret; it is sometimes possible to climb up. The **courtyard**, too, was an innovation, centered on a *şadırvan* and ringed by porphyry and marble columns pilfered from Roman buildings.

The experimental nature of the mosque is further confirmed by the **interior**, which is much wider than it is deep and covered by the largest (24-meter) diameter dome that the Turks had built at the time. To impart a sense of space the architect relied on just two free-standing columns; the other four are recessed into front and back walls to form a hexagon. Sadly, the design doesn't quite work: two smaller domes to each side, hovering over areas reserved for the dervishes favored by the ruling sultan Murat II, each had to be flanked by a pair of rather lame space-filling subsidiary domes.

The Selimiye Camii . . . and Museums

No such hesitation or awkwardness is apparent in the masterly **Selimiye Camii**, designed by the 80-year-old Sinan (for more on whom see "İstanbul," p.95) in 1569 at the command of Selim II. The work of a confident craftsman at the height of his powers, it's visible from some distance away on the Thracian plain, and is virtually the municipal symbol, reproduced on the sides of Edirne's buses, among other places.

You approach the Selimiye across the central park, Dilaver Bey, then through the **Kavaflar Arasta** (Cobbler's Arcade), attributed to Sinan's pupil Davut Ağa and nowadays given over entirely to tourist junk. Matters improve, however, as you mount steps to the **courtyard**, which is even grander than the Üç Şerefeli's, with arches in alternating red-and-white stone, the usual appropriated ancient columns, and domes of varying size above the arcades. The delicately fashioned *şadırvan* is likewise the finest in the city; the four identical slender **minarets** each have three balconies—Sinan's nod to his predecessors—and at 71m in height are the second tallest in the world after those in Mecca. The detailed carved **portal** once graced the Ulu Cami in Birgi (see p.261) and was transported here in pieces, then reassembled.

But it is the celestial interior, specifically the **dome**, that attracts and impresses visitors. Planned expressly to surpass that of Aya Sofya in İstanbul, it manages this—at 31.5m in diameter—by a bare few centimeters; Sinan doubtless benefited from a close study of the former imperial church. Supported by eight mammoth but surprisingly unobtrusive twelve-sided pillars, the cupola floats 44m above the floor, with intricate calligraphy proclaiming the glory of Allah. Immediately below sits a curious structure, a combination **şebil/gazebo** in finely wrought marble, whose waters are said to symbolize those of the mythical sacred well of Zem-Zem. The most ornate stone-carving, however, is reserved for the **mihrab** and **mimber**, backed by fine İznik faience illuminated by sunlight streaming in the many windows which the pillar support-scheme allowed.

Other than the Kavaflar Arasta, there were few dependencies of the Selimiye Camii; an associated **medrese**, at the southeastern corner of the exterior, is now the **Museum of Turkish and Islamic Arts** (Tues–Sun 8am–5:30pm, Mon 10am–2pm; 50¢), housing assorted wooden, ceramic, and martial knickknacks from the province, plus a portrait gallery of former *yağlı güreş* champions (see box on p.168). The main **Archaeological/Ethnographic Museum** (Tues–Sun 8:30am–noon & 1–5:30pm; $1), the modern building just east of the mosque precincts, contains a predictable assortment of Greco-Roman fragments; the ethnographic section focuses on carpet-weaving and other local crafts.

Peripheral Sites

Many of Edirne's monuments are north and west of town, deliberately rusticated by the early sultans to provide a nucleus for future suburbs. Because of the many depopulations the city suffered during the past three centuries, urban growth has never caught up with some of them, so many have the atmosphere of a rural English church or abbey.

Isolated to the northeast of the city center, but within easy reach, the **Muradiye Camii** is a ten-minute, down-then-up walk along Mimar Sinan Caddesi from the Selimiye mosque. According to legend, Celâleddin Rumi, founder of the Mevlevi dervish order, appeared in a dream to the pious Murat II in 1435, urging him to build a sanctuary for the Mevlevis in Edirne. The result is this pleasing, T-shaped *zaviye* crouched on a hill looking north over vegetable patches and the Tunca; a final bucolic touch is lent by the grassy entry court. Inside—and it's best to come at prayer time to guarantee admission—the mosque is distinguished by the best **İznik tiles** outside of Bursa: the *mihrab* and walls up to eye level are solid with them. Higher surfaces once bore calligraphic frescoes, but these have probably been missing since the catastrophic earthquake of 1751. The dervishes initially congregated in the *eyvans*, which form the ends of the T's cross-stroke; Murat later housed them in a separate *tekke* in the garden.

The other outlying attractions are all on the far bank of the Tunca, crossed here by the greatest concentration of **historic bridges** in Thrace, better suited to pedestrians and horsecarts than the single file of motor vehicles which barely fits on most of them. The pair farthest upstream, the fifteenth-century **Saray (Süleyman)** and **Fatih** bridges, join the left and right banks respectively of the Tunca with **Saray İçi**, an island in the river that used to support the **Edirne Sarayı**, a royal palace begun by Murat II. Unhappily it was blown to bits by the Turks themselves in 1877 to prevent the munitions stored inside from falling into Russian hands, and today nothing is left of this pleasure pavilion except the rubble of some baths, and a tower, next to which rises an incongruously modern concrete stadium, used for the Kırkpınar wrestling matches (see box on the next page).

The next bridge below the island is the **Saraçhane**; you can descend directly on foot from the Muradiye Camii to this or the preceding two, but with a vehicle you'll have to detour back to the town center. The riverbanks are officially a military zone, but you can certainly take photos of the old bridges as long as you don't do anything brazen like point your camera at soldiers or modern installations.

If time is short, cross the double-staged **Beyazit Bridge**—accessible along Horozlu Bayırı Caddesi—directly to the **İkinci Beyazit Külliyesi**, the largest Ottoman spiritual and physical-welfare complex ever constructed. Within a single irregular boundary wall, and beneath a hundred-domed silhouette familiar from many an M C Escher engraving, are assembled not only a mosque but a food storehouse, bakery, *imaret*, dervish hostel, medical school, and insane asylum, the 1484–1488 work of one Hayrettin, court architect to Beyazit II. The premises were recently renovated and are now partly occupied by the art and medicine faculties of the University of Thrace, whose students lend the place a bit of life. If they're not around you'll need to find the *bekçi* to let you in to most of the buildings.

On the east side, the **storehouse and bakery** are appropriately enough given over to ceramic kilns; the low platform in the **imaret**, around which the itinerant dervishes dined, is now surrounded by student works-in-progress. Except for its handsome courtyard and the sultan's loge inside, the **mosque** itself is disappoint-

KIRKPİNAR YAĞLİ GÜREŞ

Yağlı güreş (**grease-wrestling**) is popular throughout Turkey, but reaches the pinnacle of its acclaim at the doyen of tournaments, the annual **Kırkpınar festival**, staged early each summer on the Saray İçi islet outside Edirne. (The preferred dates are the first week of July, but the five-day event is moved back into June if Ramadan or either of the two major *bayrams* following it interfere.)

The matches have been held annually, except in times of war or Edirne's occupation, for more than six centuries, and their origins are shrouded in legend. The most commonly repeated story asserts that Süleyman, son of Orhan Gazi, was returning from a battle in 1360 with forty of his men and decided to camp at a village near Edirne. To pass the time the soldiers paired off to wrestle; the remaining two were unable to best each other after several days of tussling, and in a final elimination match expired simultaneously after midnight. Their companions buried them on the spot and, returning to visit the graves the next season, were astonished to find instead a lush meadow with forty springs (*kırk pınar* in Turkish) bubbling away. Forty is one of the sacred numbers of Islam, and the Ottomans needed little encouragement to inaugurate a commemoration.

Despite the less-than-atmospheric environment of the stadium that now hosts the bouts on Saray İçi, tradition still surrounds the event. The contestants—up to a thousand per year—are dressed only in leather briefs called *kisbet*, and slicked down from head to toe in diluted olive oil. Wrestlers are classed by height, not by weight, from toddlers up to the forty-member *pehlivan* (full-size) category. Warm-up exercises, the *peşrev*, are highly stereotyped and accompanied by *davul* (deep-toned drum) and *zurna* (single-reed Islamic oboe). Competitors, and the actual matches, are solemnly introduced by the *cazgır*, or master of ceremonies, usually himself a former champion.

The bouts, several of which are often going simultaneously, can last anywhere from a few minutes to a couple of hours, until one competitor collapses or has his back pinned to the grass; referees keep a lookout for the limited number of illegal moves or holds, and victors advance more or less immediately to the next round until, after the second or third day, only the *başpehlivan* (champion) remains. Despite the small prize purse, donated by the *Kırkpınar Ağaları*—the local boosters who put on the whole show—a champion usually makes out pretty well from appearance and endorsement fees, and you may well wonder whether he also derives some benefit from the furious on- and off-site betting. In the main, gladiators tend to be simple villagers from all over Turkey who have won regional titles, starry-eyed with the prospect of fame and escape from a rural rut.

A couple of days of folkloric exhibitions laid on by the Edirne municipality precede the gladiatorial events; if you're interested in tickets to the latter, call the tourist office (☎11518) well in advance for information. **Gypsies**, in addition to providing the music of the *peşrev*, descend on the outskirts of town in force, setting up a combination funfair, circus, and carnival for the duration.

ing, a single-dome affair disfigured by some unfortunate Ottoman Baroque mural work; the dervish hospices on either side are not generally open to the public.

West of the mosque lie the most interesting parts of the *külliye*. In the extreme northwest corner stands the **medical school**, a few of whose cells are once again low-rent (or no-rent) homes to students, at least in the summer. The school, with its central court, is conveniently linked to the *timarhane*, or asylum, built around an open garden, which in turn leads to the magnificent **darüşşifa**, or therapy center. This hexagonal, domed structure consists of a circular central space with six *eyvans* opening onto it; the inmates were brought here regularly, where a fountain—slightly elevated to drain to the rim of the chamber—and musicians played together to soothe the more intractable cases. Strange, five-sided rooms with fireplaces open off three of the *eyvans*: hardier students run modern stoves up the medieval chimneys and attempt to live and work here during the winter.

Continuing parallel to the dikes and water-meadows of the Tunca's right bank should bring you to the misnamed **Yıldırım Camii**, creditable not to Yıldırım Beyazit I but to Murat I, who built it over a Byzantine church shortly after his capture of Edirne in 1361—thus it lacks a proper *mihrab*. The mosque is reached via its own recently repaired bridge, just past the *Mihal Et Lokantası*; currently it's undergoing what appears to be an inept restoration.

Return to town over the **Gazi Mihal Bridge**, an Ottoman refurbishment of a thirteenth-century Byzantine span and hence the oldest around Edirne. Gazi Mihal was a Christian nobleman who became an enthusiastic convert to Islam—hence the epithet "Gazi," warrior for the faith. His namesake mosque, now a shambles at one end of the bridge, is probably next up for restoration. The last of Edirne's bridges, the relatively recent **Yeni Köprü**, leaps over both the Tunca and the Meriç in a 700-meter span.

Eating and Drinking

Restaurants are adequate but not especially cheap in Edirne; exceptions are the tiny *ciğerci* booths specializing in the local specialty, **deep-fried liver**.

Some of the obvious eateries on Saraçlar Caddesi aren't bad: the *Şark Köftecisi* and the *Serhad Köftecisi*, adjacent the trees on the south side of Hürriyet Meydanı, are fine if cramped. Farther down the street next to the *Otel Kent*, the *Şehir* is an acceptable steam-tray lunch place. The *Çimen Lokanta*, on one side of the Bedesten, is the same sort of thing in more evocative surroundings.

Back on Saraçlar Caddesi, the first establishment with a liquor license is the moderately expensive and rather sterile *Aile Restaurant*, upstairs in the Belediye İş Hanı, by the PTT. The *Saray Ciğer ve Çorba Salonu*, immediately adjacent, serves only liver and soups, as the name implies. Affordable food-with-booze can be had at two *meyhanes*, the *Agora* and *Emin'in Yeri*, near the *Otel Açikgöz*. Close to the *Otel Aksaray*, and just outside one gate of the Semiz Ali Paşa Çarşısı gates, you'll find the secluded *Deniz Restoran*.

For **dessert**, every imaginable kind of pudding, pastry, and ice cream is sold at various stands lining Saraçlar Caddesi. Finally, Edirne takes surprisingly little advantage of its **riverside** setting; there are just a handful of relatively expensive restaurants, and more reasonable tea gardens, out by the Yeni and Gazi Mihal bridges.

East of Edirne: Lüleburgaz

If you've become a Sinan-ophile, yet another of his substantial creations dominates the town of **LÜLEBURGAZ**, 76km east of Edirne on the main route to İstanbul. The **Sokollu Mehmet Paşa Külliyesi**, originally commissioned by that governor of Rumeli in 1549, was built in fits and starts, not being completed until 1569 during Sokollu's term as grand vizier. Today what's left is an imposing mosque/ *medrese* abutted by a covered bazaar and guarded by two isolated towers.

The **mosque** proper is peculiar, possessing only one minaret; where the others should be, three stubby, turret-like towers jut instead, all joined by a mansard crenellation. The **medrese**, still used as a children's Koran school, is arrayed around the mosque courtyard, which is entered by two tiny arcades on the east and west sides; in the middle of the vast space stands the late Ottoman caprice of a şadırvan. The mosque's **portico**, built to fit in with the *medrese*, is far more impressive than the interior, and most visitors will soon drift out the north gate to the **market promenade**, whose shops are still intact and in use. Just outside the north gate, a huge dome with a stork's nest on top shades the center of the bazaar.

Beyond, there was once a massive *kervansaray*, equal in size to the mosque/*medrese*; this was the last part to be finished, and it has all vanished save for a lone tower, balanced by another, the **Dar-ül-Kura**, at the south edge of the entire compound, beyond the mosque's *mihrab*. The former **hamam**, across the street from the complex, also constructed as an afterthought, is now jam-packed with tiny **restaurants** in its outer bays, though the main dome has collapsed.

There are a few simple but acceptable **hotels** 200m south of Sokullu Mehmet, plus the more luxurious *Hongurlar Oteli* at İstanbul Cad 73 (☎183/14500) and the *Yaman* out at the junction with the bypass road (☎183/11613). There's little point stopping over, though, as the town is otherwise utterly undistinguished and, given the frequent buses, moving on toward either İstanbul or Edirne is easy at any time.

South of Edirne: Assorted Greek Border Crossings

There's little reason to stop at any point along the E87/550 highway as it heads down from HAVSA, the turnoff point 27km southeast of Edirne. This road does, however, connect Uzunköprü and Keşan, one of which you're likely to pass through if transiting to or from Greece.

UZUNKÖPRÜ (Long Bridge) gets its name from the 173-arched Ottoman aqueduct at the north end of town. You wouldn't make a special trip to see it, though, and while Uzunköprü is an official rail entry/exit port for Turkey, the station is 4km north of town and you'd have to be pretty perverse to catch either the late-night international "express" from Greece to İstanbul or the pre-dawn train to Greece here—certainly not when connections out of Edirne are so much better. If you insist, you may end up waiting for the Greece-bound train at the one-star *Ergene Oteli* (☎189/35438), on the main square.

The main Greek-Turkish road crossing, far busier and somewhat less manic then the Edirne/Kastaniés one, is at **KİPİ/İPSALA**, astride the E25/110 highway. The two posts here are open 24 hours, but banking facilities and tourist information booths on each side only operate sporadically, so it's not a bad idea to show up with a certain amount of currency for the country you'll be entering. As at the Edirne frontier, there's a 500-meter-wide military zone that you're not allowed to cross on foot; during daylight hours at least it's fairly easy to arrange a ride across.

From the village of Kípi there are six buses daily farther into Greece; at the Turkish immigration post you'll meet only taxis. If you take one of these, a trip just to İpsala (5km away) is money wasted; for a little extra—under $10 per car if business is slow—get yourself to **KEŞAN** (30km east), a cipher as a town but with vastly more frequent bus connections to İstanbul and Çanakkale. Incidentally, long-haul bus connections out of Edirne to anywhere but İstanbul are very poor; if you're making from the former to Çanakkale, İzmir, or Bursa, you'll almost always have to change vehicles—with an hour or two layover—in Keşan.

The Thracian Coast: Tekirdağ to the Gelibolu Peninsula

Heading west from İstanbul, you don't really outrun the straggling suburbs until the junction where the Edirne-bound E5/100 splits off from the E25/110 headed for the İpsala border station. Even then the coast doesn't exactly scream at you to stop; **TEKİRDAĞ**, given its hilly setting at the head of a gently curving bay, must have once been an appealing place but now it's an eyesore, the few remaining wooden apartments swamped by the concrete, dust, and congestion of development. Down on the shore boulevard there's a **tourist information office** just next to the *TML* dock; the latter sees two weekly summer services to and from the islands of the Sea of Marmara, but you should confirm schedules in advance because Tekirdağ is no place to hang around. The most regular bus service to Şarköy (see below) plies from here as well; if you've got time to kill you might drop in at the well-marked **Rakoczi Museum**, dedicated to the Hungarian nobleman and nationalist who holed up here early in the eighteenth century after a failed uprising against the Habsburgs.

Beyond Tekirdağ the coast becomes rugged and relatively inaccessible; a rough, steep dirt road, much worse than indicated on maps and best suited for motorcycles or mountain bikes, winds through beautiful, isolated country speckled with grapevines and tumbledown villages. The hills behind are abrupt enough to deflect almost all the rivers of Thrace toward the Meriç, with few finding the sea here. Asphalt, and a bus service, reappear at GAZİKÖY, and MÜREFTE has a dock from the era when *TML* steamers were this area's only link with the outside world (the military forbade land approach), but the first place of any consequence, and the only one you'd deliberately go to, is Şarköy.

Şarköy

One of the few human-scale resorts remaining near İstanbul, **ŞARKÖY** is also one of the longest-established, having catered to İstanbul-dwellers and Thracians since the 1960s. There's an actual town behind the plane-tree esplanade fringing a kilometer of decent sand, with a few signs in English aimed at foreigners, although it's mostly 100,000-plus Turks who pour through here each summer.

The **otogar** is about a fifteen-minute walk from the beach, at the extreme northwest edge of town on the road to the E87/550 highway.

If you decide to **stay**, you should avoid the noise from various *gazinos*: the *Cennet Motel* (☎1868/1057), at the far eastern end of the beach, can be recommended. Prices, including breakfast, vary from $8–10 per person depending on the season, length of stay, and single or double occupancy, and they also offer $17–18 half-board rates. Otherwise, the nearby *Erkan* (☎1868/1233), *Şedef*, or *Tütüncü* pansiyons are similarly calm, though geared more for Turkish families on long stays. If you're inured to *arabesk* music, the *Çimen* or *Saba* motels adjoin the main shore plaza; at the extreme west end of town the *Sohbet* (☎1868/1400), overlooking the fishing harbor past the west beach, is relatively peaceful. **Eating out**, you've got the *Sevecen Restaurant*, in one of the few old buildings standing on the shore plaza; the *Çimen* and *Deniz* represent a notch up.

The Gelibolu Peninsula: Gallipoli

Burdened with a grim military history but endowed with some fine scenery and beaches, the slender **GELİBOLU PENINSULA** forms the northwest side of the **Dardanelles**. Whether you approach from Şarköy or (more likely) Keşan, the road to it is pretty, swooping down in long arcs past the Saros gulf, scene of recent friction between Greece and Turkey because of the latter's intention to prospect for undersea petroleum there.

If you're traveling under your own steam you can stop off at one of a handful of motels overlooking the gravelly Saros beaches, which are absolutely the northernmost in the Turkish Aegean.

At **BOLAYIR**, where the peninsula is a mere 4km across, you might also pause for a glance at the obvious **castle** and two **tombs**: one of Prince Süleyman—he of the Kırkpınar rites (see Edirne), killed on this spot in a riding accident in 1359—and the other of **Namık Kemal**, poet and reform advocate of the late nineteenth century who spent much of his life in exile.

Gelibolu

Principal town of the peninsula, **GELİBOLU** is a moderately inviting if slightly windy place perched just where the Dardanelles (Çanakkale Boğazı in Turkish) begin to narrow in earnest. At the heart of town is a colorful, square fishing harbor ringed by cafés and restaurants, its two pools separated by a stump of a **medieval tower**. This is the sole survivor of Byzantine Callipolis's fortifications, greatly enlarged by the Ottomans when they took the place from Catalan mercenaries in 1354. The only other significant monuments are a historic mosque in the marketplace and, well inland to the northeast, a few handsomely sturdy but otherwise unremarkable Ottoman **türbes**. Gelibolu moved briefly into the spotlight of history again during the Crimean War, when it was the Anglo-French headquarters.

Practical Details

The **ferry dock**, for regular service across to Lapseki, is right at the inner harbor entrance; the **bus terminal** is on the opposite side of the anchorage next to the old tower. Travelers **overnighting** here with the intention of visiting the nearby battlefields will find that most facilities are controlled by the brothers Sâmân and Teoman Yılmaz, who offer accommodation for every conceivable taste and budget.

Closely bunched together at one corner of the port on Liman Caddesi are the pansiyons *Yılmaz* (☎1891/1031) at no. 1 and *Anzac* at no. 2, starting at about $4 apiece, and the *Hotel Yılmaz* (☎1891/1256) at no. 6, priced at $10 single, $18 double. Out by the lighthouse, with a garden, is the brothers' *Motel Anzac* (☎1891/1256), where rooms go for $6 per person. Between the lighthouse and an army camp extends a serviceable beach, with a **campground**; there's also the *Obidi* campground at the opposite edge of town. Other alternatives to the Yılmaz cartel include the motels *Altay* and *Bilgi* (☎1891/1316), but they're inconveniently sited beyond the traffic circle at the northern outskirts of Gelibolu.

The Yılmaz clan also offers morning and afternoon **tours** of the World War I sites for about $12 per person; and runs its own bus company serving major cities

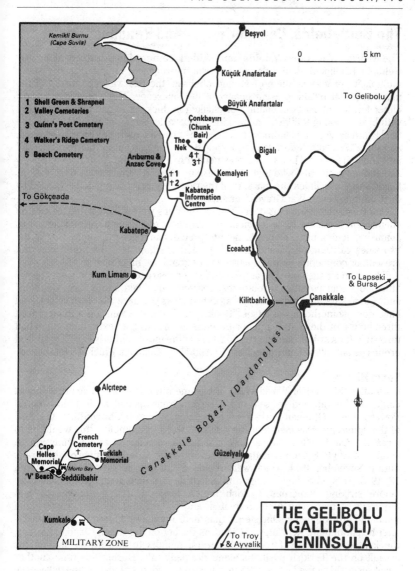

1 Shell Green & Shrapnel Valley Cemeteries
2 Valley Cemeteries
3 Quinn's Post Cemetery
4 Walker's Ridge Cemetery
5 Beach Cemetery

Kemikli Burnu
(Cape Suvla)

Beşyol

0   5 km

Küçük Anafartalar

Büyük Anafartalar

To Gelibolu

Çonkbayırı
(Chunk Bair)

The Nek

Ariburnu &
Anzac Cove

Bigalı

4†
3†

†1
5† †2

Kemalyeri

To Gökçeada

Kabatepe
Information
Centre

Kabatepe

Eceabat

Kum Limanı

To Lapseki
& Bursa

Kilitbahir

Çanakkale

Alçıtepe

Çanakkale Boğazı (Dardanelles)

French
Cemetery
†

Cape
Helles
Memorial

Turkish
Memorial

Güzelyalı

Morto Bay

'V' Beach   Seddülbahir

Kumkale

MILITARY ZONE

To Troy
& Ayvalik

**THE GELİBOLU
(GALLIPOLI)
PENINSULA**

around the Marmara. More disinterested information can be had from the occasionally open **tourist information office**, behind the park at the back of the harbor. Finally, when **eating out**, don't miss the local catch of **sardalya** (sardines), which are better grilled fresh before they find their way to Gelibolu's canneries. The *İmren Restaurant* on the waterfront is cheap, licensed to sell alcohol, and excellent.

The Battlefields, Cemeteries . . . And Beaches

The **World War I battlefields and Allied cemeteries** scattered along the Gelibolu (Gallipoli) Peninsula are by turns moving and numbing in the sheer multiplicity of graves, memorials, and obelisks, the past violence made all the more poignant by the present beauty of the landscape. The whole area is now either fertile, rolling farm country or cloaked in thick scrub and pine forest alive with birds, making it difficult to imagine the bare desolation of 1915. Recently the final 20km or so of the landmass has been designated a **national historical park**, and since 1985 some effort has been made by the Turkish authorities to mark road junctions and sites. This was complemented in 1990 by the Australian and New Zealand governments, who took the occasion of the 75th anniversary observations to add various facilities and markers of their own to join those previously placed by the Commonwealth War Graves Commission.

Unfortunately, seven-plus decades after the guns were stilled, some lessons on chauvinism seem yet to be learned: the net effect of all this plaque-laying is two confusing sets of place names to be interpreted, and a general impression of the two sides carrying on parallel monologs, acting either as if the other were not present, or competing in the construction of grandiose monuments.

The open-air sites have no admission fees or restricted hours, but since there's little public transportation through the area you should take a **tour** (see "Gelibolu" and "Çanakkale" for suggested operators)—unless you have your own vehicle and have done some homework (see "Books" in *Contexts*). Count on a minimum of three hours for the central and northern memorials, with an extra hour and a half thrown in for a swim somewhere and a look at the most southerly cape. Organized groups usually allow four hours from Çanakkale or Gelibolu, which is a bit rushed.

Some History

Soon after the start of World War I it became obvious to the Allies that Russia could not be supplied by sea, nor a Balkan front opened against the Central Powers, unless Ottoman Turkey was eliminated. **Winston Churchill**, as first lord of the admiralty, reasoned that the quickest way to accomplish this would be to force the Dardanelles with a fleet and bombard İstanbul into submission. A combined Anglo-French armada made several half-hearted attempts on the straits during November 1914, which were repulsed, but returned in earnest on March 18, 1915. This time they managed to penetrate less than 10km up the waterway before striking numerous Turkish mines, losing half a dozen vessels and hundreds of men. The Allies retreated, and command squabbles erupted as a result of Lord Kitchener's insistence that the Commonwealth armies should hereafter be paramount. Regrouped at Mudros Harbor on the Greek island of Limnos, the joint expeditionary forces took several months to prepare an amphibious assault on the Turkish positions along the peninsula. During this time another naval sprint down the Dardanelles may have succeeded, but instead the delay gave the Turks time to strengthen their own defenses.

The plan eventually formulated by the Commonwealth and French commanders called for an Anglo-French landing at Cape Helles, Seddülbahir, and Morto Bay at the mouth of the straits, and a simultaneous ANZAC (Australia-New Zealand Army Corps) assault at Kabatepe beach 13km north. The two forces were to drive toward each other, link up, and neutralise the Turkish shore batteries controlling the Dardanelles.

This rather hare-brained scheme ran into trouble from the start. At dawn on April 25, 1915, the **Anglo-French** brigades at the southernmost cape were pinned down by accurate Turkish fire; a toehold was eventually established, but it was never expanded during the rest of the campaign, and the French contingent was virtually decimated. The fate of the **ANZAC** landing was even more horrific: owing to a drifting signal buoy, the Aussies and Kiwis disembarked not on the wide, flat sands of Kabatepe, but at a cramped and Turkish-dominated cove next to Arıburnu, 2km north. Despite appalling casualties the ANZACs advanced inland in staggered parties over the next day, goaded by their commanders, to threaten the Turkish stronghold of Çonkbayırı overhead. As at the other landing, however, little permanent progress was made despite a supplementary British landing at Cape Suvla to the north; except during ferocious battles for the summit in early August, both sides settled into long-term trench warfare, which was every bit as gruesome as the north European counterpart despite the Mediterranean latitude. Finally, around Christmas 1915, the Allies gave up, with the last troops leaving Seddülbahir on January 8, 1916. Churchill's career, among others, went into temporary eclipse.

The reasons for the Allied defeat are many. In addition to the riskiness of the basic strategy, callousness and incompetence on the part of the Allied commanders—who often countermanded each other's orders or failed to press advantages with reinforcements—cannot be underestimated. With hindsight you cannot help but wonder why the Allies didn't concentrate more on Cape Suvla and the flat, wide valley behind, skirting the fortified Ottoman heights to reach the Dardanelles' northwest shore. On the Turkish side, much of the credit for the successful resistance must go to one Mustafa Kemal, then a relatively obscure lieutenant-colonel, later best known as **Atatürk**. As ranking officer at Çonkbayırı for the duration of the campaign, his role in the Turkish victory is legendary. He seemed to enjoy a charmed life, narrowly escaping death on several occasions, and, aside from his tactical skills, is credited with various other superhuman accomplishments—primarily that of rekindling morale, by threats, persuasion, or example, among often outgunned and outnumbered Ottoman infantrymen.

Ironically, both sides suffered nearly identical losses to maintain a status quo. Half a million men were deployed by defenders and attackers alike, albeit in stages; of these well over 50 percent were killed, wounded, or missing, with total deaths estimated at 160,000. The carnage among the ANZACs in particular was grossly disporportionate to the island nations' populations; indeed, the Allied top brass cavalierly regarded the "colonials" as expendable cannon fodder, an attitude that has not been forgotten in certain circles. This baptism by blood had several long-term effects: a sense of Australia and New Zealand having come of age as sovereign countries; the designation of April 25 as a solemn holiday in Australia and New Zealand to mark the event; and a healthy antipodean skepticism of joining international adventures, pending an evaluation of actual national interests.

Central and Northern Sites

Three kilometers north of ECEABAT (see below for details), a posted sideroad heads west toward "Kemalyeri" and "Kabatepe." The first stop of most tours is the **Kabatepe Orientation Center and Museum**, 6km along; this is not particularly well labeled or organized yet, although you'll be told about the series of ten informational plaques set up in the hills to the north. The first points encountered along the coast road are the **Beach**, **Shrapnel Valley**, and **Shell Green** cemeteries, followed by **Anzac Cove** and **Arıburnu**, site of the bungled ANZAC landing and ringed by more graves. Looking inland, you'll see the murderous badlands that gave the defenders such an advantage. Beyond Arıburnu, the terrain flattens out and four other cemeteries are much more dispersed.

At a fork, a left turn leads toward the beaches and salt lake at **Cape Suvla**, today renamed Kemikli Burnu; most tourists bear right for BÜYÜK ANAFARTALAR village and Çonkbayırı (Chunk Bair). The road curls up the long, flat valley partly occupied by the British during that fateful spring; if you're at the wheel you need to take another right at an inconspicuous sign facing away from you: "Çonkbayırı 6, Kabatepe 13."

The main features of **Çonkbayırı hill** are the massive New Zealand memorial obelisk and the five-monolith Turkish memorial describing Atatürk's words and deeds—chief among the latter being organizing successful resistance to the Allied attacks of August 6–10. The spot where the Turkish leader's pocketwatch stopped a fragment of shrapnel is highlighted, as is the grave of a Turkish soldier discovered in 1990 when the trenches were reconstructed.

Working your way back down toward the visitors' center, you pass the strongholds-become-cemeteries of **The Nek**, **Walker's Ridge**, and **Quinn's Post**, where the trenches of the opposing forces lay within a few meters of each other; the modern road corresponds to the no-man's-land. From here the single, perilous supply line ran downvalley to the present location of Beach Cemetery. The line of furthest ANZAC advance—for such it was—continues down a bit more to **Lone Pine (Kanlı Sırt)**, the lowest strategic position on the ridge, and the largest graveyard-memorial to those buried unmarked or at sea. Action here was considered a sideshow to the main August offensive at Çonkbayırı; a total of 28,000 men died in four days at both points.

To the Southern Cape

KABATEPE, the boarding point for the twice-weekly winter ferry to Gökçeada (Imvros), is 2km south of the orientation center. There's a good beach here—it was the intended site of the ANZAC landing—but if you're after a swim wait until reaching **KUM LİMANI**, 5km south of the museum, where an even better beach fringes a warm, clean, and unusually calm (for this far north) sea. Except for the *Kum Motel* (☎1964/1455), offering full board for $11 a head in A-frame cabins or $20 in a full-scale motel, there's been little development of this beautiful setting, but you probably won't be alone—various overland tour companies bring their clients here for a dip after battlefield sightseeing. If you're relying on public transportation, this is one place you can get to fairly easily, since dolmuşes between Eceabat and ALÇITEPE pass a junction just over a kilometer away.

The **Cape Helles** British naval obelisk adorns the nethermost tip of the peninsula, 16km beyond Kum Limanı and just past the village of **SEDDÜLBAHİR**. Views south to Bozcaada (Tenedos), west to Gökçeada (Imvros), and east to Asia are magnificent, and abundant **Ottoman fortifications** hint at the age-old importance of the place. (The Kumkale castle on the other side of the straits is still out-of-bounds to visitors.) Tucked between the medieval bulwarks is an excellent beach, the **"V Beach"** of the Allied expedition, and behind it is a **campground** and the biggest of five British cemeteries in the area. The beach partly explains the five local pansiyons such as *Fulda* and *Helles Panormama* (☎1964/1429), but so far little impact has been made on a basically sleepy hamlet.

A turning just before Seddülbahir leads to the **French cemetery** above Morto Bay and the nearby **Turkish memorial**, resembling a stark, tetrahedral footstool.

Kilitbahir and Eceabat

You'll need to retrace your steps to the Seddülbahir–Alçıtepe road to make an approximately complete circuit of the peninsula. The tiny village of **KİLİTBAHİR**, 5km south of Eceabat, is dwarfed by its massive and perfectly preserved **castle**; the road threads through it, and unpublicized, privately run **ferries** chug from it across to Çanakkale at this narrowest point (1300m) of the Dardanelles.

ECEABAT is merely a transit point, without even the limited appeal of Gelibolu or Çanakkale and nothing to detain you except the wait for the ferry to Çanakkale. There's a **PTT booth** by the jetty, which changes money and offers a metered phone until 9pm, and all kinds of snack **food** within a short distance of the dock, but you wouldn't want to patronize the handful of noisy hotels overlooking it. Local **dolmuşes** depart from in front of the *Atlanta* restaurant; there are just a couple per day, early in the morning, for Alçıtepe and Seddülbahir, and service to the Kabatepe ferry an hour before sailings to Imvros.

THE SOUTHERN MARMARA SHORE

The south coast of the Sea of Marmara is marginally more rewarding than the northern one, and you're likely to pass through it en route between İznik, Bursa and Çanakkale. The shoreline north and east of Bursa—heavily urbanized, usually polluted, primarily a dormitory community for İstanbul—is a write-off; save your energy for the two old imperial towns. As you move west, a trip to the beach becomes thinkable again, even desirable: inland presents a monotonous prospect of sunflower fields, the source of most of Turkey's cheap cooking oil. This was ancient Bithynia, renamed Mysia by the Romans, but its old cities have come so far down in the world that nothing is left of them save misleading names on the map.

Approaching Bursa: Coastal Ports and Resorts

The southern Marmara shore from İzmit to Bandırma offers little of compelling interest; for the most part this is rocky coast, with inland contours softened somewhat by ubiquitous olive groves. If you're traveling between İstanbul and Bursa, though, you're likely to catch a glimpse of at least one of the **ferry ports** that like to call themselves resorts—which they are for numbers of locals.

MUDANYA is the closest of these harbors to Bursa, but unless you have a car and a taste for dawn drives, it's the least useful transfer point to İstanbul, given the single daily steamer's early morning departure; the hydrofoil, on the days it sails, leaves an hour or so later. Despite its moment in history as the place where the provisional armistice between Turkey and the Allies was signed on

October 11, 1922, Mudanya's modern highrises are no more appealing than those blighting any other town at this end of the Marmara.

Using Mudanya as an arrival point *from* İstanbul makes a bit more sense, especially if you take the hydrofoil, but the lone normal ferry service arrives at around 10pm, making for a late hotel-search in Bursa. If you get stuck in Mudanya, you can stay at the *Koç Oteli*, right behind the ferry terminal.

KUMYAKA, 7km west of Mudanya, and **ZEYTINBAĞI**, 3km farther, both have **Byzantine churches** that are worth a look. The latter village was the Greek Trilya, and the Fatih Camii here is thought to have started life as a thirteenth-century church—a more ruinous church just out of town dates from the eighth century. Once you've seen these, you can get a good fish meal by the little harbor. Both villages are served by bus from Mudanya and Bursa.

GEMLIK, just off the Bursa–Yalova expressway, might have been attractive once with its few remaining old houses, but now its polluted gulf mocks the superfluous concrete hotels on the waterfront. The closest place for a safe swim would be **ARMUTLU**, 47km northwest of Gemlik on a dirt road, with a few hotels lining a pebble beach and sporadic ferries to and from İstanbul.

It's possible to travel all the way around the peninsula on which Armutlu sits, but you're more likely to cut straight across to **YALOVA** via the dangerous main highway from Bursa, or arrive there by water from İstanbul or Kartal. There's no reason to linger, since touts for buses to İznik, Bursa, and the nearby spa meet incoming ferries and hydrofoils. The famous hot springs at **TERMAL**, with their Ottoman *belle époque* surroundings, are 12km southwest of Yalova, just inland from ÇINARCIK. It's possible to camp by the stream that drains the spa area— ask the dolmuş driver to drop you off about 4km before the last stop in Termal itself. This is definitely the only water you'll be getting into around Yalova, as the narrowing gulf from here east is disgustingly filthy. If you miss the last hydrofoil (at 10pm) or passenger ferry (usually around 7:30pm) to İstanbul/Kartal, the acceptable hotels *Çiftlik 2*, *Mehtap*, and *Turan* are all virtually within sight of Yalova's dock; they all charge $8 single, $14 double.

Despite what you may read elsewhere there is no **car ferry** service to or from Yalova; if you're driving or are on a bus, you must cross the Gulf of İzmit via **TOPCULAR**, 15km east. Here there are regular barge-ferries over to the Eskihisar/Darica docks below **GEBZE**, on the main expressway (and suburban rail system) to İstanbul. Foot passengers get a final chance to cross the gulf at **KARAMÜRSEL–HEREKE**. It's well worth taking advantage of either service, since you'll save 80 to 120 kilometers' dull and congested drive in either direction along the gulf shore through İZMİT, the Marmara region's industrial wasteland.

East of Bursa: İznik

It's hard to believe that **İZNİK**, today a somnolent farming community at the east end of the lake of the same name, was once the seat of empires and scene of desperate battles for their control. But looking around the fertile, olive-mantled valley, you can understand the attraction for imperial powers needing a fortified base near—but not too near—the sea-lanes of the Marmara. On closer examination, İznik proves to be a pokey, even dilapidated one-horse town, slumbering away among its orchards after the exertions of history, waking only recently—and fitfully—to the demands of tourism. Compared to the sophistication of Bursans, the townspeople can seem unhelpful, and most people visit İznik as a long day out of İstanbul or Bursa, staying a night at most—which is more than enough time for the handful of mostly overrated monuments.

Founded originally by Alexander's general Antigonus in 316 BC, the city was seized and enlarged fifteen years later by his rival Lysimachus, who named it **Nicaea** after his late wife. He also gave Nicaea its first set of walls and the **grid plan** typical of Hellenistic towns; both are still evident. When the Bithynian kingdom succeeded Lysimachus, Nicaea alternated with nearby Nicomedia as its capital until bequeathed to Rome in 74 BC. Under the Roman emperors the city prospered, being capital of the province, and it continued to flourish during the Byzantine era.

Nicaea played a pivotal role in early Christianity by hosting two critically important **ecumenical councils**. The first, convened by Constantine the Great in 325, resulted in the condemnation of the Arian heresy—which maintain-ed that Christ's nature was inferior to God the Father's—and the promulgation of the Nicaene Creed, still central to Eastern Orthodox belief. The seventh council (the second to be held here) was presided over by the Empress Irene in 787; this time the Iconoclast controversy was settled by the pronouncement, widely misunderstood in the west, that icons had their proper place in the church as long as they were revered and not worshipped.

Nicaea's much-repaired walls seldom repelled invaders, and in 1081 the Selçuks took the city, only to be evicted by a combined force of Byzantines and Crusaders sixteen years later. The fall of Constantinople to the Fourth Crusade in 1204 propelled Nicaea into the spotlight once more, for the Byzantine heir Theodore Lascaris retreated here and made it the base of the improbably successful **Nicaean Empire**. The Lascarid dynasty added a second circuit of walls before returning to Constantinople in 1261, but these again failed to deter the besieging Ottomans, who, led by Orhan Gazi, the victor of Bursa, broke through in March 1331.

Renamed İznik, the city embarked on a golden age of sorts, interrupted briefly by an obligatory pillaging by Tamerlane in 1402. Virtually all the surviving monuments predate the Mongol sacking, but the most enduring contribution to art and architecture—the celebrated **İznik tiles and pottery**—first appeared during the reign of Çelebi Mehmet I, who brought skilled potters from Persia to begin the local industry. This received another boost in 1514 when Selim the Grim captured Tabriz and took more craftsmen as war booty; by the end of the sixteenth century ceramic production was at its height, with more than 300 functioning kilns. The tiles produced here adorned public buildings in every corner of the Ottoman Empire. It was to be a brief flowering, however, since within another hundred years war and politics had scattered most of the artisans. By the mid-eighteenth century the local industry had packed up completely, with products from nearby Kütahya serving as inferior substitutes. İznik began a long, steady decline, hastened by near-total devastation during the 1920–22 war.

Practical Details

With its regular street plan, İznik is easy to navigate; the main north-south boulevard **Atatürk Caddesi** and its east-west counterpart **Kılıçaslan Caddesi** link four of the seven ancient gates, dividing the town into four unequal quadrants. You'll probably arrive at the tiny **otogar** in the southeast quarter, three or

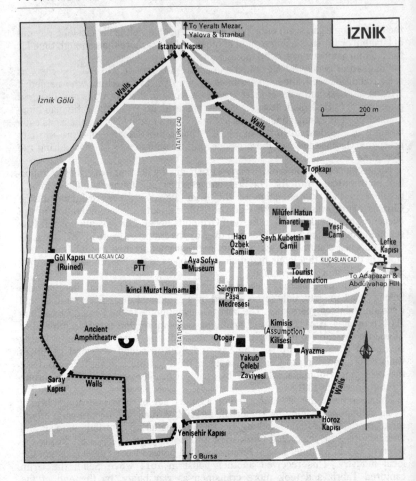

four blocks south of the **tourist information office** at Kılıçaslan Cad 168 (daily June–Aug 8:30am–noon & 1–5:30pm; closed weekends in winter), which hands out rather blurry city maps. Maple-canopied Kılıçaslan has a few good if basic **restaurants**, such as the tightly bunched *Köşk, Koru,* and *İznik*, but most outsiders will **eat** by the lakeshore, where the *Çamlık,* on the inland side of the street, has an edge in terms of prices and service on the more conspicuous *Dallas* by the water. Both serve alcohol, unlike the town-center establishments; try grilled or fried *yayın,* the excellent local catfish. For snacks or dessert there are plenty of tea gardens, cafés, and ice cream parlors overlooking the lake.

If you want to **stay**, empty beds are at a premium, single rooms even more so, and all accommodation is expensive for what you get—reservations are suggested between mid-June and mid-September. The only appealing midtown option is the *Hotel Babacan,* Kılıçaslan Cad 86 (☎252/71623), with singles for $8–14 and doubles for $12–18, depending on the plumbing arrangements; avoid the grossly overpriced *Şener* one block north. On the lakeshore south of the ancient gate, the *Çamlık Motel* (☎252/71631), like its restaurant, is the best value at $12 single, $18 double with breakfast and attached bath. The nearby *Burcum Motel* (☎252/71011), north of the old gate, has similar amenities, including a front garden, but offers only doubles for $20–28 depending on the view. Alternatives include the *Balıkçı Motel* (☎252/71152) at the extreme north end of the waterfront, with doubles going for $20, and the *Berlin* next door, with similar facilities and prices. Your only hope of anything cheaper would be the *İznik Pansiyon* (☎252/71265), 200m back from the water just before the walls veer inland, or the adjacent *Murat Cafe Pansiyon* (☎252/73300). There's also a **campground**, the *Mocamp Nicaea*, near the *Çamlık*.

The **lake** itself is quite swimmable in summer, but the town beaches are cruddy and uninviting; you really need a car to reach more attractive spots. Both men (evenings) and women (daytime) can get steam-cleaned at the **İkinci Murat Hamamı**, just southeast of İznik's central traffic circle and Aya Sofya.

The Town

In the immediate vicinity of the otogar, your likely introduction to İznik, are a few minor sites worth a passing glance. The fourteenth-century **Yakub Çelebi Zaviyesi**, one block southeast, was founded by the luckless prince slain by his brother Beyazit I at Kosovo in 1389 (see p.194); it has been compromised by too many bad restorations. One block east, nothing but foundations remain of the **Kimisis Kilisesi** (Church of the Assumption), the presumed burial place of Theodore Lascaris, which was destroyed in 1922; nearby is a dank, sunken **ayazma** (sacred spring).

It makes more sense if time is limited to head directly to the **Aya Sofa Museum** (daily 9am–noon & 1–5pm; $1), southeast of the central traffic circle, which is all that remains of the Byzantine church of Holy Wisdom, originally built by Justinian. The current structure was built after an earthquake in 1065, and as the cathedral of the provisional Byzantine capital it hosted the coronations of the four Nicaean emperors. The Ottomans converted it into a mosque immediately upon taking the city, and Mimar Sinan restored it, but the premises were already half-ruined before being reduced to their present, sorry condition in 1922. Inside there's not much to see except some damaged floor mosaics and a faint but exquisite **fresco of Christ, John, and Mary** at ground level behind a glass panel to the left as you enter.

Most of İznik's Ottoman attractions are in the northeast quarter of town. Just north of Kılıçaslan Caddesi squats the **Hacı Özbek Camii**, the earliest known Ottoman mosque, built in 1333 but much adulterated; the portico was senselessly pulled down in 1939. Three blocks due south stands the **Süleyman Paşa Medresesi**, likewise the oldest such Ottoman structure in Turkey and still used as a Koran school.

Resuming an amble along Kılıçaslan, you'll soon reach a vast landscaped park to the north dotted with İznik's most famous monuments. The **Yeşil Cami**, erected toward the end of the fourteenth century by Murat I's grand vizier, is a small gem of a building, notable for its fantastic marble relief on the portico. Tufted with a stubby minaret that harks back to Selçuk models, the mosque takes its name from the green İznik tiles that once adorned the minaret; they've long since been replaced by mediocre, tricolored Kütahya work.

Across the park sprawls the **Nilüfer Hatun İmareti**, commissioned by Murat I in 1388 in honor of his mother. Nilüfer Hatun was by all accounts a remarkable woman; daughter of a Byzantine noble (some say Emperor John VI Cantacuzenos himself), she was married off to Orhan Gazi to consolidate a Byzantine-Ottoman alliance. Her native ability was soon recognized by Orhan, who appointed her regent during his frequent absences. The T-shaped building, whose ample domes are perennially home to storks, is more accurately a *zaviye* than a mere soup-kitchen, and one of the few that never doubled as a mosque. It was originally the meeting place not of dervishes but of the Ahi brotherhood, a guild drawn from the ranks of skilled craftsmen that also acted as a community-welfare and benevolent society.

Today the *imaret* contains the **Archaeological Museum** (Tues–Sun 8:30am–noon & 1–5:30pm, Mon by discretion; admission $1), which in addition to the expected İznik ware has such Roman items as a bronze **dancing satyr**, a fine glass collection, a gold item or two, and, standing out among the nondescript marble clutter, a **sarcophagus** in near-mint condition. In the northern cross-stroke of the "T," where the Ahis put up travelers as a public service, a new exhibit highlights recent excavations at nearby kilns that have revealed a variety of previously unknown ceramic styles from the fourteenth century. They display marked Selçuk influence—and sometimes human figures.

The museum also controls the keys to the **Yeraltı Mezar**, a subterranean tomb 6km north of İznik. Either late Roman or early Byzantine, the single chamber is covered in excellent **frescoes**, including a pair of peacocks. You'll want a group for a tour, though, since the standard roundtrip taxi fare is $5–6, and you'll have to tip the key custodian at the museum $2. For a cheaper but more perilous adventure, and a fine view of Nilüfer Hatun's cupolas, climb the minaret of the adjacent **Şeyh Kubettin Camii**.

Only enthusiasts will want to walk the entire perimeter of İznik's double **walls**, now missing most of their hundred original watchtowers, but three of the seven portals are worth some time. Heavy traffic has been rerouted through modern breaches in the fortifications to prevent vibration damage to the original openings, which are now restricted to tractors and pedestrians. Closest to the Yeşil Cami is the eastern **Lefke Kapısı**, a three-ply affair including a triumphal arch dedicated to Hadrian between the inner and outer walls. Just outside is a stretch of the ancient **aqueduct** which until recently supplied the town. It's possible to get up on the ramparts here for a stroll, as it is at the northerly **İstanbul Kapısı**, the best-preserved of the gates. A Hadrianic arch is sandwiched here as well, opposite two relief **masks** in the inner portal, but the whole effect is rather dull because of the flat ground. By contrast the southern **Yenişehir Kapısı**, though the most recent gate, is in woeful condition—not least because the Selçuks, the Byzantines in 1097, and finally the Ottomans successfully stormed the city at this point.

The only tangible traces of Roman Nicaea are both in the southwestern quarter: the all-but-collapsed **amphitheater** just inside the Saray Kapısı, and an **ancient wall** delimiting the so-called "Senatus Court," extending from the surviving tower next to the gate.

If time permits you might walk or drive to the obvious **hill** 2.5km outside the Lefke Kapısı for a comprehensive view over İznik, its walls and lake. The tomb on top belongs to a certain Abdülvahap, a semi-legendary character in the Arab raids of the eighth century.

Bursa

Draped ribbon-like along the leafy lower slopes of Uludağ which towers more than 2000 meters above it, and overlooking the fertile plain of the Nilüfer Çayı, **BURSA** does more justice to its setting than any other Turkish city besides İstanbul. Gathered here are some of the finest early Ottoman monuments in the Balkans, the heart of a few neighborhoods which, despite being marooned in the midst of modern developments, remain among the most appealing in Turkey.

Industrialization over the past three decades, and an attendant quadrupling in population to over a million, means that the city as a whole is no longer exactly elegant. Silk and textile manufacture, plus patronage of the area's thermal baths by the elite, were for centuries the most important enterprises; they're now outstripped by automobile manufacture (both Renault and Murat have plants here), canneries and bottlers processing the rich harvest of the plain, and Uludağ University. Vast numbers of settlers from Artvin province have been attracted by job opportunities at the various factories, while the students provide a necessary leavening in what might otherwise be a uniformly stodgy, conservative community. Some of this atmosphere derives from Bursa's role as first capital of the Ottoman Empire and burial place of the first six sultans, whose piety as well as authority emanate from the mosques, social-welfare foundations, and tombs built at their command.

Bursa is sometimes touted as a day trip from İstanbul, but this is really doing both the city and yourself a disservice; it deserves at least an overnight, preferably two. The spirit of the place really can't be gauged amid the whisked-in tour groups gawking at the overexposed Yeşil Cami and Yeşil Türbe. And despite dire warnings in other guidebooks, Bursa is a good city for walking, whether through the hive of the bazaars, the linear parks of the Hisar district, or the anachronistic peace of the Muradiye quarter.

Some History

Although the area around Bursa had been settled at least a millennium before, the first actual city was founded here early in the second century BC by Prusias I, a king of ancient Bithynia, who in typical Hellenistic fashion named the town **Proussa** after himself. Legend claims that Hannibal helped him pick the location of the acropolis, today's Hisar.

Overshadowed by nearby Nicomedia (modern İzmit) and Nicaea (İznik), the city stagnated until the Romans, attracted by its natural hot springs, began spending lavish amounts on public baths and made it the capital of their province of Mysia. Justinian introduced silkworm culture, and Byzantine Proussa flourished until Arab raids in the seventh and eighth centuries, and the subsequent tug-of-war for sovereignty between the Selçuks and the Greeks, precipitated decline. During and after the Latin interlude in Constantinople (1204–1261) the Byzantines reconsolidated their hold on Proussa, but not for long.

The start of the fourteenth century saw a small band of nomadic Turks, led by one **Osman Gazi**, camped outside the walls of Proussa. After more than a decade of siege, the city capitulated in 1326 to Orhan, Osman's son, and the **Ottomans** ceased to be a wandering tribe of marauders. Orhan marked the acquisition of a capital and the organization of an infant state by styling himself sultan, giving the city its present name, and striking coinage. Bursa began to enjoy a second golden

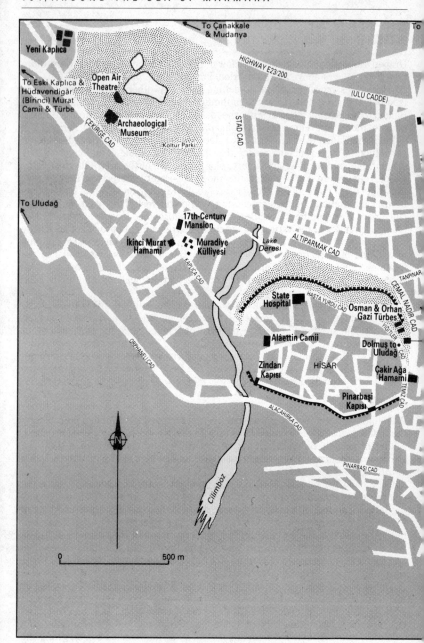

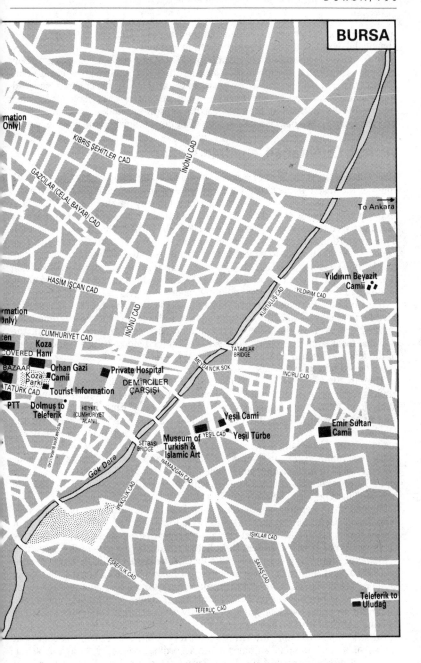

BURSA

KIBRIS SEHITLER CAD

İNÖNÜ CAD

GAZCILAR (CELAL BAYAR) CAD

To Ankara

HASIM İŞCAN CAD

İNÖNÜ CAD

YILDIRIM CAD

Yıldırım Beyazit
Camii

KURTULUŞ CAD

mation
Only)

rmation
Only)

CUMHURIYET CAD

TATARLAR
BRIDGE

İNCİRLİ CAD

en

Koza
Hanı

COVERED

BAZAAR

Koza
Parkı

Orhan Gazi
Camii

Private Hospital

DEMIRCILER
ÇARŞISI

NALBANTOĞLU CAD

TATÜRK CAD

Tourist Information

PTT

Dolmuş to
Teleferik

HEYKEL
(CUMHURIYET
ALANI)

RESSAM ŞEFİK BURSALI CAD

Yeşil Cami

Emir Sultan
Camii

YEŞİL CAD

Yeşil Türbe

SETBAŞI
BRIDGE

Museum of
Turkish &
Islamic Art

Gök Dere

NAMAZGAH CAD

İPEKÇİLİK CAD

İŞIKLAR CAD

SAVAŞ CAD

Teleferik to
Uludağ

EŞREFİLIK CAD

TEFERÜÇ CAD

age: the silk industry was expanded and the city, now outgrowing the confines of the citadel, was beautified and graced with monuments.

In the years following Orhan's death in 1362 the imperial capital was gradually moved to Edirne, a more appropriate base for the reduction of Constantinople, but Bursa's place in history, and in the hearts of the Ottomans, was ensured; succeeding sultans continued to add buildings, and be laid to rest here, for another hundred years. Disastrous fires and earthquakes in the mid-nineteenth century, and the 1920–22 war of independence, only slightly diminished the city's splendor.

Arrival, Orientation, and Information

Bursa's position at the foot of a mountain has dictated an elongated layout, with most of the major boulevards running from east to west, changing their names several times as they go. The northernmost artery is the major **E23/200 expressway** linking Çanakkale and Ankara, passing beside the **otogar** where you'll arrive unless you've flown in and taken the airport bus to the city center. The area around the otogar, with its perpetual chaos of traffic rotaries and no concessions whatsoever to pedestrians, is the worst introduction to the city imaginable; don't lose heart. There's a summer-only **tourist information booth** on the grass at the base of **Fevzi Çakmak Caddesi**, which is the quickest walking route up to the city center if you're lightly laden.

Most people, however, instantly find a dolmuş just outside the terminal on **Ulu Cadde** (officially renamed Kıbrıs Şehitleri Caddesi); the cars are prominently marked "Heykel." This is the most common alias of **Cumhuriyet Alanı**, the nominal focal point of the city; your vehicle will inch along **İnönü Caddesi**, one of the few north-south arteries besides Fevzi Çakmak to tackle the slope, sparing you a one-kilometer-plus walk.

Though Bursa is narrow, with many points of interest bunched together, it's sufficiently long that you'll want to consider **public transit** to reach the outlying attractions. Of the **city buses**, only the #1 (connecting Emir Sultan on the east side of town with Çekirge on the west) and the #3, (linking Heykel with the Uludağ *teleferik*), are of much use, but you need to buy tickets for them at designated booths. Especially if you're newly arrived, it's simpler, and well worth the extra few hundred TL, to avail yourself of Bursa's many **dolmuşes**. If your luggage won't fit in the trunk, you'll have to buy a seat for it—but for 20¢ each, it's still a lot cheaper than a private taxi. Useful routes, many starting at Heykel, are indicated in "The City," below.

Bursa's main lengthwise thoroughfare begins life just east of Heykel as **Namazgah Caddesi**, becomes **Atatürk Caddesi** west of İnönü Caddesi as it passes through the city's central bazaar and hotel district, and changes its name again to **Cemal Nadir Caddesi** right below Hisar, the nucleus of the Byzantine settlement. After being fed more traffic by **Cumhuriyet Caddesi**, which divides the bazaar, and the traffic circle at the top of Fevzi Çakmak Caddesi, the boulevard metamorphoses into **Altıparmak Caddesi**, and again into **Çekirge Caddesi** as it heads west past the Kültür Parkı. There are, though, numerous delightful secondary streets, noted in the city account, which all better suited for walking between Bursa's historical sites.

Bursa's main **tourist information office** (Mon–Fri 8:30am–5:30pm, Sat 9:30am–6:30pm; additional summer hours according to funding) is in a subterranean mall at one corner of the Koza Parkı, well-marked on the north side of

Atatürk Caddesi. Strangely, no decent city maps are available but the staff are helpful and can deal knowledgebly with specific queries. The satellite booths near the otogar and on Cemal Nadir Caddesi, below the Hisar palisade, operate only in summer; there is no longer a branch on Tanpınar Caddesi.

> The Bursa area telephone code is ☎24.

Finding a Place to Stay

There are generally enough reasonably priced **hotel** beds to go around in Bursa, even during the July festival season, thanks to the mentality that sees the city primarily as a day trip from İstanbul. Rich foreigners, particularly Arabs, gravitate toward the luxury spa-hotels at Çekirge, but there is also a cluster of modest, acceptable establishments around the Birinci Murat Camii. If you're interested in monumental Bursa, then midtown accommodation, preferably above (south of) Atatürk Caddesi, makes more sense. Hotels around the otogar are mostly pretty grim, and only a few are listed here for the benefit of late arrivals. Incidentally, Bursa's **youth hostel** is now permanently closed, whatever you may read in IYHF handbooks.

Near Atatürk Caddesi
Lâl Otel, Maksem Cad 79 (☎211710). Rambling old building, eccentric but clean rooms; about as rough as you'll want to dare in Bursa. $6 single, $8 double, bathrooms down the hall.
Saray Oteli, İnönü Caddesi, Matbaa Çıkmazı 1 (☎212820). Nothing special—downright noisy in fact—but clean enough and, overlooking Heykel, you can't get more central. Single $7, double $11.
Hotel İpekçi, Çancılar Cad 38, in the bazaar west of İnönü Caddesi (☎211935). Bright, airy rooms, quiet despite location. $8/$9 single, $12/$17 double.
Hotel Çağlayan, İnebey Cad 73 (☎211458). An old mid-range standby that's ripe for a thorough overhaul. Helpful staff partly compensate for overpriced singles at $9/$12, doubles for $14/$23.
Otel Çamlıbel, İnebey Cad 71 (☎112565). Same idea and physical condition as the preceding; rates identical as well.
Hotel Bilgiç, Ressam Şefik Bursalı (formerly Başak) Cad 30 (☎203190). The best-value establishment in town; immaculately redone in 1990, but prices haven't caught up yet— singles $10/$12, doubles $13/$21, though the lower-priced rooms without bath are rarely available.

Çekirge
Konak Palas Oteli, Birinci Murat Camii Arkası 11 (☎365113). Simple but quiet and clean rooms with spa tubs down the hall; $8 single, $13 double.
Hotel Eren, Birinci Murat Camii Aralığı 2 (☎368099). Like its neighbor above, behind the old mosque, but a bit fancier: $15 single, $21 double with attached bath.
Demirci Oteli, Hamam Cad 33 (☎365104). Noiser than the *Eren* but cheaper at $11 single, $17 double, with bath.
Hakki Paşa, Birinci Murat Cad 14, in front of the old mosque. Again somewhat noisy, but rear rooms have city panorama. Same rates as the *Demirci*.

Near the Otogar
Hotel Belkis, Gazcılar (Celal Bayar) Cad 168, within sight of Fevzi Çakmak Caddesi (☎148322). Plain but relatively calm; $6 single, $8 double for rooms without bath.

Mavi Ege, Şirin Sok 17, around the corner from the preceding (☎148420). The name's a horrible joke, since the hotel is about as un-"Blue Aegean" as you can get; stark rooms with hall shower for same prices as the *Belkis*.

Gazcılar Oteli, Gazcılar (Celal Bayar) Cad 156 (☎149477). More comfortable than the previous two; posted rates are $9/$12 single, $13/$21 double, with the higher prices for attached baths, all open to bargaining.

Camping

Two **campgrounds** straddle the Bursa–Yalova road about 8km northeast of town. *Nur Camping* is fancy and geared more for trailers; the *Mocamp* is set back a bit from the highway.

The City

There's little point in touring Bursa's monuments in strictly chronological order, though not surprisingly many of the oldest ones are clustered just outside Hisar, in today's city center. The points grouped under each heading can be visited in a leisurely morning or afternoon, adding up to two full days if you wanted to see everything comfortably. If you can't spare this much time, you could manage to see the most spectacular monuments around the Koza Parkı and at Yeşil in a rushed few hours.

Central Sites

Just across from the main tourist information office stands the **Orhan Gazi Camii**, whose 1336 foundation makes it the second-oldest mosque in Bursa. Originally built as a *zaviye* for itinerant dervishes, this is the earliest example of the T-shaped mosque with *eyvans* flanking the main prayer hall. Unfortunately it's been clumsily restored at least four times in the past four centuries, and is now mostly of use as a landmark.

The compact **Koza Parkı**, just west of Orhan Gazi, is, with its fountains, benches, strolling crowds, and outdoor cafés, the real heart of Bursa—never mind what they say about Heykel. Though animated through the day and early evening, the plaza empties soon after, with the illuminated fountains dark and still, and walkways deserted, by 11pm. On the far side of the Koza Parkı looms the tawny limestone **Ulu Cami**, built between 1396 and 1399 by Yıldırım Beyazit I, from the proceeds of booty won from the Crusaders at Macedonian Nicopolis. Before the battle Yıldırım (Thunderbolt) had vowed to construct twenty mosques if victorious. The present building of **twenty domes** supported by twelve freestanding pillars was his rather free interpretation of this promise, but it was still the largest and most ambitious Ottoman mosque of its time. The interior is dominated by a huge **şadırvan** pool in the center, whose skylight was once open to the elements, and an intricate walnut **mimber** pieced together, it's claimed, without nails or glue. Less convincing is the tradition that the main north portal was remodeled by Tamerlane when he occupied Bursa in 1402–3.

From the north porch you can descend stairs to the two-storied **Emir (Bey) Hanı**, originally a dependency of the Orhan Gazi Camii and now home to various offices and shops. A fountain plays under the trees in the court, but with no teahouse or public seating it's not a place to linger. Beyond the Emir Hanı begins Bursa's **covered market**: its assorted galleries and lesser *hans* jumbled together are a cartographer's nightmare, but a delight for shoppers hunting for clothes, silk goods ranging from scarves to jump suits, towels, bolts of cloth, and furniture, all Bursa province specialties. The whole area was devastated by fire in 1955, though, and despite careful restoration both form and function are somewhat bogus. There's more genuine continuity in the nearby **Bedesten**, another Yıldırım Beyazit foundation, today (as formerly) given over to the sale and warehousing of jewelry and precious metals.

The centerpiece of the bazaar, however, has to be the **Koza Hanı** or Silk-Cocoon Hall, flanking the park close to the Orhan Gazi Camii. Built in 1451 on two levels like the Emir Hanı, it's far grander, and still entirely occupied by silk and brocade merchants. In the middle of the cobbled courtyard, under the sycamore trees, a miniscule **mescit** perches directly over its *şadırvan*, while a U-shaped subsidiary court bulges asymmetrically to the east; there are teahouses and public benches to pause at.

The highlight of the year is the **cocoon auction** of late June and early July, when silk-breeders from around the province gather to hawk their valuable produce. Then the *han* becomes a lake of white torpedoes, each the size of a songbird's egg; the moth, when it hatches, is a beautiful, otherwordly creature with giant onyx eyes and feathery antennae. You can watch the melee from the upper arcades, or if you're careful the merchants won't mind you walking the floor. After being sent into a tailspin by French and Italian competition 200 years ago, the Bursa silk trade has recently experienced a tentative revival, though the quality of contemporary fabric cannot compare to museum pieces from the early Ottoman heyday.

Another area of the bazaar that has kept its traditions intact despite quake and blaze is the **Demirciler Çarşısı**, or Ironmonger's Market. This is just the other side of İnönü Caddesi, which is best crossed by the pedestrian underpass at Okcular Caddesi. Stall upon stall of blacksmiths and braziers attract photographers, but be advised that some expect a consideration for posing. From here you can easily continue past a small mosque and some cabinet-makers' workshops to **Fırın Sokak**, lined with some of the finest old dwellings in town. At the end of this short street a bridge spans the **Gök Dere**, one of two streams that tumble through Bursa, forming the city center's approximate eastern boundary.

East of the Gök Dere: Yeşil and Beyond

However you cross the stream, it's only a few minutes' walk up to **Yeşil**, as the neighborhood around the mosque and *türbe* of the same name is known. Designed by the architect Hacı Ivaz atop a slight but panoramic rise, the **Yeşil Cami** was begun soon after the civil war that put Çelebi Mehmet I on the throne in 1413. Despite being unfinished—work ceased in 1424, three years after Mehmet himself died—and catastrophic damage from two nineteenth-century earth tremors, it's easily the most spectacular of Bursa's imperial mosques. The incomplete entrance, faced in light marble, is all the more easy to examine for the lack of a portico; above the **stalactite vaulting** and relief calligraphy you can see the supports for arches never built.

Next you'll pass through a foyer supported by pilfered Byzantine columns to reach the interior, a variation on the T-plan usually reserved for dervish *zaviyes*. The prayer hall here is flanked by not two but six **eyvans**, and it's thought that the frontmost pair were used for councils of state and audiences rather than religious purposes. A fine **şadırvan** occupies the center of the "T," but your eye is monopolized by the hundreds of **polychrome tiles** that line not only the *mihrab* but every available vertical surface up to 5m in height, particularly two **recesses** flanking the entryway. Green and blue pigment, matching the carpets, predominates, and praying amid this dimly lit majesty must be something like worshipping inside a leaf. Tucked above the foyer, and usually closed to visits, is the **imperial loge**, the most extravagantly decorated chamber of all. Several artisans from Tabriz participated in the tiling of Yeşil Cami; the loge is attributed to a certain Al-Majnun, which translates most accurately as "intoxicated on hashish."

On the same knoll as the mosque, and immediately across the pedestrian area separating them, the **Yeşil Türbe** (daily 8:30am–noon & 1–5:30pm; free) contains the sarcophagus not only of Çelebi Mehmet I but also assorted offspring. The same Hacı Ivaz is responsible for this octagonal structure, though the outside is no longer green but blue with inferior replacement tiles applied after 1855. Inside, however, the walls and Mehmet's tomb glisten with the glorious original Tabriz material.

Regrettably, the immediate environs of the two monuments swarm with tour groups and are cutesy in the extreme; the café nearby overcharges mercilessly for the view, and a clutch of converted, vehemently repainted old houses are glutted with souvenir dross. There's not a genuine antique-seller to be found, with the possible exception of one eccentric old man next to the **medrese**, the largest surviving part of the mosque. One hundred meters below the summit, this now houses Bursa's **Museum of Turkish and Islamic Art** (daily 8am–noon & 1–5pm, except Mon 10am–1pm; $1). It's not a bad ethnographic collection, although some find the courtyard with its fountain, trees, and picnic tables equally interesting. Certain rooms may be shut due to lack of staff, but in theory you can view İznik ware, Çanakkale ceramics—in worse taste than an untalented art student's thesis project—kitchen utensils, inlaid wood articles, weapons, glass items, and the inevitable mock-up of an Ottoman *sünnet odası* (circumcision chamber).

Best of all is a wing full of **Karagöz puppets**, the painted camel-leather props used in the Turkish national shadow play, which purportedly originated in Bursa. According to legend the antics of Karagöz and his sidekick Hacıvat so entertained their fellow workmen building the Orhan Gazi Camii that Orhan had them beheaded to end the distraction. Later, missing the comedians and repenting of his deed, he arranged to immortalize the pair in the artform which now bears the name of Karagöz.

A 300-meter walk east of Yeşil leads to the **Emir Sultan Camii**, lost in extensive graveyards where every religious Bursan hopes to be buried. The mosque was originally endowed by a Bokharan dervish and trusted advisor to three sultans, beginning with Beyazit I, but it has just been restored again after enduring an Ottoman-baroque overhaul early in the last century, so you can only guess what's left of the original essence. The pious, however, seem to harbor no doubts, coming in droves to worship at the tombs of the saint and his family.

If you're short of time this is an obvious site to omit; instead, climb down steps through the graveyard and cross the urban lowlands to the **Yıldırım Beyazit Camii**, perched on a small hill at the northeast edge of the city. If you're coming directly from downtown this is a substantial hike, so you might want to take a dolmuş marked "Heykel–Beyazit Yıldırım" instead, or the more common "Heykel–Fakülte," which passes 200m below the mosque.

Completed by Beyazit I between 1390 and 1395, the Beyazit Camii is essentially the prototype for the Yeşil Cami, with little difference in the exterior marble used or the modified-T floor plan. Here, however, there's a handsome, five-arched **portico** defined by square columns. The interior is unremarkable except for a

gravity-defying **arch** bisecting the prayer hall, its lower supports apparently tapering away to end in stalactite molding. The only other note of whimsy in this spare
building is the elaborate niches out on the porch.

The associated **medrese**, exceptionally long and narrow because of its sloping
site, huddles just downhill; today it's used as a medical clinic. The **türbe** of the
luckless Beyazit, kept in an iron cage by the rampaging Tamerlane until his death
in 1403, is usually locked; perhaps the mosque custodians fear a revival of the
Ottoman inclination to abuse the tomb of the most ignominiously defeated sultan.

Around the Hisar

The **Hisar**, Bursa's original nucleus, nowadays retains just a few clusters of dilapidated Ottoman housing along its warren of narrow lanes, and some stretches of
medieval wall along its perimeter. Atop the ramparts, the city planners have scattered ribbons of park interspersed with tea gardens—excellent vantage points
over the lower town.

Heading west from the Koza Parkı and Ulu Cami toward the Hisar, you might
stop at Bursa's most central **food market**, crammed into alleys just west of İnebey
Caddesi, behind the Çakır Ağa Hamamı. This is the place to stock up for picnics,
with an excellent selection of the fruits—strawberries and cherries in spring,
peaches and pears in summer—nuts, and dairy products for which the region is
noted.

From where Atatürk Caddesi becomes Cemal Nadir Caddesi in a whirl of traffic, you can climb up to the Hisar plateau via pedestrian ramps negotiating the
ancient walls, or, less enticingly, walk along Yiğitler Caddesi, home to a rather
contrived artists' colony. Where Yiğitler stops climbing, the **türbes of Osman
and Orhan Gazi** stand side by side at the edge of the fortified acropolis that they
conquered, on the site of a Byzantine church that has long since disappeared
except for some **mosaic traces** near Orhan's sarcophagus. Unfortunately the
superstructures are post-earthquake restorations in gaudy late-Ottoman style.

Far better is the view from the cliff-top **park** sprawling around the tombs and
clocktower, with reasonable cafés at the head of the walkways down to Cemal
Nadir and Altıparmak caddesis. Most of the city's smarter shops and movie theaters line **Altıparmak**, but for now it's preferable to back away from the brink and
explore **Hisar** itself, where the wreckers took a heavy toll of the traditional
houses before preservation orders went into effect.

You must choose whether to follow signs west to Muradiye along the most
direct route, or to veer inland on a random walk around the neighborhood. At the
southernmost extreme of the citadel you'd exit at the **Pınarbaşı Kapısı**, lowest
point in the city walls and the spot where Orhan's forces finally entered the city in
1326. From there you could stroll parallel to the walls until re-entering at the
Zindan Kapısı, inside of which is the **Alâeddin Camii**, erected within a decade
of the conquest and so the earliest mosque in Bursa. It's a simple box
surmounted by a single dome, the norm for Ottoman mosques before the advent
of the T-plan *zaviye*.

A more straightforward route follows Hasta Yurdu Caddesi, the continuation of
Yiğitler, until another large park, containing several **teahouses**, opens out opposite the public hospital. The farthest ones have fine views of the Muradiye
district, and from the final café and wall, obvious stairs descend to the **Cılımboz
Deresi**, the second major stream to cut across the city, greatly shortening the
distance to the far bank.

Muradiye

Across the stream lies medieval **Muradiye**, where Bursa's best-preserved dwellings and streets are at their liveliest during the **Tuesday street market**. If you're coming directly from the city center, there are frequent dolmuşes marked "Muradiye."

The **Muradiye Külliyesi** is easy enough to find, following the district's main street past two simple lunchtime restaurants. If you were disappointed by the tourist hoopla at Yeşil, this is the place to capture the authentic early Ottoman spirit; while trinket sellers and an antique shop do fly the flag, there's no pressure to buy and no tour groups to shatter the calm. The complex, begun in 1424 by Murat II, was the last imperial foundation in Bursa, though the tombs for which Muradiye is famous were added piecemeal over the next century or so. The sultan's **mosque** is similar to the Orhan Gazi Camii in ground plan and thus does not represent any advance of imagination, but the profuse **tiles** low on the walls, spare calligraphy up high, and double dome above are satisfying. The nearby **medrese** is now a clinic, like the one at Yıldırım Beyazit.

The ten **royal tombs** are set in lovingly tended gardens, and are opened for view on a rotation schedule; to get into the locked ones you have to find the gardener-*bekçi* with the keys—no tip expected for the service. The first *türbe* encountered is that of **Şehzade Ahmet** and his brother Şehinşah, both murdered in 1513 by their cousin Selim I (the Grim) to preclude any succession disputes. The luxury of the İznik tiles within contrasts sharply with the adjacent austerity of **Murat II's tomb**, where Roman columns inside and a wooden awning out front are the only superfluities. Murat, as much contemplative and mystic as warrior-sultan, was the only Ottoman ruler ever to abdicate voluntarily, though pressures of state forced him to leave the company of his dervishes and return to the throne after just two years. He was the last sultan to be interred at Bursa, and one of the few lying here who died in his bed; in accordance with his wishes, both the coffin and the dome were originally open to the sky "so that the rain of heaven might wash my face like any pauper's."

Next along is the *türbe* of **Şehzade Mustafa**, Süleyman the Magnificent's unjustly murdered heir; perhaps indicating his father's remorse, the tomb is done up in extravagantly floral İznik tiles, with a top border of calligraphy. Nearby stands the tomb of **Cem Sultan**, his brother Mustafa, and two sons of Beyazit II, decorated with plain green tiles below as in Ahmet's, but a riot of abstract, botanical, and calligraphic paint strokes up to the dome.

Cem, the cultured and favorite son of Mehmet the Conqueror, was one of the Ottoman Empire's most interesting might-have-beens. Following the death of his father in 1481, he lost a brief dynastic struggle with the successful claimant, brother Beyazit II, and fled abroad. For fourteen years he wandered, seeking sponsorship for his cause from Christian benefactors who in all cases became his jailers: first the Knights of St. John at Rhodes and Bodrum, later the papacy. At one point it seemed that he would command a crusader army organized to re-take İstanbul, but all such plans came to grief for the simple reason that Beyazit anticipated his opponents' moves and each time bribed them handsomely to desist, making Cem a lucrative prisoner indeed. His usefulness as a pawn exhausted, Cem was probably poisoned in Italy by the pope in 1495, leaving nothing but reams of poems aching with nostalgia and homesickness.

The last ornate tomb, that of **Şehzade Mahmut** and his sons, victims of father Beyazit II and uncle Selim the Grim respectively, also sports tiles and badly deteriorated paintings; this and all the much plainer tombs near the southwestern fence are scheduled for restoration.

With such a preponderance of princes suffering unnatural deaths, it's clear that the Ottoman spirit included a broad, dark patch of bloody ruthlessness. Successful claimants of the throne who showed reluctance to murder their male relatives would be warned by Koranic scholars that rebellion was worse than fratricide; their rivals could be honored more safely in death, with magnificent *türbes*, than in life.

Directly across the street from the *külliye* is possibly your only chance to see the interior of a Muradiye house, a restored **seventeenth-century mansion** that's kept open to the public (Tues–Sun 8:30am–noon & 1–5:30pm; $1). The best room is the upstairs corner one, with carved and painted wood ceilings and cupboards, but the liberal use of foam-rubber cushions instead of authentic furniture is disconcerting.

The Kültür Parkı

From Muradiye it's just a short walk down to Çekirge Caddesi and the southeast gate of the **Kültür Parkı** (token admission charge when entry booths are staffed). Inside there's a popular tea garden, a small boating lake, a disgraceful mini-zoo that ought to be either upgraded or disbanded, and three expensive, virtually identical restaurants. As you stroll, however, it soon becomes obvious, as in similar parks in İzmir and Ankara, that there's no potential for solitude— though courting couples try their best—and no wild spots among the regimented plantations and too-broad driveways: something that speaks volumes about Turkish attitudes toward public life, conformity, and authority.

At the west end of the park, just below Çekirge Caddesi, the **open-air theater** (see "Entertainment," p.195) stands next to the **Archaeological Museum** (Tues–Sun 8:30am–noon & 1–5:30pm; $1). Inside the museum, exhibits in the "Stone Room" vary from the macabre (a Byzantine ossuary with a skull peeking out) to the homey (a Roman cavalryman figurine), but the adjacent hall featuring **metal jewelry** from all over Anatolia—watch chains, breast plates, belts, buckles, bracelets, anklets, chokers—steals the show. The left wing houses a small coin gallery and miscellaneous small ancient objects, the best of which are the **Roman glass items** and **Byzantine/Roman bronzes**. Oil lamps, pottery, a token amount of gold, and far too many ceramic figurines complete these poorly labeled exhibits; the sparseness of the collections is a shame, since the halls are well lit and could accommodate better finds. A predictable garden of sarcophagi, stelae, and other statuary fragments surrounds the building.

Çekirge

Most of the realm of the "Cicada," as **Çekirge** translates, is too remote to reach on foot except by the most avid walkers; luckily dolmuşes (marked "Çekirge") and city buses shuttle often in each direction. The **Yeni Kaplıca** (New Baths) are, however, just beyond the Kültür Parkı, accessible by a steep driveway beginning opposite the luxury *Çelik Palas Oteli*. There's actually a clutch of three facilities here, all open 6am to 10pm daily: the **Kaynarca baths**, for women only; the **Karamustafa spa**, with family rooms; and Yeni proper, dating in its present form from the mid-sixteenth century. According to legend, Süleyman the Magnificent was cured of gout after a dip in the Byzantine baths here and had his vizier Rüstem Paşa overhaul the building.

The results are not obvious in the unpromising changing rooms and *soğukluk* (cool room), but the main chamber boasts, instead of the usual *göbek taşı*, a vast **pool** of drowning depth—a sign warns non-swimmers not to enter. Fragments of mosaic paving stud the floor, and the walls are lined with once-exquisite but now blurred İznık tiles. Basic admission to this faded opulence costs a mere $2, and the full works won't exceed $7.

The multiple cupolas of the **Eski Kaplıca** or Old Baths, huddled at the far end of Çekirge Caddesi next to the *Termal Kervansaray Oteli*, are indeed Bursa's most ancient, though recently well restored. Byzantine rulers Justinian and Theodora improved a Roman spa on the site, and Murat I in turn went to work on the structure in the late fourteenth century.

The baths, with both men's and women's sections open from 7am to 10:30pm daily, are more interesting architecturally than the Yeni Kaplıca, and also much more expensive ($5 basic admission, $4.50 extra for a massage). As at the Yeni, a huge but shallow keyhole-shaped **pool** dominates the *hararet* or hot room of the men's section, whose dome is supported by eight **Byzantine columns**. Scalding (113°F) water pours into the notch of the "keyhole," and the temperature is still so taxing in the main basin that you'll soon be gasping out in the cool room, seeking relief from a fountain in the middle. Some of the natural springs on the mountainside in fact run as high as 160°F—and as low as 45°F! Afterward, the bar in the men's *camekân*, where you recuperate swaddled in towels on a chaise lounge, serves alcholic beverages should you wish to pass out completely.

On a hill just west of the thermal center stands the **Hüdavendigâr (Birinci) Murat Camii**, which with its five-arched portico and alternating bands of brick and stone seems more like a church teleported from Italy or Greece. Indeed, tradition asserts that the architect and builders were Christians, who dallied twenty years at the task because Murat, whose pompous epithet literally means "Creator of the Universe," was continually off at war and unable to supervise the work. The interior ground plan, consisting of a first-floor *medrese* above a highly modified, T-type *zaviye* at ground level, is unique in Islam. Unfortunately the upper storey, wrapped around the **courtyard** that's the heart of the place, is rarely open for visits.

Murat himself lies in the much-modified **türbe** across the street, minus his entrails which the embalmers removed before the body began its long journey back from Serbia in 1389. In June of that year Murat was in the process of winning his greatest triumph over the Serbian king Lazarus and his allies at the **Battle of Kosovo**, in today's Yugoslavia, when he was fatally stabbed in his tent by Miloš Obilič, a Serbian noble feigning desertion. His son Beyazit, later better known as Yıldırım, immediately had his brother Yakub strangled and, once in command, decimated the Christian armies. Beyazit's acts had two far-reaching consquences: the Balkans remained under Ottoman control until the early twentieth century, and a gruesome precedent of blood-letting was set for most subsequent Ottoman coronations.

Eating and Drinking

Bursa's cuisine is solidly meat-orientated, dished out in an alcohol-free environment; the most famous local recipes are *İskender kebap*, named after its supposed inventor, which is essentially *döner kebap* soaked in a rich butter, tomato, and yogurt sauce; and *İnegöl köftesi*, rich little pellets of ground meat often made even more so by being laced with cheese (*kaşarlı köfte*). You can get also fish and *soğuk meze* if you're willing to splurge, and the city is famous, too, for its chestnut-based desserts. If you're sick of Turkish sawdust-bread there are a lot of *kepekli* (whole bran) loaves about—ask at promising-looking bakeries.

Kebapcıs

Kebapcı İskender, Atatürk Cad 60. Claims to be the place where the namesake dish was invented—and that's all they serve, not even salads. Open lunchtime only, moderately expensive, and always crowded to feed-trough density.

Sultan İskender Kebap, corner of Atatürk Caddesi and Uçak Sokağı. Less mobbed and more relaxed than its neighbor above.

Çiçek İzgara, Belediye Cad 5, upper floor, behind the town hall. Flawless service despite its popularity; tablecloth elegance, extremely reasonable prices—in short, the best mid-town value. Lunch & dinner; emphasis on *İnegöl* variations.

Özömür, just west of the Ulu Cami in its *arasta*. Closes at 10pm; you pay slightly extra for historic ambience as well as for the *İnegöl köftesi*.

İnci Lokantası, in U-shaped inner court of the Koza Hanı. With its tree-canopied setting, this is the most atmospheric of a dozen *pide* ovens, tea booths, *büfes*, and tiny restaurants scattered throughout the bazaar. Lunch only.

Hacı Bey and **İskender**, two much-touted *İskender* places across from each other on Taşkapı Sokak near Heykel, are vastly overrated and expensive.

Fish

Canlı Balık, Yeni Balık Pazarı 14, about 200m below *Çiçek İzgara* in the fish market. Licensed to serve drinks, reasonably priced; can close for spring cleaning during the May spawning season.

Snacks and Desserts

Hacı İlyas, İnebey Cad 89. Good for breakfast: *Börek* and "*Kahvaltı*" as well as soups.

Şehir Lokantası, İnebey Cad 85. An alternative, with more soups, yogurt, and custards.

Öz Akay, Pars Çıkmazı, an alley off Atatürk Cad 56. Exclusive menu of *mantı* and *çiğ börek* (once-cooked, rather than twice-cooked ingredients) served lunch and dinner.

La Perla, Maksem Cad 73. A restored old house with seating on three levels. Snacks, desserts, and soft drinks served amid magenta decor.

Kıvılcım, İnönü Cad 26, above the underpass. Best desserts in town.

Bahar Muhallebecisi, Altıparmak Cad 64. A close runner-up, also with good *dondurma*.

Drinking and Hubble-Bubbles

Tino Bar, at the Setbaşı Bridge over the Gök Dere, where Atatürk Caddesi becomes Namazgah Caddesi. One of the only spots outside the Çekirge luxury hotels that serves booze. Outdoor terrace looks over the creek to the next bridge down; indoor seating too. Open noon–midnight.

Teahouse, opposite junction of İnebey and Atatürk caddesis. A good place to try a *nargile* (hubble-bubble) in an easygoing environment; see *Basics* for an introduction to *nargiles*.

Entertainment

For a city of its size Bursa has relatively few nocturnal or weekend events; the student contingent is probably responsible for the concerts that do occur. Look out for posters at the tourist information office, art galleries, and shop windows around the Koza Parkı. The most common performance **venues** are, in summer, the **open-air theater** in the Kültür Parkı, behind the archaeological museum and, in winter, the **Vefik Paşa Theater** up at Heykel. Rather tourisy musical performances and folkloric presentations form a big part of the annual July festival.

Listings

Airlines *Sönmez Holding*, c/o *Ottomantur*, Cemal Nadir Caddesi, Kızılay Pasajı, Çakırhamam district (☎210099); *THY*, Temiz Cad 16/8, Çakırhamam district (☎211167).

Airport bus Departs 45 minutes before flight time from in front of *Ottomantur* office.

Books Good stock of English-language books at the *Oxford Bookshop*, Altıparmak Cad 48–50; *Çimsel*, Altıparmak 69/A, is not as extensive.

Car rental Big international chain outlets are *Avis*, Zübeyde Hanım Cad 12/A (☎365133); *Budget*, Çekirge Cad 39/1 (☎228322); *Europcar/InterRent*, Çekirge Cad 41 (☎200016); and *Hertz*, Çekirge Cad 93 (☎363719). Two local independent agencies that offer substantial off-peak discounts are *Astoria*, Birinci Murat Caddesi, Dilen Pasajı 2/14, Çekirge (☎352502) and *Can*, Çekirge Cad 95/B (☎350571).

Festival Held the last three weeks of July annually; exhibits, open-air performances, etc.

Hamams In addition to those discussed on p.193, the *Çakır Ağa* is another more central historic one, located just below Hisar on Cemal Nadir Caddesi: open 6am–midnight for both men and women, admission $1.75. Try also *İkinci Murat* next to the Muradiye tomb complex: Fri & Sun men only, all other days women only 10am–6pm.

Hospitals *Devlet (State) Hastanesi*, on Hasta Yurdu Caddesi in Hisar district; *Özel Hayat*, on İnönü Caddesi near the underpass; and *Özel Bursa*, on Zübeyde Hanım Caddesi, Çekirge, which also has a dental clinic.

Luggage storage At the otogar, open 24hr.

PTT Main branch at corner of Atatürk and Maksem caddesis, open daily 24hr for phone service, 8am–9pm for letters.

TML agent ☎110099.

South of Bursa: Uludağ

Presiding genius of Bursa, 2543-meter **ULUDAĞ**—the "Great Mountain"—is a dramatic, often cloud-cloaked massif, its northern palisades dropping dizzyingly into the city. In ancient times it was known as the Olympos of Mysia, one of nearly twenty peaks around the Aegean so named; Olympos was possibly a generic Phoenician or Doric word for "mountain." Early in the Christian era the range became a refuge for monks and hermits, who were replaced after the Ottoman conquest by Muslim dervishes.

These days the scent of grilling meat has displaced the odor of sanctity, since Bursa natives cram the alpine campgrounds and picnic grounds to the gills on any holiday or weekend. Uludağ is considered a year-round recreation area, with a dense cluster of unplanned hotels, each with their own **ski lift**, at the 1800-meter level, though the slopes are disdained by serious skiers. Much of the dense middle-altitude forest has been designated a national park, with a pitiful few kilometers of marked hiking trails in addition to the above amenities.

As so often happens in Turkey, though, the best part of the mountain is outside the park, east of **Oteller** (as the accommodation and skiing area is known). A few hours' **walking** will bring you to some glacial **lakes** in a wild, rocky setting just below the highest summit, but don't let the relatively short distance lull you into overconfidence; because of its closeness to the Sea of Marmara, the high ridges trap moist marine air, and whiteouts or violent storms can blow up most months of the year. The best and safest seasons for a visit are May–June, when the wild-flowers are blooming, or September–October, when the mist is less.

Practical Details

Getting there is definitely half the fun if you opt for the **teleferik**, which links the Teferüç borough of Bursa with the Sarıalan picnic grounds at 1635m. To reach the lower cable car terminal, take a dolmuş labeled "Teleferik" from the corner of Ressam Şefik Bursalı and Atatürk caddesis. The unnervingly wobbly gondolas make the trip up every half-hour or so between 8am and 9pm, but are cancelled in high winds; if all goes well the trip takes just under thirty minutes, with a pause partway up at Kadıyayla. Tickets cost $2 one-way, $4 round-trip; avoid mid-afternoon and weekends, when hour-long lines at either end are the norm.

Alternatively you can take a **dolmuş**, which winds the 32km of paved road up to Oteller, beginning from Yiğitler Caddesi atop the stretch of Hisar's wall known locally as Tophane. The one-way fee for a six-seater vehicle is $6, although it can occasionally be difficult to muster the necessary number of passengers.

You'd follow the same route in your own vehicle: the road veers off above Çekirge and climbs rapidly through successive vegetation zones and past beckoning *et mangals* (barbeque restaurants) and *kendin pişin, kendin ye* (rent-a-barbecue establishments). Staff at the Karabelen **National Park gate**, 20km in, charge $2.50 per car when they're in the mood and sometimes have brochures to hand out. The final stretch of road from just below the gate to the hotels is very rough cobble, designed to prevent drivers from skidding—or speeding; so allow nearly an hour for the trip.

There's little to choose between the mostly hideous **hotels** at the end of the road, but since the national park **campgrounds** are a long way from the best hiking areas, not to mention squalid and full in summer, you might well consider a room. Out-of-ski-season rates can dip as low as $40 for a double with full board at the *Kar Otel* (☎2418/1122), the highest and quietest of them; similar rates are available at the nearby *Beceren* (☎2418/1114) or the *Yazıcı* (☎2418/1039; not to be confused with the *Grand Yazıcı*), the most consistently open in summer.

Walking Routes

The closest trailhead to the Karabelen gate is at **Kirazlıyayla**, about halfway between the gate and Oteller; you'll have to look closely for a little sign, "Patika no. 7, Kirazlıyayla–Sarıalan, 2700m," tacked onto the Uludağ University research facility sign, next to the *Genç Osman* grill. Upon reaching the end of the indicated driveway, you'll set out on what passes for a trail (*patika* in Turkish) in the ravine behind the facility building. The path is really just the way originally cleared for the overhead power lines and, now clogged with vegetation, doesn't offer quality hiking. About an hour of up-and-down progress through the trees—more with a full pack, less with a daypack—will suffice to bring you to **Sarıalan**.

Once free of the teeming parking lots, souvenir stands, and picnic meadows here—a ten-minute process—you should find another sign marked "(Trail) 3, 2565m; 1, 4135m" a few hundred meters to the east. After another half-hour under power lines, take a right fork at the signed "3385m" option. Soon you forsake the high-tension wires for a real trail through stream-creased fir forest, but the idyll is short-lived as you collide with bulldozed driveways just below Oteller, a bit less than three hours from Kirazlıyayla.

You might not be blamed for taking a car or dolmuş directly to the top of the hotel zone, where a jeep track leads to the **tungsten mine** managed by Etibank (an hour and a half on foot). An obvious path beginning behind the mine's guard-house slips up onto the broad but barren watershed ridge, just below the secondary summit of **Zirve** (2496m); follow this trail for a total of ninety minutes to a fork. Right leads to the main peak of **2543**; the left-hand choice, marked by stone cairns, is more rewarding, descending slightly to overlook the first of Uludağ's lakes, **Aynalıgöl**, reachable by its own side trail a half-hour beyond the junction.

There are some campgrounds here but none at **Karagöl**, the second and most famous lake, fifteen minutes southeast of the first one, sunk in a deep chasm and speckled with ice floes. **Kilimligöl**, the third substantial lake, is tucked away on a plateau southeast of Karagöl and offers more good high-altitude camping. Two more tarns are smaller, nameless, and difficult to find in the crags above Aynalıgöl.

Returning to Oteller, as long as the weather is good you can stay with the ridge rather than revisiting the tungsten works, passing below the ruined hut on Zirve to meet a faint trail. This soon vanishes and thereafter it's follow-your-nose downhill along the watershed as far as **Cennetkaya**, a knoll above the hotels, served by a marked trail. High above the trees, crowds, and jeep tracks here, you just might strike it lucky and glimpse patches of the distant Sea of Marmara to the north.

West of Bursa: the Mysian Lakes

The tedious 120-kilometer drive from Bursa to Bandırma is enlivened only by two large but shallow lakes: one vastly overrated, the other rarely visited. **ULUABAT (APOLLYON) GÖLÜ**, just outside Bursa, is the more rewarding lake for the casual visitor and is somewhat more accessible by public transportation, although surprisingly few people make it here. If you're driving, you'll have to keep an eye out for an inconspicuous sign, "Gölyazı," 38km west of Bursa, marking the six-kilometer side road to that village.

GÖLYAZİ proves to be an atmospheric community of half-timbered houses, with the odd daub of purple or green paint, built on an island now connected to the shore by a causeway. Remains from Roman and Byzantine **Apollonia**—thus the lake's alias—have unconcernedly been pressed into domestic service, and extensive remnants of wall ring the island's shoreline; on the mainland you can see a huge, ruined Greek **cathedral**, large enough for a few hundred parishioners.

Appearances would lead you to pronounce Gölyazı the quintessential Balkan **fishing village**: there's a lively open-air fish market each morning at the island end of the causeway, nets and rowboats are much in evidence, and the women—who don't appreciate gratuitous photos being taken of them—patiently mend traps. All this conceals the sad fact that pesticide and fertiliser runoff from surrounding fields is constantly diminishing the lake catch, and a handful of families emigrate every year. The lake itself, speckled with islets, is murky and not suitable for swimming.

All in all, Gölyazı is best visited as part of a day trip from Bursa, if **dolmuş** schedules permit. Otherwise, there's only the *Apollonia Motel*, on the landward side of the causeway, to **stay** at. It's very rough and open only in July and August. More promising is the co-managed **restaurant** of the same name at the extreme north edge of town, where you can sample inexpensive *turna* (lake pike) fresh from the tank; the staff have the key to the motel. Otherwise, there's an impromptu, mosquito-plagued **campground** across the road from the outdoor tables. There aren't yet any organized outings around the village, although you can easily arrange for one of the fishermen to take you out in a small boat to some remote ruins on the nearby islets.

MANYAS GÖLÜ, to the west, attracts visitors mainly because of the **Kuşcenneti National Park**, a bird sanctuary established in 1938 astride a stream delta and swamps at the northeast corner of the lake. The "Bird Paradise," as the name translates, is a total of 18km south of Bandırma: 13km along the Balıkesir road and then 5km on the marked side road. There's no public transportation along this last stretch.

Once you arrive, you may wonder why you bothered. The park (daily 8am–5pm; 50¢) consists mostly of a small **visitors' center** full of dioramas, labeled only in Turkish and stocked with stuffed geese, orioles, spoonbills, herons, pelicans, ducks, egrets, and owls. Supposedly you're able to view up to two million live specimens of same annually.

Next you're directed to a wooden **observation tower**, but the noise emanating from creaking timbers and screaming local weekend warriors is sufficient to frighten off every wild bird within a kilometer radius. It's a pretty pathetic excuse for a wildlife reserve, and you'll easily see more species and individuals in any unprotected Turkish river delta, on the nearby Gelibolu peninsula, or even on the rest of the lake itself—though no walkways or boats are provided to get you through or around the delta and out onto open water.

In all fairness, the park's problems have as much to do with the recent dry winters, and excessive pumping of lake water for irrigation in surrounding areas, as with planning and administration. The best months are alleged to be November (after the first rains, when various migratory species pass through on their way south) and April/May (when the swamps are full and the birds are flying north). There are no facilities in the park; closest ones are a **pansiyon** and restaurant by the roadside at Eski Sığırcı, 1.5km before the gate.

Bandırma, the Kapıdağ Peninsula, and the Marmara Islands

In the western half of the Sea of Marmara lie several inhabited islands and a large landmass that just misses being one. They're well-known to Turks—especially İstanbul people—but rarely visited by foreigners. In all honesty they're never going to attract many overseas visitors, not when the southern Turkish resorts offer more of intrinsic interest and a longer season, but they make an interesting overnight or two between İstanbul or Bursa and the north Aegean.

Except for parts of Erdek and Avşa Island, these places exist in a 1970s time warp; the resorts have all lost whatever pretenses of trendiness they once claimed, bypassed in the stampede to the south that have been made possible by increased affluence, better roads, and more frequent internal flights. The only foreigners here tend to be expatriates weekending from İstanbul, or those brought here by Turkish friends. The major settlements are nondescript, with little conscious preservation ethic, but the swimming and bicycling are fine and the scenery—the horizon studded with islets—is as close to the Greek or Yugoslav archipelagoes as you'll see in Turkey.

All the islands are easily accessible via ferry from İstanbul, Tekirdağ and especially Erdek, the main town of the Kapıdağ Peninsula and just a short bus ride from Bandırma. **BANDIRMA** itself, knocked flat during battles in 1922 and now neighbor to a NATO airbase, is a definite finalist in the ugliest town in Turkey sweepstakes. Given its status as a major transit point you may well have to spend some time here, but all you really need to know is how to get from one transport terminal to another.

The main **otogar** is at the southern outskirts of town, 800m from the **ferry port** and adjoining **train station**; if you don't want to walk up the hill or take a taxi between the two, use red-and-white city buses, labeled "Garaj/600 Evler," which depart from a tent 200m east of the harbor gate. The **dolmuş** yard, halfway between the otogar and the bay on the main thoroughfare, is not well marked: look for the *Petrol Ofisi* pump next to the entry driveway. If by some misfortune you're stranded overnight here, the *Otel Özdil*, right in front of the shoreline city-bus stand, is tolerable enough.

Erdek and Around

A leafy, cobbled, pedestrianized shore esplanade sets the tone for **ERDEK**, the easiest jumping-off point for the islands, tucked at the base of the Kapıdağ Peninsula. The closest of the islands guards the harbor entrance, and there's another islet farther out to sea, with the hills of the "mainland" looming beyond. The rest of town, with its landscaping and patches of park, is pleasant enough, but if you're going to stay any length of time you'd probably prefer to be behind the strip of beach to the northwest.

Practical Details

The **otogar** is by the road in from Bandırma, at the northeast edge of town, but many buses go all the way down to the water so ask if you want to be let off there.

Almost everything else of interest stands either along the shore promenade or just behind it—the **tourist information office**, for example, is at Hükümet Cad 54, diagonally across the street from the **PTT**, and both are one block inland from the **ferry dock**. Speaking of boats, both the big liners run by *TML* (which serve at least two of the islands daily) and the fleet of smaller private craft serving particular islands tend to depart at around 3.30 in the afternoon.

If you want to **stay** in town, start by snooping around behind Cumhuriyet Meydanı, the obvious swelling in the shore promenade. The *Ümit Hotel*, on Balıkhanı Sokak (☎1989/1092; $12 double with bath), is acceptable if you're waiting overnight for a boat, as is the nearby *Deniz Palas*. Closer to the tourist office is another concentration of inexpensive accommodation: the *Emin* (☎1989/1213) and *Günülal* pansiyons are okay; the fleabag *Saner* is not.

Standards along the beach outside of town, where there must be at least forty establishments, are a bit higher; among those enjoying quiet or panoramic positions are, in descending order of price, the *Ener Otel* (☎1989/1256), the *Kafkas Motel* (☎1989/1738), the *Aşkın* (☎1989/1024), and a **campground** (*Ay*) at the very end of the shore frontage road.

For **eating** in the town center, try either the *Durak Lokantası* near the dock or the *Uludağ Pide Salonu*, one block inland from Cumhuriyet Meydanı.

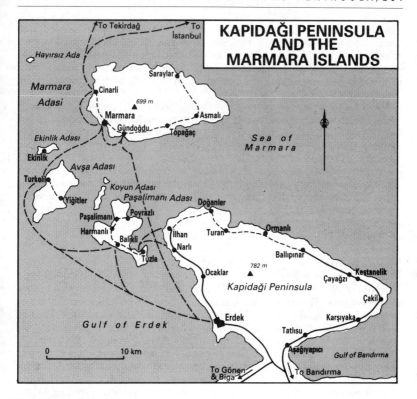

Touring the Peninsula

You'll have already seen some of Kapıdağ if you approached Erdek from Bandırma, and it's difficult to imagine a less promising preview. Between Erdek and the two-kilometer-wide isthmus that joins the peninsula to the rest of Anatolia, the shore is almost wholly given over to private and military facilities, or campgrounds geared for car campers and RVs. The ruins of ancient Kyzikos are so negligible that the archaeological service hasn't even bothered posting the usual sign; the only visible monuments are the huge array of oil storage tanks, unhappily sited opposite some of the few public beaches west of the isthmus.

On the eastern shore of the peninsula facing Bandırma things are initially even worse: despite good beaches and a motel or two at **TATLISU** and beyond, a huge fertilizer plant on the horizon discourages swimming. **KARŞIYAKA**, a few kilometers farther, has similar amenities and water that looks a little more inviting. The best thing to do here, however, would be to **cycle**: the landscape is green, the grades gentle, the road paved (if potholed) and little traveled. The sole disincentive to a complete loop of Kapıdağ would be the long dirt stretch between Ballıpınar and İlhan.

Heading the other way (northwest) out of Erdek is in most respects a better bet; from the west coast the 800-meter-high peninsula shows its green profile, tufted with olives, poplars, and willows, to full advantage. There are **dolmuş** services from the otogar to the villages of Ocaklar, Narlı, and Turan. The one-street village of **OCAKLAR**, 5km north of Erdek; is lost in vegetation; an excellent, partly shaded **beach** extends 1.5km to the north, only about half-developed with motels and restaurants, the best of which is the *Çakıl (Pir Ramis'in yeri)*, with cheap seafood.

NARLİ, 4km farther on, has more of a village feel with its ruined Greek church in the center, and an evocative setting on a slope overlooking Paşalimanı Island, but the tiny beach can't compare with Ocaklar's. There are a handful of pansiyons on the outskirts and an equal number of eateries by the jetty where dolmuşes pull up and regular launches set off for the island. Beyond Narlı there are a couple more pansiyons and new villas, but nothing overwhelming yet; the short season and the heavy military presence (patrol boats are ubiquitous) have combined to put a damper on commercialization—as have the narrow and rocky beaches between Narlı and **İLHAN**, a rickety fishing port with a more informal boat service to Paşalimanı Island. There's no set schedule; you have to go down to the dock and ask who's going out to the island next, and for how much.

The Islands

Four of the islands off Erdek are inhabited, and all can be visited with varying degrees of ease. The largest, Marmara, was a colony of Miletus in ancient times, as were Erdek (Artaki) and Kyzikos on the peninsula. A Greek identity persisted until this century, and even the wall map in the Erdek tourist office lists the old names: Elafonisos for Marmara, Ophioussa for Avşa, Haloni for Paşalimanı. As elsewhere in west Anatolia, the Greeks began leaving the archipelago at the turn of the century, with emigration acquiring a more compulsory character after some were caught cooperating with British submarine captains during World War I. Occasional elderly, forlorn Greeks still return each summer, searching for the houses they were born in, but the islanders claim they rarely find them—too much has changed.

For such a tightly bunched group, the islands are markedly different. **Avşa** is the most commercialized—some say ruined; neighboring **Ekinlik** and **Paşalimanı** are the least spoiled, with **Marmara** falling somewhere in between. Incidentally, while cars are not expressly forbidden on the islands, neither are they encouraged, making the archipelago relatively quiet by Turkish standards. The *TML* liners simply don't accept vehicles, so if you want to bring one you'll have to arrange carriage with the skippers of the private ferries—and space on these is very limited. Finally, if you show up much before June 1 or after September 30, the sea will be cool—and hardly anything will be open.

Marmara

Largest of the islands at roughly 17km by 8km, **MARMARA** acquired its present name during the Middle Ages thanks to the giant marble quarries (*ta marmara* in Greek) that are still worked on the north shore. Sailing in from the south, you'll see the rocky ridge of 700-meter İlyas Dağı, with a ruined Byzantine tower, plunging down to the west tip of the island. Except for its valley-bottom oases, Marmara is pretty bleak—downright windswept and rugged in the north—so most of its villages huddle on the southern, lee shore.

The private ferry will stop first at the pretty but facility-less port of GÜNDOĞDU; don't get off here, but wait until reaching the main town. This, simply called **MARMARA**, is backed up against a hill with steep, stepped streets penetrating inland, an enchanting setting from a distance, although seen up close its contemporary domestic architecture is nothing special. A cluster of remaining old houses at the west end of town, due to be demolished for a *gazino* complex, recently received a stay of execution, courtesy of a new historical-preservation rule.

There's a **PTT** and a **bank** in Marmara, plus a **TML agent** in a tiny booth between the mosque and its fountain that only opens when boats drop anchor. If your money's tight you might **stay** at the central *Ada Palas* (☎1984/1007), noisy but cheap at $4 a head, with occasional hot water, but the best places are at the far western end of the shore esplanade, facing the sunset. The *Marmara Otel* (☎1984/1185) has its own restaurant and provides doubles for $14; quieter and more secluded are the *Şato Motel* around the corner, with attached baths and sea-view terraces but only cold water, or (better) the *Mola Otel* (☎1984/1101), up some steps behind the *Şato*, charging $8 per person in modernized rooms. **Restaurants** are fairly unpretentious: the *Bursa* is good and cheap, as is the *Işıl*; there's also a *lahmacun* baker and a sweet shop.

Heading off around the island, you'll find that Marmara has few really good **beaches**. The rocky ones to either side of Marmara town are strictly for getting into the water and not designed to lounge around on. You'll also have to acclimatize yourself to the extremely low salinity of the Sea of Marmara, and swarms of disgusting but usually stingless white jellyfish. In cooler weather you might entertain thoughts of hiking up through the mostly barren interior, but there are only goat-trails along the ridges, and most of the time you'll be restricted to the skeletal network of dirt roads that almost completely ring the island.

The only other village equipped to handle visitors is **ÇINARLI**, 6km northwest of the main harbor by dirt road; there's no bus service, only taxis and the occasional boat (including ferries from Tekirdağ). At least two of the four sandy coves en route have public access, but Çınarlı's 700-meter beach is the best on the island by a long shot. You can try your luck staying at the *Gül Pansiyon*, the *Ketenci Pansiyon*, the *Viking Motel* or the *Alp*, behind the calmest and sandiest stretch; the phone number for the entire village—it's that sort of place—is ☎1984/1425.

Avşa (Avşar)

Low-lying and partly covered in vineyards, **AVŞA** is surrounded by beaches and crystal-clear water that are both its raison d'être and its curse. The somewhat down-at-heel resort of **TÜRKELİ** on the west coast is virtually a suburb of İstanbul in season and, unlike on Marmara where most outsiders have a villa, development here has taken the form of more than a hundred pansiyons and hotels. Prime beachfront locations were snapped up 25 years ago and built on in the spartan style of the time; if you want something more plush you'll usually have to move inland, though that's still no guarantee of much comfort.

Under the circumstances recommendations for **accommodation** are of limited value, but some names to look out for include *Motel 78*, at the extreme south end of the beach; *Otel Temizel* nearby (☎1986/1134), claiming to represent the top end of things at $12 per person; *Başarır* (☎1986/1187), again with ocean view but noiser; and the *Pansiyon Yarar* (☎1986/1248), overlooking the ferry port. There are more, slightly newer facilities behind the northern beach.

When **eating out**, be sure to sample the excellent island **wine**, whether red, rosé, or white. *Kavalleros* is the usual brand, and stores do brisk business selling souvenir bottles. Otherwise there's not much to say except that the *Yonca* is exorbitant; the sit-down ice-cream parlor run by Macedonian settlers is great; and that most people seem to eat at *Paşam* and one other nearby *pide/kebap* house.

There's no full-scale **bank** or **PTT** in Türkeli, merely a couple of porta-booths on the jetty next to the **tourist information stand** (sporadic hours geared to ferry arrivals).

The sole cultural point of interest is the abandoned Aya Triada **church**, stranded somewhere in the concrete sprawl of Türkeli. If the main town gets too much, you can stalk off past *Motel 78* toward Manastır Burnu (Monastery Cape) to find isolated, sandy coves, or try looking for others on the east coast of Avşa, near YİĞİTLER, populated almost entirely by settlers from Yugoslavia. The island is only about 7km by 3km, so no point is more than ninety minutes away on foot. It might also be possible to arrange a boat trip to **EKİNLİK**, the one-village island north of Avşa, but what you saw from the boat as you steamed into Avşa is pretty much what you'll get.

Paşalimanı

Least frequently served by ferry, and lacking enough beaches to make it the target of development, **PAŞALİMANI** is a sleepy, friendly place distinguished mainly by its giant sycamore trees. BALIKLI village is the "capital" and occasional port of call for the *TML* and private services, but the island's main link with the outside are the already-mentioned skiffs from the Kapıdağ villages which put in at TUZLA and POYRAZLI. There's no bank or PTT, so come prepared. Accommodation is likewise very basic—certainly nothing beyond a few pansiyons.

West of Bandırma: the Coast Road to Çanakkale

Once past Bandırma, the old highway—and all buses—veer sharply south to pass through **GÖNEN**, a cobble-streeted market town famous for its thermal baths and the giant *Miş* dairy on the outskirts.

A new bypass road running parallel to the coast is now 75-percent paved after a decade of work, but you probably won't see salt water again in any case until reaching **DENİZKENT**, bang on the Çanakkale/Balıkesir provincial border. It's a strange relic, the first planned resort in Turkey, laid out in the 1950s by Ankara civil servants that must have fulfilled a fantasy of American suburbia of that era. The beach is narrow but very long, with views out to the islands of the Marmara; if you want to stay there's a single motel and a separate restaurant.

Subsequently the road heads inland again, crossing the Biga Çayı, formerly the Granicus, at BIGA, where Alexander the Great won his first victory over the Persians in 334 BC. The local hill villages are populated almost entirely by Pomaks from the Rhodope Mountains of the Greek-Bulgarian frontier, who are renowned for the costumes of their women and their skill in weaving goat-hair mats—though without a prolonged acquaintance you're unlikely to see either.

Beyond Biga you eventually emerge on the southeast flank of the Dardanelles; the drive is pleasant enough, but there's really no place to stop except **LAPSEKI**, 40km east of Çanakkale. Successor to the Lampsacus of yore, it still bears a medieval fortress designed to act in concert with the one across the water at Gelibolu. Otherwise there's little to it besides the ferry jetty where all long-distance buses halt, looking for disembarking passengers.

travel details

Trains

From Edirne to İstanbul (3 daily in early am; 5hr 30min–7hr); Sofya, Bulgaria (1 daily late at night; 9hr). **From Bandırma** to İzmir (2 daily, at 2am & 2pm; 5hr 30min).

Buses and dolmuşes

From Edirne to İstanbul (half-hourly; 4hr); Keşan (hourly; 2hr); Çanakkale (2 direct daily; 4hr 30min).

From Şarköy to Tekirdağ (8 daily; 2hr 30min); Edirne (4 daily; 3hr); İstanbul (4 daily; 5hr).

From İznik to Bursa (half-hourly dolmuşes until 9pm; 1hr 30min); Adapazarı (Sakarya; hourly; 1hr 30min); Yalova (several daily; 1hr).

From Bursa to Çanakkale (hourly; 6hr); Ankara (hourly; 7hr); İstanbul with ferry transfer (hourly; 5hr); Kütahya (3 daily; 3hr); İzmir via Balıkesir and often Ayvalık (15 daily; 7hr); Yalova (half-hourly; 1hr 20min); Mudanya (half-hourly; 40min).

From **Bandırma** to Bursa (hourly; 2hr); Çanakkale (hourly; 3hr 30min); Balıkesir (hourly; 1hr 45min); İzmir (7 daily; 6hr); Manyas (passing bird sanctuary; 7 daily; 30min).

From Erdek to Bandırma (half-hourly; 25min); Bursa (8 daily; 2hr).

Ferries, short-hop

From Kilitbahir to Çanakkale (according to traffic, 6am–9pm; 10 min). Foot passengers 40¢, motorbikes $1.50, cars $6.

From Eceabat to Çanakkale (hourly 6am–midnight, plus 2 & 4am; 20min). Foot passengers 40¢, motorbikes $1.50, cars $8.

From Gelibolu to Lapseki and vice versa (15 daily, 6:30am–midnight, hourly after 4pm; 20min). Foot passengers 40¢, motorbikes $1.50, cars $8.

From Topcular to Eskihisar/Darica, car ferry (half-hourly 6am–midnight, hourly midnight–6am; 20min). Cars $10.

From Karamürsel to Hereke, passenger ferry (7 daily 7am–7pm; 30min). Foot passengers 50¢.

Ferries and hydrofoils: island & long-haul

From Tekirdağ to Marmara/Avşa/Erdek (2 *TML* liners weekly June–Sept, usually Fri/Sun pm; 2hr 30min/3hr 30min/5hr 30min).

From Kabatepe to Gökçeada (Imvros) Island (Wed & Sun afternoon Oct–Jun only; 1hr 30min). Foot passengers $1.50, motorbikes $2, cars $10.

From Mudanya to İstanbul via Armutlu (1 daily May–Sept, early am; 3hr). Foot passengers $5.50. Also hydrofoils 4 mornings weekly; 1 hr 30 min.

From Yalova, ferries to İstanbul-Kabataş (summer), İstanbul-Sirkeci (winter) via Princes' Isles—foot passengers only (3 to 5 daily; 3hr); to Kartal direct (5 daily; 1hr 15min). Fares $1–3. **Hydrofoils** to İstanbul-Kabataş or İstanbul-Karaköy (3 to 5 daily; 1hr 30min); to Kartal (8 daily on weekdays; 35min). Fares $3–7.

From Bandırma to İstanbul (2 daily May–Oct, at 2:15am & 2:15pm, 4hr 30min; in winter twice daily weekdays, 1 daily Sat/Sun). Passengers $8, cars $24.

From Erdek *TML* liners to Marmara/Avşa (daily except Sun June–Sept; 2hr 15min/3hr; daily except Wed in winter); to Paşalimanı (2 weekly June–Sept, usually Sat/Mon; 1hr). Passengers $2–6 for the above. **Private ferries** to Marmara/Avşa (daily; 2hr 30min to both); to Paşalimanı (3 weekly; 1hr). Passengers $2, cars $16.

From Marmara/Avşa to each other and İstanbul (daily each pm June–Sept, 5hr; Wed & Sat/Sun only in winter). Foot passengers $2/$10; also frequent, but doubly expensive *Deniz Otobusleri* (hydrofoils) in summer.

Flights

From Bursa to İstanbul (2 daily Mon–Fri, am & late pm, am only on Sat, none Sun; 1hr) on *Sönmez Holding*. One-way fare $30.

CHAPTER THREE

THE NORTH AEGEAN

Turkey's **North Aegean coast** sees far fewer visitors than the shoreline farther south; it's a quiet, rocky region, not over-endowed with fine beaches, and, due to the generally lower temperature of the water, with a much shorter summer season. Most of the people who come here in summer are Turks, and, although tourism is inevitably an important factor in the local economy, even in summer the number of visitors doesn't really reach mass proportions. Indeed, away from the resort towns life goes on much as it always did, with farming and fishing providing the livelihood of the bulk of the population.

The area, which roughly constitutes the ancient **Aeolia**, has been settled since Palaeolithic times. Civilization bloomed early here under the Phrygians, who arrived in Anatolia during the eighth century BC; later waves of Greek colonists established settlements along the coast, leaving the area rich in Hellenistic remains. Although the ruins of **Troy** in the north don't quite live up to their literary and legendary reputation, the ancient cities of **Assos** and **Pergamon** display some tangible reminders of the power and wealth of the greater Greek empire. The Phrygian city of **Sardis**, the ancient capital of King Croesus (and Midas before him), located a little way east of the lively town of **Manisa**, is also one of Aegean Turkey's most impressive archaeological sites.

If you're coming from İstanbul or anywhere else in northwestern Turkey, **Çanakkale** makes the most sensible port of entry—useful both as a base for the war sites at Gallipoli (detailed in Chapter Two) and the ruins at Troy. Farther south, the best stretches of beach lie near **Ayvalık**—the area's most long-established resort—and along the coastal strip running from **Assos** to **Ören**, on the northern shore of the **Gulf of Edremit**. In general there's less to write home about **inland**, where a mountainous landscape harbors a few predominantly industrial cities, with only the town of **Alaşehir** worth any kind of detour.

ÇANAKKALE TO EDREMİT

The road running from **Çanakkale** to **Edremit** is justifiably distinguished by a scenic green band on most maps—much of the route is wooded and gently hilly, giving way to a coastal strip behind which rise the mountains of the **Kaz Dağı** range. **Troy** is the obvious first stop, after which **Assos**, a few miles off the main road past **Ayvacık**, is the place to head for. Beyond Ayvacık the road follows the coast, passing a number of small resorts before reaching **Edremit**.

Çanakkale

Though celebrated for its setting on the Dardanelles, **ÇANAKKALE** has little to detain you except a good archaeological museum. However, it is the most obvious base for visiting the Gallipoli sites on the European side of the

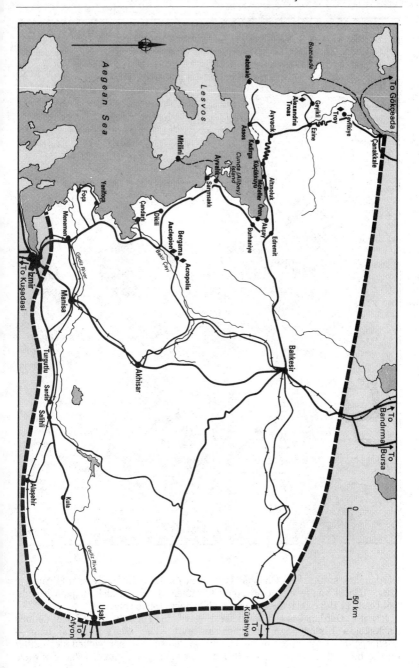

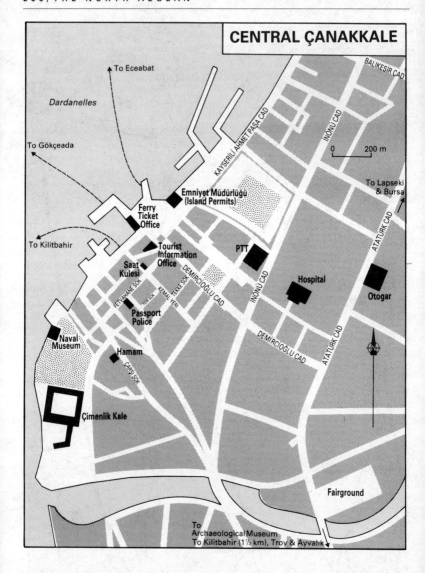

CENTRAL ÇANAKKALE

To Eceabat

Dardanelles

To Gökçeada

To Kilitbahir

BALIKESIR CAD

KAYSERILI AHMET PAŞA CAD

İNONU CAD

0   200 m

To Lapseki
& Bursa

Emniyet Müdürlüğü
(Island Permits)

Ferry
Ticket
Office

ATATÜRK CAD

Tourist
Information
Office

PTT

Saat
Kulesi

DEMİRCİOĞLU CAD

Hospital

Otogar

İNONU CAD

ÇETVAHANE SOK

KEMAL YERİ

YEN SOK

KEMAL TEKKE SOK

Passport
Police

Naval
Museum

DEMİRCİOĞLU CAD

ATATÜRK CAD

Hamam

ÇARŞ SOK

Çimenlik Kale

Fairground

To
Archaeological Museum
To Kilitbahir (1½ km), Troy & Ayvalık

Dardanelles straits (see Chapter Two), and for the admittedly sparse ruins of Troy. Also, if you're intent on going to either of the Turkish Aegean islands, Gökçeada or Bozcaada, the town is an obligatory stop for permits.

It's the Dardanelles ("Çanakkale Boğazı" in Turkish) that have defined Çanakkale's **history** and its place in **myth**. The area's classical name— "Hellespont"—is owed to one Helle, who while escaping her wicked stepmother on the back of a winged ram fell into the swift-moving channel and drowned.

From Abydus on the Asian side, the youth Leander used to swim to Sestos on the European shore for trysts with his love Hero, until one night he too perished in the current; in despair, Hero drowned herself as well. Byron narrowly escaped being added to the list of casualties on his swim in the opposite direction on May 3, 1810.

In 480 BC Xerxes' Persian hordes crossed the waters on their way to Greece; and in 411 and 405 BC the last two naval battles of the Peloponnesian War took place in the straits, the latter engagement ending in decisive defeat for the Athenian fleet. Twenty centuries later, Mehmet the Conqueror constructed the elaborate fortress of Kilitbahir, directly opposite the Çimenlik Kale in Çanakkale (which he also built), to tighten the stranglehold being applied to doomed Constantinople. In March 1915, an Allied fleet attempting to force the Dardanelles and attack İstanbul was repulsed, with severe losses, by Turkish shore batteries, prompting the even bloodier land campaign at Gallipoli. The straits are still heavily militarized and modern Çanakkale is very much a navy town.

Arrival and Information

Coming by **ferry** from European Eceabat or Kilitbahir, you'll arrive on shore near the start of **Demircioğlu Caddesi**, which barrels inland and roughly splits the town in two. Everything you'd want to see or do in Çanakkale, except for the archaeological museum, is within walking distance of the ferry docks. The **tourist information office** (Mon–Fri 8am–5:30pm; ☎196/11187), next to the main dock, is worth a stop if only to pick up their free "Turkey/Çanakkale" pamphlet, which has a map of the Gallipoli battlefields that's far more accurate than any in the various glossy booklets for sale. Arriving by **bus**, the otogar is out on **Atatürk Caddesi**, the local name for the coastal İzmir–Bursa highway, a little way north of the end of Demircioğlu Caddesi. It's a fifteen-minute walk from the waterfront, although, if you ask, most drivers will drop you off near the tourist office.

Çanakkale sees enough tourists to support a *nöbetci*, or evening and weekend **bank**, between May and October; the acting *nöbetci* changes weekly—check the schedule posted on the door of every bank. If you're seeing the **Gallipoli battlefield** from here, the principal **tour operator** in Çanakkale is *Troy Anzac Tours*, just west of the Saat Kulesi (☎196/15047), whose outings leave at 10am each day, returning around 2:30pm—cost $10–15 a head.

Finding a Place to Stay

Except during mid-August, when the Çanakkale/Troy Festival is being staged, you'll have little trouble finding a **room**. Just south of the tourist office, the Saat Kulesi (Clocktower) signals the entrance to a maze of alleys—Fetvahane Sokak, Aralık Sokak, Yeni Sokak—which is home to various inexpensive hotels and pansiyons; moving across Demircioğlu Caddesi, or closer to the water, you'll also be moving upscale hotel-wise.

Two good, adjacent budget choices are the *Kervansaray*, Fetvahane Sokak 13, and the *Otel Efes* just behind (☎196/13256), each with singles without bath for $4, doubles for $7; of the two, the *Kervansaray*, a converted 200-year-old mansion with a garden, has more character. Two streets farther inland, on Yeni Sokak, the pleasant but simple *Yetimoğlu Pansiyon* is actually an annex of the *Küçük Truva* on Fetvahane Sokak, where you should inquire if nobody's home at the pansiyon.

If you require more comfort, try the *Avrupa Pansiyon*, Matbaa Sokak 8, between Fetvahane Sokak and the water (☎196/14084), where singles with bath are $8, doubles $12. Across Demircioğlu Caddesi, behind the *Halk Bankası*, the *Otel Yıldız*, Kızılay Sokak 20 (☎196/11793), offers relative luxury and knowledgeable English-speaking staff for $19 a double, slightly less for a single. If—and only if—you arrive late at the otogar, you might consider the rather over-priced *Otel Inci*, right outside the terminal at Hasan Mevsuf Sokak 10 (☎196/ 13295), which has singles with bath for $12 and doubles for $18. The nearby *Açkin* has the same rates but also runs a much cheaper pansiyon on a side street.

If you want to **camp**, the closest site is the *Şen* at **KEPEZ**, 7km south; there are several more at **GÜZELYALI**, 12km southwest of town—the latter a rather overdeveloped place with a narrow, windswept beach. All are accessible by mini-bus but none are as good as those on the Gallipoli Peninsula or at Kilitbahir across the Dardanelles (see Chapter Two).

The Town

The name "Çanakkale" means "Pottery Castle," after the garish Çanakkale ware that finds its way into the ethnographic section of every Turkish museum. Fortunately none of this is conspicuous—the only nod to the plastic arts being a few appealing, turn-of-the-century buildings in the tiny **bazaar**, just south of the nucleus of cheap hotels. Continue past the bazaar area to **Çimenlik Park, Castle and Naval Museum** (park daily 9am–10pm; castle off-limits; museum daily except Mon & Fri 9am–noon & 1:30–5pm; free). Beached beside the park esplanade, which provides the best views of Kilitbahir fort across the way, is a replica of the minelayer **Nusrat** (same hours as museum), which stymied the Allied fleet by re-mining zones at night that the French and British had swept clean by day. It's festooned inside with fairly forgettable newspaper clippings of the era. The **museum** itself is more worthwhile, featuring archival photos—Seddülbahir in ruins after Allied shelling, Atatürk's funeral—and military para-phernelia, including (on the upper floor) Atatürk's shattered pocketwatch which stopped a shell fragment at Gallipoli and saved his life.

An hour should be enough to take in the **Archaeological Museum** (daily 8am–noon & 1–4:45pm; $1), nearly 2km from the center of town. To avoid walking there, flag down any dolmuş along Atatürk Caddesi labeled "Kepez" or "Güzelyalı." The exhibits begin with an appeal for the return of valuable loot spir-ited from Uşak to New York in the 1960s, then move on to a chronological presen-tation of area finds. The collection is strong on brass implements, delicate glass and glazed pottery, unfired lamps and figurines, and wooden objects, most of them from the nearby Bozcaada and Dardanos tumuli, and is uncluttered by the usual doorstop statuary of Turkish archaeological museums. There's also a coin case spanning all cultures from Lydian to Ottoman, although the most exquisite items are the gold and jewelry from the graves, and bone and ivory work near the exit.

Eating and Drinking

Most **places to eat** are within a block or two of the straits. Of the conspicuous waterfront restaurants south of the main ferry pier, the *Entellektüel* (sic) has the widest range of *meze* and fish—try the black bream (*karagöz*) and *mermer*. Check the freshness of the catch and the fullness of trays (and tables) when choosing.

The *Şehir Lokantası*, at the southern end of the esplanade, has the quietest and most sheltered outdoor seating.

Inland near the bazaar, the food is more modest and cheaper. Best and friendliest of the bunch is the *Yılmaz Restaurant*, one street back from the water. Farther down the same block, almost to the Çimenlik park, the *Engin Pastanesi* has the best desserts and ice cream in town, and around the corner on Çarşı Caddesi, the *Ozan Pide ve Lahmacun Salonu* is another worthy option. You can breakfast at the *Tutku Mantı ve Kahvaltı Salonu*, where Tekke Sokak meets Demircioğlu Caddesi; a little farther inland on the latter is the *Memo Pastanesi*, with more ice cream.

For **drinking**, take your cue from the Australians, who during the 75th anniversary of the Gallipoli battles in April 1990 polished off a month of normal Çanakkale beer consumption in three days at the waterfront fish-fryers and sleazy pubs near the Saat Kulesi.

The Turkish Aegean Islands

Strategically straddling the Dardanelles, the islands of **Gökçeada** and **Bozcaada** were the only Aegean islands to remain in Turkish hands after the 1923 Treaty of Lausanne, which concluded the Greek-Turkish war. Under the terms of the agreement the islands' predominantly Greek inhabitants were exempt from the population exchange of the same year, but after 1937 the islands were re-militarized along with the Greek islands of Samothraki and Limnos, and in subsequent decades the Turkish authorities began to assert their sovereignty more forcefully. A ban on foreigners visiting the islands was lifted in 1987, and even now few overseas visitors make their way here from the mainland. What they find are inexpensive though basic facilities, good beaches, and a rather uneasily shifted sense of identity.

Ferries to Gökçeada usually leave from Çanakkale but sometimes from KABATEPE on the Gelibolu Peninsula; check current schedules carefully. Ferries to Bozcaada leave from ODUN İSKELESİ, which has a couple of simple restaurants by the dock and a good beach extending south for a swim while you wait. One-way fares to both islands are 35¢ for foot passengers, $8–9 for a small car.

Since both islands are still military zones, **formal permission** is required from the authorities in Çanakkale before visiting. Go first to the Passport Police, next to the *Kervansaray* and *Efes* hotels, where you must declare which island you wish to go to and for how long; then take the paperwork to the *Emniyet Müdürlüğü*, next to the *Anafartalar Hotel*, where various stamps are applied to your application. Take this back to the Passport Police, who will give you a sealed letter addressed to the governor of the island in question, which you must present to the police upon disembarkation; often your passport will be taken, to be returned when you leave the island. There should be no charge for any of these transactions.

Gökçeada (Imvros)

The larger of the two Turkish Aegean islands, **GÖKÇEADA** hovers just northeast of the Dardanelles, tantalizingly visible from any of the Gallipoli battlefields. It's a rolling, hilly island, not unattractive, and large enough to make your own vehicle necessary. But it is heavily militarized and has a rather sad recent history.

Assigned to Turkey for its strategic value after the 1923 peace conference, the island's majority population of 6000 Orthodox Greeks was more or less left to itself for forty years, save for a token force of a hundred or so Turkish gendarmes and officials. When the Cyprus conflict first came to a head in the early 1960s, the Turkish government decided to "claim" the island more pointedly, instituting policies of forced land expropriation without compensation, heavy garrisoning, the closure of the schools for Greek children, settlement of Turkish civilians from the mainland, and the establishment of an open prison. (It was from the latter that William Hayes, of *Midnight Express* notoriety, escaped.) These measures were taken specifically to make continued residence for the ethnic Greeks impossible, and they've had the desired effect—today there are only 200–300 demoralized Greeks left, the bulk of the population having fled to Athens and farther afield.

Ferries dock at the new, functional harbor of **KUZU LİMANI**, where a small motel fails to attract much foreign business. A dolmuş meets the boat and takes you the 6km inland to **ÇINARLI**, formerly Panayia, the island's capital, which has a couple of hotels and restaurants, as well as two or three huge, shuttered Greek churches. But the streets are dusty or muddy according to season, and the grim official architecture on the main drag overwhelms the old houses on the slope. Most visitors continue another 4km by minibus to **KALE** (formerly Kastro) on the north shore, where a ruined castle built during Süleyman the Magnificent's reign overlooks a good beach and the Greek island of Samothraki. Along the waterfront are a handful of pansiyons and excellent, cheap fish tavernas with roof-terrace seating. The beach, though, is encroached upon by a huge officers' club, and the upper village around the castle is a virtual ghost town; the life of the place pretty much went out of it when the main anchorage was shifted to Kuzu Limanı.

From Kale you can easily walk the 1500m south to **BADEMLİ** (Glyki), passing on the way the hideous new prefab settlement of Yeni Bademli. Old Bademli is also virtually deserted, its 25 or so inhabitants split evenly along ethnic lines and uneasily coexisting. There's more of an illusion of normality at **ZEYTİNLİ** (Ayia Theodhori), 3km northwest of Çınarlı, where most of Gökçeada's remaining Greek Orthodox population lives, but you'll quickly notice that none are younger than 35. They're understandably bitter about the turn of events, and often reluctant to talk to—or be photographed by—outsiders.

There are three more villages in the west of the island, near the prison, but there's no transportation to them, only a rumored service van to the jail every morning. **KEFALO BURNU**, the southeastern tip of the island, has better beaches than Kale's, but again you'll need your own transportation to get to it.

Bozcaada (Tenedos)

Just a few nautical miles off Anatolia, **BOZCAADA** is a more cheerful place, if only because it's far less militarized and more architecturally consistent. It's too close to the mainland to have avoided attention by any power ruling Turkey, and the population, as evidenced by a handful of medieval mosques, has historically been about half Muslim. Covered mostly in vineyards, which are the source of the justly famous Bozcaada wine, the island is small enough to walk around—fortunately, since there's no public transportation—and has some of Turkey's best beaches.

Boats put in at the northeastern tip of the island, in the shadow of the **castle**, which has been successively enlarged by Byzantine, Genoese, Venetian, and Turkish occupiers; the most recent restoration was by the archaeological service in the 1960s. The result is one of the hugest citadels in the Aegean, easily equal to

Bodrum's; thankfully it's not a military area, so you can explore every inch—the locals use the building to graze sheep, and the lower courtyard as a soccer field.

Guarded by the castle, the single **town**, though built on a grid plan along a slight slope, is surprisingly elegant; there's a minimum of concrete and a maximum of old, overhanging upper floors and cobbled streets. The feel is much like a Greek island of twenty or thirty years ago—or a Turkish southern Aegean resort of a mere decade ago. The old Greek quarter once extended east from the church to the sea, although today less than a hundred elderly Orthodox Greeks remain, ground down by the same sort of campaign as their compatriots on Gökçeada.

The interior of the island is gently undulating country, flatter than Gökçeada and treeless except for clumps marking farms. The three best **beaches** are Ayazma, Sullubahçe, and Habbelle, all 5–6km away on the south coast; take the first right fork out of town and then two lefts. Just above Ayazma is an abandoned monastery, home of the *ayazma* (sacred spring) that gives it its name, while closer to the beach is a lone seasonal **restaurant**. From the restaurant a dirt road leads thirty minutes east (left) to **Ayiana beach**, a marvelous site if you're after complete solitude. The sea on this side of Bozcaada is incredibly clean, and warm considering how close it is to the Dardanelles.

Taking the first left fork leads to some more **beaches**—narrower and more exposed—on the eastern shore, along the 4km of asphalt ending at Tuzburnu.

Practical Details

Not surprisingly, any haven this convenient fills up in high summer, mostly with people from İstanbul and Athens visiting relatives, and **accommodation** can be in short supply—much like the water, which is drawn from deep wells and pretty salty. Advance reservations in July and August are essential. The *Koz Otel* (☎1965/1189) has two branches—one on the harbor, one giant premises way inland—and both fairly quiet. The *Gümüş Oteli* (☎1965/1252), housed in the old school, is okay if spartan at $8 per person. The *Emirgan*, behind the **PTT** and **bank**, is new but has no frills. The only approximation of luxury is the *Zafer* (☎1965/1078), on the bluff opposite the castle. Much more remote is the *Sezen Motel* (☎1965/1325), out at Tuzburnu.

The small inner fishing harbor is the spot to **eat**, where the *Liman Lokantası* vies with the *Koz Restaurant* (the latter open June–Sept, like its affiliated hotel). The local men do their heavy drinking at *Koreli'nin Yeri*; the best food, though, is probably slightly inland at *Ayazma*, which serves soup-breakfasts and commands the best view of the castle. Fish is a local fixture, accompanied by the ubiquitous **wine**; the best brands are *Doruk, Halikarnass, Talay,* and *Dimitrakopoulou*.

Troy

Although by no means the most spectacular archaeological site in Turkey, **TROY**, thanks to Homer, is probably the most celebrated. Known as *Truva* in Turkish, the remains of the ancient city lie just west of the main road about 20km south of Çanakkale. It's a scanty affair on the whole—there isn't really much to see apart from some wall remains and a few vague piles of stone with the catch-all label "Defensive Wall"—and a lot of visitors come away disappointed that the remains don't live up to the fame of their name. But if you lower your expectations and use your imagination, you may well be impressed.

Until 1871 Troy was generally thought to have existed in legend only. The Troad Plain, where the ruins now lie, was known to be associated with the Troy that Homer wrote about in the *Iliad*, but all traces of the city had vanished completely. In 1868 Heinrich Schliemann (1822–90), a German businessman who had made his fortune in America, obtained permission from the Ottoman government to start digging on a hill known to the Turks as Hisarlık, where earlier excavators had already found the remains of a classical temple and signs of further older ruins.

Schliemann himself was an interesting character. Born into a poor Mecklenburg family, he became obsessed at an early age with the myths of ancient Greece. Unable to pursue the interest professionally (although he did teach himself ancient Greek) he amassed his considerable fortune during the Californian Gold Rush of 1849, forsaking commerce at the age of 46 to become the world's most celebrated and successful amateur archaeologist.

Schliemann's work actually caused a certain amount of damage to the site, and he was also responsible for removing the so-called "treasure of Priam," a large cache of beautiful jewelry that was taken back to Berlin without Turkish government permission and subsequently lost during World War II. But the excavations uncovered nine layers of remains, representing distinct and consecutive city developments and spanning four millennia. The oldest, Troy I, dates back to about 3600 BC and was followed by four similar settlements. Troy VI and VII are thought to have been the cities described by Homer: the former is known to have been destroyed by an earthquake in about 1275 BC, while the latter shows signs of having been destroyed by fire about a quarter of a century later, around the time historians estimate the Trojan War took place. Troy VIII, which thrived from 700 to 300 BC, was a Greek city, while the final layer of development, Troy IX, was built between 300 BC and AD 300, during the heyday of the Roman Empire.

Although there's no way of being absolutely sure that the Trojan War did take place, there's a fair amount of circumstantial evidence suggesting that the city was the scene of some kind of armed conflict, even if it wasn't the ten-year battle described in the *Iliad*. It's possible that Homer's epic is based on a number of wars fought between the Mycenean Greeks and the inhabitants of Troy, who, it seems, were alternately trading partners and commercial rivals. Homer's version of events does away with these prosaic possibilities, turning the war into a full-scale epic, complete with bit parts for the gods of ancient Greece. Additionally, he gives the events a romantic turn, beginning with Paris's kidnapping of Helen of Troy from her husband Menelaus, the King of Sparta, and finishing up with the ten-year siege of Troy—finally ended by Odysseus's famous trick, when the gates were breached by soldiers hidden inside an enormous wooden horse.

The Site

The **site** (daily 8am–5:45pm; $2) is signalled by the ticket office—marked "*Gişe*"—opposite the drop-off point. From here a long, straight road leads to some more facilities and a giant wooden horse, close to which is the **house** that Schliemann stayed in while working at Troy—a small cottage basically, containing the tools the archaeologist worked with alongside pictures of his wife wearing the jewels he pillaged and other bits and pieces. Just beyond is the ruined city itself, a craggy outcrop overlooking the Troad Plain, which stretches about 8km to the sea. It's a bleak sight, and leaves you in no doubt as to the thinness of Troy's remains, but as you stand on what's left of the ramparts and look out across the plain, it's not too difficult to imagine a besieging army, legendary or otherwise, camped out below. Walking around the site, the **walls** of Troy VI are the most obvious feature, curving around in a crescent from the entrance; there are also more definite and visible remains from Troys VIII–IX, including a **bouleterion**, or council chamber, and a small **theater** a little way north.

Practical Details

Çanakkale is the most sensible base for seeing Troy, since its otogar is connected to the site by fairly frequent dolmuş—a half-hour journey through a rolling landscape of olive groves and cotton fields. Failing that you can stay in the village of TEVFIKIYE, just before Troy, although the only lodging is at the none-too luxurious *Yarol Pension*. The dolmuş to the site drops you off just beyond the village in front of a burgeoning cluster of tourist shops and restaurants, the highlight of which is the reasonably decent *Helen Restaurant*. There's also a bank, a PTT, and a parking lot.

Alexandria Troas

About 20km south of Troy is EZINE, a small wayside town from which infrequent dolmuşes run to DALYAN and the ruins of **Alexandria Troas**, a city founded in about 300BC by Antigonus I, a general of Alexander the Great and ruler of one of the successor kingdoms established when Alexander's empire broke up. Antigonus forced the inhabitants of the area to move into his city, which he named Antigonia after himself. His stab at immortality was unsuccessful. Lysimachus, king of Macedonia, conquered Antigonia, after killing Antigonus and his son Demetrius in battle, and renamed it Alexandria Troas in honor of Alexander the Great.

Apparently much of the 1000-acre city remained intact until as late as 1764, when the British traveler and antiquarian Richard Chandler visited and reported substantial city walls and fortifications enclosing what he took to be a ruined temple. Today, however, the ruins consist of only a few sections of wall and the vaults of baths perched on a rise overlooking the island of Bozcaada—all in all, not really worth bothering with. As Eric Newby wrote in *On the Shores of the Mediterranean*, "it was perfectly possible . . . to walk into it through one of the now enormous gaps in the walls and walk out through a similar gap on the far side, without, apart from tripping over some low-lying remains or else bumping into something shrouded in vegetation which loomed unidentifiable overhead, seeing much of Alexandria Troas at all."

Ayvacık and Assos

Thirty kilometers south of Ezine lies **AYVACIK**, a market town from which there's a dolmuş service to the Hellenistic settlement of Assos. It's not likely that you'll find much to detain you in Ayvacık, although you might have to wait a while for a dolmuş since there are only about four or five a day (it's worth trying to hitch if this happens). The best time to be in town is Friday—market day—when the local people (mostly settled nomads) come in from the surrounding villages to sell their produce from open-air stalls adjacent to the bus stop and ticket office.

It's a particularly noisy and colorful affair, worth spending time at between dolmuş connections: women in traditional patterned trousers and headscarves sell all kinds of fruit and vegetables, honey, cheese, and prepared *börek* pastry. In the unlikely event of your wanting to **spend the night** in Ayvacık try the *B. Hotel Restaurant*, on Assos Yolu Üzeri—the road to Assos—which has doubles from $10 (all rooms have showers).

ASSOS, 25km south, combines the two mainstays of tourism in coastal Turkey—ruins and beaches. The site of an ancient Greek settlement, it is officially called **BEHRAMKALE**, after the village that has grown up around it, but many of the locals, including dolmuş drivers, still use the name Assos. Until a few years ago the site was more or less undiscovered but now it's a well-established stopover on most itineraries, attracting a good share of visitors in summer, but most come on day trips, leaving the village relatively tourist-free by evening.

The half-hour ride, a journey of winding hill roads and impressive rocky scenery, takes you past a fourteenth-century, humpbacked **Ottoman bridge**, built with stones from the ancient settlement. Shortly after this, a left fork leads up into the village and the dolmuş drop-off point, on a small square in front of a café. From here it's only a couple of minutes' walk up to the remains of ancient Assos. The village itself has one very good **pansiyon**, the *Gök Köşe Pansiyon*, just below the ruins, although if you're staying you should get the dolmuş driver to take you down into the harbor where most of the hotels are situated.

Ancient Assos

According to some sources **ASSOS** was the site of a Hittite colony that dated as far back as the thirteenth century BC, although history only really started here around 700BC, when Greek colonists established a settlement, later building a huge temple to Athena in 540 BC. Hermias, a eunuch and disciple of Plato, was governor here and, attempting to put Plato's theories of the ideal city-state into practice, founded a branch of the Platonic academy. For three years Aristotle made his home in Assos. Later, during medieval times, the Ottomans plundered the town for stone, as did local villagers.

The chances are that one of the café patrons will offer to show you around the ruins, although it's easy enough to find the way by yourself. Follow the road up into the village past a congregation of kids and old people selling lace until you come to the **Murat Hüdavendigâr Camii**, an austere fourteenth-century mosque, built with stone quarried from the earlier settlement. Beyond is the site of the **Temple of Athena** ($1 during daylight hours) with only nine or ten columns, recently re-erected and in part reconstructed by an American university archaeological team. It's a beautiful structure, certainly, although somewhat overshadowed by the view across to Lesvos and over the Gulf of Edremit. The rest of ancient Assos is a jumble of ruins falling away from the temple, enclosed partly by the old and intermittently intact **city wall**; the most recognizable part is the old **necropolis**, littered with sarcophagi, viewable on the way down from the village to the harbor.

The Harbor and Around

Assos **harbor**, a good half-hour's walk from the upper village and archaeological site along a steep winding road, is quite different in feel. Tourism is the main means of livelihood here and there are several modern, comfortable hotels, a few campgrounds, and, at the height of summer, a lot of visitors. Also, since between here and the Greek island of Lesvos 8km away there's nothing but open water, the harbor has its own platoon of soldiers.

The harbor is very compact and you'll have no trouble finding a hotel, although during the high season free rooms are sometimes scarce. Most of the **hotels** are reasonable enough. Right on the waterfront, the *Hotel Behram* (☎081/12758) is probably the best, offering clean, comfortable rooms with bathrooms from $14 a double. It's a friendly place with a restaurant and the owner speaks German. Also recommended is the nearby *Hotel Assos Yıldız*, with a restaurant and a roof terrace, where doubles are $14. Just behind the *Behram*, the improbably named *Pension Dr No* is comparatively basic, but offers three-bed rooms for $6 with breakfast ($4 without). Showers and (squat) toilets are shared here. More upscale is the *Hotel Assos Kervansaray* (☎081/11969), a big, modern place with a huge dining area, bar, and terrace overlooking the sea. The rooms, which aren't as grand as the lobby suggests, go for $20 a double with bathroom.

All of the hotels have good **restaurants**. The one at the *Behram* overlooks the sea and is probably the most pleasant, but the owner of the *Pension Dr No* does equally good food a little cheaper. He'll also go out of his way to come up with fresh fish if you so desire.

Just to the east of the hotels are a string of **campgrounds**. *Aristo Camping* is the closest, although *Dost Camping*, just beyond, is better, charging $3 all-inclusive; it also has a restaurant and a friendly owner. Beyond here, *Assos Camping* has hot water and washing facilities; *Öz Camp*, farther on, is a little more primitive.

If you do stay here in summer, be prepared to walk a mile or two along the coast past the campgrounds to find a quiet stretch of (pebbly) **beach**. Other things to do include renting a boat to take you to **BABAKALE**, a fishing village and the most westerly point in mainland Asia, about 25km from Assos.

About 7km east of Assos, reached by taking the dirt road from the upper village (although you can walk along the coast too), is the hamlet of **KADİRGA**, where there is a good stretch of beach, some hotels, and camping facilities. Here you'll find the snazzy *Eden Beach Hotel* and the more affordable *Mercan Hotel*, the latter an inexpensive family place where you'll pay $10-plus for a double during the season. Also worth checking out is the similarly priced *Kadirğa Hotel*, which has space for campers who can use the hotel's bathroom facilities. Failing that, the *Kelfarash Pension* has single rooms from $5 in summer.

Ayvacık to Ören—and Routes Inland

From Ayvacık a mountain road winds through pine forests, offering occasional glimpses out across the Bay of Edremit, before straightening out at **KÜÇÜKKUYU**—the first of a string of resorts between here and Edremit. Küçükkuyu was originally a small harbor town, and on Fridays farmers from the surrounding villages still sell their produce in the street market while tourists swim and surf on the beaches.

Most of the **hotels** are affordable and never more than a few minutes from the beach. The *Sadık Pansiyon*, on the main road just before the bus station, has doubles for about $8. On the harbor the *Nur Motel* offers similar rates, the *Gül-tur*

Motel on the beach has doubles from about $14, and has the added attractions of a swimming pool, restaurant, disco, and surfboard rental.

After Küçükkuyu there is a series of small resort villages. **MOTELLEAR** stretches out along the road in a string of hotels and developments that merge into **ALTİNOLUK**, which isn't noticeably different, where you'll find **camping** facilities at *Camping Atandros*. There are further possibilities along the road between here and Edremit, although your best bet is probably to head for Akçay.

Akçay

From the main road, where the bus or dolmuş will drop you off, it's about a ten-minute walk into **AKÇAY**, a middle-class resort town with plenty of hotels, restaurants, and discos, filled with mainly Turkish tourists during the summer months but deadly quiet out of season.

The **tourist information office** is on Edremit Caddesi (daily 8:30am–noon & 1:30–5pm), clearly marked on the left as you walk into town, although it's not particularly helpful. If you're **staying**, the waterfront *Otel Özsoy*, Plaj Caddesi 3, will rent you a three-bedded room with adjoining bathroom from $25 (they do some good off-season bargains, too); the nearby *Hotel Linda* has rooms starting at about $8 per person. Following Etiler Caddesi, which runs south out of town parallel with the seafront, there are numerous other hotels of all shapes and sizes. One of the best is the *Otel Çimen*, fifteen or twenty minutes from the center of town at Etiler Caddesi 34, and charging $6 per person with breakfast in season. It has a restaurant, snack bar, roof bar, and a beach for guests.

There are plenty of places to **eat and drink** in town, and cheap *pide* places abound in the center. For something more substantial, head for the *Meydan Restaurant* underneath the *Linda* hotel, or the *Sarıkız Plaj Restaurant*, which overlooks the sea from Etiler Caddesi. There are also two reasonable restaurants on Turgut Reis Caddesi: the *Pinar Restaurant* and the *Faruk Restaurant*, heading east out of town. Keep on walking and you'll reach them after about ten to fifteen minutes.

Edremit and Ören

Easily reached by dolmuş from Akçay, **EDREMIT** is the Adramyttium of the *Iliad* and was sacked by Achilles. After destroying the town, Achilles kidnapped Chryseis, the daughter of the local priest of Apollo, later giving her to Agamemnon, whose refusal to return the girl to her father, despite the offer of a generous ransom, forms part of the *Iliad* story.

These days the legends far outshine the reality of the place, though if you're in dire need of lodging there are a couple of cheesy **hotels** in town. To get to these from the bus station bear right down a tree-lined street past the stadium to the town's main street—a five-to-ten-minute walk. Turn right and you'll come first to the *Otel Sato* on the left, then to the *Park Oteli* (on the right near the park), both of which have doubles for about $3. For **eating and drinking**, try the *Ömur Kebap Salonu* on Menderes Bulvarı, or the *Cumhuriyet Lokantasi*, on Inönü Caddesi (ask, because street signs are basically nonexistent).

From Edremit there are dolmuşes to **ÖREN**, about 10km to the south, another small resort popular with Turkish vacationers; during the summer you can also reach Ören by boat from Akçay. **Accommodation** possibilities include the *Villa Lale Pansiyon*, which is simple, clean, and cheap, and the *Efem Motel*, which rates as the best of the bunch, with a private beach, restaurant, bar, flower-filled garden, and doubles starting at around $12. There are plenty of other options, although, like Akçay, the town gets crowded in summer. There's an excellent **campground**, *Altın Camping*, one of the best on the Aegean coast. It has a good stretch of beach nearby, warm water, toilets, showers, and a restaurant. It also has facilities for tennis, wind-surfing, and other activities.

Balıkeşir

There are frequent bus services from Edremit to the provincial capital of **BALIKEŞİR**, about 70km to the east, but there isn't really much to take you there. The town is an important focus and market center for the surrounding area but suffers from the pollution churned into the atmosphere by the huge local cement factories. If you do pass through it will probably be on your way to somewhere else: the town is an important rail junction, with daily trains to İzmir, Bandirma, and Kütahya and Ankara, hourly buses to İzmır and Bursa, and a daily express bus to Ankara. Those stopping over might like to know that there are a few medieval mosques in town, including the sturdy and well-preserved **Zağnos Paşa Camii**, built in 1461 by one of Mehmet the Conqueror's viziers.

The best-value **hotel** is the *Molam Oteli*, on Yeşil Caddesi (☎661/18075), which lets double rooms for about $13. Further up the price scale is the *Yilmaz Otel*, Milli Kuvvetler Caddesi 37 (☎661/174933).

AYVALIK TO MANISA

Heading south from Edremit, the road follows the coastline more closely, and although the journey down to **Ayvalık** is an unspectacular one, Ayvalık itself makes an excellent place to stop for a few days. It has some good beaches and it's within easy reach of **Bergama** a little way inland, with its unmissable Hellenistic ruins. Farther down the coast there are more resorts, notably **Çandarlı** and **Foça**, although again the real attractions are inland, namely the hillside city of **Manisa** and its nearby site of **Sardis**—the ancient capital of Croesus and Midas.

Ayvalık and Around

From the Ören/Edremit junction, it's forty minutes by bus to **AYVALIK**, a couple of kilometers west of the main road. You can either take a bus all the way there or catch any bus going south and walk or hitch the rest of the way from the turnoff. A small fishing port, Ayvalık also makes a living from olive-oil production and tourism, though the latter is reasonably low-key and the town makes a nice base for beach-lounging and ruin-spotting at Bergama, 70km southeast. There are a few good beaches not far away in the recently developed resort of Sarımsaklı, and some slightly less inspiring ones on the island of Cunda. The town is just across from the Greek island of Lesvos, to which there's a regular ferry service in summer.

The Town

Founded during the fifteenth century, Ayvalık suffered a serious earthquake at the beginning of this century and another one in 1944, although the most devastating effect on the town occurred when its mainly Greek inhabitants were kicked out during the exchange of populations that followed the Greek-Turkish war of 1920–22. Greek Orthodox churches have been converted into mosques and now sport concrete minarets added in the 1950s. Ironically, some of the people resettled here were Greek-speaking Muslims from Crete and Mitilini, and many of Ayvalık's older inhabitants still speak Greek.

A few streets back from the waterfront, Ayvalık is anything but a tourist town; cobblers, toolmakers, and watch-repairers all still ply their trades from ramshackle wooden premises. The warren-like nature of the streets means you may have to ask directions to the main features, but in any case the stroll through is worthwhile. The architectural highpoint is **Taksiyarhis Kilisesi**, a nineteenth-century church that contains icons and ecclesiastical artwork painted on fish skins, although it—like all the churches—is now used as a mosque. Ayvalık's other principal mosque is the **Çınarlı Camii**, or "the mosque with the plane tree," named after the tree standing in its courtyard. Beside it is an ancient **hamam**.

Practical Details—and Ferries to Lesvos

Ayvalık is a fairly small town and most of what you'll need is concentrated around the small square with the Atatürk bust, a couple of kilometers south of the main otogar. It's in this area that you'll find the banks and the bus ticket office. Also within striking distance are most of the cheap hotels and a few restaurants. The area is also home to a fair number of tourist-oriented leather and (more occasionally) carpet shops. From the waterfront, where fishermen sell their catches, boatmen run a regular shuttle service to nearby Cunda during the summer.

Ayvalık's **tourist office** (daily 9am–noon & 1–5pm; ☎663/12122) is inconveniently located about 10–15 minutes' walk south of the town center on the main coast road. There are plenty of cheap **hotels** in the center of town. Not far from the harbor the *Özel Hotel*, Talatpaşa Caddesi, is a small family-run place with compact doubles for around $7. In the same street but farther inland, the *Elif Otel* is clean and quiet with doubles from $6, and also boasts more or less constant hot water. The *Hotel CanlıBalik*, on Gümrük Caddesi (☎663/12292), also has double rooms for about $6. At the *Kıyı Motel*, Gümrük Meydanı 18 (☎663/16677), by the harbor, you're paying mainly for a dubious sea view and sinks in the clean but spartan rooms; doubles are $14. Shower and bathroom facilities are shared. The nearby *Şehir Oteli* is (quite rightly) the cheapest place in town, with singles for $2, and hot water available down the hall.

For something a little more luxurious, head out of town to **ÇAMLIK**, a suburb of Ayvalık just beyond the tourist office, where there are a few resort-type hotels. One of the best is the *Çadır Otel*, Orta Çamlık 57 (☎663/11678), which in season lets doubles starting at $12 and three-bedded rooms for $24. All rooms have adjoining bathrooms and the price includes breakfast. Also worth investigating are the *Levent* and *Ahu* pansiyons, which have doubles for $8 and up, and the *Sözer*, which has doubles with bathrooms starting at $8. These are a few hundred meters past the *Çadır* and set back from the main road, so you'll probably have to ask directions.

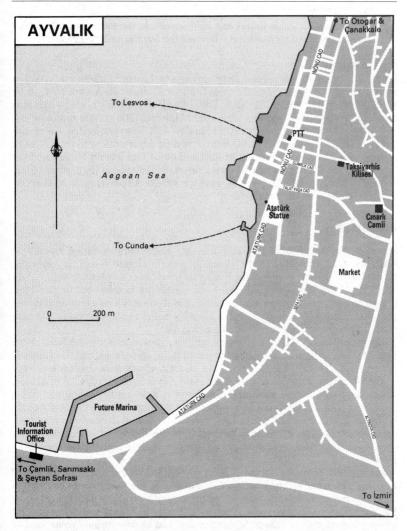

Clustered around the square with the Atatürk statue are a few **eating and drinking** possibilities, including a couple of male-only teahouses. On the waterfront are three somewhat classy restaurants: the *Öz Canlı Balık*, which has seafood and other dishes starting at about $4 per head, the similarly priced *Elif 2* restaurant, and the slightly more expensive *Kanelo*. Farther back from the water, around Talatpaşa Caddesi, are a few cheaper and more basic possibilities, notably the *Andalou Pide ve Döner Salonu* and the *Ayvalık Restaurant*, in both of which you'll be able to dine for less than $2. The restaurant in the *Canlı Balık* hotel is also worth checking out, serving excellent meals of fried fish, salad, and beer. By the water, *Café de Paris* is a popular hangout with younger people, serving alcoholic and non-alcoholic drinks and light snacks. In the town's market district you'll find an arcade of *meyhanles*; the best are the *Derdim* and the *Ege*.

Ferries to Lesvos

From Ayvalık there are regular ferry services to Lesvos. Tickets are available from a couple of agents: *Jale Turizm*, Gümrük Caddesi 41/A (☎663/12740 or 16123), and *Ayvalık Seyahat Acentası*, İnönü Caddesi 48 (☎663/11938)—who also organize group tours to various local sites of interest. The service runs approximately May 1–October 15, daily except Sunday, with only very limited winter sailings. Schedules change, but at the time of writing departures were from Ayvalık at 9am, taking two hours to reach Mitilini on Lesvos, and leaving Mitilini again at 5pm. Fares are $20 one-way for foot passengers, $30 round-trip (50 percent reduction for children under 12). Fares for cars are $50–70. All passengers are charged a Dr1000 port tax on the Greek side.

Sarımsaklı

Some of the best beaches in the area are about 6km south of Ayvalık at **SARIMSAKLI** (literally "Garlic Beach"), a fairly sizable resort development accessible by dolmuş or one of the municipal buses from the Atatürk square. You could stay here too—there are plenty of big tourist **hotels**—but, in the high season at least, most cost an arm and a leg, and if you aren't on a tour and haven't got vast amounts of cash to spare, it's probably better to stay in Ayvalık and take the bus or dolmuş to Sarımsaklı for the beach life.

If you *do* want to stay, the cheapest options in Sarımsaklı are the *Sahil Motel* (☎663/41379), which charges $24 for a double (in off-season), and the similarly priced *Motel Ahi*. Prices tend to decrease the farther back from the beach you go. At the other end of the price scale is the *Hotel Büyük Berk* (☎663/4105 or 41046), where doubles cost $62 full-board. The hotel is right on the beach and has a swimming pool and rents out windsurfers and the like. Nearby, the *Otel Ankara* is similar in character and price. The *Murat Reis Oteli*, at the end of a long road on the right as you come into Sarımsaklı, has a degree of exclusivity and a great swimming pool, though at prices that are slightly higher than the *Büyük Berk*.

Eating and drinking are not in short supply, with tourist traps like the *City of London Restaurant* and another *Café de Paris* near the beach, and slightly less tacky places farther inland. Various companies and individuals have stands along the promenade where you can arrange boat trips to Cunda and a few smaller islands. Prices start at around $7 for the day, and usually include some kind of meal.

Şeytan Sofrası

Between Ayvalık and Sarımsaklı, the headland that juts out into the Aegean leads to **Şeytan Sofrası**—the Devil's Dinner Table—a distinctive-looking rocky outcrop from which (weather permitting) you can see as far across as Lesvos. In season it's connected by regular dolmuş with Ayvalık, and it's a nice place to watch the sun go down from the café near the summit. At the top there's a small pool, supposedly Satan's footprint, into which people throw money for luck.

Cunda Island

Across the bay from Ayvalık, the island of **CUNDA**—also known as Alibey Adası—is a good day-trip destination, with a couple of stretches of beach and some seaside fish restaurants. The best way to get here in summer is by boat from Ayvalık, but at other times you'll have to rely on the roughly hourly bus service from the Atatürk square or a taxi (expensive—fix a fare first) to cross the causeway connecting the island to the mainland.

Behind the harbor is a network of dilapidated backstreets lined by decaying wooden houses and the odd remnant of life before 1922, when Cunda was known to its largely Greek-speaking inhabitants as Moskhonissi. Some way back from the waterfront is an old orthodox **church**, now deserted and home only to birds, with a few defaced and faded frescos visible inside. The church was heavily damaged in the earthquake of 1944 but is scheduled for restoration. On a small hill above town stands a small **chapel**, now used as a stable, from which you can gaze out across the bay to Ayvalık. After the Greeks were deported, the island was resettled by Cretan Muslims from the Hania area and you'll find that most people over fifty speak Greek as a matter of course. The northern half of Cunda, known as Patrica, has relatively deserted beaches.

Cunda has its own **tourist office**, which is clearly visible on the western edge of town on your way in. **Accommodation** possibilities on the island include the *Altay Pansiyon*, a couple of blocks inland, the *Ilker Pansiyon*, and the *Özlem Aile Pansiyon* (☎663/71109), all offering doubles without bath for $8. For an attached bathroom you pay fifty percent more. There's also the *Günay Motel* (☎663/71048), which has rooms starting at $14 a night. The main **campground**, *Ortunç Camping*, about 3km southwest of town, also has a restaurant and some rooms. The other site is *ADA Camping*, well marked on the way into town. The best (and most expensive) **restaurants** line the harbor, and most of them have open-air seating out front. For better value head for the nameless fish restaurant slightly inland, or the lone *pide salonu* on the corner next to the bus turnaround area.

Bergama

Though frequently touted as a day-trip destination from Ayvalık, **BERGAMA**, site of the ancient city of Pergamon, rates a couple of days in its own right. The stunning Acropolis of Eumenes II is the main attraction, but there are a host of lesser sights and an old quarter of chaotic charm to detain you a little longer. Bergama is unpromising at first: the long approach to the town center reveals a dusty modern-looking place, and the monuments to which it owes its reputation are nowhere to be seen. In fact, most of ancient Pergamon is some way away from the modern town and takes a little effort to reach.

Some History

The first recorded mention of **Pergamon** dates from 399 BC, but the town first became prominent when it became the base of Lysimachus, one of Alexander the Great's generals. He left some of his accumulated wealth in the hands of his officer, Philetarus, who inherited it all when Lysimachus was killed in battle fighting Syria for control of Asia Minor. By skilled political maneuvering Philetarus was able to hang onto his newfound wealth, passing it on to his adoptive son Eumenes, who again defeated the Syrians at Sardis and further extended the domain of Philetarus.

Eumenes, who is generally recognized as the founder of the Pergamon dynasty, was succeeded in 241 BC by his nephew, Attalus I, whose immediate task was to defeat the Gauls, which he did with the help of the sacrifice of an animal whose liver turned out to bear the word "victory." Attalus was a cunning ruler—it later emerged that he had secretly imprinted the word "victory" onto the liver with a specially made ring—and his authority was soon assured, the fame of his kingdom spreading across the Hellenistic world. Thus installed, he went on to build the temple of Athena and the library in Pergamon.

Attalus's son and successor, Eumenes II, consolidated his father's gains, allied himself with the Romans, and set about building Pergamon into a great city. He later helped the Romans defeat the Syrians at the Battle of Magnesium, extending his sphere of influence. Under Eumenes II, the gymnasium and theater were built, and the acropolis was secured with a wall. The last king of Pergamon, Attalus III, was less interested in ruling than chemistry (he spent a lot of time conducting experiments with poisons on criminals) and died after a short reign, perversely leaving his realm to the Romans, under whom Pergamon thrived, growing into a city of 150,000 people that was a renowned artistic and commercial center. With the arrival of the Goths in 262 AD, the city began a gradual decline, and passed through the hands of a succession of invaders before falling into ruin.

The German engineer Karl Humann rediscovered ancient Pergamon in 1873 when he found a strange mosaic in the possession of some local farmers, which turned out to be part of the relief from the Altar of Zeus. Humann bought the mosaic from the farmers and five years later began excavating the acropolis. Work was completed in 1886, and unfortunately much of what was found has since been carted off to Germany, including the reliefs from the Zeus altar, which you can only view in the Pergamon Museum in Berlin.

Arrival and Getting Around

The **acropolis**, the ancient city of the kings of Pergamon, is set on top of a rocky bluff towering over modern Bergama. Just out of town, to the west, is the **Asclepion**, the ancient medical center. The old town lies at the foot of the acropolis, about ten minutes' walk from the otogar. As soon as you get off the bus at the otogar you'll probably be approached by a taxi driver offering to ferry you around the ruins for $12-plus. If there are a few of you or you're in a hurry, this can make sense, but otherwise it's a bit of a racket, limiting you to one hour at the acropolis (you'll almost certainly want to spend more time there), ten minutes at the ancient basilica in Bergama town and half an hour at the Asclepion. In any case, if you're not pushed for time, it's easy enough to hit the basilica and Asclepion on foot without too much trouble, and the acropolis is easily accessible on foot by way of a path up from the old town—although this, admittedly, is one sight you may want to reach by taxi. If you set off early, however, before it gets hot, it's not a difficult trek for anyone of average fitness. Don't take the main road, though, because it's steep and not particularly direct, doubling back on itself for about 5km.

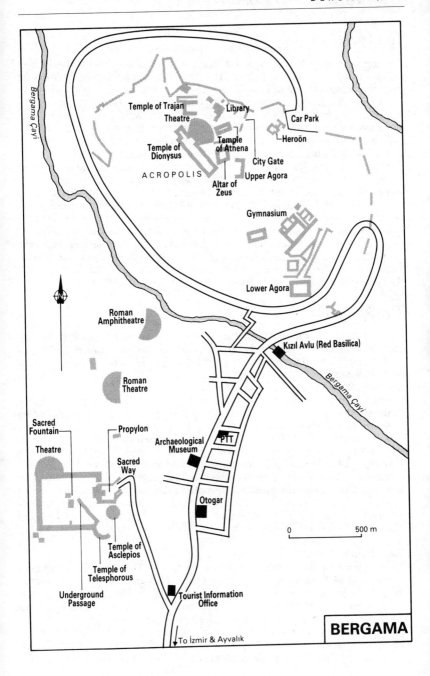

BERGAMA

The Town

The foremost attraction in Bergama itself is probably the **Kızıl Avlu**, or Red Basilica (daily 9am–noon & 1–7pm; $1), a huge brick edifice on the river not far from the acropolis, originally built as a temple to the Egyptian god Osiris and converted into a basilica by the early Christians. During its Christian phase it was one of the seven churches of Asia Minor addressed by St. John in the book of Revelation—he refers to it as home of the throne of the devil, perhaps meaning the altar of Zeus. It's now a crumbling ruin with a mosque in one of its towers and the Selinus River passing underneath the basilica via two intact tunnels.

The area around the basilica is mainly given over to the **old quarter** of the town, a jumble of ramshackle buildings, carpet shops (Bergama carpets are among the most celebrated in Turkey), mosques, and maze-like streets full of vitality and color. It's in this district that you'll find most of the cheaper hotels and restaurants. On the way from the otogar you'll pass the **Archaeological Museum** (summer daily 9am–noon & 1–7pm, winter 1–5:30pm; $1, half-price Sun and holidays), which not surprisingly has a large collection of locally unearthed booty, including a statue of Hadrian from the Asclepion and various busts of figures like Zeus and Socrates. There's also a model of the Zeus altar and the reliefs now resident in Germany.

The Acropolis

Taxis up to **the acropolis** (daily 9am–noon & 1–7pm; $2.50) pull into the site parking lot, where a ramp leads up to the former **city gate**, although this has almost completely disappeared. On your left is the **Heroön**, an ancient temple built to honor the kings of Pergamon and said to have been lined with white marble in Roman times.

From here a path leads southwest to the huge horseshoe-shaped **Altar of Zeus**, standing in the shade of an enormous pine tree. The altar was built during the reign of Eumenes II to commemorate his father's victory over the Gauls and was decorated with reliefs depicting the battle between the giants and the gods, symbolizing the triumph of order over chaos, and, presumably, that of Attalus over the Gauls. Even today its former splendor is apparent, although it has been much diminished by the removal of the reliefs to Berlin. Directly to the north of the Zeus altar lie the remains of the **Temple of Athena**, dating back to the time of Philetarus. Only part of the stepped terrace on which it was built has survived, although the entrance gate, with the inscription recording its dedication by "King Eumenes to Athena the bearer of victories," has been reconstructed in Berlin.

The Library

Directly north of the Temple of Athena is the famous **Library**, which at its peak rivaled that of Alexandria. Founded by Attalus II, it came to have a catalog of 200,000 books. Eumenes II was particularly active in building it up, to the point of augmenting the collection by borrowing books from other libraries and not returning them. He is also said to have paid for books by Aristotle and Theophrastus by offering their weight in gold. Eventually the Egyptian kings, alarmed at the growth of the Pergamon library, which they saw as a threat to the ascendancy of the library in Alexandria, banned the export of papyrus, on which all books were written at the time—and of which they were the sole producers—thereby attempting to stem the library's expansion.

In response Eumenes offered a reward to anyone who could come up with a replacement, and the old custom of writing on specially treated animal skins—parchment—was revived, leading to the invention of the codex, or paged book, since it wasn't possible to roll parchment up like papyrus. The word "parchment" is actually derived from "Pergamon." The library was broken up when Mark Antony gave the bulk of the collection to Cleopatra as a gift, and at the moment not much more than the library foundations remain, but German archaeologists, who have been here more or less continuously since 1878, are busy rebuilding it.

To the north of the library is the **Temple of Trajan**, where Trajan and Hadrian were both revered during Roman times (their busts were taken from the Temple and are also now in Berlin). The Germans are currently restoring the temple pillars. Behind the temple are mounds of rubble and collapsed walls—the remains of barracks and palaces.

The Theater

From the temple of Athena a narrow staircase leads down to the **theater**, the most spectacular part of the ruined acropolis. The theater, dating from Hellenistic times, was cut into the hillside, a visually stunning structure capable of seating 10,000 spectators. According to the architectural conventions of the day, the auditoria of Greek theaters were always greater than a semicircle, but at Pergamon, due to the steepness of the site, this was not possible and the architects compensated by building upward, creating an auditorium with eighty rows of seats. The stage was built from wood and removed after performances—the holes into which supporting posts were driven can still be seen on the terrace at the foot of the auditorium. One of the reasons for the use of a portable stage was to allow free access to the **temple of Dionysus**, built just offstage to the audience's right.

From the vantage point of the theater auditorium, the sheer scale of Pergamon, and the complexity of the social order that it represented, can best be appreciated. Sitting here and gazing out across the valley below you can't fail to wonder at the grandeur of the ancient city—and, bearing in mind the ugly sprawl of modern Bergama, it's hard not to make unfavorable comparisons.

The Upper and Lower Agoras

Just south of the Altar of Zeus is a terrace which was once the **Upper Agora** of Pergamon. There isn't much to see today, although this was once the commercial and social focal point of the city. It's here that the archaeologist Karl Humann is buried. A path leads down from here to the **Lower Agora**, where the common people lived and went about their business.

Among the remains of various houses at the foot of the path is the **Temple of Demeter**, where the so-called Eleusinian Mysteries, a cultic ritual supposed to guarantee a better life after death, were enacted. On the northern side of the temple are the remains of a building, containing nine rows of seats with space for about 1000 people, which it's thought were for spectators at the ritual. Nearby is a **gymnasium**, spread out over three terraces, where the children of the city were educated. The upper level, with its playing field, was for young men, the middle one was for adolescents, and the lower level served as a kind of playground for younger children. In the surrounding area are the remains of various houses and the **lower agora**.

The gymnasium and lower agora can be reached direct from the modern town by a direct path, and you might find it easier to take a taxi back down to the base of the acropolis and start your explorations from below.

The Asclepion

Bergama's other significant archaeological site is **the Asclepion**, (daily 9am–noon & 1–7pm; $2.50), a Greco-Roman medical center which can be reached on foot from the old aqueduct in the modern town. (Beware that it is near a large and clearly marked military zone—avoid entering this and don't take photographs away from the site itself.) The Asclepion was devoted to Asclepios, son of Apollo and the god of healing, who supposedly served as a doctor in the army of Agamemnon during the siege of Troy. According to myth, Asclepios knew how to bring the dead back to life using the blood of the Gorgon, which Athena had given to him. Zeus, worried that Asclepios's activities were endangering the natural order of things, struck him down with a thunderbolt but elevated him to the stars in compensation.

The healing methods practiced at the Asclepion were partly ritualistic in nature, with patients being required to sleep in the temple in order that Asclepios might appear to them in a dream to relay his diagnosis and suggest treatment. However, dieting, bathing and exercise also played an important part in the regime here. Galen (131–201 AD), the greatest physician of the ancient world, who laid the foundations of much of modern medical science and served as personal physician to the Emperor Marcus Aurelius, was trained here.

Much of what can be seen today was built during the time of the Emperor Hadrian (117–138), which coincided with the early stages of the first- and second-century heyday of the Pergamon Asclepion, when its function was similar to that of a nineteenth-century European spa. Some patients came here to be cured of ailments, but for others a visit to the Asclepion was simply a social amusement, part of the habitual existence of the wealthy and leisured.

From the site entrance, a long, colonnaded sacred way known as the **Via Tecta** leads to the **Propylon**, or monumental entrance gate. The propylon was built during the third century AD and postdates the earthquake that seriously damaged the complex during the previous century. To the northeast of the propylon is a square building that housed a **library** and contained the statue of the Emperor Hadrian now on display in the local museum (see above).

To the south of the propylon is the circular **Temple of Asclepios**, dating from 150 AD and modeled on the Pantheon in Rome. The domed roof of this graceful structure was 24m in diameter and had a circular opening in the center to allow light and air to penetrate. The floor and walls were decorated with mosaics, and recesses housed statues of the gods. To the west of the propylon and temple is a wide open area that was originally enclosed by colonnaded walkways, the bases of which can still be seen. At the western end of the northern colonnade is a **theater** with a seating capacity of 3500, which served to keep patients entertained. At the center of the open area is the **sacred fountain**, still gushing with harmlessly radioactive drinking water. From nearby an eighty-meter-long underground passage leads to the **Temple of Telesphorus** (a lesser deity associated with Asclepios)—a two-story circular building, which, like the Temple of Asclepios, served as a place for patients to sleep while awaiting dream diagnoses. The lower story survives and is in good repair.

Practical Details

If you're only here for the day you should be aware that the last **bus** back to İzmir leaves the otogar at 6pm, and the last dolmuş for Ayvalık departs at 3pm. If you miss it, there will be a couple more heading for Dikili, where you ought be able to pick up an Ayvalık connection. Failing that, up until 7pm you won't have any trouble picking up the Çanakkale–İzmir coastal bus service from the main road; in the opposite direction buses run until after 8pm.

Bergama's **tourist office** is on the town's main thoroughfare at İzmir Caddesi 54 (☎541/11862)—turn left out of the bus station, walk for about ten minutes and it's on the opposite side of the street near the *Asklepion Restaurant.* It doesn't, however, have much to offer. The town's bigger and more expensive **hotels** announce themselves loudly enough on the way into town, as do the local **campgrounds.** The latter are marked after an onyx shop just south of the city limits. The **best and cheapest hotels** tend to be in the old town, although there are a few reasonable possibilities in the vicinity of the otogar. Just around the corner from the otogar, the basic but comfortable *Park Otel,* Park Otel Sokak 6 (☎541/ 11246), has double rooms with bath for around $9, and good home cooking. Heading south, along the main road toward the tourist office, you'll find the *Pansiyon Aktan,* İzmir Caddesi 18 (☎541/14000), which has clean, albeit cell-like doubles for $4 and up, with intermittent hot water. A little farther along, also on the main road out of town, on the opposite side of the road to the otogar, is the *Efsane Pansiyon*—a regular tourist hotel with doubles starting at $12.

In the old town, the *Zeus Pansiyon,* near the post office above the restaurant of the same name, is very basic but has doubles starting at $4. Farther along, a side street past the hamam leads to the *Acroteria,* Bankalar Caddesi 11 (☎541/12469), offering clean, comfortable doubles for $7 ($10 for rooms with bathrooms and allegedly hot water); it also has a restaurant and terrace. Next to the police station on the same street is the *Pergamon Pansiyon,* Bankalar Caddesi 3 (☎541/ 12395), housed in an old building surrounding a courtyard—very touristy and crowded in the summer but the rooms are clean and it's nice and central, if a little noisy. The staff speak English but are said to be a little over-attentive to single women. Doubles cost $4.

The *Akropol,* Mermer Direkler Caddesi 2 (☎541/11508), has doubles starting at $8 including breakfast. A little more atmospheric (and primitive) is the *Athena,* Barbaros Mahallesi, Imam Çıkmazi 5 (☎541/ 13420), in a 150-year-old Ottoman building just behind the *Akropol.* Best of all is the *Nike Pansiyon,* Talatpaşa Mahallesi Tabak Köprü Çıkmazi 2, an old family-run pension on the far bank of a river, in the very shadow of the acropolis. There are no modern facilities but there is a marvelous garden and doubles cost just under $7, plus an additional dollar for breakfast. It's from here that the circuitous footpath leading up to the acropolis starts.

There are a few cheap, basic **places to eat and drink** in town. The *Meydan Restaurant* is the most obvious, with a terrace and foreign-language signs making it a sure draw for tourists. Next door are the *Çiçek Birahanesi* and the slightly cheaper *Yüksel Birahanesi,* where you can sit outside and have a beer with your meal. Around the corner is the *Arzum Pide Salonu.* The *Kervan Döner Salonu,* opposite the *Meydan,* also has a roof terrace but is a little less touristy. On the road out of town there are a few more European-style **cafés and bars,** including *Stop Pilsen* and the *Asklepion Restaurant.*

The Coast South of Ayvalık

The road south along the coast from Ayvalık takes you past a number of small resort towns, although the best stretch of sandy **beach** is just before these, beginning just south of Altınova and running south for about 15km to Dikili. However, it's only really accessible if you have your own wheels, and in any case it has very few facilities.

Dikili and Around

Easily reached by dolmuş from Ayvalık, **DİKİLİ**, with a population of 8500, is smaller and less touristified than many of the resorts along here. Cruise liners dock in the harbor, allowing their passengers to make day excursions to Bergama and Ayvalık or head for the beaches to the north; there's a decent beach; and in the town itself there's a sunny promenade lined with cafés and restaurants. But it's a small town, the kind of place whose possibilities are soon exhausted, and a day or two is really the most you could spend before getting itchy for somewhere else.

From the otogar turn right onto the tree-lined main street, which leads to the center of town. On the way into town there are a few **accommodation** possibilities, including the *Özdemir*, *Marti*, and *Palmiye* pansiyons, all of which have doubles starting at around $8. If you're looking for a really cheap option try the very basic *Ceylan Otel*, Onuç Sokak 19 (☎5419/1034), which has doubles for under $3—though, not surprisingly, cold water only. This is down a side road on the opposite side of the main street to the otogar.

A good upscale possibility is the *Metay Otel*, Atatürk Caddesi 25 (☎5419/2164), with doubles from $24. Rooms have attached baths and the hotel is located about five minutes from the shore. Also in this bracket is the *Perla Hotel*, Bademli Caddesi (☎5419/1849), which offers doubles for $18 and up, along with the usual tourist hotel amenities. There are plenty of **cafés and restaurants** along the shore, including the *Villa Teras* and *Liman* restaurants.

A few kilometers south of Dikili, accessible by dolmuş, **BADEMLİ** is a tiny village where there's a **campground**, the *Çamlımanı*, about 500m before the village, with a pebble beach that's ideal for snorkelling. There's also an attractive **campground** in the village itself, as well as a handful of teahouses and restaurants. A rough road runs on south from Bademli to Çandarlı, passing a number of small sandy **beaches** where it's possible to camp out—although there's no public transportation along this route. Some of the beaches even have water supplies in the form of wells used by local shepherds.

Çandarlı

About half an hour to the south of Dikili by bus, **ÇANDARLI** is a small fishing port and resort located on a promontory that caters mainly to Turkish tourists. It is the site of ancient Pitane, the northernmost Aeolian city, but nothing remains to bear witness to this. In fact, despite its august heritage, Çandarlı's oldest building is a fourteenth-century Genoese fort, one of several dotting the Turkish Aegean coast and Greek islands, a reminder of the days when the military and commercial might of Genoa dominated the North Aegean.

The beach is coarse sand, but Çandarlı is not a bad place to get away from the crowds for a day or two of relaxation. From the bus stop, you need to walk to the other side of the point for the best **pansiyons**. Don't be tempted by the *Kaya*, which you'll see when you step off the bus; try instead the *Marti Motel*, the *Philippi Pansiyon*, the *Nur Pansiyon*, or the *Senger*—all similarly priced, with doubles starting at around $12. These are all located on or near the road running along the seafront on the western side of the promontory, as are the best of Çandarlı's **restaurants**, **cafés**, and **bars**. For reasonably priced food, look no further than the *Halil'in Yeri Restaurant*; for drinking, head for the *Devil Bar*—which is as lively as it gets around here. Six or seven buses a day run each way between Çandarlı and İzmir in summer, but beware the infrequent connections during the off-season.

Foça

The resort town of **FOÇA** lies 65km south of Çandarlı, west of the main road. To reach it take an İzmır-bound bus and ask to be let off at the turnoff for Foça. From here catch a dolmuş or another bus the remaining 26km into town.

Foça is the site of the ancient town of Phocaea, founded in 600 BC by Ionian colonists. The Phoceans were renowned seafarers whose boats plied the principal trade routes of the Mediterranean, establishing (among other places) the city of Massilia, now known as Marseilles. Today, sadly, there is nothing left of their ancient settlement and the oldest building in town is a ruined Genoese fortress, built using stone from the ancient city. Foça is also home to some wonderful old Greek fishermens' cottages and its backstreets are lined with fine Ottoman houses. Just outside town, close to the main road, look out too for the **Taş Kule**, an unusual-looking tomb which is believed to date from about the eighth century BC.

These days Foça is a busy resort. Along with its sister town of **YENİFOÇA**, twenty-odd kilometers north around the coast (where there is also a Club Med), it has some good stretches of beach and hasn't yet succumbed to the highrise building boom that is afflicting so much of the rest of the Turkish coast. The local **tourist information office** is on Atatürk Mahallesi Ilçe Girişi (☎5431/1122), although you might as well head straight for the few **cheap hotels** on the street behind the seafront. The *Hanedan Oteli*, Büyük Deniz, Yalı Caddesi 1 (☎5431/1579), has doubles starting at $14 (with bathrooms) and also has a restaurant; the *Kaan Oteli* and *Evim Pansiyon* are pretty basic but have doubles for much less; or there's the fancier *İyon Pansiyon*, where doubles cost $12. For eating out, check out the numerous **restaurants** on the water, most of which do excellent fish dishes.

Menemen

Between Foça and İzmir there is very little settlement and the area is fairly inaccessible, since the main road cuts directly south to the city. Thirty kilometers or so north, **MENEMEN** is a forgettable town dominated by a ceramics works, but it's the only place besides İzmir that has decent dolmuş connections to Manisa.

Manisa and Around

The site of the ancient town of Magnesia ad Sipylus, **MANİSA** lies about 40km east of Menemen and is easily reached either from there or İzmir along pleasant mountain roads. Much of Manisa's historic core was destroyed by the Greek army during its 1922 retreat and today the town has a modern feel, but in spite of this it is an interesting place, sprawling out from the foot of the Manisa Dağı mountain range, with a few fine mosques and bustling streetlife. These in themselves might not seem worth the long detour off the İzmir road, but the nearby ruins of Sardis—the ancient capital of Croesus—provide added incentive. An overnight stop here is time well spent—you can arrive in Manisa at noon, visit Sardis in the afternoon, and spend the following morning looking around Manisa itself before moving on.

According to Homer, Manisa was founded after the Trojan War by warriors from the area. Alexander the Great passed through during his campaign, and in 190 BC there was a huge battle here between the Romans and the Syrians, led by King Antioch III. The day was decided in favor of the Romans by the cavalry of the king of Pergamon, who was given control over the city as a reward. Manisa finally came under direct Roman rule—and entered a period of great prosperity—after the death of Attalus III of Pergamon. For a short time it was capital of the Byzantine Empire, after the sacking of İstanbul by the Crusaders. In 1313 the city fell into the hands of the Selçuk prince Saruhan Bey. Later, the Ottomans used the city as a kind of training ground for princes to ready them for the rigors of İstanbul political life.

The Town

Manisa still has a lot to recommend it, although perhaps not always in the obvious sense. The area around the town's **otogar** is an old quarter undergoing extensive redevelopment where modern apartment buildings, rickety old houses, and construction sites fight for space. After arriving, walk south away from the *garaj* toward the mountains for about ten minutes until you come to **Doğu Caddesi**—the town's main commercial street, where most of the banks and larger shops are located.

The main central attractions in Manisa are three **mosques**. At the end of Ibrahim Gökçen Caddesi, the **Sultan Camii** was built in 1522 by the architect Acem Alisi for Ayşe Hafize, the mother of Süleyman the Magnificent, who lived here with her son while he was serving as governor. It comprises a hamam, theological school, primary school, hospital, and fountain. Opposite is the **Saruhan Bey Türbesi**, the tomb of Saruhan Bey, who conquered Manisa on November 13, 1313, ending Byzantine sovereignity. His army is said to have attacked Sandıkkale, the city's castle by driving a flock of goats with candles on their horns before them to give the impression that a huge army was advancing. The defenders panicked and the castle fell—an event commemorated here each November 13 by a festival. Saruhan Bey's tomb seems to have been neglected lately—the wooden door has a hole in it and you can look through to see the sarcophagus.

A little farther along on the same side of the streeet is the **Muradiye Camii**, built by Mimar Sinan for Sultan Murat III in 1583–85. The interior, with its stained-glass windows and relatively restrained decoration (despite the use of

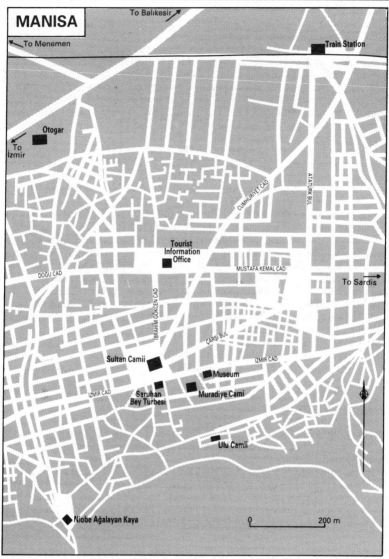

MANISA

To Balıkesir

To Menemen

Train Station

Otogar

To İzmir

CUMHURİYET CAD

ATATÜRK BUL

DOĞU CAD

Tourist Information Office

MUSTAFA KEMAL CAD

To Sardis

İBRAHİM GÖKÇEN CAD

ÇARŞI BUL

Sultan Camii

İZMİR CAD

Museum

İZMİR CAD

Saruhan Bey Türbesi

Muradiye Cami

Ulu Camii

Niobe Ağalayan Kaya

0   200 m

12kg kilos of gold), is impressive. Every year on the third or last Sunday in March, the *Mesir Şenlikleri* (Power-Gum Festival) takes place here, to commemorate the occasion when a local doctor called Merkez Effendi invented a special gum or resin to cure Ayşe Hafize, who was suffering from a mysterious ailment. The gum is scattered to the waiting crowd in the form of syrup-filled candy by the muezzin of the Muradiye Camii. People believe that the syrup will protect them from pain, in particular snake and insect bites, for the following year.

Next door to the Muradiye Camii, in the former public kitchen of the mosque, is the **Manisa Müseum** (Tues–Sun 9am–noon & 1pm–5pm; $1), where you'll find local archaeological loot from the Bronze Age onward. Most impressive are the mosaics from Sardis. There's also an ethnological section with Ottoman objects—weapons, mother-of-pearl inlaid caskets, and suchlike. Farther along the same street, the **Yeni Alaca Hamam** is one of the oldest bathhouses in town—and is still in use. Check out, too, if you're in town at the right time, the large Thursday **market**, which stretches the length of Murat Caddesi and is the source of just about any kind of vegetable or fruit you could desire, as well as cheap household items and clothing.

Manisa's oldest surviving mosque, the **Ulu Cami**, on a street above here at the base of the mountains, was built in 1366 by Işak Çelebi, the grandson of Saruhan Bey, on the site of a former Byzantine church (you can still see the remains of some of the pillars in the courtyard). The interior verges on gaudiness, with lots of maroon carpets.

Follow the maze of streets leading west from here to the foot of Mount Sipylus (Sipil Dağ; see below) and you'll eventually come to **Niobe Ağlayan Kaya** (ask for directions), the so-called "Weeping Rock of Niobe," which appears to take the form of a woman's head, and from which tears can supposedly be seen issuing every Friday. According to the legend, Niobe, the daughter of Tantalus, had seven daughters and six sons. She taunted her friend Leto, the nymph, who only had two children, a son Apollon and daughter Artemis, for her relative infertility, and Leto became jealous and ordered her own offspring to kill Niobe's. Niobe wept for a long time over the bodies of her children and eventually Zeus turned her into a rock to put an end to her suffering.

That's about it for sightseeing in Manisa, apart from the remnants of the **Sandıkkale** fortress above the town, and the **Mevlevihane**—an erstwhile *tekke* of the whirling-dervish cult, housed in a solid stone building on the southeastern edge of town.

Practical Details

Manisa's **tourist office** is on the fourth floor at Doğu Caddesi 8/14 (☎551/12541); they should be able to give you a town map, and may also be able to rustle up an English-speaker.

On the **lodging** front, Manisa leaves a little to be desired. The cheap hotels are fairly unpleasant, and the lone luxury option is overpriced. Try the *Atlas Otel*, Dumlupınar Caddesi 22 (☎551/11997), which has spartan doubles for $7, with pretty primitive plumbing. Around the corner, doubles at the *Otel Günaydin* go for $6, with dirty shared showers. The *Otel Mesran* and the *Park Otel* on Atatürk Bulvarı are also possibilities, but only if you're desperate. If you've got the money, it's worth spending it on the *Otel Arma*, on Doğu Caddesi (☎551/11980), which has modern, comfortable rooms with attached baths and intermittent hot water for $18 and up for a double.

Despite the lack of decent hotels, there are a few good **bars** and **restaurants** in town, among them a few Turkish-style "pubs" on İzmir Caddesi—although the discreet "sexy lady" pictures adorning the walls suggest they're primarily a male preserve. In the park just to the east of the Atatürk Bulvarı/Mustafa Kemal Caddesi intersection there's a pavilion with a couple of teahouses and bars that act as a kind of social focus. For **food**, the quality of the menu belies the budget prices at the *Şen Ortaklar Lokantası,* on the same street as the *Günaydin* hotel, where you'll be able to get kebabs and *sutlaç* for a little over a dollar. There are plenty of other options covering the full price spectrum: check out the *Safak Kebap Salonu,* on Cumhuriyet Caddesi (north of Doğu Caddesi), which also serves simple kebab dishes; or the more expensive *Şehir Lokantası,* near the Fatih Park just off Atatürk Bulvarı.

Ancient Sardis

About 50km east of town, the major archaeological site of **SARDİS** represents the main attraction close to Manisa, and it is easily reached by taking the Salihli dolmuş from Manisa—or the Salihli bus from İzmir. The site can also be reached by means of several daily trains from Manisa, which are a more relaxed way of doing the trip and are more useful for returning to Manisa, since they run later than the dolmuşes.

The Road to Sardis
If you're traveling by dolmuş and have the time and inclination to stop along the way, there's a 3000-year-old relief carved into the rock of **Mount Sipylus** above the road about 7km east of Manisa. This is generally believed to be an image of Cybele, the mother goddess. Ask to be dropped off at the Akpınar pool and climb a couple of hundred meters up into the rocks above the road. The image, which isn't very distinct, is carved into the rock in a niche and was probably placed here to make the valley of the Gediz River below more fertile.

Mount Sipylus, incidentally, is associated with the ancient king Tantalus, whose daughter Niobe was turned into the rock back in Manisa. According to legend, Tantalus also had two sons, Pelops and Broteas, the latter of whom supposedly carved the image of Cybele on the mountainside. Pelops ended up being served up in a dish Tantalus prepared for the gods, and narrowly escaped being eaten (apart from his shoulder). He was later brought back to life with a new ivory shoulder and Tantalus was punished by being sent to Hades, where water and food were kept eternally just out of his reach—hence the verb "to tantalize."

Continuing the journey to Sardis takes you through an uneventful landscape, not enlivened by the huge brickworks at **TURGUTLU**. Things pick up a little beyond here as the Boz Dağları mountain range rears up to the south. For Sardis get off at **SARTMUSTAFA**, a small and traditional village clustered around a group of teahouses, where local farmers like to put their feet up while their wives and daughters work the fields.

Historical and Legendary Background
Sardis is another one of those places that is so old it's difficult to separate its true history from myth. The area was probably inhabited as far back as 1200 BC and was later settled by the Lydians, who were descended from native Anatolians and Greek invaders, and who rate a bizarre sociological footnote for their promotion of prostitution as a viable way for a girl to earn her dowry. The last Lydian king, Candaules, reigned around 700 BC, and the story goes that he was so proud of his wife's beauty that he arranged for one of his bodyguards, Gyges, to glimpse her naked. The queen realized what had happened and told Gyges that he could either kill her husband and marry her, or face immediate execution. Not surprisingly Gyges opted for the former and founded a new dynasty.

Sardis grew to be an incredibly wealthy city, thanks to the gold that was washed down from the mountains and caught in sheepskins by the locals. According to legend, the source of all this gold was the Phrygian king Midas, for whom everything turned to gold on touch. Unable to eat, his burden was lifted when the gods had him wash his hands in the river Pactolus, which flowed to Sardis. Wherever the gold came from, the Lydians were happy enough and celebrated their wealth by inventing coinage.

The first coins were issued under the city's most celebrated king, Croesus, who reigned from 563 to 546 BC. Under Croesus the prosperity of the kingdom grew, attracting the attention of the Persians. Worried about the threat, Croesus consulted the Delphic oracle as to whether or not he should attack. The oracle replied that if he did he would destroy a great empire. Croesus went to war and was defeated, and after a two-week siege Sardis fell and Croesus was burned alive. As a Persian city, Sardis was sacked during the Ionian revolt of 499 BC. It made a comeback under the Macedonians, but was destroyed by an earthquake in 17 AD. The Romans rebuilt it, and the town was the site of one of seven churches of Asia mentioned in the book of Revelation. This didn't save it from destruction at the hands of Tamerlane in 1401, after which the city never really recovered, only coming to light again earlier this century, when archaeologists discovered its remains.

The Site

There are two main clusters of ruins, both easily reached on foot from the main road. The first, which is primarily made up of the gymnasium and synagogue (dawn–dusk; $1), lies just north of the main road on the eastern edge of the village and includes the **Marble Way**, a Byzantine shopping street complete with latrines (holes and drainage channels are still visible). The various shops are labeled and include a restaurant, "Jacob's Paint Shop," an office, and a hardware store. Foundations and low walls with discernible doorways are all that really remain, although in some places Greek inscriptions and engraved basins with carved crosses are visible.

A left turn leads into the **synagogue**, the walls of which are covered with impressive mosaics—although sadly these are copies, the originals being housed in the Manisa Museum. The walls and pillars are intact and covered with ornate patterned tiles, though there's little in the way of explanation. Almost adjacent to the synagogue, the highlight of the third-century AD **gymnasium** is the **Marble Court**, which has been extensively restored, with an intact eastern facade dedicated to the Roman emperor Septimus Severus and his family. Behind the court are the remains of a swimming pool and rest area. Following the main road east from here in the direction of Salihli, you'll come across more ruins, which aren't quite as impressive but include what's left of a Roman stadium, agora, basilica, and theater.

From the village teahouses, a dirt road leads up to the other main site, the **Temple of Artemis**, about ten minutes' walk from the main road. Theoretically you pay a separate fee of $1 to enter this, but it's often not collected. The temple, once numbered among the four largest in Asia Minor, was built by Croesus, destroyed by Greek raiders, and later rebuilt by Alexander the Great. Today half a dozen columns remain intact, and enough of the foundations are visible to make clear just how large the temple used to be. In the southeastern corner of the site are the remains of a small brick church.

Alaşehir

Perched between high mountains and a vine-covered valley leading down to the Gediz River, **ALAŞEHİR** is a pleasant if nondescript town easily reached from Sardis or Salihli. Founded originally by Attalus II of Pergamon, and later known as the Philadelphia of the early Christian church, (one of St. John's seven churches of the Apocalypse), its residents always astonished historians with their loyalty to the site despite repeated destruction by earthquakes. The strategic location also wasn't spared the tug of war between Turks and Byzantines, although amazingly it held out as an enclave against the Ottomans until 1390.

American church groups occasionally stop here on whirlwind tours of St. John's seven churches, although the sole evidence here consists of four squat brick stumps which once supported the seventh-century dome of the **basilica of St. John** in the Beş Eylül district. Finding it is easy enough: it faces the *Hotel Benan* on Cumhuriyet Meydanı (☎2762/1026)—which, incidentally, is the only comfortable place to stay in town, with singles for $14 and doubles for $24. Take the street leading diagonally uphill to the left, then look right just after the Atatürk obelisk. On Tuesdays the neighborhood around the church puts on a lively **street market**. If you're looking for other things to do, there's a small **Roman odeon** up on Toptepe, the hill overlooking town. The **Byzantine walls**, which only a few decades ago girded much of Alaşehir, have been allowed to crumble; what little remains can be seen at the northeast edge of town, by the bus stand.

travel details

Trains

From Manisa to Afyon 2 daily; 12hr); Balikeşehir (4 daily; 3hr); İzmir (9 daily; 1hr 30min); Sart (4 daily; 1hr 30min); Uşak 3 daily; 7hr).

Buses and dolmuşes

From Çanakkale to Bursa (16 daily; 6hr); Ayvalık/İzmir (every 1hr 30min; 3hr 30min/6hr); İstanbul (hourly via Thrace; 6hr); Lapseki (half-hourly; 45min); Ezine/Ayvacık (several daily; 1hr 30min); Odun Iskelesi (4 daily, plus a Geyikli *belediye* bus at 2:30pm, most of these connecting with the Bozcaada ferry; 1hr 10min).

From Ayvalık to Bergama (4 daily; 1hr); Bursa (10 daily; 4hr 30min); Çanakkale (hourly; 3hr 30min); Dikili (hourly; 45min); İzmir (hourly; 3hr 30min).

From Bergama to Ayvalık (4 daily; 1hr); Dikili (8 daily; 30min); İzmir (12 daily; 2hr).

From Manisa to İzmir (hourly; 1hr); Sart (5 daily; 1hr).

From Alaşehir to Denizli (4 daily; 1hr 45min); Salihli/Izmir (hourly; 2hr).

Ferries and boats

From Çanakkale to Gökçeada (5 weekly; 3hr); Eceabat (hourly on the hour 6am–midnight plus 1 & 3am; 20min); Kilitbahir (sails only when full; carries four small cars; all tickets 25 percent cheaper than the state-run service to Eceabat).

From Kabatepe to Gökçeada (Wed & Sun only; 1hr 30min).

From Odun İskelesi to Bozcaada (2 daily; 1hr 10min); Çanakkale–Odun Iskelesi dolmuşes dovetail with departures; there are also dolmuş taxis Ezine–Geyikli–jetty if the direct link fails.

From Ören to Akçay (summer numerous small boats daily; 30min).

From Ayvalık to Lesvos (1or 2 daily; 2hr).

CHAPTER FOUR

THE CENTRAL AND SOUTHERN AEGEAN

The Turkish **central and southern Aegean coast** and its hinterland have seen tourism longer than any other part of the country, if you include the first European adventurers of the eighteenth and nineteenth centuries. The territory between modern İzmir and Marmaris corresponds to the bulk of ancient **Ionia**, and just about all of old **Caria**, and it is home to a concentration of classical, Hellenistic, and Roman antiquities that is virtually unrivaled in modern Turkey. **Ephesus** (Efes in Turkish) is usually first on everyone's list of dutiful pilgrimages, but the understated charms of exquisitely positioned sites like **Priene**, **Labranda**, and **Alında** have at least as much appeal, if not more.

The landscape, too, can be compelling, most memorably at eerie **Bafa Gölü**, towering **Samsun Dağı** (more impressive from a distance), and the oasis-speckled **Bodrum Peninsula**. Towns, however—especially sprawling, polluted İzmir—are for the most part functional places, that are best hurried through on the way to more appealing destinations. But there are some pleasant surprises inland, particularly **Muğla, Birgi**, and **Şirince**: the first two are unself-conscious Ottoman museum towns, the latter a well-preserved former Greek village still just the right side of quaintness.

The biggest disappointment, however, may be the **coast** itself. Despite the tourist-brochure hype, most beaches are average at best, and west-facing shores are mercilessly exposed in the afternoon. Worse still, of the various **resort towns** on the so-called "Turkish Riviera," such as Çeşme, Kuşadası, and Marmaris, only **Bodrum** retains much intrinsic whitewashed charm, and even there it's increasingly impinged upon by shoreline villa development. Turkey has embraced mass tourism with a vengeance, and even the shortest and most mediocre sandy stretch will be dwarfed by serried ranks of resort hotels. Most of the development is aimed at Turkey's rapidly growing domestic middle-class, but the surplus can (and will) always be sold to foreigners. Runaway construction is further fuelled by the country's pernicious inflation rate: with an essentially worthless currency, real estate is a far better investment than any interest-bearing account. The only bright spot is that many local authorities—perhaps learning from the disastrous experiences of other Mediterranean countries—have imposed height limits, and most projects are only two (at most three) stories high.

It takes determination, a good map, and in some places your own vehicle to get the best out of this coast, although if you don't have your own wheels, **public transportation** is excellent; the area is also well served by **international charter flights** from various European cities to İzmir and the soon-to-open Güllük/Milas Airport. Four of the five **international ferry links** with neighboring Greek islands are found here also, making a visit to or from Greece feasible; the Turkish authorities rarely cause problems for holders of charter air tickets who wish to do this.

İZMİR AND AROUND

For most travelers, **İzmir** is an unavoidable obstacle on the way to more enticing destinations. But on closer examination the city is not without charm—and its setting and ethnological museum are unique. Should you be waiting for a flight here or otherwise be short of time or resources, it's worth having a look around. The city can also serve as a base for day-trips or short overnight jaunts, either to nearby **Çeşme** and its peninsula—a mostly stark place, but with some well-preserved villages and a beach or two—or to the valley of the **Küçük Menderes River**, where a couple of utterly untouristed old towns give a hint of what all of Turkey was like just a few decades ago.

İzmir

Turkey's third city and its second port after İstanbul, **İZMİR**—the ancient Smyrna—is home to nearly three million people. It is blessed with a mild climate and an enviable position, straddling the head of a fifty-kilometer-long gulf fed by several streams and flanked by mountains on all sides. But despite a long and illustrious history, most of the city is relentlessly modern; even enthusiasts will concede that a couple of days here is plenty.

Some History

The possibilities of the site suggested themselves as long ago as the third millennium BC, when aboriginal **Anatolians** settled at Tepekule, a hill in the modern northern suburb of Bayraklı. Around 600 BC Lydian raids sent the Bayraklı site into a long decline; it was recovering tentatively when **Alexander the Great** appeared. Spurred by a timely dream corroborated by the oracle of Apollo at Claros, Alexander decreed the foundation of a new settlement on Mount Pagos, the flat-topped hill today adorned with the Kadifekale castle. His generals Antigonus and Lysimachus carried out Alexander's plan after his death, by which time the city bore the name—Smyrna—familiar to the West for centuries after.

Under the **Romans**, who endowed it with numerous impressive buildings, the city prospered and spread north onto the plain, despite the destructive earthquakes that periodically rattle the region. It continued to do so with the advent of **Christianity**, spurred by the decline of Ephesus, its nearest rival. The martyrdom of local bishop Saint Polycarp (156 AD) occurred soon after Saint John the Evangelist's nomination of Smyrna as one of the Seven Churches of Asia Minor.

The **Arab** raids of the seventh century AD triggered several centuries of turbulence. **Selçuk** Turks held the city for two decades prior to 1097, when the **Byzantines** recaptured it; the thirteenth-century Latin tenure in Constantinople provoked another era of disruption at Smyrna, with Crusaders, Genoese, Tamerlane's Mongols, and minor Turkish emirs all jockeying for position. Order was re-established in 1415 by Mehmet I, who finally incorporated the town into the **Ottoman Empire**, his successors repulsing repeated Venetian efforts to retake it. Encouraged by the stability provided by imperial rule, and despite more disastrous earthquakes in 1688 and 1778, traders flocked to Smyrna (by this time also known as İzmir), whose population soared above the 100,000 level of late-Roman times.

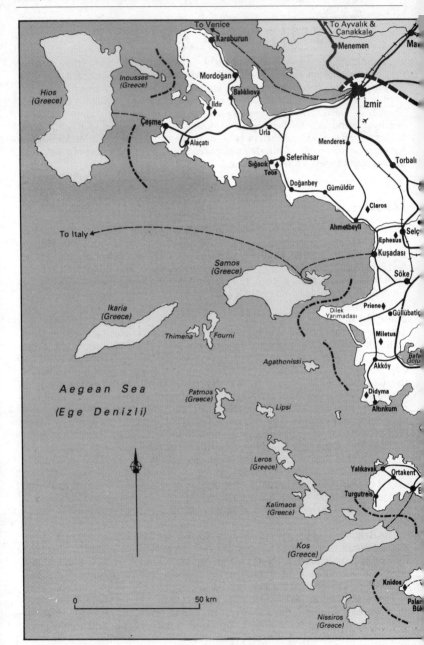

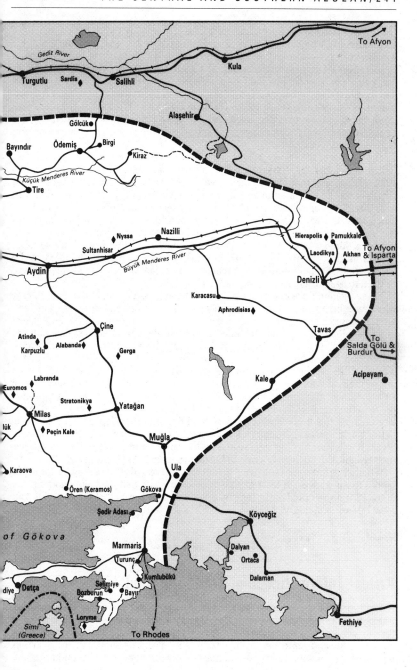

The Ottoman city was predominantly Christian, mostly Greek with a generous sprinkling of Armenians, Latins, and Sephardic Jews, and was the empire's window to the west, a cosmopolitan entrepôt in which many of the inhabitants were not even Ottoman subjects. The Ottoman ruling class habitually referred to it as *gavur İzmir*, or "infidel İzmir"—a necessary evil, within the confines of which the "heathens" enjoyed one of the most cultured lifestyles in the Mediterranean region. Following the defeat of the Ottoman Empire in World War I, Greece was given an indefinite mandate over İzmir and its hinterland. Foolishly, a huge Greek expeditonary force pressed inland, inciting the resistance of the Nationalists under Atatürk.

The climax of the two-year-long defeat of Greece and her nominal French and Italian allies was the entry into Smyrna of the Turkish army on September 9, 1922. The secular republic not having yet been proclaimed, the reconquest of the city took on the character of a successfully concluded *jihad*, or holy Muslim war, with three days of murder and plunder. Aided by civilian mobs, and in a vengeful mood after the wholesale atrocities perpetrated by the retreating Greek armies, the victors concluded their sacking by setting fire to the Armenian and Greek quarters. Almost seventy percent of the city burned to the ground in two days, and thousands of non-Muslims died; a quarter-million refugees huddled at the docks while British, American, French, and Italian vessels stood idly by and refused to grant them safe passage until a day later.

These incidents are in part attested to by the look and layout of the modern city, which was built from scratch on the ashes. The central boulevards are wide and often tree-lined, and the highrises—except for a new forty-story *Hilton*, the tallest in town—almost tasteful, but the effect seems sterile, unreal, even melancholy, an almost deliberate exercise in amnesia. Nowadays, İzmir is a booming commercial, convention and industrial center, with chemical plants, paper mills, and textile works on the outskirts. The people are generally easy-going and more willing to go out of their way for you than in Ankara or İstanbul, yet the city is also home of some of the nastier and more persistent street hustlers in Turkey, in part a product of life in the teeming shanties that line the banks of the Yeşildere River east of the city center—the grim flipside of İzmir's burgeoning development. Even in the better working-class boroughs, cloth-weaving sweatshops clank until late at night. Street hassles are further aggravated by the large numbers of American service-men around, due to the city's role as headquarters of NATO Southeast.

Whether İzmir appeals to you or not is a matter of your ability to forget or ignore the negatives, at least for the duration of your visit. Certainly nothing can detract from the grandeur of the city's setting, and it's this that may well be your most enduring memory.

> The İzmir area **telephone code** is ☎51.

Arrival, Information, and Getting Around

Arrival in İzmir can be either painless or traumatic, depending on your means of transportation. **Ferries** anchor at the **Alsancak terminal**, almost 2km north of the city center; take a taxi into town (for around $2), or walk 250m south and pick up a #2 blue-and-white bus from next to the Alsancak suburban train station. Long-distance **trains** pull in at **Basmane Station**, almost in the middle of our city plan, within walking distance of all of İzmir's affordable accommodation. If you **fly** in, use either the frequent shuttle train from the **airport to Alsancak Station** (for the #2 bus), or the special *Havaş* airport bus will let you off—somewhat more conveniently—by the *Büyük Efes* hotel on Gaziosmanpaşa Bulvarı. The half-hour journey costs about $1 and is primarily geared for arrivals of *THY* flights.

The main **otogar** is 2.5km northeast of the city center, and getting into town with luggage can be problematic. If you don't take a taxi, flag down one of the blue-and-white minibuses labeled "Çankaya–Mersinli" and be prepared to pay double for your bags. These vehicles will drop you off just opposite the *Atlantis Oteli* on Gazi Bulvarı. Red-and-white buses #50/51/52 also link the otogar with Konak Meydanı, the heart of the city, but they are extremely infrequent.

If you are coming **from points south by bus**, you should ask the driver to let you off at the "Tepecik" stop, which will spare you an unnecessary trip out to the main terminal and back. From the roadside, walk down underneath the overpass, turn left, and continue 700m more along Gaziler Caddesi until you come to Basmane Station. Arriving **from anywhere on the Çeşme peninsula**, your bus will stop at a special terminal in the coastal suburb of Güzelyalı, 6km west of downtown. From there, take any blue-and-white-minibus labeled "Konak–Balçova" to the city center; to get to Güzelyalı from Konak Meydanı, simply take the same service in reverse. If you're coming from the north on a morning train and only want to transfer to a bus for Ephesus, Kuşadası, or other more compelling attractions, get off at **Çınarlı Station** (the last stop before Basmane) and walk 300m south to the otogar.

Leaving İzmir

Leaving İzmir by bus, it's also easy to flag down southbound buses from the sidewalk along the Tepecik expressway; all buses slow down here, alert for custom. Otherwise you can catch the blue-and-white "Çankaya - Mersinli" dolmuşes back out to the otogar 300m west of the *Atlantis Oteli*, on the same side of the street; the stop is signed "Mersinli." It is not always necessary to go out to the otogar for **tickets**; many companies have sales offices on Dokuz Eylül Meydanı, the traffic circle just north of Basmane.

Information

İzmir has four **tourist information offices**—the most central and popular branch is on Gaziosmanpaşa Bulvarı next to the *THY* office (June 1–Oct 31 daily 8:30am–7pm;other times of year Mon–Sat 8:30am–5:30pm; ☎142147). Others are at Alsancak Caddesi 418, between the Alsancak train and ferry terminals, on the ferry dock itself, and in the airport arrivals hall. They can suggest hotels but don't make reservations, and they've been known to run out of the free, very useful city map. Some of the central branch staff speak English.

Getting Around

Replete with oddly angled intersections and rotaries, the modern city is somewhat confusing to negotiate. The good news is that İzmir's core is relatively compact, and most points of interest are close together. By far the quickest and most enjoyable way of exploring is on foot; when you're better off taking a bus we've said so. On the blue-and-white dolmuşes, you pay the driver in cash; for the municipality's red-and-white, numbered services you need to buy a ticket from

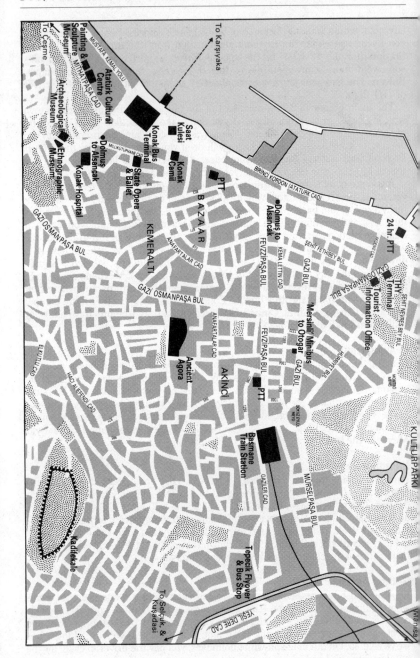

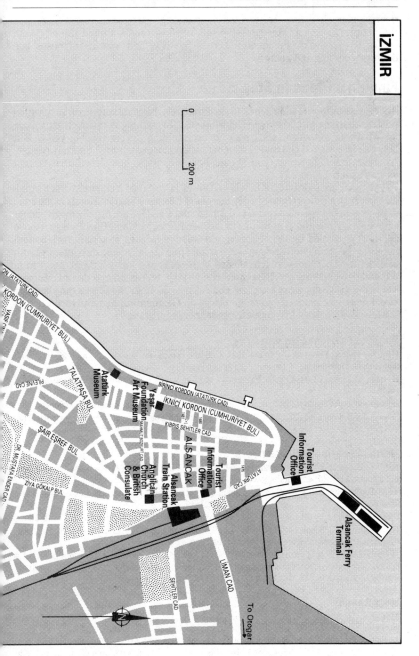

İZMİR

0
200 m

KORDON (CUMHURİYET BUL)
N (ATATÜRK CAD)

VASIF Ç

PİLEVNE CAD

TALATPAŞA BUL

Atatürk
Museum

Yaşar
Foundation
Art Museum

ŞAİR EŞREF BUL

BİRİNCİ KORDON (ATATÜRK CAD)

İKNİCİ KORDON (CUMHURİYET BUL)

MAHMUT İZMİR CAD

KIBRIS ŞEHİTLER CAD

ALSANCAK

DR. MUSTAFA ENVER CAD

ZİYA GÖKALP BUL

Anglican
Church
& British
Consulate

Information
Office

Alsancak
Train Station

ATATÜRK CAD

Tourist
Information
Office

LİMAN CAD

ŞEHİTLER CAD

Alsancak Ferry
Terminal

To Otogar

the booths on Konak Meydanı—the hub of most routes around the city, with ferries to Karşıyaka, the quarter across the bay, and swarms of buses and dolmuşes coming and going.

Finding a Place to Stay

Accommodation in İzmir tends to be either very basic or very luxurious, with a relative shortage of mid-range establishments. Everything is relatively expensive for what you get. Also, don't plan on overnighting during the big yearly fair, between late August and mid-September, when most hotels are uniformly packed. At other times, however, you should find something quickly—the city is not exactly a tourist mecca.

The main area for budget hotels is **Akinci** (also called Yenigün), which straddles Fevzipaşa Bulvarı immediately in front of Basmane Station. Hotels in the zone to the south, between Fevzipaşa and Anafartalar Caddesi, are usually much plainer and cheaper than those to the north, between Fevzipaşa and Gazi Bulvarı. Above all, don't be fooled by the charming old wooden facades of certain rock-bottom hotels in the vicinity of 1294 and 1296 sokak; they usually belie dire interiors with particleboard partitions, roach-infested bathrooms and lobby-lurkers. Apart from the noted exceptions, you'll be more comfortable on the other side of Fevzipaşa. There are also a couple of excellent choices near **Konak**, and (if you can stand the street noise) a cluster of mid-range places on **Gaziosmanpaşa Bulvarı**. Choices in each area are listed in roughly ascending order of price.

South of Fevzipaşa Bulvarı

Gümüş Palas, 1299 Sok 12 (☎134 153). Cell-like rooms, no shower in building, but clean and secure. Doubles $8.

Balıklı, 1296 Sok 18 (☎142 560). Even has a garden, which some rooms face; $8 for a double room.

Olimpiyat, 945 Sok 2 (☎251 269). $12 for room with a sink; showers charged extra.

Saray, Anafartalar Cad 635 (☎136 946); rooms surround a pleasant, glassed-in courtyard. This is where the tourist office sends impecunious backpackers; $8 for double room with sink.

North of Fevzipaşa Bulvarı

Nil, Fevzipaşa Bul 155 (☎135 228). Excellent value, but beware of street noise when choosing a room. $18 with attached shower.

Yeni Park, 1368 Sok 6 (☎135 231). Clean, quiet, but rooms vary widely; inspect with care. Doubles $17.

Işık, 1364 Sok 11 (☎131 029). On a reasonably quiet side street; good value at $17 with bath.

Güzel İzmir, 1368 Sok 8 (☎135 069, 146 693). One of the better-value mid-range hotels in this area, though singles are tiny. $18 with bath.

Bayburt, 1370 Sok 1, corner 1369 Sokak (☎122 013). Huge barn of a place built around a roofed-over courtyard café; favored by tour groups. Only drawback is street noise from nearby intersection. $19 with attached bath.

Near Konak

Meseret, Anafartalar Cad 66 (☎255 533). Clean, well-furnished rooms overlook roof of courtyard cafeteria (some noise). Baths are down the hall in this historic building. Doubles $12.

Ankara Palas, at foot of Konak pedestrian overpass (☎142 850, 137 969). Unbeatable location and set back a bit from traffic noise, this is a large hotel that's unlikely to be full. $20 with attached bath.

Gaziosmanpaşa Bulvarı

Efes, Gaziosmanpaşa Bul 48 (☎147 276). Doubles for $15 with attached shower.

Atlas, Şair Eşref Bulvarı 1 (corner of Gaziosmanpaşa; ☎144 265). The building might make New Yorkers homesick for the Flatiron Building. Elegant for the price, though street noise can be a problem. $18 with attached shower.

Babadan, Gaziosmanpaşa 50 (☎139 640). Nothing special, but mentioned here as it's the last outfit, pricewise, before the big jump up to $75 digs along the waterfront. $28 with bath.

Camping

İzmir's handiest **campground** is the *BP Mocamp* at Inciraltı 12km west of Konak (☎154 760). It's closed in winter, and not particularly cheap when it's open. *OBA Dinleme Tesisleri* (☎342 015) is open year-round and has chalets for the tentless. It's 20km out at Güzelbahçe, so you'll need a Çeşme-bound bus to get there.

The City

From Basmane Station and Dokuz Eylül Meydanı respectively, **Fevzipaşa Bulvarı** and **Gazi Bulvarı** shoot straight west toward the bay, which is clearly visible from the front steps of the station. North of these two streets lies the bulk of the largely radial modern city, wrapped around the vast expanse of the **Kültür Parkı**. From the middle of Gazi Bulvarı, **Gaziosmanpaşa Bulvarı** aims straight for Cumhuriyet Meydanı, a major intersection right by the water, and with most of İzmir's upscale tourist facilities are clustered nearby.

The waterfront itself is paralleled by two long thoroughfares: **Atatürk Caddesi**, often known as Birinci (First) Kordon, and **Cumhuriyet Bulvarı** slightly inland, commonly referred to as Ikinci (Second) Kordon. Atatürk Caddesi curls all the way around the smart district of Alsancak, merging—just south of the railroad station of the same name—with **Şair Eşref Bulvarı**, which skims the Kültür Parkı's west side on its way through two traffic circles to link up with Gaziosmanpaşa Bulvarı.

Most of the buildings that survived the 1922 fire are in the area south of Fevzipaşa Bulvari. The soul of this district is **Anafartalar Caddesi**, beginning just south of Basmane Station and snaking its way to Konak Meydanı. Once across Gaziosmanpaşa Bulvarı, the **bazaar** begins in earnest, sprawling mostly on the north side of Anafartalar, which exits inconspicuously onto **Konak Meydanı**, surrounded by government buildings and cultural facilities and bounded by the sea to the west and parkland to the south. Konak is for the moment the main urban **transportation hub**, although the municipality has big plans for the square in the form of a mega-convention/recreation/shopping center, and no one knows yet where the buses will be banished to. Birinci and Ikinci Kordon end here too, but three continuation roads—**Mithatpaşa Caddesi, Mustafa Kemal**, and **İnönü**—follow the gulf to the Güzelyalı bus stand.

Around Konak Meydanı: the Major Museums

İzmir cannot really be said to have a single center; among several possible contenders, **Konak** probably wins by default simply because it's the spot where visitors spend the most time. The ornate **Saat Kulesi** (Clocktower), dating only from 1901 but the city's official logo, stands on the opposite end of the Konak pedestrian bridge from the **Konak Camii**, which is distinguished by its facade of enamel Kütahya tiles. Both seem lost in the modernity and bustle, and will only become more obscured when the Konak redevelopment is completed.

The area southwest of Konak forms the undisputed cultural focus of İzmir, containing the **Atatürk Kültür Merkezi** (Cultural Center), **Devlet Opera ve Balesi** (State Opera and Ballet—see "Entertainment" below), and virtually all the city's **museums**.

The **Archaeological Museum** (daily 9am–5:30pm; $1) features an excellent collection of finds from all over İzmir province and beyond, housed in a building which could—and may eventually—hold more. Labeling is scant, but large explanatory posters make up for this, and the museum is well worth an hour or so of your time. The ground floor is largely given over to statuary and friezes of all eras; standouts include a rather Hebraic-looking Roman priest, a headless but still impressive archaic *kore*, and the showcased bronze statuette of a runner. The top floor, whose foyer features a large Roman mosaic from İzmir, contains smaller objects with an emphasis on Bronze Age and archaic pottery—more exciting than it sounds, particularly the so-called "orientalized" terracotta and bestiary amphoras from Pitane (Çandarlı). The section of small finds from Erythrae (Ildır) is especially good, as is a case of embossed seals, helpfully displayed with full-color enlargements. The oddest item is a unique mushroom-form column capital from the seventh century. The single best piece, though, is a graceful, if peculiar Hellenistic statuette of Eros, clenching a veil in his teeth.

The **Ethnographic Museum** (daily 9am–noon & 1–5pm; $1), immediately across from the archaeological museum, is housed in an Ottoman *belle époque* structure which was a hospital before becoming a museum in 1984. A helpful brochure with a plan of the galleries is provided at the ticket booth. In a sense it's a more enjoyable—and certainly more unique—collection than the archaeological one. One of the first exhibits on the lower floor is of the two types of İzmir area houses: the traditional wooden Turkish residence, and the more substantial "Levantine" (i.e., Christian and Jewish merchants') residences, helpfully illustrated with photographs showing the district or town where surviving mansions may still be found. There are also reconstructions of a kiln for blue beads to ward off the evil eye, and of the first Ottoman pharmacy in the area; dioramas of felt and pottery production; and a photo-and-mannikin presentation of camel-wrestling and the *Zeybeks*—the traditional warrior caste of western Anatolia. The upper floor has a more domestic focus, with recreations of a nuptial chamber, sitting room, and circumcision recovery suite, along with vast quantities of house-hold utensils and Ottoman weaponry. The galleries finish with flat weavings, saddle-bags, and fine carpets, accompanied by potted histories of the crafts.

If time is short, the **Painting and Sculpture Museum** (ground floor daily 10am–6pm, upper levels daily 10am–5pm except Sun; free) is the obvious one to miss. The lower level displays temporary exhibits; the two upstairs galleries contain almost 200 works by artists active since the foundation of the Republic. Some are awful, some decent, but most are stylistically derivative renderings of pastoral/populist themes. The modern stuff is arguably the best.

Along the Kordon to Alsancak

Cumhuriyet Meydanı, another traditional reference point, lies less than a kilometer northeast of Konak. The *meydan* itself is unremarkable except for the equestrian statue of the Gazi, depicted completing his long ride from inland Anatolia and poised in the act of chasing the infidels into the sea. Today the infidels are back, in limited measure, as evidenced by the member nations' flags undulating in amity outside the **NATO Southeast Division Headquarters** nearby.

Smart seaside apartment buildings line **Birinci Kordon** for most of its length until it doubles back on itself before the ferry terminal. For several hundred meters on either side of Cumhuriyet, the İzmir smart set convenes for drinks and snacks in the evening; by day, crowds lining up for visas gather outside the German consulate, housed in one of several substantial buildings that escaped the 1922 destruction. Another is the home of the all-but-obligatory **Atatürk Museum**, Atatürk Caddesi 248 (Tues–Fri 9am–noon & 1:30–5:30pm), occupying the building where the premier stayed on his visits to İzmir and containing a predictable assortment of Atatürkian knickknacks.

The museum more or less marks the southern margin of **Alsancak**, where the severity of the 1922 blaze was in fact less than elsewhere; just inland, particularly on **1453, 1482, 1481,** and **1480 sokaks,** plus the east side of Ikinci Kordon, are entire intact rows of sumptuous **eighteenth- and nineteenth-century mansions** that once belonged to European merchants. They add direction to wanderings out here, and for the moment remain remarkably ungentrified—most are offices and private homes. One, at Cumhuriyet Bulvarı 252, contains the **Yaşar Foundation Art Museum**, a privately run gallery that has recently been restored.

Returning from Alsancak to the city center, you unavoidably pass by or through the **Kültür Parkı** (daily 8am–midnight), built on the ruins of the pre-1922 Greek quarter, an elongated 75-acre park located midway between Alsancak Point and Kadifekale Hill. "Culture" in this case means a parachute tower, İzmir TV headquarters, permanent exhibition halls for the city's yearly trade fair, a miniature golf course and funfair, a zoo, an artificial lake, an open-air theater, plus a dozen *gazinos* and tea/beer gardens. Only the theater, which occasionally hosts summer concerts, is likely to be of interest to foreigners, plus of course the greenery and the city's quietest phone booths.

From the Bazaar to Kadifekale

İzmir's **bazaar**, though it runs a distinct second to İstanbul's, warrants a few hours' strolling, and is large enough to include several distinct city districts, notably Kemeraltı and Hisarönü. Anafartalar Caddesi, the main drag, is lined with **clothing**, **jewelry**, and **shoe shops**; Fevzipaşa Bulvarı and the alleys just south are strong on **leather** garments, which the city is famous for. (İzmir is not, however, known for its carpets.) Any distance away from the principal strips, humbler merchandise—irrigation pumps, live chickens and rabbits, tea sets, olives, rubber stamps—predominates.

In contrast to many other Turkish town bazaars, there is little of architectural interest here, though several very late Ottoman mosques are worth a glance in passing. Most of İzmir's commercial wealth resided in harbor warehouses that were wiped out in 1922; and since the pre-Republican population was two-thirds non-Muslim, there were correspondingly few historic *medreses* or mosques. Until recently there stood one handsome Ottoman *kervansaray*, that of **Kızlarağası**, near the Hisar mosque and still marked on some maps. In 1989 it was pulled down and the tradesmen evicted, with "restoration" as the excuse. In fact, a luxury hotel will likely take up the space.

Spared any such relegation is the nearby **ancient agora** (daily 9am–5pm; $1), the most accessible of İzmir's ancient sites, and also the most visited. From Anafartalar Caddesi turn south onto 943 Sokak, then west onto 816 Sokak; typical black-on-yellow signs confirm the way. The agora probably dates back to the early second century BC but what you see now are the remains of a later reconstruction, financed during the reign of the Roman Emperor Marcus Aurelius after the catastrophic earthquake of 178 AD. Principal structures, unearthed between the world wars, include a **colonnade** of fourteen Corinthian columns on the west side, and an elevated north stoa (a covered walk) resting on a vaulted basement. On the eastern part of the area sit hundreds of unsorted Ottoman gravestones and earlier fragments of sculpture, the best of which have been removed to the archaeological museum – which frankly, if time is limited, is far more worthy of a visit.

Rising just southeast of the agora, the **Kadifekale** (Velvet Castle), as visible by night as by day thanks to skillful floodlighting, is perhaps the one sight in the city you shouldn't miss. The less energetic can take a dolmuş ("Konak–Kadifekale") from in front of the archaeological museum and cover the final 300m on foot, but the best introduction to the citadel is to walk up from the agora, along a route threading through a once-elegant district of narrow streets and dilapidated pre-1922 houses that offer just a hint of what life must be like in the sprawling shanty-towns the other side of Yeşildere. Once you reach Hacı Ali Effendi Caddesi— probably via 977 or 985 Sokak—cross it and finish the climb along the pedestrian stairs opposite. The irregularly shaped fortress itself is permanently open, serving as a daytime playground for local kids but not lit inside after dark. Virtually nothing is visible of its Hellenistic foundations; the present structure dates from Byzantine and Ottoman times. Late afternoon is the best time to go, and to wait for the kindling of thousands of city lights below to match the often lurid sunsets over the bay, but the views over the city are unrivaled at any hour. In the warmer months, a **tea/beer garden** operates until late at a prime interior location under the pines; otherwise there are several more along the stretch between the castle gate and the bus stop.

Over to Karşıyaka

Karşıyaka means "the opposite shore," and that's really all it is, but it can make a nice short trip from İzmir proper. The twenty-minute ferry cruise across from Konak ends next to a waterfront park packed with pubs and snack bars that directly overhang the bay. In the evenings and on weekends, Karşıyakans turn out in force. The only monumental destination might be the **tomb of Zübeyde Hanım**, Atatürk's mother, some way inland; otherwise the cool breeze on the ride over is the main event. If you're particularly demented you can rent an airgun and blast away at hapless balloons moored in the water, thus contributing to the lead contamination and plastic litter in the bay.

STEAM TRAIN EXCURSIONS

Turkey has in captivity a large number of steam locomotives and antique parlor cars of American, British, Austrian and German make, some of which are up to eighty years old. These are generally chartered long-haul across central Anatolia by overseas train buffs, but a short, ninety-kilometer excursion from İzmir to Çamlık (south of Selçuk) is also regularly offered to groups. For reservation information contact Nurhan Arda, District Chief Manager, Alsancak Station (☎211 555), or Umur Ozanoğulları who speaks English (☎192 271).

Eating and Drinking

For a city of İzmir's size, **restaurants** are remarkably few and far between. The obvious clutch of eateries within sight of Basmane Station, usually full of transient male travelers with nowhere else to go, make for a pretty depressing—and undistinguished—meal. As is so often the case in Turkey, there's a far better selection of inexpensive establishments in the bazaar, but unfortunately most of them close by 7:30pm; also, despite their promising position in the city grid, both the Karşıyaka and Kadifekale districts offer little in the way of food besides the previously noted tea- and beer-gardens. Meals along the Birinci Kordon represent a definite notch up in price, though not always as much as you'd think, since at most establishments there the emphasis is on beer-drinking.

While **mussels** are fairly common along the Aegean in autumn, İzmir is particularly noted for them, and half a dozen of them stuffed with rice and pine-nuts make a wonderful cheap snack. The vendors are everywhere, but it's a good idea not to patronize them between late May and early September, when you run a good chance of poisoning yourself.

Akinci/Yenigün

Ömür, Anafartalar Cad 794. Cheap and friendly, serving ready-prepared dishes; no alcohol.

Çagdas, Anafartalar Cad 606. The least intimidating and cheapest of several *meyhanes* west of the station; a lot of food and a beer for $4 a person.

İnci Et Lokantası, 1369 Sokak 51/A. A meat grill, not outrageously priced, notable for being the only place on this block serving alcohol. Pink tablecloths and friendly service. About $4 for a light meal.

Bazaar

Tarihi Kemeraltı Börekcisi, Anafartalar Cad 93. Good for a breakfast of *börek* and hot milk, or dessert later; closes at 7pm.

Aksüt, 873 Sok 113, plus an annex nearby on 863 Sok. More expensive than the former, but better: shiny decor, excellent dairy products, and breakfast pastries. Closes 7:30pm.

Gülistan Pide ve Kebap Salonu, 856 Sokak, corner of 852 Sokak. Lunches only.

Yigit Çorba ve Kebap Salonu, 873 Sokak 117, upper floor. Large portions and a good view of the Başdurak Camii. Lunch only.

Halikarnass Balık Lokantası, overlooking the fountain at the junction of 870, 871, and 873 sokaks. A simple fish restaurant near the Başdurak Camii fish market, where an okay meal won't cost over $6. No alcohol. Closes at 7:30pm.

Tabaklar, 872 Sok 134. Around the corner from, and similar to, the preceding.

Doğu Karadeniz Lokantası, Yeyisel Çıkmazı 39e. A late-opening *meyhane*, just off the beginning of Anafartalar Caddesi. All male as a rule, but decorous—outdoor seating, impromptu music with your grilled items, and cold hors d'oeuvres.

Şükran Lokantası, Anafartalar Cad 61, adjacent to the *Doğu Karadeniz*. A once-premier restaurant that's come down in the world: food is average but the prices are still stiff. The big draw is the setting—outdoor seating around a fountain-courtyard of an old "Levantine" building—and the opportunity to nurse a drink until midnight unmolested by traffic.

Öz Ezo Gelin, corner of 848 Sokak and Anafartalar Caddesi, very near the two previous listings. Soups, kebabs, and pudding in an elegant dining room with a family atmosphere. No alcohol; closes at 9pm.

Bolulu Hasan Usta, 853 Sokak 13/B, behind the Kemeraltı police station. Best puddings and *dondurma* in town; shuts at 8pm.

Birinci Kordon

Eski Balıkçınız Niyazi Aydın Ensite'nin Yeri, a.k.a *Sandal Restaurant*, Ikinci Kordon 22–24, between the pedestrian overpasses. A long-established seafood chow-down, and a mouthful any way you look at it. Steeper than the bazaar fish places, but cheaper than Birinci Kordon eateries. Always mobbed, and open late.

Liman Çay Salonu, Birinci Kordon 128. Teahouse where the locals go for an evening hookah.

Gemi Lokantası, Birinci Kordon 69, Naval Station. An anchored pleasure boat with cheap fried fish and alcohol.

Çicek Pasajı, Birinci Kordon 132. A hugely successful, if hardly authentic attempt to re-create the namesake arcade in İstanbul. Always packed in the evening; *meze* plates about $1.25, draught beer a tad less.

L'Aventure, Birinci Kordon 150. A quieter, more decorous beer café just beyond *Pizza Hut*, with outdoor seating for views of the ferries coming and going.

Sirena, Birinci Kordon 194. A bar with food, okay for a mild splurge.

Sera, Birinci Kordon 206. Does Western-style breakfasts.

Palet, Birinci Kordon 79, built over the water on concrete pilings beyond the Alsancak Kordon dock. If you want to eat in style and blow a wad of bills, this is the place.

Mask, 1435 Sokak 18, Alsancak. A currently trendy bar with dancing.

Entertainment

As with the eating and drinking situation, the city's evening **entertainment** options are somewhat limited. The Atatürk Cultural Center and the State Opera and Ballet go some way to satisfying **classical music** lovers, but only between late September and May. The Atatürk is home to the local symphony orchestra, which plays regularly Friday evening and Saturday noon, and hosts random concerts of "serious" soloists. Strangely, tickets for these events are not always sold at the center; read the posters outside the building for directions, or ask at the information desk.

The Opera and Ballet, housed in a wonderful art deco building on Milli Kütüphane Caddesi, boasts a more varied program of everything from chamber music to pop and jazz. Tickets are sold on the premises.

With the onset of hot weather, events move to the open-air theater in the Kültür Parkı. The linchpin of the summer season, however, running from mid-June to mid-July, is the **International İzmir Festival**, inaugurated in 1987 and something of a misnomer since all events take place either at the Çeşme castle or various restored venues at Ephesus. Tickets tend to cost $10–18 a head, but fifty-percent student discounts are available and the acts are often world-class—past names have included Sara Vaughan, the Moscow Ballet, and Paco Peña. Get the current year's programs and tickets from the İzmir Culture Foundation at Mahmut Esat Bozkurt Caddesi 4–6, Alsancak, or the Opera and Ballet box office, the museum in Selçuk, the Festival Bureau at İnönü Cad 48/1 in Kuşadası, or the tourist office in Çeşme.

Listings

Airlines *Air France*, 1353 Cad 1 (☎259 004); *Austrian Airlines*, Şair Eşref Bul, 1371 Sok 5; (☎258 020); *British Airways*, Şehit Fethi Bey Cad 120 (☎141 788); *Istanbul Hava Yolları*, Gaziosmanpaşa Cad 2/E (☎190 541); *KLM*, Cumhuriyet Meydanı 11/2 (☎214 757);

Lufthansa, Birinci Kordon 244 (☎223 622); *Pan Am*, Ikinci Kordon 143/H (☎214 262); *Swissair*, same as *KLM*; *THY*, on the ground floor of the *Büyük Efes Oteli*, Gaziosmanpaşa Bulvarı (Mon–Sat 8:30am–7:30pm, Sun 8:30am–5:30pm; information ☎141 226; reservations ☎141 220).

Airport bus Operated by *Havaş*, this runs from in front of the *THY* office 90 minutes before each *THY* flight (non-*THY* passengers welcome). Takes 20–30 minutes to reach Menderes Airport, 18km south of town. Fare is about $1.25.

Bookstores *Dünya*, Akdeniz Cad 8/J (mostly English-language magazines); *Haşet*, Şehit Nevres Bey Bul 3/B; *NET*, Cumhuriyet Bulv 142/A, next to Dokuz Eylül Universitesi; and *Kuydaş*, Şehit Nevres Bey 9/A. All carry a range of English-language material.

Car rental One helpful local outfit, with English-speaking management, is *MAC*, Akdeniz Cad 8/B (☎192 262); other independents include *Airtour*, Şehit Fethi Bey Cad 122/B (☎131 756); *Ata*, Şehit Nevres Bey Bul 11/A (☎218 787); *Çelebi*, Şehit Nevres Bey Bul 1/1A (☎218 707); and *Nysa*, Akdeniz Cad 8/F (☎196 647). International chains include *Avis*, Şehit Nevres Bey Bul 19/A, Alsancak (☎211 226); *Budget*, Gaziosmanpaşa Bul 1/1E (☎258 012); *Europcar/ InterRent*, Şehit Fethi Bey Cad 122/F (☎254 698); and *Hertz*, Cumhuriyet Bul 123/1 (☎217 002). All of these have airport offices too.

Consulates *American*, Birinci Kordon 92/3 (☎131 369); *British* (also Canada/Australia/New Zealand), Mahmut Esat Bozkurt Cad 49, an annex of the Anglican church by Alsancak Station (☎211 795); *Netherlands*, Cumhuriyet Meydanı 11/2.

English-language library Try the library of the Turkish-American Cultural Association, Şehit Nevres Bey Bul 23/A (Mon–Fri 1:30–6:30pm).

Exchange You can change money around the clock at standard bank rates in the PTT on Cumhuriyet Meydanı; the *Babadan Oteli* is more conveniently situated but the rates are worse.

Ferries Tickets and information on international services to Venice and the domestic line to İstanbul from the *Turkish Maritime Lines* facilities at the Alsancak dock (☎210 094); the gate of the complex is on Atatürk Caddesi, opposite 1475 Sokak.

Hamams The hottest, cleanest, securest, and best-maintained baths are *Hoşgör*, on an alley inland from Mithatpaşa Cad 10, opposite Karataş Lisesi (daily 7am–11:30pm, women only in the afternoon; $1.75). Other acceptable baths include *Luks*, Anafartalar Cad 660, and *Tevfikpaşa*, 871 Sok 30—both handy if you have a no-star hotel.

Hospitals Most central are *Dokuz Eylül Universitesi Hastanesi* on Ikinci Kordon, *Çocuk Hastanesi* (Children's Hospital) on 1374 Sok 3/A, and the *Konak Hastanesi*, which includes a dental section, across the road from the ethnographic and archaeological museums.

Luggage consignment On the left-hand side of Basmane station as you face it (daily 6am–9pm).

Musical instruments Traditional Turkish ones can be bought from a long line of shops on Gaziler Caddesi, parallel to the Basmane train tracks.

Nargiles Best on the Aegean can be found at *İlhan Etike*, 906 Sok 31 in the Hisarönü district of the bazaar, or *Mehmet & Osman Kaya*, 856 Sok 7/C in Kemeraltı. See *Basics*, "Shopping," for more on nargiles.

Parcels If you don't trust the PTT for shipping souvenirs or personal effects, or can't face the bureaucracy involved, there's a *UPS* office at Akdeniz Cad 8/K, which handles air delivery to North America and elsewhere.

PTT Besides the 24-hr one on Cumhuriyet Meydanı (quiet phones), there's a branch at 859 Sokak, Kemeraltı (also with quiet phones), and another on Fevzipaşa Bulvarı, 300m west of Basmane Station—though the last has uselessly noisy phones.

Swimming Due to pollution the bay is off-limits until well beyond İnciraltı. There are pools at the *Büyük Efes Oteli*, although these are expensive; less expensive are the ones at the *Balçova Termal* resort—known also as the legendary Baths of Agamemnon—10km west of town.

Çeşme and Around

The claw-like mass of land that extends west from İzmir terminates near **Çeşme**, the most low-key of the southern Aegean's main coastal resorts. You can make detours off the eighty-kilometer highway out to visit the isolated **Karaburun Peninsula** to the north, or medieval **Sığacık** and ancient **Teos** to the south, but the several attractions within shouting distance of Çeşme, most notably **Ildır/ Erythrae**, the town of **Alaçatı**, and **Altınkum** beach, are easier ways to fill a day or two.

The immediate environs of Çeşme are bleak scrubland, with the only note of color being introduced by the deeply aquamarine sea. It's a barrenness that is deceptive: before 1922 the area, almost entirely Greek-populated, was famous for its vineyards and vegetable farms, nurtured by artesian wells surging up from hundreds of meters below ground level. After 1922, the newly arrived Muslim settlers, mostly from the Aegean islands, Macedonia, or Thrace, turned their goats loose on the farmland, and now little remains except for the occasional vine or melon patch. Agricultural reclamation is further hampered by the fact that most deep ground water is now diverted to support the ever-increasing number of villas on the peninsula's north shore.

One historical constant here is the **climate**: noticeably drier, cooler, and healthier than anywhere nearby on the Turkish coast, especially in comparison to occasionally hellish İzmir or muggy Kuşadası. These conditions, combined with the presence of several thermal springs, have made the peninsula a popular resort for over a century. This is the westernmost point of continental Turkey, and is subject to currents from the Dardanelles and maritime breezes that make the sea bracing and the nights chilly at any time of the year. For warmer, sheltered swimming on beaches unshadowed by villas, make for the **coast south of Çeşme**, where development has been restricted because most land belongs to the forestry department and various municipalities.

Çeşme

An often sleepy, two-street town of old Greek houses wrapped around a Genoese castle, **ÇEŞME** (Drinking Fountain in Turkish) doubtless takes its name from the many Ottoman fountains, some still functioning, scattered around its streets. It makes an agreeable stopover on the way to Hios in Greece, and it's hard to work up a great deal of indignation about the current scale of tourism here—although further development is likely when the town replaces İzmir as the Turkish port for *TML*'s service to Venice in 1992, sparing passengers the current four extra hours on the boat to the head of the İzmir gulf. A four-lane divided highway linking İzmir and Çeşme is to be opened simultaneously, and Çeşme's authorities are ecstatic—to put it mildly—at the prospect of increased traffic.

Arrival and Information
Coming by **ferry** from Hios, you arrive at the small dock in front of the castle. Arriving by **bus** from İzmir, you'll be let off at the **otogar**, 1km south of the ferry port. At the time of writing İzmir is the only long-distance destination served, but the otogar has obviously been built for growth, and as soon as the direct Çeşme–Kuşadası highway has opened you can expect direct services bypassing İzmir. **Dolmuşes** to Dalyan leave from next to the PTT; all others, serving Ilıca,

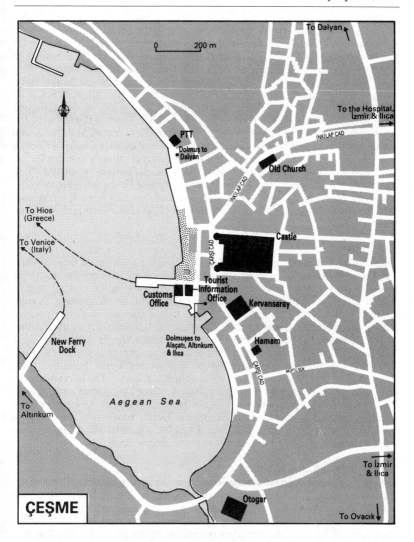

Altınkum, and Alaçatı, depart from next to customs and the **tourist information office** (June–Aug daily 8am–8pm; May & Sept Mon–Fri 8:30am–7pm, Sat & Sun 9am–5pm; Oct–Apr daily 8:30am–5pm; ☎26653), which dispenses the usual glossy brochures, town maps, and hotel listings.

Finding a Place to Stay

The most desirable location **to stay** in is the hillside above and to the right of the castle as you face it. If establishments there are full, there are other options near the intersection of Çarşı Caddesi and Müftü Sokak.

The *Anıt Pansiyon*, directly opposite the castle gate, occupies an old but well-kept house with a kitchen, shared bath, and small terrace: $6 single, $8 double for the privilege. If it's full, the *Çelik* or *Kısaoğlu*, adjacent about 100m beyond in regrettable concrete buildings, are in the same price bracket. Moving up a notch, the *Tarhan Pansiyon* (☎549/26599), behind the *kervansaray* and to the right, offers a few new rooms with bath for $12 double; the *Yalçin Otel*, Kale Sokak 38 (☎549/26981), above the *Tarhan* but reached from the *Çelik*, is new and good value at $12 for a double with bath, including breakfast. Down in the flatlands, the *Alim Pansiyon*, Müftü Sokak 3 (☎549/27828) is similarly recent, and charges $6 per person for a room with bath and breakfast served in your choice of front or rear garden. In the same neighborhood and price range, there's also the *Otel A*, Çarşı Caddesi 24 (☎549/26881), and the nearby *Memo Pansiyon* (☎549/26498). If, on the other hand, you're down to your last lira waiting for the ferry out, consider the *Yıldız*, Müftü Sok 2, with scruffy but clean beds for $4 a head. If you're serious about **camping**, see the campgrounds detailed under Ilıca and Altınkum, below.

The Town

The town's two main streets are **İnkilap Caddesi**, the main bazaar thoroughfare, and **Çarşı Caddesi**, its continuation, which saunters south along the waterfront past the castle, *kervansaray*, and most travel agencies before veering slightly inland. Unless you're a fan of nineteenth-century domestic architecture, though, Çeşme's **sights** are soon exhausted. You are free to clamber over every perilous inch of the waterfront **castle** (daily 8:30am–noon & 1–5:30pm; $1), much repaired by the Ottomans and today home of an open-air theater (see "Eating, Drinking & Nightlife", below) and a small **museum** of finds from nearby Erythrae; its collection will hopefully be supplemented by undisplayed items from the İzmir museum, and none too soon—the current exhibit is pathetic. The **kervansaray**, a few paces south, dates from the reign of Süleyman the Magnificent and has been predictably restored as a luxury hotel—managed, allegedly, by the İzmir Mafia as a money-laundering operation. The huge old **Greek basilica** in the center of town has been recently fitted with new doors but otherwise stands empty, as it has for decades, awaiting a decision as to restoration or conversion.

Eating, Drinking, and Nightlife

Doyen of Çeşme **restaurants** is the *İmren*, near the bottom of İnkilap Caddesi; the garden out back is more congenial than the garishly lit main dining room. The same folks run the *Castle Restaurant*, but there you pay—roughly $18 a couple—for the setting and view through the battlements, rather than the food, which is mediocre. Of the other waterfront eateries down by the post office, the *Rıhtım* is almost reasonable. Otherwise it's back up along İnkilap, where the *Emre Grill Café* on a side alley is just what it says. Next to the old church, the decor of *Hasan Abı*—and its eccentric proprietor—are both throwbacks to the less pretentious Turkey of the 1970s; the steam-tray grub is good and cheap, too. Just behind, with a small garden, is the *Özen Pide Salonu*, Çeşme's only *pide salonu*. Also near *Hasan Abı* on İnkilap is the *Rumeli Pastanesi*, a local legend, with some of the best ice cream on the Aegean; their home-made *reçel* (fruit preserves) are also for sale. Finally, the *Café Müller*, next to *Avis* on Çarşı Caddesi, serves waffles with whipped cream and fruit topping—a welcome respite from Turkish breakfast.

In terms of **after-dark** action, there's little middle ground between promenading on roped-off İnkilap Caddesi, and the rash of discos—*Joy, İki Buçuk*, another in the *Altınyunus* complex—well east of town. Perhaps the fact that a religious teacher was recently busted for screening porno flicks to the faithful in his living room goes some way toward explaining the locals' preference for staying in. The only relief occurs during two overlapping **summer festivals** in late June and early July, Çeşme's half of the misnamed İzmir Festival and its very own "Sea Festival"; during this season the castle is a venue for performances ranging from the painfully amateurish to top-flight.

Listings

Car rental *Sultan*, İnkilap Cad 68 (☎549/27395) is about the cheapest; they also rent motorcycles. Otherwise try *Nysa*, İnkilap Cad 8 (☎549/26508), or *Avis*, Çarşı Caddesi (☎549/27029).

Ferries You can't miss the *Ertürk* agency, the huge kiosk in front of the tourist office, which runs a morning ferry to Hios. There is another twice-weekly Turkish morning boat, the *Balina*, a fast wooden craft built originally for smuggling, which is handled by an office next to the *Sahil Restaurant*. The Greek afternoon boat is represented by *Karavan*, next to *Ertürk* at Belediye Dükkanları no. 3 (☎549/27230); in addition it's the most helpful full-service travel agency in town, with rare—and reliable—information on schedules elsewhere in Turkey. Ticket prices are $20 one-way, $25 round-trip.

Hamam On Çarşı Caddesi, 200m down from the *kervansaray*.

Hospital At the very top of İnkilap Caddesi, past the turnoff for Dalyan.

PTT 300m north of the ferry dock on the water; open daily 8am–midnight.

South of Çeşme: Alaçatı and Some Beaches

Nine kilometers southeast of Çeşme, **ALAÇATI** is a fine old Greek town, built on a slope overlooking a plain and backed by three windmills. Architecturally it's still very consistent—much like Çeşme must have been twenty years ago—and a wander through its old lanes makes for an excellent morning or afternoon. The old church has not only been turned into a mosque, but the former portico has become the heart of the meat and produce market—a strangely effective adaption. There are two or three **restaurants** between the windmills and the main square, plus one pansiyon, the *Sarı* (☎549/68315). The sea is 4km distant at **Çınar Plajı**, where a 400-meter beach is sandy enough, although lots of seaweed washes up. Facilities include one simple restaurant and the *Çark Pansiyon*.

In contrast, **OVACIK**, 5km due south of Çeşme on a road starting just east of the otogar, is dusty and half-inhabited, another ex-Greek village on a hill overlooking the straits to Hios. The pavement ends here and you'll need your own means to continue 4km down a dirt road—take a right fork at an old fountain—to the small beach at **ÇATAL AZMAK**. There's a single café there, and a better, more isolated beach five minutes' walk west, but neither can compare to the beaches at **ALTINKUM**, a series of sun-baked coves 9km southwest of Çeşme, beyond the fairly forgettable township of ÇİFTLİK, and easily accessible by dolmuş.

The **westernmost** of these is the smallest, taken up by the *Tursite* motel/camping/restaurant, whose fifty bungalows become sauna-like in summer and can only be occupied on a full-board basis at $22 per person. Between June and September the dolmuş continues a kilometer or so to the **central cove**, which is probably the best beach between Bozcaada and Dalyan, with multi-hued water

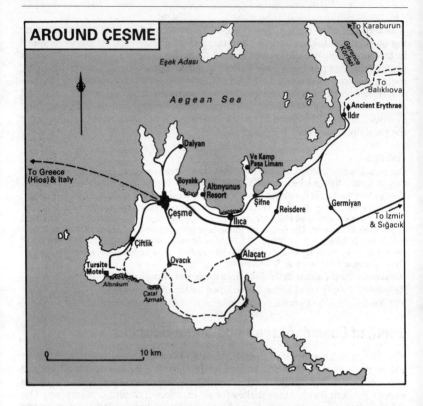

lapping hundreds of meters of sand—even dunes. You can rent kayaks and wind-surfers, and the *Ertürk* agency sometimes runs diving trips here. In high summer you have to walk pretty far east to lose the crowds—possibly over the point to the **easternmost cove**, equal in all respects to the central one. To date there are only a handful of tent/trailer/bungalow **campgrounds** scattered higgledy-piggledy in the dunes, plus a few adjoining, moderately expensive restaurants such as *Baba'nin Yeri* and *Turgut'in Yeri*. The prevailing mood is that of the last of the Hippy Daze and indeed the police have felt obliged to raid hash-smoking sessions in recent years.

Northeast of Çeşme: More Resorts ... and a Ruin

The approach to **DALYAN**, 4km north of Çeşme, is announced by a strange, four-story stone tower looming over the village's remaining Greek houses. On the whole it's a peculiar, straggly fishing settlement, built on the west shore of an almost completely landlocked harbor, which doubtless will become the area's main yacht anchorage as Çeşme becomes more crowded. There are few short-term places to stay, however, and even less in the way of sandy beach, and for most people a clutch of **fish restaurants**, appealingly set by the narrow channel to the open sea, will be the extent of Dalyan's interest.

If you can fight your way past the tangles of villas lining **BOYALIK** beach, 1500m east of town, you'll find the sand is actually okay, but painfully exposed (like most beaches on this side of the peninsula) to north winds, cold currents, and washed-up garbage. It's far better to bypass it in favor of **ILICA**, 4km due east of Çeşme, where the degree of development here—the name means "spa"— is justified by the excellent, kilometer-long beach. This can get grubby in season but is less encroached-upon east of the *Turban Ilıca* luxury hotel. If you want to **stay**, the place with the most character is definitely the *Rasim Palas* (☎549/ 31010), a century-old Greek establishment where Atatürk once took a cure. At $10 per person, with breakfast in the period-furnished dining hall, it's a bargain. Although the rooms are sparsely appointed and without attached baths, you can use the natural, 122°F thermal establishment in back. Alternatively, try the *Sahil Karabina* (☎549/31007) next door, if its restoration has been completed.

The peninsula's most luxurious **campground**, *Ve Kamp*, sprawls 3km past the east end of Ilıca beach at **PAŞA LİMANI**. At the base of the same promontory is the tiny, ugly spa of **ŞİFNE**, where you can retire for a hot mud bath should the urge seize you. But if you've come this far, you're probably on the way to Ildır and ancient Erythrae, 27km from Çeşme at the end of the paved road.

ILDIR itself is a pokey little village, its Greek houses underused and with no tourist facilities. There are, however, two fine **fish restaurants** right on the water 500m south of the village, and Ildır is built just to one side of the acropolis of **old Erythrae**, which was prominent during Hellenistic and Roman times. The city was renowned for two local cults: that of a sibyl, second in importance only to the one at Cumae in Italy, and that of Hercules, venerated in a temple containing a miraculous statue of the god. All traces of either have long since vanished, along with quite a bit of the rest of Erythrae; villagers of all subsequent eras have helped themselves to the masonry.

A well-defined path leads from the edge of Ildır up the conical hill behind the *bekçi*'s white "sentry box." If he's around he'll take you on a fifteeen-minute tour of the highlights, although the main trails lead obviously enough to most attractions. Only a few chunks of **wall** and a recent **Greek church** remain on the summit; the **theater**, disfigured by concrete stairs, spills down the north slope. North of a wheatfield/pear orchard, you'll be shown an old **tomb** and the waist-high ruins of several **houses**, including a large **Roman villa** with a fieldstone floor and storage cistern. Panoramas west over the islet-flecked gulf, and north to the mountains looming over the Gerence Körfezi, seem the main recompense for the trip up.

The Karaburun Peninsula

Until recently isolated and little-visited, the **Karaburun Peninsula**, which spears northeast of Çeşme, is the newest suburb of İzmir. While there is **bus service** as far as the town of Karaburun near the tip of the peninsula, there are few other facilities—such as pansiyons—for casual visitors; the east shore is very much villa-land, and not terrifically rewarding unless you've got your own vehicle.

The turnoff from the main highway is 12km west of URLA. The first place you'd be tempted to stop is **BALIKLIOVA**, a sheltered bay with some patches of beach and a restaurant or two. **MORDOĞAN**, about halfway up the east coast, is a proper town, but its beach is completely overshadowed by the renovated harbor and new development. The final stretch of asphalt to Karaburun is dramatic, with villages and orchards clinging to the crags of Akdağ, although **KARABURUN** itself is a letdown, with an exposed, rocky shore and port redeemed only by a few fish restaurants.

Beyond, a dirt road loops completely around the peninsula to Ildır, winding through four crumbling, half-inhabited villages that were Greek before 1922. Several pebbly **beaches** face Hios and Inousses, but they're difficult to get to without a motorcycle. The most accessible, and protected, are those in the embrace of the Gerence Körfezi, but by this point you're within 6km of Ildır, or 10km from Balıklıova via another dirt road spanning the narrow neck of the peninsula.

Sığacık and Teos

Thirty kilometers south of GÜZELBAHÇE, which is on the İzmir–Çeşme highway, **SIĞACIK** huddles inside its low-slung Genoese castle, with many of its houses built right into the perimeter. Otherwise the village is of middling architectural interest, and although you'll want to wander the maze of alleys inside, Sığacık is primarily geared up as a yacht harbor, with no decent beaches in sight. For a swim, you'll need to continue 1.5km over the hill to the west to **AKKUM**, a 150m-wide sandy cove (entry 50¢) that's gradually becoming oversubscribed.

Practical Details

Access by **bus** is complicated by loop routes and the frequent need to change vehicles. From İzmir, some, but not all, routes to ÜRKMEZ and GÜMÜLDÜR (see p.270) go through **SEFERIHISAR**, a large town 6km east of Sığacık. In Seferihisar you can catch another, red-and-white *Belediye* bus which covers the remaining distance to Akkum. A few of the Kuşadası–Seferihisar **dolmuşes** continue all the way to Sığacık, but again you'll usually have to change at Seferihisar.

If you want to **stay**, the pick of a limited bunch is the *Burg Pansiyon* (☎5448/ 1716), a new, traditional-style building right on the water; count on $6 per person with bath. Otherwise there's the *Liman* (☎5448/2019) and the *Huzur* (☎5448/ 1923), set well back from the water on the way out of town. At Akkum, there's a **campground**, the imaginatively named *Bungalow Kamping*, on the cape past the large *Neptun* windsurfing resort. As for **restaurants** around Sığacık's low-key port, the *Liman* is a bit fancier—and its food cleaner—than the *Burç*.

Teos

The same road serving Akkum continues another 4.5km to **ancient TEOS**, although if you're approaching on foot you can considerably short-cut the final series of zig-zags.

Teos was once one of the most important Ionian cities, renowned for its colossal temple of Dionysus, the deity not only of wine but also the arts and the generative forces of nature. Accordingly, in early Roman times Teos was chosen to host the Guild of Dionysus, the union of all artists, actors, and musicians throughout Asia Minor. They soon proved so insufferable that the Teans exiled them to backwaters down the coast. An earlier, more genial embodiment of the Dionysian ethic was the city's most famous son, the sixth-century poet **Anacreon**, who choked to death on a grape seed after a long life of wine, women, and song.

Appropriately, the second-century BC **temple of Dionysus** is the most interesting remain, and has been excavated—with three columns partly re-erected—in a bucolic setting of olive trees and grazing cattle. You can also pick your way 400m northeast to a hillside supporting the **Hellenistic theater**, although only the stage foundations are left of this, and it's debatable whether it's worth picking through wheat fields and buzzing flies for the view south over assorted islets to Samos. When you've finished sightseeing, a small refreshment stand operates in high season, at the road's end in front of the temple.

Inland: the Valley of the Küçük Menderes

If you have a spare day, the towns and villages of the **Küçük Menderes Valley**, inland a little way to the southeast of İzmir, are easily seen by public transportation, as connections with both İzmir or Selçuk are good. Visit **Birgi**, the most remote and unusual, first.

Birgi and Gölcük

A sleepy community of half-timbered houses tucked into a narrow valley at the foot of Boz Dağı, **BİRGİ** is an excellent example of what small-town Turkey was like before the wars and cement mania of this century. The main thing to see is the **Aydınoğlu Mehmet Bey Camii**, also called the Ulu Cami (follow the yellow signs), an engaging fourteenth-century construction on the site of an earlier church. Quite a bit of ancient Pyrgion, including a sculpted lion, is incorporated into the exterior walls; inside, it's an understated masterpiece, with the tiled *mihrab* and a single arch betraying Selçuk influence. Most impressive, though, are the carved hardwood *mimber* and shutters, some of them replacements for ones carted off to the Selimiye Camii in Edirne. The sloping, wooden roof is supported by a forest of Roman columns, the whole effect more like Spanish Andalucia than Turkey. The minaret features zigzag belts of glazed green tiles, like the Yeşil Cami in İznik, while the dome of the adjacent **Aydınoğlu clan türbe** is fashioned in concentric rings of alternating brick and the same faience.

Birgi's houses—ensembles of wood and either brick, stone, or wattle daub—run the gamut from the simple to the sumptuous. Many are crumbling, but the recently restored, eighteenth-century **Çakırağa Konağı** can be visited, and its neighbors are also well maintained. A couple of other mid- to late-Ottoman mosques perch next to or above the stream, along with some ruined baths and a *medrese*, but while they add to the atmosphere of the place none can compare to the Ulu Cami.

Down in the bazaar, there are two good **restaurants**, the *Kardeş,* offering some of the cheapest trout and best sheep yogurt in the province, and the *Çamlık*, specializing in *güveç*. If you're forced to stop over, you can get a **bed** at the inn in the Belediye building.

GÖLCÜK, 20km above Birgi, is just about the last thing you'd expect to see in the Aegean region: a six-acre **lake** in a wooded bowl tucked nearly halfway up 2129-meter Boz Dağ. The coolness and the greenery make it a favorite local summer retreat. You can come just for the day to **eat fish** at the *Rıhtım Restaurant*, on stilts over the water, or you might **stay** at the rather overpriced *Gölcük Motel* (☎545/43530)—$24 for a double with bath and breakfast; alternatively there's the *Şentürk Pansiyon*. A few summer villas are sprouting here and there, but the lakeshore itself is surprisingly undisturbed, probably because it's reedy, with no real beach and murky water.

Arrival via Ödemiş

To reach both Birgi and Gölcük you have to travel via **ÖDEMIŞ**, 9km west of Birgi. There's one **dolmuş** daily to Gölcük, but, amazingly, nothing scheduled to Birgi—although anything plying the mountain road to SALİHLİ passes within 3km of the lake and 1km of the village. Failing that, you'll have to arrange a taxi ($2 per car) to Birgi. The **train station** and **otogar/taxi stand** in Ödemiş are adjacent, and that's pretty much all you have to know about the place, which is an undistinguished market town famed mostly for the export of *salep* root—derived from a variety of orchid. Its only pretension to things cultural is the **Archaeological/Ethnographic Museum** (daily except Mon 8:30am–noon & 1–5pm; 50¢), 1.5km out on the route to Birgi. Predictable pottery vies with too many headless statues, and, in the ethnographic section, a clothed mannikin pathetically labeled "modern dress."

Tire

Thirty kilometers across the valley floor from Ödemiş, **TIRE**, clustered at the base of Güme Dağı, is an altogether different kettle of fish. Much fought-over by Byzantines and Selçuks, it eventually became one of the Aydınoğlu clan's first important strongholds, and the conservatism and religious fervour of the inhabitants is still apparent. If you've had an overdose of the touristed coast, Tire makes the perfect antidote—although being stared at may be part of the experience.

The **old quarter** with its rickety houses is uphill from the main traffic circle in the northwest of town; you might have a look at the map board outside the kitschy **museum** (same hours and price as in Ödemiş), but the best strategy is just to wander. First find the **Yeşil Imaret Zaviyesi**, also known as the Yahşı Bey Camii, built in 1442 by a general of Murat II as the core of a dervish monastery. The minaret sports the same type of faience as that of the Ulu Cami in Birgi; an unusual scallop-shell half-dome looms over the *mihrab*, as does stalactite vaulting over the front door. No other monument cries out for attention—your main impression will be of a staggering number of indifferently restored Ottoman mosques and older *türbes*, including two by the **otogar**—although Tire's atmosphere is considerably enlivened by a large gypsy presence from the surrounding villages. The gypsies are probably the source of the lace articles sold in the bazaar, and of the local horse-cart painting technique, imitated by wealthy city-dwellers on their kitchen cabinets.

THE HEART OF ANCIENT IONIA

Although old **Ionia**—including half of the league of thirteen ancient cities known as the Panionium—extended north of the Çeşme Peninsula, what the term usually evokes is the often startlingly beautiful territory around the deltas of the Küçük and Büyük Menderes rivers. Few other parts of Turkey can rival this region for the sheer concentration of ancient cities, which in their time were at the forefront of the sciences, philosophy, and the arts.

The Ionian coast was first colonized by Greek speakers in the twelfth century BC and their culture reached its zenith during the seventh and sixth centuries BC. Enormous advantages accrued to those who had chosen to settle here: an amenable climate, fertile, well-watered terrain, and a strategic location between the Aegean—with its many fine harbors—and inland Anatolia.

The Persian invasions, Alexander the Great's contrary campaigns, and the chaos following his death only temporarily hampered local development, and under the Romans and the Byzantines the region perked up again; urban life might have continued indefinitely in the old nuclei if it hadn't been for the inexorably receding coastline—thanks to the two silt-bearing rivers. By mid-Byzantine times most of the Ionian cities had been abandoned, and with the declaration of Christianity as the state religion, religious centers and oracles met a similar fate.

Contemporary inhabitants have found the silver lining to the cloud of the advancing deltas, cashing in on the rich soil brought down from the hills. Vast tracts of cotton, tobacco, sesame, and grain benefit from irrigation projects, while groves of pine, olive, and cypress, which need no such encouragement, adorn the hills and wilder reaches. And the sea, though more distant than in former times, still beckons if you get sick of ruins; indeed, tourism is threatening to outstrip agriculture as a moneyspinner.

This is nowhere more obvious than in **Kuşadası**, the unabashedly utilitarian base for excursions to the major antiquities. There are some beaches and minor sites, particularly to the north at **Pamucak** and **Claros**, to delay your progress inland, but the main show of the area is undoubtedly the ensemble of ruins farther south, spanning numerous eras: most notably at **Ephesus**; at **Priene**— perhaps the most dramatic site of all the Ionian cities; at **Milet**, farther south— probably the least impressive; and at **Didyma**, with its gargantuan temple. Oddly, considering the proximity of the river mouths, the **beaches** near these ruins unfortunately tend to be functional at best and always exposed; the immensely popular exception is **Altınkum**.

Kuşadası

KUŞADASI is Turkey's most bloated resort, a brashly mercenary coastal playground extending along several kilometers of coastline. In just three decades its population has swelled from about 6000 to almost 40,000, although how many of these are year-round inhabitants is debatable.

The town—whose name means "Bird Island"—is many people's introduction to the country: efficient ferry services link it with the Greek island of Samos, and the resort is an obligatory port of call for Aegean cruise ships, which disgorge vast numbers in summer, who delight the local souvenir merchants after a visit to the ruins of Ephesus just inland. Not to be outdone by Bodrum and Marmaris, and in a studied attempt to siphon off some business from the Greek islands opposite, the local authorities have also constructed a huge marina at the north end of town. It's the largest and best-equipped marina between Marmaris and Ayvalık, but it can't help but seem a strange venture, since the coast nearby is largely exposed leeward shore and unsuitable for sailing.

Not surprisingly, all this rapid development has affected local attitudes, to say the least. New arrivals are besieged by aggressive touts offering lodging, carpets, escort service for unaccompanied foreign women, and so forth. Stay here for the sake of the excellent connections to nearby attractions, and the adjacent beaches, rather than the town's minimal charm. Failing that, you might prefer Selçuk as a base (see p.271).

Kuşadası's origins are obscure; no proven trace has been found of any ancient settlement. The Venetians and Genoese rechristened the Byzantine anchorage of Ania as Scala Nuova when they established the harbor here to replace Ephesus's silted-up one, but only in the Ottoman era did the port acquire its current name derived from the small fortified islet—Güvercin Adası, or "Pigeon Island"—tethered to the mainland by a causeway. The little castle thereon (now home to various cafés and a disco) is actually the southernmost of several Aegean fortresses built by the Genoese during the fourteenth and fifteenth centuries.

> Kuşadası's **telepone code** is ☎636, changed recently from 6361. All local numbers should now be five digits, beginning with the orphaned "1."

Arrival and Information

Arriving by **ferry** from Samos, you'll exit customs directly onto Liman Caddesi, and walk right past the **tourist information office** (Nov–April Mon–Fri 8:30am–5:30pm; May–June & Sept–Oct daily 8am–6pm; July–Aug daily 7:30am–8pm; ☎11103), which has an excellent town map and exhaustive lists of accommodation.

The combined **dolmuş** and **long-distance bus station**, where you'll be left if coming from the south, is more than a kilometer out, past the end of Kahramanlar Caddesi on the ring road to Söke. If you're coming from the north, prevail upon the driver to leave you at the more convenient stop at the corner of İnönü Bulvarı and Atatürk Bulvarı. All northbound long-distance services, as well as dolmuşes toward Selçuk and Kadınlar Denizi, also pick up passengers here. **İzmir-bound services** are easiest to catch from the *El Birlik* office on İnönü Bulvarı, 200m south of the junction with Sağlık Caddesi.

Finding a Place to Stay

The tourist office lists nearly 300 **hotels and pansiyons** of all categories in Kuşadası, so you're spoiled for choice—except in high season. Prices within a given class are rigidly controlled, so it's more what you get for your money that's the issue. The best area for reasonably priced accommodation is just south of the core of the town, uphill from Barbaros Hayrettin Bulvarı, particularly the upper reaches of **Yıldırım, Arslanlar, and Kıbrıs caddesis**. For a relatively central location with a view of the sea, try **Bezirgan Sokak**, above Kıbrıs Caddesi, reached quickest via stairs from between the Shell station and the *Odin Restaurant* on the coast road.

Kıbrıs Caddesi

Özhan, Kıbrıs Cad 5 (☎12932). Small but immaculately kept pansiyon that's excellent value; terrace bar. $6.50 single, $13 for a double with bath, including breakfast.

Hotel Kalyon, Kıbrıs Cad 7 (☎13346). An A-class hotel, slightly quieter than the preceding. Singles $18, $25 for a double with bath and breakfast.

Otel Panorarma, Kıbrıs Cad 14 (☎14671). Some rooms live up to the name; popular with tour groups, but worth asking. Singles $18, doubles with bath $25 including breakfast.

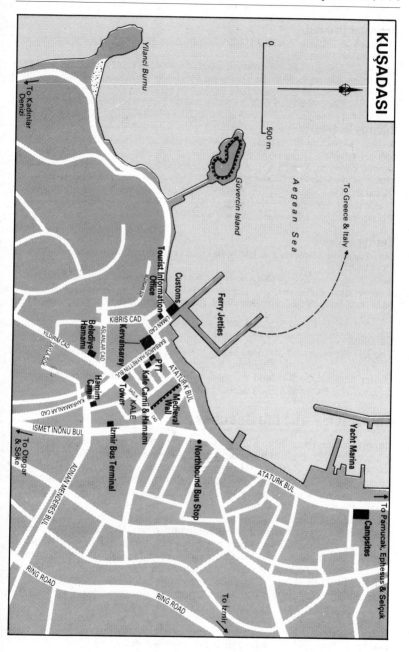

KUŞADASI

Aegean Sea

To Greece & Italy

To Kadınlar Denizi

Yılancı Burnu

Güvercin Island

0 — 500 m

Tourist Information Office

Customs

Ferry Jetties

İZCAN SOK

KIBRIS CAD

LİMAN CAD

Kervansaray

BARBAROS HAYRETTİN BUL

PTT

ATATÜRK BUL

Belediye Hamamı

ASLANLAR CAD

YILDIRIM CAD

ZAFER SOK

Kale Camii & Hamamı

SAĞLIK CAD

KALE

Medieval Wall

Hamam Camii

KAHRAMANLAR CAD

Tower

İSMET İNÖNÜ BUL

İzmir Bus Terminal

Northbound Bus Stop

ADNAN MENDERES BUL

ATATÜRK BUL

Yacht Marina

To Pamucak, Ephesus & Selçuk

Campsites

To Otogar & Söke

RING ROAD

RING ROAD

To İzmir

Arslanlar Caddesi

Su Pansiyon, Arslanlar Cad 13 (☎11453). An old budget standby. $5 single, $10 double with breakfast; baths down the hall.
Otel Rose, Arslanlar Caddesi, corner Kıbrıs Caddesi (☎11111). An older hotel where the views support the prices. $9 single, $15 double; baths down the hall.
Golden Bed, Aslanlar Caddesi, Uğurlu Çıkmazı 4 (☎18708). A new, very quiet outfit with good views; follow signs from Yıldırım Caddesi. $13 double with bath and breakfast.

Yıldırım Caddesi

Seçkin, Yıldırım Cad 35 (☎14735). Plain but acceptable for the price. $13 for a double with bath and breakfast.
Cennet Pansiyon, Yayla Sok 1, corner Yıldırım Caddesi. New and spotless, with small garden. $13 for a double with bath and breakfast.
Dülger, Yıldırım Caddesi (☎15769). Near the bazaar, hence noisy, but comfy. $19 a double.
Konak Hotel, Yıldırım Cad 55 (☎16318). A fairly new building in traditional style, popular with groups. $22 for a double with bath and breakfast.

Bezirgan Sokak

Dinç Pansiyon, Mercan Sokak, just off Bezirgan (☎14249). A 1970s-style place. $10 double with breakfast.
Şanlı, Bezirgan Sok 13 (☎13028). A new place, but with no view. $13 double with breakfast.
King (☎13128), **Enişte** (☎12171), **Hasgül** (☎13641). A cluster of places at the quiet end of Bezirgan Sokak, past the luxury *Hotel Stella*. The *Hasgül* is the newest, and most of its rooms overlook the bay.

Camping

The **BP Mocamp** out at Tusan beach is well-appointed but expensive, charging $8 for two persons and a tent; its bungalows are downright unreasonable. The **Önder** and **Yat**, both behind the marina, are marginally cheaper, well kept, and popular. The *Önder* also has a decent restaurant.

The Town—and the Beaches

Liman Caddesi runs 200m from the ferry port up to the **kervansaray**, restored as a luxury hotel before turning sharply left to become **Atatürk Bulvarı**, the main harbor esplanade. **Barbaros Hayrettin Bulvarı** is a pedestrian area beginning next to the *kervansaray* and homing in on a little stone tower, a remnant of the town's medieval walls, up the slope. To the left as you ascend is the **Kale district**, huddled inside the rest of the walls, with a mosque of the same name and some fine traditional houses that help lend the town what little appeal it has. **Sağlık Caddesi** is the perpendicular street behind the tower. Bearing left onto it takes you along the rear of Kale, where remnants of old wall, including a landscaped stretch leading down to the water, are visible; right leads up toward many of Kuşadası's more desirable pansiyons, set among the largest neighborhood of handsome old dwellings. Continuing straight ahead, the walkway (emblazoned with a sign "Old Bazaar") changes names to **Kahramanlar Caddesi**. The **marketplace** is just to the left as the street veers away from the **Hanım Camii**.

Kuşadası's most famous **beach**, the **Kadınlar Denizi** (Ladies' Beach) 2.5km southwest of town, is popular with both sexes and usually too crowded for its own good in season. Dolmuşes for this beach leave the distant terminal, and trundle south along the water past the fortified islet, alert for customers.

Güvercin Adası itself is mostly landscaped terraces within its fortifications, dotted with tea gardens and snack bars—good spots to wait for an evening ferry to Greece. One tower of the castle has been opened as a paid-admission "museum," which is something of a rip-off seeing as it's only a gallery for contemporary local crafts. Swimming off the islet is rocky; for the closest decent sand, head 500m farther south to the small beach north of Yılancı Burnu.

Tusan beach, 5km north of town, is probably more worthwhile, despite noise from the coast road; the *Tusan Motel* here rents all manner of water sports equipment. All Kuşadası–Selçuk minibuses pass by, as well as more frequent ones labeled "Şehir İçi" whose routes end near the hotel.

By far the best beach in the area is **Pamucak**, at the mouth of the Kücük Menderes River 15km north, slightly off the route to Selçuk. The only disadvantage of this exposed, four-kilometer-long stretch of sand is that it's not very pleasant when the wind is up. As yet it's little developed, with just a jail-like motel and campground at the point where the access road ends. But a couple of big luxury complexes are going up at the south end of the beach, so the writing's on the wall . . . There are regular dolmuşes from both Kuşadası and Selçuk in the high season.

Eating and Drinking

Value for money is not the order of the day as far as **food** goes in Kuşadası. A sensible impulse might be to quell rumbling stomachs until arrival in Selçuk or İzmir. Otherwise, the following are the least rapacious restaurants.

In the Kale area, two moderate eateries face each other diagonally across the intersection of Yeni and Bozkurt sokak: *Meşhur Dede Pide Salonu* and the *Kücük Ev*, both with outdoor seating. Even here, though, establish prices beforehand. Most of the more reasonable places are up on Kahramanlar Caddesi beyond the tower, where you should choose from *Ali-Bon* on the corner of Sağlık Caddesi, which serves good kebabs and desserts but no alcohol, and the *Ödemiş Çorba Salonu* and *Nazilli Döner Kebab* farther up. Just beyond these, left onto a narrow lane, the utterly budget-conscious can fill up on *saç kavurma* and sandwiches. For dessert, head for the *Ada Pastanesi*, just up from the tower on Yıldırım Caddesi.

If you want to splash out, half a dozen fish restaurants just north of the ferry landing fill the bill. *Kâzım Usta*'s mezes seem a bit fresher and more varied, but otherwise there's little to distinguish the establishments. You pick the fish you'd like, have it weighed, and you can work out the price—figure on $18 a kilo for mullet, $30 a kilo for bass, $32 for sole. If you want to eat by the water without blasting away your entire wallet, you might try the *Ada Restaurant-Plaj-Café*, on Güvercin Adası, where you can also dive off their private dock.

Nightlife

After-dark activity in Kuşadası focuses on a handful of **pubs** in the Kale district, a smattering of **discos**, and various pseudo-Turkish **singalongs** that are best avoided. For a quiet drink in congenial surroundings, try *Bebop*, Cephane Sokak 20 in the Kale; *Orient Bar*, around the corner, is similar. *Yaba*, next to the Kale Hamam, is an expensive but pleasant outdoor bar/café; *Thomas' Roof Bar*, atop the *Otel Panorama*, is as you'd imagine from the name. For more activity, the *Fame Club* and *Red Bar* at the bottom of Kıbrıs Caddesi have the loudest sound sytems in town; the *Cotton Club*, on Barbaros Hayrettin by the *Otel Pamuk Palas*, has the most elaborate videos. Finally, out on the islet, the *Disco Parisien* falls laughably short of its description, but the setting is fine and the dance floor is big.

Listings

Bookstore An exceptional one stocking English books, magazines, and papers, equal to any in İzmir, is *Kuydaş*, Kıbrıs Caddesi 10/A, at the end of the "Orient Bazaar" heading up from the kervansaray. Also good is *Art Bookstore*, Kahramanlar Cad 70, past the Hanım Camii.

Car rental Like İzmir, Kuşadası is one of the most expensive places in Turkey to rent a vehicle. Two local, non-chain agencies that may be willing to give an advantageous rate are *Daycar*, Atatürk Bul 26/B (☎11010), and *Toya Sun*, Atatürk Bul 60 (☎16849). Turkish chain outlets include *Airtour*, Atatürk Bul, Liman Apt, B Blok (☎12856); *MAC*, İnönü Caddesi, Ülgen Sok 3/2 (☎11993); *Metro*, Atatürk Caddesi, Yat Sitesi, C Blok no. 2 (☎11936); and *Nysa*, Atatürk Bul 60/4 (☎12427). Otherwise try the major chains: *Avis*, Atatürk Bul 26/B (☎11475); *Budget*, İnönü Bulvarı, Üyücü Apt 5 (☎14956); *Europcar/InterRent*, Sümbül Sokak 1, corner of Atatürk Bulvarı (☎13607); *Hertz*, Atatürk Bul 82 (☎17555).

Exchange Many booths at the corner of Liman Caddesi and Atatürk Bulvarı stay open until dark. Unwanted Greek drachmas can be changed into Turkish lira only at *İş Bankası* and *Denizcilik Bankası*—and even then at 25 percent below their actual value.

Ferries Numerous travel agencies, particularly on Liman Caddesi and Kıbrıs Caddesi, handle the Turkish morning boat to Samos—a good example is *Tekin Tur* (☎13870). Currently the sole agent for the afternoon Greek boat is *Diana*, on Kıbrıs Caddesi just above the shore road (☎14900). Ticket prices are, however, the steepest of all the Greek–Turkish ferry lines: one-way $25, day round-trip $30, open round-trip $45, plus $8 tax on the Turkish side, $6 when leaving Greece. The recently inaugurated once-weekly *Minoan Lines* ferry to Greece and Italy is handled exclusively by *Kervan*, Kıbrıs Cad 2/1 (☎11279).

Hamams *Kale Hamamı* behind the Kale Camii (very touristy); *Belediye Hamam* on Yıldırım Caddesi, just uphill from the *Otel Akdeniz* (slightly less so); both are expensive.

Hospital On Atatürk Bulvarı, near the park.

Market day Friday; stalls around Sağlık Caddesi.

PTT A few steps up Barbaros Hayrettin Bulvarı; open 24hr.

THY representatives *Osman Turizm*, Atatürk Bulvarı, Yat Limanı Karşısı (☎14205). They can sometimes make reservations and provide information, but can't actually issue tickets.

TML On the waterfront, next to the *Denizcilik Bankası* (☎11310).

North of Kuşadası: Beaches and Minor Sites

Particularly if you have your own vehicle, it's worth pressing **north** from Kuşadası toward some relatively unspoiled beaches and two archaeological sites. While neither site in itself would justify a detour, together with a chance for a swim they make a satisfying day-trip.

At the intersection where the roads from Kuşadası, Pamucak, and Selçuk meet, continue straight toward Seferihisar; the highway ahead has been newly surfaced and is no longer the narrow dirt road indicated on many maps. After 25km there's a poorly marked junction, with a sign pointing inland to Ahmetbeyli and Menderes. This is a recognized stop for buses; in your own vehicle bear seaward for the moment and park in front of the excellent beach. There is blessedly little development here to date—just a few reed shacks serving tea and kebabs, a rough campground, and, on the far side of the highway, one pansiyon.

Notion

The artificially terraced promontory bounding the beach to the east, on the opposite side of a sluggish creek, is in fact the site of ancient **NOTION**, an obscure settlement founded as the port of the ancient city of Colophon, 15km inland, as early as the eighth century BC. In time the seaside community attained greater importance than the inland one, and came to be called Neocolophon. This process was accelerated when Lysimachus punished old Colophon for its support of Antigonus in the post-Alexandrian civil wars by semi-depopulating it in 302 BC. Both settlements dwindled irreversibly as nearby Ephesus became prominent, and today Notion is ruinous in the extreme—the only recognizable monument, aside from remnants of wall visible above the stream bed, being the foundations and column fragments of a Corinthian **temple of Athina Polias** erected during the second century AD. For some it will be debatable whether the tricky scramble through the breaches in the walls is worth interrupting a tanning session, but the view from up top is superb.

Claros

The ancient oracle and temple of Apollo at **CLAROS**, 1.5km inland from Notion in a lushly vegetated valley, is more rewarding. Though overshadowed in popular imagination by the nearby oracle of Apollo at Didyma, and the more remote one at Delphi, Claros, particularly during the Roman period, equalled the other two in importance.

Though there was mention of a temple here as early as the seventh century BC, its role as a prophetic center did not begin until 300 years later, notably with its approval of the relocation of Smyrna. The sacred complex was a dependency of ancient Colophon, and was similarly punished by Lysimachus, but under Hadrian its fortunes revived spectacularly; the premises were handsomely reconstructed, and clients from throughout the Roman empire arrived to consult the oracle. Despite this, most of what is visible today—most poignantly seen at dusk—dates from early or even pre-Hellenistic times.

To get there, turn right at the yellow-and-black sign, 1km along the asphalt road up to Ahmetbeyli village, then right again once over the bridge, following more crude signs. Beyond this point the road would be impassably muddy to two-wheel-drive cars after a rain, but it's only 400m farther to the impromptu parking lot. Repeated expeditions since the turn of the century have been undertaken to keep the ruins clear of the silt deposited by the adjacent river and to pump the ruins free of the high water table. At present the site, like Notion, has unrestricted entrance, but restoration works are ongoing and the admission situation will certainly change when excavations are completed.

The complex was entered from the south via a **monumental gate,** of which a half-dozen sunken columns remain, flanked by a **semicircular bench** and a small **stoa**. Originally, a **sacred way**, now half-buried under dirt and vegetation, but still provided with statue niches and adorned with inscriptions from grateful supplicants, led some 200m to the **temple of Apollo**. This, awash in enormous toppled column drums, dates from the fourth or third century BC and—rare in Ionia—is of the Doric order. Pilgrims were admitted at night to the temple porch and their names were relayed by a priest to the prophet residing in a sunken sanctuary underneath the great hall. After the seer had drunk from a sacred spring within, his mutterings were then phrased in more artful verse by an assistant. You can still see the vaulting of the subterranean chamber's roof which supported the shrine's colossal (25-foot) statue of Apollo, of which only fragments remain. Immediately east of the temple are the remains of the sacrificial altar, while next door, on the northern side, rest the foundations of a smaller Ionic **temple of Artemis**, also with the ruins of an altar.

The Back Road to Teos and Çeşme

The coastal road **west from Claros** sweeps through magnificent scenery, with sandy coves at almost every turn, although the current minimal traffic will multiply in the near future when the new Çeşme–Kuşadası highway is completed. İzmir looms barely 70km away, and most foreigners visit the area as a day-trip, with the result that it can be difficult to find affordable short-term accommodation among the profusion of villas and motels let by the week or month, which dwarf all but the largest beaches and cater principally to Turks and sometimes Germans. Of the settlements, only **ÖZDERE** has a trace of village character, but the beach here is not that great.

The best beach is indisputably at **GÜMÜLDÜR**, 20km west of Notion and shown as Köprübaşı on some maps. A large grid of planned civil servants' vacation quarters, motels, pansiyons, and *meyhanes* has not yet managed to engulf 4km of fine sand opposite a small island. Beyond Gümüldür the road continues uneventfully to SEFERIHISAR, which is the turnoff point for Sığacık and Teos (see above) and the point to change dolmuşes if you're traveling from Kuşadası to Çeşme by public transportation. There are a few inviting beaches before **DOĞANBEY**, but most are ostentatiously tank-trapped and presumably mined against the absurdly remote possibility of an amphibious landing from Greek Samos opposite. The only other possible diversion on the way—if you can find it among the various military zones—is the islet studded with the fortifications of old **Myonessos**, tethered to the mainland by a half-submerged causeway. But you'll need your own vehicle to approach it, since dolmuşes use the faster inland bypass to Seferihisar.

South of Kuşadası

The imposing outline of **Samsun Dağ** dominates the skyline south of Kuşadası and may inspire notions of a visit. Tour operators and dolmuşes make the 28km to the national park established around the mountain—the **Dilek Yarımadaşi Milli Parkı**—easy enough to manage, and any hopes you may have of finding a wilderness will soon be dashed.

Dilek Yarımadaşi Milli Parkı

The **Dilek Yarımadaşi Milli Parkı** (daily 8am–6pm; 60¢ per person, $1 per car) was set aside in 1966 for, among other reasons, the protection of its thick forest and diverse fauna, which is said to include rare lynx, wolf, and even leopard. However, you are extremely unlikely to see any of the species in question, since over half of the 28,000-acre park is an off-limits military zone; if you try to walk out toward the tempting parts, you'll be turned back by armed sentries.

Arguably the park performs its function as a wildlife preserve far better than that of an all-purpose recreation area. Most of the decent trails or summits are in the army's turf, which is regrettable, since the terrain is undeniably beautiful, and certainly the most unspoiled along the Aegean. The unrestricted zone consists of an eight-kilometer-stretch of asphalt beyond the entrance and three mediocre, often windswept beaches along the road—Içmeler (hard sand, sycamore trees, snack bar), just beyond the gate; Aydınlık Köyü (pebbles), and Kavaklı Burun (pebbles, refreshment stand—and the first sentries). A lone jeep road saunters inland between Aydınlık and Kavaklı beaches, supposedly winding its way to the 1237-meter summit of Dilek Tepesi, but it is not clear whether access is legal.

There are no facilities for overnighting in the park; the closest pansiyons are in and around GÜZELÇAMLI, a village 1km outside the reserve boundaries. The beaches 300m below Güzelçamlı are much the same as those in the park—pebbly—but the village makes a good coastal fallback option should you find Kuşadası booked up.

Söke

Twenty-four kilometers southeast of Kuşadası, **SÖKE** holds nothing of interest to a casual traveler other than its excellent bus services. If you pass up offers in Kuşadası or Selçuk of organized tours to Priene, Miletus, and Didyma, you'll likely spend some time here making connections. This is pretty hassle-free: Kuşadası-based dolmuşes deposit you right next to other vehicles leaving for the villages adjacent to the three noted sites, as well as for Milas.

Selçuk and Around

Only two decades ago a laid-back farming town, **SELÇUK** has been catapulted into the limelight of major-league tourism by its proximity to the ruins of Ephesus—and a number of other attractions within the city limits or just outside. The flavor of tourism here, though, is markedly different from that at nearby Kuşadası, its inland location and ecclesiastical connections making it a haven for a disparate mix of collegiate backpackers and Bible-bashers from every corner of the globe.

Although evidence of settlement as early as 2000 BC has been found atop Ayasoluk Hill (Selçuk's logo), the town only really got going as a Byzantine enterprise during the fifth century AD, after the harbor of adjacent Ephesus had completely silted up. Like Birgi and Tire, the place was later a haunt of the Aydınoğlu clan, who yielded to the Ottomans in the early fifteenth century. Despite a venerable role in the events of the early church, including key events in the life of Paul, John, and (supposedly) Mary, local Christianity thereafter was restricted to the village of Kirkince (see below).

Arrival and Information

Probably the first thing you'll notice, approaching from any direction, is the huge **Hill of Ayasoluk**, ringed by a Byzantine/Selçuk **castle**. At the base of the hill and across the busy E24/550 highway, a new mock arch marks the start of a double-barrelled **pedestrian area** leading east to the **train station**. Along the way you'll pass the 24-hour **PTT** and most of the town's restaurants, while running parallel are sections of stork-nested **aqueduct**. Following the main highway a bit farther south brings you to the combined **bus/dolmuş terminal**; on the opposite side of the road, the **tourist information office** (summer daily 8:30am–6:30pm; winter Mon–Fri 9am–5:30pm; ☎5451/1945) has exhaustive lists of hotels.

Finding a Place to Stay

Overnighting in Selçuk, however, presents something of a puzzle. Prices are rigidly controlled, as in Kuşadası, but an entire category of lodging—comfortable pansiyons with attached baths—is missing, and little fills the gap between bare-bones facilities and the overpriced mid-range hotels. Most of the latter cluster around the two pedestrian streets, with the more desirable pansiyons scattered west of the base of Ayasoluk hill and behind the museum. The oldest concentration of pansiyons, tucked into the three "Spor" sokaks south of the tourist office, should be regarded only as overflow options.

Of the pedestrian-street choices, *Otel Aksoy*, Namık Kemal Caddesi 2 (☎5451/1040), is the most famous by virtue of its "stork-view" rooms. The aqueduct with its nests passes right underneath, and you pay $10 for a single with bath, $20 double, to watch. The *Hotel Subaşı*, Cengiz Topel Caddesi 10, across from the PTT (☎5451/1359), is priced the same, and clean if spartan.

Other pansiyons close to the tourist office and museum include *Barım*, Turgut Reis Sokak 34 (☎5451/1927), a restored, rambling old house; *Kırhan* (☎5451/2257), more dormitory-like at no. 7; and the *Star*, past the *Kırhan* at Ova Sokak 22 (☎5451/3858), the last of which has some rooms with attached baths for $4 a head. Another group of pansiyons worth considering is just a block west of the *Barım*, where the *Australian*, Miltner Sokak 17 (☎5451/1050), run by a family of returned Turkish-Australians, is justly proud of its new courtyard with view and the cousin's rug shop. The neighboring *İlayda* at no. 15 (☎5451/3278), and *Deniz* at Sefa Sok 9 (☎5451/1741), routinely accept the *Australian's* overflow; all charge the same per-person price of $4 for rooms with common bath.

If you want more peaceful surroundings, head toward the western edge of the town, on the way to the İsa Bey Camii, where you'll pass the *Suzan*, Kallinger Caddesi 46 (☎5451/3471), a small garden pansiyon in another restored house, and 200m before the mosque, the *Amazon*, Serin Sokak 8 (☎5451/3215), whose well-appointed rooms (though without attached baths) around a large, secluded garden and kitchen are often full with French tourists. Just over the road at No. 3 is Selçuk's best combination of calmness and affordable facilities, the *Hotel Akay* (☎5451/3009), charging $10 single, $20 double with bath.

If all of the preceding are full, one of the four pansiyons on İkinci Spor Sokak—the *Mengi* at no. 8, *Gezer* at no. 9, *Önder* at no. 7, or *Akbulut* at no. 4—should have space. These are characterless, 1960s concrete affairs but clean and serviceable enough, with good breakfasts and self-catering kitchens available, all in the $4–5 range. The closest **campground** is at the *Tusan Motel*, by the side of the road to Ephesus, but it's grim and noisy; better by far to head for *Blue Moon Camping* at Pamucak beach, 9km west, which is one of the best campgrounds on the Aegean, with wonderful sandy beaches, and where you can also camp rough.

The Town

The lodestone of settlement in every era, the **hill of Ayasoluk** (daily 8am–6:30pm; $2.50) is the first point you should head for. You enter the site through the "**Gate of Persecution**," so called by the Byzantines because of a relief of Achilles in combat that once adorned it, which was mistakenly thought to depict a martyrdom of Christians in the amphitheater of nearby Ephesus.

Traditionally St John the Evangelist—or "the Theologian," as the Greeks knew him—came to Ephesus in the middle of the first century. He died here around 100 AD and was buried on the Ayasoluk Hill, whose name is thought to be a corruption of "Ayios Theologos." The sixth-century Byzantine emperor Justinian decided to replace two earlier churches sheltering John's tomb with a basilica worthy of the saint's reputation, and until destruction by Tamerlane's Mongols in 1402 it was one of the largest Byzantine churches in existence. Today various colonnades and walls of the **basilica of St. John** have been re-erected, courtesy of a religious foundation in Lima, Ohio, which give just a hint of the building's magnificence in its prime. The tomb of the evangelist is marked by a slab at the former site of the altar; beside the nave is the baptistry, where people pose in the act of dunking for friends' cameras.

The **castle**, 200m past the church and included in the same admission ticket, is virtually empty inside but you're allowed to make a full circuit along the ramparts—worth it for the views, although if you're lazy these are available from the church.

Just behind the tourist office, the **archaeological museum** (daily 8:30am–6:30pm; $2.50) is permanently packed but well worth a visit, its galleries of finds from Ephesus arranged thematically rather than chronologically. The first, small-finds hall contains some of the most famous bronze and ceramic objects, including Eros riding a dolphin, effigies of the phallic gods Bes and Priapos (perennial postcard favorites), a humane bust of the comic dramatist Menander, and various excellent miniatures from the Roman houses at Ephesus. Beyond here—past relief work from fountains of Ephesus, a wall hoarding on oil lamp manufacture, and an ivory furniture frieze—there are a couple of courtyards containing sarcophagi and steles, leading into a hall devoted to tomb finds and mortuary practices. Just beyond this is the famous **Artemis room**, with two renditions of the goddess festooned with multiple testicles (not breasts, as is commonly believed) and tiny figurines of real and mythical beasts, honoring her role as mistress of animals. At Ephesus, Artemis adopted most of the attributes of the indigenous Anatolian mother-goddess Cybele, including a eunuch priesthood—the stone testicles possibly symbolize that supreme votive offering.

The last gallery houses friezes and busts from imperial cult temples—the strangest fragment being a giant, unlabeled forearm and head (the latter misshapen and infantile) that must have been part of a 17-foot statue.

Beyond the museum, 600m along the road toward Ephesus on the right, are the scanty remains of the **Artemision**, or sanctuary of Artemis. The archaic temple here replaced three predecessors dedicated to Cybele, and was itself burned down in 356 BC by Herostratus, a lunatic who (correctly) believed his name would be immortalized by the act. The massive Hellenistic replacement was considered to be one of the Seven Wonders of the ancient world, although this is hard to believe today: the Goths sacked it in 263 AD, and the Byzantines subsequently carted off most of the remaining masonry to Ayasoluk and Constantinople, leaving just a lone column standing amid battered foundations. Constant pumping is necessary to keep the area from flooding and in winter the ducks go for a swim here anyway.

Within sight of the Artemision stands the **İsa Bey Camii**, the most distinguished of various Selçuk monuments that give the town its name. It's a late fourteenth-century Aydınoğlu mosque, and represents, with its innovative courtyard and stalactite vaulting over the entrance, a transition between Selçuk and Ottoman styles. Although recently restored, its two minarets were snapped off long ago and the ablutions fountain in the court is missing. If you can get inside the main hall, you'll see a high, gabled roof supported by Roman columns and some fine tile work in the south dome.

Food, Drink, and Entertainment

The best and least expensive of numerous **restaurants** along pedestrianized Cengiz Topel Caddesi are *Gözde*, also known as "Köfteci Turan," near the *Otel Aksoy*, which has fish, mixed grill, and *meze*, and the *Efes* and *Bayraklı Pide Salonu*, next door to each other. The *Bayraklı* has plenty besides *pide* and all of the above serve alcohol—a concession to tourism—although prices are steeper than appearances would suggest. Sweet teeth can be satisfied at the *Sibel Pasta Salonu*, and after-hours **tippling** happens at *Stars Bar*, "the coolest place in town where everyone shines." If you'd rather not be the performer, wait until the second week of May, when the **Ephesus Festival** occurs nightly at the Ephesus amphitheater, or the middle of January, when **camel wrestling** between huge male camels in rut takes place at the edge of town.

Meryemana

Eight kilometers southwest of Selçuk, near the summit of Bülbül Dağ, stands **MERYEMANA**, a monument to piety and faith. Although most orthodox theologians maintain that the Virgin Mary died and was buried in Jerusalem, another school of thought holds that the mother of Jesus accompanied Saint John the Evangelist when he left Palestine in the middle of the first century on his way to Ephesus.

After the medieval turmoil around Ephesus, nobody from abroad was inclined to delve further into the matter until **Catherine Emmerich** (1774-1824), a German nun and seer who never left her country, recorded her visions of a small stone house, where, she claimed, the Virgin had lived her last years. In 1891 Lazarist priests from İzmir decided to follow her descriptions, and discovered a building matching them—one which, oddly enough, was already a focus of adoration by the Orthodox Greeks of nearby Kirkince, especially on the Feast of the Assumption (Aug 15). Things mushroomed predictably from there, spurred by a papal visit and imprimatur in 1967, and today the place is on the checklist of pilgrims from around the world.

The **site**, accessible only by foot or private car, is enclosed in a Selçuk municipal park (token admission) and subject to a generous dose of commercialism—although the tall trees and fountains are pleasant enough. The **house** itself, now a chapel, probably dates from early Byzantine times, but the foundations may indeed be first-century. Whatever you may believe about the historical likelihood of this being Mary's last home, it is a tribute to the tenacity of mother-goddess veneration in Anatolia.

Şirince

Kirkince itself is today called **ŞİRİNCE**, and is a well-preserved Greek hill village 7km above Selçuk, surrounded by lush orchards and vineyards and now inhabited by Muslim settlers from near Thessaloniki. They make assorted wines that pack quite a punch, and the place has not surprisingly become a target of tour groups (mostly French), but compared to Selçuk or Kuşadası it's low-key.

At the edge of Şirince as you approach stands a late nineteenth-century **church** with a pebble-mosaic floor, plaster relief work on the ceiling, and wooden vaulting—although much of it is crumbling away. Near the middle of the village there's a larger, half-collapsed stone **basilica** from 1839. But the main point of a visit is the idyllic scenery and the handsome domestic architecture.

Practical Details

Four daily **minibuses** serve Şirince, departing from next to Selçuk's station between 8:30am and 5pm. If you want to **stay** there are two pansiyons, the simple *Village of Maria* next to the wooden church, and the more elegant *Erdem* below the stone basilica. Most **restaurants** cluster around the main square; one is named after Dido Sotiriou, chronicler of the Greek Asia Minor experience and its post-1922 aftermath, in honor of a visit by her in 1990.

Ephesus (Efes)

With the exception of Pompeii in Italy, **EPHESUS** is the largest and best-preserved ancient city around the Mediterranean, and after the Sultanahmet district of İstanbul is the most visited tourist attraction in Turkey. Not surprisingly, the ruins are mobbed for much of the year, although with a little planning and initiative it's possible to tour the site in relative peace. Certainly it's a place you shouldn't miss. You'll need three or four partly shady hours to see Ephesus, and a water bottle—the acres of stone act as a grill in the heat of the day, and there are only two drinking fountains, close to the main entrance.

Some History

Situated by a fine harbor at the terminus of overland trade routes, and beneficiary of the lucrative **cults** of the Anatolian mother-goddess Cybele/Artemis, Ephesus led a charmed life from earliest times. Legends relate that Androclus, son of Kodrus king of Athens, had been advised by an oracle to settle at a place indicated by a fish and a wild boar. Androclus and his entourage arrived here to find natives roasting fish by the sea; embers from the fire set a bush ablaze, out of which charged a pig, and the city was on its way. The imported worship of Artemis melded easily with that of the indigenous cult of Cybele, and the Ephesus of 1000 BC was built on the north slope of Mount Pion (Panayır Dağı), very close to the temple of the goddess.

The Ephesians needed their commercial wealth, since they rarely displayed much common sense, military strength, or political acumen. When **Croesus** the Lydian king appeared in the sixth century, the locals could muster no other defense than to rope off the Artemis temple and retreat behind the barrier. Croesus, perhaps amused by this naivete, treated the city leniently, even contributing to the temple, but insisted on moving the population closer to the sea, north of Panayır Dağı. Still unfortified and ungarrisoned, Ephesus passed back and forth between Greek and Persian interests until the Hellenistic era.

Alexander the Great offered on his visit in 334 BC to fund the completion of the latest version of the Artemis shrine, but the city fathers tactfully demurred, saying that one deity should not support another, and dug deeper into their own pockets. Following Alexander's death his lieutenant **Lysimachus** moved the city to its present location—necessary because the sea had already receded considerably—and provided it with its first **walls**, traces of which are still visible on Panayır Dağı and Mount Koressos (Bülbül Dağı) to the south.

In subsequent confused centuries, Ephesus displayed flashes of its old fickleness, changing allegiance frequently, backing various revolts against Roman rule. Yet it never suffered for its lack of principle: during the Roman imperial period it was designated the **capital of Asia**, and ornamented with magnificent public buildings—the ones visible today—by a succession of emperors. As tolerant as it was shifty, Ephesus's quarter of a million population was swelled substantially at times by the right of sanctuary pertaining to the sacred precinct of Artemis, which at one point encompassed much of the city limits, affording shelter to large numbers of criminals. Of a somewhat less lurid cast was the more stable, mixed population of Jews, Romans, and Egyptian and Anatolian cultists.

Despite or perhaps because of this, **Christianity** took root early and quickly at Ephesus. Saint John the Evangelist arrived in the mid-first century, and Saint Paul spent the years 51 to 53 AD in the city, proselytizing foremost among the Jewish community. As usual, Paul managed to foment controversy even in this cosmopolitan environment, apparently being imprisoned for some time—in a tower near the west end of the walls—and later provoking the famous silversmiths' riot, described in Acts 19:23–20:1. Paul preached that the silver votive images of Artemis were not divine; the head of the silversmiths' guild, seeing his livelihood threatened, assembled his fellows in the amphitheater where they howled "Great is Artemis of the Ephesians!"—and for the apostle's blood. The authorities managed to calm the crowd, but Paul was obliged to depart for Macedonia.

Under the Byzantines, Ephesus was the venue of two of the **councils of the church**, including one in 431 AD at which the Nestorian heresy was anathematized. However, the general tenor of the Byzantine era was one of decline, owing to the abandoning of Artemis-worship following the establishment of state Christianity, Arab raids, and (worst of all) the final closing off of the harbor. The population began to siphon off to the nearby hill crowned by the tomb and church of St John, future nucleus of the town of Selçuk, and by the time the Selçuks themselves appeared the process was virtually complete.

The Site

Approaching the **site** (daily summer 8am–6:30pm; winter 8am–5:30pm; $5) from Kuşadası, get the dolmuş to drop you off at the *Tusan Motel* junction, from where it's another kilometer to the gate. From Selçuk it's a pleasant four-kilometer walk, the first three along a mulberry-shaded lane paralleling the busy highway. There is also a second entrance on the southern side of Ephesus on the way to Meryemana—which is perhaps more sensible in summer, since it enables you to walk downhill through the site.

Before reaching the ancient city, you can detour left off the route from Selçuk after 500m to visit the **Cave of the Seven Sleepers**, the focus of a Rip van Winkle-style legend. Seven young Ephesian Christians, refusing to sacrifice to the second-century emperor Decius, took refuge in this cave, were walled in by the imperial guard, and fell into a deep sleep. An earthquake shattered the wall and woke them; upon ambling down to town for food, they discovered that 200 years had passed and that Christianity was now the state religion. When the seven men died soon after—presumably from shock—they were re-interred in the grotto, and a commemorative church was built over their graves. The place is in fact an extensive network of catacombs, used for burial until late Byzantine times.

The first hint of the city, well before you reach the tacky parking lot with its souvenir stands and tour buses, are the rather eroded (and pilfered) remains of the **gymnasium of Vedius** and the **stadium**, funded by Nero. Once past the entry gate, take a sharp right along a path marked "Meryem Kilisesi," which leads to the **Church of St Mary**, an elongated architectural hodgepodge constructed between the second and fourth centuries AD. The building, originally a Roman warehouse, was the venue of the ecumenical council in 431 AD; its baptistry is in good condition.

Beyond the church, the **harbor baths** and **gymnasium** are prominent, but overgrown and difficult to explore. They are usually approached along the splendid **Arcadian Way**, so named after the fifth-century Byzantine emperor Arcadius who renovated it. Today tree- and bush-fringed, it's a forlorn echo of the era when it was lined with hundreds of shops and illuminated at night—although its neglect is refreshing when compared to the **ancient theater**, recently and brutally restored to provide more seating for summer festivals with material that would be more appropriate buttressing a California freeway overpass. If you bother to climb past the 20,000 sterile seats to the top, it's for the perspectives over the surrounding countryside.

The so-called **Marble Street** begins near the base of the theater and heads almost straight south; wheel-ruts in the pavement and the slightly elevated colonnade remnant to the right suggest that pedestrians and vehicles were kept neatly separated. Also to your right as you proceed is the main **agora**, currently closed for excavations, with an adjoining **temple of Serapis** where the city's many Egyptian merchants worshipped. About halfway along the Marble Street, metal stanchions protect alleged "signposting"—a footprint and a female head etched into the rock—for a **brothel**, located in the very center of the Roman city, at the junction with the Street of the Curetes (the city's other main street, named after a caste of priests at the Artemis shrine). Little remains above chest height at the house of pleasure, but there are some fine floor mosaics denoting the four seasons, and (appropriately enough) one of the priapic figurines in the Selçuk museum was found here.

Directly across the intersection of the two major streets looms the **Library of Celsus**, originally erected by the consul Gaius Julius Aquila between 110 and 135 AD as a memorial to his father Celsus Polemaeanus, still entombed under the west wall of the structure. The elegant, two-story facade was fitted with niches for statues of the four intellectual virtues, today filled with plaster copies (the originals are in Vienna). Inside, 12,000 scrolls were stored in galleries designed to prevent damage from moisture—a precaution which didn't prevent the Goths burning them all when they sacked the area in 262 AD. The library has been restored by an Austrian archaeological team and a commercial contractor, *Kallinger*, who honk

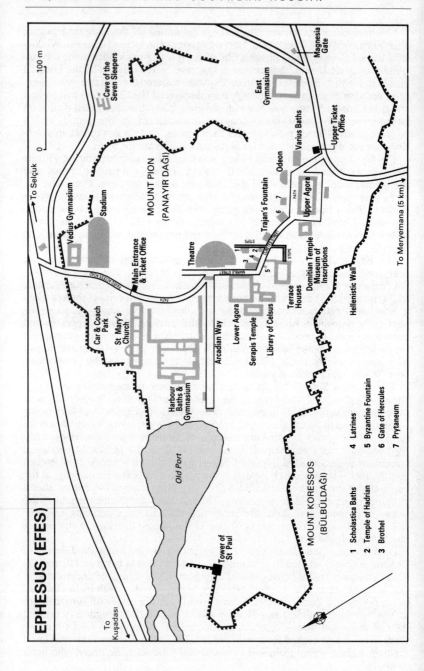

EPHESUS (EFES)

To Kuşadası

To Selçuk

To Meryemana (5 km)

Cave of the Seven Sleepers

MOUNT PION (PANAYIR DAĞI)

Vedius Gymnasium

Stadium

Main Entrance & Ticket Office

Theatre

Car & Coach Park

St Mary's Church

Harbour Baths & Gymnasium

Old Port

Arcadian Way

Lower Agora

Serapis Temple

Library of Celsus

Terrace Houses

Domitian Temple Museum of Inscriptions

Hellenistic Wall

Upper Agora

Odeon

Varius Baths

Trajan's Fountain

East Gymnasium

Magnesia Gate

Upper Ticket Office

MARBLE STREET

STEPS

MOUNT KORESSOS (BÜLBÜLDAĞI)

Tower of St Paul

1 Scholastica Baths
2 Temple of Hadrian
3 Brothel
4 Latrines
5 Byzantine Fountain
6 Gate of Hercules
7 Prytaneum

0   100 m

their horns as if the ruins were a construction site and have erected self-promoting billboards and German-only labelling. Abutting the library, and allowing (eventual) entry to the *agora*, is the triple **gate of Mazaeus and Mithridates**, restored since 1980 with a bit more taste. (Mithridates was a wealthy freedman, not to be confused with the notorious Pontic nemesis of the Roman republic).

Just uphill from the Roman city's main intersection, a **Byzantine fountain**— today pressed into service as a refreshment stand—looks across the Street of the Curetes to the **public latrines**, a favorite of visitors owing to the graphic obviousness of their function. The ancient restrooms were conveniently connected to the brothel just below. Continuing along the same side of the street, you'll come to the so-called **temple of Hadrian**, donated in 118 AD by a wealthy citizen in honor of Hadrian, Artemis, and the city in general. As in the case of the library facade, most of the relief works here are plaster copies of the originals, which reside in the Selçuk musuem. Two small heads on the arches spanning the four columns out front are of Tyche and possibly Medusa, respectively installed for luck and to ward off evil influences.

Behind and above the temple sprawl the **baths of Scholastica**, so named after a fifth-century Byzantine lady whose headless statue adorns the entrance and who restored the complex, which was actually 400 years older. There was direct access from here to the latrines and from there the brothel, although it seems from graffiti that the baths, too, were at one stage used as a bawdy house. Clay drainage pipes are still visibly lodged in the floor, as they are at many points in Ephesus.

On the far side of Curetes Street from the Hadrian shrine lies a huge pattern **mosaic**, which once fronted a series of shops. Nearby a sign points up a stepped street to the **terrace houses**, protected by an incongruous brick-and-cement structure which many initially mistake for a motel. The houses (daily 8am–5pm; separate $1 admission) give a good idea of everyday life during imperial and early Byzantine times, which appears to have been on par with that at Pompeii and Herculaneum. The first house is built around a fountained atrium paved in black-and-white mosaics; a room leading off this to the east has walls covered in murals, including one of Hercules battling the river-sprite Achelous. In the second dwelling open to view, the central court features a fine mosaic of a triton cavorting with a nereid; just south of this, in an overhead vault, Dionysus and Ariadne are depicted in an excellent, 3-D-effect glass mosaic, which, while damaged, is still recognizable.

Returning to Curetes, you pass the **fountain of Trajan**, whose ornamentation has been removed to the museum, and the street splits just above the **Hydreion** (another fountain) and the **gate of Hercules**, where a remaining column relief depicts the hero wrapped in the skin of the Nemean lion. Bearing right at the junction takes you to the **temple of Domitian**, a paranoid megalomaniac even by imperial Roman criteria; only the lower floor of the complex is left intact, housing a marginally interesting **Museum of Inscriptions** (daily 8am–5pm; free).

The main thoroughfare separates the large, overgrown **upper agora**, fringed by fountain skeletons on the side facing the Domitian foundations and by a **colonnade** to the north, opposite the civic heart of the Roman community—the **prytaneum**. This housed the inextinguishable sacred flame of Ephesus, and, despite the fact that Hestia or Vesta was the presiding goddess, two of the Artemis statues in the Selçuk museum; it also served as the reception area for official guests. The adjacent **odeon**, once the local parliament, has been as insensitively restored as the main theater, although the 27 rows of seats are presumably are the original number. The **baths of Varius** mark the end of the paved Roman street system, and also the location of the upper site entrance. Beyond the gate huddles the massive **east gymnasium**, next to which the **Magnesia gate** signals the true edge of the old city. The asphalt road here leads 5km south to Meryemana, but again you'd have to walk, hitch, or hope for a passing taxi.

Priene

Perched on a series of piney terraces graded into the southern flank of Samsun Dağ, 35km south of Kuşadası, compact but exquisite **PRIENE** enjoys a location that bears comparison with that of Delphi in Greece. The original settlement, legendarily founded by refugee Athenians and dating from perhaps the eleventh century BC, was elsewhere in the Meander basin; the townspeople, following the receding shoreline, refounded the city at the present site during the fourth century BC, just in time for Alexander to stop in and defray the cost of the principal temple of Athena.

The Pan-Ionion Sanctuary—cult center of the league of Ionian cities—had always lain in Priene's territory, just the other side of Samsun Dağ; as a result its priest was usually chosen from Priene, whose secular officials also presided over the regular meetings of the confederacy. Under Roman—and later Byzantine—rule, however, the city enjoyed little patronage from the emperors, with the result that Priene represents the best-preserved Hellenistic townscape in Ionia, without any of the usual later additions.

Arrival is by frequent dolmuş from Söke to the village of **GÜLLÜBAHÇE**, 400m east of the ruins. It is tempting to save Priene for late afternoon, when it is most beautiful, but **overnighting** can be a problem. Currently there is only one small and relatively expensive pansiyon-campground in the village—*Pension Priene* (☎6357/1249); it's prudent to reserve space first thing, or in advance. There are also just a pair of restaurants, including the *Şelale*, or "Waterfall," which cascades from the mountain-spring-fed aqueduct.

The Site

Priene (daily 8:30am–7pm; $1) was laid out by Hippodamus, an architect from nearby Miletus, who favored a grid pattern consisting of rectangular *insulae* (blocks) measuring roughly 42m by 35m. Within each rectangle stood four private dwellings; a public building had its own *insula*, sometimes two.

Once through a gap in the ancient walls, you climb a wide street, heading west, which before long is crossed by myriad smaller lanes, stepped in places. The first easily distinguished civic monument, just to the left of the main street, is the square **bouleuterion** or council house, the most intact in Turkey, consisting of seats on three sides enclosing the speakers' area, together with a sacrificial altar. Just east of the bouleuterion are the scantier remains of the **prytaneion**, or town administration offices, with traces of a dining area for the highest municipal officials. On the next terrace down lie a **Zeus temple**, the **agora**, and the sacred **stoa**, once graced by outer and inner series of Doric and Ionic columns, although nothing is left above knee-level of any of these. The commanding views, however, suggest that this was the heart of public life in the city.

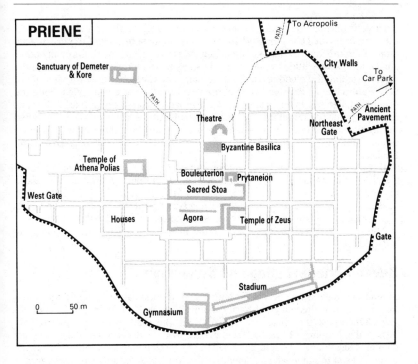

PRIENE

To Acropolis

Sanctuary of Demeter & Kore

City Walls

To Car Park

PATH

Ancient Pavement

Theatre

Northeast Gate

Byzantine Basilica

Temple of Athena Polias

Bouleuterion

Prytaneion

Sacred Stoa

West Gate

Houses

Agora

Temple of Zeus

Gate

Stadium

0 50 m

Gymnasium

Clearly visible below, reached by way of a stairway from the agora, are the **gymnasium** and **stadium**—relatively neglected parts of the site due to the shadeless climb back up that a visit entails. Some of the gymnasium walls are decorated with still-visible graffiti; nearby are **bathing basins**, complete with gutters and lion-head spouts, for use after athletics. On the west side of the stadium there are a few sets of **starting blocks** for foot races; spectators watched from the north side of the 190-by-20m area, where some seats are still discernible.

Returning to the central street and continuing down a gentle slope, you are soon in the midst of the densest surviving **residential district** in Priene. Though many of the houses, whose thick walls stand up to five feet tall, are choked by vegetation, others permit entry. The usual floor plan was a narrow passage leading to a large central court, surrounded by various rooms; the discovery of occasional stairways demonstrated that some dwellings had two stories. Priene's **west gate** marks the end of both the main street and the rows of houses.

The city's most conspicuous monument, the **temple of Athina Polias**, stands two terraces above the main residential street. This took more than two centuries to complete, and in its time was considered the epitome of Ionic perfection; a manual written by the designer Pytheos was still considered standard reading in Roman times. Five of the original thirty Ionic columns were re-erected in the 1960s, and at certain times of year they catch the sunset and glow in the dusk long after the rest of the archaeological zone is plunged in darkness.

Directly north of the Athina temple, reached by a faint trail through the pines, is the **sanctuary of Demeter and Kore**, on the highest terrace of the urban grid. Other than the foundations—a good century or two older than those of any other shrine in Priene—little is visible today besides a few Doric column stumps and a pit for catching the blood of sacificial animals. The **theater**, a little way southeast, is by contrast in an excellent state of preservation, the seats and layout being the original Hellenistic ones; prominent are five larger-than-average marble thrones for the municipal dignitaries. The stage buildings were extensively modified during the second century AD—virtually the only Roman tampering with Priene's public buildings; just behind them are the waist-high remains of a **Byzantine basilica**.

If you're keen on scrambling and the sun isn't too hot, a path beginning above the theater leads in stages to the **acropolis**, on the bluff known as Teloneia in ancient times. A good head for heights is useful because the path dwindles, after passing an aqueduct and some cisterns, to a series of paint-blazed steps and trails zigzagging steeply up the cliff. Allow an extra hour and a half for the round trip.

The mandatory exit from the site is the former **main (northeast) gate**, still mostly intact.

Beyond Priene: Eating and Swimming

Should you have a car, do not be tempted by the indication on some maps of a long beach near the village of Karine, some 17km west of Priene. In fact neither exist. Once past the village of DOĞANBEY, the road deteriorates alarmingly before dead-ending at a small rocky cove with a derelict Ottoman customs station. This, you will be told by either the fishermen camped in the ruins or the gendarmes at the modern post ahead, is **Karine**, or rather ancient Carina, whose remains are overgrown somewhere in the bushes. No further progress is permitted, should it cross your mind to storm the Dilek Yarımadaşı National Park from behind, although you're welcome to pitch a tent.

The main reason for making the bumpy journey out here is to **eat fish** at the *Karina Restaurant*, some 3km after Döganbey, which serves the best and cheapest *kefal* (gray mullet) in Turkey, compliments of the fishermen's cooperative at work in the giant lagoon to the south. The restaurant also runs a *pansiyon* nearby, but it's expensive for what you get, and the "beach"—bits of sandbar and reef at the edge of the lagoon—is all but inaccessible.

Miletus (Milet)

The position of **MILETUS**, on an eminently defendable promontory jutting out onto the ancient Gulf of Latmos, once outshone that of Priene. Its modern setting, marooned in the seasonal marshes of the Büyük Menderes, is by contrast one of the dreariest in Turkey, with little left to bear witness of the town's long and colorful past. Only the theater, visible from some distance away, hints at former glories.

Up close, the site of Miletus is an often confusing juxtaposition of relics from dissimilar eras, widely scattered and disguised by weeds or mud depending on the season. Ironically, even the grid street plan championed by native son Hippodamus has largely failed to survive, swept away by the Romans and geological processes. If you're pushed for time, this is the obvious Ionian site to miss.

Getting there by public transportation is complicated. There is no direct link with Priene, and even using Söke-based dolmuşes to the modern village of Balat (relocated after a 1958 earthquake), you still face a two-kilometer walk in. Most services head on to Didyma/Altınkum via AKKÖY, 6km distant, where there are simple **eateries** (but no accommodation). There are some expensive snack bars aimed at tour-bus clientele near the site entrance.

Some History

Miletus is at least as old as Ephesus, and far older than Priene; German archaeologists working locally since the 1890s have uncovered remnants of a Creto-Mycenean settlement from the sixteenth century BC. Ionian invaders appeared during the eleventh century, and by the seventh century BC Miletus was in the first flush of a heyday which was to last more than 200 years, when the city repulsed the advances of the Lydians and founded colonies all over Anatolia. It was also a highly evolved cultural center, with a roll call of scholars and thinkers that included the mathematician Thales and the courtesan-orator Aspasia, friend of Socrates and Pericles.

While not strong enough to completely avoid Persian domination, Miletus was able to secure favorable terms as an equal and even took the opportunity to appropriate the nearby oracle of Didyma. But with Athenian instigation, the city was unwisely persuaded to take command of the abortive Ionian revolt against the Persians between 500 and 494 BC. After the rebels' final defeat in the naval battle at Lade Island, Darius punished the ringleader severely with wholesale massacre and pillage.

Within fifty years Miletus was rebuilt some distance northeast of the original site, but it was never again to be as great—or as independent. Alexander saw fit to "liberate" the city from a new, brief occupation by Persians and their allies, whose huge fleet sat motionless offshore, perhaps in awe of the Macedonian's mystique. Later it was bequeathed to the Romans, under whose rule it enjoyed a brief renaissance—most of what you see today is a legacy of various emperors' largesse. The Byzantine town stubbornly clung to life, producing Isidorus, architect of İstanbul's Aya Sofya. Already in the ninth century, though it was dwindling, and by the time the Menteşe emirs, then the Ottomans, took control there was little left to prize.

The Site

The most obvious attraction at Miletus (daily 8:30am–7:30pm; $1), right behind the ticket booth, is the **theater**, whose Hellenistic base was modified and enlarged during the second century AD to a capacity of 15,000. The center of the front row sports two pillars which once supported the emperor's canopy; farther up, the vaulted exit passageways are enormous and virtually intact.

An eighth-century **Byzantine castle** and some contemporaneous **ramparts** surmount the theater, giving a marvelous 360° view over the floodplain, and the chance to get your bearings over the rest of the site. Visible on the plain a kilometer or so to the west is a scrubby hill, formerly the **island of Lade**.

Descending from the walls, you pass a Hellenistic **tomb** featuring a circular burial chamber in its middle. Further east, a round base is all that remains of a **naval monument**, commemorating an unknown victory of the first century BC, which once overlooked the most impressive of Miletus's four harbors, the Lion

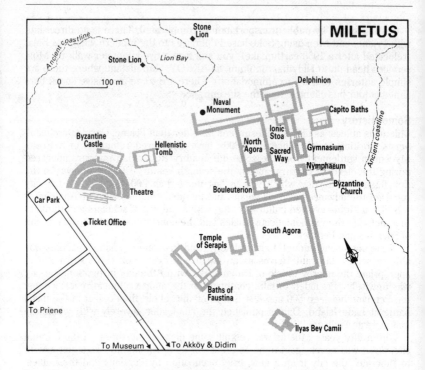

Bay, so called because of two **stone lions** that guarded the entrance—now embedded up to their haunches in the marsh.

The end of the tongue-shaped bay was lined by a colonnade which extended east to the sixth-century **Delphinion**, dedicated to Apollo Delphinius, patron of sailors, ships, and ports. Not surprisingly for such a maritime community, it was the most important religious establishment in town; today you can still see the foundations of altars or semicircular benches and the enclosing colonnade. Immediately south squat some incongruous **Selçuk baths**.

Both of these stand at the north end of a handsomely paved **processional way** which in its time linked Miletus with Didyma. On the same side of the sidewalk as you walk south stands a first-century AD Ionic **stoa**, conspicuous owing to its rather clinical partial restoration, and partly shielding the enormous **Capito baths** and a **gymnasium** of the same era. The most satisfying monument east of the sacred way is the **nymphaeum**, the largest public fountain of Miletus, once almost baroquely ornate but now standing to barely half its original height. Just south of here are the ruins of a sixth-century Byzantine **church**.

Opposite the sidewalk, beginning from the harbor, are the jumbled and overgrown remains of the so-called **north agora**; marginally more interesting is the second-century BC **bouleuterion**, which faces the nymphaeum. The processional way skirts the **south agora**, unexcavated except for a monumental gateway which was carted off to Berlin in 1908. On the west side of the agora are the recessed premises of a third-century AD **temple of Serapis**; you can make out a bas-relief representation of the deity Serapis Helios on a fallen pediment.

The Roman **baths of Faustina** (Marcus Aurelius's wife), west of here at the foot of the theater hill, are distinctive for their position at an angle to what remains of the urban grid—and for their good state of repair. The most engaging sight inside is two spouts which once fed the cold pool—one in the form of a now-decapitated statue of local river deity Meander, the other an intact lion-head.

About 200m south of the baths and marked by dense vegetation, the early fifteenth-century **İlyas Bey Camii** is arguably more interesting than anything at the ancient site except the theater. The mosque lost its minaret in the 1958 earthquake, but otherwise fared well, retaining its fine carved *mihrab*, stalactite vaulting, and Arabic inscriptions. There was once a *medrese* and *imaret* adjacent, but only a peaceful, neglected courtyard with some adjoining cells and headstones has survived. It's a serene and contemplative corner, more frequented by storks than humans.

Exactly 1km south of the ticket stall is the site **museum** (daily 8:30am–12:30pm & 1:30–7:30pm; $1), although unfortunately most of the important Miletian moveables have long since found their way to İstanbul and Berlin. The two-room collection, spanning all periods, makes do with the best of the leftovers.

Didyma (Didim)

By the time you reach **DIDYMA**, site fatigue might be beginning to set in. However, the oracular sanctuary of Apollo here, though half-ruined and besieged through the middle of the day by swarms of tour groups, rarely fails to impress. The best time to visit—and the hour when, having worked their way through either Priene or Milet (or both), many people tend to show up—is late afternoon or early evening, when the stonework glows in the sunset.

Access is probably the simplest of all the remote Ionian sites: frequent dolmuşes and the occasional full-size bus cover the route between Söke and Altınkum beach via Didim, the modern name for Didyma. The village itself is something of a tourist trap, crammed with souvenir shops and tour buses. All three of the **restaurants** across from the archaeological zone are expensive and poor in quality; for a good feed at reasonable prices you'll have to walk a kilometer south to YENİHİSAR, a much larger, less touristed village. If **staying the night** appeals, the choice is between the *Pension Oracle*, directly overlooking the ruins, and the more remote *Medusa Head*.

Some History

An oracle and shrine of some sort apparently existed at Didyma long before the arrival of the Ionian settlers in the eleventh century BC—the name itself is an ancient Anatolian word—but the imported cult of Apollo quickly appropriated whatever previous oracle, based around a sacred well and laurel tree, had worked here. Didyma remained a sacred zone, under the jurisdiction of a clan of priests originally from Delphi, and was never a town as such, although it eventually became a dependency of nearby Miletus. Every four years the sanctuary also hosted the *Didymeia*, a festival of music and drama as well as athletics.

The archaic shrine, begun during the eighth century BC, was finished within 200 years—although similar in design to the current structure, it was half the size. After their defeat of the Ionian revolt in 494 BC the Persians destroyed the first temple and plundered its treasures, including the cult statue of Apollo. The oracle sputtered along in reduced circumstances until Alexander appeared on the scene; the cult statue was retrieved from Persia and a new temple (the one existing today) was commissioned. Despite continuing subsidy from the Romans, work on this continued at a snail's pace for more than five centuries and the building was never actually completed—not entirely surprising when you consider the formidable engineering problems presented and the cost of the material; the columns alone, for example, are reckoned to have cost today's equivalent of $400 million. In the end Christianity silenced the oracle, and when the edict of Theodosius in 385 AD proscribed all pagan practices, construction ceased for good. Inhabitants of the Greek village of Yeronda (the Ottoman name for the hamlet overlooking the site) helped themselves liberally to the ancient masonry in their midst, and blocks can still be seen incorporated into some of the older village houses.

At its zenith Didyma was approached not only from Miletus but also from Panormos, a cove 6km west, via a sacred way whose final stretches were lined with statuary. Neither pavement nor statues are visible today, the latter having been abducted to the British Museum in 1858.

The Site

Entry to the **site** (daily 8:30am–7pm; $1) is now more prosaic, by way of a gate at the north end of the enclosure. At the bottom of the stairs, look out for the **Medusa head**, which fell from a Roman-era architrave and is now the unofficial logo of the place, repeated ad nauseam on posters and cards all over Turkey.

Pilgrims would first visit a **well** just below the resting place of the Medusa head to purify themselves, then approach a still-prominent **circular altar** and offer a sacrifice before proceeding to the **shrine** itself. Even in ruins this is still intimidatingly large, the surviving column stumps alone much taller than a person, and in its nearly complete state it must have inspired a proper attitude of reverence. The effect was accentuated by its positioning on a steep, stepped base and enclosure in a virtual forest of 108 Ionic **columns**—though only three of these stand to their full original height. The remaining twelve supported the roof of the entry porch, reached by a steep flight of steps, where supplicants would deliver their queries to the priest of Apollo, who would reappear after a suitable interval on a terrace some six feet higher to deliver the prophetess's oracular pronouncement. Questions ranged from the highly personal to matters of state; prophecies were stored for posterity on the premises. The cult statue of Apollo, his sacred laurel, and the sacred well were formerly enclosed in a miniature shrine of which only traces remain—although the **well** itself is still obvious, roped off to prevent accidents. As at Delphi in Greece, prophecies were formulated by a priestess, who either (accounts disagree) drank from, bathed in, or inhaled potent vapors from the waters. Her subsequent ravings were rephrased more delicately to those waiting out front.

Petitioners did not normally enter the inner sanctum, except to watch the goings-on of the Didymeia from a monumental stairway providing access to the terrace from the interior; the steps still bear spectators' graffiti, although the terrace is currently off-limits—you enter the sanctuary proper by means of twin tunnels to either side. The innermost court was never roofed, but the height of the walls once exceeded 20m; today they're half that.

North of Didyma: Some Beaches

As you drive in to Didim from Akköy, the sea—with views across to the Greek island of Agathonissi—is never far away, and the road soon parallels the water. Unfortunately the shore is scruffy and windswept, with a narrow strip of sand; at first there are just a few primitive campgrounds and the odd pansiyon just south of a new fishing port. A state-run picnic- and campground at **Tavşanburnu**, which is sandier and protected by an islet, is more appealing, and there are shops for supplies nearby. Compared to Altınkum the area is low-key, but the site heralds the start of almost continuous development south to Didyma.

South of Didyma: Altınkum

Five kilometers south of Didyma, the information board at the end of the road in **ALTINKUM** says it all—forty pansiyons and thirty hotels, arrayed behind a single kilometer of beach split by a point. Not exactly low-density, but at least the place lives up to its name (Golden Sand), a gently sloping beach with no surf, ideal for children and in total contrast to the exposed coast on the other side of Didyma.

Altınkum is essentially the shore annex of Yenihisar, 1km from Didyma, where most amenities (such as proper stores) are. However, to the right of the T-junction marked by the hotel-listings sign there's usually a mobile bank-van parked, and a permanent **bank** and **PTT** farther along. **Eating out**, you'll pay typical resort prices, though the *Duman*, just past the sporadically staffed tourist information booth, seems slightly cheaper.

The more inexpensive **pansiyons** can be found on the upper, parallel street behind the far western jetty; the *Murat, Nevim, Ömür, Kayhan*, and *Nova* are old-style establishments patronized by Turkish families, but you'd probably have to strike it lucky to find an unreserved room. In the same area are the *Samlik* and the *Gürük*, on a perpendicular lane leading back down toward the water, and a **campground**, the *Aytepe*. Accommodation to the east of the hotel-listings sign is considerably more exclusive.

ANCIENT CARIA: THE COASTAL REGIONS

In antiquity **Caria** was an isolated, mysterious region, inhabited by purportedly barbarous people indigenous to the area (a rarity in Anatolia) who spoke a language distantly related to Greek. Following the advent of Alexander, and the Hecatomnid dynasty at Halicarnassos, Hellenization proceeded apace and the differences between the Carians and their neighbors diminished. After the Byzantine period, and the fifteenth-century absorption of the local Menteşe emirate by the Ottomans, the region again assumed backwater status. Until the early Republican years internal exile to the coast here was a habitual and feared sentence for political offenders; and in a strange echo of the ancient tendency, the dialect of **Muğla province**—whose territory corresponds almost exactly to that of coastal Caria—is still one of the most eccentric and difficult to understand in the entire country.

Bafa Gölü and ancient **Heracleia ad Latmos** on its northeast shore make a suitably dramatic introduction to coastal Caria. **Euromos** and **Labranda**, slightly farther on, are two of the more satisfying minor ancient sites in Turkey, particularly the latter; both are visitable from **Milas**, the nearest substantial town and by no means devoid of interest in its own right. Southeast of Milas, **Peçin Kale** constitutes a Turkish oddity—a ruined medieval city, in this case the Menteşe capital. **Ören**, still farther southeast on the same road, is another rare beast: an attractive coastal resort that has not yet been steamrollered by industrial tourism. Southwest of Milas, however, neither **ancient Iassos** nor the small resort of **Güllük** live up to their hype. Most visitors bypass Güllük in favor of **Bodrum and its peninsula**, definitely the main tourist event on this coast, with tentacles of development creeping over every available parcel in the hinterland—although what attracted outsiders to the area in the first place still shines through on occasion.

Moving on, **Muğla** comes as a pleasant surprise: one of the best-preserved Ottoman townscapes in Turkey, it coexists with an unobtrusive and well-planned new city. Happy coexistence of old and new is about the last thing that comes to mind at nearby **Stratoniceia**, a once-untouched ancient metropolis about to be engulfed by a coal mine.

Farther south, **Marmaris** is another big—and rather crass—resort, from which the **Loryma (Hisarönü) Peninsula**, bereft of a sandy shoreline and good roads but blessed with magnificent scenery, offers the closest escape. As a compromise, **Datça** and its surroundings might fill the bill, since its remote beaches are more rewarding than the much-touted but poorly presented ruins of ancient **Knidos**.

Bafa Gölü (Lake Bafa)

The hundred square kilometers of **BAFA GÖLÜ**, one of the most entrancing spectacles in southwestern Turkey, were created when the Büyük Menderes River sealed off the Latmos Gulf from the sea. The barren, weirdly sculpted pinnacles of Mount Latmos (today Beşparmak Dağ) still loom over the northeast shore, visible from a great distance west. Numerous islets dot Bafa, most of them sporting some sort of fortified Byzantine religious establishment, dating from the lake's days as an important monastic center between the seventh and fourteenth centuries.

Bafa's separation from the ocean isn't complete: various canals link the lake's west end with an oxbow of the Büyük Menderes passing close by. As a result the water is faintly brackish, and quite a few fish species tolerant of both salt and fresh water shuttle back and forth, spawning in the lake. The most important are *levrek* (bass), *kefal* (gray mullet), *yayin* (catfish) and *yılan balığı* (eel)—all good eating and all exploited by a fishing cooperative based on the north shore (and by numerous migratory waterfowl, for whom Bafa is an important stopover).

Unhappily the lake is going through some hard times in the wake of a prolonged drought: the water level is down nearly a meter from normal, and the weeds that always hovered in the shallows have burgeoned. It's difficult to find a place not clogged by these nuisances, which is a shame since the water temperature is ideal for swimming.

Practical Details

Bus services past the lake are frequent; Söke–Milas dolmuşes are more flexible about stopping than the big buses. The southern shore of Bafa, which the main highway follows, presents a strangely deserted prospect except for olive groves—and two **campground/pansiyon/restaurants**. Heading east, the first is *Turgut*, rather sterile, regimented, and relatively expensive compared to *Ceri'nin Yeri* a few kilometers farther on. For the tentless, proprietor Ceri runs a five-room, moderately priced *pansiyon* and a three-apartment luxury outfit adjacent; it's rarely full except during May and June, when reservations (☎6131/4498) are advisable. There are no stores anywhere along the lake (although Ceri sells perishables like eggs and yogurt), so bring what you need.

Swimming is best from the back side of the monastery-capped islet joined to Ceri's restaurant by a muddy spit; some flattish rocks offer a weed-free corridor out onto the lake when the water level is back to normal. Failing that, dive off the end of the wooden jetty constructed to outrun the weeds.

Heracleia ad Latmos

Across the lake, most easily seen from *Ceri'nin Yeri*, is a stretch of irregular shoreline and a modern village whose lights twinkle at the base of Mount Latmos by night. This is also the site of **HERACLEIA AD LATMOS**, one of Turkey's most evocatively situated antiquities.

A settlement of Carian origin had existed here long before the arrival of the Ionians, and Carian habits died hard, although Latmos—as it was then known—had far better geographical communication with Ionia than with the rest of Caria. Late in the Hellenistic period the city's location was moved a kilometer or so west and the name changed to Heracleia, but despite adornment with numerous monuments and an enormous wall, it was never a place of great importance. Miletus, at the head of the then-gulf, monopolized most trade, and the inlet was already beginning to silt up.

Heracleia owes its fame, and an enduring hold on the romantic imagination, to a legend associated not with the town itself but with Mount Latmos behind. **Endymion** was a handsome shepherd who, while asleep in a cave on the mountain, was noticed by Selene, the moon goddess. She made love with him as he slept and in time bore Endymion fifty daughters without their sire ever waking once. Endymion was reluctant for all this to stop and begged Zeus, who was also fond of him, to be allowed to dream forever; his wish was granted. Later, Christian hermits who settled in the vicinity during mid-Byzantine times cleaned up Endymion's act, so to speak—in their version he was a mystic who after a lifetime of "communing" with the moon had learned the secret name of God. Once a year the anchorites, leaving their homes on the island cloisters, or in various caves on Latmos, converged on an ancient tomb believed to be Endymion's. The sarcophagus lid would be opened and the bones inside would emit a strange humming noise—the deceased saint's attempt to communicate the holy name.

The monastic communities, after producing a few minor saints, were dispersed for good early in the fourteenth century, and little is now left of any of the Byzantine monuments. But when a full moon rises over the serrated peaks across the water it is easy to suspend disbelief in all the legends pertaining to the place.

Indeed, Endymion's fate has exercised the imagination of poets down the years: Shakespeare declared "Peace, ho! The moon sleeps with Endymion/And would not be waked!," and four centuries later Keats added: "What is there in thee, Moon! that shouldst move my heart so potently?. . . Now I begin to feel thy orby power/Is coming fresh upon me."

The Site

Arriving by car, park your vehicle either next to the *Serçin* restaurant or in another area about 200m up the hill. The site is not enclosed, although you may have to pay a dollar or so admission if the warden is present. The crudely marked **bouleuterion** is 100m to the east of the first parking area, but only the retaining wall and some rows of benches are left of the second-century BC structure. The **Roman baths** visible in the valley below, and a crumbled but appealing **Roman theater** off in the olives beyond, can be reached via an unmarked trail starting between the first and second parking areas. The path up to the **hermits' caves** on Mount Latmos begins at the rear of the second parking area. Stout boots are advisable, as is a cool day in early spring or late fall—for a place still so close to the sea, Heracleia can be surprisingly hot and airless. Similar cautions apply for those wanting to trace the course of the **Hellenistic walls**, the city's most imposing and conspicuous relics, supposedly built by Lysimachus in the late third century BC.

The *Serçin* restaurant looks south over the **Hellenistic agora**, now mostly taken up by the village schoolyard; the south edge is buttressed by a row of **shops**, whose downhill side stands intact to two stories, complete with windows. From the *agora* grounds you get a good view west over the lake and assorted castle-crowned promontories. A box-like Hellenistic **temple of Athena**, perched on a hill west of the *agora*, is unmissable; its unofficial keeper will first show you an inscription to Athena, to the left of the entrance, and then his idiosyncratic collection of oddities—donations expected.

From the *agora* a wide, walled-in path descends toward the shore and the final quota of recognizable monuments at Heracleia. Most obvious is the peninsula— or, in wet years, island—studded with **Byzantine walls** and a **church**. A stone **causeway** half-buried in the "beach" here allowed entrance in what must have been drier medieval times. Follow the shore southwest to the *Zeybek* restaurant, strategically astride another promontory, and then continue along its access drive to a junction with a slightly wider road. Across the way you should see the tentatively identified Hellenistic **sanctuary of Endymion**, oriented unusually northeast to southwest. Five column stumps stand in front of the structure, which has a rounded rear wall—a ready-made apse for the later Christians, with sections of rock incorporated into the masonry.

Striking out across the pasture opposite the Endymion shrine, and skimming the base of yet another Byzantine castle, you arrive at the ancient **necropolis**, which consists of a few dozen rectangular tombs hewn into boulders on the shore. Many are partly or completely submerged, depending on the water level.

Practical Details

The most common **access** to Heracleia is by **boat** from *Ceri'nin Yeri*: figure on paying about $2 a head, round-trip, assuming a group of at least ten people and not including site admission. Tours generally depart between 9:30 and 10:30am, take twenty minutes to cross the lake, and allow just under two and a half hours at the ruins—enough for a look around and a quick meal. Alternatively, if you have your own vehicle, **drive** east to Çamiçi village (6km from *Ceri'nin Yeri*) and then turn left at the sign. The 10km all-weather dirt road leads through fields and finally a wilderness of Latmian boulders to the modern village of **KAPIKIRI**, built higgledy-piggledy among the ruins.

Scattered in and around Kapıkırı are a few simple restaurants, a campground, and rumors of a pansiyon, although the opening hours of most of the establishments are erratic to say the least. The *Zeybek Restaurant/Camping* has a good view over the lake, serves moderately priced fish, and is the most consistently open.

Milas

A small, rather nondescript town of some 35,000 people, **MİLAS** is all too often given short shrift by tourists intent on reaching the fleshpots of Bodrum as quickly as possible. This is a shame, for although it's unlikely that most foreigners would want to stay the night here, there are more than enough sights of interest to fill a few hours between buses (Milas is a major regional transport hub, with dolmuş services in every direction). First impressions are not reassuring—new highrises on the outskirts, traffic congestion in the bazaar—but opinions may improve after a stroll around.

Milas—or Mylasa, as it was formerly known—was an important Carian center (its original location was at the nearby hill of Peçin Kale—see p.296), but it was the Halicarnassos-based Hecatomnid dynasty that really put it on the map, its nearby quarries providing ample marble for numerous public monuments, and increased control over the sanctuary at Labranda bringing the city additional benefits. The city's assignment by the Roman republic to the jurisdiction of Rhodes in 190 BC was too much for the locals to stomach and they rebelled within twenty years, declaring a brief independence of two more decades before eventual incorporation into the Roman empire. Details of the Byzantine period are obscure, but the city experienced a resurgence during the fourteenth century when the Menteşe emirs, a Turcoman clan, made it the capital of their realms in southwestern Anatolia.

The Town

An elaborate early-roman tomb known as the **Gümüşkesen** (literally Silver Purse) is the most intriguing relic of ancient Mylasa, but the way there is not marked. Leave the fruit bazaar street at the corner with the *Halk Bankası* and head west up a slight incline about 400m to the landscaped site, in a slight depression south of Hıdırlık hill. There are no formal visiting hours nor regularized admission fee, but the keeper will accept a tip when he's around.

The monument consists of a square burial chamber surmounted by a Corinthian colonnade with a pyramidal roof—a design presumed to be a miniature of the now-vanished mausoleum at Halicarnassos. A small ladder has been installed on the southwest side, allowing access to the platform. The ceiling sports elaborate carvings and some flecks of paint; a hole in the floor allowed mourners to pour libations into the sepulcher below.

Milas's lively tradesmen's **bazaar** covers the western slopes of Hisarbaşı hill, which has been the focus of settlement in every era. Once past the warren of alleys perpendicular to the main longitudinal street, veer up to the summit and the late Ottoman Belen Camii. Immediately to its right stands the **Çöllühanı**, one of the last functioning, unrestored *kervansarays* in western Turkey. On many afternoons of the year the premises will be full of donkeys and carts, the former comical studies in patience while their masters drink tea in the shady galleries of the building.

Leaving the "donkey hall," go through the archways of the more modern *han* opposite and continue downhill to the grounds of the fine, pink-marble, late fourteenth-century **Firuz Bey Camii**, erected by the Menteşe emirs from bits of the ancient town.

Back past the Çöllühanı, veering southeast, there's a district of sumptuous **old houses**, the finest in Milas, behind the PTT. Watch for yellow arrow-signs with the legend "Uzunyuva" and the single Corinthian column, adorned with a stork's nest, of the first-century BC **temple of Zeus**, adjacent to which a sign cryptically reads "*Kutsal Alan* (Holy Clearing)." Much of the foundation has been incorporated into later houses.

Downhill from here you'll pass a huge stretch of **ancient wall**—possibly a fort—and at the bottom of the slope an **Ottoman bridge** with an inscribed plaque. Across the bridge, a few minutes' walk past the Orhan (Ağa) Camii, oldest of the town's mosques, stands the **Baltalı Kapı** (Gate-with-Axe)—all that remains of the ancient city walls. The axe in question, a double-headed attribute of Zeus, is faintly carved on the north-facing keystone.

The late fourteenth-century **Ulu Cami**, farther south along the canal, is perhaps more engaging, an exotically asymmetrical building incorporating a vast quantity of plundered antiquities. Kufic inscriptions adorn the lintels, and a peculiar staircase leads up over the front door to a short and stubby minaret. In addition the building has gables, buttressing, and a dome over the *mihrab* end, and the whole effect is more like that of a church than a mosque.

Across the street, the recently opened **archaeological museum** (daily 9am–noon & 1–6pm; 50¢), labeled almost exclusively in Turkish, has a sparse collection for the size of the hall—just some pottery and figurines from the immediate environs of Milas, plus two cases of mediocre gold diadems and slightly better jewelry.

Practical Details

Milas's **otogar** is way out on the northern edge of town, near the junction for Labranda. You'll be left here unless you've come from Güllük or Ören, whose dolmuşes have separate terminals in the town center. Getting into town from the otogar, take either a dolmuş marked "Şehir İçi" or a "Servis Araba" (complimentary shuttle) run by the big companies. The pick-up/drop-off point is the sidewalk south of the *Köşem* restaurant and city park; there's no fixed stand—just wait around.

If you need or want to spend the night in Milas, the only mid-range **accommodation** you'll find is grouped close together around a T-junction at the base of Hisarbaşı hill: *Otel Turan* is the oldest; the *Akdeniz* and the *Arıcan* (situated close to the produce market) are both more modern. There are a couple of *hamams* nearby if the hotel showers aren't up to standard. Between the latter two hotels there are a few shops that sell honey and carpets, the two local specialties.

Eating out, simple lunches can be had at the *Pamukkale Pide Salonu*, opposite the produce market, or several nearby holes-in-the-wall. Another good lunchtime option is the *Özcan Kebap Salonu*, halfway up the main thoroughfare threading the bazaar on Hisarbaşı hill. The *Köşem* near the park and the luxury *Sürücü Hotel* serve drinks and aren't too expensive. For dessert, there's nothing better than ice cream in the park on a hot day; or try the *Nur Pastanesi*, over on the north side of town, below the Firuz Bey Camii and across from the Bizim Birahanesi—the latter being the only other moderate establishment serving both food and booze. For **drinking** only, there's a clutch of beer halls under some trees at the base of the Zeus temple hill.

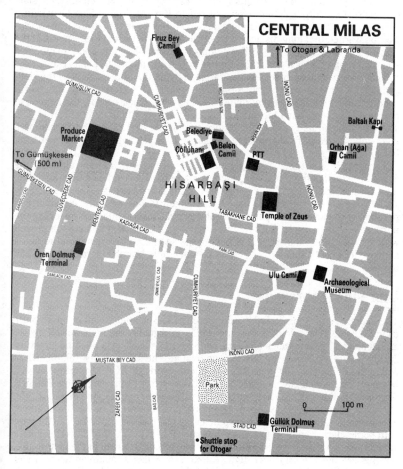

CENTRAL MİLAS

Northeast of Milas: Euromos and Labranda

A short distance north of Milas are two impressive Carian ruins that together make a good day out from the town. **Euromos** is easily reached by public transportation, although you really need your own vehicle to visit **Labranda**. If possible, try to see Labranda in the morning and Euromos in the afternoon.

Euromos

Between Bafa Gölü and Milas, 4km southeast of the town of SELİMİYE, a Corinthian **temple of Zeus**, north of the road in an olive grove, is virtually all that remains intact of the ancient city of **EUROMOS** (daily 8:30am–7pm; $1). But it is sufficiently unusual—only two other temples in Turkey are in a comparable state of repair—to justify a detour. You can get to the site from Milas by taking a dolmuş toward Selimiye, although if you're traveling back by **public transportation** be warned that long-distance buses will not stop to pick up passengers at the ruins, and even the Selimiye–Milas dolmuşes, often full by this point, may refuse you. Be prepared to walk back to Selimiye to find one at the start of its run.

There was a sanctuary to a native Carian deity on this spot as early as the sixth century BC, along with a city originally known as Kyromus. By the fourth century, under the Hellenizing influence of nearby Halicarnassos, the name had changed to Euromus and the cult of Zeus had merged with that of the earlier god. The city attained its greatest importance during the Hellenistic and Roman periods, when it nearly rivaled nearby Mylasa, but by Byzantine times it had sunk back into obscurity.

The **temple** is a legacy of the generous Roman emperor Hadrian, although the fact that several of the remaining columns are unfluted is evidence that the shrine was never finished. Of the original 32 columns, arranged six by eleven, only sixteen remain, although all of these are linked to one or more neighbors by portions of the architrave. The city itself was built several hundred meters to the northwest of the temple, but the only easily found trace of it is a stretch of **wall** with a **tower** up on the ridge overlooking the sacred area. Any attempt to find a supposedly nearby theater is likely to produce only bramble scratches and bad temper.

Labranda (Labraynda)

The sanctuary of Zeus at **Labranda**, perched in splendid isolation on a south-facing hillside overlooking the plain of Milas, is arguably the most beautifully set archaeological zone of ancient Caria, and one of its least-visited—it takes a very sturdy tour bus to brave the horrendous road in. The site lies over 15km north of Milas, but dolmuşes only go as far as the hamlet of KARGICAK, roughly halfway, beyond which you'll have to walk or thumb a ride from a passing truck. The first 6km or so is deceptively easy, but thereafter the **road** deteriorates markedly; the surface is often thick dust or mud, depending on recent weather, and the gradient is punishing at times. In summer you can normally get an ordinary car through with some alert driving in first gear, but after a heavy rain only four-wheel-drive vehicles are up to it. Rumor has it that the way in will be paved in the near future, but this has been gossip since 1987. A **taxi** from Milas, should you find a driver willing to risk his chassis, will set you back the better part of $10 round-trip.

Excavations since 1948 have turned up no finds older than the seventh century BC but it seems certain that a god was venerated here long before that. Oddly enough the agreeable climate (the elevation is 600m), and a perennial spring never prompted the founding of a city, but instead nurtured a grove of sacred syca-mores which eventually became the precinct of Zeus Stratius (the Warlike), alias Zeus Labrayndus (Axe-Bearing), after his depiction on fourth-century coins struck at nearby Mylasa. The fourth-century BC Hecatomnid rulers of Halicarnassos and Mylasa did much to promote the cult, and endowed various structures at the sanc-tuary, which may still be seen. However, the priests of Zeus retained a large degree of autonomy, exerting their independence to advantage during the chaos following Alexander's death. Roman and later Byzantine rule brought few material benefits to Labranda, and it was finally abandoned in the late eleventh century.

The Site

Just when you're beginning to wonder if you've made a wrong turn, a clump of poplars—replacements of the long-vanished sycamores—heralds the location of the springs that still supply part of the water for modern Milas. A refreshment stand and some beehives rest opposite the artificial terraces of the sanctuary (daily 8am–8pm; $1) and the rickety wooden gate giving access to them. The family of Osman the caretaker still lives on the premises, and their wandering livestock give the ruins a pastoral touch. Osman will usually escort you through the principal monuments in the following order, although he can only speak Turkish, and in any case the site is well marked and there's a helpful map-board.

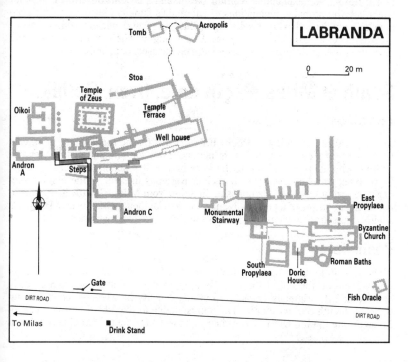

After skirting some unidentified ancient buildings, you climb up to the so-called **andron A**—one of three such constructions at Labranda that were used for sacred banquets held at the shrine; while roofless, it's otherwise complete, including a windowed niche in back. Immediately adjacent are the **oikoi** (priests' residences), fronted by four Doric column stubs. Like the andron A, this was another foundation of the Hecatomnids, although authorities disagree whether they were the actual quarters of the cult priests or merely the repository of temple records.

The temple of Zeus itself, originally laid out during the fifth century and rededicated by Idrieus, sprawls east of here. None of it stands more than knee-high, yet it is appealing, especially when viewed from the near edge of the **temple terrace**, lined with the rudiments of a stoa. From its far corner a path leads up to the ruined **acropolis** and—more importantly—a massive fourth-century **tomb** thought to be that of Idrieus and his family. This is divided in two, with three sarcophagi in the rear chamber and a damaged pair up front.

Just below the south rim of the temple terrace is the recessed **well-house**, the original exit point of the spring; just across a flat area are **andron B**, donated by Mausolus and relatively intact, and **andron C**, a Roman contribution which has not weathered the ages as well.

From the level area in front of andron C, it's a short distance to the prominent **monumental stairway** descending to the lowest terrace at the site. A right turn at the bottom of the steps leads to the **south propylaea**, one end of the long-vanished sacred way to Mylasa; straight ahead takes you to the more prominent **east propylaea**, the terminus of a processional way, also disappeared, from Alında (see p.327). Wedged in between the two *propylaeas* are the remains of a so-called **Doric house**, some adjoining **Roman baths**, and a **Byzantine church**, beyond which are the probable foundations of Labranda's famous **fish oracle**. The resident fish, bedecked with jewelry according to several ancient sources, were thrown bits of food by their custodians. Depending on whether they accepted the morsels or not, the inquirer's fortunes were on the ascendant or decline.

South of Milas: Peçin Kale, Ören, Güllük, Iassos

The original site of Mylasa at **Peçin Kale** lies just off the road leading southeast to the Gulf of Gökova, though it is better known for remains of the Menteşe emirate who appropriated the castle here and built a small settlement nearby. Farther on, travelers usually skip ancient Keramos in favor of the neighboring beach resort of **Ören**. In the opposite direction from Milas, **Güllük** is a resort in the incipient stages of a potentially massive development, while nearby **Iassos** is a fairly uninspiring ancient site close to some enticing fish restaurants.

Peçin Kale

Mylasa's shift to its current position during the fourth century BC means that its original site on the hill of **Peçin Kale** is more interesting for its **castle** (daily 8am–8pm; $1), originally Byzantine but adapted by the Menteşe emirs during their fourteenth-century tenure. The unmistakable fortified bluff lies 5km east of Milas on the road to Ören (access is via a marked 800-meter dirt side road), but the citadel, cluttered inside with the untidy ruins of the village of Mutluca, which relocated downhill twenty years ago, does not fulfill the promise of its imposing exterior, except for a view of the plain 200m below.

The Menteşe complex itself lies about 400m from the castle, up a dirt road where a left fork leads to the unusual two-storied **Kızıl Han** and the fourteenth-century **Orhan Bey Camii**, featuring a far more ancient doorjamb. Bearing right takes you to the **medrese and türbe of Ahmet Gazi**, from the same era—tombs of a Menteşe governor and his wife that are venerated as those of minor Islamic saints, with colored rags and candles. Most visitors, however, content themselves with a drink at the small reasonably priced refreshment stand, whose tables are set amid the spring-fed olives, poplars, and sycamores.

Ören

Frequented only in mid-summer despite good transportation links, **ÖREN** is an endangered Turkish species—a coastal resort that's not overdeveloped. It's virtu-ally the only sizable village on the north coast of the Gulf of Gökova, and owes its pre-tourism history to the adjacent narrow, fertile alluvial plain, and the lignite (soft coal) deposits in the mountains behind.

The route there is inauspicious, the landscape defaced by two giant power plants built with Polish aid—which accounts for the large local transient popula-tion of Polish engineers, and the occasional sign in Polish. These plants are also one of the reasons tour operators have not seen fit to develop the area, although the polluted atmosphere and open-cast mining and stack gas have not yet affected the crystalline waters offshore. Nor have they deterred the construction of a new marina beyond the beach to the east—already the frontage road has been paved and widened.

Inland Ören and Ancient Keramos

The upper village, on the east bank of a canyon mouth exiting the hills, is an appealingly homogenous settlement scattered among the ruins of **ancient Keramos**. No new works have been allowed for years, but, following a June 1989 earthquake, permission has been granted for "repairs." You can easily make out sections of wall, arches, and a boat slip, dating from the time when the sea (now a kilometer distant) lapped the town. There are no particular opening hours or admission charges—a do-it-yourself tour through the old, mostly Ottoman Greek houses should turn up various odds and ends.

The village has **shops and a post office**, but no bank; most **dolmuşes** from Milas continue the final distance to the coast.

The beach—and Practical Details

The **beach** is a more than acceptable kilometer of coarse sand, gravel, and pebbles, backed by handsome pine-tufted cliffs; in clear weather you can spy the Datça Peninsula opposite. Once there was a working harbor at the east end of town, but since the lignite is now burned locally rather than being shipped out, the loading conveyor there has been demolished to make way for the new marina. Overall the town makes a great hideout from the commercialism that has engulfed the rest of the coast, and is an excellent spot to recuperate from the rigors of overland travel. People, mostly from Ankara, come to stay for weeks on end: a single day is really pointless, and since there are less than 150 **beds** to go around, the place fills up in high season, when reservations are strongly suggested. In terms of **staying**, mid-range comfort is best represented by the *Salihağa* (☎6134/1138), on the road in from the village about 200m back from the shore. Other alternatives include the rather plain *Yıltur Motel* (☎6134/1108 or 1630), charging $5 per person in a rambling old compound at the far eastern end of the beach by the jetty; the *Keramos* (☎6134/1065), with a campground, simple cottages, and luxury motel; the fairly standard *Karya* (☎6134/1115) and *Marçalı* (☎6134/1063); or the somewhat unfriendly *Göksu* (☎6134/1112). For **eating**, there are just a handful of restaurants, some—like the good-value *Can's*, next to the *Yıltur*—affiliated with a pansiyon, and a couple of stores. **Nightlife** consists of one bar/café and a friendly, low-pressure disco/bar next to the *Yıltur*.

Güllük

GÜLLÜK, 27km southeast of Milas, began life as a small fishing and bauxite-ore port, both of which are still important enterprises. After enjoying a brief vogue among German trendies during the 1980s, it's now a rather déclassé resort. Despite a scarcity of appreciable beaches, development keeps sprouting around the old village core, the prime motivation for which is a huge vacation village to the north, along with an even larger international airport in the marsh beyond, all financed by a multinational consortium. The project is scheduled to be completed in 1992, after which you can pretty much write Güllük off.

For the moment you can still watch wooden keels being laid at the giant **boat-yards** by the main port. The miniscule town **beach**—really just a swimming plat-form—is behind the *Liman* restaurant, out toward the *Çamlık* bungalows and campground. You can continue in the same direction, past the lighthouse cape to road's end, north of town, to a final, narrow and tiny sandy beach backed by the *Urga* and *Beyaz Yunus* pansiyons.

Practical Details

Access is easy, with frequent dolmuşes from Milas pulling in at a big inland plaza near the food market. Cheap **pansiyons**, in roughly ascending order of price, include the *Yalı* (☎6137/1116), with a fine harbor view; the *Şahinler* and *Kaptan*, along the oldest part of the waterfront; the *Kemer*, on a hill at the town outskirts; and the *Meltem* and *Pelit*, out by the lighthouse with a view of the open sea. Moving up a notch, there's the *Nazar Motel* (next to the *Yalı*), the *Kordon*, and the best-sited *Motel Güllük* on the northern bay.

The rock-bottom **eating** option is the reassuringly named *Mevlana Bol Kepçç* (Mevlana Abundant Ladle) in the town's single back street. *Pelikan*, on the water, is probably the least expensive of four otherwise identical contenders. *Altesa* is a "pub" on the dolmuş square, with a pair of mid-range eateries just inland.

Iassos

Covering a headland almost completely surrounded by the Gulf of Asim, **IASSOS** would seem, from a glance at the map, to promise great things. Alas the ruins, after the first few paces, fizzle to virtually nothing, and swimming in the sumpy coves nearby is hardly an inviting prospect. Only the excellent local fish—the best reason to visit—represents an unbroken tradition from the past.

Fish stories abound at Iassos. In Hellenistic times the city's coinage even depicted a youth swimming with a dolphin who had befriended him. A more repeated tale concerns an itinerant musician who held his audience's attention until the ringing of the bell announcing the opening of the Iassian fish market. At that, the townspeople rose and trooped out, except for a partially deaf gentleman. The singer approached the man to compliment him on his manners; the deaf one, on understanding that the market had begun, hastily excused himself and fled after his peers.

The adjacent soil has always been poor, and from very early times Iassos must have attracted settlers, and made its living, by virtue of its good anchorage and fishing waters. Traces of Minoan and Mycenean habitation from as far back as 1900 BC have been found, although the city was damaged so badly during the Persian, Peloponnesian, and Mithridatic wars that it never amounted to much until Roman imperial rule. Particularly during the second century AD, Iassos recovered substantially, and most of what can be seen today dates from those years. During the Byzantine era the city ranked as a bishopric, which is reflected by the presence of two basilicas. The hilltop castle was a medieval foundation of the Knights of St John, and after the Turkish conquest the place was known as Asimkalesi (Asim's Castle), Asim being a local *ağa* (feudal lord). The poor condition of most antiquities here can be attributed to the Ottoman policy of loading all easily removable dressed stone onto waiting ships for transfer to İstanbul.

The Site

On entering the modern village of Kıyıkızacik, next to the ruins, the road does a quick bend around a Roman **mausoleum**, arguably far more interesting than anything within the city walls. Inside, a Corinthian temple-tomb rests on a stepped platform, although sadly the premises are usually locked since the archaeologists use the tomb area as a warehouse for small finds. The principal **site** ($1 admission when staff present) of Iassos is poorly marked and maintained, and it's debatable whether the entry fee is money well spent. Matters start promisingly enough as you cross the isthmus beyond the mausoleum to the **dipylon** (gate) in the **Hellenistic city wall**, repaired by the Byzantines. Once inside, the well-preserved Roman **bouleuterion**, with four rows of seats, lies immediately to your right but is currently off-limits. On your left, the **agora** has undergone a partial restoration of its Roman colonnade; at the south corner of the square is a rather obscure rectangular structure known as the **Caesarium**. Southeast of the castle there's a Roman **villa** with blurry murals and extensive floor mosaics, the latter hidden under a layer of protective sand. Nearby, a wide stairway descends to the foundations of a small **temple of Demeter and Kore**, while beyond is a partially submerged defensive **tower**.

From the tower a narrow but definite path threads past the large but dull **stoa of Artemis** on the right, before reaching the meager hillside **theater**, of which only the *cavea* walls and stumps of the stage building remain—the fine view over the northeast harbor partially compensates. Continue around, or (better) through, the **castle** here: there's little to see inside the medieval walls, although again the panorama from atop the ramparts is excellent.

Practical Details

Like Heracleia ad Latmos, Iassos has two approaches. Coming **by land**, there's a turnoff 8km west of Milas—a pretty drive, narrow but paved all the way, first across a plain planted with cotton, then through pine- and olive-studded hills over-looking the airport-to-be. There are infrequent **dolmuş** services from Milas.

Without your own car, it's better to come **by sea**. Excursion boats from Güllük provide the link in season, and almost always include a swim-stop at a beach only reachable from the water. This is certainly a bonus, since there are no beaches worthy of the name accessible by foot or vehicle anywhere near Iassos.

In Kıyıkışlacık village, four or five **restaurants**, such as the *İasos Deniz*, serve mostly fish, in particular the cheap and excellent local *çipura* (a kind of bream). If you want to **stay**, a handful of pansiyons (*Iasos, Mandalya, Gül*) can put you up for the night. Most eateries and lodgings overlook the rather murky harbor.

Bodrum and its Peninsula

In the eyes of its devotees, **BODRUM**, with its whitewashed square houses and subtropical gardens, is the longest established, most attractive, and most versa-tile Turkish resort—a real class act compared to its upstart Aegean rivals. However, its recent, almost frantic attempts to be all things to all tourists have made it hard to tell the difference, and the controlled development within the municipality—height limits and a historical-preservation code are in force—has resulted in wholesale exploitation of the until recently little-disturbed peninsula.

The Bodrum area has long attracted large numbers of Britons, both the moneyed yacht set and the charter-flight brigade. Most of the big package tour operators are active hereabouts, which can be either reassuring or dismaying, depending on your point of view.

Some History

Bodrum was originally known as **Halicarnassos**, and colonized by Dorians from the Peloponnese during the eleventh century BC. They mingled with the existing Carian population, settling on the small island of Zephysia which in later ages became a peninsula and the location of a medieval castle. Along with Knidos, Kos, and the three Rhodian cities of Lindos, Kamiros, and Ialyssos, Halicarnassos was a member of the so-called Dorian Hexapolis, whose assembly met periodically at the sanctuary of Triopian Apollo at Knidos. At some point during the sixth century BC Halicarnassos was expelled from the confederation, on the pretext that one of the city's athletes had failed to do proper reverence to the god; in reality, the increas-ing Ionian character of Halicarnassos offended the other five.

Later the city came under Persian influence, but managed to retain considera-ble autonomy. Halicarnassos' most famous son, **Herodotus** (484–420 BC), chron-icled her fortunes in his famous *Histories*. Eventually direct Persian rule was replaced by that of the **Hecatomnid satraps**, a capable if rather inbred dynasty, the most renowned of whose rulers was **Mausolus** (377–353 BC), a leader who greatly increased the power and wealth of what in effect was a semi-independent Carian principality. An admirer of Greek civilization, Mausolus spared no effort to Hellenize his cities, and was working on a suitably self-aggrandizing tomb at the time of his death—thus giving us our word "mausoleum." **Artemisia II**, his sister and wife, completed the massive structure, which came to be regarded as one of the Seven Wonders of the ancient world. Like her ancestor Artemisia I she distin-guished herself in warfare, inflicting a humiliating defeat on the Rhodians, whom she tricked into allowing her entire fleet into their port.

BODRUM IN LITERATURE AND MUSIC—AND IN DRAG

In recent years the personalities outshone the buildings, as Bodrum became something of a mecca for Turkish bohemian types. The earliest arrival was the writer-to-be **Cevat Şakir Kabaağaçlı**, who was first exiled here in 1908 for his political views, and returned compulsorily in 1923, under commuted death sentence for allegedly murdering his father, a wealthy pasha. He persistently declined all comment on the latter charge but for the balance of his long life devoted himself to the welfare of the area, in particular to the preservation of its monuments (he once wrote the British Museum demanding the return of the Halicarnassian artifacts pillaged by Charles Newton). He also recorded the lore and legends of the local seafarers, penning several collections of short stories based on these conversations. Better known as the "Fisherman of Halicarnassos," Kabaağaçlı is buried on a hill overlooking the bay of Gümbet.

Ahmet and Nesui Ertegün, two more prominent Bodrum habitues, were the sons of the Turkish ambassador to the US during the 1930s and 1940s, and caught the jazz bug while living in America. Both later became big-time recording executives, in particular establishing Atlantic's jazz label, which in the early 1960s launched the careers of (among others) Charles Mingus, John Coltrane, and The Modern Jazz Quartet. The Ertegüns were influential in the process of introducing jazz to Turkey, and their careers go a long way toward explaining the music's popularity among the Turkish middle and upper classes. Nesui died in July 1989, but his brother still occasionally visits the family villa in Bodrum. Another local villa-owner is **Zeki Müren**, the most prominent among a bevy of widely acclaimed transvestite pop singers in Turkey. In Bodrum he circulates out of drag—but has a street named after him, which, appropriately enough, leads to the biggest disco in town.

In 334 BC the rampaging Alexander's arrival coincided with a bitter succession feud between Artemisia's heirs. The Macedonian armies wreaked such havoc that the city never fully recovered, and its population was dispersed throughout Caria over the next two chaotic centuries. After a period of little importance under the Roman and Byzantine empires, and brief shuffling between Selçuk, Menteşe, and Ottoman occupiers, the **Knights of St John** slipped over from Rhodes in 1402 and erected the **castle** which is now Bodrum's most prominent landmark. Urgently needing to replace the fortress at Smyrna destroyed by the Mongols, the Knights engaged the best military engineers of the era to construct their new stronghold on the promontory. The name *bodrum*, meaning "cellar" or "dungeon" in Turkish, probably pays tribute to the stronghold's subterranean defenses. After Süleyman the Magnificent compelled the Order to depart in 1523, the castle's history was virtually synonymous with that of the town until early this century.

Arrival and Information

Both international and domestic **ferries** currently dock at the landing west of the castle, although a new international terminal will soon open across the mouth of the harbor, near the expanding marina. In the more likely event that you arrive by **bus**, you'll be left at the **otogar**, some 500m up Cevat Şakir Caddesi, which links Belediye Meydanı with the main peninsular highway and divides the town roughly in two.

Cevat Şakir's approximate continuation, Kale Caddesi, defines one edge of the bazaar, huddling in the shadow of the medieval castle. Kale Caddesi ends at İskele Meydanı, officially known as Oniki Eylül Meydanı and home of the **tourist information office** (summer Mon–Fri 8am–8pm, Sat 9am–7:30pm, closed Sun; ☎1091)—well equipped with accommodation lists, maps and transport schedules.

Northwest of Cevat Şakir is the service-orientated side of town. Most travel and car-rental agencies, plus bus-company town offices, line Neyzen Tevfik Caddesi, which takes off from Belediye Meydanı. Its most important perpendiculars, especially when accommodation-hunting, are Hamam Sokağı and Türkkuyusu Caddesi.

> The Bodrum area **telephone code** is ☎6141.

Finding a Place to Stay

Desirable **accommodation** tends to concentrate in three main areas: in Kumbahçe Mahalle, but safely away from Cumhuriyet Caddesi (where you'd get little sleep); in Tepecik district along or just off Neyzen Tevfik Caddesi (passably quiet), or the convenient and usually peaceful Türkkuyusu Caddesi, winding up from Belediye Meydanı. Advance reservations are suggested in peak season.

Driving is difficult in Bodrum, **parking** even more so; shelling out for parking fees or (worse) getting a vehicle out of impoundment is disheartening, so establishments with parking space are noted.

Kumbahçe Mahalle

Berlin, Rasathane Sokağı 18 (☎2524). On a quiet side street, with front garden. $11 double with bath.

Durak, Rasathane Sokağı, just above the former (☎1564). Similar idea, same price.

Uğur, Rasathane Sokağı, still farther up (☎2106). Similar to the preceding in all respects.

Özgün, Rasathane Sokağı, below the *Berlin* (no phone). More basic than its neighbors. $7.50 for a double without bath.

Dinç, Cumhuriyet Cad 123 (☎1141). A modestly luxurious choice overlooking the eastern bay, but subject to nighttime noise. $30 for a double with bath, including breakfast.

Türkkuyusu Caddesi

Titiz, Türkkuyusu Caddesi 12 (☎1534). Café/bar on premises. $12 for double with bath. Others on the same street, most with limited parking, include *Metin, Kocağlan, Melis, Söğüt, Dönen*, and *Çökertme*.

Tepecik

Menekşe, alley leading off Neyzen Tevfik (☎3416). Very quiet garden setting is excellent value; limited parking. Doubles with bath $8.

Mavsoleion, Turgutreis Caddesi 128 (☎2387). Roof terrace with great view; ample street parking. Singles without bath $5.50, doubles $8.50.

Belmi, Yangı Sokağı 6, off Neyzen Tevfik (☎1132). Clean rooms in this older building vary; breakfast courtyard. Singles without bath $8, doubles $11.

Ataer, alley off Neyzen Tevfik Caddesi. Nice rooms, but can be full in season with tour groups. Doubles without bath $14.

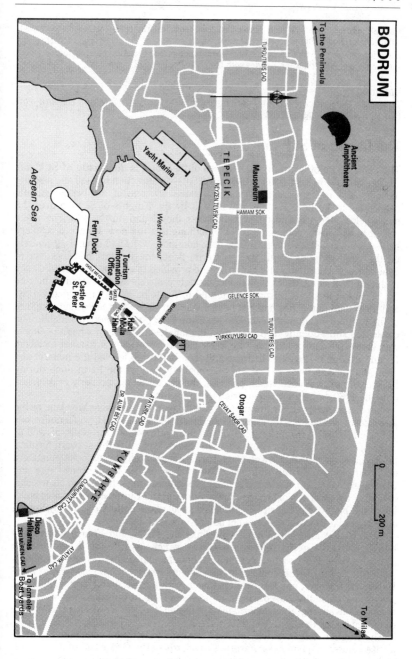

BODRUM

To the Peninsula

TURGUTREIS CAD

Ancient
Amphitheatre

TEPECIK

Mausoleum

NEYZEN TEVFIK CAD

HAMAM SOK

Yacht Marina

West Harbour

Aegean Sea

Ferry Dock

Tourism
Information
Office

ISKELE MEYD.

Castle of
St. Peter

GELENCE SOK

TURGUTREIS CAD

Hacı
Molla
Hamı

CUMHURIYET CAD

PTT

TÜRKKUYUSU CAD

DR. ALIM BEY CAD

ATATURK CAD

Otogar

CEVAT ŞAKIR CAD

KUMBAHCE

CUMHURIYET CAD

Disco
Halikarnas

ZEKI MUREN CAD

ATATURK CAD

To Icmeler
Boatyards

0

200 m

To Milas

Bahçeli Ağar, alley off Neyzen Tevfik Cad 190, behind marina (☎1648). Rooms very plain but clean; kitchen facilities provided. Doubles $11.
Herodot, Neyzen Tevfik Cad 116 (☎1093). Mid-range option recommended by tourist office; some rooms overlook harbor. Singles with bath $15, doubles $22.

Camping
There are three inconspicuous **campgrounds**—*Şenlik, Yuvam*, and *Gökhan*—on Gelence Sokağı, west of Türkkuyusu Caddesi .

The Castle of St Peter

The centerpiece of Bodrum, in all senses of the word, is the **Castle of St Peter** (daily except Mon 8am–noon & 2–6pm; $2.50)—an attraction in itself and also the location of a museum of underwater archaeology, one of the better regional collections in Turkey. The castle was built by the Knights of St John over the small Selçuk fortress and older battlements they found on the site. The initial circuit of walls was completed in 1437, although as the new science of artillery ballistics advanced, the garrison saw fit to add more walls and moats, particularly on the landward side—with their powerful fleets the Knights had less fear of attack by sea. Fourteen water cisterns were provided to guarantee self-sufficiency in the event of siege, which looked increasingly probable after 1453 when the citadel became the sole Christian stronghold in Anatolia. Work proceeded slowly, and the finishing touches had just been applied in 1522 when Süleyman's capture of the Knights' headquarters on Rhodes made their position here untenable. The castle was subsequently neglected until the nineteenth century, when the chapel was converted into a mosque, the keep into a prison, and a hamam installed. During a siege in 1915, shells from a French battleship leveled the minaret and damaged various towers. The Italians repaired most of the harm done during their brief post-war occupation, although the place was not properly refurbished until the 1960s, when it was converted to a museum.

Initial entrance is either through the **north gate**, facing İskele Meydanı, or the **west gate**, overlooking the water. Once inside the **west moat**, you'll notice bits of ancient masonry from the Mausoleum incorporated into the walls, as well as some of the 249 Christian **coats of arms**. Stairs lead up to the seaward fortifications and then into the **lower courtyard**, where strolling peacocks animate a small snack bar. To the right, the **chapel** houses the local Bronze Age and Mycenean collection, featuring artifacts recovered from three Aegean wrecks, including a new provisional case of finds from the Ulu Burun site. A smaller building at the base of the Italian tower holds a small **glass collection**, mostly Roman and early Islamic work, displayed in odd reverse illumination.

On the next level up, a **new wing** links the Italian and French towers and houses Byzantine relics retrieved from two wrecks (in the fourth and seventh centuries AD, off Yassıada), as well as a diorama explaining salvage techniques. Both the **Italian tower**, containing the coin and jewelry room plus Classical and Hellenistic statuary, and the **French tower**, with a collection of archaic bits and pieces, are currently closed except for stairs leading to the rooftop viewing platforms. Considering the rather stiff admission fee, they will hopefully have reopened by the time you read this.

The **English tower**, at the southeast corner of the castle compound, is an ill-advised study in quaintness. Assorted standards of the Order and of their adversaries compete for wall space with an incongruous array of hunting trophies;

medieval mood muzak plays as overpriced wine-by-the-glass is served at banquet tables purported to be reproductions of those from the Knights' refectory. Finish a tour by crossing the **upper courtyard**, landscaped, like much of the castle grounds. with native flora, to the **German tower** and the **Snake tower**—so named for a serpent relief plaque over the entrance. Inside is an amphora display.

The Rest of the Town

Immediately north of the castle lies the **bazaar**, most of which is pedestrianized along its two main thoroughfares of Kale Caddesi and Dr Alim Bey Caddesi; traffic enters the dense maze of streets to the southeast via Atatürk Caddesi, 200m inland. Alim Bey merges with Cumhuriyet Caddesi, the focal point of most of Bodrum's nightlife. Halfway along Kale Caddesi is Bodrum's only other substantial medieval monument apart from the castle—the eighteenth-century **han of Hacı Molla**, now host to a luxury restaurant and various souvenir shops—a pattern that is repeated throughout the lanes of the surrounding **bazaar**; most workaday tradespeople have been exiled farther inland.

From landscaped Belediye Meydanı, stroll up Türkkuyusu Caddesi, and bear left onto Turgutreis Caddesi—center of a small district of old stone houses with courtyards that give some hint of what pre-tourism Bodrum was like. Roughly 400m west along Turgutreis Caddesi lies all that's left of the **Mausoleum** (daily except Mon 8am–noon & 1–5pm; 50¢). Designed by Pytheos, architect of the Athena temple at Priene, the complete structure measured 39m by 33m at its base and stood nearly 60m high. A nine-by-eleven colonnade surmounted the burial vault and supported a stepped pyramidal roof bearing a chariot with effigies of Mausolus and his sister-wife Artemisia. Most available vertical surfaces were adorned with friezes and statues executed by some of the best sculptors of the day.

The tomb stood essentially intact for over sixteen centuries before being severely damaged by an earthquake; the Knights of St John finished the destruction between 1402 and 1522 by removing all the cut stone as building material and burning much of the marble facing for lime. Happily for posterity, they used most of the friezes for decorating their castle. When Stratford Canning, British Ambassador to the Porte, noticed them there in 1846, he obtained permission to ship them to the British Museum. Eleven years later Charles Newton discovered the site of the Mausoleum and unearthed the statues of Mausolus and Artemisia, plus portions of the chariot team, which joined the other relics in London.

Not surprisingly the Mausoleum in its present condition ranks as a disappointment, despite diligent and imaginative work by Danish archaeologists. Little is left besides the boundary wall, assorted column fragments, and some subterranean vaults, probably belonging to an earlier burial chamber. Exhibited in a shed east of the foundation cavity are plans and models as well as a copy or two of the original friezes in England. By contrast, the **ancient amphitheater**, just above the main highway bounding Bodrum to the north, has been almost overzealously restored and is used during the September festival. Begun by Mausolus, it was modified in the Roman era and originally seated 13,000, although it's present capacity is about half that. The so-called **Myndos gate**, west of the junction of Turgutreis Caddesi and Cafer Paşa Caddesi, is the sole surviving fragment of Mausolus' ambitious city wall, although stubby bits of the fortifications crop up here and there on the west side of town.

Eating and Drinking

You don't come to Bodrum to ease your budget, and **eating out** is no exception. At whatever level you dine you'll be paying above the norm, especially if you're close to the water or in a classy restaurant.

Absolute rock-bottom is the *Uslu Büfe*, a steam-tray café on Neyzen Tevfik with tables outside but no alcohol—fine for a light lunch but rather lugubrious at suppertime. Somewhat more cheerful is the *Çakır Ali*, a pizza and kebab joint, strategically placed across from the newsstand and the Adliye Camii at the foot of Cevat Şakir Caddesi. For more cheap meals, head up Cevat Şakir to either the *Uğrak Lokantası* (with the best and least expensive desserts in town) or the *Karaca*, across the street. One more inland place worth mentioning is *Can-Sa*, a grill that serves alcohol on Hamam Sokağı, around the corner from the Mausoleum.

In the Kale bazaar you might try the *Üsküdarlı* or the *Sakallı Köfteci*, and, if you can find it open, the *Kumbahçe Köftecisi* on Cumhuriyet Caddesi—which does basic inexpensive salads and kebabs. Nearby a fried *midye* and *kokoreç* stand will satisfy the urge for traditional snacks on the hoof. The *06 Lokantası*, at the end of the pedestrian area near Azmakbaşı, is surprisingly expensive for an establishment without booze but the food is pretty good and the outdoor seating always packed.

Anywhere else, especially overlooking either bay, expect a considerable jump up in price, if not always quality. If you have the inclination and wallet, there are Chinese, Italian, and even Indian restaurants, most but not all of which are along Cumhuriyet Caddesi. On the western cove, the *Reşadonya* is no cheaper or better than most of its neighbors, but is probably the quietest and least exposed to traffic fumes.

Nightlife

There must be two dozen places to **have a drink** in Bodrum. The place for the cheapest tipple has historically been the *Piknik Bar*, midway along pedestrianized Dr Alim Bey Caddesi; there's no sea view but plenty of outdoor tables and a mixed crowd. On the Cumhuriyet Caddesi strip, *Meltem* also serves Efes Pilsen at reasonabble prices—over a deafening soundtrack. Over at Neyzen Tevfik Caddesi 72, the *Mola* has a salad bar and doubles as an art gallery; the *Jazz Cafe* (Neyzen Tevfik 108) and the nearby *Cinema Bar* are both decorous and rather dull music lounges.

In terms of less sedentary **nightlife**, *Veli* is a crowded "live blues" bar at the beginning of Dr Alim Bey Caddesi. Amble along the pedestrian street past various sound systems and you'll hear everything from (usually recorded) Mexican *norteño* to hard rock. The ultimate, both in style and physical location, is *Disco Halikarnas*, at the end of Cumhuriyet Caddesi, where an $8 cover charge ($11 on weekends) and proper dress sees you in with the beautiful people. The external laser show, frequently aimed at the castle, is free.

Otherwise just join the **promenade** from the bazaar out to the east cove and back again. Everything and everybody is on display, with genuine hippie jewelry, genuine (and fake) designer jewelry, caricature artistry, and spices the principal items gaped at by veiled and skull-capped villagers and the chic set packed shoulder-to-shoulder. It's probably Turkey's most outrageous open-air circus, and, approached in this spirit, enormously amusing.

BOAT TRIPS

It's hard to miss the touts for **boat trips** in Bodrum, and if you're not planning to tour the area by land they're worth taking advantage of, since swimming anywhere near the pair of polluted town bays is inadvisable. Most of the craft are concentrated on the west harbor, and a typical day out starts between 10 and 11am, finishes between 4 and 5pm, and costs roughly $5 per person in a minimum group of seven (lunch not included). Itineraries vary little, with most boats visiting a fixed list of highlights in the following order.

First stop is usually **Kara Ada**, where you bathe in some hot springs feeding the sea at the island's shore. Next stop is the **"Akvaryum,"** a snorkellers' spot in the Ada Boğazı (Island Strait) teeming with fish, where underwater visibility can be up to 30m. The final moorings, also accessible by land and detailed below, tend to be two of the following attractions: Kargı Beach (where you can ride camels), Bağla Cove, or Karaincir Bay. Some craft head east from Kara Ada to visit **Orak Adası** and **Yalıçiftlik** Beach.

Listings

Bicycle rental *Era Turizm*, Neyzen Tevfik Cad 4.

Bookstores There are two stores which have English-language material—one in the basement of the Adliye Camii at the foot of Cevat Şakir Caddesi, the other on Dr Alim Bey Caddesi.

Car rental International chain outlets include *Avis*, Neyzen Tevfik Cad 80 (☎2333); *Budget*, Neyzen Tevfik Cad 86/A (☎3078); *Europcar/InterRent*, Neyzen Tevfik Cad 72 (☎5632); *Hertz*, Neyzen Tevfik Caddesi (☎1053). Small chains or local operators include *Airtour*, Atatürk Cad 93 (☎5927); *Bodrum Rentacar*, Azmakbaşı 22 (☎5932); *British Tour*, Cevat Şakir Cad 19 (☎3140); *Centrum*, Atatürk Cad 48 (☎6582); *Metro*, Atatürk Cad 51 (☎6148); and *Nysa*, Cevat Şakir Cad 40 (☎6658).

Exchange Late-night and weekend exchange facilities are available on a rotating schedule at *Egebank*, Dr Alim Bey Caddesi 64; *İmar Bankası*, Kale Caddesi 5/C (Belediye Meydanı); and *Dışbank*, Yeni Çarşı.

Ferry agents Several companies handle boats to Datça and Kos. Try *Motif*, Neyzen Tevfik Cad 72 (☎2309); *Karya Tur*, İskele Meydanı (☎1914); *Gino Tur*, Neyzen Tevfik Cad 200/9 (☎5026); and *Fahri Kaptan*, Neyzen Tevfik Cad 190 (☎2870). Fares are the least expensive of all the crossings to Greece: singles $9, day round-trips $13, open round-trips $17, plus $8 in taxes when leaving the Greek side.

Festival The cultural jamboree is the first part of Sept—beware accommodation shortages.

Hamam Dere Umurca Sokağı; daily 8am–5pm; Wed & Sat afternoons for women only.

Hospital The *Devlet Hastanesi* (State Hospital) is up on Turgutreis Caddesi; *Sağlık Ocağı* (Outpatient Clinic) is 300m east near the corner of Gelence Sokağı.

Market Weekly, Thurs and Fri, in the fairgrounds behind the bus station. Don't count on stupendous bargains.

Moped rental *Turqoise Tours*, Atatürk Caddesi 59; *Mylasa Hotel*, Cumhuriyet Caddesi 34.

Phone boxes The biggest concentration, with adjacent *jeton* sales, is not at the PTT but on İskele Meydanı.

Scuba diving excursions *Era Turizm*, Neyzen Tevfik Cad 4; *Motif*, Neyzen Tevfik Cad 72. A typical day excursion, including all gear, two dives, and a picnic costs about $30—remember to bring your certification card.

THY representative Neyzen Tevfik Cad 218 (☎1786).

Around the Peninsula

There is more of interest and beauty in the rest of the **Bodrum Peninsula** than the often dreary immediate environs of the town promise, and no matter how long or short your stay, some time spent there is worthwhile. The **north** side of the peninsula tends to be greener, with patches of pine forest; the **south**, studded with tall crags, is more arid, and has a sandier coast.

The population here was largely Greek Orthodox before 1923, and villages often still have a vaguely Greek feel, with ruined churches, windmills, and the old **stone houses** that even the most brazen new developments attempt to imitate. The landscape in general, with bare rock (and sometimes castles) at the higher elevations and vast **oases** along the stream beds and shore, is not unlike that of Patmos or Leros islands across the water. An otherworldly atmosphere is imparted by the big and small **islands**, both Greek and Turkish, floating out to sea, and an exotic touch is lent by the ubiquitous, white-domed *gümbetles* (cisterns), found only here and around Fethiye.

There is also a relatively high concentration of serviceable **beaches**, and virtually every resort of any importance is served by dolmuşes from Bodrum's otogar.

The South Shore

Roughly 3km west of Bodrum, **GÜMBET** is the closest real resort to the town, and the 600m, tamarisk-lined gritty beach is usually wall-to-wall loungers. It's also billed as Turkey's boardsailing mecca, and you can rent canoes and sailing dinghies as well as windsurfers. Development is slanted towards hotels and pansiyons—some fifty of them on the gradual slope behind—and there are several rather forgettable campgrounds. **BITEZ** (Ağaçlı), the next cove west and reached by a different side road, is a little classier, and seems to be overtaking Gümbet as a windsurfing center. There are quite a number of watering holes for the yachties, but the beach is negligible.

It's better to continue along the south peninsular trunk road to **ORTAKENT**, an inland village crowned by the early seventeenth-century Mustafa Paşa tower and blessed with abundant water and orchards. From both Ortakent and YAHŞİ, the next settlement, paved drives wind down several kilometers through the oases to the longest, though not necessarily the best, **beach** on the peninsula. Its two-kilometer extent is fringed by a road most of the way, and the clutter of shops, campgrounds, and motels (a score of each) behind detracts somewhat from the effect. More short-term accommodation is hidden in the orchards behind, with the vacation villas off to either side. Dolmuşes to here, incidentally, bear the legend "Ortakent Yahşi Sahil."

Beyond Yahşi, an unmarked turnoff at GÜRECE leads high above **KARGI**—a beach more easily reached from the west end of Yahşi Sahil or by boat from Bodrum, and rapidly being dwarfed by villa construction. **BAĞLA**, the next cove along, initially looks even worse, with something resembling an airport control tower planted on the cape, but keep an eye peeled for a small sign reading "Havuzbaşı." Here a dirt drive fizzles out by an old Greek church above a gushing spring feeding a fish pond; so far there's just one teahouse by the pond, and a snack bar down on the beach serving *mantı* (Turkish ravioli). The villas are encroaching on the ridges on either side, and excursion boats arrive in force by noon, but the spring-fed oasis hides much and the sand is the finest—and the water the cleanest—near Bodrum town.

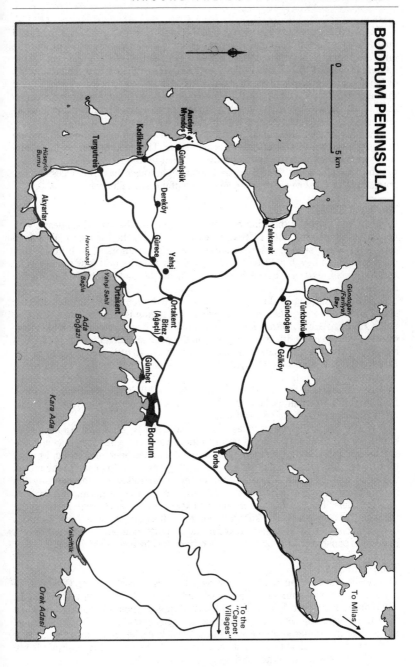

BODRUM PENINSULA

0

5 km

Ancient
Myndos
Kadıkalesi
Gümüşlük
Turgutreis
Hüseyin
Burnu
Akyarlar
Havuzbaşı
Bağla
Yahşi Sahili
Ada
Boğazı
Kara Ada
Orak Adası
Yalıçıftlik
To Milas
To the
"Carpet
Villages"
Bodrum
Gümbet
Ortakent
Ortakent
Bitez
(Ağaçlı)
Yahşi
Gürece
Dereköy
Torba
Gölköy
Gündoğan
Türkbükü
Gündoğan/
Fariyat
Bay
Yalıkavak

KARAİNCİR, the next bay with public access, is nearly as good—700m of sand guarded by a pair of promontories. Canoes and windsurfers are for rent, but the umbrellas seem to be free and there's even a wild, natural end of the beach. Of the handful of eateries, the *Ceylan* is okay, featuring roast chicken; of a similar number of motels, the *Tinaztepe* is the best. **AKYARLAR**, an old Greek port just around the bend, is more of a village, with a stone pier, mosque, many pansiyons, a campground, and a taxi stand. The beach is small, but with both Karaincir and a nameless bay in the opposite direction within walking distance, this is no great loss.

Beyond Akyarlar the coast is packed with villas and pansiyons, all staring across at nearby Kos and assorted Turkish islets. The good **beach** on the peninsula's southwestern-most cape is partly occupied by the *Armonia* resort village, but the far end, under the **Hüseyin Burnu** lighthouse, has free access and is popular with windsurfers who take advantage of the prevailing wind.

The West Shore

Once around the point the wind becomes stronger and the sand disappears, with nothing more of note until **TURGUTREIS**, usually reached by the main inland road. This is the second resort in the area after Bodrum itself, with nearly fifty pansiyons and a new bus station, but the town is a sterile grid four streets wide, and the small, exposed beach is crowded in by the luckiest half-dozen of the motels.

A side road starting by the otogar leads north to better things, through a fertile landscape of the tangerine groves for which the region is famous. After 4km you reach **KADIKALESİ**, with a long, partly protected beach and unbeatable views over to assorted islets. It's the only place on the peninsula that could be described as sleepy, and for the undemanding makes the best base on its western tip. Besides the lone luxury hotel there are just a couple of pansiyons, a campground and three or four restaurants (the two to the right of the taxi stop are reasonable by local standards). The old Greek church on the hill is the most intact around Bodrum, but of the namesake castle there seems to be no trace; any other excitement you'll have to create yourself with a rental pedalo.

If you've had a bellyful of villas, then **GÜMÜŞLÜK**, 2km past Kadıkalesi or 6km from a turnoff at Gürece, is perhaps the perfect place. It partly occupies the site of **ancient Myndos**, so most new development has been prohibited. Most of the sparse ruins litter the flat isthmus linking a giant, towering cape to the rest of the peninsula. You can scramble around the unrestricted site, assisted by the map in front of one of a half-dozen waterfront restaurants catering primarily to yacht tourists. They're drawn here by the excellent deep anchorage between the point and Tavşan Adası. The kilometer-long beach, south of the last restaurant, is less protected but still attractive, with water-sports equipment rentals; only a handful of pansiyons have been allowed, overlooked by a derelict church.

The North Shore

The north flank of the peninsula, served by a loop road out of Ortakent, in general has poor swimming and a lack of facilities. The trip over to **YALIKAVAK**, with glimpses of ocean from a windmill-dotted ridge, is possibly more worthwhile than the destination. It's the area's main sponge-fishing port, with a "working" rather than quaint harbor and a status as a "real" town, which seems to mean that prices are resort-typical but tourists are rare. A few hotels and campgrounds are available to those braving the windswept, scrappy beach.

GÜNDOĞAN (Farilya), three bays east, is an improvement; most pansiyons, and the narrow town beach, lie just west of the taxi/minibus stop. Oddly, the consistent northerly winds here and at Yalıkavak have not completely kept the developers away. If you get bored, walk inland to Gündoğan village proper, where there's a ruined monastery.

In your own vehicle, the turnoff for **GÖLKÖY** is easy to miss, and indeed development is low-rise, with the slender beach doubling as the seafront road. Swimming platforms have been erected by the hopeful motels; 500m back toward the green hills is a small lake. **TÜRKBÜKÜ**, just around the corner and on the same dolmuş route, is more picturesque, and popular with yachts, the indented local coast and island providing shelter for even more craft than at Gümüşlük. The beach is marginally better than Gölköy's; other amenities for landlubbers are much the same.

The last stop on the loop road, **TORBA** is an utterly soulless planned vacation complex, a beachless bay that might be fun for an all-inclusive windsurfing vacation, but offering little for the independent traveler or day-tripper.

East of Bodrum

The Bodrum Peninsula actually extends some distance east of the modern highway in from Milas, the twisty but paved old road winding through pine hills to Mumcular past several of the so-called "**carpet villages**" where the tawny-hued Milas carpets are woven. **ETRİN**, most famous target of special-interest tours from town, lies on the dirt road down to Çiftlik, but is also accessible via the asphalt road through ÇAMARŞI and PINARLIBELEN. Unprepossessing **MUMCULAR** has the most retail carpet shops, but all told the area's not worth the detour unless you're intent on buying a carpet—and have your own vehicle. Dolmuşes come here rarely, and tend to stick to the Milas–Mumcular stretch of road.

Muğla

MUĞLA, capital of the province containing several of the biggest resorts on the Aegean, is something of a showcase town and an exception to the Turkish rule of dire urban architecture, with a well-planned modern quarter that incorporates spacious tree-lined boulevards and accommodates some hillside **Ottoman neighborhoods** that are among the finest in Turkey. A leisurely stroll through lanes of well-maintained eighteenth-century white houses, with their tiled roofs, beaked chimneys, and ornate doors, is well worth half a day. The **bazaar**, a grid of neat alleys nestling at the base of the old residential slope to the north, is divided roughly by trade (blacksmiths predominating) and contrasts sharply with Milas' untidy jumble. Muğla is also by far the best base for visiting Stratonikya, on the road to Milas, and Gerga (see "The Çine Valley," below).

Practical Details

Muğla's almost-new **tourist information office**, on the central traffic circle sporting an Atatürk statue (Mon–Fri 8am–noon & 1–5pm), is more enthusiastic than most and may have stocks of worthwhile handouts exhausted at other branches. They also have a good map of the town.

Accommodation is somewhat limited, but since Muğla is not exactly deluged with tourists this needn't be a problem. The quietest and least expensive mid-

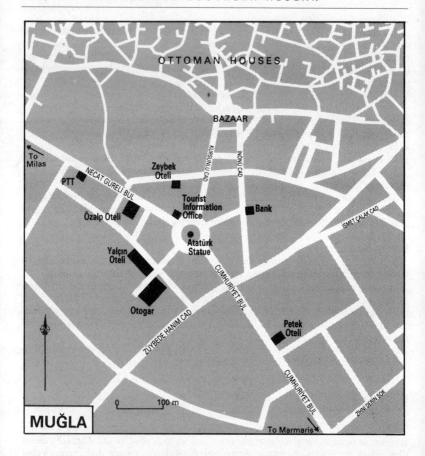

range option is the *Zeybek*, Turgutreis Caddesi 5 (☎6111/1774), with doubles for about $10. The *Yalçın*, across from the otogar, has some rooms with attached baths facing away from the traffic noise and is not bad value at $17 double. **Eating out**, either the *Ege* or the *Doyuran*, at the top of İnönü Caddesi by the entrance to the bazaar, are fine for lunch; the *Santral*, down the same street toward the new districts, serves grilled items and drinks. Muğla's **cultural festival**, held the last week in September, features nightly concerts by big Turkish names like Zülfü Livaneli and Arif Sağ, as well as films and folklore performances.

Stratonikya (Stratoniceia)

The ancient city of **STRATONIKYA**, 36km west of Muğla, would be more acclaimed if it weren't for a giant coal mine immediately west, whose noise and dust considerably reduces the peace and atmosphere of the place. The archaeological zone occupies the site of tumbledown Eskihisar village, nearly all of whose population has moved 3km west to a new settlement. Still, if you have your own vehicle or time to spare, the ruins are worth a visit. Of an afternoon many of the twenty-odd adults who have chosen to stay in Eskihisar gather at the teahouse, where you can get juice and soft drinks; it's a good idea to accept if one of them offers to escort you, as the sights are scattered and hidden, and the remaining men who work in the summer archaeological digs are quite knowledgeable.

Stratonikya was a third-century Seleucid foundation, but its heyday occurred during the Roman Imperial period, so everything you can see now dates from then. A few paces north of the teahouse is the Roman **gymnasium**, an elaborate structure with a colonnaded semicircular chamber sandwiched between three quadrangles of massive stone . At the edge of the village, overlooking the opencast mine, is the **north city gate**, flanked by a lone, unfluted Corinthian column, just outside of which is a fragment of a **sacred way** that once led to a shrine of Hecate at nearby Lagina. By the pavement stands a **subterranean tomb** in good condition, the sole survivor of a necropolis which, like the sacred way, has been sacrificed to mining interests. Parts of the substantial **city wall** are incorporated into houses on the west side of Eskihisar, with more chunks visible marching up the hillside to the south.

On the opposite side of the village is the most imposing remnant of Stratonikya, a vast rectangular space identified either as a **bouleuterion** or a **shrine of Serapis**. The first thing you'll see is an isolated, rectangular **monumental gateway** erected a few meters west, but currently entry is via twin staircases bored through the south and north side walls; the north wall's interior is covered with inscriptions. The theory that this was a council house is supported by five rows of seats, overlooking the countryside to the east. Southeast of here, the garden of an ochre-stained building serves as an impromptu **museum/warehouse** where finds from the excavation have been temporarily stored. The keeper, however, will nail you for $1 admission if you step inside, and it's really not worth the money.

Marmaris

MARMARİS rivals Kuşadası as the largest and most developed Aegean resort. Its boosters call it *Yeşil Marmaris*—"Green Marmaris"—which it certainly is, but they omit mention of the dampness, the ferocious mosquitos, and the amorphous concrete sprawl which extends for nearly 10km. According to legend, the place was named when Süleyman the Magnificent, not finding the castle here to his liking, was heard to mutter *"Mimarı as"* ("hang the architect"), later corrupted to "Marmaris"—a command that perhaps should still apply to the designers of the seemingly endless highrises.

Marmaris' newly expanded **marina**, Turkey's largest, has shaped the town's character more than anything else—this is the main base for most of the yacht-charter companies operating on the Turquoise Coast. Proximity to Dalaman Airport also means that both foreign and domestic tourists pour in non-stop during the warmer months, making Marmaris an unpleasantly tacky, loud, and expensive place to be during most of the summer. After a day or two here, you'll be relieved to move on.

Marmaris' **history** has been determined above all by the stunning local topography: a deep, fiord-like inlet surrounded by pine-cloaked hills. This did not seem to spur ancient Physcus, the original Dorian colony, to any growth or importance, but Süleyman comfortably assembled a force of 200,000 here in 1522 when launching the successful siege of the Knights of St John's base in Rhodes. Shortly after this campaign Süleyman endowed the old town nucleus with the tiny castle and a *han*. In 1798 Nelson's entire British fleet sheltered here before setting out to defeat Napoleon's French armada at the Battle of Aboukir.

Arrival and Information

The **otogar** is two blocks behind the yacht marina on the east side of town, just a few minutes' walk from the town center. The *Havaş* **airport bus** from Dalaman leaves you in front of the *THY* office on Atatürk Caddesi, the long shore road usually known as Kordon Caddesi. If you show up with your own **car**, be aware that no parking is allowed anywhere along the Kordon, and no vehicles except taxis and locals anywhere east of Ulusal Egemenlik Bulvarı. Arriving by **ferry** from the Greek island of Rhodes, the dock conveniently abuts İskele Meydanı, on one side of which stands the **tourist information office** (summer daily 8am–8pm; winter Mon–Fri 8am–noon & 1–5pm; ☎11035), dispensing town plans, bus schedules and accommodation lists.

> The Marmaris area **telephone code** is ☎612, recently changed from 6121. As at Kuşadası, the displaced "1" is now the first digit of all local numbers.

Finding a Place to Stay

Accommodation in Marmaris is generally hotel-orientated and thus expensive; there is no concentration of pansiyons or small hotels as in Turkey's other coastal resorts. Since the completion of the yacht harbor, most pansiyons have vanished from Barbaros Caddesi, as the waterfront is known east of the castle, and somewhat better value for money can be had out at the west end of the Kordon, close to where it splits into Kemal Elgin Bulvarı and Uzunyalı Beach. The listings below are in ascending order of price. One consolation: Marmaris has an excellent, IYHF-affiliated **youth hostel**.

East of Ulusal Egemenlik Bulvarı

Dilek, Hacı Mustafa Sok 108 (☎13591); **Işıksal**, Hacı Mustafa Sok 89 (☎11391). Two similar, plain pansiyons one street back from the marina, near the bus station. $8 double.

Can Pansiyon, 53 Sok 17 (☎11233). A simple, concrete affair just a few steps from the *Anadolu Turism* ferry agency. $10 a double.

Kalyon Hotel, İskele Meydanı (☎13773). Bang in the middle of everything—including the noise from the downstairs bar. $12 for a double without bath.

Otel Pina, Kemeraltı Cad 6 (☎11053). Rooms with harbor view are of course noisier. Singles $8, doubles $12.

Hotel Kaptan, Barbaros Cad 11 (☎11251). Run by the *Yeşil Marmaris* yachting agency, with plain but acceptable rooms. $12 single, $16 double with attached bath.

Hotel Anatolia, İskele Meydanı (☎12851). Next to the *Kalyon*, and no quieter, but more comfortable after a recent facelift. $24 for a double with bath.

Hotel Begonya, Hacı Mustafa Sok 101/71 (☎14095). A renovated old farm building with a pleasant garden and bar; open summer only. $32 for a double with bath and breakfast.

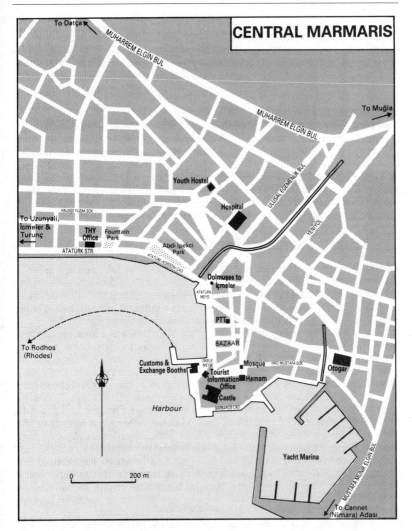

CENTRAL MARMARIS

West of Ulusal Egemenlik Bulvarı

Interyouth Hostel, 300m past the hospital on the road toward Datça (☎16432). A new three-story outfit with all modern facilities. $4–5 per person.

Suat, Hamdi Yuzak Sok 48 (☎13961); **Onay**, no. 46 (☎11330); **Emrah**, No. 51 (☎13881). These pansiyons are all inland from the park-with-fountain on the Kordon. They're old-fashioned, basic places aimed at Turkish vacationers, and are relatively quiet and inexpensive at about $8 per spartan double.

Pansiyon Honeymoon, passage off the Kordon near the *Çubuk Otel* (☎13001). Well-kept, and offering fair value at $10 single, $16 double with bath.

Sini Pansiyon, corner of Kordon and Kemal Elgin Bulvarı (☎11505). Same prices as the *Honeymoon*, a slight edge in comfort and partial sea view.

Arslan Motel, Uzunyalı Beach (☎11403). An old-style Turkish family compound built around a courtyard-restaurant. Two- or three-person "suites" with kitchenette and bath $18 per day.

Studio Anfora Pansiyon, Uzunyalı Beach (☎16733). Same concept as the preceding, but newer and pitched exclusively at foreigners. $20 per day for a two-person studio.

Otel Yavuz, Kordon Cad 10 (☎12937). Three-star comfort and service, for probably as much as you'd want to pay. $36 for a single, $46 a double with bath and breakfast.

Camping

Camping is probably not a good idea in the immediate surroundings of Marmaris. With the skyrocketing value of real estate, most campground owners expect to build villas or pansiyons on their turf, so facilities tend to be rudimentary, poorly maintained, and noisy. Your best bet is to stroll along Uzunyalı Beach and see who's operating this year between the construction sites. If you're determined to tent down for a while, it's best to head out 20km or so on the Datça road, where there are several well-equipped campgrounds, or 8km south to İçmeler, where *Karya Mocamp* and *Mustafa Camping* are permanent fixtures.

The Town . . . and Boat Excursions

Ulusal Egemenlik Bulvarı cuts Marmaris roughly in half, and the maze of narrow streets east of it contain most of the monuments and facilities—including the castle, bazaar, banks, PTT—of interest to the average tourist. Numerous travel agencies and bus company ticket offices cluster a hundred or so meters to either side of Atatürk Meydanı, the seaside plaza at the base of Ulusal Egemenlik.

Little is left of the sleepy fishing village that Marmaris was a mere two decades ago. The bazaar, including its diminutive *kervansaray*, has been ruthlessly commercialized, and only the **Kaleiçi** district, the brief tangle of streets at the base of the tiny castle, offers a pleasant wander. The **fortress** itself (daily 8am–noon & 1–5pm, 50¢) is not yet up and running as a fully stocked museum; it mostly serves as a venue for events during the May festival.

In any case, you don't come to Marmaris for cultural edification, and you swim at Kordon Beach at your peril. **Boat excursions**, whether short outings or two-week cruises, are a better way to spend time here. Day-trips usually visit highlights of the inner bay, not venturing much beyond the straits separating Cennet and Keçi islands. Most skippers will take you to a beach on the north side of Cennet Adası, and caves on the south shore, then complete the day with a visit to Kumlubükü or Turunç coves (see "Around Marmaris," below, for full descriptions). Since all of these spots are more or less difficult to reach by land, it's worth the effort—as long as you keep the price below $8 a head.

One offer that you definitely can refuse is an excursion to Kaunos from Marmaris: because of the distance involved, you'll spend six-plus hours sailing and perhaps two hours sightseeing. Kaunos (see Chapter Five, "The Turquoise Coast") is more usually reached from Dalyan or as part of a lengthy cruise.

Eating and Drinking

Getting a decent **meal** at a reasonable price is something of a challenge in Marmaris: don't expect much solace even in the bazaar, where restaurants have been uniformly gentrified. One exception is the *Ay Yıldız*, at a triple intersection just off a small plaza near the bazaar mosque, where a grilled item, two side dishes and a beer won't run much over $6. Try also the *Can Restaurant*, on the ground floor of the pansiyon of the same name, or the *İstanbul Pide Salonu* across the street. One alley farther along, the *Özyalçın Meat House* is good, particularly the bread, but a meal for two with wine will set you back $20. A small grill house at Hacı Mustafa Sokak 53 is as close to economical as you'll get near the marina, where any of the waterfront spots run to $16 apiece for a meal with wine. *Turkish Kitchen*, 100m inland from the *Çubuk Hotel* and Abdi İpekci Park, serves reasonable baked dishes. If you're staying on or near Uzunyalı Beach, you can get simple pizzas and light meals served up in an unbeatable setting for about fifteen percent less than in town.

Nightlife

Not surprisingly, most of Marmaris' **drinking** takes place along the east marina, where the yachties expand their liver capacities during happy hour at *Scorpio* or *Okimo*. The tiny *Bar Ivy* seems to get a younger, more backpacking crowd after dark. *Palm Tree*, at Hacı Mustafa Sokak 97, is fine as a garden bistro with taped music. At *Maxim's Disco* on the Kordon, where no single men are allowed between 11:30pm and 4am, you'll probably get sick on rotgut *rakı* made from figs.

Listings

Airlines *İstanbul Hava Yolları*, Kemal Elgin Bul 50/B (☎13222);*THY*, Kordon Caddesi 30/B (☎13751).

Airport Dalaman Airport, 90km east, is served both by *Marmaris Belediyesi* and *Havaş* buses departing from in front of *THY* office 2hr 45min before *THY* flights. Since there are at most three flights daily, these may not be much use if you're catching a charter.

Beach Uzunyalı, 1km or so west of the town center, is the nearest, but it's really only worth visiting if you're desperate for a swim since the water is polluted and the sand itself is used as a sidewalk by passing pedestrians, making sun-lounging difficult.

Bookstores *Şehrazat*, across from Hacı Mustafa Sok 49 behind the castle, has some used English-language books to trade. *NET*, in the bazaar, carries nautical charts of the area for use on your coastal cruise.

Car rental The majors include *Avis*, Kordon Caddesi 30 (☎12771); *Budget*, Ulusal Egemenlik Cad 6 (☎14144); *Europcar/InterRent*, Kordon Caddesi 12 (☎12001); and *Hertz*, İskele Meydanı (☎12552). Small chains and local indies include *Airtour*, Kenan Evren Bulvarı, Manolya Pansiyon Sok (☎13915); *Metro*, Şirinyer, Teke Karşısı 2 (☎15260); *Nysa*, Kısayalı 94 (☎12104); *Zafer*, Kemal Elgin Bul 50/2 (☎13222).

Consulate *British*, Hacıiman Sok 61, next to castle.

Exchange *Vakıfbank*, on the corner of the Kordon and the PTT street, stays open until 8pm daily; the booths of *Pamukbank, Şekerbank*, and *Halk Bankası*, next to customs on the ferry dock, stay open until 9:30pm.

Ferries Authorized agents for the morning Turkish ferry to Rhodes include *Yeşil Marmaris*, Barbaros Cad 11 (☎11559), *Anadolu Turizm*, corner of 53 Sokak and Kordon (☎13514), and *Engin Turizm*, Kordon 10 (☎11082). The sole agent for the evening Greek ferry to Rhodes is *All Star*, Barbaros Cad 228, near the bus station. One-way tickets cost $2; day round-trips $30, open round-trips $36, plus $8 tax when leaving the Greek side.

Festival Yachting regatta and arts presentations take place in the second week of May, when the accommodation situation gets tight.

Hamam In the rear of the bazaar on Eski Cami Arkası 3. Open daily 8am–midnight, not cheap: the works (massage, tea, etc) cost $6.

Hospital On the road to Datça, a few meters west of the landward end of Ulusal Egemenlik.

BOAT CHARTERS ALONG THE COAST

Certainly the most enjoyable thing to do in and around Marmaris is to charter a motor schooner (*gület*) or a smaller yacht, either of which will allow you to explore the convoluted coast between Bodrum and Kaş. Especially outside the high season, the daily cost isn't necessarily prohibitive—no more than renting a medium-sized car for two, for example—and in the case of a *gület*, a knowledgeable crew will be included. Virtually all of the shore described in this chapter and the next is fair game, plus many other hidden coves accessible only by sea.

You can charter a boat through specialist operators in North America (see *Basics* for details), or you can make arrangements when you arrive; although prices are always quoted in US dollars, you can pay in Turkish lira. Substantial deposits are required—usually fifty percent of the total price—so taking a cruise is not something to be indulged in lightly.

If you're uncertain about your level of commitment, or show up alone or in a very small group, the best option is what's called a **cabin charter**. Several companies set aside one schooner whose berths are let out individually; the craft departs on a certain day of the week with a fixed, "sample" itinerary of seven days. Prices in April–May and October are $320 per person, including all food and water-sports equipment—excellent value. During June–September the cost jumps to around $415.

If you can assemble a large group, and have more time at your disposal, consider a **standard charter** of a twenty-meter motorboat. In May and October a group of twelve, for example, will pay $34 each daily, not including food or sporting equipment, while a group of eight will be more comfortable and less crowded but will pay $38 a day per person. During June–Sept, count on $42–50 each per day.

Companies often offer to supply food for about $15 minimum each per day, though there's a fair mark-up hidden in this and you'd spend about the same eating three meals a day on shore. Probably the best strategy is to dine in restaurants at your evening mooring and to keep the galley stocked for breakfast and snacks; if you tip the crew appropriately they're usually be happy to shop for you.

For the greatest degree of independence, so-called **bareboat yacht charter** is the answer. This assumes that at least one of your party is a certified skipper; otherwise count on at least $130 a day extra to hire one. Prices are usually quoted by the week, and in April or October work out around $250 person. During June or September allow $320 each per week.

One of the oldest and more reliable charter **agencies** in Marmaris is *Yeşil Marmaris*, Barbaros Caddesi 11, PO Box 8, 48700 Marmaris (☎11033; fax ☎14470). Its Bodrum branch is at Atatürk Caddesi 81, 48400 Bodrum (☎6141/3091; fax ☎6141/2375). For bareboat yachts, one of the larger local operators is *Albatros Yachting*, Barbaros Caddesi 7 (☎12456; fax ☎14470), with a representative in Bodrum at Neyzen Tevfik Caddesi 72 (☎6141/2309; fax ☎6141/3522).

Around Marmaris: the Rhodian Peraea

In ancient times the peninsula extending from the head of the Gulf of Gökova to a promontory between the Greek islands of Symi and Rhodes was known as the **Rhodian Peraea**—the mainland territory of the three united city-states of Rhodes—which controlled the area for eight centuries. Despite this, and the fact that the natives were granted full Rhodian citizenship, there is little evidence of the long tenure; the peninsula was—and is—a backwater, today known as the Hisarönü, Loryma, or Daraçya Peninsula, depending on which map you look at or yacht skipper you ask. In fact, yachts have up to now been the principal means of getting around this irregular landmass, and although a new road has just been completed, the difficulty of access has until now kept development to a minimum and the locals amazingly friendly. If you're not privileged enough to have a yacht handy, the best way of seeing the area is on foot.

North: the Gökova Gulf Shore

In Marmaris you'll probably notice signs pitching an excursion to "Cleopatra's Isle." This is actually **SEDİR ADASI** (Cedar Island), an islet, near the head of the Gulf of Gökova, which still sports extensive fortifications and a theater from its time as Cedreae, a city of the Peraea. More evocative, however, is its alleged role as a trysting place of Cleopatra and Mark Antony, and the legend concerning the island's **beach**—the main goal of the day trips. The sand was supposedly brought from Africa at Mark Antony's behest, and indeed analysis has shown that the grains are not from local strata. The tour boats depart between 10am and 11am from **ÇAMLI İSKELESİ**, 6km down a side road 12km north of Marmaris, returning at 4 or 5pm; there's no public transportation to the departure point, so you must use the tour operator's shuttle bus.

The alternative approach is by boat excursion from the hamlet of **TAŞBÜKÜ**, 4km farther along the same road and just opposite the islet. Again there's no dolmuş in, but there are two motel/campgrounds with attached restaurants, the *Çamlı* and the *Sedir*. They're both reasonable, at $8 per person with bath and breakfast included, and the *Sedir* also has chalets for $4 a head. They share a reservations number in Marmaris (☎16800) and if you phone in good time will arrange to shuttle you in for free. The well-vegetated area is idyllic, if small, and the sand-and-gravel beach is not nearly as stony as the name Taşbükü (Stone Cove) implies.

Besides the obvious jaunt over to Sedir Adası, there are also boat outings available to **İNGİLİZLİMANI**—a beautiful bay reachable only by sea—and **KARACASÖĞÜT**, which is also accessible by land, via a side road 11km north of Marmaris. It's 13km (the occasional village-bound dolmuş will take you the first 11km) to this gorgeous, almost landlocked bay, girded by willows and other greenery, with the wall of mountains north of the open gulf as a backdrop. It's a big yacht haven, and you can watch the action from the tiny, ramshackle **restaurant**—cheapest of several—at the far west end of the bay. The main **beach**, alas, is muddy and has two creeks draining onto it, so you can really only swim off the functional platform jutting out into the water, well away from the boats.

South: Toward Loryma

Overland access to the bulk of the peninsula is along an initially paved road south from the main Datça-bound highway 21km west of Marmaris. The first place anyone, including dolmuşes, stops is **ORHANİYE**—but mostly for the yacht anchorage. The mere handful of pansiyons and a single campground is a reflection of the mostly muddy, shallow shore here.

SELİMİYE is the next coastal village where visitors tend to stop, again mostly by yacht, although the new direct highway from Orhanıye will bring more traffic. A hilltop Ottoman fort overlooks the port here, at the head of an all-but-landlocked arm of the giant Delikyol Bay. There's a minimal beach at the far western end of the straggly village, beyond the new villa cluster. Numerous waterfront restaurants are aimed mostly at the boat trade, and the near-absence of pansiyons or motels betrays the fact that most visitors are sleeping in cabins. Still, you may decide to stay—when the yachts are gone life passes very slowly. *Boşfer* (literally "Never Mind, Not Bothered"), the name of a fishing boat here, about sums up the mood of the place.

Bozburun and Beyond

BOZBURUN, just over the hill from Selimiye, is more of a real town, but still has a firm nautical orientation; yacht repairs and supplies are conspicuously offered, and boatyards occupy a large area. The settlement itself is undistinguished, slumbering in dusty heat six months of the year, but the setting, on a convoluted gulf with a fat islet astride its mouth and Greek Symi beyond, is startling.

The place is unlikely to go the way of Datça, even if the new road is asphalted, since there is precious little level land for development, even less fresh water, and absolutely no sand. Nonetheless Bozburun is a very "in" resort for Turks: SDP party leader Erdal İnönü has vacationed here, and various eccentrics—ex-journalists-turned bartenders, diehard Turkish hippies, recording executives-turned-restaurant-proprietors—collect in this isolated corner of coastal Turkey.

Pansiyon proprietors will collar you as you get out of the one daily dolmuş, but it's best to hold out for certain premises ten minutes' walk out of town to the left, past the primary school, as you face the bay. Top choice here, directly on the water, is the *Yalçin* (☎6126/1151), run by Behice Şengül and known locally as "Behice Hanim's," or the neighboring *Pembe Yunus* (☎6126/1154). Cement swimming platforms dot the shore here so you won't miss a beach. If you require luxury, the *Akvaryum Motel* (☎612/11434, in Marmaris) on the water is the closest you'll get.

Most of the four or five waterfront **restaurants** tender expensive delicacies to the maritime crowd; the only cheap meals are at *Başçavuş in Yeri*, on the opposite side of the Atatürk statue from the *Akvaryum*. Behind the motel is an excellent dessert shop. The trendy set, whether Turkish landlubbers or yachties, gathers beyond the *jandarma* post at either *Pizza Kekik*, the *Mariners Bar*, or the *Cafe Blanca*.

Unless you've eloped with someone, boredom could become a problem; the boat day-trips advertised rarely leave the confines of the bay. In cooler weather you could walk east one valley to SÖĞÜT, essentially a farming oasis with a minimal shore settlement boasting two restaurants, but nowhere to stay. The dolmuş serving Söğüt terminates at TAŞLICA, a hilltop village girded by almond and olive trees sprouting from a stone desert. From the square where the dolmuş leaves you, a three-to-four hour trail leads south to ancient Loryma, where a Rhodian fort overlooks the magnificent harbor of Bozukkale—which in turn holds several restaurants. If you don't want to walk back the same way you just might be able to hitch a boat ride out from here.

The East Coast

On the east coast of the peninsula, a remarkably bad road leads to two fair-sized resorts. The first, TURUNÇ, boasts a 500-meter beach and could make a pleasant alternative to Marmaris town, despite a huge luxury complex at one end of the cove. Among **pansiyons**, the *Yeşil, Zeybek, Çardak,* and *Göl* are well positioned, and the *Fidan Restaurant* on the shore is pretty good.

The road (and sometimes a dolmuş) continues south, past ancient **Amos** (only Hellenistic walls and a theater remain) to **KUMLUBÜKÜ**, another sandy bay with a half-dozen of everything. Along with **Çiftlik Bay**, a considerable distance south, dominated by a huge luxury compound, these are the only big patches of sand on the whole peninsula. At Çiftlik there's also the strangely named *Mc Cherry* **campground/motel**.

The Datça Peninsula

Once past the turnoff for Bozburun, the main highway west of Marmaris ventures out onto the elongated, narrow **Datça** (Reşadiye) Peninsula. You get glimpses through pine gullies of the sea on both sides, although the road is narrow, twisty, and inadvisable at night. With the exception of a pair of tiny villages there's nothing until Datça town except two huge campground-motels: the *Amazon*, well north of the road, and the *Aktur*, right on the road and with a decent private beach.

Datça

Too manicured and up-and-coming to be the backpackers' haven it once was, **DATÇA** is still many times calmer than either Bodrum or Marmaris. It's essentially the port of inland Reşadiye village, but under the ministrations of visiting yachtspeople and tour operators has outgrown its parent. Carpet shops are big news here—a good dozen appeal to the yacht-bound (Datça is now an official port of entry) and to the growing number of tour groups. Prices are still fifteen percent less than in Bodrum or Marmaris, and most development lies out of sight to the north—though for how much longer is difficult to predict.

Practical Details

Datça's most interesting feature is its layout: a single, kilometer-long main street meandering between two sheltered bays separated by a hill and then a narrow isthmus, finally terminating in a cape. Along the way you pass—in this order— the **PTT**, some **banks**, the tiny **tourist office**, a **dolmuş** and **taxi stand** and **ferry-ticket agencies**.

Only two **bus** companies currently serve Datça, so there's no otogar. Bodrum-bound **ferries**, operated by *Karya Tours*, run from Körmen Limanı, 9km north, connected by a short bus ride. It's worth taking the boat at least in one direction to avoid duplicating the wild bus journey in from the east. Any ferries advertised to Kos (Greece) actually go via Bodrum; there are direct services to Rhodes but they're infrequent—once a week at best.

Accommodation is barely sufficient to meet demand—you may have to try several places. The most obvious desirable location is the little hill separating the two bays, where there are four pansiyons to choose from: the *Huzur* (☎6145/1052), the most modern; the reasonable *Sadık* (☎6145/1196); the *Çagla* (☎6145/1084), the roughest but with a sea view; and the *Karaöglu* (☎6145/1079), with the best view and a pleasant café. The *Kaya* and the *Yılmaz*, nearby on the main drag, are newer, steeper, and noiser.

Another possible hunting ground is the east bay, where, just beyond the produce stalls, is the *Tokcan Pansiyon*. The *Rosi* is virtually on the beachfront, set well back from the road; the *Yalı* (☎6145/1059) and *Oya* are two older establishments. The oldest and funkiest flophouse, though not without charm, is the curiously named *Ensenada Oteli* (☎6145/1014), out on the point next to the most expensive digs, the *Dorya Motel* (☎6145/1303). The latter, if you'll treat yourself, is tastefully luxurious, with well-kept gardens and common areas. Any of the more ordinary establishments will cost about $6 single, $8 double, often with attached bath. There's also an attractive **campground**, *Camping Ilıca*, at the far end of the western beach.

When foraging for **food**, you'll find the half-dozen restaurants overlooking the west cove fairly indistinguishable in price and quality. Some imaginative dishes rarely seen elsewhere may be on display, but there are no bargains here. The *Durak*, on the main road near the bus stop, is hardly cheaper but at least the portions are bigger; if money's an issue, try the nicely decorated *Defne Pide Salonu* or the tradesmen's kitchens still farther inland. Various cafés overlooking the eastern beach can offer **breakfast** for as little as $1.25—shop around.

Things to Do

The most frantic activity you'll find in Datça is after dark at the handful of **discos and bars** along the west harbor and beyond on the west beach. Otherwise, it's a matter of picking your swimming and sunbathing spot. The **east beach**, partly hardpack sand, partly cement wharf with cafés, is quieter, and a swim initially seems tempting, but a bacteria-level gauge next to a discharging storm drain will probably put you off. The **west beach**, mixed pebble/sand, is acceptable and gets better the farther you get from the anchored yachts.

In contrast to the scenery on the drive in, the immediate surroundings of Datça are quite barren, softened only by a mineral-spring-fed **lake** halfway along the west bay. Warm water seeping up from the lakebed, 2m down, make swimming here more pleasant than in the ocean; some appealing bar/cafés overlook the stone dam that augments the water level.

With the limited swimming options in town, **local boat trips** advertised on the west harbor make a good day out. Groups generally depart between 8:30am and 9:30am, returning between 5 and 6pm. Standard stops include Palamut Bükü, Domuz Çukuru, Mesudiye Bükü, and ancient Knidos—all detailed below. The going price per person, without lunch, is $10, compared to $27 for a **taxi** to Knidos, which allows only an hour at the ruins and no opportunities for a dip.

The Way to Knidos

Beyond Datça the peninsula broadens considerably, and the scenery, almond and olive groves around somnolent villages at the base of pine-speckled mountains, is quite unlike that which came before. Of the 34km of road beyond Reşadiye village, the first six are paved, the last eight, beyond Yazıköy, are appalling, although an ordinary car with good clearance should make it in dry weather.

Some 11km out of Reşadiye, signs point down the five-kilometer side road to the shore hamlet at **MESUDİYE BÜKÜ**. Two inobtrusive **campgrounds** (*Mustafa, Ovada*) and two **motels** separate the fine sand beach from a spectacular backdrop of oasis and mountains. Prices are slightly cheaper than in Datça, but not much happens after dark. For true misanthropes, HAYIT BÜKÜ, one cove east, is even more untouched. There is an occasional **dolmuş** to Mesudiye from Datça, but this ordinarily stops in the upper village so you may have to cajole the driver into taking you the extra 3km.

A new coast road links Mesudiye with **PALAMUT BÜKÜ**, but it's no-go unless you've got a jeep. Most vehicles (but no dolmuşes) continue down the main road to the point, 18km out of Reşadiye, where a side road drops 3km south to Palamut. The stark setting is counterbalanced by a full kilometer of tiny-pebble beach with an islet offshore. Of a handful of pansiyons, the *Arçipel* and the *Bük* at the far east end of the bay are the most appealing; the only drawback is that most of the **restaurants** tend to be well to the west, by the fishing harbor.

Knidos (Cnidus)

Hard as it is to believe from its current state, **KNIDOS**, a few kilometers farther on, was one of the most fabled and prosperous cities of antiquity. With its strategic location astride the main shipping lanes of the Mediterranean, it was also a cosmopolitan city, and illustrious personalities hailing from here were legion. In its heyday it was also home of an eminent medical school, rival to the Hippocratic clinic across the straits on Kos. However, the city was most notorious for a splendid statue of Aphrodite and the cult (and sacred brothels) surrounding it.

The catch is that very little remains of this former greatness, and it's definitely not worth punishing any vehicle the full distance in from Datça. The most the site merits, at least until excavations are completed, is a short halt on a boat tour. Arriving **by boat**, you dock in the south bay, close to where there are a few expensive restaurants (the *Bora*, with a few beds too, is cheapest) and a police post. Leave **vehicles** at a small parking lot, near which a sign warns you that although the site is unrestricted you're liable to pay admission—$1 if the keeper is present.

The Aphrodisiac Cult at Knidos

Like several cities in Asia Minor, Knidos was a Peloponnesian Dorian foundation, circa 1000 BC, although the original settlement was near present-day Datça. The famous shrine of Apollo, religious focus of the Dorian Hexapolis, is thought to have been above today's Palamut Bükü. During the middle of the fourth century BC Knidos was moved to its present location—a shrewd step, taking advantage of the enforced stays of ships sheltering here from high local winds. The new town was built on both the tip of the mainland and what was then an island to the south; in ancient times the two were joined by a causeway sluiced by a bridged channel (the channel between the two has since silted up).

Undoubtedly Knidos' most famous "citizen" was an inanimate object, the **cult statue of Aphrodite** by Praxiteles, the first large-scale, freestanding nude of a woman; this adorned the new city from its earliest days and became, even more than the menacing winds, Knidos' chief source of revenue. Set up in a sanctuary so that it could be admired from every angle, the marble Aphrodite attracted thousands of ancient tourists, not all of them mere art-lovers. According to legend the statue bore a dark stain in its crotch, not a flaw in the marble but the result of a youth conceiving such a passion for it that he hid in the temple until after closing time and made love to the effigy.

After paying their respects to the image, more normal pilgrims were wont to observe the rites of love with one of the sacred prostitutes who worked in the temple area. Subsequently customers might buy tacky pornographic souvenirs, whose nature will be familiar to anyone who has browsed a postcard rack or gift shop anywhere in the modern Aegean. All this license was—perhaps predictably—too much for the Byzantine Christians, who destroyed Praxiteles' Aphrodite along with the temple, although Iris Love, chief of the American archaeological team, claims to have discovered the statue's head in a vault at the British Museum. Copies or incomplete versions of the statue still exist in New York, Rome, and Munich.

The Site

With the ruins still under excavation, the posted site-plan near the entrance is of little use. Your overwhelming impression will be of an enormous, weedy mess, virtually unlabeled and booby-trapped with deep, unguarded trenches—but you may derive some satisfaction from the windswept, dramatic setting.

Most of Knidos' public buildings were on the mainland side, and the **Hellenistic theater**, overlooking the south bay, is the best preserved. A military watchtower on the ex-island confirms that most of it is off-limits; visit instead the two **Byzantine basilicas**, one huge with extensive mosaics, overlooking the north harbor. Hellenistic Knidos was laid out in a grid pattern, although the hilly site necessitated extensive terracing, retaining walls, and stairways. Clambering along these, you'll need some luck and persistence to stumble on the agora, the bouleuterion, a Corinthian temple, a purported sundial, and an unidentified mosaic floor. Of the Aphrodite shrine, only the circular foundation remains.

INLAND CARIA

Away from the coastal regions, major settlements in ancient Caria tended to concentrate along the upper reaches of the Meander River, now the Büyük Menderes, and its tributaries, particularly the Marsyas—today the Çine Çayı.

Aydın, a pleasant if nondescript town easily reached from Kuşadası, is the preferred base of choice for visiting ancient **Nyssa**, and also **Alında, Alabanda**, and **Gerga**, the archaeological sites of the Çine Valley. Of these, only Alında is anything like required viewing and is also the easiest to reach by public transportation; the other two are pretty remote and don't repay the effort involved in driving or walking to them. Farther east, **Aphrodisias**, on a high plateau south of the Büyük Menderes, is similarly isolated but buses are more obliging since it's poised to become Ephesus' rival in southwest-Aegean tourism.

Still farther inland, the functional city of **Denizli** has transport connections in every direction, most obviously with **Hierapolis/Pamukkale**, an ancient site and geological prodigy that's the star of every other Turkish tourist poster ever produced. Whether it figures as the high or low point of your stay depends on your temperament, but if escape becomes imperative, minor attractions such as **Laodiceia** and **Akhan** are conveniently close.

Aydın and Around

AYDIN is a modern provincial capital, with clean, tree-lined main boulevards and a smattering of older buildings in the center. If you don't have a car, its excellent dolmuş services make it the obvious jumping off point for the area's ancient ruins—Nyssa to the east, the closest, and the sites of the Çine Valley, scattered either side of the picturesque road south to Muğla.

Aydın began life as Tralles, a distinguished ancient town legendarily founded by colonists from the Greek Argive and Thrace; the site of the original settlement (now a military zone requiring special permission to visit) was a plateau northwest of today's city. Despite its good natural defenses Tralles submitted, or fell, to every conqueror that ever traipsed through Asia Minor, but enjoyed a period of prosperity during the Roman Imperial period, even eclipsing neighboring Nyssa.

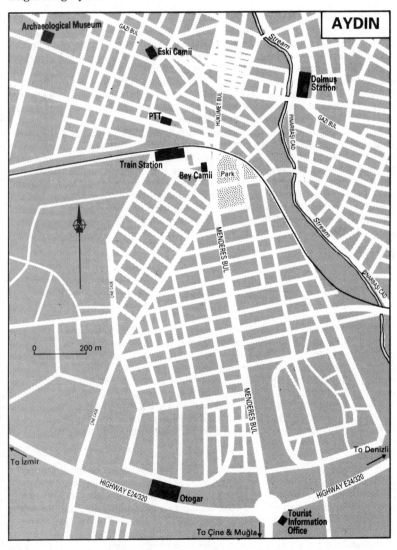

Contemporary Aydın's attractions fall mostly into the time-filling category. The oldest Turkish monument is the seventeenth-century **Bey Camii**, across from the pleasant, mosaic-paved central park. The **museum** (daily except Mon 8:30am–noon & 1:30–5pm; $1), west of the gardens, holds a wide collection of finds from around the province spanning all eras and cultures, and includes a recently added ethnographic division. Don't bother pestering the authorities for permission to visit ancient Tralles—you'll only see the barest vestiges of a Roman gymnasium.

Practical Details

The **otogar** is 600m south of the center on the main highway, just west of a large traffic circle and the **tourist office**, which has excellent city maps available; the otogar is connected with the center of town by complimetary shuttle bus. Adnan Menderes Bulvarı shoots straight up to the heart of town, where the **train station** and **PTT** face each other just west of the central square. Hükümet Bulvarı, Menderes' narrower continuation, climbs past the bulk of the hotels and restaurants before intersecting Gazi Bulvarı, Aydın's main east-west thoroughfare and location of the important **dolmuş station**.

As for **accommodation**, the *Kabaçam*, Hükümet Bulvarı 11 Sokak 2/B (☎631/12794), is the best value, with comfortable doubles with bath at $17. Runner-up is the nearby *Baltaçı*, Gazi Bulvarı, 3 Sokağı (☎631/11321), with slightly more worn facilities for the same price. Directly opposite the *Kabaçam* stands the *Vardar*, but it's a big step down in quality. There's one other four-star establishment, the *Orhan* up on Gazi Bulvarı, but it's hard to imagine both the *Kabaçam* and the *Baltaçi* being full. Various inexpensive **restaurants** are tucked into the lanes of the small bazaar west of Hükümet; the *Şanlıurfa Kebab Salonu* is representative.

Nyssa

Awash in a sea of olive groves in the hills above the Büyük Menderes Valley, ancient **NYSSA** is rarely visited—and except for its theater, *bouleuterion*, and unusual layout, there is little to interest non-specialist visitors. Most of what's left above ground are numerous arches of inferior masonry.

Originally founded by Peloponnesians, the city flourished from the first century BC until the third century AD, and remained an important Byzantine community afterward. During the Roman era it was famous as an academic center, attracting pupils from throughout Asia Minor. Strabo, while not a native, studied here and left detailed accounts of the city, which can still be partly verified even in Nyssa's present ruinous condition.

The archaeological zone lies 2km above SULTANHISAR, the modern successor to Nyssa that sits astride major bus and rail lines. There are simple eateries in Sultanhisar but nowhere to stay, and no public transportation up to the ruins.

The Site

The paved access road from the ticket office ($1 admission) balloons out into a small parking lot flanked by picnic tables, just north of which lies an excellently preserved **Roman theater**—a structure, with a capacity of well over 5000, that is slowly being taken over by wild olive saplings sprouting quaintly amid the seats. The paved road continues another 300m uphill to the start of the two-hundred meter walk to the **bouleuterion**, where twelve semicircular rows of seats face out toward an area graced with a **ceremonial basin** and **mosaics**.

Strabo described the city as built on both sides of a steep ravine, and some of the monuments he listed still cling to the banks of the canyon. A path just east of the theater descends to the mouth of a huge, 115m-long **tunnel** burrowing under the parking lot, which in Roman times was the main city square. Beyond the southern exit are the remains of two **bridges** linking the halves of Nyssa, and the virtually unrecognizable rubble of a stadium and a gymnasium, well recessed into the flanks of the gully and both currently off-limits. The tunnel, in addition to functioning as a simple storm drain, could be used to fill the stadium with water for mock naval battles.

To the west of the access road, reached by another path beginning 100m north of the guard post, stand some **baths** (adjoining the theater) and a **library**, alleged by many sources to be the second most important in Asia Minor after the one in Ephesus. You wouldn't know it from the muddled, two-story building lost in more olives.

The Çine Valley: Alinda, Alabanda, Gerga

The **Çine Çayı**, formerly the River Marsyas, is one of the largest tributaries of the Büyük Menderes. Its old name commemorates a legend concerning the satyr Marsyas, a devotee of the mother goddess Cybele. Upon finding a deer-bone flute discarded by Athena, he was enchanted by its sound as he played in Cybele's processions, and was so bold as to challenge Apollo to a musical contest. The god accepted on condition that the winner could impose the punishment of his choice on the loser. Marsyas lost; Apollo tied him to a pine tree near the source of the stream that would bear his name, and flayed him alive.

Today most travelers hurry along the modern highway that parallels the river, unaware of the legend and the three ancient sites off the main route.

Alinda

The first and best of the valley's ancient ruins, **ALİNDA**, studding a huge bluff dominating the area, is closely linked with a colorful episode in the life of Alexander the Great. Ada, sister of King Mausolus of Halicarnassos, after losing the battle of succession to the Hecatomnid throne in the mid-fourth century BC, was exiled here, then a mere fortress, to await an opportunity to reverse her fortunes. A few years later, upon the arrival of Alexander, Ada offered to surrender Alında and her personal resources in exchange for his aid in regaining her royal position. Her proposal was accepted, and Alexander holed up in Alında for some time, preparing their combined—and eventually successful—siege of Halicarnassos. During this period they became close friends, and it seems that Ada even adopted Alexander as her son. After their victory Ada was left to rule over most of Caria, but she was the last of the remarkable Hecatomnid line; little of consequence occurred locally after her death.

Although the site of Alında lies 28km off the main highway, and a total of 58km from Aydın, public-transportation connections are decent. There are direct dolmuşes from Aydın to **KARPUZLU**, the fair-sized town at the base of the ruins; if you can't get one you'll have to use an Aydın–Çine dolmuş (departing across the road from the Aydın tourist office), and change in Çine town. The last direct service back from Karpuzlu to Aydın leaves at 4pm, to Çine at 6:30pm. Don't plan to overnight in shabby **ÇINE**, where the lone hotel, *Babadan*, is an airless fleapit. In Karpuzlu there are several adequate restaurants but again only one bare-bones hotel.

The Site

From the little square where the minibuses stop, follow the signs 400m up a dirt road to the unfenced site ($1 during daylight hours) and parking lot, close by which the oldest houses of Karpuzlu merge into ancient masonry just below the monstrous **market building**. One hundred meters long, this was three-storied, with hefty interior columns; now only two floors stand, but these are in perfect condition, and, like so much Carian stonework, bear a strange resemblance to Inca construction half a world away. Cross the open agora space behind to some fragments of wall, where a serpentine path leads up to the well-preserved **theater**, retaining two galleries and most of its seats. These face south, giving superlative views over Karpuzlu and its valley. From here, continue farther north up the hill, where an impressive, two-story **Hellenistic watchtower** surveys a quiltwork of fields and trees, with rings of mountains up to 50km distant. The flat space around the tower is peppered with cistern mouths and partly collapsed tunnels, which supposedly once led to lower levels of the city. Walk west along the neck of the ridge past the foundations of **acropolis houses**, until reaching a gap in the **city walls**; just beyond are a couple of specimens from Alında's extensive **necropolis**.

Alabanda and Gerga

Both of these Carian sites are considerably more difficult to get to and will really only reward archaeological fanatics, although the walk to Gerga, providing you can reach the starting point, is enjoyable.

Alabanda

Although originally a Carian settlement, **ALABANDA** figures in history only briefly as a Roman city, notorious for its scorpions. Today there is not much to see at all, and the site, 8km west of Çine, is poorly marked and not served by any public transportation. Only the old **bouleuterion**, north of the road, is obvious, its walls standing up to 6m high. The **theater**, up in the village across the road, has almost disappeared—houses are built up against it, and vegetables are being raised in the old stage area.

Gerga

Near the headwaters of the Çine River, the valley narrows to a defile known as the Gökbel Pass. The deserted landscape, with the water far below tumbling over huge boulders, is evocative of Marsyas and his fate—and hides **GERGA**, the most mysterious site in Caria.

Twelve kilometers south of Eskiçine, the graceful **İncekemer** Ottoman bridge spans the gorge. This is a recognized bus stop (though the driver will think you're nuts), and if you have a car there is parking space. From here it's about a ninety-minute walk to Gerga. Cross the bridge, then another flimsy cement one across a tributary, and stay with the main trail, which soon becomes a dirt road. After 25 minutes you reach the village of **İNCEKEMER MAHALLE**, split in two by yet another watercourse. Change to the west bank of this, always maintaining a northerly course, and continue up the small valley between the big ridge and a smaller plug to the east. Near the top, make a hairpin left over a slight saddle to reach some stone walls and thornbush barriers for livestock. Just past this is a small farm at the base of a terraced hillside holding the remains of Gerga.

Virtually nothing is known for certain about Gerga, other than that it is of very early Carian vintage, with crude, monolithic stonework supposed to date from the Roman era. At first sight it would appear to have not been a town, but a religious sanctuary like Labranda. The most conspicuous item is a **temple or tomb** in the form of a house, visible from afar and in perfect condition despite being used as a cow shed. Its stone roof is intact and on the lintel "GERGAS" is inscribed in Greek lettering—which some archaeologists theorize is not the place name but that of an obscure Carian deity. You actually enter the site between two upright, **flattened monoliths**, irregularly shaped like African termite nests; adjacent is a large ceremonial **basin** carved from bedrock. A giant headless **statue** lies on the ground beyond the tomb-temple, and at the far edge of the main terrace are two purported **fountains**: one backed into the hillside, the other free-standing and bearing another "GERGAS" legend. While none of the individual structures is that impressive, the total effect, and the outlandish location, is unsettling.

Aphrodisias

Situated on a high plateau over 600m above sea level, ringed by mountains and watered by a tributary of the Büyük Menderes, **APHRODISIAS** is one of the more isolated and beautifully set of Turkey's major archaeological sites. Acres of marble peek out from among the poplars and vegetation that cloaks the remains of one of imperial Rome's most cultured Asian cities. Late-afternoon visits have the bonus of often dramatic cloud formations (spawned by the elevation), and the attendant dappled lighting, but both can turn murky—as can the transportation situation out.

Since 1961, excavations have been carried out with the conscious intent of rendering Aphrodisias on par with Ephesus. The eventual results will certainly be spectacular, but in the meantime the digs can be a nuisance for tourists: most of the site is off-limits to both photography and entry, and the opportunity to watch the ongoing work from a distance is small consolation. The archaeological team has a very proprietorial attitude toward unpublished inscriptions and monuments; don't even think of sneaking telephoto shots of anything—guards are everywhere and will descend in force if you're detected.

Some History

Aphrodisias was one of the earliest occupied sites in Anatolia. Neolithic and Bronze Age mounds have been found here, including the artificial hill supporting the theater. There has also been a fertility cult of some sort here for just as long, fostered by the agricultural associations of the river valley. The Assyrian goddess of love and war, Nin, became syncretized with the Semitic Ishtar, whose attributes were eventually assumed by the Hellenic Aphrodite.

Despite its strategic position near the meeting point of ancient Caria, Lydia, and Phrygia, and its proximity to major trade routes, Aphrodisias for many centuries remained only a shrine, and never really grew into a town until the second century BC. The citizens of Aphrodisias were amply rewarded for their support of

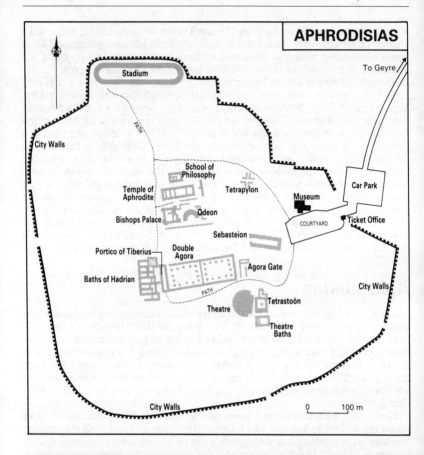

APHRODISIAS

To Geyre

Stadium

City Walls

PATH

School of Philosophy

Temple of Aphrodite

Tetrapylon

Car Park

Museum

Bishops Palace

Odeon

COURTYARD

Ticket Office

Sebasteion

Portico of Tiberius

Double Agora

Baths of Hadrian

Agora Gate

City Walls

PATH

Tetrastoön

Theatre

Theatre Baths

City Walls

0   100 m

the Romans during the Mithridatic revolt; many special privileges—including the right of sanctuary within the Aphrodite temple grounds—were granted, and the rapidly burgeoning city was heavily patronized by various emperors, becoming a major cultural center. It was renowned in particular for its school of sculpture, which benefited from nearby quarries of high-grade marble, and local works adorned every corner of the empire, including Rome itself.

Perhaps because of this fixation with graven images, not to mention the lucrative cult of Aphrodite (similar to that at Knidos), paganism lingered here for almost two centuries after Theodosius proscribed the old religions. Even after the conversion of the Aphrodite shrine to a more decorous basilica, and a change of name to Stavropolis, the Christianity professed here tended toward heretical persuasions.

The reputation of its love-cult had served to protect Aphrodisias since its inception, but by the fourth century AD a wall had become necessary. This failed singularly, however, to stave off the effect of two earthquakes and sundry raids, and decline was the dominant theme of Byzantine times. The town was abandoned completely during the thirteenth century, its former glories recalled only by the Ottoman village of Geyre—a corruption of "Caria"—among the ruins. Romantic travelers dutifully stopped, sketched, and copied inscriptions, but none suspected the wealth of relics hidden from view. First French, then Italian researchers poked desultorily below the surface early this century, but it is really the work since 1961 that has permitted a fuller understanding of the site.

The Site

A loop path around the site (daily 8am–5:30pm; $2.50), passes all the major monuments, though at the time of writing only the stadium, the baths of Hadrian, and the temple of Aphrodite were open without restriction; all other attractions were either partly or wholly closed on our two separate inspections. In light of the hefty admission fee, this situation will hopefully change soon.

The route begins inconspicuously opposite the museum with the virtually intact **theater**, founded in the first century BC but extensively modified by the Romans for their blood sports three centuries later. At the rear of the stage building are chiselled imperial decrees affecting the status of the town. Still farther behind the stage is a large square, the **tetrastoön**, originally surrounded by colonnades on all sides, which was one of several meeting places in the Roman and Byzantine city. South of the tetrastoön is a large bath complex.

The path skirts the north flank of the theater, right under the watchful eye of a guard at the hill's summit, below which you will see workmen puttering around in the **Sebasteion**—two parallel porticos erected in the first century AD to honor the deified Roman emperors—and the **double agora**, two squares ringed by Ionic and Corinthian stoas. Numerous columns still vie with the poplars, and the whole area is bounded on the southwest by the **portico of Tiberius**, which separates the agora from the fine **baths of Hadrian**, well preserved right down to the floor tiles and the odd mosaic.

North of the baths, several blue-marble columns sprout from a multi-roomed structure commonly known as the **bishop's palace**, based on its presumed use during Byzantine times. However, its ground plan, particularly the large audience chamber, is typical of a governor's residence in Roman provinces and that is certainly how the building began life. East of here huddles the appealing Roman **odeon**, with nine rows of seats. Since the many earthquakes have disrupted the local water table, the orchestra section is prone to flooding, and today frogs often croak where concerts were once given and the city council deliberated.

A few paces to the north, fourteen columns of the **temple of Aphrodite** are all that's left of the city's principal sanctuary. The Byzantines mangled not only the idol within but also the floorplan when they converted it into a basilica during the fifth century, so considerable detective work was required to re-establish the first-century BC foundations. Even these were laid atop at least two older structures, with evidence of mother-goddess-worship extending back to the seventh century BC. The Hellenistic/Roman sanctuary had forty Ionic columns arranged in an eight- by-thirteen rectangle, with the cult image erected in the main hall. The Byzantines removed the columns at each end of the temple, fashioning an apse to the east, an atrium and baptistry on the west, and it's this architectural pastiche you see today. Immediately north is the so-called **school of philosophy**, tentatively identified, like the "bishop's palace," on the basis of resemblance to other such structures elsewhere.

The northernmost feature of the site, 200m off the main path, is the 30,000-seat **stadium**, one of the largest and best-preserved in Anatolia. Under the empire, and with official encouragement, many cities of Asia Minor held periodic festivals in imitation of the major Greek competitions. Those at Aphrodisias were a version of Delphi's Pythian Games, with sporting, musical, and dramatic events. Returning to the main loop trail, the last thing you'll notice before exiting onto the museum square is the **tetrapylon**, a monumental gateway with two rows of four fluted columns. This second-century AD edifice is thought to mark the intersection of a major north-south street with a sacred way heading toward the Aphrodite shrine. The restorers apparently intend to re-erect two additional rows of columns, plus the pediments with their reliefs.

The Museum

An earthquake in 1956 damaged the old village of Geyre, giving the authorities a timely pretext to relocate the villagers 1.5km to the north and begin excavations. The old village square is now lined with the archaeologists' quarters and the attractive **museum** (same hours as site; separate $2.50 admission), whose collection consists almost entirely of sculpture recovered from the ruins. Given that Aphrodisias met most of the demand for effigies within the British empire, even what remains after the loss of originals and the spiriting away of works to city museums is considerable. The so-called "Aphrodite Hall" contains statuary related to the cult of the goddess; a rendition of Aphrodite, much defaced by Christian zealots, occupying the position of honor. In the "Penthesileia Hall," a joyous satyr carries the child Dionysus in his arms; the "Melpomene Hall" contains a wrenching version of the muse of tragedy, together with two suitably loutish-looking boxers and the completely intact, quasi-satirical portrait of Flavius Palmatus, Byzantine governor of Asia. With a small head and thick body, he was an ugly, malproportioned man, but, judging from the facial expression, one you crossed at your peril. The first (or last) notable item you'll pass is a version of Nike carrying a trophy, opposite the souvenir stand.

Practical Details

Aphrodisias is situated 13km east of KARACASU, the nearest sizable town, which lies 38km off the E24/320 highway threading through the Menderes Valley between Aydın and Denizli, and 52km from **NAZILLI**, whose otogar sits just north of the highway on the west edge of town. If coming in **by train**, exit Nazilli Station and turn right onto the main town thoroughfare, or follow the tracks southwest—they pass very close to the bus stand.

Dolmuşes leave for Karacasu, on demand, from the rear of the Nazilli otogar; during the warmer months the line may extend to Geyre, the village next to the ruins. The *Dadaş* company runs **large buses** from Nazilli Station, mostly in the early afternoon, two of which continue to Geyre and TAVAS.

If you're staying in Pamukkale, it's tempting to try to devise a loop back to Denizli through Tavas, but you have to get to Tavas in time for the last dolmuş back to Denizli, and from there to Pamukkale, which is difficult. Indeed, you're probably best off only trying to complete such an ambitious circuit under your own power, or with a tour bus out of Pamukkale.

Whatever happens, try to avoid getting stranded at Aphrodisias—a distinct possibility after 5:30pm. A **taxi** round-trip from Karacasu will cost you $7, double that if you have to take it all the way back to the Nazilli–Denizli highway. If you're going to get stuck, you're better off doing so at **GEYRE**, where there are two pansiyon/campgrounds, *Chez Mestan* and *Chez Bayar*. In **KARACASU** there is only the grimmest of dormitories built directly over the small bus terminal.

Denizli

Devastated by earthquakes in 1710 and 1899, **DENİZLİ** is a gritty agricultural town and transportation hub of almost 200,000 inhabitants, and your first and last thought will probably be to move on—most likely to Pamukkale. The **train station**, containing a **tourist information office**, lies right across the busy highway from the **otogar**, which also has an auxiliary information booth.

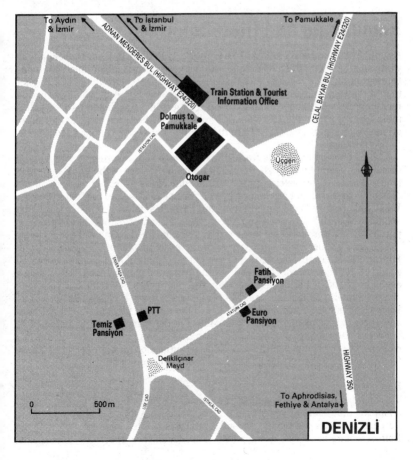

Travelers' stays in Denizli are usually measured in minutes, not hours, although if Pamukkale fills up in high season you may find yourself looking for a **place to stay** here. Unfortunately most of the conspicuous hotels are luxury outfits or cheaper places plagued by noise from the bus station, but there are a few reasonable alternatives—*Pension Temiz* (☎621/40342), on the fourth floor of the concrete building opposite the police station on Enverpaşa Caddesi, and the pansiyons *Fatih* (☎621/42107) and *Euro* (☎621/35536), near each other on Atatürk Caddesi, which descends east from Delikliçınar in the city center. Both are a short walk from the Üçgen, the traffic circle at the edge of town (follow the signs). If you're heavily laden and making for downtown, pick up a dolmuş at the stops marked with "D" signs along İstasyon Caddesi and its continuation Enverpaşa Caddesi.

You can **eat** well between buses at one of several places just southeast of the bus stand, which serve prepared dishes; there are also numerous kebab and *pide* places, plus sweet shops, around Delikliçınar, but these make more sense if you are staying in Denizli.

Pamukkale and Hierapolis

As you approach the site of **PAMUKKALE/HIERAPOLIS** from Denizli, a long white smudge along the hills to the north suggests a landslide or open-cast mine. Getting closer, this resolves into the edge of a plateau, more than 100m higher than the level of the river valley and absolutely smothered in white **travertine terraces**. Some are shaped like water lilies, others like shell-bathtubs with stalagmitic feet, with the simplest ones resembling bleached rice terraces out of an oriental engraving. The Turks have dubbed this geological fairyland *Pamukkale*, or "Cotton Castle."

The responsibility for this freak of nature rests with a spring, saturated with dissolved calcium bicarbonate, bubbling up from the base of the Çal Dağı mountains beyond. As the water surges over the edge of the plateau and cools, carbon dioxide is given off and calcium carbonate precipitates as hard chalk (travertine). What you see now has been accumulating for millennia, as slowly but surely the solidified waterfall advances southwest. Seen at sunset, subtle hues of ochre, purple, and pink are reflected in the water, replacing the dazzling white of midday.

The spring emerges in what was once the exact middle of the ancient city of **Hierapolis** but is now the garden of a motel. The ruins of Hierapolis would merit a stop even if they weren't teamed up with the natural phenomenon, but as things are you can often hardly see them for the tour buses, souvenir hawkers, and shabby motels. Pamukkale and Hierapolis are Turkey's closest equivalent to Disneyland, a tourist extravaganza in which the terraces fill in for the Matterhorn and the castle, and one "rides" the ruins (or the camels handily stationed in between). Depending on your mood, taste, and timing, it can either be a prime example of everything loathsome in modern tourism, or (in winter at least) a relatively deserted stage-set and a chance for a warm outdoor bath.

Some History
The therapeutic properties and bizarre appearance of the hot springs were known about for thousands of years before an actual town was founded by one of the Pergamene kings during the second century BC. After incorporation into the Roman empire in 129 BC development proceeded apace, spurred by minor wool

and metals industries, plus a health spa practically the equal of the present one. Hierapolis seems to have enjoyed considerable imperial favor, especially after catastrophic earthquakes in 17 and 60 AD. No less than three emperors paid personal visits, stimulating local emperor-worship alongside the veneration of Apollo and his mother Leto, who was venerated in the guise of Cybele.

The presence of a flourishing Jewish community aided the rapid and early establishment of Christianity here. Hierapolis is mentioned in Paul's Epistle to the (neighboring) Colossians, and Philip the Apostle is traditionally thought to have been martyred here along with his seven sons. However, as at Aphrodisias, paganism lingered well into the sixth century, until a zealous bishop oversaw the destruction of the remaining focuses of ancient worship and the establishment of nearly one hundred churches, several of which are still visible.

Hierapolis slid into obscurity in late Byzantine times, nudged along by Arab and Turcoman raids. After the Selçuks arrived in the 1100s, the city was abandoned, not to figure much in the Western imagination until Italian excavations began in 1957; even as recently as 1939, George Bean reported much the same landscape as the romantic travelers of the eighteenth century had witnessed. A mere three decades have sufficed to recreate, if not the monumental taste, certainly the commercialism of the Roman period.

Arrival and Practical Details

PAMUKKALE KÖYÜ, a once-sleepy village at the base of the cliff, is where most foreign travelers stay. The majority **arrive from Denizli**, where **dolmuşes** labeled "Pamukkale/Karahayıt" set off from a stand on the west edge of the Otogar; last departure in either direction is around 8pm in summer, much earlier in the cooler months. There are also red-and-white Denizli "Belediyesi" **city buses** up to Pamukkale, but these are less frequent, begin their run from downtown Denizli, and are altogether more inconvenient (though cheaper).

There are also direct **long-distance bus connections** between Pamukkale Köyü and most of the larger resorts—Kaş, Marmaris, Kuşadası, and Fethiye, among other places—twice daily. Several companies, including *Pamukkale*, have ticket offices in the village.

The village has an **after-hours bank**, *Töbank* (Mon–Sat 8:30am–11pm, Sun 4–11pm), and an *Avis* **car rental** franchise, *Durak Souvenir* (☎6218/1169), and in recent years has acquired a rash of discos, carpet shops, hustlers (on par with those near Ephesus), and wretched restaurants in its center. Despite all this, it's still a rural village, partly dependent on cotton; beyond the main drag, especially in the lower neighborhood away from the travertine, little outward change is evident. For any nocturnal peace, it's indeed better to stay on the outskirts, although this too shifts yearly as more pansiyons are erected.

Accommodation and Food

With over a hundred **pansiyons**, including "motels" and small hotels, where you end up will probably be a matter of luck and available vacancies. However, inevitably some pansiyons have an edge over the others. One of the best and friendliest is the *Kervansaray* (☎6218/1209), run by the Kaya family, whose modern doubles with bath, most overlooking greenery, cost $16; plus there's a rooftop café/restaurant. If that's full, you'll be pointed a few meters farther out of town to the *Aspawa* (☎6218/1094), a bit cheaper at $14, or the *Gül* (no phone), with a nice

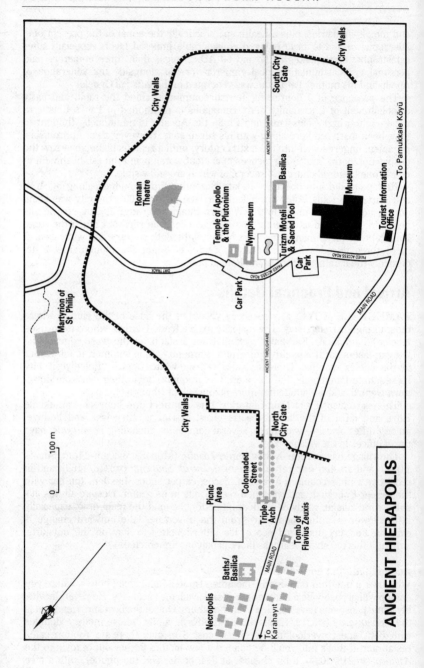

ANCIENT HIERAPOLIS

City Walls

City Walls

South City Gate

To Pamukkale Köyü

Roman Theatre

Temple of Apollo & the Plutonium

Nymphaeum

Basilica

Museum

Turizm Moteli & Sacred Pool

Tourist Information Office

Car Park

Car Park

PAVED ACCESS ROAD

PAVED ACCESS ROAD

DIRT TRACK

MAIN ROAD

ANCIENT THOROUGHFARE

ANCIENT THOROUGHFARE

Martyrion of St Philip

City Walls

North City Gate

Colonnaded Street

Picnic Area

Triple Arch

Tomb of Flavius Zeuxis

MAIN ROAD

Baths/Basilica

Necropolis

To Karahayıt

0   100 m

garden. In the northern part of the village stands the oldest pansiyon, *Ali's* (☎6218/1065), although this has expanded of late and become distinctly impersonal; prices are slightly higher than at the *Kervansaray*, but the view of the terraces compensates. For a bit of luxury, the *Çetin Motel* (☎6218/1210) is central but quiet, and offers doubles with bath and light breakfast for $14 (in low season). At the opposite end of the spectrum, the *Rose*, near the bus-company offices, is probably better as a **campground** than pansiyon. Finally, there's the *Hierapolis Motel/Camping* and the *Everybody Peace* (sic) for retro-hippies, both up by *Ali's*.

Most lodgings in the village advertise the presence of a swimming pool, but by the time the mineral water has made the long trip down from the cliff it's distinctly cool and murky—a summertime pleasure only. The conspicuous quintet of luxury motels up on the travertine brink all run in excess of $60 a double per night, quite a mark-up for the view and somewhat warmer water.

Eating out, the situation is uniformly dire. Service is slack and prices nearly double what they'd be elsewhere. You'll get better value if you arrange half board with your pansiyon. One exception is the *Kervansaray*, whose restaurant is worth a visit even if you're not staying there.

The Site

A ticket booth has recently been installed at the site (daily 9am–5pm; $1), on the road linking Pamukkale Köyü and the travertine terraces; when it's staffed you'll be liable to pay admission, whether on foot or by car. If you plan to visit Karahayıt, beyond Hierapolis, retain your ticket stub so that you don't have to pay twice when re-entering the far side of the fee zone, where there's another booth. There's still a very conspicuous path up to the plateau from the village, and you might still be able to get in free that way.

The **travertine terraces** are, deservedly, the first item on most people's agenda. Most face west-southwest, so if you can restrain yourself a late afternoon or dusk visit is most dramatic. The authorities, despairing of being able to prevent visitors from walking out on the solidified lime, have been reduced to pleading that you not wear shoes in the pools—a reasonable enough request. The main problem, other than the crowds, is that most of the pools are very shallow—mid-calf depth is about average—and a foot-soak is about all that's possible.

If you want to take a proper baths in the springs, visit the *Turism Moteli* up on the plateau, which encloses the **sacred pool** of the ancients, with mineral water bubbling from its bottom at 95° F. Time was when you could discreetly saunter in for an early-morning bath with the staff none the wiser, but admission is now highly regimented: 7am–11pm for guests, 9am–4:30pm for the public, with admission payable and a changing room by the gate. Still, the irregularly shaped pool must be one of the most delightful around the Mediterranean, with surrounding gardens and the submerged columns of a portico that once stood nearby. Come as early or late as possible; midday is the province of large tour groups.

On your way to the pool you'll pass the **tourist information office**, principally useful for its map of the site, and the **museum** (daily except Mon 9am–noon & 1:30–5pm; admission included in site fee), housed in the restored, second-century AD baths. The rather disappointing collection consists primarily of statuary, sarcophagi, masonry fragments and smaller knickknacks recovered during excavations at Hierapolis. Behind the museum is a large sixth-century **basilica**, probably Byzantine-era cathedral, with two aisles sandwiching the nave.

The Archaeological Zone

Admission to the **archaeological zone** itself is included in the original fee paid down the hill. Entrance is usually via a narrow road winding up past the north side of the *Turism Motel*. The first break in the roadside fence—it can hardly be called a gate—gives access to a **nymphaeum** or fountainhouse, the **temple of Apollo**, and the adjacent **Plutonium**. The Apollo shrine in its present, scanty form dates from the third century AD, although it was built on a second-century BC foundation. The grotto of the Plutonium, a quasi-oracular site sacred to the god of the underworld, is today a small, partly paved cavity beyond which you can hear rushing water and an ominous hissing. The latter is the emission of a highly toxic gas, probably a mixture of sulphurous compounds and carbon dioxide, capable of killing man and beast alike. In ancient times the eunuch priests of Cybele were reputedly able to descend into the chasm with no ill effect; whether this was a result of their anatomical deficiency or some less obvious ruse is unknown. Today a small, damaged grille attempts to keep daredevils out—reportedly two Germans died recently attempting to brave the cave.

The next feature—and the only monument that can really be sealed off between 5pm and 9am—is the restored **Roman theater**, dating from the second century AD. Admittedly, amphitheaters are a dime a dozen in Turkey, but this one is in exceptionally good shape, including most of the stage buildings and their elaborate reliefs. During the **Pamukkale festival** (late May or early June) performances are held here; the 46 rows of seats can still hold 6000–7000 comfortably, compared to the former capacity of 10,000.

After seeing the theater, return to the dirt track and follow it east past a stretch of the **city walls**, turning left onto a smaller path and eventually halting before the **Martyrion of St Philip**, built in honor of the apostle martyred here in 80 AD. This fifth-century structure, comprising many rectangular cells converging on a central, octagonal chamber, was almost certainly not Philip's tomb, nor even a church, but probably a site of festivals and processions on the saint's day.

Arguably the most interesting part of the city is the **colonnaded street**, which once extended for almost 1km from a gate 400m southeast of the sacred pool to another breach in the north wall. This thoroughfare, parallel to the plateau's edge, unevenly bisected the grid plan of the Hellenistic city, and terminated at each end in monumental portals a few paces outside the walls. Only the northerly one, a **triple arch** flanked by towers and dedicated to the emperor Domitian in 84 AD, still stands. The short stretch of intact pavement, flanked by various columns, was the commerical heart of the city. Immediately behind, a grove of conifers shelters a **picnic area**, which makes a possible lunch stop and good landmark to navigate toward should you wish to descend directly from the Martyrion to the colonnaded street rather than retrace your steps to the museum junction.

North of Domitian's arch, on the east side of the road, stands the squat bulk of some second-century AD baths converted 200 years later into a **basilica**. Slightly closer to the archway, west of the asphalt, you'll notice the elaborate **tomb of Flavius Zeuxis**, a prominent Hierapolitan merchant—the first of more than a thousand tombs of all shapes and sizes constituting the **necropolis**, the largest in Asia Minor and extending for nearly 2km along the road. The more sumptuous ones bear epitaphs or inscriptions warning grave-robbers of punishments awaiting those caught, and there are even forecourts with benches for visits of the deceased's relatives. Nowadays camels and their drivers, not tomb-desecrators, lurk among the tumuli.

Karahayıt

Many dolmuşes cover the 7km or so from the lower village to **KARAHAYIT**, famous for its *Kırmızı Su* (Red Water). These hot (130°F), iron-rich springs flow first into private bath cubicles and then, considerably cooled down, into two large rustic pools belonging to the small **campground** next door. Fees are payable at both the indoor and outdoor facilities, although collection can be somewhat lax. Except for the new *Club Hierapolis* development at the outskirts, Karahayıt seems a sort of cheapo Pamukkale Köyü, crammed full of pansiyons and carpet shops; local Turks and a few Germans make up the main clientele.

Around Pamukkale: Laodiceia and Akhan

Just off the road linking Pamukkale and Denizli are two minor archaeological sites, ancient **Laodiceia** and Selçuk **Akhan**—worth a short detour if you've got time or your own vehicle.

Laodiceia (Laodikya)

Thirteen kilometers south of Pamukkale, a marker points 500m west to a larger sign detailing the delights of "Laodikya," the site of ancient **LAODICEIA**, covering an elevated tableland squeezed between two river valleys; the bleak melancholy of the meager remains is accentuated by tractor furrows and high-tension wires. It's a setting redeemed principally by perennially snow-covered Honaz Dağı (2571m) to the southeast, matched in miniature by the white strip of Pamukkale to the north.

Founded by the post-Alexandrian Seleucid kings in the mid-third century BC at the junction of two major trade routes, Laodiceia came under Roman rule at the same time as the other cities of Caria. Under the empire, its prosperity—derived largely from soft, black wool—was such that (unlike Hierapolis) it needed no imperial assistance to repair the earthquake damage of 60 AD. Like at its northern neighbor, though, the presence of a large Jewish community aided in the rapid adoption of Christianity—albeit half-heartedly according to St John the Divine, whose pungent comment in Revelation 3:15-17 is notorious: "I know your works, you are neither hot nor cold. Would that you were cold or hot! So, because you are lukewarm, and neither cold nor hot, I will spew you out of my mouth"—a metaphor almost certainly derived from John's acquaintance with the springs at Pamukkale. Nonetheless Laodiceia became an important bishopric during Byzantine times, and only began its final decline after a fifth-century earthquake. Shortly after the Selçuk conquest the city was abandoned in favor of nearby Denizli.

As befits a settlement of mostly Roman importance, the visible ruins date from that era. The road starting at the orientation sign dwindles away in the center of the plateau, next to the rubble of a **nymphaeum**. Southeast of here, at the edge of the site, is the 350-meter-long **stadium**, the largest in Asia Minor but in parlous condition, constructed in the first century AD under the emperor Vespasian. Overlooking it are the fairly substantial remains of a Hadrianic **gymnasium and baths complex**. These, and the archaeological zone in general, have suffered from systematic pilferage in recent times; engravings of the 1820s show monuments standing twice their present height. Return to the nymphaeum once more and cross the rudimentary track to find the foundations of an **Ionic temple**. Continue a short distance north and begin pacing the edge of the upland to find, in quick succession, the **small theater**—facing northwest and with many seats intact—and the **large theater**, facing northeast over the modern village of Eskihisar.

Akhan

If the weather's good you might just want to walk the 3km between Laodiceia and the Selçuk *kervansaray* of **Akhan**. Upon reaching Highway E24/320, the main Denizli–Afyon road, turn left and proceed 1.5km to the lightly restored structure tucked just north of the road, on the west bank of a creek. If you enter the modern village of Akhan, you've gone too far. The rectangular structure encloses a courtyard, with arches to either side and a covered hall in back. An inscription over the front gate, which looks southeast over the stream and a peach orchard, declares that the building was completed in 1252–53, under the reign of the sultan Izzedin Kaykavuş.

travel details

Trains

From İzmir (Basmane) to Manisa–Balıkesir–Bandırma (2 daily; 5hr 30min; ferry connection at Bandırma for İstanbul's Sarayburnu dock, 4hr 15min more); to Manisa–Balıkesir–Kütahya–Ankara (2 daily, one with sleepers; 12–14hr); to Manisa–Balıkesir–Kütahya–Eskişehir (1 daily; 9hr 30min); to Selçuk–Aydın–Sultanhisar–Nazilli–Denizli (3 daily; 6hr, 2 hr to Selçuk); to Söke (1 daily; 3hr).

From İzmir (Alsancak) to Menderes Airport (24 daily, on the half-hour; return from the airport on the hour); Ödemiş (1 daily; 2hr 30min); **Tire** (1 daily; 2hr).

From Denizli to Afyon–Eskişehir–İstanbul (Haydarpaşa) (1 daily; 17hr); Afyon (1 daily; 5 hr).

Buses and dolmuşes

From İzmir to Selçuk (every 20min; 80min); Kuşadası (half-hourly; 1hr 40min); Çeşme (every 15–20 min from Güzelyalı terminal; 90min); Seferihisar (at least hourly from Güzelyalı terminal; 1hr); Ahmetbeyli/Gümüldür (at least 8 daily; 80/100min); Foça (half-hourly; 90min); Çandarlı (6 daily in season; 90min); Ayvalık (half-hourly; 2hr 30min); Bergama (hourly; 2hr); Manisa (every 15min; 45min); Salihli/Sart (hourly; 90min); Milas/Bodrum (hourly; 3hr/4hr); Muğla/Marmaris/Datça (hourly, continuing 6 times daily to Datça; 4hr/5hr/

7hr); Fethiye (12–18 daily; 6hr 40min); Aydın (half-hourly; 2hr); Denizli (hourly; 4hr); Antalya via Aydın and Burdur (8 daily; 8hr 30min); Afyon/Ankara (8 daily; 5hr 30min/9hr 30min); Bursa/İstanbul via Balıkesir (several daily; 7hr/10hr 30min); Çanakkale/Edirne (6 daily; 5hr 30min/10hr); Çanakkale/İstanbul (4 daily; 5hr 30min/11hr).

From Kuşadası to Seferihisar (hourly; 90min); Söke (half-hourly; 40min); Aydın (hourly; 75min); Dilek Yarımadası National Park (half-hourly; 40min); Bodrum (3 daily; 3hr); Pamukkale (12 daily; 3.5hr); İstanbul (6 daily; 13hr).

From Selçuk to Kuşadası (every 20min; 25min); Tire (every 20min; 40min).

From Söke to Güllübahçe/Priene (hourly; 20min); Güzelçamlı/Dilek Yarımadası National Park (half-hourly; 40min); Bafa Gölü/Milas (half-hourly; 30min/80min); Balat/Miletus (several daily; 40min); Didyma/Altınkum (hourly; 50min/60min).

From Milas to Güllük (half-hourly; 35min); Ören (at least 6 daily; 1hr); Muğla (hourly; 75min); Selimiye/Euromos (hourly; 20min/15min).

From Bodrum to Muğla (10 daily; 2hr 30min); Marmaris (8 daily; 3hr 15min); Fethiye (6 daily; 4hr 30min); İstanbul (several daily; 15hr); Ankara (several daily; 13hr); Gümbet (half-hourly; 10min); Bitez (half-hourly; 15min); Ortakent/Yahşi Sahil (half-hourly; 20min); Karaincir/Akyarlar (half-hourly; 30min); Turgutreis (half-hourly; 25min);

Yalıkavak (10 daily; 25 min); Gündoğan via Torba (hourly; 25min); Gölköy/Türkbükü via Torba (hourly; 20/25min).
From Muğla to Marmaris (half-hourly; 1hr); Köyceğiz (hourly; 50min); Fethiye (10 daily; 2hr 30min).
From Marmaris to Ortaca/Dalaman (hourly; 75min/90min); Bodrum (4 daily; 3hr 15min); Fethiye (10 daily; 2hr 45min); Turunç (hourly; 20min); Orhaniye (several daily; 35min); Selimiye/Bozburun (1 daily; 90min/100min); Söğüt/Taşlica (1 daily; 90/100min); Denizli (6 daily; 3hr); Ankara (14 daily; 13hr); İstanbul (4 daily; 16hr).
From Datça to Marmaris (13 daily; 2hr 15min); Muğla (11 daily; 3hr 15min); İstanbul (4 daily; 16hr); Ankara (3 daily; 13hr); Mesudiye (several minibuses daily; 30min).
From Aydın to Denizli (half-hourly until 7pm; 2hr); Fethiye (8 daily; 4hr 30min); Marmaris (10 daily; 2hr 45min); Ankara (several daily; 10hr); Konya (3 daily; 10hr); Çine (35min); Karpuzlu/Alında (1hr); Sultanhisar/Nazilli (30min/50min); Söke (50min).
From Nazilli to Karacasu/Geyre (6–7 daily; 40/50min).
From Denizli to Bodrum via Kale/Muğla (2–3 daily; 4hr 30min); Marmaris via Kale/Muğla (2–3 daily; 3hr 30min); Antalya via Burdur or Korkuteli (8 daily; 5hr 30min or 4hr 15min); Konya via Isparta and Eğridir (several daily; 7hr 15min). Minibuses from the same terminal to Tavas (hourly till 6pm; 40min) and Yeşilova/Salda Gölü (8 daily; 90min).

Ferries

From İzmir to İstanbul (3 weekly; 19hr). Midweek services run only early May to late Sept.
From İzmir (Konak) to Karşıyaka (half-hourly; 15min).
From Datça to Bodrum (April–Oct 2 daily; 90min). Boats actually arrive and depart from Körmen Limanı, 9km north of Datça; shuttle bus included in price.

Planes

From İzmir to İstanbul (6-9 daily on *THY*, 5 weekly on *İstanbul Hava Yolları*, 1 weekly on *Green Air*, 55min); Ankara (2 daily on *THY*; 75min); Antalya (1 weekly on *İstanbul Hava Yollari*;

50min); Dalaman (1 weekly on *İstanbul Hava Yolları*; 35min).
From Denizli to İstanbul/Ankara (2 weekly on *THT*; 1hr).

Ferries to the Greek islands

All of the ferry lines to the Greek islands are served by at least one Greek and Turkish boat each. Turkish vessels normally leave Turkey in the morning—usually between 8 and 9am—returning from Greece between 4 and 5pm, while Greek craft arrive between 9 and 10am and return between 4 and 5pm. For a morning boat you must bring your passport to agencies the evening before so that your name is recorded; for an afternoon boat it should be sufficient to hand over your papers two hours before sailing time. Bear in mind that in high season the boats can actually sell out a day or two in advance. Fares are uniform in any given port, but are consistently overpriced for the short distances involved; this is partly because any Turkish port controlled by *TML* is obliged to levy heavy docking fees on all vessels, whether *TML*-owned or not. Taking a car across costs $40–65 one-way depending on vehicle size and the port; advance reservations are essential since the boats often only hold two or three vehicles.
Çeşme–Hios (May–Oct 7–9 weekly, mid-winter 2 weekly; 1hr).
Kuşadası–Samos (early April to late Oct 2 daily, dwindling to 2 monthly mid-winter; 90 min).
Bodrum–Kos (2 daily, dwindling to 1 or 2 weekly in mid-winter; 45min).
Marmaris–Rhodes (12 weekly in season, down to 3 weekly in mid-winter; 2hr 30min).

Other international ferries

İzmir–Pireas (Greece)–Venice (Italy) (1 weekly on *TML*, usually Wed, late March to early Nov; 66hr). From mid-June to mid-Sept the boat does not call at Pireas. **NB** As of 1992 this service will switch from İzmir to Çeşme.
Bodrum–Ancona (Italy) (1 weekly, usually Wed evening; 68 hr).
Kuşadası–Samos (Greece)–Paros–Pireas–Kefallonia–Ancona (Italy) (1 weekly on *Minoan Lines*, usually Tues evening, mid-May to mid-Oct; 58hr for the full run).

CHAPTER FIVE

THE TURQUOISE COAST

The Western Mediterranean coast is dominated by the Bey range of the Taurus Mountains, the road clinging to the mountainside, winding and climbing precipitously above the sea. This is the **Turquoise Coast**, famed for its fine beaches and beautiful scenery. It is also the area covered by the ancient kingdom of **Lycia**, a land peopled by an independent race who bequeathed a legacy of distinctive rock tombs to Turkish tourism.

Until recently this was popular yachting country, many of the most attractive coves and islands being inaccessible to land-based traffic. But the roads in the area are improving at an alarming rate: last year a paved road was completed to previously secluded Kekova, and the same is planned for the ancient site of Olympos. There's a slender chance that the damage done to the area by large-scale development will be minimized by careful planning, however—already the number of floors of new buildings is being restricted, and local authorities are controlling hotel and food prices and restricting the activities of street touts. At any rate, the greater accessibility is a blessing if you happen to be backpacking without your own yacht.

The area has been opened up, above all, by the excellent **Highway 400**, which runs from Marmaris to Antalya, giving easy access to all the major sights along the way, and—hemmed in against the sea by the Bey Mountains—offering some impressively panoramic views. Accessibility to the Turquoise Coast itself has also recently been greatly improved by the construction of the **Dalaman Airport**, which handles regular direct international flights as well as domestic flights from İstanbul and Ankara.

In the east of the region, **Dalyan** is renowned for its beach—a breeding ground of loggerhead turtles—and for being a characterful small resort, run on a cooperative basis, with a concern to preserve the value of the area; it's also handy for visiting nearby **Köyceğiz Lake** and the ruins of **Kaunos**. West of here, **Fethiye**, along with the nearby "dead sea" lagoon of **Ölüdeniz**, is a full-blown vacation town, the Turquoise Coast's primary resort and worth visiting in itself, although it also serves as a base for some of the best of the region's many overgrown and crumbling ruins, leftovers from the Lycian period. Many of these, located in spectacular settings, are perhaps the real attraction of the region. **Pinara** and **Xanthos** are the closest, situated in dramatic mountainous locations; farther east, **Patara** is located close to one of the coast's best beaches, making it perfectly possible to combine a sea-and-sun vacation with the occasional cultural foray, especially bearing in mind its proximity to the region's second major resort, **Kaş**—smaller than Fethiye, although just as developed. Beyond here, **Finike** is the next major center, another resort in the incipient stages of development, and a good base for a precipitous inland route that takes in the sites of Limyra and Arykanda on the way up to **Elmalı**, whose rarefied air and marvelous setting more than repay the trip. Beyond Finike, the scenery becomes increas-

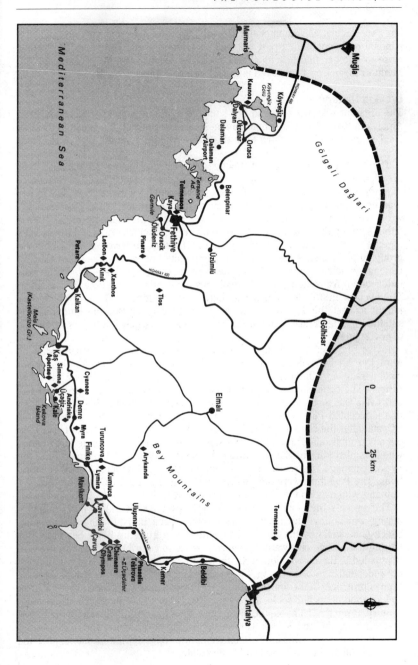

ingly spectacular as you enter the **Mount Olympos area**, officially designated a national park, continuing past the sites of **Olympos** and **Phaselis** (the former close to another fine beach) almost as far as Antalya, the main center for the Mediterranean Coast—detailed in the following chapter.

Lycia in History

The area once known as **Lycia** lies south of a line running approximately from Antalya to Köyceğiz. It is a mountainous, inaccessible land, the peaks of the Bey Dağları and the Akdağ, which form the northern borders of the region, reaching over 3000m in altitude.

The Lycian people hold a distinctive place in the history of Anatolia; their notoriously fierce desire for independence in one instance led the citizens of Xanthos to make a funeral pyre of their own city and burn themselves alive rather than be conquered. They also had their own language and customs; Herodotus wrote, for example, that (unusually) "they reckon their lineage not by their father's but by their mother's side." The main Lycian cities organized themselves together against external authority in the **Lycian Federation**, a democratic grouping that consisted of 23 cities or voting units, and was charged with electing national officials and municipal authorities—and, as long as Lycia was independent from Rome, making decisions concerning war, peace, and alliance. The Lycians' first mention in Greek literature is in Homer's **Iliad**, in which they fought against the Trojans. Later, in the sixth century BC, the kingdom was subdued by the Persian general Harpagus, but was largely left to its own means of government.

In 454 BC, after the Athenian general Cimon had cleared all Persian garrisons from the Mediterranean coast, the Lycians became members of the Delian confederacy, an Athenian maritime league that required them to pay tribute to Athens. The confederacy ceased to exist after the Peloponnesian war in 404 BC, and Lycia was again forced to pay tribute to Persia, although this did not mean that it accepted Persian domination entirely. Alexander the Great arrived in 333 BC, and after the conquest of Halicarnassos secured the surrender of Lycia without any trouble; after his death, Lycia was ruled by Alexander's general, Ptolemy, who was also king of Egypt. During the hundred years of Ptolemaic rule, the Lycian language was replaced by Greek, and the cities adopted Greek constitutions. The Ptolemies were defeated by Antiochus III in 197 BC, and later by the Romans, who handed the kingdom over to the Rhodians.

The Lycians then enjoyed a long period (over 200 years) of independence, during which time the Lycian League came back into prominence, resisting attack once again by the Pontic King Mithridates from the Black Sea in 88 BC. During the Roman civil wars, Lycian reluctance to contribute to the resources of Brutus led to the destruction of Xanthos, and although Antony later reconfirmed the independence of Lycia, in 43 AD the region was joined to Pamphylia as a Roman province. In the fourth century AD the province was divided by Diocletian and a period of decline set in, a process helped along by Arab raids in the seventh century. From this point on, the history of the region resembled that of the rest of Western Anatolia, the Selçuk Turks establishing sovereignty, and, partly under the influence of the Muslim Turkish tribes who migrated into Anatolia after the victory, establishing an Anatolian Muslim state.

Fethiye

The easternmost of the Turquoise Coast resorts, **FETHİYE** is probably the most advantageously situated for access to some of the region's most fascinating sites. And although the region's best beaches, around **Ölüdeniz** ("the Dead Sea"), are now much too crowded for comfort, Fethiye still has special qualities that set it above many other Mediteranean resorts. Unlike Kaş, which is confined by its sheer rock backdrop, Fethiye has been able to spread to accommodate the increase in tourist traffic; it also boasts other secluded beaches—**Çalış** and **Gemiler**—besides Ölüdeniz, and there seems to be a good supply of coastline left when these get out of hand. In addition, Fethiye's bay is protected by a ring of twelve islands, and one of the greatest pleasures around is to rent a boat at Fethiye harbor and tour the islands in search of secluded coves to swim, fish, and camp out in.

The town occupies the location of the ancient Lycian city of **Telmessos**, and there are some impressive rock tombs an easy stroll from the town center. A short dolmuş ride out of town is the **Kaya** "ghost town," a former Greek village that was abandoned after the exchange of populations in 1923, and whose semi-ruined houses and church conjure the sad reality of the dramatic history of the village.

Some History

Nothing much is known of the origins of Telmessos, except that it wasn't originally part of the Lycian League; indeed, in the fourth century BC the Telmessians actually fought the Lycians. It may be that Pericles, the Lycian dynast, subdued the Telmessians and allowed them into the league around this time—Lycian inscriptions have been found in the city, and it is known that during the time of the Roman Empire the city was part of the Lycian Federation.

Like most Lycian cities, Telmessos was captured by Alexander in 334–333 BC, but lost not long after; the city had to be recaptured by one of Alexander's companions by means of a famous strategem: Nearchus the Cretan asked permission to leave a number of captive women musicians and boys in the city; hidden in the womens' musical instrument cases were weapons, which were used by the prisoners' escort to seize the acropolis. In the eighth century, the city's name was changed to Anastasiopolis in honor of a Byzantine emperor. This name gave way to Makri in the following century, and became Fethiye during this century. Hardly anything now remains of the ancient city, partly because it suffered from an immense earthquake in 1957, which swept most of the town into the sea.

> The Fethiye **area telephone code** is ☎ 6151.

Arrival and Finding a Place to Stay

The **otogar** is about a kilometer from the town center to the southeast; dolmuşes to Ölüdeniz, Çalış Beach, and the village of Kaya arrive and leave from behind the PTT. The **tourist information office** (summer daily 8am–8pm; winter daily 8am–5pm; ☎11527), near the harbor at İskele Meydanı 1, have a reasonable amount of useful literature and will point you in the right direction for **hotels,** although the streets leading from the otogar into the center are lined with places, particularly Atatürk Caddesi, where the *Statüs Pansiyon* (☎11060), the *Otel Ulvi* (☎11650), and the *Kordon Oteli* (☎1834) are all reasonably priced and comfortable. Parallel to Atatürk Caddesi, Çarşı Caddesi is another good bet: the *Ilköz Aile Pansiyon* at no. 127 (☎15169) is good value at $4 a head for reasonably comfortable rooms and access to hot water; the *Holiday Pansiyon* (☎11696) at no. 91, is crowded but double rooms go for $6; more upscale, the *Hotel Üzgün* at 9/4 charges $16 for doubles with a bathroom.

Karagözler Caddesi, behind the tourist office, has a number of good pansiyons, like the *Aygen* (☎12275); farther out of town in the same area off Fevzi Çakmak Caddesi there are some very classy hotels, in Birinci and Ikinci Karagözler, including the attractive *Hotel Fethiye* on Ordu Caddesi, Ikinci Karagözler Mevkii (☎12483), with double rooms at $35. The *Ülgen Pansiyon*, 3 Merdevenli Sokak off Paspatir Caddesi (☎3491), has hot water and a pleasant roof terrace, and charges $6 single, $10 double.

Accommodation Near the Beaches
If you're here specifically for a beach vacation, and don't want to spend time traveling backwards and forwards between Fethiye and the sands to the southeast and southwest, you might find it makes sense to stay near the **beaches** themselves, either camping or staying in one of the many pansiyons.

ÇALIŞ BEACH, GÜNLÜKBAŞI
Leaving town in the opposite direction along Akdeniz Caddesi, it's 4km (dolmuşes leave from behind the PTT) to **Çalış Beach**, and, behind the beach, an area called **Günlükbaşı**, where you might find some reasonably priced accommodation. At the Fethiye end of Akdeniz Caddesi at no. 17 is the *Hotel Eine Rose* (☎14326), which charges $36 double. To get to Çalış take a left turn after 1km onto Barbaros Sokak. This road, which leads to the beach, is lined with good hotels and pansiyons, including the *Hotel Eda* (☎31143) at no. 2, $10 per person for a room with hot water; the excellent and cheap *Hotel Melis* (☎31750) at no. 67, $6 per person and a pleasant restaurant downstairs; and farther along, opposite the *Cecil* hotel are the *Oykun Pansiyon* (☎31605), which is $10 per room with breakfast (no singles), attractively decorated with a pleasant garden, and the *Beşik* (☎31418) next door, same price. Günlükbaşı itself is a string of hotels, pansiyons, and the occasional bar, separated from the sea by a road. The best of these is probably the attractive, airy *Kumsal Pansiyon* (☎31265), $12 per person, wooden floors spread with kilims and with sea views from the balconies. At the far end of the beach, continuing up a dirt road beyond the asphalt, the *Yücel Motel* (☎615/31313) has pleasant, quiet rooms for $8 per person, $20 for three.

There are a couple of excellent pansiyons off the road leading from Kaya village to Gemiler Beach, about 3km on. *Mutlu Pansiyon* (☎6156/6421) costs $4 a head for simple, basic, and quiet rooms, ideal if you have your own wheels; the *Villa Rhapsody* opposite is classier, and more expensive at $10 a head, but comfortable and family-run.

Continuing down the road, it gets substantially rougher nearer the beach, but for this reason Gemiler (or "Ships") Beach is barely visited, except by sailboats. There are a couple of good restaurants and campgrounds down here, and although the beach is a bit dirty the place has a quiet, almost forgotten air compared with teeming Ölüdeniz. Just offshore, but inaccessible unless you have your own boat, is Gemile Adasi, an island and yacht anchorage on which are the remains of a Byzantine city and necropolis.

OCAKKÖY, OVACIK, ÖLÜDENIZ
On the way to Ölüdeniz, just before the village of Ovacık, there's a turnoff to the right leading to the resort village of **Ocakköy** (contact address: Cumhuriyet Caddesi 9/2, Fethiye; ☎6151/1598, 1668), a series of self-contained stone cottages dotting the hillside around two swimming pools and the best bar and restaurant in the Fethiye region. Rooms cost $35 a night, cottages $350 a week for two people, $500 for four. Ovacık itself is less crowded than Ölüdeniz, and there is frequent transportation to the beach. There are a number of pansiyons in the village, including the reasonably priced and comfortable *Coşkun Pansiyon* (☎6156/6265, 6266), $12 for a double with breakfast.

For **camping**, one of the best sites in Ölüdeniz is on the lagoon itself—the *Ölüdeniz Campground* (☎6151/1430, 6024), with its own little beach and restaurant; it's just past the official entrance to the Ölüdeniz lagoon on the left, and costs $1 per person in a tent, $8 in a bungalow—but it gets crowded. There are other campgrounds, with bungalows, in the opposite direction, by the public beach in Ölüdeniz. One of the best is the *Belcekiz Motel* (☎6156/6009), where bungalows cost $16 for two people (no singles) and camping is $4 a head; tour groups tend to hog all the bungalows with showers, but it's worth checking the place out anyway. *Derya Camping* next door (☎6156/6097) isn't as good, but it's cheaper, $2 per person in a tent, bungalows without showers $8 per person with breakfast, and it has a motel charging $32 for a double with breakfast. Next to the *Derya* on the other side, the *Öztur Turism* campground (☎6156/1598) costs about the same but has double rooms for $20 with breakfast.

The Town

The remains of ancient Telmessos are immediately obvious as soon as you arrive in Fethiye. Covering the hillside above the bus station are a number of Lycian rock tombs, which are striking in their proximity to the city and in the grandeur of their setting. Most notable—and worth a closer inspection—is the **Amyntas Tomb**, so called because of the name "Amyntou tou Ermagiou" (Son of Hermagios), carved in Greek letters on the wall of the tomb; follow Kaya Caddesi from the bus station toward town and take a left after the fire station onto Dördüncü Amintas Yolu (marked "Kaya"), then along a path leading directly to the tomb. The tomb porch consists of two Ionic columns surmounted by a triangular pediment, and is carved in close imitation of the facade of a temple, even down to the bronze nails with which the frames were studded, and gives an excellent impression of what the original wooden temple porches would have looked like. The tomb would have been entered through the bottom right-hand sliding panel of the fake doorway, but this has now been broken by grave robbers. Traces of paint were still visible on the exterior until the nineteenth century.

There's not all that much else to see in Fethiye, although you can visit the remains of the **medieval fortress** on the hillside behind the harbor area of town. The path to the site leads off Çarşı Caddesi through backstreets up to the acropolis, affording good views of the town on the way. The fortress is attributed to the Knights of Saint John, but a variety of architectural styles suggests additional work on the part of Lycians, Greeks, Romans, Byzantines, and Turks.

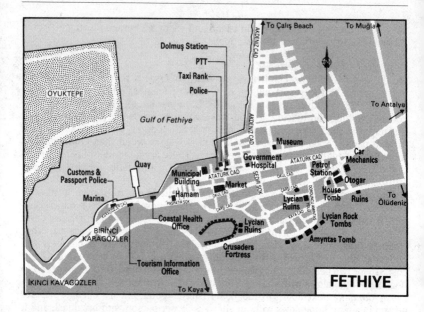

In the center of town, off Atatürk Caddesi, Fethiye's **museum** (Tues–Sun 8am–5pm; $1) is badly labeled and very small, but some of the exhibits help to enhance the nearby archaeological sights by contributing a human element. The most interesting exhibit is the stellae found at Letoön, dating from 358 BC, which was so important in translating the Lycian language. The stone slab, which is covered in a trilingual text in Lycian, Greek, and Aramaic, concerns a sanctuary to be dedicated in Xanthos to the mythical king-god, Kaunos, the supposed founder of the city of that name. Other finds include a beautiful gold-leaf head-dress dating from the third century BC, unearthed at the site of Pinara.

Kaya Köyü and the Beaches

Served by dolmuşes from behind the PTT, the ghost town of **KAYA KÖYÜ** is about 15km out of town, about 3km beyond the village of Ovacık on the road to Gemiler Beach. The deserted village is one of the most dramatic and moving of all the sites on this coast, and puts into painful relief the human suffering involved in the process of population transfer. The village has been abandoned since 1923, when its Anatolian Greek population was relocated, along with several million others, to a country that had never been their homeland, and whose language many of them couldn't speak. All you can see now is a hillside covered with ruined cottages and an attractive **basilica**, to the right of the main path about 300m up the hill from the road. The church, dated 1888, retains some of its murals, including faces of Christ and the apostles over the altar, but the general state of neglect and disrepair, plus the fact that local Turks were sympathetic enough to the situation of their neighbors never to inhabit the houses, only serves to highlight the plight of the former inhabitants of the village.

The village is located on the side of a hill, at the foot of which there is an excellent little café, the *Kardeşler*. The family that runs the café will be able to advise on the walk from Kaya Köyü to **Ölüdeniz**, and may even provide a guide, although it's not too difficult to find your own way, providing you don't lose sight of the weather-beaten red blazes that mark the route; it's about 8km in all—up through the village, over the crest of a hill and down into beautiful woods, and around the coast and down to the lagoon. This is by far the most attractive approach and is really worth attempting for its stunning views of the lagoon. Ölüdeniz itself is also served by frequent dolmuşes from Fethiye, and the warm waters of the lagoon make for pleasant swimming if you don't mind mud oozing through your toes, or paying the entrance fee of 50¢ per person, $2 per car. However, the once-beautiful lagoon, known as the "Dead Sea" in Turkish, is one of the country's best-known resorts, and in the past decade its beaches have reached saturation level.

The nearest beach to Fethiye, **Çalış**, 7km to the northeast and accessible by frequent dolmuşes from behind the PTT, is a good long stretch of sand that's cleaner and somewhat less seedy than Ölüdeniz. It's a particularly pleasant place to visit in the evenings. **Gemiler** Beach is more difficult to get to, 5km beyond Kaya Köyü along a rough and precipitous track and not served by any public transportation, but it's worth some effort if you're looking for somewhere secluded.

Food and Nightlife

There's a pleasant **restaurant** in the center of town called *Terrace*, behind the old hamam on the square between Paspatır Sokak and the tourist information office, serving fish, shish, meat, and *meze*. Another excellent option is a cheap *pide salonu*, *Nefis Pide İki*, at Tütün Sokak 21, although this gets thronged at lunchtime. It offers a range of excellent cheap kebabs and meat dishes as well as *pide*. The *Café Amyntas*, Amyntas Yolu Üzeri 1, is an excellent little cheap outdoor café up near the Amyntas tomb (take the road marked "Kaya" off to the left past the bus station). Otherwise there are a number of fairly reasonable options between Çarşı Caddesi and the harbor, including *Pizza Pepino's* at Çarşı Caddesi 26, located in a beautiful old house badly in need of restoration, and *Pizza 74* on Atatürk Caddesi, which serves European-style pizzas, grills, and hamburgers with beer.

As for **nightlife**, there are plenty of outdoor drinking places between Atatürk and Çarşi Caddesi. The most relaxed and friendly club in town is the *Entel*, opposite the *Hotel Vizion* and behind the main PTT. The *Disco Marina* is more upscale, but entrance to both is $4 including the first drink. There's also a comfortable little wooden bar on Çalış Beach—*Ali's Arche*—where you can also find out about local wildlife and arrange bird-watching tours of the region.

Listings

Boat rental One of the most pleasant experiences to be had in Fethiye is to rent a sailboat and tour some of the twelve islands that ring the bay of Fethiye. It's always possible to find deserted coves in which to swim and cook kebabs, and there are also a few really excellent little fish restaurants (notably the one on Şovalye Adası) where tables are laid out on beaches strung out with drying sponges. Boats leave from Fethiye harbor and cost $6 a day for a tour of three or four islands from 9am to 6 or 7pm; a longer trip gives you the chance to sleep on board or camp on a beach.

Car rental *Çelebi*, Hamam Sok 3/A (☎1282); *Airtour*, Atatürk Cad 55/A (☎6233). Offices of the multinational companies—*InterRent*, *Hertz*, etc—are also located on Atatürk Caddesi.

Diving The *Fethiye Diving Center* (☎16582), along from the tourist information office on Fevzi Çakmak Caddesi, offers daily trips as well as weekly courses, and includes cave and reef diving; scuba training and windsurfing.

Motorcycles/mopeds These can be rented from Atatürk Caddesi 146 (☎12439) from $14 a day for a moped to $40 a day for a BMW 650cc (insurance $4 extra).

PTT Atatürk Caddesi (Mon–Sat 8am–midnight, Sun 9am–7pm).

Shopping Fethiye is an excellent shopping town, with a marvelous food market—which is the place to stock up before boarding if you're making a trip to the islands—located between Atatürk Caddesi and Tütün Sokak in the center of town. The best place to shop for carpets, leather, and silver is Paspatır Sokak, which leads from the *Terrace* restaurant above the harbor up into the old town.

West of Fethiye

The main town west of Fethiye is **DALAMAN**, home of the southern Turkish coast's main airport and little else besides, apart from one of the country's two open prisons for the rehabilitation of long-term convicts. You may, of course arrive here, and if so it's worth knowing that the **airport**, open 24 hours a day, has a tourist information desk (also open 24 hours) and round-the-clock banking facilities. There is, however, no public transportation into town, 5km along Kenan Evren Bulvarı, so you'll have to take a taxi—count on paying about $5 for this. There are a few unexciting hotels to choose from if you are forced to stay in the town. Opposite the **otogar** is the *Karaoğlu Pansiyon*, (☎6119/2820) comfortable and clean, and costing $6 per person for a room with a shower; near the PTT, off the main street, Atatürk Caddesi, on Posthane Sokak, the little *Affable Pansiyon* guarantees hot water and charges $5 for a room with a bath. A little way east of Dalaman, toward Fethiye on Highway 400 at KÜÇÜK KARGI, there are a couple of wooded **campgrounds**, *Katrancı* and *Günlüklü*, served by the Kargı-Yanıklar–Fethiye dolmuş, and 10km farther, the peaceful, wooded village called Göçek, which also has a number of good campgrounds beside stony beaches backed by a beautiful forest.

Dalyan and Around

Westbound buses from Dalaman continue on to ORTACA, where there are plentiful dolmuşes making the twenty-minute journey to the attractive little town of **DALYAN**, 7km off Highway 400, which is a much better base for the surrounding attractions—notably the ancient site of Kaunos, upriver from Dalyan, İstuzu Beach, and the beautiful freshwater lake of Köyceğiz.

Dalyan is an exemplary tourist town, retaining a provincial Turkish identity and organized with a concern for ethical principles while more than catering to the needs of its visitors. The town achieved a measure of international fame three years ago when its "turtle controversy" blew up into a major battle against developers who wanted to build a hotel on **İstuzu Beach**, 6km south of Dalyan, which is the breeding ground of the loggerhead (or *Carretta carretta*) turtle. Conservationists succeeded in halting the development, and now the beach is carefully protected between the times the eggs are laid until they hatch (May 1–Oct 1), and those wishing to observe these processes—which occur between the hours of 10pm and 8am—are obliged (by wardens) to do so from a safe distance. During the day the beach is open to the public, and is a nice place to swim and sunbathe, although you should be careful not to disturb the turtle eggs and nests, which are easily trampled on; the tracks of the turtles in the sand where the creatures have hauled themselves up onto the beach to lay their eggs are visible in June and July. The beach is always alive with other wildlife too, including lizards, snakes, and tortoises, and its approach road is lined with profusely flowering oleander bushes.

Otherwise life in Dalyan revolves around the Dalyan River, which flows through the center of the village. The town's best pansiyons and restaurants are all located on the banks of the river, and the boats that ply up and down it are the best mode of transportation to all of the major sites in the region.

Practical Details

Pansiyon prices in Dalyan are fixed by the municipality, so that a single room without an attached bathroom is always $4 per person. There is a string of pleasant little **pansiyons** located on the river bank, reached by taking the main road past the boat cooperative office on the right and the turnoff to İstuzu on the left and continuing out of town until you come to a leafy path which ends in the area known as Maraş Mahallesi. One of the nicest of the little establishments along this lane is *Midas Camping* (☎6116/1195), which has pansiyon facilities as well as camping in the garden by the river. Another good option is the *Aktaş Pansiyon* (6116/1042), whose large picture windows offer excellent views of the temple rock tombs on the opposite bank. Rooms all have bathrooms and hot water for $16 double—no singles. Their friendly neighbors, the *Miletos Pansiyon*, have rooms for $4 a person, with shower and kitchen down the hall. If you get fed up with the fragile appeal of Dalyan village, it is possible to **camp** at İstuzu Beach between October and May. Camping is restricted to the corner of the beach at the bottom of the road from Dalyan, but there is fresh water and restroom facilities.

The best **restaurants and bars** in town are also located in this area; try, for example, the *Carreta Carreta*, which offers an excellent seafood menu, including a stew of bass and squid. Ten minutes upriver, the *Yalı* restaurant also specializes in seafood, while back in the town center, the *Baküs Bar*, down a passageway leading to the *Taşdan Hotel*, is a nice place to drink—usually to the sound of some very vocal frogs in a stream out back that's alive with them, not to mention small turtles.

Boat tour prices up and down the river to Kaunos, İstuzu Beach or to Köyceğiz Lake are fixed by the Dalyan motorboat cooperative, situated on the river between the town mosque and the turnoff to İstuzu Beach (daily 8am–7:30pm). You can either rent a whole boat, which takes eight people and costs around $28 for a half-day, or pay per person, which is around $2 for a trip to Kaunos or the beach. Many of the pansiyons along the river have their own small boats and will take you on evening trips upriver to sit and watch for bubbles and the silent dark shapes of the loggerhead turtles occasionally surfacing for air.

Around Dalyan: Köyceğiz and Kaunos

North of Dalyan, **KÖYCEĞIZ** is a sleepy little town without Dalyan's good looks that is fast being written off the tourist agenda by its quickly developing rival. Nevertheles it boasts a healthy local economy, based on local cotton, olive, and peanut cultivation, and its position on the ten-meter-deep **Köyceğiz Golü**—a onetime bay open to the Mediterranean that became dammed by deposits from mountain rivers—gives it a source of income from the fish that swim up the Dalyan Çayı from the sea to spawn here. There's no real point in staying here, but it's connected with Dalyan by a regular (Muğla-bound) bus, and you may want to stop over for a night in order to view the ruins at Kaunos (see below) on the opposite side of the lake. The **tourist information office** on the main square (Mon–Fri 8:30am–12:30pm & 1:30–5:30pm) can advise on **accommodation**, although there's nothing ultra-cheap. Choose between the good but somewhat pricey *Hotel Kaunos* at Cengiz Topel Caddesi 37 (☎1288), which charges $38 a double, and the nearby lakeside *Fulya Pansiyon* (☎2301)—clean and attractive, and costing a much cheaper $6 a head. There's also a decent forested **campground** with a beach 800m west of the town, also beside the lake.

Boat trips downriver to the ancient site of Kaunos pass a series of spectacular fourth-century **rock tombs** set into the cliff on the far bank from the village, many of which are in the temple style with two Ionic columns, similar to those in Fethiye. Ten minutes upriver, the **Ilıca thermal baths**, a series of open-air pools (free admission), are worth investigating if you don't mind slimy mud between your toes. The waters are claimed to increase male potency and cure rheumatism and gynaecological diseases, and reach temperatures of around 104° F. Whatever else they do, bathing in them certainly relieves stress, as long as you are not subjected to low-key sexual harassment while you're there—which is a distinct possibility.

The way to **KAUNOS** is navigated through swaths of reeds reflected bright green in the water. The disembarkation point is at a new fish farm that was recently opened to replace the one formerly located in the village (Dalyan means "Fish Weir"). The fish, which are served at restaurants in Dalyan, are mostly mullet and bass. A fragmentary inscription found at Kaunos suggests that the river has been fished since ancient times. From here it's a ten-minute walk up to the **site** (admission charged daily 8:30am–6pm; $1, otherwise it's unfenced).

The excavations of Kaunos began in 1967 and are still going on, using laborers from the open prison in Dalaman. The site is particularly pleasant, swarming with wildlife (and mosquitoes—take precautions if you're prone to bites), plus herons and storks in summer, flamingoes in November, small turtles, tortoises, and nodding lizards.

Kaunos was a Carian settlement thought to have been originally established as early as the ninth century BC. According to Herodotus, the people of Kaunos believed they came from Crete, although he thought it more likely they were indigenous to this region. He also said they spoke like Carians, but that their customs resembled those of Lycians; the rock tombs they cut into the cliffs near Dalyan are certainly typically Lycian in style. Above all the city was famous for the bad health of its inhabitants, who were notoriously prone to fever which at the time was attributed to the amount of fruit they ate: Kaunian figs were famous all over the Roman world, and even Galen, the greatest physician of antiquity, considered excessive consumption of fruit to be dangerous to health. The fever in question was, however, probably malaria, and no doubt had more to do with the mosquitoes hereabouts, which then were more prevalent in the marshy area around the city than figs ever were. Other famed Kaunian wares were slaves and salt; the latter was recommended by Pliny for addition to eye salves and bandages.

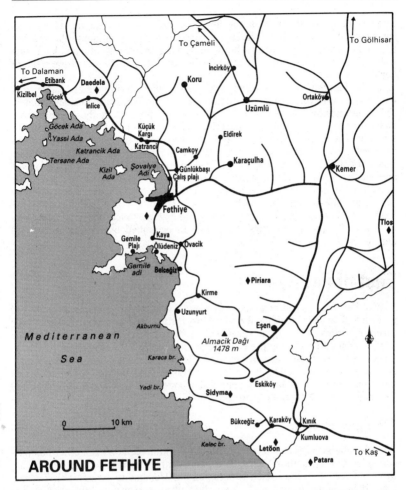

AROUND FETHİYE

There was a close relationship between Kaunos and neighboring Xanthos. The eponymous founder of Kaunos was also worshipped at Xanthos, and when the Persian Harpagus attempted to conquer the region in the sixth century BC, these two cities were the only two that resisted—something Herodotus explained as more imitation than collaboration, saying that "the Kaunians imitated the Lycians for the most part." The city began to aquire a Greek character as a result of the influence of the Hellenizing Carian ruler Mausolus—something the inhabitants readily took to, since no Carian names have been found on inscriptions. Subsequently, the city passed from one ruler to another. After Alexander's death the city was ruled by Ptolemy, then by the Rhodians, and after fierce resistance to Rhodes the city reverted to Roman rule.

Another problem Kaunos suffered was the silting of its harbor, which was a continual threat to the city's substantial commercial interests. The sea originally came right up to the foot of the acropolis hill, surrounding the city on all sides apart from an isthmus of land to the north. Since antiquity, the sea has receded by over five kilometers, however, leaving an expanse of marshland in its wake. The large lake, **Sülüklü Gölü**, is thought to mark the site of the western harbor.

Much of Kaunos is still below ground, despite the long-running excavation, and only the most obvious sites, like the **agora** and the **amphitheater**, are labeled. The **theater** is the most impressive building here, predominantly Greek in style, considerably greater than a semicircle, and resting against the hillside to the south. It retains two of its original arched entrances on the north side. Above the theater the city's **baths** and a Doric-style **temple** are also in excellent condition. The acropolis hill, crowned by a medieval and Hellenistic fortified area, completes an attractive picture. To the northwest and north of the city is a well-preserved stretch of defensive wall, some of which is thought to have been constructed by Mausolus. The ancient west harbor is now marked by a lake, Sülüklü Gölü, the Lake of the Leeches. According to Strabo, the lake was once closed off by a chain in times of danger; nowadays it's merely dive-bombed by feeding storks and herons.

East of Fethiye

East of Fethiye lies the heartland of ancient Lycia, which contains a number of archaeological sites including those of **Tlos**, **Pinara**, and **Xanthos**, all within easy reach of Fethiye. Indeed, the seventy-kilometer stretch of road as far as Kalkan, for the most part following the valley of the former River Xanthos, now known as the Eşen Çayı, is littered with beautifully located ancient cities, the lucky ones advantageously shielded to the east by the Massicytus (Akdağ) Mountains; it's an immensely fertile area too, with fields full of cotton and corn and a wide variety of fruit including pomegranates and figs.

Tlos and Pinara

The two citadel cities of **Tlos** and **Pinara** are within sight of each other on opposite sides of the Xanthos Valley. They were both important settlements, having three votes each in the Lycian Federation, but Tlos had the geographical advantage, being situated on a rich open river plain, sheltered to the east by the Massicytus range, while Pinara was surrounded by hilly terrain which was difficult to cultivate. Both cities were unearthed by the traveler Charles Fellows when he discovered the site of Xanthos, between 1838 and 1840.

Tlos

Traveling east from Fethiye, there's a turnoff after 30km to **TLOS**, one of the most ancient of the Lycian cities, situated above the modern village of KALE ASAR. It is referred to in Hittite records of the fourteenth century BC as "Dalawa in the Lukka lands," and the discovery on the site of a bronze hatchet dating from the second millennium BC confirms the long history of the place. Little else is known about its past, however, although it was numbered among the six principal Lycian cities.

Nowadays there's not a great deal to see, and what's there is hardly excavated so that the precise identification of buildings is open to question. But the site is impressive, situated on a high rocky promontory which affords excellent views of the Xanthos Valley. The acropolis hill of Tlos is dominated by a Turkish fortress from the Ottoman period, the residence of a nineteenth-century brigand, Kanlı Ali Ağa. Currently unoccupied, it has obliterated all earlier remains on the hill. To the northeast, the hill ends in almost perpendicular cliffs. On the eastern slope are traces of the Lycian city wall and a long stretch of subsequent Roman masonry, and on the same slope a group of Lycian tombs.

Between the foot of the acropolis hill and the village is a large open space thought to be the agora. Close to the base of the hill are traces of seats that formed part of the stadium. The opposite side of the agora is lined by a long building thought to be the market hall. Beyond this, to the south, lie the baths, of which two complete rooms and an apsidal projection with seven windows are intact, offering a good view of the Xanthos Valley. Between the baths and the modern road from the village are the remains of a Byzantine basilica, and to the southeast of this another open space that some believe to have been the city's basilica. To the north of a modern road that leads from the village, past the market building, is a second-century BC theater; although it's very overgrown, 34 rows of seats remain, and the stage building has a number of finely carved blocks.

Returning up the road to the acropolis, passing by the seats of the stadium and around the acropolis hill, lies the best of the ruins—the **Tomb of Bellerophon**, the facade of which was carved to resemble that of a temple, with roughly hewn columns supporting its pediment and three carved doors. On the left wall of the porch is the carving that gives the tomb its name, representing the mythical hero Bellerophon riding the winged horse Pegasus, while facing them over the door is a lion—probably meant to stand guard on the tomb. Inside are four stone benches, on which the bodies of the deceased would have been laid.

Pinara

Beyond Tlos, the road follows the course of the Xanthos Valley. The path up to the indicated site of **PİNARA**, about 5km off Highway 400, is steep and rocky; it's difficult to manage in a private car, and there is no public transportation here. It is possible to drive up as far as the village of MİNARE and hike the remaining 2km, which takes about half an hour, or you can make it to the parking lot at the top if you're prepared for substantial wear and tear on your vehicle.

Approaching the site from the road, the cliff on which the original city was founded is unmissable, since it practically blocks out the horizon—indeed, it's worth the trip up just to see the towering mass, the east face of which is covered in rectangular-cut openings, thought to be either tombs or food-storage space. They can only be reached by experienced rock climbers, and it's hard to fathom how they were ever cut in the first place.

Practically nothing is known about Pinara, inscriptions found at the site being particularly uninformative. According to the fourth-century Xanthian historian Menecrates, it was founded to accommodate the overspill from Xanthos, a kind of planned suburb for the larger city. Later on, however, Pinara—whose name means "Something Round" in the Lycian language, presumably because of the shape of the rock on which it is situated—grew to become one of the largest Lycian cities, minting its own coins and controlling three votes in the Federation.

The main part of the ruins of Pinara are situated on the lower acropolis hill, to the east of the cliff, where the city was relocated, probably quite early in its history, when it was no longer necessary to be so protected from attack. The lower acropolis is overgrown and the greater part of its buildings are unidentifiable. To the north of the hill, on its west face, is a small theater, although the site's tombs are probably its most interesting feature. On the east side of the acropolis hill, the so-called royal tomb is unique for its carvings representing four walled cities with battlements, gates, houses, and tombs, and one or two human figures on the walls of its porch. Inside there is a single bench, unusually high off the ground, suggesting that it was the tomb of a single person, probably of royal blood. In the same group of tombs, on the east face but higher up, is a house tomb with a roof in the form of a gothic arch, at the point of which is a pair of ox horns.

The Letoön

Sixteen kilometers east of Pinara the site of the **LETOÖN** (daily 8:30am–6pm; $1) is indicated off the road a kilometer before KINIK, 4km off Highway 400. It's fairly isolated, so it's a good thing the ticket collector keeps a crate of beer handy at the entrance. To get there, take a dolmuş from Fethiye to KUMLUOVA and get off just before the village at the turnoff to the Letoön, a few hundred meters' walk away.

The Letoön, the shrine of the goddess Leto, was the official sanctuary of the Lycian Federation, where national festivals were celebrated, and the extensive ruins to be seen today bear witness to its importance. The site became a center of Christian worship, and a church was consecrated here. It was not until the Arab raids in the seventh century that the site was eventually abandoned. The initial remains of the Letoön were discovered in 1840, although excavation work wasn't begun until 1962, and since then it has been systematically uncovered and labeled, making the ruins for once easily appreciated even if you don't have a knowledge of classical architecture.

Leto was loved by Zeus, and jealously pursued by Hera, his wife. Wandering about in search of a place to give birth to her children (Apollo and Artemis), she is said to have approached a fountain to relieve her thirst, only to be driven away by local herdsmen. It is said that after being driven away from the fountain, Leto was led to drink at the Xanthos River by wolves, and so changed the name of the country to Lycia, *lykos* being the Greek word for wolf. Later, after giving birth to her children on Delos, she returned to punish the herdsmen by changing them into frogs.

It is thought that the name Leto could be derived from the Lycian word, *lada*, meaning woman, and it is possible that the Anatolian mother goddess, Cybele, was worshipped on this site before her. Another similarity between the two goddesses is that they are both often mentioned in connection with mother-son incestuous unions—something historians believe might have been common in Lycian society. Most famous of all the prophecies supposed to have been given at the Letoön was that received by Alexander the Great, in which he was informed that the Persian Empire would be destroyed by the Greeks. Encouraged by this prophecy, says Plutarch, "he went on to clear the coastline of Persians as far as Cilica and Phoenicia."

The Site

Since excavations began in 1962, the remains of three temples, a nymphaeum and two porticos have been uncovered, as well as a number of interesting **inscriptions**. One of these lays down the conditions of entry to the sanctuary, including strict rules of dress stating that clothing must be simple, with the wearing of rich jewelry and elaborate hairstyles forbidden. Another important inscription found on the rock shelf to the east of the temples is a trilingual text in Lycian, Greek, and Aramaic, referring to the establishment in Xanthos of a cult of the Kaunian deity Basilens (meaning "King"), which has proved invaluable in deciphering the Lycian language.

The low ruins of the three **temples** occupy the center of the site. The westernmost of them, on the left as you stand with your back to the entrance, bears a dedication to Leto. Once surrounded by a single collonnade, with decorative half-columns around the interior walls, it dates back to the third century BC. The temple in the center is a century older, and is identified by a dedication to Artemis; its northern part incorporates a rocky outcrop. The temple to the east was similar in design to the temple of Leto, having been surrounded by a colonnade of Doric columns with half-columns around its interior. The mosaic on the floor of this temple represents a lyre, bow, and quiver, which suggest that it was dedicated to Artemis and Apollo, since the bow and quiver were symbols of Artemis, and the lyre that of Apollo. According to legend, Apollo and Artemis, Leto's chidren, were born in the Xanthos Valley, and were, apparently, the region's most revered deities. The style of the architecture and of the mosaic date it to the second and first centuries BC.

Beyond the temple, to the southwest, is a **nymphaeum**, which consisted of a rectangular building with two semicircular recesses on either side, with niches for statues. The remains of the building are bordered by a semicircular paved basin with a diameter of 27m, now permanently flooded and full of turtles and noisy frogs, a fitting reminder of the vengeance of Leto on the herdsmen who wouldn't give her a drink.

A **church** was built over the rectangular section of the nymphaeum in the fourth century, and destroyed by Arab invaders in the seventh so that only its outline is discernible.

Returning to the parking lot at the entrance there is a large, well-preserved Hellenistic **theater** on the right, entered through a vaulted passage. The southwest entrance to the passage is decorated with a row of sixteen masks. The cavea of the theater is partly cut out of the hillside.

Xanthos

The remains of the hilltop city of **XANTHOS,** with their breathtaking views of the Xanthos River—now the Eşen Çayı—and valley, are perhaps the most fascinating in the whole of Lycia.

The site first came to the attention of the Western world in 1842, when Charles Fellows, a British traveler, visited it and carried off the better part of its movable art works. It took two months to strip the site of its monuments, which were loaded into the *HMS Beacon* and shipped back to the British Museum. Buses between Fethiye and Patara will drop you off in KINIK, about 2km beyond the Letoön, and it's a twenty-minute (uphill) walk from there.

Some History

Part of the fascination of a visit to Xanthos lies in the city's history, which was dominated by the highly mercurial fortunes and unusual temperament of its inhabitants. In mythology the city was connected with the story of Bellerophon and Pegasus (see "Olympos," below). King Iobates—who originally set impossible tasks for Bellerophon and later offered him a share in his kingdom—ruled here, and the city was the home of the grandson of Bellerophon, Glaucus, who was described in the Iliad as "from the whirling waters of the Xanthos."

Archaeological finds from the site date to the eighth century BC, but the earliest historical mention of the city dates to 540 BC and the conquest of Lycia by the Persian general Harpagus. From Caria he descended into the Xanthos Valley and after some resistance succeeded in penning the citizens into their own city. Their response was the city's first holocaust: they collected together their women and children and made a funeral pyre with their household belongings. The women and children died in the flames, and the men perished fighting, the only surviving citizens being eight families who were out of town at the time.

The subsequent fate of Xanthos resembled that of the rest of Lycia, with Alexander succeeding the Persians, and in time being succeeded by his general Antigonus and then by Antiochus III. After the defeat of Antiochus, Xanthos was given to Rhodes with the rest of Lycia.

The second Xanthian holocaust occurred in 42 BC, when Brutus besieged the city, again moving the citizens to make funeral pyres of their possessions and cast themselves into the flames. The city prospered once more in Imperial times, and under Byzantine rule the city walls were renovated and a monastery built.

The Site

There is no entrance fee or restrictions to the **site** of ancient Xanthos, although sadly the most important construction discovered here—the fourth-century **Nereid Monument**, a beautifully decorated Ionic temple on a high podium—is now located in the British Museum, along with many of the other monuments and sculptures Charles Fellows pillaged in 1842. However, there is still enough to see here to require a lengthy visit.

On the way up from the road, on the left-hand side, stands a Hellenistic gateway bearing an inscription claiming that Antiochus the Great dedicated the city to Leto, Apollo, and Artemis, the national deities of Lycia; farther up, on the right-hand side of the road, the former location of the Nereid Monument is marked by a plaque. To the left of the parking lot, at the top of the path, are the Lycian acropolis and the agora, and the Roman theater, beside which are two conspicuous Lycian monuments. On the right is the so-called **Harpy Tomb**, once topped with a marble chamber that was removed by Fellows in 1842; it has since been replaced by a cement cast of the original. The figures on this, which gave the monument its name, are the pairs of bird-woman figures on the north and south sides, depicted carrying children in their arms. The figures have been identified as harpies, or, more likely, as sirens, carrying the souls of the dead (the children) to the Isles of the Blessed. Other reliefs on all four sides depict seated figures receiving gifts, which have not been identified. Beside the Harpy Tomb is a Lycian-type sarcophagus standing on a pillar tomb, an unusual structure thought to date from the third century BC. The remains of a body and some third-century pottery were found inside the tomb, along with a sixth-century relief—thought to have been brought from elsewhere—depicting funeral games.

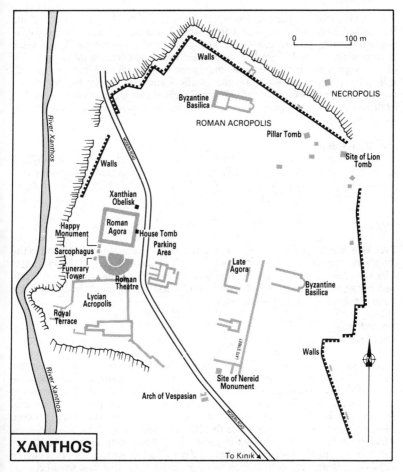

XANTHOS

Located to the northeast of the agora is an obelisk-type structure, known popularly as the **Xanthian obelisk** but in fact the remains of a pillar tomb covered on all four sides by the longest known Lycian inscription, comprising 250 lines and including 12 lines of Greek verse. Since the Lycian language hasn't been very well deciphered, understanding of the inscription is based on the verse, and on proper names appearing in the text, which tells the story of a champion wrestler in his youth who went on to sack many cities, and generally to glorify his family name.

The nearby Roman **theater** was built on the site of an earlier Greek structure and is pretty complete, only missing the upper seats which were incorporated into the Byzantine city wall. Behind the theater, overlooking the Xanthos Valley, is the Lycian acropolis, in the far southeastern corner of which are the remains of a square building thought to be the palace of the early Xanthian kings destroyed by the general Harpagus.

Returning past the parking lot, a path leads to the residential sections of the Roman and Hellenistic city, and a **Byzantine basilica,** still being excavated, is distinguished by its extensive abstract mosaics and a synthronon in the semi-circular apse. On the hill north of here is the Roman acropolis, at the eastern side of which are a number of free-standing Lycian sarcophagi, and, cut into the hill-side above, a group of picturesque tombs mainly of the Lycian house—as opposed to temple—type. A well-preserved early Byzantine monastery is located to the north of the acropolis hill, containing an open courtyard with washbasins along one side.

Practical Details

To get to Xanthos from Kalkan—by far the best base—take the Fethiye dolmuş as far as Kınık and walk up the hill. Alternatively you can rent a fourteen-seater minibus for $40. Boats are also available for group rental at the harbor, but you have to bargain for a good price.

Patara

PATARA was the principal port of Lycia, famed for its oracle of Apollo, and in the fourth century as the birthplace of Saint Nicholas, Bishop of Myra—Santa Claus—although nowadays the area is better known for its white-sand beach, which has recently given rise to some small-scale development, including a few good pansiyons, bars, and restaurants.

Some History

There are many myths concerning the Greek origins of the city of Patara, but in fact the city was Lycian from the beginning, evidenced by coins and inscriptions bearing the letters *pttara*. The city was famous for its temple and oracle of Apollo, which was supposed to rival the one at Delphi in its accuracy, probably because Apollo spent the winter months in Patara. No traces of this temple have, however, been found to date. Patara played an important part in Lycian and Roman Imperial history, being used as an important naval base during the wars between Alexander's successors. Later, in 42 BC, Brutus made his way here from Xanthos, which he had just destroyed. He threatened the Patarans with a similar fate if they didn't submit to his army, giving them a day to decide. A story told by Plutarch claims that Brutus released women hostages in the hope that they would change the minds of their menfolk, which didn't work, leading Brutus eventually to let all the hostages go free, thereby proving his charm and sensitivity and endearing himself to the Patarans, who subsequently surrendered. Whatever his tactics, his motives for taking the city at all were revealed by the fact that he took no prisoners, just ordered that all the city's gold and silver should be handed over.

The Site

The ruins can be wandered around at any time of day or night, but if there is a guard on duty he may charge you $1 admission. Down the five-kilometer-long dirt track from Highway 400 (2km from the village), the **entrance** to the city is marked by a triple-arched Roman gateway, almost completely intact, dedicated to a governor of Lycia, Mettius Modestus, in the first century AD. To the west of the gate is a little hill where a head of Apollo was discovered, and this has been supposed to be the site of the temple of Apollo.

South of this mound is a **baths complex** with a vaulted roof, and a basilica, though both are in poor state of preservation. To the west of these is a more attractive second-century temple, which while too small and simple to be identified as the city's famous temple to Apollo, is richly decorated in stucco and has a seven-meter-high door leading into its single chamber. Farther south are some better preserved **baths**, built by the emperor Vespasian (69–79 AD) and consisting of five chambers, each of which would have had a different purpose. There's a **theater** southwest of the baths of Vespasian, close to the beach—the cavea is now full of sand, but earlier visitors counted 34 rows of seats. The stage building, which is still intact, has five doors and five arched windows above them. It is also the location of an inscription ascribing the building of the stage to a woman, Vilia Procula, and her father, both of whom were citizens of Patara. The inscription states that Vilia Procula contributed the stage, its statues, and its marble revetments. The hill to the south of the theater is the city's **acropolis**, worth climbing to view the pit at the top. This unusual construction is circular, 10m in diameter, with a pillar sticking out of the top and stairs down the side of it. It was once thought to be a lighthouse, but since it's not at the summit of the hill it's more probably a cistern.

The Beach

The famous harbor of Patara silted up gradually in the Middle Ages and consequently had to be abandoned. It is now a marshy area to the northwest of the theater, bordering the superb **beach,** which is supposedly one of the longest in the world (local estimates are around 17km), twenty minutes' walk from the village—although it's hard, if you're a single women, to ever entirely shake off the groups of youths from Patara. Around the end of the road from the village, it can get a bit crowded in summer, but the walk along the dunes to the Letoön, some 7km northwest, turns up more than enough solitary spots.

Practical Details

The village of **PATARA**, 7km from Xanthos, is situated 3km off Highway 400. The turnoff to it is marked about midway between the villages of Ovaköy and Yeşilköy; Patara itself is 2km farther on, and the beach a kilometer beyond that. **Dolmuşes** leave every half hour from Kalkan. From Fethiye there are around fifteen dolmuşes a day.

All **accommodation** is in Patara village. On the right of the road leading to the beach, the *Otel Letoön* (☎3215/5216) is comfortable and has a nice bar, and rooms for $12 per person with breakfast. The *Likya Pansiyon* (☎3215/5211), in the village, costs $10 per person for rooms with showers. The best hotel in Patara is the *Ferah* (☎3215/5180), up on the hill above the village, a newly opened place that costs $8 single, $14 double. In front of the hotel is a courtyard full of olive trees where meals are served. The *Zeybek* (no phone), opposite, isn't as good, and costs $10 per room. Both hotels are within reach of the beach if you follow the road without returning to the village—a ten-minute walk.

For eating, the best established place in Patara is the *Patara Restaurant*, just before the beach on the left-hand side, after the parking lot. It's situated in a beautifully fragrant garden and serves favorite Turkish snacks like *menemen* (resembling an omelet), as well as the house specialty of *mantı*—Turkish ravioli. Also good, on the road leading out of the village up the hill to the *Ferah* hotel, is *The Lazy Frog*, a pleasant bar and restaurant with a relaxed atmosphere and a *saz*-playing proprietor who keeps guests entertained into the early hours.

Kalkan and Around

Eleven kilometers beyond the turnoff for Patara, the former Greek village of **KALKAN** appears to cling for dear life to the steep hill on which it is precariously situated. Tourism is a fairly new phenomenon in the town, and the locals who have benefited from it have been those who were too poor to go up to Kalkan's *yayla* (summer pastureland) around the mountain village of Bezirgan. The richer residents sold up their seaside property without realizing its value, and no doubt the speculators will eventually do something with the land they have bought—the worst development to date is the Patara Club, a complex of vacation villas situated to the east of the village. Meanwhile Kalkan is a relaxing place to take a break, with nothing whatsoever, not even a decent beach, to distract you from the excellent local restaurants.

Kalkan is a good base from which to explore Patara or Xanthos, or even the Letoön. It's also handy for the beach at Patara (see above for full details).

Practical Details

There are some excellent **pansiyons** located along the steep rocky paths that wind and plunge from the very top of town down to the harbor, some of which are just local homes with a room or two to rent. Most places congregate up in the residential Yalıboyu district, on the hill above the harbor, and one of the best and friendliest is the *Kalamaki Pansiyon* (☎3215/1312), on the way down to the harbor from Altıncı Nolu Sokak, the highest of the terraced streets that run parallel to the sea below. Owned by Durmuş and Christine Uşaklı, the pansiyon is one of many situated in the Greek-built houses that comprised the original village, and it takes its name from the original Greek name of the village. Spotlessly clean single and double rooms with hot water are available for $16–22, and they also serve good home cooking in the restaurant downstairs. Above the *Kalamaki*, in Altıncı Nolu Sokak, the *Şahin* (☎3215/1104), *Çelik* (☎3215/1022), and *Holiday* (☎3215/1154) each cost $12 for a double room without private bath; the comfortable and airy *Kalkan Han* (☎3215/1151), with a rooftop bar equipped with telescope, costs $36 single, $49 double. Also in Yalıboyu, another old building transformed into a hotel is the *Sultan* (☎3215/1158, 1441), where a single with bathroom goes for $10, doubles $18, and they have a restaurant upstairs. There's another lovely old Greek building on the harbor, the *Patara*, with a fabulous terrace bar serving excellent cocktails, and doubles with bath for $24, singles $20.

The *Patara* also has a decent restaurant, reasonably priced and with tasty standard fare, although good **food** isn't a problem in Kalkan. Locals recommend the *Ilyada*, which serves up to fifty different cold *meze* in a night, and serves a *günlük yemeği* ("daily food") set menu during the day for $5. It also has the usual fish and grills. The *Köşk Restaurant*, above the harbor, is noisy and good fun, with folk and oriental dancing and food served on a roofed terrace at enormous long tables. The food is very reasonably priced, too. For something a bit more special, the newly opened *Korsan* serves international dishes, including delicious crepes, at reasonable prices. Other restaurants worth trying include the *Yakamoz* by the harbor, the beautifully decorated and reasonably priced *Balıkçı Han* (☎3215/1075), which also has a cosy little bar, and the *Smile Restaurant* in

Yalıboyu Mahallesi (☎3215/1481, 1310)—a bit pricier than most of the others, but highly thought-of locally.

Wherever you eat in Kalkan, the place to end up for a **drink** later in the evening is currently the *Nostalji Bar* underneath the *Sultan Hotel*. It's not particularly cheap, but it is cosy and friendly, and well-stocked.

Out of Kalkan

Walking around the coast road west from town, you'll arrive at the **Taş Adamı** or "Stone Man," the local name for a disused **quarry** which originally provided the stone for the construction of Kalkan harbor. Beyond this is a pebbly **beach** traditionally reserved for women, although this doesn't mean you won't be followed on the way there.

It's only by exploring farther afield into the Taurus Mountains or along the coast that the real advantages of Kalkan's situation are revealed. **BEZİRGAN**, 11km inland from Kalkan by a poor road, in a green, cool valley, is the *yayla* to which richer Kalkan residents disappear in summer, and has a sprinkling of Lycian rock tombs and a Turkish flour mill. You can visit on a day-trip by donkey, on tours arranged by Süleyman Bolukbaşı (☎3215/1324). The $25 price includes a meal in one of the village's attractive wooden houses.

The road from Kalkan to Kaş follows the coastline, after a short time passing the **Kaputaş Gorge**, a deep gash leading back into the cliff face. Steps from the road lead down to the popular **Kaputaş Beach**, a small expanse of sand and pebble that is normally fairly crowded, probably as a result of the poor quality of the beaches in Kaş. A plaque on the cliff face commemorates four workers who were killed at this spot during the building of the road in 1962–63. A kilometer on toward Kaş there's a fish **restaurant**, the *Ada*, (☎3215/1424) with a **campground** just behind.

Kaş

Tourism has transformed **KAŞ**. It is beautifully situated, nestled in a curving bay—the name Kaş means "eyebrow" or "something curved"—with a backdrop of vertical, 500m-high cliffs to protect it. But what was a quaint fishing village five years ago has grown to become a large tourist metropolis before the eyes of astonished observers, with a 4000-strong population that relies on tourism to maintain a standard of living to which they have only recently become accustomed. The municipality and tourist office are aware of this. They are well organized and helpful, and keep a tight rein on hotel and restaurant prices in an effort to protect their treasured guests.

There's no beach to speak of in Kaş itself, and if you're not looking for leather and carpets, on first inspection there seems little to keep you here. The town does get lively at night, however, mainly because its shops stay open until 11pm or midnight in summer, and it's an interesting place to stroll around on a warm summer evening. By day it's a handy base from which to reach Kekova and nearby Patara if you don't have your own wheels. It's also the site of ancient Antiphellos, and the remaining ruins still litter the streets of the modern town, as well as covering the peninsula to the west.

Arrival and Accommodation

The **tourist information office** is at Cumhuriyet Meydanı 5 (Mon–Fri
8:30am–noon & 1–8pm; Sat & Sun 9am–noon & 1pm–8pm; ☎3226/1238), and has
a map of the town and hotel price lists. If you're planning to stay, their *ev
pansiyonlar* or **bed and breakfast** arrangements are a good deal, with prices
starting at $6 single, $8 double. Hotel and pansiyon prices in Kaş are in any case
strictly controlled and should be displayed in all rooms. There are a number of
cheap pansiyons near the bus station, including the *Limyra* on Meltem Sokak
(☎3226/1080) and the *Ay Pansiyon* below the mosque on Yeni Cami Caddesi
(☎3226/1020) with sea views, both charging around $12 for a double. The *Toros
Hotel*, off Üzünçarşı Caddesi (☎3226/1923), is comfortable and attractively
decorated, with a roof terrace and bar. Its owners are foremost among Turkey's
professional mountain guides, particularly regarding the Taurus Mountains, and
will be able to arrange tours or give invaluable advice on trekking in the region.
Single rooms are $16, doubles $22. Other good hotels are the *Andifli*, on Hastane
Caddesi (☎3226/1042), with beautiful views, the *Ali Baba* on the same street
(☎3226/1126) with doubles at $10, and the *Hotel Marti* on the water
(☎3226/1525), which charges $20 for one of its six double rooms, and has a bar
and restaurant.

There are two **campgrounds** close to town. The *Büyükçakıl*, on the east side
of town (☎3226/1968), rents out tents with beds for around $10 per person, and is
pleasantly shaded by olive trees. To get there from the bus station follow Elmalı
Caddesi down to the main square (Cumhuriyet Meydanı), and walk out of town
along Hükümet Caddesi, past the police station and on for about five minutes.
Kaş Camping (☎3226/1050) is on the west side of town, a kilometer out on
Hastane Caddesi, and has its own swimming pool, restaurant, and a good bar.

The Town . . . and Some Beaches

The ruins of the ancient city of **Antiphellos** are scattered around Kaş and across
the nearby peninsula. The city was the harbor of ancient Phellos, inland from
here, one of the few Lycian cities to have a Greek name (Phellos means "Stony
Ground"). Excavations here have unearthed a settlement dating back at least to
the fourth century BC, although Antiphellos only developed in importance in
Hellenistic times, when the increase in commerce meant it gained where Phellos
lost. By the Roman era, it was the most important city in the region, famous
particularly for its exported sponges, which Pliny mentioned as being exceptionally soft.

The **remains** of the ancient city are few and scattered, but what there is to see
is quite impressive. Out of town half a kilometer from the main square, along
Hastane Caddesi, is a small, almost complete Hellenistic **theater** with 26 rows of
seats. The theater didn't ever have a permanent stage building, but in recent
years a curved wall was built in the place of a stage to provide a backdrop for
local wrestling matches. Above and behind the theater, 100m away on the top of a
hill, is a unique **Doric tomb**, which is also almost completely intact. Its single
chamber is a slightly tapering cube cut from the rock on which it stands. The
two-meter-high entrance was once closed by a sliding door, but now it can be
entered in order to examine the bench in the back on which the body would have
been laid, decorated by a frieze of small female figures performing a dance.

The most interesting of the sarcophagi to have survived the locals' pillaging for building materiels is the **lion tomb** in Postane Sokak, a small street leading off the main square, to the left of the tourist information office. This towering structure had two burial chambers, the lower one forming a base for the Lycian sarcophagus above it. On the side of the lower chamber there is an undeciphered Lycian inscription, written in a poetic form similar to that of the obelisk at Xanthos. The name of the tomb is derived from the four lifting bosses (projecting bits of stonework used to remove the lid from its base) in the shape of lions' heads, resting their chins on their paws, that project from the sides of the Gothic-style lid of the tomb.

The Beaches

Considering Kaş is a major Turkish resort, its **beaches** are surprisingly awful. The nearest, Küçük Çakıl (Small Gravel) and Büyük Çakıl (Large Gravel)—the former off the main square, the latter a kilometer out of town—are, as their names suggest, stretches of dirty gravel which few people would acknowledge as beaches. Leaving town along Hastane Caddesi, the Kaş Peninsula gives good views of the Greek island Kastellorizo, but again has no beaches to speak of. The nearest decent beach is Kaputaş Beach on the way to Kalkan (see above), a small stretch of sand that gets understandably crowded.

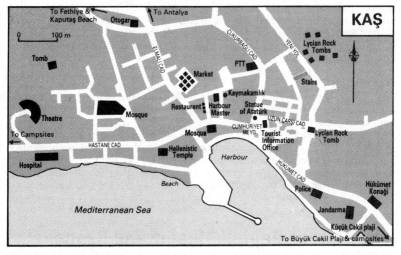

Food and Nightlife

There are a number of good **restaurants** and **bars** in Kaş, and again all prices are *belediye* controlled, and strictly policed by the *zabita* (market police). The *Çınar Restaurant*, Şube Sokak, off Çukurbağlı Caddesi, serves excellent *meze* and fish until midnight, and *gündüz yemeği,* a cheap lunchtime menu. One of the best fish restaurants in town, the *Kalamar*, on Şube Sokak, is excellently situated in an attractive garden under banana trees, with live music in the evenings. *Roosters*, on İskele Geçidi Sokak 8, serves excellent *meze*, pizza, and pasta, while the *Eriş* and the *Derya*, on the main square, are well-priced reasonable options. There are also a couple of good restaurants at the Büyük Çakıl Beach—the *Plaj Restaurant* and the *Çakıl*. The best bar in Kaş is the *Odeon Café Bar*, on Uzunçarşı Ara Sokak, opposite the *Utopia* **second-hand bookstore**, which carries some English-language novels; there's also a little enclave of **carpet shops** nearby, including the *Kaş and Carry*, housed in a stone building decorated in old-world style with wooden tables and kilims, and the excellent *Anatolian Art Gallery*. Behind here there's a **bar/nightclub** called the *Nokta Redpoint*, while for further drinking, the *FM Café Bar*, Hükümet Caddesi 12, on the way to Çakıl Beach, has good service but lousy decor. Recommended for its excellent views is the **Rock Bar** in *Kaş Camping*.

Tours, Boats . . . and Kastellorizo

Boats for rent from the local cooperative, the *Kaş Deniz Taşıyıcıları Kooperatifi*, at the harbor, start at $140 a day at the beginning of the season (April and May), $230 in high season (August and September). Otherwise, tours to Kekova cost $8 per person, Kalkan and Patara $10, and to Kastellorizo (Meis) $18. Boats to most of these destinations leave daily in the mornings, although there is an extra boat to Kastellorizo in the evening.

The *Simena Travel Agency*, İlkokul Mah 25 (☎3226/1416, 1634, 1636), offers slightly more expensive tours, including a tour to Xanthos, Letoön and Patara, a trip to Gömbe in the mountains and to Kaputaş Beach, farther along the coast toward Kalkan. *Atgen Travel* next to the Çınar Restaurant on Çukurbağlı Caddesi (3226/1534) offers donkey tours to Gömbe and Bezirgan, the mountain village above Kalkan.

Kastellorizo

The Greek island of **KASTELLORIZO**—Meis in Turkish—is just over three nautical miles off the Turkish coast. It is the smallest of the Dodecanese grouping, once supported by trade with Kaş and Kalkan, which dried up after the exchange of populations with Turkey. The subsequent explosion of an Allied arsenal in 1944 further upset the fortunes of the island, but now it has been made an official port of entry in an attempt to enhance its tourism potential, and apart from the fact that the villagers aren't too keen on English-speakers—they are still waiting for reparations for damage caused in 1944—it's not a bad place to nip across to if you need to renew your tourist visa.

The Kekova Region: Üçağız and Cyaneae

Some of the most beautifully situated ruins on the south coast are in an area known as **Kekova**—after the offshore island of that name—a stretch of rocky coastline littered with remains of Lycian settlements, some of which are now submerged under the translucent waters, which lap around these shallow coves like liquid turquoise. The central village—and most useful base for the region—is **ÜÇAĞIZ,** connected to Highway 400 by a new paved road that was only completed in 1990, and whose effects are yet to be felt. For the moment the place remains an idyllic fishing village where commerce is mainly confined to the sale of locally produced headscarves by the village girls.

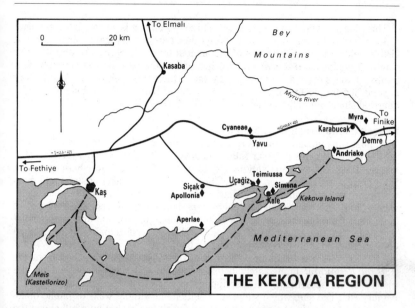

THE KEKOVA REGION

Practical Details

Üçağız's **restaurants and pansiyons** are simple and basic. Prices are reasonable but bear in mind that although fish is plentiful in Üçağız, fresh water has to be imported to the village and this can jack prices up. The friendliest **pansiyon**, located in an attractive old wood-framed building with a terrace, is the *Pansiyon Kekova* (☎3191/1037), on the main street to the harbor, run by John and Ferda. Bed and breakfast costs $8 per person, and it's the only place in town with hot, freshwater showers.

One of the most pleasant **restaurants** in the village, the *Kalealtı*, run by the Kormel family, is a short walk east along a rough path over the rocks by the sea, located just below the ruins of Teimiussa (see below). Its inaccessibilty makes it a bit cheaper than the those around the harbor; it has very basic accommodation in a single room, and camping under the eucalyptus tree outside. They can also point you in the direction of Kale and the ruins of Simena. Otherwise the *Kordon* (☎3191/1037), on a wooden terrace overlooking the harbor, serves seafood cheaper than in the larger resorts, and also has a good bar.

Boats for rent from Üçağız take ten people and cost $60 per day. A rowboat is just $2, and a tour in an outboard motorboat for part of the day is anything from $20 a boat depending on where you want to go.

Around Üçağız

Until the road was built, the Lycian ruins that surround Üçağız were visited by few apart from hardy goats and explorers. Simena and Teimiussa can be reached on foot from the village; for the other sites you need to rent a boat, either from Üçağız (probably cheapest), Kaş, or Demre.

The village (whose name means "Three Mouths") is on an inlet opposite Kekova Island, the site of the best of the ruins, most of which are submerged but visible below the sea. The ruins of the ancient town of Aperlae are on the other side of a peninsula to the west of Üçağız, and to the east are the acropolis and tombs of the site of another small Lycian settlement—Teimiussa. A little way beyond lies the village of Kale and the castle of Simena. Several small islands, quarried since antiquity to near sea level, dot the bay.

Kekova Island, Teimiussa, Simena

The most romantically situated ruins in the area are those submerged near the northern shoreline of **Kekova Island**, known as *Tersane* or "Dockyard" locally, and not identified with any antique city to date. You can get over here on a boat from Üçağiz or Demre (see below). The underwater remains of stairs and sidewalks, house walls, and a long wharf can all be observed from the boat; sadly snorkelling, and swimming in general, are banned to prevent the removal of antiquities from the area, and most skippers don't give you the option of leaving the boat. On the island itself are the well-preserved remains of an apsidal construction, possibly part of a church or a boatyard.

TEIMIUSSA is a half-hour walk east of the village, easily reached from the *Kalealtı Restaurant* immediately below it. Nothing is really known about the history of the settlement, but inscriptions indicate that it existed in the fourth century BC. The site, which suggests a settlement without walls or public buildings, consists mainly of a good scattering of rock tombs, but on a hill above the sea there is a small fort or tower about the size of a house, and below at sea level a rock-cut pier or landing stage.

The ruined medieval castle of **SİMENA**—and the village of **KALE** below it— are an hour's walk or a fifteen-minute boat ride from Üçağız. The village itself is very secluded and a lovely place to stay, if a bit pricey, with some rustic-looking **pansiyons** overlooking the sea and a few good fish **restaurants**. The climb to the castle is steep and tiring, but worth it both for the views and for the castle itself, whose castellated ramparts are in good condition, partly resting on ancient foundations. Inside the castle is a fifteen-meter-wide theater—large enough for 300 people—and on the northern slopes of the hill off the path are some well-preserved sarcophagi.

Aperlae

In the opposite direction, west of Üçağız, lies the site of **APERLAE**, a forty-minute boat ride followed by an hour's walk. The difficulty of access means that the site is practically deserted, and it's possible to swim around the sunken ruins and take a good look. Beware of sea anemones and sharp rocks. Although it's not known for certain, the assumption is that Aperlae was a Lycian city—a theory borne out in part by the Lycian coins with inscriptions "APR" and "PRL" that have been found. What is known for sure is that in Roman Imperial times Aperlae headed a league of four cities, along with Simena, Apollonia (near the village of Siçak on the road to Üçağız), and Isinda (near Belenli), and citizens of the cities were collectively termed "Aperlite." The remains of the **city walls**, which bisect the hillside and enclose a rectangular area with the sea on its southernmost side, are fairly well preserved and easily identified. Underwater are the remains of a **dock**, indented at fifteen-meter intervals for the mooring of ships, and the foundations of rows of **buildings**, divided by narrow streets.

Cyaneae

Beyond the turnoff to Kekova the road enters a stretch of wild, inhospitable countryside, whose bleak aspect seems only fit for the herds of sheep and goats that graze it. In antiquity, however, this part of the world was scattered with small settlements, the most interesting of which is currently **CYANEAE**, 23km from Kaş in the hills above the village of YAVU. Signs point the way from the center of the village up to the site, 3km above. It's a good idea to take a guide up here, either from the village or from the *Çeşme Restaurant* (see below). The hike up to the site only takes about 45 minutes but the route is fairly hazardous and difficult to follow.

The name Cyaneae derives from the Greek word meaning "dark blue"—also the origin of the word cyanide—but it's not known why the city was given this name. Nowadays it is often called "the city of sarcophagi," a more obvious epitaph, since the rows of Lycian and Roman sarcophagi to be seen at the site are the most numerous of any in the region, and are the main reason to visit.

Little is known historically about the city, apart from the fact that it was the most important in the region between Myra and Antiphellos (modern Kaş), and that it was linked by a direct road to the harbor of Teimiussa 5km away. It prospered in Roman times, and existed as the seat of a bishopric in the Byzantine age. On the left of the path up from the village are some of the oldest and most interesting of the **tombs** to be found at the site. They line either side of a passage which may have been part of an ancient road. The most impressive among the group is south of the road, a sarcophagus carved completely from the rock on which it stands. The Gothic-arch "lid," cut from the same piece of rock, has two lions' heads projecting from each side.

Below the city on the south face of the hill stands an impressive **temple tomb** whose porch has a single column, and, unusually, a recess above the pediment in which a sarcophagus has been installed. According to an inscription the sarcophagus was reserved for the bodies of the head of the household and his wife, while the rest of the family were buried in the tomb.

The top of the hill, the **acropolis**, is surrounded on three sides by a wall, the south side being so precipitous that it didn't need protection. The buildings inside are in a ruined state and covered with vegetation, but several have been identified, including a library, baths, a reservoir, and cisterns. To the west of the summit stands a moderate-sized **theater** with 25 rows of seats still visible, and, between this and the acropolis, a road lined with sarcophagi. These are mainly Roman, and are very simple, with rounded lids and crests.

Back on Highway 400, about half a kilometer in the direction of Antalya, the *Çeşme Restaurant* (☎3224/1425) is a welcoming establishment run (unusually) by a Turkish woman, and with two pansiyon rooms at $6 each, and camping space.

Demre, Myra, and Andriake

A winding forty-minute drive beyond Kaş brings you to the river-delta town of **DEMRE** (officially called Kale), a scruffy little place, too far away from the coast to be worthy of the "seaside" tag and afforded more attention by tour parties than it can really deal with. Indeed, it would be worth driving straight past the town if it weren't the location of some of the most intriguing historical sites in Turkey. As it is, it's worth spending a night here in order to see the ancient Lycian city of **MYRA** just to the north and the port of **ANDRIAKE** a little way south, not to mention the church of St. Nicholas in the town itself—best observed in peace and quiet before 9am or after 5pm, when Demre is practically empty of visitors.

Some History

Myra was one of the most prominent members of the Lycian Federation, and retained its importance throughout the Middle Ages because of its associations with the bishop St. Nicholas (Santa Claus). An ancient tradition claims that the name of the city derives from the Greek word for myrrh, the gum resin used in the production of incense. Although no record of the manufacture of this is recorded, the Emperor Constantine Porphyrogenitus described the city as the "thrice-blessed, myrrh-breathing city of the Lycians, where the mighty Nicolaus, servant of God, spouts forth myrrh in accordance with the city's name." There is also a tradition that when the tomb of St. Nicholas was opened by Italian grave robbers, they were overwhelmed by the smell of myrrh that emanated from it.

Despite Myra's importance in the Lycian Federation, there is no mention of the city in history before the first century BC, but in 42 BC Myra distinguished itself with typically Lycian defiance by refusing to pay tribute money to Brutus, and Brutus's lieutenant had to break the chain closing the mouth of the harbor at Andriake—the city's port—and force his way in. Subsequently, Myra had an uneventful if prosperous history, treated well by its imperial overlords and receiving its highest accolade when the Byzantine Emperor Theodosius II made it capital of Lycia in the fifth century.

By then the fame of the city had been much enhanced by one of its citizens, namely **Saint Nicholas**, or "Santa Claus," born in Patara in 300 AD and later appointed bishop of Myra. Saint Nicholas is supposed to have slapped the face of the Alexandrian heretic Arius at the Council of Nicaea in 325 AD, although his western identity, as a friendly old present-giver, is perhaps more familiar, based on a story of his kindness to the three daughters of a poor man who were left without a dowry. Nicholas is supposed to have thrown three purses of gold into the house one night, enabling them to find husbands. There are many miraculous occurrences connected with the saint, but little is actually known about the man. It is known, however, that on his death he was buried in the church in Demre dedicated to his name; and it is also widely believed that in 1087, his bones were carried off to Italy by a band of men from Bari (although the Venetians and Russians lay dubious claim to a similar exploit).

Practical Details

The **hotels** *Topçu* (☎3224/2200) and *Şahin* (☎3224/1686, 1687), opposite each other at the entrance to town on Finike Caddesi, cost $16 double, $10 single; both are quiet and comfortable. More centrally, the *Şahin*, on Müze Caddesi (☎3224/1686, 1687), has doubles for $16, singles for $8. Close to the Belediye building are a couple of rough but cheap pansiyons, the *Myra*, on Müze Caddesi (☎3224/1026), and the *Star* on Yeni Camii Caddesi (☎3224/3361). Better value are three pansiyons out of town on the way to Myra: the *Kent* (☎3224/2042) and the *Noel* on Yeni Cami Caddesi (☎3224/2304), and the *Lykia* (☎3224/2579) on Myra Caddesi, behind the Myra Çay Bahçesi—each of which charge around $8 single, $10 double for a room without a shower.

The best **restaurants** in the area are at the port now known as Çayağzı (previously the ancient port of Andriake), where there are also a few **campgrounds**—the *Star*, on the left of the approach road to the sea, advertised by a sorry-looking live camel, and the *Deniz*, farther down near the shore. Neither has very good facilities. It's possible to get a **boat** from here to Kekova, a 45-minute journey, but you need a boatload (15–20 people)—although some owners will take individuals for a fee of around $5. Now that the road to Kekova has been completed, the boat journey is no longer essential, but it's still a pleasant way of approaching the village, and includes a tour of the underwater ruins of Kekova Island.

The Church of St. Nicholas

The **Church of St. Nicholas** (daily 8am–6pm; $2) is in the center of town, on the right of Müze Caddesi as you head towards Kaş. The building is highly evocative of the life and times of its patron saint, even if the myths surrounding both are more romance than fact. The beatification of Nicholas occurred when visitors to his tomb made claims of miraculous occurrences and Myra became a popular place of pilgrimage. A monastery was built near the church in the eleventh century, and even after Italian merchants stole the bones of the saint, the pilgrimages continued; indeed it is thought that the monks simply designated another tomb as that of Saint Nicholas, pouring oil through openings in the top and collecting it at the bottom, selling it to pilgrims as the holy relics of the saint.

The church on the present site has little in common with the original, which dated from the third century and was first rebuilt by Constantine IX in 1043, probably after its destruction by occupying Saracens. The church is basically a basilica in form but with four aisles, one of which was added later. In 1862 Tsar Nicholas I had the church restored, when a vaulted ceiling was installed instead of a cupola in the central nave, along with a belfry—both unheard of in Byzantine architecture. Turkish archaeologists have carried out more recent restoration in order to protect the building, such as the addition of the small stone domes in the narthex.

Perhaps the most typical Byzantine structure is the synthronon, or seating for the clergy in the apse, a rare sight in Turkey since most were removed when the churches were converted into mosques. In the narthex is a **deesis** (depiction of Christ, Mary, and John the Baptist), and a mosaic floor, mainly comprising geometric designs, while the courtyard in the back is full of pieces of masonry carved with anchors and fish—Nicholas is the patron saint of sailors as well as virgins, children, merchants, scholars, pawnbrokers, and Russia. His sarcophagus, to the left of the entrance against the wall, is worth a look, although it is not considered genuine; the tomb from which the saint's bones were stolen was said to be located under a stone pavement—and, perhaps more significantly, there are marble statues representing a man and a woman (obviously a couple) on the lid.

Myra

The remains of ancient **Myra** (daily 8am–6:30pm; $1) are 2km north of the town center, and together make up one of the most easily visited, and most beautiful, Lycian sites—your imagination is captured by the immediacy with which you can walk out of the twentieth century and into a Greco-Roman theater or a Lycian rock tomb. Not surprisingly the place is crawling with people throughout the summer season, and the best times to visit are either early morning or after 5pm.

The ruins consist mainly of a large theater and some of the best examples of house-style rock tombs to be seen in Lycia. The rest of the city is still buried. The **theater** was destroyed in an earthquake in 141 AD but rebuilt shortly afterward. The rock face behind it being vertical and unable to support the cavea, the structure had to be built up with masonry on either side, although the back of the cavea rests against the cliff. The theater is flanked by two concentric galleries covering the stairs (still intact), by which spectators entered the auditorium; the outer one is two-storied. Lying around the orchestra are substantial chunks of carving that once decorated the stage building, including a carving of two theatrical masks.

The main concentration of **tombs** is to the west of the theater, and is easily accessible by of a series of iron ladders running up the cliffside. Most of the tombs are of the house type, supposed to imitate Lycian dwelling-places, even down to the wooden beams supporting the roofs. Some are decorated with reliefs, including warriors at the climax of a battle, a naked page handing a helmet to a warrior, and a funerary scene.

The second group of tombs, called the **river necropolis**, is around the side of the hill, on the right as you face the theater. Here a monument known as the "painted tomb" depicts the reclining figure of a bearded man and his family in the porch, and outside on the rock face what are presumed to be the same family but dressed in outdoor clothes. The tomb retains some traces of red and blue paint. To the east of the theater below the acropolis hill are the remains of a brick building whose identity is unknown, although it preserves an inscription on a Doric column concerning a ferry service that operated between Myra and Limyra in Roman Imperial times.

Andriake

The port of the ancient city, **Andriake**—now known as Çayağzı—lies 2.5km beyond Demre, 5km from ancient Myra. To get there, head west out of town past the bus station and the *Kıyak* and *Topcu* hotels onto the main Kaş–Antalya highway. Andriake lies where the highway turns sharp right, and is also the site of a **beach**, **campgrounds**, some good **restaurants**, and the **ferry** point for Kekova.

Andriake, built on either side of the Androkos River, was the site of **Hadrian's granary**, used to store locally grown grain and vital not only to Myra but to the whole Roman world, since its contents were sent to Rome and distributed around the empire. The substantial remains of the building are still to be seen south of the river, which runs parallel to the road from Demre—turn left 200m before the beach and continue southeast for 250m. The granary—built on the orders of Hadrian between 119 and 139 AD—consists of eight rooms constructed of well-fitting square-cut blocks. The outer walls still stand to their original full height, giving a clear idea of the impressive overall size of this structure. Above the main, central gate are busts of Hadrian and what is thought to be his wife, the Empress Sabina. Another decorative relief on the front wall, near the second door from the west, depicts two deities of disputed identity, one of whom is flanked by a snake and a griffin, while the other reclines on a couch. According to its inscription this relief was donated by a warehouse official after a dream.

Finike and Around

A winding half-hour drive beyond Demre lies **FİNİKE**, a harbor town, formerly the Lycian city Phoenicus, although there is no longer any evidence of its historical past, and precious little to suggest an illustrious future either.

Highway 400 is a double-edged sword as far as Finike is concerned. Its completion in the early 1960s provided the town with an easy shipping route for local oranges, the mainstay of the local economy. But the busy thoroughfare has also ruined Finike aesthetically by cutting its center off from the beach and disturbing the peace of this formerly attractive village. The town used to be deserted in summer as its residents headed for the hills, particularly to the *yayla* of Elmalı, but now ominous concrete constructions are beginning to obscure the view of the bay, and a very tawdry kind of development is starting to take hold of the village. The beach, too, is black and rather uninviting. The best reason to stay in Finike is that it gives easy access inland to Elmalı, and to a couple of ancient cities— Arykanda and Limyra—on the way.

Practical Details

Finike's **otogar** is centrally situated, just off Highway 400 before the turnoff for Elmalı. There are a number of good **hotels** and **pansiyons** in town, extending 8km out on the Antalya road. One of the nicest and most central is the *Kale Pansiyon* (☎3225/1457), located up on the remains of a Byzantine castle above the *Red Kit Restaurant* on the main square. The interior of the house is beautifully ornate, decorated in turn-of-the-century Ottoman splendor, and rooms cost $4 per person. For the same price, up the hill from here, is the tiny, comfortable *Şendil* (☎3225/1660, 1864), with hot-water showers in all rooms. Back through town in the direction of Antalya, up a long flight of steps on the hill above the otogar, the *Paris Hotel and Pansiyon* (☎3225/1488), is a pleasant, family-run place with rooms starting at $3 per person ($4 with bathroom) and a terrace with a good view of Finike Bay. There's a big **campground**, *Baba Camping* (☎3225/ 1568), 2km out of town on the road to Antalya, with good (if expensive) facilities, and another, cheaper place called *Kumsal*, on Highway 400. For **swimming**, there are a number of lovely rocky coves between Finike and Demre; Finike Gölü, just outside the town, also has a nice beach even if it is kind of muddy.

Into the Mountains: Limyra, Arykanda, and Elmalı

The road inland from **Finike to Elmalı** is a two-hour drive along a precipitous mountain route, made especially terrifying by the cavalier attitude of the numerous local drivers who hurtle up and down it with trucks full of produce from the local orchards. On the way up, if you trust your emergency brake, it's worth stopping to visit two beautiful mountain sites, Limyra and Arykanda.

Limyra

The site of **LİMYRA** is the less impressive of the two, but it's easily accessible if you have your own transportation. It's located about 10km outside Finike, 4km off the Finike-Elmalı road (Highway 635), turning east at the village of TUNCUROVA (the turnoff is marked). If you don't have wheels, get a dolmuş to drop you off here and walk or hitch the 4km. There's a parking lot and village at the site itself.

Limyra had a promising start: founded in the fifth century BC, the city was made capital of Lycia by Pericles in the fourth century. From then on, however, its fortunes were broadly the same as other Lycia cities, and it didn't make much of an appearance in history until 4 AD, when Gaius Caesar, grandson and adopted heir of Augustus, died here on his way home from Armenia. During Byzantine times, it became the seat of a bishop, but it suffered badly during the Arab raids of the seventh to ninth centuries and was largely abandoned.

The main settlement, and consequently most of its public buildings, lay at the foot of Tocak Dağı, but the most extensive part of the ruins consists of several hundred **tombs**. The southern slope of the mountain is covered in tombs cut into the rock face; above is a fortified acropolis. On the left of the road from Tuncurova, the western necropolis includes an impressive two-story tomb in a citrus grove. At the foot of the hill, beside the road, is a **theater** dating from 120 AD, behind which is a free-standing sarcophagus dating from the fourth century BC with an inscription in Lycian stating that it was the tomb of Xatabura, thought to have been a relative of Pericles (the founder of the Lycian Federation). It is covered in reliefs, including a funeral feast on its south side, and on its west side a scene depicting the judgment of Xatabura, depicted as a naked youth.

At the top of Tocak Dağı, to the north of the site, is the most interesting tomb of all. It's about a forty-minute climb to get there, up the path leading from behind the village, but it's worth the effort. This mausoleum is probably that of Pericles, the Lycian ruler who saved the kingdom from the ambitions of Mausolus in the fourth century BC. The style of the monument certainly dates it to that time, and Limyra was after all his capital city. The tomb is in two parts: a lower grave chamber, and the upper chamber styled like a temple, with a row of four caryatids in front and back. The figures of the frieze, which showed the hero mounting his chariot, indicate the blend of Greek and Persian influences on Lycian art.

Arykanda

ARYKANDA lies 29km from Finike, on the right side of the road; traveling by dolmuş, you should ask to be dropped off at ARIF, and from there it's a half-hour walk (follow the signs); by car the road is not currently navigable but they are working to make it so. When it is there will probably be a café at the site entrance, and a ticket office; at the moment there is just an official guide who gives tours for tips.

The ruins at Arykanda are much more extensive than those at Limyra. Finds here date back to the fifth century BC, but it's assumed that the city is much older than that because of the "anda" suffix of its name, which dates it to the second millennium BC. Although Arykanda was a member of the Lycian Federation from the second century BC, its inhabitants were chiefly renowned for their sloth and profligacy: when Antiochus III tried to invade Lycia in 197 BC, they are said to have taken his side in the hope of reaping financial benefits that could help them repay their debts. Christianity gained popularity here in the third century, which is proved by a copy of a petition by the people of Arykanda to the Emperor Maximinius requesting that the "illegal and abominable practices of the godless" be denounced and suppressed. The city continued in a much-reduced form until the eleventh century, mainly confined to the area south of the main path.

The situation of the site is breathtaking, occupying a steep rocky hillside to the south of Akdağ, part of the Bey Mountains. The most impressive sight as you arrive is the ten-meter-high facade of the **baths**, with two rows of three windows and an apse at one end. Other constructions worth seeking out include a small **temple** or tomb above the baths complex that was presumably adapted for Christian worship—on the wall is the Greek inscription "Jesus Christ is Victorious" and a cross. To the north of the track leading from the main road is a large **basilica** with mosaics and a semicircular row of benches in the apse. On to the northeast, past the agora, is an impressive **theater**, recently excavated to reveal twenty rows of seats divided by six aisles, and a well-preserved stage-building.

Elmalı

The plain of Elmalı is the most extensive stretch of arable land in southern Turkey, an important center for apples, citrus fruits, and sugar beet. The town of **ELMALI** (literally "With Apples"), dominated by nearby snow-capped Elmalı Dağı (2296m), is remarkable for its domestic architecture: a large number of its houses are beautiful Ottoman timber-framed *konaks*, some of them in excellent condition. The air is cool and fresh, with a faint smell of apples and wood smoke. There is a reasonable hotel in town, the *Belediye Otel*, run by the municipal authorities (☎3228/3137, 3139, 1043), where a single room without a bathroom costs $6, a double $10.

Elmalı has a fine classical Ottoman mosque, the **Ömerpaşa Camii**, built in 1602, and although it's only open at prayer time, the exterior is decorated with beautiful faience panels and inscriptions. The mosque *medrese* now serves as a library. Further up the main street is all that remains of a Selçuk mosque, a stubby piece of stonework that once served as a minaret, while to the west, in the street behind the former *medrese* is the sixteenth-century **Bey Hamamı**.

East to Olympos

Beyond Finike the road continues through scrubby hillsides to **KUMLUCA**, a scruffy little market town completely swamped by plastic greenhouses that has so little character it's possible to pass straight through without even realizing it. The nearest beach to Kumluca, 5km out of town, is **Mavikent**, a stony, pebbly affair backed by scrubland and ornamented by a few raggedy reed huts. There is a twenty-kilometer dirt road from here, past CAVUŞ to Olympos (see below), but it's not recommended unless you have four-wheel drive.

Half an hour's difficult drive beyond Cavuş lies the beautiful, idyllically quiet beach of **ADRASAN**—attractively lit at night, and attractively deserted in the daytime. You can reach this by dolmuş from Antalya, leaving in the evening and returning in the morning, staying at one of several **pansiyons and camp-grounds** along the length of the beach. You can also **rent boats** here to visit Olympos, a little way along the coast. The best of the **cafés**, *La Boheme* (☎3217/5083), rents out rooms for $12 for two (no singles), plus $2 for a wonderful German-style breakfast. Failing that, the *Korkmazer'in Yeri* pansiyon and restaurant (☎3217/5060) has rooms for $12, camping space for $2, as well as boats for rent ($40 a day) and windsurfing equipment.

Olympos

Two roads lead down to the ruins of the ancient Lycian city of **OLYMPOS** from Highway 400, both of which degenerate into dirt tracks in the course of their nine-kilometer length. The northernmost road is marked "Olympos and Çıralı," the other just "Olympos"—the first is by far the best road to take if you're looking to stay, or just to eat, since the village of **ÇIRALI**, on the coast, has food and accommodation. The ruins actually lie at the end of the latter road, but they're easily accessible along the beach from Çıralı. Above the village, on the slopes of nearby Tahtalı Dağ, is a natural flame, burning gases which emit from the rock face. This has been known since antiquity as the Chimaera, a name it shares with a mythical beast which is supposed to have inhabited these mountains.

Some History

Nothing is known about the origins of **Olympos**, but the city presumably took its name from nearby Mount Olympos, thought to be present-day Tahtalı Dağı, 16km north of the city—one of more than twenty mountains with the same name in the classical world. The city first appeared in history in the second century BC, when it was striking its own coins in the manner of the Lycians. Strabo wrote in 100 BC that Olympos was one of six cities in the Lycian Federation that had three votes, meaning that it was afforded top status.

The principal deity of Olympos was Hephaestos, the Roman God Vulcan, who was the god of fire and blacksmiths. He was a native of the Lycia-Caria region, and the remains of a temple dedicated to him can be found in the region of the Chimaera; fines for damage to tombs were payable to the temple treasury of Hephaestos. In the first century BC, the importance of Hephaestos diminished when Cilician pirates led by Zenicetes overran both Olympos and nearby Phaselis and introduced the worship of Mithras, a god of Indo-European origin, whose rites were performed on Mount Olympos. Zenicetes made Olympos his headquarters, but in 78 BC he was defeated by the Roman governor of Cilicia, and Olympos was declared public property. The pirates were again defeated in 67 BC by Pompey. The fortunes of Olympos revived after it was absorbed into the Roman Empire in 43 AD, and Christianity began to increase in popularity. The city was used as a trading base by the Venetians and Genoese in the eleventh and twelfth ceturies, and it was abandoned in the fifteenth century, during Turkish domination of the Mediterranean.

The Sites

About five minutes' walk south along the beach from Çıralı, the site of **Olympos** is quite idyllic, located on the banks of a stream running between the Bey Mountains and a large and beautiful bay. The area is lush with oleander and fig trees, and swarming with wildlife; turtles, ducks, and frogs swim in the stream, and it's a good place to spot rare birds and butterflies. The main part of the site is on the banks of a river which dries up in summer but is replenished by another source half a mile up the valley. On the south bank is part of a levee and a warehouse; to the east on the same side lie the walls of a Byzantine church; in the river itself is a well-preserved pillar from a former bridge. Farther back, in the undergrowth, there is a theater, most of whose seats have gone. On the north side of the river, on the hill to the left of the path to the beach, are more striking ruins, namely a well-preserved marble carved door frame built into a wall of hewn stone. At the foot of the door is a statue base dedicated by an inscription to Marcus Aurelius and bearing the dates 172–175. Beyond the door on the other side of a field is a Byzantine hamam with mosaic floors, and a Byzantine canal that carried water to the heart of the city. Above, on the hillside itself, are the remains of a Byzantine fortress.

Above the site, in the foothills of Mount Olympos, the eternal flame of the **Chimaera** is about an hour's stroll from Çıralı; it's also possible to drive to the bottom of the slope and walk from there (about twenty minutes). In any case, although the route up the hill is marked it's not easy to find its start—it's a good idea to to take a guide from the village to help you find it, and as a precaution against snakes. It also makes sense to climb up as dusk falls, since the fire is best seen in the dark; some people make rag torches and ignite them from the flames, using them to light the path on the way down.

The Chimaera is, quite simply, one of the most extraordinary sites in the whole of Lycia, a series of flames issuing out of cracks in the bare rock that can be extinguished but will always re-ignite. It's not known what causes the phenomenon; a survey carried out by oil prospectors in 1967 detected traces of methane in the gas but otherwise its makeup is completely unique to this spot. The flames can be extinguished temporarily if they are covered over, when a gaseous smell is noticeable. What is known, however, is that the fire has been burning since antiquity, and it inspired the Lycians to worship the god Hephaestos (the Roman Vulcan), who was generally celebrated in places where a natural fire sprang from the earth. The mountain was also associated with a fire-breathing monster with a lion's head and forelegs, a goat's rear, and a snake for a tail—the Chimaera. Homer relates how one Bellerophon was ordered by the King of Lycia, Iobates, to kill the monster in atonement for the supposed rape of his daughter Stheneboea, of which Bellerophon had been wrongly accused. With the help of the winged horse Pegasus, Bellerophon succeeded in this mission, killing the monster from the air by dropping lead into its mouth. Bellerophon was later deemed to have been falsely accused and avenged himself on Stheneboea by persuading her to fly away with him on Pegasus and flinging her into the sea. He later got his own just desserts when he attempted to ascend to heaven on Pegasus and was flung from the horse's back, lamed and blinded, and forced to wander the face of the earth until his death.

Practical Details

There are three buses a week from Kumluca to Çıralı, and there is also an erratic service from Kemer. Hitching is difficult because few people are prepared to venture down the dreadful road, but as soon as this is improved the way will be opened up to all kinds of traffic.

The *Palm Restaurant*, in Çıralı, run by brothers Ahmet and Mehmet Altıntaş, which has been going for several years, certainly predating large-scale tourism in the region, sells its own freshly caught fish at reasonable prices. It also has **camping** facilities and a **hotel** (the *Azur*, $20 single, $30 double with breakfast); a guide can be provided to take parties up to view the Chimaera at dusk. Tourist development has really taken off in the last few years in Çıralı, with hotels and pansiyons springing up left and right—electricity and telecommunications hot on their heels—and there should be no problem finding a room for under $5 even in the high season. If you want to rough it in style, try the German-run *Olympos Lodge* (☎081/43659), a complex of luxury cabins set in orange groves next to the beach, costing around $40 per person including breakfast and dinner.

Otherwise, Olympos is a popular place to roll out a sleeping bag on the beach, and there are a couple of shack-like cafés on the dunes that serves up Turkish breakfast for when you come around.

On to Antalya

Once past Olympos there is very little reason to stop before Antalya. The small resorts along this stretch of coast leave a lot to be desired—most are overdeveloped and overpriced—and only the ruins of the ancient city of **Phaselis** might possibly tempt you off the main road.

Tekirova

About twenty kilometers before Tekirova, marked off the road to the right, lies **ULUPINAR,** a tiny mountain hamlet in dense woods that can make either a nice stop for lunch or a good place to while away a day or two mixing beach pleasures with a little hiking—assuming you have your own transportation. There are a couple of rough-and-ready cafés serving meat *güveç*, quail, carp, and freshly grilled trout, and the so-called *Ulupınar Motel* (☎3214/1474), which rents out a few shack-type rooms on the terrace above the restaurant. It's all very rural, and the motel provides hunting, fishing, and transportation to the coast.

Apart from the occasional five-star hotel, **TEKİROVA,** a few kilometers farther along, on the opposite side of the main road, is a pretty downbeat, scruffy little village, which might be preferable to the glitzy glamor of Kemer 13km farther along, although it lacks the rusticity still evident around Olympos. The town is a convenient base for visits to Phaselis, although many of its patrons probably never make it that far. Indeed, if you want to see Turkish tourism at its most sordid, take a look around the grounds of the *Phaselis Princess*, a favored haunt of Turkish gigolos on the make with would-be millionairesses.

If you happen to be a would-be millionairess on the lookout for a Turkish gigolo, prices for a single room at the *Phaselis Princess* (☎3214/3200) start at around $60. If not, there are a number of reasonably priced **pansiyons** in the village, principally the *Marti Pansiyon* (☎3185/4163), which charges $12 single, $16 double for nice clean rooms around a swimming pool, including breakfast. The village also has two good **campgrounds**. *Rosie Camping* (no phone) is on the other side of the village on the beach road, and although it has few facilities (just cold outdoor showers on the beach), it is at least cheap—$2 per person with your own tent, $8 in theirs—and it has a restaurant and bar. Better situated is the *Sundance*, but it's some hike from the main road to get there—take a left off the main road into the village, past the *Marti Pansiyon* along the dirt road for a couple of kilometers. The campground has its own beach, and it's an easy walk around the cove to Phaselis. Facilities are again very rudimentary, but it's also only $2 per person and they have a bar and food.

Transportation in and out of Tekirova is fairly regular, connected with Antalya by half-hourly buses in season, stopping at Kemer and Phaselis on the way. *Sugar Rent-A-Car* (☎Kemer 3214/3151) has a branch in Tekirova, and *Meltour* (no phone), on the left as you enter the village, offers jeep safaris and special dolmuş tours all over the south of Turkey.

Phaselis

The ruins of ancient **PHASELIS** (daily 8am–6pm, $2) are magnificently arrayed around three small bays, providing ample opportunity to contemplate antique architectural forms from a recumbent position on one of the beaches. The natural beauty of the site, the encroaching greenery, the clear water bays, and its seclusion all make for a rewarding half-day outing—though be sure to take a supply of food and drink, as there's nowhere to buy any here.

Some History

Phaselis was not always in Lycia: it was situated at the southwest border with Pamphylia and at certain points in its history was decidedly independent. It was legendarily founded in 690 BC by colonists from Rhodes, and until 300 BC inscriptions were written in a Rhodian variety of the Dorian dialect.

The Phaselitans were great traders; they are supposed to have bought the land on which the city was founded with dried fish, and a "Phaselitan sacrifice" became proverbial for a cheap offering. There is evidence that the city's trading links stretched as far as Egypt, and its coins commonly depicted the prow of a ship on one side and the stern on the other. The Phaselitans also earned themselves a reputation as penny-pinching scoundrels, perhaps because at one point, needing funds, they put their citizenship up for sale for a hundred drachmas and attracted undesirable elements from all over Asia Minor. One story goes that the harpist Stratonicus was charged the normal price for a bath in Phaselis, whereupon the proprietor pointed out that outsiders should pay more for their baths. Stratonicus remonstrated with the attendant, saying, "You rascal, you came within a penny of making me a Phaselitan."

Phaselis was overrun along with most of the rest of Asia Minor by the Persians in the sixth century, and was not freed until 469 BC. By that time, they had begun to feel loyalty to their imperial overlord, and it was with some difficulty that the Athenian General Cimon liberated them at all. Phaselis became part of the Athenian maritime confederacy along with Olympos.

In the fourth century, Phaselis demonstrated just how independent it was from Lycia by helping Mausolus, the satrap of Caria, in his attempt to subdue the kingdom; further evidence that the Phaselitans were pragmatic in their approach to authority is their behavior toward Alexander the Great in 333 BC, when they didn't just surrender their city to him but also proffered a golden crown.

Phaselis became part of the Lycian Federation some time in the second century BC, but was later, in the first century BC, along with Olympos, overrun by Cilician pirates; although it was accepted back into the Lycian Federation afterwards, the long occupation of the city had reduced it to a mere shell, with a scanty, penniless population. After the *Pax Romana* had been signed, Phaselis distinguished itself with yet more obsequiousness in AD 129, when the Emperor Hadrian visited during a tour of the empire. Statues were erected, a forum was constructed, and a gateway was dedicated to him.

The Site

The dirt road that leads to the city from the Kemer–Tekirova highway passes a **fortified settlement** enclosed by a wall of Hellenistic stone, the northernmost section of which has a tower and three archery slits. The most obvious landmark on reaching the main site are the substantial and elegant remains of a Roman aqueduct. Supposedly one of the longest water conduits in the classical world, it brought water from a spring originating within the northern fortifications almost as far as the south harbor.

Phaselis's three **harbors** are immediately obvious, and an ideal means by which to orientate yourself, arranged around a 400-meter-long promontory on which most of the city is situated. They served the city's extensive mercantile activities, particularly the export of local timber, rose, and lily oil. The **north harbor** was too exposed to be used except in very favorable conditions, but it has the remains of an ancient dock on its south side. It offered an easy landing-point for aggressors, however, and so the crest of the cliffs above were well fortified. This 3.6-meter-wide wall now lies below the sea, but is still intact. The middle or **city harbor** has a strong sea wall since it is exposed to the north and the east, and the eighteen-meter-wide entrance could be closed off. It's a sheltered cove with an excellent beach and shallow water for bathing. The largest harbor, the **south harbor**, is protected by a 180-meter-long breakwater, most of which is under water. It gave important access for larger trading ships of up to a hundred tons.

Between the harbors the promontory is covered with the ruins of very over-grown ancient houses and of round cisterns. Important in the layout of the city is a paved avenue leading from the monumental **gateway** constructed in honor of Hadrian's visit, at the southern harbor, to the rectangular agora between the main hill and the middle harbor. The gateway, built of gray-white marble blocks, was erected in 129 or 131 BC and bears a dedication to the emperor.

The **theater**, which could hold around 1500 people, lies to the southeast of the main thoroughfare. In the second century AD it occupied a central point in the fan-shaped layout of the city. There are three large doors above the present ground level, which probably led onto the stage. Just visible below these are a row of four smaller doors that opened into the orchestra beneath the stage, possibly to admit wild animals.

Kemer

A short drive along the coast road from the Ulupınar turnoff, **KEMER** is one of the least appealing of the resorts on the Turquoise Coast, a gleaming white vacation village dominated by a swanky yacht harbor, and featuring a beach over-crowded with tour parties. It's a pricey place too, developed specifically for tour-ism, and even the staff at the tourist office admit that there's not a lot to do apart from sunbathe and swim. Most of the activity revolves around the yacht marina and the tour parties for whom the hotels were designed, but really, unless you're planning to visit the site of Phaselis, to which there are regular domuşes (and boats for rent), you'd do better to stay on the bus.

Practical Details

The **tourist information office** at Liman Caddesi 159 (daily 8:30am–6pm; ☎3214/1536), near the harbor, can provide a hotel price list—although there is no **hotel** accommodation to be had for under $10 a head—and maps. There is a reasonable **campground**, *Overland Camping*, with its own sand and stone beach in the Çınaryanı Mevkii district, where one person in a tent can stay for $2, and bungalows with hot water and breakfast cost a mere $16. Reasonable villa-style **pansiyons** along Liman Caddesi include the *Esmer* at no. 104/14 (☎3214/2506) and the *Erol* at no. 109, Sokak 21 (☎3214/1755, 1685), the former being somewhat cheaper at $25 single, $33 double. The German-run *Barbaros Pansiyon* on Kemer Caddesi (☎3214/2918) charges $20 single, $30 double, as does the nearby *Genç Pansiyon*, (3214/1653) also on Kemer Caddesi, which has balconied rooms overlooking a garden. On Liman Caddesi itself, the two-star *Ambassador Hotel* (☎3214/2626, 2627) charges $27.50 single, $37.50 double.

The **PTT** on Atatürk Bulvarı changes money (Mon–Sat 8:30am–12:30pm, 1:30–6:30pm), and sells stamps and phone *jetons* (daily 8am–midnight). Around the marina, the expensive *Dupont* **restaurant** is fairly reliable, serving pizzas and mixed grills, cakes, and beer. Some of the pansiyons are a source of cheaper food, best of which is the *Surf Pansiyon* at Hastane Caddesi 107, Sokak 5.

A few of the larger hotels, like the *Kemer* near the marina, have reasonable **discos**, and there's excellently seedy *gazino*-style entertainment, complete with oriental and folk dancers, at the *Akdeniz Restaurant* (☎3214/1219), where entrance is free but you pay through the nose for everything else. Otherwise a trip to the *Yörük Parkı*, on a small hill above the harbor, is justified by the *gözleme* (traditional Turkish sandwiches) which are cooked there, but otherwise its attempted re-creation of a nomadic tent village, complete with black goat-hair *yörük* tents, is all pretty tawdry and fake, right down to the bar installed among the tents. Even the staff appear mildly embarrassed by its existence.

Moving on from Kemer

There are **dolmuşes** to Tekirova and Phaselis from Kemer, and buses to Antalya otogar every half-hour; it's also possible to rent a **boat** to get to Phaselis from Kemer harbor, which costs around $20 a day. **Car rental** is available from *Flash Rent a Car* (☎3214/1785), İskele Caddesi, Nevzat Saygan Apt 3, or from *Orient* (☎3214/1602, 2131) at the *Orient Hotel* on Liman Caddesi; some of the major firms, including *Europcar* (☎3214/2083), *Budget* (☎3214/2809), and *Avis* (☎3214/1372) have outlets in Kemer. The German-run *Erendiz Ranch* (☎3214/2504) rents horses for tours of the surrounding mountains (minimum of 6 people, maximum 9). It also has a restaurant serving German food and beer.

Beldibi

BELDİBİ, 35km from Antalya, is really just a beach, and not a very good one at that, but it has received a lot of the overspill from Antalya in recent years resulting in a build-up of monstrous hotels and severely overpriced campgrounds. If you can avoid it, do so, but if you head out of Antalya late in the evening you may be forced to cut your losses and stay a night here.

There are a number of **pansiyons** in the village, including the simple *Kervansaray Pansiyon* (☎3184/8085), which has hot water, and charges $6 per person. The cheapest and most pleasant of the **campgrounds** is the *Orange* (3184/8072), aptly named since it's situated in an orange grove. The woman who runs it, who speaks fluent German and some English, runs a fish **restaurant** on the same premises, and arranges jeep safaris into the mountains. Pricier, but also comfortable, is *Erman Camping* (90-3214/1112), located on the far side of the village from Antalya, with just about every amenity you could imagine, including its own stretch of beach—although you certainly pay for them. It also has bungalows and tents for rent. Other sites on the Antalya side of the village charge about the same and have fewer facilities: the *Doğu Karadeniz* and *Yalçın* both have cold-water showers; the *Çelik* has hot water and is cleaner.

travel details

Buses and dolmuşes

From Dalaman to İstanbul (2 daily; 13hr); İzmir (14 daily; 6hr); Denizli (2 daily; 5hr); Fethiye (2 an hour; 1hr 30min); Marmaris (12 daily; 2hr); Bodrum (5 daily; 6hr) Antalya (2 daily in summer; 6hr) Muğla (18 daily; 2 hr); Kaş (4 daily; 4hr); Ortaca (2 an hour; 20min).

From Ortaca to İzmir (10 daily; 5hr 30min); İstanbul (3; 14hr); Ankara (3 daily; 10hr); Pamukkale (14 daily, 5/6hr); Kaş (5 daily; 5hr); Antalya (2 daily; 6hr); Bodrum (5 daily; 4hr); Dalyan (25 daily; 20min); Dalaman (2 an hour; 20min).

From Fethiye to İzmir (2 an hour; 7hr) İstanbul (3 daily; 14hr); Bodrum (6 daily; 5hr); Kaş (15 daily; 2hr 30min); Denizli (5 daily; 4hr); Patara (15 daily; 1hr 30min); Muğla (10 daily, 3hr); Aydin (6 daily; 5hr); Afyon (1 daily; 4hr); Marmaris (hourly; 3hr); Burdur (1 daily; 5hr); Ankara (2 daily; 12hr); Antalya (8 daily; 4hr); Adana (1 daily; 18hr).

From Patara to Kalkan (10 daily; 30min); Kaş (10 daily; 1hr); Fethiye (8 daily; 1hr 30min); Xanthos/ the Letoön (every hour; 30min).

From Kaş to İstanbul (2 daily; 12hr); Marmaris (4 daily; 4hr 30min); Fethiye (8 daily, 2hr 30min) Antalya (6 daily; 5hr); Pamukkale (2 daily; 10hr); Patara (two an hour; 1hr); Bodrum (3 daily; 7hr).

From Demre to İstanbul (2 daily; 11hr); Ankara (2 daily; 9hr); Alanya, (1 daily; 5hr); Adana (1 daily; 12hr); Fethiye (4 daily; 5hr); Finike (3 daily; 30min); Elmalı (3 daily; 2hr).

From Finike to Antalya (2 an hour; 2hr 15min); Adana (1 daily; 14hr); İstanbul (1 daily; 15hr) Ankara (1 daily; 13hr); Elmalı (10 daily; 1hr 30min); Kaş (3; 1hr 30min); Kalkan (2 daily; 2hr 30min); Demre (2 daily; 30min) Fethiye (13 daily; 4hr).

From Elmalı to Antalya (9 daily; 3hr); Kaş (3 daily; 3hr); Demre (6 daily; 2hr); Finike (2 an hour, 1hr 30min).

From Kalkan to Antalya (7 daily; 5hr); İstanbul (1 daily; 15hr); Ankara (1 daily; 12hr); İzmir (3 daily; 9hr); Fethiye (every half-hour; 2hr); Marmaris (2 daily; 5hr); Bodrum (1 daily; 7hr); Pamukkale (1 daily; 6hr); Adana via Alanya/Anamur/Silifke/ Mersin (1 daily; 18hr).

From Kemer to Tekirova/Phaselis (2 an hour; 30min); Antalya (2 an hour; 1hr 30min).

CHAPTER SIX

THE MEDITERRANEAN COAST

he **Mediterranean coast** of Turkey, where the Taurus Mountains sweep down to meet the sea, offers some of the country's finest unspoiled shoreline. Dominated by the mountains, the landscape is more austere than that of the Aeagean and Turquoise coasts, but it has the advantage of being quieter, and with a little effort it's always possible to escape the crowds to find a stretch of underpopulated beach or an undiscovered coastal village.

The region divides roughly into two parts. The stretch from Antalya to Alanya is the more accessible half, with the Taurus range, though always a looming presence, separated from the sea by a narrow coastal strip. East of Alanya, the mountains meet the sea head-on, making for some of Turkey's most rugged stretches of coastline, where hairpin bends and mountain roads can make travel an agonizingly slow process at times. At the eastern end of the Mediterranean the mountains recede, giving way to the flat, monotonous landscape of the Ceyhan River delta.

Antalya is most people's first experience of the Mediterranean coast, a bustling modern city whose international airport and comprehensive bus services make it a prime arrival and junction point. East of Antalya the mountains slope gently down to sandy beaches and a fertile coastal strip supporting an economy based on cotton-growing and tourism, an area largely covering the ancient region of **Pamphylia**, settled by refugees from Troy in the twelfth century BC. The ruins of four cities—**Perge**, **Sillyom**, **Aspendos**, and **Side**—testify to the sophisticated nature of the civilization that flourished here during the Hellenistic period. Perge and Aspendos are well-established day-trip destinations from Antalya, and the modern town of Side has become a mecca for organized tours, the yearly summer influx inevitably detracting somewhat from the appeal of its ancient architecture.

Seventy kilometers farther along the coast, the former pirate refuge of **Alanya** is set on and around a spectacular promontory topped by a stunning Selçuk citadel. Alanya, too, has grown in recent years into a bustling tourist center, shaking off the sleepy feel that characterizes some of the smaller Mediterranean settlements. Beyond here the coast gradually becomes wilder, the road reduced to a clifftop roller-coaster ride that descends occasionally into steep-sided valleys lush with banana plantations. Inaccessibility made this section of the coast a haven for pirates until the Romans mounted a clean-up operation during the first century BC, and in places it still has a desolate, untamed feel. The best places to break your journey are **Anamur**, where a ruined Hellenistic city abuts some of the best

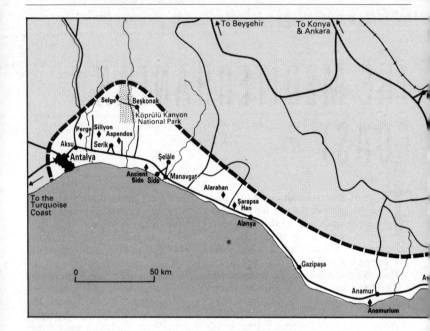

beaches in the region, and **Kızkalesi**, near **Silifke**, where a Byzantine castle of monumental proportions sits a hundred meters from the sandy shore of a crescent-shaped bay. Kızkalesi also makes a good base from which to explore the ancient city of **Uzuncaburç**, a lonely ruin set high above the sea in the Taurus Mountains.

Beyond Kızkalesi is the fertile but dull alluvial delta of the **Çukurova**, where the Ceyhan River spills down from the mountains and meanders sluggishly into the eastern Mediterranean, spawning a string of cities surrounded by medium-density industry amid low-lying cotton plantations. This end of the Mediterranean coast has less to recommend it. **Mersin** is a large, modern port only likely to be of interest to those en route to northern Cyprus, to which there are regular ferry connections; **Tarsus**, the birthplace of Saint Paul, has few surviving reminders of its long history; **Adana**, one of the country's largest urban centers, is a hectic transit point, and a staging post on journeys to the east.

ANTALYA TO ALANYA

The western part of the Turkish Mediterranean coast, between Antalya and Alanya, is not surprisingly the most popular with tourists, with long stretches of sandy beach and a rapidly developing tourist infrastructure. The cotton-rich coastal margin covers what was the ancient region of **Pamphylia**, a loose federation of Hellenistic cities established by incomers from northern Anatolia. According to ancient Greek sources, Pamphylia was settled by a "mixed multi-

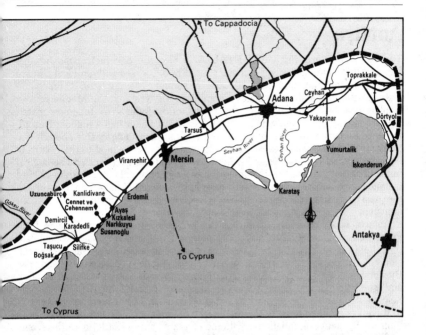

tude" of peoples after the fall of Troy in 1184 BC. It played a relatively minor role in the history of Anatolia, never even attaining local military significance, and the Pamphylian cities were fought over for centuries by stronger neighbors like the Lydians and Persians. To an extent, the Pamphylians profited from this, playing off one would-be invader against the next while continuing to run their own affairs, regardless of who exercised ultimate control of the region. In later years, Mark Antony was sent to take control of the region, treating it as his personal domain until defeated by Octavius Caesar at the Battle of Actium in 31 BC, after which Pamphylia was formally absorbed into the Roman Empire under the *Pax Romana*.

You're most likely to start your explorations at **Antalya**, a booming place that over the last five years or so has turned into a fully-fledged resort—worth visiting for its restored old town and marvelous archaeological museum. The four surviving ruined cities of Pamphylia rival the beaches as a tourist magnet, with **Perge** and **Aspendos** the best-preserved and most evocative sites. Farther along the coast, **Side** is perhaps the Mediterranean's major resort, although sadly the striking ruins of its ancient city are fast being overshadowed by the rapidly growing tourist facilities. It remains, however, the ideal place if you're after beach action and nightlife. **Alanya**, the next major center, has also seen an explosion of hotel building and tourism-related commerce over the last few years, but so far the town planners have managed to retain some sense of proportion about development. As for less-beaten tourist tracks, **Köprülü Kanyon National Park** and the ruins of ancient **Selge**, not far inland from Antalya and Side, make a delightfully untouched day excursion.

Antalya

Turkey's fastest-growing city, **ANTALYA** is also the one metropolis besides İstanbul that's simultaneously a major tourist hub. Blessed with an ideal climate (except during July and August), and a stunning setting atop a limestone plateau—the formidable Beydağları looming to the west and the Mediterranean rippling below—Antalya has seen the annual tourist influx grow to almost match its permanent population, which now stands at just under half a million. Despite the appearances of its grim concrete sprawl, Antalya is an agreeable enough city to live in, but the main area of interest for outsiders is confined to the relatively tiny and central old quarter. With the exception of the excellent archaeological museum, most attractions—including the two bus terminals—are within walking distance of each other. Three to four days here—including half-day excursions to the nearby ruins of Termessos, Perge, and Aspendos—should be more than sufficient.

Antalya was only founded during the second century BC by Attalus II of Pergamon, and named Attaleia in his honor. The Romans did not consolidate their hold on the city and its hinterland until the imperial period, at the conclusion of successful campaigns against local pirates. Christianity and the Byzantines got a similarly slow start, although because of its strategic location and good anchorage Antalya was an important halt for the Crusaders. The Selçuks supplanted the Byzantines for good early in the thirteenth century, and to them are credited most of the medieval monuments visible today (albeit some built on Byzantine foundations). Ottoman Antalya figured little in world events until 1918, when the Italians made it the focus of their short-lived Turkish colony.

> The Antalya **area telephone code** is ☎31.

Arrival and Information

Most visitors will arrive at the central **otogar**, up at the top of Kazım Özalp Caddesi, still universally referred to by its old name of Sarampol; this runs for just under a kilometer down to the Saat Kulesi (Clocktower) and the intersection with Cumhuriyet Caddesi, on the fringe of Kaleiçi—the old town, a maze of short alleys just to the south. A little way east, 800m down Ali Çetinkaya Caddesi, is the **Doğu Garaj** (Eastern Dolmuş Station), linked to the main bus terminal by a dolmuş, labeled "Sarampol/Doğu Garaj." To the west along the waterfront, down Kenan Evren Bulvarı (which becomes Akdeniz Bulvarı as it skirts Konyaltı Beach), is the dock where **ferries** arrive from Venice—5km from the center of town but connected by dolmuş. Arriving by air, Antalya's **airport** (☎217780) is about 10km northeast of the city center, and there are *THY* buses making the fifteen-minute trip into town; city-center-bound dolmuşes also pass nearby. Failing that, take a taxi—about $5 one-way.

Ther are two central **tourist information offices**, one beside *THY* on Cumhuriyet Caddesi (Mon–Fri 8am–5:30pm; Sat–Sun 9am–5pm; ☎111 747), the other in Kaleiçi next to the *Hotel Aspen* (Mon–Fri 8am–noon & 1:30–5:30pm). Both hand out city maps but neither seems to have much in the way of accommodation listings.

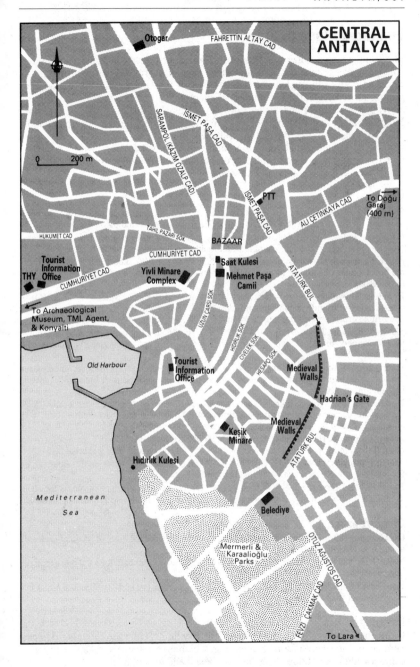

CENTRAL ANTALYA

FAHRETTIN ALTAY CAD

Otogar

İSMET PAŞA CAD

SARAMPOL KAZIM ÖZALP CAD

İSMET PAŞA CAD

ALİ ÇETİNKAYA CAD

To Doğu Garaj (400 m)

PTT

0   200 m

HÜKÜMET CAD

TAHIL PAZARI SOK

BAZAAR

CUMHURİYET CAD

Tourist Information Office

THY

CUMHURİYET CAD

Saat Kulesi

Yivli Minare Complex

Mehmet Paşa Camii

ATATÜRK BUL

To Archaeological Museum, TML Agent, & Konyaltı

UZUN ÇARŞ SOK

HIDIRLIK SOK

ÇİÇEKLER SOK

HESAPÇI SOK

Old Harbour

Tourist Information Office

Medieval Walls

Hadrian's Gate

Medieval Walls

Keşik Minare

ATATÜRK BUL

Hıdırlık Kulesi

Mediterranean Sea

Belediye

OTUZ AĞUSTOS CAD

FEIZI ÇAKMAK CAD

Mermerli & Karaalioğlu Parks

To Lara

Finding a Place to Stay

In recent years a craze for restoring dilapidated houses in Kaleiçi as modest pansiyons has gripped Antalya, and these days most travelers **stay** in this part of town, with the old nucleus of hotels between the otogar and the bazaar now getting more of a Turkish commercial clientele; you'd only want to stay there if arriving very late or for a nap between buses. In Kaleiçi, two long streets—Hıdırlık Sokak and Hesapçı Sokak—are vital when looking for accommodation; also be aware of the distinction between the redone, moderately expensive historic buildings, usually curled around a garden or courtyard with a bar/café, and the modern, cheaper, and more spartan establishments closer to the cliff edge, normally with compensating views.

Kaleiçi

Saltur Pansiyon, Hesapçı Sok 67 (☎176 238). A small, modern building next to Mermerli Park and the Hıdırlık Tower, with a fine view. $12–16 double depending on the room.

Pansiyon Falez, Hıdırlık Sok 48 (☎170 985). A tall, concrete compound; seaward rooms have the best view in Kaleiçi. $8 single with breakfast, $14 double; baths down the hall.

Adler Pansiyon, Barbaros Mahalle Civelek Sok 16 (☎117 818). The least expensive of the old-house pansiyons, owing to no attached baths—otherwise basic but clean and characterful. $6 a single, $12 a double.

Pansion The Garden, Hesapçı Sok 44, opposite the Kesik Minare (☎110 816). A ramshackle but friendly establishment; most rooms have a shower, though the main selling point (not surprisingly) is the huge garden. $8 single, $14 double, both with breakfast.

Sabah Pansiyon, Hespaçı Sok 60/A (☎175 345). An old standby that's currently expanding into a planned, mock-old house, so expect rates to inch up. $8 single, $14 double with breakfast.

Hadriyanus Pansiyon, Zeytin Çıkmazı 4, off Hıdırlık Sokak (☎112 313). A middle-aged building with one of the nicer gardens around. $12 single, $18 double, both with attached bath and breakfast.

Dedekonak Pansiyon, Hıdırlık Sok 11 (☎175 170). One of the better restoration jobs, though the garden is somewhat claustrophobic. $12 for a single, $18 double, both with attached bath and breakfast.

Erken Pansiyon, Hıdırlık Sok 5 (☎176 092). Similar to *Dedekonak*, though conversion of the rooms is a bit more patchy. Singles $12, doubles $22 for rooms with bath and breakfast.

Atelya Pansiyon, Civelek Sok 21 (☎116 416). Another mid-range choice on this quiet street. Singles $14 , doubles $24, with attached bath and breakfast.

Pansion Mini Orient, Civelek Sok 30 (☎124 417). Oddly arranged hive of rooms for about as much as you'd want to pay in Kaleiçi: $17.50 single, $24.50 double with bath and breakfast.

Otogar/Bazaar

Otel Sargin, 459 Sok 3, just off Sarampol (☎111 408). A traditional hotel of acceptable cleanliness. $6 single, $10 double.

Kaya Oteli, 459 Sok 12 (☎111 391). Tiny but clean rooms without bath for a tad more than the *Sargin*.

Kumluca Oteli, 457 Sok 21, closer to İsmet Paşa Caddesi (☎111 123). Another funky fallback, cheaper than the above.

Camping

Camping is not really advisable within the city limits. Only the *Camping Bambus*, 3km along the road to Lara, is operating, which is expensive and aimed at trailer-campers, although it does boast its own beach and decent facilities.

The City

The intersection of Cumhuriyet Caddesi and Sarampol, better known as Kalekapısı (Castle Gate), is the most obvious place to begin a tour of Antalya, dominated by the **Yivli Minare** (Fluted Minaret), erected during the thirteenth-century reign of the Selçuk sultan, Alâeddin Keykubad, and today something of a symbol of the city. The adjacent mosque is much later; the original foundation had been built on top of a church. Part of the same complex, accessible by a stairway from Cumhuriyet Caddesi, are a **türbe** from 1377 and a dervish **tekke**.

It's hard to resist continuing downhill from the Yivli Minare to the **old harbor**, restored over a decade ending in 1988. Inevitably authenticity has been sacrificed—the only fishermen left among the yachts are the sort who have radar and solar-powered TVs on board—but on balance it was a successful venture, as reflected in the fact that apparently half of Antalya chooses to do its evening promenade on what was once a gravel foreshore. By contrast once-bustling Sarampol, and even the cafés up on Cumhuriyet Caddesi, are nocturnal deserts now that the center of social gravity has shifted seaward.

Returning to Kalekapısı past souvenir and carpet shops and the eighteenth-century **Mehmet Paşa Camii**, and bearing onto Atatürk Caddesi, you'll pass the disappointing **bazaar** and soon draw even with the triple-arched **Hadrian's Gate**, recalling a visit by that emperor in 130 AD. Hesapçı Sokak, the quietest entry to **Kaleiçi**, begins here at a small park area; follow it through the old town, which, while interesting enough, is inevitably succumbing to tourist gentrification as every house—virtually without exception—has been redone as a carpet shop, café, or pansiyon. About halfway to the edge of the palisade stands the **Kesik Minare** (Broken Minaret), topping an even more ruinous structure with various pedigrees: ancient masonry is plainly visible in this converted fifth-century church.

Almost too suddenly you emerge onto the adjoining **Mermerli** and **Karaalioğlu** parks, with a number of tea gardens, plus the **Hıdırlık Kulesi** (Tower) at one corner. This is of indisputable Roman vintage but functional interpretations vary between lighthouse, bastion, or tomb; below it, steps lead down past a waterfall to a series of tamped dirt terraces and the sea. The whole area is the best place in the city to watch the often spectacular **sunsets** over the primordial, snow-capped mountains across the Gulf of Antalya.

The Archaeological Museum

The one thing you shouldn't miss while in Antalya is the city's **Archaeological Museum** (daily except Mon 9am–6pm; $2), located on the western edge of town at the far end of Kenan Evren Bulvarı. It's one of the top five archaeological collections in the country, and is well worth an hour or two of your time. To get there from the city center, take any dolmuş labeled "Konyaltı/Liman," stopping at all "D" signs along Cumhuriyet Caddesi and its continuation Kenan Evren Bulvarı.

The well-lit galleries are arranged both chronologically and thematically. Standouts of the early items are a cache of Bronze Age **urn burials** from near Elmalı, and finds from an unusually southerly **Phrygian tumulus**, with the trademark Phrygian griffon head much in evidence. Several showcased silver or ivory Phrygian figurines, with droll yet dignified expressions, date from the eighth and seventh centuries and are among the museum's worthiest treasures.

Quite a jump in time is involved to reach the next gallery of second-century (AD) statuary from Perge. A **complete pantheon** has been assembled, none of it superb but all in unusually good condition. Next is a catch-all room filled with small finds of different eras, materials, and origins, including several versions of **Eros and Aphrodite**, followed by the so-called "Empire Room," crammed with more Perge statuary honoring the various demigods and priestesses of the Roman imperial cult; the graceful **dancer** in the middle is by far the nicest piece. Best of the adjoining sarcophagus wing is an almost undamaged coffer depicting the **life of Hercules**. Mosaics in the building's corner hall, including one depicting **Thetis dunking Achilles in the Styx**, are in fair-to-good condition but crudely executed; a **gaming board** nearby, recovered from Perge, is more unusual.

A narrow room adjoining the mosaic hall is devoted to **icons** recovered from various churches in the Antalya area after 1922. They're mostly of recent date and popular in style, but unusually interesting for their rarely depicted themes and personalities. At one end is a reliquary containing some purported bones of **Saint Nicholas of Demre**. The coin gallery, next up, displays several famous hoards found in the region—more interesting than it sounds.

The collection is rounded out by an **ethnography section**, a hodgepodge of ceramics, kitsch glass lamps, smoking and writing implements, household implements, weapons, dress and embroidery, weights and locks, plus musical instruments. A diorama of nomad life is appropriately followed by socks and carpets; there's also a case on where all those wooden spoons peddled on street corners come from.

The Beaches . . . and the Düden Waterfalls

Despite earnest promotion in tourist literature, Antalya's city beaches don't rate much consideration. **Konyaltı**, 3km west of Kalekapısı, is divided into paying sections (clean) and free ones (filthy) but all are shadeless, pebbly, and sullied by industrial pollution from the nearby harbor. **Lara**, 10km distant in the opposite direction and reached by dolmuşes running along Atatürk Caddesi, has fine sand but is enclosed in a forbidding fence and accessible only for a fee.

The lower **Düden waterfalls** reach the ocean at Lara, but to get a good look at them you'll need to take a boat tour from the old harbor. The upper cascades, some 4km northeast of town, are frequently served by dolmuş from the Doğu Garaj, but beware that the surrounding parkland is often mobbed—and the falls themselves reduce to a trickle in late summer.

Eating, Drinking, and Nightlife

Since the closure or gentrification of many old favorites, Antalya's range of **restaurants** is limited—and the pressure of tourism has inevitably driven prices up. For sipping a tea or something stronger, the situation is much better, with various bistros and watering holes in Kaleiçi and around the harbor that are pleasant and affordable for most wallets.

Cumhuriyet Caddesi is the location of a number of cafés and restaurants with terraces offering excellent views of the harbor—good for leisurely breakfasts. Southwest of the junction of Cumhuriyet Caddesi and Atatürk Bulvarı, there's a covered pedestrian area called **Eski Sebzeciler İçi Sokak** that's crammed with consecutive tiny restaurants—and tourists having a feed. The local specialty is *tandır kebap*, clay-pot-roasted mutton, sold by weight and not particularly cheap. A 300-gram portion—nearly half of which will be gristle and fat—runs about $4. Vastly superior in quality, but only marginally more expensive, are the twin *Gaziantep 1 & 2* eateries, 200m from each other at the edge of the bazaar; approach them through the *pasaj* at İsmet Paşa Caddesi 3, across from the branch PTT. Here *mezes* are presented to you on a tray; choose your meat from spits lined up by the grill. Out by the archaeological museum at Kenan Evren Bulvarı 68/C, and the perfect spot for lunch after a visit, the *Develiler Kebapçisi* is considered the best carniverous chow-down in town; the bill for a meal shouldn't exceed $8. If you're determined to blow your wad—which isn't difficult in Antalya—probably the most atmospheric place to do so is the *Hisar Restaurant*, installed, as the name suggests, in a rampart of the castle directly over the old port. The sea-view terraces fill up quickly; a fish-and-wine meal under one of the old stone arches should set you back about $12 apiece.

For a lighter meal, *Cafe Gül* in Kaleiçi is a small snack bar featuring *mantı* and kebabs. *Tektat*, at Sarampol 84, has the best desserts in town, and a garden to shield you from the traffic. *Pansion Olea*, Akarçeşme Sokak 11 (a small alley off Hesapçı Sokak) often has live music at its garden bar, although for all intents and purposes **nightlife** is down at the harbor, where the *Cafe İskele*, its tables grouped around a fountain, is pleasant and not absurdly priced, with more locals than tourists. For any more stimulation, you'll have to coincide with the autumn **film and music festivals** (see below).

Listings

Airport The *Havaş* bus departs for the airport, 12km east of town, 75min before each *THY* flight from the *Büyük Oteli*, 300m east of the *THY* office. Otherwise, eastbound dolmuşes pass the side road to the airport, but it's a hot, 2-km walk away and the gate guards will view you with extreme suspicion; far better to take a taxi ($5 per car during the day, $8 at night).

Airlines *Air France*, Cumhuriyet Caddesi, 59 Sok 8; *Greenair*, Fevzi Sakmak Cad, opposite the *Tolga Hotel* (☎187 325); *İstanbul Hava Yolları*, Anafartalar Cad 2, Selekler Çarşı (☎124 888); *THY*, Özel İdare İşhanı Altı, next to tourist information (☎112 830). *Gözen Air* (☎217 780, ext 448) out at the airport represents various British charter carriers.

Bookstores Limited English-language selection at: *Ardıç Kitabevi*, Selekler Çarşı; *Universite*, next to the police station; and at *NET*, in the luxury *Dedeman Hotel*, 7km out on the road to Lara.

Car and moped rental It seems every old building in Kaleiçi that's not a pansiyon or a rug shop is a car-rental agency; most of the rest line Fevzi Çakmak Caddesi on the way to Lara Beach. Among the more prominent independents or small chains are *Airtour*, Fevzi Çakmak Cad 75/3 (☎112 713); *Grand*, Fevzi Çakmak Cad 10/2 (☎125 076); *Kavas*, Hesapçı Sok 56, Kaleiçi (☎170 359), which also rents bicycles, motorcycles, and mopeds; *Metro*, Fevzi Çakmak Cad 27/E (☎173 189); *Uno*, Lara Yolu Mezbaha Karşısı, Kurt Apt D1/2 (☎182 550); and *Urent*, Kalekapısı İmaret Aralığı 5 (☎124 574). The biggies are *Avis*, Fevzi Çakmak 2/B (☎116 693) and at the airport; *Budget*, Kenan Evren Bulvarı, İçli Apt (☎126 220) and at the airport; and *Europcar/InterRent*, Fevzi Çakmak 14/A (☎118 879) and at the airport.

Exchange Evenings and weekend exchange in the Vakıfbank booth at Kalekapısı, daily 9am–7pm; also at the central PTT.

Ferry agent The *TML* office, for the weekly ferry to Venice, is at Kenan Evren Bul 40/19 (☎111 120).

Festivals The Altın Portakal Film Festival takes place the last week of September or the first week in October, usually back-to-back with the Akdeniz Song Festival; beware tight hotel and pansiyon space.

Hamams In Kaleiçi, *Nazır* on Hamam Aralığı Sokak behind the Mehmet Paşa mosque, is open daily for men 6–10am; for women 10am–5:30pm; and for men again 5:30pm–midnight. The *Cumhuriyet*, on 403 Sokak (beginning at Sarampol 38) is open for men only continuously until 11:30pm.

Hospital Out behind the museum at the corner of Yüz Yil Bulvarı and Kâzım Karabekir Caddesi.

Luggage storage At the otogar; open until midnight.

PTT The central office at Anafartalar Cad 9 is open daily 9am–9pm for exchange and letter service; phone division open 24hr. A smaller branch on İsmet Paşa Caddesi is more convenient but keeps standard small-town hours.

Around Antalya: Termessos

After a couple of nights in Antalya you may be in a hurry to move on, heading east or west along the coast in search of better—and quieter—beaches. But before you head off, consider staying another night and having a look inland, where the ancient site of **TERMESSOS**, situated over a thousand meters above sea level, is one of Turkey's prime attractions. Indeed, its dramatic setting and well-preserved ruins, tumbling from the summit of the mountain, and enclosed within the boundaries of a national park—**Güllük Dağ Milli Parkı**—merit a considerable journey.

Despite its proximity to Lycia, Termessos was actually a Pisidian city, inhabited by the same warlike tribe of people who settled in the Anatolian Lakeland around Isparta and Eğirdir during the first millennium BC. The inhabitants of Termessos originally named themselves after the nearby mountain of Solymus (today's Güllük Dağ); their language, of which no surviving inscriptions remain, was a dialect of Pisidian, which Strabo called Solymian. The first mention of the Solymians is in the myth of Bellerophon and Pegasus, when, after defeating the monster of the Chimaera (see Chapter Five, "Olympos"), Bellerophon was sent to fight them. The first appearance of the Solymians in recorded history was in 333 BC, when Alexander the Great attacked the city and was repelled. Fourteen years later, Termessos played an interesting part in the history of the region when Antigonus—one of Alexander's successors—was challenged by Alcatus for command of the region. The Pisidians supported Alcatus, and he took refuge in Termessos. The elders of the city saw the dangers involved in defying Antigonus, and they laid a trap for Alcatus, preparing to take him captive. Alcatus committed suicide, and his body was delivered to Antigonus, but after three days it was rescued and reburied in Termessos.

Unlike that of its Lycian neighbors, much of the history of Termessos is characterized more by attack than defense, and in the third and second centuries BC the Termessians first took on the Lycian Federation, then their neighbors in nearby Isinda. In the second century BC they formed an alliance with the Pisidian city of Adada—by which time, according to inscriptions, the city was being run on democratic lines. Later, in 70 BC, Termessos signed a treaty of friendship with Rome, under which it was exempted from the jurisdiction of the governor—an independence that was proudly expressed by its never including the face or name of a Roman emperor on its coinage.

The Site

Even if you don't have to walk the final 9km through the national park (see below), the approach to the **site** of Termessos (daily 8am–5pm; $3) can seem a stiff one. Walking shoes and a supply of water are advisable, as is a sensibly timed visit to avoid the midday sun. Leaving the parking lot you'll need to climb a good twenty minutes before you reach the first remains of any interest, although on the way you'll pass a number of well-labeled ruins. These, however, are—like the aqueduct and cistern high on the cliff face to the left of the path—mainly inaccessible. The second-century AD **King's Road** was the main road up to the city, and the massive proportions of the nearby lower and upper **city walls** testify to a substantial defense system. The central part of the city is beyond the second wall, to the left of the path. Its surviving buildings, formed of square-cut gray stone, are in an excellent state of repair, their walls standing high and retaining their original mouldings—something due in part to the inaccessibility of the site; it's difficult to imagine even the most desperate forager coming up here to pillage stone.

The first building you reach is the well-preserved **gymnasium** and adjacent baths complex, although this is far overshadowed by the nearby **theater**; one of the most magnificently situated in Turkey, with the mountain soaring behind and a steep gorge dropping to its right. Greek in style, it had seating space for 4200 spectators, and wild animals were released into the orchestra from a basement under the later, Roman-built stage. Some of the seats are missing, but otherwise it's in a good state of preservation.

To the west of the theater is the **agora**, an open grassy space, at the far end of which is a **mausoleum**, approached up a broad flight of steps, with a six-meter square platform—at the back of which a grave pit is sunk into the rock. Its unusual position on the marketplace suggests that the tomb belonged to an extremely eminent citizen, and it has even been suggested that this could be the tomb of Alcatus, the pretender to the governorship of Pisidia—though the example on the hill above (see below) is generally accepted as more likely.

On the far side of the agora from the theater stands a smaller theater or **odeon**, which according to inscriptions was used for horse and foot races, races in armor, and—by far the most frequent event—wrestling. The walls of the building stand almost 10m high, although the interior doesn't amount to much more than a heap of rubble. Surrounding the odeon are four **temples**, only one of which—that of Zeus Solymus, god of war and guardian of the city of Termessos—is in a decent state of repair, with walls standing over 5m high and a bench in the back for statues. Two of the other three temples on the southeast side of the odeon—the two with portals still standing—were dedicated to the goddess Artemis.

Following the path up the hill from here leads to a fork in the road; take the left-hand path to continue to the **necropolis**, where you'll see an incredible number of sarcophagi dating from the first to the third centuries AD. Most are a simple sarcophagus on a base, though there are some more elaborate structures, many carrying inscriptions describing penalties for their violation. Fines were normally made payable to Zeus Solymus, but a portion of the money—a half or a third—was often set aside for informers.

Returning back downhill, take the left-hand fork to the **"tomb of Alcatus"**— the most widely accepted site of the general's mausoleum. The tomb itself is cavelike and undistinguished, but the carvings on its facade are remarkable—

particularly one depicting a mounted soldier—while below and to the right of the figure are carved a foot soldier's suit of armor, helmet, shield, and sword. The tomb and reliefs are consistent with the date of Alcatus's death, and the figure in the carving wears armor identical to that of Alexander the Great in a mosaic of the Battle of Issus in the Naples archaeological museum.

Practical Details

Antalya, 30km away, is the most obvious—and best—base for visiting Termessos, whether you're traveling by public transportation or your own vehicle. To **get there** by car, take the Burdur road out of Antalya, turning left after 11km toward Korkuteli. The turnoff to Termessos is marked after another 14km, and from there a dirt road leads 9km up through the forested national park (entrance 25¢ per person, 75¢ per car) to the site. Using public transportation, you need to take a dolmuş from Korkuteli as far as the beginning of the forest road, from which—if you can't hitch a ride—it's a two-hour walk to the site. There is no accommodation near the site except for a **campground** near the national-park entrance.

The Pamphylian Cities

The thirteenth century BC saw a large wave of Greek migration from northern Anatolia to the Mediterranean coast; many of the incomers moved into the area immediately east of Antalya, which came to be called **Pamphylia**, meaning "Land of the Tribes," reflecting the mixed origins of the new arrivals. Pamphylia was a remote area, cut off from the main Anatolian trade routes by mountains on all sides; nevertheless four great cities grew up here—Perge, Sillyon, Aspendos, and Side.

The first recorded mention of the region dates from the sixth century BC, when Croesus, the last king of Lydia, absorbed Pamphylia into his realm. When Croesus was defeated by the Persians in 546 BC, the Persians assumed control of the area, which alarmed the Greeks, who attempted to gain control of Pamphylia in a series of wars in which the Pamphylians fought on the side of the Persians. With the exception of Sillyon, Pamphylia eventually fell to Alexander the Great, and after his death it effectively became independent, though nominally claimed by the various successor kingdoms that inherited Alexander's realm. During the first century BC the Romans, annoyed by the activities of the Cilician pirates operating from farther along the Mediterranean, took control of the coast, ushering in three centuries of stability and prosperity, during which the Pamphylian cities flourished as never before.

Perge

About 15km east of Antalya, the ruins of **PERGE** can be reached by taking a dolmuş to the village of AKSU on the main eastbound road, from which it's a fifteen-minute walk to the site itself (you may be able to hitch a dolmuş ride if you don't want to walk). At the top of the hill is the entrance to the site (daily 9am–noon & 1:30–5pm; $2.50), which includes the largest stadium in Asia Minor. It's an enticing spot, the ruins expansive and impressive, and you could easily spend a long afternoon looking around, though in fact substantially more survived until

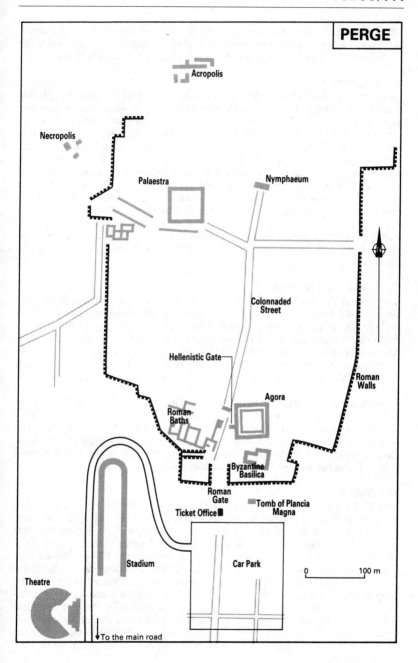

1922, when, according to some accounts, the theater was more or less intact. However, a 1920s construction boom in the nearby village of Murtunas led to the readily available supplies of stone at Perge being pillaged by local builders.

Some History

Perge was founded around 1000 BC and ranked as one of the great Pamphylian trading cities, despite the fact that it's nearly 20km inland—a deliberate defensive siting so as to avoid the unwanted attentions of the pirate bands and raiders who terrorized this stretch of the Mediterranean. Later, when Alexander the Great arrived in 333 BC, the citizens of Perge sent out guides to lead his army into the city. Alexander was followed by the Seleucids, under whom Perge's most celebrated ancient inhabitant, the mathematician Apollonius, lived and worked. A pupil of Archimedes, Apollonius wrote a series of eight books in which he described a family of curves known as conic sections, comprising the circle, ellipse, parabola, and hyperbola—theories that were developed by Ptolemy and later by the German astronomer Kepler. Most of the city's surviving buildings date from the period of Roman rule which began in 188 BC. After the collapse of the Roman Empire, Perge remained inhabited until Selçuk times, before being gradually abandoned.

The Theater and Stadium

Just beyond the site entrance, the **theater** was originally constructed by the Greeks but substantially altered by the Romans in the second century AD. Built into the side of a hill, it could accommodate 14,000 people on 42 seating levels rising up from the arena, and was used as a venue not only for theatrical entertainment but also for gladiatorial displays. Look out for the fragmentary marble reliefs running around the stage area, mainly featuring Eros and Dionysus. From the top of the auditorium you can appreciate the size and scope of the rest of the city.

Northeast of the theater is Perge's massive horseshoe-shaped **stadium**, 234m by 34m, with a seating capacity of 12,000. Because the stadium was built on level ground it was necessary to provide massive supporting pillars and arches. The spaces between these arches were divided into about thirty huge rooms (occupied by shops and businesses), many of which are still intact, giving a good impression of the scale of the whole stadium complex.

The Walled City

East of the stadium is the entrance to the city proper, marked by a cluster of souvenir and soft-drink stands. In places, stretches of the Seleucid walls have survived, giving some indication of the extent and layout of the original city. Just in front of the outer gates is the **tomb of Plancia Magna**, a benefactress of the city, whose name appears later on a number of inscriptions. Passing through the first Roman **city gate**, you'll see a ruined **Byzantine basilica** on the right, beyond which lies the fourth-century AD **agora**, around a ruined temple. To the southwest of the agora are the excavated **Roman baths**, a couple of whose original pools have been exposed; walking across the cracked surface of the inlaid marble floor, the original layout of frigidarium, tepidarium, and caldarium can—with the help of a few signs—still be discerned. Also visible in places are the brick piles that once supported the floor of the baths, enabling warm air to circulate underneath.

At the northwest corner of the agora is Perge's **Hellenistic Gate**, with its two mighty circular towers, the only building to have survived from the Hellenistic period. Behind, the horseshoe-shaped court and ornamental archway were both erected at the behest of Plancia Magna; the former was once adorned with statues—the bases of a number of these were found during excavations carried out during the mid-1950s. Beyond is the start of a 300-meter-long **colonnaded street**, with a water channel running down the middle and the shells of shops on either side. Walking along it, you'll be able to pick out the ruts made by carts and chariots in the stone slabs of the roadway. Also visible are a number of reliefs near the top of the columns of the colonnade, just beneath the capitals, one depicting Apollo and another showing a man in a toga offering a libation at an altar. At the end of the street is the **nymphaeum**, an ornamental water outlet from which a stream splashes down into the water channel below. Above here is the **acropolis hill**—probably the site of the original defensive settlement, although little of it has survived. To the west of a crossroads just before the nymphaeum is a **palaestra**, dating from 50 AD, according to an inscription found on its south wall. West of here archaeologists have found a **necropolis**; sarcophagi from this can now be seen in the Antalya museum.

Sillyon

About 7km east of Perge are the ruins of the ancient city of **SILLYON**, also dating from about 1000 BC, although much less intact than Perge—and, without your own wheels, somewhat difficult to reach.

Situated on top of a table-like hill, Sillyon's strategic position enabled it to repulse an attack by Alexander the Great, who never succeeded in capturing it. These days it doesn't seem to attract as many visitors as some of the other Pamphylian sites, perhaps because of the 1969 landslide which swept about half of it away. To get there, head back to AKSU and follow the coastal road, taking a left at a sign about 7km east of the village. From here a road leads 8km inland to the small modern settlement of ASAR KÖYÜ, where an unmarked dirt road leads to the site itself. It's possible that some of the villagers may offer to guide you around, which can be quite useful because they can steer you clear of hazardous unfenced cisterns.

The Site

You can climb up to the acropolis of Sillyon by way of a ramp leading from the **lower gate** up the western side of the hill. To the left of the gate are the foundations of a **gymnasium**, converted into a bishop's palace in Byzantine times and now used only by sheep. At the top of the ramp you'll find a large and well-preserved **city gate** and, scattered around the rest of the hilltop, a number of buildings of indeterminate age and function. The largest is a late **Hellenistic structure** with several arched windows in its upper stories that later served the Selçuks as a fortress. Just to the south is a long hall-like building, possibly a former **gymnasium**, where you can see the slots and holes used to hold wooden shutters in place in the window frames. East of here lies a building with a **37-line inscription** carved into its stone doorjamb—the only surviving written example (apart from a few coins) of Pamphylian, the Greek dialect spoken in this area until the first century AD.

The most interesting part of the acropolis is the area around the **ruined theater**, which offers graphic visual evidence of nature's gradual erosion of the man-made past. Only the top eight rows of seats remain, and the rest of the structure now lies scattered across the plain below—the huge blocks you can see were once part of the seating terraces. Farther east are the foundations of a number of houses and part of a temple, which, judging by their precarious state, seem destined to follow the theater terraces over the edge of the hill.

Aspendos

Returning to the main road, head east for **ASPENDOS**, whose theater is probably the best preserved in Asia Minor. During summer there are regular dolmuş services to Aspendos from Antalya and Side, but if you can't get there directly ask to be dropped off at the indicated turnoff just before the humpbacked Selçuk bridge a few kilometers east of the village of SERİK. From here you should be able to pick up a ride to the site, although it's only a three-kilometer walk. Just before Aspendos, the village of BELKİS has a couple of eating places, including the pleasant riverside *Belkis Restoran*. You'll find the parking lot and site entrance (daily 8am–7pm; $2) about half a kilometer northeast of the village.

Some History

Aspendos first came to prominence in 469 BC when the Greco-Persian wars of that time culminated in a huge and bloody naval battle. The Greeks won and went on to defeat the Persians again in a land battle, when, heavily outnumbered, they outwitted their opponents by coming ashore here disguised as Persians, using the element of surprise to stage a successful attack.

This wasn't the end of Persian influence in Pamphylia, since the locals, and in particular the people of Aspendos, weren't any more keen about the Greeks; in 389 BC they murdered an Athenian general sent to collect tribute, after which nominal control of the area passed to Sparta. The Spartans proved to be ineffective rulers, and by 386 the Persians were back, not to be dislodged until the arrival of Alexander the Great in 333 BC. On hearing news of Alexander's approach, the rulers of Aspendos agreed to surrender but asked Alexander not to garrison soldiers in the city. Alexander accepted their terms on the condition that they pay him a tribute of money and horses, and went off to lay seige to Sillyon. After his departure he was angered to learn that the citizens of Aspendos were busy fortifying the city, and he returned to demand a larger tribute plus hostages. His demands were met, and Aspendos had to accept a Macedonian governor as well.

After the death of Alexander in 323 BC Aspendos became part of the Seleucid kingdom, and was later absorbed into the realm of the kings of Pergamon. In 133 BC the city became part of the Roman province of Asia. Early Roman rule consisted mainly of a succession of consuls and governors demanding protection money and carting off the city's treasures. Only with the establishing of the Roman Empire did the city begin to prosper, growing into an important trade center, its wealth being based mainly on salt extracted from a nearby lake.

Aspendos remained important throughout the Byzantine era, although it suffered badly from the Arab raids of the seventh century. During the thirteenth century the Selçuks arrived, and the Ottomans who followed a couple of hundred years later ruled here until the eighteenth century, when the settlement was abandoned.

The Theater

The Aspendos **theater**, which is still occasionally used for the staging of various events, was built in the second century AD by the architect Zeno. He used a Roman rather than Greek design, with an elaborate stage behind which the scenery could be lowered, instead of allowing the natural landscape behind the stage to act as a backdrop, as had been the custom in Hellenistic times.

The stage, auditorium, and arcade above are all intact, as is the several-story-high stage building, and what you see today is pretty much what the spectators saw during the theater's heyday—a state of preservation due in part to Atatürk, who after a visit declared that it should be preserved and used for performances rather than as a museum. A dubious legend relates that the theater was built after the king of Aspendos announced that he would give the hand of his beautiful daughter to a man who built some great work for the benefit of the city. Two men rose to the challenge, one building the theater, and the other an aqueduct; both finished their works simultaneously, with the result that the king offered to cut his daughter in two, giving a half to each man. The builder of the theater declared that he would rather renounce his claim than see the princess dismembered, and he was of course immediately rewarded with the hand of the girl for his unselfishness. Later, the theater was used as a Selçuk *kervanseray*, and restoration work from that period—plasterwork decorated with red zigzags—is visible over the stage. There's also a small museum to the left of the entrance, exhibiting pictures of theater "entrance tickets" and coins.

The Acropolis

After visiting the theater many visitors leave Aspendos, not realizing that there is more to see on the hill above. Near the theater a path leads up to the **acropolis**—like that of Sillyon, built on a flat-topped hill. The site is a little overgrown and unexcavated, but a number of substantial buildings are still in place, foremost among them the **nymphaeum** and **basilica**, both 16m in height. North of the acropolis, on the plain below, stretches a Roman **aqueduct** originally 15km long, which brought water to Aspendos from the mountains above. This can also be reached by taking a left turn down a trail just outside Belkis, skirting around the western side of the hill.

Köprülü Kanyon National Park and Selge

Inland from Aspendos, **Köprülü Kanyon National Park**—protecting the Köprülü River and its Roman bridges—along with the sparse ruins of Selge in the mountains above, make a good half-day outing, provided that you have a sturdy car and something else in mind to do on the way there or back. There is no public transportation to Selge, and hardly any worth mentioning to the national park—one elusive daily dolmuş plies between Serik on the coastal highway and the isolated villages at the very top of the Köprülü Valley.

The turnoff for both the national park (*milli parkı*) and Selge is marked 48km east of Antalya on Highway 400; the asphalt on the side road ends at BEŞKONAK, a straggly village 37km in. Five kilometers or so farther on, you reach the *Kanyon Restaurant*, with treehouse-type seating under giant sycamore trees overhanging the swift-flowing river. It's a spot as popular with Turks as bused-in foreigners, but the **trout** awaiting you in the tank under one of the several gazebos is expensive, at $4 a shot, and farm-raised. Ironically the Köprülü itself teems with brown trout, but it's illegal to catch them.

Just above the treehouse-restaurant the road narrows; take the left fork, signed "Altınkaya," and inch across the first of the two Roman spans, the **Oluk Bridge**. From here it's 13km up to Selge, reached by the next right fork after Oluk, although you may want to bear left for 1km to the second **Bridge of Böğrüm**, which has a huge, popular picnic area just downstream from it. In all honesty the bridges are little different from hundreds like them in Turkey, whether Roman, Byzantine, or Selçuk, and it's only the setting that makes Köprülü any different.

The final stretch up to Selge has recently been widened and improved, so it's now passable to most cars. As you climb to an eventual altitude of 900m, the panoramas become more sweeping, the thickly wooded countryside more savage, and the 2500-meter Kuyucuk range ahead more discernible and forbidding. At the scattered hamlet of **ZERK** (also known as Altınkaya), signs beckon you to park near a pair of refreshment stands, and small boys will volunteer to show you around the adjacent ruins. It's only fair to tip them, just as correct to refuse the outrageous "parking fee" demanded by the drink-stand proprietors.

A dirt road from here, now suitable only for jeeps, continues toward the obvious theater dominating **SELGE**, but your guide will probably take you on a faint path left and south to the ancient agora and two hilltop temples. The **agora**, part of its paving still extant, occupies a saddle with 360° views downvalley and up to snow-streaked peaks; the foundations of a **Byzantine church** sit on a hill to the southeast, while the jumbled remains of a **temple of Zeus** are a bit of a slog northwest along the ridge. Returning to the jeep track via some village farmyards, you'll pass the **stadium**, of which only the western ranks of seats are left; the sporting area itself is a wheat field. The **theater**, partly cut into living rock, is impressive, but would be more so if the stage building hadn't been pulverized by lightning some decades ago, and if the highest tier of seats hadn't sustained rain damage in 1989.

Little is known for certain of the origins of Selge; it only left the realm of mythological ancestry and anecdote to enter history—and the Roman Empire—in the first century AD. The city was famous for its storax gum, made from a local shrub, and was still inhabited until early Byzantine times. The site has always been arid—only recently did modern Zerk get a permanent spring—and the ancient town must have been abandoned when the aqueduct supplying it with water collapsed. The overwhelming impression you'll have is of the determination necessary to keep a city of 20,000 thriving in such a godforsaken wilderness.

Side

About 25km east of Aspendos, **SİDE**, a ruined Hellenistic port and onetime trysting place of Antony and Cleopatra, was perhaps the foremost of the Pamphylian cities, and the ruins of the ancient port survive. Over the last few years or so, however, Side has changed almost unrecognizably; indeed, some claim it has been ruined by indiscriminate tourist development, its 24,000 hotel beds complemented by an endless array of cafés, restaurants, leather shops, jewelry shops, and one-hour film-processing laboratories. If it's sun, sand, and surf you're after, you may want to spend some time here—the beaches are superb. If you're more interested in the ruins, try to visit in the off-season when you'll at least be able to move in the streets. Failing that, arrive early in the day and do your exploring before the crowds come out in force.

Side (meaning "Pomegranate" in an ancient Anatolian dialect) was founded in the seventh century BC by colonists who were attracted by the defensive potential of its rocky cape. It grew into a rich port with an estimated 60,000 inhabitants during its second-century AD peak. Initially a significant proportion of Side's wealth rested on the slave trade, with the city authorities allowing pirates to run a slave market inside the city walls, in which thousands of human beings were bought and sold every day. This trade was later outlawed, and after the collapse of the western Roman Empire Side survived only until the Arab invasion during the seventh century AD. They put the place to the torch, driving out the last inhabitants, and Side was abandoned until the beginning of this century, when it was re-settled by Greek Muslim fishermen from Crete who built a village among the ruins. Despite attempts by the Turkish government and various archaeological agencies to evict them, these villagers clung on, and by the 1980s their children and grandchildren were starting to reap the rewards of Side's tourist boom.

Arrival and Accommodation

There are plenty of **buses and dolmuşes** running to Side from Antalya, but if you can't get one take any bus heading east and ask to be dropped off at the turn-off for Side, clearly marked next to a gas station, where it's easy to pick up a dolmuş into Side itself. The road into town is lined with hotels and signs advertising hotels—an ominous taste of what lies ahead. There is no **otogar** as such, but buses, dolmuşes, and tour buses arrive and depart from a large parking lot north of the town's main drag, just inside the monumental gateway.

Side's **tourist information office** (Mon–Fri 9am–5pm; ☎3213/1265) is on the main road into town just before the first city gate, although it won't overburden you with information. Banks and a PTT can be found on the square at the southern tip of the promontory. **Accommodation** possibilities are endless, with hundreds of hotels and pansiyons on just about every corner, many of them built against stretches of ancient stonework. At the bottom end of the price scale, the *Kader Pansiyon* and *Cizmeci Pansiyon* (☎3213/1291), both toward the top of the street parallel and west of the main street, have doubles from $12. A little more upscale are the *Hermes Pansiyon* and the *Şen Pansiyon* (☎3213/2989), just west of the square at the bottom of the main street, which start at around $14 for a double. For those with deeper pockets, the *Kleopatra Hotel* (☎3213/1033), featuring doubles with baths for $25, and the more expensive *Neptun Motel,* (☎3213/1046), whose double rooms with baths cost $45, both have prime locations on the town's western beach. As for **camping**, there are a number of campgrounds along the western beach, beginning about 500m from the theater.

Ancient Side

Ancient Side has been almost overwhelmed by the modern town, but fortunately even the inroads of mass tourism have been unable to smother the grandeur of its buildings and monuments. The road into town actually passes through the **city gate**, although this is in such bad repair you could be forgiven for not noticing it. The **city walls** have fared better—the section running east from the city gate is particularly well preserved, with a number of towers still in place.

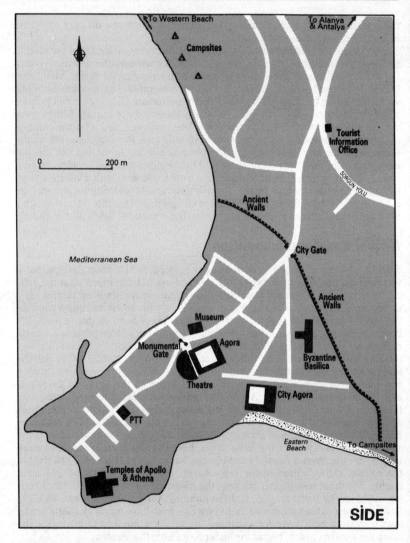

The Agora and Museum

From the city gate a colonnaded street runs down to the **agora**, once the site of
Side's second-century slave market, and today fringed with the stumps of many of
the agora's remaining columns. It's a popular spot with the nomads who hang
around trying to tempt people into taking camel rides. The circular foundation
visible at the center is all that remains of a **temple of Fortuna**, and in the
northwest corner, next to the theater, you can just about make out the outline of a
semicircular building that once served as a public latrine, seating 24 people.

Opposite the agora, on the other side of the road, is the site of the former **Roman baths,** now restored and turned into a **museum** (daily 8:30–11:45am & 1–5pm; $2.50). It retains its original floorplan and contains a cross section of locally unearthed objects—mainly Roman statuary, reliefs, and sarcophagi. If you find yourself wondering why many of the statues seem to be headless, it's because they were decapitated in an outbreak of excessive religious zeal during the early days of Christianity.

The Monumental Gate and Theater

Just south of here, the still-intact **monumental gateway** now serves as an entrance to the modern resort. To the left of the gateway is an excavated monument to Vespasian, built in 74 AD, which takes the form of a fountain with a couple of water basins in front. Inside the gate is the entrance to Side's 20,000-seat **theater** (daily 9am–noon and 1–5pm; $2.50), the largest in Pamphylia, and different from those at Perge and Aspendos in that it was built as a free-standing structure supported by massive arched vaults, and not into a hillside. The effect is stunning, and it's possible to climb to the very top of the auditorium, where you get a good sense of both the scale of the theater and the layout of ancient Side. It may seem a bit decrepit after the one at Aspendos, but restoration work is underway, and already part of the stage-building has been reconstructed. The two-meter wall surrounding the orchestra was built to protect the audience from the wild animals used during gladiatorial shows. In the back of the theater, reached via the agora, is a row of ancient **toilets,** complete with niches for statues facing the cubicles.

Other Ruins

From the gateway, modern Side's main street leads down to the old harbor and the **temples of Apollo and Athena,** both under restoration right now, but the location makes a good spot to watch the sun going down. In the days when Side was an important port, the area to the immediate west of here was a harbor. Even in Roman times it was necesary to dredge continuously to clear silt deposited by the Manavgat River, and after the city went into decline the harbor soon clogged up. Elsewhere, you'll find a number of other buildings, including the city **agora** on the eastern side of the peninsula just a stone's throw from the sea, and, a little inland from here, a ruined **Byzantine basilica,** gradually disappearing under the shifting sand of the dunes.

Eating, Drinking . . . and the Beaches

There's no shortage of places to **eat and drink** in Side, with what seem like hundreds of establishments up, down, and around the main street catering to all tastes—particularly German ones. Try the *Toros Restaurant* down near the harbor, where you can sample reasonably priced fish dishes on the terrace, or the *Aphrodite*, which has excellent swordfish. Also worth checking out is the *Sarapsi Han Restaurant*, where you should be able to get a decent meal and come away with change from $4. Turn left at the end of the main street and head west along the beach and you'll find a number of fish restaurants, including the *Apollonik*, which is small, cosy, and well-priced, with a good bar. There are also a few **discos** in town, all of which conform more or less to the usual resort stereotype. Perhaps the least awful is the *Nimfeon*, on the way out to the eastern beach.

Given Side's fine sandy **beaches**, it's not surprising the town has developed so rapidly. To the **west** the beach stretches for about 10km, lined by expensive hotels and beach clubs, and various outfits renting windsurfing boards for about $2.50 per hour; the crowds, however, can be heavy during the high season. To the **east** the sand stretches all the way to Alanya, over 60km away, although there's a little less in the way of facilities in this direction—the consolation is fewer crowds, especially if you're prepared to walk a ways.

On to Alanya: Manavgat, Alarahan, and Beyond

Fifteen minutes east of Side by dolmuş, the small town of **MANAVGAT** is not especially alluring, but it could be used as an inexpensive base for exploring the surrounding coast—the hotels here are fewer but cheaper than those in Side. The town center is five minutes' walk west of the otogar (past the PTT and over a bridge), and contains a few **restaurants** and a couple of budget **hotels**—the eccentric *Hotel Konya*, Pansiyon Lise Caddesi 11 (☎3211/3420), on the east bank of the river, which charges $4 per person, and the similarly priced but dirtier *Hotel Şelâle*, a few doors farther down the same street. There are also a couple of local firms offering river trips to the much-touted nearby Şelâle or Manavgat Waterfalls, although these are somewhat overrated.

Alanya-bound dolmuşes depart from Manavgat more frequently than from Side, although it's usually no problem to catch a ride with a bus from the Side turnoff. The road hugs the Mediterranean and there are good beaches all the way, which explains why small resorts are springing up all along this stretch of the coast.

Just under 30km east of Manavgat, a rough road spears off north to **Alarahan**, a thirteenth-century Selçuk *kervansaray* built for the benefit of traders operating between the Selçuk city of Konya and the port of Alanya. The creation of Sultan Alâeddin Keykubad—who was also responsible for the castle at Alanya (see below)—it's particularly impressive, nestling in the tranquil river valley. Farther up the same road, ranged around a pyramidal hill, there are the ruins of an ancient **castle**, scarcely discernible against the stony backdrop but accessible by way of a tunnel fifteen minutes beyond the *kervansaray*. Returning to the main road and continuing east there's another Selçuk *kervansaray*, the **Şarapsa Hanı**—now being used as a disco.

Alanya

Until a little over ten years ago **ALANYA** was a sleepy coastal town with no more than a handful of flyblown hotels to its name. Now it's one of the Mediterranean coast's major resorts, a booming place and a popular one, but one that has fortunately managed to hold on to much of its original character, and there is none of the claustrophobic atmosphere of Side. These days it is, like Side, probably best appreciated in the off-season, although it's much less crowded, even in mid-summer. Most visitors come into town from the west, an approach that reveals Alanya at its best, the road passing through verdant banana plantations on the edge of town and suddenly revealing a rocky promontory, topped by a castle, rearing out of the Mediterranean.

Little is known about Alanya's early history, although it's thought that it was founded by Greek colonists, who named it Kalonoros or "Beautiful Mountain." Things were pretty quiet until the second century BC when Cilician pirates began using the town, known by now as Coracesium, as a base to terrorize the Pamphylian coast. Eventually the Romans decided to put an end to the activities of the pirates and sent in Pompey, who destroyed the pirate fleet in a sea battle off Alanya in 67 BC. In 44 BC Mark Antony gave the city to Cleopatra as a gift. Romantic as this might sound, there was a practical reason for his choice: the area around the city was an important timber-producing center, and Cleopatra needed its resources to build up her navy. Later, in 1221, the Byzantine city fell to Selçuk sultan Alâeddin Keykubad, who gave it its present name and made it his summer residence; it's from this period that most buildings of historical importance date.

The Alanya **area telephone code** is ☎ 323.

Arrival and Accommodation

Alanya's **otogar** is about a twenty-minute walk from the town center, but if you arrive by dolmuş you'll probably be able to get a ride all the way in. The **tourist information office** is at Çarşı Mahallesi, Kalearkası (Mon–Fri 9am–5:30pm; ☎11240), opposite the town museum.

As in Side, **accommodation** possibilities are endless, taking in the full price range, although sadly the best places tend to be block-booked by tour groups from May until September. It is possible, however, to pick up some off-season bargains. The *Karasu Immobilien* agency, Damlataş Caddesi 58 (☎15260), run by Ergün Karasu, might be a good first stop, offering everything from pansiyons to furnished apartments, with prices starting at $6 a double. Otherwise budget travelers should head for İskele Caddesi, where there are a few cheap places, first of which is the *Alanya Palas*, İskele Caddesi 6 (☎11016), which has doubles only from $6 (intermittent cold water only). Next door, the *Baba Hotel*, İskele Caddesi 8 (☎11032), is similar in price and standards. Farther along, the grubby *Yayla Palas*, İskele Caddesi 48 (☎11017), isn't really worth the $6 they charge for a small double, and you'd do better to try the *Şimşel Aile Pansiyon*, Damlataş Caddesi, a simple, clean, family-run place with rooms for a dollar or so less.

Up a notch in price, there are quite a few pansiyons off Atatürk Caddesi on the way into town from the otogar. In the center of town, you might try the *Günaydın Otel*, Kültür Caddesi 30 (☎11943), charging $10 for a double with bathroom including breakfast ($8 without). The *Rio Otel*, Damlataş Caddesi 54 (☎14202), has doubles from $16; all rooms have showers and the price includes breakfast, although the place is liable to fill up in summer. On the same street, the *Hanedan Apart Otel* ("You're home in Alanya") has self-contained apartments from $16 a day. The *Üstün Aile Pansiyonu*, Meteoroloji Yanı 4, has twin rooms at $10 and triples for around $12; all rooms are a good size and have showers, although this is another one that's likely to be full in summer. The *Otel Emel*, on Bostanıca Pınar Caddesi (☎12581,12869), has doubles for about $15 with breakfast.

There are couple of good **campgrounds** west of Alanya on the Side road: the *Alanya-Motorcamp*, about 25km out just before a large hotel complex, a newly built outfit with facilities including a restaurant and shops; and the *BP-Kervansaray Motorcamp*, a little closer, where you get roughly the same deal.

Old Alanya

Most of **old Alanya** lies on the great rocky promontory that juts out into the sea, dominating the modern town. Dolmuşes from the west drop you off near the PTT on Atatürk Caddesi. From here, walk toward the harbor on the east side of the promontory to the **Kızılkule**—"The Red Tower'"—a 35-meter-high defensive tower of red stone built by Alâeddin Keykubad in 1226. Today it houses a dull **ethnographic museum** (Tue–Sun 8am–noon & 1:30–5pm; 75¢), and has a roof terrace that overlooks the town's eastern harbor. Old wooden houses cling to the slopes above the tower, and you can follow the old coastal defensive wall along the water's edge to the **Tersane**, an Ottoman shipyard, consisting of five workshops linked by an arched roof. Beyond here is small defensive tower, the **Tophane**.

Alanya Castle

Reaching **Alanya Castle** isn't quite so easy. If you have the time and inclination you can walk it; set off early in the day before it gets too hot, or better still do it in the late afternoon and catch the sunset from the top. It's a long, winding climb and will take about an hour assuming you're in reasonably good shape—if you get tired, there are plenty of restaurants and little cafés to stop off at on the way up. Often these are little more than a table and an awning in someone's front yard, but there are good views all the way up. If you can't face the walk, there's an hourly bus from just outside the tourist office on the western side of the promontory.

The castle itself is a huge fortification system, with walls snaking right around the upper reaches of the promontory. A huge archway (bearing an inscription in Persian) leads into an area which demarcated the original limits of Alanya back in Selçuk times. In among the foliage off the road is an area known as **Ehmediye**, a small village with a few old Ottoman houses clustered around the dilapidated sixteenth-century **Süleymaniye Camii**, a *kervansaray*, and the **Aksebe Türbesi**, a distinctive thirteenth-century tomb.

At the end of the road is the **İç Kale**, or Inner Fortress (daily 9am–5:30pm; $2), built by Keykubad in 1226. Inside the gates local women sell lace, and the smell of lavender hangs heavily on the air. The fortress is pretty much intact, with the shell of a **Byzantine church**, decorated with fading frescoes, in the center. Look out for the **cisterns** that supplied the fortress with water and to which it owed much of its apparent impregnability. In the northwestern corner of the fortress, a platform gives fine views of the western beaches and the mountains, although its original function was as a springboard from which prisoners were thrown to their deaths on the rocks below. These days tour guides assure their wards that it's customary to throw a rock from the platform, attempting to hit the sea rather than the rock below—an impossible feat supposed to have been set for prisoners as a chance to save their necks.

The Modern Town

Back down at sea level, apart from the hotels and restaurants, **modern Alanya** has very little to offer. On the western side of the promontory, the **Alanya Museum** (Tue–Sun 8:30am–noon & 1:30–5pm; 75¢) is filled with local archaeo-logical finds and ethnological ephemera, but the best thing about it is probably the garden, a former Ottoman graveyard in which you can take refuge from the

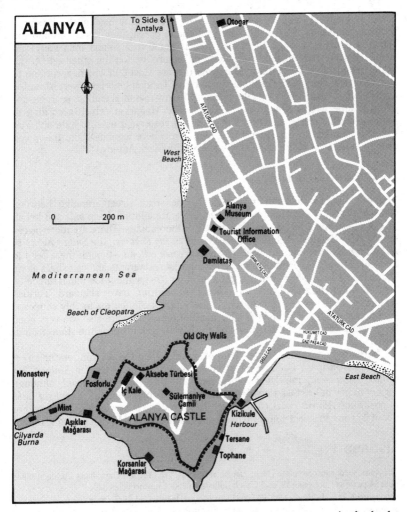

ALANYA

To Side & Antalya

Otogar

West Beach

ATATÜRK CAD

Alanya Museum

Tourist Information Office

Damlataş

Mediterranean Sea

Beach of Cleopatra

Old City Walls

HUKUMET CAD

GAZI PAŞA CAD

ISKELE CAD

ATATÜRK CAD

East Beach

Monastery

Fosforlu

Akşebe Türbesi

İç Kale

Süleymaniye Camii

Mint

Aşıklar Mağarası

ALANYA CASTLE

Kızılkule

Harbour

Tersane

Cilyarda Burna

Korsanlar Mağarası

Tophane

0   200 m

heat in summer. Don't be taken in by signs pointing to a museum in the backstreets away from the shore. They in fact lead to a house Atatürk stayed in for exactly three days in 1935 that is, frankly, not very interesting.

The Caves

Not far from the museum is the **Damlataş**, or "Cave of Dripping Stones" (daily 10am–sunset; 25¢), a stalactite- and stalagmite-filled underground cavern with a moist, warm atmosphere said to benefit asthma sufferers. It's accessible from behind the *Dalmataş Restaurant*. There are other caves, dotted around the waterline at the base of the promontory, and various local nautical entrepreneurs offer trips around them, charging about $10 per boatload and happily cramming on board as many passengers as possible. The first stop is usually the **Fosforlu** (Phosphorus Cave), where the water shimmers green; then it's on around the **Cilyarda Burnu**, a long spit of land that is home to a ruined monastery and former mint. It's not actually possible to go ashore, but on the other side of the skinny peninsula is the **Aşıklar Mağarası** (Lovers' Cave), in which, according to a bizarre local story, a German woman and her Turkish boyfriend were stranded for three months in 1965 while the police and army mounted endless searches for them. A little farther around is the **Korsanlar Mağarası**, which according to more believable stories is where the pirates of yesteryear used to hide out. You will also be taken to the **Beach of Cleopatra**, where legends claim the queen used to descend to bathe while staying here with Mark Antony.

Eating and Drinking

You won't starve to death in Alanya. In the small streets running between Gazipaşa Caddesi and Hükümet Caddesi there are a lot of cheap *pide* and kebab places where you'll be able to fill up for $2 or thereabouts. There are more places on Müftüler Caddesi, including the excellent *Saray Lokantsi*, the *Sultan Kebap ve Lahmacun Salonu*, and the *Tuna Kebap ve Yemek Salonu*—though these tend to be alcohol-free. There are plenty of cheap tourist restaurants and café/bars along Damlataş Caddesi where you can get a meal for $2–3 without too much difficulty. The *Toros Restaurant* and the *Orient Restaurant* have standard Turkish restaurant fare. Recommended, too, is the *Vitamin Station* for freshly squeezed fruit juices, milkshakes, and passable hamburgers. There are also two very good ice-cream parlors, the *Mavi Koşe* and the *Çamlıca*, both near the *Alanya Palas Hotel*.

There are better, more expensive restaurants along the seafront on the street parallel to Gazipaşa Caddesi, most of them serving fish—try the *Malperi MS Sultan Restaurant*, the *Yöret Restaurant*, and the *Janus Restaurant*, although expect to pay at least $4 a head. Another decent fish place is the *Moonlight Cafe*, opposite the *Alanya Palas Oteli*, which has a roof terrace with a good view. For about $4 you can select your own live trout from a tank and have it grilled to order.

Listings

Bicycles and motorcycles These can be rented at *"No. 39,"* on Damlataş Caddesi; bikes cost $4 per day, mopeds $12, and Czech-built Jawa 250cc motorcycles $20.

Car rental *Avis* Hükümet Cad 135 (☎3513); *Budget*, İskele Cad 68/5 (☎4400).

Excursions Try *Panel*, Kalearkası Cad 37 (☎4151) for trips to Cappadocia, Pamukkale, and the Pamphylian cities and boat excursions around Alanya.

Ferries There is a weekly Friday evening sailing from Alanya to Girne in northern Cyprus between June and September. One-way tickets cost $20; no cars taken. There is no *TML* agent in Alanya; ask at the tourist office for details.

Market For provisions, there is a small produce market on Gazipaşa Caddesi.

PTT You can't miss the main post office, in the center of town on Atatürk Caddesi. It keeps the usual small-town hours.

Shopping There is touristy silverware and carpets on sale in İskele Caddesi, and more carpets on the side streets between Gazipaşa Caddesi and Hükümet Caddesi.

Windsurfing boards $6 a day from various outlets along the western beach; you can also go water-skiing and parasailing for about $10 a pop.

ALANYA TO ADANA

The region between Alanya and Adana is ancient **Cilicia**, settled by refugees from Troy at the same time as Pamphylia farther west, although due to its physical remoteness it was never as well developed, and, despite a couple of significant centers, much of the region seems to have been wild and lawless. In ancient times it was divided between *Cilicia Tracheia* (Rough Cilicia)—from Alanya to the western edge of the Çukurova—and *Cilicia Campestris* (Smooth Cilicia), comprising the dull flatlands of the Ceyhan delta.

Rough Cilicia, with its rugged, densely wooded coastline, was a haven for pirates, whose increasingly outrageous exploits finally spurred the Romans into absorbing Cilicia into the empire in the first century BC. Today, it still retains a wild appearance, and travel through it involves some frighteningly daring bus rides along winding, mountain roads that hug the craggy coastline and skirt the rocky coves that once served as pirate hangouts. All this is to the good if you're trying to escape the crowds farther west, since far fewer people make it along here. There are some decent stretches of beach around **Anamur**, overlooked by an Armenian settlement and a partially excavated Greek settlement; at **Kızkalesi**, there are more good beaches and weird ruins—while in the mountains above **Silifke**—the next major town—the abandoned city of **Uzuncaburç** is perhaps the most extensive of the coast's ancient sites, although there are numerous more, most of them untended, between here and **Mersin**. This marks the beginning of what was Smooth Cilicia, and the end of the area's real interest, touristwise—there are ferries to Northern Cyprus but little else to stop for. Similarly, **Tarsus**, a little farther on, has little to betray its former historical importance these days; and **Adana**, Turkey's fourth-largest city, has, despite a long and venerable history, few remains of any era. Indeed, the time most travelers spend here waiting between bus connections is normally more than enough to exhaust the city's possibilities.

Alanya to Silifke

The first significant settlement after Alanya is **GAZİPAŞA**, about 50km to the east—nothing special, but it offers some reasonable beaches that are slightly less populated than those at Alanya. Beyond here the road cuts through the mountains, traversing occasional valleys planted with bananas, but rarely losing sight of the sea. On the way you'll pass the occasional little wayside restaurant and campground—at **ŞEHIR** for example—and sheltered but difficult-to-reach sandy bays, which even at the height of summer are guaranteed to be almost empty.

Anamur, İskele, and Around

Apart from the otogar there's little of interest in **ANAMUR**, although its small harbor **İSKELE** about 5km away has a few decent hotels and restaurants. It's accessible by dolmuş from the center of Anamur, and, although now picking up as a resort, is still quiet compared to Alanya.

There are quite a few reasonable **hotels** in İskele, including the *Eser Pension* (☎2322) on the beach, which has a pretty garden and terrace and double rooms starting at about $8, and the similarly priced *Yakomos Pension* just off the beach. There are **camping** facilities just west of İskele at the *Yalı Motorkamp*, where you can also rent small bungalows for $8–12, although it gets full in the summer. There are also a few very basic campgrounds in İskele itself where you'll pay less than $2 per night for all facilities.

Anemurium

A few kilometers southwest of modern Anamur is **Anemurium**, a partially exca-vated Greek settlement, on the eastern side of a peninsula formed where the Taurus Mountains jut out into the sea. An access road leads down to the site from the main road (look out for the yellow sign). Anemurium was at its peak during the third century AD, and most of what remains dates from this period. As you approach the site you'll see two parallel aqueducts running north–south along the hillside to the left. Below these a sun-baked **necropolis** contains numerous free-standing tombs whose cool interiors harbor murals of mythological scenes on the walls. The most notable of these lies near the lower aqueduct, its vault painted with scenes representing the four seasons, while on one of the walls Hermes is shown in his role as Psychopompos, conductor of the souls of the dead. To the right of the road are the hollow ruins of three **Byzantine churches**, set starkly against the blue backdrop of the Mediterranean.

At the point where the access road peters out you'll see the crumbling remains of a **bath complex** and a desolate **palestra**, or parade ground. Southwest of here is a ruined but still identifiable **theater** set into the hillside of the peninsula. Above the theater on the slope, between the lower and upper aqueduct, are the remains of a number of houses, some of which have intact vaulted roofs. East of the theater is the shell of a building containing six rows of seating, thought to have been either a **council chamber** or **concert hall** (possibly both). Beyond here some steps lead down to a courtyard, the center of a small workshop complex. Returning toward the theater and heading south, you'll come across another **baths complex**, a two-story vaulted structure that is probably the best-preserved building in Anemurium, showing easily discernible traces of decora-tion and tile-work on the interior walls.

With time, you might want to clamber up the scrubby slopes of the peninsula to what was once Anemurium **acropolis**. There isn't a lot to see here but the promontory is Turkey's southernmost point, and on a clear day gives views of the mountains of Cyprus 80km to the south.

Mamure Kalesi

In the opposite direction from Anamur, a couple of kilometers east of İskele, is **Mamure Kalesi** (daily 9am–5pm; $1), a forbidding castle built by the rulers of the Cilician kingdom of Armenia on the site of a Byzantine fort. It was later occu-pied by Crusaders, who had established a short-lived kingdom in Cyprus and used Mamure Kalesi as a kind of bridgehead in Asia. Used by successive rulers of the area to protect the coastal strip, it was most recently garrisoned by the Ottomans, who reinforced it after the British occupied Cyprus in 1878 and main-tained a strong presence here during World War I. Constructed directly above the sea, its stark facade of crenellated outer walls and watchtowers are certainly impressive, and they hide an interior of languorously decaying buildings that is quietly atmospheric—worth an hour's idling if you've got time on your hands.

Opposite is a small, family-run fish **restaurant**, and, a few kilometers east, a good forested **campground**, the *Pullu Mocamp*.

Aydıncık, Boğsak, Taşucu—and On to Cyprus

Beyond Anamur the road continues on its twisting mountainous course, passing **Softa Kalesi**—another ruined castle, again Armenian—about 10km east of Iskele. Another fifty winding kilometers beyond, the settlement of **AYDINCIK** stretches along the road for a few kilometers, offering a few cheap pansiyons, a motel, and one or two stretches of sandy beach. You could stop here for a look at relatively tourist-free Turkey, but bear in mind that people here are not as used to visitors as their neighbors to the west, and topless bathing is not advisable here. At **BOĞSAK**, about 50km farther east, there are some good beaches with camping facilities, a few small motels, and a big beach club complex, as well as another medieval **fortress** built by the Knights of Saint John. Moving on, there are a couple of quiet bays with sandy beaches, but most people push straight on to **TAŞUCU**, where there are frequent **ferry** and **hydrofoil services to Cyprus**. If you want to spend the night, you could try the *Işık Otel* on Atatürk Caddesi (☎7593/1026) near the harbor, which charges $10 a double.

On to Cyprus: Ferries and Hydrofoils

Hydrofoils depart regularly from Taşucu to **GİRNE** (Kyrenia) in the "Turkish Republic of Northern Cyprus" (TRNC) on Monday, Wednesday, and Friday at 1pm. **Fare details and departure times** are subject to change, but a one-way trip currently costs $21 per person (students $15, children under 12 $12.50), and a round-trip costs $37 per person. On Tuesday, Thursday, and Saturday at 11:30pm a **ferry** makes the same trip at a slightly more leisurely pace. Going by ferry, one-way tickets cost $16 (student $12.50, cars $12.50–$20, while round-trip tickets cost double the one-way fare. Tickets can be obtained from the *Kibris Ekspres* office on the Taşucu harbor or booked at Silifke otogar (see below); you can also buy them in Mersin. American and EC citizens don't need **visas** to visit the TRNC, although British citizens probably will—check the latest situation with the harbor authorities. Bear in mind that it's not possible to enter southern (ie, Greek-speaking) Cyprus from the TRNC.

Silifke

About 10km east of Taşucu, **SİLİFKE** is the ancient Seleucia, founded by Seleucus, one of Alexander the Great's generals, in the third century BC. Nowadays it's a quiet, fairly undistinguished town, relatively untouched by tourists—who, if they come here at all, do so only on their way to the ruins at Uzuncaburç and points north. You may want to do the same, although the very ordinariness of Silifke has its own appeal, especially after the crowds of the resorts. Many of the local men wear traditional baggy trousers and the streets are full of three-wheeled motorcycles, which appear to be the main mode of transportation in these parts. You may also notice that the food here starts getting spicier, hinting at hotter things to come in the east of the country.

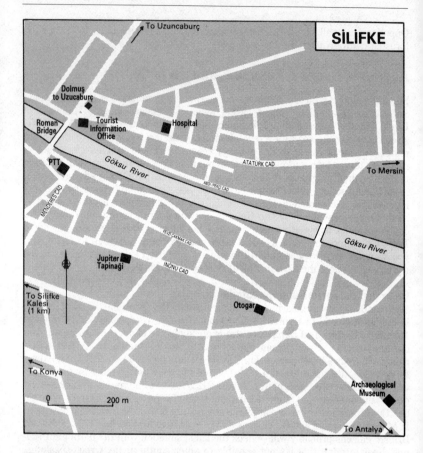

The Town

The center of town is Menderes Caddesi, about fifteen minutes' walk from the **otogar** along İnönü Caddesi. There is, however, very little to see. Signs lead up to **Silifke Kalesi**, a Byzantine castle that dominates the local skyline but looks a lot less spectacular close-up. At the top there's a café and a great view of the town. On the way up you'll pass an old **cistern**—the so-called *tekir ambarı*, or "striped depot"—which once kept Byzantine Silifke supplied with water.

Other sights include the second-century AD **Jupiter Tapınağı** (Temple of Jupiter) on İnönü Caddesi, which is little more than a pile of stones and a few pillars. On the Antalya Asfaltı on the way out of town there's an **archaeological museum** (daily 8:30am–noon & 1–5:30pm; $1), containing some locally unearthed odds and ends. Incidentally, it was near Silifke that **Frederick Barbarossa**, the Holy Roman Emperor, met his end—he drowned while fording the Göksu River about 7km north of town en route to Palestine with the Third Crusade. Today a plaque marks the spot.

Practical Details

Silifke's **tourist information office** is at Atatürk Caddesi 1/2 (Mon–Fri 8:30am–5:30pm; ☎7591/1151), reached by way of the Roman bridge spanning the Göksu River. **Hotel** possibilities are limited. The best bet is the clean, albeit spartan, *Hotel Akdeniz*, Menderes Caddesi 96 (☎7591/1285), which has double rooms starting at $6. Nearby is the slightly classier *Hotel Eren*, behind the Ziraat Bank (☎7591/1289), just north of İnönü Caddesi, with doubles starting at $6. As a last resort you could try the fairly unpleasant *Taylan Otel*, a few doors down from the *Akdeniz*, charging just $3 for two people.

There are lots of basic places to **eat and drink** but after dark most close, leaving you with only a few options. Best bet is the *Piknik Restaurant*, İnönü Caddesi 17, which is a lot cheaper than it looks, but make sure you agree on a price beforehand. Further down the scale, on the second street on the right after the *Akdeniz* hotel, is the *Dilek Restaurant*.

Inland: the Road to Uzuncaburç

Dolmuşes bound for the ancient city of Uzuncaburç depart from Silifke otogar, and from near the tourist office. If there aren't any dolmuşes around, a taxi costs about $6 one-way for the 45-minute trip.

The ride to Uzuncaburç is spectacular, taking you through a jagged gorge and a couple of villages that time seems to have forgotten. If you have your own transportation, or don't mind doing a little hitching, you might care to stop off in the village of **DEMİRCİLER**, known in ancient times as Imbriogon, where there are six **Greco-Roman tombs**, spread out on either side of the road among the olive trees. Visiting these is a rather strange experience: looking more like long-vacated houses than tombs, they are unattended and unrestored, and it's hard to believe that they have survived the depredations of time and stone plunderers. The first is a simple one-story affair just to the right of the road; a little farther along there's a larger two-story structure. To the west of the road is the **Çifte Anıt Mezarları**, or Double Mausoleum, consisting of two linked tombs, the right-hand one of which contains three sarcophagi with various decorative features—one with a relief of a lion, another featuring a man's head, the nude figures of two women, and the heads of two women.

Uzuncaburç

From Demirciler the road continues up toward the ruins of **UZUNCABURÇ**, an originally Hittite settlement that was known to the Greeks as Olba and to the Romans as Diocaesarea. A small modern settlement has grown up in haphazard fashion around the ruins, but few concessions have been made to tourism; in fact the village wasn't even connected to the electricity grid until a couple of years ago. These days it's famous for handmade rugs known as *çul*, and leather bags, examples of which you may find for sale at makeshift stalls. Local culinary specialties include *kenger kahvesi* (coffee made from acanthus) and *pekmez* (grape molasses). The *Burç Restaurant* serves simple meals and soft drinks, but there isn't anywhere to stay.

The Site

The **site** of Uzuncaburç (daily 8am–5pm; $1) lacks the size and scale of Perge and Aspendos, but is atmospheric in its own way, if only because of the relatively neglected state of most of it. Although the area was first settled by Hittite peoples, they left little in the way of souvenirs, and the most impressive surviving ruins date from Hellenistic times. It covers quite a large area and is intertwined with a modern settlement, but its core, including the centerpiece temple of Zeus Olbios, is relatively small.

The usual drop-off point is next to an overgrown Roman **theater**. From here, pass through an enormous five-columned **monumental gateway**, beyond which a colonnaded street, once the city's main thoroughfare, runs east to west: keep your eyes peeled for what look like small stone shelves on the columns, which once supported statues and busts. On the northern side of the street is a **nymphaeum**, now dried up, which once formed part of the city's water-supply system. This was part of a large network of pipes and tunnels, built by the Romans nearly two thousand years ago, that still supplies water to the modern village and others around.

To the south, the **temple of Zeus Olbios** is an early example of the Corinthian order, erected during the third century BC by Seleucus I, though with only the columns remaining intact. At the western end of the colonnaded street is the **temple of Tyche**, dedicated to the goddess of good fortune, reckoned to date from the second half of the first century AD. Five marble columns still stand, joined by an architrave bearing an inscription stating that the temple was the gift of a certain Oppius and his wife Kyria. From here a right turn leads to a large three-arched **city gate**, which according to an inscription dates from the fifth century AD.

Other Ruins

The **rest of Uzuncaburç's attractions** lie to the north of these ruins. Walk from the drop-off point as far as the *Burç Restaurant*, and turn right for the **High Tower**, a 22-meter-high, five-story Hellenistic structure that once formed part of the city wall. An ancient Greek inscription gives details of repair work carried out during the third century AD. It is believed that in addition to playing a defensive role this tower was also part of an ancient signaling network, whereby messages were relayed by flashing sunlight off polished shields. Today it looks in danger of imminent collapse.

Just outside the modern village, past the *Burç Restaurant* as far as the Atatürk bust, following the signs for the "Antık Mezar," is a **necropolis** used by Greek, Roman, and Byzantine inhabitants of the area. It has three basic types of resting place—sarcophagi, graves carved into the rock, and cave tombs housing whole families. Most of these are clearly visible, and it's even possible to enter some of the cave tombs, although they've long since been cleaned out by grave robbers.

About 1km south of Uzuncaburç, 500m west of the main road, is another **mausoleum**, this one with an eye-catching pyramid-shaped roof dating from Hellenistic times. Inside, the tombs were hidden under the floor. Another possible excursion from Uzuncaburç is to the ruins of **Ura**, a similar but less impressive ancient city 5km to the east, where the remains of some old houses, a Byzantine church, and a small fortress can be seen.

East from Silifke

About 7km east of Silifke, **KARADEDELİ**, a small village settled by former tent-dwelling Turcoman nomads, makes a good starting point for a possible walking tour of some ruined sites to the north. A series of pathways connects these sites and it's possible to rent a donkey in the village if you want to make the trek (inquire at the village café). The sites themselves are hardly breathtaking, but make an interesting enough target for some gentle hill walking. First stop, 2km north of the village, is **YALAK TAŞ**, where there are some Greco-Roman foundations, the ruins of a cistern, and what's thought to be an olive-oil factory. Another 2km north brings you to **DİLEK TAŞ** and a few more ancient cisterns. The largest ruins are at **KARAKABAKLI**, where there are a few Greco-Roman houses, some of them two stories high.

About 5km east of Karadedeli is **SUSANOĞLU**, the site of the ancient port of Corasium, and today a small resort with a good beach. A number of Roman remains are scattered through a valley running north from the beach, which is actually a silted-up Roman harbor. About half a kilometer east of the village itself is **Yapraklı Esik** (the Cove with Leaves), a quiet inlet whose waters are claimed to have curative properties.

Inland from here—reachable if you have your own transportation—the ruins of another ancient settlement signal a two-kilometer diversion to the east down a dirt road to the **Mezgit Kalesi**, or Mausoleum of the Fearless Satrap. This is similar in appearance to those at Demiricil, but a carving of a phallus adorns the exterior. The phallus represents Priapus, the well-endowed son of Dionysus and Aphrodite, and is supposed to signify that the occupant of the tomb was courageous and valiant, as well as being hung like a horse.

Heading east along the coast from Susanoğlu you'll find a number of bays with beaches, including, just past the village of **ATAKENT**, a swanky-looking *Club Scandinavia/Ertur* development. You'll probably neither want nor be able to afford to stay here, but the beach is worth checking out.

Narlıkuyu

A little way beyond Atakent, **NARLIKUYU** fringes a good bay with restaurants and a couple of pansiyons. There's a small parking lot in the center of the village, and next to it are the remains of a Roman bathhouse, known after its founder as the **Bath of Poimenius**. Inside, a mosaic depicts the well-rounded nude forms of the three graces, the daughters of Zeus. The bath was fed by an ancient Roman spring which supplied a celebrated fountain, and the waters were supposed to confer wisdom on those who drank from them. A kilometer or so down the road is **AKKUM**, again with a few pansiyons and a good stretch of beach. One pansiyon worth checking out is the *Kökler*, not far from the beach, which is clean and friendly and has an English-speaking proprieter; singles cost $8, doubles $15.

The Caves of Heaven and Hell

From Narlıkuyu a narrow paved road winds 5km north into the hills through groves of olive trees to **Cennet ve Cehennem**, or the Caves of Heaven and Hell—some of the most impressive of the many limestone caverns scattered along this coast. At the end of the road there's a parking lot, and a cluster of tea shops and souvenir stands.

There are in fact three caves, and local children are usually quick to offer their services as guides, although this isn't really necessary. Immediately adjacent to the parking area is the largest and most impressive cave, **Cennet Deresi** (Cave of Heaven)—actually a seventy-meter-deep gorge, formed when the roof of an underground canyon collapsed. It is entered via 452 steps cut into the rock on the eastern side of the ravine. When you reach the bottom, head south toward the entrance to the **Cave of Typhon**, a bona fide cave of some depth, at the end of which runs a stream of drinkable water from the same source as the spring water in Narlıkuyu.

As you go farther in, it gets difficult to breathe and it's best not to hang around too long; this fact was recorded by Strabo, the ancient geographer, leading some historians to believe that this cave may have been one of the mythical entrances to Hades. According to the legend, Typhon, after whom the cave is named, was an immense fire-breathing lizard, the father of Cerberus—the three-headed dog who guarded the entrance to Hades on the banks of the river Styx, allowing only the souls of the dead to enter and refusing to let them out. At the entrance to the cave is the **Chapel of the Virgin Mary**, a well-preserved Byzantine church containing a few frescoes.

About a hundred meters north of "Heaven," the **Cehennem Deresi** (Cave of Hell) is similar in formation to the Heaven cave but impossible to enter, as its sides are practically vertical and there's no clear way down. According to legend Zeus imprisoned Typhon here, before banishing him forever to the depths of the earth. This gorge is supposed to be another of the entrances to Hades, and local people used to tie rags to surrounding trees to placate evil spirits.

About 300m west of "Heaven" is the **Dilek Mağarası** (Wishing Cave), whose opening has been specially widened and a spiral staircase provided for ease of access. Down below, solid pathways connect a number of subterranean halls, with a total length of about 200m. The main chamber is filled with stalactites and stalagmites, and the air down below is supposed to be beneficial for asthma sufferers.

Kızkalesi and Around

A few kilometers east of Narlikuyu, **KIZKALESİ** (Maiden's Castle), is the biggest resort along this stretch of coast. It has scores of hotels, pansiyons, and restaurants, and, if you can find somewhere to stay—which isn't easy in high season—it makes a very relaxing place to spend a few days taking in the local sights and the beach.

Kızkalesi, known as Corycus in ancient times, was said by Herodotus to have been founded by a Cypriot prince called Korykos during the fourth century BC. Like most places along this coast it changed hands frequently until the arrival of the Romans in 72 BC, after which it prospered, becoming one of the most important ports along the coast. Corycus continued to thrive during the Byzantine era despite occasional Arab attacks, when the town's defenses were strengthened by the installation of two castles—constructed during the twelfth and thirteenth centuries—before falling to the Ottomans in 1482.

The Castles

Kızkalesi's most compelling feature is the thirteenth-century **sea castle** (open dawn–dusk) on an island about 200m offshore, where the legend of the so-called Maiden's Castle—examples of which are all over Turkey—is said to have originated. Supposedly, one of the Armenian kings who ruled the region in medieval times had a beautiful daughter. After it was prophesied that she would die as the result of a poisonous snakebite, the king had the castle built and moved the girl out to it, imagining that she would be safe there. One day one of the king's advisers sent a basket of fruit out to the island for her, out of which slid a snake that killed the girl. According to local stories, the snake still lives on the island, and the only people who venture out to it are tourists, for whose benefit various cheap boat services operate. The unadorned walls and sturdy towers still stand, but apart from masonry fragments and weeds there's little to see within.

Opposite the sea castle, the overgrown ruins of the mighty **land castle** at the eastern end of the beach (75¢ if there's anyone around to collect it) are easily explored, and its battlements make a good place for some sunset-watching if you can stand the mosquitoes. Look out for the main gate, constructed from ancient stones bearing various Greek inscriptions. The western gate was originally a Roman structure, built during the third century AD and later incorporated into the castle.

Practical Details

Every other building in Kızkalesi is either a **hotel or pansiyon**, and most of them are very good value. The *Mavi Pension*, 2 Plaj Yolu Üstü (☎7584/1453), run by the Keskinkaya family, offers excellent clean rooms only a stone's throw from the beach for $10 and up. More expensively, the *Motel Set*, some way back from the town beach (☎7584/1314), has a swimming pool and rooms with attached baths starting at $16. It's owned by the same people who run the best local **campground**, the *Kızkalesi Aile Plaja* (about $2.40 for a car, tent, and two people), in the shadow of the land castle. There's a restaurant here and some basic rooms that go for about $6. **Eating and drinking** possibilities are endless, and mostly fairly reasonable. The campground restaurant is good and has marvelous sea views.

Around Kızkalesi

The area **around Kızkalesi** offers a few points of interest, closest of which, immediately northeast of the village across the main road from the land castle, is a **necropolis**, dating from the fourth century AD and containing hundreds of tombs and sarcophagi, some of them beautifully carved. Many of the epitaphs give the jobs of the occupants—weavers, cobblers, goldsmiths, vintners, olive-oil manufacturers, ship owners, and midwives—who all had their last resting places here. Also scattered around this area are the remains of a number of Byzantine churches and cisterns.

Perhaps more intriguing is the series of **rock reliefs** in a valley about 6km north of the village (the turnoff is near the PTT), marked by a sign bearing the legend "People's Reliefs." Follow the path indicated from here for about a kilometer until it starts to dip down into a valley, where steps cut into the rock lead down to a kind of platform from which you can view a series of Roman men, women, and children carved into niches in the wall. There are thirteen figures in all, depicted reclining holding wine cups and standing. It's not clear who they are or why they were constructed, and the fragmentary inscriptions below most of them offer few clues.

East from Kızkalesi

East of Kızkalesi, more ruins are visible on either side of the road as far as the village of **AYAŞ**, 3km away, the site of the ancient settlement of Elaiussa Sebaste, which during the time of Augustus was important enough to coin its own money. Passing through the village, the remains of an ancient canal, a sixteenth-century Selçuk tomb, and some columns marking the site of a Roman temple are visible north of the road, although most of it is unrestored and largely unrecognizable. Beyond the remains, an aqueduct leads to a massive underground cistern, close to which you'll find a ruined theater. Scattered randomly around the area are numerous tombs, many of them richly decorated with reliefs.

Kanlıdivane

About 7km east of Kızkalesi, an indicated turnoff leads 3km north to the village of **KANLIDİVANE**, literally "Place of Blood," due to its being the site of the ancient city of Kanytelis, where locals used to believe condemned criminals were executed by being thrown into a huge chasm and devoured by wild animals. You can visit the site, which contains some significant Roman and Byzantine remains. A parking lot and ticket-sellers' hut mark the entrance (daily 8am–5:30pm; $1).

The **chasm** in question is certainly large and frightening enough to have given rise to the legends—it's 90m long by 70m wide and 60m deep, and forms the core of the ancient city. Visitors can descend into it by way of a partly eroded staircase. On the floor of the chasm there are a number of carvings in niches, representing human figures and topped by Greek inscriptions. On its southwestern edge, near the parking lot, is a seventeen-meter-high tower dating from Hellenistic times, while nearby are a number of Byzantine basilicas in various states of collapse. There's another big cluster of tombs northeast of the chasm with numerous sarcophagi and tombs.

Back on the main road, heading east toward Mersin, you can see the remains of a number of aqueducts that brought water to the various coastal and inland settlements during Roman times. The next major stop is **ERDEMLİ**—an unexciting town on the whole, with a rudimentary **campground** called *Erdemli Çamlağı*.

Viranşehir

Twenty-three kilometers east of Erdemli lies **VİRANŞEHİR**, site of the ancient Pompeiopolis, an important Roman city whose remains are signaled by a yellow sign directing you down a side road toward the sea. From the road, the first signs of previous occupation are a number of ancient canals and aqueducts on the left-hand side. About 1.5km from the main road, a second-century AD Roman **colonnaded street**, with about 40 of its 200 columns remaining, leads to the ruined ancient **harbor** where two walls project into the sea.

Viranşehir is also a popular spot with people from Mersin, who come here to swim and picnic on the beach and stay in the town's few cheap pansiyons. Whether it's worth joining them or not is debatable: the beach is drab and the proximity of Mersin casts some doubt on the cleanliness of the water.

Mersin

Turkey's largest Mediterranean port, **MERSIN** is the first of the three large cities that gird the Ceyhan delta, a modern harbor city that—aside from its regular ferry connections to Cyprus—is almost entirely without interest. Though inhabited since Hittite times, it was, until the beginning of the twentieth century, little more than a squalid fishing hamlet. Over the past eighty years or so, rapid growth and industrialization, coupled with Mersin's role as an entrepôt for the

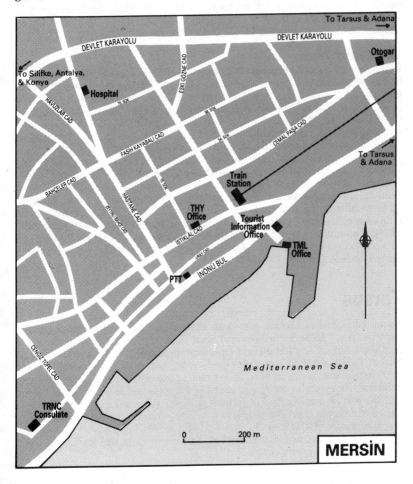

cotton-laden Çukurova hinterland, have turned it into a model—if soulless—example of contemporary Turkish urban planning.

Practical Details—and On to Cyprus

Mersin's orientation is slightly awkward; the **otogar** is some way out of town and you have to take a dolmuş from the road opposite (ask directions) to the center. The main **tourist information office** is by the harbor on İnönü Bulvari, Liman Giriş Sahası (Mon–Fri 9am–5:30pm; ☎741/16358), and there's also a smaller branch at the otogar. There are a lot of **hotels** in town and although there are a few near the otogar, the better ones tend to be located in the city center. Best of the budget possibilities is the *Emek Otel*, İstiklâl Caddesi 81, Sokak 5 (☎741/25370), situated in a dingy street but with clean rooms from $4 for one person, $6 for two. The *Büyük Otel*, Kuvayı Milliye Caddesi 40 (☎741/12606), is a big rambling warren—okay for a night but no longer, with singles for $2 and doubles for $4. Better by far is the *Hotel Ocak*, İstiklâl Caddesi 48 (☎741/15765), which has singles for $7 and doubles for $12 (with bathrooms).

On to Cyprus: Ferries

TML operates a **ferry service** to Magosa (Cyprus) on Monday, Wednesday, and Friday, departing at 10pm (journey time 10hr); on Fridays in summer the ferry goes on to Syria; at other times it returns the following day. **Tickets** are available from *Turkiye Denizlik İşletmeleri Deniz Yollari İşletmesi*, Liman Giriş Sahası on the second floor (☎741/12536). One-way fares range from $12.80 for a reclining seat to $25 for a luxury cabin; cars cost $15.40. Round-trip fares are double. There's a ten-percent reduction for students on production of an ISIC card.

Bear in mind that you can't get into southern Cyprus from the TRNC, and although American and EC citizens don't need **visas**, British citizens might (see "Taşucu," above), since as far as Turkey is concerned the TRNC is an independent state; this also means that on re-entering Turkey from it your permitted three months in the country begin again. Remember, though, that you will be refused admission to Greece with a TRNC stamp in your passport. In Mersin the **TRNC Consulate** is at Hamidiye Mahalle Karadeniz Apt (☎741/16228). You can also buy tickets for the **Taşucu–Kyrenia ferry** in Mersin from *Fergün Denizcilik Şinketi*, on İnönü Bulvarı (☎741/19960).

Tarsus

About 30km east of Mersin, across an uneventful plain dotted with occasional factories, lies **TARSUS**, birthplace of Saint Paul, and the city where Cleopatra met Mark Antony and turned him into "strumpet's fool." Saint Paul was born as Saul in Tarsus about 46 years after the meeting between Cleopatra and Antony. He returned after his conversion on the road to Damascus, fleeing persecution in Palestine. He seems to have been proud of his roots and is described as having told the Roman commandant of Jerusalem: "I am a Jew, a Tarsan from Cilicia, a citizen of no mean city." Nowadays, however, few reminders of the town's illustrious past remain. Architecturally the overriding impression is one of down-at-heel uniformity, and the majority of modern Tarsans work in the textile mills that process the locally grown cotton.

The Town

Near the bus drop-off point is the **Kancık Kapısı** (Gate of the Bitch), a Roman city gate also known as Cleopatra's Gate. Although the gate doesn't actually have any factual connection with the Egyptian queen, she is thought to have come ashore for her first meeting with Mark Antony somewhere in the vicinity (at that time Tarsus was linked to the sea by a lagoon, which has since silted up).

From Cleopatra's Gate, head north to a major junction and follow the signs to **St. Paul's Well** (left turn and then right), a walk of about ten minutes through the city's ramshackle—and in spring flower-bedecked—backstreets. There's little to see, just a hole in the ground covered by a removable lid; it's said to be on the site of Saint Paul's house, however, and therefore attracts a steady stream of visitors. Signs tell you not to tip the attendant, but after he's hauled a bucket of water up from the depths for you to drink from you might feel inclined to offer him a few lira. From the well, make your way back to the yellow sign and turn left. This leads to the old mosque, Roman baths, and a fairly mundane museum (Mon–Fri 8:30am–noon & 1–5:30pm; 50¢), which features an unexplained mummified lower arm of a woman and a few jewelry exhibits.

Practical Details

Buses on to Adana leave from near the old mosque. There's a dearth of **hotels** in Tarsus, and in any case there's no reason to stay. If you get stuck, in the town center there's the *İpekoğlu Oteli*, Adana Caddesi 90, with singles from $4 and doubles from $6, which is very basic but okay. The nearby *Hotel Zorbaz* (ask directions) is modern and clean, with singles from $8 and doubles from $9 (with bathroom).

Adana and Around

East of Tarsus sprawls **ADANA**, Turkey's fourth-largest city with 1.2 million inhabitants, a modern place which has grown rapidly since the 1918–20 French occupation. Today, as in the past, Adana owes much of its wealth to the fertile surrounding countryside of the Çukurova delta, with a textile industry that has grown up on the back of the local cotton fields. It is also an important gold-trading center.

Despite its contemporary metropolitan feel, Adana has historical roots going back to 1000BC. The arrival of the Greeks precipitated an on-off power struggle between the Greeks and the powerful Persian Empire to the east that was to last for a thousand years, ending only with the arrival of the Romans during the first century BC. Under the Romans the city became an important trading center, and afterward passed through various hands before falling to the Ottomans during the sixteenth century.

The City

Adana's most substantial ancient monument is the **Taş Köprü**, a sixteen-arched Roman bridge built by Hadrian to span the Seyhan River, just east of the city center. Not far from the bridge in the city center itself, the **Ulu Cami**, on Abidin

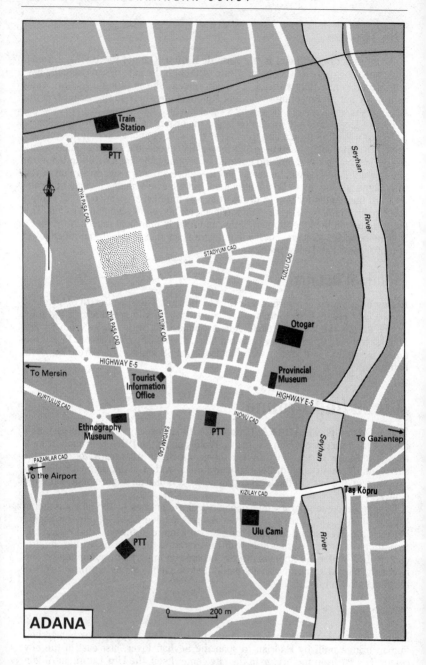

ADANA

Paşa Caddesi, was built in the Syrian style out of white and black marble in 1507, the sole legacy of Halil Bey, emir of the Ramazanoğlu Turks, who ruled Adana before the Ottoman conquest. Inside the mosque, Halil Bey's tomb has some fine tilework; it also contains some beautiful mosaics.

Another mosque, just off İnönü Caddesi, houses the **Ethnographic Museum** (Tues–Sun 9am–6pm; 75¢), full of carpets and weaponry, featuring a nomad tent and contents as an added attraction. Adana's other main museum is the **Adana Provincial Museum** (Tues–Sun 8:30am–12:30pm & 1:30–5:30pm; $2) on the road out to the otogar, an archaeological museum containing predominantly Hellenistic and Roman statuary.

Practical Details

Adana's **otogar** is located just east of Fuzuli Caddesi, about ten minutes' walk from İnönü Caddesi, and the city's train station is at the northern end of Ziya Paşa Bulvarı about twenty minutes north of the town center. The local **tourist information office** is at Atatürk Caddesi 13 (Mon–Fri 9:30am–6pm; ☎711/11323), but isn't all that much help.

There are a number of **hotels** near the otogar, but these tend to be noisy and you're better off heading into the town center. The *Mehtap Oteli*, İnönü Caddesi 123, Sokak 6 (☎711/121964), is cheap if somewhat sleazy, with doubles for $4. The *Öz Oteli*, İnönü Caddesi 34 (☎711/117844), has doubles for $6, but it gets really noisy. The *Otel Gümüş*, İnönü Caddesi 101 (☎711/114175), has singles for just over $3, doubles for a little over $6, but is pretty dreary.

On and around Saydam Caddesi and Özler Caddesi you'll find some better cheap options. The *Motel Mercan*, Ocak Meydanı 5, Melekgirmez Çarşısı (☎711/112603), is really good for the price, with doubles for around $6 with attached bath. A little cheaper is the *Ak Hotel*, Kücük Saat Cıvarı Özler Caddesi 43 (☎711/114208), with doubles from $5. The *Kristal Palas Oteli*, Özler Caddesi 19/1 (☎711/112335), has a grandiose entrance hall to compensate for its less impressive interior, and doubles for $4 (without bathrooms). The *Yeni Derya Oteli*, Saydam Caddesi Kışlık Ünal Sineması Bitişiği (☎711/112643), is a rock-bottom place with rooms for as little as $2 if you don't mind roughing it.

Back on İnönü Caddesi there are some mid-range options. At the comfortable *Otel Duygu*, İnönü Caddesi 14/1 (☎711/116741), doubles with bathrooms start at $14, while at the *Otel İpek Palas*, İnönü Caddesi 103 (☎711/118743), similar standards of accommodation and service will set you back about $15 for a double. The *Pehlivan Palas*, in a rambling old building across from the luxury *Büyuk Surineli*, has big doubles with bathrooms for $10, singles for half that.

Adana's single **campground** is on the eastern edge of town just off the main eastbound road. The place is on the small side and noisy, but the facilities, including a restaurant and pool, are reasonably priced.

In the center of Adana there are plenty of places to **eat and drink**. The local specialty is the spicy *Adana kebap*—ground lamb and pepper wrapped around a skewer and grilled—and one of the best places to try it is the *Onbaşilar Restorant* on Atatürk Caddesi opposite the tourist office, where you'll get the works for about $3. There are plenty of other possibilities up and down İnönü Caddesi, notably the *Yudum Kafeterya* on the corner of Atatürk and İnönü. The *Café Rose*, opposite the Öz Otel, is a good-value bar with food available. There are also numerous hole-in-the-wall *börek* and kebab places near the central PTT.

Around Adana

South of Adana lies the rich agricultural hinterland of the **Çukurova**, a broad delta formed by silt deposits from the Ceyhan River. It's a fertile area with extensive cotton plantations, on which much of the local economy depends, and it contains many Arabic-speaking pockets, a foretaste of the heavy Arab influence to be found farther east. About 50km south of the city sits the small resort of **KARATAŞ**, on the southernmost tip of the delta, with a pleasant stretch of beach. Easily reached by bus or dolmuş from Adana otogar, it doesn't see many tourists outside of public holidays, and most visitors tend to be Turks from Adana. It's nothing special but it would make an alternative to Adana if you're in the area. A recommended local **hotel** is the *Hotel Sidi*, with doubles for $6, and there are a couple of decent fish **restaurants**.

In the opposite direction, about 5km north of Adana, is the **Seyhan Barajı**, a huge artificial lake with bathing and sailing facilities. The reservoir supplies the area with fresh water and because of strong currents bathing is forbidden at the southern end. There's a bird sanctuary immediately to the west.

Toward Antakya

Heading east from Adana toward Antakya (referred to as "Hatay" at the otogar), the first town you reach is **YAKPINAR**, just south of the main road, where there's a small **Mosaic Museum** (Tues–Sun 9am–5pm; $1), worth a quick look for its examples of locally unearthed Roman mosaics. Beyond here you'll see a castle on top of a mountain to the south of the main road—the **Yılan Kalesi**, or "Snake Castle." If you're traveling with your own car, you can drive up to the top and admire the view.

About 12km farther on is **CEYHAN**, which, despite the colorful-looking old houses in the town center, doesn't rate more than a cursory look. South of here at the end of a winding and at times hilly road is the resort of **YUMURTALIK**—a better destination than Karataş if you're after a bit of beach action. There's a small ruined castle here, built by the Knights of St John, and the place is something of a weekend destination for the people of Adana. The best **hotel** in town is the *Hotel Öztur*, with doubles from $12.50, and there are primitive **camping facilities** on the beach.

About 40km east of Ceyhan the road forks. Due east leads to GAZIANTEP and beyond, while the southern fork heads toward ANTAKYA (for both of these see Chapter Eleven). The castle you can see towering above the road is **Toprakkale**, much fought-over by the Armenians and Crusaders during medieval times but abandoned since about 1337. You can visit Toprakkale, but be careful—much of it is very unstable and there are numerous concealed cisterns waiting for unwary people to fall into them.

The Antakya road is pretty nondescript, and the first major town, **DÖRTYOL** ("Crossroads"), does little to break the monotony. It was about 10km north of Dörtyol that Alexander the Great defeated the Persian king Darius at the **Battle of Issus** in 333 BC. Alexander's army of about 35,000 took on a Persian force of over 100,000, but despite these unfavorable odds Alexander carried the day by personally leading an attack against Darius and his entourage. Darius panicked and fled, only narrowly avoiding capture, and the route south was opened up for

Alexander and his army. Today the exact site of the engagement is uncertain, and the task of identifying it from contemporary accounts has been made harder by the fact that, due to earthquakes, the physical appearance of the landscape has changed over the intervening 2000 years.

At **YAKACIK**, about 10km south, there's a well-preserved *kervansaray* and a former crusaders' fortress that was restored during Ottoman times for some military purpose. South of here, wayside industry and pollution prepare you for the unpleasantness of İSKENDERUN.

travel details

Trains
From Mersin to Adana (6 daily; 1hr 15min).

From Adana to Ankara (4 weekly; 14hr); Gaziantep (4 weekly; 3hr); Mersin (6 daily; 1hr 15min).

Buses
From Antalya (Central Otogar) to Afyon/Ankara (almost around the clock; 5/10hr); Denizli/İzmir (6 daily; 5hr 30min/9hr 30min); Kaş (7 daily; 4hr 30min); Fethiye, by inland route (3 daily; 4hr); Konya (6 daily; 6hr 30min); Alanya (hourly; 2hr); Kemer (half-hourly; 45min).

From Antalya (Doğu Garaj) to Aksu (for Perge), red-and-white *Belediye* bus half-hourly; Gebiz (for Sillyon), same as above; Belkis (Aspendos), hourly red-and-white bus; Side/Manavgat (every 20min; 1hr 15min); plus local services to Düden Falls and Lara Beach.

From Alanya to Adana (8 daily; 10hr); Antalya (hourly; 2hr); İstanbul (4 daily; 18hr); Mersin (8 daily; 9hr); Samsun (1 daily; 24hr); Silifke via Taşucu (8 daily; 7hr).

From Silifke to Adana (3–4 an hour; 2hr); Alanya (8 daily; 7hr); Antalya (8 daily; 9hr); Konya (12 daily; 5hr); Mersin (3 an hour; 2hr).

From Adana to Adıyaman (7 daily; 6hr); Antalya (3 daily; 12hr); Alanya (8 daily; 10hr); Ankara (hourly; 10hr); Dıyabakir (3 daily; 10hr); Gaziantep (5 daily; 4hr); Kâhta (2 daily; 7hr); Kayseri (3 daily; 7hr); Konya (hourly; 7hr); Malatya (3 daily; 8hr); Şanlıurfa (4 daily; 6hr); Van (1 daily; 18hr).

Planes
From Antalya to İstanbul (3-9 daily, most on *THY* but some on *İstanbul Hava Yolları*; 1hr 5min); Ankara (1-3 daily on *THY*; 1hr); TRNC (6 weekly on *THY* and *İstanbul Hava Yolları*; 1hr).

From Adana to Ankara (1 daily; 1hr); İstanbul (1 daily; 1hr 15min); TRNC (3 weekly; 1hr).

Ferries
From Antalya to Venice (1 weekly; 71hr).

From Mersin to Magosa (TRNC) (3 weekly; 10hr), with an onward service to Syria during summer.

From Taşucu to Girne (TRNC) (3 weekly; 8hr).

Hydrofoils
From Taşucu to Girne (TRNC) (3 weekly; 2hr).

CHAPTER SEVEN

SOUTH CENTRAL ANATOLIA

Whatever your plans, the central Anatolian plateau seems at first sight to be an unpromising prospect. A large area around the lake of Tuz Gölü is virtual desert, and much more of the central plateau is steppeland, suitable only for livestock-grazing. In summer water is scarce except in the river valleys and in irrigated areas, and in winter the region is blitzed by cold and heavy snowfall. Gertrude Bell recorded the impressions of a European traveler approaching the central plateau in 1909:

> *Before him stretch wide plains, corn-growing where rainfall and springs permit, often enough barren save for a dry scrub of aromatic herbs, or flecked with shining miles of saline deposit; naked ranges of mountains stand sentinel over this feature-less expanse; the sparse villages, unsheltered from wind or sun, lie along the skirts of the hills, catching thirstily at the snow-fed streams that are barely enough for the patch of cultivated ground below; the weary road deep in dust or mud according to the season, drags its intolerable length to the horizon. It is Asia, with all its vast-ness, with all its brutal disregard for life and comfort and the amenities of exis-tence; it is the Ancient East, returned after so many millenniums of human endeavor to its natural desolation.*

The "shining miles of saline deposit" constitute the Turkish **lakeland**, the region south of Afyon and west of Konya, largely ignored by the Turkish tourist industry. These stretches of azure or silver waters stand out against the gray steppes, or appear suddenly between mountains to startling effect. Many of them, like Çavuşçu Göl or Acı Göl, have a high salt content which discourages aquatic life and human settlement alike. Others are avoided because their flat shores are liable to flood. Only the residents of **Eğirdir** and the small community on the shore of Akşehir Gölü manage to make a tenuous living out of fishing their respective lakes; Eğirdir is an increasingly popular stopover for passing tour parties.

To the east of the lakes, the plateau rises gradually toward the highlands. **Tuz Gölü** to the north is little more than a vast salt machine, and aridity in the region is increased by the underground dissipation of water. To make matters worse, the light forest that once covered this land was destroyed in the Neolithic and Classical ages by grazing herds of livestock.

Despite the inhospitable nature of the plateau, however, it has been populated as long as anywhere in Anatolia. From Paleolithic times man was drawn to the Lakeland area, which provided a livelihood for primitive hunters and fishermen, and in the Bronze Age the **Hittites**, a race who once rivaled the Egyptians, chose the plateau as their homeland. By the early historical period, the northern

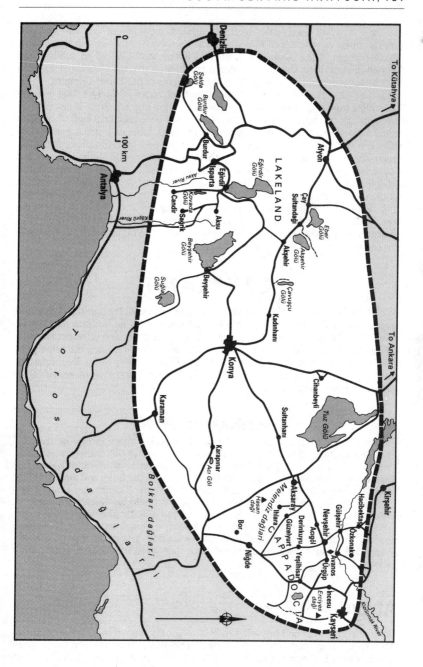

Lakeland area had been settled by the **Pisidians**, mountain people with a reputation for fierce independence who worked as mercenaries throughout the eastern Mediterranean. Their strategically situated towns were difficult to subdue, and Xenophon described them as obstinate troublemakers, who managed to keep their towns independent despite the encroachments of the Persian Empire.

Farther east, the area between the extinct volcanoes of Erciyes Dağ and the Melendiz range is **Cappadocia**, whose legacy of igneous soil (tufa) is favorable to vine-growing and horse-breeding. Water and wind have created a land of fantastic forms from the soft rock, including forests of cones, table mountains, canyon-like valleys and castle-rocks, all further hewn and shaped by civilizations that have found the region particularly sympathetic to their needs. Rain is rare, but Cappadocia is nevertheless extremely fertile compared to the rest of South Central Anatolia, and it became an important crossroads and home to a politically autonomous state between the third and first centuries BC. From the seventh to the eleventh centuries, it was a place of refuge during Arab and Turkish invasions into the area. Today its rock dwellings and unearthly landscapes make an irresistible tourist draw, and Cappadocia is certainly likely to prove the highlight of any travels in this region.

LAKELAND

One of Turkey's least visited, most underexploited areas, the Turkish **Lakeland** seems just waiting to be discovered by tourism. Until it is, facilities may not be deluxe, but the large number of beautiful, unspoiled fresh- and saltwater lakes, as well as the **nature reserves** in the Eğirdir and Burdur regions, the remains of Pisidian cities, architectural monuments to the former glory of the local emirates and the Selçuk Empire, and largely unspoiled provincial towns, all make it ideal for quiet, unhurried travels away from the seething resorts.

THE LAKES

There are three types of lakes in the Lakeland region: those in narrow, sunken basins with shores fixed by mountain borders, like Burdur Gölü; others, which are residual sheets of water resembling marshes, whose salt content varies according to the surface evaporation (that of Acı Göl is 101 grams per liter); and those that fill the depressions in the karstic plains, whose underground outlets are clogged by the clay that is produced when limestone dissolves, producing shallow stretches of fresh water like the lakes of Beyşehir, Eğirdir, and Akşehir (the last of these is so shallow that it sometimes dries out completely). Although animal life is sparse, most of the lakes contain fish of some kind—even if it's just one species—and have supported small human communities since they were first fished in the early Palaeolithic Age.

Afyon

Dominated by a tall and imposing rock strategically topped by an ancient citadel, **AFYON**'s skyline certainly leaves a vivid impression. The town remains impressive on closer inspection: it is clean and relaxed, retaining a good deal of interesting Ottoman architecture as well as a number of attractive mosques. In addition, reasonably priced hotels and restaurants make it a good choice for a night's stopover.

In honor of the fortress, and the 200-meter-high **black rock** on which it's built, the city until recently bore the impressive name of Afyon Karahisar, "**Opium Black Fortress**". The rock is believed to have first been fortified by the Hittite king Mursil II, and remains have also been found dating to the **Phrygian era**. The Romans and Byzantines—who called the city Akronium, or "High Hill"—also occupied the city, the latter building the greater part of the present-day fortress, which was subsequently used as an imperial treasury by both the Selçuks and the Ottomans.

For three weeks in the summer of 1922, Afyon took center stage in the formation of the Turkish Republic when the **Battle for Supreme Military Command** was fought with the Greeks at nearby Dumlupınar. The town's statue commemorating the Turkish victory—depicting one naked man towering over another in an attitude of victory—is one of the most moving memorials to Atatürk.

Arrival and Practicalities

Arriving in Afyon is pretty straightforward. The **train station** is at the far end of Ordu Bulvarı, about half a kilometer from the town center, while the **otogar** is about the same distance east of town on Çevreyolu. Both of them are linked with the center of town by a dolmuş service marked "Sanayı," which does a circuit taking in the archaeological museum and all the city's best hotels. It departs from central Afyon outside the main post office on Kurtuluş Caddesi. The **tourist information office** (Mon–Fri 9am–5pm) is on the right on Ordu Bulvarı as you head out of town, a few minutes walk from the town center.

The two "tourist class" **hotels** in town, the *Oruçoğlu* (☎491/20120, 20121, 20122) and the *Emek* (☎491/12323, 16070), both on Ordu Bulvarı, are central, comfortable, and overpriced at around $16 single and $24 double without breakfast. The *Oruçoğlu* has a good restaurant with views of the castle and a fixed menu at around $6 a head. Better lodging deals are the *Otel Mesut*, Dumlupınar 2 Caddesi 5 (☎491/20429, 23421), and the *Otel Hocaoğlu*, around the corner at Ambaryolu 12 (☎491/11622, 13563), where small rooms with bathrooms go for $8–10 single, $12 double, with TVs and refrigerators in some rooms.

The *Otel Naman*, close to the train station and near the Devlet Hastanesi (State Hospital) on the Ankara–İzmir road, is also fairly good value at $10 single, $15 double without breakfast; it has a pleasant terrace **restaurant** on the top floor, overlooking more black rocks, which serves a good selection of *mezes* and meat dishes. It will also serve the regional specialty of **kaymak**, thick cream supposedly made from buffalo milk, if you ask. The *Otel Karaca*, on Anbar Yolu (☎491/ 12851, 12951), is the best of a bad bunch in the area near the bus station: rooms with bathroom $7 single, $10 double. The *İkbal Lokantasi*, on Uzun Çarşı on the other side of Kurtuluş Caddesi from the *Oruçoğlu*, is a classic, old-fashioned eatery, and not too expensive.

The Town

The best way of establishing what's where on arrival is to head for the highest point in town: the **fortress** on its black rock. Happily it's now a relatively simple matter to reach the citadel by means of some 700 steps on the southern face of the rock; previously there was just a rough path. On the way up look out for

---

OPIUM

A town called **"Opium"** (the translation of Afyon) could hardly be accused of reticence concerning its more controversial claims to fame. This region produces 35 percent of the world's legal opiates: it used to be almost half, but in 1971 the United States pressured Turkey into imposing a total ban on production because of the extent of **illegal drug trafficking**. This reached a height in the late 1960s, when control was so slack that everyone from small-time users to international marketeers were converging on the area to reap the harvest for themselves. Nowadays, although poppy seeds are sprinkled liberally on bread loaves and the leaves of the plant are used in salads, all of the 20,000 tons of capsules processed around Afyon must arrive at the factory intact, and the poppy fields are regularly patrolled by government officials.

While the authorities may be circumspect about touting the city's eponymous enterprise as a tourist attraction, there are still telltale signs of civic pride in the local opiate industry: a close look at the fountain in the town square reveals that it is a graceful **bronze sculpture** of poppy seed-pods.

---

hoopoes among the varied birdlife, and at the top for rags, representing wishes, tied to trees by petitioners.

The fortress itself is thought to stand on the site of the Hittite stronghold of Khapanouwa, built around the middle of the second millennium BC. The rock was subsequently fortified by the Phrygians, Byzantines, and Turks, and the extant remains—a few crenellated walls and towers to be clambered on mainly for the views they offer—date from the latter two periods. As you look out, a fair amount of **light industry** is in evidence on the outskirts of the city, but the center is well planned and attractive.

Immediately surrounding the fortress rock is the old town, a tangle of tiny streets frequented by gangs of street urchins speaking Turkish in the peculiar local dialect and a few words of English. There are also a number of impressively old and well-preserved mosques in this area. Afyon's domestic **Ottoman architecture** is renowned in Turkey; around the citadel are the overhanging upper stories of half-timbered houses, some even complete with *kafes*, the wooden latticework on the windows designed to protect the chastity of a household's womenfolk.

Opposite the base of the steps leading up the side of the rock is Afyon's most ancient mosque, the **Ulu Cami** (open at prayer times only). This Selçuk construction, built between 1272 and 1277, has been restored, so its originally flat roof is now pitched, but it retains the original carved wooden columns with stalactite capitals and beams, as well as a wooden *mimber* carved with typical Selçuk geometric designs.

In the same area, on the way up to the citadel, the **Mevlevi Camii** is a double-domed mosque noticeable for its pyramid-roofed *son cemaat yeri*, a porch in which latecomers pray—literally the "place of last congregation." The adjoining *semahane*, or dervish ceremony hall, has a walnut-wood floor on which Mevlevi dervishes once performed their whirling ceremony. The building has now been converted into a **museum of the Mevlevi** (open at prayer times or on request to the *imam*), featuring exhibits of musical instruments and the ceremonial costumes of the dervishes. Afyon became the second-largest center of the Mevlevi order after this branch of Islamic mysticism was introduced to the city from Konya by the son of the Mevlâna, Sultan Veled.

The **Archaeological Museum** (daily 8am–5:30pm; 50¢), 1km out of town on Kurtuluş Caddesi, is labeled only in Turkish but worth a visit anyway: the collection is housed in a light, airy building and the objects are nicely displayed. The most interesting are Roman, excavated at nearby Çardalı and Kovalık Höyük, dating from the third and fourth centuries. Exhibits from this period include a small marble statue of Diana and a price list from an agora, outside in the covered gallery.

Also on Kurtuluş Caddesi but closer to the center of town, next to the *Otel Gümüş*, the **Gedik Ahmet Paşa Külliyesi** was built for one of the viziers of Mehmet the Conqueror in 1477. Adjoining it are a stone *medrese* and a functioning hamam, which, apart from the original marble floors, is in a bad state of repair.

Around Afyon

Getting out of town, perhaps the most interesting trip is to see the remains of Phrygian sculpture, dating from the sixth century BC, in the vicinity of **İHSANİYE**. There are five trains a day from Afyon to İhsaniye, as well as dolmuşes that leave from a garage at Ordu Bulvarı 11a opposite the tourist office. It's about a forty-minute journey, and after İhsaniye it's necessary to hitch, walk, or hire a dolmuş to take you to Döğer (about 10km north of İhsaniye) or Ayazin about 15km east of there (30km from Afyon, 25km from İhsaniye). You can also get a bus straight to the village of Kunduzlu, near Ayazin, from Voyvoda Gazlıgöl Caddesi, opposite the Belediye building in Afyon.

Best of all are the remains of a Phrygian town located in the modern-day village of **AYAZIN**, a right turn off the Afyon–Eskişehir road when you reach Kunduzlu. The cave houses and a well-preserved ninth-century Byzantine church are visible across fields of opium poppies on the road to the village. Closer observation reveals lion reliefs, and the scars from excavations on the part of locals and archaeologists who have found coins and other objects in the rooms. The rock-cut tomb of **Aslantaş** (Lion Stone), near the village of KAYA (formerly Hayranveli), is flanked by a relief of two lions, this time enormous and snarling at each other with bared stone teeth. A Phrygian cult monument called **Aslankaya** (Lion Rock), with a high-relief of the goddess Cybele flanked by two more enormous lions, is located near Lake Emre in the small town of DÖĞER, where the remains of a fifteenth-century Ottoman *kervansaray* can also be found.

The Afyon region is also well known for its **hot springs**, whose waters bubble up at temperatures between 60 and 80°C (140° and 176°)and have a high content of fluoride, bromide, and calcium. Mineral water from this region is bottled and sold all over Turkey. Visits to the spa town of **ÖMER**, 18km from Afyon on the Kütahya road, are arranged by the *Ece Hotel*. The **Gazlıgöl spa**, whose waters are supposed to have therapeutic value for stomach aches and kidney stones, is 3km farther on; take the Kütahya bus out of town and ask to be dropped at the *Gazlıgöl Termal*.

Sultandağı and Akşehir

Sixty-seven kilometers out of Afyon on the Konya road, **SULTANDAĞI** is a tiny village good for an overnight stop, with a ruined Selçuk *kervansaray* and easy access to the lakes of **Eber Gölü** and **Akşehir Gölü**. You can stay at the *Hotel Mehtap* (☎4996/1061; the only hotel in town), where you get a room, hot water in a shared bathroom, and breakfast for an astonishing $3. The small *kervansaray* is in a bad state of repair, but it's still possible to make out the general plan of its rooms.

If you do stay, it's well worth paying an evening visit to tiny **TAŞKÖPRÜ**, 4km from Sultandağı, past the station off the Akşehir road. There's a small fish restaurant here that stays open late to serve the local fishermen, who comprise most of the male contingent of the village's hundred-odd households. They fish the lake for bream, carp, and lobster, and catch frogs among the reeds for export to Italy. The lake is retreating from the village quite rapidly, however, and eventually the fishermen may have to resort to farming sugar cane and watermelon.

The small provincial town of **AKŞEHİR**, about halfway to Konya, has little to offer visitors. If you do end up with an hour to waste here—and you may if you're changing buses to head south toward İsparta and Eğirdir—it's worth dashing out for a visit to the *türbe* of Nasrettin Hoca, situated in a beautiful park about five minutes from the otogar. The tomb, located in a green pavillion open on three sides but with a locked gate on the fourth, commemorates the folk hero and village idiot Nasrettin Hoca. A vast body of tales and jokes are attributed to this comic figure, who is most often pictured seated backward on his equally famous donkey.

İsparta and Eğirdir

The road between Akşehir and Bağkonak on the way to İsparta and Eğirdir climbs and winds through beautiful mountainous scenery; if you have the option, give yourself the chance to admire the route rather than drive it. Beyond Bağkonak it plunges down toward Eğirdir, with beautiful views over the lake, and then follows the shore around into town.

Despite its swashbuckling name, **İSPARTA** doesn't have anything like the attractions of neighboring Eğirdir. It's a modern town whose only suggestion of romantic appeal lies in its chief industries, **roses**, which have been cultivated here for a century, and carpets. Otherwise, there's a lake—the tiniest in the region—with a picnic spot in a clearing in a forest next to it; good transportation in and out; and reasonable hotels that are better equipped to deal with Anatolian winters, and better value, than those in the vacation town of Eğirdir.

İsparta has long been an important city. In its early years it was occupied by Hittites and Lydians before being ruled briefly by the Macedonians. After Selçuk occupation in 1203, İsparta, like Eğirdir, was one of the cities that came under the control of the Hamitoğlu dynasty in the middle of the thirteenth century, and was capital of a territory delimited by the four great lakes (Beyşehir, Burdur, Akşehir, and Eğirdir). In the face of Ottoman expansion the Hamitoğlu sultan cut his losses and sold the kingdom to the Ottoman Sultan Murat I in 1381, and thereafter its star waned. Only when Eğirdir lost its importance did İsparta and neighboring Burdur regain significance as market towns in their respective areas, and more recently İsparta has also become an important carpet trading center since carpet manufacture developed in the surrounding villages during the last century.

As for spending time here, there's not a whole lot to see or do, but enough to stop you going crazy between buses. There's a simple, clean **hamam**, *Yeni Hamam* (daily 8am–5pm for men and women; $1) behind the *İsparta Hotel* in the center of town, opposite the *Muhtarlık* on the corner of Zübeyde Hanım Caddesi and Eski Tabakhane Caddesi.

The Kutlubey or **Ulu Cami** in the town center dates from 1417, and its size and grandeur attest to the importance of the town in Ottoman times. It has been badly restored, however, with terrible arabesque painting and light-green walls that don't do it justice. The town's **Archaeological Museum** (daily 8:30am–6pm; 50¢), on Kenan Evren Caddesi, has a few interesting remains from the early Bronze, Roman, and Byzantine periods, shakily labeled in English, and the rest is devoted to ethnographia, with İsparta carpets exhibited upstairs.

Practicalities

İsparta's regional **Directorate of Tourism** (*Turism Müdürlüğü*) is at Mimar Sinan Caddesi, 1742 Sok 1 (☎327/14438; Mon–Fri 9am–5pm). The **train station** is at the far end of İstasyon Caddesi from the town center, and the **otogar** a twenty-minute dolmuş ride away from the center on Mimar Sinan Caddesi. There's a useful travel agency, *Rainbow*, at Miralay Mustafa Nuri İşhanı 60 (☎327/38063), which also rents cars.

The best **hotel** in town is the *Otel Bolat* at Demirel Bul 67 (☎327/39001), which is fairly luxurious (rooms are centrally heated and have TVs) and cheap ($10 single, $16 double), though prices will no doubt increase as the hotel gains in popularity. Another good bet is the *Hotel Gülistan*, Mimar Sinan Caddesi 31 (☎327/14085, 14422), which is simple and clean, and has about a hundred rooms for $5 single, $8 double without bathrooms, $7 single, $12 double with. Otherwise the *Büyük İsparta Hotel* on the main square (Kaymakkapı Meydanı; ☎327/21017) is comfortable and plush at $24 single, $36 double with breakfast. A good cheap **restaurant** is the *Hünkar Et Lokantası*, 120 Caddesi 14, behind the *Yeni Hamam* (☎327/19692).

Changing money is best done in the jewelers' shops, but try to get there before noon on Saturday, when they close for the weekend; otherwise, the *Büyük İsparta* changes money for a commission. The **PTT** is opposite the *Atatürk Çay Bahçesi* and Ulu Cami on İstasyon Caddesi.

Around İsparta: Burdur

If the town itself isn't that exciting, İsparta does make a good base for exploring the region's lakes and resorts, the remains of ancient cities, and a few spectacular caves. Thirteen kilometers southwest, reached through fields of cultivated roses, **Gölcük** is a crater lake surrounded by trees, with a picnic area nearby. You'll need your own transportation to get there: take İsmet Paşa Caddesi out of town and on the right, you'll pass the Milas picnic spot with a little artificial lake and tables beneath the trees. They provide barbecue grills (*mangal*) and sell şiş kebab.

BURDUR may look promising on the map, but in fact it's situated some way from its lake, and there's little reason to spend time in the town itself. Despite its status as a provincial capital, flat-roofed village houses predominate, and the only impressive monument is a fourteenth-century mosque, the **Ulu Cami**, a relic of the Hamitoğlu dynasty. Frequent dolmuşes cover the scenic hour's drive from İsparta to Burdur, and there are regular onward services to the lake.

If you're driving, the **lake**, situated to the northwest of town, is most easily reached along Highway 330 to Denizli and Acıpayam. Its most popular bathing area is the five-kilometer-long Çendik Beach, 2km from Burdur, which is where the dolmuşes from town will drop you off. The 200-square-kilometer lake is extremely saline (21 grams of salt per liter) and surrounded by desert-like **badlands** developing in the clay and sand of the area.

Salda Gölü

Continuing east from Burdur, **Salda Gölü** lies about halfway to Denizli and 6km from YEŞILOVA, where you'll have to change dolmuş. The westernmost of the lakes, Salda Gölü is a crystal-green expanse, its water lightly alkaline but pleasant to swim in. A succession of campgrounds, restaurants, a motel, and a forest-service picnic area line the south shore road, with the scenery becoming more appetizing and pine-fringed as you proceed from east to west.

Sagalossos and the İnsuyu Mağarasi

One of the most impressive ancient sites in the region is the city of **SAGALOSSOS**, thought to have been the foremost Pisidian city, and also one of the oldest. In 1224 BC its inhabitants were numbered among "the people of the sea" who attacked the Egyptian coast, and according to Livy its inhabitants were "by far the most warlike in the country." The remains, most notable for their vast theater, lie due south of İsparta, some 40km by a rather roundabout road. To get there, take the bus that runs from İsparta to Antalya and ask to be dropped off in AĞLASUN, and the ruins are 7km from there (follow the signs).

The strategic position of Sagalossos, set high on a plateau against a steep rocky escarpment, compelled passing conquerors to take it; among them, both Alexander the Great and the Roman consul Manlius passed through on their way to Termessos. Today the ruins blend in with the gray rock of the cliff from which their stones originated. The **theater**, to the northeast, had a 320-foot cavea, the eastern half of which rested on rock, while the western half was supported by masonry. Cut into the cliff to the west of the city are a number of small **rock tombs**, looking almost like hand basins, which held cremated bodies. Other impressive remains include a prominently positioned **Corinthian temple** dedicated to Antonius Pius, in the south of the site and, on the other side of an **agora** from the theater, a first-century **Doric temple** with two standing walls. The original frieze from this temple, depicting Apollo playing the zither and Muses, has now been removed for safekeeping.

The **İnsuyu Mağarası**, a 600-meter-long cave, is well marked off the Burdur-Antalya road, 14km from Burdur, and easily reached by Antalya-bound bus from Burdur. The cave (daily 8:30am–6pm; $1) is well organized with lighting and foot-paths. It's nowhere near as much of an adventure to explore as the Zindan Mağarası (below), but it does have nine beautiful underwater lakes, the largest of which, Büyük Göl, measures 150m by 30m and is up to 15m deep. Its mineral-rich water is phosphorescent blue, warm, and supposedly therapeutic for diabetics.

Eğirdir

EĞİRDİR, two and a half hours from Akşehir, half an hour from İsparta, is a seaside town without the sea, with the forgotten air of a coastal resort out of season and a climate to match. The setting is astonishingly beautiful, however, clinging to the little flat land allowed by the Taurus Mountains, which appear to have squeezed half of the town onto two tiny islands in the lake beyond. The town suffers from its convenience as a lunchtime stopover for tour groups, who descend and swamp the town, only to leave it feeling all the more desolate when they take off an hour later. Even so, tourism hasn't taken any kind of significant hold, and there is enough to see and do in the region to make it worth spending some time here after the tour buses have all departed.

Eğirdir's strategic position and ease of fortification made it a place of some importance. Initially founded by the Hittites, it was taken by the Phrygians in 1200 BC. In Lydian times, when it was on the King's Highway from Ephesus to Babylon, the town became famous for its recreational and accommodation facilities. After 1071 it came under the Turkish rule of the Sultanate of Rum, based in Konya, during which time it commanded the sole eastern approach to the menacing Pisidian region. In the thirteenth century the city reached the height of its fortunes as capital of the **emirate of Felekeddin Dündar**. It remained prominent during the reign of the Hamitoğlu, and in 1331 the geographer Ibn Battutah could still describe Eğirdir as a rich and powerful city: when the Ottomans took over, however, its strategic significance disappeared, and with it the opulence of the city. The name of the town, incidentally, was originally **Eğridir** (meaning "It's Bent"), but was changed in the mid-1980s to Eğirdir, meaning "S/he's spinning", which the locals apparently thought more appropriate.

Considering the town's historical importance, monumental architecture is surprisingly scarce, but at least anything of any significance has been proudly preserved and is eagerly displayed to visistors. On a preliminary wander the most obvious remains are the nicely restored **Medrese of Dündar**, which began life in 1273 as an inn but was converted into a *medrese* by Felekeddin Dündar, and now serves as a shopping center; and the adjoining **Hizarbey Mosque**, whose roof is supported by Selçuk-style wooden pillars and which has an ornately carved door, wooden porch, and İznik-tiled *mihrab*. Nearby, straddling the entrance to the islands, are the ramparts of a Selçuk citadel (*kale*) on which an imposing cannon is still positioned, as a reminder of the importance of the trading interests that were once protected. The remains of a Byzantine church on **Yeşilada**—the farthest of the islands—are disappointingly scant, and at present it's not possible to go inside because it's closed "for restoration."

Eğirdir Practicalities

The **tourist information office** (daily 9am–noon & 1–5:30pm) is by the lake, ten minutes' walk out of town on the İsparta road. Staff can suggest hotels but aren't as informed or helpful as the *Gökuşağı* travel agency on the same road back towards town in Essan İşhani (a small shopping arcade). Here they provide information about the surrounding tourist attractions as well as **car rental**, which is cheaper here than on the south coast.

There's no shortage of **hotels** in this little town, but if you do want to stay it makes sense to head out to the "islands" by means of the government-funded causeway and stay in one of the cheap and charming pansiyons out there. Two good deals on the far side of Yeşilada are the *Sunshine Pansiyon* (☎3281/3291), $4 without bath, and the *Sunrise Pansiyon* (☎3281/3032), $5 per person with bath. Another attractive option is the *Yalı Pansiyon* (☎3281/1773) on the İsparta road, which has three rooms with kitchen facilities overlooking a garden on the lakeside, and **camping** on the lawn. They rent out their own tents for $2 per person. To get there, take a *Yazla Plaj* bus, or a taxi, to Yazla Mahallesi 4. For food, the *Ünal Hotel*'s **restaurant**, opposite the bus station on the southern lakeshore road, has a good selection of fish, and there are many decent fish restaurants serving up the local catch along the lakeside.

Altınkum Beach, about 5km out of town off the Gökçeköy road, is the best of the lake beaches, with a good restaurant (☎3281/3360) and campground.

Kovada National Park

Thirty kilometers south of Eğirdir, the beautiful forest surrounding **Kovada Gölü** has been protected as a national park; it's carefully tended and hardly visited, in or out of season. Animals found in the park supposedly include wolves and bears, more certainly wild boar and snakes. If you don't feel like risking a run-in with wildlife, there are a few good roads running through the park—one to Candır, which takes you past cultivated pistachio-nut bushes, and the other to Sağrik—and since there's no public transportation in these parts it might be worth renting a car with a local guide to point out things natural. Otherwise exploration will need to be done on foot: hitching is a doubtful option as the roads are practically empty. It's possible to **camp** beside the lake, which is well stocked with carp and bass.

The pastures around the park are used by nomads, whose goat-hair tents are frequently in evidence during the summer months. You may be lucky enough to witness *tandır* baking of *köy ekmeği* ("village bread"), or wool being spun on the simplest of wooden spindles.

Adada and the Zindan Mağarası

Indicated off the road near Sağrik is **Adada**, an antique city cut from gray stone, whose remains include Roman temples, a forum, and Hellenistic buildings with inscriptions. Off the same road, 26km from Eğirdir, is the **Zindan Cave**; to get to it, first find the village of AKSU beyond Yılanlı. Go straight up Cumhuriyet Caddesi in Aksu until you come to the Aksu River, which is crossed by an attractive Roman bridge; the entrance to the cave is in the rock face opposite.

Inside, the cave has everything from bat colonies and the stench of bat guano to stalactites and stalagmites. It's ideal for diehard spelunkers, but a flashlight and old clothes are essential if you intend to plumb all 2.5km of the cave's depths.

Beyşehir

Leaving Eğirdir in the direction of Konya, the next major lake is **Beyşehir Gölü**. The town of **BEYŞEHİR**, on its shore, sees a lot of through traffic heading in this direction, and its attractive lakeside position and historical legacy make it a good prospect for a night's stopover.

Judging by the Neolithic remains found in the region, there has been human settlement here since the sixth or seventh millennium BC. There is also extensive evidence of Hittite settlement around the lake. The town itself was originally Byzantine, known as Karallia, and in Selçuk times it was surrounded by walls and acquired a citadel as well as mosques and hamams. The local golden age, though, came under the Eşrefoğlu dynasty (1277–1326), and its best buildings all date from that time.

The attractions are not immediately obvious on a preliminary excursion. It's a scattered, rather vague-looking place, where baggy *şalvar* trousers and other traditional clothing, long since superceded by Western styles in more touristed cities, are much in evidence in the dusty streets. Once you start to explore, though, you'll soon find that there are a number of attractive monuments in the town, and a lovely Ottoman bridge, built in 1902, where you can watch locals throwing their nets out for the evening catch of *sazan* (carp).

The most obvious lure probably remains the shallow freshwater **lake**, whose 650 square kilometers average a depth of around ten meters. The exact number of islands in the lake appears to be hotly disputed among the locals, which could be explained by the fact that smaller ones appear and disappear according to the water level, but the named ones number about twenty. It's a simple matter to rent a boat and explore the islands and the lake's shore. Renting a boat is also the best way to reach the **Eflatun Pınar** ("Violet Spring"), a Hittite rock temple located on the far side of the lake, 12km out of town off the Akşehir road. The site consists of huge blocks covered with Hittite-style carved figures and winged sun discs (symbols of royalty) carried by monsters of semi-human form. To the left and right at water level are statues of a seated god and goddess. The monument is a typical Hittite sanctuary, dedicated to the divine force.

The Eşrefoğlu Camii

Back in Beyşehir itself, the most important monument is the **Eşrefoğlu Camii**, built by Eşrefoğlu Seyfeddin Süleyman between 1297 and 1299. Standing across the bridge from town, this large, flat-roofed stone building surmounted by a typical Selçuk flat-sided cone is an exceptional piece of medieval Turkish architecture, and the best surviving example of a wooden *beylik* mosque (the "beyliks" being the Turkish dynasties that ruled Anatolia before the Ottomans gained supremacy). Restoration was carried out in the 1950s, which explains the ugly concrete blocks at the base of the minaret, but otherwise the mosque is in a remarkable state of preservation, especially the beautifully carved **main portal**, typically Selçuk in its geometric ornateness. The effect inside is incredibly forest-like: not only are the columns and capitals wooden, but also the rafters, the galleries, the furniture, and the balustrades. To add to the sylvan effect, light filters through the columns from a central aperture, now glassed over, and from windows set high up in the walls. The *mihrab* is tiled in typical Selçuk style, its turquoise, black, and white tiles being almost the last of their type, and the *mimber*, also of the period, is a lovely piece of woodcarving, echoing the star motif which is apparent throughout the mosque. The floor is covered with carpets and kilims, and although the three original Selçuk carpets have now been removed to Konya, there are still some interesting and beautiful examples of later work.

The **Eşrefoğlu Türbesi**, the conically roofed building southeast of the mosque, dates from 1302, and was also built for Eşrefoğlu Süleyman Bey, who died in that year. It's worth asking the *imam* if he'll open it up for you to have a look at its beautifully tiled interior, one of the most ornate surviving examples of its type. To the southwest of the mosque there's a late thirteenth-century **clothing factory** (*dokumacilar hanı*), also built during the Eşrefoğlu period, with six domes recently restored in brick. Again, you'll need to ask permission to see it. It's one of the few remaining domed Selçuk buildings; unlike the Byzantines, they tended to use domes in business and functional buildings rather than in monuments. To the southwest of the factory there's a double **hamam**, dating from 1260, which is open to wander round. Although the building is in a fairly good state of repair, the pipes that heated the interior—using the same principle of central heating that is still employed in modern Turkish apartment buildings—have been exposed in the main room. Outside, near the door, there's a pipe that is said to have supplied milk, for bathing purposes, to the baths.

Rooms and Food

There are a few simple **hotels** in town, including the *Park Oteli*, Atatürk Caddesi, Anıt Meydanı (☎3411/4745, 3628)—$4 single, $6 double for rooms with hot water—and the *Bulvarı Oteli*, Atatürk Caddesi (☎3411/4985)—double without bath $5, with bath $8. There's also a pansiyon, or more accurately a few rooms in a family house, run by the *Göl Restaurant* (☎3411/3608), the nearer of two lakeside restaurants of that name. The other *Göl Restaurant* (owned by the same people), a couple of kilometers out of town along the shore road, has cheap local fish, rudimentary **camping** facilities, and the best possible view of the famous sunset over Beyşehir Lake. It's also considerably cheaper than its neighboring *Martı Camping*. The best **restaurant** in town is the *Beyaz Park* (☎3411/4535), next to the bridge, with very cheap food and drinks and a lovely garden outside. Opposite is one final place worth a mention, a carpet and junk shop called *Ceylanlar Ticaret* (☎3411/4433). Their carpets and kilims are reasonably priced to say the least, and they also sell Ottoman rifles and pistols and old jewelry at approximately half the price you'd expect to pay elsewhere.

Konya

Center of Sufic mystical practice and teaching in the Middle East, **KONYA** is a place of pilgrimage for the entire Muslim world. As such, this initially unattractive city on the edge of the Anatolian plateau is often spoken of by Turks with more pride than the better-known tourist resorts. This was the home of Celalledin Rumi or the **Mevlâna** (The Master), the Sufic mystic who founded the **Whirling Dervish sect**, the *Mevlevi*, and whose writings helped reshape Islamic thought and modified the popular Islamic culture of Turkey.

Konya also boasts a history as long and spectacular as any Turkish city. The earliest remains discovered here date from the seventh millennium BC, and the acropolis (now the **Alâeddin Parkı**) was inhabited successively by Hittites, Phrygians, Romans, and Greeks. The apostles Paul and Barnabas both delivered sermons here after they had been expelled from Antioch, and in 235 AD one of the earliest church councils was convened in Konya. It also took a central role during the supremacy of the western Selçuks, or the **Selçuks of Rum**. After they had defeated the Byzantine army at the Battle of Manzikert in 1071, the Selçuks attempted to set up a court in İznik, just across the Marmara Sea from İstanbul. They were driven from there by the combined Byzantine and Crusader armies, but still ruled most of eastern and central Asia Minor until the early fourteenth century.

While the concept of a capital city was somewhat alien to the nomadic Selçuks, Konya was the home of their sultans from the time of Süleyman Ibn Kutulmus, successor to Alparslan, the victor at Manzikert. Alâeddin Keykubad, the most distinguished of all Selçuk sultans, established a court of artists and scholars in Konya in the late thirteenth century, and his patronage was highly beneficial to the development of the arts and philosophy during the Selçuk dynasty. Many of the buildings constructed at this time are still standing, and examples of their highly distinctive tile work, wood-carving, carpet-making, and stonework are on display in Konya's museums. All of these art forms later served to enrich their Ottoman counterparts.

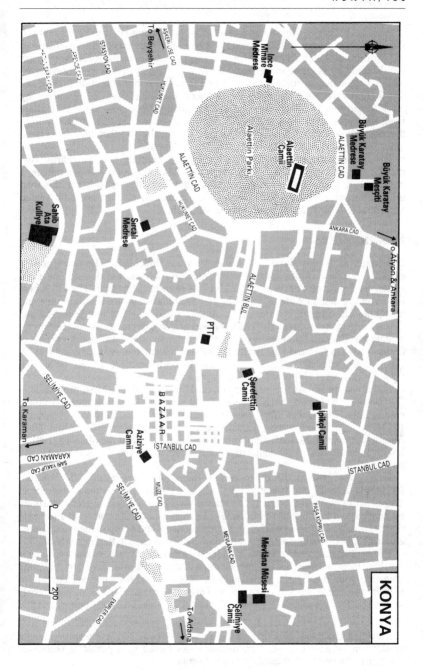

KONYA

In western Turkey, Konya has a reputation as the country's most religious and conservative city, a prejudice based on a misunderstanding of the teachings of the Mevlâna as much as on any empirical facts*. The citizens of Konya respond to this slight by pointing out to visitors that the city may appear underdeveloped and its people may seem less sophisticated than those in the west of Turkey, but this is partly because they are not allocated their fair share of resources by Ankara, and their schools are as poorly equipped as any to be found in Turkey. Even the city's statue of Atatürk is facing north—toward Ankara and away from the city center—which locals claim is symbolic of the fact that they have been ignored since the establishment of the Turkish Republic.

The "backwardness" in fact goes a long way to creating Konya's charm. This may be Turkey's eighth-largest city—with a population of a quarter of a million—but there are relatively few cars on the road and bikes have a higher profile than in İstanbul and Ankara. And despite their numbers, visitors are still treated according to Islamic dictates concerning hospitality.

Practicalities

Orientation in Konya should not present serious difficulties. The **town center** consists of a large traffic rotary—encircling the Alâeddin Parkı—and one main street, leading from the park to the Mevlâna Müzesi (Museum). The city's best hotels and restaurants are all found in this central area, as are the museums and mosques. The **otogar** is 1km out on Ankara Caddesi—take the *Konak–Otogar* dolmuş into town—and the the the **train station** is also a kilometer out at the far end of İstasyon Caddesi, connected to the city center by municipal buses every half hour, or by taxi (around $2). **Turkish airlines** is located at Alâeddin Caddesi 22, Kat 1/106 (☎112000, 112032). The **tourist information office** (Mon–Sat, 8:30am–5pm; ☎111074) is at Mevlâna Caddesi 21.

Konya's main **hotels** are also located on Mevlâna Caddesi. Most prominent is the *Dergah* (☎111197), fairly pricey at $30 single, $48 double but extremely comfortable. The *Şahin Hotel*, also conveniently located at Hükümet Alanı 6 (☎113350), is friendly and old-fashioned. The modern, well-furnished *Hotel Konya*, just behind the tourist information office on Mevlanı Meydanı (☎119212), has a pleasant restaurant and bar on the roof; rooms go for $36 single, $49 double.

Among the best at the other end of the scale is the *Çatal Aile Pansiyon* (☎114981), a small and friendly hotel, where a couple of the rooms have direct access to the roof and a kitchen. The main drawback is a single, shared bathroom; no singles, but doubles are $14, triples $18. Just around the corner at Eşârizade Sokak 13 is the *Otel Tur* (☎119825), a simple, cheap, and scrupulously clean hotel, although its $19 doubles are generally filled by tour groups in the high season.

The best **restaurant** in Konya is unquestionably the *Damla,* whose entrance is reached from a small arcade off Mevlâna Caddesi. If you have any difficulty choosing your meal you'll be led into the kitchen and the chef will attempt to explain the ingredients of a range of Turkish dishes. The bar is particularly impressive for this part of the world, stocked with wine, beer, and liquor, and you

---

*An incident which has stuck in the minds of western Turks is that of a Muslim caught smoking in the street during Ramadan who was beaten up a couple of years ago. Foreigners, however, are treated with more tolerance.

may even be offered a liqueur with your Turkish coffee. The *Koşem* on Alâeddin Bulvarı is particularly good for lunch, but closes rather early in the evenings. Despite a sign in Turkish in the window that states "Family Restaurant: No Alcohol," the waiters tend to offer foreigners a beer practically before they get a chance to sit down.

Perhaps the best breakfast to have here is the traditional Konya fare of *pide,* pieces of flat bread as long as a man's arm, covered in goats' cheese and preferably eaten straight from a coal-fired oven with butter melted over them. They're sold at bakeries throughout the day.

There is a pleasant **hamam** behind the Şerefettin Mosque on Mevlâna Meydanı. Don't be put off by the exterior—it looks a little like a garage—because inside it's everything you could ask for in a Turkish bath: white stone and marble with traditional tiny round skylights striping the steam with rays of sunlight. It has separate baths for men and women, and the masseurs are skilled and thorough.

The phone code for Konya is ☎33.

The City

Konya may be surrounded by some of Turkey's most fertile countryside (it's known locally as "the breadbasket of Turkey"), but there's hardly a blade of grass to be seen in the city itself. Extremes of temperature combine with the ubiquitous light-colored stone to create an effect of bleakness in winter and sun-bleached desiccation in summer. This rather dry and dusty appearance may not suit those who would rather head helter-skelter down to the Mediterranean, but it seems thoroughly appropriate to Konya's substantial Selçuk remains, reminiscent as they are of nomadic tents standing out on an arid plain.

The Mevlâna Müzesi

A visit to the **Mevlâna Müzesi** (Tues–Sun 9am–noon & 1–5pm, Mon 9am–noon & 3–5pm; $2.50) is among Turkey's most rewarding experiences. It's housed in a former *tekke,* the first lodge of the Mevlevi dervish sect, at the eastern end of Mevlâna Bulvarı, and can most easily be found by locating the distinctive fluted turquoise dome that rises directly above Celalledin Rumi's tomb.

The teachings of the Mevlâna were an exciting departure from Islamic orthodoxy, and they're still one of the most attractive aspects of the religion to westerners and liberal Muslims alike. Although his ideas have never been fully accepted into mainstream Islam, it's reassuring that a man who opposed religious bigotry and advocated song, dance, and humility as a means to mystic union should still have a dedicated following among devout Muslims.

The site of the *tekke* is thought to have been presented as a gift to the Mevlâna's father, Bahaeddin Veled, by the Selçuk sultans. Bahaeddin Veled was certainly buried here in 1232, and his tomb stands upended beside that of his son. According to popular myth, Veled's tomb rose until it stood upright when the Mevlâna was buried alongside in 1273, a measure of the father's respect for his son. (The custom of a son rising to his feet when his father enters a room is still prevalent in Turkey.)

The structures adjacent to the tomb were subsequently enlarged by the Çelebis ("Inheritors"), descendants of the Mevlâna who took over leadership of the order after his death. They served as a place of mystical teaching, meditation, and ceremonial dance (*sema*) from shortly after Rumi's death in 1273 until 1925, when Atatürk banned all Sufic orders, the dervishes by this time having become highly influential in political life and thus an impediment to his secular reforms.

The buildings were renovated by Beyazit II in the fifteenth century and are the finest reconstruction of a medieval *tekke* and *semahane*—the circular building in which the *sema* was performed—to be found in Turkey. Opposite the entrance is a şardivan, or fountain for ritual ablution. Along the south and east sides of the courtyard are the **cells** where the dervishes prayed and meditated, containing the waxwork figure of a dervish in the costume worn during the whirling ceremony. Before they were allowed the privilege of seclusion in the cells, the novices had to spend a period of a thousand and one days in manual labor in the soup kitchens, which are also open to the public. After the novitiate they could return to the community and take jobs, even marry, while retaining membership of the order. Next to the Sheikh's quarters, now the museum office, is a **library** of 5000 volumes on the Mevlevi and Sufic mysticism.

Across the courtyard in the main building of the museum is the **mausoleum** containing the tombs of the Mevlâna, his father, and other notables of the order. You should leave your shoes at the door and shuffle along in a line of pilgrims, for whom this is the primary purpose of their visit. Women must cover their heads, and if you're wearing shorts you'll be given a skirt-like affair to cover your legs, regardless of sex. The measure of devotion still felt toward the Mevlâna is evident in the weeping and impassioned prayer that take place in front of his tomb, but non-Muslim visitors are treated with respect and even welcomed. This is in strict accordance with Rumi's own dictates on religious tolerance:

> *Come, come whoever you are, whether you be fire-worshippers, idolators, or pagans.*
> *Ours is not the dwelling-place of despair. All who enter will receive a welcome here.*

A sentiment perhaps lacking in sophistication, some might say, but if you're a lone *gâvur* (infidel) in a center of Islamic pilgrimage then it's surely one to be cherished.

In the adjoining room, the original **semahane**, exhibits include some of the musical instruments of the original dervishes, including the *ney*. The reeds for these flutes are still grown in Hatay in southeastern Turkey and in addition to the instrument's mystical associations, it is said that the sound they make is a cry for their homeland. The instrument does indeed have the distinctive quality of a human voice, and in the hands of a virtuoso the sound is extremely poignant. A tape of dervish music plays continuously in the museum, and the "voice" of the *ney* is always clearly distinct above the other instruments.

Other exhibits include the original illuminated *Mathnawi*, the poetical work of the Mevlâna now translated into twelve languages, and silk and wool carpets, some of which form part of the great body of gifts received by Celalledin Rumi from sultans and princes. One 500-year-old silk carpet from Selçuk Persia is supposed to be the finest ever woven, having 144 knots to the square centimeter and taking five years to complete. The Selçuk carpets on display here give credence to the theory that their skills were adopted by the Ottomans, since many of the patterns and motifs, previously unique to Selçuk works, recur in subsequent carpet work throughout Asia Minor, and some of the same knots are used in Selçuk and later Ottoman examples. The latticed gallery above the *semahane* was for women spectators, a modification introduced by the followers of the Mevlâna after his death. The heavy chain suspended from the ceiling and the concentric balls hanging from it are carved from a single piece of marble. In the adjoining room, a casket containing hairs from the beard of the Prophet Mohammed is displayed alongside some finely illuminated medieval Korans.

Since Konya is the spiritual and temporal home of the Whirling Dervishes, the city plays host to the annual **Dervish Festival**, December 14–17. Unfortunately, this is not the best place to witness the dervish ceremony—members of the troupe that performs during the December festival do not profess to live as dervishes and they perform the ritual in an indoor basketball court, while Konya itself is probably at its worst at this time—the shops are filled with light-up Whirling Dervish lampstands, and hotel prices double. In addition, you will have to be prepared for temperatures as low as -15°F.

Before you fork out for the ticket (also pricey), it's worth considering that the best place to witness a *sema is* probably in the restored *semahane* in Galatasaray in İstanbul. The group performing there has official recognition as a dance troupe, but its members are practicing dervishes who have undergone the novitiate and live according to the teachings of the Mevlâna, performing ancient dervish rites and ceremonies as part of their daily routine.

TEACHINGS OF THE MEVLÂNA AND THE DERVISH CEREMONY

The Mevlâna instructed his disciples to pursue all positive manifestations of good and to practice infinite tolerance, love, and charity. He condemned slavery and advocated monogamy and a higher prominence for women in religious and public life. The Mevlâna also believed that one must strive for truth and beauty while constantly avoiding display. He did not advocate complete monastic seclusion—the Mevlevis held jobs in normal society and could marry—but believed that the contemplative and mystical practices of the dervish freed him from worldly cares and anxieties.

Contrary to the main body of Islamic belief, the Mevlâna extolled the virtues of music and dance, and the **whirling ceremony** for which the Mevlevi dervishes are renowned is a means of attaining freedom from earthly bondage and abandonment to God's love. Its ultimate purpose is to effect a union with God.

The **clothes** worn by the Mevlevi during the ceremony have symbolic significance. The camelhair hat represents a tombstone, the black cloak the tomb itself, and the white skirt the funerary shroud. During the ceremony the cloak is discarded and this denotes that the dervishes have escaped from their tombs and from all other earthly ties. The **music** symbolizes that of the spheres, and the turning dervishes represent the heavenly bodies themselves. Every movement and sound made during the ceremony has an additional significance, and is strictly regulated by detailed and specific directions. As an example, the right arms of the dancers are extended up to heaven and the left are pointing to the floor, denoting that grace is received from God and distributed to humanity, without anything being retained by the dervishes themselves.

The three **stages of the dance** are: knowledge of God, awareness of God's presence, and union with God. As the dancers turn they repeat a *zikhr*, or chant, under their breath, while the musicians sing a hymn expressing the desire for mystic union. In the final part of the ceremony, the Sheikh, the incarnation of the Mevlâna, joins the dancers and whirls with them.

More Mosques and Museums

The **Alâeddin Parkı** stands at the opposite end of Mevlâna Caddesi from the Mevlâna Müzesi, and as traffic islands go it's a nice place to stroll. The site of the original acropolis, the park has yielded finds dating back to 7000 BC as well as evidence of Hittite, Phrygian, Roman, and Greek settlers, most of which are now in the Museum of Anatolian Civilizations in Ankara. At the foot of the hill to the north are the scant remains of the Selçuk palace: two pieces of stone wall incongruously surmounted by an ugly concrete canopy.

The only other surviving building to bear witness to any of the long history of this mound is the imposing **Alâeddin Mosque**, begun by Sultan Mesut I in 1130 and completed by Alâeddin Keykubad in 1221. External features worthy of note are the irregularity of its form—probably a result of the time taken over its construction—and the use of masonry on the northeast facade from an earlier, unidentified classical construction. This masonry comprises a row of classical marble columns whose varying sizes have been cleverly compensated for in the surrounding stonework and whose diminishing heights echo the slope of the hill. The original building probably consisted of the fan-shaped hall, whose flat mud roof is supported on six more rows of Roman columns. The mosque has been closed to the public for mysteriously subliminal "restoration work" for the last three years. and there's no guarantee that it will be reopened in the immediate future. The interior is clearly visible through low windows, however, so it's possible to make out the network of wooden beams between series of low arches, both distinctly Selçuk features. The hoard of Selçuk carpets discovered here when the mosque was reopened at the beginning of this century have been relocated in the Mevlâna Müzesi, but the remains of eight Selçuk sultans, including the warrior Alparslan, are still enshrined in a *türbe* in an inaccessible interior courtyard.

The nearby **Karatay Medrese** on Alâeddin Bulvarı (Tues–Sun 8:30am–noon & 1:30–5:30pm; $1) is another important Selçuk monument. Built in 1251, the *medrese*, or school of Islamic studies, is now a museum of ceramics, but it is the building itself that is of greater interest. The main portal is a fine example of Islamic art at its most decorative, combining elements such as Arabic striped stonework and Greek Corinthian columns with a structure which is distinctly Selçuk: a tall doorway surmounted by a pointed, stalactite arch, reminiscent of the entrance of a tent. The features that distinguish Konya's two important Selçuk portals—this and the even more decorative example at the entrance of the Ince Minare Medrese—from other examples of Selçuk masonry are the use of Koranic script and interlacing, geometric patterns in the decoration.

Inside the Karatay Medrese, the most attractive exhibit is again part of the building itself. The symmetrical tiling of the famed **dome of stars** is a stylized representation of the solar system in gold, blue, and black monochrome tiles. Painted Ottoman tiles from İznik and Kütahya appear clumsy in contrast with the tiles of this delicate mosaic. The Selçuk **ceramics** on display in the museum bear witness to the fact that pious concerns were overruled by secular tastes even in the Middle Ages. The striking images of birds, animals, and even angels would all have been strictly forbidden by Islamic orthodoxy.

Behind its fine Selçuk portal the **İnce Minare Medrese**, or "School of the Slender Minaret" (Tues–Sun 8:30am–noon & 1:30–5:30; 50¢), below the park on Mevlâna Bulvarı, is now a museum of stone and woodcarving. The minaret from which it takes its name was destroyed by lightning in 1901. Most of the exhibits here, like the ceramics in the Karatay Medrese, came from the Selçuk palace once located on the present site of the Alâeddin Parkı. The finest individual item, however, is the carved wooden *mimber* (pulpit) from the thirteenth-century İplikli Camii, where the Mevlâna preached and meditated. The shell of this building can still be seen on Hükümet Caddesi.

The other notable museum is the **Museum of Archaeology** (Tues–Sun 8:30am–5pm; $1) in the south of the city. This contains the only pre-Selçuk remains in Konya, including what few Hittite artifacts from the nearby site of Çatal Höyük that have not been relocated in Ankara, and three well-preserved Roman sarcophagi from Pamphylia, one of which depicts Hercules at his twelve labors. Walking east from the museum you'll find the Sahip Ata Külliye. This mosque complex is semi-ruined but retains its beautiful brick and stone entrance portal.

Toward Cappadocia

Heading onward to Cappadocia there's very little to break the monotony of rolling wheatfields for some 150km: the Konya plain is flat, fertile, and relentless. Sights en route are sparsely scattered, and what there is to see hardly merits a half-hour detour anyway.

Çatal Höyük

The excavations at the important Neolithic site of **Çatal Höyük** have been so thorough that there's practically nothing left to see, but if you get excited by prehistoric mounds, or if you have a lively imagination, it's fairly easy to get to from Konya. Take a dolmuş or train from Konya to ÇUMRA, from which you will need to take a taxi to the site itself (10km north of the town). With your own transportation, head out of Konya on the Karaman/Mersin road, Highway 715, and take a left to Çumra 2km before İçeri Çumra. The road to the site is marked in the town.

Discovered by the British archaeologist James Mellaart in 1958, the site consists of twin flattened hills that are supposed to resemble the shape of a fork, hence the name Çatal Höyük or "Fork Tumulus." A number of exciting discoveries have been made here, giving significant clues to the lifestyle of one of the world's oldest civilizations. Thirteen strata have been identified, the earliest of which dates from 6800 BC, and the latest from 5500 BC. Evidence was found of whole complexes of houses, crammed together without streets to separate them, and entered through holes in the roof. Other finds have included wall paintings of men being eaten by vultures, animal-head trophies stuffed with squeezed clay, and human bones wrapped in straw mat and placed under the seats in a burial chamber, squatting in a fetal position. Most famous of the discoveries are statues of the mother goddess, supposed to be related to the Phrygian Goddess Cybele and the Greek Artemis. The baked earthenware or stone figures are 5–10cm tall and show a large-breasted, broad-hipped woman crouching to give birth. Today, however, all the most interesting pieces are in the Ankara Museum of Anatolian Civilizations.

Karapınar and Acı Göl

Just off Highway 330—which you can cut through to from Çatal Höyük if you're driving—there's a tiny, very beautiful crater lake just east of KARAPINAR. The lake, **Acı Göl**, is hidden from the main road, but the turnoff is on the right by a *Petrol Ofisi* and café, about 5km after the turnoff to Karapınar. If you have a tent it's an excellent place to camp, and there's good swimming, too; it's far enough from the road to afford some privacy.

Sultanhanı

The **Sultanhanı Kervansaray** (daily 7am–7pm; $1.50), 98km of dull driving from Konya on the Aksaray road, was one of the many public inns built by the Selçuks during the reign of Alâeddin Keykubad, testifying to the importance placed on social welfare by this highly cultured race. The buildings date to 1229, but have been substantially restored, first by Mehmet the Conqueror (providing evidence of the continued importance of this east–west trading route in the Ottoman period), and more recently by Turkish Radio and Television, which used the *kervansaray* in a historical television drama. Although the occasional cinder-block peeks out here and there, the restoration does serve to provide an effective model of the *kervansaray* institution.

The emphasis placed on security is clear from the high walls surrounding the complex, and by the size of the portal, which is truly massive and impressively ornate. Inside, the most prominent building is, as always, the small mosque or *mescit*, which takes a central position raised high above the courtyard on four pillars, away from the dangers of stray pack-animals. The latter were stabled in the back of the complex, opposite the entrance, in the enormous hall with five cradle-vaulted naves divided by huge pillars. The height of this room suggests accommodation for elephants rather than camels and mules, but it was meant to convey the impression of might and vigor to the foreign merchants who stayed in these provincial *hans* for up to three days free of charge. On either side of the entrance were private rooms and dormitories for servants, a hamam, workshops, a blacksmith's workshop, and storerooms.

The village that has grown up round the *kervansaray* specializes in ragamuffin children selling postcards, and also boasts a couple of **pansiyons** with camping facilities. One of these, the *Kervan*, has a decent restaurant, rooms with hot water and showers for $4 per person, and camping for $2, including use of hot water showers. The nearby *Sultanhanı Pansiyon* (☎4817/1008) charges $3 per person, $1.50 camping, but the facilities aren't as good.

CAPPADOCIA

A land created by the complex interaction of natural and human forces over vast spans of time, Cappadocia is unique to Turkey and should be visited and revisited. Its complexities cannot be understood in the time it takes a tour party to polish off a few frescoes on a photo stop-op between hotel and carpet shop.

Initially, the great expanses of bizzarely eroded, carved, and shaped volcanic matter can be disturbing. The still dryness and omnipresent dust give an impression of barrenness, and changing light takes dramatic effect to further startle and alienate the observer. Only with time comes the realization that the volcanic **tufa** that forms the land is exceedingly fertile, and that these weird formations of soft, dusty rock have accommodated, and been adapted by, many varying cultures and ways of life over the millennia. While the invading armies of great empires have generally disregarded Cappadocia, **indigenous peoples** have always exploited the region's potential, living in conditions of comparative cultural and material wealth. The most fascinating aspect of a visit to the area is the impression of continuity: rock caves are still inhabited; the fields are still fertilized with guano collected in rock-cut pigeon houses; and pottery is still made from the clay of the Kızılırmak River. **Wine** is produced locally as it has been since Hittite times, and

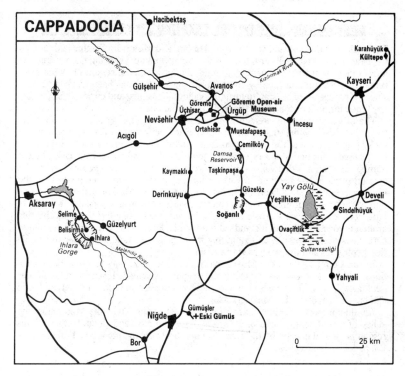

the **horses** from which the region takes its name (Cappadocia translates from the Hittite as "Land of Well-Bred Horses") are still bred and widely used, along with mules and donkeys, in transportation and agriculture.

The increase in the number of **tour groups** passing through the area has given rise to some large and ugly hotels, omnipresent carpet mafiosi, and seasonally packed museums, but these crowds are confined to a few designated areas, and tour guides ensure they don't stray too far. The essential Cappadocia is still there, waiting to be explored by travelers with time to appreciate changing forms and light, and to learn a little about how such an environment has been affected by— and has affected—the peoples who have settled there.

The **best-known sites** of Cappadocia, those most frequented by tour groups, are located within the triangle delimited by the roads connecting Nevşehir, Avanos, and Ürgüp. Within this region are the greater part of the valleys of **fairy chimneys**; the **rock-cut churches** of the Göreme Open-Air Museum, with their amazing selection of frescoes; and the Zelve monastery, a fascinating warren of **troglodyte (cave) dwellings** and churches. **Nevşehir** itself isn't much of a town, but it's an important travel center, while **Ürgüp** and its surrounding villages of **Çavuşin**, **Üçhisar**, and **Ortahisar** all make attractive bases for touring the surrounding valleys, but aren't well served by public transportation. **Avanos**, beautifully situated on the Kızılırmak River, is a center of the local pottery industry. Outside the triangle heading south, but still fairly well frequented by tour groups en route to the Mediterranean, are the underground cities of **Derinkuyu**

THE GEOLOGICAL FORMATIONS OF CAPPADOCIA

The peaks of three volcanoes—**Erciyes, Hasan,** and **Melendiz Dağları**—dominate Cappadocia. It was their eruptions some thirty million years ago, covering the former plateau of Ürgüp in ashes and mud, that provided the region's raw material: **tufa.** This soft stone formed by compressed volcanic ash has been worked on ever since by processes of erosion to form the valleys, badlands, and curious "fairy chimney" rock formations for which the region is so famous.

The original eruptions created a vast erosion basin, dipping slightly toward the Kızılırmak River, which marks an abrupt division between the fantasy landscape of rocky Cappadocia and the green farmland around Kayseri. In the south, especially, the plateau is formed of a very pure, homogenous tufa and rivers have carved out a number of straight-sided valleys. Elsewhere, where the tufa is mixed with rock, the erosion process has resulted in various formations (somewhat reminiscent of the American Southwest) collectively known as **fairy chimneys.** The stages in the creation of these extraordinary scenes can be clearly seen in many places: a block of hard rock which resists erosion, usually basalt, is left standing alone as the tufa around is worn away, until it stands at the top of a large cone. Eventually the underpart is eaten away to such an extent that it can no longer hold its capital: the whole thing collapses and the process starts again.

In the Cemil Valley, near Mustafapaşa, the cones give way to mesa-like formations—**table mountains**—caused by the deep grooves made by rivers in the harder geological layers. The area is characterized by increased amounts of water, and high cliff banks surmounted by vertical rocks.

Another important region is to the northwest of the Melendiz Mountains, the valley of the Melendiz Suyu or **Ihlara Valley.** The most individual feature of this region is the red canyon by the river, forming probably the most beautiful of all the Cappadocian landscapes.

and **Kaymaklı,** incredible **underground cities** attesting to the ingenuity of the ancient inhabitants. Less well-known sites are located to the east and west. The **Ihlara Valley** near **Aksaray,** a red canyon riddled with churches cut into its sides, is the most spectacular sight yet to feel the full force of tourism. **Kayseri** has been dropped from itineraries as a result of the development of tourism elsewhere in the region, and is now a quiet provincial capital recommended for its Selçuk architecture and the ski resort on Erciyes Dağı. To the southeast, attractions around the town of **Niğde** include the Sultansazlığı Bird Sanctuary and the nearby Eski Gümüşler Monastery, whose frescoes rival the more famous examples in Göreme.

The History of the Region

The earliest known settlers in the Cappadocia region were the **Hatti,** whose capital, Hattuşa, was located north of Nevşehir. The growth of the Hattic civilization, which was undergoing an early Bronze Age at the time, was interrupted by the arrival of large groups of Indo-European immigrants from western Europe, the **Hittites.** By 2000 BC these immigrants had imposed their rule on the region, mixing their own language and culture with that of the Hatti. The result was a rich and varied culture, and a body of laws that was remarkably humane for its time. Torture and mutilation of political prisoners, common practices of the time, were unknown to the Hittites, incest was forbidden by law, and Hittite kings were held to be "first among equals" rather than absolutist monarchs. In the Hittite

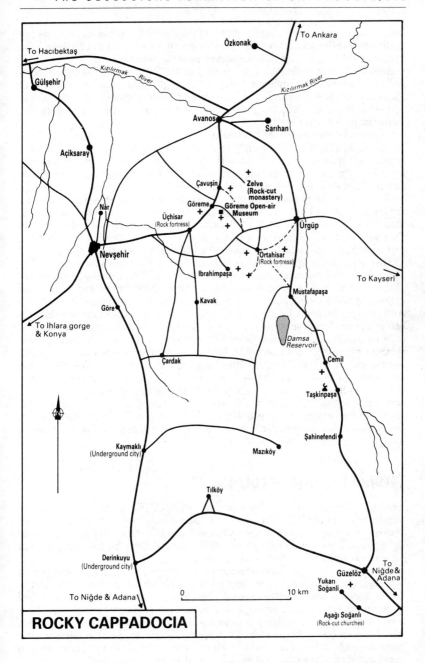

ROCKY CAPPADOCIA

laws it was written concerning the power of the monarch: "Whoever commits evil against his brothers and sisters answers for it with the royal head. Call the assembly, and if the things come to a decision he shall pay with his head."

After the fall of the Hittite Empire around 1200 BC the region was controlled to varying degrees and at different times by its neighboring kingdoms, Lydia and Phrygia in the west, Urartu in the east. This situation continued until the middle of the sixth century BC, when the Lydian king Croesus was defeated by the **Persians** under Cyrus the Great.

Cappadocia was saved from Persian rule by the arrival of **Alexander the Great** in 333 BC, and subsequently enjoyed independence for 350 years, until it became a Roman province with Kayseri as its capital. Despite this nominal annexation, de facto independence was ensured in the following centuries by the relative disinterest of the Roman and Byzantine rulers, whose only real concerns were to control the roads and thereby keep open eastern trading routes; to make the best use of the local manpower for their respective armies; and to extort tributes of local goods. Meanwhile the locals existed in very much the same way as they do now, living in rock-hewn dwellings or building houses out of local stone and relying economically on agriculture, viniculture, and livestock breeding.

This neglect, combined with the influence of an important east–west trading route, fostered a tolerance that allowed a number of faiths, creeds, and philosophies to flourish here. One of these was **Christianity**, introduced in the first century by the apostle Paul. Taking refuge from increasingly frequent attacks by Arab raiders, the new Christian communities took to the hills, where they literally carved out dwelling places, churches, and monasteries for entire communities.

In the eleventh century the **Selçuk Turks** arrived, quickly establishing good relations with the local communities. They too were interested primarily in trading routes, and their energies went into improving road systems and building the *kervansarays* that are strung along these roads to this day. The Selçuk Empire was defeated by the Mongols in the middle of the thirteenth century, and Cappadocia was controlled by the Karaman dynasty, based in Konya, before being incorporated into the Ottoman Empire in the fourteenth century. The last of the Christian Greeks left the area in the 1920s during the exchange of populations by the Greek and Turkish governments.

Nevşehir and Around

Reputedly Turkey's richest community, **NEVŞEHİR**, at the very heart of Cappadocia, can hardly be accused of an ostentatious display of wealth: the town consists of a couple of scruffy streets focused on a bus station. If you were hoping for a pleasant and comfortable town with decent amenities from which to set out on your excursions into the region, this isn't it.

The Nevşehir **otogar**, however, may start to play an irritatingly central part in your life: the most frequent services all over Cappadocia run from here, and in some cases it's necessary to make a wide detour to the city in order to travel between two neighboring towns. If you're not into hitching and don't have your own transportation then you may as well make the most of the time you'll be left with between buses. Fortunately, the longer you have to spend in the town, the more attractive it becomes, and a stroll up to the castle is all you really need to convince you that the place has merits beyond modern commerce.

Arrival and Orientation

Orientation is a simple matter in Nevşehir: the castle, which stands at the heart of the old city—to the southwest of the modern city center—is a continual landmark. The new city below is divided by two main streets: **Atatürk Bulvarı**, which contains most of the hotels and restaurants, and **Lale Caddesi**, turning into Gülşehir Caddesi to the north, where the new bus station (see below) should be located by the time of your arrival.

The **tourist information office** (Mon–Fri 8am–5pm; ☎4851/2717, 3659, 1137), on Atatürk Bulvarı on the right as you head downhill toward Ürgüp, should be your first port of call. The staff are friendly and helpful, and they can arm you with a hotel price list, a map of Nevşehir and surroundings, and advice on buses and dolmuşes in the area.

At the time of writing Nevşehir's **public transportation** is complicated by the fact that there are two dolmuş stations for local trips, situated at some distance from the long-haul bus station. There are plans to simplify this situation and relocate all three in one large terminal on the Gülşehir road: whether or not this is completed by the time of your arrival, any problems concerning public transportation can be dealt with by the tourist information staff.

The two competing **tour companies** in Nevşehir are *Tulip*, Eski Sanayi Meydanı 32 (☎4851/5519, 3339), which also owns the *Adventure* travel agency opposite, and *Neşe*, Aksaray Caddesi 5/A (☎4851/3484). Both are easily seen

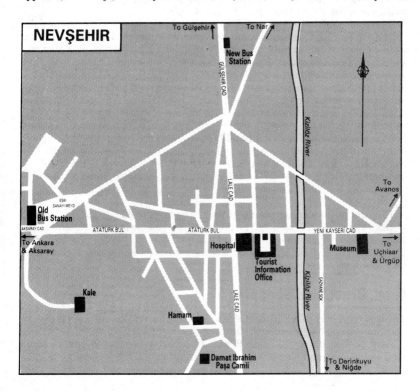

from the old bus station at the top of Atatürk Caddesi. *Neşe* is newly established and will hopefully provide healthy competition for *Tulip*, which has acquired a reputation for dishonest dealing with locals in the region. Before taking a tour from Nevşehir, it's worth phoning a few companies in Ürgüp and Göreme to compare the season's prices. **Rental cars** are obtainable from *Dede Rent a Car*, 12km out of town at the *Dedeman Hotel* (☎4851/5619), for a minimum daily rate of around $30 without tax.

Finding a Place to Stay

Pansiyons in Nevşehir are nowhere near as easily found, as cheap, or as good as elsewhere in Cappadocia. Two places near the old bus station are the reasonably priced *Hotel Kaymak*, Eski Sanayi Meydanı 11 (☎4851/5427), charging $6 single and $10 double for rooms without bathrooms, and to the north the modern and somewhat more comfortable—but gloomy—*Hısar Hotel*, Aksaray Caddesi 35 (☎4851/5672), $12 single, $20 double. A ten-minute walk away off the Ankara road is a cheap pansiyon called the *Maison du Turc*, Hasimi Sok 3 (no phone), with clean, rather spartan rooms at $6 single, $9 double. The *Hotel Şems*, single $14, double $24, on Atatürk Bulvarı above the *Aspava Restaurant*, is fairly comfortable; the only problem may be traffic noise. Ask for a room in back, where the views are better, too. The *İpek Palas* (☎4851/1478), farther north on the same street, is not as comfortable (shared bathrooms) and suffers the same problem of traffic noise, but it's cheaper: $8 single, $13 double.

If you can afford to pay more you'll be better served, since Nevşehir is a popular choice for tour companies with an eye for a good **hotel**. The *Hotel Altın Öz* (☎4851/5305), a comfortable and friendly affair with zany hi-tech glass elevators and an excellent restaurant, is situated off Kayseri Caddesi, just before the bridge as you go out of town toward Kayseri and Ürgüp: single $24, double $30. Other hotels in the same price range, but closer to the main road and farther out of town on Yeni Kayseri Caddesi, are the *Dılara* (☎4851/5441), the *Seven Brothers* (☎4851/4979) and the *Orsan* (☎4851/5329), the last of which has a swimming pool and disco (generally empty). Other hotels worth a mention are the new *Şekeryapan*, Gülşehir Caddesi 8 (☎4851/4253), comfortable and nicely furnished, with its own hamam and sauna, but a bit dark and serious, single $20, double $28; and the *Hotel Şehir Palas* (☎4851/5369), pleasantly situated next to the hamam of the İbrahim Paşa Külliyesi in the old town. It's a comfortable, quiet place with a well-stocked bar and huge terrace, and rooms costing around $26 single, $44 double.

The best of the **campgrounds** in the Cappadocia region, the *Koru Mocamp* (☎4856/1190), is indicated off to the right as you turn from Nevşehir into Üçhisar. It's quiet and green with lots of space to pitch tents under pine trees, and a good swimming pool. A tent and two people costs $6.50, parking is $1.50, and they have tents for rent.

Food, Drink, and Shopping

The best **food and drink** in town is to be found in the restaurants and bars of the good hotels, notably the *Altın Öz*, the *Şehir Palas*, and the *Şekeryapan*. Otherwise the *Aspava Restaurant*, at Atatürk Bulvarı 29, serves well-prepared, cheap *lokanta* food and kebabs, and almost opposite but farther up the hill is the slightly more expensive *Park Restaurant,* situated off the road in pleasant gardens. The *Şen* Restaurant on Lale Caddesi, toward the mosque, is a simple affair in a quiet part of town serving *tandır* kebabs, filling stews, and *pide*: all good lunchtime options.

Nevşehir's **market** is important to the region and consequently runs from Sunday night to Monday night, taking over a large area below the old bus terminal. If you're passing through Nevşehir with limited stocks of Turkish lira it's worth remembering that this is the wealthiest town in Turkey, and that its gold shops are the unofficial banks of central Anatolia. The best gold shops for **changing foreign currency** are located at Tahmis Caddesi, to the left as you walk up Atatürk Bulvarı. Sacit Uzer of *Altun Sarayi* at Tahmis Caddesi 20 gives good rates with no commission.

The only other commercial establishment worth perusal before you head on out is an excellent clothes shop, **Paco Collection**, near the tourist information office at Yeni Kayseri Caddesi 1/B. You couldn't wear a lot of their clothes in the streets of conservative Nevşehir without incurring comment, but swimwear and smart evening attire may come in useful elsewhere in Cappadocia, where Benetton is the only other outlet.

The Sights

The long walk up to the castle becomes more pleasant the closer you get: the streets get steeper and narrower, and on summer evenings the atmosphere is increasingly dominated by women working at the local handicraft of lacemaking. The remains of the Ottoman **citadel** are no big deal in themselves, being just a few crenellated walls at the top of the hill, but from this vantage point you are provided with a graphic overview of the historical development of the city. To the southeast is the small shantytown of **Muşkara**, a village of eighty houses and some three hundred people. This village was lucky enough to produce a Horatio Alger type figure who left home and went to seek his fortune in İstanbul. He found work in the Topkapı Saray, married a daughter of the sultan, and eventually became Grand Vizier **Damat İbrahim Paşa**, who profoundly affected the reign of Ahmet III, particularly in terms of its architecture.

Like all good heroes he never forgot his roots, and he returned to Muşkara to found a New Town (the meaning of "Nevşehir") based around his own mosque complex, which included *medrese, imaret,* and hamam. The town was planned with wide, western-style boulevards, for which the buildings lining them are nowhere near grand enough, and with a long, broad piazza between the market and the mosque.

The **Damat İbrahim Paşa mosque complex** (1726) is still central to the place, located on the side of the citadel hill with its *medrese* and library above it, and a tea garden directly below. It is set in a large compound made all the more impressive by the cramped streets of the surrounding residential center. The stone of the building is a pleasant, unadorned yellow, and internal painting, especially under the Sultan's loge and around the casements, is lovely. The cool, dark interior is further enhanced by small details like the fan-shaped decoration on the marble capitals, and the original carved wooden *kafes,* the screens that separated the women's balcony from the main hall. Opposite the mosque, the **Damat İbrahim Paşa Hamamı** (7:30am–9pm, open to couples after 6pm as long as you give prior warning, Saturdays women only, all other days men only; $4 with massage and towel) is also in good working order and well run.

The Museum

Nevşehir Museum, on Yeni Kayseri Caddesi (daily 8am–noon & 1–5pm; 50¢), is well worth the twenty-minute walk from the tourist information office. Well laid-out and labeled in an unusually comprehensive manner, its exhibits include three terracotta sarcophagi, dating from the third to fourth century AD, which resemble abstract mummy cases with little doors at face and knee level. Finds from the Phrygian and Byzantine periods include mirrors, pins, spoons, terracotta pots, and the like; and upstairs is an exhibition of Turkish carpets and kilims and the looms on which they were made, as well as beautiful old heavy silver Ottoman jewelry.

Underground Cities: Derinkuyu and Kaymaklı

Among the most extraordinary phenomena of the Cappadocia region are the remains of underground settlements, some of them large enough to have accommodated up to 30,000 people. A total of 36 such settlements, from villages to vast cities, have been discovered, but so far only a few have been opened to the public. The best known are Derinkuyu and Kaymaklı, on the road from Nevşehir to Niğde. There are no fairy chimneys here, but the ground consists of the same volcanic tufa, and the beleaguered, ever-resourceful Cappadocians created vast cities which are almost completely unnoticeable from ground level.

In origin, the cities are thought to date back at least to **Hittite** times (1900–1200 BC). Hittite-style seals have been found during excavations, and other Hittite remains, such as a lion statue, have turned up in the area. It is possible that the underground rooms were used as shelters during the attacks of 1200 BC, when the Hittite Empire was destroyed by invaders from Thrace. Later the complex was enlarged by other civilizations, and the presence of missionary schools, churches, and wine cellars seem to indicate that it was used by **Christian communities**. There were certainly pre-Christian underground cities in the area as early as 401 BC: they are referred to by **Xenophon**, a Greek mercenary who took charge of the Ten Thousand after the death of Cyrus, marching across Cappadocia with them:

> *The houses here were built underground; the entrances were like wells but they broadened out lower down. There were tunnels dug in the ground for the animals while the men went down by ladder. Inside the houses there were goats, sheep, cows, and poultry with their young . . . There was also wheat, beans, and barley wine in great bowls . . . When one was thirsty, one was meant to take a reed and suck the wine into one's mouth. This barley wine is exceedingly strong and is best mixed with water; but any man who is accustomed to it and drinks it undiluted enjoys its flavor to the full.*

The most thoroughly excavated of the underground cities is located in the village of **DERİNKUYU**, 29km from Nevşehir. There's a daily bus here from Aksaray, and dolmuşes from Nevşehir. A reasonable hotel in the middle of Derinkuyu, the *Ali Baba* (☎4864/1098), has rooms without showers for $4 per person, with showers for $12 double, but since the village has little to offer passing strangers there's no real point in staying unless you mistime your visit, or you want to visit the underground city before the crowds arrive.

The **underground city** of Derinkuyu, meaning "Deep Well" (daily May–Sept 8am–7pm, Oct–April 8am–5pm; entrance $2.50, students $1.25) is indicated off to the left as you approach from Nevşehir. The city is well lit and the original ventilation system still functions remarkably well, but some of the passages are small and cramped, and can get overcrowded if your visit coincides with that of a tour group. The size of this rock-cut labyrinth is difficult to comprehend even on a thorough exploration, since only part of what has been excavated is open to the public, and even the excavated part is thought to comprise only a quarter of the original city.

The area cleared to date occupies 1500 square meters and consists of a total of eight floors descending to a depth of 55 meters. What you'll see includes—on the first two floors—stables, wine presses, and a dining hall or school with two long, rock-cut tables; living quarters, churches, armories, and tunnels on the third and fourth floors; and a crucifix-shaped church, a meeting hall with three supporting columns, a dungeon, and a grave on the lower levels. In a room off the meeting hall is a circular passageway which is believed to have been a **confessional**. The **wine press** on the first floor must have had an opening to the ground above. Grapes thrown into the press were trampled and their juice collected in vats below. Dropping 70 to 85 meters, to far below the lowest floor level, were 52 large **ventilation shafts** and the deep **wells** from which the city takes its name, and the whole complex is riddled with small ventilation ducts—15,000 on the first level alone. There are also a number of escape routes from one floor to another, and passages leading beyond the city, one of which is thought to have gone all the way to Kaymaklı, 9km away. The walls of the rooms are completely undecorated, but chisel marks are clearly visible and give some idea of the work that must have gone into the creation of this extraordinary place. Most evocative of the lifestyle of former inhabitants, however, are the huge **circular doors** that could be used to seal one level from another. The doors, which were virtually impregnable from the outside, would have been closed with a pole through the circular hole in their center, and through this hole arrows could have been shot once the door was secure.

Nine kilometers before Derinkuyu on the Nevşehir–Niğde highway you'll pass **KAYMAKLI** (March–Sept 8am–7pm, Oct–Feb 8:30am–5pm; $2). Smaller and consequently less popular than Derinkuyu, only five of this underground city's levels have been excavated to date. The layout is very similar: networks of streets with small living spaces leading off them open into underground plazas with various functions, the more obvious of which are stabling, smoke-blackened kitchens, storage space, and wine presses.

Üçhisar

ÜÇHISAR, 15km east of Nevşehir on the Nevşehir–Ürgüp dolmuş run, is the first truly Cappadocian village en route to the center of the region from Nevşehir, and it makes sense to stop here if only to take your bearings from the vantage point of the sixty-meter-high rock that dominates the village. Riddled with the cave homes of villagers who lived here until it became too dangerous, the rock is now open to visitors (daily 8am–8:30pm; $1). The best time for a visit is late evening, when the views of the surrounding countryside, including Erciyes Dağı to the east and Melendiz and Hasan Dağları to the southwest, are particularly alluring. It's an excellent place to get a first impression of Cappadocia's extraordinary geology.

In the village itself there's a simple little **pansiyon**, the *Hakan* (☎4856/1080), where rooms above a café go for $3: the food downstairs is also very reasonably priced. If you're looking for scenery and solitude, however, head out of town on the old Göreme road, up a very steep hill which affords good views of the surrounding scenery. To the right about 200m out of town you'll find a group of small pansiyons including the excellent *Kaya Pansiyon* (☎4856/1441), which is clean, nicely furnished, and has a pleasant terrace restaurant with fantastic views; a buffet-style breakfast is included in the price of $15, and dinner is less than $3. The patron, who speaks some French, will pick you up from the village if you can make yourself understood on the phone. Other good bets in the same area are the *Han Pansiyon* (no phone), which has rock-cut rooms for $4 per person, and *La Maison Du Reve* (☎4856/1199), $4 per person without shower, $6 with, which is clean and attractive and has more good views.

Göreme and Around

The small town of **GÖREME**—just 3km east of Üçhisar—is of central importance to Cappadocian tourism partly because of its museum, located a couple of kilometers away on the Ürgüp road, but most importantly because it is the most famous of the few remaining Cappadocian villages whose rock-cut houses and fairy chimneys are still inhabited. The village is currently reeling a little from the effects of tourism, which has expanded remarkably in the last decade or so: its main street is given over almost entirely to servicing visitors—carpet shops, tour companies, bike- and car-rental agents—and seemingly every small dwelling now has rooms to let, and proudly proclaims itself a pansiyon, regardless of the facilities provided.

Despite the commercialization, however, the place has managed to hold onto a degree of authentic charm, and a short stroll will still take you up into tufa landscapes, vineyards which the locals cultivate for the production of *pekmez* (a breakfast syrup made from grape seeds), and the occasional rock-cut church, unknown to the hordes that frequent the nearby museum. Public transportation is adequate and hitching is relatively easy, so if you are intending to spend some time in the region this wouldn't be a bad place to base yourself.

Practicalities

Göreme's pansiyons have long been a favorite with young travelers looking for cheap lodging with a relaxed, easygoing atmosphere. Because of this the villagers are used to foreigners and their wayward ways, and single women are probably better off here than in Nevşehir or Kayseri. **Pansiyons** spring up every year in Göreme, and until recently competition was fierce: tourists were waylaid at the bus station and prices were so low that the better ones were finding it hard to maintain standards. Now the problems are being ironed out by collective price control and consequently the atmosphere in the village is substantially healthier. The price of a double room with outside shower and toilet is currently $8.

The best of the simpler pansiyons are the *Paradise* (☎4857/1248), which thrives on a constant supply of hot water and a well-deserved reputation for hospitality and friendliness (the owner is fluent in four languages, including English); the *Rock Valley Pansiyon* (☎4857/1474), comfortable and clean, with one of the best-value restaurants in town, thanks to an excellent chef and the high standards of the management; and the *Peri Pansiyon* (☎4857/1136), unique and pretty with its high-rise fairy chimneys and washing machine. The *Paradise* and the *Peri* are located at the beginning of the road to the Göreme Open-Air Museum and the *Rock Valley* is in the other direction, on the road leading past the *Gallery Ikman* carpet shop and the mosque, along the canal.

If you want an attached bathroom, the cheapest options are the *Ufuk* (☎4857/1157), between the *Peri* and the *Paradise*, which has a pleasant restaurant and bar, and the *SOS Pansiyon* up above town (walk straight past the dolmuş garage and keep going uphill, in the direction of Üçhisar), with simple, attractive rooms and breathtaking views from the terrace. Both of these have doubles at $12.

For a little more class and comfort, there are three attractive **hotels** in Göreme, the best known and nicest being the *Melek* (☎4857/1463; $12, or $3 in a dormitory; fixed menu meals $6 a head), with some rock-hewn rooms and a cool, pleasant lounge—it's all so clean even the fairy chimneys appear scrubbed. To reach it, take the road leading up into the old village, opposite *Rose Tours*—if you have problems (the secluded setting makes it a little hard to find) inquire at *Turtel Tours*, run by the same family. The newly cut *Special Cave Motel*, on the way to *Rock Valley Pansiyon*, is clean and comfortable for $6 a head, and the *Saksağan* is beautifully decorated with antiques, lace, and marble, the rooms arranged around a peaceful central courtyard. It's situated on the Üçhisar road out of town; $7 per person with breakfast.

There are several **campgrounds** on the fringes of Göreme: *Cappadocia* (no phone), on the Kayseri road, and *Dilek* (☎4857/1396), on the Ürgüp road near the *Peri Pansiyon*, the latter being more sheltered with its own water supply and a nice little restaurant; both have swimming pools and charge $3 per person in a tent, $4 in a trailer. The *Panorama* (☎4857/1352, 1434), 1km out on the Üçhisar road, works out at $4 for two with a tent, extra for vehicles. It has plenty of hot water and good facilities, but it's kind of exposed to the road, and has no trees to speak of.

Apart from the comfortable and attractive **restaurant** at *Rock Valley*, which serves vegetarian food and every conceivable egg option for breakfast, the best restaurant in Göreme, indeed among the best in Cappadocia, is the *Ataman* (☎4857/1310), straight back through the village past the *Halil* and *SOS* pansiyons. It's pricey for the village but everything is immaculately prepared and served, from local specialties like Kayseri *pastırma* (cured meat) baked in paper to French soufflés and flambées. Expect to pay anything from $5 to $15 a head. The *lokantas* on the main street are no better than average, but there's a good new **bar** next to *Rose Tours*—the *Traveler's Bar*—which is probably the best place to encounter local color and pick up information.

One of the main problems with staying in Göreme is the lack of **public transportation** in and out of the village. A taxi to Ürgüp costs $4 one-way, which really adds up if you use one every time you want to get out of town. If you are sticking around Cappadocia, you may be tempted to move to a bigger town, but there are ways to avoid this. Hitching is relatively easy in Cappadocia, since more and more Turks are taking vacations here, and Turkish hospitality seems to extend to their vehicles. Otherwise, **motorbikes** and mopeds (from $14 a day) as well as **rental cars** are available from *Rose Tours* (☎4857/1059), on the main street just before it forks to the Göreme Open-Air Museum.

If you decide to succumb to the mercies of a **tour operator**, the two best companies in Göreme are the above-mentioned *Rose Tours* and *Turtel*, on the same street in the Üçhisar direction. *Rose Tours* has a number of good basic itineraries, including some out-of-the-way destinations like Soğanlı, Ihlara Valley, and Bird Paradise (see below), from around $9. It also runs two-day tours to both Nemrut Dağ and Hattuşaş for $70. *Turtel Tours* offers a program that includes some interesting walks in the Göreme area, and can also arrange donkey and horseback trips farther afield.

The Town

The main street in Göreme is part of the highway between Nevşehir and the rest of Cappadocia. Consequently tourist-laden coaches regularly speed past a line of local businessmen who live in the forlorn hope that one day a tour guide might have a change of heart and spurn *Bazaar 54*—and his not inconsiderable commission—in favor of their more humble establishments. The **carpet shops** in Göreme are probably no better than elsewhere in Cappadocia, but a few, such as the *Gallery Ikman* (on the corner before the mosque as you head up the valley), *Rose Carpet* (in the shopping mall below the minibus station), and *Tapis de Göreme* (in the El Sanatlar Çarşısı), are well stocked and worth a browse.

After you've drunk your quota of apple tea you may be pleased to escape to the more rarefied climes of the tufa hills above town, where pride and dignity are

---

CHRISTIANITY IN CAPPADOCIA

For many centuries Anatolia was the most vital center of Christianity in the Meditteranean region. The great ecumenical councils which established the elemental doctrines of the faith were all held in Anatolia, and the region was home to some of the greatest early ecclesiastical writers. Most famously, these included the fourth-century **Cappadocian Fathers**: Basil the Great, Gregory of Nazianzuz, and Gregory of Nyssa. The religious authority of the capital of Cappadocia, Caesarea—present-day Kayseri—extended over the whole of southeast Anatolia, and it was also the birthplace of Gregory the Illuminator, the evangelizer of Armenia. The unique, creative art forms in the region are attributable to a long and complex history. Before becoming a Roman province in 18 AD the kingdom had enjoyed a 300-year period of independence, during which time small states, each with a central sanctuary and controlled by priests, had been the predominant units of power. Cappadocia's religion until the arrival of Christianity had been Semitic and Persian influenced, and its own language did not die out until the fourth century. Caesarea came under the Patriarchate of Constantinople in 381 BC, and from then on was influenced more and more by religious ideas from the capital.

Most disruptive was the **iconoclastic controversy** of 726–843, which had a profound effect on the creative life of Cappadocia. By the beginning of the eighth century, the cult of images had become extravagant, particularly noticeable in contrast to Muslim and Jewish hostility to the worship of images. In addition, the political power of the monks, whose numbers had increased considerably during the seventh century, began to cause concern. The iconoclastic movement was accompanied by the closure of monasteries and confiscation of their property. The worst period of repressive activity occurred during the reign of Constantine V, marked by the Iconoclastic Council of 754. All sacred images except the cross were forbidden, but at the same time the destruction of any religious building and its furnishings, whether or not they were decorated with idolatrous images, was prohibited.

alive and well among people who are perpetuating the traditions of centuries despite the recent changes in the village below. Pigeon droppings are still collected and used to fertilize the crops, the main mode of transportation is the donkey, and fields are irrigated with water stored in nearby caves.

There are two **churches** located in these hills, both indicated by signs from the road leading straight off the main street opposite the *Ataman Restaurant*. The **Durmuş Kadir Kilisesi** (named after the man who owns the neighboring fields) is marked "Kilise" and has a cave house with rock-cut steps next door to it, clearly visible from the path across a vineyard. It's not painted but has an impressive and unusual upstairs gallery, and cradle-shaped tombs outside.

The second church, the **Karşıbucak Yusuf Koç Kilisesi**, is also known as the "Church with Five Pillars" because its sixth was never carved. There are two domes, one of which has been damaged in the past to accommodate a pigeon coop, and frescoes in very good condition. Among them are the Annunciation, to the left; saints George and Theodore slaying the dragon, to the right; and Helena and Constantine depicted with the True Cross beside the door. In the dome above the altar are the Madonna and Child, and below, beside the altar, are depictions of the four evangelists, the only paintings in the church to have suffered substantial damage. Hasan from *Rose Carpets* is a knowledgeable guide to Göreme and its immediate vicinity, and gives informal tours on request.

From the middle of the sixth century the region had also been suffering a 300-year period of turbulence as the battleground of the Byzantines and the Arabs, and was subjected to continuous Arab raids, characterized by widespread plunder and destruction. The inhabitants responded with ingenuity: in the plains they went underground, creating subterranean cities (or extended existing complexes); and in rocky Cappadocia they took to the hills, carving monastery complexes at precarious heights in the tufa cliff faces.

After the restoration of the cult of images in 843, there was a renewed vigor in the religious activity of Cappadocia. During this period, the wealth of the church increased to such an extent that monastery-building was prohibited in 964, an edict that was only withdrawn in 1003. Meanwhile the religious communities were brought to heel, becoming controlled to a greater extent by the ecclesiastical hierarchy. Even though Cappadocia continued to be a center of religious activity well into the Ottoman period, it had lost the artistic momentum that had produced the most extraordinary works of earlier centuries.

Today, the number of churches in the Cappadocia region is estimated at well over a thousand, dating from the earliest days of Christianity to the thirteenth century. About 150 of these are decorated. Religious complexes are scattered all over Cappadocia, and despite the damage caused by time and human agencies, some of them are exceptionally well preserved. The technique of excavation, still used today, is evident in the fresh-looking pick marks on walls and ceilings. Most of the architecture is barely discernible from the outside, apart from a few small holes serving as doors, windows, or air and light shafts. Inwardly, however, the churches re-create many of the features of Byzantine buildings, especially those that were built while imperial influence was increasing in the region. Later churches have domes, barrel-vaulted ceilings and inscribed cross plans supported by pillars, capitals, and pendentives that have no structural significance whatsoever.

Göreme Open-Air Museum

The **Göreme Open-Air Museum** (daily 8:30am–5:30pm; entrance $2.50), 2km from the village up a steep hill on the road to Ürgüp, is the best known and most visited of all the monastic settlements in the Cappadocia region. It's also the largest of the religious complexes, and its churches, of which there are over thirty, contain some of the most fascinating of all the frescoes in Cappadocia. Apart from a small sixth- to seventh-century chapel, which has almost collapsed, all the churches in Göreme date from the period after the iconoclastic controversy, mainly the second half of the ninth to the end of the eleventh century.

The best preserved and most fascinating of all the churches is the **Tokalı Kilise**, the "Church with the Buckle," located away from the others on the opposite side of the road about 50m back toward the village. If it's closed, ask the curator at the ticket office to open it for you. The church is different in plan to others in the area, having a transverse nave and an atrium hewn out of an earlier church, known as the "Old Church." Most striking as you enter is the bright blue color used in the background to the paintings. The frescoes of the **Old Church**, dating from the second decade of the tenth century, portray various scenes from the life of Christ. They are classic examples of the archaic period of Cappadocian painting, which was characterized by a return to the forms of the best work of the fourth to sixth centuries: the style is linear, but like the mosaics of Aya Sofya in İstanbul, the faces are modeled by the use of different intensities of color and with the depiction of shadow.

The paintings in the **New Church** are some of the finest examples of tenth-century Byzantine art. Again they represent a return to archaic models, depicting a series of tall and elegant figures, the niches in the walls of the nave serving to give a sense of depth and substance to the paintings. The pictures represent more scenes from the life of Christ, and reflect an interpretation of the apse as the sepulchre of Christ and the altar as his tomb. The crucifix is in the conch of the apse, and the semicircular wall is used for the four scenes of Christ's Passion and Resurrection: the descent from the Cross, the entombment, the holy women at the sepulcher, and the Resurrection.

The best known of the churches in the main complex of Göreme are the three **columned churches**: the **Elmalı Kilise** (Church of the Apple), the **Karanlık Kilise** (Dark Church, currently closed for restoration) and the **Çarıklı Kilise** (Church of the Sandals). These eleventh-century churches were heavily influenced by classical Byzantine forms: each is constructed according to an inscribed cross plan, with a central dome supported on columns, in which the Pantocrator is portrayed above figures of Archangels and seraphim. The paintings of the churches, particularly in Elmalı Kilise, is notable for the skill with which the form and movement of the figures corresponds to the surfaces they cover. They are clad in drapery that follows the contours of their bodies, and their features are smoothly modeled, with carefully outlined eyes.

The facade of the **Karanlık Kilise** is carefully carved to give more of an impression of a free-standing building than elsewhere in Göreme. The expensive blue color obtained from the mineral azurite is everywhere in the church—in **Elmalı**, gray predominates.

A number of other late eleventh-century, single-aisle churches in the museum are covered in much cruder geometric patterns and linear pictures, painted straight onto the rock (unlike the frescoes of the three columned churches, which were preceded by a layer of plaster). In the Tokalı church this kind of paintwork can be seen appearing from beneath the plaster. In churches where it was not plastered over, the paintwork has become extensive. The rock-cut churches in this group include St Barbara and the Yılanlı Kilise. The predominant color of this style was red ochre, and the ubiquitous symbol was the cross, which indicated that the church had been consecrated.

The **Church of St Barbara** is named after a depiction of the saint on the north wall. Christ is represented on a throne in the apse. The strange insect-figure for which the church is also known must have had symbolic or magical significance which is now lost.

The **Yılanlı Kilise** (Church of the Snake) is most famous for the depiction of Saint Onophrius on the west wall of the nave. Saint Onophrius was a hermit who lived in the Egyptian desert in the fourth and fifth centuries, eating only dates, with a foliage loincloth for cover. According to Cappadocian guides and literature, however, the saint was originally a woman, and something of a temptress at that. When she eventually repented of her wicked ways and asked to be delivered from the desires of men, she was granted her wish, and received a beard, like that of the figure in the fresco. The story probably derives from the emphasized breasts of the figure in the picture, and from the desert foliage used by the saint as a loincloth.

Opposite Saint Onophrius, Constantine the Great and his mother Saint Helena are depicted holding the True Cross. After a vision in which she saw the True Cross, Helena traveled to Jerusalem at the age of eighty to find it. She unearthed three crosses, and to test which of them was genuine she laid them in turn on the coffin of a dead youth, who revived at the appropriate moment. Next to them, two of the "Soldier Saints," George and Theodore, are seen trampling the serpent. Saint Theodore was a Roman soldier who refused to enter into pagan worship and set fire to the temple of the mother goddess in Amasea; he was tortured and thrown into a furnace. Between the Yilanlı and Karanlık churches is a **refectory** with a rock-cut table designed to accommodate about fifty diners.

Outside the museum there are a few churches worth looking into on the road back to Göreme. These include the twelfth-century **Church of St Eustace**, reached by an iron staircase, with red and green paintings thought to have been the work of Armenian Christians. Also to the left of the road are the four-columned **Kılıçlar Kilise** (Church of the Swords), and on the right beyond Tokalı Church is the **St Daniel Chapel**, with a picture of Daniel in the lion's den. The **Saklı Kilise** (Hidden Church), about halfway between the museum and the village, uses the Cappadocian landscapes complete with fairy chimneys as a background for biblical scenes.

Çavuşin

Six kilometers from Göreme off the road to Avanos, **ÇAVUŞİN** is a small village with a good hotel and a few nice pansiyons, as well as a really beautiful church located in the hills nearby. The best approach to the village is to walk—through fabulous tufa landscapes—on a path beginning just beside *Kaya Camping* on the road from Ürgüp to Göreme. Follow the path for about half an hour, and where it takes a sudden bend through a tufa-tunnel to the left, follow the precipitous path to the right, heading down into the Kızılçukur Valley: this will lead you to Cavuşin, in the same general direction you came from, in another half hour or so.

The villagers have gradually moved out of their cave dwellings as a result of rockslides, but the old caves in the hills above the village can be explored if some care is taken. In their midst is the church of **St John the Baptist**, a large basilica thought to have been an important religious and pilgrimage center for the whole region. Its position up on the cliff face, combined with the imposing aspect of its colonnaded and molded facade, gives it prominence over the whole valley. The church was probably constructed in the fifth century, and it contains a votive pit, the only one in Cappadocia, which is thought to have contained the hand of Saint Hieron, a local saint born a few kilometers away. The walls are covered with paintings ranging in date from the sixth to the eighth centuries, probably votive offerings from grateful pilgrims.

A short distance away, located in a tower of rock in the same valley, the church known as the **"Pigeon House"** has frescoes commemorating the passage of Nicephoras Phocas through Cappadocia in 964–65, during his military campaign against Cilicia. The frescoes probably portray a pilgrimage to the Basilica of St John by the Byzantine emperor, who is known to have hankered after the monastic life and dreamed of retiring to Mount Athos with his spiritual father.

In the **village** itself, on the left as you descend to the main road, the *Çavuşin Cafeterya* (☎4861/7136) is a pleasant, tree-lined courtyard serving cold drinks and good breakfasts and snacks. Farther down on the right, the *İn Pansiyon* (☎4861/7070) has simple but comfortable rooms for $4 per person with shared bathroom (with a real bath). Across the road, the *Green Motel* (☎4861/7050) is an extremely attractive building with a pleasant garden which is also a campground. All the rooms have bathrooms and cost $8 per person. Down on the main road are a couple of good onyx shops which seem fairly priced: the *Fabrique d'Onyx* (☎4861/7069) and the *Çavuşin Onyx Factory and Silver Shop* (☎4861/7103).

Zelve

The deserted **monastery complex** located in the three valleys of ZELVE (daily 8:30am–6pm; $2.50), 3km off the Avanos–Çavuşin road, is one of the most fascinating remnants of Cappadocia's troglodyte past. The churches in Zelve date back to the pre-Iconoclastic age (ie before the ninth century) but the valley was inhabited by Turkish Muslims until about thirty years ago.

For the most part, the structure of the complex is dictated by the form of the tufa rock-faces into which it is carved: the inhabitants simply hacked out their dwellings, making few attempts—apart from the occasional dividing wall—to diversify the structure with architectural features. On the left-hand side of the first valley, about halfway up, are the remains of a small Ottoman mosque, the prayer hall and *mihrab* of which are partly hewn from the rock, showing a continuance of this ancient architectural tradition.

An exploration of the complex really requires a flashlight and old clothes, along with a considerable sense of adventure. At the top of the right-hand valley, on the right as you go up, a honeycomb of rooms are approached up metal staircases. Once you're up on the rock face the problems start: some of the rooms are entered by means of precarious steps, others by swinging up through large holes in their floors (keep an eye out for ancient hand and foot holes); and on occasions, massive leaps to a lower floor are required. Another "interesting" experience is the walk through the tunnel which leads between the two valleys on the right as you face them from the parking lot—impossible without a flashlight and nerves of steel. None of this is recommended for the infirm or claustrophobic, but it's great fun if you're reasonably energetic and have a head for heights.

A large number of chapels and medieval oratories are scattered up and down the valleys, many of them decorated with carved **crosses**. This preponderance of crosses, combined with the relatively small number of frescoes here, is thought to demonstrate a pre-Iconoclastic opposition to the cult of images. The few **painted images** found in Zelve are in the churches of the third valley, on the far right. The twin-aisled Üzümlü Kilise has pre-Iconoclastic grapevines painted in red and green on the walls, and a cross carved into the ceiling.

Ortahisar

A friendly little village located a little off the road between Göreme and Ürgüp, **ORTAHISAR** sees none of the hordes that are affecting Göreme so profoundly. Despite being surrounded by the rock-cut storehouses of Turkey's lemon mafiosi (the rock-cut caves in the region are particularly congenial to the storage of the fruit), the village itself has retained a degree of charm and innocence. After a few hours here you feel as if you know the whole populace; and they will certainly know you.

One of the chief attractions of Ortahisar is the fortress-like, 86-metre-high rock which, as at Üçhisar, once housed the entire village. It can now be explored and climbed (7:30am–8:30pm; $1.50) for excellent views of the surrounding valleys. The village itself is clustered around two squares: the first of them dominated by the bus station, the second crouched beneath the village rock.

There's plenty to explore in the valleys around Ortahisar, so if you don't have your own transportation and you want to spend time in the region it makes sense to **stay** the night. The *Göreme Hotel* (☎4869/1005; closed Nov–March), on the first village square, is old-fashioned and institutional, but very clean; $12 for a room with attached bath. The *Sarı Baba* (☎4869/1267), a small, rustic-looking pansiyon on the way to Pancarlık Kilise, might also be worth looking into. There's a good simple **restaurant**, the *Beyaz Saray*, between the two squares next to the mosque; and up near the entrance to the village, opposite the road leading to the *Öz Ay* carpet shop, the *Sinbad* **nightclub** (☎4869/1814) is located in a former lemon storage cellar. It's less expensive than the competition in Ürgüp and Avanos, and attracts a more progressive, intellectual audience. **Horses**—always an enjoyable way to get around in Cappadocia—can be rented from the French-run *Göreme Ranch* (☎4869/1763), down the hill past the *Antep Restaurant* (follow the sign off the first village square). Daily rates are $32, hourly $8.

There are also a few good **junk shops**, the best being the one run by Ahmet Yönemli (☎4869/1115), who sells old silver and copperware on the second village square, and an onyx factory, *Hisar Onyx* (☎4869/1115), where you can watch the production process from scratch.

Churches around Ortahisar

The village **guides** are two deaf-mute children, Ercan and Ahmet, who seem to know the area better than anyone. Enquire in *Hisar Onyx*: it would be almost impossible to find some of the churches in the surrounding valleys without them.

Taking the road marked "Pancarlık Kilise" off the second square, and continuing past the *Sarı Baba Pansiyon*, you'll come to the valley of the Üzenge Çay, the opposite side of which is covered with pigeon coops. If you walked down this valley to the left for a little over 2km you'd arrive in Ürgüp, but straight ahead a rough road leads across the valley to the **Pancarlık church and monastery complex**, 3km from Ortahisar. Hardly visited because of the difficulty of getting there, Pancarlık's church (free entry) has some excellent frescoes in good condition—even the faces are intact. They include the Baptism of Christ and the Annunciation, and to the left of the altar what looks like the Virgin Mary taking a bath.

Heading the other way out of Ortahisar, down Hüseyin Bey Camii Sokak and into the Ortahisar ravine, there's a group of churches that includes the **Balkanlar Kilise**, said to contain some of the oldest frescoes in Cappadocia, and the **Sarıca Kilise**, which has a dome and two free-standing pillars. Frescoes include scenes of the Annunciation and angels on the pendentives. Another church in this valley has a carving typical of the symbolism of the early Christian period. It shows a palm, representing the tree of paradise, above a cross enclosed within a crown.

Another interesting rock-cut complex which is hardly known to the public is the **Hallaç Hospital Monastery**, so called because it's thought that it was once an infirmary. This is reached by following the road leading to *Öz Ay Carpets* and continuing past the shop for about twenty minutes. The complex is carved and painted inside and out, the facade decorated with mock doors, windows, and pillars painted in green, black, and red.

Ürgüp

Above all else, **ÜRGÜP** is tourist-friendly. If you're looking for good facilities, nightlife, and shopping in a pleasant environment then Ürgüp was made for you. But unlike many resorts of this size, the place has also had the resilience and composure to accommodate its visitors without too many compromises. Before the exchange of populations in 1923, Ürgüp had a largely Greek population. There are still many distinctive and beautiful houses of Greek (and Ottoman) origin scattered around the town, many used as government buildings or hotels, while others remain domestic residences. The tufa cliffs above the town are riddled with man-made cave dwellings, now put to use as storage space and stabling for the donkeys whose braying kicks up a dawn chorus all over Cappadocia. Tourism has meant that the younger generation has moved out of the family caves and opened shops and hotels in the town below, but at least for the time being they are still in Ürgüp, and as long as they remain they will safeguard the traditions and memories of the community.

Arriving and Finding a Place to Stay

Arriving in Ürgüp, the first surprise is that the **otogar** is in the center of town. What's more, the tourist office, post office, museum, and shopping are all within walking distance, while the best hotels are at most a cheap taxi ride away.

To reach most of Ürgüp's shops and facilities, find the steps leading up from the bus station, beside *Murat's Bar*, to Cumhuriyet Meydanı. Kayseri Caddesi, the street leading downhill to the tourist information office and museum, is also the main shopping street. The **tourist information office** (☎4868/1059; daily 8:30am–5:30pm) is at Kayseri Caddesi 37, pleasantly located next to the museum in a park, complete with tea garden, where you can peruse their maps and hotel price list. The *Garanti Bankası* is open for **money exchange** every day from 8:30am to 5:30pm (other functions weekdays only), and the **post office**, on Pastane Sokak, is open until 11pm every night to sell phone tokens.

Accommodation shouldn't be a problem in high or low season, since Ürgüp is full of hotels and pansiyons. A hotel price list is posted on a board in the bus station, and this can be verified or enlarged on by the tourist office (even so, it's just as well to check the prices by phone or on arrival, as mistakes have been made). There are several attractive, well-run hotels on the roads leading in and out of Ürgüp from the Nevşehir/Göreme direction. At İstiklâl Caddesi 38 (the entrance to town) the *Hotel Asia Minor* (☎4868/1645, 2721) occupies one of Ürgüp's oldest buildings; comfortable rooms with bath are well furnished and cheap at $10. In a similar vein and price range, another stone-and-timber Ottoman building houses the *Born Hotel* (☎4868/1756) on Ahmet Refik Caddesi; it's smaller and rather chaotic but good fun, and breakfast is available for $1.50. Farther out of town on the same road is the attractive *Hotel Konak* (☎4868/1325, 1667), immaculately kept and a good choice for families—children will enjoy beds up on wooden platforms. The balconied rooms have large windows affording views of the rock-cut houses and pigeon coops opposite, from $14 including breakfast. The *Hotel Surban* (☎4868/1603, 1389), on the same road beyond the *Hanedan Restaurant*, is well decorated, modern and comfortable—$26 with breakfast.

Other cheap and central places to be recommended are the friendly and quiet *Seymen Pansiyon* (☎4868/2380; $5 double), located in another attractive building from Ürgüp's former life (although, with solar water-heating, hot water might be a problem on cloudy days), and the *Cappadoce Hotel* (☎4868/1714), an old Greek monastery building with a pleasant garden courtyard and a variety of rooms ranging from four-person with outside bathroom at $4 a head to double rooms with attached bath for $14 a room. These two hotels face each other, above the hamam on İstiklâl Caddesi.

At the other side of town, beyond the tourist information office on Kayseri Caddesi, the *Göreme Pansiyon* (☎4868/1022) is pleasant, with double rooms (some with baths) from $10, and camping space out back. Next door at No. 5 the *Peri Hotel* is an old-fashioned, comfortable kind of place with a bar downstairs; rooms with showers and toilets for $6 a person without breakfast. The *Onur Pansiyon* (☎4868/1300), Namık Kemal Caddesi 4, a backstreet behind Kayseri Caddesi, is a quiet old house with hot water and simple rooms for $4 a head.

The *Çamlık* **campground** (☎4868/1146, 1022), across the Damsa River on the Kayseri road about 1km out of town, has excellent facilities and plenty of shade, and there is also a camping area and swimming pool at the *Pınar Hotel* (☎4868/1054) at Kayseri Caddesi 24.

The Town

Ürgüp may be carefully trimmed with fancy street lighting and cobbled lanes, but before tourism awakens each morning it is very much a rural village, its streets taken over by men and women in traditional costume leading horse-drawn vehicles and donkeys out to vineyards, orchards, and vegetable plots. This is the time to explore the **old village**, whose buildings appear to be slowly emerging from the rocky hills into which they have been carved, some with stylish pillared and decorated facades of the same stone, others simple caves with doors and windows cut into the cliffs themselves.

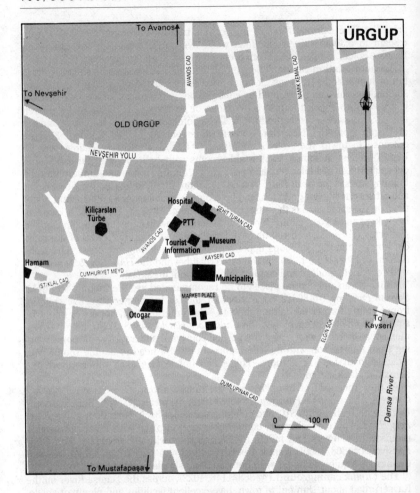

Viniculture and apple farming along the banks of the Damsa River constitute an important part of the local economy, but Ürgüp's recent wealth is largely a result of tourism, which has taken precedence as a result of adept local politicking during the past decade. Now the town's population increases from around six to nearly twenty thousand in the tourist season and traditional village shops have been replaced by banks, tour companies, and other tourist-related businesses. Perhaps the most telling of all changes, however, is that the town's **hamam**, in Yeni Cami Mahallesi, is now mixed, and women have had to refuse to be massaged by male masseurs, an unheard-of phenomenon in a traditional Turkish community.

The town's **museum** (Tues–Sun 8am–5pm; 50¢) is tiny and not particularly well labeled, but the staff are extremely helpful and prepared to explain the exhibits. These include a selection of prehistoric ceramics, figurines, lamps, stelae, statues, and ornaments found during excavations in the area.

The main **shopping** street, starting at Cumhuriyet Meydanı and continuing down Kayseri Caddesi, has some of the best **carpets, jewelry**, and **antiquities** in Turkey. It's not necessarily cheaper to buy here than in İstanbul, but Turkish traders from the east generally come to Ürgüp with carpets, silver, and antiquities before making the journey up to İstanbul, so Ürgüp's traders have first pick. Muammer Sak of *Aksa Carpets*, opposite the tourist information office on Kayseri Caddesi, carries some of the best antique carpets and kilims to be found in Turkey, and is a mine of information on ancient designs and motifs. If your budget is restricted, however, you might be better off elsewhere. Other well-stocked outlets include *Le Bazaar d'Orient*, Kayseri Caddesi 32, run by the Güzelgöz, one of Ürgüp's oldest families; *Galerie Öz* at Cumhuriyet Alanı 12, or in the *El Sanatlar Çarşısı* (beyond the tourist information office on Kayseri Caddesi); the *Antikite Bazaar*, which has a large collection of *minder, cicim,* and *kilim yastık*; and *Galerie Erhan*, a specialist in local *yahyalı* and *doşemaltı* rugs. This list is by no means comprehensive: whatever kind of carpet you're looking for, you should be able to find it somewhere in this street.

Antiques, especially silver, are also readily available in Ürgüp, collected from nomad villages in the east of Turkey by Aziz Güzelgöz (also an accomplished *saz* player) of *Antikite Aziz Baba*, Kayseri Caddesi 28, and by Veli Kırcı of *Antikite Veli Baba*, Kayseri Cad 14 (☎4868/1042). A comprehensive collection of **local wines** is available from *Mahzen Şarap Evi* on Cumhuriyet Meydanı. Wine tasting is possible at any of Ürgüp's six wineries, whose vineyards are all located in the Ürgüp area, but the best local wines are widely acknowledged to be those produced by the *Turasan* house near the *Turban Hotel* on the Nevşehir road out of Ürgüp, and the *Taşkobirlik* cooperative. It's worth remembering that white Cappadocian wines are much better than red; the reds are mixed with wines from other regions, and dyes are added.

Food and Nightlife

Ürgüp's best **restaurant** is the *Hanedan* (☎4868/1266, 1366; noon–3pm & 7pm–2am), opposite the *Türkerler Motel* on the Nevşehir road out of town. Decor includes a fish pond and stream downstairs, and upstairs a stuffed bird collection that looks as if it might take revenge on behalf of your meal. An international evening menu includes quail, snail bourguignon, and octopus stew, while the luncheon buffet of eighteen cold and twelve hot *mezes* is $5 a head. Cheaper options include a deservedly popular *lokanta* called the *Cappadocia Restaurant* at Kayseri Caddesi 16, and the *Kardeşler Pide Salonu*, Dumlupınar Caddesi 13, which serves very good nourishing *pide*. Two middle-range restaurants are the genteel *Ocakbaşı* above the bus station, and the modern *Pizza Express*, which serves reasonably priced snacks, ice cream, and wine on an open terrace above the *El Sanatlar Çarşısı* on Kayseri Caddesi.

Ürgüp's **nightlife** is excellent when you consider that this is central Anatolia and there's not a beach in sight. Entertainment combined with unlimited alcohol and an à la carte menu ($12 all-inclusive) can be found at the *Garden Coupole* (☎4868/1520) on İstiklâl Caddesi, where the folk-dancing program includes a traditional Turkish wedding ceremony (preliminaries including the shaving of the groom) and dances celebrating courtship and harvest-time, accompanied by good lively music, audible for miles around. The town's **discos** are the *Harem* on Suat Hayrı Ürgüplü Caddesi (☎4868/3359) and the *Armağan*, at the top of Kayseri

Caddesi, the latter larger with an anomalous but cosy log fire (both are closed Jan 1–Mar 30). Both have free entry but drinks are $2 each. There are also discos in most of the big hotels, the best being those in the *Otel Mustafa* (☎4868/3970), across the Damsa on the Kayseri road out of town, which also has Turkish music in the lobby, and the *Boydaş Hotel* next door (☎4868/1259). The *Halay* disco bar, İstiklâl Caddesi 31 (next to the *Garden Coupole*), is newly opened under young management and promises to be good, as does the *Piano Bar* at İstiklâl Caddesi 13. *Murat's Bar*, next to the *Magic Valley* tour company at the otogar, has a pleasant atmosphere and is quite cheap; a more upmarket alternative is the *Bar Fixe*, near the *Harem disco* on Suat Hayrı Ürgüplü Caddesi, where drinks are $4 apiece.

Exploring onward from Ürgüp there are a number of options for **transport**. A couple of good **tour companies**, *Magic Valley* (☎4868/2145) and *Kayer Tours* (☎4868/1221), have offices at the bus station; **cars, mopeds** and **motorbikes** are available for rent from *Hertz* at *Ekin*, Suat Hayrı Ürgüplü Caddesi (☎4868/2360, 2209), or from either of the above-mentioned tour companies; and, a new venture in the region, imported Italian **mountain bikes** can be rentd from *Tourbike*, İstiklâl Caddesi 10 (☎4868/3488), for $17 a day including insurance. **Dolmuşes** to the Göreme Open Air Museum, Göreme village and Kayseri leave from the otogar when they fill up, but it's generally quicker to hitch.

Around Ürgüp—Mustafapaşa to Soğanlı

The small village of **MUSTAFAPAŞA** is a pleasant bike ride from Ürgüp. The charm of the place lies in the concentration of attractive carved facades dating back to the end of the last century, when it was home to a thriving Greek community known as Sinassos: it is also central to a cluster of little-visited churches. Unfortunately Mustafapaşa makes an awkward base unless you have some way of getting around: there are a couple of municipal **buses** to and from Ürgüp, but nothing beyond that in the Cemil/Soğanlı direction.

One of the grandest of the town's old Greek residences is currently being renovated as the *Sinassos Hotel*, complete with painted and carved ceilings and fake marble trimmings. The nicest **hotel** in the region, however, is the *Natura* (☎4868/5200), an old Greek villa restored with original turn-of-the-century trimmings. It's largely taken over by German tour groups, but if you can find a room this would be a delightful place to spend some time, for $10 a double room. Another popular pansiyon, the *Manastır* (☎4868/5005), derives its name from its original function as a Greek monastery. It's clean, pleasant, and cheap, with bunk beds or mattresses on the floor for $4 per person with bathroom, $3 without. **Camping** is an attractive option at the *Pacha* campground (☎4868/5008) above the Uzengi Dere ravine—$2 per person with your tent, $3 with theirs. Turkish village food is served, and there's also a well-equipped kitchen for preparing your own.

In the center of Mustafapaşa an attractively renovated *medrese* has been converted into a **carpet workshop** and salesroom, the *Kervansaray*. Here you can watch women weaving beautiful silk carpets, but in this case beware of the word "cooperative." The women are low-waged, the work is damaging to their sight, and the carpets are overpriced.

The church of **Ayos Vasilios** is located to the north of the village, beyond the *Pasha* campground. Pick up the key from the makeshift **tourist information**

office (opening hours variable), next to the *Kervansaray* carpet shop, before setting out. The church has well-preserved frescoes, although the faces are damaged, and four rock-cut pillars. Other churches below in the Uzengi Dere ravine include the double-aisled Church of St Basil, with Iconoclastic paintings, and the Church of the Precious Cross, partly rock-cut and partly stone-built, with pre-Iconoclastic and tenth-century paintings including a very attractive "Christ of the Second Coming." On the other side of the village, passing through streets of houses cut by former Greek occupants into the tufa cliffs, is a **monastery** complex including the churches of Aya Nicola and Ayos Stefanos.

Following the Soğanlı road from Mustafapaşa—you'll have to make your own way, as there's no public transportation—the fairy chimneys give way to a landscape of **plateaus and mesas** which is no less fantastic and surreal than preceding scenery: the red canyon ridge that the road follows could be a backdrop for *Roadrunner.* About 3km from Mustafapaşa, watch out on your left for a hand-painted sign advertising *alabalık* which points to a precipitous dirt road off to the left. The road leads to a tiny **fish farm** and restaurant where fresh trout are oven-baked. To the right of the road, 5km from Mustafapaşa, lies the **Damsa Dam**, which is responsible for the fresh, green appearance of the well-irrigated fields in this area. An access road leads to a small beach on the shore, which gets crowded on summer weekends.

The next village along this road is **CEMİL,** a picturesque hamlet of tufa houses piled up against the cliffside. One and a half kilometers beyond the village, just off the road, lies the **Keşlik Monastery complex**—three churches, a wine press, and a refectory. This is believed to be one of the earliest communal monastic establishments in the region. The watchman, who speaks some English, gives a worthwhile tour of the frescoes in the churches: the first, named after a prominent picture of the angel Gabriel, includes depictions of the Last Supper, the Annunciation, and the flight to Egypt, all badly damaged and soot-blackened (a flashlight is essential); the Church of St Michael has a wine cellar downstairs; while the Church of St Stephen (seventh or eighth century) is the most beautiful of all, elaborately and unusually decorated. Non-figurative ornament includes stylized foliage and inter-laced patterns reminiscent of Turkish kilims, and figurative designs include depictions of various fruits and animals, and a peacock eating grapes.

Four kilometers farther along the same road is the village of **TAŞKINPAŞA.** Here a fourteenth-century Selçuk mosque, the **Taşkınpaşa Camii**, is flanked by two hexagonal tombs. The original marble pillars and their disparate capitals are still in place, supporting the twin domes of the mosque, and the old Selçuk minaret can be reached by a set of steps, but the intricately carved *mihrab* and *mimber* for which the building was originally famed have now been removed to Ankara, and only photographs are left in the mosque itself. To the left just beyond the village you can see the remains of another Selçuk building believed to have been a **medrese**, with an attractively carved stone portal.

One of the most spectacular of the sights this side of Ürgüp is the **Soğanlı Valley** (8am–5/6pm; $1), 5km off the road from Taşkınpaşa to Yeşilhisar, and less than 20km from either. **SOĞANLI** itself is an attractive village in two parts, Yukarı (Upper) and Aşağı (Lower) Soğanlı, set into the side of a table-top mountain. Part of the place's charm derives from its inaccessibility. It is off the tour route of all but small local companies—there are just a couple of simple restaurants, and a few stands selling the village-made rag dolls. This isolation also means that there's no public transportation, and in winter the village is often completely cut off by snow.

The Soğanlı Valley was continuously occupied from early Byzantine times to the thirteenth century, and is remarkable for the architecture of its churches and the beauty of the ninth- to thirteenth-century frescoes it contains. The name is supposed to derive from the Turkish *sona kaldı* (meaning "left to the end"), a reference to the fact that this was the last village to be taken during the Arab invasion of Cappadocia led by Battal Gazi in the sixth century.

The most interesting of the churches and monasteries are located in a side-valley on your right (as you face Yukarı Soğanlı) and are all accessible with a modicum of effort. To reach the two-storied **Kubbeli Kilise** (Church with the Dome), follow the footpath across a stream bed from the village square, and proceed uphill through the village and along the side of the valley. This has perhaps the most interesting exterior of all the Cappadocian rock churches, its form—a conical dome which is the tip of a fairy chimney, resting on a circular drum—being an imitation of a masonry structure. The **Saklı (Hidden) Kilise**, with frescoes of the apostles, is below the Kubbeli Kilise, its door facing into the valley.

Descending to the road and then up the other side of the side-valley, the **Meryem Ana Kilisesi** (Church of the Virgin) has four apsaidal chapels with frescoes and Iconoclastic decoration. The **Yılanlı Kilise** (Church of the Snake) is best seen using a flashlight, as it is blackened and damaged by Greek and Armenian graffiti from the turn of the century. It derives its name from an eleventh-century painting of St George slaying the dragon, to the left of the entrance. Returning toward the village, the **Karabaş Kilise** (Church of the Black Head) has two adjoining apsaidal chapels, the first of which has well-preserved tenth- and eleventh-century frescoes depicting scenes from the life of Christ.

In a second side-valley, reached by passing the restaurants of Yukarı Soğanlı, the **Geyikli Kilise** (Church with the Deer) has two aisles decorated in the eleventh century, and derives its name from a damaged depiction of St Eustace with a poorly defined deer. Farther up the valley the **Barbara Kilise**, a single-aisled basilica divided in two by a transverse arch, has an inscription dating it to the early tenth century.

Avanos and Around

The old city of **AVANOS** clambers up hills overlooking the longest river in Turkey, the Kızılırmak. A truly, magnificently Red River with a temper to match, the Kızılırmak appears to be on the verge of bursting its banks even in the height of summer. Avanos itself is a town of some character, separated from the rest of Cappadocia by the river and distinguished from all other towns in Turkey by the distinctive earthenware pottery made here. The same red clay that colors the river has been worked here for centuries, and techniques dating back to Hittite times are still in use. Strolling through the cobbled backstreets of the old town, you get superb views out across the river—only slightly marred by the new housing development all too evident on the south bank. Exploration of the fields and hills around the town reveals further attractions: calcium pools and thermal springs, a tiny *kervansaray*, and even an underground city, 14km away at Özkonak. Fifty kilometers to the north is the monastery complex of Hacıbektaş, founded by one of the greatest thinkers of the Islamic world.

The immediate surroundings are most comfortably explored on horseback, and the local **horses** have been bred for the terrain. They're generally even-tempered and well suited to inexperienced riders.

Practicalities

The **tourist information office** (☎4861/1360, daily 8:30am–5:30pm) has recently been moved to the other side of the river from town and is now found just across the bridge, on the right. The **PTT** is more sensibly located just beyond the pottery monument on the main street, next to the **public restrooms**.

It's easy enough to find **accommodation**, since Avanos's hotels and pansiyons cater to most tastes and requirements. One of the best small pansiyons in the region, the *Kervan* (☎4861/1483, 1879), is located in old Avanos, on the street running uphill behind Galip's workshop (see below), opposite the PTT. It's kept by the same family that runs the *Point de Rencontre* tourist agency, so inquire there about vacancies. The rooms, situated around a pleasant courtyard, are immaculately clean, well furnished, cool, and dark: $4 per person without shower, $5 with, including breakfast. Farther uphill, in Yukarı Mahalle, the *Hittite Pansiyon* is a friendly affair run by the Arikan brothers; clean, comfortable rooms with outside bathroom for $4 per person with breakfast. Dinner, possibly accompanied by a brother playing *saz*, is also provided. At the top of the hill, the *Panorama* (☎4861/1654) and the *Fantaisie* (☎4861/1947) afford beautiful views of the river and town. The *Fantaisie* has a few rooms with bathrooms, and it's possible to camp in the garden of the *Panorama*. Both charge around $3 a person.

Mesut **camping**, on the banks of the Kızılırmak near the footbridge, is a little scruffy and unfinished at the moment, but it does have a *tandır* (an oven cut into the ground) on which the proprietor's wife cooks excellent *bazlama*, a kind of *yufka* sandwich: $2 a head for camping.

Moving up in price, the *Hotel Zelve* (☎4861/1524), on the main street opposite the Hükümet Konağı, has some attractive rooms with nice views ($24 double; some are on the small side) and a good bar and restaurant, with a set menu at $4. Across the river in the Bezirhan district (follow the signs for the *Dragon Restaurant* before the bridge), the *Irmak Hotel* (☎4861/1317) is well designed to make the most of its secluded setting in extensive gardens on the banks of the river. It's geared mainly for groups, so prices are high: $36 single, $48 double.

If you have any equestrian leanings at all, the surrounding countryside should be seen from horseback, which is handy since the best stable of the region is located in Avanos. It has twenty locally bred **horses**, a couple of which are pretty sprightly (read "terrifying" if you're not of a horsey inclination), but mostly they are gentle and ideal for trekking; $30 for one day, $18 for a half day, $6 hourly.

The Town

Though the quaint, cobbled backstreets and rustic, tumbledown buildings are enjoyable, Avanos's real tourist attraction is **pottery**. The potter's square and the streets that surround it—carry on past the clay sculpture which is a memorial to this and the other local craft of weaving—contain numerous tiny workshops where the Cappadocian potter's techniques can still be observed or even attempted.

Perhaps the most famous of all the Avanos pottery workshops is Çeç, belonging to master potter **Galip**. Galip's place is generally thronged with groups, but if you arrive at a quiet time you may be shown into one of the back rooms where Galip stores hair collected from his female visitors over the past ten years or more. Countless locks trail from the ceiling and walls of the musty cave where they're displayed, and the sinister aspects of the custom are partially diminished by the fact that every year, Galip draws the names of ten of his hair-donors from a hat and gives them fifteen days' vacation in Avanos at his expense.

A tour of the workshop reveals a cellar where some fifty to sixty tons of local red earth, collected from dried-up beds of the Kızılırmak River, are stored awaiting the water that will transform them to malleable clay. The clay is worked on a wheel, turned by the foot of the potter, in natural light from the open doorway. Afterward, the polished finish on the pots is achieved by a laborious process using the rounded end of a piece of metal, a technique thought to date back to Hittite times. The pots dry slowly in a storeroom above the workshop, and later more quickly out in the open air. They are then fired in a coal furnace at 200°C for ten hours, and sometimes the firing is repeated to produce the distinctive blackened color of some of the pots. Galip's furnace is tended by his mother, the ancient and beautiful Muazzez Hanım.

Just behind the Çeç is the underground pottery workshop of Mümtaz. Here they run two-day **pottery courses** with accommodation and food for around $20.

Another local craft which deserves a mention is **knitting**. The shops in Kenan Evren Caddesi are full of beautiful, brightly colored hand-knitted sweaters as well as a good selection of şalvar (harem pants), silver, and carpets. The best selection of sweaters is at no. 66, at the *Butik Famex*, while silver, şalvar, and semiprecious stones can be found farther along toward the bridge at *Chez Efe*.

Food and Action

Sofra (☎4861/1324), on the main street near the PTT, is a reasonably priced restaurant, so popular that the food is eaten before it gets cold. The *Tafana Pide Salonu*, Kenan Evren Caddesi 47 (☎4861/1862), is also cheap, and serves a local specialty called *kiremit*, a kind of lamb stew. The *Tuvanna*, Kenan Evren Caddesi (☎4861/1497), is a slightly more expensive place that caters mostly to groups, but it's worth asking for the *günün yemeği* ("daily menu") at lunchtimes ($1.50); the *meze* are also well prepared and interesting. The *Şato Restaurant* (☎4861/1485), and the *Çeç Bar* above it, are pleasantly located on the river, near the road bridge, but again they're aimed mainly at groups rather than individual travelers.

One of the best **nightclubs** in the region, the *Dragon* (☎4861/1486, 1506), is located in the area called Bezirhane, clearly indicated by a sign off the Gülşehir road. The caves here have been painstakingly carved out of tufa by another famous local potter, Mehmet İpekdere. The evening's program is a familiar one, consisting of Turkish folk dancing and oriental (belly) dancing, followed by a disco, but the *Dragon*'s folk dancers are possibly Cappadocia's most accomplished and the management takes pains to hire the best available oriental dancers. The caves are huge, but popular with groups, so it's worth making reservations. An evening at the *Dragon* can be combined with a visit to Mehmet's large and impressive pottery workshop next door, where you can sip local wine from tiny clay vessels and watch Mehmet deftly throw another pot.

If oriental dancing is not your thing, the *Motif Restaurant* on the other side of the river, off the Nevşehir road beyond the *Irmak Hotel* at Hasan Kalesi Mevkii (☎4861/1577), has a well-established reputation for its folk-dancing program and good food; admission is $24 for a meal and entertainment in a pleasantly relaxed atmosphere. For a less organized evening, the recently opened *Bambu Bar* promises to be popular. It's well stocked—especially with local wines—friendly and comfortable, with live *saz* music in the evenings.

Hacıbektaş

The **Museum of Hacıbektaş** (daily 8am–noon & 1–5pm; $1), dedicated to one of the greatest medieval Sufic philosophers—Hacı Bektaş Veli—is located in the village of the same name, 50km north of Avanos. It may be awkward to get to—unless you have your own transportation or are prepared to hitch you'll have to take a dolmuş from Nevşehir—but it's worth the detour.

The village of **HACIBEKTAŞ** was chosen by the dervish as the location of a center of scientific study, founded there in his lifetime, and the village was renamed in his honor after his death. The tomb of Hacı Bektaş Veli is located within the monastery complex, but the main part of the complex dates from the Ottoman period, when it was the headquarters of a large community of Bektaşi dervishes.

The teachings of Hacı Bektaş Veli had reverberations throughout the Muslim world, and different sects, including the Bektaşi, the Alevi, and the Tahtacı, still follow traditions that originated in his doctrines. Little is known about his life, but he is believed to have lived from 1208 to 1270. Like other Turkish intellectuals of the time he was educated in Khorasan, where he became well versed in religion and mysticism. After journeying with his brother, who was later killed in battle, he returned to Anatolia and lived in Kayseri, Kırşehir, and Sivas. Eventually he settled in a hamlet of seven houses, Suluca Karahöyük, the present location of the monastery.

THE TEACHINGS OF HACI BEKTAŞ VELİ

While the life of Hacı Bektaş Veli may be a subject for speculation, his teachings are well known, especially his great work, the **Makalât**, which gives a valuable account of his mystical thought and philosophy.

According to Hacı Bektaş, the way to enlightenment has four stages, which he called "the Four Doors." The first is the ability to judge between clean and dirty, right and wrong, as taught by the laws of religion. Second is the duty of the dervish to pray night and day, and to call on God's name—a striving toward a future life. The third stage he called *Marifet* or "Enlightenment," claiming that enlightened mystics are like water, making other things clean, and that they are beloved of God. The last stage, *Hakikat* or "Reality," is achieved by those who practice modesty, resignation and submission, and who have effaced themselves in the presence of God and attained a level of constant contemplation and prayer.

The faults that grieved Hacı Bektaş most were those of ostentation, hypocrisy, and inconsistency: "It is of no avail to be clean outside if there is evil within your soul." This could be the origin of the unorthodox customs of later followers of the Bektaşi sect, which included drinking wine, eating during Ramadan, and—for women—uncovering the head outside the home. Hacı Bektaş's own dictum on women was unequivocal, and it is one of the most popularly quoted of all his sayings: "A nation which does not educate its women cannot progress."

As a religious leader and ethical teacher, Hacı Bektaş prepared the way for the Ottoman Empire in Asia Minor (he was the recognized spiritual leader of soldiers and peasants, promoting the Turkish language and literature among them, and helping to popularize the Islamic faith in pre-Ottoman Turkey). The Bektaşi sect grew rapidly in Anatolia after the founder's death, largely because of the demoralization and impoverishment of the monastic foundations and the similarity of many of the Bektaşi rites to Christian ones, including sprinkling the congregation in water in a ceremony resembling baptism. The Bektaşi sect was closely linked to the janissary corps, known as the sons of Hacı Bektaş, and the two were abolished at the same time.

The **complex** itself was begun during the reign of Sultan Orhan in the fourteenth century, and opened to the public as a museum in 1964, after extensive restoration. It comprises three courtyards, the second of which contains the attractive Aslanlı Çeşmesi, the **Lion Fountain**, named after a lion statue which was brought from Egypt in 1853. The sacred *karakazan*, or **black kettle** (which is actually a cauldron), can be seen in the kitchen to the right of the courtyard. Important to both the Bektaşi sect and the janissaries, the black kettle originally symbolized communality, with possible reference to the Last Supper of the Christian faith. Subsequently, as the janissaries gained power, the symbolic significance of the kettle changed: by overturning it the janissaries showed their displeasure with the sultan, and this could end in his deposition, as was the case when Selim III tried to replace the sect with his New Model Army. To the left of the courtyard is the **Meydan Evi**, bearing the earliest inscription in the complex, dated 1367. The timber roof of the Meydan Evi—where formal initiation ceremonies and acts of confession took place—has been beautifully restored, showing an ancient construction technique still in use in rural houses in central and eastern Anatolia. It's now an exhibition hall containing objects of significance to the order, including musical instruments and a late portrait of Hacı Bektaş, apparently deep in mystical reverie, with a deer in his lap and a lion by his side.

The third courtyard is the location of a **rose garden** and a well-kept graveyard, where the tombs bear the distinctive headgear of the Bektaşi order. The tomb of the prophet is also located in the third courtyard, entered through the Akkapi, a white marble entranceway decorated with typical Selçuk motifs including a double-headed eagle. Off the corridor leading to the tomb is a small room that is said to have been the cell of Hacı Bektaş himself.

The town of Hacıbektaş is also well-known for its **onyx**, which is by far the cheapest in the region. The onyx shops are found along the street leading up to the Hacı Bektaş Museum. These are the best places to buy anything of value and quality: some of the varieties they sell have been quarried locally.

Southern Cappadocia: Niğde, Aksaray, and the Ihlara Valley

The majority of Cappadocia's visitors never get beyond the well-worn Nevşehir–Avanos–Ürgüp triangle, and southern Cappadocia is far less charted and trampled. Although there's a consequent feeling of excitement about explorations made in this area, there's also less to be explored. The two major towns, Aksaray and Niğde, leave a lot to be desired as tourist centers, and the scenery is generally scrubby, barren plains, more prone to cause depression than to recharge your spirits.

The area does have its peculiarities and fascinations, however, and these are worth a degree of discomfort to experience. On the way to Niğde you can stop off at the **underground cities** of Derinkuyu and Kaymaklı (see p.454), located in a rain-washed basin between the central Anatolian plateau and the valleys of cones. Still more worthwhile is the **Ihlara Valley**. Here the **Melendiz River**, running between Aksaray and Niğde alongside the Melendiz Mountains, has created perhaps the most beautiful of all Cappadocian landscapes, a narrow ravine with almost vertical walls being cut ever deeper by the river that runs through it. Easily accessible from Niğde, too, are a small enclave of beautifully painted rock-cut churches belonging to the Eski Gümüşler Monastery, and the Sultansazlığı Bird Sanctuary (see p.484), a unique opportunity to view an astonishing variety of exotic and beautiful birds in their natural habitat.

Niğde

NİĞDE is a small provincial town which, despite a long history spent guarding the important mountain pass from Cappadocia to Cilicia, has few remaining monuments of any great interest. Apart from a Selçuk fortress perched above the main street on a hill of tufa, and a couple of medieval mosques, the town looks as if it had been thrown together by people who were more interested in nomadic wandering than town planning. Nearby, however, is the Eski Gümüşler Monastery, which will no doubt become part of the regular Cappadocia itinerary in time. For the time being it's hardly known to the tourists who flood to Göreme Open-Air Museum, even though its frescoes are in a much better state of preservation.

Niğde's history really began in the tenth century, when Tyana, the town that formerly controlled the pass between the Melendiz Mountains to the west and the Taurus Mountains to the east, was ruined by Arab incursions. From then on Niğde, a town that had been mentioned as early as Hittite times by the name of Nakida, took on the defensive role. Conquered by the Selçuks toward the end of the eleventh century, it was endowed with some attractive buildings during the reign of Alâeddin Keykubad. When the Arabian geographer Ibn Battutah visited the town in 1333, it was in ruins, probably as a result of the wars between the Mongols and the Karamanoğlu, the great rivals of the Ottoman dynasty. The Ottomans finally moved in in 1467, and since then the town has been little more than a landmark on the Kayseri–Adana road.

Practicalities

The **otogar** is 1km out from the town center off the Nevşehir–Adana Highway on Terminal Caddesi, and there are frequent dolmuşes into town; the **train station** is right on the highway, within sight of the citadel's clocktower, which makes a central landmark. To walk into town from here, cross the highway and follow İstasyon Caddesi for about ten minutes. İstasyon Caddesi is the location of a couple of reasonably comfortable **hotels**: the *Taciroğlu* (☎483/13047; $14) at no. 55, and the *Murat* (☎483/13978; $14 with bath, $10 without) at no. 46. Another good choice, the *Evim* (☎483/11860; $20 with bath), is on Atatürk Meydanı. The *Hotel Stad* (☎483/17866), next to the otogar at Terminal Caddesi 6, is also reasonable, charging $10 per person for rooms with baths.

The **tourist information office** (Mon–Sat 8:30am–noon & 1:30–5:30pm) is on the corner of İstasyon Caddesi and Bankalar Caddesi, and there is a **trekking agency** specializing in guided tours of the Taurus Mountains, run by Doğan Şafak (☎483/12117, 17866, 13374), under the *Hotel Stad* at Terminal Caddesi 6.

The Sights

The **citadel** on its tufa hill was originally founded by the Selçuk sultan Alâeddin at the end of the eleventh century but was restored by Işak Paşa in 1470, and the keep, which is all that remains today, probably dates from that time. On a mound to the south of the castle stands the **Alâeddin Camii**, dating from 1203 and restored by Sultan Alâeddin. The facade is striped gray and yellow and there is a beautiful, finely decorated portal to the east which is richly decorated with arabesques and sculpted designs. Below the mosque is the eighty-meter-long **bedesten**, a covered market street dating from the sixteenth and seventeenth centuries, and opposite this, on Nalbantlar Önüat at the foot of the citadel hill, is the fourteenth-century **Sungur Bey Camii**. Its portal is framed by geometrical moldings, and above the door to the east of the prayer hall a rose window gives the mosque a Gothic look. At the other end of this street, approaching Vali Konağı Caddesi, is the **Akmedrese**, built in the Selçuk open-courtyard style with a white marble portal. It now serves as the town's **museum** (Tues–Sun 8:30am–5pm; $1) and is most famous for the Byzantine mummy of a nun which is exhibited in a glass case to full hideous effect.

Eski Gümüşler Monastery

The real reason for coming to Niğde is the **Eski Gümüşler Monastery** (daily 8am–noon & 1:30–5:30pm; $1), 6km from town off the Yeşilhisar road. To get there, take the Gümüşler dolmuş from the otogar to the village of the same name. GÜMÜŞLER, which is indicated off to the right about 1km out of town, is an attractive little village, set in a valley surrounded by cherry orchards, but for the monastery you stay on the bus past it.

The monastery, rediscovered in 1963, has a deserved reputation for the excellent state of preservation of its paintings, which seem to have escaped the ravages of Iconoclasm and other vandalism through the ages. Even the faces are intact, providing some of the finest examples of Byzantine painting yet to be discovered in Cappadocia.

The **main church**, with its tall, elegant pillars, is entered through an almost circular arched doorway opposite the entrance to the courtyard. Decorated with black-and-white geometric designs, the church contains beautiful eleventh-century **frescoes** in the most delicate greens, browns, and blues. They include a nativity scene complete with tiny animal heads peering in at the swaddled Jesus and the Magi, off to the left; and a tall, serene Madonna, framed in a rock-cut niche. The linear stylization of the figures is marked, the features are drawn boldly and simply, and the light and shade of draperies is reduced to monochrome.

The upstairs **bedroom** was formerly reached via niches cut into the side of a shaft; now a metal ladder has been provided. The walls of the bedroom, which is complete with rock-cut beds, are decorated with dogs, deer, and birds being hunted by men with bows and arrows.

Connected to the church is a **wine press**, complete with meter-wide wine vats, and outside in the central courtyard there's a recently discovered skeleton in its grave, protected under glass. Next to the graves are round holes in which precious belongings must have been buried. Other rooms excavated to date include a kitchen and underground baths reached down a set of steps, and excavation is continuing below ground level.

Aksaray

Huddled in an oasis on the Melendiz River, on the far side of the Melendiz Mountains from Niğde, **AKSARAY** is a market town with no real interest except as a base for reaching the Ihlara Valley. Although no trace of the ancient city survives, Aksaray probably occupies the site of the Byzantine town **Archelais**. It was captured by the Selçuks in the eleventh century, then passed to the Mongols in the middle of the thirteenth century, but when the power of the Mongols began to wane the Karamanoğlu took possession in the fourteenth century. After the fall of Constantinople in 1453, part of the population of Aksaray was transferred to the capital, a repopulation program that was a measure of how weak the Byzantine city had become before the final collapse of its empire. The displaced people named the district of İstanbul in which they settled after their hometown, a name which that shabby, lively suburb still retains.

Cheap **hotels** and **restaurants** are all located behind the *Vilayet* building off the main square, and the otogar is a kilometer away from this square. There are three buses to and from Ihlara every day, and a daily dolmuş to and from Belisırma at the other end of the valley.

The Ihlara Valley

A fertile gorge cut by a deep green river between red cliffs, the **Ihlara Valley** is as beautiful a place as you could conceive. If you add some of the most attractive and interesting churches and rock-carved villages in the Cappadocia region, it's hard to believe that Ihlara hasn't been touristed off the map. It may be that the end of paradise is already in sight: telltale litter is starting to appear on the river banks, and there is talk in the village of Ihlara of luxury hotels and discos. Restraint and common sense may prevail, but if you want to be sure of seeing the place before things get out of hand, try to visit now.

At present only a few local companies—*Rose Tours* and *Turtel* from Göreme, *Kayer* and *Cappadocia Tours* from Ürgüp—make **day tours** to the valley (around $20), but there are three **buses** daily between Aksaray and Ihlara, and a daily dolmuş to Belisırma from Aksaray. It's a difficult place to hitch to because so few vehicles come this way, but once you get to either of the villages, walking is half the pleasure of the experience. **Accommodation** in the valley is a fairly straightforward matter because there are so few options. One of the best is the *Belediye Hotel* (☎4824/1242) in **IHLARA**, right in the valley with beautiful views from the balconies. Spartan but clean, it's open year-round and charges $4 per person. The nearby **hamam** (daily 10am–10pm; 50¢), reached down a set of steps behind the mosque on the road out of the village, is fed by natural hot springs. Five hundred meters out of the village on the road to the valley entrance, *Vadi Camping* can put you up for $2, but it currently has no hot water. The *Anatolia Pansiyon* (☎4824/

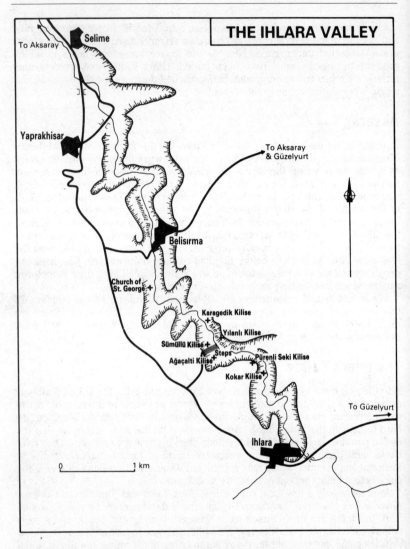

THE IHLARA VALLEY

To Aksaray

Selime

Yaprakhisar

Melendiz River

To Aksaray
& Güzelyurt

Belisırma

Church of
St. George

Karagedik Kilise

Yılanlı Kilise

Sümüllü Kilise

Melendiz River

Steps

Ağaçaltı Kilise

Pürenli Seki Kilise

Kokar Kilise

To Güzelyurt

Ihlara

0   1 km

1128; closed in winter), the green building on your right as you leave the village on the way to the valley entrance, is also fairly comfortable: rooms with bath are $8 per person, camping $1.50, showers $2 extra.

There are a couple of good, basic **restaurants** in Ihlara serving kebabs and the local meat stew, *saç kavurma* (supposed to be still bubbling when it reaches your table), and there is also a restaurant in the *Anatolia Pansiyon*.

Farther up the valley, in the exceptionally beautiful village of **BELİSIRMA**, there are two excellent **campgrounds**: *Aslan* (☎4823/1200) and *Belisırma Camping*. Both charge $1 per person to camp, and neither has hot water, but

Aslan has tents for rent, or beds for $2 per person, and the *Belisirma* offers an excellent restaurant where you can eat trout or *saç kavurma* very cheaply. The main problem here is that unless you walk the 10km up the valley from Ihlara, Belisirma can be difficult to reach. There's one **bus** every Sunday to and from Ihlara, or you can get there off the Aksaray–Güzelyurt road (there's a sign), a distance of 4km. Access from the Ihlara–Selime road is complicated by the fact that the sign is frequently removed, but there's a turnoff to the right down a kilometer-long dirt track just before the village of YAPRAKHİSAR.

The *Valley Restaurant* (☎4824/1086, 1088), at the entrance to the valley midway between Ihlara and Belisirma, is overpriced, as are the adjacent camping area and parking lot: tent and two people $5, car $1 to park, $2 if you're camping. The restaurant is open from 8am to 9pm, but closed from November 20 to March 1.

Entrance to the valley from this point costs $1.50, but if you walk from either Belisirma or Ihlara you'll get in free. Either way it takes about an hour and a half, a fairly straightforward hike that's well worthwhile for the tremendous sense of solitude afforded once you get away from the main tourist center. The villages are about 10km apart and the main concentration of churches lies between the two.

The Churches

The monastic occupation of the Ihlara Valley, or **Peristrema** as it was originally known, seems to have been continuous from early Christian times until the fourteenth century, a long period of use reflected in the numerous adaptations and restorations of the churches. It would seem from the decoration of the churches, whose development can be traced through pre- and post-Iconoclastic periods, that the valley was little affected by the religious disputes of the period. Paintings show both Eastern and Western influence, so that some figures wear Irano-Arab-type striped robes, whereas others resemble those in Byzantine frescoes in Europe.

The most interesting of the churches are located near the small bridge midway between Ihlara and Belisirma. These are made more accessible by a paved road from Ihlara to the *Valley Restaurant*, from which you can follow stairs down the valley side to the river below. It's also possible to walk from Ihlara along the southwest bank of the river to the bridge.

At the bottom of the steps is a map showing all the accessible churches, most of which are easy enough to find. To the right of the bridge, on the same side as the steps, is the **Ağaçaltı Kilise** (Church Under the Tree). Cross-shaped with a central dome, the church originally had three levels, but two of them have collapsed, as has the entrance hall. The most impressive of the well-preserved frescoes inside depict the Magi presenting gifts at the Nativity, Daniel with the lions (opposite the entrance in the west arm) and, in the central dome, the Ascension. The colors are red, blue, and gray, and the pictures are naive in their execution, and suggest influence from Sassanid Iran, particularly in the frieze of winged griffins. Only the eyes of the figures have been damaged, otherwise they are pretty well intact, and all the more curious for their seeming sightlessness.

The **Pürenli Seki Kilise** lies 500m beyond this, also on the south bank. It can be seen clearly from the river, 30m up the cliffside. The badly damaged frescoes here mainly depict scenes from the life of Christ.

Another 50m toward Ihlara, the **Kokar Kilise** is relatively easy to reach up a set of steps. Scenes from the Bible in the main hall include the Annunciation, the Nativity, the Flight into Egypt and the Last Supper. In the center of the dome there is a picture of a hand, which represents the Trinity and the sanctification.

One of the most fascinating of all the churches in the valley is located across the wooden footbridge, about 100m from the stairs. The **Yılanlı Kilise** (Church of the Snakes) contains really unusual depictions of sinners suffering in hell. Four female sinners are being bitten by snakes: one of them on the nipples as a punishment for not breast-feeding her young; another is covered in eight snakes; and the other two are being punished for slander and not heeding good advice. At the center of the scene a three-headed snake is positioned behind one of the few Cappadocian depictions of Satan. In each of the snakes' mouths is a soul destined for hell. Another depiction of the devil is just visible behind the head of Christ at the Last Supper on the north wall. Here he appears as a small gray monster with wings, the devil Selephouze, who mocked Christ saying, "Son of God, take me today as a sharer in thy banquet."

Another church worth exploring is **Sümbüllü** (Church of the Hyacinths), just 20m from the entrance stairs. The church shows Greek influence in its frescoes and has an attractive facade decorated with blind horseshoe niches. From here, staying on the same side of the river, it's about a one-and-a-half hour walk to Belisırma.

Around Belisırma, the eleventh-century **Direkli Kilise** (Church with the Columns) has fine examples of Byzantine frescoes including a beautiful long-fingered Madonna and Child on one of the columns from which the church takes its name, and a picture of St George fighting a three-headed dragon. The church has a central dome, six decorated pillars, and three altars.

The **Church of St George**, 50m up the cliffside, 3km from the stairs and 1km from Belisırma, was dedicated to the saint by a thirteenth-century Christian Emir, Basil Giagoupes, who was in the army of Mesut II. It bears an inscription expressing Christian gratitude for the religious tolerance of the Selçuk Turks. George is depicted in armor and cloak, holding a triangular shield and flanked by the donor and his wife Tamara; Tamara is handing a model of the church to the saint. To the right of this oblation scene Saint George can be seen in action, killing a three-headed serpent: the inscription above reads "Cleanse my Soul of Sins."

Continuing up the valley in the direction of Aksaray, small simple pansiyons charging around $6 a person with breakfast can be found in the villages of YAPRAKHİSAR (*Piri Pansiyon*) and SELİME (the *Hisar*).

Kayseri

Green fields and wooded hills, a snow-capped volcano and a solid-looking city built of black stone and concrete: **KAYSERİ** and its surroundings feel refreshingly familiar after the weird spookiness of Cappadocia's better-known landscapes. Tourism developed here long before the villages around Ürgüp realized the potential of the industry, and for some time it used to be the only place you could find a reasonable hotel in Cappadocia. Now there are fewer visitors, but the old-fashioned, rather jaded **hotels** are still hanging in there, and despite a reputation for **religious conservatism** there's a gentle acceptance of the waywardness of foreigners which has yet to mature in, say, Nevşehir or Niğde. In place of visitors the town has fallen back on traditional commerce, particularly raw textiles and carpets, and there is a reassuring feeling that nothing was compromised by tourism and so its decline is no great loss.

The long history and strategic importance of the town have left it with a littering of impressive **monuments**, another factor contributing to its desirability as a springboard for exploring the surrounding countryside. Two of the more obvious nearby attractions are **Sultansazlığı Bird Sanctuary** and **Mount Erciyes**, ideal for picnics in summer and skiing in winter.

Ancient civilization in the region dates back to the fourth millennium BC, as a **Chalcolithic site** at **Kültepe**, 21km from Kayseri on the road to Sivas, testifies. During the early Hittite period the site was composed of two settlements: **Kanesh**, the capital of the kingdom of the same name, probably the most powerful in Anatolia in its time; and **Karum**, which was established by Assyrian merchants as a bazaar, one of the oldest in the world.

The site of present-day Kayseri was originally called Mazaka. Its origins are unknown, but the city gained importance under the rule of the **Phrygians**. In 17–18 AD it was named Caesarea in honor of the **Emperor Tiberius**, and at the same time became the capital of the Roman province of Cappadocia. Captured by the **Persians** after the Battle of Edessa (Urfa), it was quickly regained by the Romans. As part of the **Byzantine Empire**, Caesarea was relocated 2km to the north of the ancient acropolis, allegedly around a church and monastery which had been built by Saint Basil, the founder of eastern monasticism and a bishop of Caesarea in the fourth century. The position was strategic in terms of both trade

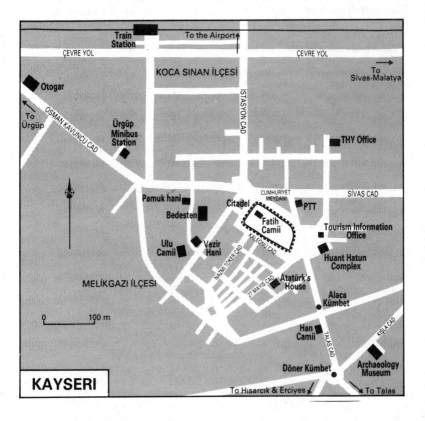

and defense, and it soon became a leading cultural and artistic center, though always vulnerable to attack from the east. The **Arab invasions** of the seventh and eighth centuries were particularly threatening, and in 1067 it finally fell to the great Selçuk leader **Kılıç Aslan II**. The town became capital of a powerful Danişmend emirate which included Cappadocia, Sivas, and Amasya. In 1097 the Crusaders were in brief possession and it was ruled equally briefly by the Mongols in 1243. Passing through the hands of various Turkish chiefs it came into the possession of Beyazit I in 1397, but when he was defeated by Tamerlane at the Battle of Angora the city was occupied by the Karamanoğlu and then the Mameluks before finally becoming part of the Ottoman Empire in 1515, under Selim the Grim.

Practicalities

To get into town from the **otogar**, at the far end of Osman Kavuncu Caddesi, take the "Merkez" (center) dolmuş. The **tourist information office** (daily 8:30am–5pm) is right at the center of things, next to the citadel at Kağnı Pazarı Honat Camii Yanı 61. They have all kinds of useful information, including train, plane, and bus times, hotel and restaurant lists, and the latest on the Mount Erciyes ski area (like "there's no snow"). The **train station** is 1km out of town at the end of Atatürk Bulvarı: "Merkez" dolmuşes into town—and to the otogar in the other direction—pass frequently. The **PTT** is near the citadel on Sivas Caddesi, as are the main banks, and **Turkish Airlines** has an office just off Sivas Caddesi (☎351/11001).

There are several good **hotels** to choose from in Kayseri, ranging from the *Turan Oteli*, Turan Caddesi 8 (☎351/112506, 11968; $50), and the very pleasant *Kadıoğlu Oteli* on İnönü Bulvarı (☎351/116320; $32), to cheaper options like the *Yeni* (☎351/18372), the *Hisar* (☎351/66644), and the *Meydan* (☎351/65135), all on Osman Kavuncu Caddesi and charging around $6. The last three are convenient for the bus station and minibuses to and from Ürgüp (the stop is also on Osman Kavuncu Cad), and are within fairly easy walking distance of the town center. They are also handy for a very good ice-cream place, the *Roma*, at the end of Osman Kavuncu Caddesi, and for the cheap *Ocakbaşı* **restaurant**, around the corner, to the right of the *Beğendik* store. The area is fairly attractive considering where bus stations are normally located in Turkish cities, but if you want to be more central take the "Merkez" dolmuş from the bus station into town: on the way you'll pass the modern, clean *Hotel Yat*, located above another *Beğendik* store near the Alaca Kümbet. If you have any problems, the tourist information office provides two numbers of organizations dealing with complaints concerning hotels: the town council's is ☎351/28960 and the hoteliers' organization is ☎351/65728.

Good **restaurants** in Kayseri include the one in the *Turan Hotel* and the pleasant little *Otağ*, in the covered market area next to Ulu Cami, which serves excellent kebabs. Otherwise a favorite option is the *Iskender Kebab Salonu* on Millet Caddesi, across from the Hunat-Hatun complex.

The City

Part of the delight of Kayseri is that so much revolves around its most beautiful old buildings, and that these still play an important part in the everyday life of the place. The nature of the buildings that have survived bears witness to the social conscience of the early Muslims, particularly of the Selçuks. Koranic teaching forbade excessive concern with private houses, and very few of them have survived. Instead the buildings of real note in the city are those that served public welfare and communal activites, especially exemplified in mosque complexes that included schools, soup kitchens, and hamams.

Other buildings that still play an important part in Kayseri's everyday life are the **covered markets**, where commercial activity—as conspicuous now as it was in the first Assyrian settlement—is most obvious. The prominence of commerce can be ascertained by the fact that there are three covered markets in the town center, all dating from different periods. The **Bedesten**, built in 1497, was originally used by cloth sellers but is now a carpet market; the **Vezirhanı**, built by Damat İbrahim Paşa in 1727, is where raw cotton, wool, and Kayseri carpets are sold, and leather is prepared for wholesale; while the recently restored **covered bazaar**, built in 1859 by natives of Kayseri, has five hundred individual shops. If you do shop here, you'll have to bargain hard: stories can be heard all over Turkey about how hard-nosed the businessmen of Kayseri can be*.

The towering crenellated walls of the **citadel**, built from black volcanic rock, are a good place to start exploring, since the life of the town seems to focus on this point. A sixth-century fortress erected in the reign of the emperor Justinian once stood here, but the citadel you see was built in 1224 by the Selçuk sultan Keykubad, and has been much restored since, particularly by Mehmet II, who also built the **Fatih Camii**, the small mosque near the southwest gate. The fact that the city walls have all but disappeared serves only to confirm the importance of this fortified nerve center: it was preserved at all costs even after the walls had lost their importance. Not surprisingly for Kayseri, there is now a modern **shopping area** located within the walls of the citadel.

Beyond the market area, on the way toward the bus station, is the first of several ancient mosques in the city, the **Ulu Cami** or Great Mosque. Constructed under the Danişmend Turkish emirs in the first half of the thirteenth century, the mosque, which can be entered from three sides, is still in remarkably good condition. Its roof is supported by four rows of stone pillars with varied marble capitals, some of them taken from other buildings, and it retains its original carved wooden *mimber*, although the central dome is modern.

Kayseri has been described as the **city of mausoleums** because of a large number of tombs: curious, squat, beautifully carved works of stone (known as *kümbet*) dating from the twelfth to fourteenth centuries, which can be found scattered about in the most unlikely places—a couple of them are on traffic islands on the main highway to Mount Erciyes. They are graceful constructions that seem out of place in such a modern environment. Examples can be found all over Persia and Turkey, an architectural form for which the Selçuk Turks were responsible: they were generally two-storied, with the burial chamber and sumptuous coffin located in the upper story. It is supposed that the design was modeled on the *yurd*, a conical tent inhabited by various tribes of the region, including the Selçuk Turks. The best-known of them in Kayseri is the **Döner Kümbet**, a typical example probably dating to around 1275, built for Sah Cihan Hatun. Mysteriously the name of the monument means "Turning Tomb," although it doesn't turn and never has. The tomb is decorated with arabesques and palmettes, and a tree of life with twin-headed eagles and lions beneath.

---

*The one about a Kayseri man stealing a donkey, painting it, and selling it back to its owner has become even more barbed in recent years: the man now abducts his mother, paints her up, and sells her back to his father.

The Museums

Near the citadel in the town center, the **külliye of Hunat Hatun** was the first mosque complex to be built by the Selçuks in Anatolia. It consists of a mosque (1237–8), the *türbe* of Princess Mahperi, wife of Sultan Keykubad, and one of the most beautiful examples of Selçuk architecture in Turkey, the thirteenth-century *medrese*. This former theological college has an open courtyard and two *eyvans* (vaulted chambers open at the front) and nowadays houses the city's **Ethnographic Museum** (Tues–Sun 8:30am–noon & 1–5:30pm; $1), with displays reflecting folk traditions of the Kayseri region.

To get to the **Archaeological Museum** (Tues–Sun 8am–noon & 1–5pm; $1) take the Erciyes road out of town past the Döner Kümbet and turn left onto Kışla Caddesi. This is certainly the best museum in the region, containing some of the most interesting artifacts to be found in Cappadocia, all extremely well labeled and explained. The first room deals with the **Hittites**, their cuneiform writing, and hieroglyphics, and includes a fascinating Hittite rock relief from Develi and the head of a sphinx. The rest of the museum is mainly dedicated to finds from the excavations of **Kültepe**. They include early Bronze Age depictions of the mother goddess, and Assyrian bowls and jugs in the shape of animals dating from the second millennium BC.

In the second room are finds from around Kayseri itself, including Hellenistic and Roman jewelry, and grave gifts from a Roman tumulus, among them highly worked pieces in gold and silver. Outside can be found a pair of lovely seventh-century BC **Hittite lions**, with all their own teeth, from Göllüdağ near Niğde.

Mount Erciyes

The 3916-meter-high extinct volcano which dominates the city to the southwest is one of the greatest pleasures the city has to offer. If you have your own wheels, take a packed lunch of local *pastırma* and *sucuk* (spicy sausage) and head for the foothills of **Mount Erciyes**, a twenty-minute drive out of town. By public transportation there's a bus to Hisarcık about every half hour, leaving from the Erciyes road 500m beyond the tourist information office. From Hisarcık, you'll need to walk or take a taxi (around $10) another 16km to the *Kayak Evi*, the ski lodge run by the Kayseri city council (beds $12 a person, breakfast $2) at Tekir Yaylası, a plateau 26km south of Kayseri at an altitude of 2150m. The ski season runs from December to May, and there's a chairlift from the *Kayak Evi* to the slopes.

Once you get beyond the foothills Erciyes is a harsh mountain, with little vegetation to soften its contours. More important for hikers is the lack of spring water, making it a tough place to climb in the height of summer. The most reasonable hike starts at the *Kayak Evi* and goes west. A guide, and equipment such as crampons and ice axes, are recommended: both should be available from the *Kayak Evi* on demand.

Sultansazlığı

Beyond Mount Erciyes the countryside around the Kayseri–Niğde road becomes flat, dull steppes which you might assume were as barren of bird or plant life as anywhere else in Cappadocia. The oasis of the **Sultansazlığı Bird Sanctuary** is easy to miss in the back lanes that wind around the tiny lakes in the region, but it's worth the effort of hunting out, if for no other reason than because there's so little else to see or do in the region.

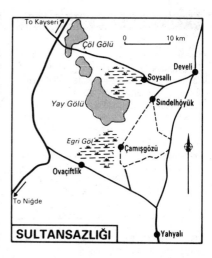

The **Sultan Marshes**, a complex of wetlands at the bottom of a closed basin, comprise two main lakes—Yay Gölü and the smaller Çöl Göllü—and around 5000 acres of surrounding marshes. The lakes are saline while the marshland is fresh water, and this particular combination of lakes, marshland, mud flats, and steppes make for an enormous variety of ecosystems. This combined with the fact that the area is positioned on the crossroads of two large migration routes make Sultan-sazlığı an important area for breeding, migrant, and wintering birds.

Although no really detailed ornithological research has been carried out so far, at least 250 species have been recorded here, 69 of which breed in the area. Most excitingly for the lay bird-watcher, visiting species include flamingos (particularly in the Yay Gölü region), pelicans, storks, golden eagles from the surrounding steppes, herons, spoonbills, and cranes.

There's a **watchtower** in Ovaçiftlik, which provides good viewing as long as the water isn't too low (as it may be in the height of summer), and a little thatched **museum** exhibiting examples of the species found in the region. This will probably be opened to coincide with your arrival. There are also good bird-watching opportunities to the northeast, near the village of SOYSALLI.

The marshes were only afforded Protected Area status in 1988. Up to then various factors threatened them and some of these—including the drainage of the marshes for agricultural purposes and hunting of certain species—have still not been completely eradicated.

Practicalities

The marshes, also known as Kuş Cenneti (Bird Paradise), are most easily accesible from the Kayseri–Niğde road, 10km from Yeşilhisar (80km from Kayseri, 60km from Niğde). Kayseri–Niğde buses pass through YEŞILHISAR every hour (flag them down at the gas station at the bottom of the village) and will take you past the end of the road to Sultansazlığı, and from there you'll need to walk (or hitch, if you're lucky) to the hamlet of OVAÇIFTLİK, near Eğri Göl, about 8km off the main road. By car, take the Adana road out of Kayseri.

Ovaçiftlik is probably the best place to base yourself if you want to explore the region, but take **camping** gear because facilities are still a bit spartan. There are a number of good little campgrounds here, particularly *Sultan Kampink* (☎3595/ 1434, 1431, 1457), where they run boat trips for about $15 and organize tours around Yay Gölü. They can also provide simple meals. If camping is impossible, the next-best bet is to stay in Yeşilhisar at the *Otel Belöz*, the municipality-run hotel near the gas station on the main road.

travel details

Trains

From Konya to İstanbul (2 daily; 13 or 14 hr); Kayseri (1 daily; 5hr); İsparta (1 daily; 4hr); Çumra (3 daily; 20min); Afyon (3 daily; 3hr).

From Afyon to İstanbul (4 or 5 daily; 8hr); Denizli (2 daily; 2hr 30min); Konya (3 daily; 3hr); Eskişehir (1 daily; 3hr); Gaziantep (3 weekly; 8hr); Diyarbakır (1 daily; 11hr).

From Kayseri to İstanbul (several daily; 12hr); İskenderun (3 weekly; 10hr); Kars (1 daily; 24hr); Konya (1 daily; 5hr); Niğde (hourly; 2hr 40min); Ankara (several daily; 7/8 hr); Van (3 weekly; 23hr).

From İsparta to Afyon (3 daily; 2hr 30min); Denizli (2 daily; 2hr 30min); İzmir (1 daily; 6hr 30min); Eğirdir (1 daily; 1hr 10min); Konya (1 daily; 4hr); İstanbul (1 daily; 13hr 30min).

Buses

Fom Beyşehir to Konya (15 daily; 1hr); İzmir (4; 8hr); İstanbul (2; 8hr); Antalya (4; 5hr); Alanya (3; 7hr); Denizli (4; 6hr); Eğirdir (8; 2hr); Gelendost (8; 1hr 30min); İsparta (8; 2hr 30min); Selçuk (4; 7hr); Aydın (4; 6hr 30min); Ankara (4; 5hr); Manavgat (4; 6hr 30min); Samsun (1; 13hr); Çorum (1; 7hr 30min); Adana (2; 7hr 30min); Antep (2; 14hr).

From Niğde to Ankara (5 daily; 4hr 30min); Konya (5; 3hr 30min); İstanbul (5; 3hr 30min); İzmir (1; 12hr); Aksaray (7; 1hr 30min); Antalya (2; 10/12hr); Alanya (1; 12hr); Adana (12; 4hr); Mersin (5; 4hr); Derinkuyu (13; 45min); Trabzon (2; 12 hr); Rise (1; 14hr); Nevşehir (13; 1hr 30min); Sivas (2; 6hr); Erzincan (2; 8hr); Kars (1; 12hr); Malatya (1; 7hr); Elaziğ (1; 9hr); Diyarbakır (1; 12hr); Kayseri (13; 1hr 30min); Kırşehir (1; 2hr 30min); Yozgat (1; 5hr); Çorum (1; 9hr); Bayburt (1; 9hr); Gümüşhane (1; 11hr); Samsun (1; 16hr).

From Nevşehir to Ankara (12 daily; 4hr); Adana (1; 5hr); İstanbul (3; 12hr); Marmaris (1; 14hr); Antalya (1; 11hr); İzmir (1; 12hr); Kayseri (7; 2hr); Konya (4; 3hr); Mersin (2; 5hr).

From Kayseri to Ankara (15; 5hr); İstanbul (6; 12hr); İzmir (2; 13hr); Antalya (4; 13hr 30min);

Adana (10; 5hr); Antakya (2; 8hr); Ürgüp (hourly; 1hr 30min); Malatya (6; 6hr); Sivas (6; 2hr 30min); Konya (12; 4hr); Aksaray (3; 2hr); Burdur (1; 11hr); Alanya (1; 13hr); Muş (2; 12hr); Diyarbakır (4; 12hr); Kars (1; 14hr); Samsun (2; 11hr); Van (3; 14hr); Mardin (1; 13hr); Siirt (2; 13hr 30min); Hakkari (3; 16hr); Erzurum (2; 14hr); Ağrı (1; 16hr); Sivas (1; 4hr 30min); Trabzon (1; 10hr 30min); Niğde (5; 1hr 30min); Ürgüp (hourly except noon; 1hr 30min).

From Ürgüp to Ankara (8 daily; 5hr); İstanbul (1; 13hr); İzmir (1; 12hr); Konya (4; 3hr); Denizli (2; 12hr); Marmaris (2; 15hr); Antalya (1; 12hr); Side (2; 13hr); Alanya (2; 14hr); Manavgat (2; 13hr) Mersin (3; 5hr); Uşak (1; 7hr); Afyon (1; 6hr); İsparta (3; 7hr); Adana (2; 5hr); Kayseri (11; 1hr 30min); Nevşehir (half-hourly; 45min); Göreme (half-hourly; 20min).

From Göreme to İstanbul (4 daily; 11hr 30min); Antalya (1; 12hr); Alanya (1; 12hr); Aydın (2; 12hr); Marmaris (1; 15hr); Selcuk (1; 12hr); Konya (6; 3hr 30min); Ankara (13; 5hr); Eğirdir (2; 5hr); Marmaris (1; 14hr 30min); Side (1; 11hr); Denizli (2; 12hr); İzmir (1; 11hr 30min); İsparta (2; 6hr); Afyon (1; 6hr); Kayseri (15; 1hr 30min).

From Derinkuyu to Aksaray (1 daily; 2hr). Dolmuşes to Niğde, Nevşehir and Kayseri.

From Afyon to Antalya (13 daily; 5hr); Alanya (5; 6hr 30min); Side (5; 5hr 30min); Manavgat (5; 5hr 45min); İstanbul (4; 8hr); Bursa (2; 5hr); Ankara (6; 4hr); Konya (3; 3hr); Adana (3; 10hr); Mersin (3; 9hr); Eskişehir (7; 2hr); Aydın (15; 5hr); Didim (4; 7hr); Marmaris (1; 9hr); Kuşadası (2; 7hr); Fethiye (2; 7hr); Bodrum (1; 10hr) Diyarbakır (1; 16hr); Samsun (1; 14hr); Rise (1; 16hr); Kutahya (5; 1hr 30min); İsparta (1; 2hr).

Planes

From Konya İstanbul (2 weekly; 1hr 15min); İzmir (2 weekly; 5hr 55min).

From Kayseri İstanbul (2 weekly; 1hr 20min); İzmir (2 weekly; 4hr 55min).

NORTH CENTRAL ANATOLIA

W
hen the first Turkish nomads arrived in Anatolia during the tenth and eleventh centuries, the landscape must have been strongly reminiscent of their Central Asian homeland. The terrain that so pleased the tent-dwelling herdsmen of a thousand years ago, however, has few attractions for modern visitors: monotonous, rolling vistas of stone-strewn grassland, dotted with rocky outcrops, hospitable only to sheep. In winter it can be numbingly cold here, while in summer temperatures rise to almost unbearable levels.

It seems appropriate that the heart of original Turkish settlement should be home to the political and social center of modern Turkey, **Ankara**, a modern European-style capital rising out of a stark landscape, symbol of Atatürk's dream of a secular Turkish republic. Though it's a far less exciting city than İstanbul, **Ankara** does make a good starting point for travels through Anatolia. And even if it's a city more important for its social and political status than for any great architectural or aesthetic merit, it does have its moments: certainly a visit to the Anatolian Civilizations Museum is essential if you want to gain some impression of how Anatolia has developed since it was first settled during Neolithic times.

North Central Anatolia also boasts the remains of one of the earliest known cities in Turkey—**Hattuşaş**, the capital of the Hittite Empire, near the village of **Boğazkale**. East of here, at **Amasya, Tokat**, and **Sivas**, later cultures and civilizations have left their respective marks. At Amasya the rock-cut tombs of the pre-Roman Pontic kings tower over a haphazard riverside settlement of Ottoman wooden houses, Tokat features a fine Selçuk seminary housing a museum and some well-preserved Ottoman houses, while Sivas boasts some of the finest examples of Selçuk architecture in Turkey. Hidden away in the mountains to the north of Ankara you'll find **Safranbolu**, an almost completely intact Ottoman town of wooden houses, tucked into a narrow gorge, where the traditions of a century or two ago are still current. North of Ankara is **Kastamonu**, home of a couple of interesting mosques which are in turn overshadowed by the town's huge citadel. In the west of the region is **Eskişehir**, of little interest as anything other than a staging post to places like Bursa, Bandırma, and the Sea of Marmara, or to **Kütahya**, 60km or so to the southwest, from where there's access to the ancient site of **Aezani**.

Oases like these, set amid the forbidding landscape of the region, bear witness to nearly 10,000 years of human settlement, and a complex and turbulent history punctuated by war and waves of conquest. Anatolia was the Roman frontline against the Persians, and in a sense it's still an arena where conflicting currents in

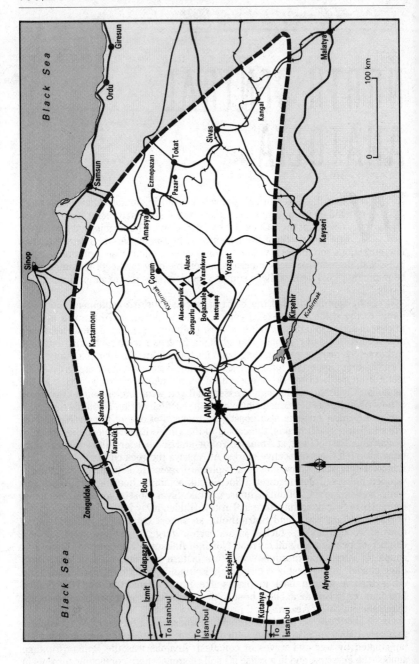

Turkish society are played off against each other; the clash of traditional and more modern ways of life in modern Turkey is immediately apparent in cities like Ankara, where sizable European-oriented middle class populations live side by side with newcomers from the countryside who only a decade or two ago were living a centuries-old peasant existence.

ANKARA AND AROUND

Modern **ANKARA** is really two cities, each seeming to exist separately and within its own time zone. It owes this double identity to the breakneck pace at which it has developed since being declared capital of the Turkish Republic in 1923.

Until then Ankara—known as **Angora**—had been a small provincial city, almost lost in the middle of the steppes, known chiefly for the production of soft, angora-goat's wool. This city still exists, in and around the old citadel that was the site of the original settlement. The other Ankara is the modern metropolis, Atatürk's capital, which has grown up around the old one, surrounding and almost swamping it. This city is a carefully planned attempt to create a seat of government worthy of a modern, western-looking state.

For visitors, Ankara is never going to be as attractive as İstanbul, and the couple of excellent museums and handful of other sights are unlikely to detain you for more than a day or two. Even so, it's worth the trip to find somewhere as refreshingly forward-looking and modern as Turkey's administrative and diplomatic center.

Some History

It was the Hittites who founded Ankara, naming it Ankuwash, around 1200 BC. Under them the town grew and prospered thanks to its position on the royal road running from Sardis to their capital at Hattuşaş. The Hittites were succeeded by the Phrygians, who called the city Ankyra (and left a significant reminder of their presence in the shape of a huge necropolis uncovered near the railroad station in 1925); Alexander the Great passed through on his way east and his successors squabbled over Ankara just as they squabbled over the rest of Anatolia; and in the third century BC, invading Gaulish tribesmen held sway for a while. Throughout it all—and through the arrival of the Romans in 25 BC—Ankara retained its importance overlooking the east–west trading routes, which by now extended into Persia and beyond.

For the first thousand years of the Christian era, Byzantine Ankara was subject to sporadic Persian and Arab attack, but it held out until 1071, when it finally fell to the Selçuks. Later, as part of the Ottoman Empire, the town went into something of a decline, with only its famous wool to prevent it from disappearing altogether.

In 1920, however, Atatürk established his provisional government here, in preference to the more vulnerable İstanbul, as the victorious World War I allies struggled to divide the dying Ottoman Empire beween them; and after Atatürk's final victory in October 1923 it was decided to make Ankara the official capital of the Turkish Republic. The services of western European architects and planners were enlisted to create today's modern city, and in the space of seventy years Ankara's population grew from 30,000 to 2,500,000.

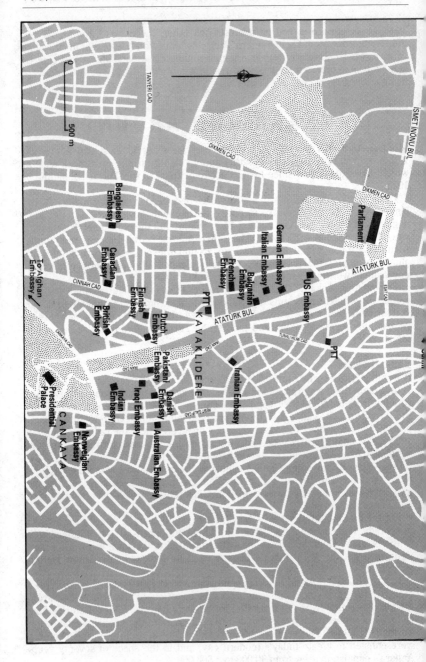

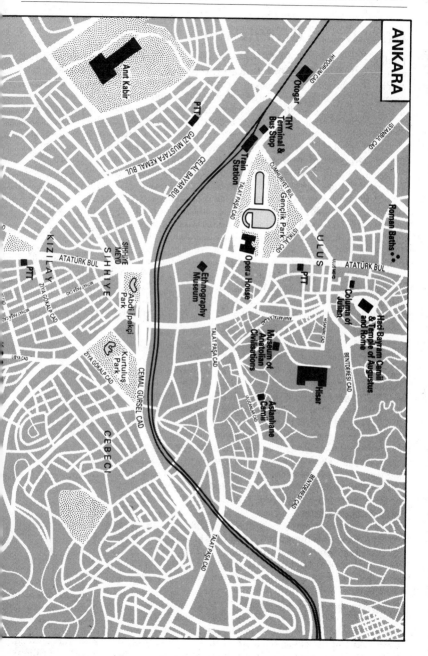

ANKARA

Anıt Kabir

PTT

GAZİ MUSTAFA KEMAL BUL.

CELAL BAYAR BUL.

HİPODROM CAD

Otogar

İSTANBUL CAD

THY Terminal & Bus Stop

Train Station

CUMHURIYET BUL.

Gençlik Park

PTT (TAKSI)

Roman Baths

ULUS

ATATÜRK BUL

PTT

ULUS MEYD

Column of Julian

Hacı Bayram Camii & Temple of Augustus and Rome

KIZILAY

ATATÜRK BUL

SIHHİYE

SIHHİYE MEYD

Abdi İpekçi Park

Opera House

Ethnography Museum

ZIYA GÖKALP CAD

Museum of Anatolian Civilisations

İstanbul Camii

Hisar

BENTDERESİ CAD

PTT

MITHAT PAŞA CAD

MITHAT PAŞA CAD

LIBYA CAD

Kurtuluş Park

ZIYA GÖKALP CAD

CEMAL GÜRSEL CAD

TALAT PAŞA CAD

TALAT PAŞA CAD

TALAT PAŞA CAD

CEBECİ

BEYTDERESİ CAD

ANAFARTALAR CAD

HİSARPARKI CAD

ULUCANLAR CAD

Arrival and Orientation

Finding your way around Ankara is fairly easy. The city is neatly bisected along its north–south axis by **Atatürk Bulvarı**. Everything you need will be within easy reach of this broad and busy street. At the northern end is **Ulus Meydanı** (usually known simply as Ulus), a large square and an important traffic intersection, marked by a huge equestrian Atatürk statue. Ulus is the point to which you'll probably gravitate on arriving in Ankara, as it's the home of the cheap hotels and handy for both otogar and train station. About 1km east of here, down Hisarparkı Caddesi, stands the **Hisar**, Ankara's old fortress and citadel, not far from the famous **Museum of Anatolian Civilisiations** (Anadolu Medeniyetleri Müzesi).

Heading south down Atatürk Bulvarı from Ulus brings you to the main west–east railroad line, beyond which lies **Sıhhıye Meydanı**. It's on this side of the tracks that modern Ankara really begins. From here **Kızılay**, the busy square that is the main transport hub of the modern city, is less than ten minutes' walk. Keep going south and you'll pass the parliament building on the right, followed by various major embassies. Atatürk Bulvarı terminates at the **Presidential Palace** (Çankaya Köskü).

There are **tourist information offices** at the otogar and the airport, as well as at İstanbul Cad 4 in Ulus (☎311 2247, 310 6818, 312 3525), and the Ministry of Tourism is at Gazi Mustafa Kemal Bulvarı 33 (☎230 1911, 231 7380), about ten minutes west of Kızılay. None of these are especially helpful, but they will be able to provide you with a map (useful) and a couple of glossy brochures (useless).

The Ankara telephone code is ☎4.

Points of Arrival

Ankara's **Essenboğa Airport** is 33km north of town and buses into town tend to depart about half an hour after flights land. Alternatively, a taxi into the center of Ankara from the airport will set you back about $15. Things are easier if you arrive at the city's **otogar** on Hipodrom Caddesi, a couple of kilometers west of the city center. From here it's usually easy enough to pick up city buses: #44, for example, will take you to **Kızılay**, #64 to Ulus. Failing this, a taxi to Ulus or Kızılay shouldn't set you back more than $3—at a push you could even walk. The **train station** is also on Hipodrom Caddesi, closer in, and the same buses pass by.

City Transportation

Getting around Ankara is no problem with plentiful **city buses** running the length of Atatürk Bulvarı. Bus #8 runs from Ulus to Çankaya, while #63 will take you from Ulus to Anıt Kabir, Atatürk's mausoleum. Bus tickets cost 20¢ and are bought in advance from kiosks next to the main bus stops. There are plenty of **taxis**, too, with 75¢ as a minimum fare and the average trip working out to about $3.

Finding a Place to Stay

There's no shortage of **hotels** in Ankara, covering the full price and quality spectrum. Most of the cheap ones are in the streets east of Atatürk Bulvarı beween Ulus and Opera Meydanı. The really cheap places tend to be fleapits, but there are plenty of decent possibilities offering singles for less than $8 and doubles for less than $16. North of Ulus, on and around Çankırı Caddesi, are a few somewhat fancier places hovering around the $16 single mark. Other hotels in various price ranges can be found along Gazi Mustafa Kemal Bulvarı in Maltepe. Another cluster is to be found on Atatürk Bulvarı south of Kızılay, with prices increasing as you move south. Bear in mind that a little haggling can sometimes go a long way, even at the more expensive places (perhaps not the *Hilton*), particularly if you visit in the low season.

Cheap Hotels

Babil Otel, Gazi Mustafa Kemal Bulvarı 66, Maltepe (☎231 7877). $8.80 single, $16 double. Not bad at all, although the rooms have no showers.

Başkent Oteli, Posta Cad 29/C, Ulus (☎311 7249). $7 double. Fairly mediocre, a last-resort kind of place.

Buhara Oteli, Sanayi Cad 13, Ulus (☎324 5245, 324 5246). $8 single, $16 double with bath. One of the better ones in this price range.

Esen Palas Oteli, Hükümet Cad 22, Ulus (☎311 2747). Singles $6 doubles $11.20 (washbasins only). No palace, but it'll do for a night. Haggle.

Hisar Oteli, Hisarparkı Cad 6, Ulus (☎311 9889, 310 8128). Singles $6, doubles $11. Washbasins only, but the rooms are clean and presentable. Recommended.

Hotel Suna, Çankırı Cad, Soğukkuyu Sok 6 (near the *Olimpiyat Otel*), Ulus (☎311 5465). Singles $10, doubles $14, with bath. Quiet and a little gloomy but the rooms are reasonable.

Hotel Zümrüt Palas, Posta Cad 16, Ulus (☎310 3210, 310 3211). $10 and $13 for rooms with bathrooms, $7 and $11 without. Good value for money.

Köprülü Palas Oteli, Sanayi Cad, Kuruçeşme Sok 3 (☎311 0870, 324 4312). Cheap at $5 and $10, but the rooms are pretty crummy.

Marmara Oteli, Denizciler Cad 17 near Opera Meydanı (☎324 2740) $4.80 and $8. Plain, waterless rooms which aren't too bad, although the smell in the corridor is disillusioning.

Nursaray Oteli, Kevgirli Cad Cediz Sok 12, Ulus (☎324 3187). Singles $5. Only if you can't find anywhere else.

Otel Avrupa, Posta Cad, Susam Sok 9, Ulus (☎311 4300). $5 and $9.50. Nothing special but bearable.

Otel Çoruh, Denizciler Cad 47 near Opera Meydanı (☎312 4113, 312 4114). Some singles with washbasins only at $6.50. Doubles with showers $14. A reasonable family hotel.

Otel Devran, Opera (İtfaiye) Meydanı (near Gazi Lisesi) (☎311 0485, 311 0486). $10 and $13 with bath. A well-run friendly place with decent, though small, rooms.

Otel Erden, İtfaiye Meydanı 23 (near Gazi Lisesi) (☎324 3191, 324 3192). $9 and $17.50 ($7 and $15 without bath). Acceptable place.

Otel Hakan, Gazi Mustafa Kemal Bulvarı 60, Maltepe (☎188 7058). $7.20 and $12. This place seems okay—the rooms are fine—but there's something indefinably dubious about it.

Otel Kösk, Denizciler Cad 56 near Opera Meydanı. (☎324 5228, 324 5229). Singles for $9 and doubles $14 with bathrooms. Not bad.

Otel Mithat, İtfaiye Meydanı, Tavus Sok 2 (☎311 5410, 311 5651). Decent rooms with attached baths for $10 and $17.

Otel Oba, Posta Cad 9, Ulus (☎312 4128, 312 4129). $10 and $14 with bath. Not bad, but a little overpriced.

Otel Pamukkale, Hükümet Cad 18, Ulus (☎311 7812). $6 and $11.20. Slightly dingy but okay for a single night.

Otel Pınar, Hisar Cad 14, Ulus (☎311 8951). $7.20 for a double with shower (toilet not attached). Occasional singles with washbasins for $4.

Otel Sıpahi, İtfaiye Meydanı, Kosova Sok 1 (☎324 0235, 324 0236). $6.50 and $8 for clean, homey rooms with washbasins.

Otel Tarabya, İtfaiye Meydanı, Kosova Sok 9 (☎311 9552). $4.80 and $8. Cheap but basic and gloomy.

Otel Turan Palas, Çankırı Cad, Beşık Sok 3, Ulus (☎312 5225, 312 5226). $6 and $11. Reasonable enough.

Otel Üçler, İtfaiye Meydanı, Kosova Sok 7. $5 and $8. Cheap but very old-fashioned place.

Otel Uğrak, İtfaiye Meydanı, Gazi Lisesi Karşisi Sanayi Cad 52 (☎311 2948). $4 and $8. Cheap but gloomy, and on the dingy side.

Otel Uğur Palas, İtfaiye Meydanı, Sanayi Cad 54. $8 and $16 for acceptable rooms with bath ($6 and $12 for rooms without).

Santral Palas, Denizciler Cad, Dibek Sok 4 (☎312 5577, 312 6588). $8 and $16 for okay rooms with bath.

Mid-range Hotels

Hotels in this range have restaurants and bars, and often quote prices in dollars. Some have star ratings. All rooms come with attached baths.

Anıt Hotel, Gazi Mustafa Kemal Bulvarı 111, Maltepe (☎231 7880). $25 and $35 although they will go lower.

Başyazicioğlu Hotel, Çankırı Cad 27, Ulus (☎310 3935). $17 and $30. One of the better ones in this price range, superior to the *Yeni Bahar* next door, for example.

Canbek Hotel, Soğukkuyu Sok 8 (☎324 3320). $23 and $32. Fancy place down a side street off Çankırı Caddesi.

Hotel As, Rüzgarlı Sok 4, Ulus (☎310 3998). Reasonable place: $20 and $25 with bath, $15 and $22 without.

Hotel Ergen, Karanfil Sok 48, Kızılay (☎117 5906). $18 and $25. Standard-issue mid-range hotel.

Hotel Taç, Çankırı Cad 35, Ulus. $18 and $22. Similarly standard.

Olimpiyat Hotel, Rüzgarlı Eşdost Sok 18, Ulus (☎243 331). $15 and $20. Good rooms for a reasonable price.

Otel Akman, Opera Meydanı, Tavus Sok 6 (☎324 4140). $18 and $25 with the usual facilities.

Otel Barınak, Koç Yurdu Yanı Onur Sok 25, Maltepe (☎231 8040). $25 and $35 but they're prepared to discount. Down a side street off Gazi Mustafa Kemal Bulvarı.

Otel Bulduk, Sanayi Cad 26 (☎310 4915). $12 and $20. A big, modern place where they're "happy to be in your service."

Otel Ersan, Meşrütiyet Cad 13, Kızılay (☎118 4092). $25 and $35. Worth the money if you have it.

Otel Kazyağdi, Sanayi Cad, Kuruçeşme Sok 4 (☎310 2440). $24 and $34. Three-star place with everything you'd expect.

Otel Örnek, Gülseren Sok 4, Maltepe (☎231 8170). $25.50 and $35.50. Down a side street just off Gazi Mustafa Kemal Bulvarı, this is fine but a little overpriced.

Otel Safir, Denizciler Cad 34 (☎324 1194). $15 and $30 but will go lower.

Otel Tuğba, Gazi Mustafa Kemal Bulvarı, Nokta Durağı 49, Maltepe (☎231 7415). $14 and $22. A friendly, quiet place.

Sembol Otel, Sümer Sok 28, Kızılay (☎231 8222). $20 and $30. Likewise.

Turist Hotel, Çankırı Cad 37, Ulus (☎310 3980). $30 and $40. Doesn't really deserve its three stars, but it's okay.

Yeni Bahar Otel, Çankırı Cad 25, Ulus (☎310 4895). $15 and $25. Reasonable enough, but you can't help feel that it would be easy to find a slightly less attractive place for a lot less cash.

Expensive Hotels

Restaurants, full-service bars, TVs in rooms, air conditioning, room service and more come as standard in these places. You can expect to pay $40-plus per night for a single.

Büyük Ankara Oteli, Atatürk Bulvarı 183 (☎125 6655). $85 and $95–$140. The city's second-best luxury hotel (after the *Hilton*), near the parliament building.

Eyuboglu Otel, Karanfil Sok 73, Kızılay (☎117 6414). $45 and $60. A typical deluxe hotel with restaurant, bar, etc. Offers laughable $2 discounts in low season.

Hilton International Hotel, Tahran Cad 12, Kavaklidere (☎168 2888). $100–125 and $115–150. You might want to stay here if you're on a generous expense account.

Hotel Bulvar Palas, Atatürk Bulvarı 141 (☎117 5020). The journalist's hotel, and very nice it is too. $32 single.

Hotel Pullman Etap Altınel, Tandoğan Meydanı (☎231 7760). $95–110 and $120–155. Swish place with a couple of restaurants (including a Japanese one).

Hotel Pullman Etap Mola, İzmir Caddesi, Kızılay. $66 and $85. Run by the same chain as the *Etap Altınel*, this one is slightly less fancy.

Otel Melodi, Karanfil Sok. 10, Kızılay (☎117 6414). $40 and $50. Very central, with all the usual comforts.

The City

Ulus Meydanı, where most of the cheap hotels are found, is, for most visitors, their first taste of Anakara. It's none too enticing; a huge equestrian staue of Atatürk towers over a busy intersection, flanked by threatening bronze soldiers in German-style army helmets.

From Ulus, Hisarparkı Caddesi leads east to the **Hisar**: on the way a quick diversion south down Susam Caddesi, followed by a fork to the left, brings you to the **Yeni Hallar**, the city's premier produce market. Just behind here on Konya Caddesi is the **Vakıf Sultan Çarşısı**, a restored *han*, now home to multitudes of cheap clothing shops.

The Citadel

If the lure of fresh produce and low-rent fashion proves less than irresistible, press on down Hisarparkı Caddesi toward the citadel, whose walls and towers loom above you. At the end of the street, steps leads up through the terraces of **İnönü Park** to a massive gateway. Beyond lies old Ankara, a village of narrow cobbled streets and ramshackle wooden houses, where women stand in door-ways gossiping and kids play in the street. For a moment, it's like stepping back a century.

It was the Gauls who built the first fortifications on this site, but most of what can be seen today dates from Byzantine times, with substantial Selçuk and Ottoman additions. From the **Ak Kale**, at the northern end of the citadel, there's a tremendous view of the rest of the city. The same goes for **Şark Kulesi**, a ruined tower rising out of the eastern walls, which is a favorite kite-flying spot with local children.

It's from here that you can best appreciate the impact of the *gecekondu* **squatter settlements** that grew up as country people, drawn to Ankara by the prospect of work and higher living standards, flocked to the city, taking advantage of an old Ottoman law stating that anyone who could build a house in a single night on an unused plot had the right to legal ownership. What began as shantytowns have since taken on a more permanent aspect: most of the *gecekondu* houses are wooden but they're relatively solid, and the city authorities, bowing to the inevitability of a development that was definitely not part of Atatürk's master plan, have

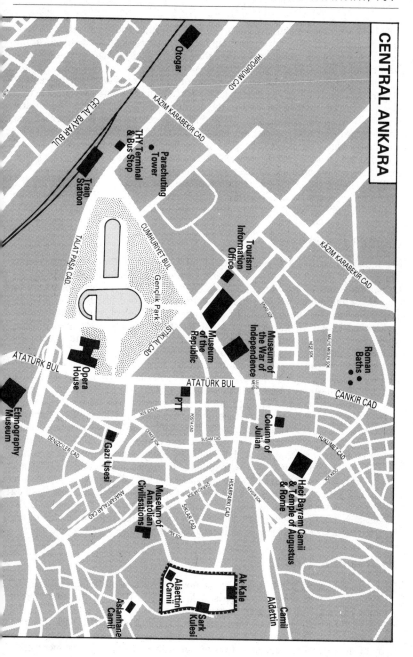

CENTRAL ANKARA

Otogar

HIPODRUM CAD

KÂZIM KARABEKIR CAD

CELAL BAYAR BUL

THY Terminal
& Bus Stop

Parachuting
Tower

Train
Station

KÂZIM KARABEKIR CAD

TALAT PAŞA CAD

CUMHURİYET BUL

Tourism
Information
Office

Gençlik Park

İSTİKLAL CAD

SIVAS SOK

Museum
of the
Republic

Museum of
the War of
Independence

MALTEPE SELER SOK

NEŞE SOK

Roman
Baths

ATATÜRK BUL

Opera
House

ATATÜRK BUL

ÇANKIR CAD

Ethnography
Museum

PTT

POSTA CAD

DENİZCİLER CAD

POS SOKAK

RESİ SOK

SUSAM CAD

Column of
Julian

HÜKÜMET CAD

Gazi Lisesi

ANKARTALAR CAD

Museum of
Anatolian
Civilisations

HISARPARKI CAD

POS ISTOSKOSU

KEVOR SOK

Hacı Bayram Camii
& Temple of Augustus
& Rome

POS SOK

SIKLAR CAD

PICK SOK

Aslanhane
Camii

Alâettin
Camii

Şark
Kulesi

Ak Kale

Camii
Alâettin

provided water and electricity and built schools. Other social amenities like tea-houses and restaurants have grown up naturally in response to the needs of the locals. Many of the inhabitants, though, cling to their village ways—growing vegetables and raising animals in their small gardens.

The Hisar has a mosque in the shape of the unexceptional twelfth-century **Alâeddin Camii**, much restored in later years. For more impressive architecture head down into the **bazaar** area to the south, where you'll find the **Aslanhane Camii**. Built by the Selçuks during the thirteenth century, this is Ankara's finest mosque, with a carved wooden ceiling supported by 24 wooden columns and a distinctive blue-tiled *mihrab*. There's a stone lion in the courtyard, and it's from this that the mosque gets its name, "Lion House." The bazaar nearby rates a little time; look out in particular for the shops selling angora wool.

If, on leaving the citadel, you follow Kadife Sokak as it curves down toward the modern city, you'll eventually come to the **Museum of Anatolian Civilizations** (see "Museums"), which for many visitors is the main reason they're here.

Roman Ankara

To the north of Ulus Meydanı you can find what's left of Roman Ankara. Just to the north of the Ulus end of Hisarparkı Caddesi, on Hükümet Meydanı, is the **Jülyanüs Sütunu** or Column of Julian, erected in honor of a visit to Ankara by the Byzantine emperor Julian the Apostate, who reigned briefly from 361–363. The stonework of the column has a strange layered effect, sort of like a long, cylindrical kebab. In the summer a pair of storks usually nests on top. After memories of the Byzantine Empire had faded the locals took to calling the column Belkız Minaresi, the Queen of Sheba's Minaret.

From here head east to Hükümet Caddesi, turn right and then right again (more or less doubling back on the direction you've been walking in), and you'll find the **Hacıbayram Camii**. Strictly speaking this is not a Roman building, but it was erected on the ruins of the **Temple of Augustus and Rome**. The temple was originally built by the Phrygians during the second century BC in honor of Cybele, and later served as a temple to the phallic god Men before being dedicated to Augustus and Rome. Today the remains of the temple wall on the square next to the mosque are about all that's left. The Hacıbayram Camii itself was built in 1400 by Hacı Bayram Veli, the founder of the Bayramiye order of dervishes, whose *türbe* in front of the mosque is a popular place of pilgrimage.

Making your way down Çiçek Caddesi to Çankırı Caddesi, and then heading north, will eventually bring you to the **Roma Hamamları**, or Roman Baths (Tues–Sun 8:30am–5:30pm; $1), just off the main road. The foundations of the baths are still visible, but you're unlikely to be overwhelmed by their splendor.

Kızılay and Around

The bus ride from Ulus to Kızılay is not an especially thrilling experience. Immediately south of Ulus you pass Ankara's main PTT, on the east side of Atatürk Bulvarı, and thereafter comes a succession of banks. Look out for the entrance to **Gençlik Parkı** on the right after the traffic circle. This park was built by order of Atatürk to provide a worthy recreational spot for the hard-toiling citizens of his model metropolis; it features an artificial lake, an amusement park, outdoor cafés, and occasional concerts. The **Opera House**, an art deco building done up in dark pink, stands near the entrance. This, too, was built at Atatürk's behest—he developed a taste for opera while serving as military attache in Sofia in 1905, and decided that Ankara, as a great modern city, needed an opera house.

Heading on down Atatürk Bulvarı you pass the **Ethnographic Museum** (see "Museums"), a grandiose white marble building on the east side of the street. To the west is an apparent industrial wasteland, but things start to improve a little farther south, beyond the rail and road overpasses, as modern Ankara suddenly begins. To the immediate east is another park, the **Abdi İpekçi Parkı**, with a small lake and teahouses, and just to the south is **Sıhhıye**, with a statue based on the Anatolian stag symbol. Here the road branches off in three directions. Along Atatürk Bulvarı the pace of street life picks up rapidly as you approach **Kızılay**, the center of modern Ankara, which turns out to be yet another immense traffic junction with a small park and a mighty Atatürk statue.

At the southeast corner of this huge junction, on the east side of Atatürk Bulvarı, is the *Gima* department store—where the merchandise smacks of the bargain basement—and a post office. Moving south from the square are numerous fancy clothing boutiques, which are impossibly expensive by Turkish standards, but reasonably affordable in dollar terms. Some of the best are in the Engürü Pasaji, a shopping center on two levels. At *Vakko*, Atatürk Bulvarı 113, and *Mudo*, Atatürk Bulvarı 125, a little farther south, you can pick up the latest fashions for men and women for about what you'd expect to pay back home.

Moving on down Atatürk Bulvarı takes you past various hotels and airline offices. A few streets east you'll see the four minarets of the **Kocatepe Camii**, a modern mosque built in Ottoman style. Its only real claim to fame is size: it's Ankara's largest mosque and one of the biggest in the world to boot. Continuing, you pass Turkey's **Parliament Building** (Büyük Millet Meclisi), a large, modern structure thoroughly in keeping with the aesthetic values of this part of Ankara. Beyond here a strip of embassies leads to **Çankaya**, the city's smartest residential district, containing the *Hilton Hotel*, the American Embassy and the **Presidential Palace** (Çankaya Köskü), in whose grounds is the **Çankaya Atatürk Museum**.

Anıt Kabir

Anıt Kabir, Atatürk's mausoleum, is a national shrine to the memory of the man who shaped modern Turkey (daily 9am–5pm, 4pm in winter; bus #63 from Ulus). The main entrance to the mausoleum is reached by traveling up Anıt Caddesi from Tandoğan Meydanı at the northwestern end of Gazi Mustafa Kemal Bulvarı, and it's this approach that reveals the place at its most impressive (you can also enter the grounds of the mausoleum from a rear entrance on Akdeniz Caddesi).

The Anıt Caddesi approach takes you through the immaculately kept grounds of the mausoleum to a parking lot. A flight of steps leads up to a colonnaded avenue leading to the courtyard of the mausoleum—at the top, the entrance to the colonnade is flanked by a couple of kiosks, the right-hand one containing a model of the mausoleum and details about its construction. The colonnade itself is lined by Hittite stone lions. In the courtyard on the right as you enter is the **sarcophagus of İsmet İnönü** (1884–1973), Atatürk's friend and prime minister, who succeeded him as president of the Republic.

On the left (northeastern) side of the courtyard another flight of steps leads up to **Atatürk's mausoleum** itself, which looks like a squared-off twentieth-century reworking of a Hellenistic temple. You pass through bronze doors (if you're wearing a hat remove it) into the marble interior, where guards keep an eye on visitors to make sure they evince an appropriate degree of respect. The interior is almost completely bare—the only decoration is some discreet mosaic work—so that all attention is focused on the 40-ton sarcophagus.

At the southeastern end of the courtyard is a **museum** containing various items of Atatürk memorabilia, including a number of the Lincoln limos that served as his official transportation.

Ankara's Museums

Ankara has one of the most prestigious museums in the country, the Museum of Anatolian Civilizations, which is arguably the highlight of the entire city. The rest of the city's museums pale by comparison, although the others listed below are all worth a visit if you have time.

Museum of Anatolian Civilizations (Anadolu Medeniyetleri Müzesi)

The Museum of Anatolian Civilizations (Tues–Sun 8:30am–5:30pm; $4, students $2) boasts an incomparable collection of Hittite and Urartian objects, all housed in a restored Ottoman *bedesten*, or covered market. Exhibits are displayed in chronological order starting with the Neolithic era, in a series of rooms built around a central hall devoted to Hittite finds. The layout is well planned, enabling you to follow the development of civilization in Anatolia effortlessly as you go around.

The exhibits in the museum are well labeled in English and German, but as you enter you may well be importuned by an official guide offering to accompany you on your tour. If you have $10 or so to spare, and like the look of whoever approaches you, this can be worth doing—many of the guides are moonlighting academics, and correspondingly well informed.

Directly adjoining the entrance area is the small **Paleolithic section**, with bone fragments and a few tools. In the **Neolithic section** (7000–5000 BC) the objects on display reflect the importance of a period in which the seeds of our civilization were sown, as settled agriculture began and tool-making techniques were refined. Much of what can be seen comes from Çatal Höyük, 52km southeast of Konya, the site of one of Anatolia's oldest human settlements. A Çatal Höyük cave dwelling has been re-created, complete with paintings of bulls' heads and other animal figures. The best-known symbols of this era are the baked-clay mother-goddess figures—female forms of ample proportions.

Next comes the **Chalcolithic section** (5500–3000 BC), with significant finds from the period when metal first began to be used. Many of these metal implements come from the sites at Hacılar and Alacahöyük, and there are also some sophisticated examples of early pottery and a number of figurines. The next section covers the **Early Bronze Age** (3000–1950 BC), a period marked by an increase in the use of metal objects. The most interesting exhibits are the bronze stag figures with their multi-pronged antlers; these have been adopted as a symbol by the Turkish Ministry of Culture and Tourism.

In the **Assyrian Trading Colony section** (1950–1750 BC) you'll find numerous pottery figures and vessels unearthed at Kültepe, the site of the Karum trading colony, established by the Assyrians near Kayseri to take advantage of Anatolia's phenomenal wealth. Next up is a section devoted to the **Old Hittite Kingdom** (1750–1200 BC). The Hittites superseded the Assyrians as masters of Anatolia and have left numerous cattle figures and sophisticated-looking vessels, most of which come from sites around Boğazkale.

The **Phrygians** (1200–700 BC) moved in when the Hittites lost their grip, and most of the finds on display in this section come from the royal tombs at Gordion. Many of them have a distinctly Hellenistic feel. Adjacent to this is the **Urartian** (1200–700 BC) section. The Urartians had a huge empire stretching from Sivas and Erzincan to Iran, and were the main rivals of the Phrygians in Anatolia. Expert masons and architects, they have left many fortresses in eastern Turkey. They were also skilled metalworkers and this section contains various examples of their art.

The central hall of the museum contains the finest examples of **Late Hittite** (1200–700 BC) carving and relief work, mostly taken from Carchemish, a city that occupied a site near the present Syrian border. The late Hittite period followed the arrival of the Phrygians, when the Hittites abandoned their old cities and took refuge in the eastern Toros Mountains in southern and southeastern Anatolia. They finally succumbed to the Assyrians in 700 BC, but their legacy forms the most compelling sections of the museum.

Other Museums

Ethnographic Museum (Etnografya Müzesi; Tues–Sun 8:30am–5:30pm; 50¢), just off Atatürk Bulvarı at the end of Talat Paşa Caddesi. Occupying a white marble building with an equestrian Atatürk statue in front, Ankara's Ethnographic Museum boasts the usual collection of folk costumes and Ottoman art and artifacts. Also features a room used as an office by Atatürk.

Painting and Sculpture Museum (Resim ve Heykel Müzesi; Tues–Sun 8:30am–5:30pm; 50¢). Basically an art museum, next door to the above. An unusual mix of European and traditional Turkish styles is displayed in the work of Turkish artists exhibited here.

Museum of the War of Independence (Kürtülüş Savaşi Müzesi; Tues–Sun 8:30am–5pm; 20¢), Cumhuriyet Bulvarı/Ulus Meydanı. Turkish captions only make it a little hard to work out the significance of the various photographs and exhibits here.

Republic Museum (Cumhuriyet Müzesi; Tues–Sun 8:30am–5pm; 25¢), Cumhuriyet Bulvarı, just down from Ulus. Located in the first headquarters of the Turkish Grand National Assembly, an ad hoc parliament founded by Atatürk in the dark days after World War I when Turkey was threatened with dismemberment, the Republic Museum has a large collection of photographs and documents. Captions are in Turkish only, though, so interest is limited.

Railroad Museum (Demiryolları Müzesi; Tues–Sun 8:30am–noon & 1–5:30pm), Ankara Railroad Station. Not always open during these times, and really of interest only to railroad buffs. The museum is located in the station near Atatürk's personal railroad coach, which is on display just off the concourse.

Eating and Drinking

Standard *pide* and kebab places can be found on just about every street in Ankara and there's an abundance of good pastry and cake shops. Really good **restaurants**, though, are surprisingly rare and, outside of the big hotel **bars**, you'll find few places to get a drink other than gloomy male-dominated "pubs."

Once again Ulus, particularly along Çankırı Caddesi, is a good place to start, with a broad range of places that are among the cheapest in town. At the Kızılay end of Karanfil Sokak and on Selânik Sokak (particularly north of Ziya Gökalp Caddesi) you'll find some slightly classier, but still easily affordable, alternatives. These streets and the places on them are the haunt of Ankara's rich kids and student types.

If you're looking to blow some cash then head for one of the big hotels, or try around Çankaya or Kavaklıdere, where there are some more expensive—but not necessarily particularly good—restaurants.

Bear in mind that many places don't serve alcohol and that they are prone to closing early, around 10pm. Decent possibilities include:

Akman Boza ve Pasta Salonu, Atatürk Bulvarı 3, Ulus. In a shopping plaza just south of the Atatürk statue, serving light meals, pastries, and *boza*, a refreshing millet-based drink.

Altın Şiş, Karanfil Sok, Kızılay. A reasonably priced kebab place that does good desserts.

Cambo, Karanfil Sok, Kızılay. Moderately priced sit-down place, good for kebabs and light snacks.

Cihan Kebap, Selânik Cad 3/B. Here you'll be able to get a two-course meal for about $3.

Çiçek Lokantası, Çankırı Cad 12/A, Ulus. On the eastern side of the street, a few hundred meters past the intersection. A good, white-tablecloth, sit-down place.

Hacı Mehmet Özlek, Sanayi Cad 7, Ulus. Named after the proprietor. A pleasant, friendly place with a decently priced menu. Ask to be seated upstairs.

Karadeniz, Karanfil Sok 11/A, Kızılay. A reasonable *pide* and *döner* place.

Kardelen, Karanfil Sok, Kızılay. Slightly fancier bar/restaurant, next door to *Karadeniz*. Alcohol served.

Kebabıstan, Karanfil Sok/Yüksel Cad, Kızılay. Plush kebab restaurant, offering all kinds of kebab including excellent mushroom *şiş*. A main course with dessert and soft drink will cost about $3.60.

Kebabıstan, Sanayi Cad, Ulus. Another branch of the above, not quite as pleasant.

Karanfil, Karanfil Sok, Kızılay. Stand-up buffet next door to *Kebabıstan* and slightly cheaper than its neighbor.

Körfez Lokantası, Bayındır Sok 24. Kebabs, fish dishes, etc. With a terrace.

McDonald's, Atatürk Bulvarı, Kızılay. Just north of Kızılay on the eastern side of the street is Ankara's *McDonald's*. It's always full of Turks trying to escape from kebabs and *köfte*. A burger will cost you about as much as a kebab with all the trimmings in a hole-in-the-wall place.

Pigalle Café Restaurant, Yüksel Cad, Kızılay. At the Kızılay (western) end of Yüksel Caddesi, the haunt of Ankara's gilded youth.

Pizza Pino, Tunalı Hilmi Cad 111/B. Upscale pizza place.

Rema Lokantası, Posta Cad/Sanayi Cad, Ulus. Basic *lokanta*, just about the cheapest eats in the area.

Salon Yüksel, Yüksel Cad, Kızılay. Near the *Pigalle* and favored by the same clientele.

Santral Kefiterya, Çankırı Cad, Ulus. A couple of hundred meters along from the Ulus intersection, on the west side of the street, this is more of a beer hall but they also do simple kebab dishes. A good place to get a drink or a bite to eat late at night when other places have closed.

Silk Road, Besteker Sok Kavaklıdere. Chinese food, after a fashion, which could make a change if you're bored with the local fare.

Uğrak Piknik and **Uğrak Lokantası**, Çankırı Cad, Ulus. Two for the price of one—a cafeteria with fixed meals for about $2.50, and a proper restaurant. After the first street on the western side of the street.

Vidar, Yüksel Cad 7/A, Kızılay. A cheapish *döner* and hamburger place.

Uludağ Kebap, Denizciler Cad 51/B, near İtfaiye Meydanı. Slightly pricey kebab place.

Wimpy, Ziya Gökalp/İnkılâp Sok, Kızılay. If you're suddenly gripped by an irresistible urge for junkfood, this is the place to come.

Nightlife

Nightlife in Ankara is extremely limited—in fact the only thing that seems to be open late are a series of seedy *gazino*-type places along Gazi Mustafa Kemal Bulvarı in Maltepe, and a few tacky **discos** in Kavaklıdere. There are some **student cafés**, bars, and discos hidden away in the backstreets of the university district, Cebeci, but you'll need to find a local to guide you to them.

Listings

Airline offices *THY*, Hipodrom Caddesi, Gar Yeni, by the train station (☎312 4900, 312 4910). Open daily 7am to 8pm, with tickets on sale beween 8:30am and 7:45pm, except on Sundays when the desk is open from 8:30am to 5:15pm. *Pan Am*, Tunus Caddesi 85/8 (☎168 2808).

Airport Esenboğa, 33km north of the city; airport buses run from the *THY* terminal on Hipodrom Caddesi.

Buses There are frequent bus connections from Ankara otogar to virtually every town of any size in Turkey. Most bus companies have their offices on Gazi Mustafa Kemal Bulvarı, Ziya Gökalp Caddesi, İzmir Caddesi, and Menekşe Sokak, where you can buy tickets in advance.

Bookshops *Tahran Kitabevi*, Sakaraya Caddesi, Kızılay, has a good selection of English, French, and German books. There are a number of other foreign-language bookshops on the same street.

Car rental *Akatur*, Cinnah Cad. 28/2, Çankaya (☎126 0603); *Atak*, Filistin Sok 9/D, Gaziosmanpaşa (☎167 9585); *Avis*, Tunus Cad. 68/2, Kavaklıdere (☎167 2313); *Hertz* Kızılırmak Sok. 1 (☎118 8440).

Cultural centers *Turkish American Association*, Cinnah Cad 20, Kavaklıdere (☎126 2644); *British Council*, İngiliz Kültür Heyeti, Adakale Sok 27, Yenişehir (☎131 7788); *French Cultural Association*, Ziya Gökalp Cad 15, Kızılay (☎131 1458); *Turkish German Cultural Institute*, Necatibey Cad, Yeşılırmak Sok, Dinçer Ap 10/16 (☎231 9237).

Embassies *American*, Atatürk Bulvarı 110, Çankaya (☎126 5470); *British*, Şehit Ersan Cad 46/A, Çankaya (☎127 4310–15); *Bulgarian*, Atatürk Bulvarı 124 (☎166 2605); *Australian*, Nenehatun Cad 83, Gaziosmanpaşa (☎136 1240–43); *Canadian*, Nenehatun Cad 75, Gaziosmanpaşa (☎136 1275–79); *Belgian*, Nenehatun Cad 109, Gaziosmanpaşa (☎136 1653); *Danish*, Kırlangiç Sok 42, Gaziosmanpaşa (☎127 5258); *Dutch*, Köroğlu Sok 6, Gaziosmanpaşa (☎136 1074); *Finnish*, Galip Dede Sok 1/20 (☎126 5921); *French*, Paris Cad 70, Kavaklıdere (☎126 1480, 125 1482); *German*, Atatürk Bulvarı 114, Kavaklıdere (☎126 5465); *Indian*, Cinnah Caddesi 77/A (☎138 2195); *Iranian*, Tehran Caddesi 10, Kavaklıdere, (☎127 4320); *Syrian*, Abdullah Cevdet Sokak 7, Çankaya (☎138 8704); *Iraqi*, Turan Emeksiz Sokak 11, Gaziosmanpaşa (☎126 6118); *Afghan*, Çinnah Caddesi 88, Çankaya (☎138 1121); *Yugoslav* Paris Caddesi 47, Kavaklıdere (☎126 2432).

Emergency Police ☎055.

Emergency Ambulance ☎077.

Emergency Fire ☎00.

Exchange Outside of normal banking hours try the cashiers in any of the big hotels, although some of them may not exchange money if you're not staying there.

Hamams *Ankara Hamamı*, Talatpaşa Bulvarı 166, Mamak Belediyesi Karşisi, men only; *Göreme Dörtyol Hamamı*, Talatpaşa Bulvarı 146, Cebeci, men only; *Yenişehir Hamamı*, Sümer Sokak 16/A, Kızılay.

Hospital If you need medical treatment head for the *Hacettepe Hastanesı*, just west of Hasırcılar Sokak in Sihhiye, where there should be an English-speaking doctor available.

Luggage consignment There's an office at the otogar where they'll charge about $1 per backpack or large bag.

PTT Ankara's main post office is the *Merkez Posta Hane*, Atatürk Bulvarı, Ulus. Come here for stamps, *jetons*, etc, and if you're having trouble getting a long-distance phone connection or want to call collect.

Tourist Police Boncuk Sokak 10/2, Kurtuluş (☎134 1756).

TML office Sakarya Caddesi, İnkılap Sokak, Deniz Apt 4/4 Kızılay (☎133 1273).

West of Ankara

There's little to see west of Ankara, with only the ruined Roman city of **Aezani** and possibly nearby **Kütahaya**, famous for its pottery, worth a real visit. If you decide to make the journey, you could also stop off in **Eskişehir** for an hour or so. Some 25km before Eskişehir are the **meerschaum quarries** which are one of that city's main claims to fame. A sign for KARATEPE leads down a dirt road, and if you follow this you'll soon see the quarries by the roadside.

Eskişehir

ESKİŞEHİR gives the impression of being little more than a modern industrial city, and indeed it's true that nowadays the place is primarily given over to the manufacture of railroad locomotives, textiles, and cement. It's also the center of the Turkish meerschaum (a fine white clayey stone) industry, so souvenir-hunters can stock up on meerschaum pipes, walking sticks, and the like, which you won't find cheaper anywhere. There are plenty of shops around town and with a little haggling it should be possible to pick up some bargains. Eskişehir's most famous pipe shop is *Işik PiPo*, Sakarya Caddesi, Konya İşhani 12/6, where you can watch the craftsmen at work.

Despite appearances, Eskişehir in fact has a long history, the modern town having been grafted onto an ancient settlement during the postwar period of rapid industrialization. Its origins go back at least to Greek times, when it was known as Dorylaeum. Some relics of this old city can be seen in the local **archae-ological museum**, or for a taste of the more recent past head for the old quarter of **Yenişehir** in the northwestern corner of town, centered around a **Selçuk castle**. On the opposite, eastern edge of the city stands the **Kurşunlu Mosque**, attributed to Mimar Sinan.

Practical Details

In the final analysis, none of the above amounts to a great deal, and Eskişehir is not a place you'd want to hang around for more than a few hours. Fortunately there are good road and rail connections, with trains running to Ankara, İzmir and İstanbul, and frequent buses and dolmuşes on the same routes. The **otogar** is on Yunus Emre Caddesi, near the river, and the **train station** is on the northwestern edge of the city center. Both are within walking distance of the not very useful **tourist information office** at Iki Eylül Cad 175a (☎221/17292). The best local hotel is the *Sale Oteli*, İnönü Cad 71, which has double rooms starting at $10.

Kütahya

Dominated by an Ottoman fortress, **KÜTAHYA** is famous above all for its fine ceramics. China, porcelain, and tiles are all manufactured in the city, and sold in stores on virtually every street. **Kütahya tiles** are used throughout Turkey, especially in restoration work on Ottoman mosques, replacing the İznik originals just as Kütahya has replaced İznik as the country's leading tile-producing center. Many modern local buildings, including the otogar, are entirely covered with tiles. These aside, there's not a great deal to detain you: most people stop just long enough to do their shopping and then head on to explore nearby Aezani.

If you're coming in by bus from Eskişehir you'll be dropped off at Kütahya **otogar** on Atatürk Bulvarı, just northwest of the city center. From the otogar it's a short walk down Atatürk Bulvarı to **Konak Meydanı**, the town's main square, distinguished by a fountain with a huge ceramic vase as its centerpiece. At the southwest corner of Konak Meydanı is the local **tourist information office** (Yeni Hükümet Konağı; ☎2311/2618). The immediate vicinity of Konak Meydanı is home to a number of attractive Ottoman houses including the **Kossuth Evi**, which provided a temporary refuge for Lajos Kossuth, the Hungarian patriot, who fled to Turkey after the suppression of the 1848 revolution. Signs point from the square along Cumhuriyet Caddesi to the **Archaeological Museum** (Tues–Sun 9:30am–noon & 1:30–5pm; 50¢), with a collection of locally unearthed archaeological odds and ends and ethnological ephemera, housed in the former Vacidiye Medrese. The *medrese* was originally part of the fine **Ulu Cami**, built by the Selçuks during the thirteenth century. If you want to see more, head up to the town's citadel for predictably good views.

The best local **hotel** is probably the *Gönen Oteli* on Menderes Caddesi (☎2311/11751, 12144), with singles from $6 and doubles from $14. Nearby are the similarly priced *Yükseli Oteli* and the slightly cheaper *Şehir Oteli* and *Nızam Oteli*. If you want to be right on Konak Meydanı, the *Gülpalas* (☎2311/11759, 11233) charges roughly twice as much. Perhaps the best place to buy Kütahaya ceramics is a small shop at Atatürk Bulvarı 39: prices start at about $10, going up to $150 for a large decorative bowl.

Aezani

The ruined Roman city of **AEZANI**, easily reached from Kütahya, is famous for its wonderfully preserved Roman temple. To get there take an Uşak- or İzmir-bound dolmuş and ask to be let out at Çavdarhisar, the nearest village. From here the site (Tues–Sun 9am–noon & 1–5pm; $2) is easily visible, just a few minutes' walk away. There isn't a great deal left of the ancient city, although you can still make out the remains of the **stadium** and **agora**. The paucity of other remains, however, is more than compensated for by the **Temple of Zeus**, probably the best-preserved ancient temple in Turkey. The roof and pediment have collapsed, but most of the columns are still standing (complete with the frieze running around the top), along with substantial sections of wall. In the cellar with its distinctive vaulted roof you'll find the **Temple of Cybele**. If you don't want to go back the way you came, pick up any dolmuş bound for UŞAK: from this unprepossessing city there are ample bus connections in all directions, in particular to İzmir and the Aegean coast in the west, and Antalya and the Mediterranean coast in the south.

North of Ankara

The mountain ranges that lie beween Ankara and the Black Sea are rugged and pine-clad—a landscape that is at times almost alpine in flavor. They are undeniably appealing, yet, scenery aside, there is little to attract the traveler. Only **Safranbolu**, with its Ottoman mansions of timber construction set in a steep-sided gorge, rates a visit on its own merits. Other places in this direction—notably **Bolu** and **Kastamonu**— are no more than attractive potential stopovers en route to other destinations.

Safranbolu

SAFRANBOLU is a stunning town of half-timbered houses some 250km north of Ankara. On the way, all roads lead to KARABÜK, a town overshadowed by a vast steelworks and perpetually shrouded in a film of industrial grime. You'll have to come here to get to Safranbolu, but you wouldn't want to stay longer than it takes to change vehicles. Safranbolu-bound dolmuşes leave from the very basic otogar on the edge of town, for a ten-kilometer (20¢) journey that seems to promise little, passing through a suffering landscape of rocks and stunted trees to arrive at an apparently modern town of five-story apartment buildings, straggling along a dusty road which doubles up and down a hillside. After about 25 minutes of switchbacking the road descends into a steep-sided valley, snakes up the other side and finally drops again into the ravine where you'll find **Eski Safranbolu**—Old Safranbolu—a town as far removed from its modern counterpart as it's possible to imagine.

Ancient houses rise up the slopes of the ravine as you descend into town, in a smudge of dirty pastel-colored timber and red-tiled roofs, and although tourism has definitely arrived—Safranbolu is already established as a summer tour-group destination—the old way of life remains remarkably intact. Apart from a bazaar of souvenir shops, few concessions have been made to the twentieth century: come here in the off-season and you might well be the only visitor in town. Various restoration and prettification projects have been discussed, but for the time being the town remains slightly run-down, and all the better for it. Wandering the narrow streets and soaking up the unique atmosphere are still the big excitements here.

The dolmuş drop-off point is a sloping square next to a **hamam**, adjoining the town square. This hamam is worth a visit if you can spare the time—its Ottoman baths have been fully restored so that you can relax in comfort in their marble splendor (separate men's and women's sections; $1). Beyond the hamam old streets lead toward the **Cincihanı**, a huge, crumbling *kervansaray* dominating the town center. At the moment this is a garbage-strewn ruin presided over by a ninety-year-old who demands outrageous amounts of money for letting you have a nose around (according to the locals 25¢ is enough, although you may want to be a little more generous), but plans are afoot to renovate it and turn it into a hotel.

Roughly north of the Cincihanı is the unexceptional seventeenth-century **Köprülü Mehmet Paşa Camii**, whose courtyard leads to its restored **arasta** (bazaar). This is where the day-trippers are brought, to browse at the well-stocked souvenir and antique shops. Southwest of the Cincihanı lies **İzzet Paşa Camii**, an elaborate, late-eighteenth-century mosque. Beyond, the town slides into dilapidation, with a lot of animals and dung in evidence; here the stream that runs through town has cut a deep fissure into the base of the ravine, now used as a household dump. Farther downstream women wash clothes in the water. If you walk down, there's a stunning view back toward the İzzet Paşa Camii, whose domes and minarets seem to hover above the surrounding houses.

Back in town, immediately beneath the southeastern walls of the Cincihanı, there's an open-air market, and from here a narrow street to the immediate left of the *Ziraat Bankasi* leads up the side of the valley to the **Kaymakamlar Evi** (Tues–Sun 8:30am–12:30pm & 1:30–5:30pm; $1), the "Governor's House," a restored Ottoman mansion typical of many around town. The house has a multitude of sparsely furnished rooms, each of which originally would have been home to an individual family unit—all members of the extended family of the owner. Each room has a carpeted floor (you'll be asked to remove your shoes for the sake of these carpets) and cushioned Ottoman couches run around the outside. By day these were used as seats, and at night they pulled out to act as beds. All the rooms feature carved wall-cupboards and storage alcoves.

If you make your way up from here to the hilltop **castle**, vantage points allow you to look down over the whole town: the palatial-looking edifice above the town on the opposite side of the ravine is an old government building, long since derelict. The castle itself is nothing special, a few walls enclosing a small *türbe* and park, but it's a pleasant place to walk.

Practical Information

Finding **somewhere to stay** can be a problem in Safranbolu. The only possibilities seem to be in the new town: the *Hotel Uz*, Misaki Milli, Mahallesi Kiranköy (☎464/21086, 20350), modern and well-equipped with singles for $10.80 and doubles (with bath) for $17.60, including breakfast; and the cheaper *Gülen Otel*, on the upper floor of an old house on the edge of the modern town, basic but clean rooms for $3 per person. To find them get off the dolmuş at the junction beyond the PTT in the new town and ask directions. There's a **tourist information office** (☎464/3046; Mon–Sat 9am–noon & 1:30–5pm) in the *arasta* but it's fairly clueless.

There are plenty of small groceries in Eski Safranbolu but **restaurants** are few and far between. The *Boncuk Cafe* in the *arasta* serves tea, coffee, soft drinks, and snacks, including hamburgers. Otherwise there are a few cheap *lokanta* places in the new town, on the main street where the PTT is.

Kastamonu

It was in **KASTAMONU** that Atatürk made his first speech attacking the fez in 1925. Little has happened here since. Today, a couple of venerable mosques, some fine old Ottoman houses and a crumbling *kale* make the place worth an afternoon or morning visit on the way to somewhere else, but not much more.

The **otogar** is about a ten-minute walk north of the town center, on the eastern bank of the river that cuts the town in two from north to south. Kastamonu's main street, Cumhuriyet Caddesi runs south from the otogar, parallel with the river.

Near the otogar on the western side of the river is the **İsmailbey Camii**, a fine-looking, twin-domed medieval mosque set atop a plug of rock. Adjacent is a small park. Heading south into town, take a right turn about five minutes after the *Otel İdrisoğlu* onto the town's main square, where you'll find the **Nasrullah Kadi**

Camii, one of Kastamonu's larger and more distinguished mosques*. At the western end of the square, the **Asirefendi Han** is still used for commercial purposes, and behind it there's an old and decrepit-looking hamam. From here a street runs south up to the **Yavapağa Camii**, a modern building screened by the ruins of a larger, much older mosque complex. The same street now curves off up to the west, in the direction of the *kale*. Along the way you'll pass the **Atabey Camii**, a rectangular stone building with a very low interior, built in 1273 but much repaired and restored in the intervening years.

Just above is the **kale**, unmarked but hard to miss. It was built by Tamerlane, who was more famous for destruction than construction, and time hasn't been especially kind to it. Only the massive walls and main gateway are wholly intact, but its grassy grounds are now a favorite spot with people indulging in Turkish-style contemplation and relaxation.

The town **museum** (Tues–Sun 8:30am–5pm; $1) is about ten minutes' walk south of the *Otel İdrisoğlu*, with the usual collection of local miscellanea.

Practical Information

Should you want to stay in Kastamonu there are quite a few **hotels**. For the budget-minded the *Otel Arslan*, Belediye Caddesi 10 (☎465/1134), offers squalid rooms for $3 single, $6 double. Nearby the *Otel Hâdi*, Belediye Caddesi 8 (☎465/11696), starts at $6 single, as does the *Otel Selvi*, Banka Sokak 10 (☎465/11831). Top of the price range, though not significantly better than the *Hâdi* or the *Selvi*, is the *Otel İdrisoğlu*, Cumhuriyet Caddesi 25 (☎465/11757), where rooms with central heating, hot water, and attached shower start at $9 single, $18 double. There aren't too many **places to eat** in town; your best bet is probably the *Uludağ Pide ve Kebap Salonu* at the corner of Belediye Caddesi and Cumhuriyet Caddesi, a white-tablecloth place that does excellent *pide*.

Bolu

The only reason you're likely to visit **BOLU** is as a stopover beween Ankara and İstanbul. It has a massive central **Ulu Cami** and a couple of **hotels** on the main street, but not much else. The *Otel Turist* is the cheapest place to stay, with singles for $5 and doubles for $7 (with shower); the *Otel Menekşe*, a few doors down, has singles for $16, doubles $26. Most **buses** seem to avoid the town center so you'll probably be dropped off on the main road, just to the north. From here it's a fifteen-minute walk into town, or you can take a taxi for about $1.50. To leave you'll have to get back to this main road and wait for a bus.

If Bolu itself is unattractive, the surrounding countryside goes some way to compensate; it's gently mountainous, with extensive deciduous forests dotted with lakes. There's an almost central European feel to this region, especially around **Aladağ** and **Kartalkaya** to the south, where there's a ski area. To the southwest lies **Abant Gölü**, a mile-high lake that's well stocked with trout. To the north, **Yedigöller National Park** is theoretically the most attractive option of all. In practice it's more trouble than it's worth, reached by an atrocious dirt road

---

*About 14km north of Kastamonu is the village of **Kasaba** (take the DADAY road and then turn right after to KASABA KÖY). Here you'll find the fourteenth-century **Mahmut Bey Camii**, a wooden building which, despite a drab exterior, has the finest Selçuk-style interior of any wooden mosque in Turkey.

with no public transportation, and turning out to be a series of muddy ponds used as trout farms, disfigured by numerous dams and diversions.

EAST OF ANKARA

Prospects improve considerably east of Ankara, where there are numerous places worth going out of your way for. Just three hours away, the ancient Hittite capital of **Hattuşaş** lies near the modern village of **Boğazkale**. The scale of the place is astonishing, more so than the ruins themselves, and it's this sheer size that makes Hattuşaş and the surrounding sites so impressive. Difficult connections and substandard, overpriced accommodation, however, mean that they're best treated as a day-trip from somewhere more congenial, like Amasya (or Ankara).

Northeast of the Hittite capital is the ancient city of **Amasya**, with its Pontic rock tombs and riverside Ottoman houses. If you visit only one place in North Central Anatolia, this should be it. South of Amasya, **Tokat** has a couple of interesting buildings, including the striking Gök Medrese, but not enough to make it worth a long stay. **Sivas**, too, is a place to visit in passing, despite what amounts to a theme park of amazing Selçuk architecture.

Sungurlu, Boğazkale, and the Hittite Sites

The Hittite sites surrounding the modern village of Boğazkale are the most impressive and significant in the whole of Anatolia. This area was once the heart of the Hittite empire, whose capital was at **Hattuşaş**, which sprawls over several square kilometers to the south of the village. A few kilometers to the east is **Yazılıkaya**, a temple site on a slightly smaller scale. **Alacahöyük**, a smaller Hittite settlement dating back to 4000 BC, 25km north of Boğazkale, is farther off the beaten track, with less to see when you get there. Many of the objects unearthed here after excavation began in earnest in 1905 are now in the Museum of Anatolian Civilizations in the capital. If you've already seen the museum, a visit to the original excavations will be doubly interesting.

How to visit the sites needs some consideration. Theoretically Hattuşaş and Yazılıkaya can be covered **on foot** from Boğazkale if you're in reasonable shape. However, it gets very hot here in the summer and there are some steep hills to climb. You might therefore want to take a tour around the sites **by taxi**: various characters in Boğazkale will offer all-inclusive deals, and in the unlikely event that they don't seek you out you'll probably be able to find them at the *Aşıkoğlu Motel*. A typical offer is $10 to visit Hattuşaş and Yazılıkaya. If you don't want to spend the night in either Boğazkale or Sungurlu (and the accommodation situation is pretty dismal in both places) then you might want to take a taxi around the three sites from Sungurlu, getting back in time for an onward bus. This will set you back about $20. It's also possible to rent a minibus to make the trip for about $40.

Sungurlu

SUNGURLU is a small town just off the main Ankara–Samsun road. You'll have to pass through if you're heading for the Hittite sites, but there's really no other reason for stopping here. Sungurlu-bound buses depart roughly every hour from

Ankara's otogar on a three-hour journey across the treeless, rolling landscape of central Anatolia.

Sungurlu's otogar is just off the main road, about 1km west of town. The departure point for Boğazkale-bound dolmuşes is the main square in Sungurlu, but you should be able to pick up the dolmuş from the main road if you're dropped off by a through bus, and a few leave from the otogar itself. The trip takes about one hour and costs $1, with the last departure at 5pm (last return from Boğazkale to Sungurlu is at about 6pm). The aforementioned taxi drivers usually hang around the square in Sungurlu and at the bus drop-off point looking for tourists. They'll ask $10 to take you to Boğazkale, although you should be able to bargain them down to $6 or even $4.

If you miss the last Boğazkale-bound dolmuş you might want to stay overnight in Sungurlu. The cheapest of the **hotels** here is the *Masatlı Oteli* (☎4557/1968) on the main square, with singles for $3 and doubles for $6. Otherwise, try the *Hittit Motel* (☎4557/1042, 1409), on the main road just east of town: $15 single, $20 double.

Boğazkale

BOĞAZKALE, about 28km to the southeast of Sungurlu, at the end of a gravel road cutting across rough pastureland, is an uneventful modern village, with the ancient Hittite capital of Hattuşaş fanning out from its southern rim. Finding your way around is fairly straightforward: it's basically a one-street town, running about half a kilometer from a welcome arch up a hill to the main square. There are several **hotels**, none of them particularly good value. The best of the bunch is the *Başkent Restoran, Pansiyon ve Camping*, Yazılıkaya Yolu Üzeri (☎4554/1037), on the road leading from Boğazkale to Yazılıkaya, at the top of a fairly steep hill. Double rooms with showers start at $12, although if you're alone and the place isn't full they might let you have one for about half that. They also have space for **camping** and tents for rent. The **restaurant**, with a view of the ruins of the Great Temple, is good value, but often block-booked by German and Austrian tour groups. Alternatively, the *Aşıkoğlu Turistik Moteli* (☎4554/1004) lies right at the entrance to the village. It has basic rooms with showers, which for $12 seem expensive for what you get (in the fall and winter they're freezing and very damp), and an outrageously overpriced restaurant. A truly uninspiring meal will set you back about $4, and although individual members of staff are friendly and helpful, the same can't be said of the management which, it seems, is only in the business to make a fast buck.

On the main square in the village the *Hattuşaş Pansiyon* is a simple but more reasonably priced place with singles for $6 and doubles for $12. It's open only during the high season (May–September). There's also a new hotel about 500m beyond the *Başkent*, but at the time of writing it was still not open. In short, you'd do well to avoid staying overnight in Boğazkale.

Hattuşaş

From 1375 to 1200 BC, **Hattuşaş** was the capital of the Hittite Empire. It was, by the standards of the time, an immense city, enclosed by walls six kilometers long. Today it consists of a series of small sites linked by road. If you're exploring on foot then the best approach is from Boğazkale's main square, and you can figure

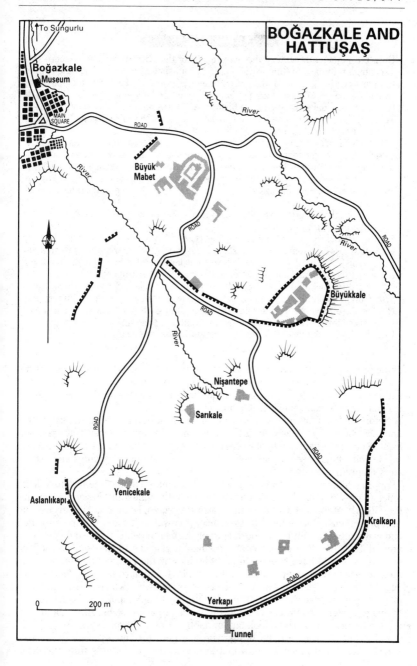

BOĞAZKALE AND HATTUŞAŞ

THE HITTITES

Until the nineteenth century the only record of the **Hittites** was an obscure Old Testament reference to King David marrying Bathsheba, widow of Uriah the Hittite. In their day, though, the Hittites ruled huge tracts of Anatolia, with an empire that rivaled the power of ancient Egypt. Somewhere in the intervening period all trace of them seems to have vanished from history, and it was not until 1834, when **Charles Texier**, a French traveler and archaeologist, discovered the ruins around Boğazkale, that the first clues of the existence of their vast empire emerged.

Initially Texier's find puzzled the archaeological community. Only when a German team began work on the Hattuşaş site in 1905 did more concrete information about the Hittites begin to emerge. The Germans unearthed thousands of **cuneiform tablets**, which when they were finally deciphered in the 1940s gave historians a complete picture of Hittite civilization and solved an archaeological mystery.

The story that emerged was of an Indo-European people who reached Anatolia in 2000 BC, grafting the culture of an indigenous people, the Hatti, onto their own. **Hittite civilization** was advanced and life was regulated by a legal code of 200 laws, according to which defiance of the state, rape, and sexual intercourse with animals were punishable by death, but which let murderers and thieves off the hook on condition that they paid compensation and returned stolen property.

The Hittite society differed from those of Mesopotamia and Egypt in that it had grown up in a mountainous region rather than in a fertile river valley. Militarily the Hittites were powerful, and at one point they even conquered Babylon; but weakened by the inroads of the Phrygians, they eventually went into decline around 1200 BC, after having dominated Anatolia for almost a thousand years.

on taking about three hours to cover the scattered remains. The spectacle is not an immediately impressive one—the various sites consist mainly of foundations and low walls, with the occasional carving here and there—but the sheer scale of it all adds up to make considerable impact.

Before taking a tour of the ruins drop in briefly at Boğazkale's **museum** (8am–noon & 1:30–5:30pm; $2.50 for a ticket which entitles you to visit Hattuşaş too), located on the left-hand side of the main street as you head up toward the square. Inside you'll find a few objects recovered from the various sites, and some explanatory diagrams.

Approaching from the direction of the main square you'll come first to a ticket office (8am–5:30pm; $2.50 if you haven't been to the museum), beyond which lies the **Büyük Mabet**, or Great Temple, also known as Temple I. The largest and best-preserved Hittite temple in existence, this was dedicated to the storm god and was probably built in the fourteenth or thirteenth century BC, and destroyed around 1200 BC. You enter via an ornamental gateway in the southeast of the site, which would have been used on holy days by the Hittite king and queen in their roles as priest and priestess of the temple. Just before the gate, look out for a large stone cistern, one side of which is decorated with two lion heads and forepaws. From the gateway a street leads into the temple, and the remnants of a drainage system are visible beneath the cracked paving slabs. After about 30m the street turns to the right; look out for another cistern here.

Following the road around brings you to where the main part of the temple stood. There's not much left now, but in the heyday of Hattuşaş this must have been the innermost sanctum. The surrounding foundations are those of 78 store-rooms in which it's thought that wine and oil were stored in huge fixed amphorae (some of these are still in place), containing beween 900 and 1750 liters of liquid each. Archaeologists also unearthed a number of cuneiform tablets in these rooms.

About 350m beyond the Great Temple, you come to a fork in the road. Bear right and follow the road as it winds up the hillside. After about half an hour of foot-slogging (this is probably the toughest stretch) you'll hit the **Yenicekale**, a fortress some 50m to the left of the road. Although little remains, its construction was clearly a considerable achievement; Hittite engineers had to create an artifi-cial platform out of the uneven and rocky terrain before they could start building.

A little higher up is the **Aslanlıkapı**, or Lion Gate. On its outer side, this gate-way is flanked by two stone lions that were supposed to defend the city from attackers and evil spirits. The lions you'll see are actually copies of the originals, which now reside in the Museum of Anatolian Civilizations in Ankara.

East of the Aslanlıkapı, the **city walls** have been partially restored, and the road leads along them to the **Yerkapı**, or Sphinx Gate. This is named after the two huge sphinxes that once guarded it, but are now kept in museums in İstanbul and Berlin. Here a **tunnel** runs for 70m through the hillside to the outer wall and a postern. The tunnel was built using the corbel-arch technique—two flat stones leaning toward each other account for its triangular profile. From the outer side two stairways lead back up to the top of the walls, and a vantage point that affords a panorama of the whole city. The foundations immediately to the north are the remnants of four temples.

About 600m to the east, heading back down the slope toward Boğazkale, are the remains of the **Kralkapı**, or King's Gate, named after the figure (actually representing a war god) carved in relief on the outer side of the gate. Again, what you see is a copy—the original is in Ankara.

Farther down the hill lies the ruined **Nişantepe**, a fortress dating back to the thirteenth century BC. Not much of the fortress itself has survived, but there's a fine Hittite inscription cut into the rock nearby, known as the **Nişantaş**. This is a memorial to king Suppiluliuma II; heavily weathered, but still discernible. To the immediate southwest of Nişantepe is **Sarıkale**, thought to be a Phrygian fort built on the foundations of an earlier Hittite structure.

From Nişantepe the road leads down to the **Büyükkale**, or Great Fortress, which served the Hittite monarchs as a palace during the thirteenth century BC. In effect it was a citadel within the city, protected by steep drop-offs on all sides and reached by a ramp. Today access is via a flight of steps, and although little has survived, the dimensions of the site (250m long by 140m wide) are awe-inspiring. It was here, in 1906, that archaeologists found 300 cuneiform tablets, including a treaty signed in 1279 BC by the Hittite king Hattusili II and Ramses II of Egypt.

Yazılıkaya

From the Hattuşaş ticket office, signs point to **Yazılıkaya**, about 3km to the east. In Turkish Yazılıkaya means "inscribed rock," and the ruins consist of an open-air temple with a number of carved reliefs. The route there dips down into a river valley then up toward the *Başkent Pension*, where more signs point the rest of the way.

The first thing you'll see as you approach the site are the remains of some foundations, which are all that's left of gateway and temple structures built during the thirteenth century BC. Behind are two open-air galleries that formed the original temple, built a couple of centuries earlier. In the larger of the two galleries, which is thought to have been the spiritual center of the Hittite religion, you'll find reliefs representing 63 gods and goddesses, the most important of a total of 1000 deities admitted by Hittite theology. Forty-two warrior gods in full battle order seem to be walking from left to right, while 21 goddesses move from right to left to meet them. The deities represented are identified by hieroglyphs, and at the center of the relief Teshub, the storm god, meets his wife Hepatu, the sun goddess.

In the smaller right-hand gallery, reached from the main one via a cleft in the rock, are more reliefs representing gods of the underworld. Opposite these is a relief of Sarumna, son of Teshub and Hepatu. This gallery is thought to have been used during the funerals of Hittite kings.

Alacahöyük

The site at **Alacahöyük**, 25km north of Boğazkale, is slightly overshadowed by its neighbors. You can reach it from Boğazkale by heading back toward Sungurlu and then turning right at the road to Alacahöyük. After about 11km take an indicated left turn for the remaining 10km to the ruins. There's no dolmuş service from Boğazkale, so you're going to have to take a taxi or hitch if you don't have your own transportation. Dolmuşes do run from Boğazkale to the village of Alaca, about 18km east of the second turn to Alacahöyük.

The hamlet of **HÖYÜK**, next to the ruins, is small, but it does have a few basic shops and a PTT. There's also a tiny **pansiyon**, but don't bank on it being open. Alacahöyük (8am–noon & 1:30–5:30pm; 50¢) dates back to the fourteenth century BC. You enter via the **Sphinx Gate**, named after the huge sphinxes that stand on either side of it. To the left of the gate are a number of reliefs depicting religious ceremonies associated with the worship of Teshub: a Hittite royal couple venerating a bull, priests in ritual costume, sacrificial rams, musicians, and acrobats all seem to have had roles to play in these lively rituals.

The Sphinx Gate opens on to a street, to each side of which are excavated areas, all clearly indicated in English. At the center of the site, set in a slight dip, are the royal tombs from which the loot on display in Ankara's ethnographic museum was taken. To the left of the Sphinx Gate, 300m across the surrounding fields, a tunnel about 25m long leads to a postern outside the original city walls.

Next to the site there's a small **museum** containing odds and ends from the excavations, most notable of which is the Hitit Çağı Banyo Teknesi, a Hittite clay bathtub. There's also an ethnographic section with costumes and carpets.

Amasya

The approach to **AMASYA** does little to prepare you for the charm of the place. Coming from Boğazkale the landscape is thoroughly uninspiring until just a few kilometers before the town itself, when you suddenly find yourself surrounded by the lush farmland and orchards of the Yeşilırmak Valley. Even arriving at the otogar or train station, both well outside the town center, Amasya doesn't seem especially impressive.

Once you've made the dolmuş trip into town, however, Amasya turns out to be one of the high points of North Central Anatolia. It occupies a point in the river valley so narrow it's almost a gorge, and has been blessed with a super-abundance of attractions. Most people come here to see the rock tombs hewn into the cliffs above town by the kings of Pontus over 2000 years ago, but Amasya also harbors some truly beautiful Selçuk and Ottoman architecture and a multitude of colorful nineteenth-century wooden houses.

History

Amasya may be tranquil now, but in the past it was the scene of battle and conquest. According to some accounts, including one by Strabo (64 BC–25 AD), the locally born geographer and historian, Amasya was founded by the Amazon queen Amasis. In reality it's more likely that the town began life as a Hittite settlement, before succumbing to Alexander the Great. When Alexander died and his empire fragmented, Amasya became capital of a Persian-ruled successor kingdom until **Mithridates**, a Greek refugee who knew an opportunity when he saw one, established the **kingdom of Pontus** here with a few followers in the third century BC. His kingdom quickly rose to prominence and eventually held sway over much of Anatolia. It was Mithridates and his descendants who were responsible for the rock tombs.

Strabo himself was born toward the end of the Pontic era. He traveled extensively in Europe, the Near East and North Africa, writing over sixty books along the way. Most of these have been lost, but Strabo was extensively quoted by other writers and so parts of his writings have survived. Of his own town he wrote:

> *My native city is located in a deep and large valley through which flows the River Iris. It has been endowed in a surprising manner by art and nature for serving the purpose of a city and fortress. For there is a lofty and perpendicular rock, which overhangs the river, having on one side a wall erected close to the bank where the town has been built, while on the other it runs up on either side to the summits of the hill. These two are connected to each other and well-fortified with towers. Within this enclosure are the royal residence and the tombs of the kings.*

Strabo's early youth coincided with the arrival of the Romans, who took over Amasya when they conquered Anatolia. Under them and through the succeeding centuries of Byzantine rule the town prospered, and it continued to do so after falling to the Selçuks—who left their distinctive architectural signature on the town—in 1071. At the end of the twelfth century Amasya was caught up in the first great Mongol incursion, led by Ghengis Khan, the self-styled "scourge of god." According to history and popular belief the Mongols terrorized Europe and the Near East, leaving a trail of death and destruction wherever they went, but in Amasya they took time off from rape and pillage to build a lunatic asylum.

The Mongols were replaced by the Ottomans, who also made a significant architectural contribution to the town: they treated Amasya (like Manisa) as a training ground for their crown princes, who served as governors of the province, to prepare them for the rigors of statesmanship at the Sublime Porte. Later in the Ottoman period Amasya was a celebrated theological center and boasted eighteen *medreses* with up to 2000 students.

Until World War I the town had a significant Armenian population, most of whom disappeared, in one way or another, after the pogroms of 1915. On June 12, 1919, Atatürk and a number of like-minded compatriots drew up the basic principles of their fight for independence in Amasya. Since then—apart from an earthquake in 1939 and a couple of bad floods—things have been quiet.

The Town

At the center of Amasya, the riverfront Atatürk square commemorates the conference/council of war that Atatürk held here on June 12, 1919 with a typical equestrian statue of the hero surrounded by admirers. The creamy yellow mosque at the eastern end of this square is the **Gümüşlü Cami**, or "Silvery Mosque," which was originally built in 1326 but which has been reconstructed at various intervals since. Its almost pavilion-like oriental exterior and carved wooden porch overlook the river, and there's an unusual tall, brick minaret.

On the southern side of the square, the **Pir Mehmet Çelebi Camii** dates from 1507. It's an extremely small example of a *mescit*, or mosque without a minaret or *mihrab*, and looks as if it was built as a pretend mosque for children. The carved facade has been decorated with ocher paint. On the street leading south from the mosque a couple of **rock tombs** have been carved into a cliff face on the far side of a small stream. They're about three or four meters above the ground, and hence inaccessible unless you happen to be traveling with a ladder.

West of the square, Atatürk Caddesi runs off through the town. A hundred meters or so along, on the southern side, is the **Kileri Süleyman Ağa Camii**, an imposing but conventionally designed Ottoman mosque built in 1489. Behind it stands the eighteenth-century **Taş Han**, a crumbling old brick-and-stone structure that now contains a metal workshop. To the rear of the Taş Han is the **Burmalı Minare Camii**—the "Twisted Minaret Mosque." Named after the spiral effect of the stonework of its minaret, this compact building was erected in 1242 but heavily restored in the eighteenth century after a fire. Inside, wooden galleries run around the walls facing the *mihrab*.

Back on Atatürk Caddesi, a *bedesten* stands opposite the Kileri Süleyman Ağa Camii, still home to various shops and businesses. Continuing west for about ten minutes brings you to the **Sultan Beyazit Camii**, just north of Atatürk Caddesi. This is Amasya's main mosque, although somehow the smaller ones are more appealing. It was built in 1486 and has a spacious garden housing a *medrese* and library.

On the other side of Atatürk Caddesi, a little to the west, is the **archaeological and ethnographic museum** (Tues–Sun 8am–noon & 1:30–5:30pm; 75¢). As Turkish municipal museums go this isn't a bad one: in addition to the obligatory amphorae, sarcophagi, and relics of ancient statues, there are interesting Ottoman carpets and inscription fragments. Center of attraction is the carved door of the Gök Medrese (see below) which was fashioned in the thirteenth century. Upstairs are more manuscripts and some writing sets, along with a few Hittite figurines and the ethnological collection—costumes and the like from Ottoman times. A curiosity is the **türbe** in the grounds, containing five mummified human husks that were found underneath the Burmalı Minare Camii. These are said to be the mortal remains of two Mongol governors and a Selçuk family (two children and a parent of indeterminate sex).

A five-to-ten-minute walk west of the museum is the **Gök Medrese Camii**, the thirteenth-century Selçuk "Mosque of the Blue Seminary," with a particularly intricate carved doorway (the door itself is in the museum). This doorway was once decorated with blue tiles—hence the name—but time seems to have taken

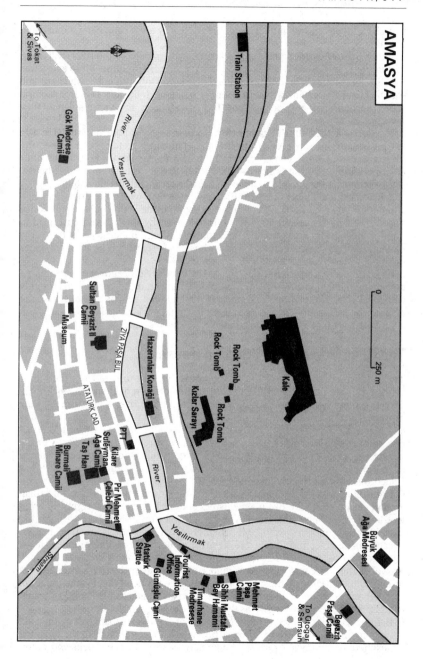

AMASYA

To Tokat & Sivas

Train Station

River Yeşilırmak

Gök Medrese Camii

Sultan Beyazit II Camii

Museum

ZIYA PAŞA BUL.

Hazeranlar Konağı

ATATÜRK CAD.

Rock Tomb

Rock Tomb

Rock Tomb

Rock Tomb

Kızlar Sarayı

Kale

0

250 m

PTT

Kilare

Süleyman Ağa Camii

Taş Han

Pir Mehmet Çelebi Camii

Burmalı Minare Camii

River

Stream

Atatürk Statue

Gümüşlü Camii

Tourist Information Office

Yeşilırmak

Timarhane Medresese

Silihi Mustafa Bey Hamamı

Mehmet Paşa Camii

Büyük Ağa Medressesi

Beyazit Paşa Camii

To Otogar & Samsun

its toll, and today there's little trace of them. Nearby are a couple of Ottoman and Selçuk tombs.

Returning to Atatürk square and heading north, parallel to the river, will bring you to the rest of Amasya's historic buildings. The **Bırmahane Medresesi** was built by the Mongols in 1308 as a lunatic asylum. Only the outer walls are still standing, but it remains a typical Mongol building, reflecting the architectural styles encountered and adapted by the Mongols in the various lands they ravaged.

Farther on is the **Sıhhı Mustafa Bey Hamamı**, very old but very much in use, as the wreaths of vapor emerging from its chimneys testify. Next comes the **Mehmet Paşa Camii**, constructed in 1486 by Mehmet Paşa, who was the tutor of Prince Ahmet, son of Sultan Beyazit. It's a sizable place with a guest house, soup kitchen, and *medrese*, and it boasts a finely decorated marble pulpit.

A little farther along is the **Şiranli Camii**, built little over a hundred years ago although it looks far older. According to a sign outside it was built using money raised by Azeri Turks, although it's not too clear why they should have paid to build a mosque in Amasya. The final mosque of any importance is the early-fifteenth-century **Beyazit Paşa Camii**, whose leafy riverbank location enhances the quiet beauty of its architecture.

From here a bridge crosses the river to the **Büyük Ağa Medrese**, a seminary/university founded in 1488 by the Chief White Eunuch of Beyazit II. This roughly octagonal structure of stone and brick is now a koran school. Although it's not open to the public, no one seems to mind if you take a look inside the courtyard, where the boys who study here play soccer beween lessons.

The Rock Tombs and Ottoman Houses

The massive **rock tombs** of the Pontic kings, thought to date from the fourth century BC, are carved into the cliff face on the northern bank of the Yeşılırmak. To reach them follow Ziya Paşa Bulvarı west along the river bank from **Atatürk Square**. After about five or ten minutes you'll come to a footbridge. Cross this and follow the signs bearing the words "Kral Kaya Mezarları", under a railroad line and through narrow streets of nineteenth-century wooden buildings, to the **Kızlar Sarayı**, or Palace of the Maidens. This erstwhile Ottoman palace is named after the harem once housed within its walls, but today little more than a few ruined walls and a crumbling tower remain.

From here a vaguely defined path leads up to the tombs, where birds flap around eerily. There are two main clusters of tombs, and bearing right will bring you to the most accessible ones. You can clamber up inside them through the raised stone doorways—although whether you'll want to is another matter, because people seem to be in the habit of using them as impromptu urinals. Passages cut out of the rock run behind two of these tombs and you can only marvel at the work that must have gone into excavating them. Bearing left will bring you to two larger tombs; beside the entrance to one of them is the mouth of a tunnel that is thought to lead to the river. Further tombs can be found with a bit of effort, but none as impressive as these.

Below the rock tombs, on the north bank of the river, is Amasya's other big attraction, the half-timbered **Ottoman houses** that add so much to the look and atmosphere of the town. Crammed into a narrow space beween rocks and water, they almost seem to be sliding into the river. In fact many of them are—owing to their parlous state of disrepair, several have succumbed to the elements or flooding over the last couple of decades, and many more have been deliberately demolished, including the majority of those on the southern bank. The fact is that, appealing as they may be to the tourist, these houses are very expensive to maintain; many owners prefer to live in prefabricated concrete apartments, which are a great deal easier to look after. Fortunately, the status of the survivors as a tourist attraction will probably preserve the examples on the north bank. One of the bigger and finer houses, the early eighteenth-century **Hazeranlar Konaği**, has been turned into an **ethnology museum and gallery** (Tues–Sun 9am–noon & 1:30–5pm; $1).

Way above the rock tombs lurks Amasya's **kale**. There's supposed to be a path leading up to it through the rocks, but if it exists it must be extremely hairy. A far easier way to get there is by road from near the Büyük Ağa Medrese. Don't worry if you can't make it—there's a magnificent panorama of the town, but not a great deal else to see beyond some ruined walls thought to date from Pontic times. A cannon is fired up here to mark the end of the daily fast during Ramadan; thanks to the acoustics of the valley, the noise down below when it's discharged is deafening.

Practical Details

Amasya's **otogar** lies well to the east of town and you'll need to take a dolmuş in. The train station is about 1km to the west, also served by dolmuşes. The **tourist information kiosk** (Mon–Fri 9:30am–noon & 1–5pm) stands on the river bank, just north of Atatürk square. As for accommodation, there's a sprinkling of pretty basic **hotels**, one expensive "tourist" hotel, and one excellent pansiyon. At the budget end, the *Aydın Oteli*, Atatürk Caddesi 86 (☎3781/2463), is probably the cheapest place to stay, but also the least appealing. Its grimy rooms go for $1.50 and up. Nearby, equally unattractive and similarly cheap, is the *Ceylan Hotel*. The *Konfor Palas*, overlooking the river on Ziya Paşa Bulvarı, offers slightly more comfort for $2 single, $4 double.

The *İlk Pansiyon*, Hittit Sokak 1 (☎3781/1689), more or less opposite the tourist information kiosk, is in a class of its own. An eighteenth-century Armenian mansion that has been faultlessly restored by Ali Yalçın, a young Turkish architect, it retains much of the original atmosphere and decor. Singles go from $8–14 and doubles from $16–22 (all rooms have bathrooms)—and it's as nice a place to stay as any in Turkey. There are only five rooms and these are often booked ahead during the season, so if you're interested try to make a reservation.

Finally there's the *Turban Hotel*, Helkis Mahallesi, Emniyet Caddesi 20, near the Büyük Ağa Medrese on the north bank of the river. You'll pay $21 for a single and $30 for a double in this squat, ugly building; but it has all the facilities you'd expect for the price, including a restaurant and bar.

The best **restaurant** in town is the *Belediye Şehir Kulubu Derneği*. This is actually the local civil-servants' club, but its restaurant seems to be open to whoever wants to try out the exceptionally good food (don't be put off by the less than exceptional decor). Also worth trying are the *Ocak Başı Aile Kebap Salonu* and the *Ali Kaya Restorant*, both near the museum. The **PTT** is on Ziya Paşa Bulvarı, opposite the bridge leading to the rock tombs.

Tokat

After Amasya, **TOKAT**—an hour and a half to the southeast by bus—comes as something of an anticlimax. There's none of Amasya's soothing riverside atmosphere and less to offer in the way of things to see. On the way down you pass a ruined *kervansaray* at **Ezinepazar**: before the modern road was built this place was a day's ride by camel from the town you left half an hour ago. If you have your own transportation or are willing to do a bit of hitching it's worth making a short detour to the village of PAZAR indicated by a sign about 26km short of Tokat. Here you'll find the **Hatun Hanı**, a well-preserved Selçuk *kervansaray* that would have been the next night's stop.

Tokat itself has two main claims to fame and only one of these carries much weight outside Turkey, or indeed outside Tokat. The internationally known one—which is no reason to stop here—is that Julius Caesar uttered the famous words *"Veni, vidi, vici"* (I came, I saw, I conquered) near the town in 47 BC, after he defeated Pharnaces II, the king of Pontus. The local claim to fame is the **Gök Medrese**, another Selçuk "Blue Seminary," now used as a museum. This is more of a reason to pause, although not necessarily for long. Tokat makes a good stop-off when traveling beween Amasya and Sivas (or vice versa)—leave Amasya in the morning, stop for something to eat and a look-see in Tokat, and aim to be in Sivas by late afternoon/early evening (you'll need to check bus times at the otogar before setting off into Tokat).

In **history**, Tokat first came to prominence as a staging post on the Persian trans-Anatolian royal road, running from Sardis to Persepolis. Later it fell to Alexander the Great and then to Mithridates and his successors. In 47 BC the Romans under Julius Caesar finally defeated the Pontic kingdom (whose rulers had foolishly been provoking Rome for years) in a five-hour battle at Zile, just outside Tokat, prompting Caesar to utter his immortal line.

Under Byzantine rule, Tokat became a frontline city in perpetual danger of Arab attack, a state of affairs that continued until the Danişment Turks took control of the city after the Battle of Manzikert in 1071. Less than a century later the İlhanid Mongols arrived, ushering in a period of war and uncertainty which finally ended in 1392 when the citizens of Tokat, tired of the endless strife, petitioned Sultan Yıldırım Beyazit to be admitted to the Ottoman Empire. Their request was granted and peace returned until the arrival of the second great Mongol wave under Tamerlane. On this occasion the town was sacked but the castle survived a lengthy siege.

With the departure of the Mongols and return of the Ottomans' life returned to normal and a period of prosperity ensued. In time, though, trade patterns shifted, the east–west routes to Persia lost their importance, and Tokat became the backwater it remains today.

The Town

Tokat's **otogar** is a little way outside town on the main road. It takes about fifteen minutes to reach the town center—head for the traffic circle near a bridge flanked by cannons and turn left down Gazi Osman Paşa Bulvarı. On the way you'll pass a couple of distinctive-looking tombs. The Mongol-built **Nurettin Bini Sentimur Türbesi**, with its hat-like pointed roof, is the most interesting of these;

the **Sümbül Baba Türbesi**, farther along the street, is a Selçuk work now incorporated into the side of a more modern building.

The first real reason to stop is the **Gök Medrese** (follow the "Müze" signs), with its painstakingly carved portal. Built in 1275 by Mu'in al-Din Süleyman, a local potentate during the era of Selçuk domination, its courtyard retains some recognizable fragments of the blue tilework that gave the place its name. Also scattered around here are Selçuk tombstones and inscriptions, and a few Roman column pedestals and capitals.

Today the Gök Medrese houses Tokat's **museum** (Tues–Sun 8:30am–noon & 1–5pm; $1), a repository for local archaeological finds and various unusual relics from the churches which served the town's sizable Greek and Armenian communities before World War I. Typical of these is a wax effigy of Christina, a Christian martyred during the rule of the Roman emperor Diocletian. The ethnographic section features examples of local *yazma*—a technique of printing on cloth using wooden blocks to produce colorful patterned handkerchiefs, scarves, and tablecloths.

Keep walking down Gazi Osman Paşa Bulvarı, past the *Belediye Oteli*, and you'll come to the **Taş Han**, originally called the Voyvoda Han, and built in 1631 by Armenian merchants. Like so many others of this sort, it's still in commercial use. Opposite is a market area, and on a street behind it is the **Hatuniye Camii**, an impressive Ottoman mosque with an adjoining *medrese*, built in 1485 during the reign of Sultan Beyazıtı II.

In the streets to the east of the Gök Medrese are Tokat's surviving half-timbered Ottoman houses, including a couple of fine mansions. The most representative of these is the **Latifoğlu Konağı**, a nineteenth-century Ottoman, Baroque building with some fine decorative carving inside. The **Madimağin Celâl'in Evi**, also of the nineteenth century, is unusual in that the interior features painted panels depicting views of İstanbul and floral motifs.

Above Tokat to the northwest is the ruined **castle**, whose original construction date is not known. Both the Selçuks and the Ottomans left their mark on this building, but today it houses only rubble.

Practical Details

Signs point the way to a **tourist information office** (☎475/15499) of sorts near Cumhuriyet Alani, the town's main square and also the location of the **banks** and **PTT**. If you want to **stay** you should have no problem finding a bed. At the bottom end of the market is the *Belediye Oteli* on Meydan Çarşısı just past the Gök Medrese (☎475/19924), where you'll pay $3.40 for a bed in a shared room, or $6 if you want privacy. You get what you pay for, but the rooms should at least be cockroach-free. Another option is the *Hotel Çamlıca*, Gazi Osman Paşa Bulvarı 85 (☎475/11269), where a clean room with bath will set you back $7 single or $12 double. The *Otel Taç*, on Gazi Osman Paşa Bulvarı on top of an office building (☎475/11331), has rooms for $6 and $12. On the same street, but farther south back toward the otogar, the *Hotel Gündüz*, Gazi Osman Paşa Bulvarı 200 (☎475/11278), charges $8 single, $16 double, with bath. Also worth checking out is the *Turist Otel* on Cumhuriyet Alani (☎475/11610), $8 single, $12 double, with bath.

There are cheap **places to eat** on practically every corner. If you want something a little more upscale try the *Belediye Lokantası*, on the ground floor of the hotel of the same name, or the slightly fancier restaurant at the *Hotel Gündüz*.

Sivas

At first sight SİVAS is grim, even intimidating. Both main arrival points, the **otogar** and **train station**, are located well outside the town center and surrounded by new concrete highrises. Indeed, this city of 200,000 people wouldn't figure on anybody's itinerary were it not for a concentration of Selçuk buildings—among the finest in Turkey—conveniently located in a park right in the center.

Sivas has been settled since Hittite times, and according to local historians was later a key center of the Sivas Frig Empire (1200 BC), an unfortunately named realm which seems to have been consigned to historical oblivion. With more certainty it can be said that under the Romans Sivas was known as Megalopolis and then Sebastaea, which in later years was corrupted to Sivas.

The town's real flowering came during Selçuk times, after the Battle of Manzikert, and ample architectural evidence of this remains. Sivas intermittently served the Selçuks as a capital during the Sultanate of Rum, before passing into Ottoman hands after a brief period of İlhanid Mongol suzerainty at the beginning of the fifteenth century.

Not until this century did Sivas enjoy fame again, when, on September 4, 1919 the Congress of Sivas was convened here when Atatürk arrived from Amasya, on his mission to rally resistance against Allied attempts to carve up the Ottoman Empire. Delegates from all over the country came to Sivas, and the congress marked an important milestone on the way to establishing modern republican Turkey.

The Town

The center of Sivas is **Konak Meydanı**, location of the main municipal buildings and PTT. You'll find a good strip of reasonably priced (but not always reasonably appointed) hotels on Atatürk Caddesi, which runs southeast out of town toward the otogar. Unfortunately there's no dolmuş service beween the otogar and Konak Meydanı so you end up having to take a taxi which will set you back about $2. You're better served if you arrive by train, as buses run down İnönü Bulvarı from the station to Konak Meydanı.

The Selçuk Legacy

The collection of **Selçuk buildings** for which Sivas is best known are nearly all grouped together in and around a small park just south of Konak Meydanı. First up is the **Bürücirde Medresesi**, built in 1271 by Muzaffer Bürücirdi and now housing his tomb. These days it's a museum, but was undergoing a long restoration at the time of writing. Even if the restoration is continuing it should be possible to have a look around the courtyard and peer at the tiled tomb of Muzaffer Bürücirde, and you won't be missing much: the museum contains nothing substantially different from what you might have already seen in the museums of Amasya and Tokat. Nearby is the **Kale Camii**, a straightforward Ottoman mosque (which strictly speaking has no right to be included in this section), built in 1580 at the behest of Mahmut Paşa, grand vizier of Sultan Murat III.

South of here is the **Çifte Minare Medrese** (Twin Minaret Seminary), also built in 1271, of which only the twin minarets themselves and an ornate facade remain. Directly opposite stands the **Şifaiye Medresesi**, an old hospital and

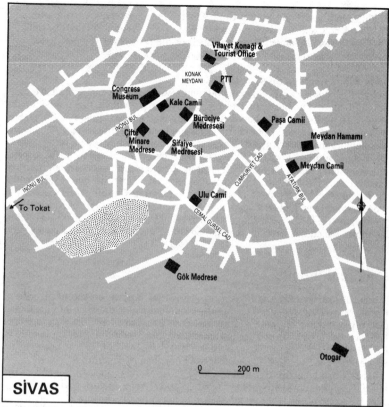

SİVAS

medical school housing the tomb of Sultan Keykâvus I. The tomb of Keykâvus features glazed tiles with swastikas and eight-pointed star motifs, and if you look carefully you'll be able to see some tile remnants clinging to the stonework. Sadly the building is not always open and you may have to content yourself with peering through the barred gate. In its heyday it was a center for the treatment of psychological disorders and apparently music therapy and hypnosis were among the healing techniques employed.

If you turn onto Cemal Gürsel Caddesi (just south of this little Selçuk theme park), you'll find the **Ulu Cami**, the oldest mosque in Sivas, built in 1179. This is a low, unattractive building, supported by fifty pillars inside and topped by an ugly corrugated-iron roof: were it not for the tall brick minaret you could almost mistake it for a factory warehouse.

A right turn from Gürsel Caddesi will take you onto Cumhuriyet Caddesi where, on the left after a couple of hundred meters, you'll find the **Gök Medrese**. This could well be the most attractive "Blue Seminary" you've yet seen, particularly if you catch it during the afternoon when the absence of shadows reveals the brickwork, carving, and tiles that embellish its stunning facade at their best. It was built in 1271 by the architect Sahip Ata, who was also responsible for buildings in Kayseri and Konya. Until 1969 the building served as a museum, but it's closed now and weeds seem to be taking over; this means that it's unlikely you'll get to see the *mescit* (prayer chapel) or the two *eyvans* (three-sided alcove-like rooms), which have some beautiful mosaic work.

Other Monuments in Sivas

Sivas has a couple of other things you might want to check out if you have time, although there's no need to feel too guilty if you neglect them. Just to the southwest of Konak Meydanı is the **Sivas Congress Museum** (Tues–Sun 8:30am–5pm; 50¢), with lots of Turkish-captioned photographs and documents commemorating Atatürk's visit. Heading east from Konak Meydanı brings you to the **Paşa Camii**, a big, yellow Ottoman structure which seems to have been squeezed into a space far too small for it by the encroachments of modern urban development. Farther along Atatürk Caddesi, set below the north side of the street and reached by a flight of steps, is the **Meydan Camii**, which was built in 1554 but looks much older thanks to its austere and angular style of construction. Nearby, up a side street leading north from Atatürk Caddesi, stands the **Meydan Hamamı**, which has been hissing and steaming for over four centuries now and is still going strong.

Practical Details

The local **tourist office** is housed in the *Vilayet Konaği*, on the north side of Konak Meydanı (Mon–Fri 9am–5pm)—go in and throw the staff into panic and disarray by asking for some information. Sivas has a small **airport** with flights to İstanbul via Ankara every Tuesday and Sunday. For more information inquire at the *THY* office, Belediye Sitesi, H Blok 7 (☎477/11147). An airport bus, costing $1, departs from the *THY* office about two hours before departure.

Hotels are plentiful, but unfortunately most of them, including some of the more expensive ones, are pretty dismal. The *Otel Evin*, Atatürk Cad 160 (☎477/12301), is one of the few exceptions, with simple rooms starting at $5 single, $7 double (cold-water basin included). A little farther east is the *Otel Çiçek* (☎477/14081), with similar rooms from $6 and $8. Opposite, the *Otel Aydın* charges $3 single, $6 double, but you'd only want to stay if the others were full. Just east of here is the *Otel Divan*, $6 single, $8 double. Closer to the town center is the *Otel Özden*, Atatürk Cad 21 (☎477/11254), where the bright lobby serves only to camouflage a gloomy and malodorous interior. You pay dearly for this deceptive reception area—rooms go for $6 single and $8 double. Other substandard budget options include the *Meydan Oteli*, Diklitaş Caddesi, Meydan Camii Yanı 3 (near the Meydan Camii; $3 and $5); the *Ak Palas*, just around the corner (same prices); and the nearby *Örnek Oteli*, Şekerbank Üstü 2, $4 and $6.

Toward Konak Meydanı, the *Otel Belde*, Atatürk Cad/Demirciler Ardı Mah, 15 Sok 37 (☎477/10736), is really rock-bottom at $3 and $6. Slightly better is the *Otel Derya*, Atatürk Caddesi/Toptancılar Çarsısı 1. Beware the *Otel Belediye*, Atatürk Cad 24 (☎477/11113), another place where a grandiose reception area belies a gloomy interior and, in this case, drab bathroomless rooms for $10 single and $16 double. The only other option is the *Otel Kösk*, Atatürk Cad 11 (☎477/11150), where rooms start at $18 (including breakfast). This is a "tourist hotel" and is consequently slightly better, but you're paying through the nose for it.

Kangal

The journey south from Sivas is fairly uneventful, although the farther south you travel the more hilly and denuded the landscape becomes. Most Malatya-bound dolmuşes call at **KANGAL**, a none-too-auspicious-looking, one-horse town about 20km east of the main road. There's nothing you'd want to see in Kangal itself, but from here you can pick up dolmuşes to a number of **thermal bath** establishments in the area. The **Balıklı Çermik** (13km from Kangal), in particular, has become a place of pilgrimage for sufferers of psoriasis and other skin ailments. Small fish eat away the affected skin as you wallow in outdoor pools. For people wanting to take the cure the *Kaplıca Oteli* in Kangal charges about $10 double. There are also **camping** facilities in this area: check current details with the Sivas tourist office.

travel details

Air

From Ankara to Adana (daily; 1hr); Antalya (2 weekly; 1hr); Diyarbakır (daily; 1hr 30min); Erzurum (daily; 1hr 45min); İstanbul (6 daily; 1hr); İzmir (daily; 1hr 30min); Malatya (4 weekly; 45min); Sivas (2 weekly; 45min); Trabzon (daily; 1hr); Van (4 weekly; 2hr).

From Sivas to İstanbul via Ankara (2 weekly; 3hr).

Buses

From Ankara to Adana (12 daily; 10hr); Amasya (hourly; 6hr); Antalya (12; 10hr); Bodrum (10; 12hr); Bursa (hourly; 7hr); Diyarbakır (5; 13 hr); Erzurum (4; 15hr); Eskişehir (4; 6hr) Gaziantep (12; 12hr); İstanbul (half-hourly; 8hr); İzmir (hourly; 9hr); Karabük (4; 5hr); Kastamonu (3; 5hr); Kayseri (14; 5hr); Konya (14; 3hr 30min); Mardin (3; 16hr); Nevşehir (12; 4hr 30min); Samsun (10; 8hr); Sivas (hourly; 8hr); Sungurlu (hourly; 3hr); Şanlıurfa (4; 15hr); Trabzon (4; 12 hr).

From Eskişehir to Ankara (4; 6hr); Bursa (6; 1hr); İstanbul (4; 4hr); Kütahya (12; 1hr).

From Kütahya to Afyon (14; 1hr 45min); Antalya (3; 5hr); Balıkeşir (4; 5hr); Bursa (12; 3hr); Eskişehir (10; 1hr); İstanbul (14; 6hr); İzmir (12; 6hr); Uşak (hourly; 1hr 15min).

From Kastamonu to Ankara (3; 5hr); İnebolu (6; 2hr); Samsun (3; 6hr).

From Amasya to Ankara (hourly; 6hr); İstanbul (12; 12hr); Kayseri (3; 8hr); Malatya (5; 9hr); Samsun (10; 3hr); Sivas (6; 4hr); Tokat (9; 2hr).

From Tokat to Amasya (12; 2hr); Ankara (12; 8hr); Sivas (10; 2hr).

From Sivas to Amasya (4; 4hr); Ankara (12; 8hr); Diyarbakır (4; 10hr); Erzurum (3; 9hr); Malatya (3; 5hr); Tokat (10; 2hr).

Trains

From Ankara to İstanbul—*Ankara Ekspresi* dep 9:40pm, arr 8am; *Mavi Tren* dep 1pm and 11pm (1st class only; journey time 8hr); *Boğaziçi Ekspresi* dep 8am, arr 6pm: to Van, Sivas, Malatya, Elaziğ and Diyarbakır or Tatvan— *Vangölü Ekspresi* dep 6:40am: to İzmir dep 6:05pm and 8:05pm: to Zonguldak dep 7:55am and 1:15pm: Erzurum dep 10:30am and 9pm: to Gaziantep dep 7pm.

From Sivas to Samsun (daily; 12hr).

CHAPTER NINE

THE BLACK SEA COAST

Extending from just east of İstanbul to the border with Soviet Georgia, the **Black Sea region** of Turkey is an anomaly, guaranteed to smash all stereotypes previously held about the country. The combined action of damp northerly and westerly winds and an almost uninterrupted wall of mountains south of the shore has resulted in a relentlessly rainy and riotously green realm, not unlike the American northwest coast. The peaks force the clouds to disgorge themselves on the ocean side of the watershed, leaving central Anatolia beyond the passes in a permanent rain shadow.

The Black Sea climate and resulting short season means there is little foreign tourism, and no overseas charters or tour operators serve the area—but when the heat's on in July and August, you'll certainly want to swim. The sea is as peculiar as the weather: fed huge volumes of fresh water by the Don, Dnieper, and Danube rivers to the north, and diminished not by evaporation but by strong currents through the Bosphorus and the Dardanelles, its upper layer is of such low salinity that you can almost drink it—and you don't need to shower after a swim.

The coastal ranges, beginning as mere humps north of Ankara but attaining world-class grandeur by the time they reach the Soviet border, have always served to keep the region isolated as well as damp. Until recently they made land access all but impossible, and provided redoubts for a patchwork of tribes and ethnic subgroups. Many of these are still there, making the Black Sea one of Turkey's most anthropologically interesting regions.

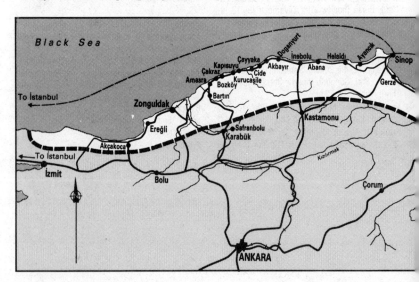

Traveling around the Black Sea consists in large part of soaking up the atmosphere (sometimes all too literally)—you don't need to worry about missing important sights, because there really aren't many. The region divides neatly into western and eastern halves, with the west comparatively lacking in character. Everything between the coal-mining town of **Zonguldak** and İstanbul is essentially a beach suburb of the latter. Between Zonguldak and **Samsun** (covered here from west to east), the largest and most featureless city of the region, only the Byzantine-Genoese harbor of **Amasra** and the historic, evocatively located town of **Sinop** reward a special trip. The **beaches** between Amasra and Sinop are admittedly magnificent, but the road along this stretch is substandard, with very poor bus and dolmuş links, and cycling (as long as you've got plenty of stamina) is likely to be more rewarding than bus rides.

East of Samsun the prospects improve along with the road; buses emerge from their inland detours, and good **beaches** continue to crop up between potentially pleasant stopovers in the old mercantile towns of **Ünye**, **Giresun**, and **Tirebolu**. Beyond **Trabzon** (Trebizond)—along with the nearby **monastery of Sumela**, the only established tourist destination on the Black Sea—beaches diminish as the scenery inland gets more imposing. Other than the **Hemşin valleys**, though, there are few specific destinations to point to.

Some History

With much trepidation, the ancient Greeks ventured onto the "Pontus Euxine" (as they called the Black Sea) at the start of the first millennium BC, sparring with the local "barbarians" and occasionally—as in the semilegendary tale of Jason and the Argonauts—getting the best of them. Between the seventh and fourth centuries numerous colonies of the Aegean cities were founded at the seaward terminus of each trade route through the Pontic mountains; these became the ancestors of virtually every modern Black Sea town. The region had its first brief appearance on the world stage when one of the home-grown Pontic

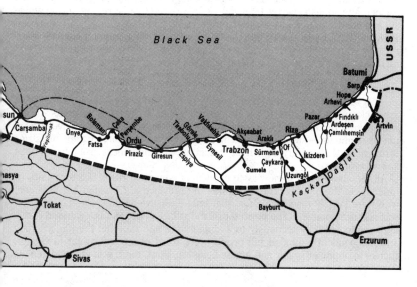

kings, **Mithridates IV Eupator**, came within a whisker of expelling the Romans from Anatolia. Even after the suppression of the several Mithridatic rebellions, the Romans concentrated on the western portion of the Black Sea and its hinterland, leaving the portion from Trabzon east in the hands of vassals. This, and the climate's heavy toll on all but the stoutest structures, accounts in part for the near absence of ancient ruins here.

With the arrival of Christianity, relations between natives and imperial overlords hardly changed at all. Only the Byzantine urban centers by the sea became thoroughly Hellenized, while subject peoples (such as the Laz) with grievances embroiled the Byzantine Empire in continual wars by appealing for aid to the neigboring Armenian and Persian empires. The Byzantine defeat at Manzikert in 1071 initially meant little to the Black Sea, safe behind its wall of mountains; the fall of Constantinople to the Fourth Crusade in 1204 had far greater immediate effects, prompting the Black Sea's second spell of global prominence. The empire-in-exile of the Grand Comneni, based around today's **Trabzon** (Trebizond), exercised influence grossly disproportionate to its size for two and a half cultured (and ultimately decadent) centuries.

Since Manzikert, Turkish chieftains had in fact begun to encroach on the coast, especially at the gap in the barrier ranges near Sinop and Samsun; the Trapezuntine dynasty even concluded alliances with them, doubtless to act as a counter to the power of the Genoese and Venetians who also set up shop in the area. Most of this factionalism was put to an end under the **Ottomans**, although even they entrusted semiautonomous administration of the Pontic foothills to feudal *derebeys* (valley lords) until the early nineteenth century. This delegation of authority, and the fact that the usual replacement of Christian populations by Muslim ones took place only in the vicinity of Trabzon, meant that the region remained remarkably poor in Ottoman monuments—and that until early this century many towns were almost half Greek or Armenian.

This equilibrium was upset when the Black Sea entered the history books for the third time as a theater of war between imperial Turkey and Russia. The two clashed four times between 1828 and 1915, with the Czarist regime giving active aid and comfort to various separatist movements in the area after 1877. Between 1918 and 1922, Greeks attempting to create a Pontic state fought it out with guerrillas loyal to Atatürk's Nationalists; with the victory of **the Republic** the Greek merchant class was expelled along with the rest of Turkey's Greek Orthodox population, and the Black Sea went into temporary economic eclipse, verging on famine during the 1930s.

Most of the credit for the recent **recovery** must go to the *hamsis*, as the locals are nicknamed after the Black Sea anchovy caught in large numbers during winter. Enterprising, voluble, and occasionally scandalous, they have set up mafias (sometimes literally) in the shipping, property, and construction industries throughout the country, much of it funded by remittances from industrious *hamsis* overseas.

All the above goes some way to explaining why most Black Sea towns are so hideous. In the old days the shore was the province of Christian businessmen, who were largely responsible for what little attractive architecture has survived war and development. The norm for inland villages was, and is, scattered dwellings connected only tenuously to a single store and mosque; the idiosyncratic and independently minded hill people were freed of any constraint to cluster, thanks to abundant water and arable fields. In short, there was little indigenous tradition of town planning, so when the boom hit, everyone did as they pleased and concrete blight was the result. The recent reopening of the Soviet border—which seems destined to end the region's backwater status—may eventually trigger a new spasm of urbanization and a possible widening of the coast highway.

BLACK SEA ROADS: A WARNING

In June 1990 a freak storm and subsequent flash flooding wrought havoc on Black Sea roads, especially along the coast between Rise and Giresun and the canyons leading inland. Literally hundreds of bridges and sections of asphalt were swept away; the most important gaps have been spanned with temporary structures, but it will take years to completely repair the damage. Particularly hard hit was the E390/885/050 trunk road between Trabzon and Erzurum, where an ongoing widening and improvement program was completely washed out, reducing the old Silk Route to an often single-laned mess of dust or mud according to season, with traffic creeping along on auxiliary, village-access roads not designed for heavy vehicles.

You should therefore expect delays in travel around the Black Sea until at least 1993; our elapsed times in the "travel details" at the end of the chapter reflect these conditions. In particular you should avoid traveling between Trabzon and Erzurum via Gümüşhane and Bayburt. The "long" way around via Hopa and Artvin ends up taking hardly any more time as matters stand (with equal or superior frequencies of public transportation), is in an excellent state, and is far more scenic anyway. Especially if you have your own vehicle, Highway 925 between Rise and Erzurum, via İkizdere and İspir, is the most direct route between the Black Sea and northeastern Anatolia. The road is in good condition (more than half is paved), connections are reasonable, and again the landscape along the way compares well with the "classic" route.

THE WESTERN BLACK SEA

The coast from Samsun west to Zonguldak is perhaps the least visited of the entire Turkish shoreline. This neglect is a joint result of poor connections and the relative lack of tourist facilities and specific attractions. While it's true that there's no pressing reason to make a special detour here, though, it's well worth fitting in some of this stretch if you're heading overland to the eastern Black Sea.

Samsun makes a dreary and discouraging gateway to the region, but matters improve as you head northwest to **Sinop**, a more interesting place than any other Black Sea town except Trabzon. Beyond Sinop the coast road west is tortuous and slow going, but spectacular scenery and scattered, unspoiled beaches and small ports provide some relief. The only place that gets much business is **Amasra**, an old medieval stronghold at the western end of this beautiful stretch. **Zonguldak** has little to detain you, and with its good train connections is of most use to travelers as an alternate entry and exit point to the region.

As a rule the **beaches** are cleaner and the weather drier along this section of the Black Sea than farther east; figs and olives are seen, attesting to the mild climate, and if you just want to laze on the sand without any other stimulation, you'll find plenty of opportunity. Sparse **bus** and dolmuş schedules are the only drawbacks; check frequencies to avoid getting stranded, or avoid them altogether with your own two-wheeler (see "Cycling" in *Basics*).

Samsun

Despite a long and turbulent history—or perhaps because of it—**SAMSUN** has absolutely no remaining historical or scenic attractions, and you won't want to stay here longer than it takes to pass through. It's a thoroughly modern city of 250,000 people laid out on a grid plan, and the center of Turkey's tobacco industry; most of the locals work directly or indirectly for the *Tekel* cigarette factory.

For the record, Samsun—like several of its neighbors—began life as a colony of Miletus in the seventh century BC. Because of its strategic location, the place changed hands frequently over the centuries; it was besieged, captured (and usually sacked) by the Pontic kings, Romans, Arabs, and several tribes of Turks. The final insult came in 1425, when the Genoese—who had a major trading station here—torched the town rather than hand it over to Ottoman control. From then until Atatürk came ashore here on May 19, 1919, after fleeing İstanbul, Samsun faded from the history books. Atatürk's arrival, though, can be said to have marked the start of the war of independence, since rather than disbanding the groups of Turkish guerrillas who had been attacking Greeks in the area, as he had been ordered to do, he began organizing them into a cohesive national resistance army.

Today, Samsun is a busy port and center for the processing of local agricultural produce, where any spare time you may have is likely to weigh heavy on your hands. At its center lies the dull **Cumhuriyet Meydanı**, with a statue of the hero on horseback and some wilting foliage, beneath which you'll find an uninspiring undergound shopping center. The rest of the town is largely concrete, although there are a couple of unremarkable fourteenth-century mosques—**Hacı Hatun Camii** and **Pazar Camii**—just off Necipbey Gazi Caddesi.

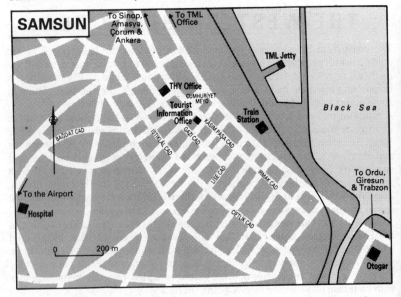

Practical Details

The **otogar** lies 2km east of the city center on the main road out of town, and the **train station** midway between the two; buses #2 and #10, as well as dolmuşes, link both with **Cumhuriyet Meydanı**, the town's hub. Tourists unable to get seats to Trabzon often fly in; the **airport** is farther out of town on the road to Amasya. On the square and in the streets immediately to the west, particularly **Kâzım Paşa Caddesi**, you'll find most of what you'll need in Samsun. The local **tourist information office** is on the second floor at 19 Mayis Bulvari 2 (☎36/110014; 9am–noon & 1–5:30pm). Should you need to stay, there are plenty of **hotels**. One of the cheapest is the *Kristal Otel*, Gaziler Meydanı, Hastane Sok 5 (☎36/111713), offering singles for $8 and doubles for $12 (with showers). The *Otel Terminal*, convenient but noisy at the otogar, has singles starting at $10, doubles $15. Other cheap possibilities include the *Bilgin Hotel*, Posthane Arkası 26 (☎36/113022), and the *Güçlük Oteli*, Pazar Camii Karsısı, with doubles from $8. Also worth checking out is the *Kent Oteli*, Necipbey Caddesi (☎36/113529), with doubles from $8.50. Quieter, more expensive alternatives include the *Gökçe Otel*, Sahil Caddesi, Ferah Sok 1 (☎36/117952), a swish place with a bar/ restaurant and rooms for $20 single, $24 double; the nearby *Burç*, Kâzım Paşa Cad 38 (☎36/115480), $19 single, $25 double with bath; and the very central *Vidinli* at Kâzım Paşa Cad 4 (☎36/116050), with slightly aging rooms for $16 single, $21 double. Probably better value than any of the foregoing is the *Tuğra*, Cumhuriyet Cad 46 (☎36/151141), with prices marginally higher than at the *Vidinli*. Top of the range is the *Turban Samsun Oteli*, Atatürk Bulvari (☎36/110750), with singles from $26 and doubles from $30.

For **food and drink** head for Saathane Meydanı, the clocktower square, where there are a number of reasonably priced possibilities. On the north side of the main, waterfront road there's a pleasure garden with numerous restaurants (great fish), ice-cream booths, and general entertainment facilities—popular with local groups.

To complete Samsun's limited list of amenities, the **THY** office is at Kâzım Paşa Cad 11/A (☎36/118260)—handy for reservations, though *THY* doesn't fly here. If you wish to fly out of Samsun, contact *THT* at ☎36/112185. There's just one **car rental** franchise, *Avis*, at Lise Cad 24/B (☎36/133288). Finally, the **TML agency** is down at the harbor, Denizcilik Koll Sti 19 (☎36/117096, 114647).

Sinop

Most people will choose to leave Samsun as soon as possible: heading west, the coast road cuts inland through extensive tobacco fields and the market town of BAFRA, in the middle of the Kızılırmak delta (with a cheap hotel and bar in the town center), before regaining the sea a few kilometers before GERZE, a low-key resort with a handful of hotels and eateries, flanked by good, not overly crowded beaches. Pleasant as this is, most people will press straight on to Sinop, 26km farther west.

Blessed with the finest natural harbor on the Black Sea, SİNOP straddles an isthmus at the foot of an exposed promontory. It's a town that does justice to its fine setting, with a clutch of monuments—above all the citadel—bestowing a real authority on the place. The port, long outstripped by those of Samsun, Trabzon, and Zonguldak, is now dominated by fishing, which along with tourism now provides most of the local income. There's also a none-too-secret NATO listening post: the Sinop Peninsula is just about the northernmost point of Anatolia, less than 200 nautical miles from Soviet Crimea, which explains why there are so many English signs and American accents in this obscure part of the world.

Sinop takes its name from the mythical **Sinope**, an Amazon queen and daughter of a minor river god. She attracted the attention of Zeus, who promised her anything she desired in return for her favors. Her request was for eternal virginity; Zeus played the gentleman and complied.

The site's natural endowments (as opposed to its namesake's) prompted Bronze Age settlement long before an actual city was founded as an Ionian colony during the eighth century BC. The first famous native son was Diogenes the Cynic: Alexander the Great is said to have visited the barrel in which he lived and been sufficiently impressed to claim, "If I were not Alexander, I would rather be Diogenes." (He had earlier asked if there was anything he could do for Diogenes, to which the cynic replied, "Yes, stand aside, you're blocking my light.")

In 183 BC the indigenous Pontic kings made Sinop one of their main cities, and later that century Mithridates Eupator, the terror of the Roman republic, was born here. The city became his capital and he adorned it with splendid monuments, but of these, and of the Roman structures built after the general Lucullus captured the place in 63 BC, virtually no trace remains.

Sinop declined during the Byzantine period, and sixth- and seventh-century attempts to revive the town's fortunes were thwarted by Persian and Arab raids. The Selçuks took the town in October 1214, converting a number of churches into mosques and erecting a *medrese*, but after the Mongols smashed the short-lived Selçuk state, Sinop passed into the hands of the İsfendiyaroğlu emirs of Kastamonu until Ottoman annexation in 1458. Thereafter the town was rarely heard of, except on November 30, 1853, when the Russians destroyed both Sinop and an Ottoman fleet anchored here, thus triggering the Crimean War, and again on May 18, 1919, when Atatürk passed through en route to Samsun.

The Town

Sinop sits astride a small peninsula jutting out into the Black Sea. It's a sleepy place whose main claim to contemporary fame is a prison (housed in part of the crumbling castle), which slightly undermines attempts to turn the place into a fully fledged resort.

The **castle** is the first thing you'll notice on entering town and, although time has inevitably taken its toll, it remains by far the most atmospheric thing about Sinop. The first defenses were probably built here by the original colonists back in the seventh century BC; during the Pontic kingdom more fortifications straddling the isthmus were added, and every subsequent occupier strengthened and adapted the whole. Most of the present structure dates from Byzantine/Genoese times, with Selçuk modifications. Considerable chunks of the walls are now missing but much is still intact, in particular the **Kumkapı**, which juts out bastion-like into the sea on the northern shore. On the south shore a hefty square tower survives (you can climb up it to look out to sea), and parts of the ramparts now surround the modern prison.

Some of Sinop's best **beaches** lie just west of Kumkapı and on the south side just west of the prison; there are more beaches at **Akliman** on the north shore just east of town.

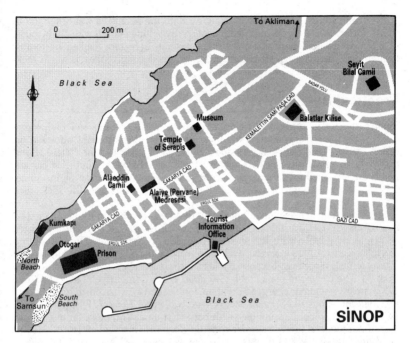

Heading east, Sakarya Caddesi leads to the **Alâeddin Camii**, a mid-thirteenth-century Selçuk mosque somewhat the worse for wear after centuries of warfare. This is the oldest mosque in town, and there's a fine *mimber* inside, but otherwise it's not very exciting. Next door is the **Alaiye Medresesi**, which also dates from the 1260s. The most notable feature is a marble-decorated entrance portal, relatively restrained by Selçuk standards. It's also known as the Pervane Medresesi after its founder, Mu'in al-Din Süleyman. The Selçuk sultans conferred the title of Pervane ("Butterfly") on their viziers, and this particular chief minister became so powerful that he did away with his sovereign in 1264, ruling as virtual autocrat of this area until dispatched in turn by the Mongols in 1278.

At the end of Sakarya Caddesi is Sinop's **museum** (Tues–Sun 8:30am–5:30pm; $1), which has the expected array of objects from the Bronze Age onwards. Many of the oldest exhibits were unearthed at KOCAGÖZ, an archaeological dig a few kilometers southwest of Sinop. Look out also for the Roman amphorae, a reminder of the days when Sinop was an important trading center, with ships unloading and loading wine and olive oil. All this, however, is fairly predictable stuff, and only the **icon display** on the top floor constitutes a departure from the usual Turkish small-town museum fare. Most of the icons are painted in Byzantine style, but actually date from the nineteenth century; scanty labeling makes their exact provenance uncertain, but it's a safe bet that they come from local Greek churches abandoned after 1923, including the Balatlar Kilise (see below). Also in the museum grounds are the sparse remains of the Hellenistic **Temple of Serapis**, excavated in 1951. A number of objects dug up on the site—including a fourth-century clay mask of Serapis (the Egyptian form of Apollo), complete with long hair and beard—are now in the museum.

Following Kemalettin Sami Paşa Caddesi onto the peninsula will bring you to the **Balatlar Kilise**, a ruined seventh-century Byzantine church with a few traces of frescoes inside. There are a few mosques out here too, flanked by tombs, though only the hilltop **Seyit Bilal Camii**, with its decorative tiles, is worth seeking out.

Practical Details

Sinop's **otogar** is conveniently adjacent to the castle, at the end of Sakarya Caddesi on the western edge of the town center. There's a **tourist information office** (☎3761/1996; 9am–5:30pm) down at the harbor between the *Hotel 117* and the *Hotel Melia Kasım*. The **TML agent** (☎3761/4021) is at the southeast harbor, and there's a small military **airport** from which scheduled civilian flights sometimes run to and from Ankara—check details and get tickets from the *THY* office (☎3761/2909).

Sinop has a good selection of **hotels** but they tend to fill up in the summer. The *Otel Uzun Mehmet*, Kurtulus Cad, Ziraat Bankası Karşısı (☎3761/2870) charges $4 single, $6 double, with hot showers available on each floor. The *Otel Meral*, Kurtulus Cad 1, offers a similar deal. Also worth checking out is the *Yılmaz Aile Pansiyon* (ask directions because it's lost in the back alleys) which has doubles from $4. The clean and presentable *Gül Palas Oteli*, Cumhuriyet Cad 13 (☎3761/1737), near the otogar, charges $6 and up double, and also has dorm rooms sleeping four for about $1.75 each. A notch or two up is *Hotel 117*, Rıhtım Cad 1 (☎3761/5117), which has doubles with bath starting at $12, more for a sea view. Top of the range is the two-star *Hotel Melia Kasım* at Gazi Cad 49 (☎3761/4210), charging $14 single, $20 double for rooms with attached baths and TV, plus a swimming pool.

There are **camping** facilities on the the southern beach at *Forestry Camping*, less than five minutes' walk from the otogar. Nearby is the *Yuvam Motel ve Camping*. East of the town center, also on the south shore, the *Karakum Holiday Village* (☎3761/2692) also has camping facilities opening onto a good stretch of beach.

For **food and drink**, there are plenty of options down by the harbor, where teahouses have chairs on the waterfront, and there are also plenty of fish restaurants (strangely, most are in the first street back from the harbor) as well as "fast food" places. Good possibilities include a restaurant run by Uzun Mehmet, proprietor of the *Otel Uzun Mehmet*, at İskele Cad 13, and the *Saray Restoran* next door, worth a stop for its good fish kebabs. For breakfast, try the café on the north side of Sakarya Caddesi, halfway up.

West of Sinop: the Coast to Amasra

Most public transportation approaches and leaves Sinop from either Samsun or Kastamonu (see Chapter Eight), but under your own steam it's rewarding enough to follow the little-traveled coast west to Amasra. Mountains, low but extending far inland, hedge the sea and force the recently paved road to wind around their knees. The region has always been a backwater, home in ancient times to the "barbarian" Paphlagonians and only lightly garrisoned by the Romans. It's still thinly populated, with many residents working overseas ten months of the year.

The coast road and the scenic but narrow inland alternative converge just south of AYANCIK, reaching the coast again only at **HELALDİ**, a pleasant fishing port with a decent beach and a couple of pansiyons. **ABANA**, a small resort 40km west, is the next place you might consider breaking the journey; it's a somnolent town with a shingle beach.

Most, however, will press on to nearby **İNEBOLU**, the biggest place between Sinop and Amasra, but still mustering only 7000 inhabitants. A few isolated Ottoman houses grace the web of narrow streets bisected by a river, wedged between the hills and the sea, and there's a long, empty shingle beach. The town's fanciest **hotel** is the *Hotel Deniz*, Zafer Yolu Cad 18 (☎4661/3448 or 3449), offering singles with bath for $9, doubles $12. Among the cheaper options the *Otel Özlü*, Cumhuriyet Cad 42 (☎4661/1198), seems about the best, with centrally heated rooms and hot showers for $4 single, $6.50 double. Otherwise try the *Otel Altınöz* at Cumhuriyet Cad 47 (☎4661/1502), with singles for $3, doubles $6. There's a **campground** between the coast road and the sea.

As for **eating and drinking**, there's a plush but not too expensive restaurant in the *Hotel Deniz*, where they're very eager to please. The *Çiçek Lokantasi*, on the street immediately east of Cumhuriyet Caddesi, does good fish for a little less money.

West of İnebolu, the cliff-top road winds its way through a succession of sleepy little havens like DOĞANYURT, ÇAYYAKA, and AKBAYIR, where you might want to break your journey for an hour or so if you're driving or cycling. Doğanyurt, just north of the road, is well off the beaten track and worth a look for precisely that reason; there's a friendly restaurant here. The constant curves mean that it takes a good two hours to drive to Cide. **CİDE** itself turns out to be a couple of kilometers inland, basically a one-street place with a **PTT, bank**, and tiny **otogar**. The *Balcıoğlu Hotel* has doubles for about $6, but most arrivals **stay** down at the beach, where the *Ece Motel* and the *Basın Mocamp* both offer singles for $6, doubles for twice that. **Camping** by the waterfront is run by the nearby restaurant; two-person huts there cost $4 a night. The **beach** is pebbly, but extends for nearly ten, uncrowded kilometers to the west.

The road continues up a few steep grades and through a number of small villages with boatyards, but the next popular stop is the village of **KAPISUYU**, an idyllic place where a mountain stream enters the Black Sea. The river's bank is shaded by trees, and at its mouth a fine stretch of sand has accumulated. It's a quiet place with just a single small pansiyon and restaurant, but many people camp along the beach.

If you need more facilities, **KURUCAŞİLE** lies just a few kilometers ahead. Long renowned as a boat-building center, its shipwrights have lately applied their skills to crafting pleasure boats for customers from all over Turkey and northern Europe, after centuries of turning out oak-timbered fishing and cargo boats. The town has a new and as yet nameless **hotel** at İskele Cad 7, near the boatyards (☎3898/1395), the biggest outfit between Cide and Amasra. Clean rooms with attached bath go for $8 single, $16 double.

A final, agonizingly slow series of switchbacks brings you to **ÇAKRAZ**, whose good beaches and scattering of pansiyons do little to disturb a splendid torpor. The best local beach is at **BOZKÖY**, nestled at the bottom of cliffs out of sight of the road, a couple of kilometers west. It can get crowded at holiday time, when perversely infrequent dolmuşes on the Kurucaşile–Amasra run are jammed to sardine-can density.

Amasra

AMASRA brazenly flaunts its charms to new arrivals. Approached from any direction, the town suddenly appears below you, swarming up onto a rocky double promontory sheltering two bays. Apart from extensive Byzantine-Genoese castles (the Genoese were here in strength, not surrendering to Mehmet the Conqueror until 1459) and a couple of churches, there isn't much to see, but Amasra's setting and sleepy atmosphere make it worth at least an overnight stop. It's thoroughly relaxing, a quiet place with a population of around 6,500, full of shady corners to sit and contemplate.

The modern town occupies an isthmus bridging the gap between the mainland and promontories, both of which are heavily fortified and their walls, pierced by several gates, still largely intact. The **inner citadel** is studded with towers and the Genoese coat of arms; of the two **Byzantine churches** which you can hunt down in the maze of alleys, the larger was converted into a mosque after the Ottoman conquest, while the ruined smaller one was apparently still used until 1923.

Amasra also boasts a small **museum** (Tues–Sun 9am–5pm; 50¢), at the far end of the western bay, containing the usual selection of local archaeological finds. Throughout town, you'll also come across the ridiculously kitsch **woodcarvings**—useless goblets, ashtrays, and back-scratchers—that local workshops churn out by the thousand for the tourist market.

The ancient breakwater of the Küçük Liman or west harbor ends at a small lighthouse, the most likely spot for a quick **swim** if the jellyfish aren't too numerous; anywhere else the water will be hopelessly polluted, particularly at the deceptively attractive town beach next to the eastern fishing port—and the even busier industrial docks. It's best to regard Amasra as a base for forays to better beaches farther east, and not the all-around resort that the city fathers would like to promote.

Practical Details

The **dolmuş and coach terminal** is on the small Atatürk Meydanı, near the middle of the main isthmus. From here everything is within easy reach, including a small, clearly marked **tourist information office**.

Accommodation possibilities are all moderate in price and fairly well-appointed. The most obvious is the *Paşa Kaptan Oteli* on the western bay, just past a small, leafy park, with singles for $4.50 and doubles for $8. Next door the *Nur Turistik Pansiyon* (☎3895/1015), a similar family-run place, charges slightly more. Overlooking the east beach, the *Huzur Pansiyon* starts at about $3 per person, as does the *Zor*, perhaps the friendliest in town, with common hot showers. Just northwest of the square, the *Çınar Restaurant-Pansiyon*, Küçük Liman Cad 1 (☎3895/1018), has singles from $3, doubles from $6. A little farther along the same street, at Küçük Liman Cad 17 (☎3895/1975), you'll find what could be Turkey's smallest pansiyon, above Mehmet Balçık's shop/soup-kitchen: three cupboard-like rooms but a fairly reliable shared hot-water shower. In the summer you can **camp** on the harbor front near the Bartın road, but be prepared to be kept awake by the noise.

For **food**, check out the *Sahil Pide Salonu* on Dereağzı Caddesi behind the *Paşa Kaptan*, where you can get Adana kebab and *ayran* for next to nothing. Also worth trying are the *Çınar Restaurant* and the *Canlı Balık* fish restaurant, both by the water on Küçük Liman Caddesi; the latter is easily Amasra's most colorful establishment, with booze and *istavrit* (Black Sea mackerel) dished up in abundance by a suitably piratical-looking type. You can drop in at the *Bedesten Bar* next door for more **drinking**, or for more dignified surroundings visit the waterfront *Cafe Kumsaal*, opposite Atatürk Meydanı.

Beyond Amasra

Southwest of Amasra, Highway 010 leaves the coast, dipping inland to **BARTIN**, a large town of rickety houses with good bus connections to Safranbolu and Ankara (see Chapter Eight); around the bazaar, especially, the old wooden houses are worth a detour. If you want to continue along the coast or catch sleeper-train to Ankara, you'll have to make for the provincial capital of **ZONGULDAK**, nearly 100km away. Bang in the heart of Turkey's main coal district, it's a large and ugly city (you can get a good breakfast at the café opposite the mosque in the main street), as is **EREĞLİ**, still farther west, whose giant steelworks consume a major fraction of the local coal output. Here boats in the harbor serve as fish restaurants—pricey but enjoyable. **AKÇAKOCA**, well on the way to İstanbul, has one last Genoese fortress, long beaches, and hotels jammed with clients from the nearby metropolis. **KARASU** is similar, a drab town 1.5km from the sea with a beach in the throes of being developed for tourism; while **KANDIRA**, a possible final stop, is amazingly provincial considering how close it is to İzmit and İstanbul; there are plenty of *lokantas* for lunch. Inland from Zonguldak, **ÇAYCUMA** is a dusty town serving the fertile valley of the Devrek river, with a great restaurant in the tiny main square.

THE EASTERN BLACK SEA

The eastern Black Sea sees far more visitors than the western half, partly because there's more of interest here, partly because it's also easier to get to. **Trabzon**, with its romantic associations and medieval monuments, is very much the main event, and given that it's located at the end of plane, ferry, and bus services it makes a logical introduction to the region. It's also the usual base for visits to **Sumela Monastery**, the only place in this chapter that you could describe as overwhelmed by tourists. Other forays inland, however, are just as rewarding if not more so—particularly to the superlatively scenic **Hemşin valleys**, inhabited by a welcoming, unusual people and the northern gateway to the lofty **Kaçkar Dağları**, covered fully in Chapter Ten.

Other than Trabzon, the coast itself between Samsun and the Georgian border offers little apart from fine scenery and swimming; **Tirebolu**, **Giresun**, and **Ünye** are the most attractive and feasible bases for exploration. All this is best appreciated with your own wheels, but even without you'll face few problems—towns are spaced close together and served by seemingly endless relays of dolmuşes, which replace the standard long-distance bus as the means of getting around here. Just about every journey is covered, and you can safely ask to be let off at an isolated beach in the near certainty that another minibus will come along to pick you up when necessary.

East of Samsun: the Coast to Trabzon

Just east of Samsun, the Black Sea coastal plain, watered by the **delta of the Yeşilırmak River**, widens to its broadest extent. The road, slightly elevated to avoid flooding, heads well inland, across one of the most fertile patches along the coast. South of the highway, tobacco is the main crop. The landscape to the north is a morass of channels, thickets, and lagoons, teeming with wildlife pursued by local hunters and fishermen; if you're interested in exploring, a canoe might be of more use than a car or local bus. ÇARSAMBA, halfway across, is a workaday town serving local agriculture: there are hotels near the bypass and restaurants on the river, but no real reason to stop.

Ünye

ÜNYE, just over 100km east of Samsun, makes a good target if you need a place to stay overnight. Inland from the busy shore highway, the town itself, with its hair-dressers, florists, and floodlit soccer field, is a world apart, tangibly more affluent than its neighbor Fatsa (see below). Much of this wealth is due to Ünye's status as a beach resort; the heaviest development is west of town, where the highway is lined by more motels and pansiyons than you'll see anywhere in Turkey outside the Aegean or the Marmara regions. The only real sight is the medieval **Fortress of Çaleoğlu** 5km inland, built on much older foundations and flanked by a **rock-cut tomb** of Pontic-kingdom vintage. The steep climb from the road rewards you with a view south over an exceptionally lush valley, and north to the Ünye coast.

Practical Details

Ünye's miniscule **otogar** is at the eastern edge of town, by the road to Niksar; a **tourist information office** operates weekdays out of the Belediye building, 300m west. If you want to **stay** in town and savor the bourgeois atmosphere, the *Rainbow Pansiyon* and adjacent *Otel Çınar* at Belediye Caddesi 20 are fine and cost $8 single, $11 double (many rooms with attached bath). At the *Otel Kılıç*, Cumhuriyet Meydanı, Hükümet Yanı 4 (☎373/11224), all rooms have attached bath for $10 single, $16 double. This is a far better deal than the identically priced but utterly decrepit *Otel Ürer*, a bad-taste relic of the 1960s, where noise from the coastal highway ruins enjoyment of the sea views.

If you're determined to stay near the water, you're better off doing it it west of town in the motel ghetto—although it's a one-to-three-kilometer walk into Ünye. Space is at a premium on weekends, and no singles are offered. Best are the *Motel Çamlık* (☎373/11333) and the more remote *Otel Kumsal* (☎373/14490), both with doubles for around $20. There are also numerous modest pansiyons in this direction (basic rooms for around $12), as well as some **campgrounds**.

Eating out, the *Deniz* or the *Dolphin* near the Belediye building in town are the fanciest places, or there are a handful of humbler diners out on the bazaar street to the east. The two listed motels out on the west beach also have their own restaurants, but of course you'll pay substantially more.

From Ünye to Giresun

FATSA, 21km east of Ünye, is a shabby mess with polluted beaches and a sad recent history. Like nearby Bolaman (see below) it is populated by Alevis, a sect closely allied to Shiism and the Bektaşi Sufi order, and during the late 1970s the inhabitants took the opportunity to put the radical political beliefs that often accompany this affiliation into action by electing a Marxist city council. A Paris-style commune, headed by a tailor popularly known as Terzi Selim, was established; in the rumblings leading up to the coup of September 1980, the army sent in tanks to close down the experiment. Locals erected barricades to no avail: an undetermined number of activists were killed or imprisoned, and Terzi Selim subsequently died in jail. Today the place is subdued as well as unattractive, with locals still reluctant to discuss these traumatic events.

At **BOLAMAN**, 9km east on the same bay, the so-called **"castle" of the Haznedaroğlu clan** sits by the harbor, with a badly decayed wooden upper story perched atop a much older medieval redoubt. The clan, de facto rulers of the area during the eighteenth and nineteenth centuries, appear to have abandoned the mansion, and it's really only worth a stop if you're in your own vehicle. Behind the castle, fringed in season by mats of drying hazelnuts, there's a less-than-pristine beach and tea garden to pause at.

The coast highway winds on northeastwards, past more sandy coves, to a yellow-and-black sign pointing toward **"Yason (Jason),"** a cape where mariners once made sacrifices at a temple of Jason (the Argonaut) before venturing further onto the temperamental waters of the Black Sea. This was replaced in due course by a **medieval church** 500m off the road, still well preserved except for a chunk missing out of the dome; these days car-campers from northern Europe have succeeded the worshipful sailors at the site.

Once past Yason, the scenery regains the drama of the stretch between Sinop and Amasra, as the hills tumble down directly into the water. **ÇAKA** has one of the prettiest beaches of the eastern Black Sea, but there's no place to overnight indoors—only Turkish-style *"kampings"* next to restaurants hiding under the greenery. Just the other side of Çam Burnu sprawls **PERŞEMBE**, the first substantial place since Fatsa, a pretty fishing port where the one-star *Hotel Vona* (☎3717/1755) fronts a small beach just east of town.

You're certainly better off staying here than in **ORDU**, 16km on. Known as Cotyora to the ancients, Ordu is now a fairly undistinguished city with just a few older houses scaling the green slopes to the west above an abandoned nineteenth-century Greek church. The **TML terminal** (agency ☎371/11013) is 600m west of this and the **otogar** is at the opposite, eastern edge of town; if you've got time to kill between connections the only other bits of history are at the **museum** in the Paşaoğlu mansion, once home to a leader of the Muslim immigrants fleeing the Caucasus in 1877–78.

Continuing east toward Giresun, there are no more appealing **beaches** until just before **PİRAZİZ**, about 15km out of Ordu; the best ones are marked at weekends by knots of parked cars.

Giresun

Tucked on both sides of a steep, fortified bluff 31km east of Ordu, **GİRESUN**, with its mix of old and new buildings and converted churches, must be a nice place to live—but you wouldn't necessarily visit unless you're intent on catching the TML ferry here, because there's precious little in the way of sights.

The town entered history as Pharnacia, a second-century BC foundation of the Pontic king Pharnace, but the name was soon changed to Cerasus, the root of the word "cherry" in virtually all Western languages. It was from here in 69 BC that the Romans first introduced the fruit to Europe, and cherry orchards still flourish all around.

The grounds of the **castle** on the bluff, which was the nucleus of the earliest settlement, are today the main city **park**. Partly overgrown, they're wild and satisfying in a way that normal, more regimented Turkish parks rarely manage. The locals picnic here on weekends, and it's a good place to wait for an evening ferry. At the northeast foot of the ramparts, a medieval **Greek church** has been recently pressed into service as the provincial museum; so far the building, with a smudged fresco in the dome, is vastly more interesting than its contents.

Still farther east, a nautical mile or so offshore, lies **Giresun Adası**, the only major island in the Black Sea. In pre-Christian times it was called Aretias, and was sacred to the Amazons who dedicated a temple to the war god Ares on it. Jason and his Argonauts supposedly stopped here to offer sacrifice, and today the islet is still the venue for suspiciously pagan spring rites every May 20, when villagers form a circle around it, cast "wishing" pebbles into the water, and then proceed to get thoroughly wasted. At other times of the year you may persuade a boatman to take you across from the little mainland anchorage just opposite; there's nothing in particular to see except the scant ruins of a Byzantine monastery.

Practical Details

Giresun's **otogar** is not just inconveniently placed 3.5km west of the center, but also poorly served: the services that originate here number in times per week rather than per day. Literally sleepy—with ticket sellers snoozing at their booths—and way too large for the current volume of traffic, it seems built for some vague future. Instead, have your bus drop you off at the west flank of the castle bluff at the Atatürk Parkı (you'll definitely pass here if you're coming from the east), behind which stand the Belediye and **tourist information office** (☎051/13560). *Ulusoy Derya*, which runs hourly minibuses to Trabzon, is just west of the nearby pedestrian overpass linking Taşbaşı Park and the **TML dock** (☎051/12382) with the main hotel district.

Of the **hotels**, the best value are the *Bozbağ*, at the junction of Eskiyağcılar Sokak and Arif Bey Caddesi (☎051/12468), with $6 singles and $10 double with attached showers, and the *Çarıkçı*, around the corner at Osman Ağa Caddesi 9 (☎051/11026), an immaculately restored old place with singles for $16 or doubles for $22, including breakfast. The *Giresun Oteli* (☎051/12469) on the ferry-dock side of the coast highway costs a little less but isn't nearly as good.

The area around the two recommended hotels swarms with decent **restaurants**; neither is it that difficult to get an alcoholic drink with your food, the town not being a fundamentalist stronghold. The *Deniz Lokantası*, next to the Belediye building, is good and popular; the *Meydan Pide Salonu*, around the corner on Köprülü Han Sokak, serves possibly the best *pide* on the entire coast. By contrast the *Kale Restaurant/Gazino*, up in the citadel, is predictably overpriced and mediocre.

Tirebolu and Around

TİREBOLU, curled above a bay enclosed by two promontories, is one of the most attractive towns on the Black Sea and the only place between Giresun and Trabzon that you'd plan to stop. A Greek Orthodox community until 1923, it's virtually unique around these parts in not having been overrun by concrete atrocities, and moreover in making at least some use of its seaside position. On the easterly promontory stands the intact **castle of St John**, built for a fourteenth-century Genoese garrison.

Above the coast road the single inland street, Gazipaşa Caddesi, contains the **PTT** and the town's three **hotels**. Most central and best of these is the clean but rather plain *Huzur*, $4 a head with common bath. Your second choice would be the *Ankara*, well to the west, with the *İnci* in the opposite direction a distinct third. **Eating** is problematic: there are no waterfront fish restaurants, so you'll have to make do with two *pide salonus* near the PTT. You can get a beer and *çerez* at *Yosun Fıçı Bira* by the fishing port, and a nocturnal **tea garden** operates on the lawn inside the castle—pleasant except for the blaring *arabesk*, and your only chance to see the fort's interior.

Tirebolu lies at the heart of the **hazelnut** (*fındık*) growing area, which extends roughly from Samsun east to the Soviet border. During late July and August you'll see vast mats of them, still in their husks, raked out to dry. Impatient locals perversely insist on eating them slightly green, when the taste resembles that of acorns.

There are decent beaches between Tirebolu and **ESPİYE**, 12km back toward Giresun; here the standard-issue Archaeological Service sign points inland to "Cağlayan Köyü, Gebe Kilisesi," but it's 40km to Cağlayan, 25 of them on a bad dirt road, and the **historic church** of Gebe is very difficult to find. Locating **Andoz Kalesi**, the westernmost of the three Genoese strongholds in the area, is far easier—a sign just west of Espiye points to the hill, less than a kilometer inland by dirt road—but it's so badly overgrown and crumbled that the climb is hardly worth the effort.

Tirebolu to Trabzon: Castles, Old Houses, and Beaches

Beyond Tirebolu you'll see more of the numerous **castles** built, mostly by the Genoese but occasionally by the Byzantines, during the thirteenth and fourteenth centuries to protect the sea approaches to Trabzon. One well-preserved stronghold lurks 15km inland, up the Harşit River at BEDRAMA; the stream, just east of Tirebolu, marks the farthest line of advance by the Czarist army in 1916. Nearby **GÖRELE** boasts a fine collection of Black Sea houses, more apparent than Akçaabat's (see below), but only really worth the effort for domestic-architecture buffs with their own cars. The town's name is an obvious corruption of nearby **Coralla** citadel, just before Eynesil. Yet another Byzantine castle at **Akçakale**, close to the road, is the best preserved between Tirebolu and Trabzon; the fortress on the point at **Fener Burnu** is less obvious.

In addition to fortresses, there's a final flurry of wide **beaches**—especially just east of Tirebolu and between Vakfıkebir and Fener Burnu—but they're generally unshaded, functional, and lacking in charm. If you're depressed by the relentless drabness of Black Sea coastal architecture, then **AKÇAABAT**, 17km west of Trabzon, may serve as a partial antidote. From the looks of the shore districts it might at first appear to be more of the same, but **Ortamahalle**, a neighborhood on the central of the three ridges behind the modern town, features a dense concentration of the wood-and-stucco houses once prevalent throughout the region. Russian shelling in 1916 devastated much of Akçaabat, however, and only one medieval church out of three dozen survived the war.

You can reach Akçaabat easily by red-and-white Belediye buses plying frequently to and from Trabzon. It's also worth knowing about the *Saray*, a one-star hotel here, in case all of Trabzon's better accommodation is full—which is not inconceivable in high summer.

Trabzon

No other Turkish city except İstanbul has exercised such a hold on the Western imagination as **TRABZON** (ancient **TREBIZOND**). Traveler-writers from Marco Polo to Rose Macaulay have been enthralled by the fabulous image of this quasi-mythical metropolis, long synonymous with intrigue, luxury, exotic customs, and fairy-tale architecture. Today the celebrated gilded roofs and cosmopolitan texture of Trebizond are long gone, replaced by the blunt reality of an initially disappointing Turkish provincial capital. But a little poking around the cobbled alleyways will still turn up tangible evidence of its former splendor—not the least of which being the monastic church of **Aya Sofya**, home to some of the most outstanding Byzantine frescoes in the world.

Some History

The city was founded during the eighth century BC by colonists from Sinope and Miletus, who settled on the easily defensible bluff isolated by today's Kuzgun and Tabakhane ravines. From the promontory's flat summit—*trapeza*, or "table" in ancient Greek—came the new town's original name, Trapezus, and all subsequent variations. Under the Romans and Byzantines the city continued to prosper, thanks to extensive patronage by Hadrian and Justinian and its location at the northeast end of a branch of the Silk Route.

But Trabzon's romantic allure is derived almost totally from a brief, though luminous, **golden age** during the thirteenth and fourteenth centuries. A scion of the royal Comnenus line, Alexius, managed to escape the Crusaders' sacking of Constantinople in 1204; shortly after, he landed at Trebizond in command of a Georgian army provided by his aunt, Queen Tamara, and proclaimed himself the legitimate Byzantine emperor. Despite the fact that there were two other pretenders, one in Epirus and the other at Nicaea (it was the latter's descendants who eventually retook Constantinople), it was the pint-sized Trapezuntine empire that was arguably the most successful.

The Trebizond kingdom owed its unlikely longevity to a number of factors. Mongol raiders of the mid-thirteenth century swept across the Middle East, accentuating the city's importance by forcing the main Silk Route to divert northward through Tabriz, Erzurum, and ultimately Trebizond. The empire's diplomats, hampered by few scruples and with the survival of the state as their only aim, arranged short- and long-term alliances with assorted Turcoman and Mongol chieftains manoeuvering at the borders. In this they were aided by the preternatural beauty of the Comneni princesses, who were given in marriage to any expedient suitor, whether Christian or Muslim; garbled tales of Christian princesses languishing in the grasp of the infidel reached western Europe and apparently inspired, among other literature, Don Quixote's quest for Dulcinea.

Someone had to transport all the goods accumulated at Trebizond's docks, and this turned out to be the **Genoese**—and soon after the Venetians as well—who each demanded and got the same maritime trading privileges from the

Trapezuntine empire as they did from the re-established Constantinople-based one. Western ideas and personalities arrived continually with the Latins' boats, making Trebizond an unexpected island of art and erudition in a sea of Turkish nomadism, and a cultural rival to the Italian Renaissance city-states of the same era.

Unfortunately the empire's factional politicking was excessive even by the standards of the age. In this respect they managed to outdo even the Medicis, lending extreme meaning to the disparaging adjective "Byzantine." The native aristocracy fought frequent battles with the transplanted courtiers from Constantinople, and the Italian contingents rarely hesitated to make it a three- or even four-sided fray. One such civil war in 1341 completely destroyed the city and sent the empire into its final decline.

It was Mehmet the Conqueror, in a campaign along the Black Sea shore, who finally finished off the self-styled empire; in 1461 the last emperor, David, true to Trapezuntine form, negotiated a more or less bloodless surrender to the sultan. Under the **Ottomans** the city became an important training ground for future rulers: Selim the Grim, while still a prince, served as provincial governor here between 1490 and 1512, and his son Süleyman the Magnificent was born and reared here until his accession in 1520. Given these early imperial associations and the sultans' vigorous local Turkification program, Trabzon, as it was renamed, was and still is a relatively devout place.

In late Ottoman times the city's Christian element enjoyed a resurgence of both population and influence; the presence of a rich merchant class justified the foundation of numerous Western consulates in Trabzon and a spate of sumptuous civic and domestic buildings. But it was a mere echo of a distant past, soon ended by a decade of world and civil war and the foundation of the Republic. Shipping dwindled after the construction of the railroad between Ankara and Erzurum and roads beyond into Iran. Today the outlook is still uncertain: though there was a brief boom during the Iran-Iraq war, both port and town have been overtaken by Samsun to the west, and in the post-*perestroika* era Trabzon may also fall behind nearby Batumi in a more autonomous Soviet Georgia.

Arrival, Orientation, and Information

Trabzon's **airport** is some 8km from the center, at the eastern edge of the town, but the **otogar** is closer—3km out near the junction of coastal Highway 010 and the damaged Route 885 heading toward Sumela and Erzurum. However, if you ask, most dolmuşes or large buses coming from the west will let you get off at the far more convenient **Çömlekçi terminal**, a row of shelters sited at the foot of the bluff on which the downtown area is built. The **TML ferry port** is also handily placed, huddled at the base of the medieval bastion pierced by the coast highway tunnel.

Whether you take a city bus in from the otogar, follow **Çömlekçi Sokak** from Çömlekçi terminal, or climb **İskele Caddesi** from the port, all roads seem to converge on **Taksim Meydanı** (Atatürk Alanı), a tree-shaded square that's the hub of Trabzon's limited social life. Bus-company ticket offices, for example those of *Ulusoy* and *Aş*, also congregate at the corners of the square. Most of Trabzon's sights are within walking distance of Taksim Meydanı, although you'll need a dolmuş to get to Aya Sofya and a bus or taxi to reach the Kaymaklı Monastery behind Boztepe.

From Taksim the city's two major longitudinal avenues lead west: **Uzun Sokak**, the pre-Republican main street, cobbled and narrow as the name implies, heads off from the southwest corner; **Kahraman Maraş Caddesi**, the modern boulevard carrying most traffic, from the northwest corner. **Şehit Sani Akbulut Caddesi** leads from the southeast angle up toward **Boztepe**, the hill dominating Trabzon. The **Sahil Yol**, or coast highway, is linked to the inland thoroughfares by a handful of strategic north-south perpendiculars like **Gazipaşa Caddesi, Cumhuriyet Caddesi**, and **Reşadiye Caddesi**.

The **tourist information office** (daily 8am–7pm March–Nov; Mon–Sat 8am–5pm in winter), at the southeast edge of Taksim Meydanı, is helpful and knowledgeable, with a stock of reasonably accurate city maps. Given that Trabzon tourism is still in its infancy, with few private operators, the staff can often be persuaded to do favors for you such as changing money outside banking hours or storing luggage; in the absence of a foreign-language bookstore in the city, they also sell a range of tourist-orientated literature in English.

> The Trabzon area telephone code is ☎031.

Finding a Place to Stay

Virtually all of Trabzon's **accommodation** is concentrated just northeast and east of Taksim Meydanı, with relatively smart places cheek by jowl with fairly basic establishments.

Most secluded of the budget places—and about as rough as you'd want to get—is the *Hotel Benli Palas*, behind the İskender Paşa Camii and the Belediye at Cami Çıkmazı 5 (☎11022), with rates ranging from $6 single to $12 for a double with attached bath. More used to foreigners, but a fair bit noisier, the *Otel Konak*, İskele Cad 27 (☎12365), advertises rooms with plumbing for $6.50 single, $13 double, but the facilities may be just a shower and sink in one corner, with the bathroom down the hall—not great value.

Better choices for just a bit more include two hotels on Güzelhisar Caddesi, which leads off İskele Caddesi: the *Erzurum Oteli* at no. 6 (☎11362), a nineteenth-century barn with doubles only for $8–10, and the *Anil* at no. 10, with singles for $9 and doubles for $15.50, both with attached baths. Unfortunately both are often full, the former because of inclusion in virtually every guidebook in whatever language, the latter by virtue of its popularity with budget overland tour operators. In that case you should try the *Otel Ural* at Güzelhisar Cad 1 (☎11414), quietest on the block with singles running from $7 and doubles from $10. A half notch up is the reasonable but extremely noisy *Hotel Kalfa*, Park Karşısı 10 (literally, "Facing the Park"; ☎12690). Prices vary from $8 for a basic single to $12 for a double with attached bath; rooms in the back are passably quiet.

If you want real comfort in Trabzon you'll have to pay substantially more. The *Horon Oteli*, Sıra Mağazalar Cad 125 (☎11199), is a one-star standby that's often (but not always) completely booked by tour groups, with decent singles for $14–17 and doubles for $22–24. The street it's on, sometimes labeled Şehit Teğmen Kalmaz Caddesi, is one block north of the central square. Also quite comfortable, but overpriced, is the *Hotel Usta*, Teleğrafhane Sok 1, just south of İskele Caddesi (☎12843), which charges $22 single, $30 double.

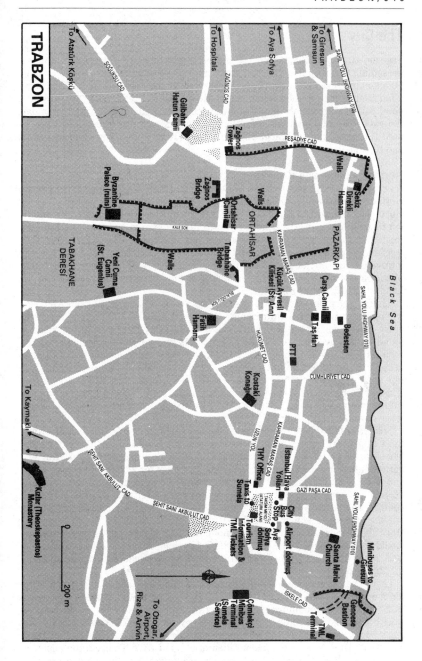

The City

Trabzon straggles along the coast and penetrates inland for several kilometers, presenting you with the choice of short rides or substantial walks to get to many points of interest—a characteristic aggravated by the modern city center's being a full kilometer from the ancient and medieval focus of settlement. Armed with a good pair of comfortable shoes, you can see most of the in-town sights in a day; the suburban monuments require both extra time and use of public transportation. If time is limited, concentrate on the two remote monasteries of Aya Sofya and Kaymaklı.

North of Taksim and Uzun Yol

An east-to-west walk along the seaward portion of town begins unpromisingly: the **Genoese bastion** straddling the coast highway tunnel, approached along Güzelhisar Caddesi, is an officers' club and off-limits to the public; detour slightly left instead to the overpass taking you to the tea garden and small park on the west flank of the castle. This seems to be Trabzon's sole acknowledgment of its seaside location, since the shoreline in general is amazingly dead and the city introverted up on its plateau. The usually locked Catholic church of **Santa Maria**, a few alleys west of the ramparts, is the last surviving reminder of the Italians' former pivotal role here.

Things get more exciting if you shift to just northwest of Taksim Meydanı, where pedestrianized **Kunduracılar Sokak** (Shoemakers' Street) is the usual entry to Trabzon's **bazaar**. Ironically just about everything *except* shoes can be found on this avenue, with a special emphasis first on pharmacies and doctors, then on gold jewelry. Once past Postahane Sokak, Kunduracılar veers right to become **Semerciler Sokak** (Saddlers' Street), equally illogically devoted to a mix of factory-made clothing and the electrically striped *keşans* and *peştemals* (see "East of Trabzon," p.555) that are standard issue for so many Black Sea women. Copper merchants and tin-platers cluster on and just off **Yalahan Sokak**, which leads downhill from Semerciler to the water.

Sooner or later you'll stumble upon the monumental heart of the bazaar, where the **Çarşı Camii**, the largest mosque in town, is handsome on the outside but late-Ottoman-garish inside. Just behind it, the sixteenth-century **Taş Han** is a fairly standard tradesmen's hall, today empty except for a couple of tailor's shops and a jeans warehouse. The **Bedesten**, below the mosque, is more interesting despite its semi-ruinous condition. Built by the Genoese in the fourteenth century, and revamped by the Ottomans, its shrub-tufted exterior seems square, but the interior, reached through the north portal, turns out to be octagonal. Once there were 48 shops on two floors, but four square pillars were evidently insufficient to support the dome which has long since fallen in. Today the *Bedesten* is used as a lumber mill, whose workers are amused by all the attention the structure gets.

Leave the bazaar going uphill, cross Maraş Caddesi, and you can't miss the ninth-century Byzantine church of **Küçük Ayvasil** on the other side. Also known as St Ann's, the diminutive shrine is permanently locked; anyway, its frescoes were obliterated sometime in the last seventy years. A stroll along Uzun Yol, just a few paces south and dotted with imposing *belle époque* mansions, may be more satisfying. There's no real concentration of old houses in Trabzon; the appeal of leisurely strolling lies partly in the unexpected confrontation with a creaking masterpiece on an otherwise unremarkable block. One of the best examples of this is the **Kostaki Konağı**, just south of Uzun Yol on Zeytin Caddesi, which is scheduled to reopen as a museum when restoration is complete.

The Old Town

Following Uzun Yol west soon brings you to the **Tabakhane Deresi** and the eponymous bridge that spans it. On the other side sprawls the fortified old town on its "table," but before crossing you should make a detour left along the east bank of the ravine, being careful to bear onto **Bilaloğlu Sokak**, away from markers pointing to the Fatih Hamamı. After about 350m you'll come to the **Yeni Cuma Camii**, formerly the thirteenth-century church of St Eugenius, patron saint of Trabzon. There may have been a shrine of sorts here as early as the third century, when Eugenius disrupted the cult of Mithra at Boztepe and was martyred by Diocletian for his pains. As so often happened in these cases, his skull was found on this spot within a few years of Alexis Comnenus' arrival, and the present church was erected to house the holy relic. The saint's intervention supposedly spared the city from the Selçuks in 1222, but he let the team down in 1461; Mehmet the Conqueror offered up his first Friday prayers here after capturing Trabzon, and immediately reconsecrated the church and added its minaret. You'll need to time your visit to the plain but relatively undisturbed interior around the daily round of prayers.

Crossing the **Tabakhane Bridge** you arrive in the **Ortahisar** (Middle Castle) district of the old town; farther upstream, at the steepest point of the gullies on either side of it, is the upper citadel, while below, tumbling off the tableland, sprawls the less defensible lower town, huddled behind a third circuit of walls that reach the sea. The **walls** are in variable condition but at their crenellated and vine-shrouded best give some idea of Trabzon's skyline in its heyday.

The highlight of Ortahisar is the former church of Panayia Khrisokefalos, now the **Ortahisar Camii** and also referred to as the Fatih Camii. As in the case of the Yeni Cuma Camii, there was almost certainly a church on this site from the third century, but the present building dates mostly from the thirteenth century, with massive renovation after a fire in the midst of the 1341 civil war. This was the main cathedral of the Trapezuntine empire, and most royal weddings, funerals and coronations took place here; the epithet *Khrisokefalos* or "Golden-Headed" recalls the zenith of the dynasty, when the Comneni could afford to plate the dome with gold. This is of course long vanished, and the Byzantine frescoes inside, smothered under layers of Islamic whitewash, and a thirteenth-century mosaic floor, recently cemented over, are equally unavailable for viewing. Today it's the volume of the barn-like basilica, with its massive interior columns, that impresses, though again as at Yeni Cuma you'll have to coincide with the conclusion of prayers or hunt down the key-keeper to get in. A handful of atmospheric teahouses and simple restaurants around the mosque ease any necessary wait.

From the apse end of the former church you can bear south, uphill, about 400m along **Kale Sokağı**, through a gateway astride the street, to enter the **upper citadel**. Of the glittering Comneni palace, in the southwest corner of the highest terrace overlooking the **Kuzgun Deresi**, nothing is left but battered masonry. From the eastern ramparts, dominating the Tabakhane Deresi, there's a fine view across to the Yeni Cuma Camii; careful navigating could get you through the maze of shacks and vegetable plots in the ravine bottom and up the other side.

Heading west from Ortahisar Camii, the **Zağnos Bridge**, built by a Greek convert who was one of Mehmet the Conqueror's chief generals, leaves Ortahisar over the Kuzgun gulch where dilapidated Greek mansions are slowly losing ground to contemporary tenements. On the far side, the **Zağnos Tower**, the southernmost dungeon in the outer enceinte of walls, has lately been restored as the *Zindan Restaurant*; you'll pay double for the rather fake atmosphere. Less bogus is the adjacent teahouse, with comically Lilliputian stools.

Across a busy boulevard and a swath of parkland from the tower squats the **Gülbahar Hatun Camii**, the most important Ottoman monument in Trabzon—although its background is more fascinating than the run-of-the-mill mosque you see now. The mother of Selim the Grim and wife of Beyazit II—known in later life as Gülbahar or "Springrose"—was originally a Comneni princess famous for her piety and good works among Christians and Muslims alike. She died in 1512, the first year of Selim's reign, and he completed the mosque and her adjoining *türbe* by 1514.

From just in front of the Gülbahar Hatun complex, Soğuksu Caddesi heads up toward the finest surviving example of the palatial bourgeois mansions that sprouted locally at the turn of the century.

The Atatürk Köşkü

Set in immaculately maintained gardens, the **Atatürk Köşkü** (daily 8am–7pm summer, 8am–5:30pm winter; small admission fee) began life in 1903 as the property of the Greek banker Karayannidhis, who was obliged to abandon it two decades later. Atatürk stayed here on the first of three occasions in 1924, and the city formally presented it to him a year before his death. As an example of patrician Black Sea architecture, the mansion, though crying out for a paint job and general maintenance, is more compelling than the contents—which include a bevy of photos of Atatürk, plus a map bearing his strategic scribbles during the Kurdish Dersim revolt of 1937.

Dolmuşes to the "Köşk" stop, and red-and-white city buses marked "Park–Köşk," both serve the site—which is 6.5km southwest of Taksim Meydanı, so you wouldn't want to walk. You can also catch the bus as it passes Gülbahar Hatun; in summer the last one down is at 7:30pm.

Aya Sofya (Haghia Sophia)

Alone on a park-like bluff overlooking the Black Sea, the monastery church of **Aya Sofya** is one of the most romantically set of Byzantine remains, and even the fact that Trabzon's suburbs have now overtaken it does little to detract from the appeal. It seems certain that there was a pagan temple here, and then an early Byzantine chapel, long before Manuel I Comnenus commissioned the present structure between 1238 and 1263. The floorplan and overall conception were revolutionary at the time, successfully assimilating most architectural trends, Christian and Muslim, prevalent in contemporary Anatolia. Aya Sofya's role as a model for many later Byzantine churches will be evident if you've already seen St Saviour (Kariye Camii) in Hora or the Pammakaristos church (Fethiye Camii) in İstanbul.

Converted into a mosque after 1461, Aya Sofya subsequently endured some even leaner and more ignominious times as an ammunition store and then as a hospital. Between 1957 and 1964, technicians working under the supervision of David Talbot Rice and David Winfield rescued the building from certain oblivion, in particular restoring dozens of **frescoes** to their former glory. Well-lit and accurately labeled in English, these are compulsory viewing even if you only have a passing interest in religious art.

The Site

From Taksim Meydanı infrequent dolmuşes labeled "Aya Sofya" cover the 3km to the monument, or more regular ones marked "BLK Sigorta" will drop you off 300m south of Aya Sofya, with the way onwards fairly well signed.

The **church** (daily 8am–6pm, closed Mon in winter; $1) is laid out along a greatly modified cross-in-square scheme, with a dome supported by four columns and three apses at the east end of what is in effect a triple nave. At the west end of the building a narthex extends the full width of the nave; barrel-vaulted porticos adorn the north, west, and south sides of the exterior. Before rushing in to view the famous frescoes, take a moment to study the finely sculpted **frieze**, illustrating Adam and Eve in the Garden, that surrounds the south portal, the only one of the three not tampered with by the Turks when they reconsecrated the church. This relief work is the most obvious evidence of the strong Armenian, Georgian, and even Syrian influence on the craftsmen—who left, in lieu of signature, the single-headed eagle of the Comneni dynasty over the biblical art.

Aya Sofya's **frescoes**, in their fluidity, warmth, and expressiveness, represented a drastic break with the rigidity of earlier painting, and compare well with the best work of their century and the next in Serbia and Macedonia as well as Constantinople itself. If you're pressed for time, the most important compositions are in the apse and the narthex, as well as in the north porch—which many people miss.

In the **apse** a serene *Ascension* hovers over *The Virgin Enthroned* between the two Archangels. The *Pantocrator* in the **dome** was unhappily beyond repair, but a host of angels swirls around him, just above the Apostles. The **narthex**, whose ceiling is divided into three sections by stone ribs, is almost wholly devoted to scenes from the life of Christ. The central zone exploits its complicated quadruple vaulting by depicting each of the Tetramorphs, symbols of the Evangelists, accompanied by seraphim. Alongside, such miraculous episodes as *The Wedding at Cana*, a decidedly adolescent *Child Jesus Teaching in the Temple* and *Healing the Canaanite's Daughter* (complete with vomited demon) fill the south vault, while *Feeding the Five Thousand* and *Calming the Storm on the Lake of Galilee* can be seen to the north. The **north portico** is taken up mostly by Old Testament scenes, including *The Sufferings of Job*.

Just north of the church an ensemble of sunken masonry was once perhaps the **baptismal font**; the square **belfry** to the west is a 1443 afterthought, indicative of the strong Italian flavor of the waning empire. If the tower is open—a rare event—the frescoes within are not nearly of the same quality as those in the church proper. The southeast apse is thought to have once been the location of Manuel I's **tomb**.

Boztepe

Boztepe, the hill dominating Trabzon on the southeast, has always been held in religious esteem; in olden days it was the site of the amalgamated cults of the Persian sun-god Mithra and the Hellenic deity Apollo—an ironic dedication when you consider how little unfiltered sun the coast receives. This reverence persisted into Christian times, when the hill was studded with churches and monasteries. Two of the latter still stand—after a fashion—and at least one is well worth the effort to visit.

The ruined former **Convent of the Panayia Theoskepastos** (The God-Protected Virgin; in Turkish the "Kızlar Manastırı") is built into the rocky slope 1.5km from Taksim Meydanı, reached by following Şehit Sani Akbulut Caddesi south and then bearing left when you see the shell of the building on the hillside. Though founded in the fourteenth century, and in continuous use by the Greek Orthodox church until 1923, few internal frescoes or other artistic details remain, and in any case the place has been securely locked for several years while the Ministry of Culture deliberates how or whether to restore it. Just above the convent, an appealing picnickers' park and grillhouse shares the view over the city with a military watchtower and the mosque and tomb of **Ahi Evren**, a target of pilgrimage among Trabzon's faithful.

The former Armenian monastery of **Kaymaklı**, 3.5km beyond the turnoff for Theoskepastos, is in an altogether higher league, containing as it does the finest frescoes in the region after those of Aya Sofya and Sumela. It's too far to walk, so take a taxi, or a bus marked "Kemik Hastane" from Taksim Meydanı. The bus will drop you off at the Mısırlı Camii, out by the local prison on the flat summit of Boztepe: 100m past the mosque, turn left (east) and down onto an unmarked dirt road; proceed 800m along this, bearing right at all forks, until you reach an informal parking lot next to an ugly, green-and-white house with a garage underneath. When the weather is dry you can get this far by car or taxi—from here it's another 250m to the monastery. After rain the dirt road is impassable, so you'll have to walk the full distance from the main road however you arrive.

What's left of Kaymaklı studs a green plateau overlooking the highway to Erzurum; today the monastery grounds are a farm, and the resident family is used to showing visitors around. Much of the place dates from the mid-fifteenth century, though the current tenants have wedged their concrete dwelling into the former cells on the east edge of the courtyard. A chapel or baptistry is bare, but the main **katholikon** is a marvel, its interior protected until now by its use as a hay-barn.

Off-season visits will be somewhat easier, since in summer the bales hide the walls to eye level and above, but at any time the best-preserved images are usually exposed, and the family is quite willing to help you dig down to get a look at the lower tier. The **south wall** bears a Bosch-like conception of Hell and the Apocalypse, complete with a *Four-Headed Cerberus* and *The Whore of Babylon Riding the Beast of the Apocalypse*; adjacent hagiographies and the admiration of angels are less lurid. In the **apse**, more frequently exposed and thus badly damaged, you can still make out a *Dormition* and the *Entry of Christ into Jerusalem*, with the Savior most definitely riding a horse rather than an ass. None of the frescoes date from earlier than the seventeenth century, and are far more sophisticated in concept and execution than you'd expect for such comparatively recent work.

Eating and Drinking

There are plenty of places to eat in central Trabzon, but few of them are really outstanding. Chicken and fish are the staple entrees, with red meat being scarce. Requests for fruit juice will be met with blank stares or offers of Fanta, strange as that may seem in this fruit-rich region. Similarly, getting a stiff drink takes some resourcefulness; Trabzon's *imams* have seen to that.

The almost uninterrupted line of **restaurants** on the north side of Taksim Meydanı get most of the tourist business, although not all of them deserve to. Among the less greasy ones are the *Eyvan Balık Restorant*, a simple fish-frier, and *Murat Balık ve Köfte*, two doors west and a bit fancier but, like the *Eyvan*, alcohol-free. If you're tired of Turkish cuisine, *Tad* has good American-style pizza—not *pide*—plus burgers and corn dogs (!) if you're feeling unadventurous. The easternmost options, edging onto İskele Caddesi opposite the *Hotel Usta*, include the *Hacıbaba İskembe Salonu*, which does fish in addition to the expected soups, and the nearby *Derya Lokantası*, strong on chicken and desserts.

Establishments on the south side of the square, while costing perhaps ten or fifteen percent more, are far more salubrious and less touristy. They don't come more obvious than the *İnan Kebap Salonu*, with tasty offerings right across from the tourist information office. The *Büryan Et Lokantası*, on Uzun Sokak across from *THY*, is also good, as is the *Çardak Pide Salonu*, 100m down Uzun Sokak on the opposite side, where you can eat outdoors under an arbor, away from the traffic. If you insist on alcohol with your meal, you'll pay dearly for it—and the stained linen tableclothes—at the much-promoted *Kıbrıs Restaurant* on the east side of Taksim Meydanı: the food, like the place in general, is stale and overpriced.

If you just want a **drink**, the best tippling is done at *Reis'in Yeri*, İskele Cad 14, down toward the *InterRent* office; here you'll sit outside with the boys, washing down *çerez* (nibble-snacks). In terms of **desserts**, everyplace has at least some pastries or goodies—the confectioners of Hemşin (see p.560) aren't far away—but the best in town by a mile is *Tatlıcı Ali Karamusa*, Bahar Sok 2/A, just off Uzun Sokak about 300m west of the square: fabulous milk-based desserts, and great *dondurma* too. The unfortunately named *Beton Helva* ("Concrete Helva"—referring to the sale of chunks cut from bigger slabs), across from the *Çardak Pide Salonu*, also has *şıra* (grape juice). There's more good *dondurma* at the *Şelale Pastanesi*, two doors down from the *Derya Lokantası* on İskele Caddesi, which also serves *acı badem* (semi-soft almond cookies). For **breakfast**, *Cafe Kuğu*, bang in the middle of Restaurant Row, approximates the atmosphere of a truck-stop dine—hearty eating if you're hungry.

Listings

Airlines *THY* is at the southwest corner of Taksim Meydanı (☎13446); *İstanbul Hava Yolları* is at the northwest corner, on the second floor of the *Ulusoy* offices (☎11367).

Airport bus A *Havaş* bus departs 90min before *THY* flights from in front of the *THY* ticket office; otherwise, there are frequent dolmuşes from a stop one block north of the Taksim Meydanı—it's signed "Havaalanı."

Bookstores None has extensive English-language stock, but many titles of interest are sold at the tourist office. One kiosk on the south side of Taksim Meydanı often has two-day-old English-language papers.

Car rental Amazingly, there are no independent operators—only major international outlets, which aren't inclined to bargain much. The addresses are: *Avis*, Gazipaşa Cad 20/B (☎23740); *Europcar/InterRent*, İskele Cad 40 (☎25844); and *Hertz*, İskele Cad 39/A (☎23234). All three outlets also have booths at the airport.

Exchange To change travelers' checks after hours, try the *Hotel Usta*. The PTT and tourist office may also oblige you.

Hamams By far the best is the ancient but newly restored *Sekiz Direkli Hamam*, Pazarkapı 8, Direkli Hamam Sok 1 (daily 6am–11:30pm; women only on Thurs, men only other days; admission $3). Second choices would be *Fatih,* 3 blocks south of Uzun Sokak east of the Tabakhane Bridge (daily 5:30am–10pm; women on Wed; admission $1.80) or the *Meydan*, just off Taksim Meydanı on Kahraman Maraş Caddesi (daily 6am–10pm; women on Sat; $1.80).

Hospitals The *Özel* (private) and *SSK* (state) hospitals are both out near Aya Sofya; *Özel* is 300m west, then 200m south of the *SSK*.

Luggage storage At the otogar, or by arrangement at the tourist information office.

PTT Located on Posthane Sokak, a tiny alley north of Kahraman Maraş Caddesi, and not on Maraş itself as incorrectly shown on most maps. Phones open 24hr; post and exchange 8am–7pm daily.

TML agent Right next door to the tourist office, on Taksim Meydanı (☎12018).

The Monastery of Sumela

At the beginning of the Byzantine era a large number of monasteries sprung up in the mountains behind Trabzon; this tendency was reinforced during the life of the Trapezuntine empire, when many of them also played a military role near the tiny realm's southern frontier.

The most important and prestigious monastery (and today the best preserved) was **Sumela**, clinging to a cliff face nearly a thousand feet above the Altındere valley, the sort of setting which has always appealed to Greek Orthodox monasticism. Despite the habitual crowds—and the poor condition of the premises—Sumela has to rate as one of the mandatory excursions along the Black Sea.

The name Sumela is a Pontic Greek shortening and corruption of *Panayia tou Melas* or Virgin of the Black (Rock), although some render it—with more grammatical liberties—as "of the Black Virgin." She had been venerated here since at least the year 385, when the Athenian monk Barnabas, acting on a revelation from the Mother of God, showed up with an icon said to have been painted by Saint Luke. He and his nephew found a site matching that of his vision—a cave on a narrow ledge partway up the nearly sheer palisade—and installed the icon in a shrine inside.

A monastery supposedly grew around the image as early as the sixth century, but most of what's visible today dates from the thirteenth and fourteenth centuries, when Sumela was intimately linked with Trebizond's Comneni dynasty, several of whose rulers conducted their coronations at Sumela rather than in the imperial capital. Over the centuries the icon was responsible for numerous miracles, and the institution housing it shared its reputation, prompting even Turkish sultans to make pilgrimages and leave offerings.

Sumela was hastily evacuated in 1923 along with all other Greek Orthodox foundations in the region; six years later it was gutted by fire, possibly set by careless squatters. In 1931 one of the monks returned secretly and exhumed a number of treasures, including the revered icon, from their hiding place. The Virgin can now be seen in the Benaki Museum in Athens; unfortunately, when the other reliquaries were opened on arrival in Greece, precious illuminated manuscripts from the Byzantine era were found to have rotted away during their eight years underground.

Practical Details

Without your own transportation, you have three ways of **getting to Sumela** from Trabzon. **Taxis** from a designated stand on the south side of Taksim Meydanı, within sight of the tourist office, charge $8 a person for a carload of four people. Slightly cheaper, but more regimented, are the **organized tours** run at 10am daily by two travel agencies, *Karden* and *Karadeniz*, at the southwest and east sides of the square respectively; cost per person is $6 for a round-trip minibus seat, with a stop for lunch thrown in on the way back. The least expensive, but chanciest, way of getting to Sumela is by **public minibus** from the Çömlekçi terminal. These theoretically leave every morning between 9:45 and 10am from beneath the canopy reading "Maçka Sivil Meryemana," but they won't go unless a minimum of seven or eight tourists present themselves, and the driver may wait around until ten or fifteen have collected. The chances of this happening are better on weekends, but in any case you shouldn't pay more than $4 a head for the round trip.

However you arrive, you should make it clear that you're interested in a very full half-day out, since the state of the roads and the final walk in dictates two and a half hours just to get there and back, and you'll want an equal amount of time at the ruins. It's 54km from Trabzon to Sumela, which signs usually indicate as "Meryemana" (Mother Mary, as Muslims call her). After 31km you turn off the chewed-up Highway 885 at MAÇKA, where there are incidentally no decent hotels. The 23-kilometer side road up the Altındere is even worse, with traffic frequently delayed for dynamiting and bulldozing of landslides. As you climb, the habitual cloud ceiling of these parts drifts down from the equally dense fir forest to meet you; in exceptional circumstances you may catch an advance glimpse of the monastery's faded, whitewashed flank soaring above the trees at the top of the valley, at an altitude of 1200m.

The environs of Sumela have been designated a national park which means a trout farm, a picnic area, and relatively expensive teahouses and kebab stalls; depending on the exact terms with your driver you may or may not have to fork over an additional $1–3 per vehicle at the park entrance booth. The monastery proper is linked to the valley bottom by a half-hour, often slippery woodland trail. Visiting hours change with daylight: 8am to 3pm from November to February; 8am to 4pm in March and October; 8am to 5pm in April and May; and 8am to 7pm from June to September. Admission—collected at the top—is $2.50, half that for students.

The Buildings

Sumela actually occupies a far smaller patch of level ground than its five-storied facade suggests. A climb up the original entry stairs, and an equal descent on the far side of the gate, deposits you in the central courtyard, with the monks' cells and guest quarters on your right overlooking the brink, and the chapel and cave sanctuary to the left. Most of the former living areas are off-limits pending restoration; the general degree of vandalism and decay is appalling, and only recently have the authorities taken strong measures to prevent further damage. Sophisticated art thieves were caught levering away large slabs of the famous frescoes in 1983, and any within arm's reach have been obliterated by graffiti-scrawlers—many of them Europeans and North Americans.

The main grotto-shrine is closed off on the courtyard side by a wall, from which protrudes the apse of a smaller chapel. A myriad of **frescoes** in varying styles cover every surface, the earliest and best ones dating from the fourteenth century, with progressively less worthwhile additions and retouchings done in 1710, 1740, and 1860. The cave paintings are in good condition—ceilings are harder to vandalise—although the irregular surface makes for some odd departures from Orthodox iconographic conventions. The Pantocrator, the Mother of God, and various apostles seem to float overhead in space; on the south (left) wall is the *Virgin Enthroned*, while *Jonah in the Whale* can be seen at the top right.

Outside on the divider wall, most of the scenes from the life of Christ are hopelessly scarred. Among the more distinct ones are a fine *Transfiguration* about ten feet up on the right; just above sits *Christ in Glory*, an oft-repeated theme with at least three renditions nearby. At the top left is *Christ Redeeming Adam and Eve*. On the apse of the tiny chapel, *The Raising of Lazarus* is the most intact image; next to it is *The Entry into Jerusalem*, with the *Deposition from the Cross* on the extreme right. When craning your neck to ogle the surviving art gets too tiring, there is (mist permitting) always the spectacular view over the valley—and the process of imagining what monastic life, or a stay in the wayfarers' quarters, must have been like here in Sumela's prime.

Other Nearby Monasteries

So many monasteries are crumbling away in the Pontic foothills that some may never be documented before they disappear forever. Two of the more famous ones, relatively close to Sumela, are best visited with your own transportation—but in all honesty they will appeal only to specialists.

To reach the cloister of **VAZELON**, dedicated to Saint John the Baptist, proceed 10km south of Maçka on the road to Erzurum; 300m past two adjacent teahouses in the unmarked village of KİREMİTLİ, bear right down a dirt road where the main road bends left. Descend south to the river and the future main highway, crossing at a ford, and climb north up the far bank to the Ortamahalle district of Kiremitli. Continue along what's now a narrow forest road, bearing right at the only fork, until a huge washout prevents further progress. From here you're looking at a forty-minute walk west to the monastery, visible in the final stretch like a mini-Sumela on the cliff-face ahead.

In fact Vazelon once ranked second to Sumela in wealth and ecclesiastical clout, but its deterioration in recent years has accelerated alarmingly. Frescoes gushed over in other literature have vanished under the ministrations of rain, campfire smoke, and vandals, and within a few more years all will have disintegrated. For the moment, the side chapel outside the walls contains a *Dormition*, a *Raising of Lazarus* and a row of angels, all dating from the sixteenth century and in fair-to-poor condition. The *katholikon*, or main sanctuary, reached by much crawling through rubble and nettles, has recently collapsed; only the northern exterior wall bears bits of a naive, eighteenth- or nineteenth-century *Last Judgment*.

The monastery of **PERISTERA**, in Turkish the Hızır İlyas Manastırı, is somewhat easier to get to but in no better condition. From Esiroğlu, 17km south of Trabzon, a rough fifteen-kilometer drive east leads first to Libova, then to the village of Şimşirli, formerly Küstül. More nettles await the intrepid scaler of the nearby crag on which the monastery walls perch. No art remains; the view is the main thing.

East of Trabzon: the Coast to the Soviet Border

The shore east of Trabzon gets progressively more extreme as you approach the Soviet border. If the Black Sea coast as a whole is wet, here's it's positively soggy; mountains increasingly impinge on the sea and soar ever steeper upward; and the people match the landscape in their larger-than-life qualities.

Natives of this area have long exercised a disproportionate influence in national politics; the best current example being Rize's **Mesut Yılmaz**, once (and future?) foreign minister, whose patronage of various local prestige projects has become the second-biggest growth industry after tea (see accompanying box). If a road is being improved or some other conspicuous public work is under way, it's probably due to his intervention; grateful supporters festoon boulevards with laudatory billboards and generally accord him a status just inferior to deity.

Civics and commerce aside, however, the coast route has remarkably little to offer travelers. Visually, the only color comes from the uniformly red-black-and-white-striped **keşans** (shawls) and multicolored **peştemals** (waistbands) worn by women between a point just west of Trabzon and Çayeli. Another exotic touch is lent by roadside signs in Georgian and Russian, aimed at tourists from the USSR— probably the first time either language has appeared publicly in print in Turkey since 1923, and a strange gesture considering that most Soviet tourists to date are Turkish-speaking Azeris. Sounds may be better: if you happen upon a summer-time singalong, the **music** will be that of the *kemençe*, the Pontic three-string spike fiddle, and the *tulum*, the slightly more versatile local goatskin bagpipe.

TEA

East of Trabzon, thanks to a climate ideal for its cultivation, **tea** is king. The tightly trimmed bushes are planted everywhere between sea level and about 600m, to the exclusion of almost all other crops. Picking the tender leaves is considered women's work, and during the six warmer months of the year they can be seen humping enormous loads of leaves in back-strap baskets to the nearest consolidation station. The tea—nearly a million raw tons of it annually—is sent more or less immediately to the fermenting and drying plants whose stacks are recurring landmarks in the region.

Oddly, tea is a very recent introduction to the Black Sea, the pet project of one Asim Zihni Derin, who imported the first plants just before World War II to a region badly depressed in the wake of the departure of its substantial Christian population in 1923. Within a decade or so tea became the mainstay of the local economy, overseen by Çaykur, the state tea monopoly. Despite the emergence of private competitors since 1985, and the Chernobyl accident which caused condemnation of the 1986 crop, Çaykur is still the major player in an industry which seems ready to expand to export volume now that the domestic market is saturated.

Trabzon to Rize

If you just want a swim and a half-day out from Trabzon, the first decent, unpolluted **beaches** are found between **ARAKLI** and **SÜRMENE**. The towns themselves are nothing to write home about, with the only point of cultural interest being the late eighteenth-century mansion of the Yakupoğlu clan, *derebeys* or feudal overlords of these parts. Otherwise known as the **Kastel**, this squats above the west bank of the Kastel Çayı, 4km east of Sürmene, opposite a seashore teahouse, the *Kastel Restaurant*. Abandoned in 1978 by the Yakupoğlus—whose ranks include one of the richest men in the country, Cevher Özden—it's locked and beginning to decay, but is still impressive. Four stone bulwarks guard the tapered center of the floorplan; the lightness of the wood and stucco work on the upper story, and the whimsical toadstool roof, seems incongruously wedded to the forbidding lower level.

It would only really be worth stopping at these places if you had your own car, and the same goes for the boatyards with their colorful, top-heavy *taka* fishing boats at **ÇAMBURNU**, 3km east. A much-touted pay beach is tucked at the base of the cliff just beyond the port, but equally good or better free **beaches** line the road to **OF** (pronounced "oaf"). If for some bizarre reason you got stranded in Of, there's a tourist-standard, one-star **hotel**, the *Çaykent* (☎0441/2424).

Rize

Yet another anonymous modern Turkish city in a grand setting, **RİZE**'s name at least will be familiar to every tourist who's bought a souvenir box of "Rize Turist Çay." Of its ancient history as Rhizus nothing survives, and of its role as the easternmost outpost of the Trapezuntine empire hardly more than a tiny castle. If you do pause it would be to visit the **Tea Institute**, a combination think-tank, botanical garden, and tasting/sales outlet on a hill overlooking the town; follow the signs to the "Çay Enstitüsü."

Otherwise, **moving on** is quickly arranged. Two separate minibus stations abut the shore road about 400m apart: the eastern one for services to Pazar, Hopa and Artvin, the westerly one for all points to Trabzon and inland to İkizdere and İspir. In between are the canopies and ticket stall for the more comfortable, red-and-white *belediye* line to Trabzon.

Rize to Hopa: Lazland

Forty or fifty kilometers beyond Rize you pass the invisible former eastern limit of the Comneni holdings and enter the territory of the **Laz**, the Black Sea's most celebrated minority group—erroneously so much of the time, since other Turks have an annoying habit of stereotypically classing anyone from east of Trabzon as "Laz." Strictly speaking the Laz are a Caucasian people speaking a language related to Georgian, 100,000 of whom inhabit Pazar, Ardeşen, Fındıklı, Arhavı and Hopa, plus certain inland enclaves. The men, with their aquiline features and often reddish hair, particularly stand out; they also distinguish themselves by an extroversion unusual even for the Black Sea, a bent for jokes—practical and verbal—and an extraordinary business acumen that's the envy of slower-witted Turks and the source of so much of the Laz-baiting and misidentification farther west. A fair chunk of Turkey's shipping is owned and operated by Laz, who recruit crews from improbably small villages. The wealth so generated makes them relatively progressive in outlook; the women can be seen wearing Western garb from Fındıklı east, and the men too seem better dressed in the latest styles, although "progress" has also been translated into making the five municipalities listed some of the ugliest on the Black Sea—which is really saying something.

From Ardeşen east the coast has absolutely no plain; imposing mountains, shaggy with tea and hazelnuts, drop directly into the sea. These natural defenses have helped the Laz maintain a semblance of independence throughout their **history**. It seems most likely that they're descendants of the ancient Colchians (from whom Jason supposedly stole the Golden Fleece). The Laz accepted Christianity in the sixth century and almost immediately got embroiled in a series of protracted wars with the Byzantines, whose governors had managed to offend them—not hard to do. No power managed to fully subdue them until the Ottomans induced conversion to Islam in the early sixteenth century. Like their neighbors the Hemşinli (see p.560) they don't lose too much sleep over their religious affiliation, although with their peripatetic habits and far-flung enterprises the Laz are now well integrated into the national fabric.

Hopa . . . and Border-Watching

HOPA, which was the end of the line until the nearby border was opened and the road to it was declassified militarily, is a grim, industrial port, devoted to the shipment of the copper mined slightly inland. The **minibus terminal** is on the east bank of the stream lapping the town on the west. If you have to stay here—and this would only happen if you were en route to the USSR and arrived too late to cross the border—there are two one-star **hotels** on the waterfront: the down-at-heel *Papila* (☎0571/1440), charging $12 per person for comfortable rooms with views over the water, or the newer, similarly priced *Cihan* (☎0571/1897). If your wallet's not up to these rates, there are a few shadier establishments near the central cluster of **restaurants, banks**, and the **PTT**, between the *Papila* and the bus terminal.

Ten cliff-hemmed, twisty kilometers northeast of Hopa, **KEMALPAŞA** is the next-to-last Turkish village on the Black Sea, with a huge pebbly **beach** and a couple of impromptu **campgrounds** a healthy distance away from the tea factory. There's no other accommodation, but you won't starve thanks to a handful of **restaurants** by the campgrounds.

Minibuses cover the entire 20km from Hopa to the **Turkish-Soviet border**, which was fixed by the respective revolutionary governments in 1921 at the stream dividing the previously insignificant village of **SARP**, rather than more logically at the Çoruh River near Batumi. The crossing was virtually inactive between 1935 and 1988—a casualty of Stalinist, then cold-war paranoia—but since the gates have opened, Turkish Sarp has taken on a carnival atmosphere, as hordes of visa-less Turks come to picnic, swim, and gawk at clearly visible Georgian Sarp on the eastern bank of the creek. If you intend to do more than just engage in Turkey's newest spectator sport, show up with your **Soviet visa** (obtainable only in İstanbul or Ankara) between the hours of 8am and 7pm daily.

Inland: The Foothills from Trabzon to Rize

While Sumela is a hard act to follow, there are a number of other possible destinations in the hills southeast of Trabzon. The valleys leading to and past them are also useful alternate routes toward Erzurum, avoiding some or all of the mess on the E390/885/915 highway.

Of to Uzungöl

The starting point for excursions up the valley of the Solaklı Çayı is Of. Both Of and **ÇAYKARA**, the unexciting main town of the lower valley, are renowned for their devoutness, with the highest ratio of *kuran kursus* (Koran schools for children) per capita in the country, and phalanxes of bearded and skull-capped *hocas* and *hacıs* striding about in the shadow of huge mosques. A further peculiarity is that anyone over forty speaks the Pontic dialect of Greek as their first language. It seems probable that the tribes of this valley were Hellenized (along with others such as those around Maçka) at some point during Byzantine rule, though they never lost their reputation as fierce brigands. Upon conversion to Islam at the end of the seventeenth century, their ferocity was transmuted into piety—as the saying goes, when the devil grows old he becomes a monk. It should come as no surprise, then, that you haven't got a prayer of finding anything stronger than a fruit juice between Of and Uzungöl.

Sixteen kilometers inland, you might persuade your dolmuş to stop at the **covered wooden bridge of Hapsiyaş** (Kiremitli), photogenically romantic despite its prosaic setting. The present structure dates only from 1935, but it seems likely there's been a span here for several centuries.

Uzungöl and Around

Beyond Çaykara, 25km along, the pavement ends and an atrocious side road climbs twenty more kilometers to **UZUNGÖL** (Long Lake), the main attraction of this area. Especially on weekends, frequent dolmuşes make the ninety-minute trip up from Of. The lake, at 1100m, is only averagely scenic, with a bazaar district clustered around its outlet; the wooden houses of the village of the same name, clustered on the slope above, are more picturesque.

The sole place to **stay** is the *İnan Kardeşler Tesisleri*, at the high end of the lake where most minibuses end their run. This is a combination trout farm/restaurant/campground/motel managed by Hüseyin and Dursun İnan, one of whom will try to wait on you personally, even on weekends when the place is mobbed. The food is simple, tasty, and very reasonable—under $6 for a medium-sized trout (sold by weight), salad, and dessert. Beds, fifty of them going for $10 each, are at a premium, so in season it's wise to phone ahead at ☎0446/6021.

Uzungöl is an ideal base for hikes up to the nearby peaks of **Ziyaret** (3111m) and **Halizden** (3193m), with a chain of glacier lakes at the base of the latter. It's a very long day's walk there and back—although you can go partway by car to save time—so take a tent and food for two days if at all possible.

The right-hand turn above Çaykara leads 3.5km to **ATAKÖY**, one of the better preserved of the Black Sea foothill villages. Don't expect a museum piece like Safranbolu (see p.506), but there are scattered clusters of half-timbered farmsteads above the main street. The municipality runs an occasional bus between here and Of. If you have your own vehicle the 70km from here to Bayburt via the 2300-meter SOĞANLI PASS makes a very scenic and reasonably easy drive.

The İkizdere Valley

The next major valley east of Uzungöl, the İkizdere Valley, holds no special attraction to stop for, but the scenery along the way is memorable and the road eventually winds up to the highest drivable pass in the Pontic ranges—one of the three highest in all of Turkey. The place is mostly worth knowing about as an alternate route to Erzurum or an approach to the Kaçkar range (see Chapter Ten for both).

İKİZDERE, with frequent minibuses from Rize, is logically enough the main town, and the transfer point for the 27-kilometer trip up the Yetimhoca Valley to BAŞKÖY, the westernmost trailhead for the Kaçkar Dağları. Watch out, though: there are at least three other Başköys or Başyaylas in a thirty-kilometer radius, so don't let yourself or your driver get confused. A better alternative, if possible, is to arrange transfer to SALER, the highest village in the valley with road access.

Beyond İkizdere, the main road soon finds itself between jagged peaks and the *yaylas* gathered at the 2600-meter **Ovitdağı Pass**, far more alpine than the over-rated Zigana Pass to the west. The col marks the limits of Rize province and, presumably, Mesut Yılmaz's patronage, since the road deteriorates markedly soon after.

The Hemşin Valleys

The most scenic and interesting of the foothill regions east of Trabzon is the drainage of the **Fırtına Çayı** and its tributaries, which tumble off the steepest slopes of the Pontic ranges, here known as the Kaçkar Dağları. Between the mountains and the sea lie a few hundred square kilometers of rugged, isolated territory that have been imperfectly controlled at best by the prevailing imperial, or regional, powers of every era.

For the less geographically minded the area is known simply as **Hemşin**, a word whose etymology encapsulates local history: *-eşen* is a local dialect suffix, derived from Armenian, meaning "population" or "settlement," as in *hamameşen*, or "the settlement around the baths" (the hot springs at today's Ayder). Over a period of time this was abbreviated to Hemşin, and came to describe the triangular zone with its base against the mountains and its apex at Pazar, and by extension the people in it.

Çamlıhemşin and Around

ÇAMLIHEMŞİN, 24km upstream from the mouth of the Fırtına Çayı, is still too low (300m) to give you a real feel for the Hemşin country. Nonetheless, it's the last real town before the mountains, utilitarian and busy, with a constant chaos of mini-buses and shoppers clogging its single main street. There's a **bank**, a **PTT**, some stores for last-minute hiking supplies, two or three **restaurants**, and a lone **hotel** (the *Hoşdere*), but it's not a place to linger when so many better things await farther up.

Above Çamlıhemşin, along both the main stream and the tributary flowing down from Ayder, you begin to see some of the many graceful **bridges** which are a regional specialty. Their age and attribution are both subject to debate, but many have been dated to the seventeenth century and credited to Armenian craftsmen.

Two of the most gravity-defying examples span the roaring Fırtına Çayı at **ŞENYUVA**, a typically dispersed community of occasionally impressive dwellings 8 to 10km above Çamlıhemşin. On the left bank of the river, usually reached by a nerve-wracking winch-and-trapeze cable bridge, the *Sisi Pansiyon ve Kamp*, run by Savaş and Doris Güney, is one of the tourist institutions of the area. Savaş, whose ancestors hail from the valley, settled here sixteen years ago with his

THE HEMŞİN PEOPLE

The **Hemşinlis** are, according to competing theories, either a very old Turkic tribe, stragglers from the original tenth-century migrations who got stuck here, or more likely natives descended from the Heptacomete tribesmen of old, who spoke a dialect of Armenian and were nominally Christian or pagan until about a century and a half ago. In support of the latter notion, there exists a group of Islamic Armenian-speakers south of Hopa who call their dialect Hemşince and claim origins in Hemşin proper.

Certainly the main body of Hemşinlis, with their strong-featured and fair-complexioned women and Caucasian-looking men, appear anything but mainstream Turkish, and these outgoing, merry, occasionally outrageous people are diametrically opposite in behavior to the more solemn central Anatolians. Quite a bit of this has to do with wearing their Islam lightly; there's none of the overt piety of the Çaykara Valley, and you're unlikely to be blasted out of bed at dawn by a *muezzin* for the simple reason that most communities are too small to support a mosque. Despite stern little signs in the country stores warning that "alcohol is the mother of all ills," the men are in fact prodigious drinkers, a tendency aggravated by the **environment**. This is by far the dampest and mistiest part of Turkey, with the sun in hiding two days out of three and up to 200 annual inches of rain in some spots. It doesn't take a genius to predict cloud forest vegetation, with everything from moss-fringed fir and alders down to marsh species and creeping vines clinging to the slopes, as well as moods swinging wildly between moroseness and euphoria among the inhabitants.

Like the nearby Laz, whom they dislike being mistaken for, the Hemşinlis are intrepid and independent. They also have a special talent as pastry and dessert chefs: the top pastry shops of major Turkish cities are usually owned and/or staffed

German-born wife in what had once been his grandfather's cornfield. A back-to-nature lifestyle mushroomed into a full-time business: bed and full board in a limited number of A-frame cabins costs $20 a day, a plot of grass for your tent $2. Trilingual Savaş, who probably knows more than anyone about the western Kaçkar, regularly organizes three-to-five-day treks through the Tatos and Verçenik ranges (see p.596 in Chapter Ten), although given that he does it as much for the fun as the money, organization can be decidedly relaxed. Try to go with him personally, rather than with one of his less experienced deputies .

If your level of commitment isn't up to camping out in the high mountains, head instead for the *yayla* of **POKUT**, where after several hours on the trail southeast from Şenyuva you can stay at the Akay family lodge. The following day you can strike out as far as Polovit *yayla* at 2300m, via Hazıntak (see below) and Amlakıt, returning the same evening to Pokut, with no need to carry any equipment heavier than a daypack and raingear. POKUT itself is fairly representative of the more substantial Black Sea *yaylas*, with handsome woodwork capped by mixed tin-and-timber roofs rising from stone foundations.

The Upper Fırtına Valley

Above Şenyuva along the main branch of the Fırtına, the road progressively worsens while the scenery just as steadily becomes more spectacular. Below, the water roils in chasms and whirlpools that are irresistible to the lunatic fringe of the by natives of these valleys. The number of Hemşinlis living in diaspora, a process begun under Russian rule last century, is far larger than the 15,000 permanently inhabiting this rather compact domain.

You know you've left the Laz zone when, a little way inland from Pazar or Ardeşen, you begin to see the brilliant leopard-skin-patterned **scarves** of the Hemşin women, skillfully worn as turbans and contrasting with the drabness of the men's garb. Curiously, the scarves are not local but imported from India, perhaps a relic of the days when Trabzon was a terminus of the Silk Route. If you buy one, a free lesson in how to wear it is usually included in the transaction; be wary, on the other hand, of the home-grown woolly booties which generally contain a very high proportion of synthetic fibers.

As in attire, Hemşinlis' **housing** comprises a mix of local and borrowed styles and materials, reflecting wealth earned outside. Some positively baronial residences preside over tea terraces and cornfields at lower elevations (Hemşin, incidentally, is one of the few places in Turkey where corn is made into food for human consumption rather than fed solely to animals). But to fully understand the Hemşin mentality you need to visit at least one **yayla**, or summer pastoral hamlet.

Yaylas are found throughout Turkey in the uplands, but in Hemşin they are at their best. These tightly bunched groups of dwellings, usually stone-built up to waist height and chalet-style in timber above, begin just at treeline and recur at intervals up to 2700m. They're inhabited only between late May and early September, when their tenants may come from as far away as Holland or Germany to renew attachments to what they consider their true spiritual homeland. Modern facilities don't come to mind—shrouded in acrid smoke, awash in mud and nettles, *yaylas* seem more part of, say, Nepal than a country bidding for EC candidacy—but if you're invited into a cabin the hospitality will be more overwhelming even by Turkish standards, and that's saying a lot.

rubber-rafting fraternity. Roughly 12km along, the single-towered castle of **ZİLKALE**, improbably sited by either the Armenians or the Genoese to control a minor trade route, appears at a bend in the road. The tree-tufted ruin, more often than not garnished with wisps of mist, today dominates nothing more than one of the most evocative settings in the Pontus. No such lonely castle would be complete without its resident ghosts, and accordingly the locals claim that after dark it's haunted by the shades of its former garrison and their horses—so don't get left behind if your minibus pauses to let you snap a picture.

Çat and Around

After another 12km or so of violent abuse to your vehicle's suspension, you'll arrive at **ÇAT**, 1250m up. This is another classic base for hiking in the western Kaçkar, and though there doesn't seem to be much to the village beyond a few scattered buildings, there's a surprisingly good **hotel/store/restaurant**, the *Otel Cancık*, asking $3 for a bed in clean rooms upstairs; there's a hot shower down the hall. If it's full, as may happen when a trek group's in town, an alternative pansiyon can be found 1km downstream.

At Çat the upper reaches of the Fırtına divide. A road paralleling the main fork heads 30km due south to ORTAKÖY, passing on the way Zilkale's sister fort of Varoş at KALEKÖY, where yet another side road winds up to an alternative **trailhead for the western Kaçkar** at KALE YAYLA. Don't try to walk any more than you have to on these roads—between Kale Yayla and Çat, for example, you're looking at a very boring three-to-four-hour slog in either direction—but wait for the one daily minibus at the junction in Çat.

The other fork above Çat bears almost due east, and is all but undrivable beyond a final, exquisite bridge leading seemingly nowhere. It eventually expires 9km later in **ELEVİT** (1800m). Somehow a Thursday-and-Friday-only **minibus** wrestles itself down from here to Pazar, descending at 8am and returning at about noon. There are actually more **shops** in Elevit than in Çat, as well as a single, crude **lodge** which should charge about the same as Çat's. Elevit, like its nearest neighbor TİREVİT, ninety minutes' walk east, is a Laz enclave in Hemşin territory.

If you're lightly equipped there are several possible day-hikes from Elevit, most rewardingly three hours up to YILDIZLI GÖLÜ at the top of the valley opening to the south of Elevit. Alternatively, with an early start, you could make a one-way dash to the safety of the lodge in Pokut (see above) via Tirevit, Polovit, Amlakıt, and Hazıntak. For more information on these places consult "The Kaçkar Dağları" in the next chapter, or *Trekking in Turkey* (listed in "Books").

Ayder

The most heavily traveled road above Çamlıhemşin ends after 17km at **AYDER** (1300m), the highest permanently inhabited settlement in the Hemşin valley system, its identity poised somewhere between village and *yayla*. Concrete shoddiness is beginning to overwhelm the indigenous wood cabins, but it doesn't matter too much as the surrounding scenery was always the most convincing attraction. In recent years Ayder has become a resort of some note, partly because of its thermal baths but more for its role as a favorite jumping-off point for hikes in the central Kaçkar Dağları. A new and predictably ugly spa complex has languished unfinished here for some time, and accommodation is still uniformly basic, but all that will doubtless change following the imminent completion of improvements to the access road.

Practical Details

In season, four or five daily **minibuses** depart Pazar for Ayder between 10am and noon; you may have to change vehicles in Çamlıhemşin. Going down to the coast from Ayder, you're pretty sure of three daily departures, at 7, 9, and 11am, and there may be one or two more after noon. The trip will take just over an hour in each direction, once the widening and asphalting of the road is completed—at the time of writing it was taking double that. In theory you can descend from Ayder to pick up the single daily minibus going up the main Fırtına valley toward Çat without having to return all the way to Pazar, but you'll need to be in Çamlıhemşin by 10am.

Among the half-dozen or so simple **hotels**, the *Otel Cağlayan*, in the upper half of the village—the oldest traditional wooden lodge in Ayder—has the most character. It's also the most used to trekkers, since Kadir Sarı, co-manager and grandson of the original owner, is an experienced local mountain guide (another good local guide is Mehmet Okumuş; PO Box 15, Hemşin, 53550 Pazar, Rize). Beds run $4 per person in double rooms; the staff also do simple but typical Hemşin dishes such as *civil* (a fry-up of butter, cornmeal, and cheese). The *Ayder Hilton* (*sic*—self-rated at four stars), a four-story concrete affair in the village center, charges the same for spartan rooms. If you prefer traditional style (though maybe a bit less comfort), and the *Cağlayan* is full, try the *Otel Saray* on the slope opposite the *Hilton*, or the neighboring *Bahar* and *Çam*, perched opposite the lower baths and the river; nobody's prices will exceed $4 per person.

In terms of **eating and drinking**, the *Hilton* is the big evening hangout; in addition to beer they have brook trout and advertise "stuffed pabes" (stuffed peppers? stuffed babies?) on their menu. Other **restaurants** serving trout are the *Şehir* and the *Viyana*, both slightly down-valley.

None of Ayder's hotels have baths on the premises, let alone attached, since it's expected that you'll patronize one of the village's two **hot springs**. The **downstream hamam**, accessible via a wobbly bridge to the far bank of the river, is open 6 to 9am for men; 9am to 5pm for women; and 5 to 7pm for men again, with the last admission thirty minutes before each changeover. Entrance costs eighty cents; mixed groups are allowed after 7pm by prior arrangement with the attendant. The scalding (close to 135°F) water is directed into a single round pool; descending trekkers will be glad to know that clothes laundering is possible. Not so at the **upper baths** (same hours and fees except men 5–11pm), where washing of any kind is discouraged and the even hotter water fills a rectangular, tiled basking pool.

There's no bank in Ayder, only a rudimentary **PTT** booth where the phone seems always to be out of order.

Hiking

Much the best day-trip from Ayder is the strenuous but rewarding **loop hike** via Hazıntak, Samistal, and Aşağı Kavron *yaylas*. This is not to be undertaken lightly—total elevation changes are 3000 meters—but you can do it in eight walking hours, excluding rest stops. The trail, beginning immediately behind the lower baths, first takes you southwest through maritime cloud forest to HAZINTAK, a handsome cluster just above treeline, and then briefly follows a majestic canyon on a cliff-face route south before veering up and southeast to the primitive rock-and-sod cottages of SAMISTAL. From the ridge above this second *yayla*, weather permitting, you'll have spectacular nose-to-nose views of the main Kaçkar summit ridge; then you face a stiff, zigzag descent east to AŞAĞI KAVRON and the end of the forest road heading north back down to Ayder.

Again, for details on the rest of the Kaçkar, refer to Chapter Ten, p.596.

travel details

Trains
From Samsun to Sivas (1 daily; 11hr).
From Zonguldak to Ankara (1 daily, overnight; 9hr 10min).

Buses
From Samsun to Sinop (3 daily; 2hr 45min); Trabzon (6; 6hr 30min); Amasya (10; 2hr 30min); Sivas (3; 6hr 30min); to Ankara (10; 7hr); to İstanbul (4; 12hr 30min).

From Sinop to Amasra (2; 6hr); Kastamonu (4; 3hr).
From İnebolu to Kastamonu (4; 1hr 30min).
From Amasra to Bartın (half-hourly; 25min); Safranbolu (4; 1hr 45min); Zonguldak (3; 1hr 45min).
From Zonguldak to İstanbul (6; 6hr); Ankara (hourly; 5hr 30min).
From Ordu to Ünye/Samsun (hourly; 1hr 30min/ 2hr 45min); Perşembe (half-hourly; 20min).

From Giresun to Tirebolu (hourly; 45min); Ordu (half-hourly; 30min).

From Trabzon to Samsun (8; 6hr 30min); Rize/ Hopa (hourly; 1hr 20min/3hr); Erzurum (3; 8hr); Bayburt (5; 5hr); Artvin/Kars (2 direct daily; 4hr 30min/12hr); İzmir (4 daily; 22hr); İstanbul (8; 19hr); dolmuş services from Çömlekçi terminal include to Rize (half-hourly; 1hr 20min); Of/ Çaykara to Uzungöl (half-hourly; 1hr/1hr 20min); Giresun (hourly; 2hr 15min).

From Rize to Erzurum via İspir (1–2 daily; 7hr); İspir (5 dolmuşes daily; 4hr); İkizdere (hourly; 1hr).

From Hopa to Artvin (hourly dolmuşes; 1hr 30min); Rize (hourly dolmuşes; 1hr 40min).

Ferries

From Trabzon/Giresun/Samsun/Sinop to İstanbul (weekly Wed/Thur mid-May to mid-Oct; 40hr/34hr/26hr 30min/20hr 30min).

Flights

From Trabzon to Ankara (1 or 2 daily on *THY*; 1hr); İstanbul (1 or 2 daily via Ankara on *THY*, 2–3hr; 4 or 5 weekly, Mon–Fri, on *İstanbul Hava Yolları*; 1hr 20min).

From Samsun to İstanbul (4 weekly with *THT*; 1hr).

CHAPTER TEN

NORTHEASTERN ANATOLIA

B leak, inhospitable and melancholy, **Northeastern Anatolia** is Turkey's Siberia, the Outback and the North Slope rolled into one. Much of it is high, windswept plateau segmented by ranks of eroded mountains that seem barely higher despite impressive altitudes on the map. Four great rivers—the Çoruh, Kura, Aras, and Euphrates (Fırat in Turkish)—rise here, beginning courses taking them to disparate ends in the Black, Caspian, and Persian seas. Their sources almost meet at the forbidding roof of the steppe near Erzurum, but as the rivers descend through warmer canyons and valleys at the edge of the uplands, oases and towns appear, lending much of the interest and attraction of the region.

A great deal of governmental attention, both military and civilian, has since been lavished on the provinces of Kars, Artvin, and Erzurum, which form the heart of the region. But despite ambitious development projects, most of the terrain will never be suited for anything except cultivating grain and sugar beets, or the grazing of livestock. Typically the only garnish you'll get with your kebab is green onions—one of the few salad vegetables able to mature in the short summer. Given the treeless landscape, the making and stacking of cow-dung patties for fuel becomes a conspicuous necessity for villagers unable to buy coal, the pie-pyramids vying in height with the equally ubiquitous haystacks. The harsh, six-month winters often dictate a troglodytic architecture of semi-subterranean burrow-houses—and sometimes an introverted, ungracious mentality to go with it, especially in Kars province, one of the poorest in the country. As a tourist, you'll feel less self-conscious in the relatively prosperous valleys around Yusufeli and Artvin; elsewhere children beg at the roadside under the guise of selling (green and warty) fruit.

Whether you approach from central Anatolia, the extreme southeast of Turkey or the Black Sea, your first stop is likely to be **Erzurum**, long a goal of armies and merchants alike and the only real urban center. Today it's the main jumping-off point to just about anywhere else in the region, with a clutch of post-Selçuk Turkish monuments to briefly distract you. To the northeast, **Kars**, the last major town before the Soviet border, is a dreary disappointment, but is the base for visits to the former Armenian capital of **Ani**, the single biggest tourist attraction in the region. North of Erzurum, the southernmost **valleys of early medieval Georgia**, now part of Turkey, hide nearly a dozen **churches** and almost as many **castles**—enchantingly set, little visited, and arguably the most rewarding targets in the area. The provincial capital of **Artvin** and the pleasant

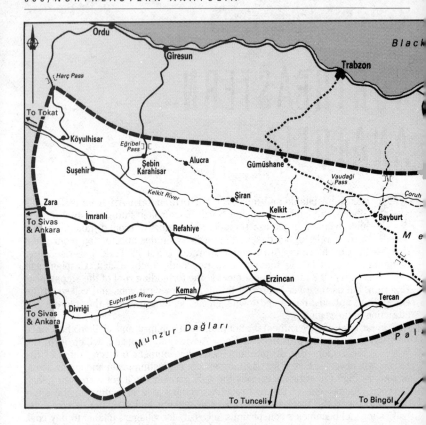

town of **Yusufeli** are the logical overnight stops while in search of Georgian monuments, and Yusufeli is also astride the most popular southern approach to the magnificent **Kaçkar Dağları**, a trekker's paradise that separates northeastern Anatolia from the Black Sea.

Some History

Perhaps because of the discouraging climate and meager resources, this corner of the country was thinly settled until the second millennium BC. The Urartians (see Chapter Twelve) had their northernmost city at today's Altıntepe, near Erzincan, between the ninth and sixth centuries, but the next real imperial power to make an appearance was the Roman Empire, succeeded by the Byzantines and Armenians. The eleventh-century undermining of the Armenian state and the Byzantine rout at Manzikert marked the start of a pattern of invasion and counterattack which was to continue until 1920. The Selçuks, their minor successor emirates and the newly ascendant Georgian kingdom jockeyed for position in the territory until swept aside by Mongol raids of the early thirteenth century, and Tamerlane's juggernaut of the next; the Ottomans finally reasserted some semblance of centralized control early in the sixteenth century.

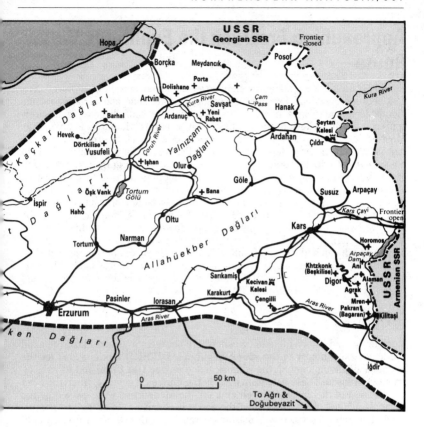

Just as the northeast had been a remote frontier of the Byzantines, so it became the border of the new Anatolian empire, confronting an expansionist Tsarist Russia, which had effectively ended what remained of Georgia's autonomy after 1783. As the Ottomans declined, Russia grew bolder, advancing out of Caucasian fortresses to lop off slices of the region on several occasions during the nineteenth century, although it got to keep its conquests only in 1829 and 1878. Until 1914 nearly half of the sites described in this chapter were under Russian rule, with additional conquests up to 1917 nullified by the Bolshevik Revolution and the collapse of the Caucasian front. Between 1915 and 1921 the area was the scene of almost uninterrupted warfare between White Russian, Armenian Dashnakist, and Turkish Nationalist armies, and massacres among the mixed civilian population which had historically been over a third Armenian and Georgian Christian.

By 1923 the northeast was all but prostrate, with ninety percent of its late Ottoman population dead or dispersed. The present international boundaries between Turkey and the Georgian/Armenian SSRs are the result of treaties between Atatürk and the Soviet Union in March and October 1921, and don't necessarily reflect historical divisions.

Approaching Erzurum: the Euphrates Valley Route

Coming from the west, many travelers cover the lonely stretch of Highway 200/ E88 between Sivas and Erzurum in one day—easily done and certainly recommendable if you're in a hurry. With more time at your disposal, a leisurely approach via the valleys of the Euphrates River and its tributaries is preferable. Most of the countryside between Kangal and Kemah is all but roadless and the railroad is still the only dependable link to the rest of Turkey; during daylight hours a **train trip** through the spectacular, ruddy river gorges, flecked with oases, is certainly the most enjoyable and scenic introduction to northeastern Turkey. The river itself, green and opaque, is warm enough above the giant Keban Dam to support carp—an anomaly in a region famed for trout.

With more advance research and a taste for adventure, you can explore the river even more thoroughly by **kayak** or **raft**, albeit in the opposite direction. The favorite stretch, with highest water between May and July, is the two-day run between Erzincan and Kemah. Continuing farther downstream is complicated by the difficulty of meeting a support vehicle on the largely roadless banks; the next place you could try might be ILIÇ, another two days' float beyond Kemah and accessible via a side road from REFAHIYE, on the E23.

Divriği

Stuck in the middle of a mountainous nowhere between Sivas and Elâzığ, on a hill overlooking a tributary of the young Euphrates, **DİVRİĞİ** merits a visit for the sake of a single monument, the whimsical and unique **Ulu Cami** and its subsidiary the Darüşşifa. These date from early in the thirteenth century, when the town was the seat of the tiny Mengüçeh emirate; the Mengüçehs were evicted by the Mongols in 1252, who demolished the castle here but left the religious foundations alone, and the place was not incorporated into the Ottoman Empire until 1516.

The main drawbacks to stopping in Divriği are the poor hotels and the limited number of options for moving on— the schedules virtually dictate an overnight stay. You'll probably arrive from either Sivas or Erzurum if you're relying on public transportation; there are no links with Elâzığ, and in any case it's most pleasant to come and go by train.

The Town

Divriği is sleepy, though dependent on the nearby iron and steel works, with a ramshackle bazaar crisscrossed by cobbled lanes and grapevines. Architecturally the town sports distinctive wooden **minarets** and old houses with inverted-keyhole windows, neither of which are seen elsewhere in Anatolia. The conspicuous **Ulu Cami** and the **Darüşşifa** (sanitorium), joined in one complex at the top of a slope 250m east of town, command a fine view. The mosque, dedicated in 1228 by a certain Ahmet Şah, is noted for its outrageous external **portals**, most un-Islamic with their wealth of floral and faunal detail. Rather far-fetched comparisons have been made to Indian Mogul art but a simpler, more likely explanation is that Armenian and Georgian craftsmen had a hand in the decoration. The north door, festooned with vegetal designs, is the most celebrated, although the northwestern one is more intricately worked—note the pair of double-headed eagles, not necessarily copied from the Byzantines since it's a very old Anatolian motif. Inside, sixteen columns and the ceiling they support are more suggestive of a Gothic cloister or a Byzantine cistern; there's rope-vaulting in one dome, while the northeastern one, at least until it's renovated, sports a peanut-brittle surface, in terms of both the relief work and variegated coloring, although the central dome has been rather tastelessly restored. The *mihrab* is plain, flanked by a more extravagant carved wooden *mimber*.

The adjoining **Darüşşifa**—or *Şifa Evi* in modern Turkish—was also begun in 1228, by Adaletli Melike Turan Melek, Ahmet Şah's wife. Its **portal** is restrained in comparison to the other two, but still bears medallions lifted almost free from their background. The gate itself is usually locked, so you have to find the caretaker to gain admission—easiest just after prayers next door. A $1 donation is requested after signing the guest register at the conclusion of the tour.

The caretaker proudly points out some of the more arcane features of the interior, which is asymmetrical in both floorplan and ornamentation, and even more eclectic than the mosque. Of four dissimilar columns surrounding a **fountain**, two are embossed; the eight-sided pool has an curlicue drain hole as well as two more conventional feeder spouts. Overhead, the dome has collapsed and been crudely replaced in the same manner as the mosque's, but four-pointed **stellar vaulting** graces the entry hall, with even more elaborate ribbing over a raised platform in the *eyvan* at the rear of the nave. The fan-reliefs on the wall behind this once formed an elaborate **sundial**, catching rays through the second-floor window of the facade; it's claimed that the suspended carved cylinder in front of this opening once revolved, though it's unclear how this helped the sundial function—perhaps there was a prism mounted in it. Musicians may once have played on the raised platform to entertain the patients, whose rather pokey bedrooms on both the ground and upper floors you're allowed to visit. One of the side rooms contains the **tombs** of Ahmet Şah and his father Sükeyman Şah.

Practical Details

The **train station**, connected with Ankara and Erzurum, is down by the river, a twenty-minute walk from the bazaar; taxis meet most arrivals, and don't cost more than a couple of dollars. The **otogar**, essentially a dirt parking lot with four or five daily departures to Sivas only, is 400m south of town on the road to Elâzığ; there's a **hamam** on the way there, which you may need to use if you spend the night here. The only two **hotels** stand across from each other on the main commercial street west of the inner bazaar: the depressingly basic *Ninni* asks $4 a single, $5.50 a double for passably clean rooms with a single hot shower on the first floor; its neighbor the *Diğer* offers still less value for money. **Eating** is a little better, with one *kebap salonu* and an oven-food place near the hotels; the *Ücler Pide Salonu* in the bazaar; and the *Belediye Restaurant* on the main square, below the Mengüçeh monuments.

The Upper Euphrates Valley

In addition to the long-distance expresses, a local "milk run" train sets out most days at 5:15am to Erzincan. If you don't mind the risk of being stranded for half a day, you might get off at **KEMAH**, a historic town perched over another picturesque reach of river. There's a complex of **tombs** from different eras perched above the river, and a huge Byzantine-Selçuk **castle**, in better shape than Divriği's, with cellars to explore. The place is even smaller than Divriği, however, and can muster just a few tiny shops and one unmarked, rudimentary hotel. Except on weekends, **dolmuşes** along the paved 50km to Erzincan are fairly regular.

Kemah used to be a trailhead for treks across the **Munzur Dağları**, which tower snow-streaked above the Euphrates' south bank, but there have supposedly been Kurdish-related troubles of late, and if you inform the *jandarma* post of your intention to climb you may be prevented from doing so. **ALPKÖY**, twenty minutes farther east along the tracks, is a better place to start—nobody will stop you here, and a giant canyon leading straight up to the heart of the mountains is very close to the station.

ERZİNCAN, once one of the most elegant cities in Turkey, with several Armenian monuments on the outskirts and dozens of mosques and *medreses* in the town, was devastated by earthquakes in 1939 and again in 1983. There's therefore no reason to linger longer than the time it takes to change buses or trains, with frequent connections on to Erzurum. Roughly halfway there, near the head of the Euphrates Valley, you might—with your own transportation—consider breaking the journey at **TERCAN**, graced by a **türbe**, **kervansaray**, and **bridge** built by the Saltuk emirs of Erzurum at the beginning of the thirteenth century. The tomb in particular is bizarre, consisting of a lobed and cone-headed cylinder enclosed in a richly decorated circular boundary wall, a design found elsewhere only in Soviet Turkestan.

Erzurum

Nearly 2000m up, its horizons defined by mountains a thousand meters above, and rocked by frequent earthquakes, **ERZURUM** is Turkey's highest and most exposed city. Because of a strategic location astride the main trade routes to Persia, the Caucausus, and western Anatolia, its sovereignty has always been contested, with the list of occupying armies reading like a Who's Who of Middle Eastern imperial powers. Today it's still a major garrison town of over a quarter of a million people, the military flavor blended with an almost stifling religous conservatism, with most women wearing gunny-sackish *çarşafs* (full-length robes with hoods and veils) in the same dun color as the surrounding steppes—and, in case you're slow to get the message the Muslim credo, *La ilaha ilallah* (There is no god but Allah), is spelled out in colored light bulbs over the main street. All told, the combination of history, climate, and earthquakes has resulted in a bleak, much-rebuilt place where sunlight seems wan even in midsummer, and where the hopefully landscaped, broad modern boulevards often end abruptly and literally in the middle of nowhere.

After years as a transit stop for overlanders on the way to Iran, Afghanistan, and India, mass tourism is just beginning in Erzurum. The city is increasingly used as a base and staging point by mountaineering expeditions bound for the Kaçkar Dağları and Ağrı Dağ, but it also deserves a full day in itself to see a compact group of very early Turkish monuments. In step with the growing number of foreign visitors, rug shops and hustlers have made their appearance near the more celebrated sites, but in general the townspeople are genuinely friendly.

Some History

Although the site had been occupied for centuries before, a city only rose to prominence here toward the end of the fourth century AD, when the Byzantine emperor Theodosius fortified the place and renamed it **Theodosiopolis**. Over the next 500 years the town changed hands frequently between Constantinople and assorted Arab dynasties, with a short period of Armenian rule.

After the Battle of Manzikert in 1071, Erzurum—a corruption of **Arz-er-Rum** or "Domain of the Byzantines" in Arabic—fell into the hands of first the Selçuks and then the Saltuk clan of Turks. These were in turn displaced by the İlhanid Mongols during the fourteenth century, forerunners of Tamerlane himself, who used the city as a springboard for his brief barnstorming of western Anatolia.

Erzurum was incorporated into the Ottoman Empire by Selim the Grim in 1515, where it remained securely until 1828, after which the Russians occupied it on three occasions. With the memory of the last Russian tenure (1916–17) still fresh in their minds, and the city now held by renegade General Karabekir, supporters of the Nationalists convened a landmark **Congress** here in July 1919, at which the present borders of the Turkish Republic were put forth as the minimum acceptable.

The Erzurum **area telephone code** is ☎011.

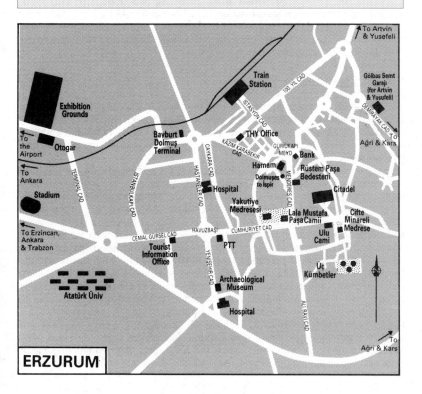

Arrival and Information

Erzurum has two bus terminals: the main long-distance **otogar**, almost 3km northwest of the center, and the **Gölbaşı Semt Garajı**, for buses to most points northeast of Erzurum, more conveniently situated just over 1km northeast of downtown. Many, though by no means all, long-distance buses stop at both stations—when it's time to **leave Erzurum**, make sure you know where your vehicle is starting from, which is easily enough checked when buying tickets at either the terminals or the numerous downtown ticket offices.

The **train station**, just over 1km directly north of the city center, is the most convenient of Erzurum's transport facilities, and also close to a major concentration of inexpensive accommodation.

If you fly into the **airport**, 10km northeast of town at the end of the same road serving the otogar, try to catch the *THY* bus ($1) into town—a taxi will set you back $5.

From the otogar a taxi fare to the city center won't exceed $2, and, aside from walking, **taxis** are really the way to get around Erzurum. There are *belediye* **buses**—particularly the #2 which links the otogar with Cumhuriyet Caddesi, the main east–west thoroughfare—but it's tedious to hunt down ticket sales points, and taxi stands are literally everywhere.

The **tourist information office** (daily June–Aug 8am–7pm; Sept–May Mon–Fri 8am–5pm; ☎15697) is on the south side of Cemal Gürsel Caddesi, 200m west of Havuzbaşı, a helpful establishment where there's normally someone who speaks English. On winter weekends there is usually a caretaker on duty who can dish out basic city maps and glossy brochures.

Finding a Place to Stay

The supply of **accommodation** in Erzurum usually exceeds demand, and in general the emphasis is on serviceable, mid-range **hotels**, with nothing horribly expensive or astoundingly cheap. If you're on a long haul overland, it's wise to break the journey here, since there's nowhere else as good to stay for hundreds of kilometers.

Several good choices line **Kâzım Karabekir Caddesi**, handy for the *THY* office and the train station, although all of them are plagued to a certain extent by traffic noise. Also be aware that the street-numbering scheme here has only recently changed and former numbers are often still posted. At the top of the street, at no. 9, just opposite the Gürcü Kapı, the *Hotel Buhara* is the best value and quietest in the area, offering comfortable singles with bath for $7.50 and doubles for $12; despite popularity with adventure-travel groups there are generally vacancies. The *Hitit Otel* at no. 26 (☎11204), a hangover from the days of the Hippy Trail to India, is about as rough and ready as you'd want to try, although passably clean, used to foreigners, and friendly—prices range from $4 for a single without bath to $12 for a double with attached bath. The *Otel Yeni San*, at no. 23 (☎15789), represents a substantial notch up in both comfort and price at $12 a single, $16 a double for attached facilities. The hotel plans to raise its prices and court tour groups in the future, and diverts solo travelers to its somewhat overpriced ($16 for single with bath) annex, the *Hotel İpek*—a green building within sight of the train station that is really only for late, desperate train arrivals.

The area immediately **south of Cumhuriyet Caddesi** is another good hunting ground for relatively quiet hotels. One block east of the PTT, the *Otel Emre* (☎37725) is a satisfactory budget option at $6 single, $8 double, with $1.50 extra for a shower down the hall. Closer to Erzurum's historic monuments—and identically priced at $11 single, $15 double with attached bath—are the *Otel Kral*, Erzincankapı 18, near the southwest corner of the central park (☎16973) and the *Otel Akçay*, Kâmil Ağa Sokak, off Cumhuriyet Caddesi 2 (☎17330). Both are comfortable enough and you can't get more central.

The City

All features of interest in Erzurum are along—or just off—Cumhuriyet Caddesi, and a leisurely tour shouldn't take more than half a day. Start at what is the de facto city park, a landscaped area with benches around the **Yakutiye Medresesi**. This was begun in 1310 by Hoca Yakut, a local governor of the İlhanid Mongols, and with its intricately worked portal, and truncated minaret featuring a knotted lattice of tilework, is easily the most fanciful building in town. The minaret in particular seems displaced from somewhere in Central Asia or Persia—not so far-fetched when you learn that the İlhanids had their seat in Tabriz. As of spring 1991 you'll be able to see the interior, since it's scheduled to open as a new ethnographic museum. A *türbe* at the east end of the building was apparently intended for Yakut but never used. Just behind the tomb squats the uninspiring, mid-sixteenth-century **Lala Mustafa Paşa Camii**; it was supposedly designed by the famous Sinan (see Chapter One, "İstanbul") but you'd never know it.

Continuing east about 300m along Cumhuriyet Caddesi, you pass the **Ulu Cami**, erected in 1179 by the third in the line of Saltuk emirs. Like most mosques of that age, it's a big square hall with dozens of columns supporting bare vaults; the one note of fancy is the central skylight, led up to by a wedding cake of stalactite vaulting. At the *mihrab* the orderly rows of columns—seven aisles by six of them—break up, yielding to an odd wooden dome built of overlapping timbers and pierced by two round windows.

Immediately adjacent stands the **Çifte Minareli Medrese**, the purported main tourist attraction in Erzurum but frankly overrated. The name—meaning "double minareted"—derives from the most conspicuous feature of the seminary, which is best admired from the park in front, although you'll be moved on by the guard if you loiter on the lawn. There is some dispute about the structure's vintage, but the majority opinion holds that Hüdavênd Hatun, daughter of the Selçuk sultan Alâeddin Keykubad II, commissioned it in 1253, making it a contemporary of the similar Gök Medrese in Sivas (see Chapter Eight, "North Central Anatolia"). In conception the Çifte Minareli was the boldest and largest theological academy of its time, but sadly it was never finished. The stalactite portal, beneath the grooved and spiral-tiled towers, gives onto a vast, bare courtyard, with stairways at the front corners leading to an upper story of cells. At the rear looms an unusual cylindrical or *kümbet*-style tomb, thought to be that of the foundress; the sarcophagus, which may be empty, lies in a separate subterranean chamber below the dome.

A cluster of less enigmatic mausoleums, the **Üç Kümbetler**, graces yet another small park about 250m directly south. The oldest of the three tombs, and the most interesting, is probably that of the first Saltuk emir and dates from the early twelfth century; its octagonal base of alternating light and dark stone breached by half-oval windows demonstrates the mutual influence of Georgian, Armenian, and early Turkish architecture. The other two *kümbets* in the ensemble date from at least a century later and aren't nearly as interesting.

On the opposite side of Cumhuriyet Caddesi from the Çifte Minareli Medrese, a narrow lane leads past some of the oldest houses in town to the signposted **Erzurum Kalesi** (daily 8am–noon & 1:30–6pm; 50¢), whose vast rectangular bulk was originally laid out by Theodosius. The interior is bare except for a shoe-box-like *mescit*, or chapel, capped by an afterthought of a dome, and a free-standing minaret, now a bell tower. Stairs on the east side lead up to the ramparts, and while the citadel is no longer the highest point in town since Erzurum began to spread to its rim of hills, it still lends the best view over the city—and the even greater, intimidating vastness of the plateau beyond.

Just northeast of the castle, but easiest reached by retracing your steps along Cumhuriyet Caddesi to Menderes Caddesi, is the **Rüstem Paşa Bedesteni**, or covered bazaar, endowed by Süleyman the Magnificent's mid-sixteenth-century grand vizier. Today it's almost totally given over to commerce in **oltutaşı**, an obsidian-like material mined near Oltu, 150km northeast. This is most frequently made into *tespih* (prayer beads) and *küpe* (earrings), and the former are a common sight throughout northeastern Turkey. Prices start at about $6 for a tiny, 10cm *tespih*; silver clasps cost $2 to $3 extra. Earrings go for anywhere between $4 and $11, depending on the size and number of stones, but most importantly whether the setting is gold or silver.

Remotest and least compelling of Erzurum's sights is the **archaeological museum** (daily except Mon 8:30am–noon & 1:30–5:30pm; $1), 400m south of Havuzbaşı. The ground floor is taken up by assorted Urartu and Caucasian pottery, plus some Roman and Hellenistic glassware and jewelry. On the upper floor, recently vacated by the ethnographic collection, is a fairly lame "massacre room," containing items recently removed from two mass graves in the province—the property, it is claimed, of Turks slaughtered by Armenians between 1915 and 1918.

Eating and Drinking

Restaurants in Erzurum aren't numerous, but they tend to be good value, with a concentration of sorts on or around Cumhuriyet Caddesi and the central park. Some of the fancier places like to style themselves as "salons"—for example the *Salon Çağın* and the *Salon Asya*, across from each other on Cumhuriyet Caddesi 150m west of the Yukutiye Medresesi. The former seems dingily subterranean but the food's good, with *mantı* on Sunday and trout daily in summer; a big meal will set you back $6 or $7. Its rival has no fish but the service is equally good and the decor cheerier. If you want **alcohol** with your food in this conservative town, you'll have to patronize the *Güzelyurt Restaurant*, directly across from the Yakutiye Medresesi on Cumhuriyet Caddesi. It looks expensive, but unless you intend to hit the wine and *rakı* it's difficult to spend more than $5 or $6. The *Park Pide Salonu*, immediately west of the *medrese* on the side street leading north from Cumhuriyet, is minuscule but serves excellent, cheap *pides*. The closest thing to a **café** in Erzurum is the *Kafe Kandil*, directly across from *Salon Asya*, where students and soldiers kill spare moments.

Listings

Airport bus Departs from in front of the *THY* office on Yüz Yıl Caddesi 90min before each flight, with a stop at the otogar en route.

Car rental *Avis*, Terminal Cad 12/A (☎18715).

Cirit This is a sort of cross between polo and warfare, with the players on horseback eliminating opponents from the field by thrusts of a blunted javelin. Ask at the tourist information office during spring and summer if a tournament is scheduled nearby.

Exchange The only relatively efficient bank that accepts travelers' checks is the main branch of *Türk Ticaret Bankası*, near the Gürcü Kapı traffic circle at the top of İstasyon Caddesi. Avoid the truly hopeless banks up on Cumhuriyet Caddesi.

Hamam *Erzurum Hamamı*, at the Gürcü Kapı end of İstasyon Caddesi (daily 6am–10:30pm, $2; men only except by prior arrangement).

Hospitals One north, one south of Havuzbaşı on the same boulevard.

Newspapers English-language publications are sold only at *Kültürsarayı*, Cumhuriyet Cad 38, although the stock is limited to week-old magazines and *Turkish Daily News*.

Skiing A possible consolation for being stuck here in winter is the Palandöken ski area, 6km away, which is supposed to be the best in the country. The single hotel and chairlift operate between December and April.

THY office Yüz Yıl Caddesi, SSK Rant Tesisleri no. 24 (☎18530).

Northwest of Erzurum: Citadels on the Çoruh River

Heading west, and then northwest, out of Erzurum toward the Black Sea, you'll follow either of two roads away from the truck route to Ankara. One, currently in a deplorable state (see Chapter Nine, "The Black Sea"), follows the old Silk Route to Trabzon via **Bayburt**; the other leads to Rize via **İspır**. After scaling the first range of peaks beyond Erzurum, both routes drop dizzyingly from 2300-meter passes to the **Çoruh River**, which flows through a deep trench well below the level of the Anatolian plateau. This remote valley, reminscent of deeper central Asia or the American southwest, was the ancestral homeland of the Bagratid clan (see below, "The Southern Georgian Valleys"), which went on to supply early medieval Armenia and Georgia with so many of their rulers.

Bayburt

BAYBURT is dwarfed by the largest **fortress** in Turkey, its history virtually synonymous with the town. Thought to have been erected during the sixth century during Justinian's skirmishes with the Laz tribe from the Black Sea, it was later appropriated by the Bagratids, until being taken and renovated by the Saltuk Turks early in the thirteenth century. The citadel was a much-coveted prize in the Russo-Turkish wars of this and the last century, so it's something of a miracle that the perimeter walls are in such good condition—although this isn't true of the interior, where there's not much to see aside from the view.

Little else redeems Bayburt other than its position astride the young Çoruh, best enjoyed at one of several riverside **restaurants** or **cafés** with views of the castle thrown in. There are **mosques** founded by Saltuk Turks and the İlhanid

Mongol governor Yakut (he of the *medrese* in Erzurum) but these fall squarely in the category of time-filling exercises, and the main reason to pause here is to break a journey between Trabzon and Erzurum; otherwise content yourself with a glance at the fort in transit.

Practical Details

Bayburt's small **otogar** is 500m south of the town center on the main highway, but buses to and from Erzurum often begin and end in the bazaar. If you need to **stay**, your best bets are two hotels on Cumhuriyet Caddesi, the main drag aiming right for the castle. The *Saracoğlu* at no. 13 (☎0291/1217) offers $5.50 singles and $9.50 doubles with attached showers (bathrooms down the hall). The *Sevil*, two doors down, is much the same.

Eating out, the enclosed *Yeni Zafer*, next to the central vehicle bridge over the Çoruh, is more appealing in winter, but the *Çoruh Lokantası* upstream, with riverbank seating, has the edge in the warm months. For summer dessert, good ice cream is dispensed on the riverside between the two.

İspir

İSPİR once rivaled Bayburt in importance, but now it has sadly declined. The setting, overlooking a bend of the Çoruh, with a monument-crowned acropolis, promises much but doesn't deliver. There's not even a proper gate left to the Bagratid **castle**, which hardly rewards a climb through the town's shanties; inside there's a squat, little-used mosque from the Saltuk era, and a badly ruined Byzantine church. The town itself is shabby, and the only foreigners passing through are those on rafting trips on the Çoruh. And the **hotels and restaurants** are among the worst in Turkey, so it's a good idea to avoid getting stuck. Least loathsome of the three places to stay is the *Arı* on the main street.

If you've arrived by bus from Rize on the way to Erzurum, or vice versa, you can get an onward bus the same day as long as you've made an early start. It's safest, though, to get a through service. If you deliberately get off here, the most interesting thing to do if you're not waterborne is to cover the rough but scenic 75km of dirt road to Yusufeli (see below, "Yusufeli and Around")—this can sometimes be done by public transportation, but more often than not by thumb.

Northeast of Erzurum: the Way to Kars

Convoys of trucks clog the most heavily traveled route beyond Erzurum, bound for both Iran and the USSR. **PASİNLER**, 40km along, is distinguished only by the crumbled citadel of **Hasankale**, originally a Bagratid stronghold taken over by the Akkoyun Turcomans during the fifteenth century. Twenty kilometers east, the graceful **Çobandede Bridge**, the finest medieval bridge in Turkey, attributed to Sinan, spans the Aras River near the beginning of its course. The road, railroad, and the river stick together until HORASAN, where the highway to Iran—via Ağrı and Doğubeyazit—peels off to the southeast, and the train tracks meander north.

Soon the river forsakes the Kars trunk road to start a sharp descent toward the Caspian Sea. The next place of any consequence, nestled among an unexpected forest of conifers, is **SARIKAMIŞ**, subject to the coldest climate in the country. The winter of 1914–15 proved lethal here for the Ottoman Third Army under the command of the megalomaniac Enver Paşa, when, in one of the worst Turkish defeats of World War I, 75,000 men froze to death or were killed attempting to halt a Tsarist force of roughly equal size; in the wake of the debacle the Russians advanced to Erzurum and beyond. Today the heavy seasonal snow supports a new and reportedly very good **ski area**, and accordingly there's a **motel**, the *Sartur*, which is the only decent place to stay on this stretch.

Beyond Sarıkamış, the scenery becomes humdrum again as the mountains level out onto the high, grassy steppes surrounding Kars. About 10km before Kars, 300m west of the road near the village of **KÜMBETLİ**, you'll see the partly crumbled Armenian church of **Kümbet Kilise**, the first of various Armenian monuments in the province.

Kars

Hidden in a natural basin by the banks of the Kars Çayı, **KARS** is arguably the most depressing town in Turkey. Although a couple of hundred meters lower than Erzurum, the climate is even more severe; the local economy is stagnant, with more street beggars in evidence than perhaps anywhere else in the country; and to top matters off hotels are substandard and overpriced. There are a few sites in town worth dallying for, but most visitors make the long trek out here for the express purpose of visiting the former Armenian capital of **Ani**. Unfortunately Kars will probably continue to take this business for granted without improving its tourist facilities.

Some History

Originally founded by the Armenians, Kars became the capital of their Bagratid dynasty early in the tenth century, when the citadel that still dominates the town was substantially improved. Later in that century the main seat of Armenian rule was transferred to nearby Ani, and Kars lost some of its importance, though the Selçuks took it along with almost everything else in the area during the mid-eleventh century. Devastating Mongol raids made a mockery of any plans the new overlords had for the place, and in 1205 the Georgians, profiting from the wane of both Selçuk and Byzantine power in the area, seized the town and held it for three centuries until displaced by the Ottomans.

Kars defends the approaches to Erzurum just as the latter is the key to the rest of Anatolia. The Russians tried repeatedly during the nineteenth century to capture the place; sieges of 1828 and 1855 were successful—the latter during the Crimean War, when a British-Turkish garrison was starved out of the citadel after five months—but on both occasions Kars reverted to Turkey by the terms of peace treaties. Not so in 1878, when after a bloody eight-month war between the two powers, Kars was finally awarded to the tsar. It remained in Russian hands until 1920, a period which bequeathed both the unusual grid layout of the city center and the incongruous *belle époque* buildings found here. Today Kars is, not surprisingly, still a major forward military position, swarming with soldiers.

Arrival and Information

The **otogar** is on the northeast side of town, on Küçük Kâzım Bey Caddesi, within walking distance of most points of interest; the **train station** is less convenient, well to the southeast off Cumhuriyet Caddesi on the way to the museum and the road to Ani.

Staff at the **tourist information office** on Ali Bey Caddesi, 100m southeast of Faik Bey Caddesi (daily 8:30am–5:30pm, ☎021/12300), worn down by the onerous task of processing Ani-visit applications, aren't very friendly, know next to nothing about anything else in the province, and speak little English to boot. City maps are usually out of stock, and it's difficult to say whether two available booklets, entitled "Kars" and "Ani," are more hilarious for their pidgin English than offensive for their abuse of historical truth.

Finding a Place to Stay

Accommodation in Kars is a dismal subject. Everything is expensive for what it is, and service often leaves much to be desired. The nominally budget hotels lining Faik Bey Caddesi are best left to the imagination, if the so-called "mid-range" establishments are anything to go by. The most basic acceptable place is the *Asya Oteli*, Küçük Kâzım Bey Caddesi 48 (☎021/12299), where doubles with bath go for $12, a few without for $10, plus a handful of singles for $6. New carpets and a paint job can't hide the many defects, but bargaining is tough since it's a sellers' market. The next notch up is filled by the nearby *Temel*, Yeni Pazar Sokak 4/A (☎021/11376), where singles with bath go for $12, doubles for $20, but again it costs nearly twice what it should. For the same price you're probably better off at the less favorably positioned but marginally friendlier *Yılmaz*, Küçük Kâzım Bey Caddesi 24 (☎021/11074), directly across from the otogar. The only relief in sight is the imminent opening of the *Paşa Motel* 2km out of town, but this still won't solve the problem of a decent room for the money within the city limits.

The Town

The Russian grid plan makes **central Kars** easy to navigate: the most important east–west streets, in addition to Cumhuriyet Caddesi and Küçük Kâzım Bey Caddesi, are **Faik Bey Caddesi**, essentially the continuation of the Erzurum–Armenian SSR highway, and **Halit Paşa Caddesi**, which contains many of Kars' restaurants. Lined with both humble and grandiose Russian structures, **Atatürk Caddesi** and **Kâzım Paşa Caddesi** lead approximately south–north to the river, on the far bank of which huddles the medieval settlement—now to all intents and purposes a shantytown.

Most items of interest cluster near this district, a few hundred meters north of the modern downtown area. The **Church of the Holy Apostles**, just the other side of the Kars Çayı on the way to the castle, was erected between 930 and 937 by the Armenian king Abbas I. Crude reliefs of the Twelve Apostles adorn the rim of the dome, but otherwise it's a squat, functional bulk of dark basalt; the belfry and portico are relatively recent additions. A church when Christians held Kars, a mosque when Muslims ruled, it briefly housed the town museum before becoming the locked warehouse of today.

Before climbing the short distance to the castle, detour slightly up the tributary of the Kars Çayı to see the **Taş Köprü**, or Stone Bridge, made of the same volcanic rock as the nearby church and restored during the 1580s by order of

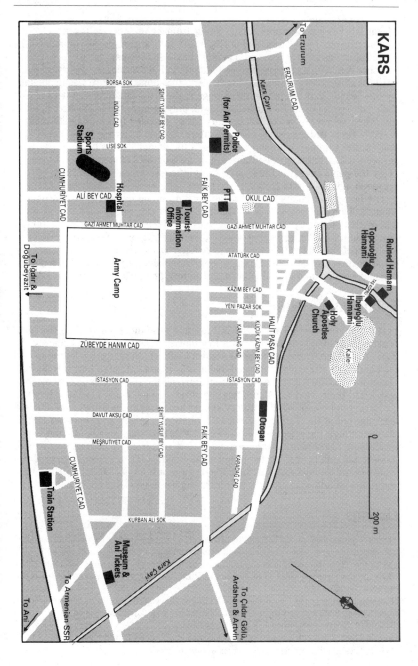

KARS

To Erzurum

ERZURUM CAD

Kars Çayı

BORSA SOK

İNÖNÜ CAD

ŞEHİT YUSUF BEY CAD

LİSE SOK

Sports Stadium

CUMHURİYET CAD

ALİ BEY CAD

Hospital

GAZİ AHMET MUHTAR CAD

FAİK BEY CAD

Tourist Information Office

Police (for Ani Permits)

PTT

OKUL CAD

GAZİ AHMET MUHTAR CAD

Topçuoğlu Hamamı

Ruined Hamam

ATATÜRK CAD

İlbeyoğlu Hamamı

KÂZIM BEY CAD

YENİ PAZAR SOK

Holy Apostles Church

Army Camp

HALİT PAŞA CAD

KÜÇÜK KÂZIM BEY CAD

KARADAĞ CAD

Kale

To Iğdır & Doğubeyazit

ZÜBEYDE HANIM CAD

İSTASYON CAD

İSTASYON CAD

DAVUT AKSU CAD

ŞEHİT YUSUF BEY CAD

MEŞRUTİYET CAD

FAİK BEY CAD

KARADAĞ CAD

Otogar

CUMHURİYET CAD

Train Station

KURBAN ALİ SOK

Museum & Ani Tickets

Kars Çayı

To Armenian SSR

To Ani

To Çıldır Gölü, Ardahan & Artvin

0   200 m

Murat III. Several **hamams**, none dating from before the eighteenth century, huddle nearby: the still-functioning **İlbeyoğlu**, the **Mazlutağa** (in ruins), and the **Topcuoğlu** (also still in use; see "Listings" below for details).

There has been a fortress of some kind on the hill overlooking the river confluence for close to two millennia. The Armeno-Byzantine structure was maintained by the Selçuks but leveled by the Mongols; the Ottomans repaired it as part of their late sixteenth-century urban renewal, only to have the Russians blast it to bits, then rebuild it in the last century. After decades as an off-limits military reserve, **Kars Kalesi**, as it's officially known, is open as a park from 9am to 7pm daily in the summer, with shorter hours in the winter. Locals come to pay their respects at the tomb of Celal Baba, a holy man of the fourteenth century, and to enjoy the panorama over Kars, but there's little else to see aside from the black-masoned military engineering.

The only other compelling attraction in Kars is the excellent **town museum** (daily 8:30am–5:30pm; $1), a fifteen-minute walk out to the east end of town, where the ethnographic section includes such curiosities as a *yayık* (butter churn) and a cradle, as well as jewelry, leatherwork, and extensive exhibits on local carpets and kilims. Downstairs is devoted to ancient pottery and ecclesiastical artifacts of the departed Russians and Armenians, particularly a huge church bell and wooden doors which graced one of the cathedrals before 1920.

Eating and Drinking

Fortunately the **restaurant** scene in Kars is a little more varied than the hotel prospects, although there are still a few tourist traps to avoid—specifically the *Şamdan* and the *Grand Manolya* on Atatürk Caddesi, where the bill for indifferent food and drink can equal or exceed that at the smartest Aegean resort. Halit Paşa Caddesi constitutes a sort of Restaurant Row; all the places listed serve alcohol, and with their wooden floors and civilized decor once matched Russian-Caucasian notions of what an eatery should be. Local businessmen and dignitaries hang out at the *Yeşilyurt* at no. 113, where the grilled and prepared food is okay, although the prices are a bit steep; try *kaymak* (clotted cream) and honey for dessert. The *Kristal Lokantası* at no. 101, across from the *İş Bankası*, is more modest but offers just as tasty fare, and the *Konak* and *Gemik*, east of the *Yeşilyurt*, are comparable. For **breakfast**, there are lots of places on Halit Paşa and Atatürk Caddesi near the otogar featuring the famous Kars honey.

Listings

Airline Contact *THT* at ☎021/19699 for information on twice-weekly flights to Ankara, and transfers to the newly opened civilian section of the military airport.

Exchange Try *not* to do this in Kars; in any case it's virtually impossible before 10:30am, when the day's rate is wired in from Ankara. *İş Bankası* might serve you earlier—but will extract a $5 commission.

Hamams Both near the Taş Köprü: the *Muradiye* (İlbeyoğlu) is open to men 8am–10am, women noon–6pm, and men again 6–11pm; admission $1.75. The *Topcuoğlu* on the far side of the bridge is for women only.

Hospital Near the south end of Okul Caddesi, corner of İnönü Caddesi.

PTT On Okul Caddesi; phone section open around the clock.

Ani

Once the capital of Bagratid Armenia, **ANİ** is today a melancholy, almost vacant triangular plateau, separated from the Armenian SSR by the Arpa Çayı (Ahuryan River) and very nearly from the rest of Turkey by two deep tributaries. It's mainly an expanse of rubble, but among this rise some of the finest examples of ecclesiastical and military architecture of its time. The Armenians were master stoneworkers, and the fortifications that defend the northern, exposed side of the plateau, and the handful of churches behind, are exquisite compositions in a blend of ruddy sandstone and darker volcanic rock. These, and the cliffs fringing the river, are the only vertical features here, dwarfed by an evocative but relentlessly horizontal landscape. Low hills on the Soviet side and muddy Turkish pastures sprawl alike under a luminous summer sky chased by clouds. It is worth putting up with the deficiencies of Kars for a night or two to make the trip out, and inconceivable that you'd venture east of Erzurum or Artvin without fitting Ani into your plans.

Some History

There was a settlement here since before Christian times, based around the citadel near the southern tip of the plateau; the name Ani is possibly a corruption of "Anahit," a Persian equivalent of Aphrodite who was one of the chief deities of the pagan Armenians. The city first came to prominence after the local installment of the Armenian Gamsarkan clan during the fifth century. Situated astride a major east–west caravan route, Ani prospered, receiving fresh impetus when Ashot III, fifth in the line of the Bagratid kings of Armenia, transferred his capital here from Kars in 961. For three subsequent generations the kingdom and its capital, under the successive rule of Ashot, Smbat II, and Gagik I, enjoyed a golden age. Beautified and strengthened militarily, with a population exceeding 100,000, Ani rivaled Bagdhad and Constantinople themselves.

By the middle of the eleventh century, however, wars of succession and the religiously motivated enmity of the Byzantines took their toll. The latter, having neutralized Bagratid power, annexed the city in 1045, but in the process they dissolved an effective bulwark against the approaching Selçuks, who took Ani with little resistance in 1064. After the collapse of the Selçuks, the Armenians returned in less than a century, this time with the assistance of the powerful Georgian kingdom. The Pahlavuni and Zakhariad clans ruled over a reduced but still semi-independent Armenia for two more centuries, continuing to endow Ani with churches and monasteries. The Mongol raids of the thirteenth century, a devasting earthquake in 1319, and realigned trade routes proved mortal blows to both Ani and its hinterland; thereafter the city was gradually abandoned, and forgotten until the last century.

Practical Details

Because of its location in a restricted zone (see below), Ani (daily 8:30am–5pm) would ordinarily be closed to visits, but in view of its artistic and historical interest both the Soviet and Turkish governments have made an exception. You'll still need a permit, routinely granted and requiring less than an hour to issue. Fill in a form at the Kars tourist information office, have this endorsed at the Security

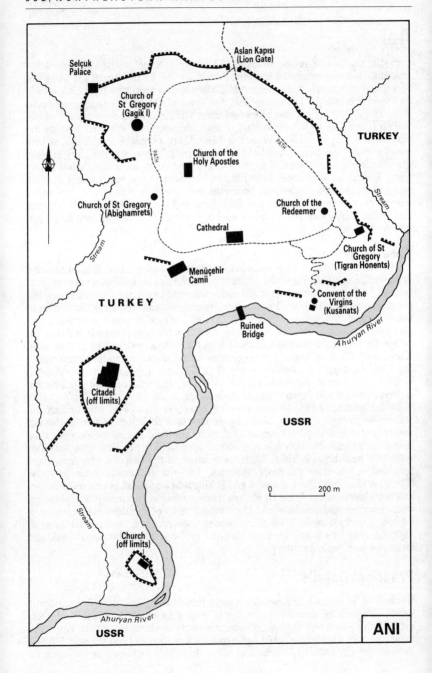

Selçuk Palace

Aslan Kapısı
(Lion Gate)

Church of
St Gregory
(Gagik I)

TURKEY

PATH

PATH

Church of the
Holy Apostles

Church of St Gregory
(Abighamrets)

Church of the
Redeemer

Cathedral

Church of St
Gregory
(Tigran Honents)

Menüçehir
Camii

TURKEY

Convent of the
Virgins
(Kusanats)

Ruined
Bridge

Ahuryan River

Stream

Stream

Citadel
(off limits)

USSR

0   200 m

Church
(off limits)

Ahuryan River

USSR

ANI

Police two blocks away, and proceed to the Kars museum to buy tickets ($2). Tickets are *not* sold at the site, a measure designed to prevent people showing up unscreened.

Ani is 43km east of Kars, just beyond the village of **OCAKLI**. Without your own vehicle, you can take an early-morning or mid-afternoon bus between Kars and the ruins, but if you use the first service you'll be stuck at the site far longer than you'd like, and the later vehicle overnights in Ocaklı, leaving you stranded. The alternatives are a minibus- or taxi-tour, arranged either by your hotel or the tourist office, for $7 to $8 per person round-trip. Solo travelers typically band together at the tourist information office; the taxis hold four people, while the minibuses carry up to nine passengers.

The ruins are scattered, and many monuments are absorbing, so allow a good two hours at Ani, plus a similar period going there and back—make sure your driver agrees to this. Prepare yourself also to be accosted, not always in a friendly manner, by hordes of village children and their elders hawking tepid Cokes, trinkets, and fake (or sometimes real) antiquities. With the lifting of the ban on photography here in 1988, mass tourism is starting to engulf Ani—as the giant parked buses at the site attest.

The Site

The vast **boundary walls** of Ani, dating from the end of the tenth century and studded with countless towers, are visible from several kilometers away as you approach past primitive villages teeming with sheep and buffalo. After handing over your ticket and permit, you enter via the **Aslan Kapısı**, so named because of a sculpted Selçuk lion on the wall just inside, and the only one of four original gates to survive.

Once inside you're confronted with the sight of the vast forlorn, weed-tufted plateau, dotted with only the sturdiest bits of masonry that have outlasted the ages. A system of **paths**, many of them remnants of the former main streets of Ani, lead to or past all of the principal remains. Bear slightly left and head first about 500m southeast to the **Church of the Redeemer**, built between 1034 and 1036. In 1957, half of the building was sheared away by lightning, so that the remainder, seen from the side, looks uncannily like a stage set.

Some 200m east, tucked down by a length of wall overlooking the Arpa Çayı, the monastery **Church of St Gregory the Illuminator (Tigran Honents)** is the best-preserved monument at Ani, and somewhat confusingly just one of three dedicated to the saint who evangelized Armenia at the beginning of the fourth century. The pious foundation of a nobleman in 1215, it's laid out, unusually, in a rectangle divided width-wise into three parts (a colonnaded narthex out front has disappeared). The layout reflects the prominent Georgian influence in thirteenth-century Ani, and the fact that the Orthodox, not the Armenian Apostolic, rite was celebrated here. The church still sports delicate exterior relief work, including extensive animal designs, and, on the south wall, a sundial, common in Armenian decoration.

But Tigran Honents is most rewarding for its **frescoes**, the only ones left at Ani, which cover most of the interior and spill out around the current entrance onto what was once the narthex wall. They are remarkable for both their high degree of realism and fluidity—especially compared to the static iconography of the neighboring Byzantines—and for the subject matter, depicting episodes in early Armenian Christianity as well as the doings of ordinary people. As you enter the first of the three nave compartments, you'll see in the lower row of images on your right *The Trial of St Gregory by King Trdat III*, *The Martyrdom of Hrpsime* (an early female convert), and *The Torture of St Gregory*. All these events took place before Trdat's repentance and conversion, the earliest sovereign to do so; to the left are secular vignettes from the life of King Trdat. The transept is taken up by scenes from the life of Christ; on the south wall are the *Annunciation*, the *Nativity*, the *Entry into Jerusalem*, and the *Descent from the Cross*. To the north is *The Raising of Lazarus*, with *The Apostles* ringing the drum of the dome.

From Tigran Honents, a narrow trail skims the tops of the cliffs dropping to the Arpa Çayı before finding a way down to the **Convent of the Virgins (Kusanats)**, perched on a ledge even closer to the river. A miniscule, rocket-like rotunda church, contemporary with Tigran Honents, is flanked by a smaller chapel or baptistry, and the whole enclosed by a perimeter wall. Just upstream are the stubs of the old **bridge** over the Arpa, relics of a time when there was far more communication between the opposite banks.

Rejoining the main plateau trail heading west from Tigran Honents, you reach the elegantly proportioned **cathedral**, completed between 989 and 1010. The architect, one Trdat Mendet, could present impressive credentials, having just previously completed restoration of the earthquake-damaged dome of Aya Sofya in Constantinople, although this is a surprisingly plain, rectangular building, with just the generic blind arcades of Armenian churches and no external apse; the dome, once supported by four massive pillars, has long since vanished. The main entrance was—unusually—not to the west, opposite the apse, but on the side of the nave, through the south wall.

To the west, within sight of the cathedral, stands what's known as the **Menüçehir Camii**, billed as the earliest Selçuk mosque in Anatolia, though its lack of *mihrab*, and the alternating red-and-black stonework, plus an inlaid mosaic ceiling, invite suspicions of mixed antecedents. Certainly the view from the ornate gallery over the border river fits more with a role as a small palace. The truncated minaret is off-limits since a tourist committed suicide by leaping off.

A narrow panhandle of land, supporting the **citadel** and yet another monastery, juts south of here, but both still fall into a forbidden zone. From the mosque you should turn north along the path to visit the **Church of St Gregory (Abughamrets)**, begun in 1040 by the same individual responsible for the Church of the Redeemer. This rotunda is like no other at Ani—instead of blind arcades, the twelve-sided exterior is pierced by functional recessed vaults alternating with the six rounded interior alcoves. The east side of the building is slowly but surely losing its dressed stone.

The nearby, so-called **kervansaray** is really the eleventh-century Church of the Holy Apostles, today badly crumbled. The main circuit continues north to the sparse ruins of the **Church of St Gregory (Gagik I)**, begun in 998 by Trdat, architect of the cathedral. Intact it would have been one of the largest rotundas in medieval Armenia, but the design, based on the seventh-century rotunda at Zvartnots in Soviet Armenia, collapsed almost immediately, so that today only man-high outer walls and giant column stumps are left. Before completing your tour at the Aslan Kapısı, you might spare a glance for the facade of the **Selçuk Palace**, the only indisputably Islamic item at Ani, tucked into the northeast extremity of the ramparts—and, interestingly, the only one to receive any degree of archaeological investigation and maintenance.

Around Ani: Other Armenian Monuments

The present-day province of Kars formed an important part of the Bagratid kingdom between the sixth and the eleventh centuries, and of the Zakhariad clan's holdings during the thirteenth century, so it's not surprising that there are numerous Armenian churches and fortresses besides Ani. Visiting them is not necessarily straightforward, however; many are in bad condition, accessible only by atrocious roads or on foot, or they lie in military security zones—sometimes all three. You'll really need your own transportation, enough Turkish to ask directions from villagers, and the *Bartholomew* "Turkey East" map. As you may have gathered at Ani, the Armenians had a particular flair for poising their churches on sheer palisades overlooking canyons, and many of the remains detailed below adhere to this pattern; even in their ruinous state they are still among the most impressive sights in northeastern Turkey.

Practical Details . . . and a Caution

Monuments known to still exist in some semblance of repair are detailed below according to whether they fall into a security area or not. The border district with the Armenian SSR is subdivided into an **outer zone**, extending 5km into Turkey from the boundary—where photography, if not your very presence, will be strongly frowned on—and an **inner zone** consisting of the final 500m to the border, where it's claimed unauthorized entry might spark off an international incident. It's worth knowing that the entire region between the Digor–Tuzluca highway and the Soviet border is off-limits after dark—even the villagers are not allowed to go there.

If you're serious about touring these churches, you'll need to contact the central military command in Ankara several weeks in advance. Neither local *jandarma* posts, nor the provincial headquarters in Kars, are authorized to grant permits, since these must be screened at the highest level and forwarded to the Soviet government for co-approval—or so it is claimed. You need to present yourself as a high-level university student of medieval art or architecture, with supporting documents, although permission is more often denied than granted. And don't just head off toward an inner-zone church hoping for the best: you'll certainly be detected by the military and turned back, and though this will be done relatively politely, with you unlikely to be detained for long, it will all add up to wasted time. Even if you do slip past the guards, the toll on your nerves will detract considerably from any enjoyment.

Above all, don't appeal to the tourist information office or other civilian authorities in Kars. At best, you'll be fed disinformation or rather curtly discouraged from setting out with such pronouncements as "If you want to see Armenian things you can go to Ani." This becomes slightly more understandable when you consider that the past treatment of these churches, not to mention their very existence, is as sensitive a topic as the alleged mistreatment of the Armenians themselves in 1895 and 1915. Officially Armenians don't exist historically, and any archaeological evidence of their past rule are non-monuments, either ignored or misattributed to Islamic builders. The continued presence of recognizable churches in this part of Turkey is a major embarrassment to the government, which sees them as the basis for potential Armenian territorial claims—and demands for reparations of the sort West Germany paid to Jewish survivors of the Holocaust.

Local authorities would rather that outsiders did not find the churches, and would probably be relieved if they disappeared altogether. In certain quarters it's charged that army demolition units have helped the process along with dynamite or bulldozers in recent years, and while this is debatable, it's certainly true that nothing is being done to preserve these monuments. Such attitudes usually contrast sharply with those of the local villagers, who are often only too happy to show you the ruins they know of; they have no ethnic axe to grind and are honored that someone should bother to visit what for them is a barn—or a quarry for building stone. Incidentally, some degree of tourism is often enough to stop any ongoing vandalism, not so much in anticipation of the monetary benefit of increased tourist traffic, but because the village elders consider that they lose face if a "cultural" institution on their turf deteriorates.

Non-restricted Monuments

Just south of the church at Kümbetli (see above), bear left on the road toward KÖTEK, and some 40–50km along there's a choice of side roads west to **KECİVAN KALESİ** (GEÇVAN). Access is via either ORTAKÖY, 3.5km off the main road, with a subsequent ninety-minute walk, or a rougher twelve-kilometer drive, the first 5km to OLUKLU and then 7km southwest from there. The castle's western ramparts and gates are in fair condition, although little else remains of the third-century Armenian fortified town sacked by the Persians after a year's siege.

At the KAĞIZMAN junction, just after the Aras River crossing, head 4km west on the road toward Karakurt, making another right on a bad dirt road. This threads through the villages of Karakuş and Karakale to reach **ÇENGİLLİ** after 15km, where there's an anomalous thirteenth-century **Georgian monastery**. Not only was the contemporary population of the area largely Armenian, but the architecture mimics the tenth- and eleventh-century styles of specimens farther north—specifically Tbeti (see "The Upper Berta Valley," below). The site can also be reached by a ninety-minute walk north from the twenty-first kilometer of the Kağızman–Karakurt highway.

There is fairly regular public transportation covering the 40km southeast of Kars to **DİGOR**, the former Armenian Tekor, where the fifth-century **church** on a hill to the south is almost completely leveled. **BEŞKİLİSE** (KHTZKONK), a ninety-minute walk upstream along the Digor Çayi, is more rewarding—though it's marked on the wrong side of the road on the Bartholomew map. If you don't want to take a local guide along, have the bus drop you off—or drive—exactly 3.5km north of town, where you turn onto a faint dirt track veering southwest from the paved road, heading some 600m toward the gorge of the Digor Çayı. Park just before a pumice quarry and walk down to the stream, following a north-bank path about half an hour to **St Sergius**, an eleventh-century rotunda that's the sole survivor of the five churches once perched at the edge of the narrow canyon here. The side walls are rent by fissures, but the dome is still intact and the west wall is covered with inscriptions.

A pair of isolated churches—not marked on the Bartholomew map—on the way to Ani are easily visited with your own vehicle; you might even convince a tour-van driver to detour to them. At SUBATAN, 25km from Kars, bear left toward BAŞGEDİKLER—about a kilometer before, turn left again for 2km to **OĞUZLU**, a half-fallen shrine of the tenth century. More intact is the thirteenth-century church of **KIZIL KİLİSE** (KARMIK VANK), reached by driving through

Başgedikler and proceeding 6km east. This cruciform-plan building was restored in the last century and still retains dome and facing stone.

Restricted Monuments

From Dolaylı on the Digor–Tuzluca road it's about 13km east to DÜZGEÇİT, and another 9km beyond to where the seventh-century cathedral of **MREN**—an outer-zone monument—overlooks the confluence of the Digor and Arpa streams. Once the focus of a town whose rubble litters the surrounding plateau, Mren exhibits marked Byzantine influence with its elongated cross-in-square layout and octagonal dome mounted on four pillars.

BAGARAN, variously known as Bekren, Pakran, or by the adjacent village name of Kilittaşı, might seem the logical next stop after Mren. However, getting to this site, which was the ninth-century Bagratid capital before the move to Kars, involves retracing your route to the main road and then, 26km southeast of Digor, taking an unmarked seven-kilometer side road to the village of KİLİTTAŞI. Final access is complicated by the terrain, but at least one early **church** is plainly visible on its pinnacle across the river.

Flanking Ani in the inner zone are the tenth-century fortress of **MAGAZBERT**, about 5km southwest, and the monastic complex of **HOROMOS**, 6km northeast, about halfway to the dam over the Arpa Çayı. Founded in the tenth century, Horomos contains four later tombs of Armenian nobility, and two churches, in a walled enclosure at the brink of the Arpa Çayı. Two kilometers northeast stands **DAYLAR**, another church of the same vintage, near the modern village of TAYLAR. Given this high concentration of other worthwhile monuments so close to potentially over-visited Ani, their current inaccessibility is regrettable.

South of Kars: the Route to Doğubeyazit

Reasonably frequent long-distance buses from Kars to Doğubeyazit follow the Kağızman–Tuzluca–Iğdır route, with the Aras River for company much of the way. East of TUZLUCA, named after some nearby rock-salt mines, the road skirts the Soviet border, whose watchtowers are plainly visible to the north, and drops sharply into a basin at an elevation of only 850m. The more temperate climate here permits the cultivation of rice, cotton, and grapes; the inhabitants are mostly Azeri Shiites, resettled here in the last century. Should you need to break the journey, IĞDIR—a pleasant though unremarkable town at the southwest corner of the valley—would be the place to do so: there are a handful of decent hotels, including the clean, mid-range *Azer*, which has singles for $6, doubles for $10, and a decent attached restaurant.

North of Kars: Around Çıldır Gölü

From Kars most travelers will want to move northwest toward Artvin without making the lengthy detour through Erzurum. Bus routes can be circuitous, however, often snaking via Susuz, Ardahan, and Göle, beyond which the scenery improves as you drop steadily, first through forest and then past some of the medieval Georgian monuments described later in this chapter.

The most northerly route between Kars and Artvin is scenically superior but requires lots of patience without your own vehicle. It's easy enough to get to Ardahan, but services take a short-cut via the dull Susuz–Hasköy route, and the unpaved stretch between Ardahan and Şavşat isn't served by buses at all.

The slate-like expanse of **ÇILDIR GÖLÜ**, nearly 2000m up, is the highest sizable lake in Turkey, although only in the summer, when hay and grain grows along the shore, is there a hint of color. Men on horseback, wielding scythes and other farming implements, canter splendidly across the steppes, but their families live like moles, the houses burrowed even deeper than the norm for the province. The shallow lake is frozen over six months of the year, and although the water is fresh, there's no obvious fishing culture—but there are plenty of birds in the summer, with handsome falcons and hawks buzzing your vehicle.

This region was an extension of medieval Georgia, despite its proximity to Ani, and most local monuments are of relatively recent vintage. At **DOĞRUYOL**, the only substantial town on the lake's eastern shore, the thirteenth-century hilltop church of **DJALA** masqueraded until recently as a mosque. A few kilometers farther on, the islet of **AKÇAKALE** (ARGENKALE) is crisscrossed by walls and linked to the semi-fortified village opposite by a half-submerged boulder causeway. There's also a badly ruined medieval chapel on the islet, but little else can be dated conclusively. At the extreme northwestern tip of the lake, the village of **GÖLBELEN** (URTA) contains another thirteenth-century church which was later a fort, and now serves as a mosque. The nearby town of ÇILDIR is an unprepossessing place north of the lake, out of sight of the water, but it's the turnoff for the five-kilometer detour north to **ŞEYTAN KALESİ**, a medieval citadel above the village of YILDIRIMTEPE. It's the only rural monument whose existence the Kars tourist authorities will admit to—probably because the Ottomans extensively overhauled it.

From Çıldır it's forty-seven fairly bleak kilometers west to **ARDAHAN**, something of a miniature Kars, with its Russian grid plan and turn-of-the-century architecture—and a pervasive military presence. There's no hotel to stay at worthy of the term, and nothing in particular to see except a fine old **bridge** over the Kura River, just opposite the massive **citadel**, originally Georgian but restored by the Ottomans early in the sixteenth century. It's still an army camp, so no photography is allowed.

Ardahan sits in the midst of a vast plateau of hayfields, swaying even in summer to winds gusting out of a livid sky. Geese waddle across the road, untamed horses gambol in the stubble, and others are lashed to wagons groaning with hay—all in all a more cheerful prospect than usual for northeastern Anatolia, as you begin the climb up to the **Çam Pass**, northeastern gateway to the Georgian valleys.

North of Erzurum: the Southern Georgian Valleys

Highway 950 heads north out of Erzurum across the steppes, aiming for an almost imperceptible gap—too trivial to call a pass—in the surrounding mountains. Almost without noticing it you're across the watershed, and as you begin a slow descent the landscape becomes more interesting, with the Tortum Çayı alongside and trees for the first time in a long while. Most buses bypass the nondescript town of TORTUM, 54km from Erzurum; in the fifteen kilometers beyond Tortum, you'll pass a pair of **castles** on the left and right, crumbling away atop well-nigh inaccessible pinnacles, and announcing more effectively than any sign that you've now reached the southern limits of medieval Georgia.

The Georgians, their Castles and Churches

Georgians have lived in the valleys of the Çoruh, Tortum, Kura, and Berta rivers, now in Turkey, since the Bronze Age. Like the neighboring Armenians, they were among the first Near Eastern nations to be evangelized, and were converted rapidly to Christianity by Saint Nino of Cappadocia in the mid-fourth century. Unlike the Armenians, they never broke with the Orthodox Patriarchate in Constantinople, and maintained good relations with Byzantium.

An effective Georgian state only entered the local stage early in the ninth century, under the auspices of the **Bagratid** dynasty. This clan contributed rulers to both the Georgian and Armenian lines, and hence the medieval history of both kingdoms overlapped to some extent. The Bagratids claimed direct descent from David and Bathsheba, which explains a preponderance of kings named David, a coat of arms laden with Old Testament symbols, and curiously Judaic Stars of David embossed on many of the churches they built.

Feudal Bagratid lords initially emerged in the nominally Byzantine-ruled districts of Tao (based around today's İspir, Yusufeli, and Oltu) and Klarjeti (Ardanuç and Ardahan), from which **Ashot I Kuropalates** began the first stages of territorial aggrandizement at the expense of Byzantium and the Arab Caliphate—and the initial wave of church-building in the area, under the guidance of the monk **Gregory Khantzeli**. Ashot's descendants included **David the Great** of Oltu, a late ninth-century ruler responsible for several of the churches described below, and Bagrat III, who in 1008 succeeded in unifying the various Georgian principalities into one kingdom with a capital at Kutaisi.

A decade or so later the Byzantines compelled Bagrat III's successor Georgi I to evacuate Tao and Klarjeti, making it an easy matter for the Selçuks to step in in 1064. They ravaged Georgia as they did all of eastern Anatolia, but as soon as they turned to confront the Crusaders a Bagratid revival began. **David the Restorer** managed by 1125 to not only expel the Selçuks, but moved the Bagratid court to newly captured Tblisi, and reunited the various feuding principalities ruled by minor Bagratid warlords.

Under the rule of David's great-granddaughter **Tamara**, medieval Georgia acquired its greatest extent and prestige, controlling most of modern Georgia, Armenia, and Azerbaijan from the Black Sea to the Caspian, as well as the ancestral Georgian valleys. The queen was not only a formidable military strategist and shrewd diplomat, but displayed a humanity and tolerance in her domestic administration unusual for the era. Many of the churches and monasteries were repaired or re-endowed by Tamara, and despite the fact that she was a woman and a non-Muslim, her name still elicits respectful compliments and even a proprietary pride in the now-Turkish valleys.

Following Tamara's death the Georgian kingdom began a slow but steady decline, precipitated by Mongol and Persian raids of the mid-thirteenth century but most of all by Tamerlane's blitz early in the next. Tamara's Georgia was effectively partitioned between the Ottoman and Persian empires, and although Bagratids continued to occupy thrones in Tblisi, they were essentially puppets.

The rise of imperial Russia was a mixed blessing: while it prevented further Muslim encroachment, it signaled the end of any viable Georgian state, and the last semi-independent king effectively surrendered what was left of his autonomy to Catherine the Great in 1783.

Tangible evidence of the Georgian heyday is still abundant in northeastern Turkey, starting with the prefix "Ar-" (as in Ardahan, Artvin, Ardanuç, etc), equivalent to "-ville" or "-burg." The Bagratids were a prolific bunch, and they stuck **castles** on just about every height; generally a passing glance is what you'll have to be satisfied with, since access to many of these eyries has long been impossible. Most remarkable, however, are the early Bagratid monastic **churches**, all dating from before the move northeast to the Caucausus proper, and most sited amidst oases at the heads of remote valleys. As a rule, the core conventions of Armenian religious architecture—domes supported on four free-standing columns, a cruciform, east-west floorplan with prominent transepts, blind exterior arcades, and intricate relief work—were borrowed wholesale, and it takes a trained eye to distinguish the two styles.

You'll need your own wheels, or a lot of time for walking and hitching, to visit most of the churches. There's usually a small village nearby, or even surrounding the monument, but invariably bus services, where they exist, arrive in the afternoon and depart for the nearest town in the morning—exactly the opposite of tourist schedules. Many of the roads in are bad, but if you can assemble a group and find a taxi driver willing to risk his undercarriage, this can end up being far cheaper than renting a vehicle in Erzurum or Trabzon.

There's not nearly the degree of official stonewalling about Georgian Christians as there is concerning Armenians, and the churches have become semi-recognized as tourist attractions. We've only detailed the most intact examples; if you have a compulsive interest in the subject, there are numerous unsung others, slowly collapsing in isolated settings, that villagers will be happy to show you. Virtually every church has suffered some damage from dynamite- and pickaxe-wielding treasure-hunters. The locals have an unshakable conviction that all of the Christians who left the area in 1923 or before secreted precious items in or under their churches before departure in the mistaken belief that they'd eventually be able to return.

Haho

Twenty-six kilometers north of Tortum, turn off west at a slightly modernized humpback bridge. Take a left fork in the first large village, then a right a few minutes later; it's 7.5km total to the main square of **BAĞBAŞI**, a large community dispersed in a fertile valley. (There are supposedly two buses a day from the Gölbaşı Semt Garajı in Erzurum to the village, but it's still a lot of toing and froing for one monument.) Beyond the *meydan*—really just a widening in the road—bear left, and exactly 8km from the highway, the dome of the late tenth-century church of **HAHO** (KHAKULI) will be seen soaring above the trees.

This is the first of several institutions constructed by David the Great, ruler of Tao between 961 and 1001. For once most of the monastery complex—the boundary wall, two satellite chapels, assorted galleries—is in good condition, the effect spoiled only by aluminum corrugated sheets on the roof, although the conical-topped dome is still covered in multicolored tiles. Over the south transept

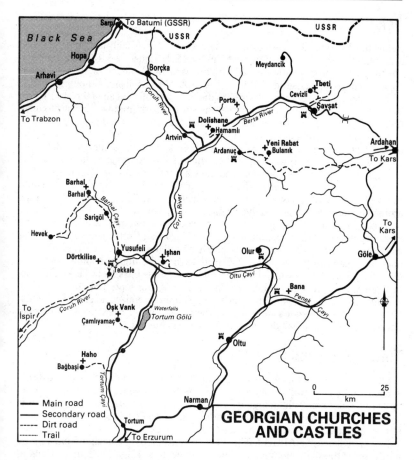

GEORGIAN CHURCHES AND CASTLES

— Main road
— Secondary road
---- Dirt road
.... Trail

0 ____ 25
km

windows, a vigilant stone eagle grasps a doe in his claws, before a fan of alternating light and dark masonry.

A narthex on the west side of the nave still exists, but the doors have been walled off; entry is now through a gallery on the south, a skillful addition of the thirteenth century that appears at first glance to be part of the original building. To the left of the old south entrance, now inside the gallery, there's a **lion and a chimera** in relief; on the right a **whale** that looks suspiciously like a dog devours **Jonah**, while below struts a **cock** (presumably the one of obstinate Pride). Inside, a small, well-executed swath of bluish **frescoed angels and Apostles** hovers over the former apse.

Haho's excellent state of repair is owed to its having served as a mosque since the eighteenth century, so you may have to wait until prayer time for admission if you can't find the warden in the village; after your visit you'll sign the "guest register" and make a donation.

Öşk Vank

Below the Haho turnoff the Tortum Valley widens appreciably, and the side road to the monastery church of **ÖŞK VANK** (OSHKHI), just over 15km beyond the one to Haho, is prominently marked with the usual black-on-yellow archaeologists' sign. It's an easy, well-graded 7km to **ÇAMLIYAMAÇ** village, although the site, with houses built up to the very walls, is the least evocative of all in the area. Given the good road in, this is also the one church regularly mobbed by bus-tours—there's even a teahouse across the lane from the nave that's used to foreigners.

None of this should deter you, since Öşk Vank is the most elaborate example of Georgian Gothic in these valleys. Another late tenth-century foundation of David the Great, it represents the culmination of Tao Georgian culture before the Bagratid dynasty's move northeast and the start of the Georgian "Golden Age."

A protruding porch shelters the main entry through the **facade** of the south transept; blind arcades, topped by scallop-shell carving, flank it, with reliefs of the archangels hovering high overhead. Alternatively you can enter from the southwest corner of the building, through a triple-arched **narthex** with an engaging zigzag roof; the interior colonnade exudes a European Gothic feel with its stellar vaulted ceiling and column capitals bearing sculpted angels. The roof over the nave, elongated to the west, has fallen in, leaving the dome stranded atop four essential pillars, two of which have their massive bases intricately worked in sinuous **geometric designs**. Halfway up the south transept wall, the vanished wooden floor of the mosque that once occupied the premises acted as protection for a stretch of **frescoes**, the best preserved in any of the Turkish Georgian churches, featuring a half-dozen ethereal saints in hieratic poses.

Tortum Gölü and Falls

A little way past the turnoff for Öşk Vank lies the inlet end of **Tortum Gölü**, a substantial body of water, roughly 10km long by 1km wide, that forces the road up onto a hair-raising cliff-hugging bypass above the western shore. The water is by turns muddy green, milky beige, or dull slate even on a bright day, so the idea of a swim isn't all that appealing, although the locals try from the stone beach below the village of **BALIKLI**. The lake was formed by a landslide blocking the north end of the valley between two and three centuries ago. The famous **Falls of Tortum** are today its natural outlet, accessible by an inconspicuous dirt side road 12km north of the Öşk Vank turnoff, or 25km south of the Su Kavuşumu junction (see below). TEK, the Turkish Electric Foundation, has supplemented the natural dam with an artifical one and a turbine; you leave the asphalted highway where you see the power plant, and then proceed as indicated by a little red-and-white sign for just over a kilometer, until glimpsing a vast rock ledge with its 48-meter cascade on your left. You'll have to scramble down a fair way to get a good look, and you won't see much except in spring, since the TEK diverts most available water for power generation later in the summer.

İşhan

Seventeen kilometers below the falls there's an important intersection in the steadily descending highway. Continuing straight leads to Yusufeli (see below); bearing right toward Olur, you reach, after 5km, an archaeological service sign pointing to **IŞHAN** (ISHKANI), a bluff-top village 6km up a dirt road through a heavily eroded, lifeless moonscape. Vehicles should be left near the central village fountain, and from there it's a final 300-meter walk down and left to the grounds of the sanctuary, where there's another fountain and nearby benches that make it a perfect spot for a picnic.

The imposing church, originally dedicated to the Virgin Mary, was constructed in stages between the seventh and eleventh centuries, ranking it among the oldest extant sacred Georgian architecture. The semicircular colonnade lining the apse is the earliest surviving portion of the building, modeled consciously after the church at Bana (see below); large chunks of the roof are missing so that the 42-meter-high dome, in a similar fashion to Öşk Vank's, rests in isolation on four columns. There are some patches of fresco high up on the surviving walls, portraying portions of the vision of Zaccharias, and in the cupola an abstract cross. The external eleventh-century **relief work** is more interesting, though, particularly on the small baptistry with its bestiary and inscriptions, opposite a bricked-up southern portal where a lion and snake are locked in combat. Sadly, Işhan in general has been messed around a lot, particularly on the northwest corner—defaced with recent, ill-advised masonry—and in the nave, which is completely blocked by a modern wall. The children from the adjacent schoolyard find the interior a convenient soccer field and volleyball court.

Backroad Castles ... and Bana

If you've already seen the Georgian churches of the Tortum Valley, and particularly if you have your own vehicle, a detour via Narman and Oltu is time well spent. Invariably dismissed or underestimated, this alternative approach compares well with similar landscapes in Afghanistan or the American southwest. Stands of poplars and green fields are juxtaposed against a cobalt sky and reddish bluffs, often crowned with crumbling Georgian **castles**. Beyond NARMAN, the river rolls past **OLTU**, with the first of the citadels—well restored by the Ottomans and again in the 1970s—overhead. Four hundred meters left of an important Y-fork, a double fort—one unit backed into the cliff, the other free-standing and flanked by a small church—looms over the river, and continuing along this option toward Işhan takes you past still another redoubt, atop a rock spur by the road to OLUR.

Bearing right instead leads toward Göle and Kars; 28km beyond Oltu (or 37km southwest of Göle) you'll see, just where the river valley narrows drastically, the seventh-century church of **BANA** on the north bank of the Penek (Irlağaç) Çayı. Perched on a knoll surveying water-meadows tufted with willows and dominated in turn by tawny crags, it's an obvious and commanding position. The Ottomans fortified Bana during the Crimean War, a century after it ceased to be used as a shrine. The Russians blasted the dome off during the 1877–78 war, and later carted off much of the stone to build a turn-of-the-century church in Oltu.

What remains—the first floor of a vast rotunda, with one talon of masonry protruding above—is still impressive, and in both architecture and setting seems a transition between Armenian shrines and the other Georgian ones. The east apse houses a colonnade virtually identical to the later one at Işhan. A dirt road limps down to the Penek, and you can cross the river, but it's only possible to approach to within 100m of Bana—unless you're willing to swim a slimy new irrigation canal of uncertain depth.

Yusufeli and Around

The area around the confluence of the Barhal and Çoruh rivers is scenically and climatically one of the most favored corners of the northeast. During the balmy summers, every sort of fruit ripens, and you're treated to the incongruous spectacle of rice paddies by the Çoruh within sight of parched cliffs overhead.

The rivers themselves are a magnet for visitors, making Yusufeli a popular base for **white-water rafters** finishing the challenging runs from İspir or Barhal upstream, or beginning the easier float down to Artvin. Highest water is from mid-June to mid-July, and the main foreign outfitter for such trips is *Sobek Expeditions*; for the address, see "Getting There" in *Basics*.

Tourism in general seems destined to grow by leaps and bounds in the future, although so far the simplicity of local facilities has appealed mostly to the hardier breed of traveler. Even if you're not an outdoor-sports enthusiast, you'll need a steady hand at the wheel—or a strong stomach if you're a passenger—for the bumpy rides out to the local Georgian churches.

If you can't get a direct **bus** service to Yusufeli from Erzurum, ask to be let off at Su Kavuşumu junction, 9km below the town center. The last through Artvin–Yusufeli bus doesn't roll past the turnoff until about 4pm, so unless you've missed it, or your heart is set on being in Barhal that evening (see below for onward schedules), don't panic and accept the offer of a **taxi** shuttle up to Yusufeli—figure on $6 per car.

Yusufeli

Straddling the Barhal Çayı just above where it meets the Çoruh, **YUSUFELİ** is an immediately likable and friendly town with all essential services—including a **bank** and a **PTT**—but a minimum of concrete. It's a fairly conservative and devout anomaly in the secular, relatively progressive province of Artvin, a situation partly explained by the fact that many of the inhabitants are descended from Bulgarian Muslim settlers of the turn of the century. Numerous travelers come to spend a night on their way to the Kaçkar Mountains and end up staying two, making a day trip up one of the nearby valleys.

Hotels are uniformly plain and inexpensive, though clean enough. The *Sefa* (☎0589/1075), next to the cement auto bridge over the river, is small (9 beds) but acceptable at $4 a single, $7 a double, with a hot shower in the hall and some rooms overlooking the water. The only other river-view accommodation is the *Aydın*, on the left-bank side of the pedestrian suspension bridge a few hundred meters upstream. The *Çiçek Palas* (☎0589/1393), conspicuous on the one main street, shouldn't be confused with the *Çelik Palas* (☎0589/1507) around the corner, though both have the same rates as the *Sefa* and neither offers any panoramas or special amenities other than multiple beds crammed into each room. Below the *Çelik*, however, there is a nice breakfast café. For more serious **eating** head for the *Mavi Köşk*, a full-menu restaurant with bar next to the *Sefa*, or the *Mahzen Fıçı Bira*, whose balcony overhangs the river on the far side of the suspension bridge from the *Aydın*. Food is secondary to the drinking and spontaneous *saz* sessions here, though, and unless you arrive early it'll be packed—often by tour groups.

Yusufeli is also the start of **dolmuş routes** to various villages farther upriver, including Barhal and Hevek. Service to these two high settlements is available daily year-round, since both are inhabited in winter, but adheres to a somewhat informal schedule. The Barhal vehicle leaves Yusufeli between 3pm and 3:30pm, while there seem to be two Hevek departures, at around 2 and 5pm. In theory all are linked to the arrival of afternoon buses from Artvin. If you miss the Barhal service, you can often plead a seat on the Hevek dolmuş which has to pass through Barhal. All dolmuşes return to Yusufeli early in the morning.

Tekkale and Dörtkilise

TEKKALE lies 7km southwest of Yusufeli on the same bank of the Çoruh, connected by dolmuşes heading to either KILIÇKAYA or KÖPRÜGÖREN, 27km upriver and the last point served by public transportation. Next to a distinctive café on stilts, bear right and away from the Çoruh, and walk or drive 6km farther to **DÖRTKİLİSE** (OTKHTA EKLESIA)—you may have to walk the final 300m since the bridge is still under construction—where the idyllic setting of this tenth-century church has been partly spoiled by the road construction. Despite the name—"Four Churches"—only one still stands intact, but it's very fine and unlike most other Georgian places of worship. Domeless, with a steep gabled roof and relatively plain exterior, it's a twin of one at nearby Barhal, though several decades older; it was later renovated by David the Great. Since the closest hamlet is 2km away, Dörtkilise was never reconsecrated as a mosque, and is now home only to bats, swallows, and occasionally livestock. Inside a double line of four columns each supports the barrel ceiling hiding under the pitched roof; with a flashlight you can also pick out traces of fresco. The large half-ruined building to the northeast was the monastery refectory, joined to the main body of the church by an equally decrepit gallery that served as a narthex.

Barhal and Hevek

The most popular route out of Yusufeli follows the valley of the Barhal Çayı north through a landscape straight out of a Romantic engraving, complete with ruined Georgian castles on assorted crags—and a terrible dirt road that hasn't changed much since the nineteenth century. After 18km, dolmuş drivers stop briefly at SARIGÖL to get the kinks out of their fingers and give their passengers a chance to eat (or just avoid being sick). Barhal, officially renamed **ALTIPARMAK** after the mountains behind, is reached 14km beyond, a total two-hour drive from Yusufeli. With its scattered wooden buildings peeking out from lush pre-alpine vegetation at 1300m, Barhal conforms more to most people's notions of a mountain village than the lower town. There are three places to **stay**: fifteen treehouse-type chalets, available by arrangement with the *Otel Karahan* in Artvin, but often filled by trekking tours; a single room let out by a family; and the very basic lodge run by Cemil Özyurt above his combination **café-restaurant**, right by the dolmuş stop and the only place to eat out. Otherwise you can hunt for spots to **camp** on the banks of the trout-rich stream.

The tenth-century church of **BARHAL** (PARKHALI), the final legacy of David the Great, is a ten-minute walk up the track toward the Kaçkar Mountains—not the main one headed toward Hevek—and then a brief scramble up a lushly vegetated slope, starting opposite a lone river-bank shed. It's virtually identical to Dörtkilise, except for being somewhat smaller—and in near-perfect condition owing to long use as the village mosque. As long as the church continues in this role it will be difficult to gain admission—you could try at prayer time—but a new mosque is nearing completion, and there is concern that the church, once abandoned, will be subject to the decay and vandalism that has beset the other Georgian monuments in Turkey. Optimistically, there also exists the possibility that the authorities might strip the church's interior whitewash to see what frescoes, if any, are hiding underneath.

HEVEK (YAYLALAR) lies another two hours' drive along a steadily worsening, twenty-kilometer road. Well above treeline at over 2000m, this substantial village is the highest trailhead for the Kaçkar, but its setting can't compare to Barhal's. So far the one place to **stay** indoors is a new, stark dormitory over one of the shops, and there's no approximation of a restaurant. Architecturally the village varies from new concrete to century-old houses, though the only specific sight is an Ottoman **bridge** just downstream. If you're determined to overnight here, it's prudent to consult Cemil Özyurt in Barhal, as he's originally from Hevek and may be able to arrange something with relatives.

The Kaçkar Dağları

A formidable barrier between the northeastern Anatolian plateau and the Black Sea, the **KAÇKAR DAĞLARI** are the high end of the Pontic coastal ranges—and Turkey's most rewarding and popular trekking area. Occupying a rough rectangle some 70km by 20km, the Kaçkars extend from the Rize–İspir road to the Hopa–Artvin highway, with the more abrupt southeast flank lapped by the Çoruh River, and the gentler northwest folds dropping more gradually to misty foothills. At 3972m, their summit ranks only third highest in Turkey after Ararat and Süphan Dağı, but in scenic and human interest they fully earn their aliases of "the Little Caucausus" and the "Pontic Alps."

"Kaçkar" is the Turkish spelling of *khatchkar*, sculpted Armenian votive crosses or gravestones once abundant in eastern Turkey—perhaps a reference to the complicated and tortured outline of the range, with multiple hanging valleys and secondary spurs. In addition to the principal summit area, several other major massifs are recognized: the Altıparmak and Marsis groups of about 3300m, at the north end of the Bulut ridge linking them with Point 3972; and the adjacent Tatos and Verçenik systems of about 3700m, at the extreme southwest of the chain. Oddly for Turkey, the Kaçkars are a young granite-diorite range instead of the usual karst, and were substantially transformed by the last Ice Age; there are still remnants of glaciers on the north slope of the highest peak, and literally hundreds of lakes spangle the alpine zone above 2600m.

Partly because of intensive human habitation, the Kaçkars support relatively few large mammals; bear and boar prefer the forested mid-altitude zones, while wolves and ibex are ruthlessly hunted in the treeless heights. Birds of prey and snow cocks are more easily seen and heard, while the summer months witness an explosion of wildflowers, butterflies—and vicious deer flies. Between May and September migration from the nearby lowlands to the *yaylas*, or summer pastures, is the norm: the lower ones are occupied first, the higher ones once the snow recedes. Upper dwellings tend to be rudimentary, made mostly of stone, but the lower, sturdy chalets cluster in proper villages, some reached by jeep tracks, others with power lines strung to them—an odd sight at 2100m.

Given the ethnic variety here, it's no surprise that local place names are similarly tangled—a discerning glance at the map will turn up plenty of Georgian and Armenian words, plus Turkified versions of same. Thus Pişkankara (the original form) has become Pişenkaya, "the Cooking Rock," while other more provocatively foreign ones like Sevcov Lake are camouflaged outright as Deniz Gölü. The recurring suffix "-evit" is a dialect-Armenian particle meaning *yayla*.

Practical Details

The four most popular **trailhead villages** are, on the Black Sea slopes, Çat and Ayder (see Chapter Nine), and on the Çoruh side, Barhal and Hevek (see above). Approach from the Black Sea hills is gentler, with clearer trails, but the paths and

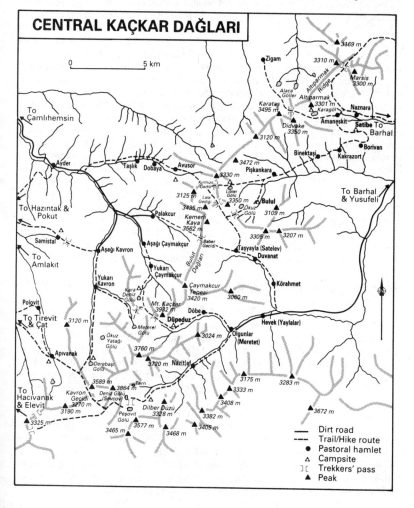

CENTRAL KAÇKAR DAĞLARI

0   5 km

To Çamlıhemşin

Zigam

▲ 3169 m
3310 m
Marsis 3300 m

Alaca Göller   Altıparmak Ridge

Karataş 3495 m   Altıparmak ▲ 3301 m
Karagöl   Naznara

Didvake 3350 m   Amaneskıt   **Satibe** To Barhal

▲ 3120 m

Binektaşi   ● Borivan

Ayder   Taşlık   Dobaya   Avusor   Pişkankara   Kakrazort

To Hazıntak & Pokut

▲ 3472 m
▲ 3330 m

Kırmızı Geçidi

3125 m   Lale Geçidi   Libler Gölü   3350 m   ● **Bulul**   To Barhal & Yusufeli

3435 m   Okuz Gölü   ▲ 3109 m

Palakcur   Kemerli Kaya 3562 m

Samistal

To Amlakıt

Aşağı Kavron   Aşağı Çaymakçur   Baber Geçidi   Taşyayla (Satelev)   ● Körahmet

3305 m   ▲ 3207 m

Duvanat

Yukarı Kavron   Yukarı Çaymakçur

Kara Deniz Gölü   Çaymakçur Tepesi ▲ 3420 m   ▲ 3060 m

Poloyit

To Tirevit & Çat   3120 m   Mt. Kaçkar ▲ 3932 m   Döbe ●

Döbe ●   **Düpeduz**   Hevek (Yaylalar)

Okuz Yatağı Gölü

Apıvanak   Meterel Gölü   ▲ 3024 m   Olgunlar (Meretet)

3760 m

Derebaşı Gölü   3720 m   Naz(t)af

3589 m   Tarn

To Hacıvanak & Elevit   Kavron Geçidi 3270 m   3864 m   Deniz Gölü (Sevcov) ◯

3190 m   Dilber Düzü 3328 m

3325 m   Pesovit Gölü   3577 m   3465 m   3468 m   ▲ 3405 m   ▲ 3382 m

▲ 3175 m   ▲ 3283 m

▲ 3333 m

▲ 3408 m

▲ 3672 m

Bulut Dağları

——   Dirt road
- - -   Trail/Hike route
●   Pastoral hamlet
△   Campsite
]⦗   Trekkers' pass
▲   Peak

villages are relatively crowded, and the almost daily mist rising up to 2800m or higher is a big problem. Hiking grades are tougher on the Çoruh flank, but the weather is more dependable. Overall the best **season** is late June to September, with the mists less of a problem as autumn approaches. If you're hardy, it gets warm enough in midsummer for a quick swim in most of the lakes. Drinkable water, available everywhere from springs, is never scarce.

In terms of **itineraries**, the Kaçkar is infinitely versatile. If you're particularly manic, you can cross from Hevek to Ayder via certain passes in a single, gruelling day, but a more reasonable minimum time to switch sides of the mountains would be three or four days, and most people are happy to spend a week or ten days.

In any case you'll need a **full trekking gear**, including heavy-duty boots, tent, stove, all-weather clothing, and food; hospitality may be offered in a *yayla*, but it cannot be counted on, as there's normally little extra to spare and they're only inhabited part-time. Otherwise, there are few specific **dangers** or warnings, besides the absolute necessity of crossing all tricky passes early in the day before they're shrouded in mist. Territorial domestic bulls are also a nuisance, far more likely to charge a tent than any wild beast. It's useful to know that the ubiquitous Pontic azalea, from whose blossoms the notorious hallucinogenic *deli bal* ("mad" honey) is made, contains sufficient flammable resin to ignite even in damp conditions. Local mountaineers consider it a pest and uproot it with little compunction.

Only two factors might detract from your enjoyment. Since the Kaçkars were first publicized in other guidebooks a few years ago, the crowds seem to increase markedly every season. There's no Nepal-style permit system yet, but such a situation is forseeable. The lack of decent large-scale **maps**, aside from the one in this book and the trekking guide detailed below, is another drawback. If this is all too daunting and you'd rather go with a **guide**, we've mentioned a couple of helpful individuals in Ayder, and we can also recommend Bunyad Dinç in İstanbul (☎1/ 332-0790), who in 1990 led a dozen Dutch on the first complete traverse from İkizdere in the west to Barhal in the east. Otherwise virtually all of the adventure-travel companies listed in *Basics* run some sort of Kaçkar group itinerary, though usually through a local subcontractor. For a rock-by-rock description of much of the following, consult the Kaçkar chapter of *Trekking in Turkey* (in "Books").

Routes in the Northern Kaçkar

Starting from **Barhal**, most trekkers head west to the top of the valley walled off by the Altıparmak chain, finishing a tough first day either near **Karagöl** or the nearby **Satibe** meadow. The following day usually involves a drop down to the Kışla Valley just south, threading through the *yaylas* of **Borivan**, **Binektaşı**, and **Pişkankara** before making camp higher up. If you choose to pitch a tent at **Libler Gölü**, near the top of the main valley, the next day will see you over the tricky **Kırmızı Gedik** saddle for an easy descent to **Ayder**—and a possible end to trekking.

Alternatively you can bear south from Pişkankara up to a camp in the **Bulul** Valley, at the head of which is the wonderful **Öküz Gölü** (Ox Lake) and an initially easy (but later steep) pass leading to the **Körahmet Valley**, still on the Çoruh side of the range. From an overnight stop next to **Satelev** *yayla*, you can choose between crossing the Bulut ridge via the **Baber Pass**, dropping down to **Palakçur** just above Ayder; or rolling downvalley to **Hevek**, with the option of ending your hike or stocking up to continue into the central Kaçkar.

Routes in the Central Kaçkar

Above Hevek, two more valleys lead up to the base of the highest Kaçar peaks. At **Meretet**, the split occurs. Bearing right takes you to camping spots near spectacular wildflowers high up in the **Düpedüz Valley**, just below the **Çaymakcur Pass**, the easiest across the entire Kaçkar. This you should leave for early the following day, and then camp at **Kara Deniz Gölü** beyond the pass, leaving plenty of time for a day-hike to **Meterel Gölü**—and from a nearby overlook, your first, spectacular nose-to-nose view of Point 3972's north face. From Kara Deniz Gölü you can reach Ayder in another long walking day, via the upper and lower **Çaymakcur yaylas.**

The main valley follows the Büyük Çay upstream to the apparent dead-end of the **Dilber meadows**, a popular (and overused) campground at the formidable base of Point 3972 itself. Despite appearances, there is a way up and out: first to the lake of **Sevcov** (Deniz Gölü), and then over the low crest just south to **Peşevit Lake**, where there's much better camping. But Sevcov is the veering-off point for the moderately difficult climb north to the summit, where the climbers' register is hidden underneath a rubble cairn.

From Peşevit Lake it's a bit of a scramble due west until meeting a trail near the top of the **Davali Valley**, aiming for the **Kavron Pass**. Once back on the Black Sea side, you can choose between descending directly to Ayder through the *yaylas* of **Apıvanak**, **Polovit**, **Amlakıt**, and **Hazıntak**, or slipping over the ridge west of Apıvanak to **Tirevit**, and the beginning of the western Kaçkar.

Routes in the Western Kaçkar

Elevit *yayla* is roughly midway between Tirevit and **Çat**, and the starting point of the march up to **Yıldızlı Gölü** (Star Lake), just across the top of the valley from **Hacıvanak** *yayla*. The lake, named for the twinkles of light that appear on its surface early in the morning, offers good camping; the nearby, gentle **Capug Pass** allows access to the headwaters of the Fırtına Çayı, although the onward route is briefly confused by the maze of new bulldozer tracks around **Başyayla** and **Kaleyayla**. At the latter, bear south up toward campgrounds by a lake at the foot of **Tatos Peak**; the following day you can cross a saddle to another lake, **Adalı**, at the base of 3711-meter **Verçenik**.

From this point you'd either descend to Çat via **Ortaköy** and **Varoş**, using a morning bus if possible part of the way, or continue walking west for another day past other lakes just below the ridge joining Verçenik to Germaniman Peak. A final 3100-meter pass just north of **Germaniman** leads to the valley containing **Saler** and **Başköy** *yaylas*, linked by daily bus to **İkizdere**.

Artvin and Around: the Northern Georgian Valleys

The northerly Georgian valleys form the heart of the **province of Artvin**, lying within a fifty-kilometer radius of the town of the same name. Nowhere else in Turkey, except for the Kaçkars, do you feel so close to the Caucasus; ornate wooden domestic and religious architecture, with green slopes or naked crags for a backdrop, clinch the impression of exoticism. Here, too, you may actually encounter native **Georgian speakers**, although they're mostly confined to the remote valleys surrounding the towns of Camili, Meydancık, and Posof. Whatever their antecedents, the people here are remarkable for their high literacy rate and left-of-center polling practices—and their seasonal presence. Disgusted by the lack of local opportunities, many have emigrated internally to work ten months of the year in the factories around Bursa and İzmir, to the extent that there are now more Artvinlis out west than in the province itself.

The region, with its wet, alpine climate, has considerable potential as a wintersports playground, but for the moment most tourists come in the summer to see the local **Georgian churches**. Individually these are not as impressive as their southern relatives, but their locations are almost always more picturesque. Visits should be uncomplicated if you follow the directions given; permits are only needed for access to points within 10km of the Soviet border—including, incidentally, all of the native-Georgian valleys listed above. Certain officious gendarmes, feeling threatened by the increased number of foreign travelers, may stop you on the way to the churches and cause problems. Be polite to them, waving passports and so forth, but politely decline unnecessary offers of escort back to headquarters to "register" or to apply for (imaginary) permits.

Artvin

As your vehicle winds up four kilometers' worth of zigzags from the Çoruh River, you begin to wonder just where **ARTVİN** is. Suddenly the town reveals itself, arrayed in sweeping tiers across a steep, east-facing slope, seeming much higher than its actual 550m of elevation. Unusually, the obligatory ruined **castle** is down low by the river; the only other buildings with a patina of history are houses from the Russian era, tucked here and there on the hill above the town. Certainly it has the least flat ground of any Turkish provincial capital, and—within the city limits at least—perhaps the fewest specific attractions. But Artvin is pleasant enough for a night or two, and becomes a destination in its own right every third week in June, when the **Kafkasör** festival takes place at a *yayla* above town. Highlight of this has traditionally been the pitting of bulls in rut against each other, but since the opening of the Soviet Georgian border the event has taken on a genuinely international character, with revelers, vendors, and performers from the Georgian SSR appearing among 75,000 locals. It's one of the last genuine folk fairs in the country, unlikely to be monkeyed around with by tourism officials, so be there if you can.

Practical Details

The **otogar** is way down by the castle, so the three main companies serving Artvin all run a *servis araba*, or shuttle van, up to town—don't get left behind, or end up getting overcharged for a taxi. Conversely, when it's time to leave, all the bus companies have ticket offices along **İnönü Caddesi**, the single main street running past the Hükümet Konağı (Government Hall) and **PTT**.

There's only one comfortable **hotel**, the *Karahan* at İnönü Caddesi 16 (☎0581/1800), a bit overpriced at $16 a single, $22 double, but all rooms have attached baths; the staff is also willing and informative, and the attached restaurant is one of two places in town serving alcohol with meals. All other accommodation represents a sharp plunge in standard and prices, to $7 a double with no bath. Choose from among the *Genya* (☎0581/1192), across from the *Karahan*; the *Yedi Mart*, also on İnönü; and the *Konak*, behind the government building, although the last-named gets some noise (and unsavory customers) from the gaming hall below it.

You may want to arrange beds at two **out-of-town establishments** while in Artvin. The *Otel Karahan* controls one inn for trekkers in Barhal (see above); they can also point you in the right direction for the municipal bungalows up at Kafkasör meadow. Both are fairly basic, with a per-person cost somewhere in between rates at the *Karahan* and Artvin's budget hotels.

Alternatives to the *Karahan* when **eating out** include the *Derya Restaurant*, up by the PTT, which serves grilled items and alcohol in an atmosphere congenial enough for unescorted foreign women, or the cheerful *Kibar Pide Salonu*, up some stairs from the main drag. The *Köşk Pastanesi*, near the top of İnönü, has breakfast-time *börek* in addition to the usual range of sweeties.

Rounding off the list of amenities are a fairly useless **tourist information office** behind the *Otel Karahan* (everyone asks questions in the hotel instead) and a fairly expensive **hamam** ($2.50 each), behind the PTT. Theoretically they shuffle clientele to accommodate either sex within the hour, but in practice this doesn't always happen.

Ardanuç and Yeni Rabat

The valleys east of Artvin are no less spectacular than their counterparts around Yusufeli. The approach to Ardanuç, once the capital of Klarjeti Georgia, is through the spectacular, high-walled "Hell's Gorge." **Dolmuşes** from Artvin do the thirty-minute trip all morning, starting at 8am, with the last one back at 3pm. The dwindling old *mahalle* of **ARDANUÇ** crouches at the foot of a giant wedding cake of crumbling orange rock, on top of which sits a giant Bagratid **castle**. With an early start to beat the heat, you can climb it, but to do that and see the church up the valley in one day you'll need your own transportation—or be willing to overnight in the newer district. This, arranged around a delightful, sycamore-shaded green, can offer a single beer bar, some restaurants, and a handful of very plain **hotels**.

Yeni Rabat

East of Ardanuç the pavement ends, and the scenery becomes ever more idyllic as the dirt road worsens. At a triple fork among the meadows and conifers 14km along, take the signed left option to Bulanık village and Yeni Rabat; most people come by car or their own two feet, but considering the rough surface there are a surprising number of Ardanuç-based dolmuşes lurching by, bound for Bulanık and Tosunlar, across the valley.

From the middle of **BULANIK**, distinguished by fine vernacular log cabins, a recent bulldozer track leads east-northeast for most of the 45-minute walk to the tenth-century monastery church of **YENİ RABAT** (SHATBERDI), nestled in the vegetable gardens of its four-house hamlet. The long-vanished monastery, founded a century earlier by Gregory Khantzeli, was renowned as a school for manuscript illuminators. The dome, nave, and transept are still virtually intact, but the exterior has been stripped of most dressed stone, and the new road in—which will be extended west to replace the river-bank route—is being run dangerously close to the foundations.

The Lower Berta Valley: Dolishane and Porta

From the Ardanuç area, retrace your steps to the junction with Highway 965 linking Artvin and Şavşat, which parallels the Berta River (Imerhevi in Georgian). Exactly 300m upstream from the Ardanuç turnoff, a fine stone **bridge** leaps over the water, and directly opposite this a sign points up a dirt road to the village of **HAMAMLI**. In theory there's a dolmuş service, but it arrives in the afternoon and returns the next morning to Artvin, which isn't very useful to tourists. After 6.5km all vehicles must park by the first house; it's two minutes more on foot to the tenth-century church of **DOLİSHANE**, now the village mosque. The vegetable garden and house of the *imam* adjoin it, and he or his family—some of them a bit jaded by a steady trickle of visitors—will show you around. There are some faded frescoes in the "basement" created when wood planking split the building into top and bottom stories; the whitewashed upper interior is of little interest. The exterior is more rewarding, the south dome window surrounded by such reliefs as the builder-king Smbat I (954–958) offering the church to Christ, a Star of David and an archangel.

Twelve kilometers above the turn for Ardanuç, a yellow metal sign—typical of those posted throughout the province by the energetic owners of the *Otel Karahan*—points to the start of the path up to **PORTA**, the modern name of the ninth-century monastery of Khantza, home to the architect-monk Gregory Khantzeli. It's an enjoyable 35-minute climb up to the **BAĞLAR** district of Pırnallı village, although you'll need good, treaded shoes, since the trail is very slippery; for the same reason reckon on the same amount of time down. The friendly hamlet, an oasis tucked into a side ravine of the main canyon running up to Pırnallı, is built higgledy-piggledy around and up against the dilapidated monuments.

The main tenth-century **church**, still impressive despite gaping holes in the dome and walls, was similar in plan to the one at Haho, with low-ceilinged aisles flanking the nave. To the west stands a separate, smaller sixteen-sided **cupola**, once part of either a belfry or a baptistry. Georgian inscriptions are chiseled profusely across its two-toned masonry, which is in near-perfect condition. Of the monastery quarters themselves, orientated west-to-east, only the southeastern corner remains. Beside the path in, the eastern wall of an isolated chapel shelters an **ayazma**, or sacred spring, which supports the local orchards—a contrast to the endemic scrub oak (*pırnal*) that gives the main village its name.

The Upper Berta Valley: Tbeti and Şavşat

The last local Georgian church lies 10km off the Artvin–Şavşat road. Turn off the side road to VELİKÖY and bear right after the river bridge. Follow the river up to a small hamlet, where an inconspicuous sign by a shop points left to the village of **CEVİZLİ**, where you'll park by the school and walk 200m more. There is a dolmuş service to and from nearby Şavşat, but as in the case of Hamamlı it inconveniently arrives in the afternoon and goes back to town the next morning.

The remains of the tenth-century monastery church of **TBETİ**, peeking out of the trees at the head of a beautiful valley, are visible at some distance to the sharp-eyed, although up close the cloister is heartbreaking—extensively damaged by local treasure-hunters a few decades ago. Tbeti was unique in its non-elongated cross-in-square floorplan, with only a church in far-off Cengilli approximating it.

Now, only the south transept retains any relief work, and a single blurry fresco of Christ is left inside, but even in this sad condition it is evocative of a ruined English or French abbey. According to tradition the great medieval Georgian poet, Shota Rustaveli, studied here for a time; he is said to have fallen hopelessly in love with Queen Tamara while serving as one of her ministers, and, being summarily rejected, ended his days in a Jerusalem monastery.

A compact **castle**, just west of the town-limits sign, heralds your arrival in ŞAVŞAT. There's little to stop for here other than the fine local **carpets** woven in a half-dozen villages of the district. You won't starve, but accommodation is even more primitive than in Artvin or Ardanuç. The road east from here through the forest to Ardahan, though nominally all-weather, deteriorates markedly as you approach the high pass at the border between Artvin and Kars provinces; just before, the tin roofs of a huge, tenement-like *yayla* glisten in the frequent mountain rain.

travel details

Trains

From Kars to Erzurum/Ankara (daily at 6 & 11am; 5–6hr/30hr).

From Erzurum to Kars (daily at 11am & 8pm; 5–6hr); to Ankara (daily at 11am & 4pm; 25hr).

Buses

From Erzurum to Bayburt (hourly; 3hr); Trabzon (5 daily; 8hr); İspir (3 daily; 2hr 30min); Rize (1 or 2 direct daily; 7hr); Kars (hourly; 3hr 30min); Yusufeli (3 direct daily; 3hr); Artvin (5 daily; 4hr); Doğubeyazit (4 daily; 4hr 30min); Van (3 or 4 daily; 7hr 30min); Sivas/Ankara (hourly; 8hr 30min/15hr).

From Kars to Erzurum (10 daily; 3hr 30min); Doğubeyazit (6 daily, last at 2pm; 3hr 30min); Digor (hourly; 45min); Iğdır (hourly; 2hr 45min); Artvin via Göle (1 daily at 7am; 7hr); Trabzon (1 daily; 12hr).

From Artvin to Erzurum (3 daily; 4hr); Kars (2 or 3 daily before noon; 7hr); Hopa/Rize/Trabzon (hourly until 3pm; 1hr 30min/3hr 15min/4hr 30min); Yusufeli (4 daily; 1hr); Ardanuç (6 daily until 2pm; 30min); Şavşat (6 or 7 daily; 1hr 15min).

Planes

From Erzurum to Ankara/İstanbul on *THY* (1 daily; 1hr/2hr 30min).

From Kars to Ankara via Elâzığ on *THT* (2 weekly; 3hr 20min).

From Erzincan to Ankara via Sivas on *THT* (2 weekly; 2hr 20min).

International trains

From Kars to Ahuryan station just inside the Armenian SSR (10am Tues & Fri summer, Tues only winter; 2hr).

CHAPTER ELEVEN

THE HATAY AND EUPHRATES BASIN

E ast of Adana, you leave tourist Turkey behind. The traveling is harder and there are fewer resorts or places of orthodox interest, with the consequence that visitors are much fewer and farther between. The area formed by the curve of the coast down toward Syria, the **Hatay**, together with the hinterland of the **Euphrates Basin**, has long been one where different civilizations and cultures have met and sometimes clashed. The towns here formed an eastern outpost of the Roman Empire, and, after the fall of Rome, experienced successive waves of conquest and counter-conquest. Almost everybody seems to have passed through at one time or another: Arabs, Crusaders, Selçuks, Mongols, and finally the victorious World War I Allies, who moved in on southeast Turkey as part of a wider attempt to break up the moribund Ottoman Empire.

Today something of this frontier atmosphere persists, and you'll notice that in many towns ethnic Turks are in the minority. It's a sometimes volatile racial mix, exacerbated by fundamentalist pressures and the separatist sympathies of some of the population, not to mention the often heavy-handed tactics of the Turkish authorities. Traveling around is, however, no problem, at least in the western part of the region, with good bus links between all the major towns. However, the roads start to deteriorate dramatically east of Gaziantep, and the hotel facilities are much more primitive.

The Hatay, which extends like a stumpy finger into Syria, is an Arab enclave and has closer cultural links with the Arab world than with the rest of Turkey. There has been some separatist tension in the area but fortunately these problems are unlikely to affect visitors, and indeed the Hatay's multi-ethnic identity gives it an extra edge of interest. **Antakya**, the largest town, is set in the valley of the Asi River separating the Nur and Ziyaret mountain ranges. The city, which dates back to Seleucid times, was an important center under the Romans, and although little has survived from the past, Antakya's Arab atmosphere and the proximity of places like **Harbiye**—the ancient resort of Daphne—and **Samandağ**, a quiet coastal town, make it worth a day or two on anyone's itinerary. The Hatay's other main center is **İskenderun**, a heavily industrialized port of minimal interest.

Following the main approach route from Adana, the **Euphrates Basin** fans out to the east and northeast, a rough triangle encroaching on the southern fringes of the Anatolian plateau, with the Euphrates itself winding its turbid way from the north into Syria. It's a backward area, where farmers scratch a living from the rocky and unrewarding land, although the government and locals alike are optimistic that the eventual completion of the massive Atatürk Dam project across the Euphrates will raise the economy above subsistence levels. Here too

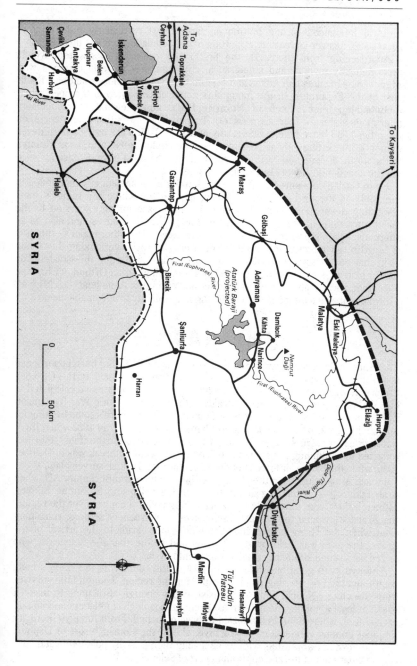

the Arab influence is strong, but moving farther east, particularly in the remoter rural areas, an ever-increasing proportion of the population is made up of Kurds.

Approaching from the west, the first major center is **Gaziantep**, which, predominantly modern and industrial in character, has more in common with Mediterranean cities like Adana and Mersin than with the more traditional towns east of the Euphrates. In the mountains north of Gaziantep is the spectacular mountain-top temple/tomb of **Nemrut Dağı**, now elevated to compulsory pilgrimage status for tourists in eastern Turkey. The towns that ring the site, on the other hand, have little to offer: **Adıyaman** and **Kâhta** are ugly modern developments, interesting only as possible bases for exploring Nemrut, as is **Malatya** to the north. **Elâzığ**, still farther north, is by far the most obvious base for visiting the abandoned city of **Harput** just outside.

From Gaziantep a pitted road leads to **Şanlıurfa**, an ancient city mentioned in the Bible as the birthplace of Abraham, and on the whole the region's most rewarding destination. Şanlıurfa makes an ideal base for an excursion to the major attractions of **Harran**, with its mud-brick beehive houses, and also as an alternative staging post for Nemrut–bound travelers. The other major destination is **Mardin**, an atmospheric place set on a crag of rock overlooking the Syrian plain that boasts some beautiful Arab houses. East of Mardin, the isolated **Tür Abdin** plateau is home to most of Turkey's remaining Syrian Orthodox Christian population and a scattering of monasteries and churches. At its heart lies **Midyat**, a town of once-elegant mansions crumbling in seemingly irredeemable decay.

THE HATAY

The **Hatay** only became part of modern Turkey in 1939, having been apportioned to the French Protectorate of Syria since the dismemberment of the Ottoman Empire. It was handed over to Turkey after a plebiscite, in a move calculated to buy Turkish support, or at least neutrality in the imminent World War. The majority of people here speak Arabic as their first language and there's some backing for union with Syria, which has led to problems—most recently in 1983 when there was serious unrest in Antakya. For its part, Syria is keen to see the Hatay returned, reflected in continuing border tension. The most recent outbreak was in October 1989, when the Syrian air force shot down an unarmed Turkish survey plane.

In fact, Arab influence in the Hatay goes back to the seventh century AD, when Arab raiders began hacking at the edges of the collapsing Byzantine Empire. Although they were never able to secure lasting political control over the region, the Arabs were able to establish themselves as permanent settlers, remaining even when the Hatay passed into Ottoman hands. Prior to the arrival of the Arabs, the area was held by the Romans and before that the Seleucids, who prized its position straddling trading routes into Syria.

Antakya, with good bus links to the rest of the country, is the Hatay's main center and the best starting point for exploring the region. Though little survives from the city's Seleucid and Roman past, it has enough attractions to make it worth at least a full day, notably an excellent archaeological museum and an odd cave church where Saint Peter is said to have preached. From Antakya there are frequent dolmuş connections to **Harbiye**, site of the Roman resort of Daphne, and the town of **Samandağ**, with its appealing though sadly polluted beach adjacent to what's left of the ancient Roman port of Seleucia ad Piera.

İskenderun and Around

South of Yakacik, the build-up of wayside industry and pollution is the signal for **İSKENDERUN**, founded by Alexander the Great as Alexandria ad Issum to commemorate his victory over the Persians. Already a major trade nexus during Roman times, under the Ottomans İskenderun became the main port for Halab (Aleppo), now in Syria, from which trade routes fanned out to Persia and the Arabian Peninsula. Today there's nothing of historical interest here, indeed there's not much of any interest at all—modern İskenderun is basically an industrial center and military and commercial harbor.

The local **tourist information office**, Atatürk Bulvarı 49/B (daily 8:30–noon & 1:30–6pm; ☎881/11620), is on the waterfront, by the town pier, in an area that's home to most of the town's cheaper **pensions and hotels**. The best of the inexpensive places is the plain *Kavaklı Pansiyon*, Şehit Pamir Caddesi 52, Sokak 14 (☎881/14606), which has singles for $8 and doubles for $12. Also worth investigating is the *Altındisler Oteli*, Sehit Paşa Caddesi 41/9 (☎881/13659), with singles from around $6 and doubles from $10. There's also a dirt-cheap **campground**, well marked, a couple of minutes' walk off Atatürk Bulvarı.

Uluçınar and South of İskenderun

Dolmuşes run from İskenderun to the small resort and fishing town of **ULUÇINAR** about 40km to the southwest, where there are some decent stretches of beach (though often charging for entry)—very popular with Syrian tourists and people from İskenderun. Of a number of **hotels** and **pensions** in the town, best is probably the *Motel Yunus*, Akdeniz Caddesi, opposite the post office, where you'll be able to get a triple room for about $15. The best **place to eat** is the waterfront *Plaj Restaurant*, which does good fish and seafood dishes. Beyond Uluçınar the road south exists more on maps than in reality, although if you can be bothered to follow it for a few kilometers you'll come across some more undiscovered **beaches**.

South of İskenderun the road rises up into the mountains, passing through the small hill town of **BELEN**, where a pair of cafés make a good place to break a long journey. It's a quiet, unspoiled place, with a few springs gushing curative water. From here the road strains and curves through the **Belen Pass**; this was of great strategic importance during Roman times, when it was known as the *Pylae Syriae* or Gates of Syria. The pass is perhaps not quite as dramatic as the name suggests—mainly bare hillside and scree slopes with few distinctive features, from which the road descends gradually into the lush Amık plain below.

About 5km beyond the Belen Pass you'll come to a major road junction, where a right turn leads toward Antakya. After a few kilometers a sign marks the road to **Bakras Kalesi**, an imposing medieval castle about 4km off the main road. The first castle to be built on this site was erected by the Arabs during the seventh century and destroyed during the First Crusade. Later the Knights Templar built a new fortress, which became an important link in their defensive system, forming the basis of what you can see today. It was much fought-over, and in 1156 a bloody battle took place here between the Knights Templar and the soldiers of Thoros, ruler of Cilician Armenia. In 1188 the castle fell to Arabs, but possession was fiercely contested until the Ottomans took over during the sixteenth century.

Antakya

ANTAKYA, 25km south, stands on the site of ancient Antioch, and although there's little sense of historical continuity, the city's laid-back pace and heavily Arab atmosphere make it unique in Turkey. Flanked by mountains to the north and south, it sits in the bed of a broad river valley planted with olive trees—a welcome visual relief if you have traveled down from the drab flatlands surrounding Adana.

The city was founded as Antioch in the fourth century BC by Seleucos Nicator, one of the four generals among whom the empire of Alexander the Great was divided. It soon grew into an important commercial center, and by the second century BC had developed into a metropolis of half a million—one of the largest cities of the ancient world, a major staging post on the newly opened trade routes leading from the Mediterranean to Asia, and a center of scholarship and learning. It also acquired a reputation as a city of all kinds of moral excess, causing Saint Peter to choose it as the location of one of the world's first Christian communities in the hope that the new religion would exercise a restraining influence.

One of the more bizarre aspects of early Christianity was the craze for pillar-sitting, which developed in Antioch during the fourth century. It began with Saint Simeon Stylites, who spent twenty-five years perched on top of a pillar meditating and making sporadic pronouncements castigating the citizens of Antioch for their moral turpitude. He attracted a lot of followers and spawned legions of imitators—250 at one point, according to ancient accounts.

Despite being razed by a series of earthquakes during the sixth century AD, Antioch was able to maintain its prosperity after the Roman era, and only with the rise of Constantinople did the city begin to decline, passing through the hands of various occupiers before finally falling to the Mamelukes of Egypt, who sacked it in 1268. By the time the Ottomans, under Selim the Grim, took over in 1516 Antioch had long since vanished from the main stage of world history, and by the turn of the last century the city was little more than a village, squatting amid the ruins of the ancient metropolis. After World War I, Antakya, along with most of the rest of the Hatay, passed into the hands of the French, who laid the foundations of the modern city.

The City

Antakya is cut in two by the Asi River, known in ancient times as the Orontes. At the heart of the city, spanning the river, is the much-renovated **Rana Köprüsü** or "Old Bridge" which dates from the third century AD. The eastern bank is home to **old Antakya**—a maze of narrow streets, backed by the rocky cliffs of the Ziyaret Dağı range. In terms of specific sights there isn't much to see, but the bazaar and market areas north of Kemal Paşa Caddesi (running from west to east just north of the Rana Köprüsü) are easily worth an hour or two of wandering. At the eastern end of Kemal Paşa Caddesi, at the junction with Kurtuluş Caddesi, is the **Habibi Naccar Camii**, a mosque incorporated into the shell of a former Byzantine church, which was in turn built on the site of an ancient temple. The distinctive pointed minaret was added during the seventeenth century and is not—as you might be tempted to imagine—a former church tower.

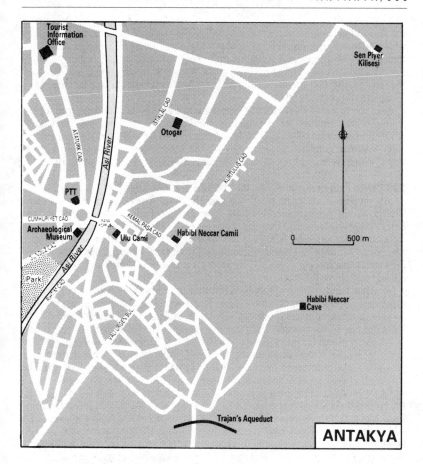

ANTAKYA

The Archaeological Museum

From the Rana Köprüsü, it's a quick hop across to the western side of the river and the **Archaeological Museum** (Tue–Sun 9am–noon & 1:30–6pm; $2), which has a collection of locally unearthed Roman **mosaics** that ranks as among the best of its kind in the world. Well laid-out and imaginatively lit in the first four rooms of the museum, they are in a state of near-immaculate preservation—bar the occasional bare patch or two where the tiles have fallen off—and mostly depict scenes from Roman mythology.

The majority were unearthed at the suburb of Daphne, now known as Harbiye (see below), which was Antioch's main vacation resort in Roman times. The finest in terms of size and scope is the so-called "**Buffet Mosaic**" in Room 2, offering a vivid depiction of the rape of Ganymede, with Zeus in the form of an eagle, while another striking mythological scene in Room 3 shows the **infant Hercules** strangling some serpents. Equally interesting are a number of the mosaics hinting at the Antochian licentiousness that so outraged the early Christians, in particular a **well-endowed hunchback** grinning wickedly (Room 3), and a **drunken Dionysus** leering at a green-clad nymph (Room 4), both of which were found in Antakya itself. A number of mosaics show scenes of theater-going and banqueting, suggesting that for the wealthier inhabitants of Antioch, at least, life was a leisured and luxurious affair.

After the mosaics, the rest of the museum is a little more mundane, with only a couple of first-century AD **statues of Venus** in the entrance hall, and some Hittite and Assyrian reliefs and idols recovered from funeral mounds on the Amık plain worth writing home about. Among the latter, look out for the two **stone lions**, which were used as column pediments during the eighth century BC.

Sen Piyer, Trajan's Aqueduct, and Habibi Neccar Cave

At the northeastern edge of Antakya is the **Sen Piyer** Kilisesi or St Peter's Church (Tues–Sun 8am–noon & 1:30–6pm; 50¢), the famous cave church of Saint Peter, from which it's said that the apostle preached to the Christian population of Antioch. It's reached by following Kurtuluş Caddesi in a northeasterly direction for about 2km until you come to a indicated right turn. Follow a dirt track toward the mountains and after about ten minutes you come to the church, set into the hillside just above the track.

Whether Saint Peter really did preach from the Sen Piyer Kilisesi is—like the exact dates of his stay in the city—open to question. All that theologians seem to be able to agree on is that he spent some time in Antioch between 47 and 54 AD, founding one of the world's first Christian communities with Paul and Barnabas. The slightly kitsch facade of the church was built by Crusaders during the twelfth century. Inside water drips down the cave walls and the cool atmosphere provides a welcome break from the heat of summer. Beneath your feet you'll be able to discern traces of mosaic-work thought to date from the fifth century AD, while to the right of the altar is a kind of font set in the floor and fed by a spring with reputed curative properties. To the left of the altar there used to be an tunnel (now blocked off), down which the early Christians could flee in the event of a raid. A special service is held here on June 29 to mark the anniversary of Saint Peter's death, attended by members of Antakya's small Christian community. More regular masses are celebrated in a nineteenth-century church just off Kurtuluş Caddesi.

Scattered around the vicinity of the church are a few sarcophagi. If you follow the track beyond the grotto you'll see scenes of a lifestyle scarcely changed in centuries. Women bake bread in outdoor ovens, while men work the fields of their farmsteads using primitive tools. On the other side of a small valley is the edge of Antakya—a sprawl of flat roofs and dirt streets.

At the southeast edge of town, near the hospital, is the **Aqueduct of Trajan**, a surviving fragment of the city's Roman water-supply system. Some way to the north of here is the **Habibi Neccar Cave,** once home to a solitary prophet.

Practical Details

From the **otogar** it's a ten-to-fifteen-minute walk to the town center. Antakya's **tourist office** is in the new town at Atatürk Caddesi 41 (daily 8am–noon & 1:30–6:30pm, ☎891/12636). You'll find most of Antakya's cheaper **hotels** in the old town, in particular the bazaar area around Kemal Paşa Caddesi. Close to the otogar on İstiklâl Caddesi, the slightly grungy *Şeker Palas Oteli* (☎891/11603) charges $3.50 for a double room without bath. A better, if somewhat more expensive, option is the nearby *Divan Oteli*, İstiklâl Caddesi 62 (☎891/11518,11735), with singles for $8 and doubles for $10. A little farther along, the unpleasant *Hotel İstanbul*, İstiklâl Caddesi 14 (☎891/11122), charges $3 for a single and $5 for a double. Slightly better is the *Hotel Kent*, also on İstiklâl Caddesi (near the bridge), which has singles from $3 and doubles from $6. With a little more money, try the *Atahan Hotel*, Hürriyet Caddesi 28 (☎891/11407,11408), where you pay $16 for a single and $21 for a double.

The best places to **eat and drink** are on Hürriyet Caddesi, notably the *Kösem Restaurant* at no. 21, though there are plenty of other options, including a number along İstiklâl Caddesi. Local delicacies and specialties worth sampling include the crystallized squashes sold by weight in many of the *pastanes*.

West of Antakya: Samandağ, Çevlik, and Around

About 25km southwest of Antakya, **SAMANDAĞ** is an Arabic-speaking resort town of about 30,000 people (though it feels smaller), decaying genteely on a sloping plain between the hills and the Mediterranean. It's a popular place, especially with Syrians and other Arab visitors, served by regular dolmuşes from Antakya otogar which will deposit you in the town's unprepossessing center, a couple of kilometers inland. Here you'll find a few stores and restaurants and a couple of banks.

To get to **the beach**, take any dolmuş heading for "*Deniz*" ("The Sea"), although it's not really recommended you swim here because of pollution from İskenderun, 50km or so up the coast. There are a couple of **hotels** close to the beach, best of which is the colonial-style *Derviş Dönmez Tesisleri* (☎8981/1656), where they charge $8 for a large clean double with bath. The hotel also has a restaurant that does good food, and acts as a social focus for the area. Next door is the *Dönmez Hotel Restaurant* (☎8981/1841), where the emphasis is more on the restaurant side of the operation, but they have six very basic rooms up on the roof, going for about $2.50 each.

Çevlik and Seleucia ad Piera

A few kilometers north of Samandağ is the village of ÇEVLİK, easily walkable along the beach—although the path is marred by a stinking refuse dump midway between the villages. You can also reach Çevlik by dolmuş from Samandağ town center. The village has a few **pensions** and a **campground**, and you can also camp on the beach, although strictly speaking this is illegal and you might get moved on. In ancient times Çevlik was the port of Seleucia ad Piera, serving Antioch, and there are still a few ruins scattered around, including the **Titus ve Vespasiyanus Tüneli** (dawn–dusk; $1)—a huge channel carved out of the hillside as part of the port's drainage system. Two inscriptions at the upper end give details of its construction. Also scattered around you'll see foundations, and sections of ruined wall. Again, swimming is probably unwise, although the village beach is popular with local fishermen.

South of Antakya: Harbiye and the Road to Syria

About 10km south of Antakya is **HARBİYE**, the ancient and celebrated suburb of Daphne, a beautiful gorge to which revelers and vacationers flocked in Roman times, drawn by shady cypress and laurel groves dotted with waterfalls and pools. Those who could afford to built villas here, while lesser mortals had to content themselves with a day-trip. Today Antakya's modern citizens follow their example, and there is a regular dolmuş service from the city otogar. From the dolmuş drop-off point follow a road uphill past modern houses until you come to a waterfall. From here follow the path down into the gorge, where a number of shady tea gardens await amid a landscape that can have hardly altered since Roman times.

The Romans built a temple to Apollo in Daphne, since it was generally held to be the setting for the god's pursuit of Daphne. According to the myth, Daphne, when seized by Apollo, prayed for deliverance; in answer to her prayers Peneus transformed her into a laurel tree. Another legend relates that the resort was where Paris gave the golden apple to Aphrodite, indirectly precipitating the Trojan War. Later, and with possibly more basis in fact, Mark Antony and Cleopatra are said to have been married here. Harbiye was also the location of the Antioch Games, which were more spectacular in their day than the ancient Olympics. In later years local Christians pulled down the Temple of Apollo and used its stone to build their churches. With the departure of the Romans the place went into decline, a process compounded by the destructive attacks of the Persians and Arabs during the sixth and seventh centuries.

About 8km south of Harbiye lies **Qalat az Zaw**, a ruined fortress originally built to defend the southern approaches to Antioch and much fought-over by Crusaders, Arabs, and Mamelukes. Twenty-odd kilometers farther on, close to the Syrian border, is the village of **YAYLADAĞI**—a quiet spot that has a pleasant **picnic area**, set in mountain woods down toward the border—a good point for a break if you're en route to the border itself.

Near Yayladaği is the 1759-meter **Djebel Akra**, the ancient Mount Cassius, a sacred summit since Hittite times. If you want to explore the mountain you need permission from the local civil and military authorities, and you have to rent a guide. Inquire at Antakya tourist office.

THE EUPHRATES BASIN

The **Euphrates Basin** is one of the most rewarding parts of Turkey, offering a number of compelling ancient sites and some fascinating isolated towns. The broad alluvial plain of the Euphrates (the Fırat in Turkish) has been inhabited for several millennia and was once a lush, fertile region. Indeed, remains of some of the world's oldest known human settlements have been discovered here. Unfortunately, centuries of continuous warfare, exacerbated by the depredations of nomadic agriculture, have reduced much of the area to dusty steppes; the soon-to-be-completed Atatürk Dam provides the only hope of life returning to the arid landscape. In the summer the harsh terrain bakes in an intense heat that can leave you regretting you ever came; to enjoy the Euphrates Basin at its best, you should visit during the spring or fall, when things cool down to more bearable levels.

Historically this has always been a frontier region, where opposing civilizations and cultures clashed. The Romans, coming up against the Persians, never really made it much farther east, and later the Byzantine Empire began to crumble here during the seventh and eighth centuries under pressure from the Arabs to the south. After World War I the victorious Allies were to strike at what was seen as the soft underbelly of the weakened Ottoman Empire when, in 1920, the French army advanced up from Syria, closing in on Gaziantep, only to be driven back after a ten-month siege by forces loyal to Atatürk.

Coming from the west, most visitors pass first through **Gaziantep**, an industrial center and last outpost of western, Europeanized Turkey that has little to recommend it. For many visitors the main attraction of the Euphrates Basin is the Commagene mountain-top temple of **Nemrut Dağı**, which is in grave danger of becoming one of Turkey's most overworked tourist clichés. Such is the appeal of this site that highly unattractive nearby towns like **Adıyaman** and **Kâhta** have also been able to carve out a piece of the action by offering overpriced and inferior accommodation to unsuspecting visitors; Nemrut Dağı is arguably better visited from Şanlıurfa, or, if you're approaching from central Anatolia, **Malatya**—a blandly inoffensive town where you'll be able to avoid the worst of the tourist rip-offs. From Malatya it's also an easy matter to make your way to **Elâzığ**, an ugly modern place interesting only for its archaeological museum and the presence of the ruined city of **Harput** just outside town.

East of Gaziantep, the road meanders across the plain of the Euphrates, crossing the river at unremarkable **Birecik** before cutting across rocky uplands to the venerable town of **Şanlıurfa** (known locally as "Urfa"), which, with a day or two's worth of sites of its own and a number of decent hotels, also makes a good base for exploring attractions like nearby **Harran**, a continuously inhabited settlement for over 6000 years—unmissable, despite swarming tour groups and suffocating summer heat.

From Şanlıurfa the by-now heavily potholed road heads due east to **Mardin**, separated from the rest of Turkey by distance and a way of life apparently frozen in the past. Here you're moving onto the fringes of the Kurdish separatist unrest that has disrupted much of eastern Turkey since the beginning of the 1980s and, although it's highly unlikely that you'll come into direct contact with trouble, you will notice heavy troop concentrations and a tangible tension in the air in isolated towns like **Midyat**. A more visible manifestation of the problems is a huge refugee camp just north of the main road between Mardin and the town of

Kızıltepe, whose inhabitants are Kurds from Iraq who fled after Saddam Hussein launched chemical warfare attacks on their communities in 1988. In Midyat you'll also find members of another minority group—Turkey's Syrian Orthodox Christian community, who split with the rest of Christendom some 1500 years ago. About 30,000 Christians live in the villages of the **Tür Abdin** plateau that fans out to the east of Midyat, dotted with ruined churches and monasteries.

Travel in the region is straightforward with good bus links operating all the way through to Mardin. You may find the dreadful roads a pain in the kidneys, but they shouldn't stop you from getting where you want to go. Bear in mind that the current political situation gives the atmosphere in Midyat, and some of the smaller villages around, a threatening edge. You may be stopped by the police at times, but if you co-operate fully this shouldn't be more than a minor inconvenience.

Gaziantep

Approaching the Euphrates Basin from the west the main road passes through **GAZİANTEP**, a modern city of half a million people, the largest in the region but with little to offer. Gaziantep can be used as a staging post on a journey to more interesting destinations to the north or farther east, and rates an overnight stop at most.

The city is known to the locals and, more importantly, to most of the bus companies as "Antep" (a corruption of the Arab *Ayn Teb* meaning "good spring"); indeed the "Gazi" prefix—meaning "warrior"—was only added in 1920, after the city withstood a ten-month French siege, when the Allies were attempting to carve up Turkey between themselves. These days the city is probably best known for its incredible pistachio nuts—*şam fıstığı*—green and full of flavor, the best you'll taste anywhere in Turkey and very cheap to boot.

The City

Gaziantep was first occupied during Hittite times and has since experienced the familiar round of conquest and counter-conquest—Assyrian, Persian, Alexandrine, Roman, Selçuk, Crusader, and Byzantine—shared by so many settlements in this part of Turkey. Industrialization, based on textiles, has brought a degree of prosperity to the city, along with an influx of country people looking for a better standard of living, many of whom live in shanty settlements similar to those found in Ankara and İzmir, spreading up the surrounding hills.

The only interesting survivor from Gaziantep's past is the **castle**, which dominates the town from a nearby hill—an artificial mound formed by layers of accumulated debris from thousands of years of human occupation. It dates back to late Roman times, but the present structure owes more to the Selçuks. To reach it, take the road running up from İstasyon Caddesi, opposite the museum. If you bear right at the top you'll eventually come to a small mosque, opposite which a ramp leads up to the main doors. It's surprisingly lively inside the citadel, with dozens of workshops and old Ottoman houses. In some of the former you might find craftsmen manufacturing the local specialty—furniture inlaid with mother of pearl, although these days it's more likely to be plastic.

The city's only other remotely worthwhile feature is **Gaziantep Museum**, on İstasyon Caddesi (Tues–Sun 8:30am–noon & 1–5:30pm; 50¢)—full of archaeological and ethnological detritus from Hittite through to Ottoman times, including a number of Hittite reliefs and a couple of reasonably well-preserved Roman mosaics.

Practical Details

Gaziantep **otogar** is on the eastern edge of the city, and you'll need to take a dolmuş (destination "*Devlet Hastanesi*") or one of the infrequent city buses from here to the town center. Get off near the junction of Suburcu Caddesi and Hürriyet Caddesi, where you'll find most of the city's hotels and restaurants.

Gaziantep does not have a true **tourism information office**, but you may be able to get ahold of some very rudimentary brochures at the *İl Turism Müdürlüğü* office on Atatürk Bulvarı, though this has more of an administrative function and the staff only speaks Turkish. If you decide to stay, there are a couple of **hotels**, although there's a dearth of real budget possibilities. The cheapest is *Hotel Şec*, Atatürk Bulvarı 4/B (☎851/15272), where you can get a reasonable, if spartan double room for about $5. Another possibility is the *Hotel Güney*, Atatürk Bulvarı 10 (☎851/16886), a few doors down, with singles from around $5 and doubles from $9. The *Türk Otel*, Hürriyet Caddesi 27 (☎851/19480), is a little fancier; it charges $14 for a double with shower, as does the *Büyük Oteli*, Karagöz Caddesi 26 (☎851/1522).

There are plenty of **restaurants**, all near the Atatürk Bulvarı/Hürriyet Caddesi junction. Best value is probably the *Keyvan Bey Restaurant* just off Hürriyet Caddesi, where you should be able to get the works for about $3. Also worth a visit is the rooftop restaurant of the *Hotel Kaleli*, which isn't as expensive as you might imagine—you should be able to eat for about $4.

Adıyaman, Kâhta, and Nemrut Dağı

One hundred and fifty kilometers northeast of Gaziantep, the mountain-top temple at **Nemrut Dağı** has, over the last five years or so, become an almost inevitable stop on the southeastern Turkey circuit, a giant tumulus set on top of one of the region's highest peaks, flanked by massive broken statues of classical gods and the local king in whose name it was erected. It's an unforgettable place, remote and grandiose, drawing countless visitors who trek up the mountainside by minibus and car. Their enthusiasm is usually rewarded, but lately the sheer numbers of people processed up to the summit by local day-trip operators has—sadly—begun to detract from the splendor of the site.

The towns of **Adıyaman** and **Kâhta**—the former served by about three daily buses direct from Gaziantep—make the most obvious bases if you've decided to spend a couple of days exploring this area, although both towns are now heavily geared for tourists and accordingly expensive. Of the two, Kâhta is probably the better bet—it's closer to Nemrut and has slightly more character than Adıyaman, which is little more than a low-rise concrete sprawl. An alternative would be to visit Nemrut Dağı from Malatya or Şanlıurfa (see below), which are generally less crowded and not as pricey.

EXCURSIONS TO NEMRUT DAĞI

It's possible to take organized **minibus trips** to Nemrut Dağı from Adıyaman, Kâhta, Malatya, and Şanlıurfa, and, given the distances involved, unless you have your own transportation, these are about the best way of getting there. However, be warned: the local operators in Adıyaman and Kâhta run a real racket, which can take much of the pleasure out a trip. Making the journey from Malatya or Şanlıurfa is relatively hassle-free but takes longer and generally ends up costing slightly more because of the necessity for overnight stops.

From Adıyaman and Kâhta

In Adıyaman, the local tourist information office charters minibuses to Nemrut, but if these are full they will be able to direct you to a local travel agent. In Kâhta, the business is in the hands of the local hotels, which run excursions (at extra cost) for their guests. The *Hotel Kommagene* offers the best organized trips while the owners of *Fortuna Camping Pansiyon* provide a slightly cheaper service (see below for details).

The excursions most in demand are those timed to get you to Nemrut for sunset or sunrise; sunset trips leave at 2pm and return at 9pm, those for the sunrise leave at 2am, returning at 11am. Expect to pay between $10 and $14 a head for an excursion taking in the subsidiary sites of Karakuş Tumulus, Cendere Bridge, and the ancient Commagene capital of Arsameia. If you're not particularly interested in catching sunset or sunrise, it's also possible to visit the site during the day, and some tours leave out the subsidiary sites (try to make sure any trip you go on *does* include them, as they're worth a visit).

Among the dodges employed by Adıyaman or Kâhta operators are last-minute jacking up of prices, and overbooking, necessitating the call-out of another minibus at extra cost. To avoid irritation, make sure that prices and numbers are firmly agreed well in advance.

From Malatya

Although visiting Nemrut from Malatya is a slightly more complicated and expensive process, it does cut out having to spend time in Adıyaman or Kâhta. The tourist information office at the city's otogar (whose main purpose is to sign up visitors for Nemrut trips) has full details, and the trips will set you back $15–20. Departures are at about 11am, reaching the summit in good time for sunset; you spend the night at one of the hotels below Nemrut, which will cost you another $15 (including breakfast)—though for hardier souls there's always the option of spending the night on the roof of the site café, which costs about $2. The return trip starts at about 6:30am, allowing you time to admire the sunrise first, reaching Malatya about 11am.

From Şanlıurfa

Visiting Nemrut from Şanlıurfa also has the advantage of cutting out Adıyaman and Kâhta, but the 260-kilometer round trip is pretty time-consuming. A number of Urfa bus companies, including *As Urfa* (☎871/11616), offer both overnight tours and day trips, usually costing about $15.

Adıyaman

If you're *not* traveling to Nemrut Dağı, **ADIYAMAN** is worth avoiding altogether, a one-street concrete eyesore that fills up with Nemrut hustlers in the summer. Most of the **hotels** in town are substandard or expensive—or both. One of the better cheaper places is the *Motel Sultan*, on Atatürk Bulvarı, with singles from $10 and doubles from $12. Nearby, the flashy-looking *Motel Beyaz Saray*, Atatürk Bulvarı 136 (☎8791/1179), has singles for $8, doubles for $12, and boasts a swimming pool and nightclub. Next door, *Arsameia Turistik Camping*, Atatürk Bulvarı 148 (☎8791/2112), has double rooms with bath for $16, as well as **camping** facilities. Many of the hotels offer organized trips to Nemrut Dağı as do various travel agents. The town has a **tourist information office** of sorts at Atatürk Bulvarı 41 (Mon–Fri 9am–noon & 1–5pm,☎8795/1008), which also offers organized tours.

Kâhta

From Adıyaman regular dolmuşes make the hour's journey to **KÂHTA**, a dusty town of low houses that looks like it's just heaved itself up out of the earth. Like Adıyaman, its only attraction is as a base for Nemrut Dağı. One of the best hotels in Kâhta is the *Hotel Kommagene*, Eski Kâhta Yolu 1 (☎8795/1098), on the western edge of town (indeed dolmuşes seem to drop passengers off here, no doubt for a commission), where rooms cost $11 for a single and $17 for a double,with bathrooms; the hotel also has a (pricey) restaurant, where alcohol is served, and camping facilities. They also arrange minibus trips to Nemrut, charging about $14 for the round trip including a few stops along the way. If you've brought a tent and there's no space at the *Kommagene*, try *Kom-Tur Camping* nearby, which also has a restaurant. The more expensive *Hotel Merhaba*, on Çarşı Caddesi (☎8795/1970) in the center of town, is a slightly faded establishment offering rooms with bath for about $18 single and $26 double. Also in the center of town are the *İpek Palas Oteli*, Mustafa Kemal Paşa Caddesi 98, and the nearby *Antiochus Pansiyon*, which both have middling rooms for around $7. At the super-budget end of the market, there's the *extremely* basic *Fortuna Camping Pansiyon* a few hundred meters east of the *Hotel Kommagene*, on the north side of the main road and clearly marked, where there is camping space and a few spartan $2-a-night cells. They also do cheaper-than-average Nemrut trips from about $8.

There are a few cheap and basic **restaurants** on Kâhta's broad main street, which represent better value for money than the hotel restaurants. Worth trying is the *Günaydın Lokanta*, where you'll be able to fill up for a dollar or two, and the *Kent Restaurant*, on the opposite side of the street, where they'll serve you beer or wine with your meal.

The Road to Nemrut Dağı

On the way to Nemrut there are a number of things to see, and it's worth making sure that any organized excursion you take stops off at these (most do). The first is about 10km north of Kâhta, where a huge mound suddenly rises up by the side of the road, just past what looks like an old-fashioned oil well. This is the **Karakuş Tumulus**, said to be the funeral mound of Antiochus's wife. It's surrounded by pillars bearing animal motifs and from the top you can look out across a valley that's due to be flooded when the Atatürk Dam, a huge project designed to harness the waters of the Tigris, is finally completed.

Beyond here the road begins to deteriorate, although it's nothing like what is to come. Nine kilometers on, the **Cendere Bridge** is a Roman structure built between 193 and 211 AD during the reign of Septimus Severus, and still in use. It's a graceful, single-arched humpbacked structure with tremendous views all around. Three of the four original columns at each end are still in place. Just beyond it are a couple of cafés and souvenir stands where your business will be solicited assiduously.

Eski Kâhta and Arsameia

After another 6km or so you come to the turnoff for **ESKİ KÂHTA**, a small village with a couple of very basic **pansiyons**, one of which, run by a family called Demirel, charges $3 a night—bring your own sleeping bag. They also serve meals and will sell you soft drinks and beer.

At the Eski Kâhta turn the road doubles back on itself: look out for a **Selçuk bridge** in the valley below you and an almost completely obliterated **Mameluke castle** perched on a rock above. Signs here point the way to the ancient site of **Arsameia**, the capital of the ancient Commagene kingdom, a kilometer away at the end of an unsurfaced road. This was excavated by German archaeologists during the 1950s, and is worth a quick detour as much for the chance to admire the mountainous local scenery as for the site itself, which amounts to little more than a few scattered fragments of masonry and worn inscriptions. Entry is $1, collected by members of a local family responsible for the site, who will also sell you soft drinks, guidebooks, and souvenirs. From a rudimentary parking area a path leads along the hillside, forking left past a finger of rock bearing a Greek inscription, to a cave with a tunnel running to a cistern. Just below the cave is another stone bearing another Greek inscription, and from there the path proceeds up the hillside to a relief depicting Hercules and Mithradates I Callinicus, the founder of the Commagene kingdom, shaking hands. Scattered around are fragments of masonry and what must have been substantial statues—look out for a giant, sandle-clad foot hiding in the grass.

Nearby is another tunnel with steps leading down into the ground, which some local people claim emerges either at the other side of the hill near the parking area, or somewhere in the valley below. In reality, as the Germans discovered after much painstaking digging, it dead-ends after about 150 meters. It's steep and roughly surfaced inside, and you'll need a flashlight if you want to take more than a cursory look. Above the tunnel entrance an inscription tells that Mithradates I Callinicus is buried in the vicinity, and that the site is consecrated to him. Just above the relief depicting Hercules and Mithradates is a kind of grassy plateau with some sketchy foundations—so sketchy, in fact, that it's difficult to determine what they might once have been. The Germans uncovered a number of mosaics here, but these have all been removed to the Museum of Anatolian Civilizations in Ankara. About 1km beyond the Arsameia turnoff is the village of **DAMLACIK**, where there's a couple of basic cafés.

Narince, Karadüt, and Some Pansiyons

Beyond Damlacik the road takes a turn for the worse, passing through a number of small villages where the local kids seem to be unsure whether to wave or throw stones. The largest of these is **NARİNCE**, a couple of kilometers after a side road to Kâhta, and 8km east of that is an indicated turnoff for Nemrut, along with the *Boğaziçi Camping ve Motel* with **camping** space and some basic rooms. Five kilometers farther on, the village of **KARADÜT** has a few **pansiyons**, including the *Apollo Pansiyon, Restaurant ve Camping* (☎8795/1246), which has beds for about $4, and the *Karadüt Motel Pansiyon* on the way out of the village, where prices are about the same.

Beyond Karadüt the road gets really bad, paved with basalt blocks that guarantee a bone-shaking ride to the summit of Nemrut Dağı. On the way up you'll pass the *Hotel Euphrat*, which offers bed, breakfast, and dinner for $14 per person, and the *Zeus Motel*, with singles from $16 and doubles from $25 (May to October only). Obviously both of these are very popular and there's no guarantee that either will have space. Advance inquiries should be directed to *Zeus Motel*, at either Mustafa Kemal Caddesi 50 (PO Box 50), Kâhta, or Atatürk Bulvarı 43, Vilayet Karşısı, Adıyaman (☎8781/2180, 3054).

Nemrut Dağı

The mighty stone heads of **Nemrut Dağı**, the temple and tomb of king Antiochus, have become one of the best-known images of eastern Turkey: they are recycled endlessly on postcards and souvenirs, and if you find yourself anywhere within a couple of hundred kilometres of the place people will naturally assume that you're here to see them.

You'll be told that the best time to visit Nemrut is dawn in order to watch the sunrise. This is true, but it will involve setting out at 2am, and on arriving at the summit you will inevitably find that at least several dozen other people are there with the same idea. You might also find that it's quite cold, so come prepared; if you're visiting in the off-season check up on weather conditions before you leave. There's often snow on the ground from November through until May, and it's not unkown for the summit roads to be blocked even as late as April.

Some History

Nemrut Dağı is the result of one man's delusions of grandeur, a great tomb/temple complex built by Antiochus I Epiphanes (64–38 BC), son of Mithradates I Callinicus, the founder of the Commagene kingdom. The Commagene dynasty was a breakaway from the Seleucid Empire, and it wouldn't rate much more than a passing mention in histories of the region were it not for the fact that Mithradates's son Antiochus chose to build this temple as a colossal monument to himself. Despite having shown early promise as a statesman by concluding a non-aggression treaty with the Romans, Antiochus later decided he was divine in nature, or at the very least an equal of the gods, declaring: "I, the great King Antiochus have ordered the construction of these temples . . . on a foundation which will never be demolished . . . to prove my faith in the gods. At the conclusion of my life I will enter my eternal repose here, and my spirit will ascend to join that of Zeus in heaven."

Antiochus's vanity knew no bounds—he also claimed descent from Darius the Great of Persia and Alexander the Great—and eventually he went too far, siding with the Parthians against Rome, and was deposed. This was effectively the end of the Commagene kingdom, which afterwards passed into Roman hands, leaving only Antiochus's massive funereal folly as a reminder of its brief existence.

Even this was forgotten by the outside world until the late nineteenth century, when Karl Puchstein, a German engineer, came across the site while making a survey in 1881. In 1883 he returned with Karl Humann (the man who removed the Pergamon altar to Berlin) to carry out a more thorough investigation, but it wasn't until 1953 that a comprehensive archaeological survey of the site began, under the direction of an American team. Since then Nemrut Dağı, hitherto only

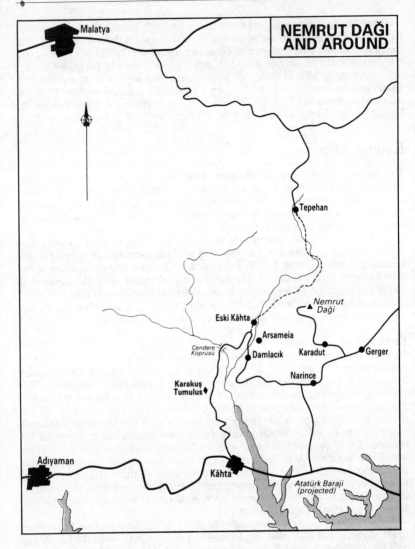

reachable after an arduous journey of several days, has been put back on the map.

The Summit

You may well find yourself traveling the last few kilometers in a convoy of minibuses, and at first sight the summit of Nemrut Dağı is a little surprising—basically a parking lot full of milling crowds. Just above are a small café, souvenir shop, and restrooms. The café provides tea, soft drinks, low-alcohol beer, and sometimes omelets, though more often than not there's nothing more than dry cookies, so it makes sense to bring your own food. They rent out dormitory beds here too, for $4, and you can also sleep on the café roof for $2—not a good idea if you can avoid it, since you wake up half frozen to death in the early hours.

The Site

Behind the parking-lot buildings is the entrance to the **site** ($5), beyond which is a vast fifty-meter tumulus of small rocks, thought to cover the tomb of Antiochus, though signs tell you that it's forbidden to climb the mound. A rocky path leads along the south side of the tumulus for a couple of hundred meters to a terrace area, on which stands the **eastern temple** with five decapitated, seated statues, each several meters in height. From left to right they represent Apollo, Fortuna, Zeus, Antiochus, and Hercules. Scattered in front of these truncated figures are the much-photographed detached heads, perhaps a little disappointing after all the hype, but remarkably intact except for the occasional missing nose, and measuring a couple of meters each in height. These were meant to incorporate several similar deities drawn from different cultures, according to the principle of syncretism, which Alexander the Great had promoted in an attempt to foster a sense of unity among the disparate peoples of his empire. On the backs of the statues are Greek inscriptions detailing Antiochus's lineage and the various rites to be observed during worship and at the dawn sacrifices once carried out at the altar in front of the statues—a space now used as a helipad for VIP visitors. The altar makes a good vantage point, where you can admire the statues and wonder at the immense effort that must have gone into the construction of this huge piece of self-aggrandizement. Scattered around are fragments of a massive stone eagle, once the symbolic guardian of the temple. Look out also for the stone lion over to one side of the temple.

A path leads around the northern base of the tumulus to the **western temple**, which has not been treated so benevolently by time. None of the statues are even partially intact, although the dispersed heads here seem less weathered than those on the other side of the tumulus. The line-up is the same, although it's harder to work out who's who. Look out for Fortuna with a garland of leaves and vines in her hair, and Apollo, claimed by some to be a dead ringer for Elvis Presley. A number of reliefs adjacent to the statuary debris have survived, however—three depicting Antiochus shaking hands with Apollo, Zeus, and Hercules, another a lion relief thought to be a planetary chart.

From the western terrace the path leads back down to the parking lot by a circuitous route—it's actually quicker, if a little harder on the feet, to scramble down over the rocks.

Malatya

From Adıyaman buses depart for **MALATYA**, a lively city with a surprisingly metropolitan atmosphere. There's little to see here, but it's a pleasant enough place for an overnight stop and it is a possible base for expeditions to Nemrut Dağı, with various day-trip deals advertised at the otogar starting at about $15.

Malatya is the center of a fertile fruit-growing region and is particularly famed for apricot production—attested to by abundant supplies of dried apricots sold at local fruit stands. Apart from that there's a university and a huge army base. It's a large city, but the downtown area is fairly compact, and though the train station and otogar are a a dolmuş-ride from the city center, most of the hotels and restaurants are within walking distance of each other.

Practical Details

There's a **tourist information office** (Mon–Sat 8:30–noon & 1–5pm,☎821/17733) in the *Vilayet* building, as well as another smaller office at the otogar whose main purpose seems to be to sign you up for a trip to Nemrut. Malatya has plenty of **hotels**, a couple of which are surprisingly good. The more expensive options are on Atatürk Caddesi, the town's main drag, while the cheaper places are on PTT Caddesi. Prices at the *Mercan Palas Oteli*, PTT Caddesi 14 (☎821/11570), start at $3 per person for rooms with washbasins only. Nearby, the *Hotel Merkez* and the *Hotel Çiçek Palas* charge similar prices. On the opposite side of the same street is the *Otel Tahran*, PTT Caddesi 20, which is a little more expensive, with singles for $6 and doubles for $12. On the main street, İnönü Bulvarı, is the basic *Park Oteli* (☎821/11691) with rooms for $3 and $5. A little farther along is the *Çınar Oteli*, Atatürk Caddesi 39 (☎821/11997), with singles for $6 and doubles for $10 or so—friendly enough but a little dingy for the price. The best budget hotel in town, comparing favorably with some of the more expensive establishments, is the *Otel Kantar*, Atatürk Caddesi 81 (☎821/11510, 13125), where clean comfortable rooms with showers (warmish water) go for $6 single ($5 without shower) and $10 double ($8 without). Another medium-price option is the *Hotel Asya*, İnönü Caddesi (☎821/14717), also with singles for $6 and doubles for $10. At the upper end of the scale is the *Hotel Sinan*, Atatürk Caddesi 16 (☎821/12907, 13007), which charges from $20 single, $25 double. Some way farther east on the same street, the *Kent Oteli*, Atatürk Caddesi 151 (☎821/12175, 12813), is not particularly good value at $14 for a single and $20 for a double.

There are plenty of **places to eat** in town. Be wary, though, of *Restaurant Melita*, next door to the *Hotel Sinan*, touted as the best restaurant in town but with a tendency to hike up the bill for unexceptional food. A better bet is the *Kışla Restaurant*, also on Atatürk Caddesi (ask directions), offering much better value for money. Also worth checking out are the *Eski Emniyet Restaurant*, behind the *Belediye* building, with good food and wine at reasonable prices, and the *Melissa Restaurant* in the park opposite the tourist information office—try the *çorba*. For breakfast and snack-type meals, try the *Kristal Kafeterya*, on Atatürk Caddesi near the *Park Otel*. *Magdalena Burger*, at Ş.Hamit Fendoğlu Caddesi 35, is a pleasant café that stays open late.

Eski Malatya

About 12km north of the modern city is **Eski Malatya**, or "Old Malatya," a ruined Roman/Byzantine town reached by dolmuşes heading for the village of Battalgazi from the center of Malatya. The old town walls are still visible, but much of the original settlement, which boasted 53 churches and a couple of dozen monasteries, has been built over by the inhabitants of the modern village. Although it looks like a factory outbuilding from the outside, the **Ulu Cami** near the school has an elegant blue-tiled interior worth a quick look. From the school follow the road to the village square where, set below the present street level, you'll find a restored *kervansaray*.

North of Malatya: Elâzığ and Harput

One hundred kilometers north of Malatya, and accessible by dolmuş, **ELÂZIĞ** was founded in 1862 by Sultan Abdül Aziz to house the overspill population of the old settlement of Harput (see below). It's an important grape-producing town, the center of an area where *okuzgözü* grapes, used to produce red *Buzbağ* wine, are harvested. Elâzığ itself is predominantly modern and soulless, but it has a decent **museum** on the campus of the Euphrates University just outside town, displaying objects from various local archaeological sites submerged by flooding after the completion of the Keban Dam north of Elâzığ in 1974. There's a remarkable collection of Urartian gold jewelry, as well as an ethnological section with some unexciting costumes and carpets.

Heading north out of Elâzığ, you can follow what was once the main Erzurum road 20km north until it disappears into the Keban Reservoir, where the fourteenth-century castle of **Eski Pertek** has been turned into a dramatic-looking island fortress. The castle is in good condition but sadly is no longer easily reached. The only realistic option is to take the infrequent car ferry to Pertek on the other side of the lake and rent a boat, although this is by no means a simple operation.

Elâzığ's **tourist information office** is at İstasyon Caddesi 35 (☎811/16572). The cheapest **hotel** in town is the *Çınar Oteli*, Hürriyet Caddesi 30 (☎811/11811) with very basic doubles for $5. A better bet is perhaps the *Erdem Hotel*, İstasyon Caddesi 19 (☎811/12212), where simple rooms go for $5 single and $8 double, although, with a little money, the two-star *Büyük Elâzığ Oteli*, Harput Caddesi 9 (☎881/14484), with doubles from about $25 a night, is much more pleasant.

A five-kilometer dolmuş ride north of Elâzığ, at the end of a road lined by military installations guarding the Keban Dam, is the abandoned city of **HARPUT**. It was a thriving commercial town of many thousands as recently as the end of the last century, but since then a series of disastrous earthquakes has led to mass emigration to Elâzığ. Only a few buildings remain, grouped around the clearly marked **castle**, built by the Byzantines. Despite its strategic location and apparent impregnablility on top of a rocky outcrop, it was captured by Tamerlane during the second Mongol wave and then by Sultan Selim the Grim in 1515. Inside the castle, of which not much more than a few crumbling walls have survived, you can visit the **Arap Baba Türbesi**, where a small stone mausoleum houses the body of a local holy man. Sometimes an attendant will raise the lid of the wooden coffin to reveal a mummified brown body. The other main survivor in town is the twelfth-century **Ulu Cami**, recognizable by its brick minaret, leaning at a precarious angle. Scattered around this are the remains of a *kervansaray* and a bathhouse.

East of Gaziantep: Toward Şanlıurfa

East of Gaziantep the landscape turns barren and arid. Most of the traffic seems to be oil tankers traveling nose to tail, to and from the oilfields around Batman and Siirt. If you're driving your own car it's worth knowing that the drivers of these vehicles don't believe in switching their headlights on until it gets *really* dark. To add to the excitement, road conditions deteriorate steadily the farther east you go, and you'll notice a disturbing number of horrifically mangled vehicles in the fields by the roadside. In the summer, when temperatures push 115°F, this route can be hellishly uncomfortable, too; if you're traveling by bus, try to make sure you get a seat in the shade when buying your ticket.

About 50km from Gaziantep, there's a turnoff for **Kargamiş**, the ancient Hittite city of Carchemish. A number of important reliefs were unearthed here by British archaeologists (including T.E. Lawrence, of *Lawrence of Arabia* fame) between 1910–15 and in 1920, complementing similar work being carried out at the ancient Hittite capital of Hattuşas near Ankara (see Chapter Eight). These days, however, the site—which is just a few kilometers north of the border with Syria—is difficult to reach, and you'll need authorization from the military authorities in Gaziantep if you want to visit it. For more details inquire at the tourist office in Gaziantep, although note that there's little to see since the reliefs mentioned above were removed to the Museum of Anatolian Civilizations in Ankara.

The main road crosses the **Euphrates River** at the shabby town of **BİRECİK**—of interest really only to ornithologists, since it's one of the few places in the world where you're likely to see a bald ibis (an ugly relative of the stork) in the wild. Birecik's ruined **castle** was founded by Frankish crusaders during the eleventh century, as a frontier outpost for the Crusader-state of Edessa (see below) but isn't really worth going out of your way to inspect closely.

Şanlıurfa

ŞANLIURFA, or "Glorious" Urfa (most of the locals just say Urfa), is a place where you could easily spend a couple of days taking in the local monuments, which include the reputed birthplace of the patriarch Abraham and a poolside mosque complex of some beauty. But just as compelling is Urfa's unique atmosphere. For visitors coming from the West, it's here that the East really seems to begin, and although by now you'll be getting used to culture shock, somehow in Urfa the differences seem more extreme. A significant proportion of the population is Kurdish, and the few women on the streets are veiled and often tattooed with henna, while the men wear baggy trousers and caps or Kurdish headdresses. Although it's a city of 200,000, sheep wander the streets, and you don't see many cars—the main means of transport are motorcycles and bikes.

In Turkey Urfa has gained some notoriety as a focus of Islamic fundamentalism—so much so that a couple of years ago the mayor of Urfa (which is also known as "the city of the prophets") was put on trial, accused of trying to undermine the secular nature of the Turkish state. Interestingly, Urfa is also famous for the high incidence of gastric complaints among visitors—something caused by the intense summer heat, which turns every plate of food into a nursery for bacteria.

Some History

Even by Turkish standards, Urfa is a truly old city. According to both Christian and Muslim sources, Abraham received his summons from God to take himself and his family to Canaan while living in Urfa. Other stories record that the prophet Job was a resident for a while, although claims that the Garden of Eden was somewhere around here are probably based more on wishful thinking than anything else.

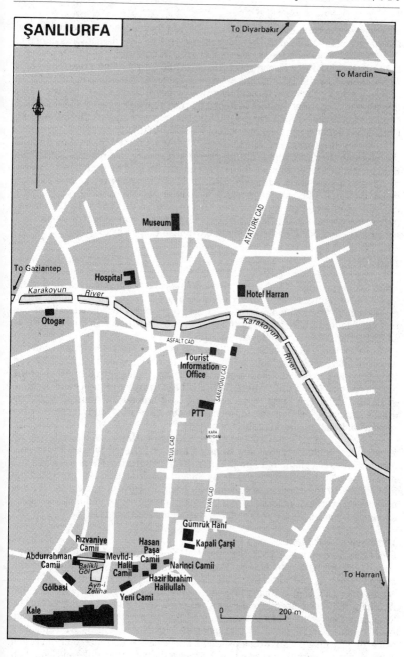

ŞANLIURFA

To Diyarbakır

To Mardin

Museum

To Gaziantep

Hospital

Karakoyun River

Otogar

Hotel Harran

ATATÜRK CAD

Karakoyun River

ASFALT CAD

Tourist
Information
Office

SARAYÖNÜ CAD

PTT

KARA
MEYDANI

EYLÜL CAD

DIVAN CAD

Gümrük Hani

Rızvaniye
Camii

Hasan
Paşa
Camii

Kapali Çarşi

Abdurrahman
Camii

Mevlid-i
Halil
Camii

Narinci Camii

Balikli
Göl

Gölbasi

Ayn-i
Zeliha

Hazir Ibrahim
Halilullah

Yeni Cami

Kale

To Harran

0   200 m

Whatever the truth of these stories, it's certain that people have been living on the site for many millennia. The first settlers were the Hurri, members of one of Anatolia's earliest civilizations, who built a fortress on the site of the present citadel around 3500 BC and controlled much of the surrounding area. The Hurri were followed by the Hittites and Assyrians, the latter remaining in control until Alexander the Great swept through after his victory at Issus. Later Urfa was—like Edessa—an important eastern outpost for the Romans against the Persians. Around about the second century AD, it became a center of the burgeoning Christian religion, and a religious school was established.

Following the collapse of Roman power the Arabs moved in, holding on until the eleventh century, when, during the First Crusade, a French count called Balduin stopped off en route to the Holy Land and decided to establish the county of Edessa, a short-lived Christian state. In 1144 the Arabs recaptured Edessa, giving the rulers of Europe a pretext to launch the Second Crusade, although the city was soon forgotten and never wrested back from the Arabs. In 1260 it was put to the sword by the Mongols and never really recovered, declining into obscurity before being absorbed into the Ottoman Empire in 1637.

Old Urfa

From Şanlıurfa **otogar** you have to take a dolmuş into the city center (a taxi if you arrive late at night). Head for the *Turban Urfa Hotel* on Sarayönü Caddesi, which makes a good orientation point. Most of the hotels and other tourist facilities can be found south of here, on or around **Sarayönü Caddesi**, which runs north to south through the center of town.

At the extreme south of Sarayönü Caddesi is **Kara Meydanı**, at the center of which stands a venerable-looking but in fact nineteenth-century mosque. Beyond Kara Meydanı, Sarayönü Caddesi turns into Divan Caddesi, east of which is the twelfth-century **Ulu Cami**, whose design is based on that of the Grand Mosque in Halab (Aleppo) in Syria. You can take a look around the courtyard with its graves and octagonal minaret. In the narrow streets nearby you can admire what remains of Urfa's medieval Arab-style houses.

At the end of Divan Caddesi is the **Gümrük Hanı**, a sixteenth-century *kervansaray*, behind which is the **Kapalı Çarşı**, or Covered Bazaar, a maze-like commercial area spilling out into the narrow streets nearby. There are stalls and hole-in-the-wall shops selling everything imaginable, from spices to guns, and the friendliness of the vendors is exceptional, even by Turkish standards. Traders sell green Diyarbakır tobacco by the kilo out of plastic sacks, and domestic appliances are occasionally auctioned off the back of horse-drawn carts.

The Cave of Abraham

From the bazaar, make your way along along Göl Caddesi, past the **Narinci Camii** and the Ottoman **Hasan Paşa Camii**, to the **Mevlid-i Halil Camii**, behind which is the entrance to **İbrahim Halilullah Dergâhı**, or "Cave of Abraham" (daily 8am–5:30pm; 40¢). According to local legend, it was here that Abraham was born, spending the first ten years of his life in hiding because a local Assyrian tyrant, Nemrut, had decreed that all new-born children be killed. As Abraham is recognized as a prophet by Muslims his birth-cave remains a place of pilgrimage and worship—there are separate entrances for men and women, shoes must be removed, and dress must be respectful—and although there isn't actually much to see inside, the atmosphere is very reverential, with plenty of praying going on. East of the cave is the **Hızır İbrahim Halilullah**, a colonnaded mosque and *medrese* complex named after the "Prophet Abraham and Friend of God" which has grown up to serve the large numbers of visitors.

Gölbasi

It's a short walk from here, via the pseudo-Ottoman new mosque, to the **Gölbaşi**—literally "At the Lakeside"—where you'll find a shady park and a couple of mosques, and three pools filled with fat carp. According to a continuation of the local legend, Abraham, after he emerged from his cave, became an implacable opponent of Nemrut and attempted to smash the idols in the local temple. The tyrant was displeased, and had Abraham hurled from the citadel battlements into a fire below. Abraham was saved when, on a command from God, the flames turned into water and the firewood into carp. The smaller of the two pools at the foot of the citadel, the **Halil-ür Rahman**, adjacent to the larger **Ayn Zeliha** pool, is the one that saved Abraham from a fiery end.

There is a teahouse beside the Ayn Zeliha where visitors like to sit in the shade and feed the carp with chickpeas bought from poolside vendors. The carp are now sacred, and it's said that anyone who eats them will go blind, a fate which supposedly befell a couple of soldiers a year or two ago (according to another story the soldiers didn't lose their sight but were sent to prison). Another pool, the **Balıklı Göl**, just to the north, is also filled with sacred carp.

At the western end of the Balıklı Göl is the seventeenth-century **Abdürrahman Camii**, which you are free to look around if you want. The present mosque replaced an older twelfth-century building whose distinctive square minaret has survived. On the north side of the pool is the **Risvaniye Camii**, built by an Ottoman governor in 1716, with some intricately carved wooden doors. Open-air stalls at the pool's edge sell religious tracts and the like—the majority of the visitors are Muslim pilgrims rather than tourists, many of whom have traveled here from all over Turkey.

The Kale

Above the Gölbaşi is Urfa's **kale**, or citadel, a massive structure whose construction is attributed to everybody who ever occupied the city. It's thought that much of what has survived probably dates from the time of the twelfth-century Frankish Crusader state. It's completely ruined now but it's worth climbing up there for the view of the mosques and pools down below. At the top are a couple of lone Corinthian columns, thought to be the remains of an early Christian chapel. They are referred to as the **Throne of Nemrut**, and local people will try to tell you that this is the spot from which Nemrut cast Abraham down into the flames.

The Museum

Şanlıurfa Museum, the city's excellent archaeological museum (Tues–Sun 8:30am–noon & 1:30–5pm, Mon 1:30–5pm; $2.50), is just north of the town center. To reach it follow Atatürk Caddesi as far as the *Vilayet* building and take a left turn. After about 200m turn right onto a side street and on your immediate left you'll see the museum garden full of stone carvings and sarcophagi, with many pieces dating back to Hittite and Assyrian times. Inside there's more of the same, with various archaeological finds ranging from gold-work to jewelry on display, plus an ethnographic section devoted to more recent local lifestyles. The collection of reliefs, dating back to Assyrian, Babylonian, and Hittite times, is particularly fascinating, thanks to the sharpness and clarity of the carvings.

Practical Details

The local **tourist information office** is at Asfalt Caddesi 3/B (Mon–Fri 9am–noon & 1–5pm, ☎8711/2467). There's a good selection of **hotels** in town, but be warned that during the summer most places fill quickly. The best option is perhaps the *Hotel İstiklâl*, Sarayönü Caddesi (☎871/11967), a fairly basic establishment with spartan rooms, built around a flower-filled courtyard. A decent room will set you back $3 single and about $5 double ($4.50 and $7 with shower). In Köprübaşı Kışla Caddesi running west from opposite the *Harran Hotel*, the *Lâle Hotel*, Köprübaşı Kışla Caddesi 11 (☎8711/31642, 28952), has singles for $4 or so and doubles for a little over $6. The same goes for the *Hotel Kervan*, on Köprübaşı Kışla Caddesi (☎8711/33712, 31367). The *Hotel Güven*, on Sarayönü Caddesi (☎8711/1700), has single rooms without bath for about $3. Just behind the *Turban Hotel*, the *Hotel İpek Palas*, Köprübaşı 4, has singles for $3 and doubles for $5 (with showers). The *Park Oteli*, Göl Caddesi 101, has less than salubrious doubles from $4, but is handy for the mosques and pools.

Up a bracket in price, the *Hotel Kapaklı* on Sarayönü Caddesi (☎8711/15230) has singles for around $7 and doubles for $13 ($10 and $16 with bathrooms), though perhaps better value is the *Turban Hotel* (☎8711/3520, 3521) with singles for $13 and doubles for $20, or the pricier *Hotel Harran*, on Atatürk Bulvarı (☎8711/34743), where a single will set you back $16, a double $24 (with bathrooms and air conditioning). These two fill up rapidly, but both have restaurants and bars—important in this heavily religious city, where you may find it difficult to get a drink in the usual places.

Otherwise, for **eating and drinking** try the *Sümer Lokantsı*, on Köprübaşı Kışla Caddesi. There are numerous others and the quality is pretty much the same wherever you go. There are a number of local specialties based on bulgar (cracked) wheat, notably *çiğ köfte*, or raw meatballs—eat at your own risk—and *dolmalı köfte*, or stuffed meatballs.

Trips to Nemrut Dağı

A number of Urfa bus companies run excursions to **Nemrut Dağı**, best of which are *As Urfa* (☎871/11616), whose office is opposite the tourist office. It offers overnight trips starting at about $10 per head.

Harran

About 40km southwest of Urfa is the village of **HARRAN**—also known as Altınbaşak—whose beehive houses, more reminiscent of Syria than Turkey, have become a major tourist attraction over recent years. Harran also has strong biblical links. In the Bible Abraham is described as having dwelt here for a while on his way from Ur to Canaan, and it's tempting to imagine the place hasn't changed much since—although the fact is visitors have made big inroads over the last decade or so.

Harran is thought to have been continuously inhabited for at least 6000 years, making it one of the oldest settlements on earth. It first came to prominence under the Assyrians, who turned it into a prosperous trading center, as well as a center for the worship of Sin, god of the moon; there was a large temple here on the site now occupied by the ruins of a Crusader fortress. Later the Romans' advance east was halted here when they were defeated by the Scythians. Despite this, the Romans later were able to turn Harran into an important center of learning, a role the town continued to play under the Byzantines and later the Arabs, who founded a university in the town. Sadly the arrival of the Mongols during the thirteenth century meant disaster, and the end of Harran as a center of anything other than archaeological importance.

Getting There

The *As Urfa* bus company in Şanlıurfa runs minibus excursions to Harran, charging $3.50 per person for groups of between five and twelve people. Departure time is 9am and the trip also takes in Han-el Barür's *kervansaray* and the ruins of Şuayb and Sagmatar (see below). It's also possible to negotiate your own departure times if you can get a group together. If you have your own vehicle, take the road south from Urfa toward Akçakale for about 37km until you reach a turnoff marked by a yellow sign; Harran is about 10km east of here. Minibuses stop at the western end of the village by the *jandarma* post (nearby are a small café and **campground**), adjacent to the ruined Ulu Cami. At the eastern end of the village is a ruined Crusader fortress.

The Village and Site

These days semi-nomadic Arabs and Kurds live amid the ruins of old Harran, surviving by farming and smuggling sheep across the Syrian border 10km to the south. It is they who have built—and live in—the mudbrick beehive-shaped buildings that dot the area, whose distinctive shape is due to the fact that no wood is used as support. Most of the people here are fairly amiable, and are amused by the fascination their way of life exerts on visitors. Many are likely to want to talk and show you around. If possible try to visit in the slow season, when the place is less likely to be crawling with tour groups. In the off-season, you may well have the place to yourself and the heat won't be quite so intense. For soft drinks head for the *Harran Tourist Coffee*—a concrete imitation beehive.

The ruins of old Harran have a kind of tragic grandeur, dwarfing and ridiculing the beehive dwellings, and it's not difficult to picture the town as it must have been before the arrival of the Mongols. The minibus stop is near a hill thought to mark the site of the original settlement. Just to the north of here is the most impressive of the ruins, the **Ulu Cami**, with its graceful square tower, built by an Arab caliph during the eighth century, and mistaken for a cathedral by T.E. Lawrence when he passed through on his way to Aleppo in 1909. Scattered around are broken pillars and remnants of the Arab university, which, judging from the surviving fragments, must have been an exceptionally beautiful complex.

It's here that you'll first be approached by the village kids who'll ask you for money and "*stilos*" (pens). If you take pictures of the little girls in traditional costume they'll demand presents, and throw tantrums if you don't cough up. At this point a couple of them will probably attach themselves to you and offer to be your guides. Some of the older ones are gifted linguists with good twenty-word vocabularies in English, German, and French. In addition to this they all speak Arabic, Turkish, and often Kurdish.

With your new entourage, make your way to the eleventh-century Crusader **fortress**, built on the site of the ancient moon temple. Here there are plenty of ruins to scramble around, although much of the structure looks in a dangerous state of near-collapse. Keep an eye out for the distinctive ten-sided tower, part of a complete defensive ring, sections of which are still visible.

Around Harran

North of Harran are the **Tek Tek Daği**, a range of mountains dotted with ruins and remains, the most accessible and interesting of which can be reached on the *As Urfa* tours. Foremost among these is the ancient site of **Sugmatar**, about 10km north of Harran, which was occupied by a star- and planet-worshipping sect until medieval times. These days there's a village with some hilltop ruins believed to have once been a temple of the sun. Also interesting to visit, though horrendously hot in summer, is **Şuayb**—an ancient, partially subterranean village. Many of the caves and chambers are still occupied.

Mardin

Seen from a distance **MARDİN** can look almost spectacular, rising up out of the flat surrounding landscape, a cluster of buildings clinging to an eerie-looking rock. Closer up, it's revealed as a provincial center of 40,000, more intriguing than beautiful, perched on a rock 1325m above sea level overlooking the Syrian plain, a mix of ugly concrete structures and fine old Arab houses. It also has a grandiose *medrese* and a couple of old mosques, and it makes a good base for excursions into the extreme eastern part of the Euphrates Basin.

Mardin has a large Arab population—mostly shopkeepers—and has recently been a focus of tension, with strong separatist and fundamentalist undercurrents at work. There were riots here at the beginning of 1990, resulting in the posting of several hundred extra policemen here from other parts of Turkey.

The Town

Mardin's origins are lost in the welter of war and conquest that forms this region's historical backdrop. The town's later history is tied up with the development of early Christianity; the first Christians to settle here were Syrian Orthodox who arrived during the fifth century AD, and today the city still has a number of churches hidden away in the backstreets.

The Christian community survived the period of Arab occupation from 640 to 1104, and was not unduly disturbed by the arrival of the Selçuks and later the Turcomans. In 1394 the Mongols captured the town, doling out death and misery in equal measures to Christian and Muslim alike, before handing Mardin over to the Karakoyun Turcoman tribe in 1408. The town fell to Ottomans under Selim the Grim in 1517 and a long era of torpor began that was not significantly disrupted until the Kurdish rebellion of 1832, when a number of public buildings were blown up. There was another small rebellion in 1840, after which the town sank back into somnolence until World War I. From 1915 onwards Mardin's Christian population was drastically reduced by massacre and emigration, and today only a thousand or so practicing Christians remain.

Although there's no shortage of featureless concrete, the architecture of Mardin's old Arab houses is stunning in places. Following Mardin's main street, **Birinci Caddesi**, east from **Cumhuriyet Meydanı** leads you to perhaps the best example of Mardin's architecture—a beautiful stone facade with three arches on the north side of the street. This is probably the finest private house in the town, and is now occupied by an extended family.

Several hundred meters beyond the house, a flight of stone steps (just before the *Hotel Buşra*) leads up to the **Sultan İsa Medresesi**, built in 1385, a striking, albeit crumbling, white structure with a magnificent Selçuk doorway, from which you can look out across the town toward Syria. If the caretaker is around it may be possible to take a look inside the eastern end of the building, which is still used as a Koran school. The *medrese* also houses the **Mardin Museum** (Tues–Sun 8:30am–5:30pm; 50¢), containing a number of Christian carvings from Midyat and Hasankeyf. One of these, housed in a chamber adjoining the museum's central courtyard, is unusual in that it features three figures carved out of a single block of stone, thought to represent Sumerian gods.

Above the Sultan İsa Medresesi is the **castle**, originally built by the Romans and extended by the Byzantines. The Arabs and then the Selçuks occupied it for a while, and from the twelfth century through until the fourteenth century it served the Artukid Turcoman tribe as a capital. From here they were able to fend off the Arabs and endure an eight-month siege during the first Mongol onslaught, only finally falling to the second Mongol wave in 1394. The Karakoyun Turcomans built the (now ruined) palace and mosque inside the walls, but sadly the only people who get to enjoy these—and the tremendous view—today are Turkish soldiers because the castle and its grounds are strictly out of bounds to civilians, thanks to the presence of three golf-ball-shaped radar domes spying on Syria.

South of Cumhuriyet Meydanı is Mardin's **Ulu Cami**, an eleventh-century Selçuk mosque with a fluted dome, which was blown up during the 1832 rebellion and has been much restored since. Nearby is the **Latifiye Camii**, dating from the fourteenth century. It has a carved Selçuk-style portal, and a courtyard with a shady garden—just the place to escape from the blinding summer heat. At the western end of town, south of the main road (you'll have to ask directions) is the the **Kasım Paşa Medresesi**, a fifteenth-century *medrese*, similar in design and execution to the Sultan İsa Medresesi.

Practical Details

Mardin can be a little confusing at first. A main road skirts the southern edge of town before heading off to the southeast and the Syrian border. The town itself lies between this road and the citadel. Mardin's principal street, **Birinci Caddesi**, branches off from the main road at the western end of town and rejoins it at the eastern end. There's a small **otogar**, on the main Syria-bound road at the eastern end of town, with frequent dolmuşes to Cumhuriyet Meydanı. Inquire here for buses to destinations elsewhere in Turkey. Incidentally, Mardin is a stop-off point on the İstanbul to Bagdhad run and, before the start of the Gulf War, you could—assuming you had the right visa—pick up buses to Iraq here.

There is no tourist office in Mardin and there are only a few **hotels** in town. There are a number of budget establishments on Birinci Caddesi, east of Cumhuriyet Meydanı, cheapest of which is the slightly dingy *Yıldız Oteli*, Birinci

Caddesi 391 (☎841/1096), which has single rooms for $3 and doubles for $5 (without bath). A couple of hundred meters farther along on the south side of Birinci Caddesi, the *Otel Kent* has reasonable singles and doubles at $4 and $6; rooms have bathrooms but don't expect hot water. Failing that, there's the *Başak Palas Oteli* on the north side of the same street (☎841/16246), where singles go for $3, doubles for $5.60—nothing special, with spartan rooms and malodorous plumbing. Similar is the *Hotel Buşra*, a little way east below the Sultan Işa Medresesi, with singles for $3 and doubles for $5, although this one does have its own hamam. Mardin's best hotel is the *Hotel Bayraktar* (☎841/1338), at the Cumhuriyet Meydanı end of Birinci Caddesı, whose plain but presentable rooms with attached baths (tepid water) go for about $10—although they tend to get filed with the extra police brought into town during times of trouble.

There are plenty of **places to eat** along Birinci Caddesi. The only vaguely upscale option is the *Hotel Bayraktar Restaurant*, where you'll pay slightly more than usual for the privilege of being able to drink alcohol with your meal. The food there is not really substantially better than at smaller places like the *06 Restaurant* on Birinci Caddesı or any other of the numerous kebab places in town. At the eastern end of town, near the white minaret just south of the main street, is a small and leafy terrace tea garden.

The Tür Abdin Plateau

Immediately east of Mardin spreads the flat plain of the **Tür Abdin**, which makes up the historical center of the Syrian Orthodox Church—a separate entity since a split with the Eastern Orthodox Church during the sixth century AD. Scattered across the area are a number of Syrian Orthodox monasteries; most of these are deserted but a couple have survived as functioning religious communities, reflecting the fact that the Tür Abdin is still home to about 30,000 Christians, who coexist uneasily with the local Kurds and account for most of Turkey's Christian minority. The Tür Abdin is a poor region, even by the standards of eastern Turkey, and in the towns and villages east of Mardin you may well see obviously undernourished and unhealthy children. The government has set up aid programs here but local people claim that the authorities neglect them deliberately.

The Syrian Orthodox Church

The area around Mardin has been a center of the **Syrian Orthodox** (or Jacobite) Church since the sixth century, when one Jacobus Baradeus, bishop of Edessa (Şanlıurfa), founded a church here after a theological dispute with the patriarch in Constantinople about the divine nature of Christ. According to the Orthodox Church, Christ had both a human and a divine nature, but Baradeus held that Christ had only a divine nature—a creed which became known as Monophysm. He was accused of being a heretic and excommunicated.

Under the Arab rulers of the day the Syrian Orthodox Christians enjoyed considerable religious freedom, and by the time of the First Crusade at the end of the eleventh century the Tür Abdin encompassed four bishoprics and eighty monasteries, the ruins of which are dotted across the plateau. Ironically it was Christian Crusaders from Edessa and Antioch (Antakya) who unleashed the first wave of persecution against what they regarded as the heretical Syrian Orthodox

Church. They were followed by the Mongols, whose motives had little to do with religion—they massacred and pillaged everybody regardless of race, color, and creed.

Under the Ottoman Empire things calmed down, and the Christian community once again enjoyed a long period of tolerance. Unfortunately, during World War I, they were tainted by association with Allied plans to dismember the Ottoman Empire and suffered presecution and massacre, a fate they shared with the Armenian and Greek minorities.

Deyr-az-Zaferan

Deyr-az-Zaferan (Saffron Monastery), 6km southeast of Mardin, is the most accessible of the area's surviving religious communities. Founded in 762, it was the seat of the Syrian Orthodox patriarch from 1160 until the 1920s—though this has since relocated to Damascus. A surprisingly large rectangular building of three stories, set on a low bluff overlooking an approach road, it wouldn't look out of place in southern Italy or Spain, and, judging by the different styles of stonework, was built in stages, with frequent pauses for restoration. These days only a handful of monks remain, running a school for orphans with the assistance of a few lay helpers.

Visiting is easy enough. You can walk to it in an hour and a half from Mardin, following the yellow signs leading southeast past the otogar. Eventually you'll come to an indicated turnoff leading you to the monastery. Failing that, pick up a taxi from Cumhuriyet Meydanı or the otogar; figure on paying $5 (possibly more if business is booming) for a return trip with waiting-time—though you'll have to bargain for this.

Approaching the monastery, you'll notice some cave-dwellings carved out of the rock on the hills behind. Scattered around are the ruined buildings of several other monasteries which didn't survive into modern times. Ancient but still intact rock channels bring water down from the hills to the Deyr-az-Zaferan, the entrance to which is a doorway bearing an inscription in Syriac, a descendant of Biblical Aramaic—the language of Christ. Some of the monks speak a smattering of English, and after being greeted and perhaps offered a glass of tea visitors are usually entrusted to one of the older orphans cared for at the monastery and taken on a guided tour.

First stop is an **underground vault**, said to have been used as a temple by sun worshippers as long ago as 2000 BC. A now-blocked window at the eastern end enabled them to watch the sunrise, while an alcove on the southern wall served as an altar (possibly a sacrificial one). The vault is enclosed by a ceiling made of self-supporting stone without the use of mortar. In the room above, entered via huge 200-year-old walnut doors, is a **mausoleum**, into whose walls are set the burial chambers of many of the Syrian Orthodox patriarchs.

Tours move on from here to the **chapel**, with its carved stone altar (replacing a wooden one destroyed by fire fifty years ago), and the **patriarch's throne**, on which are carved the names of all the patriarchs since 792 AD. Services in the chapel are held in Aramaic, and if you can manage to be here at around 6pm you may be able to attend one of them. Beyond are a couple of rooms containing sedan chairs once used to transport the patriarchs; you'll also be shown a carved walnut altar, made without using nails, and an ancient mosaic said to come from the grotto of Sen Piyer in Antakya. You may also be shown the monastery guest rooms and the patriarch's bed- and living-rooms (it is possible to stay in the rooms, but bear in mind that they are intended for people visiting for religious reasons). At the end of the tour you may want to make a donation or perhaps tip your guide, who will probably refuse your offer at first but succumb if you persist a little.

Nusaybin and Mar Augen

Returning to the main road, head southeast for about 50km to **NUSAYBİN**, on the Syrian border, from which you can reach the abandoned monastery of Mar Augen. The last 25km of the journey follows the course of the border, delineated by barbed wire and watchtowers. Nusaybin is the site of the Roman town of Nisibis, but apart from a triumphal arch there's not much left to see. More interesting is the town's ornate **train station**, built by the Germans, which was the last stop in Turkey on the Berlin–Baghdad railroad.

Unless you've got your own wheels, the monastery of **Mar Augen** is awkward to reach, and any trip will invariably involve a lot of messing around with taxis, dolmuşes, and hitching. Just before the village of GİRMERLİ (about 100km southeast of NUSAYBİN), the *Nezirhan* service station is an oasis-like motel and restaurant complex where you should be able to get a double room for about $20. About a kilometer beyond, take the turn for Gimerli, cross the bridge just past the village and take the road on the extreme right at the triple junction, traveling toward the hills for about 3km. Eventually you'll have to abandon your vehicle and make your way up to the monastery on foot—a climb of about 45 minutes.

Once home to a huge monastic community, Mar Augen is now the unlikely residence of a family that grows vegetables in its courtyard. It's the most evocative and poignant of all the abandoned monasteries in the area, although only the bare fifth-century monastery church is intact, with all traces of decoration long since erased.

Midyat

From Mardin, **MİDYAT** is an uneventful journey of just under an hour. It's actually two towns—a modern, low-roofed concrete eyesore and an old town of crumbling Arab-built mansions. In theory, Midyat, with its old churches and intricate architecture, should be a place people head for in droves. However, hostility between the predominantly Kurdish local population and the large numbers of soldiers and police who patrol the streets gives the place a very tense atmosphere. The town also lacks facilities for visitors so it's best to try to make your visit a day-trip. There is no **tourist information office**, and the town's main **hotel** is the cockroach-infested *Yavuzlar Otel*, on the main road at the foot of the old town—which also contains Midyat's only real restaurant.

There is no **otogar**, and dolmuşes stop at a junction at the foot of the old town, immediately behind which is a commercial strip of shops and businesses in narrow streets with a bazaar-like atmosphere. Behind here the town climbs up a slight hill, all cracked streets with open drains, and mysterious gateways leading to the hidden courtyards of old mansions inhabited by extended families of Kurds, Syrian Orthodox Christians, and a few Armenians.

The town's five churches are easily spotted and can all be reached on foot. Usually a priest or caretaker will show you around if you ring the bell. They aren't breathtaking, but while strolling around you can't help but wonder at the fact that they've survived intact, and many of the altars and shrines inside are touching in their naivety and simplicity.

Around Midyat

East of Midyat are a number of Syrian Orthodox monasteries and churches. To reach them you'll have to pick up a taxi in Midyat in the direction of Dargeçit. **Mar Yakoub** is the most interesting, a right-turn about 10km after the Dargeçit/ Hasankeyf junction, along a dirt road. It dates back to the fourteenth century and boasts a church with some well-preserved carvings on its facade, lintel and door-jambs. There are other monastery ruins in the vicnity, but all are fairly difficult to reach.

Hasankeyf

North of Midyat, the journey to **HASANKEYF**, the site of a ruined city built by the Artukid Turcoman tribe on the banks of the Tigris, involves a spectacular descent to the river. The original settlement was founded by the Romans as an eastern bastion of Asia Minor and later became the Byzantine bishopric of Cephe. In 640 the Arabs arrived, changing the town's name to "Hisn Kayfa." During the twelfth century the Artukid Turcomans made it the capital of their realm, until the Mongols arrived in 1260.

Unfortunately the quality of the approach doesn't match the modern town, which trails along for a couple of dreary kilometers, overshadowed by the ruined Artukid city to the west, covering two square kilometers on a clifftop site above the Tigris. The ruins are reached by turning left down a dirt track just before the modern Tigris bridge. Where the track starts to peter out you'll see a massive gateway, which marks the beginning of the city. On the other side of the gate, a stone pathway leads up a hill to the twelfth-century **palace** of the Artukid kings, perched high above the Tigris, from which you can explore the rest of the city. Although they look like standard-isssue ruins from the road, many of its skeletal houses contain intricate decorative features. Particularly impressive are the well-preserved **mosque** and a couple of domed **tombs**. Best of these is the fifteenth-century **Zeyn El-Abdin Türbesi**, a sizable cylindrical building clad in turquoise-glazed tiles and red brick.

A good overall view of ancient Hasankeyf can be gained from the northern bank of the Tigris. To get there, return to the main road and follow it north across the river. Downstream from the modern bridge are the pillars of an old **Artukid bridge** that in its day was apparently one of the finest in Anatolia.

travel details

Buses and dolmuşes

From Adıyaman to Kâhta (hourly, 1hr); Malatya (8 daily, 3hr); Şanlıurfa (4 daily, 3 hr).

From Antakya to Adana (hourly, 3hr); Aleppo (4 daily, 4hr); Gaziantep (8 daily, 5hr); Samandağ (hourly, 1hr).

From Gaziantep to Adana (4 daily, 3hr 30min); Adıyaman (3 daily, 4hr); Ankara (8 daily, 12hr); Antakya (8 daily; 4hr); Diyarbakır (10 daily, 5hr 30min); Mardin (5 daily, 6hr); Şanlıurfa (10 daily; 3hr).

From Kâhta to Adıyaman (hourly, 1hr).

From Malatya to Adana (3 daily, 8hr); Adıyaman (10 daily, 3hr); Ankara (8 daily, 12hr); Diyarbakır (8 daily, 4hr); Elâzığ (8 daily, 2hr).

From Mardin to Ankara (2 daily, 15hr); Diyarbakır (hourly, 2hr); İstanbul (2 daily, 27 hr); Midyat (5 daily, 1hr 30min); Şanlıurfa (4 daily, 3hr).

From Şanlıurfa to Adana (3 daily, 6hr); Adıyaman (3 daily, 3hr); Ankara (3 daily, 6hr); Diyarbakır (8 daily, 3hr); Gaziantep (8 daily, 3 hr); İstanbul (3 daily, 24hr); Malatya (3 daily, 7hr); Mardin (4 daily, 3hr).

Trains

From Gaziantep to Ankara (4 weekly, 15hr).

From Malatya to Adana (daily, 9hr); Ankara (daily, 18hr); Diyarbakır (several weekly, 10hr); Tatvan (daily, 12hr).

Planes

From Elâzığ to Ankara and İstanbul (4 weekly, 1hr 25min).

From Malatya to Ankara (4 weekly, 1hr); İstanbul (2 weekly, 1hr 45min), İzmir (1 weekly, 2hr).

From Gaziantep to Ankara (6 weekly, 1hr 15min); İstanbul (1 weekly, 2hr).

CHAPTER TWELVE

LAKE VAN AND THE SOUTHEAST

T he southeast of Turkey is a fascinating and challenging place to visit, despite its reputation as one of the most backward parts of Turkey. It's a rugged, sparsely populated area with a natural beauty on which man seems to have made little, if any, impression. West of Lake Van the familiar undulating steppes of central Anatolia are gradually replaced by mountains that roll all the way to the Iranian and Iraqi borders, culminating in the 5137-meter peak of Mount Ararat. At the heart of it all lies Lake Van, a vast inland sea trapped by the surrounding mountains.

Take the horror stories of terrorism and theft you'll be told in the west about this part of Turkey with a very large grain of salt. As easterners will tell you with some bitterness, the only reason westerners tell these tales is to keep the tourists and their wallets in the west. There *is* a guerrilla war going on; but most of the fighting takes place deep in the mountains a good helicopter gunship ride away from where you'll be. For the most part you can roam the east with impunity.

It is true, however, that the southeast is a little wilder than other parts of Turkey. **Getting around** takes significantly longer (you'll spend many long hours on buses), roads are badly potholed, and many of the hotels are grim. But it's worth it; this region is one of the most engaging parts of Turkey and there are fewer tourists in evidence than almost anywhere else in the country.

You're likely to approach the east through **Diyarbakır**, a populous and atmospheric city, that has been an important urban center since the earliest times. A few hours tortuous journey east will bring you to the stark hill-town of **Bitlis**, an almost eerie place that seems to have been unjustifiably overlooked by generations of travelers. From here it's only a hour or so by bus to the unseemly blot of **Tatvan**, a staging post for points east. Tatvan lies on the shores of **Lake Van** itself, about the size of Utah's Great Salt Lake. On its eastern shore is the city of **Van**, the real heart of the region, with its ruined citadel and the ghost town foundations of Old Van. Modern Van, a low-roofed sprawl of concrete and cinderblocks, lies a few kilometers inland from the lake, and makes an ideal base for exploring. From Van you can travel to **Hakkâri**, deep in the border mountains, and to **Doğubeyazit** and **Mount Ararat**.

The majority of people in this part of Turkey are **Kurds**, significant numbers of whom have strong separatist aspirations. But their situation is an anomalous one, since the Turkish government in effect refuses to acknowledge their identity as a distinct ethnic and linguistic group, claiming that the Kurds belong to the great family of Turkic peoples originating in Central Asia. The often brutal suppression of the Kurds by the modern Turkish government and a spate of arrests and

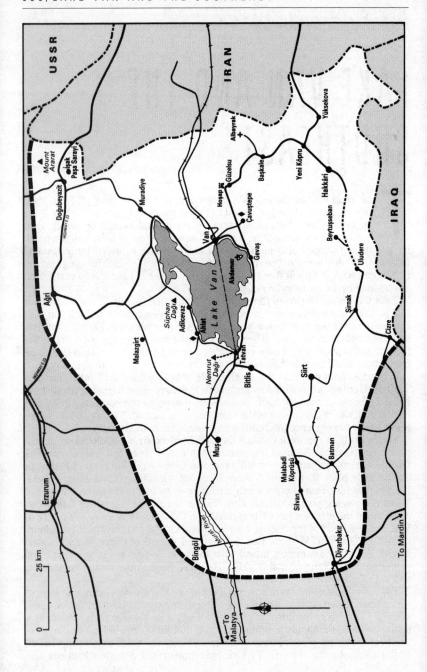

torture after the 1980 military coup led to all-out guerrilla war, with PKK, or Kurdish Workers' Party, insurgents attacking the Turkish miltary from bases in the mountains. The PKK is alleged to have murdered civilians in villages around Hakkâri (although some Kurds suggest that this was the work of the military attempting to turn people against the guerrillas), and government-armed militia groups—the so-called "village guards"—have been set up in many towns and villages to protect the local population. A new variable was added to the situation in 1988 with the influx of large numbers of Kurdish refugees from Iraq, following chemical warfare attacks by the Iraqi government. For a lucid and unbiased account of Kurdish history, explaining the background of the present conflict, read *The Kurds*, a report by the Minority Rights Group.

Today fighting continues in the mountains, principally around Hakkâri, and there is a heavy military population in most of the towns and along the major roads.

WEST OF LAKE VAN

There is little to detain you to the west of Lake Van, although the city of **Diyarbakır**, which will almost inevitably be your first taste of the region if you're traveling from the west, is worth a day or two. Some people find it a slightly intimidating place; you'll encounter a bit of street hassle here (although most of it is good natured), and it gets very hot in summer. Diyarbakır has always been a focal point of Kurdish separatist feeling, and if you have any contact at all with the locals you'll find this becomes an increasingly important issue the farther you tr 1vel into the region. East of Diyarbakır mountainous roads lead to **Bitlis**, an unusual and slightly forbidding hill-town. Travel between the two is slow and the problems caused by narrow, badly surfaced mountain roads are exacerbated by reckless local driving habits.

Diyarbakır

DİYARBAKIR is essentially a sprawl of modern buildings hiding a few beautiful mosques, and enclosed by vast Byzantine walls of black basalt. It's not particularly attractive but it does have a certain atmosphere, albeit of the kind that might start to wear on your nerves after more than a day or two.

A chaotic place with a population of a quarter of a million, Diyarbakır has something of a bad reputation in other parts of Turkey. Most of the alarming tales of terrorism and robbery can be dismissed; if you keep your head, this is no more dangerous than any other large Turkish city. The biggest hazard you're likely to encounter are the carpet-shop hustlers, many of whom turn out in practice to be school kids or "students" who will give you a guided tour of the town and won't take offense if you don't want to buy anything at the carpet shop which you'll visit—as if by chance—en route.

Talking to these young entrepreneurs is a good way to learn about Diyarbakır. You'll soon find out that it's a Kurdish city, and you may well encounter overt displays of anti-Turkish feeling for the first time. This place has long been a focus of tension and its reputation can probably be traced back to the anarchic days that preceded the 1980 coup when the city became a center of separatist activity.

Despite the fact that things are calmer now, the plight of the Kurds still makes its existence felt in Diyarbakır. The men you'll see standing around in the streets dressed in distictive headgear and battle-dress suits are Kurds from Iraq, some of the 60,000 or so who fled when Saddam Hussein's government launched chemical warfare attacks on their towns in 1988.

This influx has done nothing to alleviate Diyarbakır's already precarious economic situation. The city's only significant produce is watermelons, grown on the banks of the Tigris with pigeon droppings as fertilizer. Fifty-kilo monsters are the result, but it's claimed that in the old days Diyarbakır melons weighed as much as 100kg and had to be transported by camel and cut using a sword.

Modern Diyarbakır is a poor city; many of the streets are squalid and beggars are not an uncommon sight. Unemployment is a big problem, since there's no real industry to speak of. Recently significant sections of the city's youth have sought solace in Sufi mystical orders, which have diverted support from the separatist movement.

Given the prevailing instability it's not surprising that Diyarbakır is a big military center. Outside town is the HQ of the Turkish Seventh Army, whose job is to keep the lid down on the PKK, which keeps them busy in the mountains. To the north is a large US/Turkish airbase, and the scream of jet engines is a constant fact of life in the city.

Arrival and Orientation

Most of what you need in Diyarbakır is in the old city, within the great walls. Both the **otogar** and **train station** lie in the modern part outside the walls, but dolmuşes are on hand to ferry new arrivals downtown (don't believe any taxi drivers who tell you that there are no dolmuşes). You'll be dropped off near the Atatürk statue (under 24-hour armed guard, as the locals will gleefully tell you) in front of the Harput Kapısı, one of several vast city gateways. From here the main **hotels** on İnönü Caddesi and İzzet Paşa Caddesi are easily reached.

The town itself is straightforward enough if you keep to the main thoroughfares; from Harput Kapısı, **Gazi Caddesi** running south to the Mardin Kapısı bisects the city from north to south, and **Melek Ahmet Caddesi** running into **Yenikapı Caddesi** does the same from west to east. The backstreets, however, are a narrow maze of sometimes filthy alleys, where it's all too easy to lose your bearings.

Some History

Diyarbakır is not only the natural capital of its region, but has some claim to being one of the oldest cities on earth, so not surprisingly it has a colorful and violent history. The city is known to have existed at the time of the Hurrian Empire (see p.651), some 5000 years ago, and it subsequently saw successive periods of Urartian, Assyrian, and Persian hegemony before falling to Alexander the Great and his successors the Seleucids. The Romans appeared on the scene in 115 AD, and over the next few centuries they and the Persians squabbled violently over the town. The Romans, who knew Diyarbakır as **Amida**, built the first substantial walls around the city in 297; the ones you see today were erected in Byzantine times on top of the Roman originals. Their threatening, basalt bulwarks gave the place its popular ancient name, "Amid the Black." The modern name comes from the Arabs; in 693 the Bakr tribe of Arabs arrived and renamed the city Diyar Bakr or "Place of the Bakr." With the decline of Arab influence in the region Diyarbakır became a Selçuk and then an Ottoman stronghold.

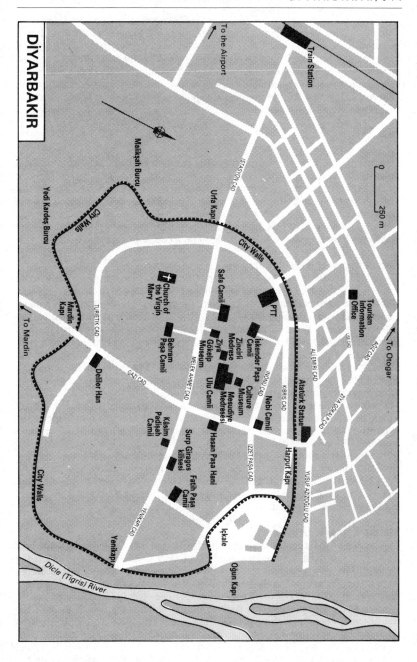

DİYARBAKIR

To the Airport

To the Otogar

To Mardin

Train Station

Tourism Information Office

Malikşah Burcu

Yedi Kardeş Burcu

City Walls

Urfa Kapı

Mardin Kapı

Deliler Han

Safa Camii

Church of the Virgin Mary

Behram Paşa Camii

Zinciri Camii

İskender Paşa Camii

Ziya Gökalp Museum

Culture Museum

Mesudiye Medresesi

Ulu Camii

Nebi Camii

PTT

Atatürk Statue

Harput Kapı

Kasım Padişah Camii

Surp Giragos Kilisesi

Hasan Paşa Hanı

Fatih Paşa Camii

İçkale

Oğun Kapı

Yenikapı

City Walls

City Walls

Dicle (Tigris) River

ISTASYON CAD

TURETIK CAD

GAZI CAD

MELEK AHMET CAD

İNÖNÜ CAD

KIBRIS CAD

İZZET PAŞA CAD

YENIKAPI CAD

ALI EMIRI CAD

US CAD

GEVRAN CAD

YUSUF AZIZOĞLU CAD

0   250 m

In 1925, after the new Republican government had finished off Kurdish hopes of autonomy, a rebellion erupted in the area around Diyarbakır. The city was besieged and Turkish troops were rushed in by train through French-occupied territory. The siege was soon lifted and hundreds of rebels were hanged on the spot, though the bloodshed didn't end here: over the next few years the lives of between 40,000 and 250,000 Kurdish villagers are thought to have been taken in reprisals.

The Walls

Diyarbakır's six-kilometer-long **city wall**, breached by four huge gateways and dotted with 72 defensive towers, is the city's most famous attraction. Most of what can be seen today dates from Byzantine times, with some Selçuk additions. The best way to explore is on foot: near Mardin Kapısı you can ascend to the ramparts, which should present no problems unless you suffer from extreme vertigo. From here onwards most sections are still intact and in circuiting the city you'll only have to descend to ground level for a couple of short stretches.

Harput Kapısı and the İç Kale

The obvious place to start is at the **Harput Kapısı**, the best preserved of the city gates—an angular and unbreachable-looking black tower. You can't actually climb up onto the battlements at this point though, so make your way down Gazi Caddesi and turn right onto İzzet Paşa Caddesi, which leads to **Saray Kapısı**, the entrance to the **İç Kale**, Diyarbakır's citadel and probably the oldest part of town. Beyond here the road dips before passing through the **Oğun Kapısı** into a slum area overlooking the Tigris, outside the city walls. The view is impressive: the broad, languid river is farther away than it looks, and spreading below you is the alluvial plain on which Diyarbakır's famous birdshit-nourished melons are cultivated in special holes dug in the sandy river banks.

The citadel itself is a military zone and its walls patrolled by soldiers, a fact which restricts your wanderings somewhat. The only accessible building is the **Hazreti Süleyman Camii**, a black stone structure with a huge square minaret built in 1160 by the Artukids, and these days looking like a grim Dickensian workhouse. The cool spring that supplies the mosque's *şadırvan* is probably the city's original water source. In the domain of the army are a couple of churches; the **Church of St George** and the **Küçük Kilise**. Not much is known about either of these, and with the former in use as a prison it could be a while before our knowledge is extended.

Mardin Kapısı to Urfa Kapısı

The stretch of wall running between **Mardin Kapısı** and **Urfa Kapısı** is the best preserved and most impressive. Head down Gazi Caddesi until you reach the **Deliler Han**, now known as the *Otel Büyük Kervansaray*. Nearby is the Mardin Kapısı. Here or at some point farther along you can ascend the wall—but if you don't feel up to the scramble it's slightly easier to go up at the Urfa Kapısı.

From Mardin Kapısı you can walk along the battlements, which most of the way are wide enough for three people walking abreast—only in a couple of places do things get slightly hair-raising. After about 400m you come to the **Yedi Kardeş Burcu** (the Tower of Seven Brothers), a huge circular tower decorated with Selçuk lions and eagles, from which there's a fantastic view out toward the

Tigris. The view over Diyarbakır itself is less inspiring, but it does enable you to appreciate the way the town has developed within the city walls. At this point they curve around to the northwest for about 300m until you reach another tower, the **Malikşah Burcu** (also known as the Ulu Badan), which again is decorated with Selçuk motifs. From here a path leads along the outside of the city walls to the Urfa Kapısı.

At the **Urfa Kapısı** you'll have to descend to street level, but you can reascend a little farther north. Continuing, the walls curve around to the northeast and in places the grassy walkway on top is wide enough to accommodate a flock of sheep: a fact which local shepherds take advantage of. From here the walls continue all the way back to Harput Kapısı but, grazing sheep aside, there isn't much to see.

The City

The Harput Kapısı also makes a good starting point for an exploration of the city proper. Immediately to the south of the gateway, at the intersection of Gazi Caddesi and İnönü Caddesi, is the **Nebi Camii**, or Mosque of the Prophet, built in 1524 by the Akkoyun Turcomans. The mosque's most distinctive feature is the alternating bands of black basalt and white sandstone used in its construction, and especially effective in the minaret—a striped effect you'll come across frequently in Diyarbakır. Both stones are quarried locally, and their combination is considerably less threatening than the unrelenting black of the walls.

Continuing down Gazi Caddesi will bring you to the **Hasan Paşa Hanı** on the left-hand (eastern) side of the street, and more bands of black and white stone. The *han* dates from the sixteenth century and is still in commercial use, mainly for carpet shops, while the city's main market area occupies the streets all around.

The Ulu Cami

Opposite the *han* is an open space and a large archway with an Arabic inscription. This leads into the courtyard of the **Ulu Cami**, Diyarbakır's most important mosque. The first of Anatolia's great Selçuk mosques, it was built in 1091 by Malik Şah, the Selçuk conqueror of the city; locals claim it as the oldest mosque in Turkey, on the basis that the first mosque here was built shortly after the original Muslim Arab conquest in 639. It was gutted by fire in 1155 and extensively refurbished, but has been little altered since: the design is thought to have been modeled on the Great Umayyad Mosque in Damascus.

On passing through the archway you find yourself in a large courtyard which is perhaps the most impressive part of the building. At the eastern and western end are two-storied arcades, constructed using pillars salvaged from earlier Roman and Byzantine buildings: on some of the columns and capitals fragments of Greek inscription are visible. The building behind you, above the arch, with storks nesting on its roof, is actually a library. In the middle of the courtyard are two *şadırvans*, and in the right-hand corner is the entrance to the **Mesudiye Medresesi**. Built in 1198 by the Artukids, this became the first university of Anatolia and is still in use as a Koran school. The mosque itself is entered via a doorway on the southern side of the courtyard. The interior is huge and there's a carved white *mimber*. The minaret is tall and angular like a church tower; in fact it's been suggested that the Ulu Cami was built on the site of an earlier Christian church.

Exiting the mosque courtyard via a door in the southwestern corner you enter a narrow alleyway. Turn left and then right, and you'll soon reach the twelfth-century **Zincirli Medresesi**, which now houses an archaeological museum (Tues–Sun 9am–noon & 1–5:30pm; 50¢). Continuing west you come to the **Ziya Gökalp Müzesi** (same hours), the former home of a turn-of-the-century Turkish nationalist that now houses sections devoted to his life and work and an unexceptional ethnographic collection. Just north of the Ulu Cami is a **Cultural Museum** with yet more ethnographic exhibits, occupying the former home of Cahit Sıtkı Tarancı, a prominent modern poet. Again, there are also exhibits about his life and work. If in doubt about directions, ask.

Diyarbakır's Other Mosques

Heading west from the Ulu Cami past the Ziya Gökalp Museum brings you to the the fifteenth-century **Safa Camii**, a mosque of notably graceful design and construction. Particularly impressive is the white minaret, which still bears traces of blue tilework. The masonry in the courtyard is of the distinctive black and white variety, and the ceiling inside has been painted and decorated with blue-and-green tile beading. Some way south of Melek Ahmet Caddesi is the **Behram Paşa Camii**, Diyarbakır's largest mosque, built in 1572 by Behram Paşa, the governor of Diyarbakır, and also featuring the by now familiar black-and-white stonework. According to local sources the mosque was constructed using a medieval form of pre-stressed concrete.

Also worth seeking out is the sixteenth-century **Kasım Padişah Camii** on Yenikapı Caddesi. This one has a tall, square minaret, set on four two-meter basalt pillars, known colloquially as the *Dört Ayaklı Minare*, or Four-Legged Minaret. According to legend if you walk around the minaret seven times and make a wish, it will be granted. Other mosques, like the **İskender Paşa Camii** and the **Fatih Paşa Camii**, both dating from the fifteenth century, are only really worth tracking down if you're a real enthusiast.

Diyarbakır's Churches

Near the Kasım Padişah Camii is the **Surp Giragos Kilisesi**, an Armenian church, called the *Kaldani Kilisesi* on signs. You enter via a doorway bearing the inscription *Aş Konak*. It's a very simple, barn-like place looked after by an ancient caretaker, a member of one of Diyarbakır's surviving Armenian families. A priest comes by once every couple of weeks to hold a service. The interior, though spartan, is also a little garish in its details—icons in boxes with colored lights are some of the more unorthodox features.

A few streets away, and almost impossible to find unless you're being escorted by one of the carpet-shop kids, is another church, in the grounds of a private house whose courtyard you have to traverse to reach it. The church is ruined, the roof has fallen in and it's been locked up, but services are still supposedly held in an outbuilding. Look out for the Armenian inscriptions and animal carvings.

Finally there's the Syrian Orthodox **Church of the Virgin Mary**, southwest of the Behram Paşa Camii. You'll probably have to ask directions to find it (look out for a belfry). A small door (keep knocking until someone comes) leads to a paved courtyard surrounded by buildings which were once part of a seventh-century monastery.

Bear in mind when visiting all these churches that Diyarbakır's Christian community keeps a fairly low profile and that the people who show you around are putting themselves out especially for you. Most of the churches have collection boxes and the least you can do is make a small contribution.

The Museum

Diyarbakır has a new **provincial museum** (Tues–Sun 8:30am–noon & 1:30–5:30pm; $1), just outside the old city. To reach it head out along Ziya Gökalp Caddesi. You'll see a fairground on the eastern (right) side of the road, and a yellow sign in the vicinity will lead you down a side street to the museum. It contains the usual archaeological and ethnological exhibits and also has a section devoted to the Karakoyun Turcoman dynasty that ruled much of eastern Anatolia and western Persia in medieval times.

Practical Details

The local **tourist office** is at Lise Caddesi 24, Onur Apartımanı (☎831/12173). To get there head north along Ziya Gökalp Caddesi, take the third turn on the left (no street name marked) and keep walking for about five minutes. They have a brochure with a street map. The **THY office** is at Kültür Sarayı Sok 15 (☎831/12314); an **airport bus** leaves from here ninety minutes before each flight.

Finding a **hotel** shouldn't be a problem, with numerous decent possibilities along İnönü Caddesi and İzzet Paşa Caddesi. Many of Diyarbakır's budget hotels are pretty grim, but the *Van Palas Oteli*, easy to find down an alley just south of İnönü Caddesi is a good bet: it's spartan, with shared showers and squat toilets, but as clean as you can expect for $2 a bed, and the backpacking contingent seems to gravitate here so the atmosphere is okay. Another budget possibility is the *Hotel Köprücü*, İnönü Caddesi, Birinci Çıkmaz (☎831/12963), down another alley to the north of İnönü Caddesi, near the Nebi Camii. Here singles go for $4.50 with showers ($3.50 without) and doubles ($6 without). Another cheap possibility is the *Hotel Nur*, Gazi Caddesi 107 (☎831/11258), with singles for $2.40 and doubles for $3.60. Similar in price and quality is the *Bal Palas Oteli*, Gazi Caddesi, Akbank Sokak (☎831/12044), down an alley to the west of Gazi Caddesi. Also worth checking out if you're looking for someplace cheap are the *Hotel Şenol*, Gazi Caddesi, Manav Sokak 6/A (☎831/23105), and the *Otel Surkent*, İzzet Paşa Caddesi 19 (☎831/16616), where reasonable rooms with bathrooms go for $4 and $6.

Moving away from the truly budget end of the spectrum the *Hotel Murat*, Balıkçılarbaşı Eski Bitişiği (☎831/10209), and the *Hotel Bingöl*, Gazi Caddesi Dörtyol Suakar Sokak 25 (☎831/11897), are similarly priced at $4.40 and $6.75 for rooms with attached baths—a little less without. The few other cheap places tend to be pretty suspect and you're better off avoiding them.

Farther up the price scale are a few decent middle-range places. The very best of these is the *Hotel Kaplan*, İnönü Caddesi, Sütçü Sokak 14 (☎831/13358), down a side street to the north of İnönü Caddesi. Here there are clean, comfortable rooms with bathrooms and seemingly constant hot water for $8 and $12. Nearby you'll find the *Hotel Malkoç*, İnönü Caddesi, Sütçü Sokak 6 (☎831/12975), charging $6 and $8 for rooms with attached baths ($5.20 and $8 without), and the nearby *Dicle Oteli*, Kıbrıs Caddesi (☎831/23068), with singles for $10 and doubles for $14; it also has a reasonable restaurant.

The *Hotel Kenan*, İzzet Paşa Caddesi 20 (☎831/16614), has singles for $12 and doubles for $16: all rooms have bathrooms and the hotel also has a hamam. Nearby, the pleasant *Otel Saraç*, İzzet Paşa Caddesi 16 (☎831/12365), offers singles for $12, doubles $16. Also worth trying is the *Amid Otel*, Gazi Caddesi, Suakar Sokak 7 (☎831/12043), where pleasant rooms with bathrooms go for $10 and $14. There's a bar on the ninth floor where they sometimes play traditional Kurdish music (this is unusual, as outward manifestations of Kurdish culture are in effect banned in Turkey). The *Hotel Derya*, İnönü Caddesi 13 (☎831/14966), has singles for $11 and doubles for $16 and is also worth checking out.

If money is no object then head for the *Demir Otel*, İzzet Paşa Caddesi 8, where singles are $25 and doubles $35. Similarly priced but slightly faded rooms are available at the *Büyük Otel*, İnönü Caddesi 4 (☎831/15832), for $25 single and $28 double. The tourist office seems to think that all visitors should stay in the two-star *Turistik Oteli*, Ziya Gökalp Bulvarı 7 (☎831/12662)—$33 single, $45 double—but if you're looking for something in this kind of range you'd probably do better to try the *Hotel Kristal*, Kıbrıs Caddesi, Sütçü Sokak 10 (☎831/40297), cheaper and better at $18 and $26 including breakfast. Finally, Diyarbakır's swankiest possibility is the *Otel Büyük Kervansaray*, Gazi Caddesi, Deliler Han (☎831/43003), where luxurious rooms in a converted *kervansaray* go for $32 and $48.

Eating and Drinking

Finding a **place to eat** should be no problem in Diyarbakır since there are kebab places on virtually every street corner. You certainly won't have any difficulty finding a cheap meal along İnönü Caddesi or İzzet Paşa Caddesi: try the *Şanlı Urfa Kebap Evi* on İzzet Paşa Caddesi for example. There are also a couple of good places on Kıbrıs Caddesi. Walking west from the Harput Kapısı you'll come to the *Kıvırcığın Sofrasi Restoran*, where you can get a decent sit-down meal for less than $2.50. A little farther along, the *Büryan Salonu*, Kıbrıs Caddesi 17, is slightly more expensive; signs in the window announce that you can pay in dollars or deutschmarks. For snacks and pastries try the *Şeymus Pastanesi*, at the corner of İzzet Paşa Caddesi and Gazi Caddesi, or the smaller but cheaper *Sinem Pastanesi* on İzzet Paşa Caddesi. For anything fancier head for one of the hotel restaurants. The same applies if you want to drink alcohol. Most of the regular places seem to be dry, but the big hotels all have **bars**.

Toward Lake Van: Bitlis and Tatvan

About 60km east of Diyarbakır, en route to Bitlis, you'll pass **SİLVAN**, a country town that has grown up around the ruins of a sixth-century Byzantine fortress. Apart from an Ulu Cami and some ruined sections of wall there's not much to see here. In fact you're probably better off bypassing Silvan altogether and heading for the **Malabadi Köprüsü**. This beautiful stone bridge with its enormous arch was built by the Artukids in 1146, and now lies just to one side of the modern road.

A few kilometers to the east is the turnoff for the oil town of BATMAN. It doesn't see too many tourists and you'll be warmly welcomed, but apart from a bizarre name it doesn't boast much of interest.

About 45km farther east is the turn for **SİİRT**, about 40km south of the main road, and some distinctive Selçuk and Arab-style architecture. Originally settled by the Babylonians, its heyday was during the period of Arab rule preceding the arrival of the Selçuks. It was the Selçuks, though, who left a lasting impression on the town. The twelfth-century **Ulu Cami** is Siirt's main landmark, and above all its tall, square, brick minaret, adorned with geometrically patterned tiling. Also worth a look are the thirteenth-century **Cumhuriyet Camii** and the Selçuk-built **Kavvan Hamam**. Look out, too, for the Arab-style mud-brick houses, hidden away in some of the backstreets behind the newer part of town.

Siirt is perhaps not a place to linger, as the provincial hinterland sees more than its fair share of guerrilla action: the town achieved particular notoriety in January 1989, when the Turkish press claimed that the security forces had been torturing and killing civilians in nearby Cizre province. A few days later the regional governor of southeast Turkey admitted that the bodies of three alleged terrorists had been buried in the Siirt municipal dump. Locals claimed that 300 people were buried here, and a left-wing periodical, *İkibin'e Doğru 2000* (Toward 2000), listed the names of 67 of them.

Bitlis

From the Siirt turnoff it's only about 50km to **BİTLİS**, although due to the neglected state of the mountain roads the journey will take over an hour. On the way you'll pass a few *hans*, the only points of interest in an otherwise bleak landscape.

A strange and atmospheric town, set in a steep-sided valley and famous for its tobacco, Bitlis itself should be a big tourist destination. A lack of facilities, however, and the slightly unwelcoming nature of the place cause most people to pass through without stopping. Nowadays the population is predominantly Kurdish, but before World War I about half the inhabitants were Armenian, and Armenian inscriptions can still be seen on many of the houses.

Modern Bitlis is essentially a one-street town (the street is called Nato Caddesi), threading its way along the banks of a river that's torrential in the winter but dries to little more than a sluggish trickle in summer. Its dark stone houses and steep valley setting give it the feel of a bleak mill town out of a D.H. Lawrence novel. Bitlis has suffered its fair share of earthquakes over the centuries; many of the buildings have wood set between the stones to act as a kind of primitive anti-quake cushioning. The most notable monument is the 1529 **Şerefiye Camii**, with a fine carved portal, echoing the Selçuk style, on the northern bank of the stream. Also of interest are the **Ulu Cami**, an unusual-looking mosque built in 1126 by the Artukids, and the **Saraf Han** *kervansaray*.

A huge **kale** built on a rock outcrop looms over the town. You reach it by following a road that snakes around its base to the far side, where a slippery path leads to the summit. The grass-covered grounds are about the size of a football field, and although there are few remains to be seen, the view is excellent.

Practical Information

Bitlis has no **tourist office**, but it does have three **hotels**. The *Turist Otel*, at the eastern end of town, has singles for $2.80 and doubles for $5.60. The rooms in this miserable dump are bare and waterless, as are those in the optimistically named *Turistik Palas Otel*, near the Şerefiye Camii, which charges roughly the same. With more money the *Hotel Hanedan* on Nato Caddesi is your best bet, with rooms for $8 and $16. It looks as if it was built for a tourist boom that never happened, but it's fairly clean (although they could stand to change the sheets more often) and the rooms have attached baths with intermittent hot water.

For **eating and drinking** the *Hanedan* also has a restaurant and a bar. The restaurant is a little pricey and you'd probably be better off trying some of the local hole-in-the-wall alternatives, like the nearby *Best Restaurant* which, while not exactly high class, is at least cheap.

Tatvan

The chances are that if you're heading for Van and points around you'll eventually end up in **TATVAN**, about 20km east of Bitlis. It will either be ankle-deep in mud or cloaked in dust, depending on what season you arrive, and has very little to recommend it other than various routes out.

As you approach the town it offers a vista of factories, lumber yards, and flat-roofed houses, squatting between Lake Van and the surrounding hills. With a few exceptions the hotels are dreadful—try to avoid spending the night here.

Getting Away

If you arrive by **bus** you'll be dropped off in the vicinity of the PTT, on Cumhuriyet Caddesi, Tatvan's long and featureless main street. Tatvan doesn't seem to have an otogar per se and you'll have to pick up onward buses from the various ticket stalls around here too. The trip to Van takes three hours and costs $3.

The most atmospheric way to get to Van, however, is by the couple of rusting **ferries** that ply the jade-green waters of Lake Van. Supposedly there are four sailings a day, but in practice there's more likely to be just one: departure times will almost invariably be a couple of hours later than advertised, so be prepared to waste a lot of time hanging around. Despite this the four-hour trip (which costs 60¢) is by far the best introduction to Van and is worth the better part of a day that it inevitably ends up wasting. Drinks and a few snacks are sold on board, but no real food. Local taxi drivers will charge $1.75 to take you to the docks—if you complain they'll tell you that they charge Turks more. **Buses** will get you to Van in three hours with a lot less drama—but far less enjoyably.

A couple of kilometers northwest of the town center on the Ahlat/Adilcevaz road is Tatvan's **train station**, served by infrequent municipal buses. The Ankara-bound *Vangölü Ekspresi* departs at 7am on Tuesday, Thursday, and Saturday, and at this time of day you'll have to take a taxi, or walk (20–25min).

Practical Details

Tatvan has a **tourist office** on a backstreet behind the *Belediye* building, and if you're lucky, you might be able to extract a totally inaccurate ferry sailing time out of the staff. With a couple of exceptions the local **hotels** are miserable places; the best of a bad selection is the *Van Gölü Hotel*, also known as the *Vangölü Denizcilik Kurumu Oteli*, originally built for the comfort of ferry passengers and not easy to find. To get there follow Cumhuriyet Caddesi for about 300m past the PTT office until you see a sign bearing a white "H" on a blue background (for *Hastane*—hospital). Turn left here and follow a winding, potholed road past an abandoned jetty on the lakeside until you reach an institutional-looking, two-story building set about 200m from the shore. This is the best hotel in Tatvan and you'll pay about $10 for a double room. It also has a restaurant.

A cheaper and more central possibility is the *Hotel Üstün*, Hal Caddesi 71/A (☎8497/1028), at the foot of a dead-end street running down from the PTT, with singles for $6 and doubles for $10. The best of the budget places, it's clean and friendly—if it's full try the *Otel Trabzon*, which is clean and reasonably quiet and has singles for $2 and doubles for $3.50. The rest of Van's hotels, like the *Otel Karaman*, Cumhuriyet Caddesi 12 (☎8497/1104), with doubles for $6.50, are dreary and dirty: use only in case of emergency.

The best place to get a bite to **eat** is the *Aşkın Pastanesi* near the Belediye, which serves good ice cream and opens at 5am for pre-train breakfasts.

The Northern Shore of Lake Van

The main road to Van, and the buses, follow the shorter route along the southern shore of Lake Van. If you have time to explore, though, there's also a road that snakes along the northern shore, taking in a couple of places of interest. If you arrive in Tatvan in the morning you could make a day-trip of it, returning to take the bus out of town in the late afternoon or early evening.

Nemrut Dağı

Immediately north of Tatvan, **Nemrut Dağı** (no relation to the one with the statues that overlooks the Euphrates Basin) rises 3050m into the clouds: a dormant volcano with a crater lake near the summit. During July and August (the roads are usually closed the rest of the year) there are dolmuş excursions for groups costing about $4 per person. If you're traveling under your own steam, take the Ahlat and Adilcevaz road out of Tatvan and make a left turn at the *Türkgas* filling station on the edge of town. From here it's about 15km along an unsurfaced road to the crater rim. Occasionally local kids and shepherds will throw stones at tourists.

From the rim it's another 3km down to the lakeside. The crater, 7km in diameter, seems to have its own micro-climate and its lush vegetation contrasts sharply with the bleak landscape outside. Despite this welcoming environment, the only inhabitants are nomads who occasionally pass through during the summer months. The lake occupies the western half of the crater and is icy cold, even in the summer, but there are some hot springs by the side if you feel like a swim.

Ahlat

Forty-two kilometers farther along Lake Van's northern shore, the town of **AHLAT** is known chiefly for its Selçuk tombs and cemetery. Originally an Armenian settlement, Ahlat fell to the Arabs during the ninth century and later both Selçuks and Kurdish Ayyubids controlled the town, followed by the Mongols who arrived in 1245. Even after the Ottoman conquest of 1533, real power in this wild region remained in the hands of the Kurdish emirs of Bitlis.

Today Ahlat's famous *kümbet* **tombs** are scattered around a modern settlement. In a typical *kümbet*, the deceased was interred in an underground chamber, beneath a prayer room reached by steps from the outside. It's thought that the traditional nomadic tent inspired the distinctive conical design. You'll see the first (and largest) of them, the two-story **Ulu Kümbet** (Great Tomb) in a field just south of the main road as you come into town. On the other side of the road is a small and rather pathetic **museum** (50¢) with some Urartian pottery and jewelry and lots of indeterminate fragments. About a kilometer farther down the road, set back some 400m, is the **Çifte Kümbet**, or Twin Tomb. The exterior isn't very inspiring, but within the larger of the two tomb-buildings are traces of stucco decoration. Nearby is the **Bayındır Türbesi**, most impressive of all with its colonnaded porch and distinctive prayer room. It was built in 1492 to house the remains of Bayındır, described by an inscription as a great king and propagator of the faith.

Toward the lake, the **Selçuk cemetery** covers almost two square kilometers, crammed with cockeyed headstones. By all accounts the cemetery was once even more impressive, having lately been encroached on by modern houses from all sides. Leaving town you'll notice a ruined **fortress** down by the lake, built during the sixteenth century by Süleyman the Magnificent. Grand as it is, not much apart from the outer walls has survived, but it's worth scrambling across the fragmented masonry to view Lake Van from the battlements.

Fifty-eight kilometers north of Ahlat is **Manzikert** (today Malazgirt), where in 1071 the Selçuks defeated the Byzantines, captured the emperor, and established for themselves a foothold in Anatolia. There's not much left here besides the remains of a black-walled fortress.

Adilcevaz

Traveling 25km east from Ahlat will bring you to **ADILCEVAZ**, set amid a fertile lakeside strip and dominated by a mighty Selçuk fortress, which is in turn somewhat overshadowed by the 4434-meter peak of **Süphan Dağı**. The mountain, which is Turkey's third-highest peak, can be climbed during the summer months: figure on a three-day trek. Look out also for the **Tuğrul Bey Camii**, a distinctive thirteenth-century mosque constructed using the dark brown stone typical of the area.

To the west of the modern village the remains of the Urartian citadel of **Kefkalesi** can be seen. The site, which lies about a thirty-minute drive along a dirt road, is not easy to reach, though you could walk there in a couple of hours or so. In the grounds of the citadel archaeologists have unearthed the foundations of a Urartian palace, and at the base of the Urartian settlement are the ruins of an Armenian monastery.

In theory you can travel on to Van following the northern shore of the lake but sparse public transportation (though dolmuşes do run in the summer) and badly surfaced roads make this a questionable undertaking; it usually makes more sense to return to Tatvan and pick up a bus or ferry from there.

VAN AND AROUND

Using the town of **Van** as a base it's possible to explore this remote corner of southeast Turkey. Highpoints after Van are the mountain town of **Hakkâri** and **Doğubeyazit**, a staging post for explorations of **Mount Ararat**. **Lake Van** itself, a huge inland sea of almost 4000 square kilometers, is one of the most unusual features of eastern Turkey. Surrounded by mountains on all sides, it sits in what was once a lowland basin later blocked off by lava flowing from Nemrut Dağı. The water is highly alkaline, rendering it slightly soapy, so local people can sometimes be seen washing clothes in it. Lately, though, high levels of **pollution**, particularly around Van, have meant that neither this nor any other lake-related activities are recommended too close to the major lakeside towns. As a result the water remains largely unexploited, with a notable absence of boat rental or water-sports facilities. There is, however, a stretch of rocky **beach** at Edremit, a few kilometers south of Van, where it's possible to swim, and it's probably safe enough to take a dip along the more sparsely populated stretches of shoreline.

Van

VAN is by turns impressive and disappointing. The most enduring image of the place is that of the Rock of Van, which eighteenth-century artists depicted as an improbable column of rock rising from the lakeside. It comes as a surprise to discover that when viewed from certain angles the rock, with the ghostly ruins of old Van at its foot, almost lives up to these flights of fancy.

Modern Van, however, with a population of 130,000, is set a few kilometers back from the lake and is something of a letdown, all concrete buildings and grid-like streets. Its only use is as a base for exploring old Van and the surrounding area, and the only point of interest is the excellent museum. Nonetheless it's an inoffensive place to spend a few days, although increasing numbers of tour groups mean carpet-sellers and occasional mild street hassle.

Some History—Van and the Armenians

From the point of view of the modern Turkish state, the history of Van and the surrounding area is sensitive, because it's inextricably bound up with the history of eastern Turkey's all-but-vanished Armenian population.

The earliest inhabitants of the Van region were the **Hurrians**, an expansionist and warlike people who established a kingdom stretching as far south as the present Syrian border between 1900 and 1260 BC. Their territorial ambitions brought them into conflict with the Hittites, with whom they fought numerous battles. Eventually the Hurrians were defeated by the Hittite king Shuppiluliuma in about 1400 BC. The fragmented kingdom later re-emerged as the Urartian Empire during the ninth century BC with Van, by then known as **Tushba**, as its capital.

At its peak, under king Arghisti I (785–753 BC), the **Urartian Empire** encompassed most of southeast Turkey, stretching into present-day Iran, Iraq, and Syria. The Urartians were great builders, and remains of their fortress-building efforts have been unearthed at several sites in eastern Turkey. They were also skilled jewelers: fine examples of their gold-working can be found in the museum of Van. Eventually centuries of fighting with the Assyrians took its toll and the Urartian Empire went into decline.

After defeating the Assyrians and capturing Ninevah in 612 BC, the **Persian** Medes moved in on the weakened Urartian Empire. At around about the same time **Armenian** settlers began to drift into the area around Van, taking advantage of the Urartian collapse. The origins of the Armenians are unclear, but it's thought that they probably came into the area from the Caucasus, although Herodotus referred to them as Phrygian colonists and Strabo suggested that they were related to the Babylonians or the Syrians.

In 331 BC Alexander the Great defeated the Persians and granted the Armenians a degree of autonomy which enabled them to build up an extensive trade network across eastern Anatolia. After Alexander's death Armenia became part of the Seleucid Empire before passing into **Roman** hands.

From 95–54 BC Armenia, under Tigranes the Great, wrested short-lived independence from the Romans. After their successful campaign against the Pontic kingdom, however, the Romans moved to reconquer the region. From this point onwards the Armenians were never able to shake off foreign domination for long, becoming a Roman, and later a Byzantine, buffer against the Persians.

Under the Romans Armenia was to play an important role in the growth of Christianity. Toward the end of the third century, during the reign of King Trdat, it became the first state to adopt Christianity as its official religion, thanks to the efforts of Saint Gregory "the Enlightener." Following the Edict of Milan in 313 Christianity became officially tolerated throughout the Byzantine Empire, enabling the Armenian church to consolidate and establish its own identity. It was about this time that the Armenian alphabet was invented.

The **Armenian Church** split from the Byzantine Church in 451 after it refused to accept the ruling of the Council of Chalcedon, declaring that Christ had two natures, human and divine. The Armenians, like the Syrian Orthodox Christians, retained their monophysite doctrine, believing that the human nature of Christ was absorbed in the divine. The ninth and tenth centuries saw perhaps the greatest flowering of Armenian culture, but in the long run the religious split led to a wider political division of the Christian population of Asia Minor. The Arabs, waiting in the wings, seized their chance and moved in on Armenia. They in turn were superceded in 1071 by the Selçuks who founded the Sultanate of Rum. Another brief Armenian revival came during the twelfth and thirteenth centuries, when they were vassals of the Georgians, but thereafter there was little respite from repeated raids by the Turcomans and the disastrous Mongol onslaughts.

The Ottomans finally took over in 1468 and several centuries of relative peace ensued. Ottoman rule was initially tolerant and the Armenians pretty much ran their own afffairs. However, in the latter half of the nineteenth century there was an upsurge of **nationalist** feeling, stirred up partly by the Russians who had an interest is fragmenting the Ottoman Empire. Even before World War I there had been outbreaks of violence against the Armenians, and with the outbreak of hostilities the situation deteriorated. What happened over the next few years is still the subject of violent dispute, but it's safe to say that by the time the fighting was over there were very few Armenians left in the Van area, or indeed anywhere else in Turkey.

It seems that although thousands of Armenians served loyally in the Ottoman army, many saw the conflict as a chance to break away from Ottoman domination and sided with the Russians. Local Turks and Kurds used this as a pretext to attack the Armenians, destroying old Van before it fell to the Russians in 1915. During the occupation years the Armenians are alleged to have attempted to force the Turks and Kurds out of Armenian territory, and as many as 600,000 Turks and Kurds are said to have been killed at this time. Certainly today the Turkish government makes much of these episodes, and news of the unearthing of massacre sites crops up regularly on Turkish TV.

The modern Turkish media is less forthcoming about what happened to Turkey's Armenian population later. In 1915 Interior Minister Talaat Bey declared that the human rights of Armenians living on Turkish soil had been "completely cancelled. . . even babies in the cradle are not to be spared"; and his partner in the ruling triumvirate, Enver Paşa, issued orders for the systematic slaughter of Turkey's Armenian population. According to numerous independent accounts the towns were emptied and their inhabitants liquidated, and Armenian soldiers serving in the Turkish army were executed. About one million people were killed and those who escaped death were driven out of the country.

When the time came to conduct the first census of the Turkish Republic, Van had a population of 6,931, compared with 80,000 before the war. So complete was the destruction of the old town that it was never rebuilt; instead modern Van was constructed a couple of kilometers away, and the foundations of the old lakeside city were left as a silent, accusatory reminder of the genocide committed against the Armenians.

Arrival and Information

Aesthetically, the ferry offers the best introduction to Van, with a view of the Rock rising out of the shoreline as you approach the docks. From the docks you'll be able to pick up a dolmuş to take you the 5km into town. You'll be dropped off at the busy junction of **Beş Yol**, at the northern end of Cumhuriyet Caddesi, the town's main drag. Beş Yol is a place you'll find yourself coming back to often, with dolmuşes leaving for most of the local attractions from streets in the immediate vicinity.

If you fly in, the **airport** is 6km south of town, and there's a bus to the very central **THY office** (Cumhuriyet Cad 196, Enver Derihanoğlu İş Merkezi; ☎061/11241). If you arrive by **bus**, the otogar is a little way northwest of downtown: dolmuşes run from here to Beş Yol and the bus company offices. All of these are reasonably handy for the **tourist information office** at Cumhuriyet Caddesi 127 (☎061/12018). During the high season there's usually an English speaker around to give you a brochure and street map, and details of ferry sailing times: the latter should be checked with the local ferry agent at ☎061/11459.

Almost everything else you'll need in Van is in the vicinity of Cumhuriyet Caddesi, too. The **banks**, **PTT**, and bus ticket offices are all here, and many of the cheaper hotels and restaurants can be found just to the west in the streets running parallel to it.

Finding a Place to Stay

After Diyarbakır, Van is the largest town in the southeast and most people who visit this part of Turkey usually end up spending at least a night here. There are therefore plenty of **hotels** in town, though some of the cheaper ones aren't all that pleasant and some of the more expensive ones could be better.

The immediate vicinity of Beş Yol is as good a place as any to start looking, especially for the cheaper options. The *Hotel Van*, across a stretch of wasteland just south of Sihke Caddesi, is basic but cheap, at $2 a night per bed. Nearby, the *Hotel Çaldıran*, on Sihke Caddesi opposite the Büyük Camii (☎061/12718), has singles for $8 and doubles for $12, with bath. The *Hotel Aslan*, also nearby at Eski Hal Civarı (☎061/12469), has reasonable, if slightly small rooms for $6 and $8. On the same street opposite Beyaz Saray is the *Otel İpek* (☎061/13033), with singles and doubles for $7 and $12.

Heading south from here you'll come to the *Hotel Tahran*, PTT Caddesi Türkoğlu Çarşısı 44 (☎061/12541), where decent rooms with attached bath go for $7 and $12. Not far from here are the *Hotel Kent*, İş Bankası Arkası (behind İş Bank; ☎061/12519), where rooms with bath go for $7 and $10, the *Otel Kahraman*, Cumhuriyet Caddesi 111 (☎061/11525), $6 and $10, and the *Bayram Oteli*, on Yani Mehmet Efendi Caddesi just past Cumhuriyet Caddesi (☎061/11116), $7 and $10. The promised hot water never seems to materialize but they do have a hamam, which is also open to the public. Another relatively cheap and reasonable possibility is the *Otel Çağ*, Hastane Caddesi 2 Sokak 39 (☎061/12717); $8 and $10 with bath, less without. Other cheap places are on the whole pretty grim.

At the upper end of the market are a number of "tourist hotels," with pleasant rooms, bars, and restaurant facilities, which tend to attract the business of tour groups. The *Büyük Asur Oteli*, Cumhuriyet Caddesi 126 (☎061/18792), has rooms for $17.50 and $27.50, while at the *Hotel Akdamar*, Kazım Karabekir Caddesi 56, they go for $23 and $32. Top of the range is the *Büyük Urartu Oteli*, Cumhuriyet Cad 60 (☎061/20660); $34 for a single and $47 to $52 for a double. Despite the address it's actually on Hastane Caddesi.

Restaurants

There's a fair selection of **places to eat** in Van. On the street west of Cumhuriyet Caddesi, near the *Hotel Tahran*, you'll find a couple of cheap *lokantas*: the *Serhat Lokantası* and the *Rumeli Lokantasi*. Also worth checking out is the *Sölen Lokantası*, on Kazım Karabekir Caddesi opposite the *Hotel Akdamar*. Best of all, however, is the *Altın Şiş Fırınlı*, just past the post office. For snacks, breakfast, and pastries try the *Güven Pastanesi* on Cumhuriyet Caddesi, near the *Belediye* building, or the *Tuşba Pastanesi* on the same street. These two seem to be the only places in town where you're likely to see unaccompanied women. East of Cumhuriyet Caddesi are a couple of cafés suitable for a hearty breakfast, serving Van's famous *otlu peynir* (herb cheese).

Slightly farther afield, near the ferry terminal, is the *Kumsal Restaurant*, which is good for fish, but where the occasional presence of a singer means you'll probably end up paying extra. Another more upscale possibility is the *Restaurant Kösk*, Maresal Cadmak Caddesi. If you want more comfort, head for the hotel restaurants.

The Rock of Van

From Beş Yol frequent dolmuşes ($1) run to the Rock of Van, on top of which sit the extensive remains of **Van Kalesi**; if it's not too hot the three kilometers also make an easy walk. The dolmuş will drop you off at the eastern end of the Rock, and from there you follow the road along the northern face toward the lake, passing a mosque and *türbe* which attract many pilgrims. Above these is a terrace, the site of a Urartian temple, of which only a couple of arched alcoves remain. It's claimed that these once contained golden statues of Urartian godesses, which were spirited away by American archaeologists during the 1930s. Cuneiform inscriptions on a statue base in one of the alcoves record the life and works of Menua, a Urartian king. Below, the road continues around to a parking lot and a teahouse. Nearby is a large stone rectangle, originally a Urartian dock. The lake once came right up to this point, but these days a fish farm stands between the erstwhile landing stage and the water.

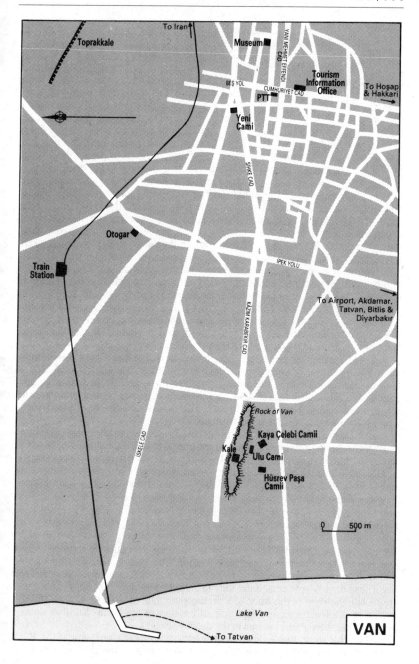

From the parking area a fragmentary stairway leads up to the *kale*, or citadel, at the top. Giving coherent directions around the Rock is almost impossible, given the lack of obvious landmarks and signs, but what follows is an attempt to guide you via the more salient features. Ascending, you come first to a kind of terrace area on the southern side of the Rock, overlooking the old town, from which steps cut into the rocks lead down to the rock-hewn **tomb of King Argistis** (790–765 BC). Around here the rock face has many Urartian cuneiform inscriptions. The tomb and inscriptions are difficult to reach, having been fenced off to prevent souvenir-hunters from chipping away the inscriptions, but if you're persistent you'll find a way. Watch out for the big hole inside the rock tomb, into which more than one unwary explorer has fallen. In front of the tomb is a footprint-like depression in the rock which inevitably is ascribed to the devil.

From the terrace area you pass through an arch onto a ramp leading up to the *kale* grounds. Exploring the jumble of ruins is easy enough, although it's not always clear exactly what you're looking at. As you climb the views get increasingly spectacular, sometimes vertiginous; many people reckon they are best appreciated at sunset. To the immediate south of the Rock of Van is the ghost town of old Van. Beware of the sheer drops on the southern side which, if you're not careful, could take you there sooner than you'd anticipated.

In Ottoman times the *kale* was garrisoned by 3000 janissaries, and today a number of recognizable architectural remnants are still visible. Most prominent of these is a **ruined mosque** with a minaret, whose partially intact steps can be climbed. Nearby are a *medrese* and barracks. The large base blocks of the *kale* date from the original Urartian fortress and a modest inscription reads "I, Sardur, the illustrious king, the mighty king, the king of the universe, the king of all lands, a king without equal, I erected these walls."

Below is another terrace overlooking Old Van where there are a couple more **rock tombs**, those of kings Ispuini (815–807 BC) and Menua (804–790 BC). A little more accessible than the tomb of Argistis, these are reached via a winding path snaking down from the citadel: each consists of a large central chamber with three smaller chambers branching off. The southern edge of the terrace is marked by the remains of mud battlements.

Retracing your steps, head for the northern side of the rock where a steep slope leads down to the outer walls. From here you can walk along what's left of the stone **battlements**. At one point a flight of steps cut into the rock, to the right, leads down to a cliff-side terrace from which you can reach another vast **rock tomb**, that of Sardur II (765–733 BC). Again, three chambers lead off from the central one.

Old Van

The destruction of **Old Van** in 1915 was so complete that only three mosques and one or two indeterminate ruins remain. The rest is an unending sea of grassy, rubble-strewn mounds, with not so much as the basic street plan discernible. These days people come here only to lounge around on the grassy knolls and appreciate the view of the Rock of Van, the silhouette of which has been likened to that of a kneeling camel. The only other sign of life is the Kurdish women washing their carpets and kilims in the nearby streams.

It's possible to scramble down to ground level at the eastern end of the Rock and walk through the dead town. The closest mosque is the thirteenth-century

Ulu Cami, with a minaret that can still be climbed. Just above, set into the cliff face high above the ground, is a huge cuneiform inscription in Persian, Medean, and Babylonian; it concerns the Persian king Xerxes. The southern limits of the old town are bounded by a road, on which a couple of sixteenth-century mosques stand. The eastern one is the **Kaya Çelebi Camii**, a mere shell whose white stone *mihrab* has unaccountably survived; the western mosque, slightly more intact, is the **Husrev Paşa Camii**. The only other significant survivors are some stretches of town wall, a couple of tombs, and a ruined hamam.

The rest has vanished forever and it's hard to believe that this was once among the most populous settlements in Anatolia, a place of which it was said that everybody should visit once before they died.

Van Museum

Back in the new town, ubiquitous yellow signs point out the way to the **Van Müzesi** (8am–noon & 1:30–5:30pm; $2), on Cengiz Caddesi just east of Cumhuriyet Caddesi, near the *Hotel Bayram*. This is the main, perhaps the only, attraction of modern Van, and it's among the best provincial museums in Turkey, certainly in the east, with far more than the usual jumble of archaeological miscellany.

In a room to the left of the ticket office on the ground floor you'll find displays of **Urartian gold jewelry**, bronze-work and terracotta figures. Also included are objects unearthed at Çavuştepe, including some ornate Urartian bronze belts. Look out also for the Urartian jewelled breastplates. Adjacent to this room is a small conservatory, containing various **rock carvings** from Mesolithic times (9000–8000 BC) through to the Bronze Age. Some of these are very primitive representations of stags, almost prototypes of the stag carvings in the Museum of Anatolian Civilizations in Ankara, while others are more sophisticated animal figures. Local ethnologists claim that some of these designs can still be found in local kilim and pottery designs. Also on display are some child sarcophagi from the fourteenth century and a number of cuneiform inscriptions.

Upstairs in the **ethnographic section** there are some fine kilims from Van and Hakkâri. There's also a prominent "Genocide Section." This, it transpires, is devoted to atrocities committed against Turks in the area and has a gory display of cracked skulls. There's little explanation but the implication seems to be that they are the remains of Turks massacred by Armenians. Nearby a cabinet contains numerous books devoted to debunking the alleged myth of the Turkish-sponsored massacres and mass expulsions of the Armenian population. In fact there's no mention whatsoever of the sufferings of Turkey's Armenians, making this a distasteful corner in an otherwise fine museum.

Toprakkale

Toprakkale, Van's only other significant site, is in a military zone and you'll need a permit from the town governor before you can visit it (inquire at the local tourist information office). It's a sizable rock outcrop, just north of town, the site of another Urartian citadel. You'll be told it's an underground palace but in reality the underground chamber is a large cistern. Other than that there's not really much to see.

Farther Out—Yedi Kilise

About 20km east of Van, in the foothills of the Varak Mountains, lies the desolate village of **YEDİ KİLİSE** (Seven Churches), also known as *Varak Vank*. The village takes its name from the seven Armenian churches that once stood here: sadly, most of these have been destroyed by earthquakes, and those that survived are now used as farm outbuildings. At the southern end of the village are the two oldest, both dating from the eighth century. One has almost completely disappeared, while the choir of the other is in use as a barn. To the north is a domed church, built on a cruciform floorplan, which was erected during the eleventh century. The porch of this church contains some intricate stone carvings, and from here an arched stone portal leads to the gutted main building. Yedi Kilise is officially off-limits to visitors so you'll need either your own transportation or the services of a helpful taxi driver to get there. Once you arrive you should have no problems—although if an army patrol happens by you'll probably be told to leave.

South of Van

The area south of Van is one of the most physically forbidding in Turkey; rugged and inaccessible mountains, dotted with isolated settlements, stretch all the way to the Iraqi and Iranian borders. The Armenian church on the island of **Akdamar**, the ancient Urartian site at **Çavuştepe**, and **Hoşap**'s Disney-on-acid castle make excellent day trips from Van, but if you want to get a real sense of this area you need to make the mountainous bus journey to the garrison town of **Hakkâri**, from which forays into the mountains themselves are possible.

Akdamar

On an island just off Lake Van's southern shore stands the tenth-century Armenian **Akdamar Kilisesi** (open during daylight hours; $2.50). The church itself is an incredible example of Armenian architecture and its island, which has always been a popular local day-trip destination, has of late also become a compulsory stop off on the tour-bus circuit. At times it gets very crowded, but once you've visited the church it's usually easy enough to find a secluded spot somewhere on the island where you can have a picnic (bring your own food because there's nothing available on the island) and start to appreciate the island's mysterious, evocative atmosphere.

It was the Armenian king Gagik Artzruni who built the church between 915 and 921 AD. He also constructed a palace and monastery here in an attempt to create a refuge from the cares of state and dynastic infighting. The palace and monastery have not survived but **the church** is still intact and justly famous: its design (similar to that of the churches found around Ani) epitomizes Armenian ecclesiastical architecture. The floorplan is small, with dimensions of only 15 by 12 meters, but the central tower is over 20 meters high.

The exterior wall is covered in marvelous **reliefs** depicting biblical scenes, idiosyncratically interpreted by Armenian masons. Three reliefs tell the story of Jonah and the Whale, one of them showing Jonah being fed to a whale with ears and teeth. Also here are the stories of Abraham and Isaac and David and Goliath, while other reliefs are of Adam and Eve (sadly damaged and defaced) and Gagik, the builder of the church. Mythical animals and inscriptions in the hook-like Armenian alphabet also abound. Inside are faded murals but unfortunately the interior is more or less gutted, and the walls daubed with graffiti.

Getting There, and Staying Nearby

Akdamar is easily visited from Van and makes an ideal day excursion. **Dolmuşes** ($1) run from near the Yeni Cami and *Çaldıran Hotel* at Beş Yol, and in the height of summer you shouldn't have too much trouble picking one up to the dock where the Akdamar-bound boats sail from. At other times the dolmuş may only run as far as the town of Gevaş, and you'll be charged another $1 for the remaining 5km to "İskele."

The departure point for the island is a **dock** by the roadside where a couple of boats ferry visitors across. The boatmen charge $20 per boatload for the round trip, and during the summer when there are plenty of passengers you'll pay about $2 per head. At quiet times you may have to wait around until the boat fills up if you don't want to end up paying extra. There's a further charge of $2.50 for admission to the island.

There's not much in the way of **hotels** near Akdamar, which most people visit from Van. Near the dock, however, stands a large wooden building with a parking lot: this is *Akdamar Camping Restaurant*, a slightly expensive establishment (which serves good fish) where the tour operators usually feed their charges before herding them across to the island. It also has some rudimentary **camping** facilities. On the shore road just outside Gevaş, the *Hotel Solul* offers basic rooms for about $3.50 single, $6 double.

Çavuştepe and Hoşap

Due south of Van, a couple more excursion possibilities take you away from the lake. Follow the signs for the Hakkâri road out of Van (not the Gevaş shore road). After a few kilometers it starts to climb, and at an altitude of about 2260 meters you traverse the Kurubaş Pass. Some 5km beyond here the road forks: a right turn takes you along the southern shore of Lake Van toward Tatvan; left leads to Hakkâri. Less than 10km in this direction, the village of **ÇAVUŞTEPE** is the site of a **Urartian royal palace**, built between 764 and 735 BC by King Sardur II. To the right of the road is a hill, on top of which the palace buildings once stood; a yellow sign leads you up an unsurfaced road to the ancient citadel.

There's usually someone on hand to show you around, and no entrance fee seems to be required. You'll be led to a temple with a number of black basalt blocks with cuneiform inscriptions; there's also a sacrificial altar and several cisterns. Beyond here is the palace itself, but even extensive excavations have failed to reveal anything much of its structure.

Continuing on the Hakkâri road from Çavuştepe will bring you, after another 10km, to the medieval Kurdish fortress of **Hoşap Kalesi** (daily 8:30am–noon & 1:30–5:30pm; $1; dolmuşes depart from the *Sevimli* office in the bazaar near the *Kent Oteli* in Van), towering above the squat modern village of GÜZELSU (a Turkish translation of Hoşap, Kurdish for "Beautiful Water"). The fortress, an extraordinary, half-ruined flight of fancy, was built at the behest of Sarı Süleyman, a local Kurdish strongman, in 1643. According to legend, he was so pleased with the result when the castle was completed that he had the architect's hands lopped off, to ensure that he would never build another to rival it.

To reach the fortress, cross the river by way of a modern bridge near a much older stone one, and follow a dirt track winding around to the far side of the hill. This will bring you to the main entrance, set in an immense round tower, where the caretaker should be on hand to let you in and relieve you of the entrance fee. The entrance opens into a tunnel leading to the interior of the fortress. Originally there were several hundred rooms, including a couple of mosques, three hamams, and a *medrese*, but there isn't really a great deal left. The best-preserved part is the keep, reached by a path from the outer fortress. Looking east from the fortress you can see the line of mud defensive walls that once encircled the village. Generations of erosion have produced a humpbacked, skeletal effect.

To Hakkâri

The four-hour bus trip to Hakkâri along the gorge of the Zab is worth it for the mountain scenery alone. The most spectacular stretches are around the 2730-meter Günzeldere Pass and in the sections of the gorge beyond the town of Başkale.

Fourteen kilometers before Başkale there's a miltary checkpoint where a soldier will board the bus and give your passport a cursory glance. From this checkpoint a road leads east to the village of ALBAYRAK, where you'll find the **Surb Bartolomeos** monastery. Many of the monastery buildings are intact and there's a fine, albeit partially collapsed church with some good stone reliefs. Unfortunately all this is now a restricted area and to visit you'll need to obtain permission from the checkpoint, which unless you speak good Turkish may be more trouble than it's worth.

At 2500m, **BAŞKALE** is the highest town in Turkey—and that's its only claim to fame. South of here the Zab gorge is at its most spectacular and photogenic, but mainly inhabited by sheep and shepherds: look out for the bridges that enable the flocks to cross the river. Here and there tracks lead off to medieval-looking settlements, and you might spot the occasional nomad encampment.

Some 60km south of Başkale, there's another checkpoint at **Yeni Köprü**. The road forks here; a left turn in the direction of the yellow sign marked "Iran" will bring you first to YÜKSEKOVA, a possible base for climbing (depending on the current level of PKK insurgency). From here the road continues to the Iranian border crossing point.

Hakkâri

HAKKÂRİ is pretty much the end of Turkey, a strange border garrison town much used as a base for trekking into the surrounding mountains, and the closest most visitors come to the guerrilla war being waged in the mountains. As a traveler it's highly unlikely that you'll come into direct contact with the trouble—the most you're likely to experience are a few checkpoints en route to Hakkâri, and a sense of the tension generated by the heavy troop presence in the town itself. One effect of the unrest in the region has been to restrict access to the mountains: climbing in the mountains around Hakkâri has been limited to select routes around Cilo Dağ since 1985.

Hakkâri itself—which has a couple of buses from Van every day—is no big deal, although it has an undeniably unique atmosphere. Most visitors simply use

NESTORIAN CHRISTIANS

Many of the settlements in the Zab gorge and surrounding mountains were home to **Nestorian Christians** until the Kurds began to massacre the men and sell the women and children into slavery during the latter half of the nineteenth century. Their fate was sealed in 1915 when the Nestorian patriarch came out in support of the Allies during the First World War. When the Russians withdrew the Nestorians deemed it wise not to hang around, and fled into Iran and Iraq.

The history of the Nestorian Church parallels that of the Syrian Orthodox Church in many ways, although their respective theological positions were completely opposite. **Nestorius** was bishop of Constantinople from 428 to 431, and formulated a doctrine which held Christ to be predominantly human in nature. In 431, however, the Council of Ephesus declared his position to be heretical. The works of Nestorius were burnt and he was deported to the Egyptian desert after suffering hideous tortures. Edessa (Şanliurfa) and Nusaybin near Mardin became important Nestorian centers, and later the focus of the faith moved to Persia. After the Mongol attacks the Nestorians relocated to the area around present-day Hakkâri.

There are a number of Nestorian churches scattered around the area, most of them very difficult to reach. Their simplicity of design, coupled with the fact that they are now mostly used as feed and dung stores, also tends to make them a bit dull. The most notable one is **Mar Şalita**, about 20km northeast of Hakkâri, but you'll need a guide to reach it and you'll have to go on foot.

the town as a starting point for exploring the mountains, in particular the 4136-meter **Cilo Dağ** facing the town to the south. There seem to be almost as many troops as civilians in the town, and commandos, in their sky-blue berets, are particularly in evidence. Patrol activity is constant, but most of the locals seem to pretend that the soldiers don't exist. They also ignore the "*Ne Mutlu Türküm Diyene*" slogans posted all over town—"How happy is he who says, 'I am a Turk'."

If you want to do any serious **trekking**, you should link up with one of the various local guides. Finding them won't be a problem as they'll probably seek you out. Salim Tuğan, based at the *Turistik Otel*, is one reliable and trustworthy possibility. He'll charge about $12 to $16 per day per person to take you into the mountains, and can also arrange group trips, taking you to nomad camps.

Even if your independent traveler's instincts rebel at the notion of hiring a guide, it makes sense to do so. In the absence of accurate maps or guidebooks you really do need someone to show you around, and on remoter routes the presence of a guide will also help avoid problems with the security forces, who can be a little testy and impulsive out in the wilds.

Practical Details

Hakkâri isn't really a normal tourist town so there is no **tourist office**, and only two **hotels**. The cheaper of them is the *Turistik Otel*, basic and none too pristine, charging $2.40 per bed: unless you're willing to pay more you may have to share a room with strangers. The better alternative is the *Hotel Ümit* on Altay Caddesi (☎1408/2467), where good, clean rooms with bathrooms (water supply intermittent) go for $10 a night double, less if business is slack. This hotel also has a restaurant. Both places are a couple of minutes' walk from the bus drop-off point, and their emissaries will doubtless pounce on you as soon as you get off.

There are a couple of reasonable places to **eat and drink**. The best-value food is at the *Derya Kebap Salonu*, Cumhuriyet Caddesi near the *Turistik Otel*, where you'll get a decent meal for less than $2. The *Elif Pastanesi*, directly beneath the *Turistik*, is good for breakfast and light snacks. The *Cilo Pub* in Altay Caddesi does slightly more expensive food and also serves beer, except during Ramadan when the town is cruelly dry. This is the town's main tourist hangout and the owner also organizes treks into the mountains to back up his catering and carpet-selling activities. The *Şehir Bira Salonu* in the same street has cheaper food and beer but a less civilized ambience.

West from Hakkâri

If you're determined to do so, it's possible to head directly back to the west from Hakkâri, although it's an involved process and only to be undertaken by the adventurous. The road is only passable during the summer months, and very bad even then. When the route is feasible, a dolmuş departs every day at 8:30am for **BEYTÜŞŞEBAN**. You need to buy your ticket a day in advance—$6 for a five-hour ride across the magnificent Altın Dağ chain. There are no hotels or other facilities here, but you can stay overnight in the local school and pick up a mini-bus to Uludere in the morning.

If you don't want to spend the night in Beytüşşeban, get out at the Beytüşşeban turnoff, near a big army camp and soft-drink store. From here you might be able to hitch a ride with a truck (although don't bank on it because traffic is scarce) or a taxi. The latter option can set you back as much as $30 for the three-hour trip, though it's worth trying to bargain this down. The road to Uludere is dotted with military checkpoints, but as a tourist you'll be treated courteously.

In **ULUDERE** you'll find the *Otel Murat*, an extremely basic hotel with three rooms where beds go from $1.50 each and the toilet is a hole out behind the house. The town also has a couple of banks, and dolmuşes to Cizre (first departure at 8am, arriving at noon) and Siirt (take the Cizre dolmuş and change at ŞIRNAK).

There's a heavy military presence again in **CİZRE**, and everything closes early, so don't leave it too late before going to eat at one of the town's two restaurants. Here the guerrilla war is very close, and you can sometimes hear gunfire from the mountains at night. There are plenty of **hotels**, though—one of the best is the two-star *Hotel Kadioğlu*. More importantly you can pick up a bus to just about any city in Turkey. You're also not far from the border crossing to Iraq.

North of Van

Heading north from Van, the town of Doğubeyazit makes an obvious starting point for any exploration of the Mount Ararat area. In theory Doğubeyazit is only 185km northeast of Van, some three hours by bus or dolmuş. Take the Ağri road and turn right at a junction marked "Muradiye," where a badly maintained road skirts the Iranian border going north. Unfortunately dolmuşes only depart a few times a week, even in the summer, and the road is officially closed after 5pm and patrolled by the army (they also patrol during the day and stop vehicles to carry out identity checks).

This means that you're more likely to end up traveling to Doğubeyazit via Ağrı, a frustrating five-hour journey, and all the more irritating because you know it's taking you far out of your way. AĞRI itself is a bleak dump, and there's no conceivable reason for stopping, although if you must there are a couple of fleapit hotels in the town center.

Doğubeyazit

DOĞUBEYAZIT itself is nothing special either, and most people come here only to see the İşak Paşa Sarayı, Mount Ararat, and a couple of other out-of-town-attractions. It's also a stop-off point for overland buses en route to the Far East, so you may well find the place is full of European and Australasian organized adventurers. As far as visitors are concerned, the action is concentrated on a few central streets where you'll find the banks, PTT, and hotels.

Practical Details

There is no **tourist information office** in town but the various travel agents and bus companies will be able to tell you all you need to know about local excursion possibilities. Cheap **hotels** include the *Hotel Gül*, Güven Caddesi 34 (☎0278/1176), with pretty horrible double rooms for $5, the similarly priced *Hotel Kıbrıs* on the same street (☎0278/1407), and the *Hotel İlhan*, Emniyet Caddesi 37 (☎0278/2055). A little more pleasant is the *Hotel Kenan*, Emniyet Caddesi 5, where you pay $7 and $10 for reasonable rooms with bathrooms. There is also a restaurant here. Another good bet is the *Hotel Tahran*, Büyük Ağri Cad 86 (☎0278/2223), charging $8 for doubles with bathrooms.

The town also has a few more expensive possibilities, most of which cater primarily to tour groups. The *İşak Paşa Hotel*, Emniyet Caddesi 10 (☎0278/1245), has plain but comfortable rooms at $12 and $22, as does the *Sim Er Tur*, Kaya Burun PK 13 (☎0278/1601), on the main road east out of town. Back in the town center, the classier *Hotel İsfahan*, Emniyet Caddesi 26 (☎0278/1138, 1139), charges $20 and $35 for facilities that include a restaurant. Both are often full.

For good food in comfortable surroundings try the hotel restaurants. Otherwise you're pretty much restricted to standard kebab places, like the *Gaziantepli Kebap Salonu* on the main street.

İşak Paşa Sarayı

Five kilometers southeast of Doğubeyazit stands the **İşak Paşa Sarayı** (8am–5pm, closed Fri; $2), a ruined seventeenth-century palace set on a 2000-meter-high plateau overlooking the town. It looks as if it could have been built for a Hollywood sound stage, epitomizing Western conceptions of Near Eastern architecture—which is doubtless what makes it so popular with the tourist crowds. Its designers seem to have taken elements from just about every architectural style extant in Anatolia and incorporated them into the palace's construction. Selçuk, Ottoman, Armenian, and Persian influences are all clearly evident once you start to search.

The strategic importance of the site was recognized as far back as Urartian times when a fortress was constructed here, and later the Selçuks and the Ottomans built castles to control east–west silk trade routes. The palace itself dates back to 1685, when work began under Çolak Abdi Paşa, a local Kurdish chieftain—his son İsak Paşa added the finishing touches a little less than a century later. According to an inevitable legend (which sounds particularly familiar if you've already visited the fortress of Hoşap), the architect had his hands cut off once he'd completed the work to prevent him from building another. By 1877 the palace was already in decline, being used by the Turkish army as a barracks. Subsequent periods of Russian occupation set the seal on its decay.

You enter via a grandiose gateway which once boasted gold-plated doors: the Russians removed these in 1917 and they're now on display at the Hermitage Museum in Leningrad. Inside a courtyard leads through to a smaller, inner courtyard. Straight ahead of you is the harem entrance, to the right the entrance to the *selâmlık*, or mens' quarters, and in the right-hand corner of the courtyard are the tombs of İsak Paşa and his wife.

The harem contains fourteen bedrooms overlooking the valley below, a kitchen, and two circular bathrooms. At its very center is a colonnaded dining hall. The *selâmlık* also contains bedrooms and a fine mosque, retaining much of its original decoration. The view across the valley takes in an old mosque and the ruins of a fortress. The mosque dates from the reign of Selim the Grim, who defeated the Persians at the Battle of Çaldıran (70km south of Doğubeyazıt) in 1514. The fortress is much older and is thought to date originally from Urartian times, although the visible remains are more recent. The foundations you can see below on the plain are all that's left of *Eski Beyazit*, "Old Beyazit," a city founded by the Urartians.

To reach the İsak Paşa Sarayı take a taxi from the central Atatürk statue for about $6 round-trip (this includes waiting time). If you're visiting in the off-season check up on the opening times as they are sometimes a little erratic. There's an extremely rudimentary **campground** attached to a farm near the palace.

Mount Ararat (Ağrı Dag)

> *Father Chantry-Pigg said that he had heard in İstanbul that a party of Seventh Day Adventist pilgrims was journeying to Mount Ararat for the second coming of Christ, which was due to occur there this summer on the summit of this mountain. It had been due in this same spot on earlier occasions, and pilgrims from all over Europe had several times traveled there to meet it, but it had been delayed, and now it was really due. If we climbed Mount Ararat, as Father Chantry-Pigg intended to do, we should find the pilgrims waiting as near the top as it was possible to get, collecting pieces of the ark, singing hymns and preparing their souls against the Coming. It seems that life on Ararat has always been immensely strange.*
>
> Rose Macaulay

Few mountains west of the Himalayas have as compelling a hold on Western imagination as **Mount Ararat**. And for once the mountain—where Noah's ark came to rest—manages to deliver some of that promise in reality. There are two peaks; the larger one at 5165m is **Büyük Ağrı** and the lesser one, weighing in at 4925m, is **Küçük Ağrı**. Traditionally Armenian monks considered Mount Ararat a sacred place and no one was allowed to climb it, so it was not until 1829 that Dr Johann Jacob Parrot, a German academic, succeeded in conquering the peak. Numerous other ascents have followed—despite the sterling efforts of US astronaut James Baldwin and others, no trace of Noah's Ark has so far been found—but even today some villagers believe that it's not possible to climb the mountain, and Turkish officials did not admit to the possibility until the 1950s.

Access to Mount Ararat

Unfortunately the mountain lies in a sensitive border zone, adjoining both the Soviet and Iranian frontiers, so access is difficult. For a long time it was closed altogether, but since 1982 **organized ascents** in the company of a guide have been permitted. Unfortunately this has made the whole process of climbing the mountain into something of a racket, and many experienced mountaineers feel that, if you want to go climbing in Turkey, there are other, easier possibilities.

In order to set up a trek to the summit of Mount Ararat you need to apply via the Turkish embassy in your own country at least three months in advance. Ask for a mountaineer's application for a trekking permit (this is quite short: make sure they don't send you a five-page "ark-hunter's" form). Your application will be forwarded to the Turkish Ministry of Foreign Affairs, which will in turn pass it on to the Ministry of Tourism and Culture. You will have to be fairly persistent, contacting your local embassy regularly for news of how your application is going, but if all goes well you should eventually receive confirmation that a permit has been issued. If not you can try contacting the Ministry of Tourism and Culture's Promotion and Sales Division (*Tanıtma ve Pazarlama Müdürglu*) in Ankara, once you're actually in Turkey. If a permit is granted the *jandarma* station in Doğubeyazit will be notified by phone, you'll be assigned a guide, and you will be free to press on with your ascent.

If you're thinking of turning up in Doğubeyazit and trying to arrange things on the spot, forget it. The military will not grant you a permit and without one the closest you'll get to Ararat will be the foothills, where you'll be picked up by an army patrol and driven back to Doğubeyazit.

However you end up doing it, the ascent of Mount Ararat can turn out to be a costly business. Guides will charge $40 per day and the minimum charge is for five days, or $200, to take a maximum of ten people to the summit. Various other costs must also be reckoned with; $24 per day for a vehicle to take you to the trail-head, $10 per day per animal for mules to carry your gear, and $10 per day for walkie-talkie rental (required by law for your guides to keep in touch with Doğubeyazit *jandarma* station).

The Ascent

The ascent starts at ELİ, a village on the southern slopes of Büyük Ağrı, a little over 10km north of Doğubeyazit. From here you'll head up to **Camp 1** at the base of the mountain proper. Figure on an afternoon start to reach Camp 1 by nightfall.

After this things start to get strenuous. **Camp 2** is at 4200m, so it's wise to take things easy to avoid the risk of altitude sickness. From here make an early start to reach the summit before cloud cover becomes too thick. Don't let your guides try to force the pace—you're paying, so take things at your own rate—and watch out for the fierce sheepdogs with spiked collars to protect them from wolves. At 4500m there's a prepared bivouac site and at around 4900m the stones give way to snow, meaning you have to use crampons. You'll pass the western summit (the lower one) from which it's easy to traverse to the higher, eastern **summit**.

Other attractions

About 35km east of Doğubeyazit and 6km west of the Iranian border is a huge **meteorite crater** that can be visited as part of an organized group. Ask in town for details. Also worth an excursion is **Balık Gölu**, a large lake about 52km northwest of Doğubeyazit, which offers walking and fishing possibilities. There are **camping facilities**, and a simple **pansiyon** on the southern shore. At **Diyadin**, 45km west of Doğubeyazit, are some good hot springs.

travel details

Trains

From Tatvan to Malatya/Kayseri/Ankara (3 a week; 11hr 30min/22hr/32hr).

From Kurtalan via Diyarbakır (2hr 30min) to Malatya/Kayseri/Ankara (4 a week; 10hr/22hr/30hr).

From Van to Kapıköy, Iranian border (3 a week; 3hr).

Buses

From Diyarbakır to Adana (4 daily; 10hr); Ankara (5; 13hr); Bitlis (5; 2hr); Malatya (8; 5hr); Mardin (4; 2hr); Şanlıurfa (6; 3hr); Sivas (4; 9hr); Tatvan (5; 4hr); Van (4; 7hr).

From Tatvan to Bitlis (hourly; 1hr); Diyarbakır (5 daily; 4hr); Van (5; 3hr).

From Van to Ağri, for Doğubeyazit (3 daily; 6hr); Doğubeyazit (3 weekly; 3hr); Erzurum (3 daily; 7hr); Hakkâri (2; 4hr); Tatvan (5; 4hr).

From Hakkâri to Diyarbakır (1 daily; 8hr); Van (2; 4hr).

From Doğubeyazit to Ağri, for Van (4; 3hr); Ankara (1; 22hr); Erzurum (5; 5hr); Kars (4; 6hr).

Ferries

From Tatvan to Van and vice versa (daily; 4hr). Timetable promises 4 daily, in practice one at most: check locally.

Flights

From Diyarbakır to İstanbul (1 or 2 daily via Ankara on *THY*; 3hr).

From Van to İstanbul (5 weekly via Ankara on *THY*; 3hr).

THE HISTORICAL FRAMEWORK

So many cultures and states have held sway on the Anatolian peninsula that a thorough unraveling of its past would demand scholars of comparative religion, linguistics, and archaeology as well as historians. The present-day Turkish Republic is but the core remnant of a vast, late-medieval empire which at one point extended from the Indian Ocean to the Atlantic—and all of these realms contributed personalities and events. What follows is only the barest outline of a complex subject.

THE EARLIEST CULTURES

Finds in the heart of modern Turkey—basically the region known historically as Anatolia or Asia Minor—suggest that there has been settled habitation since the eighth millennium BC, among the oldest on earth. The **earliest finds**, including cave deposits in the region of Antalya, and surface finds from the Ankara and Hatay regions, prove that Anatolia was inhabited in the Palaeolithic Age. More extensive discoveries from the **Neolithic** period include whole farming communities, of which the best known is **Çatal Höyük** near Konya (c.6500–5650 BC), demonstrating that early settlers lived in sizable villages consisting of networks of houses crammed one against the other and surrounded by defensive outer walls. Their tools were made from locally found obsidian and flint, and their pottery was beautifully burnished, and included stylized figures representing the mother goddess.

Oriental influence brought southeast Anatolia into the **Chalcolithic Age**. The interaction of cultures, which was probably of a commercial and technical nature, is particularly noticeable in pottery types and the use of metal tools; shared features are found through Upper Mesopotamia, northern Syria and into eastern Anatolia (especially the Lake Van region and Cilicia). Sites of this period were more like fortified towns, and frequent evidence of violent destruction suggests that they existed in a hostile environment, regularly at war with each other or with new arrivals. In central Anatolia and the Anatolian Lakeland there was less influence from the east; cultures that developed here are characterized by bright, burnished pottery and idols of local deities.

The third-millennium **Bronze Age** witnessed the rise of local dynasties, and the organization of land resources by communities inhabiting fortified settlements. The sophisticated metal equipment found in the royal cemetery of **Alaca Hüyük** suggests metallurgy was one of the principal reasons for the economic rise of the early Anatolian kings. Religious art included standards crowned with highly stylized deer and bulls; and hordes of gold jewelry as well as musical instruments were prominent among the finds in the tombs. It is thought that the Alaca dynasty originated in northeast Anatolia, since their culture shows similarities to those in the Caucasian and Pontic border zones.

Meanwhile, on the south and west **coasts**, trade was becoming increasingly important, as were the piratic activities of local rulers, whose bases appear from their architecture to have had affinities with later Indo-European cultures. On the Aegean, **Troy** was in trading contact with the Aegean islands and mainland Greece, and with other Anatolian rulers in the southeast around present-day Tarsus and Mersin. Anatolian metals, jewelry, weapons, and tableware were exported in exchange for exotic minerals such as lapis lazuli, rock crystal, and ivory. The material advantages of a coastal situation, which provided naval contacts with the Aegean and the Orient (particularly Syrian trading ports), are obvious from the comparative wealth amassed by the rulers of cities like Troy, evidenced in finds such as the so-called treasure of Priam, a third-millennium horde of jewelry and tableware discovered in the late nineteenth century.

The **Middle and Late Bronze Ages**, in the second millennium BC, began with a period of violent destruction and turbulence, out of which a race of people known as the **Hatti** emerged in central Anatolia. Their traditions and culture were later to be assimilated by the Hittites. This was an age of highly organized and regular commerce along fixed trading routes, and many Anatolian cities were annexed by colonies of Assyrian business agents. Their meticulous records have been discovered in many places, including the most famous of all these trade centers, Karum near Kaneş (modern Kültepe) in south-central Anatolia. Textiles and tin were the main imports, and the principal export was copper. The city itself was a fortified citadel with a number of large buildings surrounding open courtyards. Pottery was ornamental and showed a high degree of skill in its craftsmanship.

THE HITTITES

Perhaps the first really major civilization to emerge in Anatolia was the **Hittite** one. The Hittites seem to have first appeared moving into Hatti territory around 2000 BC, but their so-called "Old Kingdom" is believed to have been founded by King Labarnaş around 1700–1600 BC. The capital at Hattuşaş was created by his son and successor, Hattuşiliş I, remaining a power to be reckoned with (outlying territories in northern Syria and Babylonia were conquered and lost) until 1200 BC.

Hattuşaş was a huge city for its time, surrounded by a six-kilometer-long fortified wall. The kings resided in a fortified citadel located on a rock overlooking a gorge to the north of the city; within were domestic quarters, administrative buildings, storage units, and archives. The Hittites developed their artistic style from traditions of their Anatolian predecessors, and unlike their Syrian neighbors were never overwhelmed by Mesopotamian and Egyptian art. The principal examples are enormous rock-cut reliefs, including warrior gods and stylized sphinxes, adapted from the Egyptian tradition to Hittite stylistic principles.

At **Yazılıkaya**, a temple site not far from the capital, processions of gods and goddesses—one of whom is shown embracing a Hittite king, in an obvious expression of supposed kinship—are carved on the walls of an open chamber. While the warlike, imperialist nature of the Hittite rulers left an enduring impression on a previously nonaggressive Anatolia, the Hittites are also known for the humanity of their constitution and religion, and for a highly developed sense of ethics. Diplomacy was preferred to warfare, and often cemented by royal marriages. A queen ruled as an equal with her husband, and prisoners of war were not horribly tortured as they were elsewhere in the Middle East. Libraries, archives, and bureaucracy all had their place in Hittite society, and rulers were not despotic but subject to the constitution like their subjects. The Old Kingdom dynasty lasted several generations before being riven, apparently by succession struggles: after a confused interlude, the state was re-established as the Hittite Empire by Tudhaliyas II in about 1430 BC. By this time a rival power had arisen in Upper Mesopotamia. The Mitanni, ruled by an Indo-European dynasty, were basically east Anatolian Hurrians. They exerted an important cultural influence on the Hittite Empire before being defeated in battle by the Hittite ruler Suppiluliuma (1385–1345 BC).

Under Muwatallis the Hittites confirmed their military strength at the Battle of Kadesh (1290 BC), where they defeated the Egyptians under Rameses II. After the battle friendship between the two dynasties was cemented by the division of Syria and by the marriage of Rameses II to a daughter of another Hittite ruler, Hattuşiliş III, in 1250 BC. The real threat to both, however, lay with the arrival of the "**Sea Peoples**," early Greek Iron-Age merchants, which was to have widespread repercussions and eventually destroy the old order completely.

The land-bound Hittite Empire was surrounded by **smaller states**. The southern and western coasts were inhabited by tribes of Indo-European stock, with their own kings, languages, and feuds, and a major interest in maritime trade. In the southeast

Mediterranean, the land originally known as Cilicia was taken from the Hittites by Hurrians, and referred to as Kizzuwadna. They remained closely related to the Hittites, however, with regular intermarriage between the respective ruling families.

On the west coast, a greater degree of independence on the part of local dynasties meant that their activities were not well documented in Hittite records, but excavations at the site of Troy show that simultaneous with the apogee of Hittite power, Troy was being rebuilt by a new dynasty, and great supplies were amassed inside the large citadel. The second-millennium BC Trojans were serious rivals to the Greeks in the Aegean, and Troy was ultimately sacked by the Greeks around 1200 BC in the **Trojan War**, at just about the same time as the Hittite Empire finally collapsed.

THE POST-HITTITE ERA

The same factors can ultimately account for the demise of both civilizations: **migrations**, invasions, and sudden increased pressures from all sides. New tribes of Indo-European origin poured into Anatolia from east and west. The Hittite capital and other centers of Hittite rule were attacked and burnt as Anatolia entered a long cultural Dark Age.

Small city-states were founded in the southeast by the surviving Hittites and their Anatolian allies, and these **neo-Hittite** centers, for instance at Malatya, Sakça Gözü, and Karatepe, managed to salvage something of the old culture from the destruction of the empire. Cities were better fortified, with inner and outer defensive walls, but the traditional lions that stood guard at their gates were crudely carved in comparison with those which had performed the same task in the Old Hittite cities. The neo-Hittite culture was important as a bridge between the Bronze and Iron Ages, rescuing Hittite traditions and at the same time creating lively trading centers for the first Greek **Iron Age** merchants. Thus early Greek art was confronted by Hittite reliefs and statuary, and knowledge of oriental mythology and religion was also transmitted to Greece via the neo-Hittites. The neo-Hittite city-states were finally conquered and destroyed by the Greek Arameans and the Assyrians in the eighth century BC.

To the east, in the region that was later to be known as Armenia, the kingdom of **Urartu** was founded by a people thought to be descendants of the native Anatolian Hurrian race. Their cities, including the capital at Tushpa near Lake Van, were well engineered, with walled citadels and elaborate tunnel systems for escape or survival under attack. The Urartians extended their power into central Anatolia and northern Syria before they were curbed, in the second half of the eighth century BC, by the Assyrians. The Urartians specialized in metalwork, and their bronzeware was traded as far away as Greece.

To the west, a new tribe of immigrants who attained some prominence in the eighth century BC, especially under their most famous king Midas, were the **Phrygians**. Their origins are unknown, but the historical connection between Greeks and Phrygians can perhaps be ascribed to a blood relationship between them. Their capital was at Gordion, on a strategic east–west trading route, and on the river Sangarios. **King Midas**, according to Greek tradition, had a Greek wife and dedicated a throne at the sanctuary of Delphi. His kingdom reached its height during his rule, around 725 BC, but when Cimmerian horsemen came to loot and burn Gordion, he is said to have committed suicide in despair, and the Phrygian kingdom came to an abrupt end. The tumulus ascribed to king Midas bears witness to his power: nearly fifty meters high, it contained a profuse collection of artifacts, including textiles and richly carved furniture from as far away as Urartu.

The southwest coast was inhabited during the Iron Age by the **Lycians**, probably the survivors of a nation of sailors and pirates referred to as the "Lukku" in Bronze Age records. Their language and culture had a local pedigree, suggesting that they were descendants of the native Anatolian Luvians, and their architecture, timber forms copied in stone, was strikingly unique. Greek influence on the Lycians is attested to in the Bronze Age by the legend of Bellerophon and the Chimaera, and in the sixth century BC Lycia became gradually imbued by Greek influence.

The country of the **Lydians** was an inland district of western Anatolia, its capital at Sardis in the Hermus Valley. The Lydians survived the Bronze Age with a language and origin of Anatolian derivation, emerging from the turmoil of the eighth century BC to dominate western Anatolia, including areas that had previously been Phrygian. Lydian ivories, textiles, perfumes, and jewelry were exported to Greece and the east, and their refined and elegant art forms influenced those of Greek Ionia and even Persia. Their power lasted until the **Persian** conquest of Asia Minor in the sixth and fifth centuries BC ended the last vestiges of indigenous Anatolian self-rule.

ROME

Anatolia remained in Persian hands until the invasion of **Alexander the Great** in 334 BC. Under Alexander's successors, Asia Minor broke down into a number of smaller states, principally **Pergamum**, **Bithynia**, **Pontus**, and **Armenia**. Roman armies, however, were gradually spreading their influence over the territory, and by the end of the first century AD only Armenia remained unconquered as a buffer between the Roman and Persian empires.

For the next several hundred years, Anatolia ostensibly remained part of the **Roman Empire**, beset though it was by internal chaos and external attacks from all directions. In 284 AD the emperor **Diocletian** attempted a solution to both problems by dividing the empire into two administrative units, each ruled by an emperor (or *Augustus*) acting in concert with a designated successor (or *Caesar*), together comprising the so-called tetrarchy. Early in the fourth century, however, this system collapsed into civil war. The victor, **Constantine**, moved the headquarters of the eastern portion from Salonika to the minor but strategically located ancient Greek town of **Byzantium**, on the western shores of the Bosphorus straits linking the Black Sea and the Sea of Marmara. This new capital—"New Rome"—was enlarged and consciously rebuilt in imitation of the "old" Rome, and was soon renamed **Constantinople** in the emperor's honor. Not much later Constantine announced his espousal of Christianity, which by the end of the century became the state religion of an empire that had long persecuted Christians.

The unity of the empire, too unwieldy to be governed from a single center, did not survive long beyond the forceful rule of Constantine. **Theodosius the Great**, during whose 379–395 reign paganism was officially proscribed, was the last sovereign of a united empire, which upon his death was formally **divided** into two realms: the western one Latin-speaking and Rome-based, the eastern part Greek-speaking and focused on Constantinople.

THE BYZANTINE EMPIRE

The western provinces had always been financially dependent on the east, and ineffective rule in the west meant that it could not easily survive the loss of this revenue—or the invasions of "barbarian" tribes from the north. The wealthier, more densely populated **Byzantine Empire**—as the east came to be known—had abler rulers and, after a brief period of overextension, more defensible frontiers. But internal **religious disputes** would contribute heavily to weakening the empire. Rule from Constantinople was resented in the southern and eastern border provinces of Egypt, Palestine, Syria, and Armenia, not only because the indigenous cultures were so different from Classical Greece and Rome, but also because the churches in these areas embraced the **Monophysitic doctrine**, which maintained that Christ had a single divine nature. Until the thirteenth century clerics in the capital would persecute the "heretics" on the periphery, at the same time resenting claims to papal supremacy in Rome and quarrelling over points of belief with the west. All this would ultimately culminate in the separation of the eastern **Orthodox** and western **Roman Catholic** churches in 1054.

Byzantium's response to the collapse of the west, brought on by the "barbarian" raids of the fifth and sixth centuries, was vehement and expansionist—or more accurately, nostalgic. The energetic emperor **Justinian** (527–565) and his empress Theodora attempted to recapture the glory and territory of ancient Rome in a series of military campaigns throughout the Mediterranean basin. The imperial generals Narses and Belisarius reabsorbed Italy, North Africa and southern Spain into the empire, though the Byzantines were unable to stem the flow of Slavs into the Balkans, and were forced to adopt an uneasy truce with the Persian Empire after a long and inconclusive war.

After the quelling of the **Nika revolt** in 532, when Theodora saved her husband from deposition by the Hippodrome factions, Justinian was also able to carry out an ambitious

domestic agenda. He inaugurated a widespread program of construction and public works, particularly in Constantinople, which resulted in such masterpieces as the church of **Aya Sofya** (Haghia Sophia) in the capital and San Vitale in Ravenna. Justinian's streamlining and codification of the huge and often contradictory body of old Roman **law** was perhaps his most enduring achievement: the new code became the basis of the medieval legal systems of France, Germany, and Italy. In his attempts to mediate between the Monophysites of the east and the papacy, however, the emperor was less successful—the extent of the "heresy" can be judged by the fact that Theodora herself is said to have been sympathetic to the Monophysites.

Justinian's reign marked the definitive emergence of a strictly Byzantine, as opposed to Roman, identity, with institutions that were to sustain the empire for the balance of its life. Having widened its boundaries to their maximum extent and established the theocratic nature of Byzantium, he can be reckoned one of the greatest of Byzantine emperors. In the long run, though, many of his achievements proved ephemeral, and so exhausted the empire's resources that it had difficulty withstanding subsequent outside attacks.

LATER BYZANTIUM . . . AND DECLINE

In the two centuries following Justinian's death the character of the empire changed radically. All of his peripheral conquests were lost: the western realms to the Lombards and Goths, the southeastern provinces in the seventh century to the Persians and Arab raiders. By 711, the Byzantine Empire consisted only of the Balkan coasts, parts of Italy, and **Anatolia**, which would henceforth be the most important part of the empire. Equally significant, the empire had acquired a strongly Greek character, both linguistically and philosophically, and Latin influence faded as relations with Rome worsened, particularly during the reign of Irene, whom the pope refused to recognize as empress.

It was only from 867 onward that the empire regained any of its old resilience. The so-called **Macedonian** dynasty, founded by **Basil I**, a former stable boy who rendered Justinian's law code into Greek, reversed Byzantium's

fortunes. Under **Basil II** (976–1025), nicknamed "Bulgar-Slayer" for his ruthless campaigns against the Slavs, the empire again swelled its frontiers well into present-day eastern Turkey and up the Balkan peninsula, while Constantinople itself enjoyed unparalleled prosperity at the crossroads of the new Eurasian trade routes. Literature and the arts flourished, and missionaries converted many Balkan Slavs to the Orthodox church.

After the reign of the second Basil, however, the empire began its **final decline**, slow but relentless over the course of four centuries. Although by the early eleventh century the empire seemed consolidated into a stable state taking in most of the Balkans, the Aegean islands, and Anatolia, the potential for both internal and external disruption was great. For the first six decades of the new millennium, Anatolia was in a state of virtual **civil war**, with the clique of civilian bureaucrats in Constantinople pitted against the caste of landed generals out in the countryside. Each promoted their own candidates for the throne, resulting in a succession of nonentities as emperors, amenable to manipulation by either faction and utterly unequal to the external threats the empire would soon face. Simultaneously the Orthodox patriarchate renewed its vendetta against the Monophysitic churches, whose members were concentrated in the critical eastern borderlands. The warlords reduced the free peasantry to serfdom, eliminating the main source of revenue and military recruitment; the bureaucrats, usually in control at Constantinople, matched their own extravagance with stinginess toward the army—which increasingly came to be staffed by unreliable mercenaries.

The first major threats came from the west. The **Normans**, their greed excited by the reputation of Byzantine craftsmanship and splendor, invaded the Balkans late in the eleventh century and were only repulsed with help from the **Venetians**, who in return demanded extensive trading concessions within the empire—as did the **Genoese**. Government tolls and taxes plummeted as imperial monopolies were broken by the new Latin maritime powers, and western covetousness—which would culminate in the sacking of Constantinople by the Fourth Crusade in 1204—knew no bounds. Though able emperors did emerge from the twelfth-century

Comnenus dynasty and the later **Paleologus** line, without consistent western aid the Byzantines were doomed to fight a long, rearguard action against enemies from the east and north. The imperial twilight was distinguished by a final flourishing of sacred art and architecture, as Anatolia and the Balkans—as if in defiance of the political facts—were adorned with numerous beautiful **churches** that were this period's main contribution to posterity.

THE ARRIVAL OF THE TURKS

Early in the eleventh century a new people had begun raiding Byzantine territory from the east. They had originally emerged in Mongolia during the seventh or eighth century, a shamanistic, nomadic bunch whom the Chinese called *Tu-kueh* or *Dürkö*—**Turks** to the West. Driven by drought and population pressure to seek new pastures, the Turkish tribes began migrating westward, encountering the Arabs by the ninth century. The latter, recognizing their martial virtues, recruited them as auxiliaries and began converting them to Islam, a process mostly completed by the tenth century.

One branch of the Turkish tribes, followers of the chieftain **Selçuk**, adopted a settled life and **Sunni** Islam, setting down roots in Baghdad. The majority, however, referred to by the convenient catchall of "Turcoman," remained nomadic and heterodox in belief, drawing on the **Shi'ite and pagan** heritage, and rarely amenable to control by any state. The Selçuk rulers took advantage of their warrior zeal by diverting them from their own realms into those of the Byzantines.

The raiders penetrated as an advance guard deep into Byzantine Armenia, and it was as much to restrain them as to confront the Byzantines that the Selçuk ruler Alparslan marched north from Baghdad in **1071**. Meeting, almost accidentally, the motley, demoralized armies of Byzantine emperor Romanus IV Diogenes, he defeated them easily at **Manzikert** (Malazgirt). The Selçuks didn't follow up this victory, but it did leave the way open to redoubled rampages by the Turcomans across all of Anatolia. The Byzantines, alternately menaced and assisted by Latin Crusaders, managed to reoccupy the western third of Anatolia, plus the Black Sea and Mediterranean coasts, by the mid-twelfth century, by which time the Selçuks had

established a state in the area devastated by the unruly Turcomans. This was the **Sultanate of Rum**, with its capital at Konya (Iconium). After the **Battle of Myriokephalo**, nearby, in 1176, the new state came to terms with the Byzantines.

After the occupation of Constantinople by the **Fourth Crusade** in 1204, the Selçuks continued to maintain good relations with the provisional Byzantine Empire based at Nicaea; with peace assured, the Sultanate of Rum evolved into a highly cultured mini-empire in the heart of Anatolia, reaching its zenith in the first half of the thirteenth century. Their territories were endowed with a system of imposing *kervansarays*, *medreses*, bridges, and other public monuments, with the encouragement of trade being paramount. On a smaller scale, the Selçuks excelled in tile and relief work, and in the spiritual field the sultanate, despite its Sunni orientation, provided a refuge for many heterodox religous figures, including Celâleddin Rumi, founder of the Mevlevi dervish order.

Before long, however, a new scourge appeared in the form of the **Mongols**; they crushed the Selçuk armies at the battle of **Köse Dağ** in 1243, and although the sultanate lingered on until the turn of the century, the Turcoman tribes, never fully pacified, took the opportunity to swarm over the lands of both the Selçuks and the Byzantines, who had virtually abandoned Asia Minor after returning to Constantinople in 1261. There was to be a two-century gap in which there was no single political authority on the Anatolian peninsula, but during which time the process of Turkification and Islamization, begun in 1071, continued gradually nonetheless.

THE RISE OF THE OTTOMANS

In the turmoil following the collapse of the Selçuk state, Anatolia fragmented into numerous petty, mostly Turcoman **emirates**: the Saltuks and Mongol İlhanids in the northeast, the Mengüçeh near Erzincan, the Aydınoğlu clan in the central Aegean, the Menteşe in the southwest Aegean, the Karamanids in the Taurus Mountains, the Artukids in the Euphrates Basin, the Danişmendid occupying a huge swath from Malatya to Amasya, and the Hamidoğlu around the Pisidian lakes are just a few of the short-lived principalities that left monuments scattered across modern Turkey.

The emirate based around Söğüt, near Eskişehir, settled on lands granted the chieftain Ertoğrul by the Selçuk ruler Alâeddin, was not initially an important one. Ertoğrul was a typical *gazi*, a recent convert to Islam patrolling the frontier marches between Selçuk and Byzantine territory, carrying the faith ever westward in the face of infidel opposition. His son Osman, however, head of the clan from the 1290s onwards, was to give his name to a dynasty: *Osmanlı* in Turkish, **"Ottoman"** to the West. Spurred by proximity to Constantinople, the emirate began to expand under Osman's son **Orhan**, who took the important Byzantine centers of Bursa and İznik by the 1330s, and married into the Byzantine nobility, the first of several Ottoman princes who would have Greek Orthodox in-laws.

Anatolian culture had for some time been a hybrid one, with frequent intermarriage between Muslims and Christians, many descendants or converts bilingual in Greek and Turkish, and certain dervish orders— particularly the Bektaşi—effecting a synthesis between Islam and numerically declining Christianity. As Byzantine authority in a given area diminished, the assets and facilities of Christian monasteries were often appropriated by the **vakıfs** or Islamic pious foundations, which sponsored various public welfare projects; the demoralized Christian priesthood and population often converted to Islam simultaneously, though this was by no means mandatory or encouraged since it reduced tax revenue.

Complementing these processes was the **devşirme**, a custom that arose in the fourteenth century whereby a certain percentage of boys from conquered Christian districts were levied by the Ottomans to serve as an elite force, the **janissaries**. They became slaves of the sultan, were admitted to the more eclectic Bektaşi branch of Islam, and were given the best training available with an eye to their becoming not only warriors but Ottoman administrators. Free-born Muslims were expressly ineligible for elevation to the corps, and promotion was strictly on grounds of ability, so that (until abuses crept in) the Ottoman state, up to and including the office of grand vizier, was run by converts from Christianity. The only chance for advancement for those born Muslim was within the **ulema**, the body of Koranic sages

who decreed on religious matters, or as a member of the **defterdar** or "accountant" class—a huge bureaucracy overseeing the empire's various sources of revenue.

Though the janissaries formed a powerful praetorian guard, they were supplemented by a standing army, whose members were paid indirectly by assignment of a **timar**, or land-grant. All conquered territory remained the property of the sultan, who dispensed such grants with the understanding that the man's "salary" was the proceeds of the estate—and that he remained liable for armed service whenever his ruler summoned him. Initially *timars* reverted to the crown upon the holder's death, with his sons having to re-earn their portion by service. This system, based heavily on Byzantine practice, was not truly feudal, and resulted in a stability of rule that often prompted the immigration of Christian peasantry from misadministered neighboring territory. Despite religious tolerance shown to Christians of whatever rank, however, Ottoman society was **hierarchical**, with distinctions between Muslim and infidels—known as *raya*, or "cattle"—preserved in every particular from dress code to unequal status before the law. Christians were not conscripted for campaigns, and hence could not qualify for land grants; instead they paid a tax in lieu of military service, and tended to congregate in towns and cities as tradesmen.

To continue the system of *timars*, more land had to be made available for awards, and the *gazi* mentality continued. By the mid-fourteenth century the Ottomans had crossed the Sea of Marmara to Thrace, and in 1362 **Sultan Murat I** took Edirne. Constantinople was virtually surrounded by Turkish territory, and indeed the almost-vanished Byzantine Empire existed on Ottoman sufferance, reduced to vassaldom and the necessity of calling on Turkish aid to fend off challenges from Catalans, Slavs, and Hungarians. With the Latin and Orthodox Christians at each other's throats, Ottoman ascendancy was virtually assured, and Murat further isolated Constantinople with new acquistions in the lower Balkans, routing a Serbian coalition at **Kosovo** in 1389. Murdered on the battlefield by a Serbian infiltrator, he was succeeded by his elder son Beyazit I, who established an unfortunate precedent by promptly strangling his brother Yakub to assure his succession. Beyazit, nicknamed **Yıldırım** or "Lightning" for his swift deployments in battle, bested a huge Hungarian/Crusader army at Bulgarian Nicopolis in 1396, and the fall of Constantinople seemed imminent.

However, in expanding eastward into Anatolia, Beyazit—more impulsive and less methodical than his father—had both overextended himself and antagonized the great Mongol warrior **Tamerlane**. Tamerlane routed Beyazit's armies at the **Battle of Ankara** in 1402, trundling the captive sultan around in a cage for a year before his demise, and proceeded to lay waste to much of Anatolia. Even though the Mongols soon vanished, the remnant of the Byzantine Empire was granted a fifty-year reprieve, and for a decade the fate of the Ottoman line hung in the balance as Beyazit's four sons fought a civil war. The victor, Mehmet I, and his successor the mystically inclined Murat II, restored Ottoman fortunes, the latter deflecting one last halfhearted Latin Crusade in 1444.

But the greatest prize—**Constantinople**—still eluded the Ottomans. Both symbolically, as the seat of two prior empires, and practically—as a naval base controlling passage between the Black Sea and the Mediterranean—its capture was imperative. **Mehmet II**, who ascended to the throne in 1451, immediately began preparations for the deed, ringing the now half-depopulated capital with fortresses, engaging ballistics and artillery experts from Europe with an eye to breaching the city walls, and for the first time outfitting a substantial Ottoman fleet. His Byzantine adversaries hastily concluded a union with the Catholic Church, expecting Latin aid to materialize forthwith, but only a trickle of Genoese and Venetian ships and men arrived. The final siege of Constantinople, in the spring of 1453, lasted seven weeks, ending on **May 29** when the sultan's armies finally succeeded in entering the city while the last Byzantine emperor died unnoticed in the melee.

Mehmet's epithet was henceforth *Fatih*, **"the Conqueror"**; there was no longer any room for doubt that the Ottoman Empire was the legitimate successor of the Roman and Byzantine ones. The imitation of Roman and Byzantine models in Ottoman imperial practice, begun in the preceeding century and a half, increased.

MEHMET THE CONQUEROR TO SÜLEYMAN THE MAGNIFICENT

Mehmet immediately went about refurbishing the city, now renamed İstanbul, as a worthy capital of the empire, repopulating it with both Muslims and Christians from rural areas, establishing markets and public-welfare institutions, and constructing a grand palace at Topkapı. The non-Muslim communities were organized into *millets*, or "nations," headed by a patriarch or rabbi, answerable for his flock's good behavior and under whom Orthodox, Armenian, and Jew were governed by their own communal laws; this system, which tended to minimize sectarian disorder and guaranteed more freedom of worship than prevalent in contemporary Europe, persisted until 1926.

Overseas, Mehmet's mixed military record demonstrated that such a feat as the capture of Constantinople was not easily duplicated. Defeats along the Danube were followed by easier mop-up campaigns during 1458–60 in the Peloponnese and along the Black Sea, eliminating satellite Byzantine states and their Genoese cohorts. Persisting in the preconquest pattern of alternating European and Asian campaigns, Mehmet returned to the Balkans, adding Wallachia, most of present-day Greece, Bosnia/Herzegovina, and part of Albania to his domains, while simultaneously building up his navy to better counter his main rivals, the Venetians. Back in Anatolia, the Conqueror annexed the Karamanid emirate and neutralized the forces of the Akkoyun Turcomans.

Mehmet was succeeded in 1481 by his son **Beyazit II**, "the Pious," who despite a retiring disposition presided over the final relegation of Venice to secondary-power status—often by the enlistment of pirates into the Ottoman navy—and realized his father's ambition of revitalizing the core territory of the Byzantine Empire. The skills of Greek renegade statesmen and Italian mercenaries were supplemented in 1493 by the scientific knowledge of **Iberian Jews**, the ancestors of today's İstanbul Jewry, fetched by "mercy ships" sent by the sultan upon their expulsion from Spain and Portugal.

In 1512 Beyazit was forced to abdicate by his son **Selim I**, a vigorous personality in the mold of his grandfather, but with an added streak of wanton cruelty and bigotry, hence his epithet *Yavuz* (the "Fierce"—the "Grim" to the West). Both of Selim's predecessors had privately toyed with Sufic and heterodox Persian doctrines, but now religious orthodoxy was seen as vital within the Ottoman realm, since neighbor and rival Shah Ismail of Persia was starting to promote **Shi'ism** both within and without his borders. In an echo of the Catholic-Protestant bloodletting in Europe, Selim massacred 40,000 Shi'ites in Anatolia, and went on to defeat the shah at east Anatolian **Çaldıran** in 1514. Rather than press on into Persia, however, Selim turned his armies south against the Mamluks, overrunning Mesopotamia, Syria, and Egypt by 1516 and occupying most of the **holy cities** of Islam in one fell swoop. By capturing the caliph resident in Cairo and transporting him back to İstanbul, Selim essentially proved his claim to be the Defender of the (Sunni) Faith—and the **caliphate** effectively became identical with the Ottoman sultanate.

Although the empire would reach its greatest physical extent after his death, it was **Süleyman the Magnificent** who laid the foundations of this expansion during a 46-year reign that began in 1520. In his first few years on the throne, the strongholds of the Knights of St John at Rhodes and Bodrum—from which they controlled the sea lanes to Egypt—were taken, as was Belgrade, leaving the way up the Danube Valley unguarded. By 1526 Budapest, and most of Hungary, was in Ottoman hands, with the Habsburgs compelled to pay tribute for retaining a small fraction. Campaigns in Persia and the Arabian Peninsula were successful, but the first siege of Vienna in 1529 was not—nor was an attempt to drive the Portuguese out of the Indian Ocean. The Ottomans were better able to control the Mediterranean, with such admirals as Greek-born Barbaros Hayrettin (**Barbarossa**) and his protege Turgut Reis to best Venetian-Habsburg fleets. But in 1565 the siege of Malta, where the Knights of St John had retreated, failed, marking the end of the Mediterranean as an Ottoman lake. Nonetheless the Ottoman Empire, unwieldy, heterogenous, and difficult to defend, was arguably the leading power of the sixteenth century.

It was not surprisingly regarded with a mixture of terror and fascination by the states of Europe; only the **French**, under Francis I,

saw the possibility of alliance and manipulation, concluding a treaty with the Ottomans in **1536**. In addition to granting France trading advantages in the empire, the treaty's commercial clauses set forth various privileges for French nationals which came to be known as the **Capitulations**: exemption from most Ottoman taxes, and the right to be judged by their own consuls under foreign law. What began as an inducement to increased trade offered from a position of strength became, as time passed, a pernicious erosion of Turkish sovereignty, as many European nations and overseas companies secured such Capitulations for themselves, extending rights of immunity to local employees (usually Christian) provided with appropriate passports.

Domestically Süleyman distinguished himself as an administrator, legislator, builder, and patron of the arts, and indeed in Turkey he is known as *Kanuni*, "the Lawgiver". In his personal life, however, his judgment was to have enduringly harmful consequences for the Ottoman state. He became so enamored of his favorite concubine **Roxelana** that he broke with Ottoman precedent and actually married her. Scheming and ambitious, she used her influence over the sultan to turn him against his capable son and heir (by a previous liaison), **Mustafa**, inciting Süleyman to murder him and later her own son Beyazit—as well as his first grand vizier, İbrahim. Perhaps a bad conscience over these deeds heightened Süleyman's basic moroseness and introversion, and he died a lonely man on his last campaign on the Danube in 1566. With his two ablest sons gone, there were no obstacles to the succession of Roxelana's oldest son, the useless Selim.

THE CENTURIES OF DECLINE

While it's impossible to assign an exact date to the beginning of the Ottoman Empire's **decline**, the reign of the ineffectual Selim II (Selim the Sot to the West) is as good a start as any. He was followed by sixteen more, generally mediocre sultans, of whom only the bloodthirsty but resolute **Murat IV**, and the peace-loving aesthete **Ahmet II**, who instituted the cult of the tulip, did much to prevent the gradual deterioration. The decay of the empire was nonetheless almost imperceptibly gradual over a period of nearly three centuries, with spells of retrenchment and even territorial expansion.

It is far easier to catalog the **causes** of the decline. From Roxelana's time onwards the **harem** was moved onto the grounds of the Topkapı palace itself, so that the intrigues of its tenants bore directly on day-to-day government. At the start of the seventeenth century the previous, grisly custom of fratricide upon the enthronement of a new sultan was abandoned in favor of the confinement of the other heirs apparent; sequestered in the so-called **Kafes**, or **Cage**, for years (previously, heirs would serve an "apprenticeship" as a provincial governor), the next-in-line was not just inexperienced, but frequently emerged from captivity mentally and physically deranged. Few sultans campaigned overseas any longer, or presided personally over the *divan* (council of state), instead delegating most authority to their **grand viziers**.

When these viziers were able and honest, like the Albanian Köprülü clan of the seventeenth century, the downward slide of the empire was halted or reversed, but on the whole nepotism and **corruption** flourished in the decadent palace atmosphere. The early Ottoman principle of meritocracy was replaced by a **hereditary aristocracy**; the *devşirme* or levy of Christian boys was abandoned by the end of the seventeenth century, and the janissary corps was no longer celibate or religiously exclusive—sinecure passed from father to son, and the corps (with its payroll) expanded further as free Muslims rushed to enroll. Many—in direct contradiction to the institution's purpose—were artisans whose only martial act was to show up to collect pay, and demands for raises often prompted the inefficient, swollen corps to rebel, extorting money from hapless villagers and sultans alike, and on several occasions to depose and murder the latter. Similarly, land-grants to the *sipahı*, or cavalry, tended to become hereditary, and the holders evolved into a class of local warlord (the *derebeys* or "lords of the valley"). Both janissary and *sipahı* proved increasingly reluctant to fight the long wars now common, and/or when booty or pay was not forthcoming. Revolts of these and other idle, underpaid troops devastated Anatolia, which was already wracked by population pressure and land shortage; thus began a steady rural depopulation that continues today.

Much of the impetus for decline came, however, from **outside** the empire. The influx into the Mediterranean of gold and silver from the Spanish conquests in the New World set off a spiral of inflation and debased coinage. The Age of Exploration saw new sea routes forged around Africa to the East Indies, reducing the importance of overland caravan routes through Ottoman realms. Most importantly, Europe underwent the **Renaissance** and **industrialization**, while the Ottomans remained stagnant under the influence of the conservative *ulema*. The Turks had become used to easily despatching the ragtag armies of assorted principalities during the fifteenth and sixteenth centuries, and failed to grasp the reasons for their frequent defeats thereafter. New, highly centralized nation-states in the West had established rigorously trained standing armies and navies, availing themselves of the benefits of new armaments, sail-power and navigation, direct outgrowths of the Renaissance's spur to scientific inquiry. To these manifestations of European superiority the Ottomans generally reacted disdainfully, seeing no reason to learn from the infidels given the perfection of Islam.

External **evidence** of the rot took nearly a century to show: although the defeat of an Ottoman fleet at **Lepanto** (today Greek Nafpaktos) in 1571, by a combined Venetian, Spanish, and papal armada, shattered the myth of Turkish invincibility, the victory was essentially neutralized by the capture of Cyprus from Venice the same year, and the reconquest of North Africa by 1578. The 1600s proceeded well, with the successful siege of Crete and seizure of parts of Poland, but already the Ottomans were compelled to draw up treaties with their adversaries as **equals**—a far cry from the days when victorious sultans condescended to suppliant Christian kings. Worse was to follow during the second half of the seventeenth century, when the most notorious of several defeats at the hands of the Austrians and their allies was the bungled **second siege of Vienna** in 1683, where an entire Turkish army was decimated. Most of Hungary and other eastern European territory was lost as well before the **treaties of Carlowitz** (1699) and **Passarowitz** (1718) stabilized the Balkan frontier for nearly two centuries. In lieu of a formal Ottoman foreign service, necessary diplomatic initiatives were handled by the **Dragoman**, always a Christian with a knowledge of the foreign languages that Muslim Ottomans lacked.

During the eighteenth century most of the territorial attrition at the Turks' expense was to be courtesy of the **Russian Empire**, newly consolidated under Peter the Great. Russo-Turkish enmity was to be a constant in Turkish history thereafter. After a slow beginning, when French support had stiffened Ottoman resolve, Russia went on under Catherine the Great to thoroughly humiliate the Turks, presenting them with the **treaties of Küçük Kaynarca** (1774) and **Jassy** (1792), which ceded extensive territory to the tsarina, gave Russia long-coveted access to the Black Sea and the straits guarding İstanbul—and the right to interfere, anywhere in the Ottoman Empire, to protect the interests of Greek Orthodox subjects.

THE BEGINNING OF THE REFORM ERA

Selim III's accession to the throne in 1789 coincided with the advent of revolutionary regimes in France and the USA; thus the name of his proposed reforms, the **Nizam-ı-Cedid** or "New Order," was a deliberate tip of the hat to them. Though the proliferation of the *derebeys* and their defiance of central authority was the most pressing domestic problem, Selim addressed military reorganization first. With the Napoleonic wars as a background and warning, he enlisted foreign experts to set up an army trained, equipped, and attired along Western lines. This aroused the hostility of the janissary corps and their allies among the *ulema*, and Selim was deposed, then murdered, in 1808.

The new sultan, **Mahmut II**, was more tactful, moving gradually toward innovation. He managed to outlast both Russian and French designs on his realm only to be confronted by the major crisis of his reign: **full-scale rebellion in Greece**, which broke out in 1821. This proved impossible to crush, even after the Westernized army of **Mehmet Ali**, semi-autonomous ruler of Egypt, was dispatched to the scene. The destruction of an Ottoman fleet at Navarino by French, Russian, and English

ships in 1827, an overland attack by Russia on İstanbul in 1829, and a treaty in 1830 guaranteed the emergence of an **independent Greece**—the first substantial loss of Turkish territory in the southern Balkans. The French simultaneously invaded Algeria, and Mehmet Ali chose this moment for an attack on Anatolia, which went unchecked until the Russians, this time as allies of Mahmut, landed on the Bosphorus. In consideration for services rendered they extracted the **Treaty of Hunkâr İskelesi** from the sultanate, which in effect gave the tsar exclusive unimpeded access to the straits, reconfirmed the Russians' right to meddle in Ottoman internal affairs, and ensured that the British would try to act as a counter to all such intrigues.

Despite this disastrous record abroad, Mahmut II had notably more success **at home**. In 1826 the janissaries had mutinied once again, but the sultan, carefully baiting the trap, liquidated them with loyal forces—and a massive artillery bombardment—in what came to be known as the **"Auspicious Incident."** The Bektaşi sect, the "house religion" of the janissaries, was simultaneously suppressed, and a Western-style army created. During the 1830s Prussian and Austrian advisers came to train it, beginning a tradition of Teutonic involvement in Turkey's military that was to endure for nearly a century. A military academy and medical school were established, with French the language of instruction. A formal **foreign service** and a **civil service** were created, and the *ulema* was brought to heel by subordination to the secular bureaucracy. Western dress for all except clerics became mandatory—including the replacement of the turban by the more "progressive" **fez**. Along with a notably less successful attempt to introduce a uniform law code and squelch corruption, the entire program represented a quantum increase in **centralization**—and unintentionally a widening gap between the Ottoman masses and the new elite.

THE TANZİMAT AND THE YOUNG OTTOMANS

Mahmut's strenuous efforts bore more fruit posthumously when his son Sultan Abdülmecid and minister Mustafa Reşid proclaimed the **Tanzimat** or "Reorganization" in 1839, essentially an Ottoman Magna Carta which delegated some of the sultan's law-making authority to advisors, promised an end to taxation irregularities, and stipulated equal treatment of Muslim and non-Muslim before the law. Although the climate engendered by such noble sentiments permitted the founding of newspapers and private, secular schools in the ensuing decades, the proposal of infidel equality deeply offended most of the population, who were not prepared to contemplate—for example—the enlistment of Christians in the armed forces (they were in fact restricted to the navy until the twentieth century).

Foreign economic penetration of the Ottoman Empire increased suddenly, with growing commercial activity in all coastal cities; in the process the Greek, Armenian, and foreign-Christian merchant class of the ports benefited in a disproportionate manner. Simultaneously interior centers and traditional crafts went into precipitous decline, unable to compete with the results of the industrial revolution. Along with the establishment of banks and a currency reform came **loans** from overseas to the Ottoman government—the first in the 1850s, then eight more until bankruptcy ensued in the depression of 1875.

By mid-century the empire was thoroughly enmeshed in the **power struggles of Europe**—a far cry from the smug aloofness of 250 years before, and a consequence of the fact that England and France had determined that, for better or worse, the Ottomans must be propped up as a counter to Russian expansionism. Thus the empire found itself on the winning side of the 1853–56 **Crimean War**, which began as a dispute between Russia and France over the protection to be extended by each to respectively the Orthodox and Catholic church in Ottoman Palestine. The war ended with little significant territorial adjustment, but did bring a twenty-year interval of peace for the Ottomans.

Abdülmecid had been a well-meaning but weak and extravagant ruler, and was succeeded in 1861 by his brother **Abdülaziz**, who combined all of his predecessor's defects with a despotic manner. There sprung up in reaction, from the ranks of the first graduates of the empire's secular schools, the **Society of Young Ottomans**, which strove for the evolution of a constitutional monarchy along British lines. Its most enduring figure was the poet and essayist **Namik Kemal**, and it made extensive use of the newly admitted media of the press, drama, and literature to get its points across. Predictably the group aroused the ire of the sultan, who exiled the boldest; undeterred, the Young Ottomans overseas mounted a barrage of written material, much of it smuggled back into the empire to good effect.

Faced with Abdülaziz's flagrant financial irresponsibility in the years leading up to the crash of 1875, and his growing mental instability, together with new Russian mischief in İstanbul and brutally suppressed revolts in the Balkans, the Young Ottomans among the bureaucratic elite—particularly **Mithat Paşa**—deposed him on **May 30, 1876**. The crown was passed to his nephew Murat, but he shortly suffered a nervous breakdown (aggravated by the suicide of his uncle in captivity), was declared unfit to rule, and in turn placed in seclusion. The next heir apparent was his younger brother **Abdülhamid**, an unknown quantity, who was offered the throne on condition that he accept various Young Ottomans as advisers and rule under a constitution.

ABDÜLHAMİD—AND THE "YOUNG TURK" REVOLUTION

The new sultan did in fact promulgate the **constitution** drafted by the Young Ottomans, presided over the opening of the first Ottoman parliament, and retained—for a time—his hapless brother's advisers, including Mithat. But Abdülhamid soon moved to forestall a government-by-ministers, exiling Mithat (and later having him murdered).

As so often happened in late Ottoman history, the implementation of liberal reforms was interpreted by the great powers as a sign of weakness. Accordingly Russia attacked on two fronts in **1877**, at the Caucasus and in the Balkans, with an explicitly pan-Slavic agenda. The war went badly for the Ottomans, with extensive territorial losses confirmed by the ruinous peace treaty of San Stefano (at the ceasefire line just a stone's throw from İstanbul), later modified, under British pressure, at the 1878 **Conference of Berlin**. The final settlement provided for the independence of Romania, Montenegro, and Serbia; an autonomous Bulgaria; the cession of Thessaly to Greece, and Kars and Ardahan districts to Russia; and the occupation of Bosnia and Herzegovina by Austria. **Nationalism** had been unleashed—and rewarded—in the Balkans, and would be a dominant theme for the next forty years, and indeed to this day. Britain, in compensation for fending off further Russian advances, was given the right to "administer"—and fortify—**Cyprus**.

Throughout all this the young **parliament** displayed altogether too much independence for the sultan's taste, criticizing war policy and summoning certain government ministers to answer for their conduct. In early 1878, between the San Stefano and Berlin negotiation sessions, Abdülhamid finally dropped all pretense of consultative government and dissolved the Chamber of Deputies; it was not to meet again for thirty years.

With any restraining influence safely out of the way, Abdülhamid chose to rule **despotically and directly**—for the balance of his reign ministers were ciphers who rarely stayed in office for even a year. Thanks both to the circumstances of his accession and his innate character, Abdülhamid developed a fear of sedition and conspiracy bordering on paranoia. A **police state** emerged, attended by huge numbers of spies and rigorous press censorship; the introduction of a **telegraph network** provided a tremendous boost to the surveillance system. The only clause of the constitution still honored was the repeatedly invoked one that entitled the sultan to exile troublemakers.

After the disastrous wars marking the start of his reign, Abdülhamid's **foreign policy** was xenophobic and Asian-orientated, espousing Islam as a unifying force and, for the first time in centuries, emphasizing the sultan's dual role of **caliph**. This ideology didn't, however, prevent the loss of Tunis and Egypt, and had as a corollary the steadily worsening treatment of the **Armenians** of eastern Anatolia, who began to show the same nationalist sentiments as the Christians of the Balkans. The abuses culminated in the organized pogroms of **1895–96**, in which nearly 150,000 Armenians died, provoking outrage (albeit short-lived) abroad. In 1897, war with Greece and a revolt in Crete coincided; even though the Prussian-trained army defeated the Greeks in the field, the Ottomans were forced to grant the island autonomy.

Despite his political obscurantism, Abdülhamid presided over widespread **technological Westernization**; carefully cultivated ties with Germany resulted in much-needed development projects—most famously the German-built **rail system** across Anatolia, aimed at (but never reaching) Baghdad. Important investment credits were also extended, and a **Public Debt Administration** was created, which gathered revenues of the various state monopolies to service the enormous debt run up earlier in the century. At the same time, secular schooling and technical training were encouraged, as long as they didn't directly challenge the sultan's rule; but the creation of an educated elite inevitably resulted in change.

In 1889 the Ottoman Society for Union and Progress, later the **Committee for Union and Progress** (CUP) arose, mainly among army medical staff but also drawing on the talents of the huge European exile community. Soon it took strongest root in **Macedonia**, the worst-administered and most polyglot of the Ottoman provinces, and completely infiltrated the officer ranks of the Third Army at Salonika (Thessaloniki), a city where the sultan's repression was less, and where Westernizing Jews and Masons were influential. Threats of further great-power intervention in Macedonia—where disorderly Greek, Bulgarian, and other nationalist guerrilla bands were rampant—coincided with failure to pay the army, providing the spark for the revolt of the **"Young Turks,"** as the CUP plotters were nicknamed. In July 1908, the Macedonian army units demanded by telegraph that Abdülhamid restore the 1876 constitution or face unpleasant consequences. Abdülhamid's spies had either been oblivious to the threat, or he had chosen not to believe them, and on **July 24**, the sultan assented. There was widespread rejoicing on the streets of the major imperial cities, as mullahs fraternized with bishops, and Bulgarians walked arm in arm with Greeks. With the despotism over, surely the millennium was imminent.

AFTER THE REVOLUTION – THE YEARS TO WORLD WAR I

The euphoria prompted by the re-enactment of the 1876 constitution soon subsided as the **revolutionary government** fumbled for a coherent program. The coup's immediate goals had been the curbing of Abdülhamid's powers and the physical preservation of the empire—but even these limited aims proved beyond the new government's grasp. By October 1908 Bulgaria had declared full independence, and Austria had formally annexed Bosnia and Herzegovina, occupied since 1878. **Elections** for the re-convened parliament were reasonably fair, and the Young Turks, their CUP newly organized as a political party, gained a majority. Opposition to the Westernizing represented by the CUP simmered, however, and in spring 1909 a joint **revolt** of low-ranking soldiers and religious elements ousted the new government and took control of İstanbul. Abdülhamid, over-estimating the rebels' strength, unwisely came out in their support. The CUP fought back from its base in Salonika, sending Third Army general Mahmut Şevket to crush the insurrection, and topped this off by **deposing the sultan**, banishing him to house arrest in Salonika. His younger brother ascended the throne as Mehmet V, promising to respect the "will of the nation."

The revolution had been saved, but there was still no agreement on a program. Three main ideas vied for consideration. **Ottomanism**, essentially a recycled version of the Tanzimat reforms of the mid-nineteenth century, asserted that a Eurasian empire, federal in stucture, in which all ethnic and religious minorities had equal rights—and who in turn were loyal to the central government—was both viable and desirable. The adherents of **pan-Islamism**, the pet creed of Abdülhamid, stressed the Islamic nature of the Ottoman Empire and the ties between Muslim Albanians, Kurds, Arabs, and Turks. **Pan-Turanism** was more blatantly racial, dwelling on the affinities between all Turkic peoples between Central Asia and the Balkans; as time went on it was modified to a more realistic **Turkism**, or the promotion of the interests of the Turkish-speaking Muslims of Anatolia, and it was in fact this notion that would eventually carry the day.

With the lifting of the Hamidian repression, discussion of these alternatives—and cultural life in general—flourished uninhibitedly for a while. Between 1908 and 1912 the CUP, beset by internal disputes, was by no means monolithic, and parliamentary opposition was not completely quelled until 1912.

The growing **authoritarianism** of CUP rule coincided with renewed **external threats** to the empire. Italy invaded Tripolitania (today's Libya) in 1911, and the next year took all of the Dodecanese islands. In late 1912, the Balkan states of Bulgaria, Serbia, Montenegro, and Greece united for the first and last time in history, driving Turkey out of Europe in the **First Balkan War** and indeed approaching within a few miles of İstanbul by the beginning of 1913. Ottomanism as a doctrine was a dead letter, since the European minorities had opted for nationalism, leaving a far more homogeneous, truncated Asian empire. Enraged at attempts to limit the army's, and the CUP's, involvement in government, and the unfavorable terms of a pending peace treaty, key CUP officers staged a coup, murdering the minister of war and continuing the war; when the new grand vizier Mahmut Şevket was assassinated in retaliation soon after, the CUP used it as an excuse to suppress all dissent and establish a **military junta**.

The unlikely Balkan alliance soon fell apart, with Bulgaria turning on Serbia and Greece in the **Second Balkan War**, and the Ottomans taking the opportunity to regain eastern Thrace up to Edirne. This action made temporary heroes of the junta, which by now was in effect a triumvirate: **Enver Paşa**, an officer of humble origins, dashing, courageous, abstemious, as well as vain, ambitious, and megalomaniac; **Talat Paşa**, a brutal Thracian civilian who would be responsible for ordering the 1915 deportation of the Armenians; and **Cemal Paşa**, a ruthless but competent professional soldier from an old family.

CUP ideology was now resolutely Turkish-nationalist, secular, and technocratic, as well as anti-democratic—and pro-German. Public opinion, and most responsible CUP members, hoped that the Ottoman Empire would remain neutral in the obviously impending conflict, but Germanophile Enver had signed a secret agreement with the kaiser on August 2, **1914**. By coincidence Britain committed a major blunder the same day, impounding two half-built battle-ships that had already been paid for by public subscription in Turkey. The German government pulled off a major PR coup by sailing two **replacement ships** through the Allied Mediterranean blockade to İstanbul in October, presenting them to the Turkish navy—whose German commander promptly forced Turkey's hand by sending them off to bombard Russian Black Sea ports. By November Turkey was officially **at war** with the Allies, although various CUP ministers resigned in protest. "This will be our ruin," said one prophetically, "even if we win."

Despite appearances, the CUP did not become a puppet of the Germans, nor Turkey a complete satellite; although men and weaponry were diverted to the European eastern front and Anatolia was used as a granary by the Central powers, the Capitulations were unilaterally abolished over German protests (they affected the French and English more anyway), and monetary policy was determined without outside interference for the first time in sixty years—as evidenced by the inflationary printing of paper bills. But these measures needed military successes to reinforce them, and the **Turkish war effort**, carried out on five fronts simultaneously, was an unmitigated disaster. Over the four-year duration, the empire lost all of its Middle Eastern domains, as the Arabs threw their weight behind the British on the promise of subsequent autonomy, thus proving pan-Islamism as dead as Ottomanism. Enver Paşa demonstrated his incompetence by losing an entire army on the Russian front during the winter of 1914–15; the subsequent tsarist advance deep into Anatolia was only reversed after the Bolshevik Revolution.

The single bright spot from the Turkish point of view was the successful defense of the **Gallipoli Peninsula**, guarding the Dardanelles and thus the sea approaches to İstanbul. Allied armadas attempting to force the straits had been repelled in late 1914 and early 1915, after which it was decided to make an amphibious landing on the fortified promontory. This was launched on April 24, 1915, but foundered immediately, and the Allies finally withdrew just after New Year 1916. Credit for the successful Turkish resistance belonged largely to a hitherto unkown colonel named **Mustafa Kemal**, later Atatürk, the ranking

Turkish officer at the operations. Born in Salonika in 1881 of a lower-middle-class family and educated at Harbiye Military College in İstanbul, he had come of age in the midst of the pre-1908 Young Turk agitation, and like many other junior officers had been sent into exile for "disloyal" activities. Though an early member of the CUP, he had opposed its autocratic tendencies and entry into the war on Germany's side. The Turkish public craved a hero at this point, but upon Kemal's return to İstanbul the jealous Enver deprived them of this satisfaction, shuttling Kemal between various backwoods commands, until the end of the war saw him overseeing a strategic retreat to the hills on the Syrian border.

For the Ottoman Empire's **Armenians**, April 24, 1915 was also a fateful day, when the CUP authorities ordered the disarming of all Armenians serving in the Turkish army, and the round-up of Armenian civilians from Anatolian cities, towns, and villages; only those living in İstanbul and İzmir were exempted for economic reasons. Over the next ten months of deportations, the men were usually shot immediately by gendarmes, Kurdish irregulars, or bands of thugs recruited for the purpose, while women and children were forced to march, under conditions that guaranteed their abuse and death, hundreds of kilometers toward concentration camps in the Mesopotamian desert. The Armenians' homes and businesses were appropriated, often by CUP functionaries. Estimating **total casualties** is difficult and controversial, but Ottoman and foreign censuses at the turn of the century showed nearly 1.5 million Armenians living in Anatolia. Allowing for the half-million refugees who managed to escape abroad by 1923, most of the one-million difference can be assumed to have perished, making it the first deliberate, large-scale genocide of this century.

The above scenario is hotly disputed by the current Turkish government, which denies that any officially sanctioned, systematic expulsion or killing took place, and admits at most 300,000 fatalities from unspecified causes—but implying that most of these were combatants in treasonous alliance with Russia or France. While it is true that some Armenians, particularly in Van, Kars, and Adana provinces, sided with those two powers in the hopes of securing a post-war state for themselves, this happened *after* the deportation and massacre orders were issued, and can be construed as legitimate self-defense. In any event, the issue is still very much alive, and relatively clumsy Turkish propaganda has recently been developed to counter vigorous Armenian lobbying for international recognition of the tragedy.

On **October 30, 1918**, Turkish and British officers signed an armistice on the Greek island of Limnos. Two weeks later an Allied fleet sailed into İstanbul and strategic points around the Sea of Marmara were occupied by the victors, although Turkish civil adminstration was allowed to continue on condition that no "disturbances" took place. In the interim the CUP triumvirate had fled on German ships, and all met violent deaths in the following years: Talat killed in revenge by an orphaned Armenian in Berlin; Cemal assassinated in Caucasian Georgia; and Enver—dying as flamboyantly as he had lived—as a self-styled emir fighting the Bolsheviks in central Asia.

THE STRUGGLE FOR INDEPENDENCE

The Allies were now in a position to carry out their long-deferred **designs on the Ottoman heartland**, based on various secret protocols of 1915–1917. By early 1919 French troops were occupying parts of southeastern Anatolia near the present Syrian and Iraqi borders, the Italians landed on the coast between Bodrum and Antalya, and the Greeks disembarked at İzmir, where Greek civilians numbered a large part of the population. The British concentrated their strength in İstanbul and Thrace, and along with the other victors garrisoned in the capital effectively dictated policy to the defeated Ottoman regime. The new sultan **Mehmet VI** was by all accounts a collaborationist interested only in retaining his throne, and prepared to make any necessary territorial or administrative concessions to that end—including the dissolution of the last wartime parliament.

İstanbul, under de facto occupation, and with nationalist Turks forced into hiding, was a poor seedbed for a war of independence. In Thrace and Anatolia, however, various **"Committees for the Defense of (Turkish) Rights,"** patriotic Turkish guerrilla bands, had sprung up, and a substantial remnant of the Ottoman armies survived at Erzurum, under the control of **Kâzım Karabekir**. Together these would form the nucleus of the liberation forces. All that was lacking was visionary **leadership**, and further **provocations** from the Allies; neither was long in coming.

Mustafa Kemal, the hero of Gallipoli and the Syrian front, was the only undefeated Ottoman general by the end of the war; was not compromised by close association with the CUP leadership; and could hardly be accused of being pro-German. Popular and outspoken, he was considered too dangerous by the Allies to be kept idle in the capital. For his part, Kemal itched to cross over to Anatolia and begin organizing some sort of resistance to the pending imperialist schemes, but dared not do so without a suitable pretext. This was provided in the spring of 1919, when Kemal managed to wangle from the collaborationist war ministry a commission as a military inspector for all Anatolia, empowered to halt the activities of the various Committees for the Defense of Rights and seize their arms. His first stop was to be the Black Sea, where Turkish guerrillas had been fighting it out with Greeks bent on setting up a Pontic republic. On **May 19, 1919**, Mustafa Kemal landed at Samsun, four days after Greek operations began at İzmir—the last straw for many hitherto passive Turks. Contrary to his assignment, Kemal promptly began organizing and strengthening the Turkish guerrillas. The puppet government in İstanbul, realizing too late what he was up to, attempted to recall him, then summarily relieved him of duties, and finally ordered his arrest; he returned the compliment by resigning his commission. Kemal and Karabekir, along with **Rauf, Ali Fuad**, and **Refet**—three high-ranking officers of old Ottoman families—drew up a provisional plan for resistance, with the strong support of the Anatolian religious authorities. Two **ideological congresses** were scheduled, with delegates often appearing after arduous journeys in disguise: one at Erzurum in July, and another at Sivas in September. Both gatherings elected Kemal as chairman, and both ratified the so-called **National Pact**, which demanded viable Turkish borders approximating those of today; an end to the Capitulations, and a guarantee of rights to all minorities. At the same time the pact reaffirmed its loyalty to the institution of the caliphate, if not the sultan himself, who was held to be a prisoner of the Allies. It was still far too early in the game to antagonize the religious elements, and indeed secularization was still a gleam in Kemal's eye.

Throughout these maneuvers the Nationalists, as they came to be called, made good use of the **telegraph lines** installed by Abdülhamid, ensuring that telegraphists loyal to their cause manned the keys, and often conducting convoluted arguments with the İstanbul regime over the wires. By the fall of 1919, they forced the resignation of the grand vizier and the announcement of elections for a new parliament. These, in early 1920, returned a large Nationalist majority, which openly proclaimed the National Pact—and created a climate where thefts from Allied arms depots, often with the connivance of the French and Italians who opposed Greek aims in Anatolia, became a routine occurrence. At the instigation of the outraged Ottoman court, the British placed İstanbul under formal military occupation on **March 16, 1920**, raiding parliament and bundling a few score deputies into exile on Malta. Luckier members of parliament escaped to Ankara, where Kemal and others had prudently remained, and on **April 23** opened the first **"Grand National Assembly,"** in direct defiance to the Allied encroachments. Turkey's first Ankara-based parliament met in a Wild West atmosphere, lit by oil-lamps for several years, while its members tethered their horses to wooden railings out front.

The sultanate reacted vehemently to all this, securing a *fetva* (ruling) from the Islamic authorities sanctioning a holy war against the "rebels" and condemning the Nationalist leadership to death in absentia. Kemal and friends secured a counter-*fetva* from sympathetic religious figures in Ankara, and soon afterwards the head of the Bektaşi dervish order publicly commanded his followers to help the Nationalists. Such moral support was vital to the beleaguered guerrillas, who were now fighting for their lives in a **multiple-front war**: against the French in the southeast, the Italians in the southwest, Armenians in the northeast, irregular bands supporting the sultan, and—most dangerously—the Greeks in western Anatolia. The only consistent aid came from the newborn Soviet Union, which sent gold and weapons, and partitioned the short-lived Armenian republic between itself and Turkey, thus ending that theater of war by late 1920.

The Allied governments, oblivious of the new reality on the ground in Turkey, attempted to legitimize their claims to Turkish territory by presenting the humiliating **Treaty of Sèvres** to the Ottoman government in May 1920. By its terms, partly motivated by the Wilsonian Fourteen Points, but more by unalloyed greed, an independent Armenia and an autonomous Kurdistan were created; the straits of the Sea of Marmara and İstanbul were placed under international control; Thrace, İzmir, and its hinterland were given to Greece; France and Italy were assigned spheres of influence in those portions of Anatolia remaining with the Ottomans; and Turkish finances were placed under Allied supervision, with a revival of the Capitulations. By signing this treaty, the demoralized sultanate sacrificed its last shred of credibility, convinced any remaining waverers of the necessity of the Nationalist movement—and sparked a predictable Greek response.

The **Greek expeditionary armies**, acting with the authorization of Britiain, not only pressed inland from İzmir but captured Edirne, İzmit, and Bursa as well, seeking to revive notions of a Greater Greece straddling both shores of the Aegean. Only French and Italian objections caused them to halt just short of the strategic Afyon–Eskişehir railroad. In early 1921 the Greeks were on the move again, but Nationalist general İsmet Paşa stopped them twice in January and April at the defile of **İnönü**, from which he would later take his surname. Both sides had undergone subtle changes: since the fall of the republican Venizelos government in Greece and the return of the royalists, the Greek Anatolian armies had become progressively more corrupt, incompetently led, and brutal, sustained for the time being by the momentum of superior numbers and weaponry. Kemal's forces, on the other hand, had become more cohesive and professional, with irregular bands either defeated or absorbed.

But when the Greeks advanced east once more in July 1921, they swiftly captured Afyon, Eskişehir, and the vital railroad that linked them; the Nationalists strategically retreated east of the Sakarya River, less than 100km from Ankara, to buy time and extend the enemy's supply lines. Panic and gloom reigned in Ankara, with calls for Kemal's instatement as commander-in-chief at the head of the defending army, to share its fate. This was done, and soon the Greeks went for the bait, sniffing an easy chance to finish off the Nationalists. But in the ferocious, three-week **Battle of the Sakarya** beginning on August 13, they failed to make further headway toward Ankara. Although most of the Greek army survived, anything less than its capture of the Nationalist headquarters was a decisive defeat. The jubilant Grand National Assembly conferred on Kemal the title *Gazi*, or "Warrior for the Faith."

The victory at Sakarya greatly enhanced the Nationalists' international position: both the **French and Italians** soon concluded peace treaties, withdrawing from southern Anatolia; and contributions from various Asian Muslim countries poured in to finance the "holy war." With remaining support for the Greek adventure evaporating, the British tried unsuccessfully to arrange an armistice between Greece and the Nationalists. Both camps dug in and waited until, on **August 26, 1922**, Kemal launched his final offensive at **Dumlupınar** near Afyon, designed to drive the Greeks out of Anatolia. Surprised by a dawn artillery barrage, the Greek lines crumbled, and those not taken prisoner or killed fled downvalley in a disorderly rout toward waiting boats in İzmir, committing atrocities against the Turkish population, destroying the harvest, and abandoning Greek civilians to the inevitable Turkish reprisals. The latter included the **sacking and burning of İzmir** four days after the triumphant entry of the Nationalists. Never again would Greece aspire to be a Mediterranean, let alone a world, power.

Despite this resounding triumph, the war wasn't over yet, and indeed the threat of a larger conflict loomed. A large Greek army remained intact in **Thrace**, determined to fight on, and British contingents guarding the strategically vital **Dardanelles** faced off against the Nationalist army sent north to cross the straits. Some of Kemal's associates even urged him to retake western Thrace and Greek Macedonia, a sure invitation to renewed world war. Cooler heads prevailed at the last minute, however, and at Mudanya on **October 11, 1922**, an armistice was signed, accepting accomplished facts and obliging the last Greek troops to depart from eastern Thrace. A week later the British prime minister, his pro-Greek policy utterly discredited, was forced to resign.

There remained just one obstacle to full Nationalist control of Turkey: Sultan Mehmet VI still presided over a diminished realm, consisting of İstanbul alone. Few in Ankara had a good word to say about the man himself, but many expressed reluctance to abolish his office, favoring a constitutional monarchy with royalty as a stabilizing symbol. The Allies themselves helped decide the matter by extending a clumsy double invitation to a final peace conference at Lausanne—one addressed to the sultanate, the other to the Grand National Assembly. The outrage thus provoked in the latter quarters made it an easy matter for Kemal to persuade the deputies to **abolish the sultanate** on November 1, effective retroactively from March 16, 1920, the date of British direct rule in İstanbul. Within two weeks Mehmet VI, last of the House of Osman, sneaked ignominiously out of the old imperial capital on a British warship, bound for exile in Italy; his cousin Abdülmecid was sworn in as caliph, but with no temporal powers whatsoever.

The **peace conference** at Lausanne was convened immediately, with İsmet Paşa as the sole Turkish representative. If the Allies were hoping to dictate terms as at Versailles and Sèvres, they were quickly disappointed; İsmet soon proved as dogged at the negotiating table as on the battlefield, reducing seasoned diplomats to despair by his repetitive insistence on the tenets of the Erzurum-Sivas National Pact. The conference was suspended for two months in early 1923, the Allies doubtless hoping to wear İsmet down, but in the end it was they who gave in. The **Treaty of Lausanne**, signed on July 24, recognized the borders established in the recent war of independence; abolished the Capitulations; demilitarized the Dardanelles and the islands at its mouth; and postponed a decision on the status of the Mesopotamian district of Mosul.

More drastically, Greece and Turkey agreed to an **exchange of minority populations** to eliminate future outbreaks of communal conflict. Nearly half a million Muslims in Greece were sent to Turkey, and the remaining 1.3 million Greek Orthodox in Turkey were dispatched to Greece. The only exceptions were the Turkish minority in western Thrace, and Greeks with Ottoman citizenship resident in İstanbul and on Imvros and Tenedos islands at the mouth of the Dardanelles. The sole criterion was religious affiliation, and incalculable suffering was caused, especially among Turkish-speaking Christians and Greek-speaking Muslims who suddenly found themselves in a wholly alien environment.

The pact marked the end of World War I, and saw Turkey, alone of the "defeated" nations, emerge in dignity, with defendable territory and modest demands made of her. Compared to the old empire, it was a compact state—97 percent Anatolian and Muslim. Toward the end of the Lausanne conference, the first Grand National Assembly was dissolved, its work declared finished. A new political party, the **Republican People's Party** (RPP), incorporating the resources and personnel of the various Committees for the Defense of Rights, and the precepts of the National Pact, was formed, and a new parliament was swiftly created, its members drawn from the ranks of the new entity.

THE YOUNG REPUBLIC AND KEMAL ATATÜRK'S REFORMS

The Nationalists may have won the military battle for political sovereignty in Anatolia, but after ten years of constant warfare the country was physically devastated and economically a shambles. Export agriculture and urban commerce had largely been in the hands of the Greek and Armenian minorities, who had accounted for twenty percent of the pre-1914 population within the boundaries of the new state, and up to fifty percent in İzmir, İstanbul, and along the Black Sea and Sea of Marmara. With their departure or demise, and that of the foreigners who had benefited from the Capitulations, the Turks were obliged to start again commercially, which they failed to do for many years.

Kemal had little patience with or understanding of intricate economics, and preferred to emphasize sweeping social change by fiat, skillfully delivered in the maximum increments tolerable at any given moment. In October 1923 the Grand National Assembly officially moved the capital to **Ankara** and proclaimed the **Republic**, to which there was little practical obstacle since the last sultan had absconded. Kemal was designated head of state—numerous abstentions were as much as his opponents dared—and İsmet İnönü was named prime minister. Though the sultan was gone,

the caliph Abdülmecid was still around and very much a public personality—an intolerable situation for Kemal and the other Westernizers; since the war had been won they no longer felt the need of the legitimizing function of İslam. In March 1924 the caliphate was abolished and all members of the house of Osman exiled, the *medreses* and religious courts closed, and the assets of the *vakıfs* supervised by a new Ministry of Religious Affairs.

Even some of Kemal's longtime supporters were dismayed by his increasingly autocratic ways, and a few—including military men Ali Fuad, Rauf Orbay and Kâzım Karabekir—resigned from the RPP in October 1924 to form an opposition, the **Progressive Republican Party** (PRP). At first Kemal tolerated the new party as a means of blowing off steam, even replacing the unpopular İsmet as prime minister to humor them, but the RPP became alarmed when PRP speakers attracted large crowds and elements of the less supervised İstanbul press began siding with them.

Events soon provided Kemal with a basis for more action. In February 1925 the first of several **Kurdish revolts** this century erupted at Palu, near Elâzığ, under the leadership of a Naqshbandi dervish leader. The revolt was both fundamentalist Muslim and separatist-nationalist in ideology, and it took the central government two months to suppress it. (Diehards staged a comeback on Mount Ararat in 1930, and there was a major flare-up in Tunceli in 1936—both in turn related to the current troubles.) Kemal, demanding unity in a time of crisis, secured the abolition of the PRP and established a series of bloody "**Independence Tribunals**" invested with summary powers; not only the leaders of the revolt but a few minor members of the PRP found themselves on the wrong end of a rope, and freedom of the press was quickly curtailed. By autumn 1925 all the dervish orders had been made illegal throughout Turkey (though never effectively suppressed), and the veneration of saints at their tombs was forbidden. Simultaneously, Kemal embarked on a campaign against traditional headgear, in particular women's veils, the turban, and the fez. Although the caliphate had been dissolved with hardly a murmur, the sartorial laws outlawing the turban, and fez, and requiring the donning of the hated European hat, were met with stiff resistance; several offenders were hung from lampposts by the reactivated Independence Tribunals, but the secularists have never to this day fully succeeded in eliminating the cloaking of women in the rural areas.

More drastic measures followed at a dizzying pace. By 1926, the Gregorian calendar had replaced the Muslim lunar one for official use, and the şeriat or Islamic **law code** was replaced by adaptations of the western European versions. The same year, the Jewish, Armenian, and Greek minorities relinquished the last vestiges of their communal laws; henceforth all citizens of the Republic were to be judged by a uniform legal system. Parallel with the introduction of a secular law code came the relative **emancipation of women**: marriage and divorce became civil rather than religious or customary, polygamy was abolished, and within four years women were given the vote.

Not surprisingly all this inflamed the existing opposition to Kemal, and in mid-1926 a plot to assassinate him while on a visit to İzmir was uncovered. Those involved were mostly disgruntled minor deputies and ex-CUP men, but Kemal took the opportunity to charge and try most of the former Progressive Republican Party's leadership, including war hero Karabekir. Many, including all the surviving CUP leadership, were hanged, and even those acquitted were effectively barred from public life in the future. This was the last mass purge, however, and the feared Independence Tribunals were disbanded soon after, having served their purpose. There was to be no more public opposition to Kemal during his lifetime, except for a period in 1930 when a second short-lived opposition party was again judged to be a "premature experiment."

Kemal now felt secure enough to press on with his agenda, and chose as his next field **alphabet reform**. A special commission prepared a Roman script within six weeks in 1928, and by the end of the year its universal use was law, with the Gazi himself touring the country to give lessons in public parks. Reform was extended to the entire language over the next few years, with the founding of a language commission charged with the duty of purging Turkish of its Arabic and Persian accretions and reviving old Turkish words, coining new ones, or adopting French words to underline the break

with the Islamic past. Nowadays most observers admit that the process was carried too far, with the language soon as top-heavy with borrowed Western words as it had been with Eastern ones, but together with the script change the measures resulted in a massive increase in literacy and comprehension.

Less successful, and ultimately embarrassing, were programs purporting to rewrite history, in which it was variously asserted that all other languages derived from Turkish; that the Turks were an Aryan race (and other racial nonsense uncomfortably close to Nazi theories), or that they were the ancestors of the Hittites or Sumerians. After a few years these hypotheses, springing from a mix of inferiority feelings and a need for political legitimacy, were allowed to die quiet deaths. (It's perhaps worth adding that a side effect of language reform was to isolate many Turks from their own history—unable to read Ottoman Turkish, they feel isolated from the past.) More constructive, in 1934, was full **suffrage for women** in national elections and the mandatory adoption of **surnames** by the entire population; previously this had been discretionary. Kemal chose for himself **Atatürk**, "Father-Turk," dropping his first name Mustafa.

Belatedly Atatürk and his associates turned their attention to the **economic** sphere, where Turkey's weaknesses had been accentuated by the Crash of 1929. Despite public discontent at deprivation and stagnation, Kemalism, as Kemal Atatürk's ideology was named, continued to stress industrial self-sufficiency through state investment in heavy industry with a goal of complete import substitution (except for factory equipment). Development banks had been set up in 1925, and subsequently the strategically important rail network was extended and mining, steel, cement, and paper works were heavily subsidized on a pattern modeled on Italian Fascism. This paternalistic program was, however, grossly inefficient, and proceeded at the expense of the agricultural sector, which remained in abject condition until the 1950s. The eastern part of the country was effectively condemned to a subsistence existence—aggravating Kurdish feelings of neglect—a situation that remained unchanged until the massive, controversial irrigation and hydroelectric projects of the 1970s and 1980s.

Turkey's **foreign policy** during the post-independence years was rooted in non-interventionism and isolationism. Atatürk's slogan "Peace at home, peace in the world" may have had an unfortunate resemblance to appeasement policies toward Hitler at the time, but in practice secured for Turkey years of calm which were badly needed. As much as the ruling party may have admired aspects of the European totalitarian systems then prevalent, it could see clearly that on the international stage Germany, Italy, and the USSR were headed for cataclysm. Atatürk removed a remaining irritant to Anglo-Turkish relations by ceding the Mosul region to Iraq, but in 1936 began an ultimately successful campaign to annex the Hatay, part of the French Protectorate of Syria with a large Turkish population. Alliances of the 1930s, with Greece, Yugoslavia, and Romania to the west, and with Iraq, Iran, and Afghanistan to the east, tended to be opportunistic and short-lived, and nowhere near as durable as a Treaty of Friendship Turkey signed (partly for reasons of affinity between Bolshevism and Kemalism) with the Soviet Union.

Fortunately for Turkey Atatürk had accomplished the bulk of his intended life's work by **1938**, for his health was steadily worsening. He died of cirrhosis of the liver in İstanbul's Dolmabahçe Palace at 9:05am on November 10, 1938. Thousands of mourners bearing torches lined the route of his funeral cortege-train between İstanbul and Ankara.

Atatürk's legacy is a considerable one: unlike the totalitarian rulers of his day, he refrained from expansionist designs and racial/ethnic hatred, leaving behind a stable, defensible state and a guiding ideology, however uneven, expressly intended to outlive him. Personally he was a complex, even tragic figure: his charisma, energy and quick grasp of situations and people were unparalleled, but he had little liking for methodical planning or systematic study. While respected, even revered, he wasn't loved by his associates or particularly lovable—despite his sponsorship of the advancement of women, he was a callous, compulsive womanizer, with one brief spell of unhappy marriage. In his fundamental loneliness, he nursed grudges and suspicions which often had deadly consequences for those

who, as partners, might have been able to extricate Turkey from later awkward situations. By his stature and temperament Atatürk, like a giant tree that allows nothing to grow underneath, deprived Turkey of a succeeding generation of leadership. The cult of his personality—which is obvious from the silhouettes and signs on every hillside—is in some ways symptomatic of an inability to conceive of alternative ideologies or heroes, though since 1983 the economic principles of Kemalism are more talked about than observed.

WORLD WAR II & THE RISE OF MULTI-PARTY POLITICS

Atatürk was succeeded as president by his longtime general and prime minister **İsmet İnönü**, and his policy concerning the **Hatay** was posthumously vindicated in 1939, when annexation of the nominally independent Hatay republic was ratified. France, eager for Turkish support in the impending war, acquiesced, and was apparently rewarded by the Turkish signing of a treaty of alliance with France and Britain in 1939.

In the event the treaty turned out to be a dead letter: France was swiftly defeated, and German propaganda convinced the Turkish government that Britain was probably doomed as well and that the Axis would also dispatch Russia, the hereditary Turkish enemy. Entry into the war on either side became less likely as time went on, since Turkey's armed forces had become desperately antiquated, a match for neither German nor Allied weaponry. Memories of the Ottoman Empire's humiliation at the hands of the World War I Entente powers were strong too. Turkey instead remained **neutral**, selling strategically vital chromium ore to both Germany and Britain. Despite this fence-sitting, the country was essentially on a war footing, with all able-bodied men mobilized and the economy subject to the stresses of shortages, black markets, profiteering, and government budget deficits.

All these, and the partial infiltration of Nazi ideology, provoked the institution in 1942 of the so-called **Varlık Vergisi**, or Wealth Levy, a confiscatory tax applied in a discriminatory manner against businessmen of Armenian, Greek, Jewish, and *Dönme* (nominal Muslims, ex-disciples of a false Jewish messiah) descent.

It was in effect an attack by the Ankara-based nationalist bureaucrats on the remnants, in İzmir and İstanbul, of the Ottoman merchant class: there was no appeal against assessments, and sums due had to be forwarded within absurdly short time limits. Defaulters had their property confiscated and/or were deported to labor camps in the interior, where many died. The measure, having in fact raised very little money, was rescinded in 1944, but not before urban commerce had been set back a decade, and the Republic's credibility with its minorities severely damaged.

Even after the collapse of the Italians, Turkey still declined to enter the war, despite assurances of Allied support. Turkey only declared war on Germany in early 1945 to qualify for membership of the UN, and not soon enough to prevent the USSR from renewing demands for the return of the Kars and Ardahan districts, and joint control of the straits at each end of the Sea of Marmara. Though these were summarily rejected, Turkey badly needed a protective ally in the international arena, and found it in the **United States**. The arrival in İstanbul of the American warship *USS Missouri* was greeted with such euphoria that the city fathers, in a famous instance of Turkish hospitality later worked into popular literature, ordered the local bordellos thrown open for free to the sailors.

The eventual results of the mutual wooing were Turkey's participation in the Korean War, and soon after admission to **NATO** after an initial application had been rejected. This new pro-Western stance had several other consequences: the expulsion of vast numbers of ethnic Turks from Warsaw Pact Bulgaria into Turkey, a harbinger of an identical act four decades later; bad relations with neighboring Arab states, particularly after Turkey's recognition of Israel and the overthrow of the Iraqi monarchy by the Ba'ath Party; and a short-lived alliance with Greece and Yugoslavia, which was effectively dissolved by the first Cyprus crisis of the mid-1950s.

On the home front, discontent with one-party rule, secularization, and the centralized economy came to a head when four politicians—including Celâl Bayar and Adnan Menderes—having been expelled from the RPP, formed the **Demokrat Parti** in early 1946. Despite prema-

turely scheduled elections of that summer and widespread balloting irregularities, the new opposition managed to gain nearly 15 percent of the parliamentary seats. The fact that this gain was not reversed by force was due as much to the climate of changed Turkish public opinion as to any subtle pressure exerted by the United States, whose economic aid was now pouring into the country.

A showdown could not be long postponed, however, and campaigning for the nationwide **elections of May 14, 1950** was strenuous and unimpeded. The Democratic Party's platform promised something to every disgruntled element in the electorate: an end to anti-business strictures for the embryonic middle class, freer religious observance for the devout, and attention to the badly neglected agricultural sector. Though it was a safe bet that the Democrats would win, the scale of their victory—55 percent of the vote, and, by virtue of the winner-take-all, slate-of-candidates system, over 80 percent of parliamentary seats—caught everyone by surprise. Bayar replaced İnönü as president, and **Menderes** took office as prime minister.

"POPULIST" GOVERNMENT

Virtually the first act of the new government was to permit, after a seventeen-year gap, the recitation of the call to prayer in Arabic—a decree neatly coinciding with the start of Ramadan. Simultaneously rashes of fez- and turban-wearing, polygamy, and use of the Arabic script were noted in the provinces. There followed far-reaching programs of rural loans and public works, an end to various government monopolies and restrictions on investment by foreigners, and massive imports of luxury goods and farm machinery, based on the assumption that Turkey's allies would quietly subsidize all this. Many projects, including a Soviet-sponsored oil refinery on the Aegean, were controversial, although in retrospect Menderes can be credited with opening up a country where for three decades very little in the way of people, capital, or goods had moved in or out. Despite lip service paid to private enterprise, however, much of this development was unplanned, uncoordinated investment in state enterprises, and most of it took the form of expensive rewards to supporters—a mere continuation of the old RPP system of patronage. Menderes himself, a largely self-taught farmer/lawyer, had his colossal vanity fed by the adulation of the peasants, who not only sacrificed livestock in his honor at his public appearances, but went so far as to name children after him.

The honeymoon with the electorate continued through the first years of the 1950s, aided by bumper harvests, although by 1954 clouds loomed on the horizon: the **national debt** and trade deficit were enormous, and the black-market value of the Turkish lira was one-fourth the official exchange rate. But the increasingly sensitive Democrats would not tolerate even mutterings of criticism: in 1953 assets and institutions of the ousted RPP had been expropriated and abolished, and the small, right-wing/religious National Party, with its handful of seats in parliament, was proscribed. The first of a series of **repressive press laws** was passed in early 1954, further poisoning the atmosphere just before the May elections. These the Democrats won even more easily than four years previously, but instead of imbuing them with more confidence, they took the result as a mandate to clamp down harder on dissent and to run the country ever more shamelessly for the benefit of their clientele. The economy continued to worsen, with the first bouts of **inflation** which was thereafter to be a constant feature of Turkish life. During 1955 the government, looking for a distraction from, and scapegoats for, domestic problems, found both in the form of the Cyprus issue and minorities—especially İstanbul Greeks. DP-orchestrated street demonstrations got out of hand, ending in destructive **riots** aimed at the wealthy and foreigners in all three major cities.

In the wake of all this, support for the government tumbled, but probably not enough so that it would have lost honestly contested elections in 1957. These, however, were heavily rigged, and the results—trimming the Democrats' strength to just over two-thirds of the total—were never officially announced. Turkey thus approached the end of the decade in a parlous state, with a huge, dangerous gulf between the rural population and the intellectual/commercial elite in the towns—and, more dangerously, an alienated, antagonized military.

THE FIRST MILITARY INTERVENTION—AND THE 1960S

Nowhere had dismay over the intentions and policies of the Democratic government been felt more keenly than in the military, which considered itself the guardian of Atatürk's secular reforms (and indeed was enshrined as such in the military code of the Republic). The officers, debarred from voting and watching the value of their fixed salaries erode in the face of inflation, felt betrayed and neglected as the new middle class and Democrat apparatchiks surpassed them economically and socially. Cliques of officers had begun to formulate plans for action as far back as 1954, but it was not until May 27, 1960 that middle-ranking and commanding officers, working in concert, staged a **coup**. The month preceding the action was marked by student demonstrations in İstanbul and Ankara, which were fired on with some loss of life by elements of the army and police still loyal to Menderes.

The coup was bloodless, swift, and complete. Democrat members of parliament and ministers were jailed, and there was rejoicing in the streets of the larger cities. For the next sixteen months, a **National Unity Committee** (NUC) ruled the country and oversaw the preparation of a new, extremely liberal constitution to supersede the one of 1924. The ruling committee, however, was an uneasy marriage of convenience, incorporating not only idealistic top brass hoping for a speedy return to civilian rule, but junior officers who wished for an indefinite period of authoritarian military government, and who in fact embarked on disruptive purges of university faculties and the officer corps themselves. Committee chief and acting head of state **Cemal Gürsel** adroitly outflanked this element, exiling their representatives to minor overseas posts and lifting the ban on political activity early in 1961. The new constitution, which provided for a bicameral legislature, proportional representation in the lower house, and a supreme court, was submitted to public referendum in July, with elections scheduled for October.

The **referendum**, which was essentially a vote of confidence in the NUC, showed just 62 percent in favor of the new constitution. This was hardly gratifying to the junta, which panicked at the display of lingering support for the DP. Since the coup, several hundred leading members, including Menderes and Bayar, had been imprisoned on the bleak island of Yassıada in the Sea of Marmara and tried on charges of undermining the 1924 constitution, corruption, and complicity in the riots of 1955—among others. Upon the return of guilty verdicts and fifteen death sentences, the NUC hastily ratified three of these—against Menderes, foreign minister Zorlu, and finance minister Polatkan—while commuting the others, including that of Bayar, to life imprisonment. The three hangings, carried out a month before the elections, backfired badly, making Menderes a martyr and ensuring a long electoral life for the Justice Party, the new incarnation of the now-banned Democratic Party.

The inconclusive **parliamentary elections** proved a further disappointment to the NUC; neither the Justice Party nor a refurbished RPP gained a majority, with the balance of power held by splinter groups. Under threat of another coup, the two major parties were induced to form a coalition, with Cemal Gürsel as president and İnönü again prime minister for the first time since 1938. These compromises rankled certain disaffected junior officers who had hoped to get rid of the Democrats once and for all, and they resolved to clean up the "mess" with two subsequent coup attempts, one in February 1962 and another fourteen months later. The latter, involving the occupation of the state radio station by veterans of May 27, was quelled and its leader executed. There would be no more putsches from below.

Civilian political life settled into a semblance of **normality**, with more unstable coalitions until 1965. In terms of standards of living, the promised economic reforms of the NUC had not borne fruit; the import-substitution policies of the old RPP, whereby industrial/manufacturing self-sufficiency, however uneconomic, was subsidised, were quietly revived, while land reform and rural development was again deferred. The first wave of **emigration** to Germany and other western European countries acted as a social safety valve, and the "guest workers" would return to Turkey for vacations with cars, consumer durables, and—to a limited extent—European notions and wives. For the first time, independent labor unions began organizing and recruiting inside Turkey, and the right to strike

was finally confirmed in 1963. The new urban proletariat found a political voice in the newly formed Turkish Workers Party, whose very existence nudged the RPP, now led by future prime minister **Bülent Ecevit**, leftward into a social-democratic mold. In 1964 **Süleyman Demirel**, who was to emerge as one of the country's most enduring political figures over the next three decades, became leader of the JP, which was obliged to come out strongly in favour of free enterprise and foreign investment. In October 1965, Demirel's Justice Party gained a majority of votes in the national elections, with the RPP and TWP together tallying less than a third.

But international events were to assume increasing importance in the Turkish domestic scene. Neighboring **Cyprus** had gained independence in 1960 by terms of a treaty between the new republic and the "guarantors" Britain, Greece, and Turkey. Incorporated in the Treaty of Guarantee and the Cypriot constitution were extensive concessions to the Turkish Cypriot minority, which constituted roughly one-fifth of the island's population. By 1963 Cypriot president Makarios declared these clauses unworkable, and sought to limit the veto power of the Turkish community. Members of EOKA, the right-wing paramilitary force of the Greek population, took this as a cue to commence attacks on Turkish settlements, who replied in kind. Virtual civil war beset the island through much of 1964, with the ranks of both sides swelled by illegal, smuggled-in Greek and Turkish troops. A full-scale Greco-Turkish war was only narrowly avoided. The Turkish government had to confine its response to retaliations against the Greek population of its two Aegean islands and İstanbul, while ethnic violence recurred sporadically across Cyprus, despite the imposition of a UN-supervised truce for the rest of the decade.

Turkey was also not immune from the spirit of May 1968, which here took the form of increased **anti-Americanism** and leftist sentiments, particularly on and around university campuses. At the height of the Vietnam War the US was easily labeled an imperialist power, a diagnosis confirmed by the delayed publication of a secret 1964 letter from President Johnson to İnönü warning Turkey against military intervention in Cyprus. Many Turks felt betrayed by the US's lack of support on the Cyprus issue, having followed the American lead on foreign policy issues since the end of World War II. Even the establishment found the obviousness of American tutelage offensive to sentiments of national independence, and most of the half-dozen US military installations were quietly transferred either to Turkish sovereign control or at worst that of NATO. Relations with the Soviet Union improved dramatically. Ironically, perhaps the most lasting American legacy to Turkey was swarms of automobiles and 110-volt household appliances, provided as part of Marshall Plan assistance during the 1950s or sold off by departing diplomatic and military personnel throughout the 1960s.

Demirel was re-elected in **1969** to a second term as prime minister, but his majority and authority were soon eroded by the loss of a crucial budget vote and the defection of sixteen percent of the JP to legally reform the Democrat Party. More ominous was the upsurge in **political violence** in the streets and around the universities, which was to be a pervasive feature of Turkish life until 1980. Extreme left-wing groups, which had emerged in response to the impotence and subsequent break-up of the TWP, fought it out with right-wing and/or Islamic activists, who had set up paramilitary training camps as far back as 1966.

THE SECOND MILITARY INTERVENTION & THE 1970S

Against this backdrop of domestic unrest, lingering corruption, and continued non-productive parliamentary maneuvers, the generals acted again. On March 12, 1971, they issued a proclamation forcing Demirel and his cabinet to resign in favor of an "above-party" government composed of reformist technocrats. This measure, often called the **"coup by memorandum,"** allowed parliament to continue functioning, while stealing the wind from the sails of a considerable body of restive NCOs who had hoped for a full-scale military regime. Martial law was, however, imposed on the major cities and the ever-troublesome southeast, and thousands from the university community, the press, and broadcasting were arrested and tried, mostly on charges of inciting violence or class conflict, in a wave of **repression** every bit as comprehensive as the more publicized one of 1980. In September

amendments were promulgated to limit the freedoms granted by the 1961 constitution, but soon the "above-party" regime, effectively stymied by JP operatives in the Grand National Assembly, was forced to resign. Despite, or because of, the threat of another coup, acting premier Nihat Erim managed to cobble together a merry-go-round of successively less radical and more acceptable cabinets, and preserved a semblance of civilian rule for two more years.

The surprise winners of the freely contested **elections in October 1973** were Bülent Ecevit and his RPP, although it was soon forced into uneasy alliance with the Islamic National Salvation Party (NSP), which gained control of several ministries. During Ecevit's short but momentous period of office, the economy was savaged by OPEC's oil price hike, which preceded the Turkish **military intervention in Cyprus**.

The military junta then ruling Greece had ousted President Makarios and replaced him with extremists supporting union with Greece. The Turkish Cypriot population, mainly concentrated in the north of the island, was under serious threat, although by now they had fielded guerrilla bands to challenge the violence of the Hellenistic paramilitary group EOKA. Ecevit's appeal to Britain to intervene in accordance with the Treaty of Guarantee went unheeded, so he gave the order for Turkish troops to invade the island in July. Failure to secure concessions on behalf of the Turkish Cypriots at negotiations in London led to subsequent Turkish occupation of the northern third of the island.

Nearly two decades later, the situation remains essentially unchanged, with a negotiated settlement as elusive as ever. The **ceasefire** (hostilities haven't formally ended) is policed by a UN peace-keeping force sandwiched in a buffer zone called the "Green Line" between the Greek Cypriot-controlled south and the self-proclaimed Turkish Republic of Northern Cyprus. There is great unity of opinion in Turkey on the Cyprus issue, in that the status quo is seen as the only viable option at present. Large numbers of Turkish troops remain in Cyprus, and Ankara shows no intention of withdrawing them, nor of ceasing to play a part in local politics or stop the flow of Anatolian settlers, despite the damage that this does to Turkey in international organizations—especially the European Community.

Back on the domestic front, Ecevit, riding a tide of post-Cyprus popularity, resigned to call a snap election and campaign for a workable parliamentary majority. For various reasons, however, the poll was delayed until April 1975, when Süleyman Demirel was able to assemble a coalition government along with the Islamic NSP and the neo-fascist Nationalist Action Party, and hung onto power after inconclusive elections two years later.

All this served only to further polarize feelings in the country, which from 1976 onward was beset by steadily increasing political **violence** by extremists at either end of the political spectrum. Death tolls escalated from 300 during 1976–77, to over 3000 during 1980, with the number of wounded and bomb explosions during this period well into five figures. While the perpetrators initially confined their activities to each other, a steady deterioration of parliamentary decorum and the politicization of trade unions and the civil service meant that incidents were soon almost universal.

Ecevit regained power for about eighteen months beginning at the close of 1977 and attempted to address the **dire economic situation**, which had been aggravated not only by the endemic disorder, but by successive governments' public spending, trade deficits, and other inflationary policies. International assistance was secured, but on condition that the budget was balanced, protectionism reduced, and the lira devalued, and in the event the political resolve to apply such strict controls was lacking. In December 1978, street battles in the southern city of Maraş between right-wing, fundamentalist Sunni gunmen and left-wing Alevîs claimed more than a hundred lives within a week; the neo-fascist NAP was blamed by many for having orchestrated the clashes. Martial law was declared in many provinces, but this failed to prevent the establishment of an Alevî commune in the Black Sea town of Fatsa, where the army eventually sent in tanks against street barricades. Against such a background of events, Demirel regained power in 1979, but also failed to halt the slide into **civil and economic chaos**. Random, tit-for-tat murders in İstanbul reached twenty per day, with some neighborhoods run by various factions—entry to these with the wrong newspaper in hand guaranteed a beating or worse.

THE 1980 COUP AND ITS AFTERMATH

The armed forces, at first reluctant to act because of the apparent ineffectiveness of the 1960 and 1971 interventions, soon decided that the Republic was facing its gravest crisis yet. A planning group for a military takeover apparently existed as early as 1978, but public rumblings first surfaced in the form of a warning letter to the two major political parties at New Year 1980. By this time **martial law** was in force in all of the major cities as well as in the southeast. Also, an economist and engineer named **Turgut Özal** had been appointed as head of the State Planning Organization, in which capacity he ditched the import-substitution policies prevalent since the founding of the Republic for an **export-orientated economy**.

Now international events intervened. Turkey's strategic importance to the West had been emphasized by the Iranian revolution and the Soviet invasion of Afghanistan, and the US was particularly anxious to secure a stable base in the Middle East. After five years of cool relations, prompted by an embargo of arms to Turkey in the wake of the Cyprus action, rapprochement feelers were put forth. By the time the Iran-Iraq war began in April 1980, these began to include signals of tacit approval for a coup. Some sources have also alleged that, given the existing martial-law controls, the continued escalation of domestic violence was inconceivable without the military's toleration of it—even to the extent of using agents provocateurs to guarantee a solid pretext for a full-scale takeover.

This occurred bloodlessly on **September 12, 1980**, to the initial relief of the vast majority of the population. The frenzied killings ceased; Demirel and Ecevit were both detained; all political parties were disbanded shortly after; and all trade unions and associations were closed down. Turgut Özal was, however, left in charge of the economy, since his reforms were seen as both effective and essential to Western support.

It soon became apparent that this coup represented a drastic break from the pattern of the previous two. A **junta** of generals, not junior officers, was firmly in control from the start, and the return to civilian rule would be long delayed, and within a new framework.

Meanwhile, bannings, indictments, and purges punctuated the early 1980s, and while the radical right was by no means immune from prosecution, it became clear that the left would bear the brunt of the crackdown. Nationalist right-wing beliefs, as long as they were not explicitly fascist, were compatible with the generals' agenda—they were more critical of extreme fundamentalist influence, though inconsistent in their reaction to it.

The principal **targets** of the new rulers, and ones that had been relatively untouched in previous coups, were labor syndicates, internationalist or separatist groups, and the left-leaning intelligentsia, all previously influential in Turkish politics. DİSK, the radical trade-union confederation, had 1477 of its members put on trial after its dissolution; 264 were convicted, despite lack of evidence of advocacy of violence, although the proceedings dragged on for so long—until 1990, in fact—that many defendants qualified for immediate release on the basis of time already served. Even more controversial was the six-year court case against the Turkish Peace Association, in which twelve defendants, including an ex-ambassador, were convicted. An example of the relatively lenient treatment of the right was the acquittal, on appeal, of fundamentalist National Salvation Party leader Necmettin Erbakan on charges of attempting to create an Islamic state; Erbakan subsequently founded an influential Islamic successor, the Refah (Welfare) Party. The neo-fascist National Action Party, however, was decimated by eight death sentences and dozens of longer prison terms for its members. The military attacked the universities less directly, purging 1475 academic staff as of 1984 by outright dismissal, placement on non-renewed short-term contracts, or transfer to less desirable positions. All campuses were put under the control of a new body, the Higher Education Council, subject to the direct authority of the acting head of state.

In a process somewhat akin to the drafting of the 1960 constitution, a 160-strong Consultative Committee of carefully screened applicants was convened, which promulgated a new, highly **restrictive constitution** in 1982. This was ratified by ninety percent of the Turkish electorate in a controversial referendum which was also an election for the presidency. No campaigning against was allowed;

the only candidate was **General Kenan Evren**, military chief of staff and coup leader; and it was presented as an all-or-nothing package.

RETURN TO CIVILIAN RULE AND THE RISE OF ANAP

Civilian authority was tentatively re-established in the general **election of November 1983**, although severe controls were placed on parties and candidates. Pre-coup parties and their leaders remained excluded from politics, and only three of the fourteen newly formed parties were allowed to contest the elections. Nonetheless, the centrist slate backed by the generals came last, and Turgut Özal's center-right Anavatan Partisi (ANAP, Motherland Party) won just under half the votes and just over fifty percent of the parliamentary seats.

ANAP was and still is a party of uneasy alliance, incorporating a range of opinion from economic liberals and Islamists. Özal, as party leader and prime minister, managed—despite his own former membership in the fundamentalist National Salvation Party—the almost impossible task of balancing the opposing forces in the new party. Simultaneously he set a scorching pace of **economic reform** during his first term, with exports reaching record levels and growth rates averaging more than six percent during the period 1983–1988. Inflation, however, continued to soar, as public expenditure was beefed up to buy support, especially among the farmers and civil servants, and by 1986 foreign indebtedness and spiraling prices were again critical issues.

In local elections of 1984 and 1986, opposition parties gained some ground, particularly Erdal İnönü's Sosyal Halkçi (Social Democrat) Party, and the Doğru Yol (True Path) and Demokratik Sol (Democratic Left) parties, fronts respectively for the activities of still-proscribed Demirel and Ecevit. Popular pressure grew for a **lifting of the ban** on pre-coup politicians, which was narrowly approved in mid-1987. Parliamentary elections in November of that year showed just 36 percent support for ANAP but, because of a non-proportional-representation system put into effect for the occasion, it took nearly two thirds of the seats in the Grand National Assembly. The SHP emerged as the main opposition, with nearly a quarter of the seats; the DYP did badly; and Ecevit, his DSP party failing to poll the ten-percent nationwide required for representation, announced his retirement—temporarily, as it turned out—from politics.

THE LATE 1980S: TRENDS AND PROBLEMS

Özal's two prime-ministerial terms were marked by a dramatic increase in **Islamic activity**. The Department of Religious Affairs received extra staffing and funding, and the teaching hours devoted to Muslim issues in schools saw a similar rise. Much of this can be attributed to a conscious effort to offset or channel the influence of Iranian-style funda-mentalism, but there also seems to have been a deliberate policy of promoting moderate Islamic sentiment as a safeguard against the resurgence of communist ideology. Outside of the government apparatus, the *vakıfs* or pious endowments have also grown spectacularly, supported largely by donations from Saudi Arabia. Educational and welfare programs run by the *vakıfs* offer some hope and relief to those trapped in the burgeoning *gecekondus* of the principal cities, where life is most precari-ous, but the assistance has also encouraged fanatical and intolerant elements.

Kurdish separatism, an intermittent issue since the foundation of the Republic, re-surfaced in a violent form in the southeastern provinces. The main group involved is the Kurdish Workers' Party (PKK), a Marxist-Leninist group founded in 1971, and partly based in Syria, Iraq, and Iran. Its paramilitary war of attri-tion, resumed against the Turkish government and its representatives in 1984, does not appear to have won it widespread support, but its posi-tion has undoubtedly been strengthened by the frequent over-zealous actions and policies of the Turkish authorities. These include the continued ban on public use of the Kurdish language (which isn't even recognised), Kurdish child-names, the public performance of Kurdish music, and the forced relocation of village popu-lations and the provision of arms to an indige-nous security force, the "village guards." The PKK has retaliated by targeting not only these guards but any representative of the central government (e.g., teachers and other civil servants), and by making it impossible for the rural population to remain neutral.

Turkey's relations with most of its neighbors remain uneasy. **Ties with Greece** have been strained not only by the Cyprus issue but by ongoing disputes over airspace, seabed exploi-tation rights, and territorial waters in the Aegean, and by the Greek government's maltreatment of and denial of full civil rights to the Turkish-speaking minority in Greek Thrace. **Bulgarian-Turkish relations** made interna-tional headlines throughout the summer of 1989, as the Bulgarian communist regime's policy of forced Slavification of the Bulgarian Turkish minority resulted in dozens of deaths and ultimately escalated into the largest European mass emigration since World War II. Between May and August, over 300,000 ethnic Turks fled Bulgaria for Turkey, which initially welcomed them (the government had in fact invited them as part of the war of words with Bulgaria) and attempted to some extent to capi-talize politically on the exodus. When the real-ity of the number of refugees to be settled hit home, however, the border was closed, and by 1990 the new government in Sofia had formally renounced the heavy-handed assimilationist campaign of its predecessor, while up to a third of the new arrivals decided to return to Bulgaria.

In direct contrast to the Turkish govern-ment's concern for the rights of Turkish minori-ties abroad, there has been a pattern of continued **human-rights violations** at home. This has principally taken the form of inhumane conditions in prisons but more importantly the torture of suspects by law-enforcement agen-cies, and continual harassment of the press. At various times government spokesmen have admitted that torture was practiced during the 1980–83 period of military rule, when hundreds of thousands of individuals were taken into custody, but until recently they declined to comment on, or denied, allegations of continu-ing incidents. Lately a few cases of official torture during the period of civilian rule have been admitted, and some prosecutions of those responsible conducted, but their numbers have thus far been token, and the guilty have often been quietly promoted out of harm's way rather than being jailed. Abuses continue today, partic-ularly in police stations during the initial periods of detention, although the extent is difficult to establish, as is the question of whether it is sanctioned at the highest levels. Amnesty

International claims that torture is still widespread and systematic, while other monitoring organizations maintain that, while admittedly widespread, it is no longer officially condoned.

If torture may eventually cease to be a feature of Turkish civic life, restrictions on the press show no signs of abating yet. The record number of prosecutions of journalists, editors, and publishers between 1984 and 1990 may paradoxically be a result of the media's growing boldness in testing the limits of censorship. An unsettling echo of the Menderes years is the extreme sensitivity of Turgut Özal to even the mildest criticism in print, with dozens of libel and slander suits filed by government prosecutors.

Meanwhile, in not entirely unrelated developments, Turkey's European-oriented foreign policy suffered various setbacks toward the end of the decade. Turkey had been an associate member of the **European Community** since 1964, but its 1987 application for full membership was shelved indefinitely by the Community shortly after, ostensibly because of the need to concentrate on increased integration of the existing twelve member states. At the same time substantial public-relations efforts were devoted to beating back repeated proposals by the US, sponsored by the international Armenian lobby, designating April 24 as a day of "national remembrance" for the alleged genocide perpetrated against the Armenian community in 1915. This marked an increase in the sophistication of the more extreme Armenian advocates, who appear to have mostly abandoned the policy of terrorist attacks on Turkish diplomats and installations that characterized the late 1970s. Finally, the dramatic changes in eastern Europe further marginalized the country, as Soviet influence in the region collapsed and doubts were cast on the future strategic importance of a post-Cold War NATO in general and Turkey in particular. In short, Turkish foreign policy was foundering by the late 1980s, deprived of a coherent position and often reduced to reacting to, rather than influencing, events.

THE 1990S AND BEYOND

Turgut Özal's **elevation to the presidency** in November 1989 set the stage for him and his circle of family and friends to extend their hold on Turkish political life. As prime minister, he had skillfully maintained a balance between the religious and secular wings of ANAP, and now, as president, he has been doing the same on a nationwide scale. Despite his official description as being "above-party," Özal is still widely perceived as the real leader of ANAP. He was instrumental in choosing the next prime minister, Yıldırım Akbulut, an extremely lackluster yes-man. Akbulut has thus far been unable to command much respect either within the party or in the general population, where the repetition and even publishing of jokes at his expense has become a favorite pastime. His position has repeatedly been undermined by Özal himself, who has—in apparent contravention of the constitution—assumed many of the executive functions of the prime minister. Özal's interference has also prompted the resignations of several other cabinet ministers, including foreign minister Mesut Yılmaz.

Iraq's **invasion of Kuwait** in August 1990 reinforced Özal's position, and also reminded NATO and the US of Turkey's continuing strategic position. Özal, and not Akbulut or Yılmaz, contacted other heads of state and was central in defining Turkey's stance as an enthusiastic adherent of the UN sanctions—perhaps in anticipation of tangible rewards from the West for such support. The Gulf crisis provided a needed boost to Özal's popularity, which had slumped following his election as head of state, widely seen as self-aggrandizement, by a compliant and ANAP-dominated parliament. Much of the public is in fact grateful that he, and not Akbulut, is effectively in control.

However, a nationwide **political vacuum** in terms of maturity and substance is growing. ANAP, beset by resignations, defections, and factions, has lost its original energy and direction, but the opposition parties have not yet been able to turn this to their advantage. The SHP, rent by a recent internal power struggle in which chairman Erdal İnönü ousted general secretary Deniz Baykal, confines itself to making critical comments on every government move. Bülent Ecevit's DSP rebounded from a nadir in its fortunes by doing extremely well at the SHP's expense in the August 1990 municipal elections; İnönü renewed his oft-repeated call for a merger of the two parties but was rebuffed by Ecevit, who perhaps thinks he can sustain momentum until the next national elections, which must be held by August 1992.

Demirel's DYP took a drubbing in the local polls, and overall the electorate is uninspired by the politics of personalities, and in the absence of a national agenda and policy statements has little idea of what the various parties stand for. The only consensus that seems to have developed is the full **rehabilitation of Menderes** and his cronies, an act of contrition that has taken the form of a spate of streets and public facilities named after Menderes—and, on the thirtieth anniversary of the hangings of the three executed ministers, their solemn reburial in a special mausoleum.

Turkey is in fact at a critical juncture where almost anything seems possible. A sharp increase in urban terrorism during 1990, with more than a dozen **political assassinations** perpetrated by both Islamic fundamentalists and far-leftists, could herald a return to the civil strife of the past; and Turkey's involvement in the war against Iraq cannot help. However, a coup appears unlikely in the immediate future, and the completion of another ten-year cycle in 1990 without tanks on the streets was greeted with relief. In many respects the country is booming, and both the economy and improved electronic communications have reached levels of sophistication sufficient to make control by martial law difficult—it seems very unlikely that a fresh military intervention would have either public or Western support. On the down side, numerous destabilizing factors persist: the domestic inflation and foreign debt is demoralizing, the troubles in the southeast continue more or less unabated, and most important of all, **Islamic militancy** continues to increase.

A December 1989 decree empowering individual universities to allow, at their discretion, women to wear headscarves is perhaps just the thin edge of a wedge of increased religiosity*, a development mirrored by the growing electoral strength of the fundamentalist Welfare Party. Özal and ANAP have in fact been fostering an uneasy synthesis of techno-cratic Westernization and Islam, but the stability of such a hybrid is debatable. The *Sharia* (the Islamic law code operating in Iran, Saudi Arabia, Sudan, etc) is clearly incompatible with Western norms of civil and human rights. The imposition of such a code would have far-reaching effects within Turkey, where—for example—women, after seven decades of nominal Kemalist emancipation, would find themselves unable to hold public office or drive, and where a ban on banking interest would decouple Turkey from the world economy.

Finally, and perhaps most importantly, a full-scale fundamentalist revival would sink any chance of **admission to the EC**, although this remains a moot point and at best will not occur before the new millennium. Already sixteen million East Germans have leapfrogged past Turkey, and it's not inconceivable that Austria, Norway, and Hungary will do likewise. Other formidable obstacles to full membership include Turkey's spotty human-rights record, many clauses of the 1982 constitution, the seemingly intractable under-development of the east, and the continued partition of Cyprus, but above all a quasi-racist attitude in Europe that sees Turkey as a Third World country inherently unsuitable for membership in a "white, Christian" club. For their own part, some Turkish intellectuals regard full EC membership as a reward for past services rendered to NATO, or imagine that Turkey will thus be passively insured against further rule by its military. They might gently be reminded that three newer EC members—Spain, Portugal, and Greece—with previous authoritarian regimes had disposed of them and their legacy in advance of joining, and that more active remedial measures on the part of Turkey are expected.

There is the very real danger that if Turkey is kept waiting too long or rejected outright by the EC, the fundamentalists will be able to crow that they were right all along to reject the West, and the country may well go through a period of obscurantist regimes. On the other hand alternative directions may exist. A closer relationship to the US, the development of a Black Sea trading block, and a new sense of self-confidence could all serve to foster a sense of identity that would help insulate the country from fundamentalism.

---

*It may seem strange that the freedom to wear Islamic dress is opposed by many "secularists," but in Turkey secularism has always been a matter of suppressing the public expression of religion and keeping it out of politics, as opposed to the Western notion of freedom of belief and equal treatment for all religions.

MUSIC OF TURKEY

There's a tremendous variety of music in Turkey, and arriving at your first Turkish cassette shop you'll be confronted by a vast choice, and probably won't have a clue where to start. The best advice is to keep your ears and eyes open as you travel.

Probably the first sort of music you'll hear will be either **arabesk** or **taverna**, which account for around 80 percent of the country's cassette sales. If you don't like them, don't despair—there's plenty of good music to be had, but, as everywhere, there is also a lot of junk. During your stay, you'll hear tapes playing in buses, teahouses, and shops. Don't be afraid to ask someone what they're listening to—it's the best way to discover what you like. Tapes are cheap (around $2 at the current rate of exchange) and generally of adequate quality.

To see **live music**, the likeliest spots are city restaurants. Venues are listed in the weekly music paper **Müzik Magazin** under the section *Türkiye'deki Tüm Gazinolar*. The magazine also carries six charts, which are useful for reference. The categories are: **Türk müziği** (*sanat*, or "art" music); **halk müziği** (folk music); **arabesk**, **taverna**; **özgün** (protest music); and **pop müziği** (Turkish and Western pop).

HALK MÜZİĞİ

Folk music (*halk müziği*) is still a living tradition in Turkey, but there are signs of decline, caused partly by the broadcasting and recording industries. Recently folklore groups have been founded in many areas to preserve a slowly dying art. *Halk müziği* can be divided into four rough categories: Turkish rural music; Kurdish music; *ozan*; and *türkü*.

TURKISH RURAL MUSIC

In general, the folk music styles of all the Turkish provinces are very similar; striking differences are found only around the eastern Black-Sea, close to the Syrian border, and in the predominantly Kurdish eastern region.

In Turkish villages, music is made primarily at **celebrations** such as weddings or annual festivals. Weddings can often last for three days, and from mid-morning to midnight loud dance music of the *davul* and *zurna* or *klarnet* (see box for an introduction to these instruments) is audible some distance away. **Dances** are performed by segregated groups of men or women, who link hands and arms to form a long line—if you're watching you will invariably be asked to join in. Wedding music, together with dance tunes, children's songs, and game songs, are all forms of *kırık hava* or "broken melody," and are characterized by incessant but very danceable rhythms.

In the area around Trabzon and Rise on the Black Sea, *kemençe* music is the most popular. The *kemençe* is not only played at weddings and other festivities, but also for personal enjoyment, and you'll often see shopkeepers or barbers fiddling away when there are no customers around. *Kemençe* music is played at an exceptionally fast tempo, marked out by drums or stamping feet. Two good cassettes of *kemançe* music are "*Kayana/Laziko*" by **Yusuf Cemal Keskin** and "*Muhabbet Alemi/1*" by **Hüseyin Köse**. At celebrations in the area between Rise and the Soviet border you may also hear the *tulum* (bagpipe); a good example of this music can be heard on "*Peştamallı Kız*" by **Riseli Mustafa Sırtlı**.

OZAN

Ozan is the music of the folk-poets of Anatolia, who are usually referred to as *aşıks*, meaning "the ones in love." The *aşıks* have wandered the plains of Anatolia since around the tenth century, putting music to the words of legendary poets like Yunus Emre, Pir Sultan Abdal, and Sefil Ali, as well as writing their own songs. *Aşıks* belong to the **Bektaşi/Alevî** faith, which combines wisdom with warmth and stresses unity, understanding, and equality between all men and women. Despite this, many *aşıks* have been the subject of mistrust and contempt from orthodox Sunni Muslims. *Aşıks* accompany themselves on the *saz*, a long-necked lute with three sets of strings, representing the fundamental trinity of their faith: Allah, Mohammed, and Ali.

Today a large number of *aşıks* still make cassettes, and even more play in the villages and towns of central Anatolia. One of the greatest in recent years was **Aşık Veysel**, a blind singer who died in 1974. There are still several tapes of his available, and many of his songs, such as "*Bülbül*" (The Nightingale) and "*Kara Toprak*" (My Faithful, Beloved Black Earth), are sung by other *aşıks* and singers of *türkü* (see below). His best recordings are available on the French *Ocora* label, and are the only ones made in a village setting—those cut in the sterile environment of the Radio Ankara studios are like hearing a caged bird sing.

A group worth looking out for is **Muhabbet**, which combines the talents of some of the best *aşıks* in Turkey today. **Arif Sağ**, **Musa Eroğlu**, **Muhlis Akarsu**, and **Yavuz Top** alternate between releasing solo cassettes and playing with Muhabbet. As a group they have released seven tapes and there are dozens more solo offerings. Of the many other *aşıks* with tapes available, **Ali Ekber Çiçek**, **Murat Çobanoğlu**, **Feyzullah Çınar**, and **Mazlumi ve Asım Mırık** are all worth hearing.

KURDISH MUSIC

Around ten million Kurds live within the political boundaries of Turkey. Their folklore and national identity is preserved with the help of *dengbej* (bards), *stranbej* (popular singers), and *cirokbej* (storytellers). A *dengbej* is a singer with an exceptional memory, in effect the guardian of the Kurdish national heritage, since he must know hundreds of songs for which there is no written notation. *Dengbejs* sing about the Kurdish myths and legends, the struggle for freedom and the successive rulers and occupiers of their land, love songs, and music for entertainment.

Sadly, some of the best Kurdish *dengbejs*, like **Şivan Perwer** and **Temo**, now live in exile in Europe.

The main instruments used in Kurdish music are wind instruments, such as the *blur* and the *düdük*, found in the mountainous regions where the echo from the hills is taken advantage of; and string instruments, such as the *tembur* and the *saz*, used in the towns of the plains.

TÜRKÜ

Türkü is folk-based urban popular music. It takes its melodies from the folk tradition, playing them on a mixture of folk, Western, and Arabic instruments. The weekly *Halk Müziği* chart prominently features *türkü* music, and stars like **Belkis Akkale**, **Burhan Çaçan**, and **Nuray Hafiftaş** are constantly battling for top positions. Other artists worth hearing include **Beşir Kaya** and **İzzet Altımeşe**.

URBAN MUSIC

ÖZGÜN

Özgün is the protest music of Turkey, sounding quite somber on first impression, but often very moving and sometimes danceable. The lyrics are central to *özgün* music, so for non-Turkish-speakers a lot of the impact is lost. The music mixes elements of folk, *türkü*, and *sanat* (see below), with considerable variation between artists. **Ruhi Su** plays in a style that has much in common with music of the *aşıks*, whereas **Selda** shows more *türkü* influence. Stalwarts **Zülfü Livaneli** and **Fatih Kısparmak** are prone to lushly arranged orchestral backing.

ARABESK AND TAVERNA

Arabesk and *taverna* represent the disposable side of popular music, full of catchy choruses that have you humming the tune in five minutes and forgetting it in ten. If you go to a tape shop, either *arabesk* or *taverna* will invariably be playing and, if you like it, the shopkeeper will show you hundreds of other new releases to tempt you. *Arabesk* mixes the insipid side of Arabic *chabbi* (pop music) with the gaudiness of Western showbiz. Long-established stars like **Coşkun Sabah**, **İbrahim Tatlıses**, and **Orhan Gencebay**, and up-and-coming stars like **Küçük Emrah**, sell tapes by the millions.

Taverna is a fairly recent innovation, the offspring of Greek taverna music and Turkish cabaret, drawing to some extent on folk music and *arabesk*. Even more disposable than the

INSTRUMENTS

PERCUSSION

Davul or *ramzalla:* Large double-sided drum. Each side is used with different-sized sticks to create a bass-and-snare-drum-like effect.

Def: Kurdish bass drum.

Deblek, *dümbelek*, or *dar(a)buka:* Goblet-shaped drum made of pottery, wood, or metal and played with the hands. In Kurdish it's called a *demblik*.

Küdüm: Small kettledrums usually played in pairs, with sticks.

Bendit: Frame drums of assorted sizes.

Tef: Frame drum with added snares or metal rings inside the frame.

Zil: Pair of small cymbals.

Kaşık: A set of wooden or metal spoons, often brightly painted, that are manipulated like chopsticks by placing the handles of the spoons between the fingers.

Erbane: Kurdish tambourine.

WIND INSTRUMENTS

Zurna: A very loud double-reed oboe-type instrument with seven finger-holes, made of wood with a conical body ending in a large bell. In Kurdish it's called a *zirne*.

Tulum: A bagpipe found in Rise and Artvin provinces, near the Soviet border. It generally has two pipes, each with five finger-holes, inserted into a goatskin bag which the player inflates before he begins. In Turkish Thrace, a nearly identical instrument is called *gayda*.

Ney: An end-blown flute requiring enormous skill to play, despite its simple design. It is made from bamboo, calamus reed, or hardwood, with six finger-holes in front and a thumb-hole in the back.

Kaval: An end-blown flute made of wood, with seven finger-holes in the front and one thumb-hole behind. A favorite instrument of Turkish shepherds.

Klarnet: Clarinet.

Mey and *düdük:* These are essentially the same, being called *mey* in western Turkey and *düdük* in eastern Turkey and neighboring Soviet Republics. Both are small, oboe-like instruments with a very large reed and a much sweeter tone than the *zurna*. The *düdük* is also the name given to a simple duct flute that you see for sale in markets throughout the country.

Çifte or *arghul:* A double instrument sounding similar to the clarinet, with two mouthpieces and two sets of finger-holes on a pair of bamboo pipes. Often one set is used as a continuous drone. The *arghul* is found only in a small area near the Syrian border, and is related to the *arghoul* played in Egypt and Syria. The *çifte* is peculiar to the environs of Ereğli on the western Black Sea.

Blur: A Kurdish shepherd's flute made from a branch of either mulberry or walnut, with seven or nine finger-holes.

STRING INSTRUMENTS

Kemençe (or *kemançe*): A fiddle with three strings, originally used by the shepherds of the Black Sea coast. It has an oblong wooden body and a short neck. *Kemençe* are held vertically and played with a bow of horsehair or, more recently, nylon.

Keman: Originally a round-bodied version of the *kemençe*; now the name more commonly refers to a standard violin, often preferred for its tone.

Rebab: A pear-shaped relative of the *kemençe* used in classical and Mevlevi dervish music.

Saz: Long-necked lute, usually with seven strings (two pairs, and one set of three) played with a very thin plectrum. Several variations include the *divan saz*, with eight strings; the *cura saz*, with six strings; and the *bağlama*, with seven strings on a shorter neck and a large bulbous body.

Ud: A fretless lute with eleven strings (five pairs and one single), and nearly identical to the *oud* found throughout the Arab world.

Cümbüş: A fretless banjo-type lute that substitutes for the *ud* when playing with louder instruments. It has a large resonating metal bowl covered with skin or plastic.

Saz tambur: Smaller fretted version of the *cümbüş*.

Tambur or *tembur:* A very long-necked lute with three strings and a large, almost rectangular body, noted for its very deep tone.

Yaylı tambur: Bowed version of the above, its tone somewhere between a cello and double bass.

Kanun: A trapezoidal zither with between forty and a hundred strings, and a system of levers for tuning to different scales quickly.

latter, it could easily be used as elevator or supermarket muzak. In recent years sales have been catching up with *arabesk*, and stars like **Cengiz Kurtoğlu**, **Metin Kaya**, and **Karışık** are constantly topping the chart. Not long ago, **Karışık** managed to have eight cassettes in the top 25 at once.

SANAT

Sanat means "art," and fifteen to twenty years ago the term accurately described the music. Times have changed, however, and the once-great **Zeki Müren**, **Bülent Ersoy**, **Emel Sayın**, and their contemporaries are now just crooning their way into old age. The cassette-buying public, hungry for new sounds, has all but forgotten the days of other top singers like **Münir Nurettin Selçuk**, **Müzeyyen Senar**, and Atatürk's favorite, **Safiye Ayla**, and the rich textures of their orchestral backing.

You might find an old **Zeki Müren** tape in cassette stores but you'll be better off trying junk shops for old records. Zeki is a gay transvestite with a status in Turkey roughly equivalent to Frank Sinatra, and has topped the *sanat* chart consistently for the past twenty years. Earlier in his career, his music was based on classical style with room for his voice to flourish; although he still reaches number one, he is now definitely past his prime.

CLASSICAL AND RELIGIOUS MUSIC

OTTOMAN AND MEVLEVI MUSIC

Turkish classical music, which includes the music of the Mevlevi, is the product of the Ottoman civilization. It is based on modal systems or *makams*, an analogue to the western scale system formulated over five centuries ago, and the traditional classical repertoire in Turkey today is selected almost entirely from notated sources preserving the works of such composers as **Abdülkadir Meragi** (died 1435), **Prince Cantemir** (17th–18th century) and **Sultan Selim III**.

The Mevlevi order of dervishes has provided its own, related body of ritual music that contains many of the most highly regarded compositions from the sixteenth to the twentieth centuries. The best-known Mevlevi composers are **Köçek Derviş Mustafa Dede** (17th century), **Dede Efendi** (18th–19th century), and **Rauf Yekta** (19th–20th century).

Public concerts are given in theaters, concert halls, and in radio broadcasts, often with large ensembles of over thirty instrumentalists and singers. One of the most famous ensembles is the İstanbul Municipal Conservatory's **Klâsik İcra Heyeti**, which often gives concerts around İstanbul, and on Sunday mornings these and other such performances may be broadcast live on Radio İstanbul. The instruments normally used by classical ensembles include *tambur*, *ney*, *rebab* or *kemençe*, *keman*, *kanun*, *ud*, and *küdüm*.

The single most important Mevlevi musical event of the year is the annual **Mevlana festival**, held in Konya during the two weeks preceding December 17. Compositions for the ceremony are called *ayin*, and the musicians are collectively known as the *mutrip*. The *mutrip* predominantly play the two traditional Mevlevi instruments, *ney* and *küdüm*, although *tambur*, *kanun*, and *rebab* are sometimes used.

FASLI

The *faslı*, or semi-classical, style can be described as a nightclub version of classical Turkish music, essentially a vocal suite of light orchestral pieces. The music has a distinctly gypsy flavor, and every short rest is filled with flourishes and improvisations from the stars of the orchestra, which would be frowned upon in strictly classical circles. The main instruments used are *klarinet*, *keman*, *ud*, *cümbüs*, *kanun*, *darabuka*, and *yaylı tambur*.

Currently the best-known artists of this genre are *klarnet* player **Mustafa Kandıralı**, *kanun* player **Ahmet Yatman**, *ud* player **Kardi Şençalar**, and vocalists **Suzan Bizimer** and **Kemal Gürses**.

Dave Muddyman

SELECTED DISCOGRAPHY

Şivan Perwer: *Vol. 9 & 11* (Kurdistan Yekitiya Hunermenden 9 & 11). Arguably the finest Kurdish singer. Both collections contain Şivan's powerful voice and *saz* accompaniment, backed by *düdük* and *blur*, with Western keyboards and classical Arabic instruments like *ud* and *kanun*.

Aşık Veysel: One disc of *Voyages d'Alain Gheerbrant en Anatolie* (Ocora 558634). The only recording of Veysel in a village. Wonderfully supported by his constant companion Küçük Veysel, who sings in imitating unison with the master. Produced in France and easily available.

Aşık Veysel: *Dostlar Beni Hatırasın* (Diskotür DTK 503). The best of his Radio Ankara recordings; rather sterile sound, but contains many of his most treasured songs.

Muhabbet: *5* (Zirve 1008) & *88* (Pınar 003). Combined talent of four of the greatest *saz* players. All have deep, resonating voices, which add soulful respite to the wash of fine *saz* interludes.

Arif Sağ: *Halay* (Nora 001). Arif Sağ has been one of Turkey's favorite singers for many years, releasing dozens of records and tapes, both solo and with Muhabbet. This tape features complex rhythms, superb *saz* playing, and solos from many Turkish folk instruments.

Yavuz Top: *Deyişler-1* (Sembol plak 1048). A fast and vibrant tape from another member of Muhabbet. The flutes and *saz* play melodic interchanges over pulsating rhythms.

Mazlumi ve Asım Mırık: *Şölende Sohbet-2* (Şölen 013). Two relatively unknown *saz* players accompanied by the *mey*. An atmospheric and melodic collection of songs.

Özalarımızla 90 Dakika: (Harika 4052). A ninety-minute compilation of different *aşıks* that include **Murat Çobanoğlu**, **Ali Ekber**, **Feyzullah Çır**, and **Reyhani**. A good introduction to *ozan* music.

Türküler Gecidi: (Türküola 2265). Another wonderful ninety-minute hit-parade from the world of *türkü*, featuring **Belkis Akkale**, **Burhan Çaçan**, **Mahmut Tunçer**, and others.

Diyarbakırlı Beşir Kaya: *Derman Kalmadı* (Özdemir 023). The sound of *düdük*, *saz*, and *mey* blend beautifully with bass guitar, kit drums, and Beşir's soaring voice. The modern sound of eastern Turkey and very danceable.

Belkis Akkale: *Türkü Türkü Türkiyem* (Sembol plak 1011). Possibly the greatest *türkü* singer at her best. Almost all traditional instruments of Turkey are in here somewhere.

Sümeyra: *Kadınlarımızın Yüzleri* (Yeni Dünya). Female *özgün* singer with one of the most soulful voices in Turkey, accompanying herself on the *saz*.

Selda: (Uzelli 1155). Selda is equally at home singing *türku* and *özgün*. This collection features both and includes the wonderful "*Dost Merhaba.*"

Ruhi Su: *Zeybekler* (IMECE 27). One of the greatest *özgün* singers with a collection of old western Anatolian ballads sung in Ruhi's characteristical forceful style.

Boğaziçi: *Türk Müziğinde Rum Bestekârlar* (Columbia TCP 2239). A mixture of Greek and Turkish musicians playing music of the Byzantine, Ottoman, and Mevlevi traditions. Beautiful recording of courtly classical, "art", and sacred music.

Ancient Turkish Music in Europe: (Diskotür HDK 5034). Ottoman music from the sixteenth to eighteenth centuries recorded by the Bakfark Balint lute trio of Hungary. A mixture of vibrant dances and sedate court music.

Mevlana: *Mistik Türk Müziği Şaheserleri serisi*, Vol 1–6 (Kent). One of the best sets of Mevlevi music. Any of them will provide a good introduction to the beautiful and soothing music of the Mevlevi, though volumes 1 and 2 may prove difficult to find.

Folk Music of Turkey: (Topic 12 TS 333). An excellent selection of many styles of Turkish folk music. Produced in Britain as part of a series covering Balkan music.

TURKISH FILMS

The work of Yılmaz Güney aside, Turkish films are little known outside Turkey, perhaps a result of its preoccupations with what most foreign critics perceive as strictly local issues like rural to urban population drift and the dislocation of traditional lifestyles. However, throughout the 1970s and 80s Turkish directors produced a number of powerful movies worthy of wider recognition. Now that the artistic restrictions that followed the 1980 coup show some signs of relaxing, there is every chance that the 1990s will be a rich decade for Turkish cinema.

Filmmaking as an art form in Turkey has only emerged over the last couple of decades or so, although the local motion-picture industry has been churning out low-budget melodrama for the better part of seventy years, and indeed continues to do so. All forms of filmmaking have been handicapped by lack of financing and technical resources, and filmmakers wishing to address social or political issues also have to contend with state censorship. While this has put constraints on directors and writers, however, it has also meant that some recent films deal with aspects of everyday life in Turkey in a lyrical, almost mythic way, attempting to allegorize a reality that cannot always be dealt with directly.

THE GROWTH OF THE INDUSTRY

The history of film in Turkey began in 1897 when **Sigmund Weinberg**, a Romanian café owner in the Pera district of İstanbul, screened the city's first motion picture. This did not, however, lead to a moving-picture boom and it was not until World War I that the government, realizing the propaganda value of film, set up several **army film units**. These units put together a number of documentaries, although the first movie ever produced under Turkish government auspices (recording the demolition of a Russian monument in İstanbul) was shot under the direction of an Austrian military crew. A Turkish projectionist, **Fuat Uzkınay**, took the largely symbolic role of holding the camera, under close Austrian supervision.

By the end of the war Turkish military filmmakers had mastered their trade sufficiently to go on and make a documentary record of the War of Independence. With the end of hostilities a number of **production companies** were set up, including one owned jointly by Sigmund Weinberg and Fuat Uzkınay, the cameraman at that first documentary shoot, and Turkey's feature-film industry came into existence.

During the 1920s a trend of awkward adaptations of works by seventeenth-century French playwrights like Molière was established, a field that was dominated by two companies, İpek Film and Kemal Film. The leading director of the period was **Muhsin Ertuğrul**, who made 29 movies between 1922 and 1953. His resume also includes a couple of War of Independence features: *Ateş'ten Gömlek* (*The Shirt of Fire*; 1923) and *Bir Millet Uyaniyor* (*The Awakening of a Nation*; 1932). These movies did refer to actual events, rather than offer a distorted vision of life in the France of Louis XIV, but they never sought to challenge the official line of Kemalist Turkey; nor did they break any new ground artistically.

Any attempts to do either would have probably foundered against the government's rigorous **censorship** laws. All films faced a three-tiered process; first, scripts were censored before filming began, then the police controlled sequences as they were shot, and finally government censors inspected the finished work, excising contentious material.

Governmental stifling of creativity was exacerbated by a chronic lack of cash and equipment, with the result that by World War II the staple fare of Turkish picture houses was Hollywood productions and laughable B-movies churned out in Egypt by a Turkish producer, **V.O. Bengü**.

In quantitative terms the output of the Turkish film industry picked up significantly in the 1950s with the establishment of a genre of mass-entertainment **melodrama** that continues to this day. These films had a very basic premise that was to prove successful time and time again: rural boy meets rural girl, the world tries to keep them apart (in more sophisticated variants one is temporarily blind to the virtues of the other) but, ultimately, they triumph over tragedy and live happily ever after, having achieved fame and fortune along the way. Unsophisticated and sometimes illiterate rural and small-town audiences are still lapping up these films, and ensuring the continuing financial, if not artistic, wellbeing of hundreds of actors and directors.

One positive effect of this increased cinematic activity was that it enabled a **new generation** of young filmmakers to master the skills of cinematography, among them Yılmaz Güney and a number of others who, in the 1960s and 1970s, would go on to develop a homegrown Turkish cinematic identity.

THE NEW WAVE: YILMAZ GÜNEY

It was during the 1960s that the first attempts were made to produce films that moved away from melodrama into the realm of social criticism. A leading director of the period was **Lüfti Ö. Akad** who, having cut his teeth on melodramas and a few derivative gangster pictures during the 1940s and 1950s, went on to direct *Tanrı'nın Bağışı Orman* (*The Forest, God's Gift*) in 1964, a documentary study of the feudal hierarchy in Anatolia. In 1966 he made *Hudutların Kanunu* (*The Law of the Frontier*), a dramatic treatment of similar issues, dealing specifically with the stranglehold of wealthy landlords on the rural population in the southeast. He later directed *Kızılırmak-Karakoyun* (*Red River, Black Sheep*), based on a play by poet Nazim Hikmet. Between 1973 and 1975

Akad produced an important trilogy, exploring the drift of population from rural Anatolia to the cities and the conflict between traditional lifestyles and modern, Westernized city life: *Gelin* (*The Bride*), *Düğün* (*The Wedding*), and *Diyet* (*The Retaliation*).

In the 1970s **Yılmaz Güney** took over as Turkey's leading serious director and became, in the process, the only Turkish director to gain real recognition outside his native land. After serving his apprenticeship on the melodramas of the 1950s, Güney had scripted *Hudutların Kanunu* for Akad and took the lead acting role in *Kızılırmak-Karakoyun*. His first major film was *Umut* (*Hope*; 1970); the story of a cabdriver who loses his house and stakes his remaining money on a mad treasure-hunting venture. Though not an outstanding film, it is indicative of the thematic direction that Güney's later films were to take, and certain scenes, notably the final one where the maddened hero circles a hole in the ground blindfolded, are echoed in later films.

Umut was followed in 1971 by *Ağıt* (*The Elegy*), in which a man is forced to resort to smuggling by economic circumstance, and *Acık* (*Sorrow*), a film about lost love and revenge. Güney was imprisoned after the 1971 coup, and remained in jail until 1974. On his release he made *Arkadaş* (*The Friend*), which, like the earlier *Umutsuzlar* (*The Hopeless*) and *Baba* (*The Father*), dealt with the lot of Turkey's urban poor, an area in which Güney was less confident as a director. In the same year Güney was imprisoned again, accused of murdering a judge. He began directing **films from his cell**—writing scripts and passing on instructions to fellow-directors; paradoxically, some of his finest work was produced in this period.

In 1979 *Sürü* (*The Herd*), written by Güney and directed by **Zeki Ökten**, was released. Like Güney's earlier films the theme is that of rural dislocation. Life among feuding nomadic families in the south is the starting point; with their traditional grazing lands threatened by development, a Kurdish family decides to take its sheep to the markets of Ankara. Visually the film is dominated by the road and rail journey of the shepherds and their flocks, and this is used to highlight the dichotomy between their lifestyle and city ways. The political turmoil that surrounds them, but which they are barely aware of, is suggested by characteristic Güney touches: almost impressionistic sequences of manacled prisoners and a youth being shot for distributing pamphlets.

Güney also worked on his most famous film, **Yol** (*The Road*), from his prison cell, with the outside directorial assistance of **Serif Gören**. It's an extraordinary film, taking an allegorical look at the state of the nation by following the fortunes of five prisoners who have been allowed a week's parole. Even when temporarily released they are unable to make their own way through a society that seems unreal to them, and their behavior is determined by social conditions over which they have no control. One prisoner, Ömer, returns to his Kurdish village and is faced with a choice between returning to prison or taking to the hills. He eventually opts for the latter but there is the sense that he doesn't really make the decision himself, but rather that it's forced on him. The film focuses, though, on Seyit Ali, who returns to his village to find that his wife, who has become a prostitute, is being held by his brothers, who expect him to kill her. He rebels against this, refusing to murder her, but abandoning her in the snow—after a change of heart he returns to save her, only to find that she is dead. The scenes in which he strides through the snow are among the most powerful in any Güney film. Güney, having escaped from jail, was able to edit this film himself in exile in France, and the final result, released in 1982, is permeated by a strong sense of longing for his homeland.

Güney's last film was *Duvar* (*The Wall*), made during his French exile and released in 1983. It's a composite portrait of Turkish prison life, focusing on the experiences of a group of young detainees, who are little more than children. The prison of the film becomes a microcosm of Turkish society as seen through the eyes of the men, women, and children who are its inmates. The prison hierarchy, with the prison governor at the top, is shown as unmerciful and inflexible; complaints are responded to with violence and the prisoners have no possible chance of redress for the wrongs done to them. This is graphically demonstrated by the fate of Şabah, one of the young inmates; he is sexually assaulted by one of the guards and, encouraged by his fellow inmates, decides to report the incident to the prison doctor. At the last moment his nerve fails him. His friends duly ostracize him, and in despair Şabah attempts to escape and is killed. Güney himself died of cancer, aged 46, the year after *Duvar*'s release.

An important contemporary of Güney was **Ömer Kavur**. His first film, *Emine*, was released in 1974. Set in a small provincial town at the turn of the century, the film looked at the role of women in traditional society. In 1979 Ömer directed *Yusuf ile Kenan* (*Yusuf and Kenan*), the story of two young boys forced to leave their village after their father is killed in a blood feud. An increasingly important element of modern Turkish life, the experience of the migrant worker, was explored in **Tunç Okan**'s *Otobüs* (*The Bus*,1977). The film examines the dislocating effect of having to leave the homeland in search of work through the eyes of a group of Turks who, having come to Sweden in search of work, find themselves abandoned in Stockholm, ripped off by a fellow countryman.

THE 1980s AND BEYOND

With the political turmoil and violence of the late 1970s there was a severe reduction in the output of the Turkish cinema, although 1980 saw the release of *Hazal*, directed by **Ali Özgentürk**, a dramatic depiction of life in a spectacularly isolated, semi-feudal village, where a young woman attempts to escape from an arranged marriage to a ten-year-old boy in order to be with her lover. Retribution is swift and harsh and the film is played out in the evocative setting of a terraced mountain village. In the wake of the 1980 coup, the work of many directors was banned, and the Turkish film industry was effectively driven into exile.

The early to mid-1980s saw something of a revival. In 1982 Ali Özgentürk made *At* (*The Horse*), a co-production with West Germany which has been described as a harsher reworking of *The Bicycle Thieves*. The film tells the story of a peasant and his son who arrive in İstanbul in search of a better life. The father hopes to be able to earn enough as a street trader to put his son through school, but is inevitably overwhelmed by life in the big city.

Hakkâri'de bir mevsim (*A Season in Hakkâri*), directed by **Erdan Kıral** in another co-production with West Germany, was released in 1983. Arguably the best Turkish film of the decade, and certainly the one that won most international acclaim, it's a visually stunning film examining the experiences of a young teacher sent to a distant Kurdish village to take over the local school. He is shocked by the poverty and isolated from the locals by a language and culture gap. Gradually, however, through his relationship with two local orphans, the girl Zazi and her brother Halit (a smuggler, also excluded from village life), he comes to identify with his surroundings, a process helped when the locals call on his aid during an epidemic. When he receives notice from the authorities that he can leave the village he is reluctant to go, having found a stability hitherto unknown in his rootless existence.

Although many recent Turkish films have been notably subdued, often skirting or totally avoiding any attempts at political comment, a number have been made from the middle of the decade on that address issues of social hypocrisy and the position of women in Turkish society. *Bir Yudum Sevgi* (*A Sip of Love*), directed by **Atif Yılmaz** in 1984, looks at one woman's struggle to win her personal independence. Related themes emerge in *Asiye*, an unusual musical adapted from a play, lambasting the notion of the woman as male property through the tale of a peasant woman who becomes a prostitute and later a brothel-madam.

The director **Başar Sabuncu** chalked up a number of noteworthy films during the decade. *Çıplak Vatandaş* (*The Naked Citizen*, 1986) is a fairly light-hearted satire, following the fortunes of a man who, while temporarily deranged by economic misfortune and confrontation with bureaucracy, runs almost naked through his home town, only to be subsequently exploited by an advertising firm that uses him in a TV commercial for bath salts. *Kupa Kızı* (*Queen of Hearts*), released the following year, is an acidic reworking of *Belle de Jour*, telling the story of a woman who turns part-time prostitute and uses sex as a means of revenge. In *Asılacak Kadın* (*A Woman to be Hanged*), a young woman becomes a judicial scapegoat for the murder of an old man who has sexually abused her. The film fell foul of the censor and its release resulted in the banning of the novel that inspired it for

"offending national morality." Sabuncu's next film, in 1988, was *Zengin Mutfağı* (*Kitchen of the Rich*), an adaptation of a play set among the servants in the kitchen of a wealthy family, intended as an allegory of the situation immediately before the 1971 military coup.

Other 1980s films worthy of mention include **Nesli Çölgecen**'s 1986 effort *Ağa* (*Landlord*) and Ömer Kavur's 1986 return to the director's chair, *Anayurt Oteli* (*Motherland Hotel*). The former examines the struggles of a wealthy landlord in the southeast, unable to come to terms with changes in rural life. Here a severe drought is substituted for the socio-economic forces that might have caused these changes had the film been made a decade earlier. Kavur's film is set in a small town near İzmir where an obsessive and lonely hotel owner's life falls apart when an attractive female guest breaks a promise to make a return visit. The film breaks new ground for Turkish cinema, exploring psychological and emotive issues with a previously unknown depth. Another important late-1980s film was *Kırk Metre Kare Almanya'da* (*Forty Square Meters of Germany*), directed by **Tevfik Başer** in 1987, which looks at the experience of Turkish migrant workers through the eyes of a village woman brought to Hamburg and confined in a dismal apartment while her husband goes off to work.

Recent efforts seem to indicate that Turkish directors once again feel secure enough to question openly the way their society functions and refer to political conditions within Turkey. Tunç Başaran's *Uçurtmayı Vurmasınlar* (*Don't Let them Shoot the Kite*, 1989), about the relationship that develops in jail between a sensitive inmate and the five-year-old son of a woman doing time for drug-dealing, touches on an area of Turkish life that, earlier in the decade, would have been out of bounds to filmmakers. *Blackout Nights* (1990), by **Yusuf Kürçenli**, goes even further. Based on an autobiographical novel by the poet Rıfat Ilgaz, who was arrested as a suspected communist at the end of World War II, it questions the need for censorship and attacks political oppression.

It is significant that a recent film should be preoccupied by subject matter like this. It indicates that as far as directors are concerned these remain big issues, a reflection perhaps on the broader state of Turkish society.

TURKISH WRITERS

Turkish literature, like so much else about the country, is virtually unknown abroad except for the epic works of Yaşar Kemal. This is regrettable, because Turkish authors particularly excell in the genre of short stories and memoirs. On the whole, writing in the country is heavily biased toward accounts of city life, particularly İstanbul—a reflection, perhaps, of the cultural dominance of the city. The pieces below, however, show more of a cross section of Turkish society.

İRFAN ORGA

İRFAN ORGA was born into a wealthy Ottoman family in old İstanbul in 1908. Family life was irrevocably shattered by World War I and the Nationalist revolution. Brought up in extreme poverty after 1915, Orga was enrolled as a cadet in the Kuleli Military Academy, which was seen by his widowed mother as the only way of advancement. Later, as an officer of the air force, he arrived in wartime England in 1941 speaking no English, and soon began living with a married woman. Despite the unhappiness and dislocation this precipitated—court cases, trouble with the immigration authorities, the loss of his officers' commission, and eventually a permanent ban on return to Turkey—Orga quickly learned English and within eight years had penned the memoir excerpted below, currently in print and published in the US by Hippocrene Books. This was phenomenally well received, a success he was never to repeat despite producing numerous subsequent works on Turkish subjects. Orga was able to live in some semblance of comfort only in his later years; he died in 1970.

PORTRAIT OF A TURKISH FAMILY

I had become very restless at home and was often insubordinate. My mother worried incessantly about my education, but all the schools were still disorganised and many teachers had never come back from the war. I used to haunt the streets, playing a corrupted version of football near the gardens of the Mosque, for I had nothing to keep my mind constantly occupied. My mother and I used to have fierce and bitter quarrels and, because I could not bear being confined to the house, I took to roaming farther and farther away from home. No doubt had I had a father to discipline me I should never have dared to do these things, but I would not listen to my mother or grandmother, flying into a passion if they attempted to interfere with me.

My mother was rebelling against life too—but for a different reason. Her rebellion was, unexpectedly enough, against wearing the veil, for she had noticed that none of the foreign women wore them and that even a few of the more daring Turkish women from good families had ceased the practice also. She used to complain about it to my grandmother, declaring she was sick and tired of keeping her face covered, and I would interrupt, with lordly ten-year oldness, saying I would not have her going about the streets with her face open. I would chastise her too for her many goings-out.

"You are never at home," I would declare and although usually I was told to mind my own affairs, one day I was very surprised when my grandmother actually agreed with me.

"It is quite true," she said heatedly. "You are always out these days. And it is not right for you to complain that you have to wear the veil. Why, many women are still behind the kafes and they never see the colour of the sky, excepting from behind their veils. But at least you cannot complain of that for you tore the kafes from here and it is a wonder to me that you were ever accepted in this street, for you behaved exactly like a fast woman looking for another husband or like a prostitute. Yes, you did!" she assured my mother's astonished face. "And now you talk of leaving aside your veil. Why, I lived for thirty years with my husband and I never went out without his permission and I had to keep my face covered all the time. If I went out in the carriage with Murat, immediately all the windows were closed and sometimes the blinds were drawn too. I say it is a scandal that women are today revealing their faces. God will punish them! Do not let me hear another word from you, my daughter, for surely the sky will open on you for such impiety."

Never had I heard my grandmother talk at such length or with such obvious passion. My mother replied:

"You are talking a great deal of old-fashioned nonsense, mother! My place is not in the home these days. If I were to sit at home all day, or you either for that matter, who would go to market for us? Do you expect me to stay here all day, reading the Koran and wearing my veil for fear the passers-by should see me from the street? I tell you again, from now on I shall go without my veil!"

And she angrily tore the pretty veil from her face and threw it petulantly on the floor.

My grandmother lifted her hands to heaven.

"I never thought I should live to see this day," she said.

"Times are changing," said my mother.

"They will say you are a prostitute!" wailed my grandmother, genuinely distressed, totally incapable of accepting such a fierce gesture as the "opening" of the face.

"If they do, it will not worry me," retorted my mother. "Their words will not bring bread to me. And from now on, you will throw aside your veil too, mother."

"Oh no, no, no!" said my grandmother in superstitious horror. "God forbid I should invite punishment upon me!"

But the next morning when my mother went into Beyoğlu, with a box of embroidered articles under her arm and her lovely face naked to the world, she was stoned by some children near Bayazit and received a nasty cut on the side of her head. After that she was cautious about going anywhere alone, but was adamant about not re-veiling herself; Mehmet or I would go with her to Beyoğlu, my grandmother steadfastly refusing to be seen with her. The reaction to her in the street was mixed. The older ones were stricken with horror, more especially since they had always recognised my mother as a good woman, and now their faith in her was sadly battered. She was still young and attractive—she was twenty-five—and despite the shadows that lingered now and then in her eyes, was so unusually beautiful that people could not help but stare at her, and certain sections of the street wondered if she were trying to catch a husband. They came in their droves, the old men as well, to remonstrate with my grandmother, urging her to put a stop to this terrible thing, and my grandmother, thoroughly enjoying herself, would groan to them that she had no authority left in this wayward family of

hers. But the younger women sided with my mother, and some of them even began to follow her example. Their fathers, however, in the absence of dead husbands, took a stick to them muttering piously that no woman in their family would so disgrace themselves. So they put on their veils again in a hurry.

Not a few wished to apply the chastening stick to my mother also. They gave my grandmother sympathy until she was sick of it and prophesied gloomily—but with a little bit of anticipatory relish too, I think—that my mother would come to a bad end.

And indeed she very nearly did !

For one day in Bayazit, when she was alone, an impressionable Frenchman attempted to flirt with her. She tried walking hurriedly on but this had no effect at all, or if anything a worse effect, for the gallant Frenchman became more than ever aware of the swing of her silk skirts and the little dark curls that twined so coquettishly at the nape of her neck. Naturally he followed her. And all the little boys of the district became aware, as is the way of all little boys, of the one-sided flirtation which was in progress. And naturally enough they followed the tall Frenchman, so there was that day in Bayazit the very, very unusual sight of a young Turkish woman, with open face, followed by a foreigner and an innumerable number of small, dirty-nosed boys. When my mother made the mistake of stopping, trying to explain in her totally inadequate French that the gentleman was making a great mistake, he took off his hat, bowed elegantly and declared with obvious feeling:

"Vous êtes ravissante!"

And all the small boys who could not understand a word of what he said, cheered or jeered, according to their several temperaments, and my mother—very properly—hurried on, blushing and breathless and perhaps wishing a little bit for the security of her veil.

So it was that when she came down our street, with her procession behind her, the neighbours were more than ever scandalised and ran into their houses to tell the ones inside. But when my mother called out to them in Turkish that she was being followed, and very much against her will, they set to with a vengeance and brought out sticks and brooms and shooed off the gallant representative of Gallicism in no uncertain manner. Mehmet and

I, who were watching the whole proceedings from the window, were bursting with laughter but my poor grandmother was quite ready to die with shame.

"Such a disgrace!" she kept saying. "We shall never be able to live in this street again."

But in this she was wrong for when the street had finally disposed of the amorous Frenchman, and a few old men had in fact chased him half-way to Bayazit with tin buckets in their hands, to break his head, the street settled down again to lethargy, exonerating my mother from all blame. All excepting the old women, that is.

Reprinted by permission of Eland Books.

SAİT FAİK

SAİT FAİK was born in 1906, the son of a wealthy Adapazarı businessman, but spent most of his later years at the family villa on Burgaz, one of the Princes' Islands. He was fortunate in being able to rely on a small inheritance, because he was intrinsically unsuited for conventional employment, never holding any job longer than a few weeks. Nor did he spend much time away from the İstanbul area, except for a brief period of study and travel in Switzerland and France, where he failed to graduate from university. Instead he spent most of his life strolling the waterfront and back-streets of his beloved city, cultivating friendships with all sorts of people, who were astonished to learn, after his death, of his profession and class, since he kept both a secret—along with his homosexuality. His stories, available in English in the collection A Dot on the Map, *first published in 1983, are rarely strong on plot, often verging on the indulgent; but they have an unerring eye for characterization, dialog and description. Faik died in 1954 of cirrhosis of the liver, doubtless prompted by long hours spent drinking with the fishermen, bootblacks, and idlers of İstanbul's* meyhanes *and coffee houses.*

THE SILK HANDKERCHIEF

The broad façade of the silk factory was bathed in moonlight. Several people hurried past the gate. As I was moving listlessly with steps that did not know where they were heading, the gatekeeper called after me, "Where are you going?"

"Just taking a stroll," I said.

"Aren't you going to the circus?"

When I didn't answer, he added, "Everyone is going. Nothing like this has ever come to Bursa before."

"I don't feel like going at all," I said.

He begged and begged, and persuaded me to guard the factory. I sat a little while, smoked a cigarette, sang a song. Then I became bored. "What should I do?" I wondered, got up, took the spiked stick from the gatekeeper's room, and started making the rounds of the factory.

As soon as I passed through the shop where the girls process the silk cocoons, I heard the sound of rapid footsteps. I turned on the flashlight I had been carrying in my pocket and scanned the place. In the bright beam of the flashlight there appeared two bare feet that were trying to run away. I hurried after them and caught the fugitive.

We entered the gatekeeper's room together, the thief and I. I turned on the yellow light. Oh, what a little thief this was! The hand that I squeezed to the verge of crushing was minute. His eyes were shining. After a while I let go of his hand because I had to laugh—to laugh my head off. At this point the tiny fellow rushed at me with a penknife. The rascal wounded my little finger. I firmly grasped the scamp and searched his pockets. I found a handful of illicit tobacco, some contraband cigarette paper, and a fairly clean handkerchief. I pressed some of the tobacco on my bleeding finger, tore the handkerchief, and made him bind my hand. With the remaining tobacco we rolled two thick cigarettes and had a friendly chat.

He was fifteen. Now this kind of thing was not his habit, but there you are, sin of youth. You understand, my friend, someone wanted a silk handkerchief from him, his sweetheart, his beloved, the girl next door. He of course didn't have the money to go and buy it at the market. He thought and thought and in the end hit upon this solution. I said, "All right, but the manufacturing plant is over there, what were you doing over here?" He laughed. How was he to know the location of the manufacturing plant?

Both of us smoked my cheap-brand cigarettes and became good friends. A genuine native of Bürsa, born and bred there, he had never been to İstanbul, and just once to Mudanya in his long life—you should have seen his face as he said this.

At Emir Sultan, where we used to go sledding in the moonlight, I had other friends of this same type. I was sure that the skin of this one, just like theirs, turned dark in the pools of Gökdere, whose sound I could hear from afar. I know how they turn the same color as the skin of the fruits according to the season.

I looked and saw that he had a complexion as swarthy as a walnut whose green peel has fallen off. He also had white and brittle teeth like the white meat of a fresh walnut. I know that from the beginning of the summer until the walnut season only the hands of Bursa children smell like plums and peaches, and only the chests that appear through the holes left by the torn buttons of their striped shirts smell like hazelnut leaves.

At that point the gatekeeper's clock chimed midnight. The circus was going to be over any minute.

"I must be off," he said.

As I was thinking, troubled that I had sent him away without giving him a silk handkerchief, I was startled by a noise from outside. The gatekeeper was coming in grumbling. Behind him, the thief. . .

This time I pulled his ears and the gatekeeper gave him a searing whipping with a slender willow branch on the soles of his feet. Thank God the boss wasn't there. Otherwise he would surely have handed him over to the police with the words, "A child this young, and a thief! Sir, let him sit in jail and wise up!"

However much we tried to scare him he did not cry. His eyes took the expression of the eyes of children ready to cry, but not even the slightest tremor appeared on his lips, and his eyebrows remained just as firmly set; they were just a little dishevelled.

When he was let go, he shot out like a swallow that has been set free. Like a sharp wing that swipes at the moonlight and the corn field, he dashed off.

At that time I lived in the upper level of the manufacturing plant where the goods were stored. My room was really beautiful, especially pleasant on moonlit nights. There was a mulberry tree right in front of my window. Moonlight would slip through the foliage of the tree and pour in shafts over the room. Almost invariably, summer and winter, I left my window open. How cool and strange were the gusts that blew in! Because I had often worked on ships, I

could tell from their smell which were the southwest, the northeast, the northwest, and the west winds—I knew them all. What winds passed over my blankets, each like an erotic dream!

I was sleeping lightly as usual. Morning was approaching. I could hear a noise from outside. It was as if someone were on the mulberry tree. I must have been frightened, for I did not get up or shout. At this very moment a shadow appeared in the window.

It was the boy, quietly slipping through the window. As he passed by me, I shut my eyes. He rummaged in the closets, searching for quite a while through the stacked goods. I didn't make a sound. To tell the truth, faced with this daring, I wasn't going to utter a word even if he had taken all the goods. I knew that the next day the boss would say, "Idiot, were you a corpse in a grave? You bastard!" He would kick me in the rear and fire me. But I didn't make a peep.

The boy, however, slipped away through the window emptyhanded just as he had come, without a sound. At this moment I heard the cracking sound of a branch. He fell to the ground. As I came down, the gatekeeper and a few other people had gathered around him.

He was dying. The gatekeeper wrenched open his fist, which was tightly clenched. From inside its palm, a silk handkerchief spurted out like water.

Yes, genuine, pure silk handkerchiefs are all like that. No matter how much you squeeze and crease them inside your palm, once the fist has opened, they spurt out of your hand like water.

Translated by Svat Soucek; reprinted by permission of Indiana University Press

EDOUARD RODITI

EDOUARD RODITI *was born of Turkish Sephardic Jewish parents, but left İstanbul relatively early in life. Though now dividing his time between Paris and California, he still retains an obvious affection for his roots. Roditi is above all a versatile writer, having translated some of Yaşar Kemal's work into English and penned a history of Magellan's circumnavigation of the globe, in addition to being an important surrealist poet. The following piece, taken from a collection called* The Delights of Turkey, *first published in the 1970s, demonstrates that he is also an elegant prose stylist.*

THREE FAITHS, ONE GOD

In one of the boxes of secondhand books that the Latin Quarter dealers of Paris display on the parapets of the embankments of the Seine, I once picked up an old guidebook of Istanbul. It attracted my attention because it contained more explanatory text and fewer illustrations than those that are now published for hasty semiliterate and camera-clicking tourists who know things only by sight, and, no longer finding enough time for reading, generally remain a mine of misinformation about all that they have seen. To prepare myself for a more thorough exploration of the Byzantine and Ottoman monuments of the former Turkish capital, I therefore began to read this book a couple of months before I was actually able to leave Paris for Turkey. Somewhere among the learned author's very factual descriptions of Byzantine churches and other Greek-Orthodox monuments, I found a story that fascinated me because it contrasted so oddly with the otherwise sober tone of his historical explanations.

In 1453, when the besieged Byzantine capital finally fell to the Turks, it had been resisting their attacks for so long that most of the surrounding territory was already living fairly peacefully behind the Turkish lines. Close to the besieged city, a Greek-Orthodox monastery thus went about its daily business without ever being disturbed by constant warfare which seemed to have become part of the natural order of things. Among its bearded and black-robed brethren, it harbored a particularly lazy, gluttonous, and ignorant monk who never displayed much interest in anything but the immediate satisfaction of his own gross appetite. Brother Dositheos, since we must give him a name, happened one day to be preparing to fry himself some fish in a pan when a breathless messenger reached the monastery, bringing news that the Imperial city had at long last fallen to the Turks.

"Impossible," Brother Dositheos replied, calmly continuing to season his fish, perhaps even sprinkling a pinch of oregano herbs in the pan while the rest of the monastery interrupted their occupations to listen in dismay to the messenger's account of bloodshed, plunder, and rape. "Impossible," Brother Dositheos repeated. "Haven't we all seen them displaying every day for weeks, on their rounds along the top of the city's battlements, all the miraculous

ikons under whose protection the city has been placed by our saintly Patriarch Gennadios? Haven't we all heard that the Patriarch has revolted against the usurping authority of the new Roman Legate and proclaimed again the full independence of our Church? How can you believe that the Most Holy Virgin and all our Saints have deserted a city thus placed under their protection?"

The messenger and the other monks continued to argue with Brother Dositheos while he began to fry his fish as if nothing of any importance had happened. Finally, he rebuked them: "I'll believe you if the fish that I'm now frying come back to life in my pan."

Immediately, the three fish that he was frying jumped out of the pan, live and unharmed, and fell into the waters of a nearby pool that was fed by a natural spring. But all three fish bore, on one side, black marks where their skin had already been charred by the pan, whereas their other side remained silvery and unharmed. Ever since, there has always been, in the monastery's pool, which has thus become a *haghiasma* of waters that perform miraculous cures, the same number of fish that continue to display the same unique markings.

I decided to investigate this tale in Istanbul and, shortly after my arrival there, repeated it to a friend, a well-known Turkish historian. He too was fascinated by it, but admitted that he had never yet heard of the monastery and its miraculous pool. Inquiries made in various quarters then revealed that a few older people could remember having once heard the legend of the miraculous fish, but nobody that I knew had ever seen them or could tell me where the monastery and its pool might still be found.

In my wanderings in the more distant section of Old Istanbul where the last Byzantine Emperors had lived in the Vlachernae Palace, I asked again and again, in the following weeks, whether anyone there knew where I might find the *balikli kilisi*, the Church of the Fish. Many had heard of it and informed me that it was somewhere beyond the city's battlements, but nobody could tell me near which gate I might find it along the great fortified stretch that protected the city from land attacks all the way from the shores of the Golden Horn to those of the Sea of Marmara, where the city was then defended against attacks from the sea by the sinister Fortress of the Seven Towers.

Though I still failed to find the object of my search, the search itself proved fruitful, however, in that it now led me to discover a number of little-known mosques and Byzantine monuments which I might otherwise have neglected. I was thus encouraged to continue my explorations, especially as the spring weather was ideal for such long walks in little-frequented neighborhoods on the outskirts of Old İstanbul, where the fruit trees were blossoming in the many gardens scattered among almost rural slums and the ruins of abandoned monuments.

Among other monuments, I then discovered, close to the Fortress of the Seven Towers where I had just visited the dungeons and deciphered on their walls some of the messages left there by desperate prisoners, the ruins of what is now called Imrahor Djami, the Mosque of the Executioner. Situated among unidentifiable Byzantine ruins which an old Turkish woman with a passion for flowers, cats, and caged songbirds had transformed into a fantastic garden that she watered diligently with rain from a well-head that still communicated with vast underground Byzantine cisterns, this abandoned Byzantine church had once been rebuilt as a mosque by the pious executioner employed at the nearby fortress. It had previously been attached to the Monastery of Saint John of Studion, reputed in ecclesiastical history to have been the first Christian monastic community endowed with a rule, as opposed to earlier communities of hermits grouped together without having a common rule of life.

One day, close to one of the gates of the Old City, I then discovered another old mosque that was not listed in any of my guidebooks. It had been built to commemorate a holy man who, on the day that Baghdad had fallen to the armies of the Sultan, had stood there proclaiming the great news by the gate of the city, having been vouchsafed a vision of the fall of Baghdad, though the messengers sent to the Ottoman capital to bring the news of victory reached İstanbul only several weeks later, having come all the way from Baghdad by camel or on horseback.

In any other city, this little mosque might have attracted the tourist's attention. Though its proportions were modest, its architecture was in the same delicately classical style as the famous Baghdad Kiosk in the gardens of the Imperial Palace of Top Kapu. Its decoration was more simple, but in exquisite taste, and its *mihrab*, toward which the Faithful turn when they must face the east in prayer, was of finely carved marble and flanked with beautiful flowered panels of brightly colored İznik ceramic tiles. As I was quietly admiring all this, I was approached by the mosque's *Imam*, a surprisingly young Moslem ecclesiastic for these days of weakened faith when so few men of his generation choose a religious way of life. As he greeted me, he seemed to be proud to discover a foreigner visiting his otherwise deserted mosque. In broken Turkish, I told him that I found the *mihrab* truly beautiful, *chok güzel*. Seeing that I was bareheaded but wore an embroidered cap that I always carry in my pocket for such occasions, and that I had dutifully removed my shoes before entering the sacred precincts, he asked me if I was a Moslem. When I told him without further ado that I'm a Jew, an American poet, he remarked that we are all brothers if we still believe in one and the same God, especially in days when all too many men have lost their faith.

Suddenly, it occurred to me that he might know where I could find the *balikli kilisi*. To my inquiry, he replied that he knew it well. One of the Greek priests there was his friend. I would find the monastery only about half a mile from here, just beyond the nearest gate in the Old City's battlements. He then decided to lock the door of his mosque and accompany me to the gate, where he pointed out to me, in the suburban countryside beyond it, a few buildings that were almost concealed behind a slight tree-capped rising that was skirted by a rough road leading from the walled city's gate.

Together, we followed this road till we reached a group of monumental buildings that appeared to have been built in the early nineteenth century, in the Russian neo-Classical style of many Greek Orthodox monasteries that I had already visited on Mount Athos or elsewhere in Greece. Wealthy and pious Russians once devoted vast sums to the task of rebuilding such hallowed ecclesiastical monuments which, since the fall of Byzantium, had slowly been allowed to go to rack and ruin. But these particular buildings now seemed to have fallen on evil days again. At first, they appeared to be deserted, left almost in a state of ruin.

Suddenly, a black-robed Greek ecclesiastic appeared in a doorway. Recognizing my guide, he greeted him cordially and volubly in fluent Turkish. I was then introduced to him somewhat abruptly as an American Jew, a poet who believed in God and who had come to visit the *haghiasma*.

The Greek priest led us through a paved yard where grass grew between the disjointed stone flags, to a huge church built in neo-Classical Russian imitation of a pillared Greek temple. Unlocking its main door, he revealed to me its once majestic and splendidly decorated aisles, which now offered every evidence of having but recently been wrecked by a mob of sacrilegious Vandals. From the vaulted ceilings, heavily wrought brass lamps had been torn and still lay scattered on the floor. The painted *iconostasis*, or icon screen, with its neo-Gothic woodwork and its saints depicted in the "Pre-Raphaelite" manner of Russian Romantic painters who studied in Rome instead of remaining faithful to traditional Byzantine styles, was sorely battered. Though much had already been hastily repaired, I could see that great effort and expense would still be necessary in order to restore all that had been so wantonly destroyed or damaged.

We stood there for a while, embarrassed by what we saw and by the Greek priest's silent sorrow as he contemplated the ruin of the splendid church of which he had once been so proud. Then he sighed, shrugged his shoulders and, through another door, led us into a small walled churchyard where all the marble tombs had been desecrated, disfigured, or overturned. From their Greek inscriptions, I was able to read the names of a couple of nineteenth-century Patriarchs of Constantinople as well as of several formerly aristocratic Phanariot families: Photiadis, Zarifi, Eliasco, Mavrogordato. In a corner of the yard, a pile of human bones had been gathered, after the Turkish mob had torn them from their sepulchers and scattered them to the winds during the anti-Greek riots which the Menderes government encouraged, a few years earlier, as an expression of protest against Greek oppression of the Turkish minority in Cyprus.

The Greek priest patted the young *Imam's* shoulder affectionately, then explained to me in Turkish: "When he heard that the mob was coming here, he came and fetched us and hid us all in his mosque. God will remember what he did for us on that dreadful day."

Returning to one of the other buildings of the almost deserted monastery, the Greek priest opened a small and nondescript door, then led us down some steps to a marble-lined and quite undamaged crypt that had escaped the attentions of the mob. In the marble basin of a fountain into which the waters of the natural spring now flowed, the three fish were swimming. They had black markings on one side, as if they had been burned, but their other side was immaculately silvery. The miraculous fish seemed to have lived over four hundred years, ever since the fall of Byzantium, and only recently to have escaped by another miracle the destructive frenzy of a rioting Turkish mob. I felt down my spine a shiver, like the devastating touch of the finger of God in a poem by Gerard Manley Hopkins. We stood there, all three, in silence, each one of us confirmed in his own different faith, but united in our common respect for all who try sincerely to be worthy of their faith.

Reprinted by permission of New Directions Publishing.

AYSEL ÖZAKIN

AYSEL ÖZAKIN was born in Urfa in 1942, and educated in Ankara, teaching French in İstanbul before beginning her career as a novelist and short-story writer. Shortly after the 1980 coup, Özakin moved to Germany where she has lived ever since. The following extract is from the novel she wrote shortly before leaving Turkey, The Prizegiving *(published only in the UK by The Women's Press)—in part an autobiographical work that was one of the first Turkish works of literature to question the institution of marriage.*

THE PRIZEGIVING

"Is this Polatlı?" asked the young girl sitting next to Nuray.

All the women in the compartment looked outside simultaneously, at the soldiers sitting in groups on the flat ground.

"Yes," said Nuray, "it's Polatlı."

The woman of thirty or thirty-five, with short, blonde hair, who was sitting on the other side of Nuray, next to the window, looked at the soldiers too, in an absent-minded way, and nodded her head. Of all the occupants of the compartment she was the one who had spoken least. She had either leant her head back and slept, or opened and read the notebook which she was holding on her knees. While she was reading she would hold the notebook upright, with the blue plastic cover facing towards Nuray, trying to hide what was written inside. Nuray respected this effort on her part, and refrained from looking into the notebook. Is it a diary? she wondered. Or the draft of a novel? For a moment Nuray looked at her pale face, turned towards the window. It seemed as if deep thoughts and anxieties lay hidden in that face. It looked tired but meaningful . . . From such observations Nuray began to imagine that she and the silent woman sitting next to her had qualities in common. From time to time the woman would raise her head from the notebook and scrutinize the other women in the compartment.

The women had acquired small pieces of information about one another. They had found out in which district of Ankara or İstanbul each lived. In the process, each of them had expressed her views on Istanbul or Ankara as a city. İstanbul was chaotic, dirty, out of control and so on . . . Ankara, for its part, had polluted air, but on the other hand was orderly and easy to live in . . . The conversation dragged on along these lines. The women were more or less equally divided into two camps: those who favoured İstanbul in spite of everything, and those who would not exchange Ankara for any other city. Eventually they tired of this discussion, and remained silent for a long while.

The train stopped at many stations along the way. Village women and men would get on to the train with their baskets, string bags and sacks and would open the doors of the compartments to ask if there were any seats free. The city-dwelling passengers sitting inside would say there were no seats free, even if there were. The villagers would either, with silent stubbornness, come in and sit down, or else travel quietly in the corridors, keeping themselves to themselves. They would get off at another intermediate station. A village girl, wearing a long, loose-fitting coat, *şalvar* of floral-printed cotton material and a traditional head-covering, had come in and perched herself beside Nuray. The man waiting outside, with the sun-tanned face, wearing a

cloth cap and aged about thirty-five, was her father. The girl was sixteen. She had bound her *yemeni* tightly round her brow. She had a tiny nose, and sparkling, black, childlike eyes. Her father had taken her to a *hoca*. They were on their way back. She pointed to her forehead and the back of her neck. Her head ached constantly. The *hoca* had written her an amulet. She put her henna-dyed, chapped hand down inside her clothing, brought out the amulet, and showed it to them. A small, triangular-shaped object, wrapped in a piece of flannel cloth, had been hung around her neck. One of the women, who was about Nuray's age, immediately reproached the girl.

"What good is a *hoca* going to do your headache? Tell your father to take you to a good doctor." Then, addressing herself to the other women in the compartment, she said, "What age are we living in? They still haven't managed to break away from these absurd things . . . "

The village girl, sitting with her back hunched, like an old woman, looked at her in bewilderment. After that, she did not speak at all until her father opened the door and said to her, "Come on, now." As she left she turned back towards them with a shy smile and said, "Have a good journey."

The train stopped for quite a long time at that station. Was there a mechanical fault, or did the crowd of people on the opposite platform mean another train was expected? Some cloth-capped, dark-skinned, poorly dressed men had gathered round a pillar and were talking idly, puffing at their cigarettes. Two women in black *feraces*, their heads covered in finely embroidered *yemenis,* carrying baskets in their hands and their children on their backs, walked quickly away on to the road behind the station, which led to a village. Three other women, dressed in *çarşafs,* and a man wearing a wide cloth cap and loose-fitting trousers, were squatting on the ground at the foot of the wall, eating food laid out on newspaper. There was a little girl standing waiting, her back leant against the station wall. Like the other women, she was fully covered. Only her small, red-cheeked face was exposed. She was about eleven or twelve. The people who were taking most interest in the train were some thin village youths in blue jeans. They were smoking and walking up and down in front of the windows. One of them was peering impatiently into the women's compartment where Nuray was sitting, as if he wanted to say something, or was waiting for something. He had a pale, spotty face and narrow shoulders. There was a shameless desire and a sad longing in his gaze. A very old man with a white beard, wearing *şalvar* and a green skull-cap, walked on bow legs away from the station, carrying a *heybe* on his back.

The young girl sitting on Nuray's right took out of her bag a hardback book with gold lettering on the cover and began to read it. Nuray had a daughter the same age as her; she gave the girl a motherly smile, and asked what she was reading. It was a novel. The title was *When You Choose Freedom*. Nuray looked at the cover of the book. She had never heard of the author before.

The girl was wearing tight-fitting jeans. Her fingernails were painted dark red, and she would frequently insert one of them into her mouth and nibble at it. After discovering the train had arrived at Polatlı, she put the book back in her bag and took out a black metal box, which she opened. There was a mirror in the lid, and the compartments inside contained blue, green, black and grey eyepencils, lipsticks of various shades, powder compacts, tweezers, toilet water and a hairbrush. She started to clean her dark-skinned face with a piece of cotton wool wetted with toilet water. She worked in a bank, and lived in the Ayrancı district of Ankara.

Nuray folded her arms and heaved a sigh. She thought about her daughter, who carried no make-up articles in her bag apart from a comb and a cheap mirror bought from a street stall, and who merely washed her face with soap every morning before going out with a large canvas bag full of books and papers hanging from her shoulder. Nuray felt the pain of her love for her daughter.

Translated by Celia Kerslake; reprinted by permission of The Women's Press

BOOKS

There are a massive number of books about every aspect of Turkey in English, many of them published or re-issued in the past few years, paralleling a renewed interest in the country. Books with Turkish publishers are rarely available outside of Turkey, and the prices, where quoted, should be regarded as approximate.

ANCIENT AND MEDIEVAL HISTORY

Seton Lloyd *Ancient Turkey—A Traveler's History of Anatolia* (University of California Press; $25). Written by a former head of the British Archaeological Institute in Ankara, this is indispensable on the ancient civilizations. Without sacrificing detail and convincing research, it's written in an accessible, compelling style, avoiding the dull, encyclopedic approach of most writing on the subject.

Ekrem Akurgal *Ancient Civilizations and Ruins of Turkey* (Türk Tarih Kurum Basımevi; $15). Excellent detailed survey of Anatolian sites from prehistoric times to the end of the Roman Empire. Includes site plans and interesting graphic reconstructions of monuments, and dated photos of a few monuments.

Otto F. A. Meinardus *St. John of Patmos and the Seven Churches of the Apocalypse* (Caratzas; $6.95). The Seven Churches were all in western Anatolia, and this volume, though mostly ecclesiastical history, is also a practical handbook to the sites.

John Julius Norwich *Byzantium—the Early Centuries* (Knopf; $29.95). First of three volumes, this is an astonishingly detailed, well-informed and above all readable account of a fascinating period of world history.

Cyril Mango *Byzantium: The Empire of the New Rome* (Scribners; $17.50). A single volume that makes a good, accessible introduction to Byzantium, covering daily life, economic policy and taxation, scholarship and universities, cosmology, and superstition, among other topics.

Steven Runciman *Byzantine Style and Civilization* (Viking Penguin; $8.95). Eleven centuries of the art of the Byzantine world in one small paperback, and still fascinating. Facts are presented in interesting contexts and theories are well argued. His *The Fall of Constantinople, 1453* (CUP; $10.95) is the classic study of the event.

Michael Psellus *Fourteen Byzantine Rulers* (Viking Penguin; $7.95). Covers the turbulent period between 976 and 1078, when the scholarly author was advisor to several of the emperors of whom he writes.

Procopius *The Secret History* (University of Michigan; $7.50). Extraordinarily raunchy account of the murkier side of the reigns of Justinian and his procuress empress, Theodora, from no lesser authority than the emperor's official war historian. Bitterly dirt-digging; compulsive reading.

Anna Comnena *The Alexiad of Anna Comnena* (AMS Press; $48). The daughter of Emperor Alexius I, perhaps the first woman historian, wrote a history of the First Crusade from the other side. Accounts of military campaigns predominate, and it's all a bit dry, but holds its own historical interest.

Speros Vryonis, Jr *The Decline of Medieval Hellenism in Asia Minor and the Process of Islamization from the Eleventh through the Fifteenth Century* (University of California Press; $18.95) Heavy, footnoted stuff, but the definitive study of how the Byzantine Empire culturally became the Ottoman Empire.

OTTOMAN AND MODERN HISTORY

Lord Kinross *The Ottoman Centuries* (Morrow; $14.95). Readable, balanced summary of Ottoman history from the fourteenth to the twentieth century; *Atatürk: A Biography of Mustafa Kemal, Father of Modern Turkey*, by the same author (Morrow; $7.50), is considered the definitive English biography—as opposed to hagiography—of the father of the Republic.

Roderic Davison *Turkey, a Short History* (Prentice Hall; o/p). Non-chronological text that touches on everything, particularly good for late Ottoman and early Republican events. Widely available.

Geoffrey L. Lewis *Turkey* (Praeger; o/p). Hard to find, but a much more witty and readable choice—a little uneven, though, and coverage ceases at 1965.

Bernard Lewis *The Emergence of Modern Turkey* (OUP; $13.95). Analysis of the roots of the Republic in the reform movements of the late Ottoman Empire, as well as Republican history.

F. W. Hasluck *Christianity and Islam under the Sultans* (Octagon Books, 2 vols; o/p). Invaluable if you can find it; includes ample material on the influence of pagan and Christian practice on the Bektaşi dervish order.

Yaşar Nuri Öztürk *The Eye of the Heart: An Introduction to Sufism and the Tariqats of Anatolia and the Balkans* (Redhouse Press, İstanbul; $6). A frustratingly brief description of the tenets of mystical Islam and the main dervish orders in Turkey; lavishly illustrated.

Alan Moorehead *Gallipoli* (Ballantine; $4.95). Coffee-table format, but with a good text—the most "popular" history of the battles, in all senses.

Tezer Taşkıran *Women in Turkey* (IBD Ltd; o/p). Pro-Republican, non-feminist review of the history of women in Turkish political and public life.

Pars Tuğlacı *The Ottoman Palace Women* (Cem Yayınevi; $20). Bilingual (English and Turkish) account of life in the palace harem, with loads of bizarre illustrations.

Christopher Walker *Armenia: The Survival of a Nation* (St. Martin; $35). A far-reaching if partisan history, with extended discussion on Armenian relations with the Turks—particularly the 1895–96 and 1915 massacres.

Alexis Alexandris *The Greek Minority of İstanbul and Greek Turkish Relations 1918–1974* (Center for Asia Minor Studies, Athens; $11). Effectively illustrates how the treatment of this community, whose rights were guaranteed by the Treaty of Lausanne, has functioned as a gauge of general relations between Greece and Turkey during the period in question.

Faik Okte *The Tragedy of the Turkish Capital Tax* (Longwood Pub. Group; $34.50). Short, remorseful monograph on the discriminatory World War II tax, written by the İstanbul director of finance who was responsible for its implementation.

Çağlar Keyder *State and Class in Turkey: A Study in Capitalist Development* (Verso; $16.95). Intertwined with the Marxist and academic rhetoric is a very useful economic history of the Republic.

Metin Heper *The State Tradition in Turkey* (Humanities; $35) and *State, Democracy, and the Military: Turkey in the 1980s* (De Gruyter $49.95). Heavy-going but up to date.

TRAVEL

Freya Stark *Ionia—a Quest* (o/p), *Alexander's Path* (Overlook Press; $10.95). Some of the most evocative travel writing available on Turkey.

John A. Cuddon *The Owl's Watch-song* (Random Century; $11.95). Backstreet and *meyhane* İstanbul of the 1950s, on the eve of the first Cyprus crisis.

John Freely *Stamboul Sketches* (o/p). Lyrical rendering of the author's personal impressions of Istanbul, combined with fascinating historical detail.

Michael Pereira *East of Trebizond* (o/p). Travels between the Black Sea and Northeastern Anatolia during the late 1960s, interspersed with readable history of the area. Common in second-hand travel-bookshops.

Lord Kinross *Europa Minor* (Morrow; o/p). Good yarns interspersed with a comprehensive coastal ramble from the Hatay to İstanbul during the early 1950s.

Christina Dodwell *A Traveler on Horseback—in Eastern Turkey and Iran* (Walker & Co; $18.95). Hard to believe that just because you're on a horse you're not going to meet other tourists, but Christina Dodwell does seem to have found a couple of useful travel companions: loads of money and eternal optimism.

ART, ARCHITECTURE, AND ARCHAEOLOGY

Godfrey Goodwin *A History of Ottoman Architecture* (Thames and Hudson; $24.95).

Definitive guide to Ottoman architecture, covering the whole of Turkey and providing a sound historical and ethno-geographical context for any Ottoman construction you care to name.

T. A. Sinclair *Eastern Turkey: An Archaeological and Architectural Survey* (Pindar Press, 4 vols; UK only, £165 each). The standard reference, covering just about every monument east of Cappadocia, but prohibitively priced. Try a specialist library.

Metin Sözen *The Evolution of Turkish Art and Architecture* (Haşet Kitabevi; $25). Lavishly illustrated, erudite survey of major Turkish monuments by period, followed by detailed discussion of the fine arts.

Spiro Kostoff *Caves of God—Cappadocia and its Churches* (OUP; $17.95). Dry rendering of a fascinating subject, but there's no rival, and it is thorough.

David Talbot Rice, et al *The Church of Hagia Sophia in Trebizond* (Edinburgh University Press; UK only, £30). The last word, from the team that restored the frescoes in this landmark church.

Metin And *Turkish Miniature Painting—the Ottoman Period* (Dost Yayınları). Attractive, interesting account of the most important Ottoman art form. Loads of color plates, mostly excellent production.

Philip Mansel *Sultans in Splendor—the Last Years of the Ottoman World* (Vendome; $35). The illustrations are the makings of this book: a collection of rare photos depicting unbelievable characters from the end of the Ottoman Empire. It's also well written, and contains a good deal of information not available in other sources.

David Talbot Rice *Islamic Art* (OUP; $9.95). Covers an enormous timescale and geographical area, giving useful perspectives on Ottoman and Selçuk art forms alongside those of Persia and Muslim Spain.

Jean Jenkins and Poul Rovsing Olsen *Music and Musical Instruments in the World of Islam* (Horniman Museum, London; o/p). Interesting introduction, not too technical but usefully illustrated with photos and line drawings.

W. Ziemba, A. Akatay, and S.L. Schwartz *Turkish Flatweaves: an Introduction to the Weaving and Culture of Anatolia* (o/p). Beautifully produced, well-researched primer with a useful guide to the meanings of recurrent symbols and geographical origins of Turkish rugs.

GUIDES

George E. Bean *Turkey's Southern Shore* (John Murray 1989; $19.95), *Turkey Beyond the Maeander* (John Murray 1980; $24.95), *Lycian Turkey* (John Murray 1978; $24.95), *Aegean Turkey* (John Murray 1989; $22.95). A series of scholarly guides to the archaeological sites of Turkey written from the original research of Professor Bean, much of which has never been superseded.

Fatih Çimok *Cappadocia* (A Turism Yayınları 1987). Attractively illustrated coffee-table-type format, more detailed and better researched than its competitors.

Betsy Harrell and Evelyn Lyle Kalças *Mini Tours near İstanbul* (Redhouse Press 1975, o/p). Invaluable if you're living in the city and need to know how to get out.

Dr. Ü. Önen *Lycia—Western Section of the Southern Anatolian Coast* (Dr U. Önen 1984, o/p). Useful little volume, easy to carry around the sites, giving you a good idea of what's worth visiting in the region.

Laurence Kelly, ed. *İstanbul, a Traveler's Companion* (Macmillan 1989; $9.95). Well-selected historical documents concerning various aspects of the city, and fascinating eye-witness accounts of historical events such as the Crusaders' sack of Constantinople.

Simon Cole *Coping With Turkey* (Basil Blackwell, 1989; $9.95). If you're in Turkey long enough to need this book you'll probably pick up most of the information by other means, but it's well researched and some of it is useful.

Engin Ural *Turkish Law for Foreigners* (Engin Ural, Kennedy Cad 33/3, Kavaklidere, Ankara; $5). Covers topics such as prohibited occupations, ages of consent, rape and antiquities; invaluable if you're settling in Turkey.

Hilary Sumner-Boyd and John Freely *Strolling through İstanbul—A Guide to the City* (Routledge Chapman & Hall 1987; $19.95). Thorough, but covers much of the same ground as the Blue Guide.

John Freely *Blue Guide to İstanbul* (Norton 1987; $18.95). Thorough but a bit pompous.

Jane Taylor *Imperial Istanbul; İznik-Bursa-Edirne* (Weidenfeld and Nicholson, 1989; UK only, £9.95). An excellent stone-by-stone, fresco-by-fresco guide to the Byzantine and Ottoman monuments of the four listed cities. Invaluable floorplans of the more complicated buildings.

Marc Dubin and Enver Lucas *Trekking in Turkey* (Lonely Planet; $8.95). Long and short walks in every Turkish mountain range, plus the Turquoise coast, by one of the authors of this Real Guide.

Haldun Aydıngün *Aladağlar: An Introduction* (Redhouse Press, İstanbul; $5). Details approaches and scrambling routes in this compact karst range near Niğde.

Sally Taylor *A Traveler's Guide to the Woody Plants of Turkey* (Redhouse Press, İstanbul; $3). Coverage of all native trees and shrubs of Turkey, with keying sections and especially useful glossary of Turkish species names.

Pete Raine *Mediterranean Wildlife* (Harrap/Rough Guide; UK only, £7.95). Excellent place to start for what to see in the way of bird, animal, and plant life, and where and when to find it.

FICTION AND POETRY

Yaşar Kemal The best-known Turkish novelist in the West, thanks to English translations by his wife of virtually every one of his titles. Some however, are available only in the UK, published by Collins and Harvill. Oldest are the epics, somewhat turgid and folky, set in inner Anatolia: *Mehmed My Hawk* (Pantheon; $6.95), its sequel *They Burn the Thistles* (Writers and Readers; $4.95) and *The Lords of Akchasaz: Murder in Ironsmith's Market* (Collins and Harvill; £6:50). The trilogy *The Wind from the Plain* (Collins and Harvill; £6.95), *Iron Earth, Copper Sky* (Collins and Harvill; £5.95) and *The Undying Grass* (Collins and Harvill; £6.95) is strong on human observations and detail rather than a plot that will compel you to read to the end. Better are some later novels, mostly set in and around İstanbul, including *The Sea-Crossed Fishermen* (Braziller; $16.95), a psychological drama set against a background of an Istanbul sea-fishing village, and contrasting an old man's struggle to save the dolphins of the Marmara Sea with the fortunes of a desperate

hoodlum at bay in the city, *The Saga of a Seagull* (Pantheon; $11.95), and *The Birds Have Also Gone* (Collins and Harvill; £9.95) a symbolic, gentle story about bird-catchers on the Çukurova plain.

Fatma Mansur *Phoenix in Her Blood* (Eothen; UK only, £9.95). Describing itself as a historical entertainment, this wacky, off-beat fantasy of divine power games in Asia Minor has nice allegorical twists but it can be a bit obscure to say the least.

İrfan Orga *Portrait of a Turkish Family* (Eland; UK only, £5.95). Heartbreaking story follows the Orga family from an idyllic existence in late Ottoman İstanbul through grim survival in the early Republican era; some of it is excerpted on p.708.

Aziz Nesin *Istanbul Boy* (Univ. of Texas, 2 vols; $10 each). Set in the same era and milieu as Orga's work, and strong on local color, but not such a good read.

Aysel Özakın *The Prizegiving* (The Women's Press; UK only, £4.95) Interesting insights into Turkish society, but lacks momentum as a novel, and it can be a bit predictable. The opening passage is given on p.714.

Daniel de Souza *Under a Crescent Moon* (Consort Book Sales; $10.95). Turkish society seen from the bottom looking up—an excellent volume of prison vignettes by a jailed foreigner, and in its compassion the antithesis of *Midnight Express*. Compellingly written, sympathetic and spiced with interesting prejudices on the part of the writer.

Geoffrey L. Lewis, trans. *The Book of Dede Korkut* (Penguin; $6.95). The Turkish national epic, set in the age of the Oğuz Turks: by turns racy, formulaic, elegant, and redundant.

Haldun Taner *Thickhead and Other Turkish Stories* (Forest Books; $18.95). Mostly set in İstanbul from the 1950s to 1970s, translated by Geoffrey L. Lewis.

Sait Faik *A Dot on the Map* (Indiana University Turkish Studies; $12.95). A large collection of short stories, translated by various scholars, from the acknowledged Turkish master of the genre; most are set in and around İstanbul and the Sea of Marmara during the early Republican years. One of these tales is reproduced on p.710.

Edouard Roditi *The Delights of Turkey* (New Directions; $4.45). Twenty short stories, by turns touching and bawdy, set in rural Turkey and Istanbul, by a Sephardic Jew of Turkish descent now resident in Paris and California. One of the best is reproduced on p.711.

Rose Macaulay *The Towers of Trebizond* (Carroll & Graf; $8.95). Classic parody of church intrigue, British ethnocentricity, and proselytizing naivete, with generous slices of Turkey in the 1950s.

Maureen Freely *The Life of the Party* (Warner Books; $4.50). Salacious cavortings of Bosphorus University faculty during the 1960s, including a thinly disguised amalgam of the author's father John Freeley and others. An excellent read.

Orhan Pamuk *The White Castle* (Carcanet; UK only, £12.95). Historical caper in which a seventeenth-century Italian scholar is captured by pirates and sold to an Ottoman astronomer.

Pierre Loti *Aziyade* (Routledge, Chapman & Hall; $12.95). For a romantic tale set in nineteenth-century Ottoman Istanbul this is surprisingly racy, with lots of fascinating insights into Ottoman life and Western attitudes to the Orient.

Hüseyin Avni Dede *Byzantine Coffin Nails* (Gümüş Basınevi). Translator Richard McKane calls Avni a "poet of the people," and his works are certainly accessible even to an audience that knows nothing of the poverty-riven life of an Istanbul coin-seller.

Talat S. Halman *Living Poets of Turkey* (Dost Yayınları). A wide selection of modern Turkish poetry, with an introduction giving the sociopolitical context. Halman also edited *Yunus Emre and his Mystical Poetry* (Indiana University Press; o/p), the works of a significant Islamic folk poet and medieval Turkish humanist, with explanatory essays.

Nazim Hikmet *A Sad State of Freedom* (o/p) Gentle, moving poems—many of which were written in prison—from the internationally renowned Turkish poet who died in exile in 1963.

LANGUAGE

It's worth learning as much Turkish as you can while you're there; if you travel far from the tourist centers you may well need it, and Turks will always appreciate foreigners who show enough interest and courtesy to learn at least basic greetings. The main advantages of the language from the learner's point of view are that it's spelled phonetically, and grammatically regular. The disadvantages are that the vocabulary is completely unrelated to any language you're likely to have ever studied, and the grammar, which relies heavily on suffixes, gets more alien the deeper you delve into it. Concepts like vowel harmony, beyond the scope of this brief primer, complicate matters further. Trying to grasp at least the basics, though, is well worth the effort.

PRONUNCIATION

Pronunciation in Turkish is worth mastering, since once you've got it the phonetic spelling and regularity helps you progress fast. The following letters differ significantly from English pronunciation.

A, a short a similar to that in far.
Â, â softly aspirated a, can sound as if preceded by a faint y or h.
E, e as in bet.
İ, i as in pit.

I, ı unstressed vowel similar to the a in probable.
O, o as in pot.
Ö, ö like oo in boot, but with the tongue held near the roof of the mouth.
U, u as in blue.
Ü, ü like ew in few.
C, c like j in jello.
Ç, ç like ch in chat.
G, g hard g as in get.
Ğ, ğ generally silent, but lengthens the preceding vowel and between two vowels can be a y sound.
H, h as in hen, never silent.
J, j like the s in pleasure.
S, s as in six.
Ş, ş like sh in shape.
V, v soft, between a v and a w.

DICTIONARIES AND PHRASEBOOKS

If you want to learn more than you would from a straightforward phrasebook, Hugo's Phrasebooks' *Turkey* (Hunter $3.25) still probably has a slight edge over Yusuf Mardin's *Colloquial Turkish* (Routledge $14.95); or buy both, since they complement each other well. Alternatively, there's Geoffrey Lewis's *Turkish Grammar* (OUP $28), a one-volume solution. If you're serious about learning Turkish when you get there, the best series published in Turkey is a set of three textbooks and tapes, *Türkçe Öğreniyoruz* (Engin Yayınevi), available in good bookshops in İstanbul and Ankara.

Among widely available Turkish **dictionaries**, the best are probably those produced by Langenscheidt ("Lilliput", $2.95) or the *Concise Oxford Turkish Dictionary* ($39.95; distributed in Turkey by ABC Kitabevi, $15), a hardback suitable for serious students. In Turkey, locally produced Redhouse dictionaries are the best value: the four-and-a-half-inch *Mini Sözlük* ($4) has the same number of entries as the seven-and-a-half-inch desk edition and is adequate for most demands; the definitive, two-tome version even gives Ottoman Turkish script and etymologies for each word, but it costs the earth and isn't exactly portable.

WORDS AND PHRASES

BASICS

Good morning	*Günaydın*	I live in . . .	*. . .'de/da oturuyorum*
Good afternoon	*İyi Günler*	Today	*Bugün*
Good evening	*İyi Akşamlar*	Tomorrow	*Yarın*
Good night	*İyi Geceler*	The day after	*Öbür gün/Ertesi gün*
Hello	*Merhaba*	tomorrow	
Goodbye	*Allahaısmarladık*	Yesterday	*Dün*
Yes	*Evet*	Now	*Şimdi*
No	*Hayır*	Later	*Sonra*
No (there isn't any)	*Yok*	Wait a minute!	*Bir dakika!*
Please	*Lütfen*	In the morning	*Sabahleyin*
Thank you	*Teşekkür ederim/Mersi/*	In the afternoon	*Öğleden sonra*
	Sağol	In the evening	*Akşamleyin*
You're welcome,	*Bir şey değil*	Here/there/over there	*Burda/Şurda/Orda*
that's OK		Good/bad	*İyi/Kötü*
How are you?	*Nasılsınız? Nasılsın? Ne*	Big/small	*Büyük/Küçük*
	haber?	Cheap/expensive	*Ucuz/Pahalı*
I'm fine (thank you)	*(Sağol) İyiyim/İyilik Sağlık*	Early/late	*Erken/Geç*
Do you speak	*İngilizce biliyormusunuz?*	Hot/cold	*Sıcak/Soğuk*
English?		Near/far	*Yakın/Uzak*
I don't understand	*Anlamadım/Anlamıyorum*	Vacant/occupied	*Boş/Dolu*
I don't know	*Bilmiyorum*	Quickly/slowly	*Hızlı/Yavaş*
I beg your pardon,	*Affedersiniz*	With/without (milk)	*(Sut)lu/(Sut)suz*
sorry		. . . (meat)	*(Et)li/(Et)siz*
Excuse me (in a	*Pardon*	Enough	*Yeter*
crowd)		Mr . . .	*. . . Bey*
I'm sightseeing	*Geziyorum/Dolaşıyorum*	Mrs . . .	*. . . Hanım*
I'm American/	*Amerikan/*	Miss . . . (Used with	*Bayan . . .*
Canadian	*Kanadalı*	first name)	

DRIVING

Left	*Sol*	No entry	*Araç giremez*
Right	*Sağ*	Dead end alley	*Çıkmaz sokak*
Straight ahead	*Direk*	Slow down	*Yavaşla*
Turn left/right	*Sola dön/Sağa dön*	Road closed	*Yol kapalı*
Parking	*Park edilir*	Crossroads	*Dörtyol*
No parking	*Park edilmez*	Military area	*Askeri bölge*
One-way street	*Tek yön*	Pedestrian crossing	*Yaya geçidi*

SOME SIGNS

Entrance/exit	*Giriş/Çıkış*	Ticket office	*Gişe*
Free/paid entrance	*Giriş ücretsiz/Ücretli*	Beware	*Dikkat*
Gentlemen	*Baylar*	First aid	*İlk yardım*
Ladies	*Bayanlar*	No smoking	*Sigara İçilmez*
Restrooms	*WC/Tuvalet/Umumî*	Keep off	*Çimenlere basmayınız*
Open/closed	*Açık/Kapalı*	the grass	
Arrivals/departures	*Varış/Kalkış*	Stop	*Dur*
Pull/push	*Çekiniz/İtiniz*	No entry (women/	*(Biletsiz/Damsız)*
Out of order	*Arızalı*	without a ticket)	*girilmez*
Drinking water	*İçilebilir su*	Please take off your	*Lütfen ayakkabılarınızı*
To let/for rent	*Kiralık*	shoes	*çıkartınız*
Foreign exchange	*Kambiyo*	No entry on foot	*Yaya giremez*

WORDS AND PHRASES

ACCOMMODATION

Hotel	Hotel/Otel	For one/two weeks	Bir/İki haftalık
Pension, boarding house	Pansiyon	With an extra bed	İlave yataklı
Campground	Kamping	With a double bed	Çift kişilik yataklı
Hostel	Yurt	With a shower	Duşlu
Tent	Çadır	Hot water	Sicak su
Is there a hotel nearby?	Yakinda otel var mı?	Cold water	Soğuk su
Do you have a room?	Boş odanız var mı?	Can I see it?	Bakabilirmiyim?
Single/double/triple	Tek/Çift/Üç kişilik	I have a reservation	Reservasyonım var
Do you have a double room for one/two/three nights?	Bir/İki/Üç gecelik çift yataklı odanız var mı?	Can we camp here?	Burda kamp edebilirmiyiz?

QUESTIONS AND DIRECTIONS

Where is the . . . ?	. . . Nerede?	How far is it to . . . ?	. . . 'a/e ne kadar uzakta?
When?	Ne zaman?	Can you give me a ride to . . . ?	Beni . . . 'a/e götürebilirmisiniz?
What (what is it?)	Ne (ne dir?)		
How much (does it cost?)	Ne kadar/Kaça?	What time does it open?	Kaçta açılıcak?
How many?	Kaç tane?		
Why?	Niye?	What time does it close?	Kaçta kapanacak?
What time is it?	(polite) Saatınız var mı? (informal) Saat kaç?	What's it called in Turkish?	Türkcesi ne dir? Turkçe nasıl söylersiniz?
How do I get to . . . ?	. . . 'a/e nasıl giderim?		

TRAVELLING

Airplane	Uçak	What time does it leave?	Kaçta kalkıyor?
Bus	Otobus	When is the next bus/train/ferry?	Bir sonraki otobus/Tren/Vapur kaçta kalkıyor?
Train	Tren		
Car	Araba	Do I have to change?	Aktarma var mı?
Taxi	Taksi	Where does it leave from?	Nereden kalkıyor?
Bicycle	Bisiklet		
Ferry	Vapur/Feribot		
Ship	Gemi	What platform does it leave from?	Hangi perondan kalkıyor?
Hitchhiking	Otostop		
On foot	Yaya	How many kilometers is it?	Kaç kilometerdir?
Bus station	Otogar		
Train station	Tren İstasyonu	How long does it take?	Ne kadar sürerbilir?
Ferry terminal/dock	İskele	Which bus goes to . . . ?	Hangi otobus . . . 'a gider?
Port	Liman		
A ticket to . . .	. . . 'a bir bilet	Which road leads to . . . ?	A hangi yol . . . 'a çıkar?
Round-trip	Gidiş-dönüş		
Can I reserve a seat?	Reservasyon yapabilirmiyim?	Can I get out at a convenient place?	Müsait bir yerde inebilirmiyim?

DAYS OF THE WEEK AND MONTHS

Sunday	Pazar	January	Ocak	July	Temmuz
Monday	Pazartesi	February	Şubat	August	Ağustos
Tuesday	Salı	March	Mart	September	Eylül
Wednesday	Çarşamba	April	Nisan	October	Ekim
Thursday	Perşembe	May	Mais	November	Kasım
Friday	Cuma	June	Haziran	December	Aralık
Saturday	Cumartesi				

SEASONS

Spring	*İlkbahar*	Summer	*Yaz*	Fall	*Sonbahar*	Winter	*Kış*

NUMBERS

1	*Bir*	8	*Sekiz*	30	*Otuz*	100	*Yüz*
2	*İki*	9	*Dokuz*	40	*Kırk*	140	*Yüz kırk*
3	*Üç*	10	*On*	50	*Elli*	200	*İki yüz*
4	*Dört*	11	*On bir*	60	*Altmış*	700	*Yedi yüz*
5	*Beş*	12	*On iki*	70	*Yetmiş*	1000	*Bin*
6	*Altı*	13	*On üç*	80	*Seksen*	9000	*Dokuz bin*
7	*Yedi*	20	*Yirmi*	90	*Doksan*	1,000,000	*Bir milyon*

Compounded numbers tend to be run together in spelling:

50,784 *Ellibinyediyüzseksendört*

The most important ordinals, as in class of train, restaurant, etc, are:

First *Birinci*   Second *İkinci*   Third *Üçüncü*

TIME CONVENTIONS

(At) 3 o'clock	*Saat üç(ta)*	It's 8:10	*Sekizi on geçiyor*
2 hours (duration)	*İki saat*	It's 10:45	*On bire çeyrek var*
Half hour (duration)	*Yarım saat*	At 8:10	*Sekizi on geçe*
Five-thirty	*Beş büçük*	At 10:45	*On bire çeyrek kala*

GLOSSARY

Many of the Turkish terms below will change their form according to where they appear (i.e. *ada*, island, but Eşek Adası, Donkey Island); the genitive suffix is appended in parentheses, or the form written separately when appropriate .

ARCHAEOLOGICAL, ARTISTIC, AND ARCHITECTURAL TERMS

ACROPOLIS Ancient fortified hilltop.

AGORA Marketplace and meeting area of an ancient Greek city.

APSE Curved or polygonal recess at the altar end of a church.

BOULEUTERION Council hall of a Hellenistic or Roman city.

CAMEKÂN Changing rooms in a *hamam*.

CAPITAL The top of a column, often ornamented.

CAVEA The seating-curve of an ancient theater.

DEISIS Portrayal of Christ with the Virgin Mary and John the Baptist.

EYVAN Domed side-chamber of an Ottoman religious building.

EXEDRA A semicircular niche.

GÖBEK TAŞI Literally "navel stone"—the hot central platform of a *hamam*.

HARARET The hottest room of a *hamam*.

KAABA Shrine at Mecca containing a sacred black stone.

KATHOLIKON Central shrine of a monastery.

KEMER Series of vaults, or an aqueduct.

KUBBE Dome, cupola—as in *Kubbeli Kilise* (the Domed Church).

KULE(Sİ) Tower, turret.

KÜLLIYE(Sİ) Building complex—term for a mosque and associated buildings taken as a whole.

KÜMBET Vault, dome; by analogy the cylindrical "hatted" Selçuk tombs of central Anatolia.

MİHRAB Niche in mosque indicating the direction of Mecca and prayer.

NAOS The inner sanctum of an ancient temple.

NARTHEX Vestibule or entrance hall of a church; also *exonarthex*, the outer vestibule when there is more than one.

NAVE The principal lengthwise aisle of a church.

NECROPOLIS Place of burial in an ancient Greek or Roman city.

NYMPHAEUM Ornate, multistoried facade, often with statue niches, surrounding a public fountain in an ancient city.

PENDENTIVE Curved, triangular surface enabling a dome to be supported over a square floorplan.

PIER A mass of supportive masonry.

PORPHYRY A hard red or purple rock containing mineral crystals.

REVETMENT Facing of stone, marble, or tile on a wall.

SON CEMAAT YERİ Literally "place of the last congregation"—a mosque porch where latecomers pray.

STOA Colonnaded walkway in ancient Greek marketplace.

SYNTHRONON Semicircular seating for clergy, usually in the apse of a Byzantine church.

TABHANE A hospice for traveling dervishes or *ahis*, often housed in an *eyvan*.

TRANSEPT The "wings" of a church, perpendicular to the nave.

TUFA Soft, carvable rock formed from volcanic ash.

TYMPANUM The surface, often adorned, enclosed by the top of an arch on churches or more ancient ruins.

VERD ANTIQUE A type of green marble.

VOUSSOIR Stripes of wedge-shaped blocks at the edge of an arch.

COMMON TURKISH TERMS

ADA(SI) Island.

AĞA A minor rank of nobility in the Ottoman Empire, and still a term of respect applied to a local worthy—follows the name (e.g., Ismail Ağa).

AHİ Medieval Turkish apprentice craftsmens' guild, with religious overtones.

ARABESK Popular form of Turkish *sanat* or "art" music, which plagues travelers on long bus rides and at nightspots.

ARASTA Marketplace built into the foundations of a mosque, a portion of whose revenues goes to the upkeep of the latter.

AYAZMA Sacred spring.

BAHÇE(Sİ) Garden.

BEDESTEN Covered market hall, often lockable.

BEKÇİ Caretaker at an archaeological site or monument.

BELEDİYE(Sİ) Municipality—both the corporation and the actual town hall.

BEY Another minor Ottoman title like *ağa*, still in use.

CAMİ(İ) Mosque.

ÇARŞAF 1) a bedsheet 2) the full-length, baggy dress-with-hood worn by religious Turkish women.

ÇARŞI(SI) Bazaar, market.

ÇAY(I) 1) tea, the national drink 2) a stream or torrent.

ÇEŞME(Sİ) Streetcorner fountain.

ÇIKMAZ(I) Dead-end alley.

DAĞ(I), DAĞLAR(I) "Mount" and "mountains," respectively.

DOLMUŞ Literally "filled"—the shared taxi system in larger Turkish towns; there's some confusing overlap with "minibus," since not all of the latter are *dolmuşes*, and vice versa.

ENTEL Short for *entelektüel*—the arty, trendy crowd that patronizes western-style bars in the larger cities.

ESKİ "Old"—frequent modifier of place names.

EZAN The Muslim call to prayer.

GAZİ Warrior for the (Islamic) faith; also a common epithet of Atatürk.

GAZİNO An open-air nightclub, usually adorned with colored lights and featuring live or taped *arabesk* music.

GECEKONDU Literally "founded-by-night"—a reference to the Ottoman law whereby houses begun in darkness which had acquired a roof and four walls by dawn were inviolable. The continuance of the tradition is responsible for the huge *gecekondu* shantytowns around all large Turkish cities.

GİŞE Ticket window or booth.

GÖL(Ü) Lake.

HACI Honorific of someone who has made the pilgrimage to Mecca; precedes the name.

HAMAM(I) Turkish bath.

HAN(I) Traditionally a tradesmen's hall or an urban inn; now can also mean office building.

HANIM "Lady"—polite title from Ottoman times, and still in use; follows the first name.

HARABE Ruin; *harabeler* in the plural, abbreviated "Hb" on maps.

HAREM The women's quarters in Ottoman residences.

HASTANE(Sİ) Hospital.

HİCRÎ The Muslim dating system, beginning with Muhammad's flight to Medina in 622 AD, and based on the thirteen-month lunar calendar; approximately six centuries behind the *Miladî* calendar. Abbreviated "H" on monuments and inscriptions.

HİSAR Same as *kale*.

HITTITE First great civilization (c.1800–1200 BC) to emerge in Anatolia.

HOCA Teacher in charge of religious instruction for children.

ILICA Hot spring.

IRMAK River, e.g., Yeşilırmak (Green River).

İL(İ) Province, the largest administrative division in Turkey, subdivided into *ilces* (counties).

İMAM Usually just the prayer leader at a mosque, though it can mean a more important spiritual authority.

İMARET(İ) Soup kitchen and hostel for dervishes and wayfarers, usually attached to a *medrese*.

İSKELE(Sİ) Dock, jetty.

KALE(Sİ) Castle, fort.

KAPI(SI) Gate, door.

KAPLICA Developed hot springs, spa.

KERVANSARAY(I) Strategically located "hotel," usually Selçuk, for pack animals and men on Anatolian trade routes; some overlap with *han*.

KİLİM Flat-weave rug without a pile.

KİLİSE(Sİ) Church.

KONAK Large private residence, also the main government building of a province or city; the possessive form is *konağı*.

KÖŞK(Ü) Kiosk, pavilion, gazebo, folly.

MABET Temple, at ancient sites; possessive is *mabedi*.

MAĞARA(SI) Cave.

MAHALLE(Sİ) District or neighborhood of a larger municipality or postal area.

MEDRESE(Sİ) An Islamic theological academy.

MESCIT Small mosque with no *mimber*, Islamic equivalent of a chapel; possessive is *mescidi*.

MEYDAN(I) Public square or plaza.

MEYHANE Tavern where alcohol and food are both served; tend to be male preserves.

MEZAR(I) Grave, tomb; thus *mezarlık*, cemetery.

MİLÂDÎ The Christian year-numbering system; abbreviated "M" on inscriptions and monuments.

MİMBER Pulpit in a mosque, from which the *imam* delivers homilies; often beautifully carved in wood or stone.

MİNARE(Sİ) Turkish for "minaret," the tower from which the call to prayer is delivered.

MUEZZIN Man who pronounces call to prayer from the minaret of a mosque; the call is often taped these days.

MUHTAR Village headman; *muhtarlık* is the office, both in the abstract and concrete sense.

NAMAZ The Muslim rite of prayer, performed five times daily.

NEHİR (NEHRİ) River.

OTOGAR Bus station.

OVA(SI) Plain, plateau.

ÖREN Alternate term for "ruin;" common village name.

PANSİYON Typical guesthouse in Turkish resorts.

RAMADAN The Muslim month of fasting and prayer; spelled *Ramazan* in Turkish.

SARAY(I) Palace.

SAZ Long-necked, fretted stringed instrument central to Turkish folk ballads and Alevî/Bektaşi devotional music.

SEBİL Public drinking fountain, either free-standing or built into the wall of an Ottoman structure.

SELÂMLIK Area where men receive guests in any sort of dwelling.

SELÇUK The first centralized, Turkish state based in Antolia, lasting from the eleventh to the thirteenth centuries.

SEMA A dervish ceremony; thus *semahane*, a hall where such ceremonies are conducted.

SUFİ Dervish—more properly an adherent of one of the heterodox mystical branches of Islam. In Turkey the most important sects were (and to some extent still are) the Bektaşi, Mevlevi, Helveti, and Kadiri orders.

SULTAN VALİDE The Sultan's mother.

ŞADIRVAN Ritual ablutions fountain of a mosque.

ŞEHZADE Prince, heir apparent.

ŞEREFE Balcony of a minaret.

ŞEYH Head of a Sufi order.

TAPINAK Alternate term for "temple" at archaeological sites; the possessive is *tapınağı*.

TATİL KÖYÜ or **SİTESİ** Resort development, either for Turkish civil servants or a private co-operative—not geared for foreign tourists.

TEKKE(Sİ) Gathering place of a Sufi order.

TEKEL The government monopoly, now no longer exclusive, on alcohol, cigarettes, matches, etc.

TERSANE(Sİ) Shipyard, dry-dock.

TUĞRA Monogram or seal of a sultan.

TÜRBE(Sİ) Free-standing tomb.

ULEMA The corps of Islamic scholars and authorities in Ottoman times.

USTA Another honorific, often half-jokingly bestowed on any tradesman, meaning "master craftsman;" follows the first name.

VAKIF Islamic religous trust or foundation, responsible for social welfare and upkeep of religious buildings.

VİLÂYET Formal word for province; also a common term for the provincial headquarters building itself.

VIZIER The principal Ottoman minister of state, responsible for the day-to-day running of the empire.

YALI Ornate wooden residence along the Bosphorus.

YAYLA Pastoral mountain hamlet occupied only in summer.

YENİ "New"—common component of Turkish place names.

ZAVİYE A mosque built specifically as a convent or hospice for dervishes, usually along a T-plan.

ACRONYMS AND ABBREVIATIONS

A. Ş. Initials of "*Anonim Şirket,*" Turkish equivalent of "Inc."

ANAP *Anavatan Partisi* or Motherland Party: the ruling center-right party founded, and to a great extent still controlled, by President Turgut Özal.

BUL Standard abbrevation for *bulvar(ı)* (boulevard).

CAD Standard abbreviation for *cadde(si)* (avenue).

DSP *Demokratik Sol Partisi* or Democratic Left Party: leftist party headed by Bülent Ecevit.

DYP *Doğru Yol Partisi* or True Path Party: center-right party headed by Süleyman Demirel.

KDV Acronym of the Turkish sales tax.

PTT *Post Telefon ve Telegraf,* the joint postal and phone service in Turkey, and by extension its offices.

SHP *Sosyal Halkçı Partisi* or Social Democratic Party: center-left party headed by Erdal İnönü.

SOK Abbreviation for *sokak* (*sokağı*) or street.

THT *Türk Hava Transporu,* a domestic air service spun off from THY and run by the *Türk Hava Kurumu,* or Turkish Aviation Club.

THY *Türk Hava Yolları,* Turkish Airways.

TL Standard symbol for Turkish lira.

TML English Acronym of *Turkish Maritime Lines.*

TRT Acronym of *Türk Radyo ve Televisyon,* the Turkish broadcasting corporation.

INDEX